African Statistical Yearbook

Annuaire statistique pour l'Afrique

2015

African Development Bank Group
Immeuble du Centre de Commerce
International d'Abidjan CCIA
Avenue Jean-Paul II
01 BP 1387
Abidjan 01, Côte d'Ivoire
Tél. (Standard) : +225 20 26 10 20
Email: Statistics@afdb.org
www.afdb.org

African Union Commission
P.O. Box 3243
Roosevelt Street (Old Airport Area)
W21K19 Addis Ababa Ethiopia
Tel: (251) 11 518 26 74
Fax:(251) 11 551 78 44
Email: austatdivision@africa-union.org
www.au.int

Economic Commission for Africa
P.O. Box 3001
Addis Ababa Ethiopia
Tel: +251 11 551 7200
Fax: +251 11 551 0365
Email: ecainfo@uneca.org
www.uneca.org

Groupe de la Banque africaine de développement
Immeuble du Centre de Commerce
International d'Abidjan CCIA
Avenue Jean-Paul II
01 BP 1387
Abidjan 01, Côte d'Ivoire
Tél. (Standard) : +225 20 26 10 20
Email: Statistics@afdb.org
www.afdb.org

Commission de l'Union africaine
P.O. Box 3243
Roosevelt Street (Old Airport Area)
W21K19 Addis Abeba,
Éthiopie
Tel: (251) 11 518 26 74
Fax:(251) 11 551 78 44
Email: austatdivision@africa-union.org
www.au.int

Commission économique pour l'Afrique
P.O. Box 3001 Addis Abeba,
Éthiopie
Tel: +251 11 551 7200
Fax:+251 11 551 0365
Email: ecainfo@uneca.org
www.uneca.org

Design/layout by Phoenix Design Aid

ISO 14001 certified and EMAS-approved.

ISSN 1561-2805

Production team
Équipe de production

2015

The African Statistical Yearbook 2015 was prepared under the aegis of the African Statistical Coordination Committee set up by major continental organizations dealing with statistical development, namely: the African Development Bank (AfDB), the African Capacity Building Foundation (ACBF), the African Union Commission (AUC), and the United Nations Economic Commission for Africa (ECA) within the framework of the implementation of the Reference Regional Strategic Framework for Statistical Capacity Building in Africa (RRSF).

It was prepared under the overall guidance of Dr. Chukwudozie Ezigbalike, Officer-in-Charge of the African Center for Statistics (ACS) of ECA, Dr. Charles Leyeka Lufumpa, Director of the Statistics Department of the AfDB, Dr. René N'Guettia Kouassi, Director of Economic affairs (AUC), and the leadership of Mr. Kokil Beejaye, Division Manager at the AfDB, Mr. Yeo Dossina, Acting Head of Statistics Division at AUC, and Mr. Molla Hunegnaw, statistician from ECA.

The joint AfDB-AUC-UNECA Technical Team comprised the following personnel. *From the AfDB*: Mr. Chaouch Anouar, Mr. Christophe Baradandikanya, Mr. Mohamed Ben M'Barek, Mr Mustapha Bouzaiene, Mr. Kadisha Mbiya Hilaire, Mr. Louis Kouakou, Ms Amel Kchouk, Ms Nesrine Ressaissi, Mr. Slaheddine Saidi, and Mr. Jerbi Slim. *From the ECA:* Mr. Yared Bekele, Ms. Meaza Bekele, Mr. Tesfaye Belay, Mr. Elias Fisseha, Mr. Molla Hunegnaw, Mr. Haile Mulualem, Mr. Thomas Sinmegn, and Mr. Léandre Ngogang Wandji. *From the AUC:* Mr. Jose Awong Alene, Mr. Nougbodohoue Samson Bel-Aube, Mr. Paul Kutoati, Mrs Selamawit Mussie, Ms. Theresa Watwi Ndavi, Mr. Gildas C. Nzingoula, Mr. Brighton Mutasa (ADEA) and Mr Abdoulaye Oueddo (AFREC).

The following National Data Focal persons provided useful data for their respective countries: Benin: l'Inspecteur d'Etat Monsieur Edouard Alexandre Daga; Botswana: Ruth K. Mothibi; Burkina Faso:

L'annuaire statistique pour l'Afrique 2015 a été élaboré sous l'égide du Comité africain de coordination de la statistique adopté par les principales organisations du continent en charge du développement de la statistique, à savoir, la Banque africaine de développement (BAD), la Fondation africaine de renforcement des capacités (ACBF), la Commission de l'union africaine (CUA), et la Commission économique pour l'Afrique des Nations Unies (ECA) dans le cadre de la mise en œuvre du Cadre stratégique régional de référence pour le renforcement des capacités statistiques en Afrique (CSRR).

Il a été conçu sous la direction générale du Dr. Chukwudozie Ezigbalike, Directeur par intérim du Centre africain pour les statistiques (CAS) de la CEA, de Dr. Charles Leyeka Lufumpa, Directeur du Département des statistiques de la BAD, de Dr. René N'Guettia Kouassi, Directeur des affaires économiques de la CUA et sous la conduite de M. Kokil Beejaye, Chef de Division à la BAD, et M. Yeo Dossina, Chef par Intérim de la Division Statistique à la CUA et M. Molla Hunegnaw, statisticien à la CEA.

L'équipe technique conjointe BAD, CUA, CEA a été composée du personnel suivant. *Pour la BAD* : M. Chaouch Anouar, M. Christophe Baradandikanya, M. Mohamed Ben M'Barek M. Mustapha Bouzaiene, M.. Kadisha Mbiya Hilaire, M. Louis Kouakou, Mme Amel Kchouk, Mme Nesrine Ressaissi, M. Slaheddine Saidi, et M. Jerbi Slim. *Pour la CEA* : M. Yared Bekele, Mlle Meaza Bekele, M. Tesfaye Belay, M. Elias Fisseha, M. Molla Hunegnaw, M. Haile Mulualem, M. Thomas Sinmegn, et M. Léandre Ngogang Wandji. *Pour la CUA* : Messieurs Jose Awong Alene, M. Nougbodohoue Samson Bel-Aube, Paul Kutoati, Mme Selamawit Mussie, Mlle Theresa Watwi Ndavi, M. Gildas C. Nzingoula, M. Brighton Mutasa (ADEA) et M. Abdoulaye Oueddo (AFREC).

Les Correspondants Nationaux des Données (CND) suivants ont fourni des données pour leur pays :

Production team
Équipe de production

Pascal Nakelse; Cameroon: Olivier Tchamago / Joseph Tamche/ Barnabé Okouda; Chad: Tinro Raoul Mbaïogoum; Comoros: Achirafi Anfaita; Congo, Dem. Rep.: Félix Mpaka Ebun'be; Côte d'Ivoire: Koto Ehou N'Boya; Djibouti: Mohamed Mohamed; Equatorial Guinea: Ciriaco Edjang Esono; Gabon: Tangui Gaëtan Bakolosso; Gambia: Ousman Dibba; Ghana: Edward Asuo Afram; Kenya: Mary Wanyonyi; Lesotho: Matlhoeko M. J. Thaisi; Malawi: Lameck Million/ Clement S. Mtengula; Mali: Mohamed Kanambaye; Morocco: Kada Sakina; Mozambique: Nilton Chaúque; Namibia: Aloysius Tsheehama; Niger: Ahamed Daouda Baoua; Nigeria: Elisha Fafunmi; Rwanda: Alice Uwimana; South Sudan: David Thiang; Sudan: Suheir Mohamed; Swaziland: Hanson Dlamini; Tanzania: Gregory Millinga; Togo: Tchilabalo Bozobendo Telou; Tunisia: Walid Mourou; Uganda: John Bonaventure Musoke; Zimbabwe: Godfrey Makware.

Benin : l'Inspecteur d'État M. Edouard Alexandre Daga; Botswana : Ruth K. Mothibi ; Burkina Faso : Pascal Nakelse ; Cameroun : Olivier Tchamago / Joseph Tamche / Barnabé Okouda ; Comores : Achirafi Anfaita ; Congo, Rep. Dem. du : Félix Mpaka Ebun'be ; Côte d'Ivoire : Koto Ehou N'Boya ; Djibouti : Mohamed Mohamed ; Guinée Equatoriale : Ciriaco Edjang Esono ; Gabon : Tangui Gaëtan Bakolosso ; Gambie : Ousman Dibba ; Ghana : Edward Asuo Afram ; Kenya : Mary Wanyonyi ; Lesotho : Matlhoeko M. J. Thaisi ; Malawi : Lameck Million / Clement S. Mtengula ; Mali : Mohamed Kanambaye ; Maroc : Kada Sakina ; Mozambique : Nilton Chaúque ; Namibie : Aloysius Tsheehama ; Niger : Ahamed Daouda Baoua ; Nigeria : Elisha Fafunmi ; Rwanda : Alice Uwimana ; Soudan du Sud : David Thiang ; Soudan : Suheir Mohamed ; Swaziland : Hanson Dlamini ; Tanzanie : Gregory Millinga ; Tchad : Tinro Raoul Mbaïogoum ; Togo : Tchilabalo Bozobendo Telou ; Tunisie : Walid Mourou ; Uganda : John Bonaventure Musoke ; Zimbabwe : Godfrey Makware.

Table of Contents
Table des matières

2015

Table of Contents
Table des matières

2015

2015

Foreword

Avant-propos

Foreword
Avant-propos

2015

The African Statistical Yearbook (ASYB) 2015 is the seventh edition jointly produced by the African Development Bank (AfDB), the African Union Commission (AUC), and the United Nations Economic Commission for Africa (ECA). It is a result of the fruitful collaboration that exists among the three pan-African organizations within the field of statistics. This synergistic collaboration has two principal benefits: (1) it minimizes the risk of inconsistent information being produced by the three organizations, and (2) it reduces the reporting burden on member states, who might otherwise be obliged to submit data separately to each institution.

As with the previous six editions, this 2015 edition presents a time series showing how African countries performed on several economic and social indicators over the period 2006–2014.

As our collective efforts to build the capacity of national statistical systems bear fruit, we are able to use more national data for the country tables, in some cases even to source data directly from online dissemination facilities of national statistical offices (NSOs) – as the custodians of countries' official statistics and coordinators of the National Statistical Systems.

Invariably, there are some data sets that have to be sourced from international organizations that have been designated to compile comparable statistics on specific themes for the whole world, including Africa. Still it is important that such series are confirmed by the countries so that any variations resulting, for instance from methodological differences, are reconciled before compiling the final figures in the ASYB. We have therefore continued to emphasize the importance of involving our member states in the validation process. In that regard, each country received a draft of the country tables to review and correct as necessary. Thereafter, representatives of selected NSOs were convened in

L'édition 2015 (de l'Annuaire Statistique pour l'Afrique (ASA) est la septième à être produite conjointement par la Banque Africaine de Développement (BAD), la Commission de l'Union Africaine (CUA) et la Commission Économique des Nations Unies pour l'Afrique (CEA). C'est le fruit du renforcement continu de la collaboration qui existe entre ces trois institutions panafricaines dans le domaine statistique. La production conjointe à travers un mécanisme panafricain donne à cette publication un sceau continental. Cette collaboration permet aux trois institutions de réduire : (1) le risque de publier des données incohérentes sur l'Afrique, et (2) le fardeau sur nos États membres qui, autrement, auraient à soumettre les mêmes données à trois reprises.

Comme pour les six éditions précédentes, cette édition 2015 présente des séries temporelles montrant les performances des pays africains dans plusieurs domaines économiques et sociaux sur la période 2006–2014.

Nos efforts collectifs pour renforcer les capacités des systèmes statistiques africains ayant commencé à porter des fruits, nous sommes maintenant en mesure d'utiliser plus de données de sources nationales pour les profils statistiques des pays ; dans certains cas, nous sommes même en mesure de collecter des données directement à partir des systèmes de diffusion en ligne des Instituts Nationaux de la Statistique (INS) – en tant que dépositaires des statistiques officielles des pays et coordinateurs des Systèmes Statistiques Nationaux.

Inévitablement, certaines données doivent être collectées à partir de sources internationales qui ont été mandatées pour produire des statistiques comparables dans des domaines spécifiques pour le monde entier, y compris l'Afrique. Néanmoins, il est important que de telles séries soient confirmées par les pays de telle sorte que toutes les a validation workshop for further discussion and clarification of outstanding issues.

Users of this publication may observe differences between figures published here and those published elsewhere. These are unavoidable as a result, for instance, of different release dates and associated stages of the datasets in the compilation process at the time of the respective releases. As a result of these differences, one may observe apparent discrepancies between values published in the 2015 edition of the ASYB, as member states or international data providers recompute data series based on improved or otherwise revised data points and/or models. Differences may also be observed between data from national sources and those published and disseminated by international organizations due to the fact that the latter may have been adjusted for comparability between countries.

The African Statistical Yearbook continues to serve the intended purpose of bringing together, in one volume, data on African countries for policy-makers, researchers and other users. We are therefore committed to continue producing, jointly, the African Statistical Yearbook on an annual basis. And bearing in mind that the original collection of the statistics takes place at the national level, we shall continue in our efforts, again jointly, to continuously reinforce the capacities of the national structures to produce quality and credible statistics, first for their development needs, and then to feed into appropriate continental and global databases and repositories.

divergences, résultant par exemple de l'application de méthodologies différentes, soient réconciliées avant la diffusion des données définitives dans l'annuaire statistique. Nous avons par conséquent continué à souligner l'importance d'impliquer nos états membres dans le processus de validation. Dans cette optique, chaque pays a reçu une copie de la version initiale de son profil statistique afin d'en faire la revue et de réaliser des corrections le cas échéant. Ensuite, des représentants d'instituts nationaux de la statistique choisis ont été invités à un atelier de validation pour continuer la discussion et apporter des éclaircissements sur des questions en suspens.

Les utilisateurs de cette publication ne manqueront pas d'observer des différences entre les données publiées ici et celles fournies par d'autres sources. Ceci est inévitable en raison, entre autres, des différentes dates de publications des données et des différentes versions des données qui sont publiées selon les étapes du processus de compilation. Comme résultats de ces différences, l'on peut avoir l'impression qu'il y a des divergences entre les données publiées dans l'édition 2015 de l'annuaire statistique et celles publiées dans la présente édition. Ceci est dû au fait que les pays membres et les fournisseurs internationaux de données recalculent les séries en tenant compte de nouvelles informations et/ou de modèles plus récents. Des différences peuvent aussi apparaître entre les données issues de sources nationales et celles issues de sources internationales car ces dernières ajustent dans certains cas les données pour les rendre comparables sur le plan international.

L'annuaire statistique pour l'Afrique continue de servir sa mission qui est de regrouper en un seul volume des données sur les pays africains à l'usage des décideurs politiques, des chercheurs ainsi que d'autres catégories d'utilisateurs. Nous réaffirmons notre engagement à produire conjointement cette publication sur une base annuelle. Compte tenu du fait que la production de statistiques a lieu essentiellement au niveau national, nous continuerons nos efforts conjoints pour renforcer les capacités des structures nationales afin qu'elles soient en mesure de produire des statistiques fiables et de qualité, d'abord pour leurs propres besoins de développement, ensuite pour alimenter les bases de données continentales et mondiales.

Dr. Charles Leyeka Lufumpa
Director
Statistics Department
African Development Bank

Dr. René N'Guettia Kouassi
Director
Economic Affairs
African Union Commission

Dr. Chukwodozie Ezigbalike
Officer in Charge
African Centre for Statistics
United Nations Economic Commission for Africa

Introduction

2015

The Yearbook series is a result of joint efforts by major African regional organizations to set up a joint data collection mechanism of economic and social data on African countries as well as the development of a common harmonized database. The Joint African Statistical Yearbook aims to break with the practices of the past where each regional/ sub-regional organization was publishing statistical data on African countries of the continent in an inefficient way, leading to duplication of efforts, inefficient use of scarce resources, increased burden on countries and sending different signals to users involved in tracking development efforts on the continent. It is expected that the joint collection and sharing of data between regional institutions will promote wider use of country data, reduce costs and significantly improve the quality of the data and lead to better monitoring of development initiatives on the continent.

The data in this issue of the Yearbook are arranged generally for the years 2006 to 2014 or for the last nine years for which data are available.

The Yearbook is published in one volume consisting of two parts: a set of summary tables followed by country tables.

La série de publication de l'annuaire est le résultat des efforts conjoints des principales organisations régionales africaines pour disposer d'un mécanisme commun de collecte des données économiques et sociales et d'une base de données commune et harmonisée sur les pays africains. L'annuaire statistique commun marque le début d'une rupture avec les pratiques du passé où chaque organisation régionale/sous régionale éditait des données statistiques sur les pays africains d'une manière inefficace. En effet, ces anciennes pratiques conduisaient à la duplication des efforts, à une mauvaise utilisation des ressources rares et à l'accroissement des fardeaux sur les pays. En même temps, elles envoyaient des messages disparates aux utilisateurs impliqués dans les efforts de suivi du développement du continent. On s'attend à ce que la collecte et le partage communs des données entre les institutions régionales favorisent une utilisation plus large des données des pays, réduisent leurs coûts d'accès, améliorent de manière significative leur qualité et conduiront à un meilleur suivi des initiatives de développement du continent.

Le présent annuaire présente généralement les données sur la période allant de 2006 à 2014 ou sur les neuf dernières années pour lesquelles des données sont disponibles.

L'annuaire est édité en un volume composé de deux parties : un ensemble de tableaux synoptiques et un ensemble de profils-pays.

2015

Abbreviations and Acronyms

Abréviations et acronymes

Abbreviations and Acronyms

Abréviations et acronymes

2015

ACBF	African Capacity Building Foundation / Fondation pour le renforcement des capacités en Afrique
AEO/PEA	African Economic Outlook / Perspectives de l'Économie Africaine
AfDB/BAD	African Development Bank / Banque Africaine de Développement
AfDF/FAD	African Development Fund / Fonds Africain de Développement
AFREC	African Energy Commission / Commission africaine sur l'énergie
ACS/CAS	African Centre for Statistics / Centre africain pour la statistique
AUC/CUA	African Union Commission / Commission de l'Union Africaine
ADEA/ADEA	Association for the Development of Education in Africa / Association pour le Développent de l'Education en Afrique
CPC/CCP	Central Product Classification / Classification Centrale des Produits des Nations Unies
CPI/IPC	Consumer Price Index / Indice des prix à la consommation
COMTRADE	United Nations Commodity Trade Statistics Database / Base de données des statistiques du commerce des Nations Unies
ECA/CEA	Economic Commission for Africa / Commission Économique pour l'Afrique
FAO	Food and Agriculture Organisation / Organisation des Nations Unies pour l'Alimentation et l'Agriculture
F.O.B/F.À.B.	Free On Board / Franco à bord
IDA	International Development Association / Association Internationale de Développement
ILO/BIT	International Labor Organization / Bureau International du Travail
IMF/FMI	International Monetary Fund / Fonds Monétaire International
ISIC/CITI	International Standard Industrial Classification / Classification Internationale Type par Industrie
ITU/UIT	International Telecommunication Union / Union Internationale des Télécommunications
M1	Broad Money / Masse monétaire
M2	M1 + quasi money / M1+ «quasi monnaie»
MDG/OMD	Millennium Development Goals / Objectifs du Millénaire pour le Développement
NEPAD	New Partnership for Africa's Development / Nouveau Partenariat pour le Développement de l'Afrique
ODA/APD	Official Development Assistance / Aide Publique au Développement
OECD/OCDE	Organization for Economic Co-operation and Development / Organisation de Coopération et de Développement Economique
PRS/SRP	Poverty Reduction strategy / Stratégie de Réduction de la Pauvreté
RRSF/CSRR	Regional Reference Strategic Framework / Cadre Strategique Regional de Reference
SDR/DTS	Special Drawing Rights / Droits de Tirage Spéciaux
SHaSA	Strategy for the Harmonization of Statistics in Africa / Stratégie pour l'Harmonisation des Statistiques en Afrique
SNA/SCN	System of National Accounts / Système de Comptabilité Nationale
UN/ONU	United Nations / Organisation des Nations Unies
UNCTAD/ CNUCED	United Nations Conference on Trade and Development / Conférence des Nations Unies sur le Commerce et le Développement
UNDATA	United Nations Statistical Databases / Bases des données statistiques des Nations Unies
UNESCO	United Nations Educational, Scientific and Cultural Organization / Organisation des Nations Unies pour l'Education, la Science et la Culture
US/EU	United States / Etats-Unis d'Amérique
WTO/OMC	World Trade Organization / Organisation Mondiale du Commerce

2015

General notes

Notes générales

General notes

The statistics presented in the Yearbook are, as far as possible in accordance with international recommendations and definitions. Where important deviations are known to exist, they are indicated in footnotes at the end of each country's table. Owing to the rounding of figures, the totals shown in tables do not always correspond exactly to the sum of their component items.

I. SOCIAL AND DEMOGRAPHIC INDICATORS

Population

Data presented in this section are derived mainly from the following publications: "World Population Prospects: estimates and projections of the UN Secretariat Population Division", "World Urbanisation Prospects" and "Labour Force Estimates and Projections, 1980-2020" prepared by the International Labour Organisation (ILO). National sources have been used to supplement missing data when comparable with the UN series.

Mid-year population

Unless otherwise stated, the figures shown relate to de facto population. Population (Urban) refers to the number of persons living in areas defined as urban, according to national definitions of this concept. Since national definitions differ, cross-country comparisons should be made with care.

Average annual growth rate

The number of people added to (or subtracted from) a population in a year due to natural increase and net migration expressed as a percentage of the population at the beginning of the time period. Average annual population growth is the exponential rate of growth of midyear population from year t-1 to t, expressed as a percentage.

Crude birth rate

Number of births over a given period divided by the person-years lived by the population over that period. It is expressed as the number of births per 1,000 populations.

Crude death rate

Number of deaths over a given period divided by the person-years lived by the population over that period. It is expressed as the number of deaths per 1,000 population.

Population by age groups

Three age groups are used in order to highlight the proportion of active population vis-à-vis the dependent population. Population aged 15-64 is the number of people who could potentially be economically active, excluding children.

Economically active population

The economically active population comprises all persons of either sex who furnish the supply of labor for the production of goods and services during a specified time-reference period.

Life expectancy, crude birth and death rates

Life expectancy at birth is the average number of years a new-born infant would live if prevailing patterns of mortality of the total population at the time of his/her birth were to stay the same throughout his/her life. Crude birth and death rates represent the number of live births and the number of deaths respectively per 1000 people. Death is the permanent disappearance of all evidence of life at any time after live birth has taken place (postnatal cessation of vital functions without capability of resuscitation). This definition excludes foetal deaths.

Net reproduction rate

The net reproduction rate is the average number of daughters that would be born to a woman if she passed through her lifetime conforming to the age -specific fertility and mortality rates of a given year. This rate is similar to the gross reproduction rate but takes into account that some women will die before completing their childbearing years.

Total fertility rate
The total fertility rate is the average number of children that would be born per woman if she experiences no mortality and were subject to a given set of age-specific fertility throughout her lifetime.

Health

Percentage of mothers provided at least one antenatal care
Antenatal care visit coverage (at least one visit) is the percentage of women aged 15-49 with a live birth in a given time period that received antenatal care provided by skilled health personnel at least once during their pregnancy.

Percentage of deliveries attended by skilled health personnel
Percentage of births attended by skilled health personnel (doctors, nurses or midwives) is the percentage of deliveries attended by health personnel trained in providing lifesaving obstetric care, including giving the necessary supervision, care and advice to women during pregnancy, labor and the post-partum period; conducting deliveries on their own; and caring for new-borns. Traditional birth attendants, even if they receive a short training course, are not included.

Births registered (%)
The percentage of births registered during a specified time period for a country or designated region.

Deaths registered (%)
The percentage of deaths registered during a specified time period for a country.

Physicians (per 10 000 population)
Practicing physicians, practicing general practitioners, practicing specialists refers to the number of physicians, general practitioners and specialists (including self-employed) who are actively practicing medicine in public and private institutions. The data should exclude dentists, stomatologists, qualified physicians who are working abroad, working in administration, research and industry positions. Data should include foreign physicians licensed to practice and actively practicing medicine in the country. Data should be calculated to represent full-time equivalents.

Nurses (per 10 000 population)
Nurses refers to the total number of nurses certified or registered and who are actively practicing in public and private hospitals, clinics and other health facilities, including self-employed. Nursing assistants and midwives should be included. Data should exclude nurses who are working abroad, working in administrative, research and industry positions. The figures for physicians and nurses relate to those registered at the government offices.

Hospital beds - Total (per 10 000 population)
The number of hospital beds is calculated for public and private hospitals.

Percentage of children provided the vaccines (BCG, DPT3, Polio, Measles)
Child immunization measures the percentage of children aged 12-23 months who received specific vaccinations before 12 months or at any time. A child is considered adequately immunized against:

- diphtheria, pertussis (or whooping cough), and tetanus (DPT) after receiving three doses of vaccine;
- measles after receiving one dose of measles vaccine;
- tuberculosis after receiving Bacille Calmette-Guérin vaccine (BCG);
- polio after receiving the three doses of polio vaccine.

Access to safe water
It is measured by the number of people who have a reasonable means of getting an adequate amount

of clean water, expressed as a percentage of the total population.

Education

The sources of the data on education, reported in this publication, consist of national publications and the UNESCO Statistical Yearbook. Data presented generally relate to the public (official) and private (independent) schools. The indicated years refer to the beginning of school year. Adult education, apprenticeship courses and correspondence schools are excluded. Owing to variations in school systems, caution needs to be exercised when comparing the data across countries.

Student enrolment at specific level

First level student enrolment is the number of pupils enrolled at the primary level of education, regardless of age. Second level student enrolment is the total number of students enrolled at the secondary level of education, regardless of age.

Adult Illiteracy Rate

Percentage of persons aged 15 and over who cannot read and write.

Pupil-Teacher ratio

Pupil-teacher ratio is the average number of pupils (students) per teacher at a specific level of education in a given school-year.

Gender Parity Index

Gross rate of registration for girls/boys, expressed as having a value of one when there is gender parity. Parity index between gender (PIG) measures progress in achieving gender parity in education participation and / or learning opportunities available to female compared to those available to males. This is a comparison of values assigned to females and males for a given indicator in a given year. It also reflects the level of development of women in society. This indicator should be disaggregated by level of education (pre-primary, primary and secondary).

II. NATIONAL ACCOUNTS

National accounts data provide essential information on the economic performance of African countries in terms of growth and structure of output, investments and savings. National accounts data are obtained from various national sources and supplemented with data from international sources such as the UN Yearbook of National Accounts and AfDB and ECA African Centre for Statistics estimates. Where necessary, official figures have been adjusted to conform to the System of National Accounts (SNA). Many countries continue to compile their national accounts in accordance with the 1968 SNA, but more and more are adopting the 1993 SNA while others are migrating to SNA 2008. A few countries still use concepts from older SNA guidelines, including valuations such as factor cost, in describing major economic aggregates.

Gross Domestic Product (GDP)

Gross Domestic Product is an aggregate measure of production equal to the sum of the gross values added of all resident institutional units engaged in production (plus any taxes, and minus any subsidies, on products not included in the value of their outputs).

GDP by kind of economic activity (by sector)

GDP by sector gives value-added by the broad categories of the ISIC classification. Value added is evaluated at basic prices or factor cost or at producer prices, depending on the current practice in the country. Data are provided at current prices and in terms of growth rates over the previous year based on data at constant prices.

Expenditure on GDP

General government final consumption

General government final consumption expenditure comprises all current expenditure for purchases of goods and services by all levels of government, as well as capital expenditure on national defense and security.

Private final consumption
Household final consumption expenditure represents the final consumption of households and non-profit institutions. It includes imputed rent for owner-occupied dwellings but excludes purchases of dwellings and it also includes any statistical discrepancy.

Gross capital formation
Gross capital formation consists of gross domestic fixed capital formation plus net changes in the level of inventories.

Exports and imports of goods and services
Exports and imports of goods and services refer to the value of goods and non-factor services provided to or from the rest of the world. They do not include receipts and payments for factor services such as investment income, interest and labor income. The data are generally estimated on the basis of foreign trade statistics and are not directly comparable with those from the balance of payments.

III. INFLATION

Inflation is measured by the annual percentage changes in the Consumer Price Index (CPI). The CPI shows the cost of acquisition of a basket of goods and services purchased by the average consumer. Weights for the computation of the index numbers are obtained from household budget surveys. CPI data are provided by the national statistical systems, mainly by the National Statistical Office or central banks.

IV. AGRICULTURAL PRODUCTION

Agricultural production
The data on major crops produced are obtained from the National Statistical Offices of the following countries; Burkina Faso, Burundi, Cameroon, Congo, Côte d'Ivoire, Democratic Republic of Congo, Gabon, Gambia, Guinea-Bissau, Kenya, Lesotho, Madagascar, Malawi, Mali, Mauritania, Mauritius, Morocco, Mozambique, Nigeria, Senegal, Sudan, Swaziland, Zambia, and Zimbabwe. For the remaining countries the data are obtained from the online database of the Food and Agricultural Organization (FAO). For those countries, the five major crops per country are obtained by calculating the average yearly production of each crop produced by a given country (considering only years when the crop is produced) and ranking them in descending order.

Agricultural and food production index
The various indices of agricultural production illustrate the relative level of the aggregate volume of agricultural production for each year, in comparison with the base period 2004-2006. These indices of agricultural production obtained from the FAO online database are computed using the Laspeyres formula, using the price weighted sum of the production of various commodities less seed and feed. The price used for weighting the production quantity of each commodity is the average price during the years indicated as the base year.

V. MINING PRODUCTION

The sources of the data reported are national statistical offices (for those countries responding to the AfDB, AUC and ECA questionnaire) the United Nations Industrial Commodity Database accessed through UNDATA (at http://data.un.org/) and the United Nations Industrial Commodity Yearbook. Data for some of the minerals were also obtained from the British Geological Survey, and the United States Geological Survey website.

Mining production
For a detailed description of the minerals included

in this publication, the user may refer to the Central Product Classification (CPC) Ver.1.1, Statistical Papers, Series M, No.77, Ver.1.1 (United Nations publication, Sales No. E.03.XVII.3). It was difficult to identify the three major commodities for each country due to the reference period being too narrow and commodities varying from one country to another. First, we obtained the export values of minerals for the years 2005 through 2013. We then considered the average value (considering only years when the commodity was available) to help us decide which commodity to include in the publication. In addition, we decided to choose strategic commodities (such as oil, gas and diamonds) when the country produces them.

VI. ENERGY

The data provided for this section are from the United Nations Energy Statistical Yearbook and the Energy Database which may be accessed through UNDATA (at http://data.un.org/), also from African Energy Commission (AFREC).

Electricity production

The figures reported for production refer to the gross generation of electricity. These include the consumption by station auxiliaries and any losses in transformers as well as electricity generated by pumping stations without deducting the electric energy consumed by the pumps. The production of electricity may fall into public utilities, whose primary purpose is to generate and transmit electric energy for use by the public, and self-producers, undertakings which produce electric energy intended, in whole or in part, for their own uses.

VII. TOURISM AND INFRASTRUCTURE

Tourism

Data on tourism have been primarily collected from national sources, and where national sources are not available, from the online databases UNWTO and Tourism Decision Metrics of Tourism Economics. The indicators published are the number of arrivals in the country, the number of hotel rooms, overnight stays, tourism receipts, tourism's total contribution to GDP and tourism's total contribution to employment. The number of tourists to a country, unless otherwise stated, refers to all persons (checked at the frontier) traveling for pleasure, health, business, meetings or studies and stopping in that country for 24 hours or more. The figures exclude immigrants and residents in a frontier zone.

Infrastructure

Paved Roads (% of total)

Paved roads are those surfaced with crushed stone (macadam) and hydrocarbon binder or bituminized agents, with concrete, or with cobblestones, as a percentage of all the country's roads, measured in length.

Total Network (Railways-km)

Rail lines are the length of railway route available for train service, irrespective of the number of parallel tracks.

Main Telephone Lines

Telephone lines are fixed telephone lines that connect a subscriber's terminal equipment to the public switched telephone network and that have a port on a telephone exchange. Integrated services digital network channels and fixed wireless subscribers are included.

Mobile Cellular Subscribers

Mobile cellular telephone subscriptions are subscriptions to a public mobile telephone service using cellular technology, which provide access to the public switched telephone network. Post-paid and prepaid subscriptions are included.

VIII. FINANCIAL AND MONETARY STATISTICS

Monetary Statistics

Data for this section are essentially obtained from the IMF International Financial Statistics Database and central banks.

Money supply (M1)

Money supply comprises transferable deposits and currency outside deposit money banks.

Quasi money

Quasi money comprises time, savings and foreign currency deposits.

Net foreign assets

Net foreign assets equal the sum of foreign assets, less the sum of foreign liabilities of monetary authorities and deposit money banks.

Domestic credit

Domestic credit includes all domestic assets of the banking system. It is the sum of claims on the central government (net), on official entities and the private sector. Credit to the private sector is shown separately but as a subset of domestic credit.

International reserves

International reserves consist of the country's holding of monetary gold, Special Drawing Rights (SDRs) and foreign exchange, as well as its reserve position in the International Monetary Fund (IMF).

Exchange rates

Exchange rates expressed in national currency unit per US dollar unit are reported as end period and period averages of market exchange rates and official rates. The market rate is defined as the rate determined largely by market forces; and the official rate is that determined by the authorities.

Public Finance

Data for this section have been primarily collected from National Authorities such as National Statistics Offices, Ministries of Finance and central banks. Where national sources are not available, data from IMF publications (Country Reports) are used.
For countries: Botswana, Egypt, Ethiopia, Kenya, Malawi, Mauritius, Namibia, South Africa and Swaziland, the data were compiled following their respective fiscal period as annual data. Therefore, the years 2006-2014 represent the ending calendar year according to the fiscal period of each country.

Revenue and grants

Includes all non-repayable receipts, requited and unrequited, current and capital, and non-compulsory, non-repayable, unrequited receipts from other governments (domestic or foreign) and international institutions.

Tax revenue

Includes compulsory, unrequited, non-repayable contributions exacted by a government for public purposes.

Non-tax revenue

It includes requited receipts from property incomes, fees and charges, non-industrial and incidental sales, the cash operating surpluses of departmental enterprises and unrequited receipts such as fines, forfeits and current private donations.

Grants

Unrequited, non-repayable, non-compulsory government receipts from other governments or international institutions.

Expenditure and net lending

Includes all non-repayable payments by government, whether requited or unrequited and whether current or capital, as well as government transactions in debt and equity claims upon others acquired for purposes of public policy.

Current expenditure
It includes all non-repayable payments by government, whether requited or unrequited, other than capital expenditure or grants.

Capital expenditure
Expenditure for acquisition of fixed capital assets, stocks, land or intangible assets plus unrequited transfers for the purpose of permitting the recipient to acquire such assets. In order to be classified as a capital asset, an asset acquired must exceed a minimum value and be intended for use for more than one year in the process of production.

Net lending
Net lending (lending minus repayments) comprises government transactions in claims upon others acquired for purposes of public policy rather than for the management of government liquidity or earning a return. It covers both debt and equities and both payments and receipts.

Fiscal balance
Fiscal balance or government overall surplus/deficit is defined as total revenue and grants received less total expenditure and net lending.

Balance of Payments
The balance of payments is a statistical statement that summarizes, for a specific period, the economic transactions of an economy with the rest of the world. Transactions for the most part between residents and non-residents consist of those involving goods, services, and income; those involving financial claims on, and liabilities to, the rest of the world; and those classified as transfers which involve offsetting entries to balance, in an accounting sense, one-sided transactions. Data in this section are obtained from African central banks and where data are not available from national sources or if country data do not meet the required quality, IMF Country Reports are also used. Data from international sources relate to the following countries: Equatorial Guinea, Liberia, Lesotho, Sierra Leone, and Libya.

Trade balance
Trade balance is equal to exports less imports of goods, both measured on the free-on-board (f.o.b.) basis that is, by the value of the goods at the border of the exporting country. Goods cover general merchandise, goods for processing, repairs on goods, goods procured in ports by carriers, and non-monetary gold.

Services balance
Services include transportation (freight and passenger transportation); travel; communication services; construction services; insurance services; financial services; computer and information services; royalties and license fees; personal, cultural, and recreational services; government services. Services balance is defined as exports minus imports of services.

Net income
Income includes compensation of employees which covers wages, salaries, and other benefits; investment income which consists of direct investment income, portfolio investment income and other investment income. Net income is income received from investments abroad less income paid to foreigners investing in the country.

Compensation of employees
Compensation of employees includes salaries, wages, salaries paid by non-resident employers to their resident employees, and vice versa.

Investment income
Investment income covers direct investment income, portfolio investment income (equity and debt) and other investment income (interest from other financial transactions).

Current transfers
Current transfers consist of all transfers that do not

involve: (i) transfers of ownership of fixed assets; (ii) transfers of funds linked to the acquisition or disposal of fixed assets; (iii) forgiveness, without any counterparts being received in return, of liabilities by creditors.

Net official transfers

It comprises net transfer payments between governments of the reporting country and the rest of the world.

Workers' remittances

Workers' remittances return amounts transferred abroad by resident workers and vice versa.

Other private transfers

Other private transfers comprise net transfer payments between private persons and non-official organizations of the reporting country and the rest of the world, which carry no provisions for repayments.

Current account balance

Current account balance is the sum of net exports of goods and services, net income, and net current transfers.

Capital account

The capital account covers international capital transfers (e.g. debt forgiveness) and the acquisition/disposal of non-produced, nonfinancial assets (such as patents).

Financial account

The financial account deals with transactions involving financial claims on, or liabilities to, the rest of the world, including international purchases of securities, such as stocks and bonds.

Errors & omissions

Net errors & omissions are derived residually as the difference between total of receipts and payments (both current and capital together with the financial account)

Overall balance

The balance of payments is a record of a country's international transactions with the rest of the world. Transactions are organized in two different accounts, the current account and the capital and financial account.

External Debt and Financial Flows

Data in this section are mainly obtained from the following international sources: IMF World Economic Outlook database, OECD online database and UNCTAD online database. However, a few countries have submitted their data and they are published in this edition of the African Statistical Yearbook. The purpose of the Yearbook is to include data from national sources to the extent possible when the data quality is acceptable. Data from national sources relate to the following countries: Benin, Burkina Faso, Cameroon, Equatorial Guinea, Lesotho, and Niger.

External debt

External debt (total outstanding debt) is the amount, at any given time, of disbursed and outstanding contractual liabilities of residents of a country to non-residents to repay principal, with or without interest, or to pay interest with or without principal. It is the sum of public and publicly guaranteed short and long-term debt, private non-guaranteed short and long-term debt and the use of IMF credit.

External debt service

Total external debt service is the sum of principal repayments and interest actually made. It is debt service payment on short- and long-term debt (public and publicly guaranteed and private non-guaranteed) and the use of IMF credit.

Present value of external debt

Present value of debt is the sum of short-term external debt plus the discounted sum of total debt service payments due on public, publicly guaranteed, and private nonguaranteed long-term external debt over the life of existing loans.

Total government domestic debt

The total government domestic debt consists of liabilities that are owed by a country's citizens and government.

Foreign direct investment

Foreign direct investment refers to investments made to acquire or add to a lasting management interest (usually 10 percent of voting stock) enterprise operating in a country other than that of the investor. It is the sum of equity capital, reinvestment of earnings and other short- and long-term capital as shown in the balance of payments.

Official development assistance

ODA relates to grants or concessional loans (i.e. with a grant element of at least 25 percent) undertaken by the official sector, whose main objective is the promotion of economic development and welfare. Data in this section are net disbursements of ODA.

IX. EXTERNAL TRADE

Data for this section are mainly obtained from national sources. This is the case for the following countries: Algeria, Benin, Burkina Faso, Burundi, Cameroon, Côte d'Ivoire, Egypt, Ethiopia, Gambia, Guinea-Bissau, Kenya, Malawi, Mali, Morocco, Mozambique, Namibia, Niger, Nigeria, Rwanda, Sudan, Swaziland, Tanzania, Togo, Zambia and Zimbabwe. Where national data were not available, we have used the UNCTAD online database. The names of major export and import commodities have been selected by the reporting countries themselves. For the data obtained from UNCTAD, the harmonized system (rev1) classification is used to determine the list of main exported and imported commodities. Unless otherwise indicated, the import statistics are reported on a CIF valuation base while exports are reported on FOB.

Notes générales

Les statistiques présentées dans cet Annuaire sont, autant que possible, conformes aux recommandations et définitions internationales. Lorsque des divergences importantes sont connues, elles sont indiquées dans les notes figurant à la fin du tableau de chaque pays concerné. A cause des chiffres arrondis, les totaux indiqués dans certains tableaux ne correspondent pas toujours exactement à la somme de leurs composantes.

INDICATEURS SOCIAUX ET DÉMOGRAPHIQUES

Population

Les données présentées dans cette section sont tirées principalement des publications: «Perspectives d'avenir de la population mondiale, estimations et projections», «Perspectives d'Urbanisation Mondiale» de la Division de la Population du Secrétariat de l'ONU, «Estimations et Projections de la Main d'Œuvre, 1980-2020» du Bureau International du Travail (BIT). Les sources nationales ont été utilisées pour compléter les données non disponibles, dans la mesure où elles étaient comparables aux séries de l'ONU.

Population en milieu d'année

Sauf indication contraire, les chiffres indiqués se rapportent à la population de fait. La population urbaine est le nombre des personnes vivant dans les zones considérées comme urbaines selon les définitions de ce concept dans chaque pays. Etant donné que cette définition varie quelque peu d'un pays à un autre, la prudence s'impose lorsqu'on procède à des comparaisons entre pays.

Taux de croissance annuel moyen

Le nombre de personnes ajouté (ou soustrait) à une population en un an en raison de l'accroissement naturel et la migration nette exprimée en pourcentage de la population au début de la période de référence. La croissance annuelle moyenne de la population est le taux de croissance exponentielle de la population en milieu d'année de l'année t-1 à t, exprimée en pourcentage.

Taux brut de natalité

Nombre de naissances sur une période donnée divisée par la population totale moyenne au cours de cette période. Elle est exprimée en nombre de naissances pour 1 000 habitants.

Taux brut de mortalité

Nombre de décès sur une période donnée divisée par la population totale moyenne au cours de cette période. Elle est exprimée en nombre de décès pour 1 000 habitants.

Groupes d'âges

Trois groupes d'âge sont utilisés dans le but de mettre en lumière la proportion du groupe d'âge actif par rapport aux dépendants. La population âgée de 15-64 ans est le nombre de personnes qui peuvent potentiellement être économiquement actives, et exclut les enfants.

Population économiquement active

La population active comprend toutes les personnes qui, durant une période de référence spécifiée, sont considérées comme pourvues d'un emploi ou au chômage, c'est-à-dire qui constituent la main-d'œuvre.

Espérance de vie, taux bruts de natalité et de mortalité

L'espérance de vie à la naissance indique le nombre moyen d'années que vivrait un nouveau-né si les tendances de la mortalité observées pour l'ensemble de la population au moment de sa naissance restaient inchangées tout au long de sa vie. Les taux bruts de natalité et de mortalité représentent respectivement le nombre annuel moyen de naissances et de décès pour 1 000 habitants. La mortalité est le fait d'une disparition permanente de toute évidence de vie, à tout moment, après que la naissance ait eu lieu. Cette définition exclut les morts nés.

Taux net de reproduction

Le taux net de reproduction est le nombre moyen de filles qui seraient nés d'une femme si elle a traversé sa vie conformément à la fécondité spécifique par âge et au taux de mortalité pour une année donnée. Ce taux est similaire au taux brut de reproduction, mais prend en compte le fait que certaines femmes mourront avant d'avoir terminé leurs années de procréation

Indice synthétique de fécondité

L'indice synthétique de fécondité est le nombre moyen de naissances qu'une femme soumise à un ensemble de fécondités spécifiques par âge, pourrait avoir au cours de sa période de procréation.

Santé

Pourcentage de mères ayant reçu au moins un soin prénatal

La couverture des soins prénatals (au moins une visite) est le pourcentage de femmes de 15-49 ans, avec une naissance vivante dans une période de temps donnée, qui a reçu des soins prénatals dispensés par un personnel de santé qualifié au moins une fois pendant leur grossesse.

Pourcentage d'accouchements assistés par du personnel de santé qualifié

Pourcentage d'accouchements assistés par un personnel de santé qualifié (médecins, infirmiers ou sages-femmes) est le pourcentage d'accouchements assistés par du personnel de santé qualifié dans la pratique des soins obstétricaux vitaux (y compris les contrôles nécessaires, les soins et les conseils aux femmes pendant la grossesse, le travail et le période post partum), des accouchements; et des soins aux nouveau-nés. Les accoucheuses traditionnelles, même si elles reçoivent une formation de courte durée, ne sont pas incluses.

Naissances enregistrées (%)

C'est le pourcentage des naissances enregistrées au cours d'une période de temps spécifiée pour un pays ou une région désignée.

Décès enregistrés (%)

C'est le pourcentage des décès enregistrés pendant une période de temps spécifiée pour un pays.

Les médecins (pour 10 000 habitants)

Se réfèrent au nombre de médecins, généralistes et spécialistes (y compris les travailleurs indépendants) qui pratiquent activement la médecine dans les établissements publics ou privés. Les données devraient exclure les dentistes, les stomatologues, les médecins qualifiés qui travaillent à l'étranger, ou qui occupent des postes dans l'administration, dans l'industrie ou dans recherche. Les données devraient inclure des médecins étrangers autorisés à exercer et à pratiquer activement la médecine dans le pays. Les données doivent être calculées pour représenter l'équivalent du temps plein de travail.

Les infirmières (pour 10 000 habitants)

Nombre total d'infirmières certifiées ou enregistrés et qui exercent activement dans les hôpitaux publics et privés, les cliniques et autres établissements de santé, y compris les travailleurs indépendants. Les infirmières auxiliaires et sages-femmes devraient être incluses. Les données devraient exclure les infirmières qui travaillent à l'étranger, qui travaillent dans des postes administratifs, la recherche et dans l'industrie.

Les chiffres pour les médecins et les infirmières se rapportent à ceux enregistrés dans les bureaux du gouvernement.

Les lits d'hôpitaux - total (pour 10 000 habitants)

Le nombre de lits d'hôpitaux se calcule pour les hôpitaux publics et privés.

Pourcentage d'enfants a fourni les vaccins (BCG, DTC3, polio, rougeole)
La vaccination des enfants mesure le pourcentage des enfants âgés de 12 à 23 mois qui ont reçu certains vaccins spécifiques avant 12 mois ou à tout moment avant. Un enfant est considéré suffisamment immunisé contre :

- la diphtérie, la coqueluche et le tétanos (DCT) après avoir reçu trois doses de vaccin ;
- la rougeole après avoir reçu une dose de vaccin ;
- la tuberculose après avoir reçu le Bacille Calmette-Guérin (BCG) ;
- la poliomyélite après la troisième dose du vaccin de la polio.

Accès à l'eau potable
Elle est mesurée par le nombre de personnes qui ont un moyen raisonnable d'obtenir une quantité suffisante d'eau potable, exprimée en pourcentage de la population totale.

Education
Les sources des données sur l'éducation présentées dans cette publication sont les publications nationales et l'Annuaire statistique de l'UNESCO. Les données présentées portent en général sur les écoles de l'Etat (publiques) et les écoles indépendantes (privées). Les années indiquées se rapportent au commencement de l'année scolaire. Sont exclus la formation des adultes, les stages d'apprentissage et les cours par correspondance. Compte tenu des différences des systèmes scolaires, la comparaison des données présentées est sujette à caution.

Elèves inscrits selon le degré
La scolarisation dans le premier degré est le nombre d'enfants de tous âges inscrits à l'école primaire. La scolarisation dans le second degré est le nombre d'élèves de tous âges inscrits dans le cycle d'enseignement secondaire.

Taux d'analphabétisme des adultes
C'est le pourcentage des adultes âgés de plus de 15 ans qui ne savent ni lire ni écrire.

Ratio élèves-enseignants
Le rapport élève-maître est le nombre moyen d'élèves (étudiants) par enseignant dans un degré d'enseignement déterminé dans une année scolaire donnée.

Indice de Parité de Genre
Le taux Brut d'Inscription des Filles relative à celui des Garçons, prend la valeur un quand il y a parité entre les genres. L'indice de parité entre les genres (GPI) mesure les progrès effectués dans la réalisation de la parité de genre dans la participation à l'éducation et/ou aux opportunités d'apprentissage offertes aux femmes par rapport à celles offertes aux hommes. Il s'agit d'une comparaison entre des valeurs attribuées aux femmes et aux hommes pour un indicateur donné au cours d'une année donnée. Il reflète aussi le niveau d'épanouissement des femmes dans la société. Cet indicateur doit être désagrégé par niveau d'enseignement (enseignement pré-primaire, primaire et secondaire).

II. COMPTES NATIONAUX
Cette section présente des informations sur la comptabilité nationale. Les données de la comptabilité nationale fournissent des indications essentielles sur la performance économique des pays africains en termes de croissance et de structure de production, d'investissement et d'épargne. Les données de la comptabilité nationale proviennent de diverses sources nationales et complétées par d'autres sources internationales telles que l'Annuaire de Comptabilité nationale de l'ONU et les estimations de la BAD et du Centre africain pour la statistique de la CEA. Les chiffres officiels ont été ajustés en fonction du Système de Comptabilité Nationale (SCN) quand cela s'est avéré nécessaire. De nombreux pays continuent d'élaborer leurs

comptes nationaux à partir du SCN 1968. Mais de plus en plus de pays sont en train de migrer vers le SCN 1993 ou même 2008. Certains pays continuent encore d'utiliser les concepts provenant des anciennes recommandations du SCN incluant la comptabilisation des agrégats économiques aux coûts des facteurs.

Produit intérieur brut (PIB)

Le produit intérieur brut est une mesure globale de la production qui est égale à la somme des valeurs ajoutées brutes de toutes les unités institutionnelles résidentes engagées dans le processus de production (plus les taxes indirects/impôt sur les produit et moins les subventions).

Le PIB par branche d'activité (par secteur)

Le PIB par secteur donne la valeur ajoutée pour les grandes catégories de la classification CITC. La valeur ajoutée est évaluée aux prix de base ou aux coûts des facteurs ou encore au prix du producteur selon la pratique en vigueur du pays. Les données nominales sur les valeurs ajoutées sont fournies aux prix courants et les taux de croissance annuels pour chaque catégorie sont calculés à partir des données à prix constants.

Emplois du PIB

La consommation finale des administrations publiques

La consommation finale des administrations publiques comprend toutes les dépenses courantes consacrées à l'achat de biens et de services par les administrations de tous les niveaux, ainsi que les dépenses en capital au titre de la défense et de la sécurité nationale.

La consommation finale privée

La consommation finale privée représente la consommation finale des ménages et des institutions à but non lucratif. Elle ne comprend pas les achats de logement mais elle inclut le loyer imputé des logements occupés par leur propriétaire. Elle comprend aussi tout écart statistique.

La formation brute de capital

La formation brute de capital comprend les dépenses consacrées à l'accroissement du capital fixe de l'économie, majorées des variations nettes du niveau des stocks.

Les exportations et importations de biens et services

Les exportations et importations de biens et services représentent la valeur des biens et services non facteurs fournis au reste du monde ou reçus de celui-ci. La valeur des revenus et des paiements des services facteurs comme le produit des placements, les intérêts et le revenu du travail, en est exclue. Les données sont généralement estimées sur la base des statistiques du commerce extérieur et ne sont pas directement comparables à celles de la balance des paiements.

III. INFLATION

L'inflation est mesurée par la variation moyenne annuelle de l'indice des prix à la consommation (IPC). L'IPC montre le coût d'acquisition par un consommateur moyen d'un panier de biens et services. Les coefficients de pondération pour le calcul des indices sont obtenus à partir d'enquêtes sur les dépenses des ménages. Les données de l'IPC proviennent des systèmes statistiques nationaux, et essentiellement des Instituts nationaux de statistique ou des Banques centrales.

IV. PRODUCTION AGRICOLE

Production agricole

Les données sur les principales productions agricoles sont obtenues via les instituts nationaux de statistiques des pays suivants : Burkina Faso, Burundi, Cameroun, Congo, Côte d'Ivoire, République démocratique du Congo, Gabon, Gambie, Guinée-Bissau, Kenya, Lesotho, Madagascar, Malawi, Mali, Mauritanie, île Maurice, Maroc, Mozambique, Nigeria, Sénégal, Soudan, Swaziland, Zambie, et Zimbabwe. Pour les autres pays les données sont tirées de la base de données en ligne de l'Organisation pour l'Alimentation et l'Agriculture (FAO). Pour ces pays, les cinq principales productions agricoles sont obtenues en calculant la production annuelle moyenne de chaque produit du pays (seules les années où le produit est récolté sont retenues) et en rangeant ces productions par ordre décroissant.

Indices de la production agricole et alimentaire

Les différents indices de la production agricole illustrent le niveau du volume global de production agricole chaque année, relativement à la période de base 2004-2006. Ces indices sont obtenus à partir de la base de données en ligne de la FAO et calculés en utilisant la formule de Laspeyres somme pondérée par les prix des productions des différents produits hors semences et graines d'alimentation. Le prix utilisé pour pondérer la quantité de chaque produit est le prix moyen au cours des années de référence

V. PRODUCTION MINIERE

Les sources des données présentées sont soit : les instituts nationaux de statistiques, pour les pays auxquels le questionnaire conjoint BAD - CUA - CEA a été envoyé, soit : la base des données sur les produits industriels des Nations Unies, accessible via UNDATA (à http://data.un.org/) ou l'annuaire des produits industriels des Nations Unies. Pour certains minerais, les données ont également été obtenues à partir de l'enquête géologique britannique et sur le site internet de l'enquête géologique des Etats-Unis.

Production minière

Pour les descriptions détaillées des produits miniers inclus dans cette publication, le lecteur peut se référer à la Classification Centrale des Produits (CCP), Papiers statistiques, Séries M, N077, Ver 1.1 (Publication des Nations Unies, Ventes N0. E.03. XVII.3). Il était difficile d'identifier les trois principaux produits puisque la période de référence était très variable et courte pour plusieurs produits et aussi les produits varient d'un pays à un autre. Dans un premier temps, nous avons obtenu les valeurs des exportations des produits miniers pour les années 2005 à 2013. Nous avons ensuite agrégé sur la période où le produit est disponible avant de calculer la moyenne pour pouvoir décider quel produit à inclure dans la publication. Finalement, nous avons décidé de choisir les produits stratégiques (tels que le pétrole, le gaz et le diamant) lorsque le pays continue de les produire.

VI. ENERGIE

Les sources des données publiées proviennent de l'Annuaire statistique sur l'énergie des Nations Unies et de la base de données sur l'énergie accessible à travers UNDATA (http://data.un.org) et aussi de la Commission africaine sur l'Energie (AFREC).

Production d'électricité

Les chiffres publiés pour la production sont relatifs à la production brute d'électricité, qui inclut la consommation des stations auxiliaires et toutes pertes dans la transformation et aussi l'électricité produite par les stations de pompage sans déduction de l'énergie consommée par ces mêmes pompes. La production d'électricité comprend, d'une part, les installations publiques, dont le but primaire est la génération et la transmission de l'énergie électrique pour la consommation publique, et d'autre part, les producteurs privés qui produisent l'énergie électrique, totalement ou en partie, pour leur propre consommation.

VII. TOURISME ET INFRASTRUCTURE

Tourisme

Les données sur le tourisme ont été principalement collectées auprès de sources nationales ; quand les sources nationales ne sont pas disponibles, les données sont tirées des bases des données en ligne UNWTO et Tourism Decision Metrics (TDM) de Tourism Economics.

Les indicateurs publiés sont le nombre d'arrivées dans, le nombre de chambres d'hôtel, le nombre de nuitées, les recettes touristiques, la contribution totale du tourisme au PIB et la contribution totale du tourisme à l'emploi. Le nombre de touristes d'un pays se rapporte, sauf indication contraire, à toutes les personnes contrôlées à la frontière et voyageant pour le plaisir, la santé, les affaires, les réunions ou les études, s'arrêtant dans le pays pour vingt-quatre heures ou plus. Les données excluent les immigrés et résidants frontaliers.

Infrastructure

Routes pavées (% du total)

Les routes pavées sont celles dont la surface est construite avec de la pierre concassée (macadam) et de liant hydrocarboné ou d'agents bitumineux, du béton ou de pavés. Le dénominateur est l'ensemble des routes du pays, mesurées en longueur.

Réseaux total (Railways-km)

Le total des lignes ferroviaires est la longueur de l'itinéraire disponible pour le service de train de chemin de fer, quelque soit le nombre de pistes parallèles.

Lignes téléphoniques principales

Les lignes téléphoniques sont les lignes téléphoniques fixes qui relient l'équipement terminal d'un abonné au réseau public commuté téléphonique et qui ont un port sur un central téléphonique. Les réseaux de canaux de service numérique intégrés et les abonnés fixes sans fil sont inclus.

Les abonnés au réseau cellulaire mobile

Les abonnements téléphoniques mobiles sont les abonnements à un service de téléphonie public mobile utilisant la technologie cellulaire, qui fournissent un accès au réseau téléphonique public commuté. Les abonnés post-payés et prépayés sont inclus.

VIII. FINANCES ET STATISTIQUES MONETAIRES

Statistiques monétaires

Les données de cette section proviennent essentiellement des banques centrales africaines et de la base de données sur les Statistiques financières internationales du FMI.

Monnaie (M1)

La masse monétaire au sens strict (M1) comprend les dépôts transférables et la circulation fiduciaire hors banques.

Quasi-monnaie

La quasi-monnaie englobe les dépôts à terme, les dépôts d'épargne et les dépôts en devises.

Avoirs extérieurs nets

Les avoirs extérieurs nets sont égaux à la somme des avoirs extérieurs moins la somme des engagements extérieurs des autorités monétaires et des banques créatrices de monnaie.

Crédits intérieurs

Le crédit intérieur est égal à la somme des créances nettes sur l'Etat, sur les entreprises publiques et le secteur privé. Le crédit au secteur privé est présenté séparément mais en tant que sous-groupe du crédit intérieur.

Réserves internationales

Les réserves internationales comprennent les avoirs du pays en or monétaire, droits de tirage spéciaux

(DTS) et devises, ainsi que ses réserves auprès du Fonds monétaire international (FMI).

Taux de change
Les taux de change, exprimés en unité de monnaie nationale par rapport au dollar EU, sont indiqués comme des taux de fin de période et des moyennes sur la période des taux de change du marché et des taux officiels. Le taux du marché est défini comme le taux déterminé grosso modo par les forces du marché ; et le taux officiel est celui fixé par les autorités.

Finances publiques
Les données de cette section sont principalement collectées par les autorités nationales, telles que les instituts nationaux de statistiques, les ministères des finances et les banques centrales ; quand les sources nationales ne sont pas disponibles, les données des publications du FMI (rapports des pays) sont employées.

Pour le Botswana, l'Égypte, l'Éthiopie, le Kenya, le Malawi, les îles Maurice, la Namibie, l'Afrique du Sud et le Swaziland, les données ont été compilées selon l'année fiscale, comme données annuelles. Ainsi, les années 2006 à 2014 représentent bien l'année civile selon la période fiscale de chaque pays.

Recettes totales et dons
Les recettes publiques incluent toutes les recettes non remboursables de l'Etat, avec ou sans contrepartie, provenant d'autres administrations (locales ou étrangères) et des institutions internationales.

Recettes fiscales
Les recettes fiscales regroupent les impôts, taxes, droits et autres transferts obligatoires autres que les cotisations de sécurité sociale. Elles sont la principale source de revenu de la plupart des administrations publiques et constituent des transferts obligatoires vers ce secteur.

Recettes non fiscales
Elles regroupent les impôts sur les revenus de la propriété, les droits et taxes non industrielles et les ventes de biens existants, les amendes, les pénalités, les confiscations, les indemnisations accordées par un tribunal, et les transferts volontaires autres que les dons.

Dons
Les dons sont des transferts non obligatoires courants ou en capital qu'une administration publique peut recevoir d'une autre administration publique ou d'une organisation internationale.

Dépenses et prêts nets
Ils comprennent tous les paiements non remboursables effectués par l'Administration publique, avec ou sans contrepartie, y compris les dépenses courantes et en capital, les transactions au titre de la dette publique et les participations au capital pour des raisons de politique publique.

Dépenses courantes
Elles comprennent tous les paiements non remboursables effectués par l'Administration publique, avec ou sans contrepartie, autres que les dépenses en capital ou les subventions.

Dépenses en capital
Il s'agit des dépenses pour l'acquisition d'immobilisations, des stocks, des terrains ou des actifs incorporels ainsi que les transferts sans contrepartie dans le but de permettre au bénéficiaire d'acquérir ces actifs. Pour être classé comme un capital, un bien acquis doit dépasser une valeur minimale et être destiné à plus d'un an d'utilisation dans le processus de production.

Prêts nets
Les prêts nets (total des prêts moins les remboursements) comprennent les transactions de l'Etat relatives aux créances sur des tiers obtenues à des fins de politique publique plutôt que d'en tirer

profit. Ce chiffre porte à la fois sur les paiements et les recettes.

Déficit fiscal

L'excédent/déficit global des finances publiques est la différence entre, d'une part, les recettes courantes, les recettes en capital et les dons publics reçus et, d'autre part, les dépenses totales et les prêts moins les remboursements.

Balance des paiements

La balance des paiements est un état statistique où sont résumées, pour une période donnée, les transactions économiques d'une économie avec le reste du monde. Les transactions, pour la plupart entre résidents et non-résidents, sont celles qui portent sur les biens, services et revenus; celles qui font naître des créances financières sur le reste du monde ou des engagements financiers envers celui-ci et celles qui sont considérées comme des transferts, pour lesquels il y a lieu de passer des contre-écritures de manière à solder les transactions à sens unique. Les données de cette section proviennent des Banques centrales africaines. Lorsque ces données ne sont pas disponibles ou de mauvaise qualité, les Rapports pays du FMI ont été utilisés en remplacement. Les données provenant de sources internationales portent sur les pays suivants : Guinée Equatorial, Libéria, Lésotho, Sierra Leone et Libye.

Balance commerciale

Elle est égale à la différence entre les exportations et les importations de biens, évalués sur la base f.à.b (franco à bord) c'est-à-dire à la frontière du pays exportateur. Le poste des biens englobe les marchandises générales, les biens importés ou exportés pour subir une transformation, la valeur des réparations de biens, les biens achetés dans les ports par les transporteurs non-résidents, et l'or non monétaire.

Balance des services

Les services recouvrent les transports (fret et transport international des passagers), la rubrique des voyages, les services de communication, les services des bâtiments et travaux publics, les services d'assurance, les services d'informatique et d'information; les redevances et droits de licence: les services personnels, culturels et relatifs aux loisirs; les services fournis ou reçus par les administrations publiques. La balance des services est définie par les revenus moins les paiements au titre des services.

Revenus nets

Le poste revenus enregistre deux types de flux : ceux qui relèvent de la rémunération des salariés qui comprend les salaires, traitements et autres prestations ; et ceux qui correspondent au revenu des investissements qui comprend les revenus des investissements directs, des investissements de portefeuille et d'autres investissements.

Rémunération des salariés

Les rémunérations des salariés comprennent les salaires, gages, traitements versés par des employeurs non résidents à leurs salariés résidents et inversement.

Revenus des investissements

Les revenus des investissements couvrent les revenus des investissements directs, les revenus des investissements de portefeuille (participation au capital et titres de créance) ainsi que les autres revenus d'investissement (intérêts provenant d'autres opérations financières).

Transferts courants

Les transferts courants sont tous ceux qui ne font pas intervenir : i) le transfert de propriété d'un actif fixe, ii) le transfert de fonds lié ou subordonné à l'acquisition ou à la cession d'un actif fixe, iii) la remise, sans contrepartie, d'une dette par un créancier.

Transferts officiels nets

Transferts officiels nets comprennent les paiements

de transfert net entre les gouvernements du pays déclarant et le reste du monde.

Envois de fonds des travailleurs
Les envois de fonds des travailleurs comprennent les montants transférés à l'étranger par des travailleurs résidents et vice-versa.

Autres transferts privés
Autres transferts privés comprennent les paiements de transfert net entre personnes privées et des organisations non officielles du pays déclarant et le reste du monde qui ne transportent aucune provision pour les remboursements.

Solde du compte courant
La balance des comptes des opérations courantes est la somme des exportations nettes des biens et services, du revenu net et des transferts courants nets.

Compte de capital
Le compte de capital reprenant les transferts internationaux de capitaux (ex. annulation de dette) et l'acquisition/ la cession d'actifs non produits et non financiers.

Compte financier
Le compte financier reprenant les opérations impliquant un transfert de propriété de parties de l'actif et du passif d'une économie par rapport au reste du monde, parmi lesquelles les achats internationaux de titres tels que des actions ou des obligations.

Erreurs et omissions
Erreurs et omissions nettes sont calculées de façon résiduelle comme la différence entre le total des recettes et des dépenses (courantes et en capital ainsi que le compte financier).

Balance générale
La balance des paiements est un registre des transactions internationales d'un pays avec le reste du monde. Les opérations sont organisées dans deux comptes différents, le compte courant et le compte capital et financier.

Dette extérieure et flux financiers

Les données de cette section proviennent essentiellement des sources internationales suivantes: la base de données sur les «Perspectives de l'économie mondiale » du FMI, les bases de données en ligne de l'OCDE et de la CNUCED. Cependant, quelques pays ont fourni leurs données pour cette édition de l'annuaire. L'objectif de l'annuaire est d'inclure les données fournies par les pays eux-mêmes dans la mesure du possible pourvu que la qualité des données le permette. Les données nationales proviennent des pays suivants : Bénin, Burkina Faso, Cameroun, Guinée Equatoriale, Lésotho et Niger.

Dette extérieure totale
La dette extérieure totale est le montant dû mais non remboursé, à un moment donné, par les résidents d'un pays à des non-résidents, et qui se sont engagés à rembourser le principal, avec ou sans intérêt, ou à payer les intérêts avec ou sans le principal. Elle est la somme de la dette publique, de la dette garantie publique, de la dette privée non garantie à long terme, du recours au crédit du FMI et de la dette à court terme.

Service de la dette extérieure
Le service total de la dette (extérieure) est la somme des remboursements du principal et des paiements des intérêts. Il s'agit du service de la dette à court terme et de la dette à long terme (dette publique, dette privée à garantie publique et dette non garantie privée) et du recours au crédit du FMI.

Valeur actuelle de la dette extérieure
La valeur actualisée de la dette est la somme de la dette extérieure à court terme plus la valeur actualisée du total des paiements du service de la dette

dus sur la dette extérieure à long terme publique et garantie par l'État et la dette extérieure à long terme privée non garantie au cours de la vie des prêts existants.

Dette publique intérieure
La dette publique intérieure : détenue par les agents économiques résidents de l'État émetteur et libellée en monnaie nationale.

Investissements directs étrangers
L'investissement direct étranger représente l'investissement effectué pour acquérir ou accroître une participation durable au capital d'une entreprise (généralement 10 pourcent du pouvoir de vote) opérant dans un pays autre que celui de l'investisseur. C'est la somme du capital social, du réinvestissement des bénéfices et d'autres capitaux à court et à long termes comme il est indiqué dans la section traitant de la balance des paiements

Aide publique au développement
L'APD représente les dons et les prêts accordés à des conditions financières privilégiées (c'est-à-dire avec un élément de libéralité d'au moins 25 pour cent) au secteur public dans le but principal de promouvoir le développement économique et le bien-être social. Il s'agit des décaissements nets d'APD.

IX. COMMERCE EXTERIEUR

Les données pour cette section proviennent majoritairement des sources nationales. C'est le cas des pays suivants : Algérie, Bénin, Burkina Faso, Burundi, Cameroun, Côte d'Ivoire, Égypte, Éthiopie, Gambie, Guinée Bissau, Kenya, Malawi, Mali, Maroc, Mozambique, Namibie, Niger, Nigeria, Rwanda, Soudan, Swaziland, Tanzanie, Togo, Zambie et Zimbabwé. Dans le cas où des données nationales n'ont pu être trouvées, nous avons eu recours à la base de données en ligne de la CNUCED. Les noms des principaux produits d'exportation et d'importation ont été choisis par les pays eux-mêmes. Pour les données obtenues de la CNUCED la nomenclature du système harmonisé (rev1) a été employée pour déterminer la liste des produits principaux d'exportations et d'importation. Sauf indication contraire, les statistiques d'importation sont valorisées sur la base CAF tandis que les exportations sont valorisées FOB.

Remittances to Africa: Dynamics, opportunities and challenges

2015

For several years, the African Bank of Development (AfDB), in collaboration with the African Union Commission and the Economic Commission for Africa, has raised the issue of Domestic Resource Mobilization, particularly in the 2010 edition of its *African Economic Outlook (AEO)*, which focused on this theme in a keynote article. The aim was to sensitize African decision-makers and public authorities on the need for better channeling of domestic saving, to optimize national resources, both public and private, and to focus allocations to economically and socially productive investments. In raising the profile of Domestic Resource Mobilization as a developmental issue, the AfDB Group and its partners were motivated in particular by the major financial challenges confronting the continent in order to achieve the Millennium Development Goals (MDGs).

The debate about Domestic Resource Mobilization has tended to focus on the efficiency and the optimization of tax resources and on ways of channeling domestic saving held by the banking and financial system towards productive investment. On occasion, the discussions extended to exploring other possible forms and mechanisms of financial flows to foster sustainable and inclusive development and ensure Africa's structural transformation. Accordingly, flows from migrants' remittances can constitute an invaluable support mechanism for Africa in order to loosen its reliance on foreign assistance, reduce levels of external debt, improve the balance of payments, and build resilience and competitiveness into national economies.

In this context, the analysis presented here focuses on the importance of remittance flows for development in Africa. As a first step, the study presents a comprehensive picture of the dynamics of these kinds of flows, recent trends, and characteristics. As a second step, this study aims to synthesize the impact of these flows from a number of different economic and social viewpoints. The analysis examines the positive and negative externalities which these financial flows give rise to; it also looks at ways to improve the mobilization of these flows to accelerate sustainable, inclusive, and green development across the continent.

Preliminary aspects

Before analyzing the various issues surrounding remittance flows (sometimes termed "workers' remittances"), we need to look more deeply at the definition of this economic concept. The need to revisit this concept was brought to the fore in the sixth edition of the *Balance of Payments Manual* prepared by the IMF. In the past it was common for these types of remittance to be referred to as "migrant remittances" or "migrant workers' transfers". However, the new definition retained since 2005 is broader, simpler, and more closely aligned to the classification of such data in many economies. Now personal transfers are defined independently of the source of revenue of the households, and this extends to the sending of funds, the relation between these households, and the migrants' objectives leading to the transfers. Thus, even if it is recognized that the personal transfers come mainly from a migrant worker who sends part of their savings back to their country of origin, the personal transfers – according to the new approach set out in the Manual – are not limited solely to migrants' transfers.

Although the themes of migration and remittances are not new topics, they still generate a growing interest within the international community, in academia and research institutes, as well as in destination countries and countries of origin. In many African countries, there is a general consensus that the region needs to capitalize on these human and financial resources in order to address the vast challenges posed by the development agenda. Such challenges include environmental constraints and the problem of climate change, food insecurity, poor access to health services, infrastructural deficits, high levels of poverty and social inequality. In some destination countries in Europe, however, which are still feeling the effects of austerity measures in the wake of the global financial crisis, and which are struggling to reduce massive sovereign debt, capital outflows of this type are not always welcomed.

The controversy surrounding this subject may be explained in more than one way. This becomes evident if one looks at the high volume of the transfers, and their expected increase in the years to come. Moreover, on the basis of official projections, the flow of remittances bound for Africa will double in 2015 compared to their level in 2005, to reach, according to World Bank, around US$ 64 billion. To appreciate fully what this means for the continent, one needs to grasp that this sum is equivalent to half of the Gross Domestic Product (GDP) of Angola, twice the national revenue of Côte d'Ivoire or Tanzania, and four times the GDP of Botswana or Equatorial Guinea.

Concept of Remittances in the balance of payments

Remittances represent household income from foreign economies arising mainly from the temporary or permanent movement of people to those economies. In fact, the balance of payments framework defines remittances in a somewhat broader sense because it does not tie remittances to the concepts of migration, employment, or family relationships.

Remittances are mainly derived from two items in the balance of payments framework: income earned by workers in economies where they are not resident (or from nonresident employers) and transfers from residents of one economy to residents of another. The two items in the balance of payments framework that principally refer to remittances are "compensation of employees" and "personal transfers" and both of these standard components are recorded in the current account.

Compensation of employees
"Compensation of employees" refers to the income of border, seasonal, and other short-term workers who are employed in an economy where they are not resident, as well as to the income of residents employed by nonresident entities. It represents remuneration paid in return for the labor input to the production process contributed by an individual within an employer-employee relationship.

Personal transfers
Personal transfers consist of all current transfers in cash or in kind made or received by resident households to or from nonresident households. Personal transfers thus include all current transfers between resident and nonresident individuals. Therefore, personal transfers are a subset of current transfers and cover all current transfers between individuals.

"Personal transfers" replaces an item called "workers' remittances" in the standard presentation of the fifth edition of the IMF's Balance of Payments Manual. According to that definition, workers' remittances are current transfers by migrants who are employed in new economies and considered residents there.

The impact of the high volume of remittances, both at macroeconomic and microeconomic levels, is generally recognized today. It is often cited in support of various initiatives advocating for a better mobilization of such resources. Moreover, the high volume of the transfers lends weight to the argument calling for more evidence-based knowledge, to assist African governments to formulate practical policy options and optimize the use of such flows for development.

The aspects examined in this study, both on the migratory flux and on remittance flows, are based on official statistics produced by international organizations, but where data are not yet available, recourse is made to their expert projections. However, this exploratory analysis cannot be considered to be exhaustive, insofar as a portion of the migratory flux or flows escape statistical recording due to their informal nature; or are misrepresented by the current tools of statistical observation.

Thus, a considerable share of remittance flows is transmitted through non-official means or channels. This constitutes a major challenge for the public authorities in order to integrate it into the formal channels and official records. These non-official flows, according to the World Bank, represent 35–75% of the amounts dispatched officially in the developing countries. In fact, African countries top the rankings for unofficial remittance inflows, while East Asian countries, on the other hand, rank much lower down the scale for this form of transmission. In general, the formal sector – whose network includes big money transfer operators like Western Union or MoneyGram as well as local commercial banks – is much more highly developed in Latin America and in the Asian countries than in the African continent.

The analysis of this category of unofficial transfers opens up the discussion to a series of related issues which require special attention, which this study will try to clarify. In particular, we examine the quality of the official statistics on the migratory flux and the transmission of funds; the need to reinforce countries' capacities in these fields; the impact of remittances for the recipient economies; the behavior of the beneficiary households; financial channels supporting these transfers; the channeling of flows towards productive investments and the reduction of poverty; the management of some negative externalities; and the selection of measures or policies to promote a greater involvement of the African Diaspora in the development dynamic or process.

The key role of migratory flows

The stock of African migrants settling out of their country of origin recorded a strong growth during the decade 2000-2010, compared to the two previous decades.

During the first decade of the current century, the number of migrants increased by 56.2%, rising from 19.594 million in 2000 to 30.603 million in 2010. That is equivalent to an annual growth rate of 4.6% (compared to an increase of 1.9% per annum over the period 1980-2000). Conflicts and political instability in some countries account in large part for this rise.

This trend was also due to the *high population growth in the continent during the 1980s (3.1% per annum, against 2.6% and 2.5% respectively in the 1990s and decade 2000–2010)*. The generation born during the 1980s would have reached 20 to 30 years of age by the decade 2000-2010, which is the age when most youth choose to emigrate in search of better job opportunities.

Figure 1: Afican migrants' distribution by destination (in % of total stock)

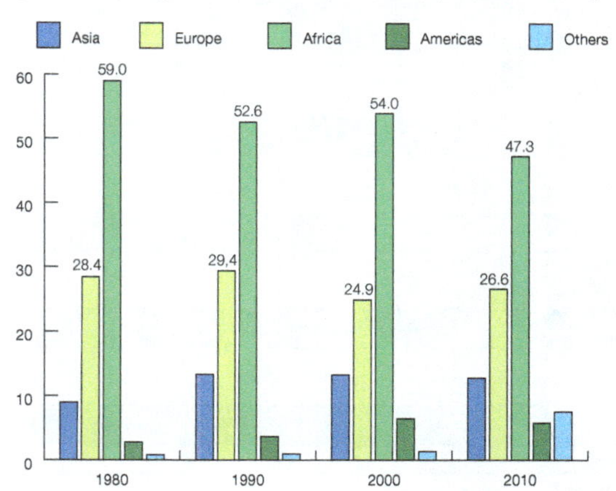

Source: World Bank

Figure 1 examines the movement of African migrants to different destinations over a 30-year period, from 1980 to 2010. Over this period, approximately half of the African migrants moved to another country within the continent, although this proportion has dropped recently in favor of other destinations. The second most popular destination during the 30-year period was Europe, with more migrants settling there in 2010 (26.6%) than in 2000 (24.9%), although those percentages are slightly lower than in 1980 (28.4%) and 1990 (29.4%).

By contrast, the destination of the Americas registered a moderate increase from 1980 to 2000 but dropped slightly in 2010. Other destinations (Australia, New Zealand, Reunion Island, Mayotte, etc.) manifest higher growth, reaching 7.5% in 2010 compared with approximately 1% during the previous decades.

If we next look at the migrants' countries of origin (Figure 2), it is clear that *two major subregions of the continent (West Africa and North Africa) provide the dominant quota of African migrants around the world.* West Africa accounts for 30% of the total migrant stock and North Africa for 29%. During the last three decades, the share of West Africans as a proportion of the total migrants remained stable, while that of North African migrants diminished slightly. The share of East Africa and Southern Africa regions relatively progressed to account respectively for 18.2% and 16.8% of the total stock in 2010.

Figure 2: African migrants' distribution by region of origin (in % of total stockl)

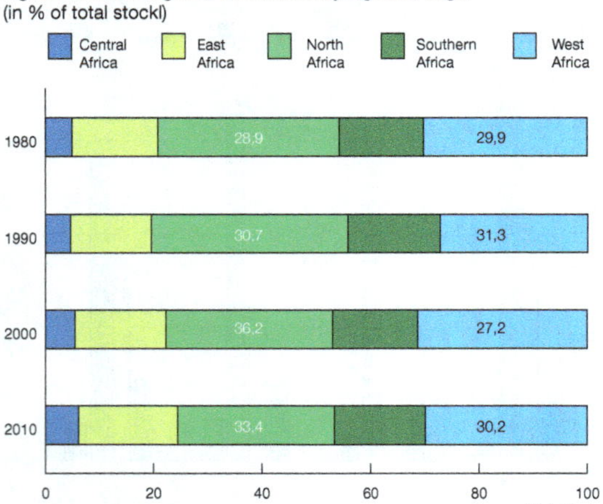

Source: World Bank

On the whole, approximately *3% of the African total population is established out of its country of origin.* This ratio has remained stable for several decades. The main countries feeding the migratory outflow from Africa are Egypt, Morocco, and Burkina Faso. During the last decade 2000-2010, in addition to a strong growth in the number of African migrants, another noteworthy characteristic has emerged. This is the rise of Zimbabwe and Côte d'Ivoire among the top countries of origin. Migrants totaled more than one million for each country in 2010. Political developments that occurred in these countries during this decade largely explain this evolution.

Probably, for various reasons relating to the extent of territories, economic motivations, and especially the historical links (attributed to cultural and social proximity between populations), intra-Africa migration seems to take place within the same subregions of the continent, mainly between the countries of West Africa, those of Southern Africa and East Africa.

On the basis of 2010 data, 40.4% of the African migrants installed in a host country of the continent originate from West Africa and reside in a country of the same subregion. To a lesser extent, the Southern Africa and the East Africa subregions present a similar configuration.

In terms of the gender split, female migration progressed marginally during the last decade to reach 44.3% of total migrant stock (compared to 42.5% in the 1980s and 1990s). This would henceforward shape the remittance flow profile, by supposing that the female migrants are more likely to remain attached to their countries and subregions of origin than migrants of the opposite sex.

Table 1. Intra-Africa migration (in thousands, 2010)

	Region of establishment					
Subregion of origin	**Central Africa**	**East Africa**	**North Africa**	**Southern Africa**	**West Africa**	**Total**
Central Africa	491	597	1	57	68	1 216
East Africa	41	2 923	45	41	0	3 049
North Africa	12	15	516	4	89	636
Southern Africa	11	227	0	2 931	4	3 174
West Africa	377	37	88	48	5 852	6 402
Total	932	3 799	651	3 081	6 015	14 477

Source : World Bank

To some extent, assessments around population movements are related to the immigration policies in the host countries. However, research work has shown that the migratory flux throughout the world is mainly affected by four economic and demographic factors: (i) income disparity between the global areas (or between countries); (ii) the share of youth in the economically active population in the host country and in the country of origin; (iii) the stock of migrants already established in the host countries (emergence of networks); and (iv) the impact of poverty in the country of origin (rather as a constraint factor on the capacity to migrate). And the rise in clandestine immigration in 2014 indicates that such movements of people may well intensify in the years to come. This will be driven by high population growth in Africa and by those seeking to escape from areas of conflict that have recently emerged.

It will be recalled that the data on international migration examined previously do not cover the years after 2010. As a result, the political volatility that occurred in some regions of the continent, in particular in North Africa and West Africa, during the four last years, may have slightly increased the volume of migratory stocks. However, as described above, this should not impact the projections and findings significantly. This point will though be taken into account in our analysis of remittance flows (for which the available data extend beyond the year 2010).

Remittance flows to Africa: an important and stable source of external capital

Since the 1980s, the debate has focused on the importance of remittance flows from destination countries to countries of origin. This has often been seen as a form of compensation for the human resources loss in developing countries due to migratory outflow movements. Furthermore the potential of remittance flows to stimulate economic growth in the countries of origin has also been underscored.

A debate began on a raft of issues related to these migrant transfers, which are now subject to more thorough studies. The topics selected include: the determinants of transfer flows; the circuits used to operate these transfers; and the economic impact of these funds on countries of destination. In recent years, research on these questions has intensified, partly because of the strong growth in the volume of transfers. In fact, this trade in transfers has expanded to become a real "market," sharpening the appetite of certain financial operators and leading to an increase in the research literature surrounding the subject.

Figure 3: Regional share in global remittance flows (in %)

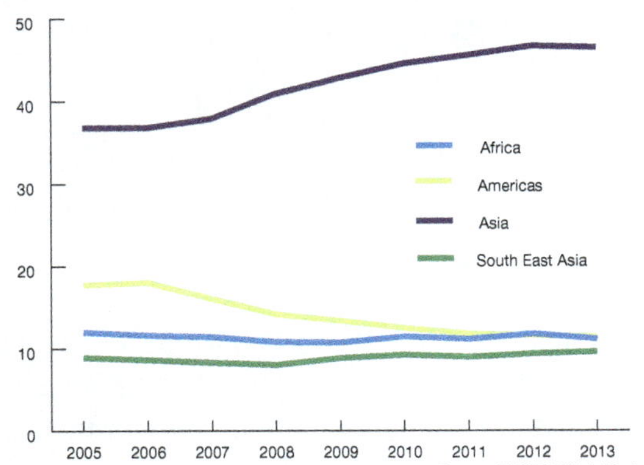

Source: UNCTAD,World Bank

Indeed, the global volume of remittances is projected to reach, according to the last estimates of the World Bank, US$ 586 billion in 2015 compared with approximately US$ 583 billion in the previous year. *According to the same source, the flows intended for the African continent will rise in 2015 to US$ 63.8 billion* against a provisional estimate of US$ 62.7 billion in 2014, *reflecting an increase of about 1.5%,* following an increase of 4% in 2014. The weaker growth rate of remittances in 2015 is attributed to a high base effect (high level recorded in 2014), also due to economic developments in the Euro Zone and particularly to the depreciation of the euro against the US dollar, which will slow remittances growth to main recipient regions in Africa.

During the last decade of 200–2010, the share of remittances to Africa as a proportion of the total global volume remained *relatively stable at around 11.3%.* The share intended for countries of South America lost approximately 6.4 percentage points and fell from 17.7% in 2005 to 11.3% in 2013 (almost on the same level as Africa). In parallel, flows destined for Asia appreciably increased, reaching 46.4% in 2013 compared with 36.8% in 2005, which meant that Asia topped the rankings of the beneficiary areas. That is hardly surprising because Asia is not only the most populated area of the world but also the one with the largest Diaspora.

The volume of remittances to Africa, which has been marked by a steady and sustained growth, as elaborated in the following section, constitutes a major support for many African countries. On the macroeconomic level, remittances have been a welcome source of foreign exchange earnings. This has helped African governments to improve current account balances, fiscal fragility and the stability of external accounts' sovereign creditworthiness. At the microeconomic (household) level, these remittances have provided a welcome supplementary income for certain strata of society which are the most usually the most disadvantaged.

Official remittance flows to the African continent as a whole have *exceeded flows of Foreign Direct Investment (FDI) since 2010 and currently represent twice the amount of Official Development Assistance (ODA).* That said, there is significant variation between different subregions and countries. For example, the ODA to Sub-Saharan Africa remains equivalent to the volume of migrant remittances, whereas the ODA to North Africa accounts for only about 7% of remittance flows.

At the country level, these flows represent remarkable external resources of capital compared with the levels of the national income, the international reserves, or the external debt stock. Over the period 2005–2013, the *average annual volume of remittances to Africa equated to approximately 3.5% of GDP, 8.5% of imports in current prices, almost 12% of external debt, and 11% of gross international reserves.* This indicates the significant value of these flows to African governments.

Figure 4: External financial flows to Africa (in billions of US$)

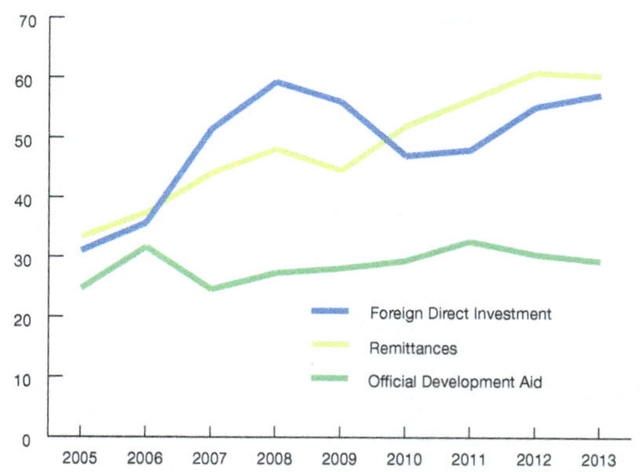

Source: OECD, World Bank

Again, this analysis masks some heterogeneity across African countries, as illustrated by quartile statistics (Table 2). Indeed, while official transfers represent 3.2% of Africa's overall GDP, *this ratio reaches 10.7% in Senegal, 9.8% in Nigeria and 5.7% in Egypt.* Compared to international reserves, or external debt, official transfers represent much higher ratios in many countries, particularly those countries less endowed with natural resources or classified as low-income. This is indeed the case for Lesotho and Uganda, where the ratio transfers of funds compared to gross reserves stand at 53.3% and 32.1% respectively.

The impacts of financial transfers on private consumption, savings and investment, is only one of the facets of their contribution to economic growth and development in migrants' countries of origin. These resources not only increase household incomes but also help to improve the balance of payments (BoP) situation. The transfers thus partly offset the chronic balance of payments deficits in many countries by contributing to foreign exchange earnings. Their impact on this balance is more appreciable than that of other financial flows (such as official and private aid, foreign direct investment or external loans) since their use is not subject to donors' preconditions relating to particular investment areas; they do not require interest repayments, nor do they have to be refunded sometime in the future.

African governments have long recognized the positive effect of workers' monetary transfers on their balance of payments situation, and have taken measures to encourage and increase these flows. However, these measures have to be applied with prudence because, although the transfers positively affect the BoP equilibrium in migrants' countries of origin, they do not always have a positive impact on production, inflation and imports, as will be elaborated later in this study.

Table 2. Remittances ratio to selected economic aggregates (in %, 2005-2013)

	in % of GDP	in % of external debt	in % of imports	in % of reserves
1st quartile (25% of countries post a ratio below ...)	0.8	2.8	2.0	3.2
Median (50% of countries post a ratio below...)	1.5	6.2	4.1	16.4
3rd quartile (75% of countries post a ratio below ...)	5.4	19,6	11.9	39,7
Africa	3.2	11.7	8.5	10,8

Source : AfDB, OECD, UNCTAD

The stability of remittances confers to these flows the *character of a precautionary saving and insurance* device in the case of an adverse shock to a household (e.g. loss of the livelihood of the main breadwinner) or any occurring hazard (natural disaster, flood, civil conflict).

It is important to mention too the use of these resources to fund some public services and utilities. Indeed, at the societal level, remittances constitute *a vital source of income for a large part of the population* and contribute to the financing of its health and education expenditure. In the next section, the discussion turns to how transfers can address inequalities and poverty reduction; this is examined through the lens of recent economic literature.

Recent trends: Sustained dynamic of remittance flows

The analysis of remittances development over the period 2005-2013 reveals that flows to Africa progressed at the annual average rate of 7.7% per annum in current prices (but at the rate of 6.5% per annum if expressed in constant 2010 $). This growth rate, which was slightly less than that of global remittances (8.7% per annum), was much higher than that observed in South America (+4.0%) but on the other hand much less vigorous than that recorded for Asia (approximately 12% per annum), which as previously discussed, benefited from its high stock of migrants.

This strong growth in remittance flows to Africa during 2005–2013 resulted not only from the increase in the number of migrants, but also from a more accurate recording of these financial flows. This was due in large part to an increase in the use of official or formal channels in the operation of transfers. This last evolution is the consequence of recent technological advances which allow rapid transfers of modest amounts (through mobile telephony), a relative reduction in transaction costs, and a stricter control on previously unregulated capital movements at the international level. However, a considerable proportion of remittance flows (estimated at about 40% of the official transfers, according to reliable sources) continues to go through informal channels. This constitutes a major challenge for the public authorities in order to encourage formalization of these transfers so that they can be recorded as part of the official economy.

Figure 5: Remittances to Africa over time (in billions of US$)

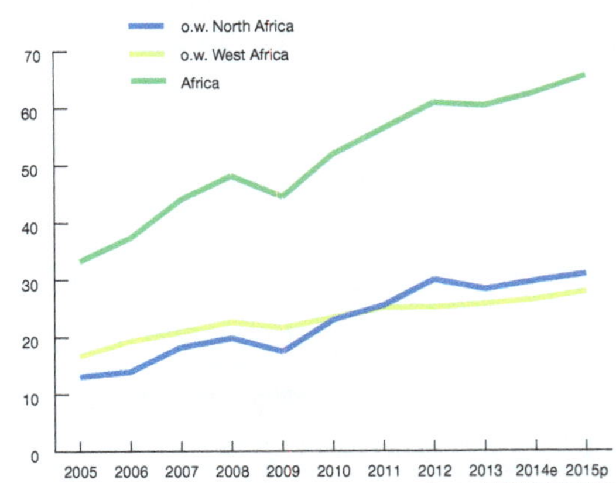

Source: UNCTAD, World Bank

The trajectory of remittances over time closely parallels developments in the global economy, in particular in the destination countries where the migrants have moved. The global financial crisis of 2008-2009 clearly affected the volume of remittances from such countries to Africa, since transfers dropped by 7.4% in 2009, although this was reversed after 2010, by recording an increase of 16.7%.

Polarization of remittances on two subregions

The dynamic of remittances to Africa is largely dictated by the inflows recorded in two subregions of the continent, North Africa and West Africa, which constitute the principal beneficiary subregions. Over the period 2005–2013, flows to North Africa grew by 10.2% per annum, whereas in West Africa the annual increase was posted at 5.6%.

However, political events that occurred in North Africa since 2011 (the so-called "Arab Spring") had a mitigating impact on remittances insofar as this region recorded substantial rises of transfer flows in 2011 and 2012 followed by a fall in 2013. The North African subregion was particularly hard-hit by the drop in transfers to Egypt (-9.1%). However, we have already observed that remittances can often provide an important support for the beneficiary countries during periods of crisis and conflict, and thus serve a countercyclical function.

Figure 6: Remittances to Africa over time (% subregional share, 2010-2013)

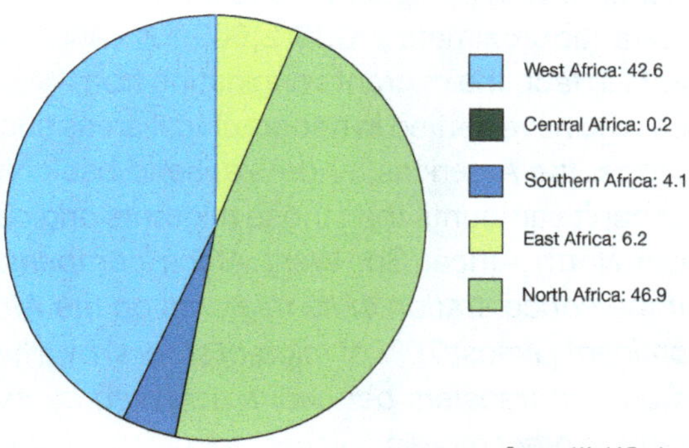

Source: World Bank

The two main beneficiary subregions mentioned above (West Africa and North Africa) jointly represent the vast majority (almost 90% on average over the three last years) of the total flows intended for Africa. Indeed, North Africa draws approximately 47% of the total flow and thus slightly outstrips West Africa, which receives around 42% of the annual amount. The East Africa and the Southern Africa subregions on average receive respectively 6.2% and 4.1% of formally recorded flows to the continent.

The concentration of flows to the two subregions of North and West Africa is characterized by a structural feature.

Figure 7: Remittances by sub-regions (share in %, 2005-2010-2013)

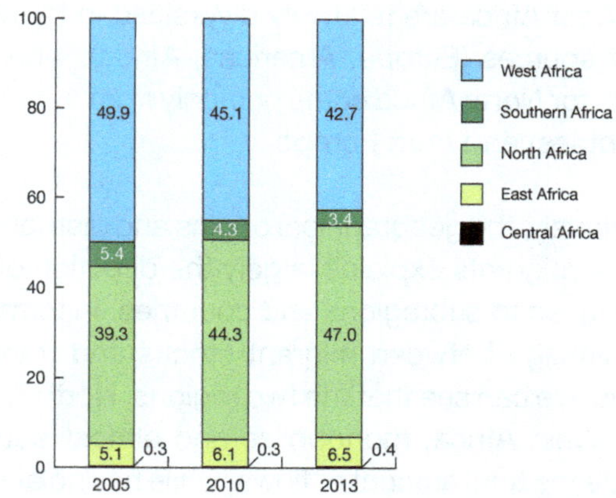

Source: World Bank

Despite the large volume of intra-African migration, the amount of remittances this generates ranks only third in terms of the total volume. On the other hand, Europe, which constitutes the second most popular destination for African migrants (approximately 25% of the migrant stocks), accounts for almost 40% of the total volume of transfers. Asia, which is the third in terms of migratory flows, contributes a little more than 20% of the total annual flow to Africa.

Figure 8: Combined distribution of migrants' origin and remittances by sub-region (%, 2010)

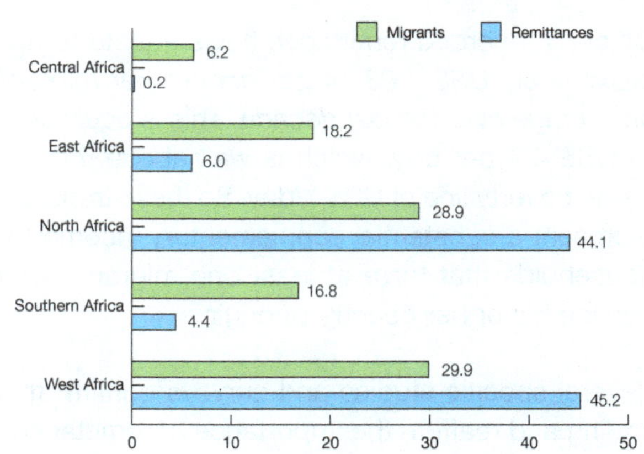

Source: World Bank

Regarding the two subregions where remittance flows are concentrated (North Africa and West Africa), it should be noted that the flows intended for West Africa are relatively diversified in terms of their sources (Europe, Americas, Africa), whereas flows for North Africa come primarily from Asia (Gulf countries) and from Europe.

Obviously, the geographical origins and distribution of the migrants explains largely the direction of remittances to subregions and countries. In terms of the linkage between migrant stocks and transfer flows, we can see that the two regions, North Africa and West Africa, monopolize and almost equally divide the total amount of flows, while having almost the same volume of migrants.

However, compared to West Africa, the concentration of migratory flows originating from North Africa's countries to countries with higher income does not confer to this region any substantial advantage. As an illustration, and in spite of a less significant number of migrants residing in Europe (15.3% compared to 50.4% for North Africa), West Africa succeeds in gathering a remittances volume flow coming from Europe equivalent to that received by North Africa (38% and 39%).

Per capita remittance flows to Africa compared to other global regions and transfer costs

Officially recorded remittance flows equate to approximately *US$ 1,631.4 per annum per migrant on average over the last decade.* This is equivalent to US$ 4.7 per day, which is well above the extreme poverty line of US$ 1/day. So these transfers represent a substantial supplementary income for households that have at least one migrant living outside his or her country of origin.

Several specific studies and surveys confirm this finding and reaffirm the importance of remittances as an instrument to reduce poverty. This is particularly relevant if we take into account the amount of informal flows that bypass the statistical recording; indeed, many serious assessments compute them at 40% of the official figures included in balance of payments of some countries.

However, *the transfers to Africa seem relatively limited compared to the average annual amount of US$ 2,770 per migrant sent back to the Asia region.* This can largely be explained by the fact that most African migrants are concentrated in less economically advanced areas than Asian migrants; they therefore have less disposable incomes to send money home.

The two subregions of North Africa and West Africa post on a whole the same amount of transfers per capita (approximately US$ 2,600 for each subregion). In fact, the migrants originating from West Africa who have settled in geographical areas such as Europe, the Americas, and Asia, send back higher per capita amounts than those migrants originating from North Africa. So, *West Africa compensates for the concentration of its migrants on the African continent (almost 70% of migrant stocks) by a higher amount of transfers per capita achieved by its migrants in other more advanced country destinations.*

In addition to the other factors that could limit the volume of remittances through formal channels (situation of the migrant in the host country, his or her attitude or motivation and level of income), the cost of making these transfers appears to be one of the major hurdles to the expansion of these flows. Although the average costs dropped in recent years at the international level, the charges and commissions deducted for transfers to Sub-Saharan Africa remain among the highest, with charged services accounting on average for 12% of the transferred amount.

Elsewhere, the cost of transfers to the countries of North Africa increased during 2014 to surpass the world average costs. In addition, among the countries of G20, the costs of transfers issued from South Africa are the highest (approximately 19.8%), which is expected to have limited the volume of transfers to other countries in the Southern African subregion, which are closely linked to South Africa in terms of migration patterns.

Figure 9: Transfer costs by recipient region (average %)

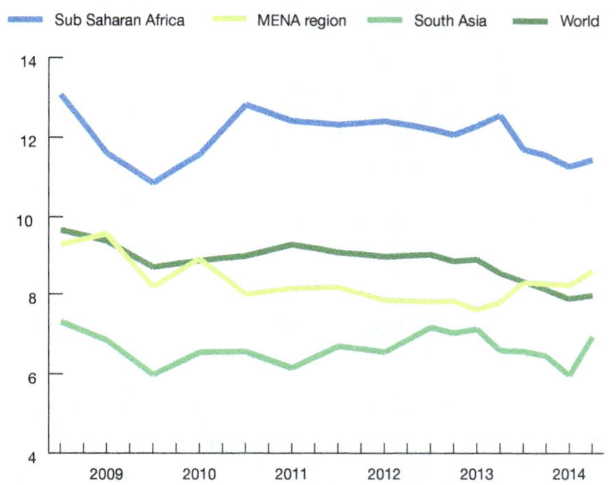

Source: World Bank

High concentration of flows by countries

Analysis of the annual data by country over the last decade highlights the strong inequality and high dispersion of remittances among the African nations. This uneven pattern has become accentuated since the global financial crisis of 2008. The processing of some selected statistical indicators over time (median, first and third quartiles) reflects the skewness of statistical distributions of remittances with a widening spread on the right side since 2005 (see Figure 10).

To illustrate this aspect differently, we can note that five African countries alone accumulated 82% of the total amount of remittances received by the continent during the period 2010–2013. This strong concentration of remittance flows to just five countries can be illustrated in another way by the curve displaying the cumulative percentage of countries

Figure 10: Statistical indicators on annual remittances to Africa (in millions of US$)

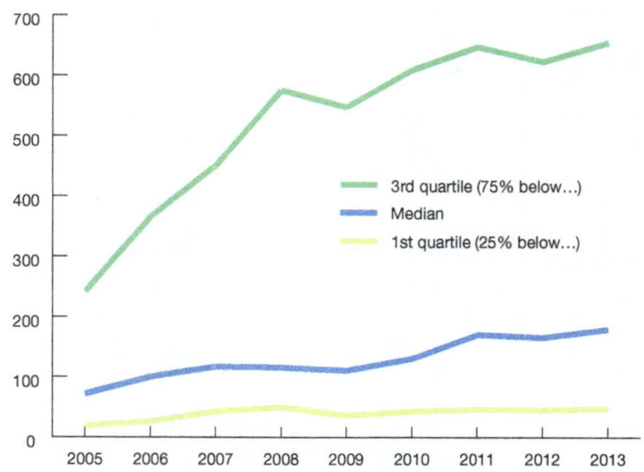

Source: UNCTAD, author calculation

on the horizontal axis and the cumulative corresponding percentage of remittances on the vertical axis, known as the Lorenz curve (Figure 11). In such a diagram, the distance (area) which separates the curve and the first bissectrix measures the degree of inequality in the remittance flow distribution among countries.

Figure 11: Lorenz curve of annual remittances in African countries (2010-2013)

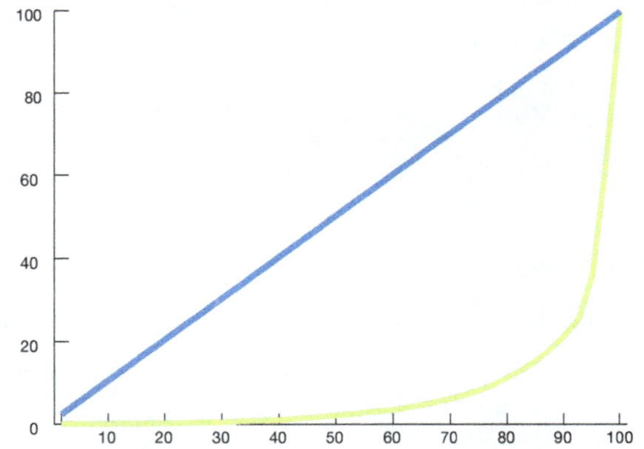

Source: UNCTAD, author calculation

Table 3. Remittances : Top 10 African recipient countries (data in millions of US$)

Country	2005	Rank	Country	2010	Rank	Country	2013	Rank
Nigeria	14 640.1	1	Nigeria	19 817.8	1	Nigeria	21 000.0	1
Egypt	5 017.3	2	Egypt	12 453.1	2	Egypt	17 468.6	2
Morocco	4 589.2	3	Morocco	6 422.5	3	Morocco	6 619.4	3
Algeria	2 060.0	4	Tunisia	2 063.3	4	Tunisia	2 299.6	4
Tunisia	1 392.7	5	Algeria	2 044.4	5	Algeria	2 000.0	5
Senegal	788.8	6	Senegal	1 477.7	6	Senegal	1 652.2	6
Sudan	703.8	7	Sudan	1 100.1	7	Kenya	1 334.2	7
South Africa	613.6	8	South Africa	1 069.6	8	South Africa	1 123.4	8
Lesotho	599.4	9	Uganda	770.8	9	Uganda	1 042.2	9
Kenya	425.0	10	Kenya	685.8	10	Mali	842.2	10

Source : UNCTAD

The inequality of the remittances distribution by country seems to be accentuated over time and benefits the two large and most populated countries of the continent (Egypt and Nigeria). So, it is no surprise to find that the country benefiting the most from remittance flows is Nigeria, followed by Egypt, then by three other countries of North Africa. Since 2005, the classification of countries in this ranking of the top 10 beneficiaries has changed little, with eight countries (Nigeria, Egypt, Morocco, Algeria, Tunisia, Senegal, South Africa and Kenya) making a regular appearance.

Parallel to remittance inflows, it is also interesting to examine the characteristics of outflows from Africa. Indeed, the volume of remittance outflows from African countries equates on average to approximately 21% of total annual inflows (a little more than US$ 14 billion in 2014). Most of these outflows benefited other African countries, since Africa holds almost 84% of the annual outflow transfers, followed by Europe (10.7%) and Asia (5.0%).

Table 4. Intra-Africa remittance flows (data in millions of US$, 2012)

	Sending region					
Recipient region	Central Africa	East Africa	North Africa	Southern Africa	West Africa	Total
Central Africa	26.5	31.5	0.3	0.0	2 807.5	2 865.8
East Africa	0.0	1 205.4	56.4	21.2	419.2	1 702.2
North Africa	0.2	6.6	2 376.4	0.2	115.8	2 499.3
Southern Africa	0.0	7.1	5.6	970.7	29.3	1 012.8
West Africa	6.1	0.0	48.6	0.0	3 336.8	3 391.6
Total	32.8	1 250.7	2 487.3	992.2	6 708.7	11 471.7

Source : World Bank

This finding is consistent with the migration patterns analyzed in the preceding sections. We have seen that almost half of African migrants moved within the continent, more precisely in their respective subregion. The matrix of the intra-Africa remittances flows reflects the current situation, in which West Africa receives almost all intra-Africa inflow transfers from countries in the subregion, but simultaneously feeds an almost equivalent volume of outflow remittances to other regions such as Central Africa.

By excluding Libya (which was certainly one of the major African countries in terms of remittance outflows before 2010, but which has recently recorded a massive exodus of migrants due to the prevailing political situation), the major African countries in terms of remittance outflows over recent years are South Africa, Côte d'Ivoire, Angola, and Uganda.

Lastly, in an infra-annual reading (monthly or quarterly series) of the data, we can note the seasonal character of transfers in certain countries. This results in a massive surge of migrant transfers over one month or a given quarter of the year. This kind of phenomenon can induce a constraint on the foreign exchange earnings at the macroeconomic level, and may cause volatility in the total flow of transfers and sudden changes in the value of the local currencies. This implies the need for the authorities to take measures to "de-seasonalize" these flows and to spread them out in a more uniform way over the entire year.

Do remittances act as a development lever?

The impact of the remittances on the economic development of countries of origin is the subject of a debate that still flourishes in the economic literature. The conclusions drawn remain largely debatable and mitigated. Indeed, although a correlation between the level of development in a country and volumes of international migration is generally admitted, the question of the consequences of migration and related financial transfers on the economies of origin proves more complex.

A review of the literature suggests that financial transfers resulting from migration do not act in a systematic and obvious way in terms of the development process. Nonetheless there seems to be a direct impact from transfer flows on the distribution of income, poverty reduction and individual wellbeing. Some researchers have focused on the effects of remittances on the economy as a whole, by examining the effect on employment, productivity and growth. Others have looked at the effect on the external trade balance and current account deficit reduction.

Figure 12: African countries : remittances ratio to GDP (in %) and HDI

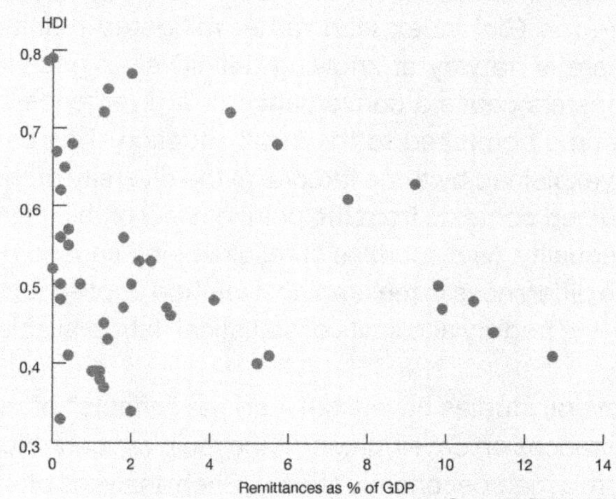

Source: UNCTAD / UNDP

Many studies come to more positive conclusions on the macroeconomic repercussions of transfers. They point to their stability over a long period, their capacity to act as a "shock absorber" in some critical situations, and their relatively uniform distribution within the population. Thus, remittances would have no negative impact on growth via real exchange rate, unlike other flows of external financing.

These findings can be explained by migrants' behavior as regards money transfer, in particular their reactivity in the event of an overvaluation of their country of origin's currency. Moreover, since remittances sent by migrants are generally compared to export incomes, they can help to improve the solvency score allotted by international banks and credit rating agencies. In this respect, they make it possible for beneficiary countries to have more flexible access to international financial and capital markets.

Research about the effects of money transfers on the local distribution of income tends to focus on social equity and justice; it does not deal in depth with the consequences for the domestic economy. In the empirical evaluations, the majority of impact studies of remittances on the distribution of income use the Gini index with rather mitigated results. There is no way of knowing definitively if migrant transfers cause a convergence or a divergence of income compared to the initial situation. This can be explained by three factors: (i) the diversity of the studied contexts from the point of view of the initial inequality; (ii) disparities of results being caused by the differences in the empirical method applied; and (iii) the fragility and limits of statistical data available.

Several studies have examined the "effects" of remittances on development in the recipient countries from a macroeconomic stance. Such analyses often address the subject in a rather general or theoretical manner and struggle to provide satisfactory empirical validation of macroeconomic interactions. This may be due to a lack of appropriate data. By contrast, empirical case studies focusing on the microeconomic scale impacts are generally localized, with relatively limited examples dealing with the African country context.

Those studies that deal with the effects that migrant remittances can have on economic development at the national and local levels show that these transfers are intended firstly for family consumption, education and health expenditure and increasingly for small investments. Other uses are cited, such as specific expenditure that coincides with family events (marriage) and religious festivals. Accordingly, it appears that the transfers are used partly for consumption and partly for small investments.

Remittances do not always have positive effects on the economies of recipient countries; in fact, they may be damaging. This is especially the case for countries receiving for example a large volume of remittances (with distinguished seasonality), as this may create volatility in the exchange rate of the local currency, which may affect interest rates and their balance of payments. In fact, like any important source of foreign currency inflows (e.g. powerful exporting sectors; discovery of large oil reserves), remittances are likely to start a phenomenon similar to the "Dutch disease", resulting in an appreciation of the national currency but potential loss of competitiveness as a corollary and an increase in the price of imported goods.

However, the question of migrant contributions to the economies and development of their countries of origin should not be judged solely in terms of monetary remittances. Other benefits include the transmission of know-how and expertise gained in other countries, the building up of a network of business contacts in other lands, and the influence of alternative ideas on social and political matters. All these present a wealth of research topics, which deserve to be taken up but which fall outside the parameters of this study.

To sum up, the impact of migrant transfers to beneficiary African countries needs to be assessed by looking at the way in which these transfers are used. The channeling of these funds for the accumulation of productive capital and entrepreneurial investment can have a direct and positive impact on employment and growth. However, some researchers have demonstrated that even if money transfers are allocated exclusively to consumption and housing purchase or construction, this can still have various indirect effects on economic growth. In this context, one can mention the freeing up of other potential resources for investment and the activation of the multiplier effect.

Challenges connected with the promotion of remittance flows

The debate surrounding remittances raises a series of challenges to which public authorities and other stakeholders need to pay special attention:

• *Improvement of statistical data on remittances and associated issues.*
This is essential from a number of angles, and highlights the need for reliable and harmonized data. For this to happen, it is essential to build capacity in administrative units responsible for monitoring remittance flows for better data quality (in particular within central banks). As a parallel activity, other statistical instruments need to be mobilized to increase knowledge on the patterns of migration, the profiles of migrants, as well as the dynamics of transfer flows.

Household surveys in migrants' countries of origin constitute a very useful data source to refine the estimate of remittance flows received. The reliability of the estimate depends of course on the way in which the module of the questionnaire relating to migration is designed and the income resources associated. It depends too on the way in which this module is perceived by the questioned units and on the representativeness of the sample.

Another option, in spite of its methodological difficulties, consists in directly questioning the migrants in the host countries. This method makes it possible to collect detailed information on incomes, savings, amount of money sent, and migrant preferences or practices in terms of transfer channels. It also makes it possible to connect the behaviors of individuals to their characteristics and to those of their families who remain in the country of origin.

A third combined approach consists in carrying out household surveys counting the individuals in migration in a given country and carrying out a second stage survey using a matched sample of the same migrants and their home families. This kind of survey is of course complex and tends to be expensive, but the produced data can considerably refine the estimate of the total bilateral volume of remittances between countries.

• *Enhancing and efficient monitoring of remittances.* African countries can potentially use future remittances (and other future receivables) as collateral to raise finance from international capital markets for development projects. However, the seasonality of migrant transfers to Africa described above may affect the ability to raise finance. Moreover, another challenge to efficient monitoring of remittances is posed by the high share of the transfers carried out via informal circuits. This calls for government efforts to encourage formalization of money transfers so that they may be recorded and counted officially.

Furthermore, it is known that the manner of spending these transfers is fundamental to the unlocking of a virtuous process to reduce poverty and spur inclusive growth. According to this logic, the intervention of the public policy is more than ever essential, by implementing regulating tools to foster and securitize transfers, and to integrate them in the development framework of the countries. This implies a set of public measures and coherent interventions geared to optimize their impact on social and economic development, for example: the adjustment of certain regulations; increasing the role of post offices and microfinance institution in money transfers; further engagement of the financial and banking system; the design of specific programs for migrants, etc. The intervention of public authorities is also necessary to correct and overcome negative externalities caused by these transfers.

Africa can learn from the experiences of other countries, which can provide useful insights. Thus, a number of developing countries, in particular Brazil, Mexico, India and Philippines, adopted incentive measures aiming at channeling remittances towards savings accounts and local investment funds. These countries set up various plans, including: encouraging migrants to save for retirement; extending credit at preferential rates; assisting the companies that had been established as a result of the transfers of funds; and allowing the immigrants recently returned to their country of origin to have flexible access to capital.

The large proportion of informal flows constitutes a concern for African countries, which they must address by promoting the formal transfers network through various incentives and measures, and by encouraging the recipients to save more within the framework of the official banking system. To make official transfers more attractive, the countries could also offer favorable exchange rates and level the banking systems. The remittance landscape in Africa is rapidly changing with the introduction of innovative, mobile money transfers and branchless banking technologies. Although the adoption of these technologies has been limited largely to domestic money transfers, these technologies have the potential to vastly improve access to both remittances and broader financial services, including low-cost savings and credit products, for African migrants and remittance recipients in African countries.

• *Support a reduction in the cost of transfers and greater access to formal financial channels*. Although they have fallen in recent years, the cost of money transfers to and within Africa, remains relatively high and is extremely volatile. By contrast, the cost of making a transfer from the United States is among the lowest, followed by the transfer costs emanating from Europe. It is paradoxical that the cost of sending money intra-continent is much higher in Africa, despite the fact that the flow of transfers carried out between African countries is very large, even between countries of the same subregion. For example, the sending of funds from South Africa to other African countries generally costs more than a transfer from another continent. Although remittances are extremely useful, particularly in times of crisis, in Africa they are remarkably expensive, especially when they are intended for rural areas of Africa weakly served in terms of banking networks. Some measures and actions are essential to relieve this situation. This could be done through the intervention of public authorities with respect to the financial intermediaries, to sensitize them on the importance of the growing remittances market and the opportunity of regional coordination and integration. Other measures could also be taken in the countries issuing the transfers: to support an equitable and efficient market for the execution of the transfers; to promote transparency in the establishment of tariffs; to sensitize migrants on the different choices available to them; to tolerate opening bank accounts for the clandestine migrants; and to give them access to less expensive financial services transfers. Such measures would thus promote higher volume transfers through the formal financial circuit.

• *Harnessing the Diaspora to development strategies.* Very often, the debate on emigration stresses the leakage of competences and labor force from poor countries towards rich ones. In particular, the flight of highly skilled and trained human resources deprives the countries of origin of essential competences. However, remittances are the central and most tangible link between migration and development. Instead of focusing on the negative aspects of emigration, remittance flows should be seen as an opportunity for African countries to benefit from their citizens who choose to live and work abroad.

In addition, the loss of human resources for migrants' economies of origin, especially those with a higher education level or professionally skilled, is not always equally compensated by remittance flows, insofar as this category of migrants is sometimes less inclined to transfer money. Adapted mechanisms and instruments should be devised in order to build bridges between migrants and their countries of origin and to connect the Diaspora to the development dynamics in the continent.

• *Generating a "platform" of knowledge on various subjects associated with migration and remittances in Africa.* This article on remittances has in addition the modest ambition to sensitize the various stakeholders on the need to delve further into the analysis of these kinds of flows. The aim is to foster the implementation of a large knowledge platform around remittance issues. Initiatives such as the project "AIR" (African Institute for Remittances) sponsored by the African Union Commission in partnership with other institutions, namely the European Commission (EC), the World Bank (WB), the African Development Bank (AfDB) and the International Organization for International Migration (OIM), constitutes an anchoring point to link different contributions, reflections and research tasks in this field in Africa. The aim is to create a space to share experiences and material knowledge for greater inclusion /understanding of the migratory phenomenon and its dimensions. This includes all the aspects relating to migrant transfers and proposing, for the public and private decision makers of the continent, a panoply of instruments and measures to promote effective and inexpensive remittance flows.

Conclusion

This analysis has shown remittances to be a considerable and very important source of funds for African countries, especially to address a plethora of development challenges that require high levels of funding. Currently, the total remittances volume to African countries exceeds foreign direct investment flows and in some countries is equal in size to official development assistance. In addition, these flows tend to be regular and stable sources of external capital, with a promising future prospect. Their positive impact on issues related to the human development (inclusive growth, poverty reduction, employment, education and health) in the African continent is largely recognized.

Nevertheless, the impact of remittances on the economic development process in African countries is not always optimal. It depends on the monitoring of these kinds of transfers, on the way in which they are mobilized and effected, so that they can be channeled to productive capital accumulation and investment, and so respond to various challenges facing African countries.

The analysis presented in this article has shown the role of migration as crucially underpinning an expansion of remittances. Indeed, the nature of population movements during the last decades, whereby half the migration takes place within the continent, has configured the current features and the profile of remittance flows. It has led to a concentration of transfers to two major subregions of the continent – North and West Africa – and predominantly to a limited number of countries. Our analysis has also revealed the relatively weak amount of transfers by migrants to Africa, compared with other global regions, and the exorbitant cost of operational transfers to/within African countries.

However, in spite of their importance, many facets of these financial flows (accurate volumes, features, motivation, uses, etc.) remain poorly appraised. Many aspects still remain relatively under-researched, for example the structure of the remittances market, the allocation of these resources, and the externalities induced. The African Development Bank (AfDB) and its partners (AUC & AEC) recognize the value of these types of transfers and the contribution they can make to drive the development process in Africa. Notwithstanding, the AfDB is at the same time cognizant that these remittances do not constitute a panacea and cannot replace sound economic policies at the country level.

The efficient mobilization of remittances faces a series of challenges which need to be addressed in parallel, given their complementarity. One of the major challenges relates to improving statistical and data quality with respect to migration and remittances by building statistical capacity in the relevant ministries and departments.

The other axes for the promotion of formal transfer channels require public authorities to create a synergy between different actors associated with remittances issues (African financial systems and banks, post offices and international partners), in terms of regulation and coordinated economic policy measures. Although the rapid adoption of innovative money transfer technologies is transforming the landscape for remittances and broader financial services, remittance markets in Africa remain relatively underdeveloped in terms of their financial infrastructure and the regulatory framework. In this context, interventions could include the integration of informal flows into the formal financial sphere; simplified access for individuals to financial circuits; and a reduction in transfer costs to beneficiary African countries.

In parallel, improving the inter-linkage between remittances and development by more efficient channeling of these external financial resources to productive investment represents the other major challenge facing African countries. In this regard, several other options can be considered: the involvement of the African Diaspora in national development strategies; institutional coordination between African financial intermediaries (in particular at the subregional level) to expand and improve the operation of the remittances market; and the establishment of adapted saving and investment services, even connected to specific or local development projects.

Envois de fonds en Afrique: Dynamique, opportunités et défis

2015

Depuis plusieurs années, la Banque Africaine de Développement (BAD), en collaboration avec la Commission de l'Union Africaine et la Commission Economique pour l'Afrique, a mis en avant la question de la mobilisation des ressources domestiques (MRD), notamment à l'occasion de l'édition 2010 de ses « Perspectives Economiques en Afrique » (PEA), qui a consacré un article à cette thématique. Le but était de sensibiliser les décideurs et les pouvoirs publics africains à la nécessité de mieux canaliser l'épargne intérieure, d'optimiser les ressources nationales, qu'elles soient publiques ou privées, et orienter leur allocation à des investissements économiquement et socialement productifs. En adoptant la mobilisation des ressources domestiques comme une des thématiques du développement, le Groupe de la BAD et ses partenaires étaient motivés notamment par les défis financiers majeurs dans la réalisation des Objectifs du Millénaire pour le Développement (OMD) en Afrique.

Le débat autour de la mobilisation des ressources domestiques s'est parfois focalisé sur l'efficience et l'optimisation des ressources fiscales et la manière d'orienter davantage l'épargne intérieure détenue par les secteurs bancaires et financiers vers l'investissement productif. A l'occasion, les discussions se sont étendues à l'exploration de nouvelles formes et mécanismes de flux financiers comme alternatives réelles pour alimenter les schémas de développement et assurer la transformation structurelle en Afrique. A ce titre, les envois de fonds peuvent constituer un recours précieux pour l'Afrique afin de s'affranchir davantage de l'aide extérieure, de réduire les niveaux d'endettement, améliorer les comptes extérieurs et renforcer la résilience et la compétitivité des économies nationales.

Dans ce contexte, l'analyse présentée dans ce document met en avant l'importance des flux d'envois de fonds pour le développement en Afrique. Au préalable, l'étude s'attache à présenter un état des lieux sur la dynamique de ces flux, leur tendance récente et leur physionomie. Dans une seconde étape, il s'agira de fournir une synthèse de l'impact de ces flux sur plusieurs aspects économiques et sociaux. L'analyse examinera les externalités positives ou négatives qu'elles soulèvent et fournira des pistes pour une meilleure mobilisation de ces flux afin d'accélérer le développement durable, inclusif et vert du continent.

Aspects préliminaires

Avant d'aborder les différents aspects relatifs aux flux d'envois de fonds (désignés parfois par remises), il convient de fournir quelques précisions sur ce concept économique. Ses contours ont été revus avec l'élaboration de la sixième édition du « Manuel de la balance des paiements » élaboré par le FMI. Auparavant, on désignait souvent ces flux par envois de fonds de migrants ou de travailleurs émigrés. Mais, la nouvelle définition retenue depuis 2005 est plus large, plus simple et plus cohérente avec les pratiques d'établissement des données dans de nombreux pays. Dorénavant, les transferts personnels sont définis indépendamment de la source de revenus des ménages qui procèdent aux envois de fonds, de la relation entre ces ménages, et du but dans lequel le transfert est effectué. Ainsi, même si l'on admet que les transferts personnels proviennent principalement de travailleurs migrants qui envoient une partie de leur épargne vers leur économie d'origine, les transferts personnels dans la nouvelle approche du manuel ne se limitent pas uniquement aux transferts réalisés par les migrants.

Bien que les thématiques de la migration et des remises des migrants ne soient pas des sujets nouveaux, ils ne cessent de susciter un intérêt croissant de la part de la communauté internationale, du milieu académique et des instituts de recherche, mais également des pays concernés. Dans plusieurs pays africains, l'intérêt porté sur le sujet part du principe que l'Afrique doit capitaliser ces ressources humaines et financières en vue de remédier aux défis que pose le processus de développement. Ces défis incluent les contraintes environnementales et les changements climatiques, la sécurité alimentaire, l'accès aux services de santé, le déficit en infrastructure, la pauvreté et les inégalités sociales. En revanche, pour certains pays de destination des migrants en Europe, qui continuent encore de pâtir des mesures d'austérité instaurées suite à la crise mondiale et qui doivent réduire leur endettement public, ce type de flux de capitaux sortants n'est souvent pas vu d'un bon œil.

Les controverses autour du sujet s'expliquent à plus d'un titre. Surtout, au regard de l'ampleur et l'importance des montants transférés, et notamment par rapport aux perspectives prometteuses de leur progression dans les années à venir. En effet, sur la base des statistiques officielles disponibles, *les envois de fonds à destination de l'Afrique devraient déjà doubler en 2015 comparés à leur niveau de 2005, pour atteindre, selon les projections de la Banque Mondiale, 64 milliards de dollars.* Pour situer les choses, il suffit de remarquer que ces flux l'Afrique représentent par exemple environ la moitié du PIB de l'Angola, ou encore deux fois le revenu national de la Côte d'Ivoire ou de la Tanzanie et quatre fois le PIB du Botswana ou de la Guinée Equatoriale.

Concept des envois de fonds dans la balance des paiements

Les envois de fonds (ou remises) représentent les revenus de ménages qui proviennent d'économies étrangères et dont l'origine est principalement liée au déplacement, temporaire ou permanent, de personnes vers ces économies. En fait, les définitions des comptes envois de fonds dans la balance des paiements (BdP) sont un peu plus larges que celles relatives aux mouvements de personnes, car elles ne sont pas fondées sur des concepts de migration, d'emploi ou sur des relations familiales.

Les remises proviennent principalement de deux composantes de la balance des paiements : le revenu gagné par les travailleurs dans des économies dont ils ne sont pas résidents (ou provenant d'employeurs non résidents) et les transferts de résidents d'une économie au profit de résidents d'une autre économie. Les deux postes de la BdP qui se rapportent substantiellement aux envois de fonds sont la « rémunération des salariés » et les «transferts personnels» et sont enregistrées au compte courant.

Rémunération des salariés

La rémunération des salariés désigne le revenu de travailleurs frontaliers, saisonniers et autres travailleurs à court terme qui sont employés dans une économie dont ils ne sont pas résidents, et le revenu de résidents employés par des entités non résidentes. La rémunération des salariés représente la rémunération versée en échange du facteur travail qu'un particulier consacre au processus de production dans le cadre d'une relation employeur-employé.

Transferts personnels

Les transferts personnels comprennent tous les transferts courants en espèces ou en nature effectués ou reçus par des ménages résidents au profit ou en provenance de ménages non résidents. Ils englobent tous les transferts courants entre particuliers résidents et non résidents. Ainsi, les transferts personnels sont un sous-ensemble des transferts courants et regroupent tous les transferts courants effectués par des particuliers au profit de particuliers.

Les transferts personnels remplacent un poste appelé « envois de fonds de travailleurs » dans la présentation type de la cinquième édition, et dans laquelle les envois de fonds de travailleurs étaient constitués par les transferts courants effectués par des migrants employés dans de nouvelles économies où ils sont considérés comme résidents.

L'impact, à la fois au niveau macroéconomique que microéconomique des envois de fonds et bien que parfois mitigé sur certains volets, est aujourd'hui largement reconnu et souvent mis en avant pour soutenir les différentes initiatives visant à promouvoir les stratégies d'une meilleure mobilisation de telles ressources. En outre, l'importance du volume des transferts réalisés donne toute sa pertinence à la nécessité de constituer un ensemble de connaissances et de savoir sur les déterminants et les problématiques annexes à ces flux pour appuyer les gouvernements africains dans la formulation de mesures opérationnelles permettant d'optimiser ces flux pour le développement.

Les éléments développés dans ce document, tant sur les flux migratoires que sur les envois de fonds, se fondent sur les statistiques officielles et, le cas échéant, sur des estimations réalisées par les services d'organisations internationales. Sauf que cette analyse exploratoire demeure relativement incomplète, dans la mesure où une partie des flux migratoires ou de fonds échappe à l'enregistrement statistique ou est mal « cernée » par les outils d'observation statistique actuels.

Ainsi, une part non négligeable des envois continue de transiter par des voies informelles et constitue un défi majeur pour les autorités publiques afin de l'intégrer au circuit formel. Elle représenterait selon les travaux de la Banque Mondiale 35 à 75 % des montants expédiés par voie officielle dans les pays en développement. En l'occurrence, les pays d'Afrique se situeraient dans le haut de la fourchette, tandis que ceux d'Asie de l'est seraient en revanche plutôt alignés sur le seuil bas. En général, le secteur formel, dont le réseau formé par opérateurs de transferts de fonds, comme Western Union ou MoneyGram, avec les banques commerciales locales, se partagent le gros du marché, est bien plus développé en Amérique latine et dans les pays asiatiques que sur le continent africain.

L'étude de cette catégorie de transferts ouvre la voie sur une série de sujets et aspects connexes qui méritent une attention particulière et que l'analyse sous revue tentera de soulever, dont en particulier la question de la qualité des statistiques officielles sur les flux migratoires et les envois de fonds et la nécessité de renforcer les capacités des pays dans ces domaines, approfondir l'analyse de l'impact des envois sur les économies bénéficiaires, le comportement des ménages bénéficiaires, les circuits financiers supportant ces transferts, la canalisation des flux vers des investissements productifs et la réduction de la pauvreté, la gestion de certaines externalités négatives et les mesures à adopter afin d'impliquer davantage la diaspora dans la dynamique et le processus de développement.

Le rôle déterminant des flux migratoires

Le stock de migrants africains installés hors de leur pays d'origine a enregistré une forte croissance durant la décennie 2000-2010, comparativement aux deux décennies précédentes.

Sur la première décennie du siècle en cours, le nombre de migrants aurait augmenté de 56,2 %, passant de 19,594 millions en 2000 à 30,603 millions en 2010, soit une croissance annuelle de 4,6 % sur cette période (contre une augmentation de 1,9 % par an sur la période 1980-2000). Les conflits et l'instabilité de la situation politique dans certains pays seraient à l'origine de ce phénomène.

Cette évolution bénéficierait également de la *forte croissance démographique du continent durant les années quatre vingt (3.1 % par an, contre 2.6 % et 2.5 % respectivement dans les années 90 et 2000)*. La génération née dans les années 80 aurait eu entre 20 et 30 ans en atteignant la décennie 2000-2010 et donc à un âge où les jeunes choisissent d'émigrer en quête de meilleures opportunités d'emploi.

Graphique 1 : Répartition des migrants africains selon leur destination (en % du stock total)

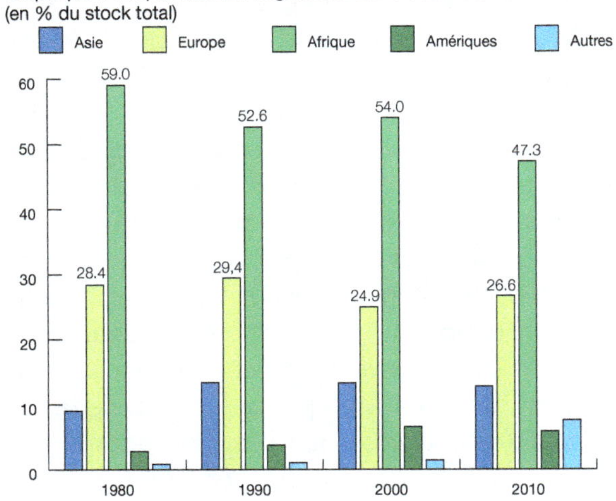

Source : Banque Mondiale

Le graphique 1 décrit le mouvement des migrants africains vers différentes destinations sur une période de 30 ans, de 1980 à 2010. Sur cette période, environ *la moitié des migrants africains s'est établie sur un autre pays du continent*, bien que cette proportion ait baissé récemment au profit d'autres destinations. La deuxième destination de prédilection sur cette période de 30 ans a été l'Europe, avec une proportion de migrants plus élevée en 2010 (26,6 %) qu'en 2000 (24,9 %), bien qu'en légère baisse par rapport à 1980 (28,4 %) et à 1990 (29,4 %).

Alors que la destination Amériques a enregistré une augmentation modérée entre 1980 et 2000 mais cette proportion marque un repli en 2010. La part de migrants vers d'autres territoires de destination (Australie, Nouvelle Zélande, Réunion, Mayotte....) se montre beaucoup plus remarquable puisque elle atteint 7,5 % en 2010 contre en gros 1 % durant les décennies précédentes.

Ensuite, lorsqu'on examine les flux de migrants selon le pays d'origine (graphique 2), il apparait que *deux principales sous régions du continent fournissent le contingent de migrants africains : l'Afrique de l'Ouest (30 %) et l'Afrique du Nord (29 %)*. Depuis une trentaine d'années, la part de l'Afrique de l'Ouest est stable mais celle de l'Afrique du Nord est en baisse. La part des sous région Afrique de l'Est et Afrique Australe ont relativement progressé entre temps pour se situer respectivement à 18,2 % et 16,8 % en 2010.

Graphique 2 : Répartition des migrants africains selon leur origine (en % du stock total)

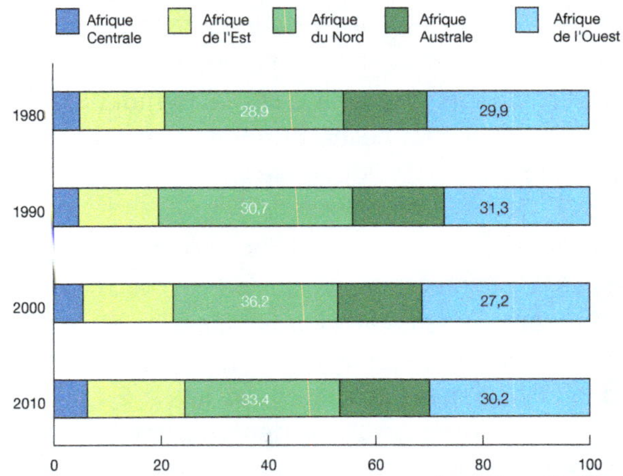

Source : Banque Mondiale

Au total, environ 3 % de la population totale africaine est établie hors de son pays d'origine. Ce ratio demeure stable depuis plusieurs décennies. Les principaux pays alimentant les flux migratoires au départ de l'Afrique sont respectivement l'Égypte, le Maroc et le Burkina-Faso.

Durant la dernière décennie 2000-2010, outre le fait que le nombre total de migrants africains ait marqué une forte croissance, le classement des pays africains selon le stock de migrants hors de leurs pays d'origine enregistre l'apparition du Zimbabwe et la Côte d'Ivoire au pelletons des pays fournissant plus d'un million de migrants chacun en 2010. Les évènements politiques survenus dans ces pays au cours de cette décennie expliqueraient largement cette évolution.

Vraisemblablement, pour des raisons relatives à l'étendue des territoires, à des motifs économiques

Tableau 1. Migration intra-Afrique (stocks de migrants en milliers, 2010)

	Région d'installation					
Région d'origine	Afrique Centrale	Afrique de l'Est	Afrique du Nord	Afrique Australe	Afrique de l'Ouest	Total
Afrique Centrale	491	597	1	57	68	1 216
Afrique de l'Est	41	2 923	45	41	0	3 049
Afrique du Nord	12	15	516	4	89	636
Afrique Australe	11	227	0	2 931	4	3 174
Afrique de l'Ouest	377	37	88	48	5 852	6 402
Total	932	3 799	651	3 081	6 015	14 477

Source : Banque Mondiale

et surtout aux liens historiques (donc liées à une certaine proximité entre les populations, qu'on pourrait qualifier de culturelle et sociale), la migration intra-Afrique semble s'effectuer fondamentalement à l'intérieur des mêmes sous régions du continent, principalement entre les pays d'Afrique de l'Ouest, ceux de l'Afrique Australe et de l'Afrique de l'Est.

Ainsi, et sur la base des données de 2010, 40,4 % des migrants africains installés dans un pays d'accueil du continent sont originaires de pays de l'Afrique de l'Ouest et établis dans un pays de cette même sous région. Avec des proportions moindres, l'Afrique Australe et l'Afrique de l'Est présentent une configuration quasiment analogue.

Examinée par genre, *la migration féminine a légèrement progressé durant la dernière décennie pour atteindre 44,3 % du stock total de migrants* (contre 42,5 % dans les années 80 et 90). Ceci pourrait façonner à l'avenir le profil des flux d'envois de fonds, en admettant que les migrants de sexe féminin afficheraient un sentiment d'attachement plus prononcé à leurs pays ou régions d'origine que chez les migrants de l'autre sexe.

A certains égards, les appréciations autour du mouvement de personnes sont liées aux politiques d'immigration dans les pays d'accueil. Toutefois, les travaux conduits sur cet aspect s'accordent à ce que les flux migratoires à travers le monde sont principalement déterminés par quatre facteurs économiques et démographiques : (i) le différentiel de revenu entre les régions du globe (ou entre les pays) ; (ii) la part des jeunes dans la population active dans le pays d'accueil et le pays d'origine, (iii) le stock de migrants déjà établis dans les pays d'accueil (émergence de réseaux) et (iv) l'impact de la pauvreté dans le pays d'origine (plutôt comme élément pesant sur la capacité à migrer). Et le bond des statistiques récentes sur l'immigration clandestine en 2014 indique que les mouvements de personnes pourraient s'intensifier davantage dans les années à venir. D'autant plus que la croissance démographique en Afrique demeure relativement élevée, alors que certaines populations seraient poussées à mouvoir pour échapper à des zones ou des poches récemment ouvertes de conflits.

On retiendra que les données relatives à la migration internationale examinées précédemment ne couvrent pas les années postérieures à 2010. Du coup, les évolutions politiques intervenues dans certaines sous régions du continent, notamment en Afrique du Nord et en Afrique de l'Ouest au cours des quatre dernières années, pourraient avoir influencé légèrement une partie de la configuration des stocks migratoires. Néanmoins, comme décrit plus haut, ceci ne devrait pas pour autant bouleverser ou affecter complètement la représentation qui ressort de l'analyse effectuée. Ce point sera pris en considération lors de l'analyse des flux d'envois de fonds (dont les données disponibles vont au-delà de l'année 2010).

Les envois de fonds en Afrique : une source potentielle importante et stable de capitaux extérieurs

Déjà, depuis les années 80, on admettait l'importance de ce type de transferts pour compenser la perte de capital humain des pays en développement du fait des mouvements migratoires. Mais on connaissait aussi leur potentiel de stimulation de la croissance économique dans les pays d'origine des migrants.

Un débat s'est engagé sur une large palette de questions liées à ces transferts, qui font désormais l'objet d'études plus poussées. Les thèmes retenus incluent les déterminants des transferts de fonds, les circuits empruntés pour opérer ces transferts, et l'impact économique de ces opérations sur les pays destinataires. Ces dernières années, la recherche sur ces questions s'est intensifiée, en partie à cause de la très forte augmentation du volume des transferts, qui en fait un véritable marché aiguisant l'appétit de certains opérateurs financiers et a conduit parallèlement à un foisonnement de la littérature scientifique sur le sujet.

En effet, le montant des envois de fonds au niveau mondial atteindrait, selon les dernières estimations de la Banque Mondiale, 586 milliards de dollars EU en 2015 comparé à environ 583 milliards pour l'année 2014. *Selon la même source, les flux destinés au continent africain s'afficheraient en 2015 à 63.8 milliards de $ EU* contre une estimation provisoire à 62,7 milliards en 2014, *soit une progression de 1,5 % environ*, après une croissance de presque

Graphique 3 : Part dans le total mondial des envois de fonds (en %)

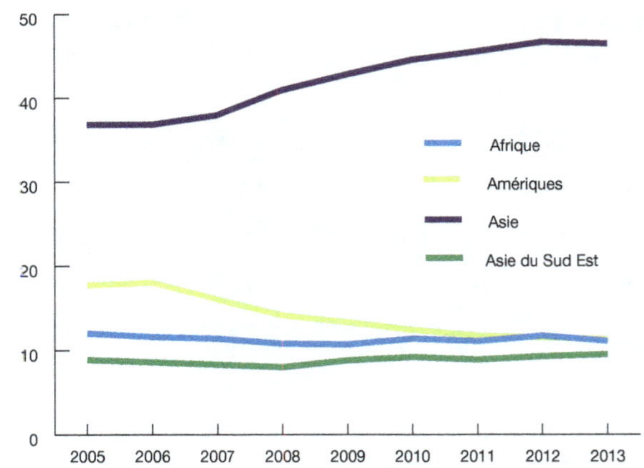

Source : CNUCED, Banque Mondiale

4 % en 2014. La croissance plus faible des remises en 2015 est expliquée par un effet de base (niveau élevé enregistré en 2014), ainsi qu'aux développements économiques en zone euro et surtout à la dépréciation de la monnaie unique face au dollar E.U. qui devrait peser sur les envois de fonds vers les principales régions bénéficiaires en Afrique.

Durant la dernière décennie, la part des envois de fonds dont a bénéficié l'Afrique dans le flux total mondial est demeurée *relativement stable en moyenne à 11,3 %.* La part destinée aux pays d'Amérique du Sud a perdu environ 6,4 points de pourcentages et est passée de 17,7 % en 2005 à 11,3 % en 2013 (quasiment au même niveau que l'Afrique). Parallèlement, les flux à destination de l'Asie ont sensiblement augmenté, puisque leur part a atteint 46,4 % en 2013 contre 36,8 % en 2005 et place ce continent en tête des régions bénéficiaires des envois de fonds. Cela n'a rien de surprenant car l'Asie est la région du monde la plus peuplée et c'est aussi celle qui compte la diaspora la plus nombreuse sur la planète.

La stabilité des envois vers l'Afrique et leur progression soutenue au cours du temps (comme cela sera développé dans la section suivante) constituent un soutien majeur pour de nombreux pays africains, aussi bien au niveau macroéconomique, à travers, entre autres, les entrées de devises qui permettent de soutenir l'équilibre de la balance courante et pallier à la vulnérabilité des comptes extérieurs, que au niveau microéconomique en fournissant un supplément de revenu pour certaines couches sociales.

Vu sous un autre angle, les flux officiels d'envois de fonds pour l'ensemble du continent *dépassent ceux des investissements directs étrangers (I.D.E) depuis 2010 et représentent actuellement deux fois le montant de l'aide publique au développement (APD).* Toutefois, l'analyse de la situation selon les régions est un peu plus mitigée, puisque l'aide publique au développement en Afrique Subsaharienne demeure encore équivalente au volume des transferts officiels de migrants alors que l'APD ne représente qu'environ 7 % des transferts réalisés vers l'Afrique du Nord.

A l'échelle des pays, ces flux représentent des ressources extérieures remarquables en capitaux lorsqu'elles sont comparées aux niveaux du revenu national, des réserves internationales ou à l'encours de l'endettement extérieur. Sur la période 2005-2013, *le montant annuel moyen des remises extérieures vers l'Afrique atteint environ 3,5 % du PIB,*

Graphique 4 : Evolution des flux financiers extérieurs vers l'Afrique (en milliards de $ E.U)

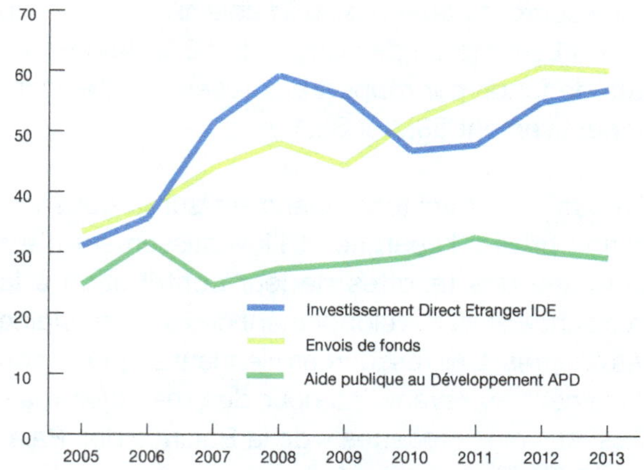

Source : OCDE, Banque Mondiale

couvre environ 8,5 % des importations en valeur courante, symbolise respectivement presque 12 % et 11 % de l'encours de la dette extérieure et des réserves internationales brutes.

De nouveau, cette description masque une certaine hétérogénéité de ces ratios selon les pays et illustrée par les statistiques des quartiles (tableau.2). En effet, si les envois représentent dans l'ensemble 3,2 % du produit intérieur brut, *ce ratio atteint 10,7 % au Sénégal, 9,8 % au Nigéria et 5,7 % en Égypte*. Rapportés aux réserves internationales,

Tableau 2. Ratios des envois de fonds à certains agrégats (en %, 2005-2013)

	en % du PIB	en % de la dette extérieure	en % des importations	en % des réserves internationales
1er quartile (25% des pays affichent un ratio inférieur à…)	0,8	2,8	2,0	3,2
Médiane (50% des pays affichent un ratio inférieur à…)	1,5	6,2	4,1	16,4
3ième quartile (75% des pays affichent un ratio inférieur à…)	5,4	19,6	11,9	39,7
Afrique	3,2	11,7	8,5	10,8

Source : BAD, OCDE, CNUCED

ou à l'encours de la dette extérieure, ce ratio prend des proportions beaucoup plus élevées dans bon nombre de pays relativement moins lotis en termes de ressources naturelles ou à faible revenu. C'est le cas du Lesotho ou de l'Ouganda où le ratio transferts de fonds par rapport aux réserves atteignent respectivement 53,3 et 32,1 %.

L'impact des transferts financiers sur la consommation privée, l'épargne et l'investissement n'est que l'une des facettes de leur contribution à la croissance et au développement des pays d'origine des émigrés. Ces ressources viennent s'ajouter non seulement au revenu intérieur des ménages mais aussi au volet « recettes » de la Balance des Paiements (BdP). Les transferts compensent ainsi en partie les déficits chroniques de la balance des paiements dans certains pays en palliant au manque de devises. Leur impact sur cette balance est plus appréciable que celui des autres flux financiers (tels que l'aide publique et privée, l'investissement direct ou les emprunts extérieurs) puisque leur utilisation n'est pas soumise aux conditions des donateurs ou liées à des projets d'investissement particuliers, ne sont pas générateurs d'intérêts et n'ont pas à être remboursés.

Les pays africains ont depuis longtemps pris conscience de l'effet positif des transferts d'argent sur leur balance des paiements, et ont pris des mesures pour encourager et accroître cet afflux de devises. Mais ces mesures devaient être appliquées avec prudence parce que, mis à part leurs effets positifs sur l'équilibre de la balance des paiements, les transferts ont une influence sur l'activité économique du pays d'origine. Selon la manière dont cet argent est dépensé ou investi, il n'aura pas le même impact sur la production, l'inflation et les importations.

La stabilité de ces flux leur confère *le caractère d'une épargne de précaution* et assurent ainsi un rôle efficace d'assurance en cas de choc imprévu pour les ménages (perte de revenu pour le chef de famille) ou face à la survenue de tout aléa (catastrophe naturelle, sècheresse, conflit civil.

Il est important de signaler également l'utilisation de ces ressources pour financer parfois des équipements collectifs et services d'utilité ou de proximité. En effet, sur le terrain social, les *remises constituent une source vitale de revenus pour une bonne partie de la population* et contribuent au financement de ses dépenses de santé et d'éducation. Les paragraphes qui vont suivre permettront de d'ailleurs mieux discuter l'impact sur la réduction des inégalités et de la pauvreté à travers une revue rapide de la littérature économique.

Dynamique soutenue des flux d'envois de fonds

L'analyse de l'évolution des transferts de fonds sur la même période 2005-2013 montre que ces *flux vers l'Afrique ont progressé en moyenne au taux annuel de 7,7 % l'an en valeurs courantes* (mais au rythme de 6,5 % l'an s'ils sont exprimés en $ constant de 2010). Cette croissance, qui est en phase avec celle des envois au niveau mondial (8,7 % l'an), s'affiche à un rythme supérieur à celui

Graphique 5 : Evolution d'envois de fonds en Afrique, 2005-2015 (en milliards de $ EU)

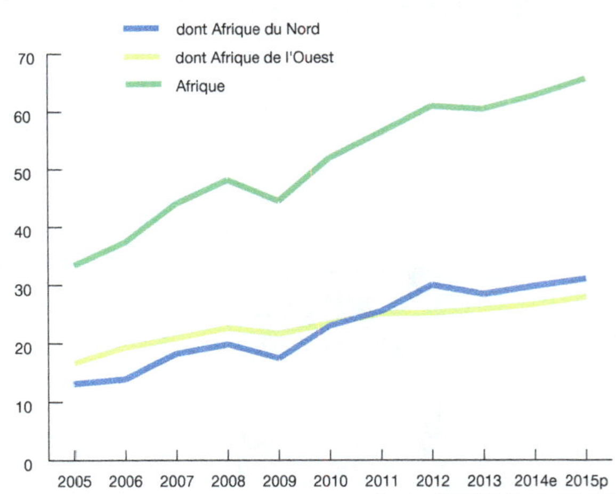

Source : CNUCED, Banque Mondiale

observé au niveau de l'Amérique du Sud (+4,0 %) mais en revanche bien moins vigoureux que celui enregistré pour l'Asie (environ 12 % l'an), qui bénéficie évidemment d'un avantage majeur en termes de stocks de migrants.

La forte augmentation des envois de fonds au cours de dernière décennie résulte non seulement de l'accroissement du nombre des migrants, mais également d'un meilleur enregistrement de ces flux financiers, en raison notamment d'une utilisation accrue des circuits formels lors des opérations de transferts. Cette dernière évolution est elle-même le fruit des avancées technologiques permettant de transférer rapidement de modestes sommes, de la réduction relative des coûts de transaction et du fait d'un contrôle plus strict sur les mouvements de capitaux informels opérée au niveau international. Toutefois, une proportion non négligeable des envois de fonds (estimée certaines sources autour de 40 % des transferts officiels) continue néanmoins de transiter par des voies informelles et constitue un défi majeur pour les autorités publiques afin de l'intégrer au circuit formel.

L'évolution des envois de fonds dans le temps est en outre sensiblement liée aux développements de la conjoncture internationale, en particulier dans les pays à partir desquels sortent ces flux. A cet effet, la dernière crise internationale de 2008-2009 a nettement marqué le cheminement des flux vers l'Afrique, puisque les envois de fonds ont baissé de 7,4 % en 2009, pour marquer par la suite un rattrapage dès 2010 en enregistrant une augmentation de 16,7 %.

Polarisation des transferts autour de deux régions

La dynamique des envois destinés vers l'Afrique est largement dictée par celle enregistrée dans deux sous régions du continent, l'Afrique du Nord et l'Afrique de l'Ouest, qui constituent sans conteste les principales régions réceptrices. Sur la période 2005-2013, la croissance des flux vers l'Afrique du Nord a atteint 10,2 % l'an, alors qu'en Afrique de l'Ouest la progression annuelle s'affiche à 5,6 %.

Toutefois, les évènements politiques survenus en Afrique du Nord depuis 2011 (désignés par printemps arabe) ont eu un impact mitigé sur les flux d'envois de fonds, dans la mesure où la sous région a connu des hausses substantielles des flux en 2011 et 2012 suivies d'une baisse en 2013. Ce repli des flux vers l'Afrique du Nord s'explique surtout par la baisse des flux observée en Égypte (-9,1 %). Mais, comme signalé précédemment, les remises peuvent souvent constituer un soutien important pour les pays bénéficiaires durant des épisodes de crises et ont ainsi un caractère contra-cyclique.

Graphique 6 : Répartition des remises en Afrique par région (en %, 2010-2013)

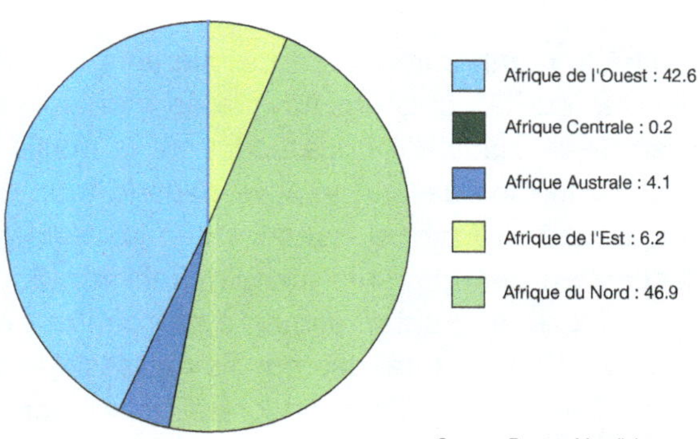

Source : Banque Mondiale

Les deux principales sous régions bénéficiaires de transferts du continent évoquées plus haut (Afrique du Nord et Afrique de l'Ouest) accaparent à elles seules une proportion majeure (presque 90 % en moyenne sur les trois dernières années) du flux total destiné à l'Afrique. En effet, l'Afrique du Nord capte environ 47 % du flux total et devance ainsi légèrement l'Afrique de l'Ouest qui bénéficie en moyenne d'un peu plus de 42 % du montant annuel. L'Afrique de l'Est et l'Afrique Australe retiennent en moyenne respectivement 6,2 % et 4,1 % des flux formels reçus par l'Afrique.

La concentration des flux sur les deux sous régions mentionnées se distingue par un caractère structurel.

Graphique 7 : Envois de fonds par région (part en %, 2005-2010-2013)

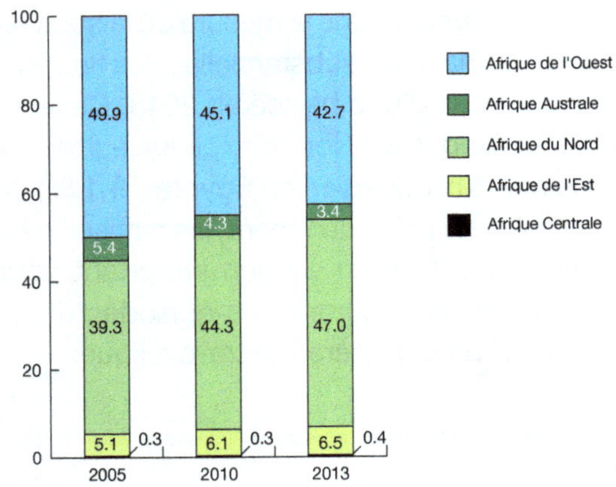

Source : Banque Mondiale

Malgré le nombre important de migrants africains installés sur le continent Afrique, le montant des « remises » issus d'Afrique occupent le troisième rang en termes de part relative dans le total des flux annuels. L'Europe, qui constitue la deuxième destination des migrants africains (environ 25 % du stock de migrants), alimente par contre pour presque 40 % le total des envois réalisés. L'Asie, troisième en termes de flux migratoires, « reverse » vers l'Afrique un peu plus de 20 % de l'ensemble des montants annuels.

Pour les deux régions où se concentrent les flux (Afrique du Nord et Afrique de l'Ouest), il faut signaler que *l'origine des flux destinés à l'Afrique de l'Ouest est relativement plus diversifiés* (Europe, Amériques, Afrique) que celle dont bénéficie l'Afrique du Nord où les flux proviennent essentiellement d'Asie (Pays du Golfe) et d'Europe.

Evidemment, la nature de la répartition des migrants explique largement la physionomie des flux des

Graphique 8 : Répartition des migrants et des envois de fonds en Afrique (%, 2010)

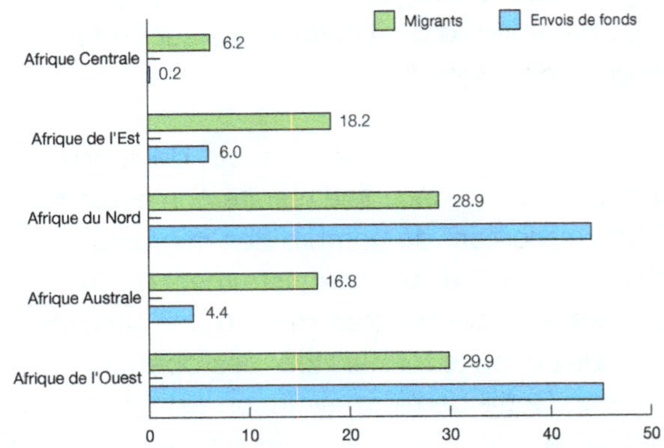

Source : Banque Mondiale

envois de fonds et leur distribution selon les sous régions ou les pays du continent. A cet effet, le rapprochement stock de migrants et flux d'envois, montre d'abord que les deux sous région Afrique du Nord et Afrique de l'Ouest accaparent et se partagent en gros le montant total des flux, tout en ayant quasiment le même nombre de migrants.

Cependant, on notera à ce niveau que, comparativement à l'Afrique de l'Ouest, la concentration des flux migratoires à partir des pays d'Afrique du Nord sur des pays à revenu élevé ne confère pas à cette région un avantage particulièrement conséquent. A titre d'illustration, et en dépit d'un nombre de migrants moins important installés en Europe (15,3 % comparativement à 50,4 % pour l'Afrique du Nord), l'Afrique de l'Ouest réussit à bénéficier d'un flux de remises provenant d'Europe équivalent à celui reçu par l'Afrique du Nord (38 et 39 %).

Flux des remises par migrant vers l'Afrique comparé à d'autres régions du globe et coûts des transferts

Les montants des envois officiels atteignent environ *1 631,4 $ EU par an par migrant en moyenne sur la dernière décennie.* Ce montant est équivalent 4,7 $ par jour, donc au-delà du seuil de pauvreté extrême correspondant à 1 $EU/jour, ce qui est déjà un supplément de revenu important pour les ménages qui ont au moins un migrant installé hors de son pays d'origine.

Plusieurs études et enquêtes spécifiques confirment ce constat et démontrent l'importance des remises comme facteur de réduction de la pauvreté. Ceci est d'autant plus pertinent, sachant que ses évaluations ne prennent pas en considération le montant des flux informels qui échappent à l'enregistrement statistique et que nombres d'estimations sérieuses les placent dans certains pays à 40 % des chiffres officiels retenus par la balance des paiements.

Toutefois, *ce montant s'avère relativement faible comparativement au montant moyen de 2 770 $EU par tête de migrant enregistré dans la région Asie.* Ceci s'expliquerait en grande partie par la concentration relative des migrants africains sur des zones géographiques économiquement moins avancées comparés aux migrants asiatiques ; et donc bénéficient d'un plus faible revenu disponible à rapatrier.

Les deux sous régions Afrique du Nord et Afrique de l'Ouest affichent dans l'ensemble des niveaux de transferts par tête identiques (environ 2 600 $EU pour chacune des sous région). En fait, les migrants africains originaires d'Afrique de l'Ouest et installés sur des zones géographiques comme l'Europe, les Amériques et l'Asie effectuent des envois par migrant bien supérieurs à ceux réalisés par les migrants issus d'Afrique du Nord. Du coup, *l'Afrique de l'Ouest compense la concentration de ses migrants sur le continent africain (presque 70 % du stock) par un montant plus élevé des envois par tête réalisés par ses migrants à partir d'autres pays avancés.*

Outre les autres facteurs qui pourraient limiter le volume des envois par voie officielle (situation du migrant dans le pays d'accueil, comportement ou motivation et niveau de revenu), le coût des transferts figure parmi les obstacles majeurs à l'expansion de ces flux. Certes, le coût moyen a nettement baissé au niveau international au cours des dernières années, mais les charges et commissions imputées lors des transferts vers l'Afrique Sub-saharienne restent relativement les plus élevés, avec des services de transfert comptabilisés en moyenne à 12 % du montant effectué.

Ailleurs, les coûts des transferts vers les pays d'Afrique du Nord ont augmenté au cours de l'année 2014 et se placent au dessus du coût moyen mondial. D'autre part, parmi les pays du G20, les coûts de transferts au départ de l'Afrique du Sud sont les plus élevés (environ 19.8 %), ce qui limiterait probablement le volume des remises vers les autres pays d'Afrique Australe, qui sont étroitement liés à l'Afrique du Sud en termes de flux migratoires et de transferts.

Graphique 9 : Coût moyen des transferts selon la région réceptrice (en %)

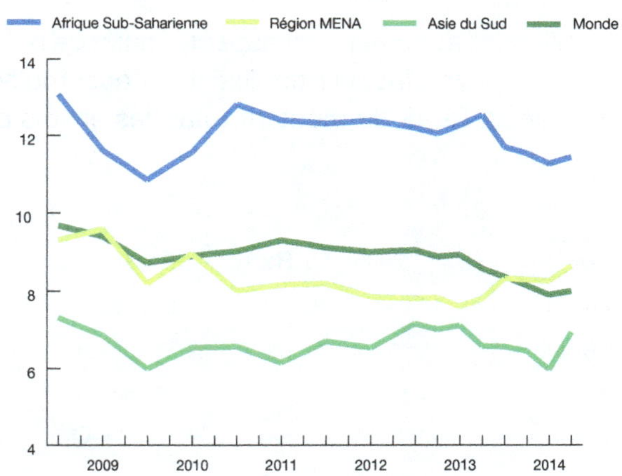

Source : Banque Mondiale

Forte concentration selon les pays

L'exploration des données annuelles par pays durant la dernière décennie met en évidence un aspect important, à savoir la forte inégalité et la dispersion élevée des transferts entre les pays africains et qui s'est particulièrement accentuée depuis 2008.

L'évolution de certains indicateurs statistiques au cours du temps (médiane, premier et troisième quartile) traduit des distributions statistiques des envois selon les pays étalées à droite avec un étalement croissant depuis 2005 (c.f. graphique 10).

Graphique 10 : Statistiques sur les envois de fonds par pays en Afrique (en millions de $EU)

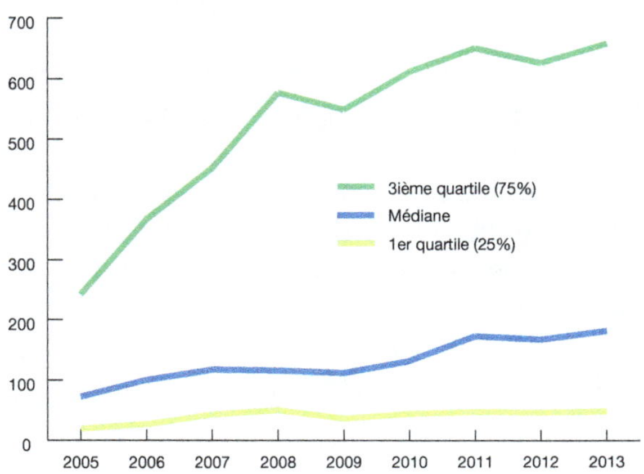

Source : CNUCED, calcul auteur

Pour illustrer autrement cet aspect, il suffit de noter que cinq pays africains totalisent ou accumulent à eux seuls 82 % du montant total des envois de fonds reçu par le continent durant les trois dernières années. La caractérisation de cette forte concentration des flux d'envois de fonds selon les pays peut être traduite d'une autre manière plus éloquente par la courbe qui retrace la proportion cumulée du nombre de pays sur l'axe horizontal et la proportion cumulée correspondante en flux de transferts, dite encore courbe de Lorenz (graphique 11). Sur un tel diagramme, la distance (superficie)

Graphique 11 : Courbe de concentration des flux annuels des envois de fonds en Afrique (2010-2013)

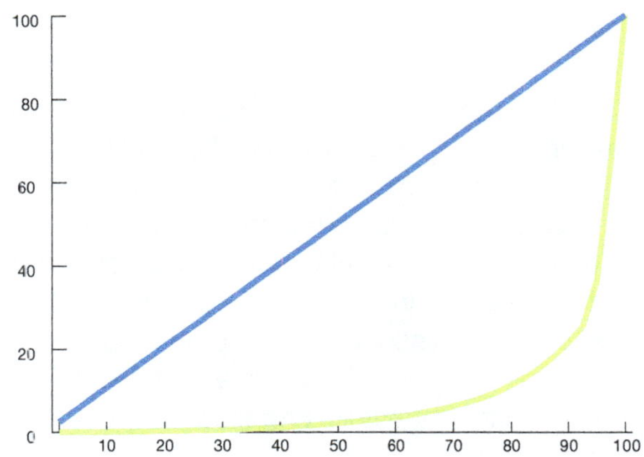

Source : CNUCED, calcul auteur

Tableau 3. Top 10 des pays africains bénéficiant des envois de fonds (montants en millions de $ EU)

Pays	2005	Rang	Pays	2010	Rang	Pays	2013	Rang
Nigéria	14 640,1	1	Nigéria	19 817,8	1	Nigéria	21 000,0	1
Égypte	5 017,3	2	Égypte	12 453,1	2	Égypte	17 468,6	2
Maroc	4 589,2	3	Maroc	6 422,5	3	Maroc	6 619,4	3
Algérie	2 060,0	4	Tunisie	2 063,3	4	Tunisie	2 299,6	4
Tunisie	1 392,7	5	Algérie	2 044,4	5	Algérie	2 000,0	5
Sénégal	788,8	6	Sénégal	1 477,7	6	Sénégal	1 652,2	6
Soudan	703,8	7	Soudan	1 100,1	7	Kenya	1 334,2	7
Afrique du Sud	613,6	8	Afrique du Sud	1 069,6	8	Afrique du Sud	1 123,4	8
Lesotho	599,4	9	Ouganda	770,8	9	Ouganda	1 042,2	9
Kenya	425,0	10	Kenya	685,8	10	Mali	842,2	10

Source : CNUCED

Tableau 4. Envois de fonds intra-Afrique (données en millions de $ EU, 2012)

	Région émettrice					
Région réceptrice	Afrique Centrale	Afrique de l'Est	Afrique du Nord	Afrique Australe	Afrique de l'Ouest	Total
Afrique Centrale	26,5	31,5	0,3	0,0	2 807,5	2 865,8
Afrique de l'Est	0,0	1 205,4	56,4	21,2	419,2	1 702,2
Afrique du Nord	0,2	6,6	2 376,4	0,2	115,8	2 499,3
Afrique Australe	0,0	7,1	5,6	970,7	29,3	1 012,8
Afrique de l'Ouest	6,1	0,0	48,6	0,0	3 336,8	3 391,6
Total	32,8	1 250,7	2 487,3	992,2	6 708,7	11 471,7

Source : Banque Mondiale

qui sépare la courbe et la première bissectrice mesure le « degré d'inégalité » de la distribution des envois reçus par les pays.

L'inégalité de la distribution des envois officiels entre les pays semble également s'accentuer au cours du temps et profite finalement aux deux pays parmi les plus peuplés que compte le continent (l'Égypte et le Nigéria). Rien d'étonnant de retrouver dans le top 10 des pays africains bénéficiant des flux d'envois figure au premier rang le Nigéria suivi par l'Égypte, elle même talonnée par trois autres pays d'Afrique du Nord. Depuis 2005, le classement des pays dans ce top 10 a peu changé avec huit pays (Nigéria, Égypte, Maroc, Algérie, Tunisie, Sénégal, Afrique du Sud, Kenya) qui font régulièrement partie du top 10.

Parallèlement aux flux entrants, il est également intéressant de signaler les principaux traits relatifs aux flux de fonds sortants d'Afrique. En effet, le montant des transferts de même type sortant des pays africains représentent en moyenne environ 21 % des flux annuels entrants (un peu plus de 14 milliards de $ EU en 2014). L'essentiel de ces flux bénéficie à d'autres pays africains, puisque l'Afrique conserve presque 84 % des montants annuels sortants suivie par l'Europe (10.7 %) et l'Asie (5.0 %).

Ce constat est en cohérence avec la situation examinée dans le précédent document relatif aux flux migratoires. On sait que presque la moitié des migrants d'origine africaine sont installés sur le continent, plus précisément dans leur sous région respectives. La matrice des envois intra-Afrique ci-dessous traduit finalement la situation actuelle dans laquelle l'Afrique de l'Ouest perçoit la quasi-totalité des transferts intra-Afrique entrants à partir des pays de la sous région, mais alimente simultanément d'un volume presque équivalent en flux sortants de remises la d'autres sous régions comme l'Afrique Centrale.

En excluant la Libye (qui était certes l'un des pays majeurs en termes de flux sortants avant 2010, mais qui a enregistré un départ massif des migrants compte tenu de la situation politique qu'il traverse depuis plus de quatre ans), les principaux pays africains en matière de flux d'envois de fonds sortants sur les dernières années sont respectivement l'Afrique du Sud, la Côte d'Ivoire, l'Angola et l'Ouganda.

Enfin, dans une lecture infra-annuelle (série mensuelle ou trimestrielle) des données, on notera le caractère saisonnier plus ou moins marqué des transferts dans certains pays, qui se traduit par un afflux massif des envois sur un mois ou un trimestre déterminé de l'année. Ce genre de phénomène peut induire une contrainte sur le mouvement du taux de change au niveau macroéconomique et la stérilisation des flux importants et soudains de devises. Ceci implique l'identification de mesures par les autorités publiques afin de « désaisonnaliser » ces flux pour les étaler de manière plus uniforme sur l'ensemble de l'année.

Les envois de fonds, un levier pour le développement ?

L'impact des transferts sur le développement économique des pays d'origine fait l'objet d'un débat nourri dans la littérature économique et dont les résultats demeurent largement discutables et mitigés. En effet, bien que l'existence d'interactions fortes entre le développement et la migration internationale soit en général admise, la question des conséquences des flux migratoires et des transferts financiers qui leur sont associés sur les économies d'origine s'avère plus complexe et mérite d'être approfondie.

Une revue de la littérature disponible sur le sujet suggère *que les transferts financiers issus de l'émigration n'agissent pas de façon systématique et de manière évidente comme des leviers déclencheurs d'un processus de développement.* Généralement, les analyses menées au niveau international relèvent souvent l'impact direct des transferts de fonds sur la répartition du revenu, la réduction de la pauvreté et le bien-être individuel. Certains travaux se concentrent sur les effets des transferts sur l'économie en général, en examinant les incidences sur l'emploi, la productivité et la croissance. D'autres articles traitent du rôle des transferts d'argent dans l'optique de l'allègement et la réduction des déficits du solde commercial et celui de la balance des opérations courantes.

De nombreux travaux aboutissent à des conclusions plus positives sur les retombées macroéconomiques des transferts, liées selon eux à leur stabilité sur longue période, leur caractère d'amortisseur de certaines crises, ou encore leur répartition relativement uniforme au sein de la population. Ainsi, les envois de fonds n'auraient pas d'impact négatif sur la croissance via le taux de change réel, à la différence d'autres flux de financement extérieur.

Graphique 12 : Ratio des envois de fonds au PIB (en %) et IDH

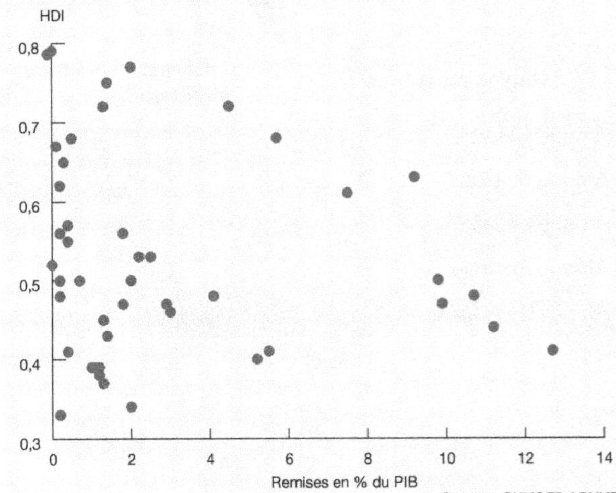

Source : CNUCED / PNUD

Ces résultats s'expliqueraient par le comportement des migrants en matière de transfert, en particulier leur réactivité en cas de surévaluation de la monnaie de leur pays d'origine. En outre, les envois de fonds des migrants étant généralement assimilés à des revenus d'exportation, ils contribueraient à améliorer la note de solvabilité attribuée par les banques internationales et les agences de notation, et permettraient ainsi aux pays récipiendaires de disposer d'un accès plus souple aux marchés internationaux de capitaux.

Les recherches sur les effets des transferts d'argent sur la répartition du revenu au niveau local se focalisent sur la justice sociale et l'égalité mais ne traitent pas des conséquences pour l'économie intérieure. Dans les évaluations empiriques, la plupart des études de l'impact des transferts de fonds sur la répartition du revenu utilisent l'indice de Gini avec des résultats plutôt mitigés. Rien ne permet de répondre clairement à la question de savoir si les transferts effectués par les émigrés provoquent une convergence ou une divergence du revenu par rapport à la situation initiale, et cela pour trois raisons principales : (i) la diversité des contextes étudiés du point de vue de l'inégalité initiale ; (ii) les disparités de résultats pouvant être provoquées par les différences de méthode empirique appliquée et (iii) la fragilité et des limites des matériaux statistiques disponibles.

Plusieurs études de type macro-économiques se sont intéressées aux « effets » des envois de fonds sur le développement dans les pays bénéficiaires. Toutefois, ces analyses abordent le sujet de manière souvent générale ou plutôt théorique et peinent à fournir une validation empirique satisfaisante des interactions macroéconomiques, en partie pour manque de données appropriées ; alors que les études de cas empiriques privilégiant les impacts à l'échelle microéconomiques sont relativement localisées et peu nombreuses sur les exemples de pays africains.

Celles qui ont porté sur les incidences que les transferts de fonds des migrants peuvent avoir sur le développement économique à l'échelle nationale et locale montrent principalement que les envois d'argent des migrants sont destinés prioritairement à la consommation familiale, à l'éducation et aux dépenses de santé et de plus en plus vers la réalisation de petits investissements. D'autres utilisations sont évoquées comme par exemple les dépenses ponctuelles qui coïncident avec les fêtes familiales et religieuses. Dans cette optique, il apparait évident que l'impact des transferts de fonds est lié à leur affectation et, plus particulièrement, à la répartition entre consommation et investissement.

Les envois de fonds n'ont pas que des effets positifs sur les économies des pays bénéficiaires et peuvent être à l'origine de certaines externalités négatives. C'est surtout le cas pour les pays qui reçoivent un volume important d'envois de fonds (avec parfois une forte saisonnalité) par exemple font généralement face à de fortes variations de leur taux de change pouvant affecter leurs taux d'intérêt et leurs balances des paiements. En fait, à l'instar de toute source importante de devises (ressources naturelles, secteurs exportateurs performants), les envois de fonds sont susceptibles de déclencher un phénomène similaire à ce qui désigné par la « maladie hollandaise » (Dutch disease), se traduisant par une appréciation de la monnaie nationale avec pour corollaire une perte de compétitivité et une hausse des produits importés. Différents travaux vont dans ce sens et montrent qu'une augmentation du montant des sommes expédiées par les travailleurs émigrés ferait apprécier le taux de change du pays bénéficiaire.

Cependant, la question de l'impact des transferts financiers sur le développement ne se résume pas au seul aspect économique. La transmission de savoir-faire, l'influence des idées en matière sociale et politique constituent autant de questions qui mériteraient à elles seules d'être analysées à part. De nombreuses études apportent des éclairages, au niveau de régions bien déterminées, et les conclusions auxquelles elles parviennent sont rarement généralisables.

Au total, l'ampleur de l'impact sur le développement des transferts d'argent dans les pays bénéficiaires dépend de la manière dont ces transferts sont utilisés. Il est ainsi évident que l'allocation de ces fonds à l'accumulation du capital productif et l'investissement entrepreneurial influe directement et de façon positive sur l'emploi et la croissance. Toutefois, certains chercheurs ont démontré que même si l'argent transféré est affecté exclusivement à la consommation et à l'achat ou la construction immobilière, il peut avoir divers effets indirects ou d'entrainement sur la croissance économique. Parmi ces effets, on peut évoquer la libération d'autres multiples sources potentielles d'investissement et l'activation de l'effet multiplicateur.

Défis associés à la promotion des envois de fonds

Compte tenu de ce qui précède, le constat et le débat autour des transferts de fonds soulèvent une série de défis que les autorités publiques et les différents intervenants sur cette thématique doivent accorder une attention particulière :

• *Amélioration de l'observation statistique sur les transferts et les phénomènes qui leurs sont associés.* Cet aspect est essentiel à plus d'un titre et repose sur la nécessité de disposer de données fiables et harmonisées. Parallèlement au renforcement des capacités des services chargés de la comptabilisation des envois de fonds sur la qualité des données (notamment au niveau des banques centrales), la mobilisation d'autres instruments statistiques permettrait de fournir des éléments de connaissances précieux, à la fois sur les profils de la migration que sur la dynamique des envois de fonds.

Le recours aux enquêtes auprès des ménages dans les pays de départ des migrants peuvent constituer une source de données très utile pour affiner l'estimation des envois de fonds reçus au cours d'une année. La fiabilité de l'estimation dépend bien sûr de la façon dont est conçu le module du questionnaire relatif à la migration et aux revenus qui lui sont associés, de la manière dont ce module est perçu par les personnes interrogées et de la représentativité de l'échantillon.

Une autre option, en dépit des difficultés méthodologiques qu'elle suscite, consiste à interroger directement les migrants dans les pays d'arrivée. Cette méthode permet de collecter des informations détaillées sur les revenus, l'épargne et les transferts ainsi que sur les pratiques bancaires des immigrés. Elle permet également de relier les comportements de transfert des individus à certaines de leurs caractéristiques et à celles de leurs familles restées au pays.

Une troisième approche combinée consiste à mener des enquêtes ménages recensant les individus en migration dans un pays donné et à réaliser dans un second temps une enquête auprès de ces mêmes individus sur leur lieu de résidence, de façon à construire une base de données « appariées » migrants-familles d'origine. Ce type de collecte est bien sûr complexe et vraisemblablement coûteux, mais les données produites peuvent permettre de considérablement affiner l'estimation du volume global des envois de fonds transitant d'un pays à un autre.

• *Consolidation des flux et canalisation efficiente des transferts.* Les pays africains peuvent potentiellement utiliser à l'avenir les envois de fonds (et autres ressources financières) comme une garantie à des financements sur les marchés internationaux de capitaux vers des projets de développement. Cependant, la saisonnalité des transferts des migrants vers l'Afrique décrit ci-dessus peut affecter la capacité de lever des fonds. Par ailleurs, un autre défi posé à une gestion efficace des envois de fonds réside dans la part élevée des transferts effectués via des circuits informels. Cela demande des efforts de la part des pouvoirs publics pour favoriser l'enregistrement et la comptabilisation officielle de ces transferts d'argent.

En outre, on sait que la manière de « dépenser » ces transferts est fondamentale dans l'enclenchement d'un processus vertueux et porteur de croissance inclusive. Dans cette logique, l'intervention de la politique économique, en tant qu'outil régulateur dans le but de booster les transferts, leur canalisation et leur intégration dans les schémas de développement des pays, est plus que jamais indispensable. Ceci implique un ensemble de mesures et interventions cohérentes vers l'optimisation de son impact sur le développement économique et social : ajustement de certaines réglementations, promouvoir le rôle des services postaux et les institutions de la micro-finance, implication des secteurs financiers et bancaires, conception de programmes spécifiques, etc. L'intervention des pouvoirs publics est également nécessaire pour corriger et palier les externalités négatives occasionnées par ces transferts.

Les expériences tentées dans d'autres pays peuvent fournir des enseignements utiles dans ce domaine. Ainsi, un certain nombre de pays en développement, notamment le Brésil, le Mexique, l'Inde et les Philippines, ont adopté des mesures incitatives visant à canaliser les envois de fonds dans des comptes d'épargne et des fonds d'investissement locaux. Ces pays ont mis en place des plans d'épargne-retraite pour les émigrés, octroient des prêts à des taux préférentiels ou des aides aux entreprises créées grâce à des transferts de fonds et permettent aux immigrés récemment rentrés dans leur pays d'avoir un accès plus flexible aux capitaux.

La part importante des flux informels constitue un souci auquel les pays africains doivent remédier et promouvoir davantage les réseaux de transfert officiels, en encourageant par diverses mesures incitatives les bénéficiaires à épargner davantage dans le cadre des circuits financiers formels. Pour rendre les transferts formels plus attirants, les pays pourraient également offrir des taux de change préférentiels et notamment moderniser les systèmes bancaires. La situation en matière de « remises » en Afrique évolue rapidement avec l'introduction d'innovations technologiques (transferts d'argent via le mobile et la banque à distance). Bien que l'adoption de ces innovations a été limité en grande partie aux transferts à l'échelle nationale, ces technologies ont le potentiel d'améliorer considérablement, à la fois, la mobilisation des envois de fonds et un accès plus large aux services financiers (incluant des produits d'épargne et crédits à faible coût), pour les migrants africains et les bénéficiaires de transferts de fonds dans les pays d'origine.

• *Favoriser la réduction des coûts de transferts et l'accès aux circuits financiers.* Bien qu'ils aient baissé au cours des dernières années, les coûts des transferts de fonds en Afrique restent relativement élevés et sont extrêmement volatiles. A titre d'illustration, les coûts de transfert depuis les États-Unis sont généralement parmi les moins élevés, suivis par les coûts de transfert émanant d'Europe. Pour paradoxal que ca puisse paraître, le coût d'envoi de fonds intra-continent est beaucoup plus élevé, alors que l'analyse avait montré plus haut qu'un large flux des transferts s'effectue entre les pays du même continent, voire de la même région. Ainsi, l'envoi de fonds depuis l'Afrique du Sud vers d'autres pays africains revient généralement plus cher qu'un transfert depuis un autre continent. Les envois de fonds sont particulièrement utiles, mais particulièrement onéreux, notamment lorsqu'ils sont destinés aux zones rurales de l'Afrique mal desservies en termes de réseaux bancaires.

Certaines mesures et actions sont indispensables pour remédier à cette situation, moyennant l'intervention des pouvoirs publics au niveau africain vis-à-vis des intermédiaires financiers, leur sensibilisation à l'importance de se positionner sur un « marché » en expansion et l'opportunité d'envisager une coopération et intégration régionale dans ce domaine. D'autres mesures serait également envisageables dans les pays d'où partent les transferts : favoriser une concurrence équitable et efficiente des marchés dans l'exécution des transferts, transparence dans l'établissement des tarifs, sensibilisation des migrants quant aux choix qui s'offrent à eux, tolérer l'ouverture de comptes bancaires pour les immigrés clandestins et leur donner ainsi accès à des services de transfert moins coûteux. De telles mesures permettraient du coup à un volume de transferts plus importants d'emprunter le circuit financier formel.

• *Association et implication de la diaspora dans les stratégies de développement.* Trop souvent, les débats sur l'émigration mettent l'accent sur la fuite des compétences et de la main d'œuvre des pays pauvres vers les pays riches. Notamment, le départ de ressources humaines hautement formées et qualifiées prive les pays de compétences essentielles. Mais, les envois de fonds forment le lien central et tangible entre la migration et le développement. Donc, au lieu de se concentrer sur les aspects négatifs de l'émigration, les remises devraient être considérées plutôt comme une opportunité pour les pays africains de bénéficier de leurs citoyens qui ont choisi de vivre et de travailler à l'étranger.

D'autre part, la perte de capital humain pour les économies d'origine, surtout celles avec des migrants dotés d'un niveau de formation supérieur ou professionnellement qualifiés, n'est pas forcément autant compensée par les flux de transferts dans la mesure où les travailleurs hautement qualifiés sont parfois moins enclins à transférer de l'argent. Des mécanismes adaptés et des instruments pourraient être imaginés afin de maintenir les ponts entre les migrants et leurs pays d'origine et d'associer la diaspora à la dynamique de développement du continent.

• *Mise en place d'une « plateforme » de connaissance sur les différents sujets associés aux transferts en Afrique.* Cette étude sur les envois de fonds a par ailleurs cette modeste ambition de sensibiliser les différents intervenants sur la nécessité d'approfondir l'analyse de ces flux. L'objectif étant d'accélérer la mise en place d'une large plateforme de connaissance autour de la thématique des « remises ». Des initiatives telles que le projet « AIR » (African Institute for Remittances) parrainé par la Commission de l'Union Africaine en partenariat avec d'autres institutions, à savoir la Commission européenne (CE), la Banque mondiale (BM), la Banque africaine de développement (BAD) et l'Organisation internationale pour les migrations (OIM), constitue un point d'ancrage pour mailler les diverses contributions, réflexions et travaux de recherche dans ce domaine en Afrique. Le souci est de constituer un espace de partage de savoir ou de connaissances pour mieux comprendre, d'un côté les phénomènes migratoires et leur dimension, et de l'autre tous les aspects relatifs aux transferts et proposer une panoplie de mesure de promotion efficace et à moindre coût des envois de fonds.

Conclusion

L'analyse sous revue a montré que les remises ou envois de fonds constituent une source de fonds extérieurs très importante pour les pays africains, surtout dans un contexte où le continent est confronté à une série de défis en matière de développement et le volume élevé des financements requis. Actuellement, le montant des envois de fonds vers l'Afrique dépasse le flux des investissements directs étrangers et équivaut à l'aide publique au développement dans certains pays. Par ailleurs, ces transferts forment une source de capitaux extérieurs régulière et stable, avec un potentiel de progression prometteur. Leur impact positif sur les problématiques liées au développement humain (croissance inclusive, réduction de la pauvreté, l'emploi, l'éducation et la santé) du continent est largement reconnu.

Néanmoins, l'ampleur de l'impact des transferts sur la dynamique de développement dans les pays africains bénéficiaires n'est pas souvent optimale. Elle dépend de la manière dont ces transferts sont mobilisés et affectés, sachant surtout que l'allocation optimale de ces fonds à l'accumulation du capital productif et l'investissement contribue à répondre aux différents enjeux auxquels sont confrontés les pays africains.

L'analyse présentée dans ce document a remis sur la table le rôle de la migration comme facteur déterminant dans la dynamique et l'expansion des transferts. En effet, la nature du mouvement de population durant les dernières décennies, et dont la moitié s'opère sur le continent, a dessiné la configuration actuelle et le profil des flux d'envois de fonds. L'étude révèle la polarisation des « remises » sur deux sous régions majeures du continent – Afrique du Nord et Afrique de l'Ouest – et leur concentration sur un nombre limité de pays. Elle met en avant également le montant relativement faible des transferts par migrant comparé à d'autres régions du globe et le coût exorbitant des opérations de transfert vers/entre les pays africains bénéficiaires.

Cependant, malgré leur poids, plusieurs aspects relatifs à ces flux financiers générés en direction des pays africains (volume exact, caractéristiques, motivations, utilisations, etc.) demeurent relativement mal connus. De nombreuses zones d'ombres subsistent encore quant à la structure du marché ou à l'allocation de ces ressources et les externalités générées. La Banque africaine de développement (BAD) et ses partenaires (CUA et CEA) reconnaissent l'utilité de ce type de transferts et accordent une haute priorité à leur promotion et à leur intégration dans le processus de développement en Afrique. Néanmoins, la BAD reste en même temps convaincue que ces envois ne constituent pas une panacée et ne sauraient se substituer à de saines politiques économiques au niveau des pays.

La consolidation et la mobilisation efficiente des remises se heurtent à une série de défis qu'il faudra relever de manière simultanée, étant donné leur complémentarité. L'un des principaux points est relatif à la qualité des données et statistiques rattachées aux phénomènes migratoires et les envois de fonds, à travers le renforcement des capacités statistiques des ministères et départements concernés. Bien que l'adoption rapide des nouvelles technologies en matière de transfert d'argent continue de façonner le paysage des envois de fonds et plus largement les services financiers, le marché des « remises » en Afrique demeure relativement peu développé en termes d'infrastructure financière et de réglementation. Dans ce contexte, les interventions pourraient inclure l'intégration des flux informels dans la sphère financière formelle; un accès simplifié pour les individus aux circuits financiers; et une réduction des coûts de transfert aux pays africains bénéficiaires.

Parallèlement, l'amélioration d'interaction entre les envois de fonds et la question du développement à travers l'orientation efficiente des ressources financières extérieures vers l'investissement productif constitue l'autre défi majeur auquel sont confrontés les pays africains. Dans ce sens, plusieurs autres pistes peuvent être envisagées : association de la diaspora africaine aux schémas de développement, coordination institutionnelle entre les intermédiaires financiers africains (en particulier au niveau sous régional) pour mieux conquérir le marché des transferts, la création de produits d'épargne et de placement adaptés, voire reliés à des projets locaux ou spécifiques de développement.

Part
Partie
1

Summary Tables

Tableaux résumés

Section 1

Social and Demographic Indicators

Indicateurs démographiques et sociaux

POPULATION

1-1. Total mid-year population – Population totale au milieu de l'année

Thousands / *Milliers*

Country	2005	2006	2007	2008	2009	2010	2011	2012	2013	2014	Pays
Algeria	33 961	34 507	35 097	35 725	36 383	37 063	37 763	38 482	39 208	39 929	Algérie
Angola	16 544	17 122	17 713	18 314	18 927	19 549	20 180	20 821	21 472	22 137	Angola
Benin	8 182	8 444	8 707	8 973	9 241	9 510	9 780	10 051	10 323	10 600	Bénin
Botswana	1 876	1 896	1 915	1 934	1 952	1 969	1 987	2 004	2 021	2 039	Botswana
Burkina Faso	13 422	13 822	14 235	14 660	15 095	15 540	15 995	16 460	16 935	17 420	Burkina Faso
Burundi	7 770	8 043	8 328	8 624	8 927	9 233	9 540	9 850	10 163	10 483	Burundi
Cabo Verde	479	482	484	485	486	488	491	494	499	504	Cabo Verde
Cameroon	18 138	18 612	19 098	19 595	20 104	20 624	21 156	21 700	22 254	22 819	Cameroun
Central African Republic	3 961	4 032	4 107	4 185	4 266	4 350	4 436	4 525	4 616	4 709	République Centrafricaine
Chad	10 014	10 357	10 694	11 031	11 371	11 721	12 080	12 448	12 825	13 211	Tchad
Comoros	601	617	633	649	666	683	700	718	735	752	Comores
Congo	3 543	3 647	3 759	3 876	3 995	4 112	4 225	4 337	4 448	4 559	Congo
Congo. Dem. Republic	54 028	55 591	57 188	58 819	60 486	62 191	63 932	65 705	67 514	69 360	Rép. Démocratique du Congo
Côte d'Ivoire	17 394	17 662	17 949	18 260	18 601	18 977	19 390	19 840	20 316	20 805	Côte d'Ivoire
Djibouti	777	788	799	810	822	834	847	860	873	886	Djibouti
Egypt	71 778	72 991	74 230	75 492	76 775	78 076	79 392	80 722	82 056	83 387	Égypte
Equatorial Guinea	604	622	640	658	677	696	716	736	757	778	Guinée Equatoriale
Eritrea	4 854	5 035	5 210	5 382	5 558	5 741	5 933	6 131	6 333	6 536	Érythrée
Ethiopia	76 167	78 291	80 441	82 621	84 838	87 095	89 393	91 729	94 101	96 506	Éthiopie
Gabon	1 379	1 413	1 447	1 483	1 519	1 556	1 594	1 633	1 672	1 711	Gabon
Gambia	1 437	1 482	1 529	1 578	1 628	1 681	1 735	1 791	1 849	1 909	Gambie
Ghana	21 384	21 948	22 526	23 110	23 692	24 263	24 821	25 366	25 905	26 442	Ghana
Guinea	9 576	9 799	10 047	10 315	10 593	10 876	11 162	11 451	11 745	12 044	Guinée
Guinea Bissau	1 422	1 453	1 484	1 517	1 551	1 587	1 624	1 664	1 704	1 746	Guinée-Bissau
Kenya	35 786	36 757	37 752	38 773	39 825	40 909	42 028	43 178	44 354	45 546	Kenya
Lesotho	1 926	1 940	1 956	1 972	1 990	2 009	2 030	2 052	2 074	2 098	Lésotho
Liberia	3 270	3 385	3 522	3 673	3 821	3 958	4 080	4 190	4 294	4 397	Libéria
Libya	5 594	5 686	5 782	5 877	5 964	6 041	6 103	6 155	6 202	6 253	Libye
Madagascar	18 290	18 826	19 371	19 927	20 496	21 080	21 679	22 294	22 925	23 572	Madagascar
Malawi	12 925	13 308	13 714	14 138	14 573	15 014	15 458	15 906	16 363	16 829	Malawi
Mali	11 941	12 326	12 726	13 138	13 559	13 986	14 417	14 854	15 302	15 768	Mali
Mauritania	3 146	3 238	3 330	3 423	3 516	3 609	3 703	3 796	3 890	3 984	Mauritanie
Mauritius	1 213	1 217	1 220	1 223	1 227	1 231	1 235	1 240	1 244	1 249	Maurice
Morocco	30 125	30 395	30 667	30 955	31 277	31 642	32 059	32 521	33 008	33 493	Maroc
Mozambique	21 010	21 587	22 171	22 763	23 361	23 967	24 581	25 203	25 834	26 473	Mozambique
Namibia	2 027	2 053	2 081	2 111	2 143	2 179	2 218	2 259	2 303	2 348	Namibie
Niger	13 184	13 680	14 197	14 738	15 303	15 894	16 511	17 157	17 831	18 535	Niger
Nigeria	139 586	143 315	147 187	151 208	155 381	159 708	164 193	168 834	173 615	178 517	Nigéria
Rwanda	9 429	9 661	9 928	10 223	10 530	10 837	11 144	11 458	11 777	12 100	Rwanda
São Tomé & Principe	155	159	163	168	173	178	183	188	193	198	São Tomé & Príncipe
Senegal	11 271	11 583	11 905	12 239	12 587	12 951	13 331	13 726	14 133	14 548	Sénégal
Seychelles	87	88	89	90	91	91	92	92	93	93	Seychelles
Sierra Leone	5 120	5 281	5 416	5 532	5 641	5 752	5 865	5 979	6 092	6 205	Sierra Leone
Somalia	8 467	8 688	8 911	9 140	9 381	9 636	9 908	10 195	10 496	10 806	Somalie
South Africa	48 235	48 919	49 603	50 267	50 890	51 452	51 949	52 386	52 776	53 140	Afrique du Sud
South Sudan	8 039	8 377	8 737	9 118	9 521	9 941	10 381	10 838	11 296	11 739	Soudan du Sud
Sudan	31 586	32 398	33 218	34 040	34 853	35 652	36 431	37 195	37 964	38 764	Soudan
Swaziland	1 105	1 118	1 135	1 154	1 174	1 193	1 212	1 231	1 250	1 268	Swaziland
Tanzania	38 824	39 942	41 120	42 354	43 640	44 973	46 355	47 783	49 253	50 757	Tanzanie
Togo	5 540	5 686	5 835	5 987	6 144	6 306	6 472	6 643	6 817	6 993	Togo
Tunisia	10 051	10 160	10 274	10 391	10 511	10 632	10 753	10 875	10 997	11 117	Tunisie
Uganda	28 725	29 711	30 729	31 779	32 864	33 987	35 148	36 346	37 579	38.845	Ouganda
Zambia	11 470	11 782	12 110	12 457	12 825	13 217	13 634	14 075	14 539	15 021	Zambie
Zimbabwe	12 711	12 724	12 740	12 784	12 889	13 077	13 359	13 724	14 150	14 599	Zimbabwe
Africa	**910 129**	**932 643**	**955 848**	**979 740**	**1004 303**	**1 029 516**	**1 055 383**	**1 081 889**	**1 108 966**	**1 136 526**	**Afrique**

1-2. Female (as % of Total) - Population féminine (% de la population totale)

Percentage / *Pourcentage*

Country	2005	2006	2007	2008	2009	2010	2011	2012	2013	2014	Pays
Algeria	49.5	49.5	49.5	49.4	49.4	49.4	49.4	49.4	49.4	49.5	Algérie
Angola	50.6	50.5	50.5	50.5	50.5	50.5	50.4	50.4	50.4	50.4	Angola
Benin	50.5	50.5	50.4	50.3	50.3	50.2	50.2	50.2	50.2	50.1	Bénin
Botswana	50.2	50.1	50.1	50.0	50.0	49.9	49.8	49.8	49.7	49.6	Botswana
Burkina Faso	50.7	50.6	50.6	50.5	50.5	50.4	50.4	50.3	50.3	50.2	Burkina Faso
Burundi	50.5	50.5	50.6	50.6	50.6	50.6	50.6	50.6	50.6	50.6	Burundi
Cabo Verde	51.0	50.9	50.8	50.6	50.5	50.4	50.3	50.3	50.2	50.1	Cabo Verde
Cameroon	50.1	50.1	50.1	50.1	50.0	50.0	50.0	50.0	50.0	50.0	Cameroun
Central African Republic	50.9	50.9	50.9	50.8	50.8	50.8	50.8	50.8	50.8	50.8	République Centrafricaine
Chad	50.1	50.0	50.0	50.0	50.0	50.0	49.9	49.9	49.9	49.9	Tchad
Comoros	49.8	49.7	49.7	49.7	49.7	49.7	49.6	49.6	49.6	49.6	Comores
Congo	50.1	50.0	50.0	50.0	50.0	50.0	50.0	50.0	50.0	50.0	Congo
Congo. Dem. Republic	50.4	50.3	50.3	50.3	50.3	50.3	50.3	50.3	50.3	50.3	Rép. Démocratique du Congo
Côte d'Ivoire	48.6	48.7	48.8	48.8	48.9	48.9	48.9	49.0	49.0	49.1	Côte d'Ivoire
Djibouti	49.7	49.7	49.7	49.8	49.8	49.8	49.8	49.8	49.8	49.8	Djibouti
Egypt	49.7	49.7	49.8	49.8	49.8	49.8	49.8	49.8	49.8	49.8	Égypte
Equatorial Guinea	48.7	48.7	48.7	48.7	48.7	48.7	48.8	48.8	48.8	48.8	Guinée Equatoriale
Eritrea	50.3	50.3	50.3	50.2	50.2	50.2	50.2	50.1	50.1	50.1	Érythrée
Ethiopia	50.0	50.0	50.0	50.0	50.0	50.0	50.0	50.0	50.0	50.0	Éthiopie
Gabon	50.1	50.0	50.0	49.9	49.9	49.8	49.8	49.8	49.7	49.7	Gabon
Gambia	50.5	50.5	50.5	50.5	50.5	50.5	50.5	50.5	50.5	50.5	Gambie
Ghana	50.0	50.2	50.3	50.4	50.5	50.5	50.5	50.5	50.4	50.4	Ghana
Guinea	50.0	50.0	50.0	50.0	50.0	49.9	49.9	49.9	49.9	49.9	Guinée
Guinea Bissau	50.3	50.3	50.3	50.3	50.3	50.3	50.3	50.3	50.3	50.3	Guinée-Bissau
Kenya	50.1	50.1	50.1	50.1	50.1	50.1	50.1	50.1	50.1	50.1	Kenya
Lesotho	51.2	51.2	51.1	51.0	51.0	50.9	50.8	50.7	50.7	50.6	Lésotho
Liberia	49.9	49.8	49.8	49.8	49.7	49.7	49.7	49.7	49.6	49.6	Libéria
Libya	48.6	48.6	48.7	48.8	48.9	49.1	49.3	49.6	50.0	50.3	Libye
Madagascar	50.2	50.2	50.2	50.2	50.2	50.2	50.2	50.2	50.2	50.2	Madagascar
Malawi	50.2	50.1	50.1	50.0	50.0	50.0	49.9	49.9	49.9	49.9	Malawi
Mali	49.9	49.8	49.8	49.7	49.7	49.7	49.6	49.6	49.6	49.6	Mali
Mauritania	49.8	49.7	49.7	49.7	49.7	49.7	49.7	49.6	49.6	49.6	Mauritanie
Mauritius	50.5	50.5	50.5	50.5	50.5	50.6	50.6	50.6	50.6	50.7	Maurice
Morocco	50.6	50.7	50.8	50.8	50.8	50.8	50.8	50.7	50.6	50.5	Maroc
Mozambique	51.6	51.5	51.5	51.4	51.3	51.3	51.2	51.2	51.1	51.1	Mozambique
Namibia	51.2	51.3	51.3	51.4	51.5	51.5	51.5	51.5	51.5	51.4	Namibie
Niger	49.8	49.8	49.8	49.7	49.7	49.7	49.7	49.6	49.6	49.6	Niger
Nigeria	49.3	49.2	49.2	49.2	49.2	49.2	49.1	49.1	49.1	49.1	Nigéria
Rwanda	51.3	51.3	51.3	51.3	51.2	51.2	51.2	51.2	51.2	51.2	Rwanda
São Tomé & Príncipe	50.8	50.8	50.7	50.7	50.7	50.7	50.7	50.6	50.6	50.6	São Tomé & Príncipe
Senegal	51.0	51.0	51.0	51.0	51.0	51.0	51.0	51.0	51.0	50.9	Sénégal
Seychelles	50.0	49.9	49.6	49.3	49.1	49.0	48.9	49.0	49.1	49.2	Seychelles
Sierra Leone	50.6	50.5	50.5	50.5	50.5	50.4	50.4	50.4	50.3	50.3	Sierra Leone
Somalia	50.3	50.3	50.3	50.3	50.3	50.3	50.3	50.3	50.3	50.2	Somalie
South Africa	51.3	51.3	51.4	51.4	51.5	51.5	51.5	51.5	51.5	51.4	Afrique du Sud
South Sudan	50.1	50.1	50.1	50.1	50.0	50.0	50.0	50.0	50.0	50.0	Soudan du Sud
Sudan	49.8	49.8	49.8	49.8	49.8	49.8	49.8	49.8	49.8	49.8	Soudan
Swaziland	51.1	51.1	51.0	50.9	50.9	50.8	50.8	50.7	50.7	50.6	Swaziland
Tanzania	50.1	50.1	50.1	50.1	50.0	50.0	50.0	50.0	50.0	50.0	Tanzanie
Togo	50.9	50.9	50.9	50.8	50.8	50.8	50.7	50.7	50.7	50.7	Togo
Tunisia	50.1	50.2	50.2	50.2	50.3	50.3	50.4	50.4	50.4	50.5	Tunisie
Uganda	50.0	49.9	49.9	49.9	49.9	49.9	49.9	49.9	49.9	49.9	Ouganda
Zambia	50.1	50.1	50.1	50.1	50.1	50.1	50.1	50.1	50.1	50.1	Zambie
Zimbabwe	50.5	50.6	50.6	50.7	50.7	50.7	50.7	50.7	50.6	50.6	Zimbabwe
Africa	**50.1**	**50.1**	**50.1**	**50.1**	**50.0**	**50.0**	**50.0**	**50.0**	**50.0**	**50.1**	**Afrique**

POPULATION

1-3. Economically active population- Population active

Country	Total (000)						Female / Femmes (%)						Pays
	2009	2010	2011	2012	2013	2014	2009	2010	2011	2012	2013	2014	
Algeria	11 333	11 643	11 926	12 196	12 453	12 693	16.7	16.8	17.0	17.1	17.2	17.3	Algérie
Angola	6 849	7 115	7 366	7 627	7 899	8 182	45.6	45.9	46.0	46.0	46.1	46.2	Angola
Benin	3 784	3 915	4 045	4 177	4 311	4 449	46.8	46.9	46.9	46.9	47.0	47.0	Bénin
Botswana	977	991	1 004	1 018	1 031	1 045	47.0	46.9	46.8	46.7	46.6	46.5	Botswana
Burkina Faso	6 794	7 013	7 234	7 464	7 702	7 947	47.7	47.6	47.5	47.4	47.4	47.3	Burkina Faso
Burundi	4 111	4 257	4 400	4 536	4 666	4 797	51.3	51.3	51.3	51.4	51.4	51.4	Burundi
Cabo Verde	216	221	226	232	238	243	38.4	38.4	38.4	38.4	38.4	38.4	Cabo Verde
Cameroon	7 904	8 155	8 405	8 662	8 927	9 200	45.5	45.6	45.6	45.6	45.7	45.7	Cameroun
Central African Republic	1 980	2 031	2 081	2 134	2 188	2 243	47.1	47.2	47.2	47.2	47.2	47.2	République Centrafricaine
Chad	4 156	4 293	4 437	4 588	4 744	4 906	45.0	45.0	45.0	45.0	44.9	44.9	Tchad
Comoros	220	227	233	239	245	252	30.0	30.2	30.3	30.4	30.6	30.7	Comores
Congo	1 626	1 676	1 723	1 767	1 810	1 854	48.7	48.7	48.7	48.7	48.7	48.7	Congo
Congo. Dem. Republic	23 645	24 386	25 146	25 930	26 741	27 580	49.9	49.9	49.9	49.8	49.8	49.8	Rép. Démocratique du Congo
Côte d'Ivoire	7 268	7 437	7 617	7 814	8 023	8 239	37.1	37.3	37.5	37.6	37.8	37.9	Côte d'Ivoire
Djibouti	274	281	288	295	301	307	34.6	34.8	34.8	34.8	34.9	34.9	Djibouti
Egypt	25 371	25 970	26 576	27 179	27 776	28 365	23.9	24.0	24.1	24.2	24.2	24.2	Égypte
Equatorial Guinea	354	366	378	390	402	414	44.6	44.7	44.7	44.8	44.8	44.9	Guinée Equatoriale
Eritrea	2 674	2 765	2 859	2 956	3 055	3 155	48.1	48.1	48.1	48.1	48.1	48.1	Érythrée
Ethiopia	39 279	40 599	42 045	43 570	45 163	46 807	47.0	47.0	47.0	47.1	47.1	47.1	Éthiopie
Gabon	557	574	591	608	626	644	46.2	46.2	46.2	46.1	46.1	46.1	Gabon
Gambia	682	704	727	751	775	801	47.7	47.8	47.8	47.9	47.9	47.9	Gambie
Ghana	9 907	10 199	10 486	10 772	11 058	11 349	50.0	50.1	50.1	50.0	49.9	49.7	Ghana
Guinea	4 321	4 461	4 597	4 737	4 881	5 029	45.6	45.7	45.7	45.7	45.7	45.8	Guinée
Guinea Bissau	656	674	693	712	732	753	46.9	47.0	47.0	47.0	47.0	47.0	Guinée-Bissau
Kenya	15 138	15 631	16 149	16 686	17 239	17 804	46.6	46.6	46.6	46.6	46.6	46.7	Kenya
Lesotho	807	822	838	855	872	890	46.3	46.2	46.1	45.9	45.8	45.7	Lésotho
Liberia	1 322	1 372	1 421	1 466	1 510	1 555	47.7	47.7	47.6	47.5	47.4	47.4	Libéria
Libya	2 246	2 274	2 295	2 308	2 316	2 327	27.5	27.6	27.8	28.2	28.6	28.9	Libye
Madagascar	10 227	10 623	10 969	11 327	11 696	12 075	49.4	49.4	49.4	49.4	49.4	49.4	Madagascar
Malawi	6 557	6 763	6 979	7 206	7 442	7 686	51.7	51.5	51.4	51.3	51.2	51.0	Malawi
Mali	4 592	4 892	5 036	5 178	5 324	5 479	37.8	38.3	38.4	38.4	38.5	38.6	Mali
Mauritania	1 112	1 150	1 186	1 221	1 258	1 295	26.2	26.4	26.5	26.5	26.6	26.7	Mauritanie
Mauritius	557	570	575	580	585	591	36.6	37.5	37.6	37.7	37.9	38.0	Maurice
Morocco	11 296	11 374	11 592	11 812	12 031	12 243	26.4	26.8	26.9	26.9	27.0	27.0	Maroc
Mozambique	10 841	11 089	11 347	11 614	11 893	12 184	53.5	53.4	53.2	53.1	52.9	52.8	Mozambique
Namibia	827	831	835	839	869	901	48.4	48.5	48.6	48.6	48.6	48.5	Namibie
Niger	4 977	5 158	5 349	5 551	5 763	5 986	31.0	31.0	31.1	31.1	31.1	31.2	Niger
Nigeria	48 364	49 748	51 183	52 668	54 205	55 798	42.6	42.6	42.5	42.5	42.5	42.4	Nigéria
Rwanda	4 995	5 166	5 354	5 563	5 785	6 005	52.5	52.4	52.4	52.4	52.3	52.3	Rwanda
São Tomé & Principe	60	62	65	67	69	71	37.8	37.9	38.0	37.9	38.0	38.1	São Tomé & Principe
Senegal	5 401	5 570	5 744	5 925	6 113	6 307	44.9	45.0	45.0	45.0	45.0	44.9	Sénégal
Seychelles	...	...	...	...	...	...	...	...	...	...	...	...	Seychelles
Sierra Leone	2 181	2 234	2 289	2 344	2 401	2 459	49.7	49.6	49.5	49.4	49.3	49.2	Sierra Leone
Somalia	2 749	2 827	2 915	3 010	3 112	3 218	33.4	33.5	33.6	33.6	33.7	33.8	Somalie
South Africa	18 892	18 566	18 761	19 108	19 414	19 703	44.3	44.2	44.7	44.6	44.5	44.4	Afrique du Sud
South Sudan	...	...	...	...	...	...	...	...	...	...	...	...	Soudan du Sud
Sudan	10 707	11 024	11 333	11 643	11 960	12 294	29.0	29.1	29.2	29.3	29.3	29.4	Soudan
Swaziland	402	413	425	436	447	457	39.6	39.6	39.5	39.4	39.2	39.1	Swaziland
Tanzania	21 525	22 155	22 813	23 502	24 219	24 964	49.8	49.8	49.8	49.7	49.7	49.7	Tanzanie
Togo	2 868	2 953	3 038	3 124	3 212	3 303	51.4	51.3	51.2	51.1	51.0	50.9	Togo
Tunisia	3 760	3 835	3 901	3 962	4 019	4 071	26.8	26.8	26.8	26.9	26.9	26.9	Tunisie
Uganda	13 059	13 516	14 002	14 511	15 041	15 592	49.1	49.0	49.0	49.0	49.0	48.9	Ouganda
Zambia	5 417	5 581	5 761	5 954	6 159	6 375	46.2	46.2	46.2	46.3	46.3	46.3	Zambie
Zimbabwe	6 499	6 622	6 821	7 085	7 394	7 717	49.5	49.5	49.5	49.4	49.3	49.2	Zimbabwe
Africa	**382 310**	**392 774**	**404 057**	**415 896**	**428 092**	**440 599**	**42.4**	**42.5**	**42.5**	**42.5**	**42.5**	**42.5**	**Afrique**

1-4. Adult Illiteracy Rate (%) - Taux d'analphabétisme des adultes (%)

Percentage | *Pourcentage*

Country	1990-2002			2005-2012			2015 (*)			Pays
	MF	M	F	MF	M	F	MF	M	F	
Algeria	30.1	20.4	39.9	27.4	18.7	36.1	19.8	12.8	26.9	Algérie
Angola	32.6	17.1	45.8	29.6	17.4	41.4	28.9	18.0	39.3	Angola
Benin	65.3	52.1	76.7	71.3	59.4	81.6	61.6	50.1	72.7	Bénin
Botswana	31.4	34.6	28.7	14.9	15.4	14.4	11.5	12.0	11.1	Botswana
Burkina Faso	87.2	81.5	91.9	71.3	63.3	78.4	64.0	57.0	70.7	Burkina Faso
Burundi	40.7	32.7	47.8	13.1	11.2	15.4	14.4	11.8	16.9	Burundi
Cabo Verde	37.2	25.2	47.0	15.1	10.3	19.7	12.4	7.9	16.9	Cabo Verde
Cameroon	31.6	20.8	41.3	28.7	21.7	35.2	25.0	18.8	31.1	Cameroun
Central African Republic	49.4	33.2	64.7	43.4	30.4	55.8	63.2	49.3	75.6	République Centrafricaine
Chad	74.3	59.2	87.2	64.6	54.4	74.6	59.8	51.5	68.1	Tchad
Comoros	31.5	25.5	36.5	24.5	19.5	29.4	22.2	18.2	26.3	Comores
Congo	...	...	...	20.7	13.6	27.1	20.7	13.6	27.1	Congo
Congo. Dem. Republic	32.8	19.1	45.9	38.8	23.1	53.9	36.2	21.9	50.0	Rép. Démocratique du Congo
Côte d'Ivoire	51.3	39.1	61.4	43.1	34.4	52.4	56.9	46.9	67.5	Côte d'Ivoire
Djibouti	...	...	...	...	...	...	...	...	...	Djibouti
Egypt	44.4	32.8	56.4	26.1	18.3	34.2	26.2	17.8	34.6	Égypte
Equatorial Guinea	11.7	5.2	18.4	5.8	2.9	8.9	4.7	2.6	7.0	Guinée Equatoriale
Eritrea	47.5	34.6	59.8	31.1	20.5	41.0	26.2	17.6	34.5	Érythrée
Ethiopia	73.0	64.0	81.5	61.0	50.9	71.1	50.9	42.8	58.9	Éthiopie
Gabon	27.8	20.6	34.7	11.0	7.7	14.4	16.8	14.7	19.0	Gabon
Gambia	63.2	51.0	74.9	48.9	39.1	58.1	44.5	36.1	52.4	Gambie
Ghana	42.1	33.6	50.2	28.5	21.7	34.7	23.4	18.0	28.6	Ghana
Guinea	79.4	67.1	90.3	74.7	63.2	87.8	69.6	61.9	77.2	Guinée
Guinea Bissau	58.6	42.4	72.5	44.7	31.1	57.9	40.1	28.2	51.7	Guinée-Bissau
Kenya	17.8	12.5	22.1	27.8	21.9	33.1	22.0	18.9	25.1	Kenya
Lesotho	13.7	20.0	8.0	24.2	34.5	15.0	20.6	29.9	11.7	Lésotho
Liberia	56.5	44.8	68.0	57.1	39.2	73.0	52.4	37.6	67.2	Libéria
Libya	22.8	11.7	35.0	10.5	4.2	16.7	9.0	3.3	14.4	Libye
Madagascar	29.3	23.5	34.7	35.5	32.6	38.4	35.3	33.3	37.4	Madagascar
Malawi	35.9	25.1	46.0	38.7	27.9	48.7	34.2	27.0	41.4	Malawi
Mali	81.0	73.3	88.1	66.6	56.9	75.4	61.3	51.8	70.8	Mali
Mauritania	48.8	40.5	56.6	41.4	34.7	48.0	47.9	37.4	58.4	Mauritanie
Mauritius	15.7	11.8	19.5	11.2	8.9	13.3	9.4	7.1	11.5	Maurice
Morocco	58.4	44.8	71.3	32.9	23.9	42.4	31.5	21.4	41.2	Maroc
Mozambique	61.3	45.2	75.0	49.4	32.6	63.5	41.2	26.7	54.6	Mozambique
Namibia	15.0	13.2	16.5	23.5	25.7	21.6	18.1	20.8	15.5	Namibie
Niger	90.6	90.6	90.6	71.3	57.1	84.9	80.9	72.7	89.0	Niger
Nigeria	44.6	32.3	56.3	48.9	38.7	58.6	40.4	30.8	50.3	Nigéria
Rwanda	35.1	28.6	40.2	34.1	28.9	38.5	29.5	26.8	32.0	Rwanda
São Tomé & Príncipe	15.1	7.8	22.1	30.5	19.7	39.9	25.1	18.2	31.6	São Tomé & Príncipe
Senegal	60.7	48.9	70.8	50.3	38.2	61.3	42.3	30.3	53.4	Sénégal
Seychelles	8.2	8.6	7.7	8.2	8.6	7.7	...	...	...	Seychelles
Sierra Leone	...	...	...	56.7	45.3	67.4	51.9	41.3	62.3	Sierra Leone
Somalia	...	...	...	...	...	...	...	...	...	Somalie
South Africa	17.6	15.9	19.1	7.0	6.1	7.8	5.7	4.5	6.9	Afrique du Sud
South Sudan	...	...	...	...	...	...	...	...	...	Soudan du Sud
Sudan	38.7	28.4	47.9	28.1	19.3	36.8	24.1	16.7	31.4	Soudan
Swaziland	18.3	16.8	19.7	12.2	11.6	12.7	12.5	12.6	12.5	Swaziland
Tanzania	30.6	22.5	37.8	32.2	24.5	39.2	29.4	24.1	34.6	Tanzanie
Togo	46.8	31.3	61.5	39.6	25.9	52.0	33.5	21.7	44.7	Togo
Tunisia	40.8	29.8	51.8	20.9	12.6	28.9	18.2	10.4	25.8	Tunisie
Uganda	31.9	21.7	41.1	26.8	17.4	35.4	21.6	14.7	28.5	Ouganda
Zambia	30.9	19.1	38.2	38.6	28.1	48.2	36.6	29.1	44.0	Zambie
Zimbabwe	16.5	11.1	21.5	16.4	12.2	19.9	13.5	11.5	15.4	Zimbabwe
Africa	**41.3**	**32.5**	**49.4**	**34.9**	**27.2**	**42.2**	**32.3**	**25.7**	**38.7**	**Afrique**

*** Estimation UNESCO 2015**

1-5. Gross Enrolment Ratio in primary - Taux brut de scolarisation au primaire

Percentage / *Pourcentage*

Country	2000			2005			2010-2015			
	MF	M	F	MF	M	F	MF	M	F	
Algeria	103.2	107.8	98.5	106.7	110.9	102.4	117.4	120.7	114.0	Algérie
Angola	...	...	...	...	...	...	140.5	171.2	109.6	Angola
Benin	81.2	97.5	65.0	98.5	111.3	85.8	122.8	129.5	115.9	Bénin
Botswana	103.7	103.7	103.7	105.2	105.9	104.5	...	...	...	Botswana
Burkina Faso	45.0	52.5	37.3	58.3	64.6	51.8	85.0	87.3	82.6	Burkina Faso
Burundi	57.1	63.8	50.5	80.2	87.0	73.5	137.4	138.0	136.9	Burundi
Cabo Verde	83.1	89.7	76.5	100.3	109.1	91.4	110.6	117.9	107.0	Cabo Verde
Cameroon	122.8	125.2	120.3	114.2	117.3	111.2	112.0	116.9	103.2	Cameroun
Central African Republic	...	...	...	66.5	78.9	54.3	95.2	109.3	81.3	République Centrafricaine
Chad	64.1	79.2	48.7	72.1	85.8	58.2	95.4	108.2	82.4	Tchad
Comoros	116.8	126.0	107.3	...	...	...	117.4	122.9	111.7	Comores
Congo	87.8	91.2	84.3	110.3	114.2	106.3	109.4	105.5	113.4	Congo
Congo. Dem. Republic	...	...	...	...	...	...	110.9	118.2	103.6	Rép. Démocratique du Congo
Côte d'Ivoire	77.3	88.2	66.4	...	...	...	94.2	101.8	86.6	Côte d'Ivoire
Djibouti	30.8	35.3	26.1	43.6	47.7	39.3	67.9	72.5	63.2	Djibouti
Egypt	101.3	105.3	97.2	105.5	108.7	102.1	113.4	115.7	111.1	Égypte
Equatorial Guinea	107.6	118.4	96.8	100.7	103.1	98.3	90.7	91.8	89.6	Guinée Equatoriale
Eritrea	50.4	54.9	45.8	60.2	65.9	54.3	42.5	46.0	38.8	Érythrée
Ethiopia	54.9	66.3	43.4	79.2	86.3	72.1	...	...	...	Éthiopie
Gabon	...	...	...	...	...	...	164.9	167.3	162.4	Gabon
Gambia	90.5	96.8	84.2	90.8	89.5	92.1	85.2	83.4	87.0	Gambie
Ghana	86.0	89.0	83.0	90.4	92.1	88.6	106.9	106.9	106.8	Ghana
Guinea	57.5	68.8	46.0	80.1	88.9	71.2	90.8	98.4	83.1	Guinée
Guinea Bissau	76.0	91.1	61.0	114.0	...	...	116.2	120.2	112.3	Guinée-Bissau
Kenya	95.6	96.3	94.9	107.0	109.2	104.8	...	...	...	Kenya
Lesotho	117.6	114.7	120.6	117.1	116.8	117.5	111.0	112.4	109.6	Lésotho
Liberia	112.7	129.6	95.4	...	...	...	95.7	99.6	91.6	Libéria
Libya	...	...	...	106.8	107.4	106.2	...	...	...	Libye
Madagascar	99.6	101.6	97.6	138.3	141.4	135.3	145.2	146.1	144.2	Madagascar
Malawi	137.5	139.9	135.2	126.8	125.2	128.4	141.3	138.7	143.9	Malawi
Mali	62.2	70.8	53.3	80.1	88.9	70.9	88.5	93.8	82.9	Mali
Mauritania	82.7	84.0	81.3	91.3	89.9	92.7	96.7	94.2	99.2	Mauritanie
Mauritius	104.6	105.0	104.1	105.7	106.0	105.3	108.2	108.9	107.4	Maurice
Morocco	91.6	98.8	84.0	104.6	109.5	99.4	117.5	120.3	114.6	Maroc
Mozambique	74.4	84.9	64.0	100.5	109.1	91.9	105.1	110.3	99.9	Mozambique
Namibia	114.4	114.2	114.5	109.1	109.2	108.9	109.5	111.2	107.7	Namibie
Niger	33.6	39.8	27.1	50.0	58.0	41.8	71.1	77.1	64.9	Niger
Nigeria	98.4	108.2	88.1	100.9	108.9	92.6	84.8	88.4	81.0	Nigéria
Rwanda	110.6	114.0	107.3	120.0	120.1	120.0	133.7	132.3	135.1	Rwanda
São Tomé & Príncipe	...	...	...	128.8	130.5	127.1	116.6	118.0	115.1	São Tomé & Príncipe
Senegal	68.1	72.9	63.2	80.5	82.1	79.0	83.6	80.2	87.1	Sénégal
Seychelles	108.0	106.4	109.8	112.8	114.3	111.3	106.9	104.4	109.6	Seychelles
Sierra Leone	68.7	71.6	65.9	...	...	...	131.5	132.2	130.8	Sierra Leone
Somalia	...	...	...	...	...	...	...	...	...	Somalie
South Africa	106.5	109.5	103.5	107.0	110.1	104.0	101.6	104.3	98.9	Afrique du Sud
South Sudan	...	...	...	...	...	...	...	81.4	54.5	Soudan du Sud
Sudan	...	...	...	...	...	...	...	...	...	Soudan
Swaziland	95.2	97.5	92.8	103.1	106.3	99.9	115.0	121.2	108.8	Swaziland
Tanzania	68.2	68.6	67.7	105.0	106.9	103.1	93.0	91.5	94.5	Tanzanie
Togo	112.8	127.0	98.6	113.3	122.6	104.1	132.8	138.2	127.4	Togo
Tunisia	115.9	119.0	112.6	110.0	112.1	107.8	109.7	110.9	108.4	Tunisie
Uganda	129.4	133.5	125.3	119.8	120.3	119.3	109.8	108.9	110.6	Ouganda
Zambia	84.3	87.7	80.9	117.3	120.8	113.9	113.6	113.9	113.3	Zambie
Zimbabwe	101.2	102.7	99.7	...	...	...	...	...	...	Zimbabwe
Africa	**89.5**	**95.7**	**83.1**	**99.6**	**104.5**	**94.5**				**Afrique**

1-6. Gross Enrolment Ratio in secondary - Taux brut de scolarisation au secondaire

Percentage | *Pourcentage*

Country	2000			2005			2010-2015			
	MF	M	F	MF	M	F	MF	M	F	
Algeria	61.9	60.5	63.4	76.7	73.5	80.1	97.6	95.7	99.5	Algérie
Angola	14.9	16.4	13.4	...	...	...	31.5	38.3	24.8	Angola
Benin	21.6	30.0	13.4	34.6	44.8	24.4	47.7	59.2	36.1	Bénin
Botswana	74.7	72.7	76.6	76.9	75.1	78.8	...	...	...	Botswana
Burkina Faso	10.4	12.5	8.2	14.3	16.7	11.8	25.9	28.6	23.2	Burkina Faso
Burundi	...	...	...	12.8	14.9	10.7	28.5	33.0	24.2	Burundi
Cabo Verde	27.3	...	...	26.6	29.8	23.5	50.4	84.7	100.9	Cabo Verde
Cameroon	67.2	...	...	72.2	68.2	76.2	92.7	54.3	46.4	Cameroun
Central African Republic	...	...	...	...	...	...	17.8	23.6	12.1	République Centrafricaine
Chad	10.8	16.7	4.8	15.7	23.2	8.1	22.8	31.2	14.3	Tchad
Comoros	31.8	35.0	28.6	...	...	...	73.5	75.0	71.9	Comores
Congo	35.8	42.0	29.6	...	...	...	53.7	57.5	49.8	Congo
Congo. Dem. Republic	...	...	...	...	...	...	43.3	54.5	32.2	Rép. Démocratique du Congo
Côte d'Ivoire	...	...	...	...	...	...	...	...	...	Côte d'Ivoire
Djibouti	14.0	16.8	11.1	22.2	26.6	17.8	47.7	52.6	42.7	Djibouti
Egypt	85.8	89.1	82.4	...	...	...	86.3	87.1	85.5	Égypte
Equatorial Guinea	31.3	43.4	19.1	28.2	32.8	23.6	...	...	...	Guinée Equatoriale
Eritrea	22.2	26.0	18.4	26.2	32.7	19.6	29.8	33.0	26.4	Érythrée
Ethiopia	13.6	16.4	10.9	25.0	31.2	18.7	...	...	...	Éthiopie
Gabon	...	...	...	...	...	...	...	...	...	Gabon
Gambia	...	...	...	...	...	...	57.5	59.0	56.0	Gambie
Ghana	41.0	45.0	36.9	47.3	51.7	42.9	67.1	69.2	64.9	Ghana
Guinea	...	...	...	29.3	39.0	19.4	38.1	46.6	29.4	Guinée
Guinea Bissau	17.9	23.2	12.6	32.4	...	...	...	...	...	Guinée-Bissau
Kenya	39.3	40.3	38.3	47.9	49.0	46.7	...	...	...	Kenya
Lesotho	32.4	27.5	37.6	39.6	34.5	44.9	53.3	44.5	62.3	Lésotho
Liberia	35.2	40.7	29.6	...	...	...	37.9	33.1	42.5	Libéria
Libya	...	...	...	99.1	90.6	108.0	...	...	...	Libye
Madagascar	...	...	...	21.1	21.6	20.7	38.0	38.9	37.1	Madagascar
Malawi	32.0	36.6	27.5	27.8	30.5	24.9	34.2	36.1	32.4	Malawi
Mali	18.5	23.5	13.3	27.6	33.7	21.1	50.6	58.3	42.6	Mali
Mauritania	18.0	20.7	15.3	22.3	23.7	20.8	26.8	29.0	24.5	Mauritanie
Mauritius	76.8	78.1	75.5	90.7	92.0	89.5	95.9	93.9	97.8	Maurice
Morocco	38.1	42.3	33.8	49.6	53.5	45.6	68.9	74.1	63.4	Maroc
Mozambique	6.1	7.4	4.7	13.1	15.6	10.7	25.9	27.4	24.4	Mozambique
Namibia	60.2	56.8	63.5	63.5	59.8	67.2	...	...	...	Namibie
Niger	7.0	8.9	5.3	10.1	12.5	7.8	15.9	19.1	12.8	Niger
Nigeria	24.5	26.4	22.4	34.7	37.6	31.7	43.8	46.4	41.2	Nigéria
Rwanda	10.5	11.1	10.0	16.7	18.1	15.4	31.8	30.8	32.8	Rwanda
São Tomé & Principe	...	...	...	43.2	41.8	44.6	80.4	76.2	84.6	São Tomé & Principe
Senegal	15.9	19.2	12.5	22.6	25.9	19.3	41.0	42.9	39.1	Sénégal
Seychelles	100.2	97.4	103.0	111.3	107.9	115.0	101.3	97.0	106.1	Seychelles
Sierra Leone	...	...	...	...	...	...	...	...	...	Sierra Leone
Somalia	...	...	...	...	...	...	...	...	...	Somalie
South Africa	84.3	80.1	88.6	91.0	88.5	93.6	101.9	100.3	103.5	Afrique du Sud
South Sudan	...	...	...	...	...	...	...	5.6	2.6	Soudan du Sud
Sudan	...	...	...	...	...	...	...	...	...	Soudan
Swaziland	41.9	41.7	42.1	46.6	46.2	47.1	59.9	60.8	59.1	Swaziland
Tanzania	...	...	...	...	...	...	35.0	37.3	32.6	Tanzanie
Togo	32.1	44.5	19.8	45.0	58.8	31.2	54.9	...	...	Togo
Tunisia	74.9	73.1	76.8	85.8	81.9	89.8	91.1	89.0	93.3	Tunisie
Uganda	16.4	18.5	14.2	19.1	21.2	17.0	...	...	...	Ouganda
Zambia	...	...	...	...	...	...	100.8	107.5	94.1	Zambie
Zimbabwe	42.7	45.4	40.0	...	...	...	...	...	...	Zimbabwe
Africa	**38.5**	**39.8**	**35.4**	**39.8**	**42.3**	**37.3**	**53.6**	**56.6**	**50.5**	**Afrique**

1-7. Pupil-teacher ratios - Ratios élèves-enseignants

Per teacher	*Primary - Primaire*				*Secondary - Secondaire*				*Par enseignant*
Country	2000-04	2005	2007	2008-14	2000-04	2005	2007	2008-14	Pays
Algeria	26.5	25.4	23.9	23.2	...	...	...	...	Algérie
Angola	...	...	41.0	42.5	19.0	...	...	27.4	Angola
Benin	51.6	46.8	...	44.1	23.9	...	...	...	Bénin
Botswana	25.8	25.6	25.2	25.4	14.4	13.8	13.9	...	Botswana
Burkina Faso	48.7	47.2	47.7	48.2	31.5	...	28.2	26.3	Burkina Faso
Burundi	51.2	48.7	52.0	47.1	21.2	22.8	28.0	29.7	Burundi
Cabo Verde	26.9	26.0	24.9	23.0	22.7	23.5	19.0	16.8	Cabo Verde
Cameroon	53.9	47.8	44.4	45.6	16.4	16.2	21.9	21.4	Cameroun
Central African Republic	...	88.6	91.1	80.1	...	...	...	68.1	République Centrafricaine
Chad	68.7	63.2	60.4	61.3	34.2	33.5	32.9	29.8	Tchad
Comoros	35.0	...	...	27.7	13.8	...	...	...	Comores
Congo	82.8	...	58.5	44.4	34.3	...	...	18.7	Congo
Congo. Dem. Republic	34.3	...	38.3	34.7	...	...	15.7	15.3	Rép. Démocratique du Congo
Côte d'Ivoire	42.4	...	41.0	41.7	...	...	...	...	Côte d'Ivoire
Djibouti	34.5	...	35.5	33.2	31.9	...	34.3	24.5	Djibouti
Egypt	21.9	25.6	27.1	27.7	17.1	...	...	12.1	Égypte
Equatorial Guinea	32.0	...	...	26.2	23.2	19.2	...	...	Guinée Equatoriale
Eritrea	46.7	47.5	47.9	40.9	47.8	51.3	49.3	37.9	Érythrée
Ethiopia	67.3	...	...	53.7	...	...	...	39.7	Éthiopie
Gabon	36.0	...	...	24.5	...	...	...	...	Gabon
Gambia	38.5	36.6	35.2	33.9	...	...	...	...	Gambie
Ghana	32.3	32.8	32.0	30.1	18.8	18.9	17.7	15.8	Ghana
Guinea	45.2	44.9	45.4	43.6	31.8	34.4	...	33.1	Guinée
Guinea Bissau	44.1	...	...	51.9	15.0	...	...	...	Guinée-Bissau
Kenya	39.5	44.8	45.6	46.8	26.1	24.8	26.6	29.7	Kenya
Lesotho	42.7	41.6	37.2	34.1	25.1	27.0	25.4	24.7	Lésotho
Liberia	38.3	...	...	26.5	...	...	...	14.9	Libéria
Libya	...	...	...	...	...	...	...	...	Libye
Madagascar	52.4	53.6	48.7	43.1	...	21.6	24.4	27.6	Madagascar
Malawi	72.1	71.0	78.1	74.1	37.3	37.8	38.5	41.5	Malawi
Mali	52.2	54.4	51.7	48.5	29.0	...	24.0	24.7	Mali
Mauritania	40.8	40.3	42.5	40.1	28.4	31.0	...	...	Mauritanie
Mauritius	22.0	22.3	21.5	20.9	17.6	17.4	16.1	14.7	Maurice
Morocco	27.6	27.1	27.4	25.7	18.7	...	...	...	Maroc
Mozambique	65.2	66.3	64.8	54.8	...	32.2	36.8	33.1	Mozambique
Namibia	33.1	30.8	29.9	40.7	22.4	25.1	24.6	...	Namibie
Niger	43.7	43.7	39.7	38.8	30.9	27.4	...	34.7	Niger
Nigeria	35.8	36.9	46.1	37.6	40.6	40.2	28.4	33.1	Nigéria
Rwanda	62.0	69.0	69.3	59.3	26.3	28.7	22.0	22.9	Rwanda
São Tomé & Príncipe	32.1	30.8	...	31.4	21.7	21.7	...	19.8	São Tomé & Príncipe
Senegal	43.2	41.7	34.2	31.6	26.4	26.4	...	27.4	Sénégal
Seychelles	13.5	13.7	12.5	13.3	12.6	13.4	13.3	11.8	Seychelles
Sierra Leone	37.3	...	...	33.0	26.6	...	...	...	Sierra Leone
Somalia	...	...	35.5	...	...	...	19.3	...	Somalie
South Africa	33.8	29.6	31.0	29.5	30.8	32.9	29.2	25.0	Afrique du Sud
South Sudan	...	...	...	...	...	...	...	...	Soudan du Sud
Sudan	29.6	29.0	36.7	38.4	22.5	21.5	18.5	22.2	Soudan
Swaziland	32.3	32.9	32.4	29.3	18.1	16.7	19.0	16.4	Swaziland
Tanzania	58.3	55.9	53.1	45.6	...	...	...	26.4	Tanzanie
Togo	39.1	33.6	39.1	41.7	34.0	30.5	35.5	26.2	Togo
Tunisia	20.6	20.0	18.2	17.1	17.6	17.2	16.2	13.6	Tunisie
Uganda	50.1	49.9	49.6	47.8	18.5	19.1	18.5	18.5	Ouganda
Zambia	53.5	56.5	55.4	49.2	...	...	...	...	Zambie
Zimbabwe	38.6	...	...	...	22.3	...	...	...	Zimbabwe
Africa	**38**	**39**	**40**		**23**	**27**	**23**		**Afrique**

1-8. Gender Parity Index, Primary, Total - Indice de Parité de Genre, Primaire, Total

Country	2006	2007	2008	2009	2010	2011	2012	2013	2014	Pays
Algeria	0.926	0.935	0.939	0.938	0.939	0.938	0.944	...	...	Algérie
Angola	...	...	0.858	0.849	0.813	0.640	...	...	...	Angola
Benin	0.800	...	0.841	0.860	0.877	0.881	0.895	0.904	...	Bénin
Botswana	0.979	0.972	0.973	0.965	...	...	...	...	...	Botswana
Burkina Faso	0.818	0.839	0.866	0.886	0.909	0.926	0.946	0.966	...	Burkina Faso
Burundi	0.894	0.913	0.932	0.948	0.966	0.982	0.992	1.006	...	Burundi
Cabo Verde	0.837	0.859	0.859	0.865	0.864	0.869	0.876	...	...	Cabo Verde
Cameroon	0.949	0.942	0.938	0.927	0.928	0.924	0.915	0.920	...	Cameroun
Central African Republic	0.687	0.697	0.705	0.709	0.711	0.726	0.743	...	...	République Centrafricaine
Chad	0.682	0.700	0.707	0.710	0.735	0.753	0.762	0.767	...	Tchad
Comoros	...	0.897	0.920	...	...	0.847	...	0.944	...	Comores
Congo	0.906	0.933	0.933	0.933	0.946	0.944	1.074	...	...	Congo
Congo. Dem. Republic	0.797	0.798	0.797	0.817	...	0.838	0.850	0.866	...	Rép. Démocratique du Congo
Côte d'Ivoire	...	0.815	0.838	0.855	0.866	0.865	0.876	...	...	Côte d'Ivoire
Djibouti	0.819	0.866	0.892	0.900	...	0.909	0.901	0.883	0.872	Djibouti
Egypt	0.942	0.949	...	0.957	0.959	0.942	0.960	...	...	Égypte
Equatorial Guinea	...	...	0.951	0.959	0.971	0.979	0.976	...	...	Guinée Equatoriale
Eritrea	...	...	...	...	...	...	...	...	...	Érythrée
Ethiopia	0.861	...	...	...	...	...	...	...	...	Éthiopie
Gabon	...	...	...	...	...	0.971	...	...	...	Gabon
Gambia	1.045	1.046	1.060	...	1.025	1.037	1.043	1.042	...	Gambie
Ghana	0.982	0.982	0.982	0.982	...	0.991	0.964	0.998	0.999	Ghana
Guinea	0.826	0.841	0.838	0.842	0.825	0.853	0.845	...	...	Guinée
Guinea Bissau	...	...	...	...	0.934	...	...	...	...	Guinée-Bissau
Kenya	0.972	0.985	0.979	0.978	...	...	1.004	...	...	Kenya
Lesotho	1.004	0.997	0.995	1.001	0.981	0.972	0.975	0.981	...	Lésotho
Liberia	0.924	...	0.911	0.896	...	0.916	...	...	0.920	Libéria
Libya	0.960	...	...	...	...	...	...	...	...	Libye
Madagascar	0.961	0.968	0.971	0.978	0.982	0.981	0.987	0.993	...	Madagascar
Malawi	1.036	1.035	1.027	1.029	1.037	1.040	1.037	1.034	...	Malawi
Mali	0.818	0.831	0.845	0.856	0.868	0.880	0.884	...	...	Mali
Mauritania	1.024	1.031	1.044	1.050	1.047	1.056	1.053	1.050	...	Mauritanie
Mauritius	0.992	0.992	0.985	0.990	0.989	0.990	0.986	0.993	...	Maurice
Morocco	0.906	0.911	0.918	0.931	0.940	0.948	0.952	0.953	0.952	Maroc
Mozambique	0.859	0.867	0.878	0.893	0.897	0.903	0.906	0.909	...	Mozambique
Namibia	0.996	0.987	0.983	0.979	0.976	...	0.969	...	...	Namibie
Niger	0.730	0.740	0.776	0.793	0.816	0.829	0.841	...	...	Niger
Nigeria	0.866	0.889	0.895	0.904	0.916	...	...	...	...	Nigéria
Rwanda	1.029	1.023	1.029	1.029	1.026	1.029	1.021	1.022	...	Rwanda
São Tomé & Príncipe	...	0.997	0.981	1.007	0.994	0.971	0.968	0.976	...	São Tomé & Príncipe
Senegal	0.984	1.000	1.023	1.041	1.055	1.064	1.079	...	1.087	Sénégal
Seychelles	...	1.028	1.042	1.039	1.039	1.051	1.033	...	...	Seychelles
Sierra Leone	...	...	...	...	...	0.948	0.989	1.000	...	Sierra Leone
Somalia	...	0.553	...	...	...	...	...	...	...	Somalie
South Africa	0.945	0.951	0.952	0.951	0.950	0.948	0.948	0.949	...	Afrique du Sud
South Sudan	...	...	...	...	...	0.662	...	...	...	Soudan du Sud
Sudan	0.865	0.841	0.869	0.892	0.899	0.886	0.892	...	...	Soudan
Swaziland	0.935	0.933	...	0.921	0.918	0.898	0.917	...	...	Swaziland
Tanzania	0.860	0.866	0.878	0.853	0.902	0.909	0.922	0.892	...	Tanzanie
Togo	0.962	0.961	0.963	0.969	0.970	0.972	0.978	0.972	...	Togo
Tunisia	1.003	1.004	1.007	1.010	1.014	1.016	...	1.016	...	Tunisie
Uganda	0.975	0.984	0.986	0.999	1.016	...	1.032	1.039	...	Ouganda
Zambia	0.968	0.957	0.965	0.975	0.998	0.980	0.994	0.992	...	Zambie
Zimbabwe	...	...	...	...	...	...	0.986	...	...	Zimbabwe
Africa	**0.901**	**0.844**	**0.836**	**0.846**	**0.852**	**0.859**	**0.867**	**0.870**	**...**	**Afrique**

1-9. Gender Parity Index, Secondary, Total - Indice de Parité de Genre, Secondaire, Total

Country	2006	2007	2008	2009	2010	2011	2012	2013	2014	Pays
Algeria	1.089	1.078	1.036	1.010	1.037	1.040	...	...	...	Algérie
Angola	...	...	0.769	0.765	0.685	0.648	...	...	...	Angola
Benin	...	...	...	...	...	0.610	...	0.657	...	Bénin
Botswana	1.057	1.054	1.065	...	...	...	...	...	...	Botswana
Burkina Faso	0.724	0.733	0.742	0.745	0.764	0.780	0.811	0.846	...	Burkina Faso
Burundi	0.719	0.696	...	0.693	0.688	0.706	0.735	0.784	...	Burundi
Cabo Verde	0.791	0.775	0.799	0.834	...	0.845	0.856	...	...	Cabo Verde
Cameroon	1.166	1.199	1.118	1.196	1.199	1.184	1.191	1.159	...	Cameroun
Central African Republic	...	...	...	0.557	...	0.550	0.513	...	...	République Centrafricaine
Chad	0.360	0.449	0.413	0.413	0.423	0.438	0.457	...	...	Tchad
Comoros	...	...	...	...	...	...	...	1.035	...	Comores
Congo	...	...	...	...	...	...	0.867	...	...	Congo
Congo. Dem. Republic	...	...	...	...	...	...	...	0.678	...	Rép. Démocratique du Congo
Côte d'Ivoire	...	0.533	0.555	0.561	0.576	0.586	0.590	...	...	Côte d'Ivoire
Djibouti	0.676	0.706	0.702	0.738	...	0.803	0.771	0.769	0.811	Djibouti
Egypt	...	...	...	0.981	0.964	0.980	0.981	...	...	Égypte
Equatorial Guinea	...	...	...	...	...	...	...	...	...	Guinée Equatoriale
Eritrea	...	...	...	...	...	...	...	...	...	Érythrée
Ethiopia	0.628	...	...	...	...	...	...	...	...	Éthiopie
Gabon	...	...	...	...	...	...	...	...	...	Gabon
Gambia	...	...	0.927	0.955	0.948	...	...	...	...	Gambie
Ghana	0.845	0.873	0.881	0.887	...	0.899	0.895	0.910	0.938	Ghana
Guinea	0.523	...	0.578	...	...	0.631	...	...	...	Guinée
Guinea Bissau	...	...	...	...	...	...	...	...	...	Guinée-Bissau
Kenya	0.934	0.874	0.916	0.903	...	...	0.929	...	...	Kenya
Lesotho	1.306	1.353	1.378	1.415	1.422	1.412	1.399	...	...	Lésotho
Liberia	...	...	...	...	...	0.820	...	...	0.780	Libéria
Libya	1.176	...	...	...	...	...	...	...	...	Libye
Madagascar	0.949	0.951	0.942	0.939	...	0.950	0.954	0.962	...	Madagascar
Malawi	0.843	0.835	0.849	0.876	0.909	0.915	0.899	0.910	...	Malawi
Mali	0.627	0.672	0.660	0.671	0.703	0.715	...	0.800	...	Mali
Mauritania	0.844	...	0.882	0.838	0.853	0.847	0.847	0.939	...	Mauritanie
Mauritius	1.026	1.025	1.029	1.036	1.039	1.040	1.042	...	...	Maurice
Morocco	0.866	0.872	0.867	0.865	0.870	0.863	0.856	...	...	Maroc
Mozambique	0.714	0.727	0.747	0.786	0.816	0.864	0.889	0.912	...	Mozambique
Namibia	1.149	1.157	...	...	...	...	...	...	...	Namibie
Niger	0.626	0.613	0.605	0.600	0.671	0.643	0.668	...	...	Niger
Nigeria	0.827	0.782	0.846	0.883	0.888	...	...	...	...	Nigéria
Rwanda	0.868	0.854	0.858	0.906	0.976	1.024	1.065	1.071	...	Rwanda
São Tomé & Príncipe	...	1.079	1.076	1.125	1.030	1.153	1.136	1.109	...	São Tomé & Príncipe
Senegal	0.758	...	0.789	...	0.870	0.912	...	...	...	Sénégal
Seychelles	...	1.092	1.112	1.097	1.063	1.073	1.007	...	...	Seychelles
Sierra Leone	...	...	...	...	...	0.749	0.858	0.874	...	Sierra Leone
Somalia	...	0.460	...	...	...	...	...	...	...	Somalie
South Africa	1.049	1.034	1.023	1.030	1.034	1.029	1.032	1.069	...	Afrique du Sud
South Sudan	...	...	...	...	...	...	...	...	...	Soudan du Sud
Sudan	0.956	0.914	0.899	0.867	0.866	0.915	0.913	...	...	Soudan
Swaziland	1.024	0.907	...	1.011	0.999	0.972	0.988	...	...	Swaziland
Tanzania	0.546	0.529	...	...	...	...	...	...	...	Tanzanie
Togo	1.096	...	1.080	1.076	1.072	1.049	...	...	...	Togo
Tunisia	0.813	0.819	0.850	0.832	0.859	0.854	...	0.870	...	Tunisie
Uganda	...	...	...	...	0.816	...	0.875	0.921	...	Ouganda
Zambia	...	...	...	...	...	...	...	...	...	Zambie
Zimbabwe	...	...	...	...	...	...	0.973	...	...	Zimbabwe
Africa	**0.844**	**0.836**	**0.846**	**0.852**	**0.859**	**0.867**	**0.870**	**...**	**...**	**Afrique**

HEALTH - SANTE

1-10. Primary health care - Soins de santé primaire

Percentage	*Access to safe water - Accès à l'eau potable*		*Immunization / Vaccination (%)* Tuberculosis - Tuberculose		*Diphtheria (DPT3) - Diphtérie*		*Measles - Rougéole*		*Pourcentage*
Country	**1990**	**2012**	**1990**	**2013**	**1990**	**2013**	**1990**	**2013**	**Pays**
Algeria	94	84	99	99	89	95	83	95	Algérie
Angola	42	54	48	85	24	93	38	91	Angola
Benin	57	76	92	88	74	69	79	63	Bénin
Botswana	92	97	93	99	92	96	87	94	Botswana
Burkina Faso	44	82	95	96	66	88	79	82	Burkina Faso
Burundi	69	75	97	95	86	96	74	98	Burundi
Cabo Verde	...	89	97	94	88	93	79	91	Cabo Verde
Cameroon	49	74	76	82	48	89	56	83	Cameroun
Central African Republic	58	68	96	37	82	23	82	25	République Centrafricaine
Chad	40	51	59	62	20	48	32	59	Tchad
Comoros	87	...	99	78	94	83	87	82	Comores
Congo	...	75	90	92	79	69	75	65	Congo
Congo. Dem. Republic	43	46	65	78	35	72	38	73	Rép. Démocratique du Congo
Côte d'Ivoire	76	80	62	84	54	88	56	74	Côte d'Ivoire
Djibouti	75	92	81	86	85	82	85	80	Djibouti
Egypt	93	99	89	98	87	97	86	96	Égypte
Equatorial Guinea	...	...	94	71	77	3	88	42	Guinée Equatoriale
Eritrea	43	...	...	97	...	94	...	96	Érythrée
Ethiopia	14	52	64	71	49	72	38	62	Éthiopie
Gabon	...	92	96	92	78	79	76	70	Gabon
Gambia	74	90	98	98	92	97	86	96	Gambie
Ghana	53	87	71	98	58	90	61	89	Ghana
Guinea	51	75	50	66	17	63	35	62	Guinée
Guinea Bissau	36	74	90	94	61	80	53	69	Guinée-Bissau
Kenya	43	62	92	79	84	76	78	93	Kenya
Lesotho	80	81	89	87	82	96	80	92	Lésotho
Liberia	...	75	...	87	...	89	...	74	Libéria
Libya	54	...	90	99	84	98	89	98	Libye
Madagascar	29	50	67	77	46	74	47	63	Madagascar
Malawi	42	85	97	96	87	89	81	88	Malawi
Mali	28	67	82	87	42	74	43	72	Mali
Mauritania	30	50	79	95	33	80	38	80	Mauritanie
Mauritius	99	100	87	99	85	98	76	99	Maurice
Morocco	73	84	96	99	81	99	79	99	Maroc
Mozambique	34	49	59	93	46	78	59	85	Mozambique
Namibia	64	92	...	94	...	89	...	82	Namibie
Niger	35	52	50	49	22	70	25	67	Niger
Nigeria	47	64	80	80	56	58	54	59	Nigéria
Rwanda	62	71	92	99	84	98	83	97	Rwanda
São Tomé & Príncipe	...	97	99	97	92	97	71	91	São Tomé & Príncipe
Senegal	60	74	90	97	51	92	51	84	Sénégal
Seychelles	96	96	98	99	99	98	86	97	Seychelles
Sierra Leone	37	60	...	99	...	92	...	83	Sierra Leone
Somalia	...	...	31	33	19	42	30	46	Somalie
South Africa	83	95	57	84	72	65	79	66	Afrique du Sud
South Sudan	...	57	...	52	...	45	...	30	Soudan du Sud
Sudan	67	55	77	93	62	93	57	85	Soudan
Swaziland	39	74	96	98	89	98	85	85	Swaziland
Tanzania	55	53	85	99	78	91	80	99	Tanzanie
Togo	130	60	99	97	77	84	73	72	Togo
Tunisia	82	97	96	97	93	98	93	94	Tunisie
Uganda	41	75	75	93	45	78	52	82	Ouganda
Zambia	48	63	97	82	91	79	90	80	Zambie
Zimbabwe	79	80	91	95	88	95	87	93	Zimbabwe
Africa	**56**		**77**		**61**		**61**		**Afrique**

Section 2

Economic Statistics

Statistiques économiques

NATIONAL ACCOUNTS – COMPTES NATIONAUX

2-1. GDP at Current market prices – PIB aux prix du marché (courant)

Million US$ | *Million $ EU*

Country	2006	2007	2008	2009	2010	2011	2012	2013	2014	Pays
Algeria	118 700	134 793	170 041	137 445	162 366	199 288	207 679	208 681	224 123	Algérie
Angola	52 381	65 266	88 539	73 158	83 369	110 891	125 430	142 738	147 552	Angola
Benin	4 705	5 511	6 647	6 600	6 570	7 297	7 548	8 309	8 741	Bénin
Botswana	10 127	10 939	11 113	10 107	13 747	15 365	14 537	14 778	13 404	Botswana
Burkina Faso	5 845	6 761	8 368	8 368	9 004	10 766	11 620	12 883	12 639	Burkina Faso
Burundi	1 273	1 356	1 612	1 775	1 984	2 073	2 291	2 684	2 832	Burundi
Cabo Verde	1 237	1 515	1 793	1 716	1 666	1 866	1 744	1 817	2 020	Cabo Verde
Cameroon	17 953	20 432	23 322	23 381	23 623	26 587	26 472	29 568	31 899	Cameroun
Central African Republic	1 461	1 698	1 985	1 982	1 986	2 196	2 170	1 538	1 711	République Centrafricaine
Chad	7 422	8 639	10 352	9 253	10 670	12 156	12 626	12 843	13 739	Tchad
Comoros	403	467	530	536	544	611	596	657	708	Comores
Congo	7 731	7 435	10 176	9 339	12 281	14 798	13 656	13 796	14 705	Congo
Congo. Dem. Republic	17 275	20 360	24 276	24 335	24 915	25 406	27 117	31 069	33 884	Rép. Démocratique du Congo
Côte d'Ivoire	14 297	16 364	19 206	18 263	20 523	23 832	27 453	29 886	34 474	Côte d'Ivoire
Djibouti	769	848	984	1 049	1 129	1 239	1 354	1 455	1 625	Djibouti
Egypt	107 585	132 171	164 841	187 968	214 623	231 222	260 153	255 199	274 654	Égypte
Equatorial Guinea	8 537	10 836	16 408	11 149	13 408	18 009	19 161	16 856	16 828	Guinée Equatoriale
Eritrea	1 211	1 318	1 380	1 857	2 117	2 608	3 092	3 444	3 870	Érythrée
Ethiopia	14 501	17 637	24 757	27 464	26 083	30 479	42 210	46 558	53 939	Éthiopie
Gabon	10 563	12 509	15 686	12 031	14 568	18 795	17 847	19 260	20 203	Gabon
Gambia	653	797	962	904	961	933	936	979	1 119	Gambie
Ghana	20 410	24 758	28 528	25 978	32 174	39 565	41 939	48 586	33 454	Ghana
Guinea	2 932	4 134	4 516	4 610	4 730	5 155	5 737	6 401	7 300	Guinée
Guinea Bissau	592	696	866	828	849	1 105	1 073	1 158	1 143	Guinée-Bissau
Kenya	25 812	31 921	35 315	37 022	39 701	40 832	49 617	54 443	72 542	Kenya
Lesotho	1 407	1 587	1 670	1 736	2 242	2 561	2 495	2 268	1 929	Lésotho
Liberia	745	949	1 101	1 155	1 292	1 538	1 734	1 936	2 053	Libéria
Libya	54 641	67 513	87 143	63 027	74 774	34 701	81 908	73 374	40 974	Libye
Madagascar	5 413	7 407	9 380	8 454	8 636	9 883	9 901	10 559	10 935	Madagascar
Malawi	3 998	4 431	5 321	6 195	6 864	7 335	5 631	4 518	5 965	Malawi
Mali	6 227	7 151	8 756	8 986	9 412	10 658	10 348	10 945	11 825	Mali
Mauritania	3 010	3 307	3 950	3 650	4 335	5 119	4 845	5 035	5 461	Mauritanie
Mauritius	6 732	7 792	9 641	8 835	9 718	11 252	11 442	11 929	14 201	Maurice
Morocco	65 625	75 011	89 074	90 089	90 683	99 071	95 726	103 718	116 808	Maroc
Mozambique	7 816	9 352	10 369	12 147	12 545	11 337	14 596	16 582	16 531	Mozambique
Namibia	7 978	8 741	8 487	8 876	11 282	12 412	13 037	13 113	11 733	Namibie
Niger	3 647	4 281	5 397	5 405	5 712	6 384	6 663	7 309	7 800	Niger
Nigeria	244 136	265 697	332 123	270 534	369 062	411 744	460 954	514 965	549 910	Nigéria
Rwanda	3 110	3 775	4 797	5 309	5 699	6 407	7 220	7 522	7 149	Rwanda
São Tomé & Príncipe	136	144	183	196	201	248	264	311	346	São Tomé & Príncipe
Senegal	9 358	11 294	13 414	12 796	12 928	14 371	14 043	14 795	14 520	Sénégal
Seychelles	1 016	1 034	967	847	970	1 066	1 134	1 410	1 450	Seychelles
Sierra Leone	1 865	2 130	2 454	2 421	2 578	2 932	3 789	4 913	5 695	Sierra Leone
Somalia	...	...	...	...	...	...	...	...	...	Somalie
South Africa	271 636	299 417	286 769	295 936	375 349	416 802	397 348	366 060	333 008	Afrique du Sud
South Sudan	...	...	...	...	...	15 064	14 712	11 933	14 900	Soudan du Sud
Sudan	45 252	59 431	64 820	60 562	69 665	69 960	68 126	66 748	86 111	Soudan
Swaziland	2 950	3 050	3 023	3 175	3 891	4 153	4 050	3 795	3 788	Swaziland
Tanzania	18 278	21 502	27 258	28 543	29 990	32 477	38 262	44 779	49 017	Tanzanie
Togo	2 219	2 531	3 168	3 163	3 173	3 757	3 897	4 179	4 181	Togo
Tunisia	34 377	38 910	44 855	43 456	44 051	45 837	45 029	46 274	46 152	Tunisie
Uganda	11 010	13 548	17 917	18 921	19 687	21 685	24 412	25 512	26 147	Ouganda
Zambia	12 757	14 057	17 911	15 328	20 265	23 732	24 940	26 821	30 512	Zambie
Zimbabwe	6 108	5 646	5 221	8 157	9 422	10 956	12 393	13 490	10 582	Zimbabwe
Africa	**1 285 822**	**1 478 849**	**1 737 372**	**1 625 019**	**1 928 016**	**2 136 512**	**2 302 959**	**2 380 377**	**2 458 790**	**Afrique**

NATIONAL ACCOUNTS – COMPTES NATIONAUX

2-2. GDP growth Rates at Constant Market Prices - Taux de croissance du PIB

Percentage | *Pourcentage*

Country	2006	2007	2008	2009	2010	2011	2012	2013	2014	Pays
Algeria	1.7	3.4	2.4	1.6	3.6	2.8	3.3	2.8	4.0	Algérie
Angola	11.5	14.0	11.2	2.4	3.4	3.9	5.2	6.8	4.5	Angola
Benin	3.8	4.6	5.0	2.7	2.6	3.3	5.4	5.6	5.5	Bénin
Botswana	8.0	8.7	3.9	- 7.8	8.6	6.2	4.3	5.9	4.8	Botswana
Burkina Faso	6.3	4.1	5.8	2.9	8.4	6.6	9.0	6.6	3.4	Burkina Faso
Burundi	5.4	3.4	4.9	3.8	5.1	4.2	4.0	4.5	4.7	Burundi
Cabo Verde	9.1	9.2	6.7	- 1.3	1.5	4.0	1.2	0.7	2.0	Cabo Verde
Cameroon	3.2	3.3	2.9	1.9	3.3	4.1	4.6	5.5	5.3	Cameroun
Central African Republic	4.8	4.6	2.1	1.7	3.0	3.3	4.1	- 36.0	1.0	République Centrafricaine
Chad	0.6	3.1	2.5	2.8	13.6	0.1	8.9	3.9	7.3	Tchad
Comoros	2.6	0.8	0.6	1.1	2.2	2.5	3.0	3.5	3.5	Comores
Congo	6.2	- 1.6	5.9	7.5	8.7	3.4	3.8	3.3	6.0	Congo
Congo. Dem. Republic	0.7	1.6	2.3	3.8	2.4	- 4.7	9.8	8.7	8.3	Rép. Démocratique du Congo
Côte d'Ivoire	5.6	6.3	6.2	2.8	7.2	6.9	7.2	8.5	8.9	Côte d'Ivoire
Djibouti	4.8	5.1	5.8	5.0	3.5	4.5	4.8	5.0	5.9	Djibouti
Egypt	6.8	7.1	7.2	4.9	4.8	1.8	2.2	2.1	2.2	Égypte
Equatorial Guinea	1.3	13.1	12.3	- 8.1	- 1.3	5.0	3.2	- 4.8	- 2.8	Guinée Equatoriale
Eritrea	...	...	...	...	...	...	...	...	...	Érythrée
Ethiopia	11.5	11.8	11.2	10.0	10.6	11.4	8.8	9.7	10.3	Éthiopie
Gabon	1.2	4.8	5.3	- 2.7	6.9	7.0	5.3	5.6	5.1	Gabon
Gambia	1.1	3.6	5.7	6.4	6.5	- 4.3	5.3	6.3	- 0.7	Gambie
Ghana	6.1	6.5	8.4	4.0	3.4	14.0	9.3	7.3	4.2	Ghana
Guinea	2.5	1.8	4.9	- 0.3	1.9	3.9	3.8	2.3	1.3	Guinée
Guinea Bissau	2.3	3.2	3.2	3.3	4.4	9.0	- 2.2	0.9	2.6	Guinée-Bissau
Kenya	6.7	7.1	7.4	6.0	7.0	6.4	6.9	7.0	4.5	Kenya
Lesotho	4.1	4.9	5.1	4.5	5.6	4.3	6.0	5.7	4.3	Lésotho
Liberia	8.9	13.2	6.2	5.3	6.1	7.9	8.3	8.1	2.6	Libéria
Libya	6.5	6.4	2.7	- 0.8	5.0	- 62.1	104.5	- 13.6	- 4.7	Libye
Madagascar	5.4	6.5	7.2	- 3.5	0.1	1.5	2.5	2.4	3.2	Madagascar
Malawi	7.7	5.5	8.6	7.6	9.5	3.8	2.1	6.1	5.7	Malawi
Mali	5.3	4.3	5.0	4.5	5.8	2.7	0.0	1.7	5.8	Mali
Mauritania	18.9	2.8	1.1	- 1.0	4.8	4.4	6.0	5.7	6.4	Mauritanie
Mauritius	3.9	5.4	5.5	3.1	4.2	3.9	3.2	3.2	3.2	Maurice
Morocco	7.8	2.7	5.6	4.8	3.6	5.0	2.7	4.4	2.7	Maroc
Mozambique	8.7	7.3	6.8	6.5	7.1	7.4	7.1	7.4	7.5	Mozambique
Namibia	7.1	5.4	2.6	0.3	6.0	5.1	5.1	5.1	5.3	Namibie
Niger	5.8	3.1	9.6	- 0.7	8.4	2.3	11.1	4.1	6.5	Niger
Nigeria	6.0	6.4	6.0	7.0	10.6	4.9	4.3	5.4	6.3	Nigéria
Rwanda	9.2	7.6	11.2	6.2	6.3	7.5	8.8	4.7	6.0	Rwanda
São Tomé & Principe	12.6	2.0	9.1	4.0	4.5	4.9	4.0	4.0	4.9	São Tomé & Principe
Senegal	2.5	4.9	3.7	2.4	4.2	1.7	3.4	3.5	4.5	Sénégal
Seychelles	9.4	10.4	- 2.1	- 1.1	5.9	7.9	6.0	6.6	2.5	Seychelles
Sierra Leone	4.2	8.0	5.2	3.2	5.3	6.0	15.2	20.1	6.0	Sierra Leone
Somalia	2.4	2.6	2.6	2.6	2.6	2.6	2.6	2.6	...	Somalie
South Africa	5.6	5.4	3.2	- 1.5	3.0	3.2	2.2	2.2	1.4	Afrique du Sud
South Sudan	...	...	...	5.0	5.5	- 4.6	- 46.1	13.1	...	Soudan du Sud
Sudan	7.7	5.8	3.8	4.5	6.5	0.9	0.5	3.6	3.4	Soudan
Swaziland	3.3	3.5	2.4	1.3	1.9	- 0.6	1.9	3.0	2.5	Swaziland
Tanzania	6.7	7.1	7.4	6.0	7.0	6.4	6.9	7.3	7.4	Tanzanie
Togo	3.9	2.1	2.4	3.4	4.0	4.8	5.8	5.4	5.5	Togo
Tunisia	5.7	6.3	4.5	3.1	2.6	- 1.9	3.9	2.3	2.4	Tunisie
Uganda	7.0	8.1	10.4	4.1	6.2	6.4	3.6	4.7	7.0	Ouganda
Zambia	7.9	8.4	7.8	9.2	10.3	7.6	6.3	6.7	5.7	Zambie
Zimbabwe	- 3.5	- 3.7	- 17.7	5.3	11.4	11.9	10.6	4.5	3.1	Zimbabwe
Africa	**5.8**	**6.0**	**5.4**	**3.4**	**5.7**	**2.8**	**6.7**	**3.5**	**3.9**	**Afrique**

2-3 . Per Capita GDP – PIB par habitant

US Dollars — *Dollars EU*

Country	2006	2007	2008	2009	2010	2011	2012	2013	2014	Pays
Algeria	3 440	3 841	4 760	3 778	4 381	5 277	5 397	5 322	5 613	Algérie
Angola	3 059	3 685	4 834	3 865	4 265	5 495	6 024	6 648	6 665	Angola
Benin	557	633	741	714	691	746	751	805	825	Bénin
Botswana	5 341	5 712	5 747	5 178	6 980	7 734	7 255	7 312	6 575	Botswana
Burkina Faso	423	475	571	554	579	673	706	761	726	Burkina Faso
Burundi	158	163	187	199	215	217	233	264	270	Burundi
Cabo Verde	2 566	3 132	3 699	3 532	3 417	3 805	3 527	3 642	4 010	Cabo Verde
Cameroon	965	1 070	1 190	1 163	1 145	1 257	1 220	1 329	1 398	Cameroun
Central African Republic	362	413	474	465	457	495	479	333	363	République Centrafricaine
Chad	717	808	938	814	910	1 006	1 014	1 001	1 040	Tchad
Comoros	654	738	817	804	796	873	830	895	942	Comores
Congo	2 120	1 978	2 625	2 338	2 987	3 502	3 149	3 102	3 226	Congo
Congo. Dem. Republic	978	1 134	1 329	1 308	1 313	1 310	1 367	1 529	1 629	Rép. Démocratique du Congo
Côte d'Ivoire	257	286	327	302	330	373	418	443	497	Côte d'Ivoire
Djibouti	976	1 061	1 214	1 277	1 353	1 464	1 575	1 667	1 833	Djibouti
Egypt	1 474	1 781	2 184	2 448	2 749	2 912	3 223	3 110	3 294	Égypte
Equatorial Guinea	13 736	16 941	24 936	16 472	19 260	25 152	26 024	22 266	21 629	Guinée Equatoriale
Eritrea	241	253	256	334	369	440	504	544	592	Érythrée
Ethiopia	185	219	300	324	299	341	460	495	559	Éthiopie
Gabon	7 476	8 642	10 578	7 920	9 361	11 791	10 932	11 521	11 805	Gabon
Gambia	440	521	609	555	572	538	522	529	586	Gambie
Ghana	930	1 099	1 234	1 097	1 326	1 594	1 653	1 876	1 265	Ghana
Guinea	299	411	438	435	435	462	501	545	606	Guinée
Guinea Bissau	407	469	571	534	535	680	645	680	655	Guinée-Bissau
Kenya	702	846	911	930	970	972	1 149	1 227	1 593	Kenya
Lesotho	725	811	847	873	1 116	1 262	1 216	1 093	920	Lésotho
Liberia	220	269	300	302	326	377	414	451	467	Libéria
Libya	9 609	11 676	14 828	10 567	12 379	5 686	13 308	11 832	6 552	Libye
Madagascar	288	382	471	412	410	456	444	461	464	Madagascar
Malawi	300	323	376	425	457	474	354	276	354	Malawi
Mali	505	562	666	663	673	739	697	715	750	Mali
Mauritania	930	993	1 154	1 038	1 201	1 382	1 276	1 294	1 370	Mauritanie
Mauritius	5 533	6 387	7 881	7 201	7 897	9 112	9 231	9 586	11 368	Maurice
Morocco	2 159	2 446	2 878	2 880	2 866	3 090	2 944	3 142	3 488	Maroc
Mozambique	362	422	456	520	523	461	579	642	624	Mozambique
Namibia	3 886	4 201	4 021	4 141	5 178	5 597	5 770	5 693	4 997	Namibie
Niger	267	302	366	353	359	387	388	410	421	Niger
Nigeria	1 703	1 805	2 196	1 741	2 311	2 508	2 730	2 966	3 080	Nigéria
Rwanda	322	380	469	504	526	575	630	639	591	Rwanda
São Tomé & Príncipe	857	883	1 090	1 134	1 128	1 355	1 406	1 610	1 746	São Tomé & Príncipe
Senegal	808	949	1 096	1 017	998	1 078	1 023	1 047	998	Sénégal
Seychelles	11 523	11 596	10 759	9 356	10 635	11 610	12 283	15 188	15 540	Seychelles
Sierra Leone	353	393	444	429	448	500	634	806	918	Sierra Leone
Somalia	…	…	…	…	…	…	…	…	…	Somalie
South Africa	5 553	6 036	5 705	5 815	7 295	8 023	7 585	6 936	6 267	Afrique du Sud
South Sudan	…	…	…	…	…	1 451	1 357	1 056	1 269	Soudan du Sud
Sudan	1 397	1 789	1 904	1 738	1 954	1 920	1 832	1 758	2 221	Soudan
Swaziland	2 638	2 687	2 620	2 705	3 261	3 426	3 290	3 037	2 988	Swaziland
Tanzania	458	523	644	654	667	701	801	909	966	Tanzanie
Togo	390	434	529	515	503	580	587	613	598	Togo
Tunisia	3 383	3 787	4 317	4 134	4 143	4 263	4 141	4 208	4 152	Tunisie
Uganda	371	441	564	576	579	617	672	679	673	Ouganda
Zambia	1 083	1 161	1 438	1 195	1 533	1 741	1 772	1 845	2 031	Zambie
Zimbabwe	480	443	408	633	721	820	903	953	725	Zimbabwe
Africa	**1 379**	**1 547**	**1 773**	**1 618**	**1 873**	**2 024**	**2 129**	**2 146**	**2 163**	**Afrique**

2-4. Structure of Output (at current market prices) – Structure du PIB (aux prix courants du marché)

Share of GDP (%)	*Agriculture*		*Industry*		*Manufacturing*		*Services*		*Part du PIB (%)*
Country	2006	2013	2006	2013	2006	2013	2006	2013	Pays
Algeria	8.0	10.6	62.5	48.0	4.5	9.7	29.5	41.4	Algérie
Angola	5.2	5.4	58.2	54.6	3.6	10.2	36.6	40.1	Angola
Benin	36.0	36.5	14.4	14.0	8.4	16.5	49.5	49.5	Bénin
Botswana	2.3	2.6	48.0	36.9	5.8	9.4	49.8	60.5	Botswana
Burkina Faso	36.7	34.7	17.6	24.9	11.3	13.4	45.7	40.5	Burkina Faso
Burundi	44.3	42.9	16.7	16.6	11.3	26.4	39.0	40.5	Burundi
Cabo Verde	9.4	9.4	18.1	19.6	3.7	9.1	72.5	71.0	Cabo Verde
Cameroon	20.6	23.2	32.0	30.2	18.7	31.7	47.4	46.6	Cameroun
Central African Republic	55.2	54.7	14.2	13.8	6.5	20.7	30.6	31.5	République Centrafricaine
Chad	28.0	24.1	38.9	43.1	6.4	29.6	33.1	32.8	Tchad
Comoros	41.0	35.9	11.7	11.1	4.0	12.8	47.4	53.0	Comores
Congo	41.0	35.9	11.7	11.1	4.0	12.8	47.4	53.0	Congo
Congo, Dem. Republic	25.3	24.5	26.3	26.1	15.9	30.0	48.5	49.4	Rép. Démocratique du Congo
Côte d'Ivoire	22.3	20.9	31.3	44.8	16.3	48.6	46.3	34.3	Côte d'Ivoire
Djibouti	3.6	3.6	16.8	19.5	2.6	4.1	79.6	76.8	Djibouti
Egypt	14.1	14.5	38.4	39.1	17.0	33.8	47.5	46.4	Égypte
Equatorial Guinea	2.0	1.6	95.5	94.7	0.1	3.2	2.6	3.7	Guinée Equatoriale
Eritrea	26.1	17.6	19.3	23.5	6.4	10.3	54.6	58.9	Érythrée
Ethiopia	47.9	45.0	12.7	11.9	4.5	9.4	39.4	43.0	Éthiopie
Gabon	5.2	3.6	62.4	55.2	4.6	15.3	32.4	41.2	Gabon
Gambia	24.3	24.0	16.2	15.8	7.6	9.9	59.6	60.2	Gambie
Ghana	30.4	22.4	20.8	28.8	10.2	11.2	48.8	48.8	Ghana
Guinea	23.8	21.2	39.9	40.4	6.2	20.7	36.3	38.5	Guinée
Guinea Bissau	43.9	48.9	14.0	14.8	12.6	36.2	42.1	36.2	Guinée-Bissau
Kenya	27.2	29.7	19.1	21.0	11.8	25.1	53.7	49.3	Kenya
Lesotho	8.0	7.6	35.9	30.7	21.4	17.7	56.1	61.7	Lésotho
Liberia	70.5	70.7	10.4	11.4	6.3	32.2	19.1	17.9	Libéria
Libya	2.3	0.9	75.4	67.3	5.1	11.5	22.3	31.8	Libye
Madagascar	27.5	26.4	19.9	19.4	14.8	26.7	52.7	54.2	Madagascar
Malawi	34.4	27.5	18.2	16.3	13.8	16.3	47.4	56.2	Malawi
Mali	37.6	42.0	24.1	22.4	9.9	19.7	38.2	35.5	Mali
Mauritania	20.8	25.2	41.8	39.4	25.0	15.1	37.4	35.4	Mauritanie
Mauritius	5.2	3.2	26.6	24.6	19.5	23.6	68.2	72.2	Maurice
Morocco	16.9	16.6	27.2	28.5	15.9	28.1	56.0	54.9	Maroc
Mozambique	27.9	28.7	26.4	21.2	16.0	22.4	45.7	50.2	Mozambique
Namibia	10.5	6.1	34.6	33.4	15.6	21.7	54.9	60.5	Namibie
Niger	46.2	39.9	12.1	20.9	5.8	16.7	41.6	39.2	Niger
Nigeria	32.0	21.0	41.9	26.0	2.6	17.1	26.1	53.0	Nigéria
Rwanda	41.8	35.1	12.3	15.7	5.6	11.1	45.9	49.2	Rwanda
São Tomé & Príncipe	18.8	22.0	17.8	18.0	7.1	14.4	63.4	60.0	São Tomé & Principe
Senegal	15.0	16.2	23.9	22.2	14.5	20.4	61.1	61.7	Sénégal
Seychelles	3.5	2.9	19.1	15.1	10.5	11.1	77.4	82.0	Seychelles
Sierra Leone	53.6	49.7	11.2	23.0	2.8	6.3	35.2	27.2	Sierra Leone
Somalia	60.2	60.2	7.4	7.4	2.5	7.7	32.4	32.5	Somalie
South Africa	2.6	2.3	29.4	29.9	16.4	19.5	68.0	67.8	Afrique du Sud
South Sudan	...	...	...	...	...	...	...	...	Soudan du Sud
Sudan	32.2	34.5	24.1	19.9	8.3	19.8	43.7	45.6	Soudan
Swaziland	7.8	7.5	46.7	51.1	41.4	108.9	45.5	41.4	Swaziland
Tanzania	30.4	33.0	22.9	22.6	8.6	16.2	46.7	44.4	Tanzanie
Togo	40.3	44.8	20.3	21.1	10.2	21.2	39.4	34.1	Togo
Tunisia	10.2	9.4	29.6	30.0	17.4	27.3	60.2	60.7	Tunisie
Uganda	24.5	27.0	24.1	22.2	7.5	20.8	51.4	50.8	Ouganda
Zambia	18.4	13.2	35.8	34.9	11.2	18.3	45.8	51.9	Zambie
Zimbabwe	15.6	12.0	56.7	31.1	28.4	22.5	27.6	56.9	Zimbabwe
Africa	**16.5**	**15.6**	**38.9**	**34.4**	**10.3**	**19.2**	**44.6**	**49.9**	**Afrique**

2-5. Structure of Demand (at current market prices) – Structure de la demande (aux prix courants du marché)

Share of GDP (%)	*Household Final Cons. Expenditure / Dep. des menages en cons. finale*		*General Government Final Cons. Expenditure / Dep. Generale du gouv. en cons. finale*		*Gross Capital Formation/ Formation brute de capital*		*Exports of Goods and Non Factor Services / Exportations de biens et services non facteurs*		*less Imports of Goods and Non Factor Services/ Moins Importations de biens et services non facteurs*		Part du PIB (%)
Country	**2006**	**2013**	**2006**	**2013**	**2006**	**2013**	**2006**	**2013**	**2006**	**2013**	**Pays**
Algeria	31.7	34.8	11.2	19.0	30.2	43.3	48.8	33.4	21.9	30.5	Algérie
Angola	29.0	29.6	15.3	26.1	23.3	23.7	63.5	48.6	31.2	28.0	Angola
Benin	76.6	76.7	12.1	11.3	20.6	27.3	18.5	18.3	27.7	33.5	Bénin
Botswana	38.9	50.4	17.0	20.5	25.9	33.9	52.3	55.2	34.1	59.9	Botswana
Burkina Faso	71.6	58.1	21.6	20.1	20.6	29.2	11.5	24.7	25.3	32.0	Burkina Faso
Burundi	94.0	78.0	16.9	15.4	16.9	32.6	7.3	8.5	35.1	34.5	Burundi
Cabo Verde	81.6	63.8	19.5	17.7	38.7	35.9	19.9	34.9	59.7	52.3	Cabo Verde
Cameroon	71.5	77.2	9.6	11.6	16.8	19.5	23.0	20.7	21.0	28.9	Cameroun
Central African Republic	87.7	88.9	9.2	7.4	10.1	15.0	14.9	12.7	22.0	23.9	République Centrafricaine
Chad	69.7	52.9	6.6	8.7	22.8	32.8	47.7	36.4	46.8	30.8	Tchad
Comoros	98.9	103.6	13.3	27.1	11.3	7.5	14.8	17.0	38.3	55.0	Comores
Congo	24.0	27.7	9.1	14.4	28.7	53.5	79.3	76.2	41.2	71.8	Congo
Congo, Dem. Republic	69.2	65.2	13.6	13.2	7.6	19.0	52.4	43.7	42.7	41.1	Rép. Démocratique du Congo
Côte d'Ivoire	85.8	76.1	9.3	12.5	14.6	15.4	46.4	37.2	56.1	41.3	Côte d'Ivoire
Djibouti	59.4	77.6	29.4	23.7	34.2	28.6	40.6	32.9	63.6	62.7	Djibouti
Egypt	69.9	80.9	12.0	11.7	18.3	14.2	30.6	18.1	30.9	24.8	Égypte
Equatorial Guinea	6.9	8.0	2.9	5.1	26.9	36.9	96.9	91.8	33.6	41.8	Guinée Equatoriale
Eritrea	91.9	77.0	25.9	19.2	13.7	8.8	6.9	17.1	38.4	22.0	Érythrée
Ethiopia	85.3	72.5	12.2	8.3	25.2	35.8	13.8	12.5	36.5	29.1	Éthiopie
Gabon	30.1	30.9	13.3	17.4	24.0	29.5	60.6	49.6	28.1	27.4	Gabon
Gambia	95.5	85.7	6.3	7.5	30.7	20.7	1.4	19.7	33.9	33.6	Gambie
Ghana	82.6	66.2	11.3	16.4	21.6	22.4	25.2	41.7	40.7	46.7	Ghana
Guinea	74.6	91.4	7.1	11.1	23.2	19.1	38.2	25.5	43.1	47.1	Guinée
Guinea Bissau	93.5	93.6	14.9	9.0	6.3	4.6	12.8	14.4	27.6	21.7	Guinée-Bissau
Kenya	76.3	81.2	14.4	14.3	18.6	20.2	23.0	18.0	32.3	33.7	Kenya
Lesotho	109.6	92.7	36.0	34.4	21.0	32.4	54.4	39.6	121.0	99.1	Lésotho
Liberia	83.4	49.7	12.9	23.5	31.6	57.2	21.2	28.8	49.1	59.2	Libéria
Libya	17.1	19.7	10.6	41.9	21.4	21.2	78.7	62.9	27.8	45.7	Libye
Madagascar	81.8	87.7	9.0	9.7	25.3	15.6	29.7	30.1	45.8	43.1	Madagascar
Malawi	88.7	...	10.9	...	20.3	...	16.8	...	36.7	...	Malawi
Mali	68.9	63.7	16.9	16.3	22.0	21.7	25.0	26.7	32.9	28.4	Mali
Mauritania	74.2	92.8	11.9	15.9	20.4	10.2	58.0	48.7	64.5	67.7	Mauritanie
Mauritius	69.7	73.8	14.1	14.4	26.7	24.0	60.4	54.3	70.9	66.5	Maurice
Morocco	57.5	60.1	18.5	19.0	29.4	34.2	34.2	33.6	39.7	46.9	Maroc
Mozambique	79.5	70.5	12.3	22.2	17.0	17.6	30.4	27.8	39.3	38.2	Mozambique
Namibia	54.3	66.0	19.5	27.6	22.3	24.5	45.5	43.0	41.6	61.1	Namibie
Niger	72.9	70.1	15.0	13.6	23.6	34.4	18.1	23.3	29.5	41.4	Niger
Nigeria	63.3	72.1	6.9	8.1	8.3	14.7	43.1	18.0	21.5	13.0	Nigéria
Rwanda	78.1	74.3	18.2	14.2	16.7	26.5	12.4	15.6	25.3	30.7	Rwanda
São Tomé & Príncipe	113.7	86.8	10.3	27.2	17.4	27.3	15.9	12.3	57.2	53.6	São Tomé & Príncipe
Senegal	79.1	78.4	13.6	15.5	24.7	27.2	25.6	28.0	43.1	49.1	Sénégal
Seychelles	49.9	44.6	39.4	28.2	26.9	37.6	84.4	78.2	100.5	88.6	Seychelles
Sierra Leone	87.6	79.7	10.2	8.7	10.4	12.7	17.1	44.7	25.3	45.8	Sierra Leone
Somalia	72.4	72.7	8.7	8.7	20.3	20.0	0.3	0.3	1.7	1.7	Somalie
South Africa	61.8	60.6	18.2	20.3	21.8	21.4	29.3	31.0	31.0	33.2	Afrique du Sud
South Sudan	...	89.7	...	23.0	...	11.9	...	18.2	...	42.8	Soudan du Sud
Sudan	61.8	60.6	18.2	20.3	21.8	21.4	29.3	31.0	31.0	33.2	Soudan
Swaziland	84.9	84.5	13.9	15.4	12.8	8.0	66.0	50.8	77.6	58.7	Swaziland
Tanzania	68.0	68.2	17.5	16.2	27.6	28.9	22.6	17.5	35.7	30.8	Tanzanie
Togo	93.7	81.8	13.6	15.1	17.4	24.0	43.7	46.0	68.4	67.0	Togo
Tunisia	61.7	68.9	16.7	18.8	23.4	21.8	46.0	46.9	47.9	56.5	Tunisie
Uganda	80.0	72.5	13.4	8.2	20.7	29.0	14.9	20.3	29.0	29.9	Ouganda
Zambia	72.4	64.2	15.4	8.0	15.9	28.0	36.0	34.6	39.8	34.8	Zambie
Zimbabwe	97.0	102.4	1.8	15.7	7.8	13.0	35.3	26.0	42.0	57.1	Zimbabwe
Africa	58.5	62.1	13.2	15.9	19.9	22.7	39.4	29.7	31.0	30.5	**Afrique**

2-6. Inflation (Average annual Growth Rates) (%) - Inflation (Taux de Croissance moyenne annuel) (%)

Country	2006	2007	2008	2009	2010	2011	2012	2013	2014	Pays
Algeria	1.8	4.3	5.1	6.5	4.1	5.8	9.7	4.1	3.9	Algérie
Angola	13.3	12.3	12.4	13.7	14.5	13.5	10.3	8.8	7.3	Angola
Benin	3.8	1.3	7.9	0.4	2.1	2.7	6.7	1.0	- 1.1	Bénin
Botswana	11.6	7.1	12.6	8.1	6.9	8.5	7.5	5.9	4.4	Botswana
Burkina Faso	2.4	- 0.3	10.7	0.9	- 0.6	2.8	3.8	0.5	-0.3	Burkina Faso
Burundi	2.8	8.4	24.4	10.5	6.5	9.6	18.2	7.9	4.4	Burundi
Cabo Verde	4.8	1.7	6.8	1.0	2.1	4.5	2.5	1.5	- 0.2	Cabo Verde
Cameroon	5.1	0.5	5.7	3.0	0.9	3.3	2.4	2.3	1.9	Cameroun
Central African Republic	6.7	0.9	9.3	3.6	1.5	1.8	5.3	1.5	8.2	République Centrafricaine
Chad	8.1	- 7.4	8.3	10.1	- 2.1	2.0	7.5	0.2	1.7	Tchad
Comoros	4.5	4.4	4.9	- 2.9	3.8	1.8	6.3	1.6	2.7	Comores
Congo	4.9	2.6	4.5	5.8	0.3	2.1	6.1	6.0	-0.1	Congo
Congo, Dem. Republic	2.5	1.9	6.3	0.5	1.7	4.9	1.3	2.6	0.5	Rép. Démocratique du Congo
Côte d'Ivoire	21.4	22.3	44.7	29.0	17.2	12.6	3.7	1.3	1.3	Côte d'Ivoire
Djibouti	3.5	5.0	12.0	1.7	4.0	5.1	3.7	2.4	3.2	Djibouti
Egypt	7.7	9.5	18.3	11.8	11.1	10.1	7.1	9.5	10.1	Égypte
Equatorial Guinea	4.4	2.8	6.0	5.5	4.7	7.3	3.6	3.6	3.6	Guinée Equatoriale
Eritrea	15.1	9.3	19.9	34.7	20.5	13.3	12.3	12.3	11.4	Érythrée
Ethiopia	12.3	17.0	25.5	36.4	2.8	33.2	23.0	7.7	7.4	Éthiopie
Gabon	- 1.4	5.0	5.3	1.9	1.4	1.3	2.7	0.5	4.5	Gabon
Gambia	2.1	5.4	4.4	4.6	5.0	4.8	4.3	5.7	5.7	Gambie
Ghana	11.7	10.7	16.5	19.2	10.7	8.7	9.2	11.8	16.0	Ghana
Guinea	34.7	22.9	18.4	4.7	15.5	21.4	15.2	8.0	13.6	Guinée
Guinea Bissau	2.0	4.6	7.9	- 2.8	2.2	4.8	2.3	1.2	- 1.5	Guinée-Bissau
Kenya	6.0	4.3	16.2	9.5	4.1	14.0	9.4	5.7	6.9	Kenya
Lesotho	6.1	8.0	10.7	7.3	3.6	5.0	6.0	5.0	5.4	Lésotho
Liberia	6.1	11.4	17.5	7.4	7.3	8.5	6.8	7.6	9.7	Libéria
Libya	1.5	6.3	10.4	2.5	2.5	15.9	6.1	2.6	2.7	Libye
Madagascar	10.8	10.3	9.2	9.0	9.2	9.5	5.7	5.8	6.1	Madagascar
Malawi	13.9	8.0	8.7	8.4	7.4	7.6	21.3	27.3	23.8	Malawi
Mali	1.5	1.4	9.2	2.4	1.2	3.0	5.3	- 0.6	0.9	Mali
Mauritania	6.2	7.3	7.3	2.2	5.7	6.2	4.9	4.1	3.5	Mauritanie
Mauritius	8.9	8.8	9.7	2.5	2.9	6.5	3.9	2.9	4.2	Maurice
Morocco	3.3	2.0	3.7	1.0	0.9	0.9	1.3	1.9	0.4	Maroc
Mozambique	13.6	9.2	14.5	3.8	12.4	11.2	2.6	4.3	2.6	Mozambique
Namibia	5.0	6.6	9.1	9.5	4.9	5.0	6.7	5.6	5.4	Namibie
Niger	0.0	0.1	11.3	0.5	0.9	2.9	0.5	2.3	- 0.9	Niger
Nigeria	8.2	5.4	11.6	12.5	13.7	10.8	12.2	8.5	8.1	Nigéria
Rwanda	8.9	9.1	15.4	10.3	2.3	5.6	6.3	4.2	1.8	Rwanda
São Tomé & Príncipe	23.1	18.6	32.0	17.0	13.3	14.3	10.6	8.1	6.3	São Tomé & Príncipe
Senegal	2.1	5.9	5.8	- 1.0	1.2	3.4	1.4	0.7	- 1.1	Sénégal
Seychelles	- 1.9	5.3	37.0	31.7	- 2.4	2.6	7.1	4.3	1.4	Seychelles
Sierra Leone	9.7	11.6	14.8	9.3	17.8	18.5	13.8	9.9	8.3	Sierra Leone
Somalia	...	...	...	...	...	...	...	...	...	Somalie
South Africa	3.2	6.2	9.9	7.2	4.1	5.0	5.6	5.7	6.1	Afrique du Sud
South Sudan	...	...	25.8	8.9	12.8	47.3	45.1	0.0	1.7	Soudan du Sud
Sudan	7.2	8.1	14.3	11.3	13.0	18.0	35.6	36.4	37.0	Soudan
Swaziland	5.3	8.1	12.6	7.6	4.5	6.1	8.9	5.6	5.7	Swaziland
Tanzania	7.3	7.0	10.3	12.1	8.2	12.7	16.0	7.9	6.1	Tanzanie
Togo	2.2	0.9	8.7	3.7	1.5	3.6	2.6	1.8	0.2	Togo
Tunisia	4.1	3.4	4.9	3.5	4.2	3.5	5.1	5.8	4.9	Tunisie
Uganda	7.2	6.1	12.1	13.0	4.0	18.7	14.0	5.5	4.3	Ouganda
Zambia	9.0	10.7	12.4	13.4	8.5	8.6	6.6	7.0	7.8	Zambie
Zimbabwe	184101	12562581	5.3	11.5	3.0	3.3	3.9	1.6	- 0.2	Zimbabwe
Africa	**5.6**	**6.9**	**10.7**	**9.7**	**8.0**	**9.2**	**9.2**	**7.0**	**7.2**	**Afrique**

2-7. Agricultural and Food Production Index – Indice de la production agricole et alimentaire

2004 - 2006 = 100

	Agricultural Production/ Procuction agricole				Food Production/ Production alimentaire				2004 - 2006 = 100
Country	2010	2011	2012	2013	2010	2011	2012	2013	Pays
Algeria	124.98	134.70	143.81	158.41	125.07	134.86	144.05	158.78	Algérie
Angola	171.96	188.61	157.37	211.55	172.67	189.56	157.65	212.71	Angola
Benin	114.98	126.06	131.74	144.91	122.35	130.70	137.75	150.28	Bénin
Botswana	123.72	142.46	129.86	129.82	124.03	142.93	130.26	130.22	Botswana
Burkina Faso	115.98	104.84	122.21	123.15	122.63	112.53	128.77	124.13	Burkina Faso
Burundi	107.90	102.42	95.22	129.35	113.67	112.18	98.77	144.72	Burundi
Cabo Verde	113.02	88.74	91.28	89.71	113.03	88.59	91.07	89.56	Cabo Verde
Cameroon	139.18	143.04	149.90	154.46	142.94	148.42	154.99	159.41	Cameroun
Central African Republic	113.99	119.13	120.85	122.79	113.27	118.35	119.39	121.24	République Centrafricaine
Chad	104.32	96.94	120.03	115.21	110.14	101.17	124.20	119.54	Tchad
Comoros	113.63	109.59	112.28	113.51	113.66	109.56	112.25	113.48	Comores
Congo	122.97	125.45	131.82	135.50	123.35	125.77	132.15	135.83	Congo
Congo, Dem. Republic	106.47	110.55	115.74	116.98	106.54	110.63	115.88	117.21	Rép. Démocratique du Congo
Côte d'Ivoire	107.45	110.61	120.33	123.46	109.47	114.35	121.86	124.38	Côte d'Ivoire
Djibouti	118.55	132.33	134.50	134.40	118.55	132.33	134.50	134.40	Djibouti
Egypt	109.27	113.54	118.66	118.39	110.13	114.16	119.89	119.63	Égypte
Equatorial Guinea	110.94	112.39	115.84	116.55	112.51	113.50	116.81	118.16	Guinée Equatoriale
Eritrea	106.41	108.77	110.93	110.25	106.34	108.71	110.87	110.18	Érythrée
Ethiopia	137.33	139.16	146.47	147.02	136.88	138.43	147.55	148.11	Éthiopie
Gabon	116.99	118.42	121.20	122.32	114.51	115.54	118.49	119.68	Gabon
Gambia	133.53	88.25	107.55	98.24	133.58	88.19	107.55	98.22	Gambie
Ghana	124.64	131.46	138.84	143.47	124.65	131.38	138.79	143.45	Ghana
Guinea	113.36	116.48	122.27	122.81	113.21	116.27	122.16	123.43	Guinée
Guinea Bissau	121.67	128.01	137.42	140.38	121.98	128.40	137.94	140.94	Guinée-Bissau
Kenya	122.93	117.58	121.37	122.67	123.97	118.54	122.69	123.00	Kenya
Lesotho	110.44	108.88	99.25	111.48	110.88	108.76	98.57	111.50	Lésotho
Liberia	100.49	104.19	104.36	100.82	120.47	125.48	125.71	120.55	Libéria
Libya	109.74	110.49	111.50	110.61	109.90	110.70	111.71	110.81	Libye
Madagascar	123.59	124.67	129.63	118.88	124.48	125.20	130.25	119.28	Madagascar
Malawi	155.15	164.38	173.41	186.61	156.74	166.56	181.87	193.20	Malawi
Mali	142.42	136.28	146.33	141.29	153.92	144.63	154.41	149.79	Mali
Mauritania	112.51	111.47	120.28	120.26	112.51	111.47	120.28	120.26	Mauritanie
Mauritius	98.62	98.34	95.84	93.90	98.62	98.18	95.81	93.85	Maurice
Morocco	126.40	130.61	124.10	134.35	126.65	130.91	124.30	134.69	Maroc
Mozambique	147.94	157.53	151.46	156.59	153.35	162.48	155.48	161.41	Mozambique
Namibia	90.15	88.37	91.39	89.79	90.74	88.94	91.98	90.36	Namibie
Niger	145.11	127.77	138.10	132.35	145.31	127.79	138.16	132.39	Niger
Nigeria	103.88	96.29	106.33	109.89	103.81	96.60	106.75	110.51	Nigéria
Rwanda	144.92	156.11	166.27	170.22	145.93	157.15	167.89	172.01	Rwanda
São Tomé & Príncipe	102.48	100.35	102.26	111.15	102.46	100.44	102.36	111.26	São Tomé & Príncipe
Senegal	150.71	108.28	128.15	125.94	152.35	108.90	128.80	126.42	Sénégal
Seychelles	91.25	101.59	104.91	109.86	94.38	105.45	108.87	114.01	Seychelles
Sierra Leone	148.67	155.51	160.95	169.30	148.77	155.38	160.78	169.27	Sierra Leone
Somalia	104.31	107.47	110.59	117.11	104.31	107.47	110.59	117.12	Somalie
South Africa	117.68	116.73	120.43	122.31	118.33	117.19	121.01	122.99	Afrique du Sud
South Sudan	116.38	115.82	119.10	120.89	117.01	116.28	119.67	121.56	Soudan du Sud
Sudan	98.91	106.99	102.23	113.49	100.14	108.43	102.21	115.07	Soudan
Swaziland	103.55	105.75	111.27	112.13	103.88	106.09	111.67	112.53	Swaziland
Tanzania	128.92	139.30	148.18	153.83	130.75	140.34	149.39	155.03	Tanzanie
Togo	123.04	136.26	132.59	120.65	129.16	140.52	136.96	124.53	Togo
Tunisia	106.53	106.65	118.78	118.01	106.61	106.70	118.86	118.12	Tunisie
Uganda	111.56	113.62	110.88	111.82	111.58	112.90	110.51	111.30	Ouganda
Zambia	162.10	173.10	180.80	178.56	170.00	181.35	183.45	186.87	Zambie
Zimbabwe	101.19	104.50	105.90	107.04	95.92	99.75	99.31	97.55	Zimbabwe

2-8. Industrial, Mining and Manufacturing Production Index – Indice de la production industrielle, minière et manufacturière

Country	Base	*Industrial Production/ Procuction Industrielle*				*Mining Production/ Production minière*				*Manufacturing Production/ Production manufacturière*				Pays
		2010	2011	2012	2013	2010	2011	2012	2013	2010	2011	2012	2013	
Algeria	2010=100	100.0	100.4	102.0	102.9	100.0	90.5	85.4	90.5	100.0	98.7	98.8	100.5	Algérie
Angola	2010=100	100.0	95.7	101.2	...	100.0	95.0	100.3	...	100.0	99.5	103.2	...	Angola
Benin	2010=100	100.0	107.3	109.9	114.2	...	...	...	...	...	...	...	...	Bénin
Botswana	2010=100	...	...	...	...	100.0	100.2	92.5	108.5	...	...	...	...	Botswana
Burkina Faso	2010=100	100.0	92.5	96.5	101.2	100.0	101.3	99.4	...	100.0	88.3	91.6	...	Burkina Faso
Burundi	2010=100	100.0	108.5	118.3	119.5	100.0	114.5	155.4	88.3	100.0	107.4	114.9	113.6	Burundi
Cabo Verde	...	...	...	...	...	...	...	...	...	...	...	...	...	Cabo Verde
Cameroon	2010=100	100.0	102.3	105.0	116.3	...	...	...	...	100.0	102.1	104.7	119.9	Cameroun
Central African Republic	2010=100	100.0	107.7	114.1	68.2	100.0	111.4	123.8	39.3	100.0	106.9	111.1	77.3	République Centrafricaine
Chad	2005=100	100.0	96.2	93.1	82.4	...	...	...	...	...	...	...	...	Tchad
Comoros	2011=100	...	...	100.0	91.3	...	...	...	...	...	...	...	...	Comores
Congo	...	...	...	...	...	...	...	...	...	...	...	...	...	Congo
Congo, Dem. Republic	...	...	...	...	...	...	...	...	...	...	...	...	...	Rép. Démocratique du Congo
Côte d'Ivoire	2010=100	100.0	92.6	124.4	130.2	...	...	...	...	...	...	...	...	Côte d'Ivoire
Djibouti	...	...	...	...	...	...	...	...	...	...	...	...	...	Djibouti
Egypt	2010=100	...	...	...	...	...	...	...	...	100.0	99.5	100.3	99.8	Égypte
Equatorial Guinea	...	...	...	...	...	...	...	...	...	...	...	...	...	Guinée Equatoriale
Eritrea	...	...	...	...	...	...	...	...	...	...	...	...	...	Érythrée
Ethiopia	...	...	...	...	...	...	...	...	...	...	...	...	...	Éthiopie
Gabon	2005=100	116.6	116.6	125.8	...	...	...	...	...	...	...	...	...	Gabon
Gambia	...	...	...	...	...	...	...	...	...	...	...	...	...	Gambie
Ghana	2010=100	100.0	157.0	170.4	181.8	100.0	306.5	356.6	402.2	100.0	117.0	119.3	119.9	Ghana
Guinea	2006=100	130.5	130.5	115.3	114.5	...	...	...	...	...	...	...	...	Guinée
Guinea Bissau	...	...	...	...	...	...	...	...	...	...	...	...	...	Guinée-Bissau
Kenya	...	...	...	...	...	...	...	...	...	...	...	...	...	Kenya
Lesotho	...	...	...	...	...	...	...	...	...	...	...	...	...	Lésotho
Liberia	...	...	...	...	...	...	...	...	...	...	...	...	...	Libéria
Libya	...	...	...	...	...	...	...	...	...	...	...	...	...	Libye
Madagascar	...	...	...	...	...	...	...	...	...	...	...	...	...	Madagascar
Malawi	...	...	...	...	...	...	...	...	...	...	...	...	...	Malawi
Mali	2010=100	100.0	111.2	113.1	116.5	...	...	...	...	...	...	...	...	Mali
Mauritania	2010=100	100.0	99.6	103.7	115.4	100.0	97.6	100.6	...	100.0	105.6	126.9	...	Mauritanie
Mauritius	2010=100	100.0	101.2	103.3	107.6	100.0	81.0	74.3	70.9	100.0	101.4	103.3	107.7	Maurice
Morocco	2010=100	...	...	...	...	100.0	105.2	101.8	99.9	100.0	103.4	104.5	104.8	Maroc
Mozambique	...	...	...	...	...	...	...	...	...	...	...	...	...	Mozambique
Namibia	...	...	...	...	...	...	...	...	...	...	...	...	...	Namibie
Niger	2010=100	100.0	105.6	112.2	127.6	100.0	98.1	109.5	...	100.0	133.5	115.4	...	Niger
Nigeria	2010=100	100.0	107.5	109.0	109.4	100.0	102.4	97.5	85.0	100.0	117.8	133.7	162.8	Nigéria
Rwanda	...	...	...	...	...	...	...	...	...	...	...	...	...	Rwanda
São Tomé & Príncipe	...	...	...	...	...	...	...	...	...	...	...	...	...	São Tomé & Príncipe
Senegal	2010=100	100.0	106.5	105.9	101.0	100.0	118.2	114.8	92.6	100.0	107.1	105.5	100.4	Sénégal
Seychelles	...	...	...	...	...	...	...	...	...	...	...	...	...	Seychelles
Sierra Leone	...	...	...	...	...	...	...	...	...	...	...	...	...	Sierra Leone
Somalia	...	...	...	...	...	...	...	...	...	...	...	...	...	Somalie
South Africa	2010=100	...	...	...	...	100.0	99.1	96.0	100.0	100.0	102.8	105.2	106.7	Afrique du Sud
South Sudan	...	...	...	...	...	...	...	...	...	...	...	...	...	Soudan du Sud
Sudan	...	...	...	...	...	...	...	...	...	...	...	...	...	Soudan
Swaziland	...	...	...	...	...	...	...	...	...	...	...	...	...	Swaziland
Tanzania	...	...	...	...	...	...	...	...	...	...	...	...	...	Tanzanie
Togo	2010=100	100.0	107.7	114.4	101.4	100.0	126.0	158.2	191.2	100.0	115.6	117.4	112.8	Togo
Tunisia	2010=100	100.0	96.3	98.3	100.0	100.0	78.8	78.9	76.3	100.0	98.9	100.6	102.9	Tunisie
Uganda	2010=100	...	...	...	...	...	...	...	...	100.0	103.9	107.6	110.8	Ouganda
Zambia	2010=100	100.0	105.6	107.6	111.8	100.0	100.9	99.0	100.8	100.0	110.6	117.3	123.1	Zambie
Zimbabwe	...	...	...	...	...	...	...	...	...	...	...	...	...	Zimbabwe

Source: UN, Monthly Bulletin of Statistics Online Database and Afristat

Source: NU, Bulletin mensuel des statistiques (base de données en ligne) et Afristat

2-9. Electricity Production by Type – Production d'electricité par categorie

	Total electricity generation (GWh)			of which: Total hydro production (GWh)			Total production from fossil fuels (GWh)			
Country	2000	2010	2013	2000	2010	2013	2000	2010	2013	Pays
Algeria	25 412	42 834	56 149	54	171	99	25 358	42 663	55 819	Algérie
Angola	1 445	5 448	6 370	912	3 703	4 588	533	1 745	1 778	Angola
Benin	134	152	162	2	1	1	132	150	160	Bénin
Botswana	947	430	2 626	0	0	0	947	430	2 617	Botswana
Burkina Faso	406	565	731	98	118	106	302	448	625	Burkina Faso
Burundi	100	241	184	98	230	179	2	11	4	Burundi
Cabo Verde	138	287	297	0	0	0	130	280	290	Cabo Verde
Cameroon	3 130	5 958	6 523	3 092	4 260	4 783	38	1 580	1 613	Cameroun
Central African Republic	107	160	192	84	135	159	23	25	28	République Centrafricaine
Chad	92	100	269	0	0	0	92	100	269	Tchad
Comoros	20	37	66	2	5	5	18	32	60	Comores
Congo	299	781	1 407	298	426	864	1	355	543	Congo
Congo, Dem. Republic	6 020	7 600	7 278	6 001	7 591	7 235	19	9	38	Rép. Démocratique du Congo
Côte d'Ivoire	4 807	6 052	9 102	1 764	1 602	1 914	3 036	4 278	7 016	Côte d'Ivoire
Djibouti	180	325	82	0	0	0	180	325	80	Djibouti
Egypt	76 463	146 795	157 930	14 659	13 046	13 840	61 667	132 045	142 468	Égypte
Equatorial Guinea	42	410	413	2	14	18	40	396	396	Guinée Equatoriale
Eritrea	210	311	404	0	0	0	209	309	398	Érythrée
Ethiopia	1 818	4 931	8 461	1 790	4 882	7 306	23	31	564	Éthiopie
Gabon	1 147	1 776	2 113	809	912	1 082	331	855	1 017	Gabon
Gambia	111	205	238	0	0	0	111	203	236	Gambie
Ghana	7 220	10 096	12 871	6 606	6 925	8 233	614	3 171	4 635	Ghana
Guinea	743	969	1 183	406	519	580	337	450	598	Guinée
Guinea Bissau	20	67	75	0	0	0	20	67	75	Guinée-Bissau
Kenya	4 103	7 467	8 989	1 325	3 393	2 498	2 129	2 287	3 405	Kenya
Lesotho	288	694	385	288	694	385	0	0	0	Lésotho
Liberia	31	30	40	0	0	0	31	30	40	Libéria
Libya	15 300	32 753	31 183	0	0	0	15 300	32 753	31 174	Libye
Madagascar	780	1 196	2 422	540	711	858	240	478	1 542	Madagascar
Malawi	1 204	1 943	2 442	1 023	1 733	2 380	181	210	43	Malawi
Mali	814	1 691	1 736	245	695	820	517	944	864	Mali
Mauritania	230	701	391	32	116	123	198	585	268	Mauritanie
Mauritius	1 685	2 689	2 886	95	101	95	1 176	2 035	2 291	Maurice
Morocco	14 153	23 637	26 689	718	3 433	2 990	13 371	19 545	22 483	Maroc
Mozambique	8 849	16 658	15 026	8 836	16 640	14 542	13	18	318	Mozambique
Namibia	1 414	1 293	1 496	1 380	1 235	1 442	34	58	41	Namibie
Niger	205	250	452	0	0	0	205	250	448	Niger
Nigeria	14 727	26 057	25 200	5 628	6 310	5 267	9 099	19 747	19 934	Nigéria
Rwanda	113	280	769	110	110	214	3	170	256	Rwanda
São Tomé & Príncipe	15	25	28	7	5	11	8	20	18	São Tomé & Príncipe
Senegal	1 528	3 032	2 952	0	253	311	1 476	2 724	2 586	Sénégal
Seychelles	178	283	409	0	0	0	178	283	408	Seychelles
Sierra Leone	89	298	332	15	253	287	74	45	45	Sierra Leone
Somalia	235	310	362	0	0	11	235	310	351	Somalie
South Africa	210 384	245 840	283 728	3 648	5 091	7 858	193 419	227 552	260 017	Afrique du Sud
South Sudan	...	...	271	...	...	21	...	...	250	Soudan du Sud
Sudan	3 079	8 009	11 599	1 183	6 202	7 884	1 386	1 297	3 504	Soudan
Swaziland	451	653	700	192	288	212	259	260	315	Swaziland
Tanzania	2 479	5 080	6 051	2 145	2 548	1 560	334	2 532	4 385	Tanzanie
Togo	175	132	208	100	98	95	75	32	111	Togo
Tunisia	10 095	16 521	18 369	64	50	60	10 008	15 907	17 944	Tunisie
Uganda	1 557	2 406	3 203	1 551	1 485	2 393	6	821	613	Ouganda
Zambia	7 830	11 304	11 917	7 782	11 273	11 134	48	31	781	Zambie
Zimbabwe	6 996	8 160	8 800	3 260	6 001	5 844	3 736	2 089	2 917	Zimbabwe
Africa	**439 998**	**655 922**	**744 162**	**76 844**	**113 257**	**120 285**	**512 537**	**513 386**	**546 690**	**Afrique**

Section 3

Monetary and Financial Statistics

Statistiques monétaires et financières

MONETARY STATISTICS - STATISTIQUES MONETAIRES

3-1. Broad Money Supply (M2) / Masse monétaire (M2)

Country	*Amount (billions nat. currency) / Montant (milliards de mon. nat.)*			*Annual % Growth / Acr. Annuel en %*			*Income Velocity of Money (GDP/M2) / Vitesse de circ. de la monnaie (PIB/M2)*			Pays
	2012	2013	2014	2012	2013	2014	2012	2013	2014	
Algeria	11 012.7	11 941.5	13 626.5	10.9	8.4	14.1	1.1	1.1	1.0	Algérie
Angola	3 876.0	4 431.5	5 366.7	6.0	14.3	21.1	2.2	2.2	2.0	Angola
Benin	1 720.0	2 017.2	2 362.1	9.0	17.3	17.1	1.7	1.5	1.4	Bénin
Botswana	51.7	56.2	64.9	13.9	8.6	15.5	1.2	1.3	1.1	Botswana
Burkina Faso	1 740.2	1 924.6	2 201.5	15.9	10.6	14.4	2.4	2.3	2.0	Burkina Faso
Burundi	745.2	833.8	943.9	10.9	11.9	13.2	3.8	3.9	3.6	Burundi
Cameroon	3 074.1	3 407.5	3 611.8	1.4	10.8	6.0	3.2	3.1	3.2	Cameroun
Cabo Verde	123.4	137.5	144.2	6.3	11.4	4.8	0.8	0.7	0.7	Cabo Verde
Central African Republic	214.8	220.1	226.9	4.2	2.5	3.1	4.4	2.9	3.1	République Centrafricaine
Chad	784.3	852.1	932.8	13.4	8.6	9.5	7.7	6.9	6.7	Tchad
Comoros	87.4	89.9	96.3	16.0	2.8	7.2	1.9	2.0	2.0	Comores
Congo	2 303.0	2 318.6	2 559.0	21.1	0.7	10.4	2.7	2.6	2.5	Congo
Congo. Dem. Republic	2 093.4	2 297.3	2 596.9	- 7.6	9.7	13.0	3.7	3.7	3.5	Rép. Démocratique du Congo
Côte d'Ivoire	2 930.1	3 255.3	3 654.4	21.1	11.1	12.3	6.9	6.6	6.5	Côte d'Ivoire
Djibouti	206.2	220.4	244.4	15.0	6.9	10.9	0.9	0.9	0.9	Djibouti
Egypt	1 094.4	1 295.7	1 517.4	8.3	18.4	17.1	0.8	0.8	0.7	Égypte
Equatorial Guinea	1 688.6	1 812.0	1 975.2	57.8	7.3	9.0	5.2	4.2	3.7	Guinée Equatoriale
Eritrea	52.5	60.8	69.4	14.1	15.8	14.2	0.6	0.6	0.6	Érythrée
Ethiopia	188.8	234.3	293.2	32.9	24.1	25.1	...	...	...	Éthiopie
Gabon	2 033.6	2 260.9	2 472.9	15.7	11.2	9.4	3.3	3.2	3.1	Gabon
Gambia	15.9	18.3	21.1	7.8	15.2	15.0	1.2	1.2	1.2	Gambie
Ghana	22.6	26.9	35.4	24.3	19.1	31.2	2.5	2.7	1.8	Ghana
Guinea	11 450.2	13 067.4	14 384.7	1.0	14.1	10.1	...	...	...	Guinée
Guinea Bissau	162.8	186.9	206.9	- 6.0	14.8	10.7	2.8	2.6	2.4	Guinée-Bissau
Kenya	1 727.4	1 996.2	2 376.2	14.1	15.6	19.0	1.6	1.6	1.8	Kenya
Lesotho	7.2	8.7	9.9	7.0	21.1	14.5	1.9	1.6	1.4	Lésotho
Liberia	0.6	0.7	0.6	- 3.1	7.9	- 13.2	9.2	8.6	8.9	Libéria
Libya	65.6	70.2	73.0	13.2	6.9	4.0	1.5	1.2	0.7	Libye
Madagascar	2 612.1	2 452.8	5 894.4	9.8	- 6.1	140.3	4.8	5.2	3.0	Madagascar
Malawi	386.5	522.0	626.6	22.9	35.1	20.0	2.3	2.0	2.5	Malawi
Mali	1 718.1	1 845.4	2 025.4	15.2	7.4	9.8	2.5	2.3	2.3	Mali
Mauritania	413.4	469.7	527.8	10.5	13.6	12.4	3.1	...	...	Mauritanie
Mauritius	345.6	365.6	390.2	8.2	5.8	6.7	0.6	0.6	0.7	Maurice
Morocco	992.2	1 020.4	1 066.3	4.5	2.8	4.5	0.6	0.6	0.7	Maroc
Mozambique	132.7	160.8	191.4	25.6	21.2	19.0	2.2	2.0	1.8	Mozambique
Namibia	67.1	73.9	81.6	17.1	10.2	10.5	1.0	1.2	1.1	Namibie
Niger	802.5	882.3	1 000.5	31.2	9.9	13.4	3.5	3.5	3.2	Niger
Nigeria	15 480.4	15 612.2	16 162.9	29.1	0.9	3.5	3.1	3.2	3.3	Nigéria
Rwanda	889.9	1 028.2	1 161.1	14.0	15.5	12.9	...	...	...	Rwanda
São Tomé & Príncipe	1 879.5	2 140.4	2 369.5	20.3	13.9	10.7	2.0	2.1	2.1	São Tomé & Príncipe
Senegal	2 894.7	3 127.1	3 366.7	6.8	8.0	7.7	1.8	1.7	1.5	Sénégal
Seychelles	7.6	9.3	10.5	- 0.7	23.7	12.4	1.8	1.6	1.5	Seychelles
Sierra Leone	3 623.2	4 161.2	4 900.2	22.5	14.8	17.8	3.4	3.9	3.9	Sierra Leone
Somalia	...	...	...	...	...	...	...	...	...	Somalie
South Africa	2 372.2	2 518.1	2 714.3	5.2	6.2	7.8	0.8	0.9	0.8	Afrique du Sud
South Sudan	6.6	6.5	7.0	37.7	- 1.7	8.3	...	...	...	Soudan du Sud
Sudan	58.8	66.5	79.1	40.3	13.0	19.1	3.0	3.4	4.5	Soudan
Swaziland	9.7	11.2	12.5	10.0	15.9	11.2	2.1	2.0	2.0	Swaziland
Tanzania	14 647.1	16 106.8	18 812.2	12.5	10.0	16.8	2.9	3.2	3.0	Tanzanie
Togo	905.6	978.2	1 062.8	8.9	8.0	8.7	1.5	1.4	1.3	Togo
Tunisia	51.2	54.6	60.1	8.4	6.6	10.2	0.9	0.9	0.8	Tunisie
Uganda	12 123.1	13 270.5	14 767.3	14.9	9.5	11.3	3.6	3.6	3.2	Ouganda
Zambia	25.7	31.0	37.0	17.9	20.8	19.1	3.7	3.4	3.7	Zambie
Zimbabwe	3.7	3.9	4.0	19.0	5.4	3.3	...	...	...	Zimbabwe
Africa	**...**	**...**	**...**	**...**	**...**	**...**	**...**	**...**	**...**	**Afrique**

MONETARY STATISTICS - STATISTIQUES MONETAIRES

3-2. Exchange Rate - Taux de change

Average Exchange (National Currency per US $) - Taux de change (Moyen) (monnaie nationale par dollar)

Country	2006	2007	2008	2009	2010	2011	2012	2013	2014	Pays
Algeria	71.6	69.4	64.9	72.5	73.9	72.9	77.6	79.4	78.4	Algérie
Angola	80.4	76.7	75.0	79.3	91.9	93.9	95.5	96.5	97.6	Angola
Benin	522.9	478.9	446.9	471.1	494.7	471.4	510.2	493.9	493.3	Bénin
Botswana	5.8	6.1	6.8	7.2	6.8	6.8	7.6	8.4	9.0	Botswana
Burkina Faso	522.9	478.9	446.9	471.1	494.7	471.4	510.2	493.9	493.8	Burkina Faso
Burundi	1 028.7	1 081.9	1 185.7	1 230.2	1 260.8	1 441.7	1 575.0	1 539.1	1 516.7	Burundi
Cameroon	522.9	479.3	447.8	472.2	495.3	471.9	510.5	494.0	493.9	Cameroun
Cabo Verde	87.9	80.5	75.1	79.2	83.2	79.3	85.8	83.1	83.0	Cabo Verde
Central African Republic	522.9	479.3	447.8	472.2	495.3	471.9	510.5	494.0	493.9	République Centrafricaine
Chad	522.9	479.3	447.8	472.2	495.3	471.9	510.5	494.0	493.9	Tchad
Comoros	392.2	359.2	335.2	353.3	371.0	353.6	382.6	370.5	370.3	Comores
Congo	522.9	479.3	447.8	472.2	495.3	471.9	510.5	494.0	493.4	Congo
Congo. Dem. Republic	468.3	516.7	559.3	809.8	905.9	919.5	919.8	919.8	925.3	Rép. Démocratique du Congo
Côte d'Ivoire	522.9	478.9	446.9	471.1	494.7	471.4	510.2	493.9	493.8	Côte d'Ivoire
Djibouti	177.7	177.7	177.7	177.7	177.7	177.7	177.7	177.7	177.7	Djibouti
Egypt	5.7	5.6	5.4	5.5	5.6	5.9	6.1	6.9	7.1	Égypte
Equatorial Guinea	522.9	478.9	446.9	471.1	494.7	471.4	512.4	500.7	496.0	Guinée Equatoriale
Eritrea	15.4	15.4	15.4	15.4	15.4	15.4	15.4	15.4	15.4	Érythrée
Ethiopia	8.7	9.0	9.6	11.8	14.4	16.9	17.7	18.6	19.7	Éthiopie
Gabon	522.9	479.3	447.8	472.2	495.3	471.9	510.5	494.0	493.4	Gabon
Gambia	28.2	24.9	22.3	26.6	27.7	28.4	31.1	33.4	32.5	Gambie
Ghana	0.9	0.9	1.1	1.4	1.4	1.5	1.8	2.0	2.6	Ghana
Guinea	5 148.8	4 197.8	4 601.7	4 801.1	5 726.1	6 658.0	6 986.1	6 995.9	7 004.6	Guinée
Guinea Bissau	522.9	478.9	446.9	471.1	494.7	471.4	510.2	493.9	493.8	Guinée-Bissau
Kenya	72.1	67.3	69.2	77.4	79.2	88.8	84.5	86.1	87.8	Kenya
Lesotho	6.8	7.1	8.3	8.4	7.3	7.3	8.2	9.6	10.9	Lésotho
Liberia	58.0	61.3	63.2	68.3	71.4	72.2	73.5	75.5	76.9	Libéria
Libya	1.3	1.3	1.2	1.3	1.3	1.2	1.3	1.3	1.3	Libye
Madagascar	2 182.8	1 857.7	1 714.5	1 978.4	2 112.6	2 027.1	2 199.1	2 218.3	2 268.0	Madagascar
Malawi	136.0	140.0	140.5	141.1	150.5	156.9	253.1	370.2	405.7	Malawi
Mali	522.9	478.9	446.9	471.1	494.7	471.4	510.2	493.9	493.8	Mali
Mauritania	271.3	262.5	243.1	263.2	276.1	281.3	296.6	302.1	306.0	Mauritanie
Mauritius	31.7	31.3	28.5	32.0	30.8	28.7	30.0	30.7	30.6	Maurice
Morocco	8.8	8.2	7.7	8.1	8.4	8.1	8.6	8.4	8.3	Maroc
Mozambique	23.1	25.4	25.8	24.3	27.5	34.0	29.1	28.4	30.1	Mozambique
Namibia	6.8	7.0	8.3	8.5	7.3	7.3	8.2	9.7	10.8	Namibie
Niger	522.8	479.6	448.3	471.5	495.9	473.7	512.4	500.7	496.0	Niger
Nigeria	128.7	125.8	118.5	148.9	150.3	154.7	157.5	157.3	165.2	Nigéria
Rwanda	551.7	547.0	546.8	568.3	583.1	600.3	614.3	646.6	679.0	Rwanda
São Tomé & Príncipe	12 364.9	13 536.8	14 695.2	16 208.5	18 498.6	17 622.9	19 068.4	18 450.0	18 447.7	São Tomé & Príncipe
Senegal	522.9	478.9	446.9	471.1	494.7	471.4	510.2	493.9	493.8	Sénégal
Seychelles	5.5	6.7	9.5	13.6	12.1	12.4	13.7	12.1	12.3	Seychelles
Sierra Leone	2 961.9	2 985.2	2 981.5	3 385.7	3 978.1	4 349.2	4 344.0	4 332.5	4 434.1	Sierra Leone
Somalia	...	...	...	...	...	...	...	...	...	Somalie
South Africa	6.8	7.0	8.3	8.5	7.3	7.3	8.2	9.7	10.8	Afrique du Sud
South Sudan	...	...	...	...	...	3.0	3.0	3.0	3.0	Soudan du Sud
Sudan	2.2	2.0	2.1	2.3	2.3	2.7	3.6	4.8	5.7	Soudan
Swaziland	6.8	7.1	8.3	8.4	7.3	7.3	8.2	9.7	10.4	Swaziland
Tanzania	1 251.9	1 245.0	1 197.2	1 320.3	1 410.2	1 571.1	1 571.7	1 597.6	1 642.0	Tanzanie
Togo	522.9	479.3	447.8	472.2	495.3	471.9	510.5	494.0	493.9	Togo
Tunisia	1.3	1.3	1.2	1.4	1.4	1.4	1.6	1.6	1.7	Tunisie
Uganda	1 831.5	1 723.5	1 720.4	2 030.5	2 177.6	2 522.7	2 504.6	2 586.9	2 557.1	Ouganda
Zambia	3.6	4.0	3.7	5.0	4.8	4.9	5.1	5.4	6.2	Zambie
Zimbabwe	164.55	9 686.77	6 723 052 073.34	...	...	...	...	...	...	Zimbabwe

3-3. Government Finance - Finances Publiques

% of GDP	Revenue / Recette			Expenditure / Depense			Fiscal Balance / Solde budgetaire			% du PIB
Country	2011	2013	2014	2011	2013	2014	2011	2013	2014	Pays
Algeria	39.9	35.9	33.5	41.0	37.4	40.6	- 1.2	- 1.5	- 7.0	Algérie
Angola	45.8	35.2	33.5	37.7	34.9	35.7	8.1	0.3	- 2.2	Angola
Benin	20.1	21.3	21.6	21.9	23.2	22.7	- 1.8	- 1.9	- 1.1	Bénin
Botswana	30.4	33.6	35.1	36.6	32.8	29.9	- 6.2	0.7	5.2	Botswana
Burkina Faso	19.5	21.6	19.9	23.0	26.0	23.6	- 3.5	- 4.4	- 3.7	Burkina Faso
Burundi	26.0	30.8	28.9	34.3	30.4	30.1	- 8.3	0.4	- 1.2	Burundi
Cameroon	18.2	18.0	17.7	21.7	22.0	22.8	- 3.6	- 4.1	- 5.2	Cameroun
Cabo Verde	25.6	24.9	26.1	33.1	33.9	34.1	- 7.5	- 9.0	- 8.0	Cabo Verde
Central African Republic	13.3	8.4	18.8	15.7	14.7	22.0	- 2.4	- 6.3	- 3.2	République Centrafricaine
Chad	24.8	20.4	18.7	22.4	23.1	24.3	2.4	- 2.7	- 5.6	Tchad
Comoros	23.6	43.7	25.6	22.1	25.5	26.2	1.4	18.2	- 0.6	Comores
Congo	41.4	45.8	38.4	25.4	37.5	43.8	16.0	8.3	- 5.4	Congo
Congo. Dem. Republic	18.0	17.4	16.4	19.1	19.2	20.0	- 1.2	- 1.7	- 3.7	Rép. Démocratique du Congo
Côte d'Ivoire	14.4	19.8	19.6	18.4	22.1	21.8	- 4.0	- 2.3	- 2.2	Côte d'Ivoire
Djibouti	34.5	35.0	33.4	35.6	38.1	35.9	- 1.1	- 3.1	- 2.6	Djibouti
Egypt	19.3	20.0	22.7	29.1	33.7	35.4	- 9.8	- 13.7	- 12.8	Égypte
Equatorial Guinea	33.6	23.9	23.3	32.6	28.4	30.4	1.0	- 4.5	- 7.2	Guinée Equatoriale
Eritrea	18.4	18.3	18.6	34.6	30.8	30.3	- 16.2	-12.5	- 11.6	Érythrée
Ethiopia	16.6	15.9	15.1	18.2	17.8	17.7	- 1.6	- 1.9	- 2.6	Éthiopie
Gabon	27.8	26.8	25.1	25.6	29.9	31.8	2.3	- 3.2	- 6.6	Gabon
Gambia	21.2	18.3	20.7	26.0	26.8	26.7	- 4.7	- 8.4	- 6.0	Gambie
Ghana	18.7	16.8	18.2	24.4	26.3	28.5	- 5.7	- 9.5	- 10.4	Ghana
Guinea	19.9	24.3	24.8	20.2	26.3	29.0	- 0.3	- 2.1	- 4.2	Guinée
Guinea Bissau	16.7	10.5	19.5	18.1	11.9	21.7	- 1.4	- 1.4	- 2.1	Guinée-Bissau
Kenya	20.3	20.4	21.6	24.0	26.0	29.6	- 3.7	- 5.6	- 8.0	Kenya
Lesotho	50.0	58.7	55.4	50.5	53.9	54.4	- 0.5	4.8	1.0	Lésotho
Liberia	31.6	28.9	29.2	29.2	30.5	30.2	2.5	- 1.6	- 1.1	Libéria
Libya	39.1	58.7	45.1	55.0	64.9	94.2	- 15.9	- 6.2	- 49.1	Libye
Madagascar	11.7	10.9	12.4	14.1	14.9	14.4	- 2.4	- 4.0	- 2.0	Madagascar
Malawi	24.9	30.5	36.9	27.0	30.7	41.2	- 2.1	- 0.2	- 4.3	Malawi
Mali	21.8	18.6	21.7	25.2	25.5	27.3	- 3.4	- 6.9	- 5.6	Mali
Mauritania	20.9	33.5	30.9	21.6	28.7	29.6	- 0.7	4.8	1.2	Mauritanie
Mauritius	21.1	21.4	21.3	24.6	24.9	24.9	- 3.5	- 3.5	- 3.6	Maurice
Morocco	26.5	26.6	27.3	33.6	32.1	32.3	- 7.0	- 5.5	- 4.9	Maroc
Mozambique	27.3	32.2	31.4	32.4	35.0	41.4	- 5.1	- 2.9	- 10.0	Mozambique
Namibia	27.5	34.0	37.9	34.5	35.1	32.9	- 6.9	- 1.1	5.0	Namibie
Niger	20.8	22.6	24.7	22.6	24.9	30.4	- 1.9	- 2.3	- 5.7	Niger
Nigeria	17.4	16.3	14.9	19.3	15.2	14.8	- 1.9	1.1	0.1	Nigéria
Rwanda	23.6	23.5	26.0	27.1	28.7	30.3	- 3.5	- 5.2	- 4.3	Rwanda
São Tomé & Príncipe	40.3	26.0	26.3	52.9	37.3	35.7	- 12.6	- 11.3	- 9.4	São Tomé & Príncipe
Senegal	21.9	22.2	21.7	28.7	27.7	26.8	- 6.7	- 5.5	- 5.1	Sénégal
Seychelles	38.3	34.2	33.5	44.1	33.2	32.5	- 5.8	0.9	1.0	Seychelles
Sierra Leone	17.0	13.3	13.0	21.6	15.7	14.2	- 4.6	- 2.4	- 1.2	Sierra Leone
Somalia	...	...	...	...	...	...	...	...	...	Somalie
South Africa	27.3	29.2	28.1	30.7	33.0	31.5	- 3.4	- 3.9	- 3.4	Afrique du Sud
South Sudan	...	...	...	...	...	...	...	...	...	Soudan du Sud
Sudan	17.3	9.9	9.6	17.1	12.2	10.5	0.2	- 2.3	- 0.9	Soudan
Swaziland	23.0	33.5	33.0	30.7	32.6	33.4	- 7.7	0.9	- 0.3	Swaziland
Tanzania	19.2	20.8	20.7	25.1	27.7	24.5	- 6.0	- 6.9	- 3.8	Tanzanie
Togo	22.6	25.3	25.1	23.7	29.7	30.0	- 1.1	- 4.5	- 4.9	Togo
Tunisia	26.0	26.5	26.8	28.4	31.2	31.5	- 2.4	- 4.6	- 4.7	Tunisie
Uganda	18.7	15.9	15.4	23.0	18.5	20.3	- 4.3	- 2.6	- 4.9	Ouganda
Zambia	17.6	18.4	17.2	19.3	25.1	22.7	- 1.7	- 6.7	- 5.5	Zambie
Zimbabwe	26.7	27.7	28.1	29.0	30.2	30.5	- 2.4	- 2.4	- 2.4	Zimbabwe
Africa	**25.0**	**24.6**	**23.1**	**28.0**	**28.0**	**28.1**	**- 3.0**	**- 3.5**	**- 5.0**	**Afrique**

3-4. External Debt - Dette extérieure

Country	Debt outstanding (% of GDP) / Encours de la dette (% du PIB)						Debt service (% of Exports) / Service de la dette (% des exportations)						Pays
	2009	2010	2011	2012	2013	2014	2009	2010	2011	2012	2013	2014	
Algeria	4.1	3.5	2.2	1.8	1.6	1.3	2.2	0.4	1.8	1.6	2.3	2.3	Algérie
Angola	20.8	21.4	19.0	18.1	19.2	22.2	9.0	6.4	5.6	6.4	7.0	10.6	Angola
Benin	16.2	18.1	16.9	16.9	19.0	19.2	3.6	3.8	6.0	6.3	5.5	6.8	Bénin
Botswana	26.2	21.3	26.9	27.9	25.3	27.6	6.6	3.7	4.8	8.5	5.8	5.9	Botswana
Burkina Faso	25.6	26.6	22.7	22.2	21.0	23.8	4.3	2.7	2.2	2.7	3.0	3.4	Burkina Faso
Burundi	21.2	22.9	23.0	21.2	19.0	19.0	1.4	1.5	2.3	7.2	12.2	8.8	Burundi
Cameroon	5.3	6.2	7.0	9.0	12.3	14.8	4.[illegible]	3.1	2.1	2.5	3.0	3.7	Cameroun
Cabo Verde	59.2	64.6	67.8	91.6	104.9	102.7	9.3	8.3	8.3	8.7	9.4	9.7	Cabo Verde
Central African Republic	16.7	20.0	22.1	25.8	38.8	34.7	12.4	5.1	3.7	9.0	9.1	11.0	République Centrafricaine
Chad	18.5	20.2	21.4	20.4	23.7	30.2	2.0	1.6	2.2	3.2	6.8	9.2	Tchad
Comoros	52.0	48.9	44.7	40.6	17.9	16.6	10.5	11.4	10.0	10.3	2.1	2.7	Comores
Congo	58.9	19.7	21.7	26.2	32.3	32.4	8.0	1.5	1.1	1.2	2.9	3.3	Congo
Congo. Dem. Republic	75.0	24.3	21.4	20.1	22.3	23.8	3.8	2.0	1.5	1.9	1.8	1.5	Rép. Démocratique du Congo
Côte d'Ivoire	71.6	66.2	66.7	44.1	40.1	39.1	17.2	14.1	22.7	9.7	12.4	8.2	Côte d'Ivoire
Djibouti	59.8	56.1	52.3	49.2	48.4	50.4	8.0	7.8	7.9	8.5	8.4	12.6	Djibouti
Egypt	16.8	15.7	15.1	15.0	17.4	19.4	11.7	9.7	11.6	11.7	12.4	26.3	Égypte
Equatorial Guinea	5.6	5.4	6.9	8.8	8.3	6.4	0.2	0.3	0.1	0.8	2.9	2.7	Guinée Equatoriale
Eritrea	49.1	45.8	35.8	29.1	25.6	23.1	35.9	33.5	13.1	8.3	8.3	6.7	Érythrée
Ethiopia	15.1	20.6	22.9	18.1	20.3	20.8	2.4	3.2	4.3	6.6	8.5	11.3	Éthiopie
Gabon	17.9	15.7	13.2	15.4	18.0	19.0	8.3	8.3	4.4	6.9	15.8	5.6	Gabon
Gambia	43.1	42.3	43.2	44.4	43.4	39.2	31.3	33.4	30.9	32.9	29.6	27.4	Gambie
Ghana	26.9	27.2	25.1	25.2	28.6	40.8	4.2	3.9	3.2	3.8	4.5	6.3	Ghana
Guinea	69.9	66.7	62.3	22.8	23.1	20.5	7.2	4.0	9.0	235.6	3.6	16.1	Guinée
Guinea Bissau	128.9	23.6	31.8	39.2	36.5	37.4	8.7	648.7	0.6	0.1	0.0	2.8	Guinée-Bissau
Kenya	20.9	21.7	22.8	18.3	17.9	16.7	4.6	4.4	3.4	3.8	4.2	10.7	Kenya
Lesotho	39.4	32.6	225.2	290.8	387.8	484.1	5.1	3.8	3.4	3.5	4.2	4.9	Lésotho
Liberia	145.4	8.8	12.0	11.6	14.1	20.1	355.5	170.5	3.8	4.6	2.3	4.5	Libéria
Libya	8.8	7.5	16.1	6.8	7.6	13.6	0.0	0.0	0.0	0.0	0.0	0.0	Libye
Madagascar	56.2	59.5	39.4	44.3	44.1	43.2	10.2	14.4	22.9	24.6	23.9	21.5	Madagascar
Malawi	12.9	12.6	12.4	17.1	26.2	19.9	1.3	1.3	1.5	2.0	1.2	2.1	Malawi
Mali	22.1	26.8	23.2	26.2	26.9	29.8	4.7	4.5	5.9	4.6	4.8	5.9	Mali
Mauritania	87.6	79.2	73.2	87.2	90.4	70.1	6.7	5.6	4.1	6.0	5.7	9.2	Mauritanie
Mauritius	23.2	22.5	83.3	87.9	102.7	93.4	3.1	4.4	3.7	3.8	3.7	4.3	Maurice
Morocco	24.7	25.9	25.2	29.9	31.2	31.7	7.5	6.5	6.3	7.0	8.0	7.8	Maroc
Mozambique	57.3	60.1	65.8	54.9	58.1	77.5	18.8	33.9	17.3	10.9	11.1	11.5	Mozambique
Namibia	28.2	30.9	39.2	37.6	37.6	42.7	15.5	14.2	19.6	31.0	20.9	21.2	Namibie
Niger	39.9	50.0	48.9	52.6	50.9	67.7	2.3	2.3	4.4	2.4	3.9	4.4	Niger
Nigeria	1.5	1.4	1.4	1.4	1.6	1.8	0.9	0.6	0.5	0.5	0.7	0.7	Nigéria
Rwanda	13.9	13.6	15.7	14.2	19.9	24.4	1.7	2.3	3.8	9.4	17.7	5.5	Rwanda
São Tomé & Príncipe	69.2	78.2	73.3	83.8	74.3	75.0	18.9	11.2	8.0	7.3	14.3	22.5	São Tomé & Príncipe
Senegal	52.0	53.1	53.0	63.3	69.4	79.1	6.2	6.4	13.7	7.6	7.2	10.3	Sénégal
Seychelles	89.9	49.3	46.0	45.1	36.9	37.9	11.2	7.3	2.3	2.4	3.8	3.9	Seychelles
Sierra Leone	28.6	30.4	32.6	25.9	21.3	21.7	4.7	3.8	4.2	1.9	1.6	1.9	Sierra Leone
Somalia	...	...	...	...	...	...	...	...	...	...	...	...	Somalie
South Africa	26.5	27.8	28.4	35.7	37.3	43.3	50.0	31.7	27.9	32.2	38.5	42.4	Afrique du Sud
South Sudan	...	...	0.0	0.0	0.0	0.0	...	...	0.0	0.0	0.0	0.0	Soudan du Sud
Sudan	57.6	56.7	59.2	63.4	67.4	53.9	3.1	2.9	2.4	4.2	2.8	3.3	Soudan
Swaziland	12.6	13.2	15.5	14.2	17.2	17.9	1.5	2.5	19.5	7.3	12.4	9.3	Swaziland
Tanzania	21.0	23.9	25.7	25.9	26.4	28.0	3.6	3.4	3.2	2.8	3.6	4.8	Tanzanie
Togo	55.3	17.2	15.4	18.5	20.7	23.3	4.6	4.7	1.9	2.3	3.6	3.4	Togo
Tunisia	49.5	48.5	48.1	54.0	54.9	59.4	11.7	10.3	55.5	57.7	65.3	64.9	Tunisie
Uganda	18.8	20.6	26.6	26.4	27.1	30.5	11.5	10.2	10.6	12.8	14.7	15.3	Ouganda
Zambia	41.8	30.3	14.9	17.1	16.4	18.4	13.8	3.9	2.1	5.6	2.7	3.7	Zambie
Zimbabwe	97.2	84.6	75.1	73.1	79.0	121.2	40.7	14.4	...	...	...	...	Zimbabwe
	...	...	...	...	...	...	...	...	...	...	...	...	
Africa	**21.9**	**20.1**	**20.3**	**20.7**	**21.6**	**23.1**	**13.5**	**9.1**	**10.3**	**10.9**	**12.2**	**14.5**	**Afrique**

3-5. Balance of payments - Balance des paiements

% of GDP	Trade balance / Solde commercial					Current account balance / Solde du compte courant					% du PIB
Country	2010	2011	2012	2013	2014	2010	2011	2012	2013	2014	Pays
Algeria	11.2	14.0	9.7	4.5	2.3	7.6	8.9	5.9	0.4	- 4.0	Algérie
Angola	39.7	42.5	37.4	29.2	26.4	9.0	11.8	11.0	5.8	2.7	Angola
Benin	- 9.5	- 7.1	- 12.3	- 18.4	- 12.8	- 7.3	- 3.5	- 7.9	- 14.5	- 15.2	Bénin
Botswana	- 6.8	- 4.8	- 13.3	1.6	- 4.1	- 6.0	- 0.6	- 3.9	10.4	7.9	Botswana
Burkina Faso	- 1.4	0.0	- 1.3	- 3.1	- 4.1	- 3.6	- 1.3	- 0.7	- 10.4	- 10.7	Burkina Faso
Burundi	- 31.1	- 31.2	- 32.8	- 29.5	- 28.1	- 14.8	- 12.0	- 9.4	- 8.3	- 9.5	Burundi
Cameroon	- 0.9	- 2.2	- 1.0	- 1.1	- 1.1	- 3.4	- 2.8	- 3.3	- 3.8	- 4.2	Cameroun
Cabo Verde	- 40.1	- 45.1	- 40.2	- 34.2	- 32.6	- 12.4	- 16.3	- 11.5	- 3.5	- 9.0	Cabo Verde
Central African Republic	- 9.5	- 5.7	- 6.0	- 8.4	- 18.4	- 10.1	- 7.6	- 4.6	- 3.0	- 5.2	République Centrafricaine
Chad	6.9	10.9	7.5	6.1	7.4	- 9.0	- 5.6	- 8.5	- 9.9	- 9.3	Tchad
Comoros	- 28.5	- 28.6	- 33.4	- 32.3	- 30.0	- 5.1	- 11.2	- 8.2	- 5.7	- 7.8	Comores
Congo	49.4	47.9	44.6	35.4	31.9	0.1	4.7	- 2.4	- 4.7	- 6.3	Congo
Congo. Dem. Republic	4.7	2.8	- 0.2	- 0.2	3.4	- 9.9	- 5.9	- 8.1	- 10.2	- 8.4	Rép. Démocratique du Congo
Côte d'Ivoire	12.1	23.5	12.7	10.8	9.9	1.0	12.3	- 1.1	- 1.6	- 3.1	Côte d'Ivoire
Djibouti	- 26.1	- 33.7	- 39.3	- 41.2	- 49.9	- 5.4	- 13.7	- 18.4	- 23.8	- 19.6	Djibouti
Egypt	- 11.7	- 11.7	- 13.1	- 13.0	- 12.4	- 2.0	- 2.6	- 3.9	- 2.4	- 0.8	Égypte
Equatorial Guinea	24.8	34.4	38.6	34.9	35.5	- 13.1	- 14.1	- 16.0	- 8.1	- 9.9	Guinée Equatoriale
Eritrea	- 19.6	- 10.3	- 4.6	- 5.5	- 5.5	- 5.6	0.6	2.3	0.3	0.2	Érythrée
Ethiopia	- 24.8	- 18.1	- 18.6	- 18.0	- 17.6	- 6.2	- 0.7	- 7.3	- 6.0	- 8.6	Éthiopie
Gabon	34.7	36.9	35.8	34.6	33.8	8.7	13.2	14.0	12.1	6.7	Gabon
Gambia	- 22.5	- 23.9	- 28.0	- 25.3	- 22.9	- 16.0	- 9.5	- 16.7	- 14.4	- 10.7	Gambie
Ghana	- 9.2	- 7.7	- 10.0	- 7.9	- 5.0	- 8.6	- 9.0	- 11.7	- 11.9	- 9.2	Ghana
Guinea	0.6	- 9.4	- 11.2	- 9.1	- 8.7	- 1.9	- 20.5	- 23.8	- 22.0	- 26.2	Guinée
Guinea Bissau	- 8.3	- 0.2	- 4.7	- 3.5	- 2.7	- 8.3	- 1.3	- 7.8	- 4.1	- 0.5	Guinée-Bissau
Kenya	- 17.3	- 22.0	- 20.4	- 19.4	- 17.0	- 6.0	- 9.4	- 8.6	- 2.9	- 7.5	Kenya
Lesotho	- 48.8	- 43.2	- 46.5	- 48.3	- 58.6	- 5.7	- 11.0	- 5.9	- 7.9	- 3.4	Lésotho
Liberia	- 35.8	- 40.5	- 33.9	- 30.3	- 37.2	- 59.6	- 57.4	- 50.6	- 43.5	- 36.5	Libéria
Libya	32.2	22.7	43.3	27.2	- 13.7	19.5	9.1	29.1	13.6	- 23.3	Libye
Madagascar	- 12.6	- 10.1	- 11.1	- 7.8	- 7.6	- 9.7	- 6.9	- 6.7	- 5.4	- 2.3	Madagascar
Malawi	- 12.3	- 8.6	- 11.7	- 10.5	- 8.0	- 13.2	- 9.2	- 15.7	0.0	- 23.8	Malawi
Mali	- 9.8	- 3.1	1.1	- 3.3	- 7.7	- 12.8	- 6.2	- 2.6	- 1.8	- 6.2	Mali
Mauritania	3.2	5.5	- 11.0	- 7.8	- 4.2	- 7.4	- 5.4	- 25.3	- 22.9	- 13.1	Mauritanie
Mauritius	- 19.5	- 20.9	- 21.5	- 19.0	- 18.5	- 7.7	- 9.0	- 6.3	- 8.9	- 8.2	Maurice
Morocco	- 16.4	- 19.5	- 21.0	- 19.6	- 18.2	- 4.1	- 11.4	- 11.1	- 7.6	- 6.0	Maroc
Mozambique	- 9.4	- 19.8	- 27.7	- 26.5	- 30.7	- 7.3	- 27.0	- 44.4	- 37.2	- 39.2	Mozambique
Namibia	- 4.8	- 9.9	- 12.5	- 15.0	- 19.2	0.9	- 1.2	- 2.6	- 4.8	- 4.0	Namibie
Niger	- 11.3	- 14.5	- 6.5	- 5.0	- 13.8	- 19.8	- 22.3	- 15.3	- 16.6	- 20.3	Niger
Nigeria	8.3	7.6	9.2	8.5	7.4	3.9	3.0	4.1	3.9	2.6	Nigéria
Rwanda	- 13.4	- 17.2	- 19.1	- 15.3	- 19.8	- 7.3	- 7.5	- 11.4	- 7.1	- 11.8	Rwanda
São Tomé & Principe	- 42.4	- 42.2	- 36.5	- 37.1	- 37.2	- 23.0	- 26.6	- 22.5	- 18.3	- 17.0	São Tomé & Principe
Senegal	- 14.9	- 17.5	- 20.5	- 21.0	- 22.4	- 4.5	- 8.0	- 10.9	- 10.8	- 9.3	Sénégal
Seychelles	- 39.4	- 41.1	- 41.4	- 30.1	- 37.5	- 22.1	- 29.3	- 26.3	- 15.2	- 12.3	Seychelles
Sierra Leone	- 17.5	- 42.5	- 21.0	7.4	6.6	- 22.1	- 57.6	- 33.1	- 37.3	- 35.6	Sierra Leone
Somalia	...	...	...	...	...	...	...	...	...	...	Somalie
South Africa	1.8	1.6	- 1.2	- 2.1	- 2.7	- 1.5	- 2.2	- 5.0	- 5.8	- 5.8	Afrique du Sud
South Sudan	...	56.1	- 19.1	15.8	14.0	...	...	9.5	- 18.0	7.7	Soudan du Sud
Sudan	3.5	3.9	- 5.0	- 6.2	- 3.9	- 2.5	- 1.9	- 9.6	- 8.7	- 8.4	Soudan
Swaziland	- 3.8	- 1.1	1.9	7.0	5.7	- 10.0	- 8.2	3.8	5.3	2.4	Swaziland
Tanzania	- 10.5	- 12.6	- 13.2	- 12.4	- 12.7	- 5.3	- 8.8	- 6.3	- 10.0	- 11.1	Tanzanie
Togo	- 14.2	- 22.4	- 21.2	- 22.6	- 25.3	- 6.3	- 9.1	- 9.6	- 8.8	- 5.9	Togo
Tunisia	- 10.4	- 10.5	- 13.6	- 12.8	- 13.6	- 4.8	- 7.4	- 8.3	- 8.4	- 7.9	Tunisie
Uganda	- 11.3	- 11.4	- 9.6	- 8.7	- 9.7	- 8.4	- 9.6	- 6.7	- 7.5	- 5.2	Ouganda
Zambia	13.3	9.3	5.8	5.4	6.7	5.9	3.0	3.1	0.7	0.0	Zambie
Zimbabwe	- 19.6	- 28.7	- 23.4	- 25.1	- 31.7	- 22.7	- 29.8	- 24.6	- 25.4	- 23.1	Zimbabwe
Africa	**2.7**	**2.9**	**1.8**	**0.5**	**- 1.3**	**0.2**	**- 0.7**	**- 1.1**	**- 2.2**	**- 3.7**	**Afrique**

3-6. Financial Flows - Flux financiers

US $ per Capita	Official development assistance (ODA) / Aide publique au développement (APD)							Foreign direct investment (FDI) inflows / Investissement direct étranger (IDE) entrant							$ EU par habitant
Country	2007	2008	2009	2010	2011	2012	2013	2007	2008	2009	2010	2011	2012	2013	Pays
Algeria	11.2	9.1	8.8	5.4	5.0	3.8	5.3	49.7	73.7	75.5	62.1	68.3	39.0	43.1	Algérie
Angola	14.0	20.1	12.6	12.2	9.6	11.6	13.4	-50.4	91.7	116.5	-165.1	-149.8	-331.3	-199.6	Angola
Benin	54.5	71.5	73.8	72.5	70.6	50.9	63.2	29.3	18.9	14.5	18.6	16.5	28.0	31.0	Bénin
Botswana	56.2	372.5	143.0	79.3	60.5	36.9	53.6	258.2	269.4	66.0	69.1	550.1	73.4	93.1	Botswana
Burkina Faso	66.8	68.3	71.7	68.4	62.2	70.4	61.4	24.1	7.2	6.7	2.2	9.0	20.0	22.1	Burkina Faso
Burundi	57.5	60.6	62.9	68.2	60.3	53.1	53.8	0.1	0.4	0.0	0.1	0.4	0.1	0.7	Burundi
Cabo Verde	100.9	28.0	32.2	26.2	28.9	27.5	33.1	9.9	1.1	36.8	26.1	30.8	24.2	25.7	Cabo Verde
Cameroon	341.5	457.6	402.7	672.5	514.1	497.9	487.8	393.6	544.7	358.9	324.6	312.3	115.9	37.5	Cameroun
Central African Republic	43.1	61.5	56.7	60.0	60.6	50.2	41.0	13.8	28.0	9.9	14.1	8.3	15.7	17.3	République Centrafricaine
Chad	33.6	38.2	49.3	41.5	38.1	38.4	31.1	-30.1	42.3	33.0	26.7	23.3	27.5	42.0	Tchad
Comoros	70.8	63.9	75.4	97.8	73.4	94.7	102.4	12.1	7.1	20.6	12.1	32.7	14.3	17.4	Comores
Congo	31.6	125.1	70.9	319.0	61.5	32.0	33.8	605.3	651.5	466.0	537.7	723.2	635.9	458.3	Congo
Congo. Dem. Republic	23.7	30.0	39.0	56.1	86.6	43.5	38.1	31.6	29.4	11.0	47.3	26.4	50.4	31.1	Rép. Démocratique du Congo
Côte d'Ivoire	9.5	34.3	129.1	44.5	74.1	132.8	62.1	23.8	24.4	20.3	17.9	15.6	16.2	18.3	Côte d'Ivoire
Djibouti	141.0	173.8	202.8	158.6	167.4	170.5	167.4	244.6	282.6	121.2	32.1	92.1	128.0	313.0	Djibouti
Egypt	15.4	23.2	13.1	7.6	5.1	21.9	65.1	157.2	126.3	87.2	81.2	-6.0	83.4	65.6	Égypte
Equatorial Guinea	49.0	48.8	46.5	121.7	33.9	19.3	7.6	1 942.9	-1 206.4	2 417.4	3 927.2	2 758.4	2 736.7	2 528.4	Guinée Equatoriale
Eritrea	30.4	26.7	25.9	28.0	21.9	21.8	13.2	1.4	7.2	16.4	15.9	6.6	6.7	6.9	Érythrée
Ethiopia	31.8	40.3	45.0	40.5	39.6	35.6	40.7	2.8	1.3	2.6	3.3	7.0	3.0	10.1	Éthiopie
Gabon	35.3	41.8	50.8	66.8	45.5	44.8	54.4	186.1	521.3	377.2	320.6	436.6	426.3	512.1	Gabon
Gambia	64.1	60.5	79.7	73.1	80.0	75.0	59.7	50.4	45.2	24.8	22.6	21.3	13.6	13.6	Gambie
Ghana	51.7	56.6	66.8	69.8	72.9	71.3	51.4	38.0	52.8	122.3	104.2	129.8	129.8	124.5	Ghana
Guinea	22.7	31.8	20.2	20.0	18.3	29.7	42.5	38.4	37.0	13.3	9.3	85.7	53.0	2.1	Guinée
Guinea Bissau	86.1	93.3	101.1	85.9	81.3	53.1	69.1	13.1	3.6	12.0	22.8	17.0	4.5	9.7	Guinée-Bissau
Kenya	35.4	35.5	47.1	42.3	62.8	65.3	77.4	19.4	2.5	3.0	4.6	8.5	6.4	12.3	Kenya
Lesotho	68.2	76.3	64.8	135.4	139.6	148.6	167.6	55.3	103.0	94.0	27.0	28.0	26.3	23.1	Lésotho
Liberia	199.1	340.6	134.1	358.0	187.5	136.3	124.4	37.4	77.3	57.0	113.7	124.5	235.0	247.1	Libéria
Libya	3.4	12.6	6.9	1.4	105.2	14.2	20.9	665.8	541.1	555.0	316.0	0.0	231.5	113.2	Libye
Madagascar	46.2	42.3	21.7	22.3	20.4	17.0	21.8	39.9	58.7	52.0	38.3	37.4	36.4	36.5	Madagascar
Malawi	54.2	65.3	52.9	68.1	51.7	73.8	68.8	9.1	13.8	3.4	6.5	8.3	8.1	7.2	Malawi
Mali	72.7	66.7	67.8	72.3	82.1	62.0	83.1	5.2	12.5	51.5	27.0	35.7	24.6	24.5	Mali
Mauritania	104.3	132.1	106.2	103.7	103.2	107.6	74.9	41.9	100.1	-0.9	36.2	159.0	364.4	296.7	Mauritanie
Mauritius	56.5	89.6	126.3	101.8	150.1	143.5	119.2	277.9	313.0	202.0	349.4	350.9	475.2	207.8	Maurice
Morocco	39.8	46.9	29.7	31.4	45.4	45.5	59.6	91.4	80.3	62.4	49.7	80.1	83.9	101.7	Maroc
Mozambique	50.5	52.5	68.7	70.0	69.9	68.6	73.7	18.0	26.0	38.5	42.5	144.8	223.4	239.0	Mozambique
Namibia	104.5	99.6	151.9	117.7	131.0	117.2	113.6	352.3	341.2	243.6	363.9	368.0	381.3	303.5	Namibie
Niger	38.3	41.5	30.7	46.8	39.3	52.6	43.4	9.1	23.1	51.7	59.2	64.5	49.0	35.4	Niger
Nigeria	13.3	8.5	10.7	12.9	10.8	11.3	14.6	41.4	54.6	55.7	38.2	54.3	42.2	32.3	Nigéria
Rwanda	72.8	91.3	88.7	95.3	113.4	76.7	91.8	8.3	10.0	11.3	3.9	9.5	13.9	9.4	Rwanda
São Tomé & Príncipe	312.7	281.3	176.1	278.0	0.0	0.0	0.0	220.3	470.1	89.5	138.0	98.3	0.0	0.0	São Tomé & Príncipe
Senegal	73.1	87.3	80.7	71.6	79.5	78.7	69.5	25.0	32.5	25.4	20.5	25.4	20.1	21.1	Sénégal
Seychelles	123.9	139.3	251.3	614.4	240.7	385.3	273.6	2 676.9	1 444.3	1 892.3	2 311.4	2 258.8	1 794.3	1 913.0	Seychelles
Sierra Leone	101.5	68.4	79.5	81.2	72.5	74.1	72.8	17.8	10.4	19.6	41.5	162.0	91.7	95.1	Sierra Leone
Somalia	44.2	83.8	70.5	51.6	110.6	98.0	94.5	15.8	9.5	11.5	11.6	10.3	10.5	10.2	Somalie
South Africa	16.3	22.4	21.1	20.0	27.0	20.4	24.5	114.8	183.2	147.4	70.7	81.7	87.0	155.1	Afrique du Sud
South Sudan	0.0	0.0	0.0	0.0	104.8	151.9	133.0	0.0	0.0	0.0	0.0	0.0	0.0	0.0	Soudan du Sud
Sudan	63.8	75.4	67.5	58.2	30.2	26.2	30.6	73.3	76.4	73.8	81.2	73.9	66.9	81.5	Soudan
Swaziland	44.6	60.6	47.7	76.6	103.0	71.6	92.8	33.0	91.6	56.0	113.7	76.9	72.9	53.6	Swaziland
Tanzania	68.6	55.0	67.2	65.8	52.8	59.3	69.6	14.1	32.7	21.8	40.3	26.5	37.7	38.0	Tanzanie
Togo	21.0	55.1	81.1	64.1	83.9	36.3	32.4	8.4	4.0	7.9	13.6	112.4	14.1	12.4	Togo
Tunisia	31.3	36.1	47.8	51.8	85.7	93.5	64.9	157.3	265.5	160.6	142.3	106.7	147.4	99.6	Tunisie
Uganda	56.5	51.7	54.3	50.7	44.9	45.5	45.0	25.8	22.9	25.6	16.0	25.4	33.2	30.5	Ouganda
Zambia	83.2	89.6	98.8	69.2	75.9	68.0	78.6	109.3	75.4	54.2	130.8	81.3	123.0	124.6	Zambie
Zimbabwe	37.5	47.9	57.1	56.0	53.6	73.0	57.3	5.4	4.0	8.1	12.7	29.0	29.1	28.3	Zimbabwe
Africa	**36.6**	**40.3**	**41.6**	**41.5**	**43.8**	**42.1**	**45.8**	**53.7**	**60.5**	**55.9**	**45.7**	**46.4**	**51.0**	**51.8**	**Afrique**

3-7. Intra-African Trade by Economic Grouping in 2013 - Commerce intra-africain par zone économique en 2013

Economic Grouping	AMU UMA	CAEMC CEMAC	COMESA	ECCAS CEEAC	ECOWAS CEDEAO	FRANC ZONE ZONE FRANC	SADC	WAEMU UEMOA	AFRICA AFRIQUE	WORLD MONDE	Zone économique
Exports to →			*(Millions of US $)*	/	*(Millions de $ EU)*						**← Exportations vers**
AMU	5 524	359	1 353	449	1 353	1 139	147	779	8 549	143 575	UMA
CAEMC	52	635	420	755	420	770	643	134	1 769	40 495	CEMAC
COMESA	423	2 706	11 937	2 929	11 937	9 044	4 972	6 338	20 127	129 013	COMESA
ECCAS	61	660	393	794	449	804	4 286	144	5 543	109 809	CEEAC
ECOWAS	423	2 706	11 937	2 929	11 937	9 044	4 960	6 338	20 127	129 013	CEDEAO
FRANC ZONE	323	1 830	6 392	2 073	6 392	4 570	977	2 739	9 583	59 527	ZONE FRANC
SADC	557	297	1 890	4 290	1 890	752	24 549	437	29 334	183 083	SADC
WAEMU	270	1 195	5 972	1 318	5 972	3 799	331	2 604	7 810	18 985	UEMOA
AFRICA	9 051	4 115	16 013	9 201	16 013	11 963	32 107	7 818	68 463	513 493	AFRIQUE
WORLD	141 780	20 440	123 932	47 919	106 753	61 281	179 817	40 657	569 221	18 227 586	MONDE
Exports to →											**← Exportations vers**
AMU	3.8	0.3	0.9	0.3	0.9	0.8	0.1	0.5	6.0	100.0	UMA
CAEMC	0.1	1.6	1.0	1.9	1.0	1.9	1.6	0.3	4.4	100.0	CEMAC
COMESA	0.3	2.1	9.3	2.3	9.3	7.0	3.9	4.9	15.6	100.0	COMESA
ECCAS	0.1	0.6	0.4	0.7	0.4	0.7	3.9	0.1	5.0	100.0	CEEAC
ECOWAS	0.3	2.1	9.3	2.3	9.3	7.0	3.8	4.9	15.6	100.0	CEDEAO
FRANC ZONE	0.5	3.1	10.7	3.5	10.7	7.7	1.6	4.6	16.1	100.0	ZONE FRANC
SADC	0.3	0.2	1.0	2.3	1.0	0.4	13.4	0.2	16.0	100.0	SADC
WAEMU	1.4	6.3	31.5	6.9	31.5	20.0	1.7	13.7	41.1	100.0	UEMOA
AFRICA	1.8	0.8	3.1	1.8	3.1	2.3	6.3	1.5	13.3	100.0	AFRIQUE
WORLD	0.8	0.1	0.7	0.3	0.6	0.3	1.0	0.2	3.1	100.0	MONDE
← Imports from											**→ Importations de**
AMU	5519	52	302	61	302	191	585	139	8 672	152 926	UMA
CAEMC	396	700	2 177	727	2 177	2 014	344	1 314	3 745	21 725	CEMAC
COMESA	1 262	372	13 120	405	13 120	6 923	2 108	6 550	17 308	143 850	COMESA
ECCAS	495	835	2 417	878	2 417	2 279	4 737	1 445	1 445	52 004	CEEAC
ECOWAS	1 262	372	13 120	405	13 120	6 923	2 108	6 550	17 308	139 889	CEDEAO
FRANC ZONE	1 028	848	9 130	886	9 130	5 010	835	4 161	12 114	59 537	ZONE FRANC
SADC	187	663	5 277	4 670	5 277	838	24 426	172	32 674	191 871	SADC
WAEMU	631	149	6 954	160	6 954	6 954	470	2 847	8 336	37 561	UEMOA
AFRICA	8 189	1 806	20 982	5 958	20 982	4 766	29 734	8 231	69 946	563 408	AFRIQUE
WORLD	126 542	43 065	137 783	119 286	137 783	63 040	237 374	19 925	609 774	18 685 082	MONDE
← Imports from											**→ Importations de**
AMU	3.6	0.0	0.2	0.0	0.2	0.1	0.4	0.1	5.7	100.0	UMA
CAEMC	1.8	3.2	10.0	3.3	10.0	9.3	1.6	6.1	17.2	100.0	CEMAC
COMESA	0.9	0.3	9.1	0.3	9.1	4.8	1.5	4.6	12.0	100.0	COMESA
ECCAS	1.0	1.6	4.6	1.7	4.6	4.4	9.1	2.8	2.8	100.0	CEEAC
ECOWAS	0.9	0.3	9.4	0.3	9.4	4.9	1.5	4.7	12.4	100.0	CEDEAO
FRANC ZONE	1.7	1.4	15.3	1.5	15.3	8.4	1.4	7.0	20.3	100.0	ZONE FRANC
SADC	0.1	0.3	2.8	2.4	2.8	0.4	12.7	0.1	17.0	100.0	SADC
WAEMU	1.7	0.4	18.5	0.4	18.5	18.5	1.3	7.6	22.2	100.0	UEMOA
AFRICA	1.5	0.3	3.7	1.1	3.7	0.8	5.3	1.5	12.4	100.0	AFRIQUE
WORLD	0.7	0.2	0.7	0.6	0.7	0.3	1.3	0.1	3.3	100.0	MONDE

Section 4

Economic Infrastucture and Investment Climate

Infrastructures économiques et climat des affaires

ECONOMIC INFRASTRUCTURE / INFRASTRUCTURE ECONOMIQUE

4-1. Tourism and Infrastructure / Tourisme et Infrastructure

Country	*Arrival of tourists (Thousands) / Arrivée des touristes (Milliers)*		*Paved Roads (% of total) / Routes asphaltées (% du total)*		*Main Telephone Lines per 100 inhabitants / Lignes téléphoniques fixes pour 100 habitants*		*Mobile Cellular Subscribers per 100 inhabitants / Abonnés aux téléphones mobiles pour 100 habitants*		Pays
	2012	2014	Year / Année	%	2006	2013	2006	2013	
Algeria	2 634	3 157	2010	77.1	8.2	8.0	60.9	100.8	Algérie
Angola	528	641	2001	10.4	0.6	1.0	17.8	61.9	Angola
Benin	220	238	2004	9.5	0.9	1.5	12.5	93.3	Bénin
Botswana	2 374	2 594	2005	32.6	7.0	8.6	43.4	160.6	Botswana
Burkina Faso	263	282	2011	20.6	0.7	0.8	7.4	66.4	Burkina Faso
Burundi	205	157	2004	10.4	0.3	0.2	2.5	25.0	Burundi
Cabo Verde	533	622	2000	69.0	14.9	13.3	22.6	100.1	Cabo Verde
Cameroon	492	485	2010	10.1	0.7	3.6	16.8	70.4	Cameroun
Central African Republic	65	65	2010	6.8	...	0.0	2.7	29.5	République Centrafricaine
Chad	86	86	2000	1.0	0.2	0.2	4.5	35.6	Tchad
Comoros	21	23	2000	76.5	3.1	3.1	6.0	47.3	Comores
Congo	256	252	2009	7.1	0.4	0.4	25.2	104.8	Congo
Congo. Dem. Republic	167	199	2004	1.8	0.0	...	7.9	41.8	Rép. Démocratique du Congo
Côte d'Ivoire	361	396	2007	7.9	1.5	1.3	23.0	95.4	Côte d'Ivoire
Djibouti	...	...	2000	45.0	1.4	2.4	5.7	28.0	Djibouti
Egypt	11 196	9 756	2010	92.2	14.8	8.3	24.7	121.5	Égypte
Equatorial Guinea	...	...	...	...	1.6	2.0	19.3	67.5	Guinée Equatoriale
Eritrea	...	...	2000	21.8	0.7	1.0	1.2	5.6	Érythrée
Ethiopia	596	693	2007	13.7	0.9	0.8	1.1	27.3	Éthiopie
Gabon	517	571	2007	12.0	2.6	1.2	63.6	214.8	Gabon
Gambia	157	178	2004	19.3	3.1	3.5	27.3	100.0	Gambie
Ghana	1 234	1 123	2009	12.6	1.6	1.0	23.7	108.2	Ghana
Guinea	96	104	2003	9.8	0.2	...	...	63.3	Guinée
Guinea Bissau	...	...	2002	27.9	0.5	0.3	10.8	74.1	Guinée-Bissau
Kenya	1 619	1 257	2011	7.0	0.8	0.5	20.0	71.8	Kenya
Lesotho	422	457	2005	53.0	2.7	2.8	18.4	86.3	Lésotho
Liberia	...	...	2001	6.2	...	0.1	8.3	59.4	Libéria
Libya	79	91	2001	57.2	16.0	12.7	69.1	165.0	Libye
Madagascar	256	218	2011	16.3	0.7	1.1	5.6	36.9	Madagascar
Malawi	751	756	2003	45.0	1.0	0.2	4.7	32.3	Malawi
Mali	32	...	2009	24.6	0.7	0.8	12.3	129.1	Mali
Mauritania	...	...	2011	34.6	1.1	1.4	32.7	102.5	Mauritanie
Mauritius	965	1 036	2009	98.0	29.4	29.2	63.5	123.2	Maurice
Morocco	9 375	10 398	2011	70.6	4.2	8.9	52.7	128.5	Maroc
Mozambique	2 113	2 060	2009	20.8	0.3	0.3	10.8	48.0	Mozambique
Namibia	1 063	1 072	2010	14.5	6.6	8.0	29.7	118.4	Namibie
Niger	85	84	2008	20.6	0.2	0.6	3.5	39.3	Niger
Nigeria	768	834	2004	15.0	1.2	0.2	22.6	73.3	Nigéria
Rwanda	815	944	2004	19.0	0.2	0.4	3.3	56.8	Rwanda
São Tomé & Príncipe	12	22	2001	68.1	4.8	3.6	11.6	64.9	São Tomé & Príncipe
Senegal	989	1 039	2010	35.5	2.4	2.4	25.8	92.9	Sénégal
Seychelles	208	232	2011	96.5	23.4	23.4	79.7	147.3	Seychelles
Sierra Leone	60	50	2002	8.0	0.5	0.3	...	65.7	Sierra Leone
Somalia	...	...	2001	11.8	1.2	0.6	6.3	49.4	Somalie
South Africa	9 188	10 070	2001	17.3	10.0	7.3	81.1	145.6	Afrique du Sud
South Sudan	...	...	...	...	...	...	...	25.3	Soudan du Sud
Sudan	814	792	2001	36.3	1.3	1.1	11.9	72.9	Soudan
Swaziland	1 093	1 132	2002	30.0	4.0	3.7	22.4	71.5	Swaziland
Tanzania	1 043	1 192	2009	14.9	0.4	0.3	14.0	55.7	Tanzanie
Togo	235	263	2007	21.0	1.4	0.9	12.5	62.5	Togo
Tunisia	5 950	6 069	2011	76.3	12.5	9.3	72.2	115.6	Tunisie
Uganda	1 197	1 306	2003	23.0	0.4	0.6	6.8	44.1	Ouganda
Zambia	859	929	2001	22.0	0.8	0.8	14.1	71.5	Zambie
Zimbabwe	1 673	1 848	2002	19.0	2.6	2.1	6.7	96.3	Zimbabwe
Africa	**60 883**	**62 323**			**3.1**	**2.3**	**21.5**	**74.2**	**Afrique**

DOING BUSINESS IN 2014 / CLIMAT DES AFFAIRES EN 2014

4-2. Doing Business in 2014 (Rankings for 189 countries)
Climat des affaires en 2014 (Rang sur 189 pays)

Country	*Ease of Doing Business* / *Facilité de faire des affaires*	*Dealing with Licenses* / *Agréments*	*Enforcing Contracts* / *Exécution des contrats*	*Registering Property* / *Enregistrement de biens*	*Getting Credit* / *Obtention de crédits*	*Protecting Investors* / *Protection des investisseurs*	*Paying Taxes* / *Paiement des impôts*	*Trading across Borders* / *Commerce transfrontalier*	*Closing a Business* / *Fermeture d'une entreprise*	Pays
Algeria	154	127	120	157	171	132	176	131	97	Algérie
Angola	181	67	187	164	180	94	144	167	189	Angola
Benin	151	64	167	165	116	135	178	121	115	Bénin
Botswana	74	93	61	51	61	106	67	157	49	Botswana
Burkina Faso	167	75	153	147	131	122	152	174	115	Burkina Faso
Burundi	152	133	158	48	171	94	124	169	144	Burundi
Cabo Verde	158	166	159	172	116	117	181	160	123	Cabo Verde
Cameroon	122	114	39	62	104	170	91	101	189	Cameroun
Central African Republic	187	145	182	150	131	135	185	186	152	République Centrafricaine
Chad	185	123	149	166	131	146	186	182	152	Tchad
Comoros	159	31	177	105	131	122	167	144	189	Comores
Congo	178	102	151	168	104	146	182	181	117	Congo
Congo. Dem. Republic	184	111	176	142	131	146	168	175	189	Rép. Démocratique du Congo
Côte d'Ivoire	147	180	72	124	131	146	175	158	85	Côte d'Ivoire
Djibouti	155	146	171	154	180	162	75	56	70	Djibouti
Egypt	112	142	152	84	71	135	149	99	126	Égypte
Equatorial Guinea	165	94	67	145	104	122	171	143	189	Guinée Equatoriale
Eritrea	189	189	68	176	185	166	174	172	189	Érythrée
Ethiopia	132	28	50	104	165	154	112	168	74	Éthiopie
Gabon	144	76	156	181	104	146	154	135	125	Gabon
Gambia	138	71	49	113	160	162	180	77	102	Gambie
Ghana	70	106	96	43	36	56	101	120	161	Ghana
Guinea	169	159	133	122	131	162	184	141	119	Guinée
Guinea Bissau	179	165	169	160	131	122	150	119	189	Guinée-Bissau
Kenya	136	95	137	136	116	122	102	153	134	Kenya
Lesotho	128	161	115	93	151	106	109	147	120	Lésotho
Liberia	174	143	174	177	160	181	77	149	169	Libéria
Libya	188	189	126	189	185	188	157	139	189	Libye
Madagascar	163	177	146	153	180	87	65	109	129	Madagascar
Malawi	164	72	154	76	151	132	103	170	166	Malawi
Mali	146	97	128	133	131	146	145	163	108	Mali
Mauritania	176	77	86	66	171	166	187	151	189	Mauritanie
Mauritius	28	117	44	98	36	28	13	17	43	Maurice
Morocco	71	54	81	115	104	122	66	31	113	Maroc
Mozambique	127	84	164	101	131	94	123	129	107	Mozambique
Namibia	88	25	53	173	61	87	85	136	81	Namibie
Niger	168	119	132	95	131	146	155	179	128	Niger
Nigeria	170	171	140	185	52	62	179	159	131	Nigéria
Rwanda	46	34	62	15	4	117	27	164	101	Rwanda
São Tomé & Príncipe	153	46	179	148	185	183	162	111	162	São Tomé & Príncipe
Senegal	161	151	142	167	131	122	183	79	99	Sénégal
Seychelles	85	48	103	78	171	56	43	42	61	Seychelles
Sierra Leone	140	120	109	158	151	62	130	133	143	Sierra Leone
Somalia	...	...	...	...	...	...	...	...	...	Somalie
South Africa	43	32	46	97	52	17	19	100	39	Afrique du Sud
South Sudan	186	167	94	180	171	173	98	187	189	Soudan du Sud
Sudan	160	160	163	46	165	174	139	162	156	Soudan
Swaziland	110	55	173	129	61	110	74	127	80	Swaziland
Tanzania	131	169	45	123	151	141	148	137	105	Tanzanie
Togo	149	170	134	182	131	122	163	112	93	Togo
Tunisia	60	85	78	71	116	78	82	50	54	Tunisie
Uganda	150	163	80	125	131	110	104	161	98	Ouganda
Zambia	111	99	98	152	23	83	78	177	95	Zambie
Zimbabwe	171	176	157	94	104	87	143	180	148	Zimbabwe

Section 5

Millennium Development Goals

Objectifs du millénaire pour le développement

MILLENIUM DEVELOPMENT GOALS
OBJECTIFS DU MILLENAIRE POUR LE DEVELOPPEMENT

Goal 1. Eradicate Extreme Poverty and Hunger / Eradiquer la pauvreté extrême et la faim

	Population below $1.25 (PPP) per day, percentage Proportion de la population disposant de moins de 1,25 dollar par jour en parité du pouvoir d'achat		Poverty gap ratio at $1.25 a day (PPP), percentage Ecart de pauvreté au seuil de 1.25$ par jour (%)		Poorest quintile's share in national income or consumption, percentage Part du quintile le plus pauvre de la population dans la consommation nationale		Population undernourished, percentage Prévalence de la malnutrition dans la population totale (%)		
Country	year	%	year	%	year	%	2010-2012	2013	Pays
Algeria	1995	6.8	1995	1.4	1995	7.0	5	5.0	Algérie
Angola	2009	43.4	2009	16.5	2009	5.4	27.4	18.0	Angola
Benin	2003	47.3	2003	15.7	2003	7.0	8.1	9.7	Bénin
Botswana	1994	31.2	1994	11.0	1994	3.1	27.9	26.6	Botswana
Burkina Faso	2009	44.6	2009	14.7	2009	6.7	25.9	20.7	Burkina Faso
Burundi	2006	81.3	2006	36.4	2006	9.0	73.4	...	Burundi
Cabo Verde	2002	21.0	2002	6.1	2002	4.5	8.9	9.9	Cabo Verde
Cameroon	2007	9.6	2007	1.2	2007	6.7	15.7	10.5	Cameroun
Central African Republic	2008	62.8	2008	31.3	2008	3.4	30.0	37.6	République Centrafricaine
Chad	2003	61.9	2003	25.6	2003	6.3	33.4	34.8	Tchad
Comoros	2004	46.1	2004	20.8	2004	2.6	70.0	...	Comores
Congo	2005	54.1	2005	22.8	2005	5.0	37.4	31.5	Congo
Congo. Dem. Republic	2006	87.7	2006	52.8	2006	5.5	...	...	Rép. Démocratique du Congo
Côte d'Ivoire	2008	23.8	2008	7.5	2008	5.6	21.4	14.7	Côte d'Ivoire
Djibouti	2002	18.8	2002	5.3	2002	6.0	19.8	18.9	Djibouti
Egypt	2008	1.7	2008	0.4	2008	9.2	5	5.0	Égypte
Equatorial Guinea	...	...	...	...	...	...	...	...	Guinée Equatoriale
Eritrea	...	...	...	...	...	...	65.4	...	Érythrée
Ethiopia	2011	30.7	2011	8.2	2011	8.0	40.2	35.0	Éthiopie
Gabon	2005	4.8	2005	0.9	2005	6.2	6.5	5.0	Gabon
Gambia	2003	33.6	2003	11.7	2003	4.8	14.4	6.0	Gambie
Ghana	2006	28.6	2006	9.9	2006	5.2	5	5.0	Ghana
Guinea	2007	43.3	2007	15.0	2007	6.4	17.3	18.1	Guinée
Guinea Bissau	2002	48.9	2002	16.6	2002	7.3	8.7	17.7	Guinée-Bissau
Kenya	2005	43.4	2005	16.9	2005	4.8	30.4	24.3	Kenya
Lesotho	2003	43.4	2003	20.8	2003	3.0	16.6	11.5	Lésotho
Liberia	2007	83.8	2007	40.9	2007	6.4	31.4	29.6	Libéria
Libya	...	...	...	...	...	...	< 5	...	Libye
Madagascar	2010	81.3	2010	43.3	2010	5.4	33.4	30.5	Madagascar
Malawi	2010	61.6	2010	26.2	2010	5.6	23.1	21.8	Malawi
Mali	2010	50.4	2010	16.4	2010	8.0	7.9	5.0	Mali
Mauritania	2008	23.4	2008	6.8	2008	6.0	9.3	6.5	Mauritanie
Mauritius	...	...	...	...	...	...	5.7	5.0	Maurice
Morocco	2007	2.5	2007	0.5	2007	6.5	5.5	5.0	Maroc
Mozambique	2008	59.6	2008	25.1	2008	5.2	39.2	27.9	Mozambique
Namibia	2004	31.9	2004	9.5	2004	3.2	33.9	37.2	Namibie
Niger	2008	43.6	2008	12.4	2008	8.1	12.6	11.3	Niger
Nigeria	2010	68.0	2010	33.7	2010	4.4	8.5	6.4	Nigéria
Rwanda	2011	63.2	2011	26.6	2011	5.2	28.9	33.8	Rwanda
São Tomé & Principe	2001	28.2	2001	7.9	2001	5.2	7.7	6.8	São Tomé & Principe
Senegal	2011	29.6	2011	9.1	2011	6.1	20.5	16.7	Sénégal
Seychelles	2007	0.3	2007	0.1	2007	3.7	8.6	...	Seychelles
Sierra Leone	2011	51.7	2011	16.6	2011	7.8	28.8	25.5	Sierra Leone
Somalia	...	...	...	...	...	...	...	...	Somalie
South Africa	2009	13.8	2009	2.3	2009	2.7	5	5.0	Afrique du Sud
South Sudan	...	...	2009	23.7	...	...	...	...	Soudan du Sud
Sudan	2009	19.8	2009	5.5	2009	6.8	...	...	Soudan
Swaziland	2010	40.6	2010	16.0	2010	4.1	27.0	26.1	Swaziland
Tanzania	2007	67.9	2007	28.1	2007	6.8	38.8	34.6	Tanzanie
Togo	2011	28.2	2011	8.8	2011	6.0	16.5	15.3	Togo
Tunisia	2010	1.1	2010	0.4	2010	6.7	5	5.0	Tunisie
Uganda	2009	38.0	2009	12.2	2009	5.8	34.6	25.7	Ouganda
Zambia	2010	74.5	2010	41.9	2010	3.6	47.4	48.3	Zambie
Zimbabwe	...	...	...	...	1995	4.6	32.8	31.8	Zimbabwe
Africa	...	...	...	...	...	...	**20.7**	...	**Afrique**

Sources: countries report, UNSD MDGs & WB

MILLENIUM DEVELOPMENT GOALS
OBJECTIFS DU MILLENAIRE POUR LE DEVELOPPEMENT

Goal 2. Achieve universal primary education / Assurer l'éducation primaire pour tous

	Net Primary Enrolment Ratios / *Taux net de scolarisation au primaire*			*Proportion of pupils starting grade 1 who reach last grade of primary* / *Proportion d'écoliers ayant commencé la première année d'études primaires qui terminent l'école primaire*			*Literacy rate of 15-24 year-olds. women and men* / *Taux d'alphabétisation des 15-24 ans. femmes et hommes*			
Country	**1990**	**value**	**year**	**1990**	**value**	**year**	**1990**	**value**	**year**	**Pays**
Algeria	83.4	99.1	2012	75.6	92.8	2011	...	91.8	2006	Algérie
Angola	...	85.7	2011	...	31.9	2009	...	73.0	2012E	Angola
Benin	39.3	94.9	2012	21.5	59.3	2011	...	42.4	2006E	Bénin
Botswana	85.4	84.0	2009E	66.2	93.0	2008E	...	96.0	2012E	Botswana
Burkina Faso	...	66.8	2012	48.6	69.0	2011	...	39.3	2007	Burkina Faso
Burundi	...	94.1	2010	50.0	43.8	2011	53.6	88.9	2008	Burundi
Cabo Verde	98.2	97.3	2012	...	89.3	2010	88.2	98.1	2012	Cabo Verde
Cameroon	72.0	91.5	2012	56.7	69.8	2011	...	80.6	2010	Cameroun
Central African Republic	57.5	72.2	2012	36.5	46.6	2011	...	36.4	2010E	République Centrafricaine
Chad	...	63.8	2011	25.5	38.1	2011	...	48.9	2012E	Tchad
Comoros	...	83.3	2007	...	55.4	2003	...	86.4	2012E	Comores
Congo	...	91.6	2012	...	70.3	2007E	...	80.9	2011E	Congo
Congo. Dem. Republic	...	36.2	1999	...	70.7	2011	...	65.8	2007E	Rép. Démocratique du Congo
Côte d'Ivoire	...	61.9	2009	56.0	82.2	2011	...	48.3	2012E	Côte d'Ivoire
Djibouti	27.5	58.3	2013	...	75.9	2012	...	...		Djibouti
Egypt	...	97.3	2011E	...	96.1	2009	...	89.3	2012	Égypte
Equatorial Guinea	...	62.2	2012	...	72.1	2011	...	98.1	2012E	Guinée Equatoriale
Eritrea	...	34.2	2012	...	69.0	2009	...	91.0	2012E	Érythrée
Ethiopia	...	68.7	2006	...	36.6	2011	...	55.0	2007	Éthiopie
Gabon	...	92.1	1997	...	59.8	2002E	...	88.5	2012E	Gabon
Gambia	47.8	73.7	2012	...	82.8	2011	...	69.4	2012E	Gambie
Ghana	...	87.6	2013	...	72.2	2008	...	85.7	2010	Ghana
Guinea	26.1	75.5	2012	46.7	58.6	2011	...	31.4	2010	Guinée
Guinea Bissau	...	70.8	2010	...	...		...	74.3	2012E	Guinée-Bissau
Kenya	...	83.0	2009E	...	77.6	2004E	...	82.4	2007E	Kenya
Lesotho	71.8	82.1	2012	47.4	63.9	2011	...	83.2	2009E	Lésotho
Liberia	...	40.9	2011	...	67.8	2008	...	49.1	2007E	Libéria
Libya	...	...		...	...		...	99.9	2012E	Libye
Madagascar	66.8	77.4	2003	34.0	40.7	2011	...	64.9	2009E	Madagascar
Malawi	...	97.5	2009	24.4	49.1	2011	...	72.1	2010E	Malawi
Mali	...	73.3	2012	...	61.6	2011	...	47.1	2011	Mali
Mauritania	...	70.4	2012	53.4	81.2	2008	...	56.1	2007E	Mauritanie
Mauritius	97.2	97.9	2012	...	97.3	2011	91.2	98.1	2011	Maurice
Morocco	55.3	98.7	2013	68.9	91.6	2012	...	81.5	2011	Maroc
Mozambique	44.0	86.4	2012	33.8	30.6	2011	...	67.1	2009	Mozambique
Namibia	79.4	88.5	2012	...	84.5	2009	...	87.1	2007E	Namibie
Niger	24.0	63.6	2012	50.1	69.3	2010	...	23.5	2012E	Niger
Nigeria	...	65.7	2010E	...	79.3	2009E	...	66.4	2008E	Nigéria
Rwanda	...	98.7	2012	40.9	35.6	2011	...	77.3	2010E	Rwanda
São Tomé & Principe	96.6	97.0	2013	64.7	66.1	2009	...	80.2	2008E	São Tomé & Principe
Senegal	44.7	79.4	2012	69.1	61.4	2011	...	66.0	2011	Sénégal
Seychelles	...	93.9	2011	...	94.0	2010	...	99.1	2012E	Seychelles
Sierra Leone	...	...		...	...		...	62.7	2012E	Sierra Leone
Somalia	...	...		...	...		...	...		Somalie
South Africa	...	90.5	2012E	...	77.0	2003	...	98.9	2012	Afrique du Sud
South Sudan	...	41.4	2011E		...		...	...		Soudan du Sud
Sudan	...	51.5	2011	...	75.8	2009	...	87.9	2012E	Soudan
Swaziland	74.3	84.9	2007	48.8	67.3	2010	...	93.5	2010E	Swaziland
Tanzania	51.3	97.8	2008	...	81.4	2009	...	74.6	2010E	Tanzanie
Togo	64.5	92.8	2008	35.3	67.1	2011	...	79.9	2011	Togo
Tunisia	91.8	99.9	2012	71.8	94.8	2009	...	97.3	2011	Tunisie
Uganda	...	91.0	2011	...	24.8	2010	...	87.4	2010	Ouganda
Zambia	...	97.9	2012E	...	53.1	2008	66.4	64.0	2007E	Zambie
Zimbabwe	...	83.5	2003	...	62.1	2002E	...	90.9	2011E	Zimbabwe
Africa	**61.9**	**78.3**	**...**	**56.1**	**71.2**	**...**	**...**	**81.3**	**...**	**Afrique**

Sources: UNSD MDG (http://mdgs.un.org/unsd/mdg/Data.aspx)

MILLENIUM DEVELOPMENT GOALS
OBJECTIFS DU MILLENAIRE POUR LE DEVELOPPEMENT

Goal 3. Promote gender equality and empower women
Promouvoir l'égalité des sexes et l'autonomisation des femmes

	Primary / Primaire Girls to Boys Ratio / Rapport Filles-garçons (%)		*Secondary /Secondaire Girls to Boys Ratio Rapport Filles-garçons*		*15-24 Year Olds Literacy Female to Male Ratio / Ratio d'alphabétisation des jeunes de 15-24 ans : femmes/hommes*		
Country	**1990**	**2010-12**	**1990**	**2010-12**	**1990**	**2015**	**Pays**
Algeria	84.0	94	77.0	99.8	78.6	89.5	Algérie
Angola	92.0	...	65.8	65.1	...	99.9	Angola
Benin	50.0	89	41.2	61.0	40.9	85.6	Bénin
Botswana	107.0	...	111.0	...	110.5	67.9	Botswana
Burkina Faso	63.0	95	53.2	81.0	39.1	103.6	Burkina Faso
Burundi	80.0	99	61.0	73.0	77.1	90.9	Burundi
Cabo Verde	97.0	91	107.0	119.0	88.2	92.3	Cabo Verde
Cameroon	86.0	88	68.0	86.0	94.9	100.5	Cameroun
Central African Republic	63.0	74	40.0	51.0	60.0	100.4	République Centrafricaine
Chad	44.0	76	22.0	46.0	64.5	55.2	Tchad
Comoros	70.0	91	67.6	96.0	81.1	90.7	Comores
Congo	94.0	107	76.0	87.0	95.2	101.6	Congo
Congo. Dem. Republic	70.4	87.2	48.0	58.7	71.8	68.2	Rép. Démocratique du Congo
Côte d'Ivoire	71.0	85	47.3	84.5	68.4	89.8	Côte d'Ivoire
Djibouti	74.0	90	68.7	77.0	78.1	71.9	Djibouti
Egypt	84.0	96	78.0	98.0	71.9	...	Égypte
Equatorial Guinea	...	98	...	97.7	91.9	95.0	Guinée Equatoriale
Eritrea	94.0	84	93.3	80.0	68.0	101.1	Érythrée
Ethiopia	66.0	90.9	76.9	89.0	76.1	97.2	Éthiopie
Gabon	...	95.4	...	97.0	...	95.3	Gabon
Gambia	...	104	47.0	95.2	66.5	103.1	Gambie
Ghana	84.0	94	66.0	90.0	85.0	93.8	Ghana
Guinea	45.0	84	32.0	61.9	...	98.4	Guinée
Guinea Bissau	...	93.6	45.3	93.0	30.8	110.4	Guinée-Bissau
Kenya	97.0	...	73.3	...	93.4	...	Kenya
Lesotho	125.0	97	157.0	140.0	126.2	91.2	Lésotho
Liberia	...	88.4	39.8	78.7	52.5	121.3	Libéria
Libya	...	...	103.0	...	83.9	68.0	Libye
Madagascar	96.0	99	94.0	95.0	85.6	100.0	Madagascar
Malawi	87.0	104	58.0	90.0	67.6	99.1	Malawi
Mali	61.0	88	50.0	69.9	67.8	100.4	Mali
Mauritania	73.0	105	46.0	85.0	63.1	75.4	Mauritanie
Mauritius	101.0	99	100.0	104.0	100.0	78.5	Maurice
Morocco	68.0	95	72.0	86.0	61.7	100.7	Maroc
Mozambique	76.0	91	57.0	89.0	47.7	84.2	Mozambique
Namibia	109.0	97	126.0	97.5	103.7	83.3	Namibie
Niger	60.0	84	37.0	67.0	37.3	108.0	Niger
Nigeria	79.0	87.5	78.0	84.6	81.5	47.1	Nigéria
Rwanda	99.0	102	81.0	107.0	86.1	81.8	Rwanda
São Tomé & Principe	91.0	97	...	114.0	...	104.7	São Tomé & Principe
Senegal	73.0	108	51.0	90.2	60.3	98.0	Sénégal
Seychelles	...	100.5	...	100.8	...	87.2	Seychelles
Sierra Leone	68.0	99	52.0	97.0	...	...	Sierra Leone
Somalia	...	...	53.3	...	...	78.2	Somalie
South Africa	99.0	95	116.0	103.0	99.7	...	Afrique du Sud
South Sudan	...	...	...	...	...	100.8	Soudan du Sud
Sudan	...	...	79.7	...	71.3	...	Soudan
Swaziland	100.0	88.7	99.3	96.0	101.0	96.2	Swaziland
Tanzania	64.0	92	34.0	86.9	86.9	100.5	Tanzanie
Togo	87.0	98	76.0	91.0	56.0	102.7	Togo
Tunisia	80.0	93.1	58.0	99.3	81.0	91.6	Tunisie
Uganda	99.0	103	57.1	88.0	75.7	99.4	Ouganda
Zambia	...	99	60.7	88.2	88.1	98.8	Zambie
Zimbabwe	99.0	...	88.0	...	94.6	103.9	Zimbabwe
Africa	**81.4**	**93.2**	**69.2**	**87.7**	**76.9**	**90.1**	**Afrique**

Sources: countries report, UN MDGs database, UIS, World Bank

MILLENIUM DEVELOPMENT GOALS
OBJECTIFS DU MILLENAIRE POUR LE DEVELOPPEMENT

Goal 4. Reduce child mortality / Réduire la mortalité infantile

Country	*Infant Mortality / Mortalité infantile Current Status / Statut actuel* (per/pour 1000)		Target / Cible	*Under 5 Mortality / Mortalité des < 5 ans Current Status / Statut actuel* (per/pour 1000)		Target / Cible	Pays
	1990	2013	2015	1990	2013	2015	
Algeria	39.9	21.6	13.3	47.1	25.2	15.7	Algérie
Angola	133.4	101.6	44.5	225.9	167.4	75.3	Angola
Benin	107.9	56.2	36.0	179.4	85.3	59.8	Bénin
Botswana	38.9	36.3	13.0	49.5	46.6	16.5	Botswana
Burkina Faso	102.5	64.1	34.2	202.2	97.6	67.4	Burkina Faso
Burundi	103.4	54.8	34.5	170.8	82.9	56.9	Burundi
Cabo Verde	48.4	21.9	16.1	63.0	26.0	21.0	Cabo Verde
Cameroon	84.8	60.8	28.3	136.4	94.5	45.5	Cameroun
Central African Republic	115.3	96.1	38.4	176.9	139.2	59.0	République Centrafricaine
Chad	115.9	88.5	38.6	214.7	147.5	71.6	Tchad
Comoros	88.1	57.9	29.4	125.4	77.9	41.8	Comores
Congo	60.1	35.6	20.0	92.2	49.1	30.7	Congo
Congo. Dem. Republic	114.7	86.1	38.2	176.0	118.5	58.7	Rép. Démocratique du Congo
Côte d'Ivoire	104.3	71.3	34.8	151.6	100.0	50.5	Côte d'Ivoire
Djibouti	92.1	57.4	30.7	118.6	69.6	39.5	Djibouti
Egypt	62.5	18.6	20.8	85.1	21.8	28.4	Égypte
Equatorial Guinea	124.4	69.3	41.5	184.0	95.8	61.3	Guinée Equatoriale
Eritrea	92.6	36.1	30.9	150.6	49.9	50.2	Érythrée
Ethiopia	121.8	44.4	40.6	205.0	64.4	68.3	Éthiopie
Gabon	60.3	39.1	20.1	92.7	56.1	30.9	Gabon
Gambia	79.9	49.4	26.6	169.8	73.8	56.6	Gambie
Ghana	80.3	52.3	26.8	128.2	78.4	42.7	Ghana
Guinea	140.4	64.9	46.8	237.6	100.7	79.2	Guinée
Guinea Bissau	132.8	77.9	44.3	224.8	123.9	74.9	Guinée-Bissau
Kenya	63.9	47.5	21.3	98.7	70.7	32.9	Kenya
Lesotho	69.5	73.0	23.2	86.3	98.0	28.8	Lésotho
Liberia	165.3	53.6	55.1	248.0	71.1	82.7	Libéria
Libya	36.2	12.4	12.1	42.4	14.5	14.1	Libye
Madagascar	98.1	39.6	32.7	160.8	56.0	53.6	Madagascar
Malawi	143.4	44.2	47.8	245.3	67.9	81.8	Malawi
Mali	130.5	77.6	43.5	254.2	122.7	84.7	Mali
Mauritania	77.8	67.1	25.9	117.8	90.1	39.3	Mauritanie
Mauritius	19.9	12.5	6.6	23.1	14.3	7.7	Maurice
Morocco	63.5	26.1	21.2	80.7	30.4	26.9	Maroc
Mozambique	158.0	61.5	52.7	237.0	87.2	79.0	Mozambique
Namibia	49.6	35.2	16.5	73.6	49.8	24.5	Namibie
Niger	137.7	59.9	45.9	327.3	104.2	109.1	Niger
Nigeria	126.3	74.3	42.1	213.2	117.4	71.1	Nigéria
Rwanda	92.8	37.1	30.9	151.8	52.0	50.6	Rwanda
São Tomé & Príncipe	70.3	36.7	23.4	110.4	51.0	36.8	São Tomé & Príncipe
Senegal	70.5	43.9	23.5	141.1	55.3	47.0	Sénégal
Seychelles	14.2	12.2	4.7	16.5	14.2	5.5	Seychelles
Sierra Leone	158.1	107.2	52.7	267.7	160.6	89.2	Sierra Leone
Somalia	108.1	89.8	36.0	179.7	145.6	59.9	Somalie
South Africa	47.0	32.8	15.7	61.0	43.9	20.3	Afrique du Sud
South Sudan	149.5	64.1	49.8	252.9	99.2	84.3	Soudan du Sud
Sudan	80.2	51.2	26.7	128.0	76.6	42.7	Soudan
Swaziland	55.4	55.9	18.5	73.9	80	24.6	Swaziland
Tanzania	90.3	55.8	30.1	146.4	84.7	48.8	Tanzanie
Togo	41.0	13.1	13.7	52.2	15.2	17.4	Togo
Tunisia	107.2	43.8	35.7	178.7	66.1	59.6	Tunisie
Uganda	101.3	36.4	33.8	167.0	51.8	55.7	Ouganda
Zambia	114.5	55.8	38.2	192.5	87.4	64.2	Zambie
Zimbabwe	50.4	55.0	16.8	74.6	88.5	24.9	Zimbabwe
Africa	**91.4**	**52.5**	**30.5**	**148.3**	**77.0**	**49.4**	**Afrique**

Sources: UN MDGs database & World Bank for Sudan and South Sudan

MILLENIUM DEVELOPMENT GOALS
OBJECTIFS DU MILLENAIRE POUR LE DEVELOPPEMENT

Goal 5. Improve maternal health / Améliorer la santé maternelle

Country	*Births Attended by Skilled Health Staff / Naissances assistées par un personnel de santé qualifié* (%)			*Contraceptive Prevalence Rate / Taux de prévalence contraceptive* (% of women ages 15-49 / % des femmes agées de 15 à 49 ans)		*Maternal Mortality / Mortalité maternelle* (per / pour 100 000)		Target / Cible	Pays
	1990-99	2000-04	2009-12	1990	2013	1990	2013	2015	
Algeria	77.0	95.9	...	46	63.9	220	89	55	Algérie
Angola	22.5	44.7	...	4	15.2	1200	460	300	Angola
Benin	59.8	65.5	84.1	11	21.6	770	340	193	Bénin
Botswana	87.0	94.2	...	35	55.1	140	170	35	Botswana
Burkina Faso	30.9	37.8	65.9	7	19.0	700	400	175	Burkina Faso
Burundi	...	25.2	60.3	8	25.6	1100	740	275	Burundi
Cabo Verde	88.5	...	...	29	63.6	670	53	168	Cabo Verde
Cameroon	58.2	61.8	63.6	12	27.8	200	590	50	Cameroun
Central African Republic	45.9	44.1	48.8	12	29.1	930	880	233	République Centrafricaine
Chad	15.0	14.4	22.7	2	6.9	920	980	230	Tchad
Comoros	51.6	61.8	82.2	14	43.5	440	350	110	Comores
Congo	...	...	93.6	25	46.7	420	410	105	Congo
Congo. Dem. Republic	...	60.7	80.4	14	21.9	930	730	233	Rép. Démocratique du Congo
Côte d'Ivoire	47.1	68.0	59.4	8	20.0	710	720	178	Côte d'Ivoire
Djibouti	...	60.6	...	3	28.8	290	230	73	Djibouti
Egypt	55.2	69.4	...	43	62.7	230	45	58	Égypte
Equatorial Guinea	5.0	64.6	...	8	22.0	1200	290	300	Guinée Equatoriale
Eritrea	20.6	28.3	...	5	18.4	880	380	220	Érythrée
Ethiopia	...	5.6	10.0	3	32.4	950	420	238	Éthiopie
Gabon	...	85.5	89.3	21	40.9	270	240	68	Gabon
Gambia	44.1	54.7	56.6	10	23.0	700	430	175	Gambie
Ghana	44.3	47.1	68.4	15	26.3	580	380	145	Ghana
Guinea	34.8	55.5	45.3	2	12.9	1200	650	300	Guinée
Guinea Bissau	25.0	34.7	43.0	5	15.7	1100	560	275	Guinée-Bissau
Kenya	44.3	41.6	43.8	29	50.7	400	400	100	Kenya
Lesotho	60.9	55.4	61.5	21	50.9	520	490	130	Lésotho
Liberia	...	50.9	...	7	14.8	1200	640	300	Libéria
Libya	99.0	...	...	38	57.8	99	15	25	Libye
Madagascar	47.3	51.3	43.9	14	44.0	640	440	160	Madagascar
Malawi	54.8	56.1	71.4	12	49.1	1100	510	275	Malawi
Mali	40.0	40.6	56.1	4	11.0	1100	550	275	Mali
Mauritania	40.0	56.9	65.1	3	14.6	760	320	190	Mauritanie
Mauritius	98.5	98.4	...	75	76.0	68	73	17	Maurice
Morocco	39.6	62.6	73.6	40	66.7	300	120	75	Maroc
Mozambique	44.2	47.7	54.3	4	15.2	910	480	228	Mozambique
Namibia	68.2	75.5	...	30	57.8	200	130	50	Namibie
Niger	17.6	15.7	29.3	4	14.3	1200	630	300	Niger
Nigeria	41.6	35.2	48.7	7	15.9	1100	560	275	Nigéria
Rwanda	25.8	31.3	69.0	18	52.3	910	320	228	Rwanda
São Tomé & Príncipe	...	76.4	81.7	21	40.2	150	210	38	São Tomé & Príncipe
Senegal	48.3	58.0	65.1	7	14.6	670	320	168	Sénégal
Seychelles	...	...	...	...	...	...	...	...	Seychelles
Sierra Leone	...	41.7	62.5	3	9.1	1300	1100	325	Sierra Leone
Somalia	34.2	24.8	...	4	22.8	890	850	223	Somalie
South Africa	84.4	91.2	...	50	64.7	250	140	63	Afrique du Sud
South Sudan	...	...	19.4	0.6	6.7	1800	730	...	Soudan du Sud
Sudan	69.4	...	23.1	9	14.3	1000	360	250	Soudan
Swaziland	56.0	74.0	82.0	22	64.1	300	310	75	Swaziland
Tanzania	35.8	...	48.9	11	38.4	870	410	218	Tanzanie
Togo	50.5	60.8	59.4	25	19.0	620	450	155	Togo
Tunisia	80.5	89.9	98.6	53	65.1	130	46	33	Tunisie
Uganda	37.8	39.0	57.4	7	32.9	600	360	150	Ouganda
Zambia	47.1	43.4	...	15	47.1	470	280	118	Zambie
Zimbabwe	72.5	...	63.2	44	60.6	450	470	113	Zimbabwe
Africa	**50.9**	**51.2**	**59.3**	**19.4**	**34.9**	**708**	**420**	**177**	**Afrique**

Sources: countries report, UNSD MDGs & WB

MILLENIUM DEVELOPMENT GOALS
OBJECTIFS DU MILLENAIRE POUR LE DEVELOPPEMENT

Goal 6. Combat HIV/AIDS, Malaria and other diseases / Combattre le VIH/Sida , le paludisme et d'autres maladies

Country	*Number of women (15+) living with HIV ('000) Nombre de femmes (+15) vivant avec le VIH ('000)*	*Incidence of Tuberculosis (per 100 000 population) Incidence de la tuberculose pour 100 000*		*HIV Prevalence among population 15-24 years Taux de prévalence du VIH dans la population âgée de 15*			Pays
	2012	2000	2012	2011	2012	2013	
Algeria	0.0	87.0	89.0	0.1	0.1	0.1	Algérie
Angola	101.0	250.0	316.0	2.2	2.3	2.4	Angola
Benin	80.0	86.0	70.0	1.2	1.1	1.1	Bénin
Botswana	0.0	918.0	408.0	22.8	22.4	21.9	Botswana
Burkina Faso	103.0	71.0	54.0	1.0	1.0	0.9	Burkina Faso
Burundi	64.0	288.0	130.0	1.2	1.1	1.0	Burundi
Cabo Verde	0.0	160.0	144.0	0.5	0.5	0.5	Cabo Verde
Cameroon	65.0	310.0	238.0	4.5	4.4	4.3	Cameroun
Central African Republic	115.0	1071.0	367.0	4.3	4.1	3.8	République Centrafricaine
Chad	153.0	151.0	151.0	2.8	2.7	2.5	Tchad
Comoros	70.0	39.0	34.0	...	...	...	Comores
Congo	104.0	353.0	381.0	2.8	2.6	2.5	Congo
Congo. Dem. Republic	107.0	327.0	327.0	1.2	1.1	1.1	Rép. Démocratique du Congo
Côte d'Ivoire	71.0	369.0	172.0	3.0	2.8	2.7	Côte d'Ivoire
Djibouti	28.0	619.0	620.0	1.2	1.1	0.9	Djibouti
Egypt	...	26.0	17.0	0.1	0.1	0.1	Égypte
Equatorial Guinea	69.0	101.0	139.0	...	...	...	Guinée Equatoriale
Eritrea	4.0	157.0	93.0	0.7	0.7	0.6	Érythrée
Ethiopia	48.0	421.0	247.0	1.4	1.3	1.2	Éthiopie
Gabon	67.0	527.0	428.0	4.3	4.1	3.9	Gabon
Gambia	84.0	225.0	284.0	1.3	1.2	1.2	Gambie
Ghana	67.0	152.0	72.0	1.4	1.4	1.3	Ghana
Guinea	105.0	234.0	178.0	1.7	1.7	1.7	Guinée
Guinea Bissau	96.0	192.0	242.0	3.9	3.8	3.7	Guinée-Bissau
Kenya	50.0	286.0	272.0	6.1	6.1	6.0	Kenya
Lesotho	...	553.0	630.0	22.8	22.9	22.9	Lésotho
Liberia	69.0	242.0	304.0	1.3	1.2	1.1	Libéria
Libya	...	40.0	40.0	...	...	...	Libye
Madagascar	41.0	293.0	234.0	0.5	0.4	0.4	Madagascar
Malawi	63.0	467.0	163.0	11.4	10.8	10.3	Malawi
Mali	92.0	77.0	60.0	1.0	0.9	0.9	Mali
Mauritania	67.0	277.0	350.0	...	...	...	Mauritanie
Mauritius	...	24.0	21.0	1.2	1.2	1.1	Maurice
Morocco	...	117.0	103.0	0.1	0.2	0.2	Maroc
Mozambique	71.0	513.0	552.0	11.1	10.9	10.8	Mozambique
Namibia	0.0	1407.0	655.0	14.6	14.5	14.3	Namibie
Niger	131.0	191.0	104.0	0.5	0.5	0.4	Niger
Nigeria	107.0	172.0	108.0	3.4	3.3	3.2	Nigéria
Rwanda	33.0	325.0	86.0	3.0	2.9	2.9	Rwanda
São Tomé & Príncipe	43.0	114.0	93.0	0.8	0.7	0.6	São Tomé & Príncipe
Senegal	59.0	155.0	137.0	0.5	0.5	0.5	Sénégal
Seychelles	...	37.0	30.0	...	...	...	Seychelles
Sierra Leone	109.0	264.0	674.0	1.6	1.6	1.6	Sierra Leone
Somalia	33.0	285.0	286.0	0.5	0.5	0.5	Somalie
South Africa	2.0	576.0	1003.0	18.8	18.9	19.1	Afrique du Sud
South Sudan	...	...	146.0	2.3	2.3	2.2	Soudan du Sud
Sudan	...	144.0	114.0	0.2	0.2	0.2	Soudan
Swaziland	1.0	803.0	1349.0	27.4	27.4	27.4	Swaziland
Tanzania	50.0	72.0	73.0	5.4	5.2	5.0	Tanzanie
Togo	83.0	236.0	165.0	2.6	2.5	2.3	Togo
Tunisia	...	25.0	31.0	0.1	0.1	0.1	Tunisie
Uganda	58.0	427.0	179.0	7.2	7.4	7.4	Ouganda
Zambia	79.0	713.0	427.0	13.0	12.8	12.5	Zambie
Zimbabwe	18.0	726.0	562.0	15.7	15.4	15.0	Zimbabwe
Africa	**63. 6**	**313. 4**	**262. 1**	**4. 8**	**4. 8**	**4. 7**	**Afrique**

Source: UN MDGs database

MILLENIUM DEVELOPMENT GOALS
OBJECTIFS DU MILLENAIRE POUR LE DEVELOPPEMENT

Goal 7. Ensure environmental sustainability/ Assurer un environnement durable

Country	Proportion of urban population living in slums / Proportion de citadins vivant dans des taudis		% Population with Access to an Improved Water Source / % de la population ayant accès aux sources d'eau potable	Forest Area (% of land area) / Superficie forêstière (% des terres)	Terrestrial protected areas (% of total land area) / Surfaces des terres protégées (% du total des terres)	CO_2 Emissions per Capita (Metric tons) / Emissions de CO_2 par habt (T. métrique)		Pays
	1990	2009	2012	2012	2012	2006	2010	
Algeria	...	...	84.0	0.6	7.5	3.0	3.3	Algérie
Angola	...	65.8	54.0	46.7	12.4	1.3	1.6	Angola
Benin	79.3	69.8	76.0	39.6	26.1	0.5	0.5	Bénin
Botswana	...	...	97.0	19.6	37.2	2.5	2.7	Botswana
Burkina Faso	78.8	...	82.0	20.2	15.2	0.1	0.1	Burkina Faso
Burundi	...	...	75.0	6.6	4.9	0.0	0.0	Burundi
Cabo Verde	...	...	89.0	21.3	2.5	0.6	0.7	Cabo Verde
Cameroon	50.8	46.1	74.0	41.2	11.0	0.2	0.4	Cameroun
Central African Republic	87.5	95.9	68.0	36.2	18.0	0.1	0.1	République Centrafricaine
Chad	98.9	89.3	51.0	9.0	16.6	0.0	0.0	Tchad
Comoros	65.4	...		1.2	10.1	0.2	0.2	Comores
Congo	...	49.9	75.0	65.6	30.4	0.4	0.5	Congo
Congo. Dem. Republic	...	61.7	46.0	67.7	12.0	0.0	0.0	Rép. Démocratique du Congo
Côte d'Ivoire	53.4	57.0	80.0	32.7	22.9	0.4	0.3	Côte d'Ivoire
Djibouti	...	...	92.0	0.2	0.1	0.6	0.6	Djibouti
Egypt	50.2	13.1	99.0	0.1	11.2	2.4	2.6	Égypte
Equatorial Guinea	...	...		57.1	20.6	7.6	6.7	Guinée Equatoriale
Eritrea	...	...		15.1	5.0	0.1	0.1	Érythrée
Ethiopia	95.5	76.4	52.0	12.0	18.4	0.1	0.1	Éthiopie
Gabon	...	...	92.0	85.4	19.9	1.4	1.7	Gabon
Gambia	...	...	90.0	47.8	4.8	0.2	0.3	Gambie
Ghana	65.5	40.1	87.0	20.7	15.1	0.4	0.4	Ghana
Guinea	80.4	...	75.0	26.3	28.1	0.1	0.1	Guinée
Guinea Bissau	...	...	74.0	71.2	16.3	0.1	0.2	Guinée-Bissau
Kenya	54.9	54.7	62.0	6.1	11.6	0.3	0.3	Kenya
Lesotho	...	53.7	81.0	1.5	0.5	...	0.0	Lésotho
Liberia	...	68.3	75.0	44.3	2.5	0.2	0.2	Libéria
Libya	...	...		0.1	0.1	9.5	9.8	Libye
Madagascar	93.0	76.2	50.0	21.4	5.0	0.1	0.1	Madagascar
Malawi	66.4	68.9	85.0	33.6	18.3	0.1	0.1	Malawi
Mali	94.2	65.9	67.0	10.1	6.0	0.0	0.0	Mali
Mauritania	...	...	50.0	0.2	0.6	0.5	0.6	Mauritanie
Mauritius	...	...	100.0	17.3	4.5	3.0	3.2	Maurice
Morocco	37.4	13.1	84.0	11.5	21.5	1.6	1.6	Maroc
Mozambique	75.6	80.5	49.0	49.1	17.6	0.1	0.1	Mozambique
Namibia	34.4	33.5	92.0	8.7	43.2	1.1	1.5	Namibie
Niger	83.6	81.7	52.0	0.9	16.7	0.1	0.1	Niger
Nigeria	77.3	62.7	64.0	9.0	14.1	0.7	0.5	Nigéria
Rwanda	96.0	65.1	71.0	18.4	10.5	0.1	0.1	Rwanda
São Tomé & Príncipe	...	...	97.0	28.1		0.5	0.6	São Tomé & Príncipe
Senegal	70.6	38.8	74.0	43.6	24.8	0.4	0.5	Sénégal
Seychelles	...	...	96.0	88.5	42.0	8.8	7.8	Seychelles
Sierra Leone	...	...	60.0	37.2	10.5	0.1	0.1	Sierra Leone
Somalia	...	73.6		10.5	0.6	0.1	0.1	Somalie
South Africa	46.2	23.0	95.0	7.6	6.2	8.9	9.2	Afrique du Sud
South Sudan	...	...	56.5	..	...	...	...	Soudan du Sud
Sudan	...	...	55.5	..	4.2	0.3	0.3	Soudan
Swaziland	...	...	74.0	33.2	3.0	0.9	0.9	Swaziland
Tanzania	77.4	63.5	53.0	36.8	32.2	0.1	0.2	Tanzanie
Togo	...	...	59.0	4.9	24.7	0.2	0.2	Togo
Tunisia	...	...	96.0	6.7	5.4	2.3	2.5	Tunisie
Uganda	75.0	60.1	72.0	14.1	11.5	0.1	0.1	Ouganda
Zambia	57.0	57.3	62.0	66.1	37.8	0.2	0.2	Zambie
Zimbabwe	4.0	24.1	80.0	38.7	27.2	0.8	0.7	Zimbabwe
Africa	**62**	**50**	**74.0**	**26.8**	**14.4**	**1.2**	**1.2**	**Afrique**

Sources: countries report. UNSD MDGs & WB

Part
Partie
2

Country Tables
Tableaux par pays

ALGERIA — ALGÉRIE

AREA (km2)	2 381 741		SUPERFICIE (km2)
CAPITAL CITY	Algiers	Alger	CAPITALE
CURRENCY	Algerian Dinar	Dinar algérien	MONNAIE

I SOCIAL AND DEMOGRAPHIC INDICATORS — INDICATEURS DEMOGRAPHIQUES ET SOCIAUX

	Year / Année	Value / Valeur	
POPULATION			**POPULATION**
Population ('000)			Population ('000)
Both sexes	2014	39 929	Les deux sexes
Male	2014	20 183	Masculin
Female	2014	19 746	Féminin
Average annual growth rate	2014	1.8	Taux de croissance annuel
Active Population ('000)	2014	12 110	Population active ('000)
Population by age group ('000)			Population par groupe d'âge ('000)
0-14 years	2014	11 198	0-14 ans
15-64 years	2014	26 893	15-64 ans
65+ years	2014	1 838	65+ ans
Economically. active population. in agriculture (%)	2014	26.3	Participation de la population active agricole (%)
Crude birth rate	2014	23.9	Taux brut de natalité
Crude death rate	2014	5.9	Taux brut de mortalité
Total fertility rate	2014	2.8	Indice synthétique de fécondité
Proportion of urban population	2014	75.5	Part de la population urbaine
Life Expectancy at Birth - Total (years)	2014	71.1	Espérance de vie à la naissance - Totale (ans)
Dependency Ratio - Total (%)	2014	45.6	Taux de dépendance - Total (%)
HEALTH			**SANTÉ**
Percentage of children under-five and underweight	2005	3.7	% d'enfants de moins de cinq ans avec insuffisance pondérale
Prevalence of undernourishment	2013	5.0	Prévalence de la malnutrition
Under five mortality rate (both sexes, per 1000)	2013	25.2	Taux de mortalité de moins de 5 ans (les deux sexes, pour 1000)
Infant mortality rate (both sexes) per 1000	2013	21.6	Taux de mortalité infantile (les deux sexes) par 1000
Percentage of children provided the vaccines :			Pourcentage d'enfants vaccinés :
BCG	2013	99.0	BCG
DPT3	2013	95.0	DTC3
Polio	2012	95.0	Polio
Measles	2013	95.0	Rougeole
Percentage of mothers provided at least one antenatal care (%)	2006	89.4	Pourcentage de mères ayant au moins reçu un soin prénatal (%)
Percentage of deliveries attended by skilled health personnel	2006	95.2	% d'accouchements assistés par un personnel de santé qualifié
Number of doctors (per 10 000 population)	2007	12.1	Nombre de médecins (pour 10 000 habitants)
Number of nurses (per 10 000 population)	2007	19.5	Nombre d'infirmières (pour 10 000 habitants)
Hospital beds - Total (per 10 000 population)	2004	17.0	Nombre de lits d'hôpitaux - Total (pour 10 000)
Births registered (per 1 000)	2014	23.9	Naiss.s enregistrées (pour 1 000)
Deaths registered (per 1 000)	2014	5.9	Décès enregistrés (pour 1 000)
Public expenditure on Health (% of budget)	2009	10.6	Dépenses publiques consacrées à la santé (% du budget)
EDUCATION			**EDUCATION**
Enrolment in primary education (both sexes) (000)	2012	3 452	Scolarisation dans le primaire (les deux sexes) (000)
Female	2012	1 641	Féminin
Enrolment in secondary education (both sexes) (000)	2011	4 573	Scolarisation dans le secondaire (les deux sexes) (000)
Female	2011	2 285	Féminin
Enrolment in tertiary education (both sexes) (000)	...	...	Scolarisation dans le tertiaire (les deux sexes) (000)
Female	2012	713.5	Féminin
Literacy rate (both sexes)	2006	72.6	Taux d'alphabétisation (deux sexes)
Male	2006	81.3	Masculin
Female	2006	63.9	Féminin
Pupil-teacher ratio	...	...	Ratio élève-enseignant
Public expenditure on education (% of budget)	2008	11.4	Dépenses publiques consacrées à l'enseignement (% du budget)
POVERTY			**PAUVRETÉ**
GNI Per Capita (US$)	2013	5 330.0	RNB par habitant ($EU)
Human Poverty Index (HPI-1) Value (%)	2007	17.5	Valeur de l'Indice de pauvreté (IPH-1) (%)
Population below International Poverty Line ($2/day) (%)	...	...	Population sous le seuil international de pauvreté (2$/J) (%)
Share of Income Held by Richest 10%	...	...	% de revenu des 10% plus riches
Share of Income Held by Poorest 10%	...	...	% de revenu des 10% plus pauvres
Gini index	...	...	Indice de Gini

Charts / Graphiques

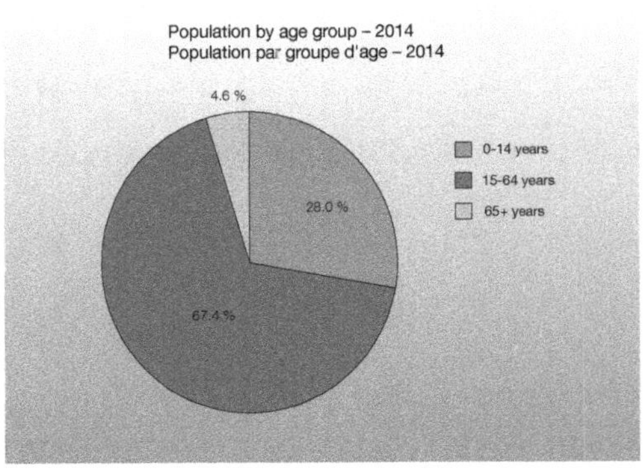

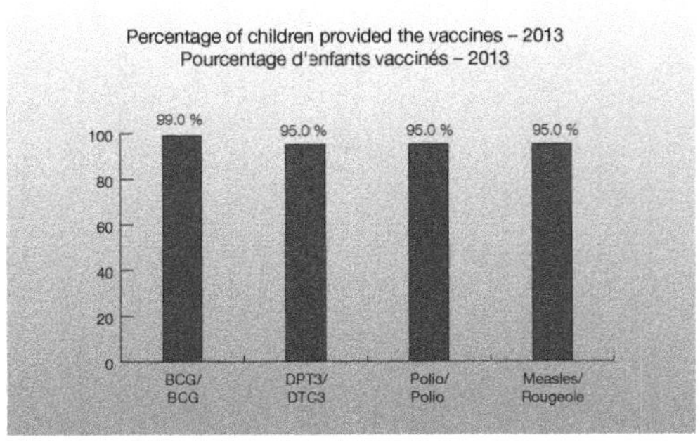

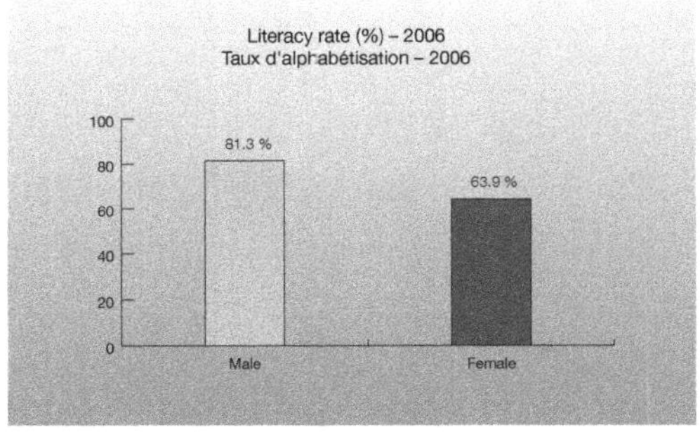

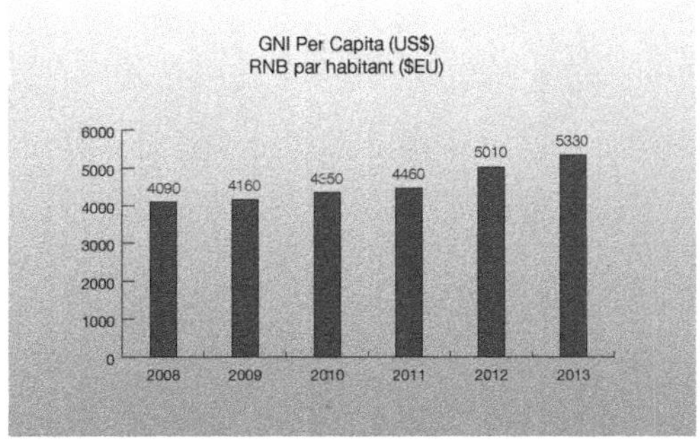

II NATIONAL ACCOUNTS — COMPTES NATIONAUX	2006	2007	2008	2009	2010	2011	2012	2013	2014	
GROSS DOMESTIC PRODUCT BY KIND OF ECONOMIC ACTIVITY AT CURRENT PRICES *ALGERIAN DINAR (MILLIONS)*										**PRODUIT INTÉRIEUR BRUT PAR BRANCHE D'ACTIVITÉ ÉCONOMIQUE AUX PRIX COURANTS** *DINAR ALGÉRIEN (MILLIONS)*
Agriculture, hunting, forestry and fishing	641 285	708 073	727 413	931 341	1 015 258	1 183 216	1 421 694	1 627 762	...	Agriculture, chasse, sylviculture et pêche
Mining and quarrying	3 955 086	4 192 301	5 101 333	3 216 901	4 261 874	5 332 750	5 639 183	5 048 595	...	Industries extractives
Manufacturing	358 332	381 476	408 868	466 054	500 581	533 610	583 311	617 175	...	Industries manufacturières
Electricity, gas & water	82 658	87 691	93 706	91 211	98 622	110 602	122 554	125 822	...	Electricité, gaz et eau
Construction & public works	610 071	732 721	869 989	1 000 055	1 194 113	1 262 567	1 411 160	1 562 105	...	Bâtiments et travaux publics
Wholesale & retail trade, restaurants, hotels	803 569	944 325	1 094 243	1 270 747	1 404 044	1 580 312	1 801 208	2 044 680	...	Commerce de gros et de détail, restaurants et hôtels
Finance, insurance, real estate, etc.	359 183	482 346	599 899	631 527	673 622	702 864	738 898	775 465	...	Banques, assurances, affaires immobilières
Transport and communications	730 238	808 381	830 341	865 215	933 707	1 003 545	1 095 278	1 443 123	...	Transport(s) et communications
Public administration and defense	652 257	777 113	1 057 430	1 180 794	1 569 007	2 368 273	2 634 958	2 506 435	...	Administrations publiques et défense
Education	...	...	...	...	...	...	...	...	...	Education
Health and Social Work	...	...	...	...	...	...	...	...	...	Santé et actions sociales
Other services	86 778	95 131	105 047	114 542	125 832	138 445	154 480	167 114	...	Autres services
Less Imputed Service Charges	- 269 356	- 389 125	- 498 494	- 516 523	- 532 785	- 544 210	- 564 798	- 584 910	...	Moins services d'intermédiation financière
Gross domestic product at factor cost / basic prices	8 010 101	8 820 432	10 389 775	9 251 863	11 243 875	13 671 974	15 037 925	15 333 367	...	Produit intérieur brut aux couts des facteurs / prix de base
Plus: indirect taxes / taxes on products, less subsidies	491 535	532 454	653 929	716 162	747 689	854 636	1 077 506	1 235 904	...	Plus taxes indirectes/impôts sur les produits, moins les subventions
EXPENDITURE ON GROSS DOMESTIC PRODUCT AT CURRENT PURCHASER'S VALUES *ALGERIAN DINAR (MILLIONS)*										**EMPLOI DU PRODUIT INTÉRIEUR BRUT AUX PRIX COURANTS D'ACQUISITION** *DINAR ALGÉRIEN (MILLIONS)*
Government final consumption	954 868	1 089 003	1 458 510	1 609 366	2 065 755	3 015 170	3 293 396	3 153 693	...	Consommation finale des administrations publiques
Private final consumption	2 695 580	2 963 820	3 333 286	3 743 918	4 115 566	4 548 234	5 210 992	5 769 783	...	Consommation finale privée
Gross fixed capital formation	1 969 458	2 462 124	3 228 343	3 811 419	4 350 922	4 620 307	4 992 412	5 638 369	...	Formation brute de capital fixe
Change in inventories	595 525	761 767	896 307	861 238	617 218	857 173	1 250 894	1 529 813	...	Variation des stocks
Exports of goods and services	4 149 707	4 402 232	5 298 034	3 525 855	4 610 103	5 658 617	5 979 810	5 528 757	...	Exportations de biens et services
Less imports of goods and services	1 863 501	2 326 059	3 170 777	3 583 772	3 768 000	4 172 893	4 612 074	5 051 145	...	Moins importations de biens et services
GDP at purchasers' values	8 501 636	9 352 886	11 043 704	9 968 025	11 991 564	14 526 608	16 115 430	16 569 271	...	PIB aux prix d'acquisition
GROSS DOMESTIC PRODUCT BY KIND OF ECONOMIC ACTIVITY AT CONSTANT PRICES *ANNUAL GROWTH RATES (%)*										**PRODUIT INTÉRIEUR BRUT PAR BRANCHE D'ACTIVITÉ ECONOMIQUE AUX PRIX CONSTANTS** *TAUX DE CROISSANCE ANNUEL (%)*
Agriculture, hunting, forestry and fishing	8.1	2.5	- 3.8	21.1	4.9	11.6	7.2	8.8	...	Agriculture, chasse, sylviculture et pêche
Mining and quarrying	- 2.3	- 0.5	- 3.0	- 7.8	- 2.0	- 3.1	- 3.3	- 5.3	...	Industries extractives
Manufacturing	3.1	3.0	6.3	9.7	2.7	3.6	4.3	4.3	...	Industries manufacturières
Electricity, gas & water	3.4	4.5	7.5	9.7	5.4	7.4	10.2	4.3	...	Electricité, gaz et eau
Construction & public works	12.5	8.3	9.5	0.1	9.6	5.2	8.6	6.9	...	Bâtiments et travaux publics
Wholesale & retail trade, restaurants, hotels	6.9	13.3	9.3	10.5	7.6	7.9	5.4	9.9	...	Commerce de gros et de détail, restaurants et hôtels
Finance, insurance, real estate, etc.	11.3	17.1	12.8	8.9	10.6	16.2	6.0	4.4	...	Banques, assurances, affaires immobilières
Transport and communications	6.0	8.0	7.5	4.0	6.2	6.2	8.7	5.0	...	Transport(s) et communications
Public administration and defense	3.2	2.8	6.3	7.6	5.7	5.2	4.1	4.0	...	Administrations publiques et défense
Education	...	...	...	...	...	...	...	...	...	Education
Health and Social Work	...	...	...	...	...	...	...	...	...	Santé et actions sociales
Other services	4.4	4.3	4.8	3.3	4.1	2.9	2.1	4.8	...	Autres services
Less Imputed Service Charges	13.5	21.2	13.1	9.0	10.4	17.2	5.9	4.2	...	Moins services d'intérmediation financière
Gross domestic product at factor cost / basic prices	2.2	3.1	1.7	1.0	3.6	3.1	- 1.5	0.0	...	Produit intérieur brut aux couts des facteurs / prix de base
Plus: indirect taxes / taxes on products, less subsidies	- 3.4	7.5	11.5	9.0	3.8	0.0	19.7	12.9	...	Plus taxes indirectes/impôts sur les produits, moins les subventions
Gross domestic product at market prices	1.7	3.4	2.4	1.6	3.6	2.8	3.3	2.8	...	Produit intérieur brut aux prix du marché
EXPENDITURE ON GROSS DOMESTIC PRODUCT AT CONSTANT PURCHASERS' VALUES *ANNUAL GROWTH RATES (%)*										**EMPLOIS DU PRODUIT INTÉRIEUR BRUT AUX PRIX CONSTANTS D'ACQUISITION** *TAUX DE CROISSANCE ANNUEL (%)*
Government final consumption	6.2	12.1	12.1	8.5	5.8	9.8	2.8	0.8	...	Consommation finale des administrations publiques
Private final consumption	3.3	4.5	6.9	6.2	5.7	6.1	5.1	5.1	...	Consommation finale privée
Gross fixed capital formation	6.2	13.5	12.4	8.8	7.0	2.9	7.2	8.6	...	Formation brute de capital fixe
Exports of goods and services	- 2.1	7.2	- 2.4	- 10.1	-	- 2.7	- 3.8	- 5.8	...	Exportations de biens et services
Less imports of goods and services	- 1.5	11.9	15.4	12.8	4.5	- 4.6	13.9	9.8	...	Moins importations de biens et services
Notes	2012 Semi-Final-2013:provisional						2012 Semi-Définitive-2013:provisoire			Notes

III INFLATION	2006	2007	2008	2009	2010	2011	2012	2013	2014	
ANNUAL GROWTH RATES (%)										**TAUX DE CROISSANCE ANNUEL (%)**
All items	1.8	4.3	5.1	6.5	4.1	5.8	9.7	4.1	3.9	Ensemble
of which:										dont:
Food and Non-alcoholic beverages	2.6	6.8	7.5	9.3	4.2	5.9	13.0	3.0	4.5	Alimentation et boissons non alcoolisés
Alcoholic beverages & tobacco	...	...	...	...	...	...	...	...	...	Boissons alcoolisées et tabacs
Clothing and Footwear	0.3	2.2	2.2	4.9	5.0	6.2	8.1	8.6	7.5	Habillement et chaussures
Housing, Water, Electricity, Gas and Other Fuels	3.3	2.9	1.3	2.6	1.7	1.6	4.1	2.7	2.8	Logement, eau, electricité, gas et autres combustibles
Furnishing, household equipment	0.7	1.1	2.0	2.5	3.5	5.9	5.3	3.7	3.8	Meubles, articles de ménage et entretien courant
Health	1.8	2.8	2.7	4.2	3.3	5.1	5.8	6.2	5.3	Santé
Transport	-0.5	1.0	3.9	3.3	3.3	4.1	4.6	7.6	-0.5	Transport
Communication	...	...	...	...	...	...	...	...	...	Communication
Recreation & culture	...	...	...	...	...	...	...	...	...	Loisirs et culture
Education	-0.8	0.0	2.4	2.8	0.6	0.2	3.5	1.7	6.2	Enseignement
Restaurants & hotels	...	...	...	...	...	...	...	...	...	Restaurants et hôtels
Miscellaneous goods & services	2.4	3.6	5.4	5.8	8.8	13.2	11.0	4.5	1.8	Biens et services divers

IV AGRICULTURAL PRODUCTION - PRODUCTION AGRICOLE	2006	2007	2008	2009	2010	2011	2012	2013	2014	
TONNES *(THOUSAND)*										**TONNES** *(MILLIERS)*
Potatoes	2 181	1 507	2 171	2 636	3 300	3 862	4 219	4 928	...	Pommes de terre
Wheat	2 688	2 319	1 111	2 953	2 605	2 555	3 432	3 299	...	Blé
Dates	491	527	553	601	645	725	789	848	...	Dates
Olives	265	209	254	475	311	611	394	579	...	Olives
Tomatoes	796	567	559	641	718	772	797	975	...	Tomates

V MINING PRODUCTION - PRODUCTION MINIERE	2006	2007	2008	2009	2010	2011	2012	2013	2014	
Crude petroleum, metric tons (thousands)	66 037	66 265	63 680	59 054	57 588	56 393	52 800	52 029	...	Pétrole brut, tonnes métriques (milliers)
Natural gas, terajoules (thousands)	...	...	7 493	7 332	7 158	7 080	6 800	...	...	Gaz naturel, térajoules (milliers)
Iron ores and concentrates, metric tons (thousands)	...	...	2 077	1 307	1 469	1 320	1 560	...	...	Minerai de fer et concentrés, tonnes métriques (milliers)

VI ENERGY - ENERGIE	2006	2007	2008	2009	2010	2011	2012	2013	2014	
Total electricity generation (GWh)	35 226	37 196	40 036	42 769	42 834	51 313	56 985	56 149	...	Production d'électricité totale (GWh)
of which:										dont:
Production of electricity from fossil fuels (GWh)	35 008	36 970	39 753	42 427	42 663	51 062	56 776	55 819	...	Production d'électricité à partir de combustibles fossiles (GWh)
Production of hydro electricity (GWh)	218	226	283	342	171	173	126	99	...	Production d'électricité d'origine hydraulique (GWh)
Production of electricity from solar, wind, tide, wave and other sources (GWh)	...	...	...	...	...	78	83	231	...	Production d'électricité d'origine solaire, éolienne, marée motrice et autres (GWh)

VII TOURISM AND INFRASTRUCTURE - TOURISME ET INFRASTRUCTURE	2006	2007	2008	2009	2010	2011	2012	2013	2014	
VII-1 TOURISM										**VII-1 TOURISME**
International tourist arrivals (thousands)	1 638	1 743	1 772	1 912	2 070	2 395	2 634	2 902	3 157	Arrivées de touristes internationaux (milliers)
Rooms in hotels and similar establishments (thousands)	...	...	...	...	...	...	...	...	...	Chambres d'hotels et établissements assimilés (milliers)
Overnight stays (thousands)	5 916	6 706	7 538	7 400	7 976	11 614	11 041	14 014	15 340	Nuitées (milliers)
Tourism receipts (US$ thousand)	219 698	218 300	322 400	246 000	219 800	209 100	217 000	249 900	263 909	Recettes touristiques (milliers de $ EU)
Total contribution to GDP (%)	8.2	7.6	6.8	7.7	7.3	6.6	6.6	6.6	6.7	Contribution totale au PIB (%)
Total contribution to Employment (%)	6.9	6.4	5.6	6.3	5.9	5.7	5.8	5.9	6.0	Contribution totale à l'emploi (%)
VII-2 INFRASTRUCTURE										**VII-2 INFRASTRUCTURE**
Paved roads (% of total)	...	...	73	74	77	...	...	...	...	Routes asphaltées (% du total)
Total Network (Railways-km)	3 572	3 572	3 572	4 723	3 512	4 691	4 691	...	...	Réseau total voies ferrées-Km
Main Telephone Lines (per 100 inhabitants)	8	9	9	7	8	8	9	8	...	Lignes téléphoniques fixes (pour 100 habitants)
Mobile Cellular Subscribers (per 100 inhabitants)	61	79	76	90	88	94	98	101	...	Abonnés aux téléphones mobiles (pour 100 habitants)

VIII EXTERNAL TRADE - COMMERCE EXTERIEUR	2006	2007	2008	2009	2010	2011	2012	2013	2014	
US$ (MILLIONS) EXPORTS, FOB										**$ E.U (MILLIONS) EXPORTATIONS, FÀB**
Exports - Total	54 741	60 585	78 581	45 181	57 089	72 882	71 736	64 378	...	Exportations - Total
Exports to AFRICA	...	...	...	...	...	...	...	...	...	Exportations vers l'AFRIQUE
Main Products										**Principaux produits**
Crude Oil	22 697	25 374	30 514	16 856	20 725	28 745	27 750	24 327	...	Pétrole brute
Natural gas	8 877	8 625	14 481	8 225	11 942	13 576	15 802	12 824	...	Gaz naturel
Liquefied natural gas	6 383	6 725	9 092	5 598	5 879	6 671	6 500	6 042	...	Gaz naturel liquifié
Condensate	7 268	8 498	1 090	5 146	4 269	5 496	4 698	4 839	...	Condensat
Refined petroleum products	4 756	5 838	7 310	5 373	9 220	11 972	11 045	10 906	...	Produits pétroliers raffinées
Main Destinations										**Principales destinations**
United States	14 857	18 091	18 952	10 365	13 827	15 127	10 778	5 341	...	États-Unis
Italy	9 314	7 967	12 294	5 702	8 779	10 441	11 513	9 017	...	Italie
Spain	5 983	5 338	9 093	5 402	5 909	7 186	7 809	10 344	...	Espagne
France	4 570	4 100	6 370	4 424	3 776	6 534	6 124	6 786	...	France
Netherlands	2 845	4 528	6 111	3 265	4 164	4 916	5 257	4 824	...	Pays-Bas
IMPORTS, CIF										**IMPORTATIONS, CAF**
Imports - Total	21 456	27 631	39 475	39 258	41 000	47 220	50 369	54 910	...	Importations - Total (millions)
Imports from Africa	...	...	...	...	...	...	...	...	...	Importations en provenance de l'Afrique
Main Products										**Principaux produits**
Iron and steel	2 778	3 424	5 850	6 065	5 235	4 473	3 441	3 255	...	Fer et acier
Road vehicles	2 375	3 556	4 800	4 781	4 044	4 978	...	...	...	Véhicules routiers
Other industrial machinery and parts	1 459	1 889	2 440	3 550	4 610	4 621	4 551	2 395	...	Autres machines industrielles et pièces détachées
Cereals and cereal preparations	1 404	1 988	4 051	2 362	1 996	4 073	3 259	3 273	...	Céréales et préparations à base de céréales
Electrical machinery, apparatus and appliances, n.e.s.	1 016	1 210	1 903	2 247	2 173	2 587	3 253	4 007	...	Machines et appareils électriques, n.d.a.
Main Origin										**Principales provenances**
France	4 370	4 614	6 504	6 160	6 120	7 115	6 433	6 258	...	France
China	1 708	2 389	4 067	4 751	4 605	4 737	5 965	6 828	...	Chine
Italy	1 881	2 407	4 309	3 660	4 113	4 675	5 191	5 653	...	Italie
Spain	1 027	1 588	2 915	2 971	2 644	3 427	4 343	5 084	...	Espagne
Germany	1 477	1 788	2 411	2 765	2 382	2 558	2 591	2 861	...	Allemagne

IX FINANCIAL AND MONETARY STATISTICS - FINANCES ET STATISTIQUES MONETAIRES										
	2006	2007	2008	2009	2010	2011	2012	2013	2014	
IX-1 MONETARY STATISTICS *ALGERIAN DINAR (MILLIONS)*										**IX-1 STATISTIQUES MONÉTAIRES** *DINAR ALGÉRIEN (MILLIONS)*
Money supply (M1)	4 870 070	5 994 610	6 955 970	7 292 690	8 280 740	9 929 190	11 012 700	11 941 510	13 626 500	Masse monétaire (M1)
Quasi-money	1 809 265	1 926 836	2 160 771	2 229 057	2 524 281	2 732 489	3 194 644	3 615 397	4 019 318	Quasi-monnaie
of which Demand Deposit	...	...	...	...	...	...	...	...	...	dont Monnaie scripturale
Net foreign assets	5 501 570	7 397 800	10 246 823	10 758 043	11 871 426	13 795 216	14 810 906	15 099 127	15 602 160	Avoirs extérieurs nets
Domestic credit	310 157	- 340 075	-1 402 359	- 892 479	- 794 639	- 658 563	- 342 269	500 028	3 078 925	Crédit intérieur
of which claims on private sector	1 030 152	1 214 950	1 413 130	1 621 380	1 823 706	2 000 952	2 273 446	2 746 556	3 150 784	dont créances sur le secteur privé
of which claims on government sector, net	-1 673 651	-2 601 728	-4 091 776	-4 079 485	-4 143 004	-4 458 146	-4 707 890	-4 741 928	-3 512 025	dont créances nettes sur le gouvernement
International reserves (millions US$)	78 208	110 626	143 544	149 347	162 915	183 122	191 597	195 013	183 788	Réserves internationales (millions $EU)
Average Exchange Rate (National Currency per US$)	71.62	69.39	64.95	72.52	73.85	72.89	77.60	79.40	78.43	Taux de change (moyen) (monnaie nationale par $ EU)
IX-2 PUBLIC FINANCE *ALGERIAN DINAR (BILLIONS)*										**IX-2 FINANCES PUBLIQUES** *DINAR ALGÉRIEN (MILLIARDS)*
Total Revenues and Grants	3 640	3 688	5 191	3 676	4 393	5 790	6 395	5 951	5 641	Recettes totales et dons
Tax Revenue	3 520	3 564	5 054	3 559	4 203	5 507	6 149	5 697	5 370	Recettes fiscales
Non Tax Revenue	120	116	137	117	190	283	246	254	270	Recettes non fiscales
Grants	0	8	0	-	0	-	-	-	250	Dons
Total Expenditures and Net Lending	2 489	3 231	4 284	4 389	4 571	5 959	7 197	6 197	7 128	Dépenses totales et prêts nets
Current expenditure	1 438	1 674	2 218	2 300	2 659	3 879	4 791	4 309	4 684	Dépenses courantes
Of which Wages and Salaries	448	616	839	911	1 213	1 775	1 988	1 778	1 967	Dont rémunérations et salaires
Capital expenditure	1 015	1 435	1 973	1 946	1 808	1 974	2 276	1 888	2 094	Dépenses d'équipement
Net Lending	36	123	93	143	104	105	130	-	350	Prêts nets
Fiscal Balance	1 151	457	907	- 713	- 178	- 169	- 802	- 246	- 1 238	Solde global y compris les dons
IX-3 BALANCE OF PAYMENTS *ALGERIAN DINAR (BILLIONS)*										**IX-3 BALANCE DES PAIEMENTS** *DINAR ALGÉRIEN (MILLIARDS)*
Trade balance	2 474	2 376	2 637	565	1 345	1 890	1 550	739	...	Balance commerciale
Services Balance	- 160	- 256	- 451	- 630	- 503	- 639	- 550	- 537	...	Balance des services
Net Income	- 329	- 128	- 84	- 95	- 130	- 154	- 300	- 330	...	Revenus nets
Compensation of employees	...	...	...	...	...	...	...	...	...	Rémunération des salariés
Investment Income	...	...	...	...	...	...	...	...	...	Revenus des investissements
Current transfers, net total	117	153	175	191	190	193	245	191	...	Transferts courants
Net official transfers	...	...	...	...	...	...	...	...	...	Transferts officiels nets
Workers' remittances	...	...	...	...	...	...	...	...	...	Envois de fonds des travailleurs
Other private transfers	...	...	...	...	...	...	...	...	...	Autres transferts privés
Current account balance	2 102	2 146	2 276	31	902	1 290	945	63	...	Solde du compte courant
Capital & financial account	...	- 64	189	250	243	38	...	86	...	Comptes de capital et financier
Capital account	...	0	0	0	0	0	1	...	...	Compte de capital
Financial account	...	41	123	281	291	69	71	...	...	Compte financier
Errors & omissions	...	- 105	66	- 31	- 48	- 31	- 83	- 140	...	Erreurs et omissions
Overall balance	...	2 041	2 380	281	1 150	1 467	934	9	...	Balance générale

X DEBT AND FINANCIAL FLOWS - DETTE ET FLUX FINANCIERS	2006	2007	2008	2009	2010	2011	2012	2013	2014	
X-1 DEBT *US$ (MILLIONS)*										**X-1 DETTE EXTÉRIEURE** *$ E.U (MILLIONS)*
Total external debt	5 612	5 795	5 921	5 687	5 681	4 405	3 637	3 396	2 864	Dette extérieure totale
Private	2 000	2 100	3 769	3 520	3 649	2 590	2 344	2 402	1 965	Privée
Public	3 612	3 695	2 152	2 167	2 032	1 815	1 293	994	898	Publique
Total external debt service	13 630	1 510	1 457	1 059	218	1 412	1 195	1 593	1 515	Service de la dette extérieure
Present value of External debt	...	...	...	...	...	...	...	...	...	Valeur actuelle de la dette extérieure
Total government domestic debt (in local currency)	...	...	...	...	...	...	...	...	...	Dette publique intérieure
X-2 FINANCIAL FLOWS *US$ (MILLIONS)*										**X-2 FLUX FINANCIERS** *$ E.U (MILLIONS)*
Net Foreign Direct Investment Inflows	1 888	1 743	2 632	2 746	2 301	2 581	1 499	1 691	...	Investissement étranger direct (flux nets entrants)
Main origin of FDI Inflows										**Principales origines de l'IDE entrant:**
United States	1 781	1 117	- 401	578	715.0	582.0	- 753.0	...	...	États-Unis
Italy	- 9	4	110	309	1 476.0	1 645.8	1 684.8	...	...	Italie
France	64	25	329	674	268.9	360.7	266.1	...	...	France
Spain	324	193	355	158	113.9	...	78.4	...	...	Espagne
Germany	45	86	13	86	53.0	...	...	...	...	Allemagne
African countries	...	...	...	...	...	...	...	...	...	Pays africains
Net total Official Development Assistance	240	394	325	319	198	190	145	208	...	Aide publique au développement (nette totale)
Main origin of Net ODA										**Principales origines de l'APD nette**
France	173	185	122	94	69.8	73.3	57.9	84.0	...	France
Spain	43	61	64	54	9.5	- 0.6	2.0	- 16.1	...	Espagne
Italy	11	5	10	4	4.9	6.1	0.7	0.4	...	Italie
Belgium	13	13	10	11	10.3	7.5	3.4	5.6	...	Belgique
United Arab Emirates	35	11	1	11	- 2.9	- 0.2	- 4.6	...	...	Emirats arabes unis

AREA (km²)	1 246 700		SUPERFICIE (km²)
CAPITAL CITY	Luanda	Luanda	CAPITALE
CURRENCY	Angolan Kwanza	Kwanza Angolais	MONNAIE

I SOCIAL AND DEMOGRAPHIC INDICATORS – INDICATEURS DEMOGRAPHIQUES ET SOCIAUX

	Year / Année	Value / Valeur	
POPULATION			**POPULATION**
Population ('000)			Population ('000)
Both sexes	2014	22 137	Les deux sexes
Male	2014	10 979	Masculin
Female	2014	11 158	Féminin
Average annual growth rate	2014	3.0	Taux de croissance annuel
Active Population ('000)	2014	7 941	Population active ('000)
Population by age group ('000)			Population par groupe d'âge ('000)
0-14 years	2014	10 462	0-14 ans
15-64 years	2014	11 144	15-64 ans
65+ years	2014	531	65+ ans
Economically. active population. in agriculture (%)	2014	82.0	Participation de la population active agricole (%)
Crude birth rate	2014	43.5	Taux brut de natalité
Crude death rate	2014	13.6	Taux brut de mortalité
Total fertility rate	2014	5.8	Indice synthétique de fécondité
Proportion of urban population	2014	61.5	Part de la population urbaine
Life Expectancy at Birth - Total (years)	2014	52.3	Espérance de vie à la naissance - Totale (ans)
Dependency Ratio - Total (%)	2014	91.0	Taux de dépendance - Total (%)
HEALTH			**SANTÉ**
Percentage of children under-five and underweight	2007	15.6	% d'enfants de moins de cinq ans avec insuffisance pondérale
Prevalence of undernourishment	2013	18.0	Prévalence de la malnutrition
Under five mortality rate (both sexes, per 1000)	2013	167.4	Taux de mortalité de moins de 5 ans (les deux sexes, pour 1000)
Infant mortality rate (both sexes) per 1000	2013	101.6	Taux de mortalité infantile (les deux sexes) par 1000
Percentage of children provided the vaccines :			Pourcentage d'enfants vaccinés :
BCG	2013	85.0	BCG
DPT3	2013	93.0	DTC3
Polio	2012	88.0	Polio
Measles	2013	91.0	Rougeole
Percentage of mothers provided at least one antenatal care (%)	2009	67.6	Pourcentage de mères ayant au moins reçu un soin prénatal (%)
Percentage of deliveries attended by skilled health personnel	2007	47.3	% d'accouchements assistés par un personnel de santé qualifié
Number of doctors (per 10 000 population)	2009	1.7	Nombre de médecins (pour 10 000 habitants)
Number of nurses (per 10 000 population)	2009	16.6	Nombre d'infirmières (pour 10 000 habitants)
Hospital beds - Total (per 10 000 population)	2005	8.0	Nombre de lits d'hôpitaux - Total (pour 10 000)
Births registered (per 1 000)	2014	43.5	Naiss.s enregistrées (pour 1 000)
Deaths registered (per 1 000)	2014	13.6	Décès enregistrés (pour 1 000)
Public expenditure on Health (% of budget)	2009	8.4	Dépenses publiques consacrées à la santé (% du budget)
EDUCATION			**EDUCATION**
Enrolment in primary education (both sexes) (000)	2011	5 027	Scolarisation dans le primaire (les deux sexes) (000)
Female	2011	1 956	Féminin
Enrolment in secondary education (both sexes) (000)	2011	885	Scolarisation dans le secondaire (les deux sexes) (000)
Female	2011	349	Féminin
Enrolment in tertiary education (both sexes) (000)	...	...	Scolarisation dans le tertiaire (les deux sexes) (000)
Female	2011	39.1	Féminin
Literacy rate (both sexes)	2012	70.6	Taux d'alphabétisation (deux sexes)
Male	2012	82.5	Masculin
Female	2012	59.1	Féminin
Pupil-teacher ratio	...	...	Ratio élève-enseignant
Public expenditure on education (% of budget)	2010	8.7	Dépenses publiques consacrées à l'enseignement (% du budget)
POVERTY			**PAUVRETÉ**
GNI Per Capita (US$)	2013	5 170.0	RNB par habitant ($EU)
Human Poverty Index (HPI-1) Value (%)	2007	37.2	Valeur de l'Indice de pauvreté (IPH-1) (%)
Population below International Poverty Line ($2/day) (%)	2009	67.4	Population sous le seuil international de pauvreté (2$/J) (%)
Share of Income Held by Richest 10%	2009	32.4	% de revenu des 10% plus riches
Share of Income Held by Poorest 10%	2009	2.2	% de revenu des 10% plus pauvres
Gini index	2009	42.7	Indice de Gini

Charts / Graphiques

Population by age group – 2014
Population par groupe d'age – 2014

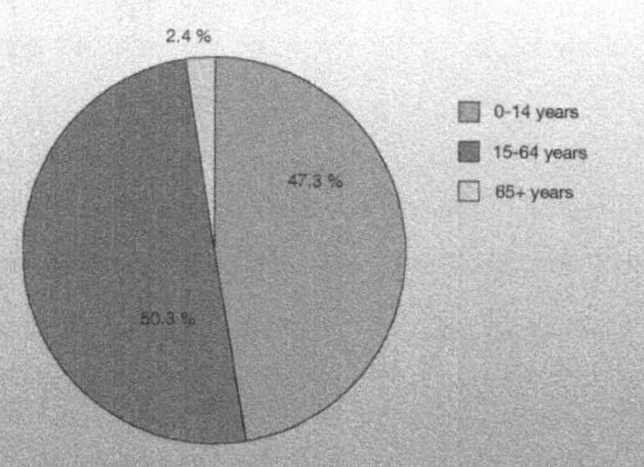

Percentage of children provided the vaccines – 2013
Pourcentage d'enfants vaccinés – 2013

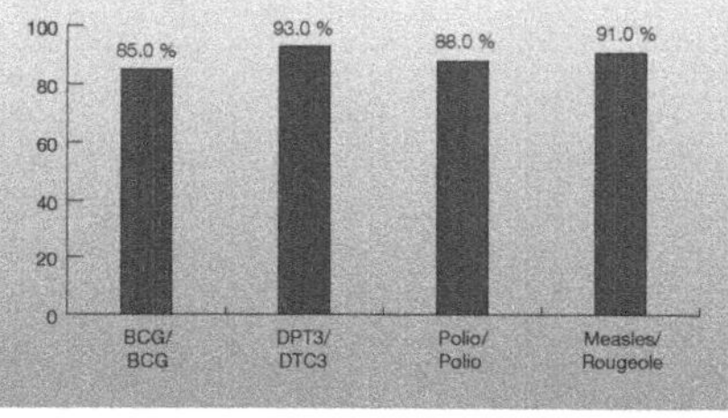

Literacy rate (%) – 2012
Taux d'alphabétisation – 2012

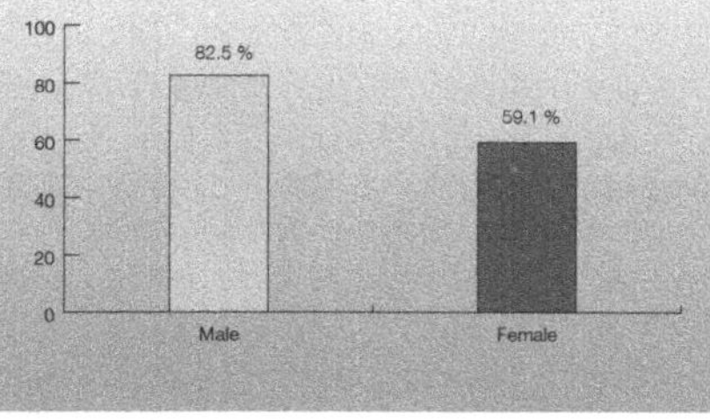

GNI Per Capita (US$)
RNB par habitant ($EU)

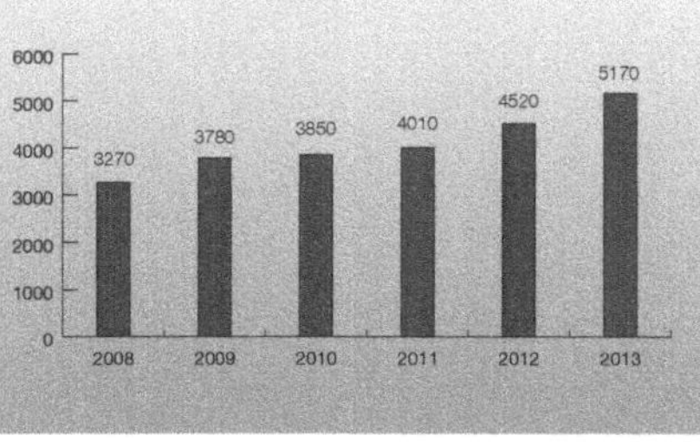

ANGOLA

	2006	2007	2008	2009	2010	2011	2012	2013	2014	
II NATIONAL ACCOUNTS — COMPTES NATIONAUX										
GROSS DOMESTIC PRODUCT BY KIND OF ECONOMIC ACTIVITY AT CURRENT PRICES *ANGOLAN KWANZA (MILLIONS)*										**PRODUIT INTÉRIEUR BRUT PAR BRANCHE D'ACTIVITÉ ÉCONOMIQUE AUX PRIX COURANTS** *KWANZA ANGOLAIS (MILLIONS)*
Agriculture, hunting, forestry and fishing	218 541	262 446	319 236	361 604	458 257	564 062	627 707	748 425	...	Agriculture, chasse, sylviculture et pêche
Mining and quarrying	1 971 092	2 499 640	3 300 632	2 250 260	3 365 810	5 045 875	5 559 425	5 501 231	...	Industries extractives
Manufacturing	152 091	170 190	229 975	211 004	306 237	401 026	487 768	568 187	...	Industries manufacturières
Electricity, gas & water	34 449	55 163	36 483	59 687	63 585	82 999	98 457	103 859	...	Electricité, gaz et eau
Construction & public works & public works	288 632	373 105	435 850	467 355	666 011	811 977	1 238 087	1 444 553	...	Bâtiments et travaux publics
Wholesale & retail trade, restaurants, hotels	394 520	473 149	584 056	560 750	660 904	725 987	844 816	993 788	...	Commerce de gros et de détail, restaurants et hôtels
Finance, insurance, real estate, etc.	235 769	300 370	358 955	418 906	463 878	508 951	619 257	763 776	...	Banques, assurances, affaires immobilières
Transport and communications	132 891	169 312	260 390	272 743	317 302	451 820	530 750	608 569	...	Transport(s) et communications
Public administration and defense	362 442	446 990	626 644	763 134	811 569	1 252 218	1 447 449	2 455 728	...	Administrations publiques et défense
Education	...	...	...	...	...	...	...	...	...	Education
Health and Social Work	...	...	...	...	...	...	...	...	...	Santé et actions sociales
Other services	438 593	342 967	451 164	413 339	582 138	671 113	806 857	1 026 550	...	Autres services
Less Imputed Service Charges	- 28 384	- 52 355	- 89 941	- 111 407	- 117 216	- 152 059	- 150 984	- 258 902	...	Moins services d'intermédiation financière
Gross domestic product at factor cost / basic prices	4 200 636	5 040 975	6 513 443	5 667 375	7 578 474	10 363 969	12 109 589	13 955 765	...	Produit intérieur brut aux coûts des facteurs / prix de base
Plus: indirect taxes / taxes on products, less subsidies	9 126	- 34 640	129 910	136 109	83 656	52 509	- 135 032	- 178 975	...	Plus taxes indirectes/impôts sur les produits, moins les subventions
EXPENDITURE ON GROSS DOMESTIC PRODUCT AT CURRENT PURCHASER'S VALUES *ANGOLAN KWANZA (MILLIONS)*										**EMPLOI DU PRODUIT INTÉRIEUR BRUT AUX PRIX COURANTS D'ACQUISITION** *KWANZA ANGOLAIS (MILLIONS)*
Government final consumption	645 850	777 831	1 117 054	1 116 238	1 332 860	1 933 459	2 179 894	3 598 601	...	Consommation finale des administrations publiques
Private final consumption	1 222 807	1 551 012	1 913 019	2 303 263	2 646 397	3 304 895	3 806 437	4 077 501	...	Consommation finale privée
Gross fixed capital formation	980 907	1 288 159	2 046 422	2 436 365	2 222 440	2 935 397	3 533 436	3 264 516	...	Formation brute de capital fixe
Change in inventories	...	...	...	...	...	...	...	...	...	Variation des stocks
Exports of goods and services	2 671 846	3 399 591	4 814 772	3 696 401	4 739 836	6 370 916	6 838 653	6 696 059	...	Exportations de biens et services
Less imports of goods and services	1 311 648	2 010 258	3 247 914	3 748 783	3 279 403	4 128 189	4 383 863	3 859 887	...	Moins importations de biens et services
GDP at purchasers' values	4 209 762	5 006 335	6 643 353	5 803 484	7 662 130	10 416 478	11 974 557	13 776 790	...	PIB aux prix d'acquisition
GROSS DOMESTIC PRODUCT BY KIND OF ECONOMIC ACTIVITY AT CONSTANT PRICES *ANNUAL GROWTH RATES (%)*										**PRODUIT INTÉRIEUR BRUT PAR BRANCHE D'ACTIVITÉ ECONOMIQUE AUX PRIX CONSTANTS** *TAUX DE CROISSANCE ANNUEL (%)*
Agriculture, hunting, forestry and fishing	16.3	5.6	4.8	5.2	3.3	- 0.6	5.1	7.8	...	Agriculture, chasse, sylviculture et pêche
Mining and quarrying	13.8	21.7	9.9	- 4.8	- 0.4	- 7.0	5.2	- 0.5	...	Industries extractives
Manufacturing	6.5	2.0	5.9	7.0	19.2	139.5	10.8	12.6	...	Industries manufacturières
Electricity, gas & water	33.5	9.5	8.1	23.7	9.5	- 0.3	11.7	3.5	...	Electricité, gaz et eau
Construction & public works	11.6	17.7	8.9	12.8	26.0	8.4	25.4	3.4	...	Bâtiments et travaux publics
Wholesale & retail trade, restaurants, hotels	4.1	13.6	17.6	2.3	- 9.7	- 4.0	7.7	4.9	...	Commerce de gros et de détail, restaurants et hôtels
Finance, insurance, real estate, etc.	8.4	4.9	10.4	6.2	5.1	4.3	14.2	5.1	...	Banques, assurances, affaires immobilières
Transport and communications	9.2	9.0	27.5	14.1	8.1	39.8	7.4	4.6	...	Transport(s) et communications
Public administration and defense	11.5	9.6	8.0	9.6	10.0	1.7	3.4	10.1	...	Administrations publiques et défense
Education	...	...	...	...	...	...	...	...	...	Education
Health and Social Work	...	...	...	...	...	...	...	...	...	Santé et actions sociales
Other services	12.1	- 5.5	7.9	11.9	9.0	1.5	6.8	14.9	...	Autres services
Less Imputed Service Charges	17.2	7.8	8.8	- 5.5	10.1	- 14.3	- 3.9	6.6	...	Moins services d'intermédiation financière
Gross domestic product at factor cost / basic prices	11.7	13.9	10.5	2.0	4.6	5.3	7.8	4.0	...	Produit intérieur brut aux couts des facteurs / prix de base
Plus: indirect taxes / taxes on products, less subsidies	82.3	85.9	- 89.3	8.5	- 39.9	- 312.3	- 19.9	- 17.0	...	Plus taxes indirectes/impôts sur les produits, moins les subventions
Gross domestic product at market prices	11.5	14.0	11.2	2.1	3.6	1.9	7.6	4.2	...	Produit intérieur brut aux prix du marché
EXPENDITURE ON GROSS DOMESTIC PRODUCT AT CONSTANT PURCHASERS' VALUES *ANNUAL GROWTH RATES (%)*										**EMPLOIS DU PRODUIT INTÉRIEUR BRUT AUX PRIX CONSTANTS D'ACQUISITION** *TAUX DE CROISSANCE ANNUEL (%)*
Government final consumption	9.8	8.5	12.3	6.5	9.9	8.8	2.1	9.9	...	Consommation finale des administrations publiques
Private final consumption	6.4	6.0	8.2	6.1	5.9	- 22.3	6.0	8.5	...	Consommation finale privée
Gross fixed capital formation	4.2	12.1	26.4	14.2	- 9.1	16.0	7.5	3.9	...	Formation brute de capital fixe
Exports of goods and services	14.3	16.6	10.6	- 7.5	- 4.3	13.0	5.2	- 1.2	...	Exportations de biens et services
Less imports of goods and services	6.4	7.6	18.2	- 0.7	- 9.1	11.0	- 0.1	2.1	...	Moins importations de biens et services
III INFLATION										
	2006	2007	2008	2009	2010	2011	2012	2013	2014	
ANNUAL GROWTH RATES (%)										**TAUX DE CROISSANCE ANNUEL (%)**
All items	13.3	12.3	12.4	13.7	14.5	13.5	10.3	8.8	7.3	Ensemble
of which:										dont:
Food and Non-alcoholic beverages	...	...	...	...	...	...	...	...	...	Alimentation et boissons non alcoolisés
Alcoholic beverages & tobacco	...	...	...	...	...	...	...	...	...	Boissons alcoolisées et tabacs
Clothing and Footwear	...	...	...	...	...	...	...	...	...	Habillement et chaussures
Housing, Water, Electricity, Gas and Other Fuels	...	...	...	...	...	...	...	...	...	Logement, eau, electricité, gas et autres combustibles
Furnishing, household equipment	...	...	...	...	...	...	...	...	...	Meubles, articles de ménage et entretien courant
Health	...	...	...	...	...	...	...	...	...	Santé
Transport	...	...	...	...	...	...	...	...	...	Transport
Communication	...	...	...	...	...	...	...	...	...	Communication
Recreation & culture	...	...	...	...	...	...	...	...	...	Loisirs et culture
Education	...	...	...	...	...	...	...	...	...	Enseignement
Restaurants & hotels	...	...	...	...	...	...	...	...	...	Restaurants et hôtels
Miscellaneous goods & services	...	...	...	...	...	...	...	...	...	Biens et services divers

	2006	2007	2008	2009	2010	2011	2012	2013	2014	
IV AGRICULTURAL PRODUCTION - PRODUCTION AGRICOLE										
TONNES *(THOUSAND)*										**TONNES** *(MILLIERS)*
Cassava	9 037	9 730	10 057	12 828	13 859	14 334	10 636	16 412	...	Manioc
Bananas	1 100	1 398	1 723	1 985	2 048	2 646	2 991	3 095	...	Banane
Maize	526	616	702	970	1 073	1 262	454	1 549	...	Mais
Cabbages and other brassicas	-	69	621	1 042	1 067	1 171	1 051	1 135	...	Choux et autres choux
Beans, dry	85	104	124	247	250	304	96	312	...	Haricots, sec
V MINING PRODUCTION - PRODUCTION MINIERE										
	2006	2007	2008	2009	2010	2011	2012	2013	2014	
Crude petroleum, metric tons (thousands)	...	...	...	...	...	...	...	...	...	Pétrole brut, tonnes métriques (milliers)
Natural gas (terajoules)	...	...	...	...	...	...	...	...	...	Gaz naturel (térajoules)
Diamonds and other precious stones, unworked, carat (thousands)	...	...	...	...	...	...	...	...	...	Diamants et autres pierres précieuses, brut, carat (milliers)
VI ENERGY - ENERGIE										
	2006	2007	2008	2009	2010	2011	2012	2013	2014	
Total electricity generation (GWh)	2 959	3 217	3 930	4 172	5 448	5 654	6 000	6 370	...	Production d'électricité totale (GWh)
of which:										dont:
Production of electricity from fossil fuels (GWh)	294	720	796	999	1 745	1 644	1 710	1 778	...	Production d'électricité à partir de combustibles fossiles (GWh)
Production of hydro electricity (GWh)	2 665	2 497	3 134	3 173	3 703	4 007	4 287	4 588	...	Production d'électricité d'origine hydraulique (GWh)
Production of electricity from solar, wind, tide, wave and other sources (GWh)	...	...	...	...	...	3	3	4	...	Production d'électricité d'origine solaire, éolienne, marée motrice et autres (GWh)
VII TOURISM AND INFRASTRUCTURE - TOURISME ET INFRASTRUCTURE										
	2006	2007	2008	2009	2010	2011	2012	2013	2014	
VII-1 TOURISM										**VII-1 TOURISME**
International tourist arrivals (thousands)	121	195	294	366	425	481	528	650	641	Arrivées de touristes internationaux (milliers)
Rooms in hotels and similar establishments (thousands)	...	...	...	...	...	...	...	...	...	Chambres d'hotels et établissements assimilés (milliers)
Overnight stays (thousands)	231	340	386	1 899	2 856	1 436	1 429	1 754	2 028	Nuitées (milliers)
Tourism receipts (US$ thousand)	72 590	217 965	276 115	517 630	702 630	630 030	690 030	1204 940	1032 040	Recettes touristiques (milliers de $ EU)
Total contribution to GDP (%)	3.7	3.8	3.5	4.5	4.0	3.3	3.2	3.7	3.6	Contribution totale au PIB (%)
Total contribution to Employment (%)	3.5	3.9	3.5	4.9	4.3	3.4	3.2	3.9	3.8	Contribution totale à l'emploi (%)
VII-2 INFRASTRUCTURE										**VII-2 INFRASTRUCTURE**
Paved roads (% of total)	...	...	...	...	...	...	...	...	...	Routes asphaltées (% du total)
Total Network (Railways-km)	...	...	...	...	...	...	...	...	...	Réseau total voies ferrées-Km
Main Telephone Lines (per 100 inhabitants)	1	1	1	2	1	1	1	1	...	Lignes téléphoniques fixes (pour 100 habitants)
Mobile Cellular Subscribers (per 100 inhabitants)	18	28	37	43	48	60	61	62	...	Abonnés aux téléphones mobiles (pour 100 habitants)
VIII EXTERNAL TRADE - COMMERCE EXTERIEUR										
	2006	2007	2008	2009	2010	2011	2012	2013	2014	
US$ (MILLIONS) *EXPORTS, FOB*										**$ E.U (MILLIONS)** *EXPORTATIONS, FÀB*
Exports - Total	31 862	44 396	63 914	40 828	50 595	67 310	71 093	70 045	...	Exportations - Total
Exports to AFRICA	...	...	...	...	...	...	...	...	...	Exportations vers l'AFRIQUE
Main Products										**Principaux produits**
Crude oil	29 929	42 352	61 666	39 271	48 629	64 539	68 871	...	...	Pétrole brut
Diamonds	1 155	1 182	1 210	814	976	1 205	1 160	...	...	Diamonds
Refined oil	295	324	400	314	423	676	515	...	...	Pétrole raffiné
Gas	260	328	392	218	300	376	330	...	...	Gaz
Coffee	0	0	1	1	1	1	1	...	...	Café
Main Destinations										**Principales destinations**
United States	12 092	13 965	18 331	10 004	11 710	10 282	6 024	...	...	États-Unis
China	10 859	13 925	21 043	15 131	21 754	25 712	34 421	...	...	Chine
France	1 543	2 561	3 770	3 372	2 027	2 092	1 135	...	...	France
India	200	899	1 271	3 625	4 665	6 880	6 926	...	...	Inde
China, Taiwan	1 854	2 292	1 892	1 091	2 727	5 314	4 215	...	...	Taiwan, Chine
IMPORTS, CIF										**IMPORTATIONS, CAF**
Imports - Total	8 008	11 095	16 970	23 643	18 143	20 228	23 717	22 282	...	Importations - Total (millions)
Imports from Africa	...	...	...	...	...	...	...	...	...	Importations en provenance de l'Afrique
Main Products										**Principaux produits**
Floating or submersible drilling or production platforms	23	58	719	830	353	2 165	...	...	...	Flottantes ou submersibles de forage ou de production des plates-formes
Parts of boring or sinking machinery, whether or not self-propelled	1 323	2 909	2 930	3 353	3 129	2 707	...	...	...	Pièces du forage ou de fonçage, qu'ils soient ou non autopropulsés
Petroleum oils & oils obtained from bituminous minerals,o/than crude etc	71	145	696	3 644	3 105	2 419	...	...	...	Huiles de pétrole, bitumineux, distilles, sauf brut
Aircraft nes of an unladen weight exceeding 15.000 kg	108	184	256	194	281	334	...	...	...	Aéronefs nda d'un poids à vide > 2.000 kg mais pas sup 15.000 kg
Diesel powered trucks with a GVW exceeding twenty tonnes	89	180	379	204	...	...	...	...	...	Diesel chariots de manutention d'un PTAC supérieure à vingt tonnes
Main Origin										**Principales provenances**
Portugal	1 392	1 884	...	3 658	2 607	3 455	3 879	...	...	Portugal
United States	807	1 113	1 485	1 500	1 679	1 748	1 774	...	...	États-Unis
Korea, Rep.	1 037	1 128	215	198	203	2 351	...	...	...	Corée, Rép
China	534	1 042	1 795	1 807	1 829	1 837	2 189	...	...	Chine
Brazil	807	771	1 410	1 674	964	940	1 042	...	...	Brésil

IX FINANCIAL AND MONETARY STATISTICS - FINANCES ET STATISTIQUES MONETAIRES	2006	2007	2008	2009	2010	2011	2012	2013	2014	
IX-1 MONETARY STATISTICS *ANGOLAN KWANZA (MILLIONS)*										**IX-1 STATISTIQUES MONÉTAIRES** *KWANZA ANGOLAIS (MILLIONS)*
Money supply (M1)	688 210	1 027 450	2 097 450	2 547 960	2 728 390	3 657 020	3 875 990	4 431 540	5 366 680	Masse monétaire (M1)
Quasi-money	174 542	263 641	590 200	736 250	964 612	1 409 778	1 620 181	1 809 217	2 006 750	Quasi-monnaie
of which Demand Deposit	...	...	...	...	...	...	...	...	...	dont Monnaie scripturale
Net foreign assets	891 291	1 022 738	1 509 141	1 181 572	1 731 026	2 927 440	3 165 722	3 115 369	3 126 011	Avoirs extérieurs nets
Domestic credit	- 168 213	86 875	596 858	1 747 767	1 460 323	1 627 397	1 705 104	2 261 543	3 015 809	Crédit intérieur
of which claims on private sector	273 708	492 519	801 048	1 285 702	1 532 272	1 973 568	2 451 384	2 819 717	2 852 043	dont créances sur le secteur privé
of which claims on government sector, net	- 458 434	- 429 270	- 267 510	397 233	- 222 513	- 446 380	- 942 291	- 665 549	69 065	dont créances nettes sur le gouvernement
International reserves (millions US$)	8 599	11 197	17 869	13 664	19 749	28 786	33 415	32 780	27 289	Réserves internationales (millions $EU)
Average Exchange Rate (National Currency per US$)	80.37	76.71	75.03	79.33	91.91	93.93	95.47	96.52	97.59	Taux de change (moyen) (monnaie nationale par $ EU)
IX-2 PUBLIC FINANCE *ANGOLAN KWANZA (MILLIONS)*										**IX-2 FINANCES PUBLIQUES** *KWANZA ANGOLAIS (MILLIONS)*
Total Revenues and Grants	1 685 031	2 124 712	3 217 433	2 069 733	3 295 490	4 775 555	5 055 160	4 848 100	4 817 595	Recettes totales et dons
Tax Revenue	1 589 521	2 052 808	3 070 233	1 988 221	3 094 470	4 527 745	4 832 560	4 699 400	4 662 119	Recettes fiscales
Non Tax Revenue	95 510	69 632	145 329	79 266	199 093	245 987	221 000	148 700	155 476	Recettes non fiscales
Grants	0	2 273	1 872	2 246	1 927	1 823	1 600	-	-	Dons
Total Expenditures and Net Lending	1 288 353	1 908 798	3 573 055	2 510 282	3 034 517	3 927 632	4 548 500	4 809 300	5 134 055	Dépenses totales et prêts nets
Current expenditure	852 387	1 240 727	2 103 177	1 767 008	2 166 517	2 934 632	3 192 500	3 372 300	3 596 708	Dépenses courantes
Of which Wages and Salaries	311 292	364 456	542 953	665 000	713 759	877 330	1 031 000	1 155 000	1 236 543	Dont rémunérations et salaires
Capital expenditure	435 966	668 071	1 469 878	743 275	868 000	993 000	1 356 000	1 437 000	1 537 347	Dépenses d'équipement
Net Lending	-	-	-	-	-	-	-	-	-	Prêts nets
Fiscal Balance	396 677	215 914	- 355 623	- 440 549	260 973	847 923	506 660	38 800	- 316 460	Solde global y compris les dons
IX-3 BALANCE OF PAYMENTS *ANGOLAN KWANZA (MILLIONS)*										**IX-3 BALANCE DES PAIEMENTS** *KWANZA ANGOLAIS (MILLIONS)*
Trade balance	1 856 910	2 470 647	3 333 741	1 447 184	3 042 536	4 422 618	4 522 922	4 044 363	...	Balance commerciale
Services Balance	- 484 374	- 945 981	-1 636 470	-1 471 232	-1 644 881	-2 154 635	-2 037 206	-2 078 109	...	Balance des services
Net Income	- 496 503	- 582 892	-1 029 274	- 541 268	- 743 229	- 908 833	- 994 944	- 955 537	...	Revenus nets
Compensation of employees	...	...	...	...	...	...	...	...	...	Rémunération des salariés
Investment Income	...	...	...	...	...	...	...	...	...	Revenus des investissements
Current transfers, net total	- 15 267	- 17 022	- 15 762	- 29 376	- 40 226	- 127 670	- 168 229	- 204 947	...	Transferts courants
Net official transfers	...	...	...	...	...	...	...	...	...	Transferts officiels nets
Workers' remittances	...	...	...	...	...	...	...	...	...	Envois de fonds des travailleurs
Other private transfers	...	...	...	...	...	...	...	...	...	Autres transferts privés
Current account balance	860 765	924 751	652 235	- 594 691	614 199	1 231 479	1 322 543	805 770	...	Solde du compte courant
Capital & financial account	...	...	...	...	...	...	- 848 102	- 792 349	...	Comptes de capital et financier
Capital account	...	...	...	...	...	...	...	...	...	Compte de capital
Financial account	...	...	...	...	...	...	- 848 122	- 792 349	...	Compte financier
Errors & omissions	...	...	...	...	...	...	- 31 164	- 5 293	...	Erreurs et omissions
Overall balance	...	...	...	...	...	...	443 277	8 128	...	Balance générale

X DEBT AND FINANCIAL FLOWS - DETTE ET FLUX FINANCIERS										
	2006	2007	2008	2009	2010	2011	2012	2013	2014	
X-1 DEBT *US$ (MILLIONS)*										**X-1 DETTE EXTÉRIEURE** *$ E.U (MILLIONS)*
Total external debt	7 823	9 929	13 987	15 213	17 859	21 060	22 749	27 396	32 821	Dette extérieure totale
Private	4 536	5 974	9 072	8 946	10 698	13 197	13 952	17 929	17 850	Privée
Public	3 287	3 956	4 915	6 267	7 161	7 863	8 798	9 466	14 971	Publique
Total external debt service	4 809	4 406	2 037	3 730	3 251	3 790	4 576	4 880	7 156	Service de la dette extérieure
Present value of External debt	...	...	...	...	...	...	...	...	...	Valeur actuelle de la dette extérieure
Total government domestic debt (in local currency)	...	...	...	...	...	...	...	...	...	Dette publique intérieure
X-2 FINANCIAL FLOWS *US$ (MILLIONS)*										**X-2 FLUX FINANCIERS** *$ E.U (MILLIONS)*
Net Foreign Direct Investment Inflows	- 38	- 893	1 679	2 205	- 3 227	- 3 024	- 6 898	- 4 285	...	Investissement étranger direct (flux nets entrants)
Main origin of FDI Inflows										**Principales origines de l'IDE entrant:**
France	694	694	518	- 478	1 511.3	980.5	953.7	...	...	France
Norway	...	...	854	2 282	908.1	...		...	...	Norvège
United States	280	- 99	789	54	1 974.0	707.0	- 3 011.0	...	...	États-Unis
Denmark	...	...	...	- 75	203.9	250.7	253.9	...	...	Danemark
Germany	-	31	19	11	30.5	...	...	...	...	Allemagne
African countries	...	...	...	...	...	...	...	...	...	Pays africains
Net total Official Development Assistance	164	248	369	239	238	194	242	288	...	Aide publique au développement (nette totale)
Main origin of Net ODA										**Principales origines de l'APD nette**
Global Fund	12	14	30	10	25.9	3.8	10.9	...	...	Fonds mondial
United States	33	40	43	42	54.8	66.5	78.2	62.1	...	Etats-Unis
Japan	12	23	18	7	37.6	11.4	13.8	15.2	...	Japon
Norway	23	21	18	18	13.2	13.1	12.1	10.0	...	Norvège
IDA	28	28	22	20	3.9	7.3	36.3	...	...	IDA

BENIN — BÉNIN

AREA (km²)	114 763		SUPERFICIE (km²)
CAPITAL CITY	Porto Novo	Porto-Novo	CAPITALE
CURRENCY	CFA Franc	Franc CFA	MONNAIE

I SOCIAL AND DEMOGRAPHIC INDICATORS – INDICATEURS DEMOGRAPHIQUES ET SOCIAUX

	Year / Année	Value / Valeur	
POPULATION			**POPULATION**
Population ('000)			Population ('000)
Both sexes	2014	9 988	Les deux sexes
Male	2014	4 908	Masculin
Female	2014	5 081	Féminin
Average annual growth rate	2014	2.7	Taux de croissance annuel
Active Population ('000)	2014	3 930	Population active ('000)
Population by age group ('000)			Population par groupe d'âge ('000)
0-14 years	2014	4 462	0-14 ans
15-64 years	2014	5 263	15-64 ans
65+ years	2014	263	65+ ans
Economically. active population. in agriculture (%)	2014	42.1	Participation de la population active agricole (%)
Crude birth rate	2014	39.7	Taux brut de natalité
Crude death rate	2014	8.0	Taux brut de mortalité
Total fertility rate	2014	5.4	Indice synthétique de fécondité
Proportion of urban population	2014	47.3	Part de la population urbaine
Life Expectancy at Birth - Total (years)	2014	59.5	Espérance de vie à la naissance - Totale (ans)
Dependency Ratio - Total (%)	2014	89.8	Taux de dépendance - Total (%)
HEALTH			**SANTÉ**
Percentage of children under-five and underweight	2006	20.2	% d'enfants de moins de cinq ans avec insuffisance pondérale
Prevalence of undernourishment	2013	9.7	Prévalence de la malnutrition
Under five mortality rate (both sexes, per 1000)	2013	85.3	Taux de mortalité de moins de 5 ans (les deux sexes, pour 1000)
Infant mortality rate (both sexes) per 1000	2013	56.2	Taux de mortalité infantile (les deux sexes) par 1000
Percentage of children provided the vaccines :			Pourcentage d'enfants vaccinés :
BCG	2013	88.0	BCG
DPT3	2013	69.0	DTC3
Polio	2011	56.2	Polio
Measles	2013	63.0	Rougeole
Percentage of mothers provided at least one antenatal care (%)	2011	85.8	Pourcentage de mères ayant au moins reçu un soin prénatal (%)
Percentage of deliveries attended by skilled health personnel	2012	84.1	% d'accouchements assistés par un personnel de santé qualifié
Number of doctors (per 10 000 population)	2008	0.6	Nombre de médecins (pour 10 000 habitants)
Number of nurses (per 10 000 population)	2008	7.7	Nombre d'infirmières (pour 10 000 habitants)
Hospital beds - Total (per 10 000 population)	2013	5.0	Nombre de lits d'hôpitaux - Total (pour 10 000)
Births registered (per 1 000)	2014	36.0	Naiss.s enregistrées (pour 1 000)
Deaths registered (per 1 000)	2014	9.4	Décès enregistrés (pour 1 000)
Public expenditure on Health (% of budget)	2013	7.1	Dépenses publiques consacrées à la santé (% du budget)
EDUCATION			**EDUCATION**
Enrolment in primary education (both sexes) (000)	2013	2 064	Scolarisation dans le primaire (les deux sexes) (000)
Female	2013	972	Féminin
Enrolment in secondary education (both sexes) (000)	2013	869	Scolarisation dans le secondaire (les deux sexes) (000)
Female	2013	344	Féminin
Enrolment in tertiary education (both sexes) (000)	2010	82.0	Scolarisation dans le tertiaire (les deux sexes) (000)
Female	2011	23.4	Féminin
Literacy rate (both sexes)	2006	28.7	Taux d'alphabétisation (deux sexes)
Male	2006	40.6	Masculin
Female	2006	18.4	Féminin
Pupil-teacher ratio	2012	44.0	Ratio élève-enseignant
Public expenditure on education (% of budget)	2010	26.1	Dépenses publiques consacrées à l'enseignement (% du budget)
POVERTY			**PAUVRETÉ**
GNI Per Capita (US$)	2013	790.0	RNB par habitant ($EU)
Human Poverty Index (HPI-1) Value (%)	2007	43.2	Valeur de l'Indice de pauvreté (IPH-1) (%)
Population below International Poverty Line ($2/day) (%)	2012	74.3	Population sous le seuil international de pauvreté (2$/J) (%)
Share of Income Held by Richest 10%	2012	34.9	% de revenu des 10% plus riches
Share of Income Held by Poorest 10%	2012	2.7	% de revenu des 10% plus pauvres
Gini index	2012	43.5	Indice de Gini

Charts / Graphiques

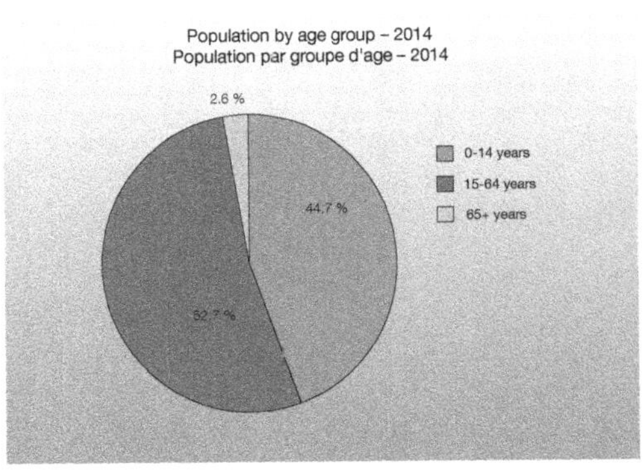

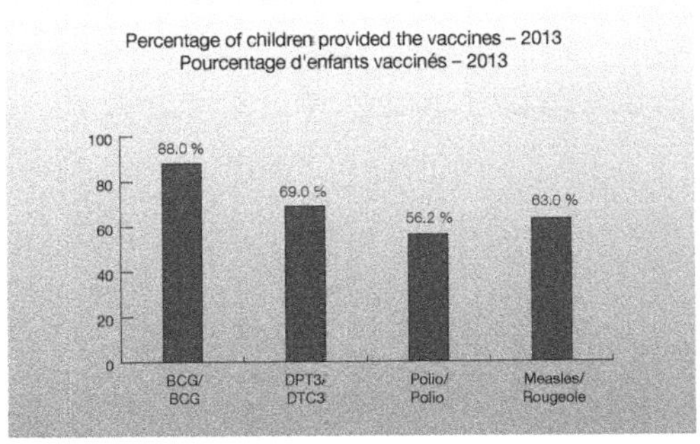

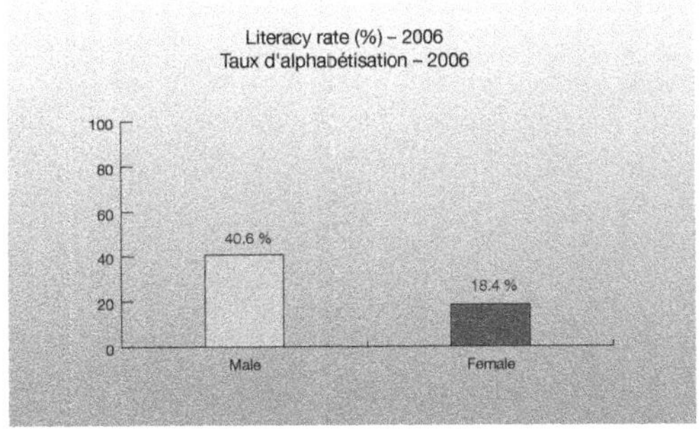

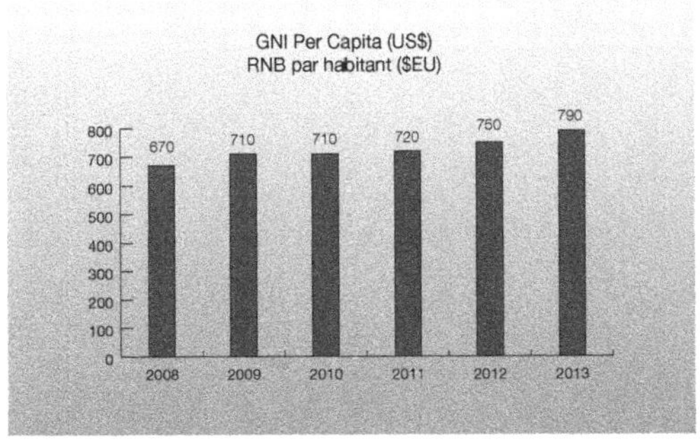

II NATIONAL ACCOUNTS — COMPTES NATIONAUX

	2006	2007	2008	2009	2010	2011	2012	2013	2014	
GROSS DOMESTIC PRODUCT BY KIND OF ECONOMIC ACTIVITY AT CURRENT PRICES *CFA FRANC (MILLIONS)*										**PRODUIT INTÉRIEUR BRUT PAR BRANCHE D'ACTIVITÉ ÉCONOMIQUE AUX PRIX COURANTS** *FRANC CFA (MILLIONS)*
Agriculture, hunting, forestry and fishing	798 012	826 887	958 389	1 006 899	1 054 845	1 144 825	1 255 121	1 355 001	1 420 120	Agriculture, chasse, sylviculture et pêche
Mining and quarrying	5 762	6 289	6 928	7 278	7 439	8 043	8 532	9 007	9 738	Industries extractives
Manufacturing	185 427	198 387	213 118	232 048	250 834	264 803	289 237	302 984	327 300	Industries manufacturières
Electricity, gas & water	28 391	28 125	28 666	31 033	33 661	35 919	38 800	41 487	44 860	Electricité, gaz et eau
Construction & public works	100 448	109 848	124 806	134 985	137 661	148 846	157 780	166 410	179 931	Bâtiments et travaux publics
Wholesale & retail trade, restaurants, hotels	412 852	448 739	521 126	526 737	537 602	555 513	614 408	652 911	711 484	Commerce de gros et de détail, restaurants et hôtels
Finance, insurance, real estate, etc.	271 635	294 751	321 695	340 614	358 320	379 734	406 310	436 944	473 907	Banques, assurances, affaires immobilières
Transport and communications	195 076	222 429	250 070	256 415	263 939	273 401	401 394	414 801	455 526	Transport(s) et communications
Public administration and defense	259 220	281 611	300 743	320 188	330 858	352 188	375 005	397 261	423 152	Administrations publiques et défense
Education	...	...	...	...	...	...	...	...	...	Education
Health and Social Work	...	...	...	...	...	...	...	...	...	Santé et actions sociales
Other services	...	...	...	...	...	...	...	...	...	Autres services
Less Imputed Service Charges	- 41 991	- 45 572	- 50 618	- 52 353	- 54 080	- 57 313	- 62 669	- 66 735	- 72 834	Moins services d'intermédiation financière
Gross domestic product at factor cost / basic prices	2 214 834	2 371 493	2 674 923	2 803 844	2 921 078	3 105 959	3 483 917	3 710 071	3 973 183	Produit intérieur brut aux couts des facteurs / prix de base
Plus: indirect taxes / taxes on products, less subsidies	245 410	267 482	295 621	305 290	328 810	333 812	367 133	394 036	428 973	Plus taxes indirectes/impôts sur les produits, moins les subventions
EXPENDITURE ON GROSS DOMESTIC PRODUCT AT CURRENT PURCHASER'S VALUES *CFA FRANC (MILLIONS)*										**EMPLOI DU PRODUIT INTÉRIEUR BRUT AUX PRIX COURANTS D'ACQUISITION** *FRANC CFA (MILLIONS)*
Government final consumption	297 902	323 720	351 916	374 464	385 434	400 039	436 358	461 719	491 550	Consommation finale des administrations publiques
Private final consumption	1 884 542	2 002 999	2 232 294	2 364 709	2 491 328	2 631 387	2 962 097	3 148 286	3 495 945	Consommation finale privée
Gross fixed capital formation	481 079	526 031	602 519	651 625	665 987	712 864	766 206	1 078 327	863 151	Formation brute de capital fixe
Change in inventories	24 613	18 980	13 124	8 133	17 014	29 532	33 314	40 768	7 629	Variation des stocks
Exports of goods and services	454 530	515 773	587 634	490 792	490 792	490 636	589 114	749 935	812 804	Exportations de biens et services
Less imports of goods and services	682 423	748 529	816 944	780 590	800 667	824 687	936 039	1 374 928	1 268 923	Moins importations de biens et services
GDP at purchasers' values	2 460 244	2 638 975	2 970 544	3 109 134	3 249 888	3 439 771	3 851 050	4 104 106	4 402 156	PIB aux prix d'acquisition
GROSS DOMESTIC PRODUCT BY KIND OF ECONOMIC ACTIVITY AT CONSTANT PRICES *ANNUAL GROWTH RATES (%)*										**PRODUIT INTÉRIEUR BRUT PAR BRANCHE D'ACTIVITÉ ECONOMIQUE AUX PRIX CONSTANTS** *TAUX DE CROISSANCE ANNUEL (%)*
Agriculture, hunting, forestry and fishing	5.6	4.2	3.6	2.5	1.5	5.2	6.4	6.3	5.2	Agriculture, chasse, sylviculture et pêche
Mining and quarrying	6.0	7.0	8.0	3.0	0.2	6.0	4.0	3.5	6.0	Industries extractives
Manufacturing	- 3.6	2.6	3.3	2.6	4.3	1.0	3.0	4.8	6.0	Industries manufacturières
Electricity, gas & water	2.4	- 1.2	1.0	7.7	7.9	4.6	5.9	4.8	6.0	Electricité, gaz et eau
Construction & public works	6.0	7.2	8.2	3.0	0.0	6.0	3.9	3.4	6.0	Bâtiments et travaux publics
Wholesale & retail trade, restaurants, hotels	3.0	5.8	8.4	- 0.1	1.6	0.7	5.6	6.4	6.6	Commerce de gros et de détail, restaurants et hôtels
Finance, insurance, real estate, etc.	3.7	5.4	5.9	3.1	3.5	3.5	4.6	4.8	6.3	Banques, assurances, affaires immobilières
Transport and communications	4.0	6.0	7.0	8.6	3.1	3.3	6.6	5.8	6.6	Transport(s) et communications
Public administration and defense	4.8	4.6	5.0	4.7	3.3	2.9	4.5	4.4	1.5	Administrations publiques et défense
Education	...	...	...	...	...	...	...	...	...	Education
Health and Social Work	...	...	...	...	...	...	...	...	...	Santé et actions sociales
Other services	...	...	...	...	...	...	...	...	...	Autres services
Less Imputed Service Charges	5.0	6.4	6.8	1.4	3.3	3.9	7.2	4.4	7.0	Moins services d'intermédiation financière
Gross domestic product at factor cost / basic prices	3.8	4.6	5.0	2.9	2.3	3.6	5.4	5.6	5.3	Produit intérieur brut aux couts des facteurs / prix de base
Plus: indirect taxes / taxes on products, less subsidies	3.3	4.9	5.0	- 0.5	5.9	- 0.3	5.3	5.8	6.2	Plus taxes indirectes/impôts sur les produits, moins les subventions
Gross domestic product at market prices	3.8	4.6	5.0	2.7	2.6	3.3	5.4	5.6	5.4	Produit intérieur brut aux prix du marché
EXPENDITURE ON GROSS DOMESTIC PRODUCT AT CONSTANT PURCHASERS' VALUES *ANNUAL GROWTH RATES (%)*										**EMPLOIS DU PRODUIT INTÉRIEUR BRUT AUX PRIX CONSTANTS D'ACQUISITION** *TAUX DE CROISSANCE ANNUEL (%)*
Government final consumption	3.5	4.1	4.9	4.6	2.9	2.7	4.3	4.2	1.7	Consommation finale des administrations publiques
Private final consumption	0.4	2.6	3.6	3.0	3.1	3.1	4.7	4.8	13.9	Consommation finale privée
Gross fixed capital formation	17.9	6.0	8.3	2.7	- 5.9	5.4	4.6	45.0	- 24.3	Formation brute de capital fixe
Exports of goods and services	- 5.0	13.3	11.0	- 5.0	3.0	- 1.1	9.0	12.0	7.4	Exportations de biens et services
Less imports of goods and services	2.0	8.0	7.0	- 3.0	0.8	- 1.0	10.0	27.5	5.4	Moins importations de biens et services

III INFLATION

	2006	2007	2008	2009	2010	2011	2012	2013	2014	
ANNUAL GROWTH RATES (%)										**TAUX DE CROISSANCE ANNUEL (%)**
All items	3.8	1.3	7.9	0.4	2.1	2.7	6.7	1.0	-1.1	Ensemble
of which:										dont:
Food and Non-alcoholic beverages	-0.5	-0.8	18.0	2.4	4.0	5.7	4.7	2.6	-0.9	Alimentation et boissons non alcoolisés
Alcoholic beverages & tobacco	0.7	1.0	3.5	5.4	-0.1	1.2	2.5	0.8	0.9	Boissons alcoolisées et tabacs
Clothing and Footwear	1.6	-1.1	0.2	-0.1	2.4	1.4	0.5	0.8	0.5	Habillement et chaussures
Housing, Water, Electricity, Gas and Other Fuels	7.0	-0.4	4.9	4.7	5.4	2.1	1.6	-0.5	1.0	Logement, eau, electricité, gas et autres combustibles
Furnishing, household equipment	-2.3	1.3	3.1	0.5	-0.1	1.1	1.6	1.2	-0.1	Meubles, articles de ménage et entretien courant
Health	-1.4	1.1	2.4	0.6	1.8	0.3	1.4	0.3	-0.1	Santé
Transport	11.6	8.9	5.1	-7.1	3.0	2.4	31.7	-0.3	-6.9	Transport
Communication	161.1	-	0.5	-14.7	-3.3	-5.9	-2.0	0.0	-0.8	Communication
Recreation & culture	4.7	-1.1	-2.2	-2.8	0.2	0.6	-0.4	-0.7	-0.1	Loisirs et culture
Education	-2.8	-	0.2	2.2	-1.5	0.6	0.3	0.0	-0.3	Enseignement
Restaurants & hotels	-1.2	2.6	0.8	5.8	0.3	2.7	3.0	0.9	1.6	Restaurants et hôtels
Miscellaneous goods & services	2.0	-0.2	0.9	5.7	-3.5	2.2	9.5	0.8	0.3	Biens et services divers

IV AGRICULTURAL PRODUCTION - PRODUCTION AGRICOLE	2006	2007	2008	2009	2010	2011	2012	2013	2014	
TONNES *(THOUSAND)*										**TONNES** *(MILLIERS)*
Cassava	2 809	2 284	3 611	3 996	3 445	3 915	3 296	3 796	4 627	Manioc
Yams	1 577	1 682	2 529	2 374	2 624	2 934	2 739	3 178	3 601	Ignames
Maize	864	932	978	1 205	1 013	1 437	1 175	1 401	1 577	Maïs
Seed cotton	250	269	210	166	137	174	240	306	423	Graines de coton
Sorghum	133	117	142	123	157	158	134	115	403	Sorgho

V MINING PRODUCTION - PRODUCTION MINIERE	2006	2007	2008	2009	2010	2011	2012	2013	2014	
Gold ores and concentrantes (Kilograms)	...	19	20	20	20	20	...	...	...	Minerais d'or et concentrés (kilogrammes)
Salt and pure sodium chloride, metric tons (thousands)	15	15	...	...	...	...	...	...	...	Sel et chlorure de sodium pur, tonnes métriques (milliers)
	...	...	...	...	...	...	...	...	...	

VI ENERGY - ENERGIE	2006	2007	2008	2009	2010	2011	2012	2013	2014	
Total electricity generation (GWh)	329	410	233	140	152	155	162	162	...	Production d'électricité totale (GWh)
of which:										dont:
Production of electricity from fossil fuels (GWh)	324	406	229	138	150	153	160	160	...	Production d'électricité à partir de combustibles fossiles (GWh)
Production of hydro electricity (GWh)	1	1	1	1	1	1	1	1	...	Production d'électricité d'origine hydraulique (GWh)
Production of electricity from solar, wind, tide, wave and other sources (GWh)	...	...	...	...	...	...	...	...	...	Production d'électricité d'origine solaire, éolienne, marée motrice et autres (GWh)

VII TOURISM AND INFRASTRUCTURE - TOURISME ET INFRASTRUCTURE	2006	2007	2008	2009	2010	2011	2012	2013	2014	
VII-1 TOURISM										**VII-1 TOURISME**
International tourist arrivals (thousands)	180	186	188	190	199	209	220	232	238	Arrivées de touristes internationaux (milliers)
Rooms in hotels and similar establishments (thousands)	20.32	20.32	20.32	20.32	20.32	...	...	...	...	Chambres d'hotels et établissements assimilés (milliers)
Overnight stays (thousands)	3 991	4 225	4 488	4 720	5 163	5 473	6 264	6 521	6 606	Nuitées (milliers)
Tourism receipts (US$ thousand)	115 800	206 400	235 500	131 000	148 900	177 000	169 600	193 964	205 933	Recettes touristiques (milliers de $ EU)
Total contribution to GDP (%)	6.7	8.1	7.8	6.5	6.5	7.1	6.6	6.5	6.6	Contribution totale au PIB (%)
Total contribution to Employment (%)	5.9	7.1	6.8	5.7	5.6	6.2	5.7	5.7	5.8	Contribution totale à l'emploi (%)
VII-2 INFRASTRUCTURE										**VII-2 INFRASTRUCTURE**
Paved roads (% of total)	30	30	30	35	36	...	...	...	...	Routes asphaltées (% du total)
Total Network (Railways-km)	758	758	758	...	...	...	...	...	...	Réseau total voies ferrées-Km
Main Telephone Lines (per 100 inhabitants)	1	1	1	1	1	2	2	2	...	Lignes téléphoniques fixes (pour 100 habitants)
Mobile Cellular Subscribers (per 100 inhabitants)	13	24	40	54	74	79	84	93	...	Abonnés aux téléphones mobiles (pour 100 habitants)

VIII EXTERNAL TRADE - COMMERCE EXTERIEUR	2006	2007	2008	2009	2010	2011	2012	2013	2014	
CFA FRANC (MILLIONS) Exports, fob										**FRANC CFA (MILLIONS) EXPORTATIONS, FÀB**
Exports - Total	116 706	130 844	188 197	199 231	264 902	184 033	234 366	286 675	466 910	Exportations - Total
Exports to AFRICA	49 753	50 156	93 147	116 135	170 609	84 325	103 519	102 191	192 838	Exportations vers l'AFRIQUE
Main Products										**Principaux produits**
Cotton, not carded, or combed	47 118	60 660	70 000	60 101	56 000	52 678	76 042	116 202	143 709	Coton, non cardé ni peigné
Cashew	8 602	8 347	12 493	13 838	47 047	24 627	30 657	38 038	49 906	Noix de cajou
Palm oil	2 128	1 194	3 387	7 607	4 522	6 864	7 159	9 950	10 741	Huile de palme
Palm kernel cake	...	...	14 852	17 694	17 862	20 321	19 093	17 130	40 771	Tourteaux de palmiste
Cottonseed meal	2 094	2 977	3 939	2 822	16 111	6 992	9 977	10 588	23 663	Tourteaux de coton
Main Destinations										**Principales destinations**
China	28 026	31 363	31 317	36 864	112 146	28 711	58 943	59 336	70 510	Chine
India	10 078	15 313	17 163	16 390	26 535	21 827	30 477	35 007	46 680	Inde
Chad	1 872	2 175	8 702	10 720	12 317	19 211	26 284	25 855	40 598	Tchad
Nigeria	10 160	18 152	39 491	79 504	10 731	18 050	20 528	21 531	27 740	Nigéria
Indonesia	2 041	4 321	10 989	4 071	10 454	13 098	16 364	19 112	20 778	Indonésie
IMPORTS, CIF										**IMPORTATIONS, CAF**
Imports - Total	526 948	781 792	767 122	731 436	1 055 127	976 446	1 180 017	1 446 100	1 761 197	Importations - Total (millions)
Imports from Africa	...	...	...	...	205 094	230 529	264 920	276 032	312 211	Importations en provenance de l'Afrique
Main Products										**Principaux produits**
Meat, fresh, chilled or frozen poultry	23 025	36 832	55 294	68 302	156 014	91 003	182 351	294 297	503 855	Viandes et abats comestibles, volailles frais, refrigérés ou congelés
Petroleum oils & oils obtained from bituminous minerals,o/than crude etc	80 523	127 206	76 195	72 322	142 467	87 270	160 778	128 693	171 716	Huiles de pétrole ou de minéraux bitumineux
Rice	58 889	101 025	82 661	43 200	80 133	71 542	111 590	113 936	120 952	Riz
Electricity	29 570	29 069	33 264	45 742	63 338	58 957	62 246	67 609	74 743	Energie électrique
Palm oil and its fractions refined but not chemically modified	15 383	27 593	34 440	31 711	56 058	48 682	51 624	48 873	68 815	Huile de palme et ses fractions, raffinées, mais non chimiquement modifiées
Main Origin										**Principales provenances**
France	91 513	136 287	128 949	128 211	155 040	149 212	162 180	169 447	235 521	France
Togo	57	63	54	80	108	111	117	164	224	Togo
China	45	78	102	98	91	89	98	146	146	Chine
Netherlands	14	24	30	37	84	48	61	146	136	Pays-Bas
United Kingdom	33	43	23	28	60	44	56	97	127	Royaume-Uni

IX FINANCIAL AND MONETARY STATISTICS - FINANCES ET STATISTIQUES MONETAIRES	2006	2007	2008	2009	2010	2011	2012	2013	2014	
IX-1 MONETARY STATISTICS *CFA FRANC (MILLIONS)*										**IX-1 STATISTIQUES MONÉTAIRES** *FRANC CFA (MILLIONS)*
Money supply (M1)	805 060	947 030	1 219 970	1 295 920	1 446 120	1 578 410	1 719 980	2 017 150	2 362 080	Masse monétaire (M1)
Quasi-money	223 606	279 472	350 100	424 330	466 744	507 543	590 633	638 182	761 576	Quasi-monnaie
of which Demand Deposit	...	...	...	...	...	...	...	...	...	dont Monnaie scripturale
Net foreign assets	525 485	671 945	700 332	657 785	735 182	719 363	792 007	910 536	1 070 079	Avoirs extérieurs nets
Domestic credit	255 069	231 973	442 261	599 334	593 701	747 748	760 412	880 445	968 088	Crédit intérieur
of which claims on private sector	415 821	519 922	624 350	698 548	757 818	844 960	924 440	1 022 582	1 084 250	dont créances sur le secteur privé
of which claims on government sector, net	- 160 752	- 287 949	- 182 089	- 99 214	- 164 117	- 97 212	- 164 028	- 142 137	- 116 162	dont créances nettes sur le gouvernement
International reserves (millions US$)	912	1 209	1 263	1 230	1 200	887	713	695	894	Réserves internationales (millions $EU)
Average Exchange Rate (National Currency per US$)	522.90	478.89	446.87	471.07	494.68	471.42	510.18	493.94	493.28	Taux de change (moyen) (monnaie nationale par $ EU)
IX-2 PUBLIC FINANCE *CFA FRANC (MILLIONS)*										**IX-2 FINANCES PUBLIQUES** *FRANC CFA (MILLIONS)*
Total Revenues and Grants	472 597	626 940	633 300	675 800	651 100	692 700	797 470	873 600	928 000	Recettes totales et dons
Tax Revenue	378 797	446 740	512 200	500 315	525 900	534 700	598 170	668 100	732 000	Recettes fiscales
Non Tax Revenue	38 100	101 300	69 100	75 384	77 100	70 900	124 400	127 300	90 700	Recettes non fiscales
Grants	55 700	78 900	52 000	100 100	48 100	87 100	74 900	78 200	105 300	Dons
Total Expenditures and Net Lending	483 800	622 356	684 538	809 000	702 200	754 700	815 760	952 000	942 940	Dépenses totales et prêts nets
Current expenditure	369 200	423 756	465 038	494 000	504 400	515 600	592 430	651 400	648 100	Dépenses courantes
Of which Wages and Salaries	135 000	143 100	182 438	225 900	238 700	253 200	279 360	300 300	310 000	Dont rémunérations et salaires
Capital expenditure	113 400	198 400	174 700	302 300	177 200	226 600	217 300	288 100	294 840	Dépenses d'équipement
Net Lending	1 200	200	44 800	12 700	20 600	12 500	6 030	12 500	-	Prêts nets
Fiscal Balance	- 11 203	4 584	- 51 238	- 133 200	- 51 100	- 62 000	- 18 290	- 78 400	- 14 940	Solde global y compris les dons
IX-3 BALANCE OF PAYMENTS *CFA FRANC (MILLIONS)*										**IX-3 BALANCE DES PAIEMENTS** *FRANC CFA (MILLIONS)*
Trade balance	- 257 300	- 378 900	- 406 400	- 351 000	- 308 900	- 355 000	- 472 800	- 754 300	...	Balance commerciale
Services Balance	- 44 844	- 34 088	9 300	- 63 200	- 34 000	- 22 000	- 7 300	- 26 300	...	Balance des services
Net Income	- 15 400	- 4 300	- 5 100	- 15 500	- 26 500	- 7 000	- 24 600	- 29 600	...	Revenus nets
Compensation of employees	...	...	...	...	...	...	...	...	...	Rémunération des salariés
Investment Income	...	...	...	...	...	...	...	...	...	Revenus des investissements
Current transfers, net total	154 900	148 700	162 000	152 100	132 300	115 000	200 400	216 100	...	Transferts courants
Net official transfers	...	...	...	...	...	...	...	...	...	Transferts officiels nets
Workers' remittances	...	...	...	...	...	...	...	...	...	Envois de fonds des travailleurs
Other private transfers	...	...	...	...	...	...	...	...	...	Autres transferts privés
Current account balance	- 162 644	- 268 588	- 240 200	- 277 600	- 237 100	- 269 000	- 304 300	- 594 100	...	Solde du compte courant
Capital & financial account	...	...	...	...	...	...	...	...	...	Comptes de capital et financier
Capital account	...	...	...	...	...	...	...	...	...	Compte de capital
Financial account	...	...	...	...	...	...	...	...	...	Compte financier
Errors & omissions	...	...	...	...	...	...	...	...	...	Erreurs et omissions
Overall balance	...	...	...	...	...	...	...	...	...	Balance générale

X DEBT AND FINANCIAL FLOWS - DETTE ET FLUX FINANCIERS	2006	2007	2008	2009	2010	2011	2012	2013	2014	
X-1 DEBT *US$ (MILLIONS)*										**X-1 DETTE EXTÉRIEURE** *$ E.U (MILLIONS)*
Total external debt	544	698	1 040	1 070	1 187	1 233	1 278	1 580	1 679	Dette extérieure totale
Private	-	-	-	-	-	-	-	-	-	Privée
Public	544	698	1 040	1 070	1 187	1 233	1 278	1 580	1 679	Publique
Total external debt service	66	94	27	39	48	55	71	79	104	Service de la dette extérieure
Present value of External debt	...	...	...	...	...	...	...	...	...	Valeur actuelle de la dette extérieure
Total government domestic debt (in local currency)	...	...	...	...	...	...	...	...	...	Dette publique intérieure
X-2 FINANCIAL FLOWS *US$ (MILLIONS)*										**X-2 FLUX FINANCIERS** *$ E.U (MILLIONS)*
Net Foreign Direct Investment Inflows	53	255	170	134	177	161	282	320	...	Investissement étranger direct (flux nets entrants)
Main origin of FDI Inflows										**Principales origines de l'IDE entrant:**
France	6	...	...	...	...	...	...	...	...	France
United States	6	- 8	2	- 10	...	...	...	...	...	États-Unis
Korea	...	...	...	...	...	...	...	...	...	Corée
Denmark	...	8	- 2	...	...	...	...	...	...	Danemark
Sweden	...	...	- 1	- 3	- 0.1	9.7	9.0	9.0	...	Suède
African countries	...	...	...	...	...	...	...	...	...	Pays africains
Net total Official Development Assistance	399	474	641	682	689	690	511	653	...	Aide publique au développement (nette totale)
Main origin of Net ODA										**Principales origines de l'APD nette**
France	74	56	66	50	48.8	41.5	41.4	38.1	...	France
IDA	43	28	62	93	90.3	85.3	64.5	73.5	...	IDA
United States	20	25	35	59	98.9	206.2	44.1	24.2	...	Etats-Unis
Denmark	33	45	48	51	39.1	36.2	31.7	16.7	...	Danemark
AfDF	30	70	48	32	46.1	46.5	40.9	18.0	...	FAfD

BOTSWANA

BOTSWANA

AREA (km²)		**581 730**	**SUPERFICIE (km²)**
CAPITAL CITY	**Gaborone**	**Gaberone**	**CAPITALE**
CURRENCY	**Botswana Pula**	**Pula Botswanais**	**MONNAIE**

I SOCIAL AND DEMOGRAPHIC INDICATORS — INDICATEURS DEMOGRAPHIQUES ET SOCIAUX

	Year / Année	Value / Valeur	
POPULATION			**POPULATION**
Population ('000)			Population ('000)
Both sexes	2014	2 144	Les deux sexes
Male	2014	1 036	Masculin
Female	2014	1 109	Féminin
Average annual growth rate	2014	1.9	Taux de croissance annuel
Active Population ('000)	2014	1 071	Population active ('000)
Population by age group ('000)			Population par groupe d'âge ('000)
0-14 years	2014	800.0	0-14 ans
15-64 years	2014	1 304	15-64 ans
65+ years	2014	141	65+ ans
Economically. active population. in agriculture (%)	2014	25.0	Participation de la population active agricole (%)
Crude birth rate	2014	25.7	Taux brut de natalité
Crude death rate	2014	6.3	Taux brut de mortalité
Total fertility rate	2014	2.7	Indice synthétique de fécondité
Proportion of urban population	2014	63.0	Part de la population urbaine
Life Expectancy at Birth - Total (years)	2014	68.0	Espérance de vie à la naissance - Totale (ans)
Dependency Ratio - Total (%)	2014	60.0	Taux de dépendance - Total (%)
HEALTH			**SANTÉ**
Percentage of children under-five and underweight	2008	11.2	% d'enfants de moins de cinq ans avec insuffisance pondérale
Prevalence of undernourishment	2013	26.6	Prévalence de la malnutrition
Under five mortality rate (both sexes, per 1000)	2012	46.4	Taux de mortalité de moins de 5 ans (les deux sexes, pour 1000)
Infant mortality rate (both sexes) per 1000	2013	35.0	Taux de mortalité infantile (les deux sexes) par 1000
Percentage of children provided the vaccines :			Pourcentage d'enfants vaccinés :
BCG	2014	91.0	BCG
DPT3	2014	95.0	DTC3
Polio	2014	89.0	Polio
Measles	2014	91.0	Rougeole
Percentage of mothers provided at least one antenatal care (%)	2007	94.4	Pourcentage de mères ayant au moins reçu un soin prénatal (%)
Percentage of deliveries attended by skilled health personnel	2007	94.6	% d'accouchements assistés par un personnel de santé qualifié
Number of doctors (per 10 000 population)	2006	3.4	Nombre de médecins (pour 10 000 habitants)
Number of nurses (per 10 000 population)	2006	28.4	Nombre d'infirmières (pour 10 000 habitants)
Hospital beds - Total (per 10 000 population)	2011	26.0	Nombre de lits d'hôpitaux - Total (pour 10 000)
Births registered (per 1 000)	2012	23.0	Naiss.s enregistrées (pour 1 000)
Deaths registered (per 1 000)	2012	13.5	Décès enregistrés (pour 1 000)
Public expenditure on Health (% of budget)	2009	16.7	Dépenses publiques consacrées à la santé (% du budget)
EDUCATION			**EDUCATION**
Enrolment in primary education (both sexes) (000)	2012	337	Scolarisation dans le primaire (les deux sexes) (000)
Female	2012	165	Féminin
Enrolment in secondary education (both sexes) (000)	2012	173	Scolarisation dans le secondaire (les deux sexes) (000)
Female	2012	89	Féminin
Enrolment in tertiary education (both sexes) (000)	2010	51.2	Scolarisation dans le tertiaire (les deux sexes) (000)
Female	2011	22.6	Féminin
Literacy rate (both sexes)	2012	86.7	Taux d'alphabétisation (deux sexes)
Male	2012	86.3	Masculin
Female	2012	87.1	Féminin
Pupil-teacher ratio	2012	24.0	Ratio élève-enseignant
Public expenditure on education (% of budget)	2009	16.2	Dépenses publiques consacrées à l'enseignement (% du budget)
POVERTY			**PAUVRETÉ**
GNI Per Capita (US$)	2013	7 770.0	RNB par habitant ($EU)
Human Poverty Index (HPI-1) Value (%)	2007	22.9	Valeur de l'Indice de pauvreté (IPH-1) (%)
Population below International Poverty Line ($2/day) (%)	2009	27.8	Population sous le seuil international de pauvreté (2$/J) (%)
Share of Income Held by Richest 10%	2009	49.6	% de revenu des 10% plus riches
Share of Income Held by Poorest 10%	2009	1.1	% de revenu des 10% plus pauvres
Gini index	2009	60.5	Indice de Gini

Charts / Graphiques

Population by age group – 2014
Population par groupe d'age – 2014

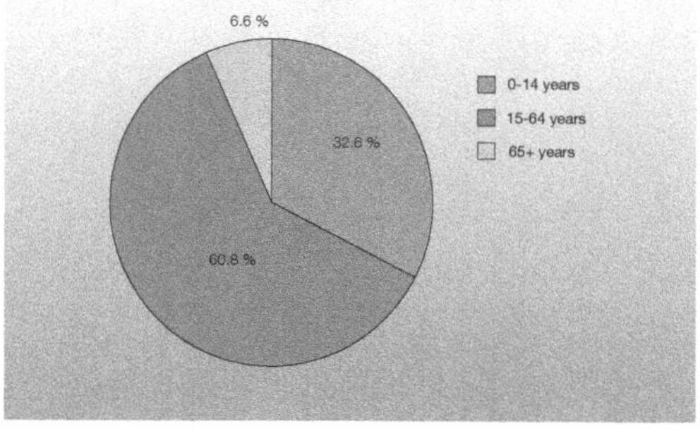

Percentage of children provided the vaccines – 2014
Pourcentage d'enfants vaccinés – 2014

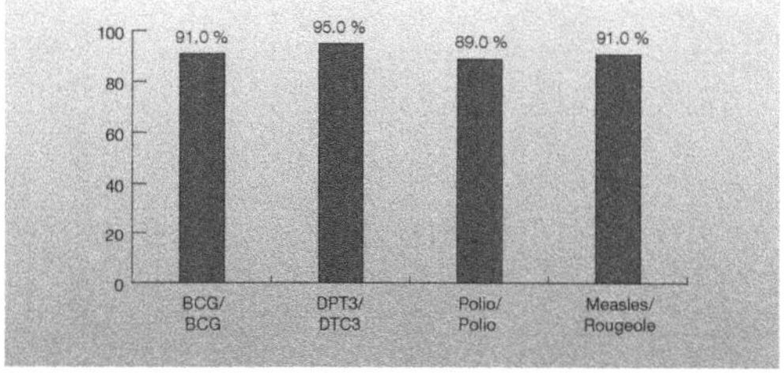

Literacy rate (%) – 2012
Taux d'alphabétisation – 2012

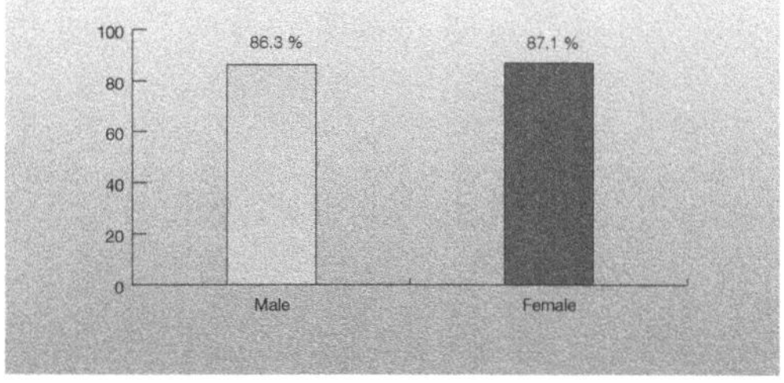

GNI Per Capita (US$)
RNB par habitant ($EU)

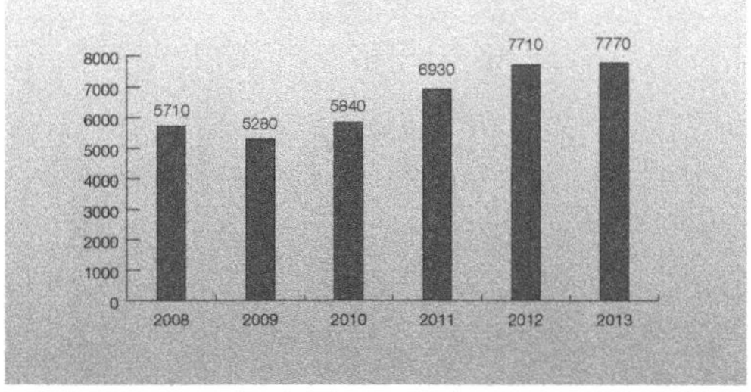

II NATIONAL ACCOUNTS — COMPTES NATIONAUX

	2006	2007	2008	2009	2010	2011	2012	2013	2014	
GROSS DOMESTIC PRODUCT BY KIND OF ECONOMIC ACTIVITY AT CURRENT PRICES *BOTSWANA PULA (MILLIONS)*										**PRODUIT INTÉRIEUR BRUT PAR BRANCHE D'ACTIVITÉ ÉCONOMIQUE AUX PRIX COURANTS** *PULA BOTSWANAIS (MILLIONS)*
Agriculture, hunting, forestry and fishing	1 211	1 505	1 888	2 071	2 161	2 636	2 961	2 877	3 045	Agriculture, chasse, sylviculture et pêche
Mining and quarrying	19 019	19 568	18 644	11 210	16 661	26 792	21 998	27 568	32 557	Industries extractives
Manufacturing	3 123	4 207	4 279	4 662	5 548	6 074	6 523	7 285	7 736	Industries manufacturières
Electricity, gas & water	785	752	654	317	412	- 59	- 675	- 350	- 144	Electricité, gaz et eau
Construction & public works	2 838	3 544	3 727	4 495	5 056	6 247	7 465	7 998	8 690	Bâtiments et travaux publics
Wholesale & retail trade, restaurants, hotels	7 032	8 244	10 047	11 163	13 084	15 595	16 897	18 535	21 033	Commerce de gros et de détail, restaurants et hôtels
Finance, insurance, real estate, etc.	6 675	7 653	9 317	9 695	11 610	13 979	16 645	17 948	19 813	Banques, assurances, affaires immobilières
Transport and communications	2 251	2 697	3 304	3 993	4 471	5 114	6 325	6 906	7 787	Transport(s) et communications
Public administration and defense	7 819	8 887	10 900	12 316	13 377	14 778	16 924	17 731	20 055	Administrations publiques et défense
Education	...	...	...	...	...	...	...	...	...	Education
Health and Social Work	...	...	...	...	...	...	...	...	...	Santé et actions sociales
Other services	2 939	3 256	3 847	4 593	5 243	5 881	6 750	7 344	8 139	Autres services
Less Imputed Service Charges	...	...	...	...	...	...	...	...	...	Moins services d'intermédiation financière
Gross domestic product at factor cost / basic prices	53 692	60 312	66 606	64 515	77 623	97 038	101 812	113 841	128 710	Produit intérieur brut aux couts des facteurs / prix de base
Plus: indirect taxes / taxes on products, less subsidies	5 415	6 841	8 116	8 947	9 244	10 205	10 892	11 969	13 232	Plus taxes indirectes/impôts sur les produits, moins les subventions
EXPENDITURE ON GROSS DOMESTIC PRODUCT AT CURRENT PURCHASER'S VALUES *BOTSWANA PULA (MILLIONS)*										**EMPLOI DU PRODUIT INTÉRIEUR BRUT AUX PRIX COURANTS D'ACQUISITION** *PULA BOTSWANAIS (MILLIONS)*
Government final consumption	10 071	11 815	15 207	15 493	17 162	19 407	21 196	23 463	23 488	Consommation finale des administrations publiques
Private final consumption	22 983	25 307	36 486	41 921	43 543	54 638	66 602	61 534	65 565	Consommation finale privée
Gross fixed capital formation	15 487	19 062	22 852	25 646	29 202	33 641	39 867	40 999	42 157	Formation brute de capital fixe
Change in inventories	- 175	1 616	4 188	2 954	6 772	6 856	2 947	- 116	1 495	Variation des stocks
Exports of goods and services	30 886	36 609	34 128	25 566	33 377	47 621	47 833	68 291	70 695	Exportations de biens et services
Less imports of goods and services	20 144	27 256	38 139	38 116	43 188	54 920	65 740	68 362	61 457	Moins importations de biens et services
GDP at purchasers' values	59 107	67 153	74 721	73 462	86 868	107 243	112 705	125 810	141 942	PIB aux prix d'acquisition
GROSS DOMESTIC PRODUCT BY KIND OF ECONOMIC ACTIVITY AT CONSTANT PRICES *ANNUAL GROWTH RATES (%)*										**PRODUIT INTÉRIEUR BRUT PAR BRANCHE D'ACTIVITÉ ECONOMIQUE AUX PRIX CONSTANTS** *TAUX DE CROISSANCE ANNUEL (%)*
Agriculture, hunting, forestry and fishing	13.3	12.2	2.0	6.4	5.8	0.2	- 8.5	1.3	- 0.3	Agriculture, chasse, sylviculture et pêche
Mining and quarrying	5.1	- 4.8	0.3	- 42.4	20.4	- 6.5	- 4.6	23.9	4.5	Industries extractives
Manufacturing	20.0	25.7	- 2.6	5.0	3.9	11.4	3.7	6.5	0.4	Industries manufacturières
Electricity, gas & water	3.0	- 4.9	6.6	- 5.2	12.0	- 34.2	- 32.2	12.0	- 18.5	Electricité, gaz et eau
Construction & public works	15.9	23.2	0.8	12.3	3.6	23.1	14.4	5.1	2.8	Bâtiments et travaux publics
Wholesale & retail trade, restaurants, hotels	27.4	15.2	18.0	3.9	9.3	13.8	6.8	7.7	7.1	Commerce de gros et de détail, restaurants et hôtels
Finance, insurance, real estate, etc.	4.9	11.2	11.7	1.5	11.5	7.7	10.7	7.2	3.1	Banques, assurances, affaires immobilières
Transport and communications	13.8	15.4	10.2	14.8	6.4	6.1	10.9	5.4	7.4	Transport(s) et communications
Public administration and defense	- 2.2	5.6	0.2	2.8	7.5	6.3	2.8	6.0	5.2	Administrations publiques et défense
Education	...	...	...	...	...	...	...	...	...	Education
Health and Social Work	...	...	...	...	...	...	...	...	...	Santé et actions sociales
Other services	13.8	8.2	15.2	11.3	6.2	8.3	10.7	8.0	4.2	Autres services
Less Imputed Service Charges	...	...	...	...	...	...	...	...	...	Moins services d'intérmediation financière
Gross domestic product at factor cost / basic prices	8.7	6.5	5.5	- 9.1	10.2	6.1	4.9	9.5	4.4	Produit intérieur brut aux couts des facteurs / prix de base
Plus: indirect taxes / taxes on products, less subsidies	5.4	25.5	12.6	3.4	- 2.8	5.8	4.3	7.7	4.9	Plus taxes indirectes/impôts sur les produits, moins les subventions
Gross domestic product at market prices	8.4	8.3	6.2	- 7.7	8.6	6.0	4.8	9.3	4.4	Produit intérieur brut aux prix du marché
EXPENDITURE ON GROSS DOMESTIC PRODUCT AT CONSTANT PURCHASERS' VALUES *ANNUAL GROWTH RATES (%)*										**EMPLOIS DU PRODUIT INTÉRIEUR BRUT AUX PRIX CONSTANTS D'ACQUISITION** *TAUX DE CROISSANCE ANNUEL (%)*
Government final consumption	- 4.0	3.5	5.0	3.0	3.7	5.0	15.1	14.0	- 1.9	Consommation finale des administrations publiques
Private final consumption	21.8	17.6	23.4	9.5	- 5.8	7.1	19.9	- 0.8	- 7.3	Consommation finale privée
Gross fixed capital formation	7.0	11.3	3.3	9.5	9.2	12.2	13.6	- 6.8	15.3	Formation brute de capital fixe
Exports of goods and services	3.1	8.5	- 2.5	- 37.7	16.0	27.5	4.2	30.0	0.6	Exportations de biens et services
Less imports of goods and services	0.0	25.0	17.5	- 10.9	6.5	19.2	28.7	1.6	- 5.8	Moins importations de biens et services
Notes	NA Data: 2013-2014 estimates are provisional					Données CN: 2013-2014 les estimations sont provisoires				Notes

III INFLATION

	2006	2007	2008	2009	2010	2011	2012	2013	2014	
ANNUAL GROWTH RATES (%)										**TAUX DE CROISSANCE ANNUEL (%)**
All items	11.6	7.1	12.6	8.1	6.9	8.5	7.5	5.9	4.4	Ensemble
of which:										dont:
Food and Non-alcoholic beverages	12.5	11.2	20.2	14.7	3.6	6.9	8.0	5.4	3.0	Alimentation et boissons non alcoolisés
Alcoholic beverages & tobacco	13.0	10.1	13.2	35.2	7.1	8.4	7.6	10.3	9.0	Boissons alcoolisées et tabacs
Clothing and Footwear	1.0	1.6	2.0	8.4	8.0	8.9	7.5	6.3	6.0	Habillement et chaussures
Housing, Water, Electricity, Gas and Other Fuels	4.9	4.8	8.1	4.8	6.4	8.4	7.7	4.3	3.9	Logement, eau, electricité, gas et autres combustibles
Furnishing, household equipment	9.7	6.8	6.0	11.9	9.4	9.0	7.3	4.9	5.0	Meubles, articles de ménage et entretien courant
Health	8.8	7.5	11.3	5.5	2.7	4.5	5.9	5.5	8.3	Santé
Transport	15.1	5.5	21.1	-8.4	12.1	13.2	10.8	7.3	1.2	Transport
Communication	...	...	-0.3	-0.3	1.2	-3.0	-1.4	0.3	0.3	Communication
Recreation & culture	2.8	-0.2	2.3	5.0	6.0	8.3	5.8	4.5	4.2	Loisirs et culture
Education	24.9	6.0	3.9	3.9	5.8	10.6	6.4	4.7	7.4	Enseignement
Restaurants & hotels	...	...	12.7	18.8	9.0	9.3	8.4	7.9	7.6	Restaurants et hôtels
Miscellaneous goods & services	3.5	2.8	4.9	3.8	7.0	5.3	2.0	1.2	5.2	Biens et services divers

IV AGRICULTURAL PRODUCTION - PRODUCTION AGRICOLE										
	2006	2007	2008	2009	2010	2011	2012	2013	2014	
TONNES *(THOUSAND)*										**TONNES** *(MILLIERS)*
Sorghum	26	27	24	30	33	45	25	23	...	Sorgho
Maize	15	2	9	20	11	29	20	15	...	Maïs
Sunflower seed	6	3	8	2	5	6	6	7	...	Tournesols
Groundnuts, with shell	1	0	1	2	2	5	6	6	...	Arachides, avec coquille
Cotton lint	1	0	1	0	0	0	0	0	...	Fibre de coton

V MINING PRODUCTION - PRODUCTION MINIERE										
	2006	2007	2008	2009	2010	2011	2012	2013	2014	
Hard Coal, metric tons (thousands)	962	828	910	738	988	788	1 454	1 496	1 712	Houille, tonnes métriques (milliers)
Coal, tons (thousands)	34 293	33 639	32 595	17 734	22 018	22 901	20 619	22 693	24 237	Cuivre, tonnes (milliers)
Diamonds and other precious stones, unworked, carat (thousands)	26	23	23	24	26	22	26	49	47	Diamants et autres pierres précieuses, bruts, carat (milliers)

VI ENERGY - ENERGIE										
	2006	2007	2008	2009	2010	2011	2012	2013	2014	
Total electricity generation (GWh)	1 042	659	583	444	430	699	2 257	2 626	...	Production d'électricité totale (GWh)
of which:										dont:
Production of electricity from fossil fuels (GWh)	1 042	659	583	444	430	694	2 250	2 617	...	Production d'électricité à partir de combustibles fossiles (GWh)
Production of hydro electricity (GWh)	...	...	...	...	...	...	...	...	...	Production d'électricité d'origine hydraulique (GWh)
Production of electricity from solar, wind, tide, wave and other sources (GWh)	...	...	...	...	...	5	8	9	...	Production d'électricité d'origine solaire, éolienne, marée motrice et autres (GWh)

VII TOURISM AND INFRASTRUCTURE - TOURISME ET INFRASTRUCTURE										
	2006	2007	2008	2009	2010	2011	2012	2013	2014	
VII-1 TOURISM										**VII-1 TOURISME**
International tourist arrivals (thousands)	1 426	1 736	2 101	2 103	2 145	2 244	2 374	2 498	2 594	Arrivées de touristes internationaux (milliers)
Rooms in hotels and similar establishments (thousands)	...	...	4.9	6.4	6.7	7.1	7.5	8.4		Chambres d'hotels et établissements assimilés (milliers)
Overnight stays (thousands)	12 580	9 049	11 058	11 715	12 054	12 593	13 333	13 782	14 089	Nuitées (milliers)
Tourism receipts (US$ thousand)	537 210	546 070	552 710	450 140	456 650	516 030	547 522	582 283	618 203	Recettes touristiques (milliers de $ EU)
Total contribution to GDP (%)	11.9	11.9	10.7	9.1	8.3	7.2	8.2	8.3	8.5	Contribution totale au PIB (%)
Total contribution to Employment (%)	12.8	13.1	12.6	10.7	9.8	8.5	9.7	9.8	10.1	Contribution totale à l'emploi (%)
VII-2 INFRASTRUCTURE										**VII-2 INFRASTRUCTURE**
Paved roads (% of total)	71	72	73	76	76	37	37	37	...	Routes asphaltées (% du total)
Total Network (Railways-km)	891	891	891	891	891	891	...	891	...	Réseau total voies ferrées-Km
Main Telephone Lines (per 100 inhabitants)	7	7	7	7	7	8	8	9	...	Lignes téléphoniques fixes (pour 100 habitants)
Mobile Cellular Subscribers (per 100 inhabitants)	43	60	77	96	120	146	154	161	...	Abonnés aux téléphones mobiles (pour 100 habitants)

VIII EXTERNAL TRADE - COMMERCE EXTERIEUR										
	2006	2007	2008	2009	2010	2011	2012	2013	2014	
US$ (MILLIONS) EXPORTS, FOB										**$ E.U (MILLIONS) EXPORTATIONS, FÀB**
Exports - Total	30 886	36 906	34 128	25 566	33 378	47 622	47 839	68 290	77 593	Exportations - Total
Exports to AFRICA	603	833	1 218	711	874	1 110	1 166	1 266	1 495	Exportations vers l'AFRIQUE
Main Products										**Principaux produits**
Diamonds	3 413	3 359	3 139	2 176	3 206	4 995	4 010	7 339	6 612	Diamants
Copper Nickel	650	905	885	514	618	510	708	550	333	Nickel de Cuivre
Beef	61	96	79	69	128	68	351	119	134	Bœuf
Soda ash	80	77	75	73	75	77	97	36	116	Carbonate de soude
Textiles	156	453	267	196	164	264	83	43	85	Textiles
Main Destinations										**Principales destinations**
United Kingdom	3 105	3 333	2 697	1 835	2 609	3 662	3 878	4 317	2 078	Royaume-Uni
Norway	435	553	193	334	438	280	319	339	1 236	Norvège
Zimbabwe	250	377	215	152	176	174	121	128	828	Zimbabwe
United States	87	51	48	45	57	63	78	122	685	États-Unis
South Africa	303	422	867	466	619	801	836	851	491	Afrique du Sud
IMPORTS, CIF										**IMPORTATIONS, CAF**
Imports - Total	19 577	29 064	38 140	38 116	43 189	54 920	65 740	68 361	76 548	Importations - Total (millions)
Imports from Africa	2 700	3 478	4 145	3 689	4 242	4 996	6 021	...	5 833	Importations en provenance de l'Afrique
Main Products										**Principaux produits**
Petroleum, petroleum products and related materials	451	538	819	528	953	1 043	2 113	1 294	2 502	Pétrole et produits dérivés
Road vehicles	256	450	558	428	435	624	634	562	1 212	Véhicules routiers
Non metallic mineral manufactures, n.e.s.	127	208	403	366	484	670	427	30	564	Articles minéraux non métalliques manufacturés, n.d.a.
Manufactures of metal, n.e.s.	150	202	246	200	239	362	355	351	562	Articles manufacturés en métal, n.d.a.
Electrical machinery, apparatus and appliances, n.e.s.	114	167	212	198	221	394	237	300	353	Machines et appareils électriques, n.d.a.
Main Origin										**Principales provenances**
Zimbabwe	48	52	48	38	38	49	46	38	49	Zimbabwe
China	37	72	151	154	306	797	240	110	882	Chine
United States	25	49	68	102	75	157	169	193	751	États-Unis
Sweden	19	23	29	29	10	23	45	16	312	Suède
United Kingdom	42	56	317	287	525	721	1 445	965	119	Royaume-Uni

IX FINANCIAL AND MONETARY STATISTICS - FINANCES ET STATISTIQUES MONETAIRES	2006	2007	2008	2009	2010	2011	2012	2013	2014	
IX-1 MONETARY STATISTICS *BOTSWANA PULA (MILLIONS)*										**IX-1 STATISTIQUES MONÉTAIRES** *PULA BOTSWANAIS (MILLIONS)*
Money supply (M1)	24 570	32 230	39 230	38 720	43 530	45 420	51 720	56 170	64 870	Masse monétaire (M1)
Quasi-money	19 411	26 058	31 459	31 609	33 596	36 088	38 247	38 250	40 815	Quasi-monnaie
of which Demand Deposit	...	...	...	...	...	...	...	...	...	dont Monnaie scripturale
Net foreign assets	48 773	60 545	72 780	59 270	52 550	63 610	63 682	71 886	86 316	Avoirs extérieurs nets
Domestic credit	- 8 817	- 12 383	- 10 233	- 818	9 440	8 381	16 412	16 861	11 034	Crédit intérieur
of which claims on private sector	12 108	15 220	19 268	21 254	23 622	28 781	35 091	39 800	45 346	dont créances sur le secteur privé
of which claims on government sector, net	- 21 224	- 27 833	- 29 730	- 22 404	- 14 580	- 22 726	- 21 096	- 26 909	- 37 893	dont créances nettes sur le gouvernement
International reserves (millions US$)	7 992	9 790	9 119	8 704	7 885	8 082	7 628	7 726	8 698	Réserves internationales (millions $EU)
Average Exchange Rate (National Currency per US$)	5.84	6.14	6.83	7.16	6.79	6.84	7.62	8.40	8.96	Taux de change (moyen) (monnaie nationale par $ EU)
IX-2 PUBLIC FINANCE *BOTSWANA PULA (MILLIONS)*										**IX-2 FINANCES PUBLIQUES** *PULA BOTSWANAIS (MILLIONS)*
Total Revenues and Grants	22 267	27 398	28 629	30 455	30 023	31 909	38 486	41 658	48 951	Recettes totales et dons
Tax Revenue	11 980	15 919	17 267	20 454	20 045	20 505	24 846	29 792	32 053	Recettes fiscales
Non Tax Revenue	10 174	11 030	10 785	9 378	9 209	11 076	13 107	11 359	16 573	Recettes non fiscales
Grants	113	448	577	623	769	329	533	507	326	Dons
Total Expenditures and Net Lending	17 632	19 737	24 822	35 151	39 489	38 417	38 667	40 736	41 730	Dépenses totales et prêts nets
Current expenditure	14 155	15 954	18 579	23 889	25 732	27 089	28 836	32 106	33 220	Dépenses courantes
Of which Wages and Salaries	5 216	5 801	6 850	8 701	9 252	11 899	12 941	14 548	13 348	Dont rémunérations et salaires
Capital expenditure	3 783	4 055	6 548	11 458	13 905	11 438	10 019	8 682	8 909	Dépenses d'équipement
Net Lending	- 306	- 272	- 305	- 197	- 147	- 110	- 188	- 52	- 399	Prêts nets
Fiscal Balance	4 635	7 660	3 808	- 4 696	- 9 466	- 6 508	- 181	922	7 222	Solde global y compris les dons
IX-3 BALANCE OF PAYMENTS *BOTSWANA PULA (MILLIONS)*										**IX-3 BALANCE DES PAIEMENTS** *PULA BOTSWANAIS (MILLIONS)*
Trade balance	10 159	7 094	- 2 574	- 9 480	- 6 825	- 4 982	- 14 772	2 027	...	Balance commerciale
Services Balance	1 151	747	- 1 438	- 3 070	- 2 985	- 2 317	- 3 129	- 2 098	...	Balance des services
Net Income	- 4 511	- 4 531	- 4 314	- 1 703	- 3 733	- 770	175	- 892	...	Revenus nets
Compensation of employees	- 361	- 468	20	- 97	- 114	- 139	- 256	71	...	Rémunération des salariés
Investment Income	- 4 150	- 4 063	- 4 335	- 1 606	- 3 619	- 631	431	- 963	...	Revenus des investissements
Current transfers, net total	4 615	6 837	8 302	6 101	7 942	7 463	13 395	13 853	...	Transferts courants
Net official transfers	...	...	...	...	...	...	...	...	...	Transferts officiels nets
Workers' remittances	...	...	...	...	...	...	...	...	...	Envois de fonds des travailleurs
Other private transfers	628	535	183	- 107	- 341	- 29	611	291	...	Autres transferts privés
Current account balance	11 414	10 147	- 25	- 8 152	- 5 602	- 605	- 4 331	12 890	...	Solde du compte courant
Capital & financial account	- 874	- 1 526	4 914	1 409	- 1 863	6 286	- 667	- 7 715	...	Comptes de capital et financier
Capital account	- 48	- 51	-	-	23	3	-	-	...	Compte de capital
Financial account	- 826	- 1 475	4 914	1 409	- 1 886	6 284	- 667	- 7 715	...	Compte financier
Errors & omissions	- 284	2 072	2 563	2 181	954	- 2 251	4 136	- 3 835	...	Erreurs et omissions
Overall balance	10 256	10 693	7 452	- 4 563	- 6 511	3 430	- 862	1 340	...	Balance générale

X DEBT AND FINANCIAL FLOWS - DETTE ET FLUX FINANCIERS										
	2006	2007	2008	2009	2010	2011	2012	2013	2014	
X-1 DEBT *US$ (MILLIONS)*										**X-1 DETTE EXTÉRIEURE** *$ E.U (MILLIONS)*
Total external debt	1 411	1 257	1 103	2 650	2 928	4 130	4 062	3 736	3 695	Dette extérieure totale
Private	1 055	939	825	1 258	976	1 260	1 246	1 264	1 252	Privée
Public	355	317	278	1 392	1 952	2 870	2 816	2 473	2 443	Publique
Total external debt service	909	980	237	244	183	333	536	469	509	Service de la dette extérieure
Present value of External debt	...	...	...	...	...	...	...	...	...	Valeur actuelle de la dette extérieure
Total government domestic debt (in local currency)	1 750	1 750	2 200	3 600	4 649.9	18 790.0	6 483.8	6 357.9	7 018.3	Dette publique intérieure
X-2 FINANCIAL FLOWS *US$ (MILLIONS)*										**X-2 FLUX FINANCIERS** *$ E.U (MILLIONS)*
Net Foreign Direct Investment Inflows	486	495	521	129	136	1 093	147	188	...	Investissement étranger direct (flux nets entrants)
Main origin of FDI Inflows										**Principales origines de l'IDE entrant:**
United Kingdom	88	88	86	108	43.3	...	...	...	...	Royaume-Uni
United States	...	...	2	3	4.0	4.0	...	...	...	États-Unis
Luxembourg	...	...	4	1	8.7	3.3	...	...	...	Luxembourg
France	...	...	...	...	...	...	...	...	...	France
Germany	...	...	...	...	4.0	...	...	...	...	Allemagne
African countries	...	...	...	...	...	...	...	...	...	Pays africains
Net total Official Development Assistance	69	108	720	279	156	120	74	108	...	Aide publique au développement (nette totale)
Main origin of Net ODA										**Principales origines de l'APD nette**
United States	25	45	232	214	77.0	78.5	50.2	75.4	...	Etats-Unis
Germany	3	2	439	2	2.4	2.0	0.3	...	...	Allemagne
France	1	9	2	1	6.5	0.7	0.5	0.5	...	France
Norway	2	2	3	2	0.6	0.5	0.5	0.2	...	Norvège
Sweden	2	4	4	3	4.7	2.1	7.2	6.4	...	Suède

AREA (km²)	274 000		SUPERFICIE (km²)
CAPITAL CITY	Ouagadougou	Ouagadougou	CAPITALE
CURRENCY	CFA Franc	Franc CFA	MONNAIE

I SOCIAL AND DEMOGRAPHIC INDICATORS – INDICATEURS DEMOGRAPHIQUES ET SOCIAUX

	Year Année	Value Valeur	
POPULATION			**POPULATION**
Population ('000)			Population ('000)
Both sexes	2014	18 450	Les deux sexes
Male	2014	9 198	Masculin
Female	2014	9 253	Féminin
Average annual growth rate	2014	3.0	Taux de croissance annuel
Active Population ('000)	2014	8 324	Population active ('000)
Population by age group ('000)			Population par groupe d'âge ('000)
0-14 years	2014	8 777	0-14 ans
15-64 years	2014	9 127	15-64 ans
65+ years	2014	546	65+ ans
Economically. active population. in agriculture (%)	2014	95.2	Participation de la population active agricole (%)
Crude birth rate	2014	40.3	Taux brut de natalité
Crude death rate	2014	10.8	Taux brut de mortalité
Total fertility rate	2014	5.5	Indice synthétique de fécondité
Proportion of urban population	2014	29.0	Part de la population urbaine
Life Expectancy at Birth - Total (years)	2014	56.7	Espérance de vie à la naissance - Totale (ans)
Dependency Ratio - Total (%)	2014	89.7	Taux de dépendance - Total (%)
HEALTH			**SANTÉ**
Percentage of children under-five and underweight	2010	26.2	% d'enfants de moins de cinq ans avec insuffisance pondérale
Prevalence of undernourishment	2013	20.7	Prévalence de la malnutrition
Under five mortality rate (both sexes, per 1000)	2013	97.6	Taux de mortalité de moins de 5 ans (les deux sexes, pour 1000)
Infant mortality rate (both sexes) per 1000	2013	64.1	Taux de mortalité infantile (les deux sexes) par 1000
Percentage of children provided the vaccines :			Pourcentage d'enfants vaccinés :
BCG	2013	96.0	BCG
DPT3	2013	88.0	DTC3
Polio	2012	109.4	Polio
Measles	2013	82.0	Rougeole
Percentage of mothers provided at least one antenatal care (%)	2012	87.2	Pourcentage de mères ayant au moins reçu un soin prénatal (%)
Percentage of deliveries attended by skilled health personnel	2010	65.9	% d'accouchements assistés par un personnel de santé qualifié
Number of doctors (per 10 000 population)	2010	0.5	Nombre de médecins (pour 10 000 habitants)
Number of nurses (per 10 000 population)	2010	5.7	Nombre d'infirmières (pour 10 000 habitants)
Hospital beds - Total (per 10 000 population)	2010	4.0	Nombre de lits d'hôpitaux - Total (pour 10 000)
Births registered (per 1 000)	2014	40.3	Naiss.s enregistrées (pour 1 000)
Deaths registered (per 1 000)	2014	10.8	Décès enregistrés (pour 1 000)
Public expenditure on Health (% of budget)	2013	12.5	Dépenses publiques consacrées à la santé (% du budget)
EDUCATION			**EDUCATION**
Enrolment in primary education (both sexes) (000)	2014	2 594	Scolarisation dans le primaire (les deux sexes) (000)
Female	2014	1 256	Féminin
Enrolment in secondary education (both sexes) (000)	2014	762	Scolarisation dans le secondaire (les deux sexes) (000)
Female	2013	343	Féminin
Enrolment in tertiary education (both sexes) (000)	2012	55.6	Scolarisation dans le tertiaire (les deux sexes) (000)
Female	2013	24.1	Féminin
Literacy rate (both sexes)	2007	28.7	Taux d'alphabétisation (deux sexes)
Male	2007	36.7	Masculin
Female	2007	21.6	Féminin
Pupil-teacher ratio	2013	52.2	Ratio élève-enseignant
Public expenditure on education (% of budget)	2013	15.9	Dépenses publiques consacrées à l'enseignement (% du budget)
POVERTY			**PAUVRETÉ**
GNI Per Capita (US$)	2013	670.0	RNB par habitant ($EU)
Human Poverty Index (HPI-1) Value (%)	2007	51.8	Valeur de l'Indice de pauvreté (IPH-1) (%)
Population below International Poverty Line ($2/day) (%)	2009	72.4	Population sous le seuil international de pauvreté (2$/J) (%)
Share of Income Held by Richest 10%	2009	32.2	% de revenu des 10% plus riches
Share of Income Held by Poorest 10%	2009	2.9	% de revenu des 10% plus pauvres
Gini index	2009	39.8	Indice de Gini

Charts
Graphiques

Population by age group – 2014
Population par groupe d'age – 2014

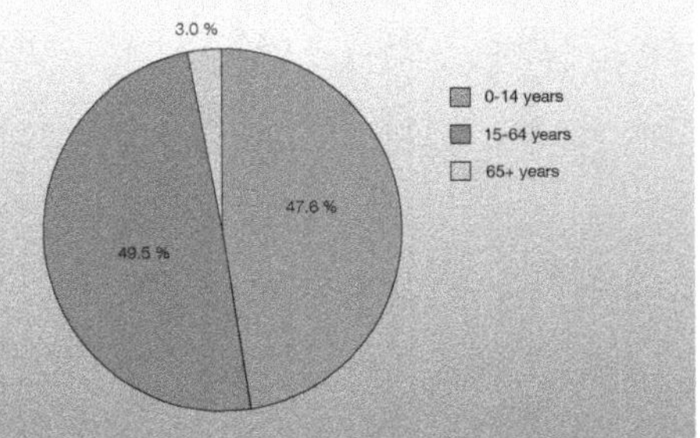

Percentage of children provided the vaccines – 2013
Pourcentage d'enfants vaccinés – 2013

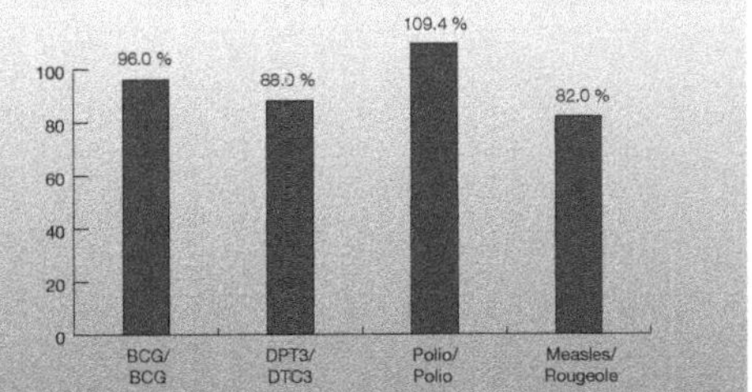

Literacy rate (%) – 2007
Taux d'alphabétisation – 2007

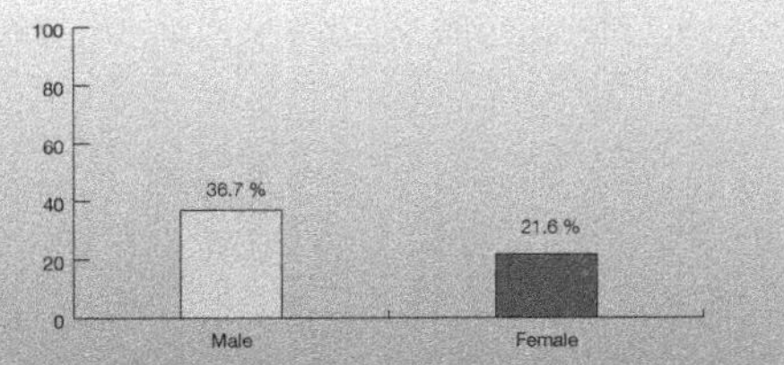

GNI Per Capita (US$)
RNB par habitant ($EU)

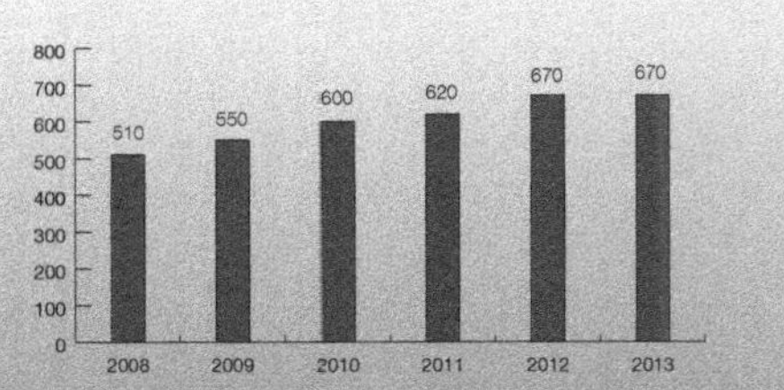

II NATIONAL ACCOUNTS — COMPTES NATIONAUX

	2006	2007	2008	2009	2010	2011	2012	2013	2014	
GROSS DOMESTIC PRODUCT BY KIND OF ECONOMIC ACTIVITY AT CURRENT PRICES *CFA FRANC (MILLIONS)*										**PRODUIT INTÉRIEUR BRUT PAR BRANCHE D'ACTIVITÉ ÉCONOMIQUE AUX PRIX COURANTS** *FRANC CFA (MILLIONS)*
Agriculture, hunting, forestry and fishing	1 032 784	971 481	1 384 987	1 279 151	1 443 795	1 555 834	1 836 951	1 980 679	2 088 385	Agriculture, chasse, sylviculture et pêche
Mining and quarrying	11 145	15 204	29 473	108 753	287 827	512 436	629 401	593 286	509 526	Industries extractives
Manufacturing	318 941	328 247	286 380	317 059	303 786	342 715	301 491	310 608	307 664	Industries manufacturières
Electricity, gas & water	25 473	35 278	40 538	45 407	32 864	42 336	41 586	47 234	53 638	Electricité, gaz et eau
Construction & public works	140 028	178 844	179 034	177 513	208 679	280 294	363 920	467 882	555 670	Bâtiments et travaux publics
Wholesale & retail trade, restaurants, hotels	320 447	358 562	421 035	509 111	606 068	597 733	715 405	722 923	539 150	Commerce de gros et de détail, restaurants et hôtels
Finance, insurance, real estate, etc.	251 657	259 846	259 063	282 446	289 422	299 510	313 585	361 936	384 361	Banques, assurances, affaires immobilières
Transport and communications	157 130	171 905	189 413	176 263	174 765	171 524	176 935	194 179	212 208	Transport(s) et communications
Public administration and defense	532 780	626 685	635 064	663 347	685 078	787 316	911 009	987 873	1 287 114	Administrations publiques et défense
Education	...	...	...	...	...	...	...	...	...	Education
Health and Social Work	...	...	...	...	...	...	...	...	...	Santé et actions sociales
Other services	65 519	68 564	69 666	80 399	83 493	86 455	100 038	108 478	141 338	Autres services
Less Imputed Service Charges	- 43 618	- 48 081	- 53 204	- 50 894	- 46 095	- 57 619	- 60 460	- 65 932	- 71 137	Moins services d'intermédiation financière
Gross domestic product at factor cost / basic prices	2 812 286	2 966 535	3 441 449	3 588 555	4 069 682	4 618 534	5 329 862	5 709 146	6 007 917	Produit intérieur brut aux couts des facteurs / prix de base
Plus: indirect taxes / taxes on products, less subsidies	243 834	271 307	298 043	353 330	384 185	456 651	598 322	654 312	690 982	Plus taxes indirectes/impôts sur les produits, moins les subventions
EXPENDITURE ON GROSS DOMESTIC PRODUCT AT CURRENT PURCHASER'S VALUES *CFA FRANC (MILLIONS)*										**EMPLOI DU PRODUIT INTÉRIEUR BRUT AUX PRIX COURANTS D'ACQUISITION** *FRANC CFA (MILLIONS)*
Government final consumption	659 270	774 069	800 731	854 895	917 992	1 040 672	1 183 309	1 276 766	1 599 892	Consommation finale des administrations publiques
Private final consumption	2 187 054	2 214 115	2 608 552	2 711 238	2 798 645	3 020 514	3 528 084	3 697 598	3 863 629	Consommation finale privée
Gross fixed capital formation	584 442	687 869	771 976	887 362	1 014 309	1 284 812	1 412 347	1 627 671	1 763 566	Formation brute de capital fixe
Change in inventories	45 281	17 689	176 004	79 349	108 034	78 599	122 404	229 883	127 076	Variation des stocks
Exports of goods and services	352 030	351 349	369 566	504 541	930 904	1 328 100	1 558 765	1 569 537	1 508 997	Exportations de biens et services
Less imports of goods and services	771 957	807 249	987 337	1 095 501	1 316 017	1 677 512	1 876 725	2 037 997	2 164 261	Moins importations de biens et services
GDP at purchasers' values	3 056 120	3 237 842	3 739 492	3 941 885	4 453 867	5 075 185	5 928 184	6 363 458	6 698 899	PIB aux prix d'acquisition
GROSS DOMESTIC PRODUCT BY KIND OF ECONOMIC ACTIVITY AT CONSTANT PRICES *ANNUAL GROWTH RATES (%)*										**PRODUIT INTÉRIEUR BRUT PAR BRANCHE D'ACTIVITÉ ECONOMIQUE AUX PRIX CONSTANTS** *TAUX DE CROISSANCE ANNUEL (%)*
Agriculture, hunting, forestry and fishing	10.6	- 4.2	19.6	- 9.1	11.1	- 3.0	10.6	3.4	4.1	Agriculture, chasse, sylviculture et pêche
Mining and quarrying	26.3	24.5	30.6	166.9	71.8	38.1	0.1	7.9	10.0	Industries extractives
Manufacturing	- 16.6	12.7	- 18.7	- 1.8	- 4.7	12.7	4.8	6.8	3.7	Industries manufacturières
Electricity, gas & water	- 1.1	6.0	37.7	4.6	- 23.6	59.0	4.1	8.3	7.9	Electricité, gaz et eau
Construction & public works	12.0	5.0	- 5.3	3.9	9.7	41.6	8.0	6.6	0.0	Bâtiments et travaux publics
Wholesale & retail trade, restaurants, hotels	- 2.3	12.7	9.4	20.4	11.3	- 9.4	1.7	11.8	2.4	Commerce de gros et de détail, restaurants et hôtels
Finance, insurance, real estate, etc.	27.0	2.0	4.0	0.4	- 2.1	- 1.3	3.6	7.8	1.5	Banques, assurances, affaires immobilières
Transport and communications	47.5	5.3	6.5	- 6.2	29.1	12.8	4.3	8.3	6.9	Transport(s) et communications
Public administration and defense	9.2	6.8	- 1.3	3.3	- 0.7	9.8	12.8	5.5	8.6	Administrations publiques et défense
Education	...	...	...	...	...	...	...	...	...	Education
Health and Social Work	...	...	...	...	...	...	...	...	...	Santé et actions sociales
Other services	- 3.4	5.5	2.1	5.7	5.6	3.5	12.8	5.5	8.6	Autres services
Less Imputed Service Charges	14.7	9.8	11.1	- 5.1	- 9.3	25.4	3.1	7.0	5.9	Moins services d'intérmediation financière
Gross domestic product at factor cost / basic prices	8.0	3.7	5.9	1.5	8.2	5.8	7.7	6.3	4.9	Produit intérieur brut aux couts des facteurs / prix de base
Plus: indirect taxes / taxes on products, less subsidies	- 11.2	9.0	5.0	19.4	10.9	15.0	20.8	9.1	5.5	Plus taxes indirectes/impôts sur les produits, moins les subventions
Gross domestic product at market prices	6.3	4.1	5.8	2.9	8.4	6.6	9.0	6.6	5.0	Produit intérieur brut aux prix du marché
EXPENDITURE ON GROSS DOMESTIC PRODUCT AT CONSTANT PURCHASERS' VALUES *ANNUAL GROWTH RATES (%)*										**EMPLOIS DU PRODUIT INTÉRIEUR BRUT AUX PRIX CONSTANTS D'ACQUISITION** *TAUX DE CROISSANCE ANNUEL (%)*
Government final consumption	- 5.5	5.7	3.4	0.5	6.5	6.1	11.9	6.0	6.3	Consommation finale des administrations publiques
Private final consumption	2.2	1.1	10.7	- 2.5	6.2	- 6.5	14.7	8.0	5.8	Consommation finale privée
Gross fixed capital formation	22.7	8.5	10.1	15.7	10.4	35.9	3.6	10.1	0.4	Formation brute de capital fixe
Exports of goods and services	29.8	6.0	4.6	21.0	60.6	26.7	3.6	3.5	3.6	Exportations de biens et services
Less imports of goods and services	1.9	3.0	20.0	8.9	25.1	20.7	10.1	10.1	1.9	Moins importations de biens et services
Notes	NA Data : 2012-2013-2014: Provisional					Données CN:2012- 2013-2014:Provisoires				Notes

III INFLATION

	2006	2007	2008	2009	2010	2011	2012	2013	2014	
ANNUAL GROWTH RATES (%)										**TAUX DE CROISSANCE ANNUEL (%)**
All items	2.4	-0.3	10.7	0.9	-0.6	2.8	3.8	0.5	-0.3	Ensemble
of which:										dont:
Food and Non-alcoholic beverages	-0.3	-1.3	23.3	3.5	1.5	6.1	5.4	-0.4	-3.2	Alimentation et boissons non alcoolisés
Alcoholic beverages & tobacco	2.1	1.7	4.9	-1.4	-0.9	1.9	5.3	-1.4	-2.9	Boissons alcoolisées et tabacs
Clothing and Footwear	2.3	2.1	2.9	0.4	-0.3	0.6	1.0	0.2	-	Habillement et chaussures
Housing, Water, Electricity, Gas and Other Fuels	5.0	-1.6	12.1	0.7	1.5	3.8	4.1	2.8	2.8	Logement, eau, electricité, gas et autres combustibles
Furnishing, household equipment	0.5	0.5	7.0	-0.5	-1.3	0.4	-0.1	0.1	0.2	Meubles, articles de ménage et entretien courant
Health	2.3	0.1	1.7	-0.4	0.2	0.6	0.1	0.4	-	Santé
Transport	6.0	-1.9	5.7	-1.7	-1.2	2.3	4.5	1.9	6.9	Transport
Communication	-	-	-	-5.1	-18.9	-18.6	1.0	0.6	0.8	Communication
Recreation & culture	0.2	-0.4	1.1	-0.8	-0.3	0.2	-0.6	-1.4	-0.8	Loisirs et culture
Education	5.8	6.8	0.4	0.4	1.7	0.4	0.5	1.4	0.9	Enseignement
Restaurants & hotels	4.1	2.5	2.7	0.5	2.2	6.6	4.7	0.9	-2.0	Restaurants et hôtels
Miscellaneous goods & services	-0.1	0.2	6.5	2.3	-0.7	0.7	0.9	0.6	0.8	Biens et services divers

IV AGRICULTURAL PRODUCTION - PRODUCTION AGRICOLE

	2006	2007	2008	2009	2010	2011	2012	2013	2014	
TONNES *(THOUSAND)*										TONNES *(MILLIERS)*
Sorghum	1 516	1 507	1 875	1 521	1 990	1 506	1 924	2 116	1 836	Sorgho
Millet	1 175	966	1 255	971	1 148	829	...	...	1 038	Millet
Maize	867	534	1 014	895	1 133	1 077	1 556	1 712	1 420	Maïs
Cotton lint	760	377	721	484	530	441	549	620	813	Fibres de coton
Cow pea	436	253	538	454	626	730	641	705	797	Niébé

V MINING PRODUCTION - PRODUCTION MINIERE

	2006	2007	2008	2009	2010	2011	2012	2013	2014	
Gold ores and concentrates (Kilograms)	225	2 250	6 033	11 581	22 939	31 774	...	...	...	Minerais d'or et concentrés (Kilogrammes)
Natural phosphates, P205 content, metric tons (thousands)	2	2	2	2	2	2	...	...	...	Phosphates, naturels, teneur en P205, tonnes métriques (milliers)
Abrasives, natural, metric tons (thousands)	...	...	...	...	...	...	...	...	...	Abrasifs naturels, tonnes métriques, (milliers)

VI ENERGY - ENERGIE

	2006	2007	2008	2009	2010	2011	2012	2013	2014	
Total electricity generation (GWh)	548	611	619	700	565	612	479	731	...	Production d'électricité totale (GWh)
of which:										dont:
Production of electricity from fossil fuels (GWh)	468	501	483	567	448	530	382	625	...	Production d'électricité à partir de combustibles fossiles (GWh)
Production of hydro electricity (GWh)	80	110	136	132	118	82	97	106	...	Production d'électricité d'origine hydraulique (GWh)
Production of electricity from solar, wind, tide, wave and other sources (GWh)	...	...	...	...	...	...	...	...	...	Production d'électricité d'origine solaire, éolienne, marée motrice et autres (GWh)

VII TOURISM AND INFRASTRUCTURE - TOURISME ET INFRASTRUCTURE

	2006	2007	2008	2009	2010	2011	2012	2013	2014	
VII-1 TOURISM										**VII-1 TOURISME**
International tourist arrivals (thousands)	264	289	272	269	274	238	263	266	282	Arrivées de touristes internationaux (milliers)
Rooms in hotels and similar establishments (thousands)	...	5.8	...	...	5.8	...	8.4	...	...	Chambres d'hotels et établissements assimilés (milliers)
Overnight stays (thousands)	1 584	1 826	1 587	1 570	1 576	1 407	1 595	1 618	1 717	Nuitées (milliers)
Tourism receipts (US$ thousand)	52 400	55 800	62 200	66 400	71 600	92 668	99 287	106 461	119 532	Recettes touristiques (milliers de $ EU)
Total contribution to GDP (%)	3.6	4.2	3.9	4.1	3.7	3.3	3.5	3.4	3.3	Contribution totale au PIB (%)
Total contribution to Employment (%)	3.1	3.7	3.5	3.6	3.1	3.0	3.1	2.9	2.9	Contribution totale à l'emploi (%)
VII-2 INFRASTRUCTURE										**VII-2 INFRASTRUCTURE**
Paved roads (% of total)	15	15	15	15	15	21	...	...	...	Routes asphaltées (% du total)
Total Network (Railways-km)	622	622	622	622	622	622	622	...	...	Réseau total voies ferrées-Km
Main Telephone Lines (per 100 inhabitants)	1	1	1	1	1	1	1	1	...	Lignes téléphoniques fixes (pour 100 habitants)
Mobile Cellular Subscribers (per 100 inhabitants)	7	13	21	25	37	48	61	66	...	Abonnés aux téléphones mobiles (pour 100 habitants)

VIII EXTERNAL TRADE - COMMERCE EXTERIEUR

	2006	2007	2008	2009	2010	2011	2012	2013	2014	
CFA FRANC (MILLIONS) EXPORTS, FOB										**FRANC CFA (MILLIONS) EXPORTATIONS, FÀB**
Exports - Total	307 638	298 542	310 407	382 950	650 279	1 110 414	1 111 507	1 162 519	1 227 182	Exportations - Total
Exports to AFRICA	88 716	98 902	96 385	120 725	155 578	...	...	...	...	Exportations vers l'AFRIQUE
Main Products										**Principaux produits**
Cotton, not carded, or combed	161 418	144 633	87 902	108 094	110 320	125 642	151 183	216 840	244 371	coton, non cardé ni peigné
Gold (including Gold Platinum), unwrought	4 676	4 615	55 643	136 571	438 729	85 217	805 741	732 774	722 368	or (y compris l'or platine), sous formes brutes ou mi
Other seeds and fruits oleaginous, even crush	4 847	16 545	7 392	5 962	7 276	14 896	10 155	21 541	24 143	Autres graines et fruits oleagineux, meme concasses
Live bovine	2 430	1 233	8 074	5 386	4 030	4 241	2 532	195	714	Animaux vivants de l'espèce bovine
Cigars (including those with cut ends)	3 773	4 703	4 291	2 540	3 573	3 062	2 029	406	325	Cigares (y compris ceux a bouts coupés)
Main Destinations										**Principales destinations**
Switzerland	57 695	60 901	86 795	114 606	403 948	762 113	700 522	683 151	701 236	Suisse
France	39 368	32 219	19 259	41 860	15 512	27 458	23 440	27 156	40 736	France
Belgium, Luxembourg	19 912	25 674	8 605	18 799	8 929	24 184	1 568	631	13 421	Belgique, Luxembourg
Singapore	11 694	15 985	23 790	19 576	31 011	53 977	25 028	67 245	95 647	Singapour
Ivory Coast	8 152	9 203	13 467	5 619	10 120	11 622	44 115	23 110	62 775	Côte d'Ivoire
IMPORTS, CIF										**IMPORTATIONS, CAF**
Imports - Total	689 455	717 780	873 042	976 988	1 067 259	1 214 026	1 747 187	2 057 088	1 662 376	Importations - Total (millions)
Imports from AFRICA	343 648	277 145	390 615	431 235	463 798	350 560	479 446	545 146	878 024	Importations en provenance de l'AFRIQUE
Main Products										**Principaux produits**
Petroleum oils & oils obtained from bituminous minerals	144 217	150 687	188 092	144 816	210 189	253 258	403 496	465 504	451 189	Huiles et préparations de pétrole ou minéraux bitumin
Rice	37 807	33 096	40 889	20 956	31 517	44 575	58 796	61 946	48 956	Riz
Medicaments (excluding goods n° 3002)	23 182	28 093	40 127	31 572	39 679	56 057	51 104	87 398	76 726	Medicaments (a l'exclusion des produits des n° 3002,
Hydraulic cement (including cement not pulver	23 812	27 443	30 977	23 409	36 490	34 612	47 540	53 771	...	Ciments hydroliques (y compris les ciments non pulver
Motor cars and other vehicles	20 921	22 729	28 584	23 444	34 310	35 741	43 519	49 206	...	Voitures de tourisme et autres vehicules automobiles
Main Origin										**Principales provenances**
Ivory Coast	136 246	126 903	131 181	94 400	163 049	122 440	160 224	162 054	240 941	Côte d'Ivoire
France	117 582	116 096	122 388	89 109	116 832	144 111	153 929	183 785	193 819	France
China	31 595	62 687	89 544	67 009	99 850	117 178	156 791	20 033	143 258	Chine
United States of America	25 259	49 619	59 830	50 194	49 195	58 174	126 857	134 246	41 019	Etats-Unis
India	31 108	49 459	50 012	30 179	27 799	42 648	58 540	87 551	53 754	Inde

IX FINANCIAL AND MONETARY STATISTICS - FINANCES ET STATISTIQUES MONETAIRES										
	2006	2007	2008	2009	2010	2011	2012	2013	2014	
IX-1 MONETARY STATISTICS *CFA FRANC (MILLIONS)*										**IX-1 STATISTIQUES MONÉTAIRES** *FRANC CFA (MILLIONS)*
Money supply (M1)	678 020	839 190	937 310	1 107 490	1 319 510	1 501 100	1 740 230	1 924 580	2 201 470	Masse monétaire (M1)
Quasi-money	248 518	295 423	354 139	432 994	591 273	630 901	744 716	849 263	971 380	Quasi-monnaie
of which Demand Deposit	...	...	...	...	...	...	...	...	...	dont Monnaie scripturale
Net foreign assets	236 206	423 480	382 184	574 706	657 749	681 958	680 015	547 674	413 646	Avoirs extérieurs nets
Domestic credit	466 976	403 317	551 607	583 578	718 269	864 380	1 055 593	1 454 362	1 784 072	Crédit intérieur
of which claims on private sector	541 378	545 641	662 390	671 077	769 405	950 539	1 180 112	1 491 476	1 738 430	dont créances sur le secteur privé
of which claims on government sector, net	- 75 392	- 143 313	- 111 773	- 88 489	- 52 346	- 87 219	- 125 579	- 37 952	45 643	dont créances nettes sur le gouvernement
International reserves (millions US$)	555	1 029	928	1 296	1 068	957	1 025	628	388	Réserves internationales (millions $EU)
Average Exchange Rate (National Currency per US$)	522.90	478.89	446.87	471.07	494.68	471.42	510.18	493.94	493.76	Taux de change (moyen) (monnaie nationale par $ EU)
IX-2 PUBLIC FINANCE *CFA FRANC (BILLIONS)*										**IX-2 FINANCES PUBLIQUES** *FRANC CFA (MILLIARDS)*
Total Revenues and Grants	554	643	623	762	867	988	1 176	1 374	1 240	Recettes totales et dons
Tax Revenue	355	398	437	485	552	636	790	925	878	Recettes fiscales
Non Tax Revenue	29	35	39	45	116	98	108	125	123	Recettes non fiscales
Grants	170	210	147	232	199	254	278	324	239	Dons
Total Expenditures and Net Lending	738	835	792	887	1 044	1 167	1 453	1 653	1 471	Dépenses totales et prêts nets
Current expenditure	387	450	455	463	497	629	829	819	874	Dépenses courantes
Of which Wages and Salaries	160	188	199	228	246	281	332	356	387	Dont rémunérations et salaires
Capital expenditure	366	383	325	430	552	535	625	859	602	Dépenses d'équipement
Net Lending	- 15	1	12	- 6	- 6	3	- 1	- 25	- 6	Prêts nets
Fiscal Balance	- 184	- 192	- 169	- 126	- 177	- 179	- 277	- 279	- 231	Solde global y compris les dons
IX-3 BALANCE OF PAYMENTS *CFA FRANC (BILLIONS)*										**IX-3 BALANCE DES PAIEMENTS** *FRANC CFA (MILLIARDS)*
Trade balance	- 257	- 293	- 416	- 217	- 140	12	108	- 329	- 256	Balance commerciale
Services Balance	- 167	- 174	- 212	- 192	- 262	- 342	- 408	- 459	- 482	Balance des services
Net Income	- 1	- 1	- 1	- 3	- 3	- 9	5	- 93	- 90	Revenus nets
Compensation of employees	11	4	4	5	6	1	15	- 14	- 15	Rémunération des salariés
Investment Income	- 12	- 5	- 5	- 8	- 9	- 10	- 11	- 80	- 75	Revenus des investissements
Current transfers, net total	133	193	183	243	244	272	255	217	232	Transferts courants
Net official transfers	...	...	...	...	...	...	...	...	...	Transferts officiels nets
Workers' remittances	...	...	...	...	...	...	...	...	...	Envois de fonds des travailleurs
Other private transfers	...	...	...	...	...	...	...	...	...	Autres transferts privés
Current account balance	- 292	- 275	- 445	- 169	- 161	- 68	- 39	- 665	- 596	Solde du compte courant
Capital & financial account	269	458	407	406	174	152	77	521	353	Comptes de capital et financier
Capital account	...	...	...	...	...	...	...	...	...	Compte de capital
Financial account	...	...	...	...	...	...	...	...	...	Compte financier
Errors & omissions	70	5	5	- 12	2	1	-	- 4	-	Erreurs et omissions
Overall balance	47	188	- 33	225	15	85	37	- 147	- 242	Balance générale

X DEBT AND FINANCIAL FLOWS - DETTE ET FLUX FINANCIERS

	2006	2007	2008	2009	2010	2011	2012	2013	2014	
X-1 DEBT *US$ (MILLIONS)*										**X-1 DETTE EXTÉRIEURE** *$ E.U (MILLIONS)*
Total external debt	1 216	1 579	1 757	2 146	2 393	2 444	2 581	2 708	3 005	Dette extérieure totale
Private	-	-	-	-	-	-	-	-	-	Privée
Public	1 216	1 579	1 757	2 146	2 393	2 444	2 581	2 708	3 005	Publique
Total external debt service	41	46	46	51	52	63	79	90	106	Service de la dette extérieure
Present value of External debt	...	...	...	1 394	1 704.4	1 787.0	1 960.2	...	...	Valeur actuelle de la dette extérieure
Total government domestic debt (in local currency)	...	...	...	259	314.5	438.0	554.8	...	...	Dette publique intérieure
X-2 FINANCIAL FLOWS *US$ (MILLIONS)*										**X-2 FLUX FINANCIERS** *$ E.U (MILLIONS)*
Net Foreign Direct Investment Inflows	34	344	106	101	35	144	329	374	...	Investissement étranger direct (flux nets entrants)
Main origin of FDI Inflows										**Principales origines de l'IDE entrant:**
France	13	...	...	...	...	...	...	...	...	France
Norway	...	...	- 45	69	6.8	...	...	...	...	Norvège
Netherlands	...	...	...	...	...	...	...	...	...	Pays-Bas
Luxembourg	...	...	...	0	...	...	...	...	...	Luxembourg
Spain	...	...	...	...	...	...	...	...	...	Espagne
African countries	...	...	...	...	...	...	...	...	...	Pays africains
Net total Official Development Assistance	901	950	1 001	1 083	1 062	995	1 159	1 040	...	Aide publique au développement (nette totale)
Main origin of Net ODA										**Principales origines de l'APD nette**
IDA	159	170	179	224	191.2	219.2	215.4	...	...	IDA
France	131	115	142	77	63.8	78.5	65.3	62.8	...	France
AfDF	117	63	82	83	80.8	86.8	69.6	...	...	FAfD
Netherlands	55	66	89	66	54.4	53.9	41.2	42.8	...	Pays-Bas
Germany	29	40	45	48	52.5	43.8	51.4	67.7	...	Allemagne

AREA (km²)	27 834		SUPERFICIE (km²)
CAPITAL CITY	Bujumbura	Bujumbura	CAPITALE
CURRENCY	Burundi Franc	Franc Burundais	MONNAIE

I SOCIAL AND DEMOGRAPHIC INDICATORS – INDICATEURS DEMOGRAPHIQUES ET SOCIAUX

	Year / Année	Value / Valeur	
POPULATION			**POPULATION**
Population ('000)			Population ('000)
Both sexes	2014	9.530	Les deux sexes
Male	2014	4.680	Masculin
Female	2014	4.851	Féminin
Average annual growth rate	2014	3.2	Taux de croissance annuel
Active Population ('000)	2014	4 584	Population active ('000)
Population by age group ('000)			Population par groupe d'âge ('000)
0-14 years	2014	4.192	0-14 ans
15-64 years	2014	5.120	15-64 ans
65+ years	2014	218	65+ ans
Economically. active population. in agriculture (%)	2014	85.7	Participation de la population active agricole (%)
Crude birth rate	2014	42.7	Taux brut de natalité
Crude death rate	2014	13.7	Taux brut de mortalité
Total fertility rate	2014	5.8	Indice synthétique de fécondité
Proportion of urban population	2014	11.8	Part de la population urbaine
Life Expectancy at Birth - Total (years)	2014	54.5	Espérance de vie à la naissance - Totale (ans)
Dependency Ratio - Total (%)	2014	66.8	Taux de dépendance - Total (%)
HEALTH			**SANTÉ**
Percentage of children under-five and underweight	2011	29.1	% d'enfants de moins de cinq ans avec insuffisance pondérale
Prevalence of undernourishment	...	...	Prévalence de la malnutrition
Under five mortality rate (both sexes, per 1000)	2013	82.9	Taux de mortalité de moins de 5 ans (les deux sexes, pour 1000)
Infant mortality rate (both sexes) per 1000	2013	54.8	Taux de mortalité infantile (les deux sexes) par 1000
Percentage of children provided the vaccines :			Pourcentage d'enfants vaccinés :
BCG	2013	95.0	BCG
DPT3	2013	96.0	DTC3
Polio	2013	83.6	Polio
Measles	2013	98.0	Rougeole
Percentage of mothers provided at least one antenatal care (%)	2010	98.9	Pourcentage de mères ayant au moins reçu un soin prénatal (%)
Percentage of deliveries attended by skilled health personnel	2010	60.3	% d'accouchements assistés par un personnel de santé qualifié
Number of doctors (per 10 000 population)	2004	0.3	Nombre de médecins (pour 10 000 habitants)
Number of nurses (per 10 000 population)	2004	1.9	Nombre d'infirmières (pour 10 000 habitants)
Hospital beds - Total (per 10 000 population)	2013	16.0	Nombre de lits d'hôpitaux - Total (pour 10 000)
Births registered (per 1 000)	2014	44.3	Naiss.s enregistrées (pour 1 000)
Deaths registered (per 1 000)	2014	12.5	Décès enregistrés (pour 1 000)
Public expenditure on Health (% of budget)	2013	12.1	Dépenses publiques consacrées à la santé (% du budget)
EDUCATION			**EDUCATION**
Enrolment in primary education (both sexes) (000)	2014	2.117	Scolarisation dans le primaire (les deux sexes) (000)
Female	2014	1.073	Féminin
Enrolment in secondary education (both sexes) (000)	2014	550	Scolarisation dans le secondaire (les deux sexes) (000)
Female	2014	253	Féminin
Enrolment in tertiary education (both sexes) (000)	2013	0.0	Scolarisation dans le tertiaire (les deux sexes) (000)
Female	2010	10.4	Féminin
Literacy rate (both sexes)	2008	86.9	Taux d'alphabétisation (deux sexes)
Male	2008	88.8	Masculin
Female	2008	84.6	Féminin
Pupil-teacher ratio	...	...	Ratio élève-enseignant
Public expenditure on education (% of budget)	2013	17.1	Dépenses publiques consacrées à l'enseignement (% du budget)
POVERTY			**PAUVRETÉ**
GNI Per Capita (US$)	2013	260.0	RNB par habitant ($EU)
Human Poverty Index (HPI-1) Value (%)	2007	36.4	Valeur de l'Indice de pauvreté (IPH-1) (%)
Population below International Poverty Line ($2/day) (%)	2006	93.5	Population sous le seuil international de pauvreté (2$/J) (%)
Share of Income Held by Richest 10%	2006	28.0	% de revenu des 10% plus riches
Share of Income Held by Poorest 10%	2006	4.1	% de revenu des 10% plus pauvres
Gini index	2006	33.3	Indice de Gini

Charts / Graphiques

Population by age group – 2014
Population par groupe d'age – 2014

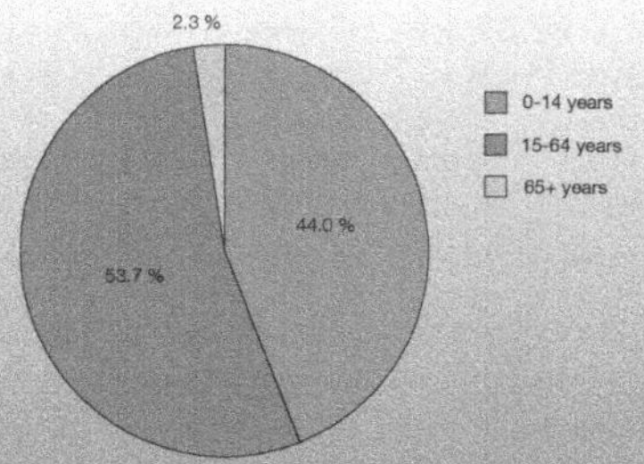

Percentage of children provided the vaccines – 2013
Pourcentage d'enfants vaccinés – 2013

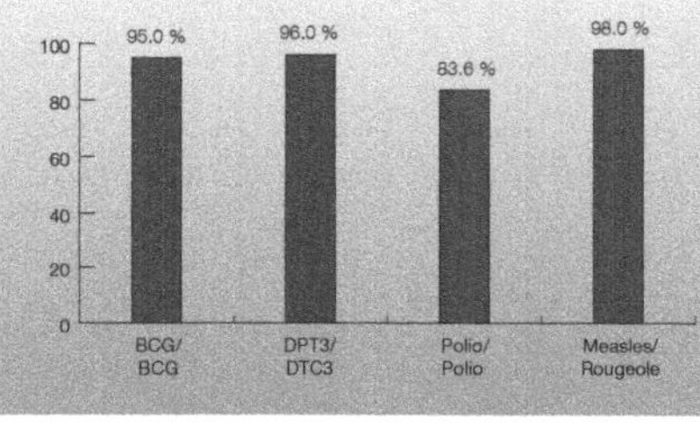

Literacy rate (%) – 2008
Taux d'alphabétisation – 2008

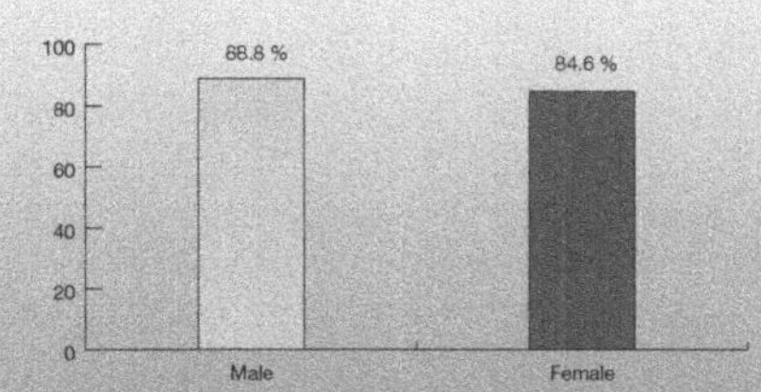

GNI Per Capita (US$)
RNB par habitant ($EU)

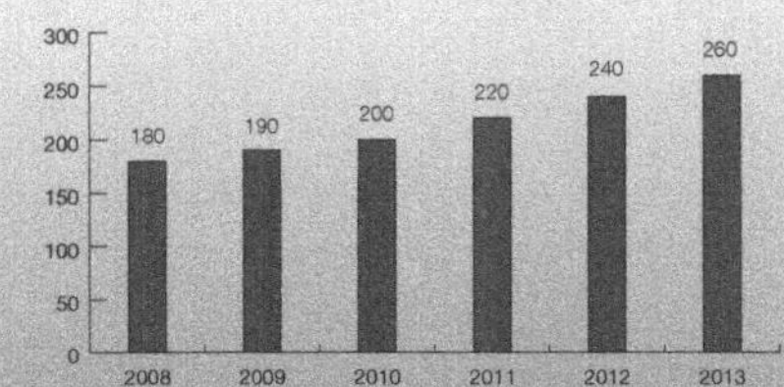

II NATIONAL ACCOUNTS — COMPTES NATIONAUX	2006	2007	2008	2009	2010	2011	2012	2013	2014	
GROSS DOMESTIC PRODUCT BY KIND OF ECONOMIC ACTIVITY AT CURRENT PRICES *BURUNDI FRANC (MILLIONS)*										**PRODUIT INTÉRIEUR BRUT PAR BRANCHE D'ACTIVITÉ ÉCONOMIQUE AUX PRIX COURANTS** *FRANC BURUNDAIS (MILLIONS)*
Agriculture, hunting, forestry and fishing	532 313	512 565	726 325	797 420	961 166	1 034 898	1 337 251	1 586 717	1 792 923	Agriculture, chasse, sylviculture et pêche
Mining and quarrying	10 428	10 121	11 852	12 334	12 153	10 419	20 349	24 571	30 518	Industries extractives
Manufacturing	135 759	170 917	205 185	248 042	256 177	282 775	358 337	394 756	461 363	Industries manufacturières
Electricity, gas & water	8 512	12 431	16 639	16 053	11 762	14 698	16 183	19 015	20 467	Electricité, gaz et eau
Construction & public works	45 916	58 252	60 930	94 364	104 723	109 672	153 333	175 463	210 275	Bâtiments et travaux publics
Wholesale & retail trade, restaurants, hotels	298 289	290 226	397 053	415 991	454 534	512 982	660 240	768 590	896 079	Commerce de gros et de détail, restaurants et hôtels
Finance, insurance, real estate, etc.	26 546	49 478	56 076	65 280	93 005	108 267	129 977	150 015	168 542	Banques, assurances, affaires immobilières
Transport and communications	40 816	70 361	62 172	91 401	88 414	90 230	132 126	149 934	168 787	Transport(s) et communications
Public administration and defense	62 959	103 149	127 721	150 068	142 743	159 270	178 482	202 855	216 253	Administrations publiques et défense
Education	44 734	55 005	78 343	85 089	140 966	184 670	193 210	221 032	260 348	Education
Health and Social Work	10 285	17 684	17 048	25 475	38 386	66 971	70 919	82 607	99 463	Santé et actions sociales
Other services	19 514	46 302	49 573	53 601	57 228	54 865	68 712	79 532	91 495	Autres services
Less Imputed Service Charges	- 35 479	- 46 503	- 55 610	- 57 650	- 91 111	- 105 997	- 130 596	- 158 282	- 176 335	Moins services d'intermédiation financière
Gross domestic product at factor cost / basic prices	1 200 592	1 349 988	1 753 307	1 997 468	2 270 146	2 523 720	3 188 521	3 696 805	4 240 177	Produit intérieur brut aux couts des facteurs / prix de base
Plus: indirect taxes / taxes on products, less subsidies	109 308	117 243	157 832	186 709	230 901	295 814	335 850	377 488	428 732	Plus taxes indirectes/impôts sur les produits, moins les subventions
EXPENDITURE ON GROSS DOMESTIC PRODUCT AT CURRENT PURCHASER'S VALUES *BURUNDI FRANC (MILLIONS)*										**EMPLOI DU PRODUIT INTÉRIEUR BRUT AUX PRIX COURANTS D'ACQUISITION** *FRANC BURUNDAIS (MILLIONS)*
Government final consumption	221 501	261 210	357 600	415 700	479 300	521 800	568 564	627 085	679 506	Consommation finale des administrations publiques
Private final consumption	1 231 200	1 333 300	1 786 500	1 903 000	2 038 000	2 158 380	2 782 143	3 176 056	3 580 867	Consommation finale privée
Gross fixed capital formation	276 299	271 922	274 207	267 312	478 400	613 851	836 196	1 266 802	1 558 915	Formation brute de capital fixe
Change in inventories	- 55 190	- 24 203	16 042	91 851	29 664	193 439	152 439	62 450	70 816	Variation des stocks
Exports of goods and services	95 840	96 970	181 380	145 590	222 430	297 190	356 050	346 600	464 444	Exportations de biens et services
Less imports of goods and services	459 750	471 968	704 590	639 276	746 747	965 126	1 171 020	1 404 700	1 685 640	Moins importations de biens et services
GDP at purchasers' values	1 309 900	1 467 231	1 911 139	2 184 177	2 501 047	2 819 534	3 524 371	4 074 294	4 668 908	PIB aux prix d'acquisition
GROSS DOMESTIC PRODUCT BY KIND OF ECONOMIC ACTIVITY AT CONSTANT PRICES *ANNUAL GROWTH RATES (%)*										**PRODUIT INTÉRIEUR BRUT PAR BRANCHE D'ACTIVITÉ ECONOMIQUE AUX PRIX CONSTANTS** *TAUX DE CROISSANCE ANNUEL (%)*
Agriculture, hunting, forestry and fishing	3.2	- 9.3	2.0	- 1.2	1.6	- 1.4	4.1	8.4	0.4	Agriculture, chasse, sylviculture et pêche
Mining and quarrying	- 1.5	- 6.0	- 28.5	8.0	- 1.4	14.3	2.0	15.0	8.0	Industries extractives
Manufacturing	6.4	3.2	5.0	1.6	3.3	2.3	8.5	1.3	4.4	Industries manufacturières
Electricity, gas & water	- 18.1	44.2	2.7	- 12.8	- 27.0	- 21.7	5.0	17.5	4.5	Electricité, gaz et eau
Construction & public works	9.6	22.3	10.8	34.4	1.5	2.1	5.2	3.0	7.0	Bâtiments et travaux publics
Wholesale & retail trade, restaurants, hotels	- 0.5	- 8.5	- 5.0	- 12.9	2.3	3.8	4.8	3.4	6.2	Commerce de gros et de détail, restaurants et hôtels
Finance, insurance, real estate, etc.	11.5	56.9	41.3	18.2	6.7	13.4	5.3	5.5	7.0	Banques, assurances, affaires immobilières
Transport and communications	9.3	53.1	- 33.0	32.6	- 7.0	1.5	5.1	4.6	7.3	Transport(s) et communications
Public administration and defense	16.7	59.9	26.2	19.8	- 5.0	12.6	2.5	2.3	3.5	Administrations publiques et défense
Education	37.3	20.2	26.6	13.7	73.3	22.0	7.0	10.0	12.5	Education
Health and Social Work	- 30.2	- 21.0	- 3.6	29.9	34.4	43.3	11.0	12.0	15.0	Santé et actions sociales
Other services	24.3	115.9	35.2	2.1	2.4	- 16.0	3.8	4.3	4.8	Autres services
Less Imputed Service Charges	- 6.5	31.3	19.6	4.7	40.1	18.9	14.0	20.0	6.0	Moins services d'intermédiation financière
Gross domestic product at factor cost / basic prices	5.2	3.8	4.5	3.6	3.4	3.2	4.4	4.6	4.6	Produit intérieur brut aux couts des facteurs / prix de base
Plus: indirect taxes / taxes on products, less subsidies	8.0	- 0.5	9.0	5.7	23.5	12.8	0.6	4.1	5.4	Plus taxes indirectes/impôts sur les produits, moins les subventions
Gross domestic product at market prices	5.4	3.5	4.9	3.8	5.1	4.2	4.0	4.5	4.7	Produit intérieur brut aux prix du marché
EXPENDITURE ON GROSS DOMESTIC PRODUCT AT CONSTANT PURCHASERS' VALUES *ANNUAL GROWTH RATES (%)*										**EMPLOIS DU PRODUIT INTÉRIEUR BRUT AUX PRIX CONSTANTS D'ACQUISITION** *TAUX DE CROISSANCE ANNUEL (%)*
Government final consumption	11.6	- 15.4	36.0	41.9	13.0	9.6	20.0	7.7	5.9	Consommation finale des administrations publiques
Private final consumption	10.6	- 0.8	2.9	- 5.1	- 1.9	4.4	4.1	4.3	5.0	Consommation finale privée
Gross fixed capital formation	- 4.6	- 2.0	- 9.6	4.3	66.4	17.2	11.6	23.4	2.1	Formation brute de capital fixe
Exports of goods and services	- 20.4	- 3.9	54.7	- 26.4	26.0	21.9	1.4	31.5	17.6	Exportations de biens et services
Less imports of goods and services	28.8	- 1.7	26.7	- 14.4	20.7	17.0	5.3	2.8	5.1	Moins importations de biens et services
Notes	NA Data : 2012-2014:Estimates are provisional					Données CN: 2012-2014:Donéées provisoires				Notes

III INFLATION	2006	2007	2008	2009	2010	2011	2012	2013	2014	
ANNUAL GROWTH RATES (%)										**TAUX DE CROISSANCE ANNUEL (%)**
All items	2.8	8.4	24.4	10.5	6.5	9.6	18.2	7.9	4.4	Ensemble
of which:										dont:
Food and Non-alcoholic beverages	0.1	8.6	33.0	10.1	6.9	9.6	14.1	9.5	2.3	Alimentation et boissons non alcoolisés
Alcoholic beverages & tobacco	...	...	...	...	...	...	...	7.3	-0.9	Boissons alcoolisées et tabacs
Clothing and Footwear	-0.6	-5.4	4.2	9.3	0.8	16.7	24.5	0.0	8.7	Habillement et chaussures
Housing, Water, Electricity, Gas and Other Fuels	8.2	10.5	16.0	11.9	9.9	6.2	31.7	6.4	7.0	Logement, eau, electricité, gas et autres combustibles
Furnishing, household equipment	1.2	5.7	12.8	24.2	8.7	6.3	7.1	14.4	17.3	Meubles, articles de ménage et entretien courant
Health	8.7	8.5	11.2	10.8	0.2	30.8	3.8	2.9	8.3	Santé
Transport	7.0	10.7	27.4	-8.7	2.6	19.8	3.1	8.3	6.4	Transport
Communication	...	...	...	...	...	...	...	-	0.4	Communication
Recreation & culture	...	...	...	...	...	...	...	2.8	4.5	Loisirs et culture
Education	1.2	6.3	-0.6	7.2	4.5	5.3	0.3	-	1.0	Enseignement
Restaurants & hotels	...	...	...	...	...	...	...	5.4	6.0	Restaurants et hôtels
Miscellaneous goods & services	0.0	4.8	18.2	15.0	2.0	11.6	17.7	18.0	10.4	Biens et services divers

IV AGRICULTURAL PRODUCTION - PRODUCTION AGRICOLE	2006	2007	2008	2009	2010	2011	2012	2013	2014	
TONNES *(THOUSAND)*										**TONNES** *(MILLIERS)*
Maize	117	116	118	120	126	128	110	162	138	Maïs
Sweet potatoes	837	874	900	484	303	300	1 167	840	663	Patates douces
Cassava	571	559	577	235	188	160	580	2 234	2 056	Manioc
Beans	209	205	190	203	202	199	802	225	250	Haricots
Banana	1 608	1 701	1 760	1 806	137	132	276	2 236	1 707	Banane

V MINING PRODUCTION - PRODUCTION MINIERE	2006	2007	2008	2009	2010	2011	2012	2013	2014	
Gold ores and concentrates - Production (Kilograms)	4	2	2	1	0	1	2	3	1	Minerais d'or et leurs concentrés - Production (Kilogrammes)
Tin ores and concentrates, includes Cassiterite - Production (metric tons)	22	52	84	44	67	159	259	74	106	Minerais d'étain et leurs concentrés - Production (Tonnes métriques)
Colombo-tantalite (kg) - Production (Kilograms)	...	51	48	28	29	52	117	31	...	Colombo-tantalite (kg) - Production (Kilogrammes)

VI ENERGY - ENERGIE	2006	2007	2008	2009	2010	2011	2012	2013	2014	
Total electricity generation (GWh)	94	118	113	122	241	153	184	184	...	Production d'électricité totale (GWh)
of which:										dont:
Production of electricity from fossil fuels (GWh)	2	2	2	2	11	2	4	4	...	Production d'électricité à partir de combustibles fossiles (GWh)
Production of hydro electricity (GWh)	92	116	111	120	230	150	179	179	...	Production d'électricité d'origine hydraulique (GWh)
Production of electricity from solar, wind, tide, wave and other sources (GWh)	...	...	...	...	...	1	1	1	...	Production d'électricité d'origine solaire, éolienne, marée motrice et autres (GWh)

VII TOURISM AND INFRASTRUCTURE - TOURISME ET INFRASTRUCTURE	2006	2007	2008	2009	2010	2011	2012	2013	2014	
VII-1 TOURISM										**VII-1 TOURISME**
International tourist arrivals (thousands)	214	192	202	212	142	189	205	149	157	Arrivées de touristes internationaux (milliers)
Rooms in hotels and similar establishments (thousands)	...	...	...	...	...	...	...	...	...	Chambres d'hotels et établissements assimilés (milliers)
Overnight stays (thousands)	1 301	1 187	1 269	1 274	874	1 162	912	923	973	Nuitées (milliers)
Tourism receipts (US$ thousand)	1 200	1 200	1 200	1 400	1 700	2 400	1 400	2 200	2 182	Recettes touristiques (milliers de $ EU)
Total contribution to GDP (%)	2.1	3.2	4.0	4.9	5.5	5.1	4.7	4.5	4.3	Contribution totale au PIB (%)
Total contribution to Employment (%)	1.8	2.8	3.4	4.2	4.8	4.6	4.3	3.9	3.7	Contribution totale à l'emploi (%)
VII-2 INFRASTRUCTURE										**VII-2 INFRASTRUCTURE**
Paved roads (% of total)	11	...	...	15	16	16	17	15	...	Routes asphaltées (% du total)
Total Network (Railways-km)	...	...	...	...	...	...	...	...	...	Réseau total voies ferrées-Km
Main Telephone Lines (per 100 inhabitants)	0	0	0	0	0	0	0	0	...	Lignes téléphoniques fixes (pour 100 habitants)
Mobile Cellular Subscribers (per 100 inhabitants)	2	3	6	10	18	20	23	25	...	Abonnés aux téléphones mobiles (pour 100 habitants)

VIII EXTERNAL TRADE - COMMERCE EXTERIEUR	2006	2007	2008	2009	2010	2011	2012	2013	2014	
US$ (MILLIONS) **EXPORTS, FOB**										**$ E.U (MILLIONS)** **EXPORTATIONS, FÀB**
Exports - Total	60 400	63 653	82 581	84 162	124 596	197 836	242 700	205 749	...	Exportations - Total
Exports to AFRICA	9 105	9 785	13 710	14 664	15 097	...	...	...	...	Exportations vers l'AFRIQUE
Main Products										**Principaux produits**
Sugars and sugar confectionery	...	...	...	...	...	...	...	...	...	Sucres et sucreries
Cigarettes containing tobacco	807	986	1 796	1 774	1 685	1 646	4 002	5 516	...	Cigarettes, contenant du tabac
Beer made from malt	604	873	1 822	1 596	2 222	2 802	3 838	3 212	...	Bière maltée à base de malt
Coffee, coffee husks and skins and coffee substitutes	40 372	41 684	47 184	48 733	85 814	95 282	100 999	32 604	...	Café
Tea	10 238	9 925	15 531	18 946	21 920	28 324	36 643	29 049	...	Thé
Main Destinations										**Principales destinations**
Switzerland	20 339	19 590	23 019	20 803	39 140	...	46 373	...	...	Suisse
United Kingdom	7 393	6 917	9 108	7 599	22 705	...	25 034	...	...	Royaume Uni
Rwanda	3 212	2 367	4 104	3 745	2 033	...	6 141	...	...	Rwanda
Netherlands	314	323	827	1 227	800	...	1 379	...	...	Pays bas
Kenya	1 220	233	1 768	488	1 866	...	4 294	...	...	Kenya
IMPORTS, CIF										**IMPORTATIONS, CAF**
Imports - Total	442 511	346 100	477 781	494 829	626 271	1 127 650	1 003 121	721 660	...	Importations - Total (millions)
Imports from AFRICA	96 177	111 416	133 171	149 295	181 836	276 611	338 738	...	...	Importations en provenance de l'AFRIQUE
Main Products										**Principaux produits**
Pharmaceutical products	28 984	26 990	36 491	37 671	49 499	64 859	74 935	66 214	...	Produits pharmaceutiques
Vehicles other than railway, tramway	25 566	15 657	14 858	16 375	36 166	21 308	25 915	8 783	...	Voitures automobiles, tracteurs, cycles & autres véhicules terrestres, leur parties
Gas oils - bunker oil, No.1 furnace, motor diesel	26 578	29 206	57 003	24 704	61 041	101 908	99 403	89 399	...	Gasoil
Gasoline Engine	23 631	25 160	37 545	18 073	46 167	78 513	99 737	89 642	...	Essence pour moteur
Machinery and app. mechanical or electrical	18 713	16 876	47 580	33 102	33 087	75 244	68 411	...	...	Machine et app. électrique
Main Origin										**Principales provenances**
Belgium	52	48	61	56	60	87	109	84	...	Belgique
Kenya	36	32	36	42	38	58	65	76	...	Kenya
China	19	15	29	41	63	79	99	92	...	Chine
France	20	12	26	21	30	41	37	26	...	France
Tanzania	8	11	20	22	33	61	70	104	...	Tanzanie

IX FINANCIAL AND MONETARY STATISTICS - FINANCES ET STATISTIQUES MONETAIRES										
	2006	2007	2008	2009	2010	2011	2012	2013	2014	
IX-1 MONETARY STATISTICS *BURUNDI FRANC (MILLIONS)*										**IX-1 STATISTIQUES MONÉTAIRES** *FRANC BURUNDAIS (MILLIONS)*
Money supply (M1)	301 560	330 080	443 120	530 770	633 490	672 130	745 210	833 800	943 930	Masse monétaire (M1)
Quasi-money	89 835	89 709	103 537	118 264	145 692	183 918	196 551	229 915	249 338	Quasi-monnaie
of which Demand Deposit	...	...	...	...	...	...	...	...	...	dont Monnaie scripturale
Net foreign assets	80 800	130 568	256 060	264 043	254 447	204 477	197 824	230 618	180 547	Avoirs extérieurs nets
Domestic credit	374 320	349 443	377 751	498 115	626 362	784 629	884 717	952 125	1 121 218	Crédit intérieur
of which claims on private sector	207 369	216 776	261 117	320 624	420 869	561 036	635 177	686 682	734 968	dont créances sur le secteur privé
of which claims on government sector, net	156 347	124 203	93 962	167 944	195 969	218 131	241 687	254 561	370 078	dont créances nettes sur le gouvernement
International reserves (millions US$)	131	176	266	322	331	294	307	328	316	Réserves internationales (millions $EU)
Average Exchange Rate (National Currency per US$)	1 028.68	1 081.87	1 185.69	1 230.18	1 260.77	1 441.69	1 575.03	1 539.10	1 516.71	Taux de change (moyen) (monnaie nationale par $ EU)
IX-2 PUBLIC FINANCE *BURUNDI FRANC (BILLIONS)*										**IX-2 FINANCES PUBLIQUES** *FRANC BURUNDAIS (MILLIARDS)*
Total Revenues and Grants	288	366	463	412	635	778	1 137	1 274	1 241	Recettes totales et dons
Tax Revenue	163	183	233	279	342	424	492	540	555	Recettes fiscales
Non Tax Revenue	15	15	29	26	22	33	35	39	41	Recettes non fiscales
Grants	109	169	201	107	271	321	610	694	645	Dons
Total Expenditures and Net Lending	362	408	490	508	816	1 027	1 131	1 255	1 294	Dépenses totales et prêts nets
Current expenditure	245	273	364	416	552	675	786	786	819	Dépenses courantes
Of which Wages and Salaries	94	114	158	185	215	258	282	296	334	Dont rémunérations et salaires
Capital expenditure	118	135	127	93	264	352	478	540	548	Dépenses d'équipement
Net Lending	- 1	0	- 1	- 1	-	-	- 133	- 70	- 73	Prêts nets
Fiscal Balance	- 74	- 42	- 27	- 97	- 181	- 248	6	18	- 53	Solde global y compris les dons
IX-3 BALANCE OF PAYMENTS *BURUNDI FRANC (BILLIONS)*										**IX-3 BALANCE DES PAIEMENTS** *FRANC BURUNDAIS (MILLIARDS)*
Trade balance	- 191	- 215	- 315	- 338	- 415	- 540	- 831	- 909	...	Balance commerciale
Services Balance	- 173	- 164	- 208	- 156	- 109	- 128	- 171	- 160	...	Balance des services
Net Income	- 9	- 6	- 5	- 21	- 13	- 22	- 9	3	...	Revenus nets
Compensation of employees	...	...	...	...	...	...	...	...	...	Rémunération des salariés
Investment Income	...	...	...	...	...	...	...	...	...	Revenus des investissements
Current transfers, net total	236	261	221	316	167	332	644	673	...	Transferts courants
Net official transfers	...	...	...	...	...	...	...	...	...	Transferts officiels nets
Workers' remittances	...	...	...	...	...	...	...	...	...	Envois de fonds des travailleurs
Other private transfers	...	...	...	...	...	...	...	...	...	Autres transferts privés
Current account balance	- 137	- 124	- 308	- 198	- 370	- 358	- 368	- 394	...	Solde du compte courant
Capital & financial account	137	161	246	214	363	351	363	389	...	Comptes de capital et financier
Capital account	64	138	167	1 261	96	122	222	162	...	Compte de capital
Financial account	73	22	79	- 1 048	267	229	141	228	...	Compte financier
Errors & omissions	1	- 37	61	- 15	8	7	5	5	...	Erreurs et omissions
Overall balance	...	...	...	...	...	...	...	...	...	Balance générale

X DEBT AND FINANCIAL FLOWS - DETTE ET FLUX FINANCIERS	2006	2007	2008	2009	2010	2011	2012	2013	2014	
X-1 DEBT *US$ (MILLIONS)*										**X-1 DETTE EXTÉRIEURE** *$ E.U (MILLIONS)*
Total external debt	1 472	1 468	1 518	376	455	476	487	511	539	Dette extérieure totale
Private	6	1	-	-	-	-	-	-	-	Privée
Public	1 466	1 467	1 518	376	455	476	487	511	539	Publique
Total external debt service	11	6	3	2	3	5	16	25	23	Service de la dette extérieure
Present value of External debt	...	...	...	...	...	...	...	...	...	Valeur actuelle de la dette extérieure
Total government domestic debt (in local currency)	...	258	256	335	387.4	450.0	521.6	596.3	...	Dette publique intérieure
X-2 FINANCIAL FLOWS *US$ (MILLIONS)*										**X-2 FLUX FINANCIERS** *$ E.U (MILLIONS)*
Net Foreign Direct Investment Inflows	...	1	4	...	1	3	1	7	...	Investissement étranger direct (flux nets entrants)
Main origin of FDI Inflows										**Principales origines de l'IDE entrant:**
Netherlands	5	4	...	...	...	...	...	...	...	Pays-Bas
Belgium	...	1	1	...	2.6	1.4	...	...	...	Belgique
France	- 1	...	...	...	...	...	...	...	...	France
Germany	1	...	...	...	...	...	...	...	...	Allemagne
United States	...	...	...	...	...	...	...	...	...	États-Unis
African countries	...	...	...	...	...	...	...	...	...	Pays africains
Net total Official Development Assistance	431	479	522	561	630	575	523	546	...	Aide publique au développement (nette totale)
Main origin of Net ODA										**Principales origines de l'APD nette**
IDA	101	84	68	47	107.7	94.7	103.1	...	...	IDA
United States	47	26	30	48	43.5	51.8	43.3	26.5	...	Etats-Unis
Belgium	33	26	58	52	56.9	98.0	31.6	79.9	...	Belgique
Netherlands	17	23	32	18	19.1	19.6	17.2	32.7	...	Pays-Bas
Germany	15	23	23	28	29.5	5.7	4.8	4.2	...	Allemagne

AREA (km²)		4 033	SUPERFICIE (km²)
CAPITAL CITY	Praia	Praia	CAPITALE
CURRENCY	Escudo	Escudo	MONNAIE

I SOCIAL AND DEMOGRAPHIC INDICATORS — INDICATEURS DEMOGRAPHIQUES ET SOCIAUX

	Year Année	Value Valeur	
POPULATION			**POPULATION**
Population ('000)			Population ('000)
Both sexes	2014	504	Les deux sexes
Male	2014	251	Masculin
Female	2014	252	Féminin
Average annual growth rate	2014	1.5	Taux de croissance annuel
Active Population ('000)	2014	243	Population active ('000)
Population by age group ('000)			Population par groupe d'âge ('000)
0-14 years	2014	145	0-14 ans
15-64 years	2014	332	15-64 ans
65+ years	2014	26	65+ ans
Economically. active population. in agriculture (%)	2014	12.3	Participation de la population active agricole (%)
Crude birth rate	2014	19.9	Taux brut de natalité
Crude death rate	2014	5.1	Taux brut de mortalité
Total fertility rate	2014	2.3	Indice synthétique de fécondité
Proportion of urban population	2014	64.9	Part de la population urbaine
Life Expectancy at Birth - Total (years)	2014	75.4	Espérance de vie à la naissance - Totale (ans)
Dependency Ratio - Total (%)	2014	51.9	Taux de dépendance - Total (%)
HEALTH			**SANTÉ**
Percentage of children under-five and underweight	...	...	% d'enfants de moins de cinq ans avec insuffisance pondérale
Prevalence of undernourishment	2013	9.9	Prévalence de la malnutrition
Under five mortality rate (both sexes, per 1000)	2013	26.0	Taux de mortalité de moins de 5 ans (les deux sexes, pour 1000)
Infant mortality rate (both sexes) per 1000	2013	21.9	Taux de mortalité infantile (les deux sexes) par 1000
Percentage of children provided the vaccines :			Pourcentage d'enfants vaccinés :
BCG	2013	94.0	BCG
DPT3	2013	93.0	DTC3
Polio	2010	96.9	Polio
Measles	2013	91.0	Rougeole
Percentage of mothers provided at least one antenatal care (%)	2010	87.4	Pourcentage de mères ayant au moins reçu un soin prénatal (%)
Percentage of deliveries attended by skilled health personnel	2005	77.5	% d'accouchements assistés par un personnel de santé qualifié
Number of doctors (per 10 000 population)	2010	3.0	Nombre de médecins (pour 10 000 habitants)
Number of nurses (per 10 000 population)	2010	4.5	Nombre d'infirmières (pour 10 000 habitants)
Hospital beds - Total (per 10 000 population)	2010	21.0	Nombre de lits d'hôpitaux - Total (pour 10 000)
Births registered (per 1 000)	2014	19.9	Naiss.s enregistrées (pour 1 000)
Deaths registered (per 1 000)	2014	5.1	Décès enregistrés (pour 1 000)
Public expenditure on Health (% of budget)	2009	10.2	Dépenses publiques consacrées à la santé (% du budget)
EDUCATION			**EDUCATION**
Enrolment in primary education (both sexes) (000)	2013	67	Scolarisation dans le primaire (les deux sexes) (000)
Female	2013	32	Féminin
Enrolment in secondary education (both sexes) (000)	2013	60	Scolarisation dans le secondaire (les deux sexes) (000)
Female	2013	32	Féminin
Enrolment in tertiary education (both sexes) (000)	2010	10.1	Scolarisation dans le tertiaire (les deux sexes) (000)
Female	2013	7.7	Féminin
Literacy rate (both sexes)	2012	85.3	Taux d'alphabétisation (deux sexes)
Male	2012	90.5	Masculin
Female	2012	80.5	Féminin
Pupil-teacher ratio	2011	23.3	Ratio élève-enseignant
Public expenditure on education (% of budget)	2012	13.8	Dépenses publiques consacrées à l'enseignement (% du budget)
Poverty			Pauvreté
GNI Per Capita (US$)	2013	3 620.0	RNB par habitant ($EU)
Human Poverty Index (HPI-1) Value (%)	2007	14.5	Valeur de l'Indice de pauvreté (IPH-1) (%)
Population below International Poverty Line ($2/day) (%)	2007	53.2	Population sous le seuil international de pauvreté (2$/J) (%)
Share of Income Held by Richest 10%	2007	31.8	% de revenu des 10% plus riches
Share of Income Held by Poorest 10%	2007	2.7	% de revenu des 10% plus pauvres
Gini index	2007	40.7	Indice de Gini

Charts
Graphiques

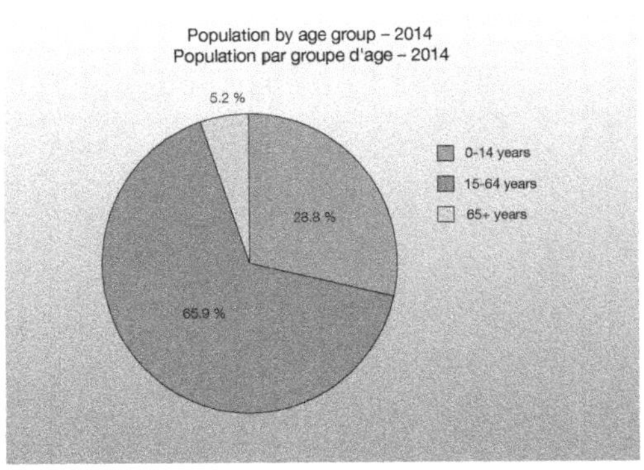

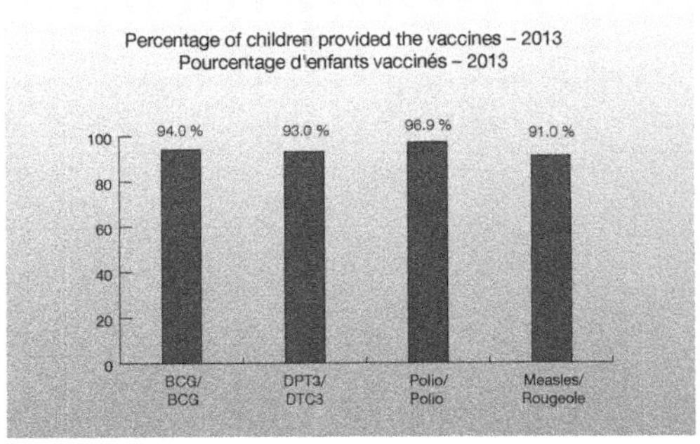

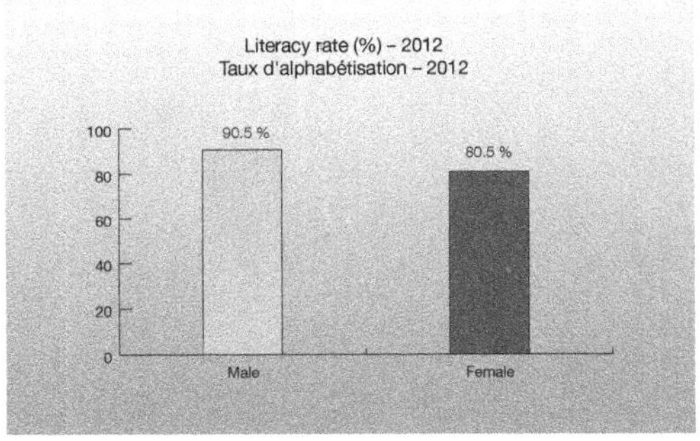

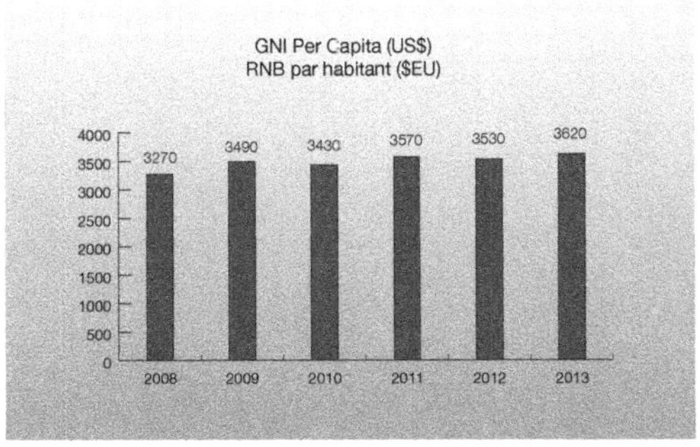

II NATIONAL ACCOUNTS — COMPTES NATIONAUX

	2006	2007	2008	2009	2010	2011	2012	2013	2014	
GROSS DOMESTIC PRODUCT BY KIND OF ECONOMIC ACTIVITY AT CURRENT PRICES *ESCUDO (MILLIONS)*										**PRODUIT INTÉRIEUR BRUT PAR BRANCHE D'ACTIVITÉ ÉCONOMIQUE AUX PRIX COURANTS** *ESCUDO (MILLIONS)*
Agriculture, hunting, forestry and fishing	8 120	10 389	10 442	11 304	11 071	11 602	12 388	...	...	Agriculture, chasse, sylviculture et pêche
Mining and quarrying	3 035	802	1 014	774	708	612	587	...	...	Industries extractives
Manufacturing	3 178	5 541	6 527	6 689	7 528	8 054	8 541	...	...	Industries manufacturières
Electricity, gas & water	338	900	1 318	2 125	1 940	2 157	3 021	...	...	Electricité, gaz et eau
Construction & public works	9 067	13 376	16 409	16 584	14 973	15 455	13 712	...	...	Bâtiments et travaux publics
Wholesale & retail trade, restaurants, hotels	20 494	19 644	20 252	21 486	22 402	24 899	27 465	...	...	Commerce de gros et de détail, restaurants et hôtels
Finance, insurance, real estate, etc.	9 873	17 466	19 983	19 360	20 027	22 949	23 581	...	...	Banques, assurances, affaires immobilières
Transport and communications	20 555	19 929	22 083	20 917	21 035	20 283	20 447	...	...	Transport(s) et communications
Public administration and defense	12 521	15 504	16 181	17 947	19 018	18 949	22 192	...	...	Administrations publiques et défense
Education	...	...	...	...	...	...	...	...	...	Education
Health and Social Work	...	...	...	...	...	...	...	...	...	Santé et actions sociales
Other services	2 546	1 812	2 012	2 071	2 268	2 565	-	...	...	Autres services
Less Imputed Service Charges	- 3 323	...	...	...	...	...	...	...	...	Moins services d'intermédiation financière
Gross domestic product at factor cost / basic prices	86 404	105 362	116 219	119 258	120 970	127 525	131 935	-	-	Produit intérieur brut aux couts des facteurs / prix de base
Plus: indirect taxes / taxes on products, less subsidies	10 981	16 612	18 479	16 621	17 598	20 399	18 789	...	...	Plus taxes indirectes/impôts sur les produits, moins les subventions
EXPENDITURE ON GROSS DOMESTIC PRODUCT AT CURRENT PURCHASER'S VALUES *ESCUDO (MILLIONS)*										**EMPLOI DU PRODUIT INTÉRIEUR BRUT AUX PRIX COURANTS D'ACQUISITION** *ESCUDO (MILLIONS)*
Government final consumption	19 002	21 296	22 739	24 708	25 536	27 401	26 625	...	...	Consommation finale des administrations publiques
Private final consumption	79 513	76 770	81 864	86 839	87 328	92 864	96 188	...	...	Consommation finale privée
Gross fixed capital formation	38 241	53 944	57 285	52 337	62 625	69 128	53 034	...	...	Formation brute de capital fixe
Change in inventories	- 595	6 787	8 091	7 164	3 399	1 149	1 093	...	...	Variation des stocks
Exports of goods and services	19 401	38 470	43 242	36 699	40 059	46 555	52 638	...	...	Exportations de biens et services
Less imports of goods and services	58 176	75 294	78 523	71 867	80 379	89 173	78 855	...	...	Moins importations de biens et services
GDP at purchasers' values	97 384	121 974	134 698	135 879	138 569	147 924	150 724	-	-	PIB aux prix d'acquisition
GROSS DOMESTIC PRODUCT BY KIND OF ECONOMIC ACTIVITY AT CONSTANT PRICES *ANNUAL GROWTH RATES (%)*										**PRODUIT INTÉRIEUR BRUT PAR BRANCHE D'ACTIVITÉ ECONOMIQUE AUX PRIX CONSTANTS** *TAUX DE CROISSANCE ANNUEL (%)*
Agriculture, hunting, forestry and fishing	0.3	0.0	1.0	10.5	- 3.6	4.4	6.7	...	...	Agriculture, chasse, sylviculture et pêche
Mining and quarrying	15.4	9.6	23.9	- 23.7	- 7.9	- 13.5	- 30.4	...	...	Industries extractives
Manufacturing	- 1.6	6.2	12.2	- 1.0	10.3	4.9	3.6	...	...	Industries manufacturières
Electricity, gas & water	22.4	- 16.8	41.3	15.8	13.2	- 2.4	45.2	...	...	Electricité, gaz et eau
Construction & public works	16.2	8.5	19.1	- 7.7	- 11.0	0.6	- 9.8	...	...	Bâtiments et travaux publics
Wholesale & retail trade, restaurants, hotels	8.6	18.7	- 1.6	3.5	0.9	6.1	6.5	...	...	Commerce de gros et de détail, restaurants et hôtels
Finance, insurance, real estate, etc.	11.7	13.7	10.2	- 4.5	0.9	14.2	- 0.8	...	...	Banques, assurances, affaires immobilières
Transport and communications	- 5.2	7.0	6.7	- 4.0	6.6	- 7.4	7.7	...	...	Transport(s) et communications
Public administration and defense	2.7	2.3	1.8	9.0	4.5	12.8	16.5	...	...	Administrations publiques et défense
Education	...	...	...	...	...	...	...	...	...	Education
Health and Social Work	...	...	...	...	...	...	...	...	...	Santé et actions sociales
Other services	9.6	4.3	6.5	- 1.2	6.0	...	...	...	...	Autres services
Less Imputed Service Charges	18.5	...	...	...	...	...	...	...	...	Moins services d'intermédiation financière
Gross domestic product at factor cost / basic prices	4.9	8.4	6.7	0.1	1.2	3.0	3.0	...	...	Produit intérieur brut aux couts des facteurs / prix de base
Plus: indirect taxes / taxes on products, less subsidies	76.7	11.4	6.2	- 9.8	3.7	10.6	- 10.0	...	...	Plus taxes indirectes/impôts sur les produits, moins les subventions
Gross domestic product at market prices	10.1	8.6	6.7	- 1.3	1.5	4.0	1.2	...	...	Produit intérieur brut aux prix du marché
EXPENDITURE ON GROSS DOMESTIC PRODUCT AT CONSTANT PURCHASERS' VALUES *ANNUAL GROWTH RATES (%)*										**EMPLOIS DU PRODUIT INTÉRIEUR BRUT AUX PRIX CONSTANTS D'ACQUISITION** *TAUX DE CROISSANCE ANNUEL (%)*
Government final consumption	- 2.8	11.4	3.8	7.3	2.0	6.0	- 3.5	...	...	Consommation finale des administrations publiques
Private final consumption	7.0	3.7	1.6	6.1	- 1.2	2.2	1.6	...	...	Consommation finale privée
Gross fixed capital formation	18.3	37.0	2.5	- 8.5	19.0	5.6	- 23.3	...	...	Formation brute de capital fixe
Exports of goods and services	13.8	14.7	7.4	- 17.5	9.1	11.5	9.4	...	...	Exportations de biens et services
Less imports of goods and services	7.0	23.7	- 1.2	- 6.5	9.5	4.6	- 14.7	...	...	Moins importations de biens et services
Notes	NA : 2012:Semi-Final							CN: 2012:Semi-Définitif		Notes

III INFLATION

	2006	2007	2008	2009	2010	2011	2012	2013	2014	
ANNUAL GROWTH RATES (%)										**TAUX DE CROISSANCE ANNUEL (%)**
All items	4.8	1.7	6.8	1.0	2.1	4.5	2.5	1.5	-0.2	Ensemble
of which:										dont:
Food and Non-alcoholic beverages	6.5	5.0	9.0	2.0	2.2	5.2	2.6	0.7	-1.2	Alimentation et boissons non alcoolisés
Alcoholic beverages & tobacco	0.3	-1.0	2.0	1.9	2.3	2.6	6.4	4.3	1.3	Boissons alcoolisées et tabacs
Clothing and Footwear	-5.6	4.1	10.6	-1.8	3.0	2.3	0.3	1.3	1.5	Habillement et chaussures
Housing, Water, Electricity, Gas and Other Fuels	12.1	9.4	4.3	-	2.7	6.4	5.5	4.9	-0.2	Logement, eau, electricité, gas et autres combustibles
Furnishing, household equipment	1.1	4.5	7.9	6.7	2.3	3.0	2.1	3.5	1.2	Meubles, articles de ménage et entretien courant
Health	0.4	0.3	5.3	6.2	2.4	0.4	0.4	0.7	1.3	Santé
Transport	8.2	2.7	7.9	-6.0	2.7	7.4	4.3	-3.7	-1.7	Transport
Communication	-0.3	-19.4	-2.1	-2.8	-8.6	-	-14.2	3.7	0.7	Communication
Recreation & culture	-0.9	-3.8	12.6	-2.2	-1.7	0.2	-2.0	-5.6	-1.2	Loisirs et culture
Education	-0.1	0.1	0.7	-	0.1	-	-0.3	-	-0.7	Enseignement
Restaurants & hotels	2.3	17.7	9.1	1.2	5.7	3.4	8.1	6.5	-0.1	Restaurants et hôtels
Miscellaneous goods & services	0.8	2.6	5.1	9.7	4.5	0.6	1.8	4.9	4.8	Biens et services divers

IV AGRICULTURAL PRODUCTION - PRODUCTION AGRICOLE	2006	2007	2008	2009	2010	2011	2012	2013	2014	
TONNES *(THOUSAND)*										**TONNES** *(MILLIERS)*
Tomatoes	13	13	14	14	12	17	14	14	...	Tomates
Bananas	7	7	7	7	7	9	10	10	...	Bananes
Onions, dry	3	3	3	3	3	5	7	7	...	Oignons sec
Carrots and turnips	6	6	6	6	6	6	6	5	...	Carottes et navets
Mangoes, mangosteens, guavas	7	6	6	7	7	2	2	3	...	Mangues, mangoustans, goyaves

V MINING PRODUCTION - PRODUCTION MINIERE	2006	2007	2008	2009	2010	2011	2012	2013	2014	
Salt and pure sodium chloride, metric tons (thousands)	2	2	2	2	2	2	...	...	...	Sel et chlorure de sodium pur, tonnes métriques (milliers)
Abrasives, natural, metric tone (thousands)	...	...	...	...	...	...	...	...	...	Abrasifs naturels, tonnes métriques (milliers)
	...	...	...	...	...	...	...	...	...	

VI ENERGY - ENERGIE	2006	2007	2008	2009	2010	2011	2012	2013	2014	
Total electricity generation (GWh)	236	253	270	281	287	287	297	297	...	Production d'électricité totale (GWh)
of which:										dont:
Production of electricity from fossil fuels (GWh)	229	246	264	274	280	280	290	290	...	Production d'électricité à partir de combustibles fossiles (GWh)
Production of hydro electricity (GWh)	...	...	...	...	...	...	...	...	...	Production d'électricité d'origine hydraulique (GWh)
Production of electricity from solar, wind, tide, wave and other sources (GWh)	7	7	6	7	7	7	7	7	...	Production d'électricité d'origine solaire, éolienne, marée motrice et autres (GWh)

VII TOURISM AND INFRASTRUCTURE - TOURISME ET INFRASTRUCTURE	2006	2007	2008	2009	2010	2011	2012	2013	2014	
VII-1 TOURISM										**VII-1 TOURISME**
International tourist arrivals (thousands)	242	267	285	287	336	428	492	503	485	Arrivées de touristes internationaux (milliers)
Rooms in hotels and similar establishments (thousands)	4.8	5.4	6.2	6.4	5.9	7.9	8.5	...	...	Chambres d'hotels et établissements assimilés (milliers)
Overnight stays (thousands)	2 515	2 580	3 337	3 758	4 288	5 374	6 379	6 829	6 556	Nuitées (milliers)
Tourism receipts (US$ thousand)	208 900	303 900	351 800	286 000	278 200	368 300	413 700	462 500	428 930	Recettes touristiques (milliers de $ EU)
Total contribution to GDP (%)	6.2	6.0	5.3	6.0	5.6	5.4	5.2	5.5	...	Contribution totale au PIB (%)
Total contribution to Employment (%)	31.3	33.4	39.2	36.3	36.1	36.9	38.0	40.3	36.6	Contribution totale à l'emploi (%)
VII-2 INFRASTRUCTURE										**VII-2 INFRASTRUCTURE**
Paved roads (% of total)	...	...	...	...	...	...	29	...	...	Routes asphaltées (% du total)
Total Network (Railways-km)	...	...	...	...	...	...	...	...	...	Réseau total voies ferrées-Km
Main Telephone Lines (per 100 inhabitants)	15	15	15	15	15	15	14	13	...	Lignes téléphoniques fixes (pour 100 habitants)
Mobile Cellular Subscribers (per 100 inhabitants)	23	31	57	60	76	81	86	100	...	Abonnés aux téléphones mobiles (pour 100 habitants)

VIII EXTERNAL TRADE - COMMERCE EXTERIEUR	2006	2007	2008	2009	2010	2011	2012	2013	2014	
ESCUDO (MILLIONS) EXPORTS, FOB										**ESCUDO (MILLIONS) EXPORTATIONS, FÀB**
Exports - Total	8 429	6 545	8 640	7 365	4 656	6 889	5 577	6 923	...	Exportations - Total
Exports to AFRICA	...	...	...	...	...	...	...	...	...	Exportations vers l'AFRIQUE
Main Products										**Principaux produits**
Fish, including fresh and chilled	889	564	1 421	1 855	2 831	4 388	...	2 603	...	Poissons, y compris frais et réfrigérés
Clothes	522	537	541	517	412	464	...	355	...	Vêtements
Footwear and footwear parts	264	375	341	309	368	376	...	420	...	Chaussures et ses parties
Spirits and liqueurs	38	48	51	61	58	55	...	59	...	Spiritueux et liqueurs
Lobsters, including fresh and/or frozen	37	31	34	34	36	70	...	260	...	Homards, y compris frais et/ou congélés
Main Destinations										**Principales destinations**
Portugal	906	902	980	928	840	975	...	946	...	Portugal
Spain	497	323	896	1 710	2 685	3 795	...	3 828	...	Espagne
United States	25	22	9	30	60	29	...	62	...	Etats-Unis
Morocco	161	113	66	...	...	...	...	...	...	Maroc
France	0	0	0	80	23	337	...	196	...	France
IMPORTS, CIF										**IMPORTATIONS, CAF**
Imports - Total	47 579	59 829	62 311	56 225	73 077	96 126	75 476	72 637	...	Importations - Total (millions)
Imports from Africa	...	...	...	...	...	...	...	...	...	Importations en provenance de l'Afrique
Main Products										**Principaux produits**
Diesel oil	2 361	3 964	4 004	3 606	4 107	8 479	...	12 645	...	Gas-oil
Iron, steel	2 454	3 057	4 357	2 473	2 747	3 348	...	2 623	...	Fer, Acier
Cement	2 149	2 461	2 828	2 355	2 361	2 341	...	3 195	...	Ciment
Vehicles for transport of people	1 620	1 771	1 934	1 342	1 329	1 485	...	2 053	...	Véhicules de transport de personnes
Plastics and articles thereof	1 575	1 566	1 962	1 916	1 847	1 927	...	3 602	...	Matières plastiques et ouvrages associés
Main Origin										**Principales provenances**
Portugal	23 878	27 059	31 370	27 171	31 796	33 601	...	24 224	...	Portugal
Netherlands	5 316	9 771	10 576	9 412	10 374	14 391	...	12 058	...	Pays-Bas
Spain	2 668	2 667	4 533	5 531	6 578	7 423	...	4 782	...	Espagne
Brazil	2 977	3 743	3 528	2 508	2 300	2 056	...	2 117	...	Brésil
Italy	2 267	2 275	1 696	1 738	1 075	3 345	...	930	...	Italie

IX FINANCIAL AND MONETARY STATISTICS - FINANCES ET STATISTIQUES MONETAIRES										
	2006	2007	2008	2009	2010	2011	2012	2013	2014	
IX-1 MONETARY STATISTICS *ESCUDO (MILLIONS)*										**IX-1 STATISTIQUES MONÉTAIRES** *ESCUDO (MILLIONS)*
Money supply (M1)	85 440	94 630	101 780	105 310	111 000	116 090	123 410	137 490	144 150	Masse monétaire (M1)
Quasi-money	44 879	49 043	55 671	60 768	62 877	70 756	75 662	82 523	86 568	Quasi-monnaie
of which Demand Deposit	...	...	...	...	...	...	...	...	...	dont Monnaie scripturale
Net foreign assets	25 189	30 998	28 991	27 376	28 482	19 986	25 375	33 541	42 698	Avoirs extérieurs nets
Domestic credit	72 983	78 555	91 381	99 192	105 489	121 514	125 018	129 209	131 775	Crédit intérieur
of which claims on private sector	43 683	55 559	70 443	78 761	85 815	97 248	96 712	98 668	97 737	dont créances sur le secteur privé
of which claims on government sector, net	27 545	21 358	19 530	18 550	17 196	20 456	24 928	26 856	29 681	dont créances nettes sur le gouvernement
International reserves (millions US$)	254	364	361	398	382	339	376	475	511	Réserves internationales (millions $EU)
Average Exchange Rate (National Currency per US$)	87.91	80.51	75.13	79.20	83.17	79.26	85.77	83.05	83.01	Taux de change (moyen) (monnaie nationale par $ EU)
IX-2 PUBLIC FINANCE *ESCUDO (MILLIONS)*										**IX-2 FINANCES PUBLIQUES** *ESCUDO (MILLIONS)*
Total Revenues and Grants	30 743	34 838	39 116	36 540	39 679	37 915	36 688	37 580	43 739	Recettes totales et dons
Tax Revenue	22 238	25 824	29 254	24 970	26 241	29 581	27 573	27 863	30 621	Recettes fiscales
Non Tax Revenue	2 716	3 442	3 433	4 720	3 998	3 993	4 913	5 766	6 387	Recettes non fiscales
Grants	5 789	5 572	6 430	6 850	9 440	4 342	4 203	3 950	6 731	Dons
Total Expenditures and Net Lending	36 252	35 986	39 911	44 615	59 246	48 973	52 004	51 202	57 124	Dépenses totales et prêts nets
Current expenditure	23 837	23 749	24 452	26 670	33 099	34 329	34 262	35 525	40 649	Dépenses courantes
Of which Wages and Salaries	11 547	12 491	13 518	14 844	14 810	15 679	15 886	16 479	18 306	Dont rémunérations et salaires
Capital expenditure	12 415	12 237	15 460	17 946	26 147	14 644	17 742	15 677	16 475	Dépenses d'équipement
Net Lending	-	-	-	-	-	-	-	-	-	Prêts nets
Fiscal Balance	- 5 509	- 1 148	- 795	- 8 076	- 19 567	- 11 058	- 15 316	- 13 622	- 13 385	Solde global y compris les dons
IX-3 BALANCE OF PAYMENTS *ESCUDO (MILLIONS)*										**IX-3 BALANCE DES PAIEMENTS** *ESCUDO (MILLIONS)*
Trade balance	- 40 694	- 53 243	- 57 233	- 53 735	- 56 822	- 67 206	- 56 176	- 51 801	- 53 603	Balance commerciale
Services Balance	11 612	15 762	18 404	12 782	16 529	20 449	25 012	30 393	24 374	Balance des services
Net Income	- 3 515	- 2 530	- 3 540	- 3 442	- 6 710	- 5 655	- 6 448	- 5 137	- 7 547	Revenus nets
Compensation of employees	...	...	...	...	...	...	...	...	...	Rémunération des salariés
Investment Income	...	...	...	...	...	...	...	...	...	Revenus des investissements
Current transfers, net total	25 383	24 224	23 902	24 596	28 281	28 469	22 233	22 257	23 586	Transferts courants
Net official transfers	...	...	...	...	...	...	...	...	...	Transferts officiels nets
Workers' remittances	...	...	...	...	...	...	...	...	...	Envois de fonds des travailleurs
Other private transfers	...	...	...	...	...	...	...	...	...	Autres transferts privés
Current account balance	- 7 214	- 15 787	- 18 467	- 19 800	- 18 722	- 23 943	- 15 379	- 4 288	- 13 190	Solde du compte courant
Capital & financial account	7 972	15 587	22 912	22 301	25 659	24 008	19 754	10 744	...	Comptes de capital et financier
Capital account	1 540	2 148	2 084	3 670	3 311	985	1 122	533	...	Compte de capital
Financial account	6 432	13 439	20 828	18 631	22 348	23 023	18 631	10 210	...	Compte financier
Errors & omissions	- 6 432	- 13 439	- 20 828	- 18 631	- 22 348	- 23 023	- 18 631	- 10 211	...	Erreurs et omissions
Overall balance	- 5 674	- 13 639	- 16 383	- 16 130	- 15 411	- 22 958	- 14 257	- 3 755	...	Balance générale

X DEBT AND FINANCIAL FLOWS - DETTE ET FLUX FINANCIERS	2006	2007	2008	2009	2010	2011	2012	2013	2014	
X-1 DEBT *US$ (MILLIONS)*										**X-1 DETTE EXTÉRIEURE** *$ E.U (MILLIONS)*
Total external debt	783	884	905	1 015	1 076	1 266	1 598	1 906	2 073	Dette extérieure totale
Private	197	246	261	242	252	320	435	543	574	Privée
Public	586	638	644	773	824	946	1 163	1 363	1 499	Publique
Total external debt service	56	51	60	53	53	65	68	81	90	Service de la dette extérieure
Present value of External debt	...	...	...	...	...	...	...	...	...	Valeur actuelle de la dette extérieure
Total government domestic debt (in local currency)	...	...	...	...	29 518.8	32 016.2	...	...	...	Dette publique intérieure
X-2 FINANCIAL FLOWS *US$ (MILLIONS)*										**X-2 FLUX FINANCIERS** *$ E.U (MILLIONS)*
Net Foreign Direct Investment Inflows	131	190	264	174	158	153	57	19	...	Investissement étranger direct (flux nets entrants)
Main origin of FDI Inflows										**Principales origines de l'IDE entrant:**
Italy	6	11	50	- 36	8.4	0.5	- 4.8	...	...	Italie
France	1	...	...	...	...	...	...	...	...	France
Luxembourg	1	1	1	1	...	...	1.8	...	...	Luxembourg
Germany	...	-	-	-	-	...	...	...	...	Allemagne
Hungary	0	-	-	-	-	-	...	...	...	Hongrie
African countries	...	...	...	...	...	...	...	...	...	Pays africains
Net total Official Development Assistance	138	165	222	196	328	252	246	243	...	Aide publique au développement (nette totale)
Main origin of Net ODA										**Principales origines de l'APD nette**
Portugal	47	44	62	53	142.1	146.7	168.2	159.1	...	Portugal
IDA	21	21	18	-	21.7	- 2.0	11.8	...	...	IDA
United States	7	7	24	36	37.1	9.4	3.8	5.2	...	Etats-Unis
Luxembourg	14	16	19	14	16.9	15.2	18.2	19.0	...	Luxembourg
Spain	5	21	20	21	21.2	15.5	5.5	5.0	...	Espagne

AREA (km²)	**475 650**		**SUPERFICIE (km²)**
CAPITAL CITY	**Yaounde**	**Yaoundé**	**CAPITALE**
CURRENCY	**CFA Franc**	**Franc CFA**	**MONNAIE**

I SOCIAL AND DEMOGRAPHIC INDICATORS — INDICATEURS DEMOGRAPHIQUES ET SOCIAUX

	Year / Année	Value / Valeur	
POPULATION			**POPULATION**
Population ('000)			Population ('000)
Both sexes	2014	22 819	Les deux sexes
Male	2014	11 408	Masculin
Female	2014	11 410	Féminin
Average annual growth rate	2014	2.5	Taux de croissance annuel
Active Population ('000)	2014	8 736	Population active ('000)
Population by age group ('000)			Population par groupe d'âge ('000)
0-14 years	2014	9 756	0-14 ans
15-64 years	2014	12 328	15-64 ans
65+ years	2014	734	65+ ans
Economically. active population. in agriculture (%)	2014	40.9	Participation de la population active agricole (%)
Crude birth rate	2014	36.8	Taux brut de natalité
Crude death rate	2014	11.5	Taux brut de mortalité
Total fertility rate	2014	4.7	Indice synthétique de fécondité
Proportion of urban population	2014	53.8	Part de la population urbaine
Life Expectancy at Birth - Total (years)	2014	55.5	Espérance de vie à la naissance - Totale (ans)
Dependency Ratio - Total (%)	2014	77.5	Taux de dépendance - Total (%)
HEALTH			**SANTÉ**
Percentage of children under-five and underweight	2011	15.1	% d'enfants de moins de cinq ans avec insuffisance pondérale
Prevalence of undernourishment	2013	10.5	Prévalence de la malnutrition
Under five mortality rate (both sexes, per 1000)	2013	94.5	Taux de mortalité de moins de 5 ans (les deux sexes, pour 1000)
Infant mortality rate (both sexes) per 1000	2013	60.8	Taux de mortalité infantile (les deux sexes) par 1000
Percentage of children provided the vaccines :			Pourcentage d'enfants vaccinés :
BCG	2013	82.0	BCG
DPT3	2013	89.0	DTC3
Polio	2014	79.1	Polio
Measles	2013	83.0	Rougeole
Percentage of mothers provided at least one antenatal care (%)	2011	89.8	Pourcentage de mères ayant au moins reçu un soin prénatal (%)
Percentage of deliveries attended by skilled health personnel	2011	63.6	% d'accouchements assistés par un personnel de santé qualifié
Number of doctors (per 10 000 population)	2011	0.8	Nombre de médecins (pour 10 000 habitants)
Number of nurses (per 10 000 population)	2011	13.1	Nombre d'infirmières (pour 10 000 habitants)
Hospital beds - Total (per 10 000 population)	2010	13.0	Nombre de lits d'hôpitaux - Total (pour 10 000)
Births registered (per 1 000)	2014	36.8	Naiss.s enregistrées (pour 1 000)
Deaths registered (per 1 000)	2014	11.5	Décès enregistrés (pour 1 000)
Public expenditure on Health (% of budget)	2014	5.0	Dépenses publiques consacrées à la santé (% du budget)
EDUCATION			**EDUCATION**
Enrolment in primary education (both sexes) (000)	2013	4 146	Scolarisation dans le primaire (les deux sexes) (000)
Female	2012	1 784	Féminin
Enrolment in secondary education (both sexes) (000)	2013	2 039	Scolarisation dans le secondaire (les deux sexes) (000)
Female	2012	785	Féminin
Enrolment in tertiary education (both sexes) (000)	2013	334.4	Scolarisation dans le tertiaire (les deux sexes) (000)
Female	2011	103.1	Féminin
Literacy rate (both sexes)	2010	71.3	Taux d'alphabétisation (deux sexes)
Male	2010	78.3	Masculin
Female	2010	64.8	Féminin
Pupil-teacher ratio	2013	38.0	Ratio élève-enseignant
Public expenditure on education (% of budget)	2012	14.5	Dépenses publiques consacrées à l'enseignement (% du budget)
POVERTY			**PAUVRETÉ**
GNI Per Capita (US$)	2013	1 290.0	RNB par habitant ($EU)
Human Poverty Index (HPI-1) Value (%)	2007	30.8	Valeur de l'Indice de pauvreté (IPH-1) (%)
Population below International Poverty Line ($2/day) (%)	2008	34.7	Population sous le seuil international de pauvreté (2$/J) (%)
Share of Income Held by Richest 10%	2008	34.9	% de revenu des 10% plus riches
Share of Income Held by Poorest 10%	2008	2.5	% de revenu des 10% plus pauvres
Gini index	2008	43.8	Indice de Gini

Charts
Graphiques

Population by age group – 2014
Population par groupe d'age – 2014

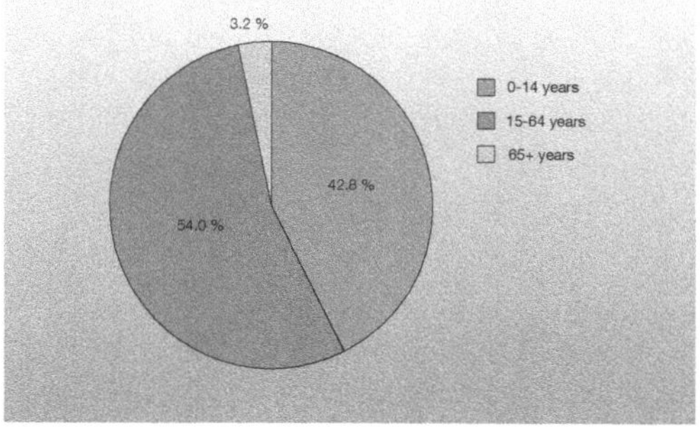

Percentage of children provided the vaccines – 2013
Pourcentage d'enfants vaccinés – 2013

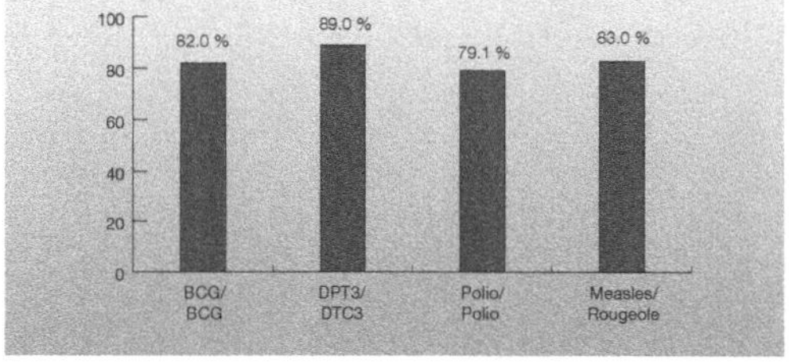

Literacy rate (%) – 2010
Taux d'alphabétisation – 2010

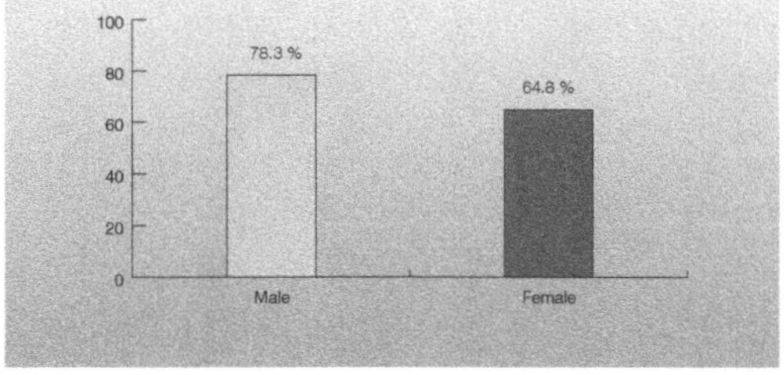

GNI Per Capita (US$)
RNB par habitant ($EU)

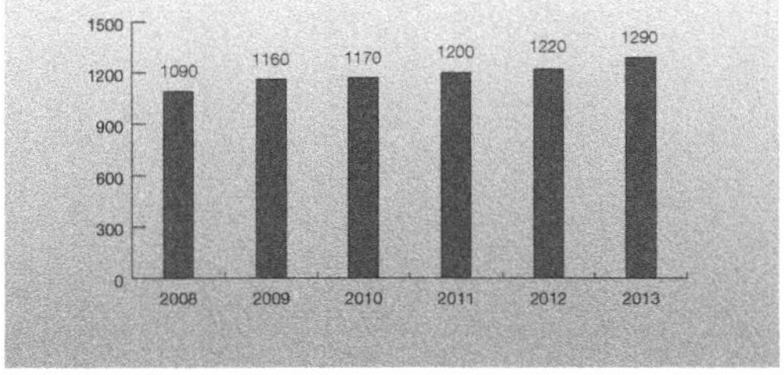

II NATIONAL ACCOUNTS — COMPTES NATIONAUX

	2006	2007	2008	2009	2010	2011	2012	2013	2014	
GROSS DOMESTIC PRODUCT BY KIND OF ECONOMIC ACTIVITY AT CURRENT PRICES *CFA FRANC (BILLIONS)*										**PRODUIT INTÉRIEUR BRUT PAR BRANCHE D'ACTIVITÉ ÉCONOMIQUE AUX PRIX COURANTS** *FRANC CFA (MILLIARDS)*
Agriculture, hunting, forestry and fishing	1 816	2 066	2 257	2 391	2 535	2 728	2 894	3 089	3 378	Agriculture, chasse, sylviculture et pêche
Mining and quarrying	966	958	1 086	807	778	961	1 100	1 090	1 384	Industries extractives
Manufacturing	1 536	1 340	1 532	1 653	1 756	1 679	1 845	1 942	2 091	Industries manufacturières
Electricity, gas & water	95	99	102	100	110	120	121	135	156	Electricité, gaz et eau
Construction & public works	274	293	275	485	598	663	710	865	916	Bâtiments et travaux publics
Wholesale & retail trade, restaurants, hotels	1 926	2 064	2 146	2 143	2 196	2 349	2 536	2 791	2 908	Commerce de gros et de détail, restaurants et hôtels
Finance, insurance, real estate, etc.	678	677	731	759	806	877	946	1 021	1 296	Banques, assurances, affaires immobilières
Transport and communications	535	595	621	659	758	819	863	965	1 030	Transport(s) et communications
Public administration and defense	315	342	458	507	532	569	623	699	741	Administrations publiques et défense
Education	295	356	360	406	462	488	513	537	570	Education
Health and Social Work	82	85	90	102	127	134	141	154	163	Santé et actions sociales
Other services	181	194	221	232	242	256	268	293	311	Autres services
Less Imputed Service Charges	- 59	- 47	- 61	- 60	- 64	- 68	- 74	- 81	- 88	Moins services d'intermédiation financière
Gross domestic product at factor cost / basic prices	8 642	9 021	9 818	10 185	10 836	11 573	12 485	13 498	14 857	Produit intérieur brut aux couts des facteurs / prix de base
Plus: indirect taxes / taxes on products, less subsidies	746	772	811	856	864	973	1 030	1 110	1 226	Plus taxes indirectes/impôts sur les produits, moins les subventions
EXPENDITURE ON GROSS DOMESTIC PRODUCT AT CURRENT PURCHASER'S VALUES *CFA FRANC (BILLIONS)*										**EMPLOI DU PRODUIT INTÉRIEUR BRUT AUX PRIX COURANTS D'ACQUISITION** *FRANC CFA (MILLIARDS)*
Government final consumption	901	994	1 127	1 243	1 358	1 457	1 548	1 691	1 813	Consommation finale des administrations publiques
Private final consumption	6 715	7 180	7 910	8 304	8 776	9 519	10 404	11 273	11 972	Consommation finale privée
Gross fixed capital formation	1 565	1 729	1 862	1 965	2 220	2 583	2 600	2 834	3 260	Formation brute de capital fixe
Change in inventories	14	- 8	60	80	8	1	19	15	-	Variation des stocks
Exports of goods and services	2 160	2 343	2 470	1 771	2 030	2 307	2 540	3 018	3 467	Exportations de biens et services
Less imports of goods and services	1 967	2 446	2 801	2 322	2 693	3 321	3 596	4 223	4 430	Moins importations de biens et services
GDP at purchasers' values	9 387	9 792	10 629	11 040	11 700	12 546	13 515	14 608	16 083	PIB aux prix d'acquisition
GROSS DOMESTIC PRODUCT BY KIND OF ECONOMIC ACTIVITY AT CONSTANT PRICES *ANNUAL GROWTH RATES (%)*										**PRODUIT INTÉRIEUR BRUT PAR BRANCHE D'ACTIVITÉ ECONOMIQUE AUX PRIX CONSTANTS** *TAUX DE CROISSANCE ANNUEL (%)*
Agriculture, hunting, forestry and fishing	3.0	5.9	5.2	2.9	6.0	3.1	2.7	3.7	4.1	Agriculture, chasse, sylviculture et pêche
Mining and quarrying	7.6	- 7.7	- 1.8	- 13.1	- 11.9	- 6.7	3.7	8.7	21.4	Industries extractives
Manufacturing	- 0.6	0.5	3.5	- 1.0	2.7	2.3	5.1	3.6	5.6	Industries manufacturières
Electricity, gas & water	3.3	4.5	5.7	- 0.6	3.9	3.6	- 0.1	8.8	11.4	Electricité, gaz et eau
Construction & public works	4.0	0.5	- 8.2	12.5	9.1	9.6	6.7	12.9	7.8	Bâtiments et travaux publics
Wholesale & retail trade, restaurants, hotels	1.8	2.0	- 3.5	- 0.1	1.9	4.9	5.4	5.7	5.7	Commerce de gros et de détail, restaurants et hôtels
Finance, insurance, real estate, etc.	1.0	3.2	19.3	6.9	7.3	5.2	2.9	6.2	7.2	Banques, assurances, affaires immobilières
Transport and communications	11.9	9.2	8.6	7.5	5.2	8.2	8.1	7.9	3.6	Transport(s) et communications
Public administration and defense	6.0	10.6	1.6	3.5	3.7	4.3	6.1	5.8	3.7	Administrations publiques et défense
Education	5.0	5.0	4.0	6.2	8.9	4.5	3.7	6.3	3.7	Education
Health and Social Work	2.0	2.0	3.5	7.7	24.7	3.9	3.4	5.3	5.4	Santé et actions sociales
Other services	- 0.8	10.3	- 11.2	1.8	- 1.7	4.5	7.3	3.5	4.7	Autres services
Less Imputed Service Charges	- 3.8	- 7.7	6.3	- 6.0	4.3	3.7	6.8	7.8	8.0	Moins services d'intérmediation financière
Gross domestic product at factor cost / basic prices	2.9	3.3	2.6	1.7	3.5	3.9	4.7	5.4	5.8	Produit intérieur brut aux couts des facteurs / prix de base
Plus: indirect taxes / taxes on products, less subsidies	7.3	2.9	6.0	4.9	0.4	6.7	3.7	7.4	5.8	Plus taxes indirectes/impôts sur les produits, moins les subventions
Gross domestic product at market prices	3.2	3.3	2.9	1.9	3.3	4.1	4.6	5.6	5.8	Produit intérieur brut aux prix du marché
EXPENDITURE ON GROSS DOMESTIC PRODUCT AT CONSTANT PURCHASERS' VALUES *ANNUAL GROWTH RATES (%)*										**EMPLOIS DU PRODUIT INTÉRIEUR BRUT AUX PRIX CONSTANTS D'ACQUISITION** *TAUX DE CROISSANCE ANNUEL (%)*
Government final consumption	3.0	9.1	6.3	4.6	8.4	5.5	5.5	6.5	4.1	Consommation finale des administrations publiques
Private final consumption	3.7	4.6	3.2	3.1	4.6	5.3	5.4	5.5	3.1	Consommation finale privée
Gross fixed capital formation	0.2	11.7	4.6	3.5	10.7	12.1	1.4	5.2	12.6	Formation brute de capital fixe
Exports of goods and services	1.3	5.3	- 3.7	- 12.5	7.8	2.2	- 1.3	26.0	9.9	Exportations de biens et services
Less imports of goods and services	2.3	15.2	4.0	- 2.1	15.7	13.2	1.2	18.3	5.6	Moins importations de biens et services
Notes	2013-2014:Provisional							2013-2014: Provisoire		Notes

III INFLATION

	2006	2007	2008	2009	2010	2011	2012	2013	2014	
ANNUAL GROWTH RATES (%)										**TAUX DE CROISSANCE ANNUEL (%)**
All items	5.1	0.5	5.7	3.0	0.9	3.3	2.4	2.3	1.9	Ensemble
of which:										dont:
Food and Non-alcoholic beverages	6.9	-1.7	9.1	5.8	1.2	4.8	3.5	4.0	0.8	Alimentation et boissons non alcoolisés
Alcoholic beverages & tobacco	3.3	-0.2	...	...	...	...	-5.9	2.9	1.4	Boissons alcoolisées et tabacs
Clothing and Footwear	-1.4	-	...	...	...	...	2.2	2.6	1.6	Habillement et chaussures
Housing, Water, Electricity, Gas and Other Fuels	15.3	0.5	1.7	-4.2	-0.1	3.1	3.0	2.1	2.0	Logement, eau, electricité, gas et autres combustibles
Furnishing, household equipment	5.1	0.4	...	...	...	...	4.0	1.4	0.4	Meubles, articles de ménage et entretien courant
Health	2.3	1.2	1.0	0.1	-0.5	-0.7	2.4	0.6	0.8	Santé
Transport	8.5	2.4	0.4	-0.7	0.9	0.3	2.1	2.3	7.7	Transport
Communication	...	...	...	...	...	...	...	-2.5	-2.5	Communication
Recreation & culture	-0.9	0.1	...	...	...	...	-7.1	0.1	0.7	Loisirs et culture
Education	...	...	...	...	...	...	...	3.2	1.1	Enseignement
Restaurants & hotels	...	...	...	...	...	...	...	2.4	3.6	Restaurants et hôtels
Miscellaneous goods & services	...	...	...	...	...	...	...	0.8	-0.1	Biens et services divers

IV AGRICULTURAL PRODUCTION - PRODUCTION AGRICOLE	2006	2007	2008	2009	2010	2011	2012	2013	2014	
TONNES *(THOUSAND)*										**TONNES** *(MILLIERS)*
Cassava	2 838	2 939	2 883	2 941	3 808	4 083	4 287	4 396	...	Manioc
Plantain	1 723	2 280	2 501	2 550	3 182	3 426	3 569	3 692	...	Banane-Plantain
Taro	1 267	1 398	1 482	1 491	1 632	1 569	1 614	1 552	...	Macabo/Taro
Maize	1 250	1 355	1 395	1 625	1 670	1 572	1 810	1 847	...	Maïs
Palm oil	122	114	124	109	116	135	99	122	...	Huile de palme

V MINING PRODUCTION - PRODUCTION MINIERE	2006	2007	2008	2009	2010	2011	2012	2013	2014	
Crude petroleum, barils (thousands)	32	31	31	27	23	22	23	24	30	Pétrole brut, barilss (milliers)
Gold ores and concentrates, Kilograms	104 459	79 109	2 919	-	-	-	-	...	...	Minerais d'or et concentrés, Kilogrammes
Marble, travertines, etc., metric tons (thousands)	0	0	0	0	0	-	0	...	...	Marbles, travertins, etc., tonnes métriques (milliers)

VI ENERGY - ENERGIE	2006	2007	2008	2009	2010	2011	2012	2013	2014	
Total electricity generation (GWh)	4 018	5 252	5 690	5 874	5 958	5 874	6 167	6 523	...	Production d'électricité totale (GWh)
of which:										dont:
Production of electricity from fossil fuels (GWh)	235	1 320	1 372	1 716	1 580	1 537	1 574	1 613	...	Production d'électricité à partir de combustibles fossiles (GWh)
Production of hydro electricity (GWh)	3 719	3 847	4 232	4 016	4 260	4 217	4 470	4 783	...	Production d'électricité d'origine hydraulique (GWh)
Production of electricity from solar, wind, tide, wave and other sources (GWh)	64	76	77	71	59	59	60	64	...	Production d'électricité d'origine solaire, éolienne, marée motrice et autres (GWh)

VII TOURISM AND INFRASTRUCTURE - TOURISME ET INFRASTRUCTURE	2006	2007	2008	2009	2010	2011	2012	2013	2014	
VII-1 TOURISM										**VII-1 TOURISME**
International tourist arrivals (thousands)	451	477	487	498	573	545	533	577	622	Arrivées de touristes internationaux (milliers)
Rooms in hotels and similar establishments (thousands)	23.7	28.1	26.9	27.2	...	...	...	...	...	Chambres d'hotels et établissements assimilés (milliers)
Overnight stays (thousands)	890	1 018	1 064	1 126	1 268	1 167	1 353	1 717	1 952	Nuitées (milliers)
Tourism receipts (US$ thousand)	175 000	219 300	150 700	259 500	154 400	404 100	345 600	367 349	419 629	Recettes touristiques (milliers de $ EU)
Total contribution to GDP (%)	6.2	6.0	5.3	6.1	5.7	6.1	6.4	6.1	6.2	Contribution totale au PIB (%)
Total contribution to Employment (%)	5.5	5.2	4.6	5.6	5.3	5.3	5.6	5.4	5.5	Contribution totale à l'emploi (%)
VII-2 INFRASTRUCTURE										**VII-2 INFRASTRUCTURE**
Paved roads (% of total)	58	60	10	...	10	23	...	...	...	Routes asphaltées (% du total)
Total Network (Railways-km)	982	974	977	977	977	977	977	...	...	Réseau total voies ferrées-Km
Main Telephone Lines (per 100 inhabitants)	1	1	1	2	3	3	3	4	...	Lignes téléphoniques fixes (pour 100 habitants)
Mobile Cellular Subscribers (per 100 inhabitants)	17	24	31	40	42	50	60	70	...	Abonnés aux téléphones mobiles (pour 100 habitants)

VIII EXTERNAL TRADE - COMMERCE EXTERIEUR	2006	2007	2008	2009	2010	2011	2012	2013	2014	
CFA FRANC (MILLIONS) EXPORTS, FOB										**FRANC CFA (MILLIONS) EXPORTATIONS, FÀB**
Exports - Total	1 588 000	1 721 000	1 694 000	1 582 864	1 924 213	2 133 608	2 182 512	2 230 681	2 557 858	Exportations - Total
Exports to AFRICA	...	...	...	...	...	...	...	...	...	Exportations vers l'AFRIQUE
Main Products										**Principaux produits**
Petroleum oils, crude	188 323	202 837	47 452	681 814	698 362	761 239	936 334	1 087 464	1 223 668	Huiles brutes de pétrole
Fuel, lubricant	212 212	266 444	99 874	93 488	247 347	345 922	269 308	127 403	159 108	Carburants et lubrifiants
Woods	169 134	210 557	149 179	99 821	123 044	135 922	142 823	135 517	149 004	Bois sciés
Cocoa beans	172 453	223 862	234 159	255 012	301 410	241 596	201 567	223 738	279 324	Cacao brut en fèves
Aluminium, crude	339 372	537 027	32 657	32 146	48 437	44 515	26 871	31 821	73 281	Aluminium brut
Main Destinations										**Principales destinations**
Spain	686	854	759	1 146	1 774	2 396	2 575	2 855	...	Espagne
Italy	139	143	148	54	237	186	589	625	...	Italie
France	131	226	118	...	...	...	1 135	1 071	...	France
Netherlands	176	112	107	65	68	75	247	234	...	Pays bas
USA	143	139	92	73	46	32	76	65	...	USA
IMPORTS, CIF										**IMPORTATIONS, CAF**
Imports - Total	2 577 000	3 442 000	2 832 000	2 073 492	2 864 689	2 859 644	2 748 399	3 285 082	3 747 276	Importations - Total (millions)
Imports from Africa	...	...	...	...	...	...	...	...	...	Importations en provenance de l'Afrique
Main Products										**Principaux produits**
Hydrocarbons	305 392	335 116	345 591	369 846	662 490	835 972	1 009 430	772 723	1 051 977	Hydrocarbures
Cereals	136 125	224 713	305 695	181 530	161 403	222 876	264 257	314 505	241 718	Céréales
Machinery, mechanical	125 957	163 333	401 399	197 899	216 598	269 221	272 792	299 649	338 790	Machines et app. Mécaniques
Vehicles; tractors	136 221	171 650	121 994	146 442	192 052	216 731	194 770	186 027	213 690	Véhicules automobiles; tracteurs
Machinery, electrical	101 395	251 549	184 853	137 306	134 169	201 301	181 187	214 063	266 608	Machines et appareils électriques
Main Origin										**Principales provenances**
Nigeria	1 065	1 195	1 689	4 809	2 820	4 833	5 919	4 533	...	Nigéria
France	253	370	219	246	216	204	392	401	...	France
China	136	203	133	128	320	371	346	466	...	Chine
USA	369	-	-	7	13	23	116	128	...	USA
Belgium	48	105	93	275	744	589	558	...	...	Belgique

IX FINANCIAL AND MONETARY STATISTICS - FINANCES ET STATISTIQUES MONETAIRES	2006	2007	2008	2009	2010	2011	2012	2013	2014	
IX-1 MONETARY STATISTICS *CFA FRANC (MILLIONS)*										**IX-1 STATISTIQUES MONÉTAIRES** *FRANC CFA (MILLIONS)*
Money supply (M1)	1 713 380	2 031 940	2 303 280	2 462 430	2 741 080	3 032 870	3 074 100	3 407 490	3 611 810	Masse monétaire (M1)
Quasi-money	724 466	744 690	821 851	883 223	1 038 490	1 104 879	1 147 735	1 257 690	1 315 678	Quasi-monnaie
of which Demand Deposit	...	-	...	...	...	...	...	...	...	dont Monnaie scripturale
Net foreign assets	1 015 623	1 503 506	1 736 298	1 780 800	1 849 441	1 629 648	1 541 390	1 552 978	1 604 804	Avoirs extérieurs nets
Domestic credit	874 752	682 732	699 466	866 188	1 202 407	1 670 682	1 939 998	2 261 673	2 471 436	Crédit intérieur
of which claims on private sector	887 428	948 877	1 142 116	1 266 887	1 466 950	1 779 274	1 910 943	2 159 135	2 353 542	dont créances sur le secteur privé
of which claims on government sector, net	- 114 844	- 381 647	- 585 874	- 558 227	- 496 171	- 373 849	- 162 092	- 155 097	- 108 326	dont créances nettes sur le gouvernement
International reserves (millions US$)	1 718	2 908	3 088	3 676	3 643	3 199	3 381	...	...	Réserves internationales (millions $EU)
Average Exchange Rate (National Currency per US$)	522.89	479.27	447.81	472.19	495.28	471.87	510.53	494.04	493.91	Taux de change (moyen) (monnaie nationale par $ EU)
IX-2 PUBLIC FINANCE *CFA FRANC (BILLIONS)*										**IX-2 FINANCES PUBLIQUES** *FRANC CFA (MILLIARDS)*
Total Revenues and Grants	4 473	1 963	2 215	1 925	1 940	2 280	2 426	2 623	2 783	Recettes totales et dons
Tax Revenue	1 635	1 700	1 970	1 680	1 705	2 048	2 179	2 355	2 488	Recettes fiscales
Non Tax Revenue	174	161	153	158	164	172	191	222	239	Recettes non fiscales
Grants	2 664	102	92	87	71	60	56	46	55	Dons
Total Expenditures and Net Lending	1 367	1 537	1 984	1 932	2 067	2 728	2 757	3 218	3 599	Dépenses totales et prêts nets
Current expenditure	1 096	1 147	1 395	1 491	1 611	1 922	1 923	2 151	2 428	Dépenses courantes
Of which Wages and Salaries	418	435	561	629	634	698	706	790	880	Dont rémunérations et salaires
Capital expenditure	271	389	589	441	456	807	834	1 067	1 170	Dépenses d'équipement
Net Lending	-	-	-	-	0	-	-	-	-	Prêts nets
Fiscal Balance	3 105	426	231	- 7	- 127	- 449	- 331	- 595	- 816	Solde global y compris les dons
IX-3 BALANCE OF PAYMENTS *CFA FRANC (BILLIONS)*										**IX-3 BALANCE DES PAIEMENTS** *FRANC CFA (MILLIARDS)*
Trade balance	351	335	206	- 184	- 104	- 274	- 140	- 186	...	Balance commerciale
Services Balance	- 204	- 189	- 424	- 251	- 271	- 58	- 255	- 285	...	Balance des services
Net Income	- 132	- 240	- 185	- 225	- 131	- 143	- 227	- 271	...	Revenus nets
Compensation of employees	...	...	...	...	...	...	24	22	...	Rémunération des salariés
Investment Income	...	...	...	...	...	...	- 251	- 293	...	Revenus des investissements
Current transfers, net total	132	229	278	132	110	122	134	162	...	Transferts courants
Net official transfers	...	...	...	...	...	...	...	...	...	Transferts officiels nets
Workers' remittances	...	...	...	...	...	...	...	...	...	Envois de fonds des travailleurs
Other private transfers	...	...	...	...	...	...	...	...	...	Autres transferts privés
Current account balance	147	135	- 125	- 528	- 396	- 353	- 488	- 580	...	Solde du compte courant
Capital & financial account	100	223	307	475	408	235	617	45	...	Comptes de capital et financier
Capital account	829	94	66	87	73	...	...	...	...	Compte de capital
Financial account	- 729	129	241	388	335	...	...	...	...	Compte financier
Errors & omissions	96	86	58	77	87	- 46	- 82	48	...	Erreurs et omissions
Overall balance	297	446	163	24	99	- 164	48	- 487	...	Balance générale

X DEBT AND FINANCIAL FLOWS - DETTE ET FLUX FINANCIERS	2006	2007	2008	2009	2010	2011	2012	2013	2014	
X-1 DEBT *US$ (MILLIONS)*										**X-1 DETTE EXTÉRIEURE** *$ E.U (MILLIONS)*
Total external debt	1 161	1 180	1 200	1 230	1 462	1 863	2 395	3 633	4 735	Dette extérieure totale
Private	156	91	1	1	1	1	1	1	1	Privée
Public	1 005	1 089	1 199	1 229	1 460	1 862	2 394	3 632	4 734	Publique
Total external debt service	418	342	258	215	176	162	183	238	321	Service de la dette extérieure
Present value of External debt	...	...	...	...	...	...	...	...	...	Valeur actuelle de la dette extérieure
Total government domestic debt (in local currency)	9	10	9	10	10.1	12.1	12.4	1 409.6	...	Dette publique intérieure
X-2 FINANCIAL FLOWS *US$ (MILLIONS)*										**X-2 FLUX FINANCIERS** *$ E.U (MILLIONS)*
Net Foreign Direct Investment Inflows	59	189	21	740	538	652	526	572	...	Investissement étranger direct (flux nets entrants)
Main origin of FDI Inflows										**Principales origines de l'IDE entrant:**
France	120	84	- 66	57	103.3	- 330.1	84.8	...	...	France
United States	- 11	- 52	2	- 50	48.0	- 4.0	6.0	...	...	États-Unis
Netherlands	1	...	...	...	1.3	...	...	...	...	Pays-Bas
United Kingdom	- 9	- 8	7	- 3	18.5	- 6.4	11.1	...	...	Royaume-Uni
Italy	...	...	3	1	21.1	3.9	- 4.0	...	...	Italie
African countries	...	...	...	...	...	...	...	...	...	Pays africains
Net total Official Development Assistance	1 719	1 926	549	648	541	612	596	737	...	Aide publique au développement (nette totale)
Main origin of Net ODA										**Principales origines de l'APD nette**
Germany	228	755	110	91	90.5	2.0	0.3	0.5	...	Allemagne
France	244	596	113	91	82.1	148.9	88.5	174.3	...	France
Austria	443	1	1	0	0.3	0.3	0.4	0.3	...	Autriche
IDA	53	32	29	48	82.8	73.0	87.8	...	...	IDA
Canada	207	12	12	7	7.2	12.2	5.0	2.7	...	Canada

AREA (km²)	622 984		**SUPERFICIE (km²)**
CAPITAL CITY	Bangui	Bangui	**CAPITALE**
CURRENCY	CFA Franc	Franc CFA	**MONNAIE**

I SOCIAL AND DEMOGRAPHIC INDICATORS – INDICATEURS DEMOGRAPHIQUES ET SOCIAUX

	Year / Année	Value / Valeur	
POPULATION			**POPULATION**
Population ('000)			Population ('000)
Both sexes	2014	4 709	Les deux sexes
Male	2014	2 318	Masculin
Female	2014	2 391	Féminin
Average annual growth rate	2014	1.9	Taux de croissance annuel
Active Population ('000)	2014	2 142	Population active ('000)
Population by age group ('000)			Population par groupe d'âge ('000)
0-14 years	2014	1 861	0-14 ans
15-64 years	2014	2 668	15-64 ans
65+ years	2014	180	65+ ans
Economically. active population. in agriculture (%)	2014	60.5	Participation de la population active agricole (%)
Crude birth rate	2014	33.9	Taux brut de natalité
Crude death rate	2014	14.5	Taux brut de mortalité
Total fertility rate	2014	4.3	Indice synthétique de fécondité
Proportion of urban population	2014	39.8	Part de la population urbaine
Life Expectancy at Birth - Total (years)	2014	50.8	Espérance de vie à la naissance - Totale (ans)
Dependency Ratio - Total (%)	2014	76.2	Taux de dépendance - Total (%)
HEALTH			**SANTÉ**
Percentage of children under-five and underweight	2011	23.5	% d'enfants de moins de cinq ans avec insuffisance pondérale
Prevalence of undernourishment	2013	37.6	Prévalence de la malnutrition
Under five mortality rate (both sexes, per 1000)	2013	139.2	Taux de mortalité de moins de 5 ans (les deux sexes, pour 1000)
Infant mortality rate (both sexes) per 1000	2013	96.1	Taux de mortalité infantile (les deux sexes) par 1000
Percentage of children provided the vaccines :			Pourcentage d'enfants vaccinés :
BCG	2013	37.0	BCG
DPT3	2013	23.0	DTC3
Polio	2012	47.0	Polio
Measles	2013	25.0	Rougeole
Percentage of mothers provided at least one antenatal care (%)	2006	57.3	Pourcentage de mères ayant au moins reçu un soin prénatal (%)
Percentage of deliveries attended by skilled health personnel	2010	53.8	% d'accouchements assistés par un personnel de santé qualifié
Number of doctors (per 10 000 population)	2004	0.9	Nombre de médecins (pour 10 000 habitants)
Number of nurses (per 10 000 population)	2009	2.6	Nombre d'infirmières (pour 10 000 habitants)
Hospital beds - Total (per 10 000 population)	2011	10.0	Nombre de lits d'hôpitaux - Total (pour 10 000)
Births registered (per 1 000)	2014	33.9	Naiss.s enregistrées (pour 1 000)
Deaths registered (per 1 000)	2014	14.5	Décès enregistrés (pour 1 000)
Public expenditure on Health (% of budget)	2009	11.0	Dépenses publiques consacrées à la santé (% du budget)
EDUCATION			**EDUCATION**
Enrolment in primary education (both sexes) (000)	2012	662	Scolarisation dans le primaire (les deux sexes) (000)
Female	2012	285	Féminin
Enrolment in secondary education (both sexes) (000)	2012	126	Scolarisation dans le secondaire (les deux sexes) (000)
Female	2012	43	Féminin
Enrolment in tertiary education (both sexes) (000)	...	...	Scolarisation dans le tertiaire (les deux sexes) (000)
Female	2012	3.4	Féminin
Literacy rate (both sexes)	2010	36.8	Taux d'alphabétisation (deux sexes)
Male	2010	50.7	Masculin
Female	2010	24.4	Féminin
Pupil-teacher ratio	...	...	Ratio élève-enseignant
Public expenditure on education (% of budget)	...	...	Dépenses publiques consacrées à l'enseignement (% du budget)
POVERTY			**PAUVRETÉ**
GNI Per Capita (US$)	2013	320.0	RNB par habitant ($EU)
Human Poverty Index (HPI-1) Value (%)	2007	42.4	Valeur de l'Indice de pauvreté (IPH-1) (%)
Population below International Poverty Line ($2/day) (%)	2008	8.9	Population sous le seuil international de pauvreté (2$/J) (%)
Share of Income Held by Richest 10%	2008	46.1	% de revenu des 10% plus riches
Share of Income Held by Poorest 10%	2008	1.2	% de revenu des 10% plus pauvres
Gini index	2008	56.3	Indice de Gini

Charts / Graphiques

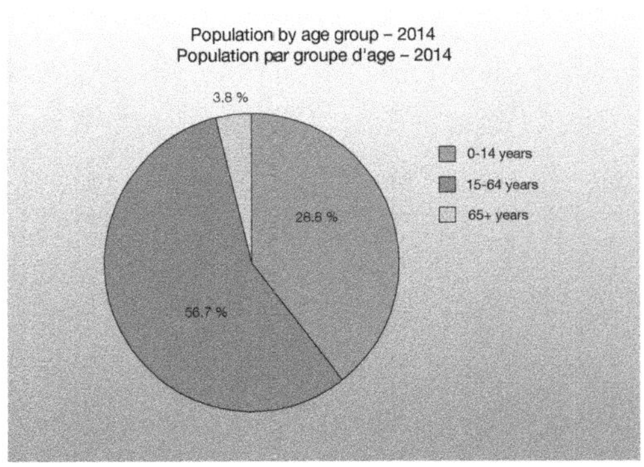

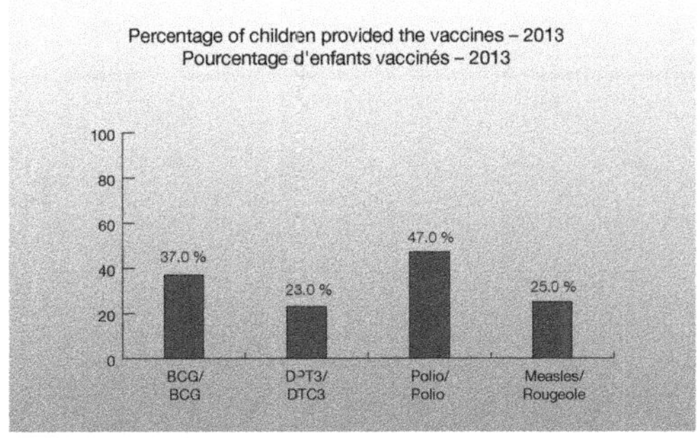

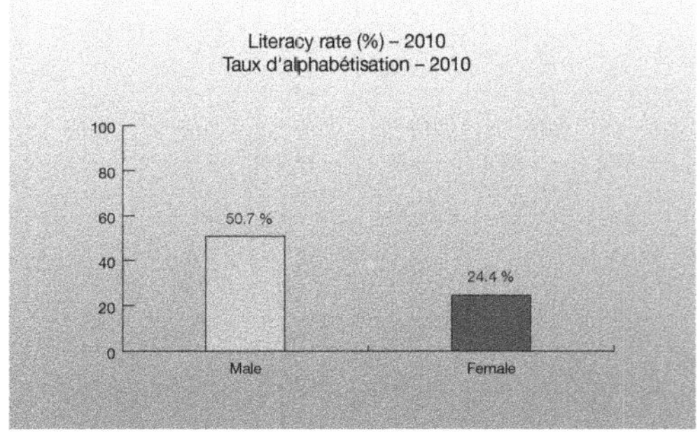

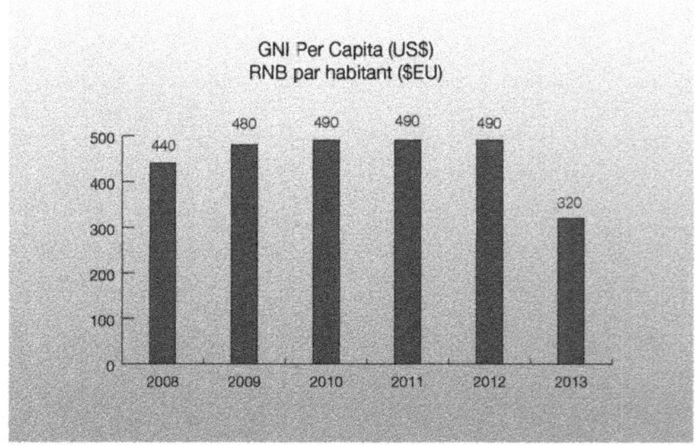

II NATIONAL ACCOUNTS — COMPTES NATIONAUX	2006	2007	2008	2009	2010	2011	2012	2013	2014	
GROSS DOMESTIC PRODUCT BY KIND OF ECONOMIC ACTIVITY AT CURRENT PRICES *CFA FRANC (MILLIONS)*										**PRODUIT INTÉRIEUR BRUT PAR BRANCHE D'ACTIVITÉ ÉCONOMIQUE AUX PRIX COURANTS** *FRANC CFA (MILLIONS)*
Agriculture, hunting, forestry and fishing	401 521	416 571	467 271	478 020	494 655	542 519	571 357	350 417	374 361	Agriculture, chasse, sylviculture et pêche
Mining and quarrying	20 333	21 197	13 878	16 231	18 009	20 484	22 473	7 465	4 601	Industries extractives
Manufacturing	47 531	50 959	56 230	59 446	61 549	64 735	68 122	60 901	64 540	Industries manufacturières
Electricity, gas & water	6 523	6 770	5 939	6 152	6 443	6 761	6 702	5 871	5 900	Electricité, gaz et eau
Construction & public works	29 246	31 290	36 067	38 076	40 002	44 107	47 112	40 238	48 988	Bâtiments et travaux publics
Wholesale & retail trade, restaurants, hotels	88 963	98 970	108 602	114 321	120 694	127 436	134 259	111 548	118 454	Commerce de gros et de détail, restaurants et hôtels
Finance, insurance, real estate, etc.	44 602	49 618	54 448	57 315	61 396	68 929	71 707	55 716	55 909	Banques, assurances, affaires immobilières
Transport and communications	38 275	42 580	46 724	49 185	52 180	59 658	62 363	51 399	51 782	Transport(s) et communications
Public administration and defense	37 200	36 300	36 900	39 500	43 900	46 000	49 000	26 000	26 026	Administrations publiques et défense
Education	...	...	...	...	...	...	...	...	...	Education
Health and Social Work	...	...	...	...	...	...	...	...	...	Santé et actions sociales
Other services	13 500	13 200	12 600	16 700	13 800	-	11 400	8 700	65 000	Autres services
Less Imputed Service Charges	...	...	...	...	...	...	...	...	...	Moins services d'intermédiation financière
Gross domestic product at factor cost / basic prices	727 694	767 455	838 659	874 945	912 627	980 629	1 044 494	718 255	815 561	Produit intérieur brut aux couts des facteurs / prix de base
Plus: indirect taxes / taxes on products, less subsidies	42 900	46 400	50 400	60 800	71 000	55 400	63 200	41 450	29 300	Plus taxes indirectes/impôts sur les produits, moins les subventions
EXPENDITURE ON GROSS DOMESTIC PRODUCT AT CURRENT PURCHASER'S VALUES *CFA FRANC (MILLIONS)*										**EMPLOI DU PRODUIT INTÉRIEUR BRUT AUX PRIX COURANTS D'ACQUISITION** *FRANC CFA (MILLIONS)*
Government final consumption	71 264	69 577	69 577	78 995	81 103	82 297	81 994	76 790	133 912	Consommation finale des administrations publiques
Private final consumption	675 486	724 230	806 804	862 362	883 440	941 216	984 343	705 437	810 267	Consommation finale privée
Gross fixed capital formation	78 160	81 450	103 163	105 575	138 771	126 204	165 857	65 869	86 004	Formation brute de capital fixe
Change in inventories	...	...	...	...	...	...	...	...	...	Variation des stocks
Exports of goods and services	115 011	123 142	103 995	89 289	102 333	139 412	140 200	108 300	37 878	Exportations de biens et services
Less imports of goods and services	169 327	184 544	194 480	200 476	222 020	253 100	264 700	196 691	223 200	Moins importations de biens et services
GDP at purchasers' values	770 594	813 855	889 059	935 745	983 627	1 036 029	1 107 694	759 705	844 861	PIB aux prix d'acquisition
GROSS DOMESTIC PRODUCT BY KIND OF ECONOMIC ACTIVITY AT CONSTANT PRICES *ANNUAL GROWTH RATES (%)*										**PRODUIT INTÉRIEUR BRUT PAR BRANCHE D'ACTIVITÉ ECONOMIQUE AUX PRIX CONSTANTS** *TAUX DE CROISSANCE ANNUEL (%)*
Agriculture, hunting, forestry and fishing	4.3	2.2	1.5	- 0.9	2.3	6.8	2.9	- 45.1	- 14.1	Agriculture, chasse, sylviculture et pêche
Mining and quarrying	8.0	0.5	- 9.3	- 8.3	- 2.9	6.4	10.7	- 67.7	- 35.1	Industries extractives
Manufacturing	6.5	7.0	5.5	3.0	2.5	3.0	3.0	- 13.3	3.2	Industries manufacturières
Electricity, gas & water	5.5	2.9	- 6.7	1.1	2.5	4.0	- 1.4	- 13.3	1.0	Electricité, gaz et eau
Construction & public works	4.0	6.0	5.5	3.5	3.0	8.1	3.5	- 17.2	3.6	Bâtiments et travaux publics
Wholesale & retail trade, restaurants, hotels	5.0	8.0	5.0	2.2	3.0	9.0	7.4	- 20.9	1.5	Commerce de gros et de détail, restaurants et hôtels
Finance, insurance, real estate, etc.	20.1	23.5	5.5	2.2	3.0	9.7	- 9.2	- 23.0	40.7	Banques, assurances, affaires immobilières
Transport and communications	17.9	8.0	5.0	2.2	3.0	11.0	1.0	- 20.0	1.4	Transport(s) et communications
Public administration and defense	- 10.4	- 4.3	- 3.2	2.9	7.4	1.7	2.4	- 48.6	- 10.7	Administrations publiques et défense
Education	...	...	...	...	...	...	...	...	...	Education
Health and Social Work	...	...	...	...	...	...	...	...	...	Santé et actions sociales
Other services	- 5.9	- 4.1	- 9.1	27.4	- 20.2	...	...	- 33.9	566.5	Autres services
Less Imputed Service Charges	...	...	...	...	...	...	...	...	...	Moins services d'intérmédiation financière
Gross domestic product at factor cost / basic prices	5.2	4.5	2.1	0.8	2.3	5.4	3.8	- 36.0	3.2	Produit intérieur brut aux couts des facteurs / prix de base
Plus: indirect taxes / taxes on products, less subsidies	- 2.0	6.2	1.5	16.6	14.5	- 24.1	9.7	- 37.2	- 37.2	Plus taxes indirectes/impôts sur les produits, moins les subventions
Gross domestic product at market prices	4.8	4.6	2.1	1.7	3.0	3.3	4.1	- 36.0	1.0	Produit intérieur brut aux prix du marché
EXPENDITURE ON GROSS DOMESTIC PRODUCT AT CONSTANT PURCHASERS' VALUES *ANNUAL GROWTH RATES (%)*										**EMPLOIS DU PRODUIT INTÉRIEUR BRUT AUX PRIX CONSTANTS D'ACQUISITION** *TAUX DE CROISSANCE ANNUEL (%)*
Government final consumption	- 7.9	- 4.1	18.4	51.1	10.0	- 2.4	- 16.6	- 3.0	12.2	Consommation finale des administrations publiques
Private final consumption	4.4	6.3	- 0.3	0.3	3.0	1.9	3.0	- 31.3	3.8	Consommation finale privée
Gross fixed capital formation	7.8	2.3	21.6	5.4	12.2	- 12.6	29.0	- 57.5	15.9	Formation brute de capital fixe
Exports of goods and services	17.1	5.2	- 12.7	- 17.0	9.8	5.2	10.1	- 24.4	6.0	Exportations de biens et services
Less imports of goods and services	6.1	7.0	- 2.3	5.5	13.4	- 13.3	9.1	- 15.6	23.0	Moins importations de biens et services
Notes	NA data : 2011:Provisionnal;2012-2014: Projections				Données des CN: 2011:Provisoire; 2012-2014: Projections					Notes

III INFLATION	2006	2007	2008	2009	2010	2011	2012	2013	2014	
ANNUAL GROWTH RATES (%)										**TAUX DE CROISSANCE ANNUEL (%)**
All items	6.7	0.9	9.3	3.6	1.5	1.8	5.3	1.5	8.2	Ensemble
of which:										dont:
Food and Non-alcoholic beverages	7.1	1.5	12.2	3.5	1.4	1.1	7.4	1.5	10.8	Alimentation et boissons non alcoolisés
Alcoholic beverages & tobacco	...	1.0	7.2	6.8	-0.1	1.6	-0.2	1.9	6.1	Boissons alcoolisées et tabacs
Clothing and Footwear	...	-2.6	2.5	3.2	0.9	-1.3	5.1	-1.0	1.7	Habillement et chaussures
Housing, Water, Electricity, Gas and Other Fuels	8.2	3.3	11.6	3.8	4.6	7.1	1.2	0.6	-0.7	Logement, eau, electricité, gas et autres combustibles
Furnishing, household equipment	...	-1.8	8.5	5.2	-1.4	3.8	6.0	-4.9	-5.5	Meubles, articles de ménage et entretien courant
Health	...	-1.7	1.3	0.2	-	-	0.5	-1.4	5.1	Santé
Transport	...	1.4	1.8	1.6	0.3	-1.2	2.7	0.8	-0.4	Transport
Communication	...	-	-	-	-	-	1.2	-1.1	-1.1	Communication
Recreation & culture	...	2.2	8.7	1.7	8.2	0.5	-4.8	-4.3	7.9	Loisirs et culture
Education	...	...	...	...	...	...	...	...	...	Enseignement
Restaurants & hotels	...	-1.1	4.9	2.1	-0.9	-1.2	13.8	9.2	21.3	Restaurants et hôtels
Miscellaneous goods & services	...	2.2	3.2	5.3	7.6	6.3	6.0	20.4	23.6	Biens et services divers

	2006	2007	2008	2009	2010	2011	2012	2013	2014	
IV AGRICULTURAL PRODUCTION - PRODUCTION AGRICOLE										
TONNES *(THOUSAND)*										**TONNES** *(MILLIERS)*
Cassava	572	598	622	643	679	706	684	700	...	Manioc
Yams	370	387	402	416	435	452	460	470	...	Ignames
Maize	131	140	147	151	150	160	162	165	...	Maïs
Groundnuts in shells	146	156	160	163	140	160	149	162	...	Arachides en coques
Taro (cocoyam)	101	106	110	114	118	123	125	130	...	Taro
V MINING PRODUCTION - PRODUCTION MINIERE										
	2006	2007	2008	2009	2010	2011	2012	2013	2014	
Diamonds, industrial, carat (thousands)	416	418	377	310	...	...	...	...	...	Diamants, industriels, carat (milliers)
Diamonds and other precious stones, unworked, carat (thousands)	420	...	...	...	...	...	...	...	...	Diamants et autres pierres précieuses, brut, carat (milliers)
Gold ores and concentrates (Kilograms)	9	13	37	61	...	...	...	...	...	Minerais d'or et concentrés (kilogrammes)
VI ENERGY - ENERGIE										
	2006	2007	2008	2009	2010	2011	2012	2013	2014	
Total electricity generation (GWh)	168	160	160	159	160	165	176	192	...	Production d'électricité totale (GWh)
of which:										dont:
Production of electricity from fossil fuels (GWh)	29	24	24	24	25	25	27	28	...	Production d'électricité à partir de combustibles fossiles (GWh)
Production of hydro electricity (GWh)	139	136	136	135	135	139	149	159	...	Production d'électricité d'origine hydraulique (GWh)
Production of electricity from solar, wind, tide, wave and other sources (GWh)	...	...	...	...	...	1	1	5	...	Production d'électricité d'origine solaire, éolienne, marée motrice et autres (GWh)
VII TOURISM AND INFRASTRUCTURE - TOURISME ET INFRASTRUCTURE										
	2006	2007	2008	2009	2010	2011	2012	2013	2014	
VII-1 TOURISM										**VII-1 TOURISME**
International tourist arrivals (thousands)	14	17	31	52	54	61	65	64	65	Arrivées de touristes internationaux (milliers)
Rooms in hotels and similar establishments (thousands)	...	...	...	...	...	...	...	...	...	Chambres d'hotels et établissements assimilés (milliers)
Overnight stays (thousands)	84	91	175	103	95	50	57	125	128	Nuitées (milliers)
Tourism receipts (US$ thousand)	8 000	8 400	9 000	4 500	5 500	6 136	6 811	6 363	6 880	Recettes touristiques (milliers de $ EU)
Total contribution to GDP (%)	4.4	4.2	4.5	4.2	4.2	3.7	3.7	4.0	4.0	Contribution totale au PIB (%)
Total contribution to Employment (%)	3.9	3.7	4.0	3.7	3.8	3.4	3.2	3.4	3.4	Contribution totale à l'emploi (%)
VII-2 INFRASTRUCTURE										**VII-2 INFRASTRUCTURE**
Paved roads (% of total)	...	...	...	7	7	...	...	...	...	Routes asphaltées (% du total)
Total Network (Railways-km)	...	...	...	...	...	...	...	...	...	Réseau total voies ferrées-Km
Main Telephone Lines (per 100 inhabitants)	...	...	...	0	0	0	0	0	...	Lignes téléphoniques fixes (pour 100 habitants)
Mobile Cellular Subscribers (per 100 inhabitants)	3	8	14	20	23	22	25	29	...	Abonnés aux téléphones mobiles (pour 100 habitants)
VIII EXTERNAL TRADE - COMMERCE EXTERIEUR										
	2006	2007	2008	2009	2010	2011	2012	2013	2014	
CFA FRANC (MILLIONS) EXPORTS, FOB										**FRANC CFA (MILLIONS) EXPORTATIONS, FÀB**
Exports - Total	82 422	85 418	66 100	61 000	71 700	94 800	99 935	89 562	...	Exportations - Total
Exports to AFRICA	...	...	...	...	...	...	...	...	...	Exportations vers l'AFRIQUE
Main Products										**Principaux produits**
Diamonds	32 667	29 755	22 198	23 310	25 862	28 944	...	24 327	...	Diamants
Rough lumber	39 800	41 947	34 906	24 727	29 596	38 399	...	12 824	...	Bois grume
Cotton	764	529	927	585	2 339	4 746	9 175	6 042	...	Coton
Coffee	794	4 189	1 147	1 993	2 689	4 296	...	4 839	...	Café
Gold	75	77	246	453	716	970	...	10 906	...	Or
Main Destinations										**Principales destinations**
Belgium	20 416	15 059	11 712	23 187	20 895	22 342	27 312	16 134	...	Belgique
China	3 738	4 446	8 803	6 697	7 894	12 603	15 337	8 937	...	Chine
Indonesia	4 774	13 332	6 141	2 341	5 303	4 612	...	...	...	Indonésie
France	5 179	5 077	5 000	4 208	5 070	5 259	9 758	5 429	...	France
Morocco	1 727	5 278	6 051	4 824	5 852	3 934	5 348	...	...	Maroc
IMPORTS, CIF										**IMPORTATIONS, CAF**
Imports - Total	105 900	119 300	134 500	127 900	151 100	179 309	217 529	129 727	...	Importations - Total (millions)
Imports from Africa	...	...	...	...	...	...	...	...	...	Importations en provenance de l'Afrique
Main Products										**Principaux produits**
Petroleum, petroleum products and related materials	17 584	15 866	43 836	11 857	27 088	32 770	...	...	...	Pétrole et produits dérivés
Cereals and cereal preparations	3 799	8 484	9 974	12 040	13 735	19 251	...	...	...	Céréales et préparations à base de céréales
Medicinal and pharmaceutical products	4 079	7 106	6 316	10 263	9 413	10 232	...	...	...	Produits médicinaux et pharmaceutiques
Road vehicles	4 303	8 471	5 871	6 917	8 651	8 837	...	...	...	Véhicules routiers
Telecommunication and sound recording apparatus	1 120	5 254	6 743	5 105	6 372	6 728	...	...	...	Équipements pour les télécommunications et le son
Main Origin										**Principales provenances**
France	15 610	24 069	26 219	26 150	31 147	36 734	19 112	32 042	...	France
Cameroon	8 363	12 218	13 728	14 540	16 846	19 946	10 803	8 229	...	Cameroun
United States	8 961	7 630	8 364	17 279	16 154	19 626	4 951	...	...	États-Unis
Netherlands	14 552	14 606	9 345	12 854	14 390	16 821	22 268	11 464	...	Pays-Bas
Korea, Republic of	107	54	29 635	151	10 996	12 784	50 360	124	...	Corée, République de

IX FINANCIAL AND MONETARY STATISTICS - FINANCES ET STATISTIQUES MONETAIRES

	2006	2007	2008	2009	2010	2011	2012	2013	2014	
IX-1 MONETARY STATISTICS *CFA FRANC (MILLIONS)*										**IX-1 STATISTIQUES MONÉTAIRES** *FRANC CFA (MILLIONS)*
Money supply (M1)	122 970	118 490	138 060	156 970	197 560	206 120	214 750	220 050	226 870	Masse monétaire (M1)
Quasi-money	17 349	19 346	24 359	25 253	30 674	40 127	39 508	44 024	44 871	Quasi-monnaie
of which Demand Deposit	...	...	...	...	...	...	...	...	...	dont Monnaie scripturale
Net foreign assets	37 339	25 741	24 400	28 664	10 568	13 326	- 11 408	8 614	50 929	Avoirs extérieurs nets
Domestic credit	139 287	145 771	161 672	187 133	222 854	263 552	292 845	278 458	265 209	Crédit intérieur
of which claims on private sector	51 212	55 204	62 413	67 695	88 087	105 474	138 049	113 428	122 722	dont créances sur le secteur privé
of which claims on government sector, net	82 894	85 222	95 959	116 532	132 255	154 628	151 063	159 848	137 814	dont créances nettes sur le gouvernement
International reserves (millions US$)	126	83	122	211	181	155	158	...	...	Réserves internationales (millions $EU)
Average Exchange Rate (National Currency per US$)	522.89	479.27	447.81	472.19	495.28	471.87	510.53	494.04	493.91	Taux de change (moyen) (monnaie nationale par $ EU)
IX-2 PUBLIC FINANCE *CFA FRANC (MILLIONS)*										**IX-2 FINANCES PUBLIQUES** *FRANC CFA (MILLIONS)*
Total Revenues and Grants	176 200	117 000	134 800	150 300	168 800	138 100	181 300	63 900	158 719	Recettes totales et dons
Tax Revenue	60 400	45 000	48 500	81 100	92 000	87 100	109 300	39 800	43 182	Recettes fiscales
Non Tax Revenue	12 900	38 600	44 000	19 800	22 300	24 700	18 000	3 400	3 788	Recettes non fiscales
Grants	102 900	33 400	42 300	49 400	54 500	26 300	54 000	20 700	111 749	Dons
Total Expenditures and Net Lending	107 200	104 300	133 700	155 700	182 900	162 700	181 200	111 900	185 605	Dépenses totales et prêts nets
Current expenditure	69 500	77 600	97 600	109 400	123 400	121 600	113 000	99 200	145 919	Dépenses courantes
Of which Wages and Salaries	37 200	37 400	38 600	42 100	43 300	46 000	50 800	53 700	58 270	Dont rémunérations et salaires
Capital expenditure	37 700	26 700	36 100	46 300	59 500	41 100	68 200	12 700	15 072	Dépenses d'équipement
Net Lending	-	-	0	-	-	-	-	-	24 614	Prêts nets
Fiscal Balance	69 000	12 700	1 100	- 5 400	- 14 100	- 24 600	100	- 48 000	- 26 887	Solde global y compris les dons
IX-3 BALANCE OF PAYMENTS *CFA FRANC (MILLIONS)*										**IX-3 BALANCE DES PAIEMENTS** *FRANC CFA (MILLIONS)*
Trade balance	- 23 497	- 33 867	- 68 300	- 67 000	- 79 400	- 59 000	- 68 300	- 55 100	...	Balance commerciale
Services Balance	- 35 867	- 41 489	- 43 515	- 42 961	- 56 302	- 54 600	- 58 000	- 24 000	...	Balance des services
Net Income	- 7 830	- 7 457	- 9 900	- 2 600	- 1 600	4 600	5 900	2 800	...	Revenus nets
Compensation of employees	...	...	...	...	...	...	...	...	...	Rémunération des salariés
Investment Income	...	...	...	...	...	...	...	...	...	Revenus des investissements
Current transfers, net total	42 231	30 500	34 100	36 900	39 600	30 700	69 500	53 600	...	Transferts courants
Net official transfers	...	...	...	...	...	...	...	...	...	Transferts officiels nets
Workers' remittances	...	...	...	...	...	...	...	...	...	Envois de fonds des travailleurs
Other private transfers	...	...	...	...	...	...	...	...	...	Autres transferts privés
Current account balance	- 24 963	- 52 313	- 87 615	- 75 661	- 97 702	- 78 300	- 50 900	- 22 700	...	Solde du compte courant
Capital & financial account	...	...	...	...	...	...	...	...	...	Comptes de capital et financier
Capital account	...	...	...	...	...	...	...	...	...	Compte de capital
Financial account	...	...	...	...	...	...	...	...	...	Compte financier
Errors & omissions	...	...	...	...	...	...	...	...	...	Erreurs et omissions
Overall balance	...	...	...	...	...	...	...	...	...	Balance générale

X DEBT AND FINANCIAL FLOWS - DETTE ET FLUX FINANCIERS										
	2006	2007	2008	2009	2010	2011	2012	2013	2014	
X-1 DEBT *US$ (MILLIONS)*										**X-1 DETTE EXTÉRIEURE** *$ E.U (MILLIONS)*
Total external debt	1 087	986	1 073	331	397	485	560	597	594	Dette extérieure totale
Private	55	60	67	...	...	...	...	...	...	Privée
Public	1 032	926	1 005	331	397	485	560	597	594	Publique
Total external debt service	41	36	44	23	11	11	25	20	22	Service de la dette extérieure
Present value of External debt	...	...	...	...	...	...	...	...	...	Valeur actuelle de la dette extérieure
Total government domestic debt (in local currency)	...	...	...	...	...	...	...	...	...	Dette publique intérieure
X-2 FINANCIAL FLOWS *US$ (MILLIONS)*										**X-2 FLUX FINANCIERS** *$ E.U (MILLIONS)*
Net Foreign Direct Investment Inflows	35	57	117	42	62	37	71	80	...	Investissement étranger direct (flux nets entrants)
Main origin of FDI Inflows										**Principales origines de l'IDE entrant:**
France	...	...	...	...	...	...	...	...	...	France
Korea	...	...	...	...	...	...	...	...	...	Corée
Portugal	...	...	...	...	...	...	...	...	...	Portugal
Chile	...	...	...	...	...	...	...	...	...	Chili
Sweden	...	...	...	...	...	...	...	...	...	Suède
African countries	...	...	...	...	...	...	...	...	...	Pays africains
Net total Official Development Assistance	134	177	257	242	261	269	227	189	...	Aide publique au développement (nette totale)
Main origin of Net ODA										**Principales origines de l'APD nette**
France	27	54	26	26	24.5	21.4	18.5	22.6	...	France
United States	21	18	34	31	20.5	11.9	15.4	19.2	...	Etats-Unis
IDA	34	- 2	12	27	17.8	53.3	42.5	...	...	IDA
Japan	0	3	12	6	8.1	38.3	13.6	5.5	...	Japon
IMF (Concessional Trust Funds)	- 6	24	21	40	13.2	-	10.7	...	...	FMI (Fonds fiduciaires concessionnels)

CHAD — TCHAD

AREA (km²)	1 284 000		**SUPERFICIE (km²)**
CAPITAL CITY	N'Djamena	N'Djamena	**CAPITALE**
CURRENCY	CFA Franc	Franc CFA	**MONNAIE**

I SOCIAL AND DEMOGRAPHIC INDICATORS – INDICATEURS DEMOGRAPHIQUES ET SOCIAUX

Indicator	Year / Année	Value / Valeur	Indicateur
POPULATION			**POPULATION**
Population ('000)			Population ('000)
Both sexes	2014	13 201	Les deux sexes
Male	2014	6 548	Masculin
Female	2014	6 653	Féminin
Average annual growth rate	2014	3.4	Taux de croissance annuel
Active Population ('000)	2014	4 745	Population active ('000)
Population by age group ('000)			Population par groupe d'âge ('000)
0-14 years	2014	6 719	0-14 ans
15-64 years	2014	6 113	15-64 ans
65+ years	2014	340	65+ ans
Economically. active population. in agriculture (%)	2014	65.3	Participation de la population active agricole (%)
Crude birth rate	2014	48.2	Taux brut de natalité
Crude death rate	2014	13.8	Taux brut de mortalité
Total fertility rate	2014	7.0	Indice synthétique de fécondité
Proportion of urban population	2014	23.2	Part de la population urbaine
Life Expectancy at Birth - Total (years)	2014	51.6	Espérance de vie à la naissance - Totale (ans)
Dependency Ratio - Total (%)	2014	90.9	Taux de dépendance - Total (%)
HEALTH			**SANTÉ**
Percentage of children under-five and underweight	2010	30.3	% d'enfants de moins de cinq ans avec insuffisance pondérale
Prevalence of undernourishment	2013	34.8	Prévalence de la malnutrition
Under five mortality rate (both sexes, per 1000)	2013	147.5	Taux de mortalité de moins de 5 ans (les deux sexes, pour 1000)
Infant mortality rate (both sexes) per 1000	2013	88.5	Taux de mortalité infantile (les deux sexes) par 1000
Percentage of children provided the vaccines :			Pourcentage d'enfants vaccinés :
BCG	2013	62.0	BCG
DPT3	2013	48.0	DTC3
Polio	2011	31.0	Polio
Measles	2013	59.0	Rougeole
Percentage of mothers provided at least one antenatal care (%)	2004	38.9	Pourcentage de mères ayant au moins reçu un soin prénatal (%)
Percentage of deliveries attended by skilled health personnel	2010	22.7	% d'accouchements assistés par un personnel de santé qualifié
Number of doctors (per 10 000 population)	2006	0.4	Nombre de médecins (pour 10 000 habitants)
Number of nurses (per 10 000 population)	2006	1.9	Nombre d'infirmières (pour 10 000 habitants)
Hospital beds - Total (per 10 000 population)	2005	4.3	Nombre de lits d'hôpitaux - Total (pour 10 000)
Births registered (per 1 000)	2014	45.3	Naiss.s enregistrées (pour 1 000)
Deaths registered (per 1 000)	2014	13.9	Décès enregistrés (pour 1 000)
Public expenditure on Health (% of budget)	2009	13.8	Dépenses publiques consacrées à la santé (% du budget)
EDUCATION			**EDUCATION**
Enrolment in primary education (both sexes) (000)	2013	2 331	Scolarisation dans le primaire (les deux sexes) (000)
Female	2013	1 003	Féminin
Enrolment in secondary education (both sexes) (000)	2012	458	Scolarisation dans le secondaire (les deux sexes) (000)
Female	2012	143	Féminin
Enrolment in tertiary education (both sexes) (000)	2010	22.1	Scolarisation dans le tertiaire (les deux sexes) (000)
Female	2010	3.3	Féminin
Literacy rate (both sexes)	2012	37.3	Taux d'alphabétisation (deux sexes)
Male	2012	46.9	Masculin
Female	2012	27.8	Féminin
Pupil-teacher ratio	2013	62.2	Ratio élève-enseignant
Public expenditure on education (% of budget)	2011	10.1	Dépenses publiques consacrées à l'enseignement (% du budget)
POVERTY			**PAUVRETÉ**
GNI Per Capita (US$)	2013	1 020.0	RNB par habitant ($EU)
Human Poverty Index (HPI-1) Value (%)	2007	53.1	Valeur de l'Indice de pauvreté (IPH-1) (%)
Population below International Poverty Line ($2/day) (%)	2011	60.54	Population sous le seuil international de pauvreté (2$/J) (%)
Share of Income Held by Richest 10%	2011	32.6	% de revenu des 10% plus riches
Share of Income Held by Poorest 10%	2011	1.8	% de revenu des 10% plus pauvres
Gini index	2011	43.3	Indice de Gini

Charts / Graphiques

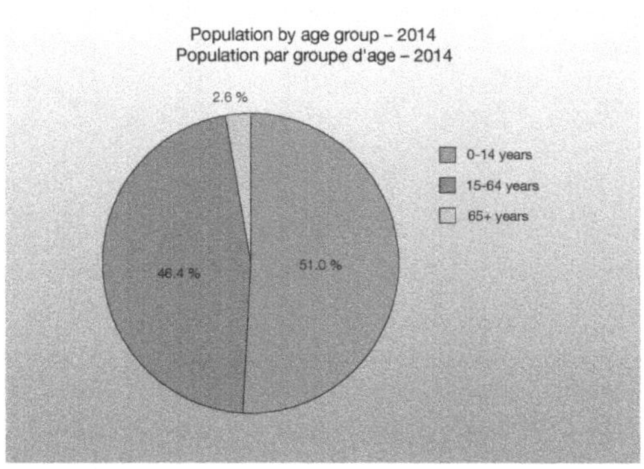

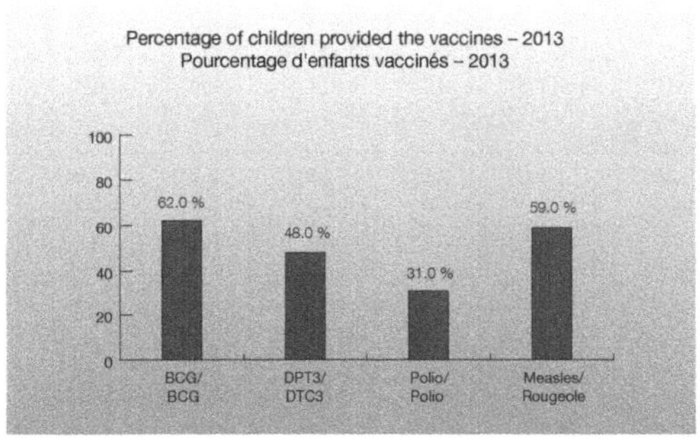

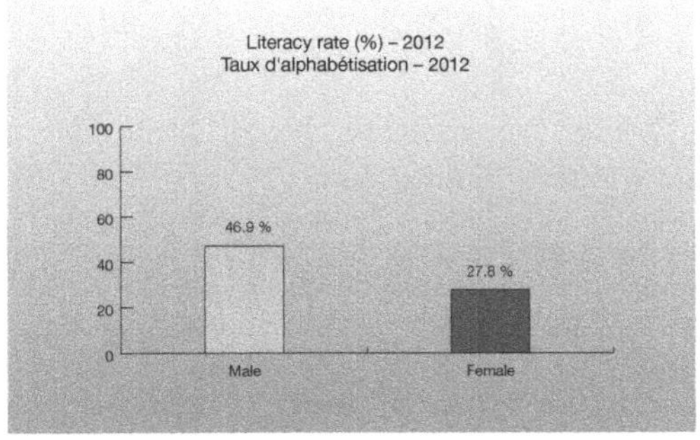

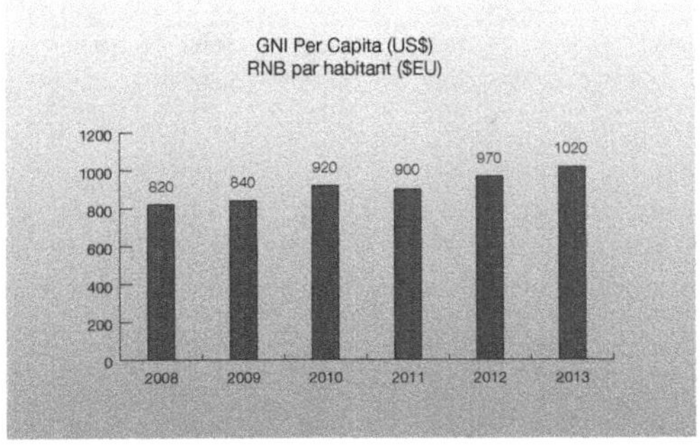

II NATIONAL ACCOUNTS — COMPTES NATIONAUX	2006	2007	2008	2009	2010	2011	2012	2013	2014	
GROSS DOMESTIC PRODUCT BY KIND OF ECONOMIC ACTIVITY AT CURRENT PRICES *CFA FRANC (BILLIONS)*										**PRODUIT INTÉRIEUR BRUT PAR BRANCHE D'ACTIVITÉ ÉCONOMIQUE AUX PRIX COURANTS** *FRANC CFA (MILLIARDS)*
Agriculture, hunting, forestry and fishing	1 068	1 115	1 115	1 132	1 422	1 208	1 447	1 497	1 629	Agriculture, chasse, sylviculture et pêche
Mining and quarrying	1 096	1 149	1 414	867	1 355	1 714	1 890	1 678	1 450	Industries extractives
Manufacturing	243	240	295	330	359	413	447	602	765	Industries manufacturières
Electricity, gas & water	1	- 1	4	5	3	9	13	13	16	Electricité, gaz et eau
Construction & public works	146	163	186	231	268	289	337	377	438	Bâtiments et travaux publics
Wholesale & retail trade, restaurants, hotels	675	706	582	596	641	655	688	806	943	Commerce de gros et de détail, restaurants et hôtels
Finance, insurance, real estate, etc.	302	345	282	331	373	413	440	522	561	Banques, assurances, affaires immobilières
Transport and communications	121	146	105	105	117	117	119	149	200	Transport(s) et communications
Public administration and defense	180	200	370	461	440	478	569	618	665	Administrations publiques et défense
Education	...	...	...	...	...	...	...	...	...	Education
Health and Social Work	...	...	...	...	...	...	...	...	...	Santé et actions sociales
Other services	...	...	...	...	...	...	...	...	...	Autres services
Less Imputed Service Charges	- 16	- 20	- 32	- 37	- 42	- 46	- 50	- 62	- 76	Moins services d'intermédiation financière
Gross domestic product at factor cost / basic prices	3 816	4 042	4 321	4 022	4 936	5 249	5 900	6 200	6 590	Produit intérieur brut aux couts des facteurs / prix de base
Plus: indirect taxes / taxes on products, less subsidies	65	98	158	102	120	171	176	210	255	Plus taxes indirectes/impôts sur les produits, moins les subventions
EXPENDITURE ON GROSS DOMESTIC PRODUCT AT CURRENT PURCHASER'S VALUES *CFA FRANC (BILLIONS)*										**EMPLOI DU PRODUIT INTÉRIEUR BRUT AUX PRIX COURANTS D'ACQUISITION** *FRANC CFA (MILLIARDS)*
Government final consumption	257	258	495	458	528	427	560	558	613	Consommation finale des administrations publiques
Private final consumption	2 705	2 907	2 624	2 323	2 645	2 655	2 975	3 388	4 257	Consommation finale privée
Gross fixed capital formation	877	949	755	1 235	1 570	1 639	1 897	2 141	2 331	Formation brute de capital fixe
Change in inventories	7	39	- 6	3	- 10	5	- 37	- 37	- 242	Variation des stocks
Exports of goods and services	1 850	1 842	1 976	1 574	2 063	2 379	2 458	2 334	2 116	Exportations de biens et services
Less imports of goods and services	1 815	1 855	1 366	1 467	1 741	1 684	1 776	1 973	2 229	Moins importations de biens et services
GDP at purchasers' values	3 881	4 140	4 479	4 124	5 056	5 421	6 076	6 410	6 846	PIB aux prix d'acquisition
GROSS DOMESTIC PRODUCT BY KIND OF ECONOMIC ACTIVITY AT CONSTANT PRICES *ANNUAL GROWTH RATES (%)*										**PRODUIT INTÉRIEUR BRUT PAR BRANCHE D'ACTIVITÉ ECONOMIQUE AUX PRIX CONSTANTS** *TAUX DE CROISSANCE ANNUEL (%)*
Agriculture, hunting, forestry and fishing	23.2	1.5	- 0.6	- 2.8	32.9	- 17.6	21.2	2.1	7.2	Agriculture, chasse, sylviculture et pêche
Mining and quarrying	5.0	- 3.8	- 10.0	- 3.8	3.8	- 2.4	- 6.4	- 10.8	0.1	Industries extractives
Manufacturing	- 0.5	10.4	10.9	8.4	10.3	8.4	1.8	27.0	28.9	Industries manufacturières
Electricity, gas & water	- 98.9	32.0	- 436.2	- 13.4	10.1	10.1	25.3	16.1	24.4	Electricité, gaz et eau
Construction & public works	- 4.5	8.7	6.9	15.0	13.0	2.0	18.0	15.0	11.9	Bâtiments et travaux publics
Wholesale & retail trade, restaurants, hotels	- 0.2	5.2	- 12.9	6.6	18.6	1.0	14.8	16.9	16.3	Commerce de gros et de détail, restaurants et hôtels
Finance, insurance, real estate, etc.	- 15.9	13.9	- 18.6	14.2	10.7	7.6	4.5	14.5	5.1	Banques, assurances, affaires immobilières
Transport and communications	241.5	13.5	- 22.5	8.7	13.2	12.6	- 2.9	14.7	23.2	Transport(s) et communications
Public administration and defense	- 1.9	2.6	75.4	23.4	- 2.8	10.7	18.5	6.8	5.7	Administrations publiques et défense
Education	...	...	...	...	...	...	...	...	...	Education
Health and Social Work	...	...	...	...	...	...	...	...	...	Santé et actions sociales
Other services	...	...	...	...	...	...	...	...	...	Autres services
Less Imputed Service Charges	27.8	27.9	57.1	13.0	14.2	8.0	8.0	17.0	19.2	Moins services d'intérmediation financière
Gross domestic product at factor cost / basic prices	6.8	2.9	- 3.2	4.3	14.9	- 2.9	10.2	7.2	10.3	Produit intérieur brut aux couts des facteurs / prix de base
Plus: indirect taxes / taxes on products, less subsidies	- 0.1	21.8	59.7	- 43.4	17.1	18.7	3.3	16.0	15.7	Plus taxes indirectes/impôts sur les produits, moins les subventions
Gross domestic product at market prices	6.7	3.3	- 1.9	2.6	14.9	- 2.4	10.1	7.4	10.4	Produit intérieur brut aux prix du marché
EXPENDITURE ON GROSS DOMESTIC PRODUCT AT CONSTANT PURCHASERS' VALUES *ANNUAL GROWTH RATES (%)*										**EMPLOIS DU PRODUIT INTÉRIEUR BRUT AUX PRIX CONSTANTS D'ACQUISITION** *TAUX DE CROISSANCE ANNUEL (%)*
Government final consumption	- 43.7	82.5	- 8.5	14.3	- 17.9	31.4	- 2.3	8.0	3.9	Consommation finale des administrations publiques
Private final consumption	20.3	- 4.1	- 13.7	- 2.7	28.3	- 8.9	20.3	13.5	7.8	Consommation finale privée
Gross fixed capital formation	7.4	- 24.5	58.0	24.0	2.2	15.8	11.0	7.1	4.3	Formation brute de capital fixe
Exports of goods and services	- 4.2	- 12.2	1.9	2.8	- 2.1	- 7.6	- 6.0	- 2.7	17.2	Exportations de biens et services
Less imports of goods and services	- 0.7	- 30.4	5.6	14.6	- 7.3	4.3	8.3	10.8	1.5	Moins importations de biens et services
Notes	The serie is revised from 2008					La série a été révisée à partir de 2008				Notes

III INFLATION	2006	2007	2008	2009	2010	2011	2012	2013	2014	
ANNUAL GROWTH RATES (%)										**TAUX DE CROISSANCE ANNUEL (%)**
All items	8.1	-7.4	8.3	10.1	-2.1	2.0	7.5	0.2	1.7	Ensemble
of which:										dont:
Food and Non-alcoholic beverages	14.4	-12.1	16.4	8.9	-3.8	1.9	11.8	-1.8	2.5	Alimentation et boissons non alcoolisés
Alcoholic beverages & tobacco	4.0	-2.8	-1.6	9.1	-4.7	5.9	-2.6	-0.3	12.7	Boissons alcoolisées et tabacs
Clothing and Footwear	-1.2	-6.9	1.7	0.8	-1.5	0.3	1.8	1.0	1.9	Habillement et chaussures
Housing, Water, Electricity, Gas and Other Fuels	8.6	-0.4	1.6	37.5	-1.1	1.3	2.8	2.4	-13.8	Logement, eau, electricité, gas et autres combustibles
Furnishing, household equipment	-1.7	-3.8	-1.1	3.8	-1.9	3.5	5.6	4.6	5.8	Meubles, articles de ménage et entretien courant
Health	0.6	2.4	0.8	0.3	-1.0	2.8	2.1	3.7	0.2	Santé
Transport	1.6	0.4	1.7	-0.6	4.7	0.6	5.3	7.6	-4.8	Transport
Communication	-	-	-	-5.1	-3.4	-5.5	-3.2	-	-	Communication
Recreation & culture	-3.2	-7.5	-0.1	-1.5	-1.0	1.8	1.4	2.8	2.4	Loisirs et culture
Education	-9.9	-10.6	0.2	-5.9	4.1	2.1	6.3	6.8	7.6	Enseignement
Restaurants & hotels	10.0	-4.7	3.5	8.1	-0.9	4.1	5.1	-4.7	2.6	Restaurants et hôtels
Miscellaneous goods & services	-0.5	-6.0	5.2	-1.6	12.1	18.4	24.2	4.9	1.4	Biens et services divers

TCHAD

IV AGRICULTURAL PRODUCTION - PRODUCTION AGRICOLE

	2006	2007	2008	2009	2010	2011	2012	2013	2014	
TONNES *(THOUSAND)*										**TONNES** *(MILLIERS)*
Sorghum	694	577	685	685	570	870	512	1 171	...	Sorgho
Millet	590	495	523	523	298	300	577	341	...	Millet
Groundnuts in shells	450	450	...	403	517	993	570	1 298	...	Arachides en coques
Cereals, nec	338	584	406	448	303	594	329	847	...	Céréales, nda
Yams	275	320	325	330	415	400	420	430	...	Ignames

V MINING PRODUCTION - PRODUCTION MINIERE

	2006	2007	2008	2009	2010	2011	2012	2013	2014	
Crude petroleum, metric tons (thousands)	7 874	7 190	46 549	43 625	44 704	41 880	37 173	34 310	...	Pétrole brut, tonnes métriques (milliers)
	...	...	...	...	...	...	...	...	...	
	...	...	...	...	...	...	...	...	...	

VI ENERGY - ENERGIE

	2006	2007	2008	2009	2010	2011	2012	2013	2014	
Total electricity generation (GWh)	104	99	97	97	100	203	235	269	...	Production d'électricité totale (GWh)
of which:										dont:
Production of electricity from fossil fuels (GWh)	104	99	97	97	100	203	235	269	...	Production d'électricité à partir de combustibles fossiles (GWh)
Production of hydro electricity (GWh)	...	...	...	...	...	...	...	...	...	Production d'électricité d'origine hydraulique (GWh)
Production of electricity from solar, wind, tide, wave and other sources (GWh)	...	...	...	...	...	...	...	...	...	Production d'électricité d'origine solaire, éolienne, marée motrice et autres (GWh)

VII TOURISM AND INFRASTRUCTURE - TOURISME ET INFRASTRUCTURE

	2006	2007	2008	2009	2010	2011	2012	2013	2014	
VII-1 TOURISM										**VII-1 TOURISME**
International tourist arrivals (thousands)	46	77	61	70	71	77	86	87	86	Arrivées de touristes internationaux (milliers)
Rooms in hotels and similar establishments (thousands)	...	...	...	...	...	2.4	...	...	...	Chambres d'hotels et établissements assimilés (milliers)
Overnight stays (thousands)	84	128	156	125	72	117	140	142	140	Nuitées (milliers)
Tourism receipts (US$ thousand)	50 620	57 040	70 360	72 340	76 800	87 429	74 312	77 323	78 228	Recettes touristiques (milliers de $ EU)
Total contribution to GDP (%)	3.3	3.3	2.9	3.5	3.4	3.7	3.5	3.6	3.4	Contribution totale au PIB (%)
Total contribution to Employment (%)	2.8	2.8	2.5	3.0	3.2	3.4	3.0	3.1	2.9	Contribution totale à l'emploi (%)
VII-2 INFRASTRUCTURE										**VII-2 INFRASTRUCTURE**
Paved roads (% of total)	...	...	...	...	...	...	...	...	...	Routes asphaltées (% du total)
Total Network (Railways-km)	...	...	...	...	...	...	...	...	...	Réseau total voies ferrées-Km
Main Telephone Lines (per 100 inhabitants)	0	0	0	1	0	0	0	0	...	Lignes téléphoniques fixes (pour 100 habitants)
Mobile Cellular Subscribers (per 100 inhabitants)	5	9	15	20	25	30	35	36	...	Abonnés aux téléphones mobiles (pour 100 habitants)

VIII EXTERNAL TRADE - COMMERCE EXTERIEUR

	2006	2007	2008	2009	2010	2011	2012	2013	2014	
US$ (MILLIONS) EXPORTS, FOB										**$ E.U (MILLIONS) EXPORTATIONS, FÀB**
Exports - Total	3 378	3 632	4 189	2 891	3 713	4 540	4 294	6 438	...	Exportations - Total
Exports to AFRICA	...	...	...	...	...	...	...	...	...	Exportations vers l'AFRIQUE
Main Products										**Principaux produits**
Crude Oil	2 925	3 160	3 820	2 397	3 222	3 947	3 721	2 433	...	Pétrole brute
Cattle	204	220	242	242	226	241	228	1 282	...	Bovins
Cotton	84	76	71	38	32	70	52	604	...	Coton
Sheep and goats	19	22	26	29	27	31	30	484	...	Ovin-caprins
Gum arabic	27	17	22	19	18	24	23	11	...	Gomme arabique
Main Destinations										**Principales destinations**
United States	2 706	3 166	3 706	2 442	2 498	3 415	...	...	...	États-Unis
China	357	136	61	89	588	290	...	...	...	Chine
France	22	15	61	130	57	228	...	...	...	France
Japan	...	130	202	...	...	...	...	...	...	Japon
United Kingdom	16	20	16	12	15	15	...	...	...	Royaume-Uni
IMPORTS, CIF										**IMPORTATIONS, CAF**
Imports - Total	1 795	2 217	2 654	2 835	3 347	3 251	2 992	2 156	...	Importations - Total (millions)
Imports from Africa	...	...	...	...	...	...	...	...	...	Importations en provenance de l'Afrique
Main Products										**Principaux produits**
Metal working machinery	164	215	219	214	230	210	...	...	...	Machines et appareils pour le travail des métaux
Gas, natural and manufactured	94	136	161	134	171	194	...	...	...	Gaz naturel et gaz manufacturé
Office machines and automatic data processing machines	92	112	119	124	169	110	...	...	...	Matériels informatique et bureautique
Non-ferrous metals	76	82	113	162	134	110	...	...	...	Métaux non ferreux
Other transport equipment	77	107	116	118	108	99	...	...	...	Autres matériels de transport
Main Origin										**Principales provenances**
France	323	427	472	449	458	471	...	...	...	France
United States	199	247	263	248	268	241	...	...	...	États-Unis
Cameroon	161	204	232	216	244	269	...	...	...	Cameroun
Portugal	81	107	118	112	114	121	...	...	...	Portugal
Germany	88	117	121	98	99	97	...	...	...	Allemagne

IX FINANCIAL AND MONETARY STATISTICS - FINANCES ET STATISTIQUES MONETAIRES	2006	2007	2008	2009	2010	2011	2012	2013	2014	
IX-1 MONETARY STATISTICS *CFA FRANC (MILLIONS)*										**IX-1 STATISTIQUES MONÉTAIRES** *FRANC CFA (MILLIONS)*
Money supply (M1)	379 270	400 760	506 400	482 880	605 280	691 330	784 280	852 110	932 760	Masse monétaire (M1)
Quasi-money	20 644	25 655	31 983	33 002	36 563	58 899	57 548	67 509	78 006	Quasi-monnaie
of which Demand Deposit	...	...	...	...	...	...	...	...	...	dont Monnaie scripturale
Net foreign assets	259 528	406 801	617 183	238 851	303 111	456 016	558 057	537 690	522 689	Avoirs extérieurs nets
Domestic credit	168 941	33 980	- 58 891	313 930	403 596	349 593	347 576	465 364	760 382	Crédit intérieur
of which claims on private sector	85 975	99 271	141 954	171 761	223 636	278 119	367 320	389 561	537 007	dont créances sur le secteur privé
of which claims on government sector, net	30 874	- 94 582	- 238 787	104 834	149 447	39 613	- 40 879	35 702	165 562	dont créances nettes sur le gouvernement
International reserves (millions US$)	626	956	1 346	617	632	951	1 156	...	...	Réserves internationales (millions $EU)
Average Exchange Rate (National Currency per US$)	522.89	479.27	447.81	472.19	495.28	471.87	510.53	494.04	493.91	Taux de change (moyen) (monnaie nationale par $ EU)
IX-2 PUBLIC FINANCE *CFA FRANC (BILLIONS)*										**IX-2 FINANCES PUBLIQUES** *FRANC CFA (MILLIARDS)*
Total Revenues and Grants	636	810	1 014	652	1 069	1 422	1 542	1 295	1 270	Recettes totales et dons
Tax Revenue	567	748	948	521	989	1 313	1 359	1 169	1 114	Recettes fiscales
Non Tax Revenue	6	13	9	16	11	18	16	13	14	Recettes non fiscales
Grants	63	49	57	115	69	91	167	113	142	Dons
Total Expenditures and Net Lending	542	731	874	987	1 289	1 284	1 512	1 464	1 652	Dépenses totales et prêts nets
Current expenditure	343	464	611	634	767	736	725	823	966	Dépenses courantes
Of which Wages and Salaries	85	153	185	201	216	250	283	333	359	Dont rémunérations et salaires
Capital expenditure	199	245	296	353	522	548	787	641	686	Dépenses d'équipement
Net Lending	-	21	- 32	-	-	-	-	-	-	Prêts nets
Fiscal Balance	94	79	140	- 335	- 220	138	30	- 169	- 382	Solde global y compris les dons
IX-3 BALANCE OF PAYMENTS *CFA FRANC (MILLIONS)*										**IX-3 BALANCE DES PAIEMENTS** *FRANC CFA (MILLIONS)*
Trade balance	1 059 634	901 781	937 544	36 414	191 117	619 557	687 204	310 636	...	Balance commerciale
Services Balance	-1 032 494	- 724 811	- 700 847	- 436 327	- 734 815	- 725 868	- 775 330	- 997 006	...	Balance des services
Net Income	110 013	- 75 929	- 120 029	- 326 084	- 177 830	- 191 207	- 322 768	- 156 953	...	Revenus nets
Compensation of employees	- 43 289	1 929	3 430	6 516	4 295	4 629	1 908	...	...	Rémunération des salariés
Investment Income	153 302	- 77 858	- 123 459	- 332 600	- 182 125	- 195 837	- 324 676	...	...	Revenus des investissements
Current transfers, net total	70 953	287 857	216 144	345 600	153 490	163 017	172 924	417 340	...	Transferts courants
Net official transfers	...	...	...	...	...	...	...	...	...	Transferts officiels nets
Workers' remittances	- 39 859	- 11 957	- 18 655	- 20 500	- 23 841	- 24 226	- 26 746	...	...	Envois de fonds des travailleurs
Other private transfers	...	...	...	...	...	...	...	...	...	Autres transferts privés
Current account balance	208 106	388 898	332 812	- 380 397	- 568 039	- 134 500	- 237 969	- 425 983	...	Solde du compte courant
Capital & financial account	- 9 169	- 215 128	6 803	488 756	434 566	383 780	448 660	...	...	Comptes de capital et financier
Capital account	52 116	57 742	45 811	49 500	57 268	82 346	75 383	...	...	Compte de capital
Financial account	- 61 285	- 273 470	- 35 454	444 784	377 298	301 434	373 277	...	...	Compte financier
Errors & omissions	- 39 415	- 49 672	- 130 025	-	-	-	-	...	...	Erreurs et omissions
Overall balance	159 522	124 098	209 590	108 359	- 133 472	249 280	210 690	...	...	Balance générale

X DEBT AND FINANCIAL FLOWS - DETTE ET FLUX FINANCIERS	2006	2007	2008	2009	2010	2011	2012	2013	2014	
X-1 DEBT *US$ (MILLIONS)*										**X-1 DETTE EXTÉRIEURE** *$ E.U (MILLIONS)*
Total external debt	1 805	1 765	1 625	1 711	2 150	2 602	2 570	3 043	4 145	Dette extérieure totale
Private	-	-	-	-	-	-	-	-	-	Privée
Public	1 805	1 765	1 625	1 711	2 150	2 602	2 570	3 043	4 145	Publique
Total external debt service	71	57	157	65	62	109	153	297	526	Service de la dette extérieure
Present value of External debt	...	...	...	...	...	...	...	...	...	Valeur actuelle de la dette extérieure
Total government domestic debt (in local currency)	...	...	...	...	...	...	...	...	...	Dette publique intérieure
X-2 FINANCIAL FLOWS *US$ (MILLIONS)*										**X-2 FLUX FINANCIERS** *$ E.U (MILLIONS)*
Net Foreign Direct Investment Inflows	- 278	- 322	466	376	313	282	343	538	...	Investissement étranger direct (flux nets entrants)
Main origin of FDI Inflows										**Principales origines de l'IDE entrant:**
France	16	26	19	10	- 4.0	- 4.2	- 3.9	...	...	France
Netherlands	...	...	...	...	...	...	...	...	...	Pays-Bas
Germany	...	...	...	...	...	...	...	...	...	Allemagne
Italy	...	...	4	- 4	...	...	...	...	...	Italie
Korea	...	...	...	...	...	...	...	...	...	Corée
African countries	...	...	...	...	...	...	...	...	...	Pays africains
Net total Official Development Assistance	289	359	422	561	486	460	479	399	...	Aide publique au développement (nette totale)
Main origin of Net ODA										**Principales origines de l'APD nette**
United States	37	60	81	170	134.6	113.9	118.7	53.3	...	Etats-Unis
France	42	48	39	41	40.7	35.5	36.4	39.7	...	France
IDA	32	18	- 49	4	- 3.8	3.9	- 2.1	...	...	IDA
Germany	27	29	33	28	20.1	32.9	24.1	24.8	...	Allemagne
AfDF	30	16	13	21	11.7	29.7	16.3	...	...	FAfD

COMOROS — COMORES

AREA (km²)	2 235		SUPERFICIE (km²)
CAPITAL CITY	Moroni	Moroni	CAPITALE
CURRENCY	Comoros Franc	Franc Comorien	MONNAIE

I SOCIAL AND DEMOGRAPHIC INDICATORS — INDICATEURS DEMOGRAPHIQUES ET SOCIAUX

	Year / Année	Value / Valeur	
POPULATION			**POPULATION**
Population ('000)			Population ('000)
Both sexes	2014	774	Les deux sexes
Male	2014	387	Masculin
Female	2014	387	Féminin
Average annual growth rate	2014	2.7	Taux de croissance annuel
Active Population ('000)	2014	262	Population active ('000)
Population by age group ('000)			Population par groupe d'âge ('000)
0-14 years	2014	303	0-14 ans
15-64 years	2014	428	15-64 ans
65+ years	2014	32	65+ ans
Economically, active population, in agriculture (%)	2012	94.6	Participation de la population active agricole (%)
Crude birth rate	2014	33.7	Taux brut de natalité
Crude death rate	2014	6.5	Taux brut de mortalité
Total fertility rate	2014	4.6	Indice synthétique de fécondité
Proportion of urban population	2014	36.8	Part de la population urbaine
Life Expectancy at Birth - Total (years)	2012	61.5	Espérance de vie à la naissance - Totale (ans)
Dependency Ratio - Total (%)	2014	78.5	Taux de dépendance - Total (%)
HEALTH			**SANTÉ**
Percentage of children under-five and underweight	2000	25.0	% d'enfants de moins de cinq ans avec insuffisance pondérale
Prevalence of undernourishment	2012	23.0	Prévalence de la malnutrition
Under five mortality rate (both sexes, per 1000)	2012	87.3	Taux de mortalité de moins de 5 ans (les deux sexes, pour 1000)
Infant mortality rate (both sexes) per 1000	2012	64.0	Taux de mortalité infantile (les deux sexes) par 1000
Percentage of children provided the vaccines :			Pourcentage d'enfants vaccinés :
BCG	2011	76.0	BCG
DPT3	2011	83.0	DTC3
Polio	2011	85.0	Polio
Measles	2011	72.0	Rougeole
Percentage of mothers provided at least one antenatal care (%)	2000	74.0	Pourcentage de mères ayant au moins reçu un soin prénatal (%)
Percentage of deliveries attended by skilled health personnel	2000	61.8	% d'accouchements assistés par un personnel de santé qualifié
Number of doctors (per 10 000 population)	2006	2.0	Nombre de médecins (pour 10 000 habitants)
Number of nurses (per 10 000 population)	2006	7.0	Nombre d'infirmières (pour 10 000 habitants)
Hospital beds - Total (per 10 000 population)	2006	22.0	Nombre de lits d'hôpitaux - Total (pour 10 000)
Births registered (per 1 000)	2012	36.1	Naiss.s enregistrées (pour 1 000)
Deaths registered (per 1 000)	2012	8.4	Décès enregistrés (pour 1 000)
Public expenditure on Health (% of budget)	2009	8.0	Dépenses publiques consacrées à la santé (% du budget)
EDUCATION			**EDUCATION**
Enrolment in primary education (both sexes) (000)	2008	111	Scolarisation dans le primaire (les deux sexes) (000)
Female	2008	52	Féminin
Enrolment in secondary education (both sexes) (000)	2005	43	Scolarisation dans le secondaire (les deux sexes) (000)
Female	2005	18	Féminin
Enrolment in tertiary education (both sexes) (000)	2010	5.1	Scolarisation dans le tertiaire (les deux sexes) (000)
Female	2010	2.1	Féminin
Literacy rate (both sexes)	2010	74.9	Taux d'alphabétisation (deux sexes)
Male	2010	80.2	Masculin
Female	2010	69.7	Féminin
Pupil-teacher ratio	2011	27.7	Ratio élève-enseignant
Public expenditure on education (% of budget)	2002	24.1	Dépenses publiques consacrées à l'enseignement (% du budget)
POVERTY			**PAUVRETÉ**
GNI Per Capita (US$)	2013	840.0	RNB par habitant ($EU)
Human Poverty Index (HPI-1) Value (%)	2007	20.4	Valeur de l'Indice de pauvreté (IPH-1) (%)
Population below International Poverty Line ($2/day) (%)	2004	65.0	Population sous le seuil international de pauvreté (2$/J) (%)
Share of Income Held by Richest 10%	2004	55.2	% de revenu des 10% plus riches
Share of Income Held by Poorest 10%	...	...	% de revenu des 10% plus pauvres
Gini index	2004	64.3	Indice de Gini

Charts / Graphiques

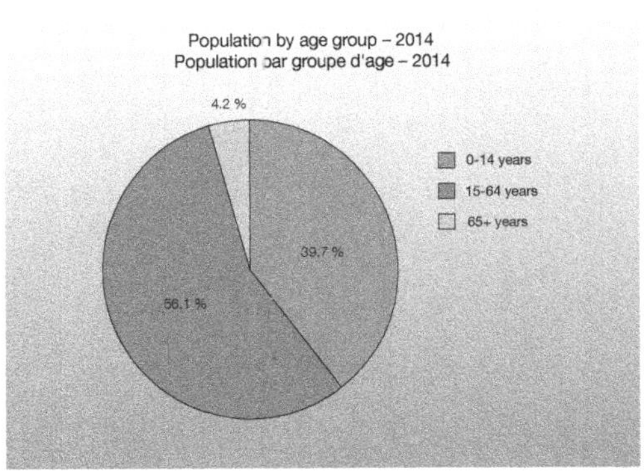

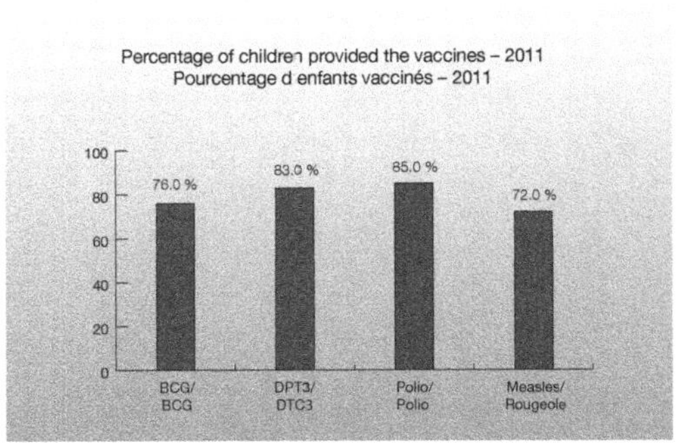

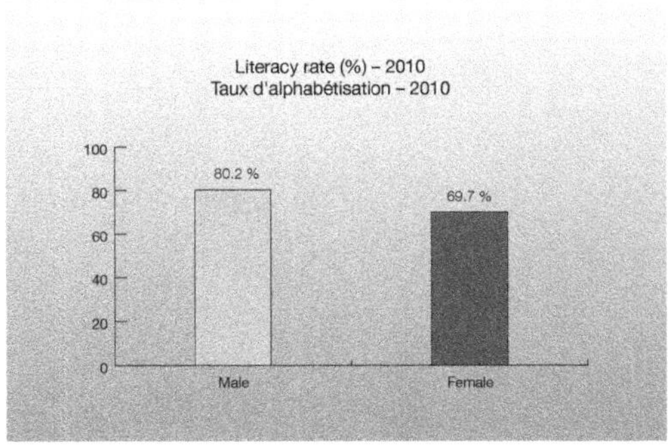

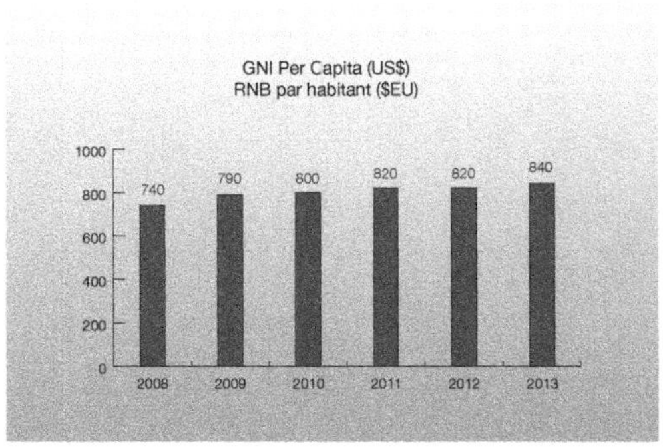

II NATIONAL ACCOUNTS — COMPTES NATIONAUX

	2006	2007	2008	2009	2010	2011	2012	2013	2014	
GROSS DOMESTIC PRODUCT BY KIND OF ECONOMIC ACTIVITY AT CURRENT PRICES *COMOROS FRANC (MILLIONS)*										**PRODUIT INTÉRIEUR BRUT PAR BRANCHE D'ACTIVITÉ ÉCONOMIQUE AUX PRIX COURANTS** *FRANC COMORIEN (MILLIONS)*
Agriculture, hunting, forestry and fishing	65 254	67 874	74 783	79 065	77 983	80 477	80 587	82 286	82 926	Agriculture, chasse, sylviculture et pêche
Mining and quarrying	...	...	...	...	...	...	...	...	...	Industries extractives
Manufacturing	6 441	6 780	6 653	9 356	10 292	12 406	13 735	15 587	17 090	Industries manufacturières
Electricity, gas & water	2 767	2 676	2 504	2 913	3 027	3 338	3 517	3 784	3 993	Electricité, gaz et eau
Construction & public works	9 348	8 639	12 792	9 607	9 942	7 930	7 483	5 993	5 198	Bâtiments et travaux publics
Wholesale & retail trade, restaurants, hotels	42 361	45 830	46 362	50 634	54 153	58 174	61 860	65 770	69 530	Commerce de gros et de détail, restaurants et hôtels
Finance, insurance, real estate, etc.	6 918	6 882	7 233	7 930	12 552	14 557	18 307	20 894	24 256	Banques, assurances, affaires immobilières
Transport and communications	7 934	8 352	8 154	8 594	9 062	9 511	9 973	10 427	10 886	Transport(s) et communications
Public administration and defense	21 409	22 534	21 164	21 504	24 372	25 555	27 861	29 418	31 475	Administrations publiques et défense
Education	...	...	...	...	...	...	...	...	...	Education
Health and Social Work	...	...	...	...	...	...	...	...	...	Santé et actions sociales
Other services	827	869	602	944	994	1 239	1 354	1 555	1 699	Autres services
Less Imputed Service Charges	- 3 996	- 4 206	- 4 550	- 4 922	- 5 321	- 5 702	- 6 095	- 6 480	- 6 870	Moins services d'intermédiation financière
Gross domestic product at factor cost / basic prices	159 264	166 229	175 697	185 625	197 056	207 485	218 582	229 234	240 182	Produit intérieur brut aux couts des facteurs / prix de base
Plus: indirect taxes / taxes on products, less subsidies	...	...	...	...	...	...	...	...	...	Plus taxes indirectes/impôts sur les produits, moins les subventions
EXPENDITURE ON GROSS DOMESTIC PRODUCT AT CURRENT PURCHASER'S VALUES *COMOROS FRANC (MILLIONS)*										**EMPLOI DU PRODUIT INTÉRIEUR BRUT AUX PRIX COURANTS D'ACQUISITION** *FRANC COMORIEN (MILLIONS)*
Government final consumption	21 255	21 455	27 636	31 737	41 199	47 087	55 358	62 040	69 781	Consommation finale des administrations publiques
Private final consumption	157 535	169 463	171 419	186 325	197 940	211 749	224 095	237 417	250 088	Consommation finale privée
Gross fixed capital formation	18 920	16 269	31 457	30 460	20 452	16 451	8 446	3 110	- 4 005	Formation brute de capital fixe
Change in inventories	- 977	2 128	6 273	459	8 826	7 739	12 955	13 968	17 783	Variation des stocks
Exports of goods and services	23 579	25 696	24 664	26 450	30 276	32 743	36 115	38 884	42 055	Exportations de biens et services
Less imports of goods and services	61 048	68 781	85 752	89 806	101 637	108 284	118 387	126 185	135 520	Moins importations de biens et services
GDP at purchasers' values	159 264	166 229	175 697	185 625	197 056	207 485	218 582	229 234	240 182	PIB aux prix d'acquisition
GROSS DOMESTIC PRODUCT BY KIND OF ECONOMIC ACTIVITY AT CONSTANT PRICES *ANNUAL GROWTH RATES (%)*										**PRODUIT INTÉRIEUR BRUT PAR BRANCHE D'ACTIVITÉ ECONOMIQUE AUX PRIX CONSTANTS** *TAUX DE CROISSANCE ANNUEL (%)*
Agriculture, hunting, forestry and fishing	2.6	2.3	8.3	- 3.1	- 0.7	4.1	4.1	4.1	3.8	Agriculture, chasse, sylviculture et pêche
Mining and quarrying	...	...	...	...	...	...	...	...	...	Industries extractives
Manufacturing	3.0	- 7.4	- 4.1	36.3	5.7	2.0	2.0	2.0	1.9	Industries manufacturières
Electricity, gas & water	2.1	- 10.5	- 12.5	17.8	19.4	2.3	2.3	2.3	2.2	Electricité, gaz et eau
Construction & public works	3.1	- 0.8	13.5	- 19.2	17.6	4.2	4.2	4.2	3.9	Bâtiments et travaux publics
Wholesale & retail trade, restaurants, hotels	3.3	1.7	- 14.1	13.7	1.2	4.2	4.2	4.2	3.9	Commerce de gros et de détail, restaurants et hôtels
Finance, insurance, real estate, etc.	3.1	1.8	4.8	3.8	3.2	3.4	3.4	3.4	3.2	Banques, assurances, affaires immobilières
Transport and communications	3.1	- 4.5	- 14.7	11.2	22.8	3.3	3.3	3.3	3.1	Transport(s) et communications
Public administration and defense	0.6	- 0.7	- 4.9	4.8	0.3	2.0	2.0	2.0	1.9	Administrations publiques et défense
Education	...	...	...	...	...	...	...	...	...	Education
Health and Social Work	...	...	...	...	...	...	...	...	...	Santé et actions sociales
Other services	1.7	- 0.2	- 5.1	0.7	22.7	8.2	8.2	8.2	7.2	Autres services
Less Imputed Service Charges	0.6	- 0.8	12.0	13.6	12.1	43.8	22.0	8.3	13.7	Moins services d'intermédiation financière
Gross domestic product at factor cost / basic prices	2.6	0.8	0.4	2.0	2.2	2.6	3.0	3.5	3.0	Produit intérieur brut aux couts des facteurs / prix de base
Plus: indirect taxes / taxes on products, less subsidies	...	...	...	...	...	...	...	...	...	Plus taxes indirectes/impôts sur les produits, moins les subventions
Gross domestic product at market prices	11.1	0.8	0.4	1.9	2.2	2.6	3.0	3.5	3.0	Produit intérieur brut aux prix du marché
EXPENDITURE ON GROSS DOMESTIC PRODUCT AT CONSTANT PURCHASERS' VALUES *ANNUAL GROWTH RATES (%)*										**EMPLOIS DU PRODUIT INTÉRIEUR BRUT AUX PRIX CONSTANTS D'ACQUISITION** *TAUX DE CROISSANCE ANNUEL (%)*
Government final consumption	0.0	14.3	25.0	14.8	11.3	2.0	2.2	2.2	2.1	Consommation finale des administrations publiques
Private final consumption	9.6	- 5.8	2.9	2.8	0.3	4.0	4.5	4.5	4.2	Consommation finale privée
Gross fixed capital formation	23.0	- 9.1	56.7	9.8	- 16.3	6.0	7.0	7.0	6.3	Formation brute de capital fixe
Exports of goods and services	383.1	62.2	- 3.5	- 6.9	27.3	2.0	2.0	2.0	1.9	Exportations de biens et services
Less imports of goods and services	42.6	16.7	35.4	- 0.5	19.3	5.5	5.8	5.0	5.1	Moins importations de biens et services
Notes	NA Data: 2013:Provisional;2014:Estimates					Données des CN: 2013:Provisoire;2014:Estimée				Notes

III INFLATION

	2006	2007	2008	2009	2010	2011	2012	2013	2014	
ANNUAL GROWTH RATES (%)										**TAUX DE CROISSANCE ANNUEL (%)**
All items	4.5	4.4	4.9	-2.9	3.8	1.8	6.3	1.6	2.7	Ensemble
of which:										dont:
Food and Non-alcoholic beverages	3.9	7.0	4.9	-7.7	3.1	2.0	7.9	2.0	3.8	Alimentation et boissons non alcoolisés
Alcoholic beverages & tobacco	...	...	...	...	...	...	...	...	...	Boissons alcoolisées et tabacs
Clothing and Footwear	0.6	-4.1	4.8	-17.5	21.6	0.6	2.2	1.6	1.2	Habillement et chaussures
Housing, Water, Electricity, Gas and Other Fuels	...	...	4.9	16.3	2.3	2.1	3.7	-0.1	0.8	Logement, eau, electricité, gas et autres combustibles
Furnishing, household equipment	...	...	4.7	-5.1	10.4	1.6	2.5	1.4	0.3	Meubles, articles de ménage et entretien courant
Health	0.8	-14.7	4.8	20.8	0.7	-0.5	4.1	6.6	4.7	Santé
Transport	-1.5	4.5	4.8	7.5	14.8	-11.6	6.1	-1.1	-1.6	Transport
Communication	...	...	...	...	...	...	...	...	-	Communication
Recreation & culture	...	...	4.6	-15.1	-3.2	-0.1	0.3	1.0	1.0	Loisirs et culture
Education	...	...	4.8	-4.4	0.1	1.8	0.4	0.4	-	Enseignement
Restaurants & hotels	...	...	4.9	40.2	13.7	-5.7	9.9	5.4	1.1	Restaurants et hôtels
Miscellaneous goods & services	...	...	5.0	-18.1	20.5	17.2	7.2	5.3	1.6	Biens et services divers

IV AGRICULTURAL PRODUCTION - PRODUCTION AGRICOLE										
	2006	2007	2008	2009	2010	2011	2012	2013	2014	
TONNES *(THOUSAND)*										**TONNES** *(MILLIERS)*
Coconuts	80	80	79	73	83	85	90	92	...	Noix de coco
Cassava	60	62	64	65	62	68	69	70	...	Manioc
Bananas	70	62	59	72	74	64	66	65	...	Bananes
Rice, paddy	20	17	20	22	24	27	27	29	...	Riz
Taro (cocoyam)	10	9	10	10	13	12	12	13	...	Taro

V MINING PRODUCTION - PRODUCTION MINIERE										
	2006	2007	2008	2009	2010	2011	2012	2013	2014	
	...	...	...	...	...	...	...	...	...	
	...	...	...	...	...	...	...	...	...	
	...	...	...	...	...	...	...	...	...	

VI ENERGY - ENERGIE										
	2006	2007	2008	2009	2010	2011	2012	2013	2014	
Total electricity generation (GWh)	9	52	38	37	37	60	62	66	...	Production d'électricité totale (GWh)
of which:										dont:
Production of electricity from fossil fuels (GWh)	4	47	33	32	32	55	57	60	...	Production d'électricité à partir de combustibles fossiles (GWh)
Production of hydro electricity (GWh)	5	5	5	5	5	5	5	5	...	Production d'électricité d'origine hydraulique (GWh)
Production of electricity from solar, wind, tide, wave and other sources (GWh)	...	...	...	...	...	...	...	...	...	Production d'électricité d'origine solaire, éolienne, marée motrice et autres (GWh)

VII TOURISM AND INFRASTRUCTURE - TOURISME ET INFRASTRUCTURE										
	2006	2007	2008	2009	2010	2011	2012	2013	2014	
VII-1 TOURISM										**VII-1 TOURISME**
International tourist arrivals (thousands)	29	15	15	11	15	19	21	22	23	Arrivées de touristes internationaux (milliers)
Rooms in hotels and similar establishments (thousands)	0.164	0.164	...	...	5.1	5.1	5.1	...	...	Chambres d'hotels et établissements assimilés (milliers)
Overnight stays (thousands)	136	106	103	79	107	131	151	159	169	Nuitées (milliers)
Tourism receipts (US$ thousand)	14 600	15 500	14 600	13 700	13 700	15 410	16 257	16 598	18 021	Recettes touristiques (milliers de $ EU)
Total contribution to GDP (%)	8.8	8.3	7.0	6.6	6.9	6.8	6.9	6.5	6.7	Contribution totale au PIB (%)
Total contribution to Employment (%)	7.7	7.2	6.0	5.8	6.0	6.0	6.0	5.7	5.8	Contribution totale à l'emploi (%)
VII-2 INFRASTRUCTURE										**VII-2 INFRASTRUCTURE**
Paved roads (% of total)	...	...	...	77	...	...	...	...	...	Routes asphaltées (% du total)
Total Network (Railways-km)	...	...	...	...	...	...	...	...	...	Réseau total voies ferrées-Km
Main Telephone Lines (per 100 inhabitants)	3	4	4	5	3	3	3	3	...	Lignes téléphoniques fixes (pour 100 habitants)
Mobile Cellular Subscribers (per 100 inhabitants)	6	10	14	18	24	31	40	47	...	Abonnés aux téléphones mobiles (pour 100 habitants)

VIII EXTERNAL TRADE - COMMERCE EXTERIEUR										
	2006	2007	2008	2009	2010	2011	2012	2013	2014	
COMOROS FRANC (MILLIONS) EXPORTS, FOB										**FRANC COMORIEN (MILLIONS) EXPORTATIONS, FÀB**
Exports - Total	4 089	4 912	2 190	5 297	7 655	8 908	7 215	3 751	4 213	Exportations - Total
Exports to AFRICA	...	...	...	...	...	...	...	...	...	Exportations vers l'AFRIQUE
Main Products										**Principaux produits**
Vanilla	1 009	1 222	654	645	309	350	552	1 210	413	Vanille
Nails of girofle	2 054	2 866	615	3 221	5 410	6 361	5 494	1 574	239	Clous de giroffe
Ylang-Ylang	913	711	815	762	881	745	-	418	290	Ylang-Ylang
Other products	60	60	74	643	1 055	1 434	503	549	3 271	Autres produits
Main Destinations										**Principales destinations**
Turkey	202	1 947	670	1 591	2 365	2 719	...	...	...	Turquie
France	603	1 096	512	1 111	1 622	1 883	...	...	...	France
Netherlands	1 485	68	257	535	695	839	...	...	...	Pays-Bas
India	542	389	227	494	701	820	...	...	...	Inde
Saudi Arabia	360	478	219	496	717	833	...	...	...	Arabie saoudite
IMPORTS, CIF										**IMPORTATIONS, CAF**
Imports - Total	45 189	49 716	60 323	74 532	84 280	97 935	104 676	56 181	...	Importations - Total (millions)
Imports from Africa	...	...	...	...	...	...	...	...	...	Importations en provenance de l'Afrique
Main Products										**Principaux produits**
Rice	2 092	3 044	5 756	8 297	7 254	12 168	11 395	13 980	...	Riz
Meat, fish	2 588	1 700	3 799	3 821	5 184	5 285	5 284	2 737	...	Viande, poisson
Petroleum Products	3 329	225	13	12	20	22	26	14	...	Produits Pétroliers
Iron and Steel	2 627	1 015	1 856	3 332	2 919	3 406	3 745	2 476	...	Fer et Acier
Flour	2 899	4 293	1 250	1 634	1 739	2 240	2 763	1 143	...	Farine
Main Origin										**Principales provenances**
France	10 234	8 397	11 410	13 989	15 730	18 332	...	...	...	France
United Arab Emirates	7 163	10 190	11 427	14 258	16 189	18 764	...	...	...	Émirats arabes unis
South Africa	2 987	3 657	4 436	5 450	6 180	7 178	...	...	...	Afrique du Sud
India	3 275	3 053	3 783	4 725	5 317	6 183	...	...	...	Inde
Pakistan	2 565	2 954	3 548	4 395	4 974	5 776	...	...	...	Pakistan

IX FINANCIAL AND MONETARY STATISTICS - FINANCES ET STATISTIQUES MONETAIRES	2006	2007	2008	2009	2010	2011	2012	2013	2014	
IX-1 MONETARY STATISTICS *COMOROS FRANC (MILLIONS)*										**IX-1 STATISTIQUES MONÉTAIRES** *FRANC COMORIEN (MILLIONS)*
Money supply (M1)	41 040	45 540	50 790	57 570	68 750	75 330	87 370	89 860	96 310	Masse monétaire (M1)
Quasi-money	13 184	13 400	16 024	21 817	26 097	26 506	30 871	32 985	34 348	Quasi-monnaie
of which Demand Deposit	...	...	...	...	...	...	...	...	...	dont Monnaie scripturale
Net foreign assets	40 166	43 156	40 203	44 114	45 974	53 860	62 709	56 567	56 027	Avoirs extérieurs nets
Domestic credit	17 367	19 413	27 503	37 172	43 704	45 845	49 366	59 694	67 193	Crédit intérieur
of which claims on private sector	13 449	15 282	19 460	28 048	35 304	38 431	47 062	52 946	55 604	dont créances sur le secteur privé
of which claims on government sector, net	2 871	2 938	5 246	7 266	5 743	6 016	1 604	5 511	7 718	dont créances nettes sur le gouvernement
International reserves (millions US$)	94	117	112	150	145	155	194	173	170	Réserves internationales (millions $EU)
Average Exchange Rate (National Currency per US$)	392.18	359.16	335.15	353.30	371.01	353.56	382.64	370.45	370.32	Taux de change (moyen) (monnaie nationale par $ EU)
IX-2 PUBLIC FINANCE *COMOROS FRANC (MILLIONS)*										**IX-2 FINANCES PUBLIQUES** *FRANC COMORIEN (MILLIONS)*
Total Revenues and Grants	29 533	33 945	41 853	44 776	57 911	50 907	65 962	106 460	67 198	Recettes totales et dons
Tax Revenue	17 260	16 678	18 176	20 515	22 479	23 520	26 849	29 407	35 475	Recettes fiscales
Non Tax Revenue	4 295	4 482	5 091	5 887	6 368	11 273	17 287	7 518	8 105	Recettes non fiscales
Grants	7 978	12 785	18 586	18 374	29 064	16 114	21 826	69 535	23 618	Dons
Total Expenditures and Net Lending	32 970	37 314	46 338	43 627	48 300	47 793	57 803	62 019	68 730	Dépenses totales et prêts nets
Current expenditure	25 392	27 040	29 855	34 240	33 155	35 785	41 898	45 648	46 711	Dépenses courantes
Of which Wages and Salaries	13 250	15 052	15 690	17 034	17 864	18 409	18 278	18 605	20 251	Dont rémunérations et salaires
Capital expenditure	7 578	10 274	16 484	8 939	15 145	11 708	15 444	16 371	22 019	Dépenses d'équipement
Net Lending	-	-	-	448	-	300	461	0	-	Prêts nets
Fiscal Balance	- 3 437	- 3 369	- 4 485	1 149	9 611	3 114	8 159	44 441	- 1 532	Solde global y compris les dons
IX-3 BALANCE OF PAYMENTS *COMOROS FRANC (MILLIONS)*										**IX-3 BALANCE DES PAIEMENTS** *FRANC COMORIEN (MILLIONS)*
Trade balance	- 34 288	- 40 039	- 56 009	- 53 361	- 57 488	- 61 466	- 75 941	- 76 743	...	Balance commerciale
Services Balance	- 3 181	- 3 047	- 5 080	- 8 928	- 10 820	- 11 172	- 12 933	- 11 260	...	Balance des services
Net Income	- 663	557	- 598	- 439	- 316	- 277	- 648	- 786	...	Revenus nets
Compensation of employees	...	...	...	...	...	...	...	...	...	Rémunération des salariés
Investment Income	- 579	- 566	- 919	- 616	- 672	- 852	- 854	- 786	...	Revenus des investissements
Current transfers, net total	29 301	31 178	38 375	48 836	54 027	53 301	73 770	66 685	...	Transferts courants
Net official transfers	7 240	22 883	16 009	16 595	26 445	20 974	19 246	63 578	...	Transferts officiels nets
Workers' remittances	...	...	...	...	...	...	...	...	...	Envois de fonds des travailleurs
Other private transfers	...	...	...	...	...	...	...	...	...	Autres transferts privés
Current account balance	- 8 831	- 11 350	- 23 311	- 13 892	- 14 597	- 19 615	- 15 753	- 22 104	...	Solde du compte courant
Capital & financial account	8 173	11 150	27 927	12 448	13 328	15 601	15 220	24 317	...	Comptes de capital et financier
Capital account	7 240	23 044	16 677	16 532	26 445	20 972	19 256	63 578	...	Compte de capital
Financial account	933	- 11 875	11 249	- 4 084	- 13 117	- 5 371	- 4 036	- 39 260	...	Compte financier
Errors & omissions	658	201	- 4 849	1 444	1 269	4 014	533	- 2 213	...	Erreurs et omissions
Overall balance	...	...	...	...	...	...	...	...	...	Balance générale

X DEBT AND FINANCIAL FLOWS - DETTE ET FLUX FINANCIERS	2006	2007	2008	2009	2010	2011	2012	2013	2014	
X-1 DEBT *US$ (MILLIONS)*										**X-1 DETTE EXTÉRIEURE** *$ E.U (MILLIONS)*
Total external debt	283	349	365	278	266	273	242	117	118	Dette extérieure totale
Private	-	-	-	6	6	6	2	15	1	Privée
Public	283	349	365	272	260	267	240	102	117	Publique
Total external debt service	4	9	4	8	10	10	9	2	3	Service de la dette extérieure
Present value of External debt	...	...	...	197	199.6	208.9	79.8	...	...	Valeur actuelle de la dette extérieure
Total government domestic debt (in local currency)	...	...	...	...	...	...	...	...	...	Dette publique intérieure
X-2 FINANCIAL FLOWS *US$ (MILLIONS)*										**X-2 FLUX FINANCIERS** *$ E.U (MILLIONS)*
Net Foreign Direct Investment Inflows	1	8	5	14	8	23	10	14	...	Investissement étranger direct (flux nets entrants)
Main origin of FDI Inflows										**Principales origines de l'IDE entrant:**
United States	...	...	...	...	...	...	...	...	...	États-Unis
Luxembourg	...	...	...	...	...	...	...	...	...	Luxembourg
Norway	...	...	...	...	...	...	...	...	...	Norvège
Turkey	...	...	...	...	...	...	...	...	...	Turquie
Slovenia	...	...	...	...	...	...	...	...	...	Slovénie
African countries	...	...	...	...	...	...	...	...	...	Pays africains
Net total Official Development Assistance	32	45	42	50	67	52	69	82	...	Aide publique au développement (nette totale)
Main origin of Net ODA										**Principales origines de l'APD nette**
France	19	18	19	22	20.9	21.8	23.8	38.5	...	France
IDA	1	3	-	- 1	3.3	- 0.5	- 0.3	...	...	IDA
United Arab Emirates	1	-	4	-	16.1	0.5	7.9	...	...	Emirats Arabes Unis
UNDP	1	1	2	2	1.5	0.7	0.8	...	...	PNUD
IMF (Concessional Trust Funds)	-	-	4	7	2.4	2.5	4.8	...	...	FMI (Fonds fiduciaires concessionnels)

AREA (km²)		342 000	SUPERFICIE (km²)
CAPITAL CITY	Brazzaville	Brazzaville	CAPITALE
CURRENCY	CFA Franc	Franc CFA	MONNAIE

I SOCIAL AND DEMOGRAPHIC INDICATORS — INDICATEURS DEMOGRAPHIQUES ET SOCIAUX

	Year / Année	Value / Valeur	
POPULATION			**POPULATION**
Population ('000)			Population ('000)
Both sexes	2014	4 559	Les deux sexes
Male	2014	2 279	Masculin
Female	2014	2 280	Féminin
Average annual growth rate	2014	2.7	Taux de croissance annuel
Active Population ('000)	2014	1 786	Population active ('000)
Population by age group ('000)			Population par groupe d'âge ('000)
0-14 years	2014	1 939	0-14 ans
15-64 years	2014	2 465	15-64 ans
65+ years	2014	154	65+ ans
Economically. active population. in agriculture (%)	2014	29.7	Participation de la population active agricole (%)
Crude birth rate	2014	37.1	Taux brut de natalité
Crude death rate	2014	10.0	Taux brut de mortalité
Total fertility rate	2014	4.9	Indice synthétique de fécondité
Proportion of urban population	2014	64.9	Part de la population urbaine
Life Expectancy at Birth - Total (years)	2014	59.2	Espérance de vie à la naissance - Totale (ans)
Dependency Ratio - Total (%)	2014	78.7	Taux de dépendance - Total (%)
HEALTH			**SANTÉ**
Percentage of children under-five and underweight	2012	11.8	% d'enfants de moins de cinq ans avec insuffisance pondérale
Prevalence of undernourishment	2013	31.5	Prévalence de la malnutrition
Under five mortality rate (both sexes, per 1000)	2013	49.1	Taux de mortalité de moins de 5 ans (les deux sexes, pour 1000)
Infant mortality rate (both sexes) per 1000	2013	35.6	Taux de mortalité infantile (les deux sexes) par 1000
Percentage of children provided the vaccines :			Pourcentage d'enfants vaccinés :
BCG	2013	92.0	BCG
DPT3	2013	69.0	DTC3
Polio	2011	90.0	Polio
Measles	2013	65.0	Rougeole
Percentage of mothers provided at least one antenatal care (%)	2005	85.8	Pourcentage de mères ayant au moins reçu un soin prénatal (%)
Percentage of deliveries attended by skilled health personnel	2012	93.6	% d'accouchements assistés par un personnel de santé qualifié
Number of doctors (per 10 000 population)	2007	1.0	Nombre de médecins (pour 10 000 habitants)
Number of nurses (per 10 000 population)	2007	8.2	Nombre d'infirmières (pour 10 000 habitants)
Hospital beds - Total (per 10 000 population)	2005	16.0	Nombre de lits d'hôpitaux - Total (pour 10 000)
Births registered (per 1 000)	2014	37.1	Naiss.s enregistrées (pour 1 000)
Deaths registered (per 1 000)	2014	10.0	Décès enregistrés (pour 1 000)
Public expenditure on Health (% of budget)	2009	5.3	Dépenses publiques consacrées à la santé (% du budget)
EDUCATION			**EDUCATION**
Enrolment in primary education (both sexes) (000)	2012	734	Scolarisation dans le primaire (les deux sexes) (000)
Female	2012	378	Féminin
Enrolment in secondary education (both sexes) (000)	2012	339	Scolarisation dans le secondaire (les deux sexes) (000)
Female	2012	157	Féminin
Enrolment in tertiary education (both sexes) (000)	...	...	Scolarisation dans le tertiaire (les deux sexes) (000)
Female	2013	15.8	Féminin
Literacy rate (both sexes)	2011	79.3	Taux d'alphabétisation (deux sexes)
Male	2011	86.4	Masculin
Female	2011	72.9	Féminin
Pupil-teacher ratio	...	...	Ratio élève-enseignant
Public expenditure on education (% of budget)	2010	29.0	Dépenses publiques consacrées à l'enseignement (% du budget)
Poverty			Pauvreté
GNI Per Capita (US$)	2013	2 590.0	RNB par habitant ($EU)
Human Poverty Index (HPI-1) Value (%)	2007	38.0	Valeur de l'Indice de pauvreté (IPH-1) (%)
Population below International Poverty Line ($2/day) (%)	2011	57.3	Population sous le seuil international de pauvreté (2$/J) (%)
Share of Income Held by Richest 10%	2011	29.9	% de revenu des 10% plus riches
Share of Income Held by Poorest 10%	2006	2.3	% de revenu des 10% plus pauvres
Gini index	2006	44.4	Indice de Gini

Charts / Graphiques

Population by age group – 2014
Population par groupe d'age – 2014

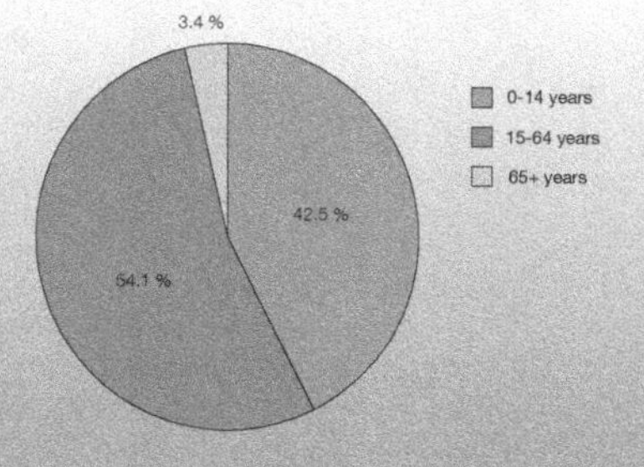

Percentage of children provided the vaccines – 2013
Pourcentage d'enfants vaccinés – 2013

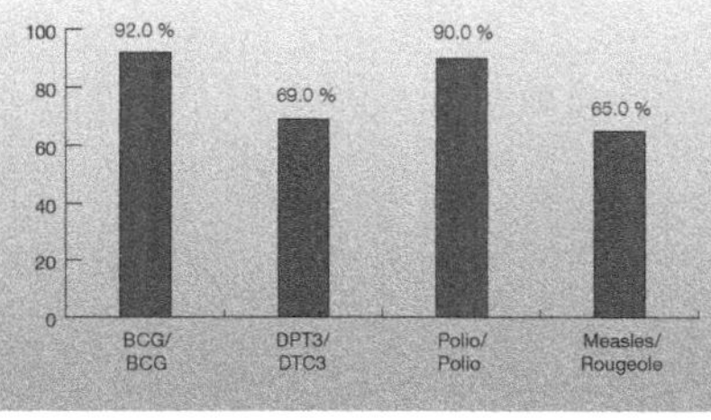

Literacy rate (%) – 2011
Taux d'alphabétisation – 2011

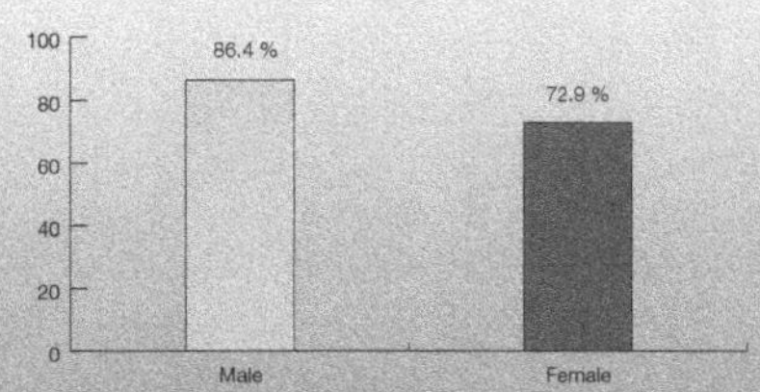

GNI Per Capita (US$)
RNB par habitant ($EU)

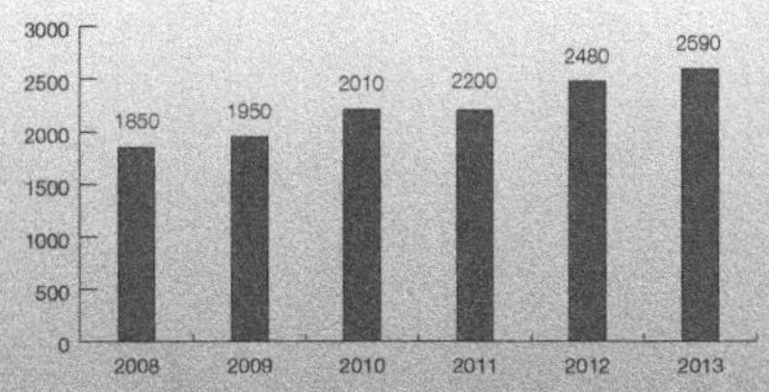

II NATIONAL ACCOUNTS — COMPTES NATIONAUX

	2006	2007	2008	2009	2010	2011	2012	2013	2014	
GROSS DOMESTIC PRODUCT BY KIND OF ECONOMIC ACTIVITY AT CURRENT PRICES *CFA FRANC (BILLIONS)*										**PRODUIT INTÉRIEUR BRUT PAR BRANCHE D'ACTIVITÉ ÉCONOMIQUE AUX PRIX COURANTS** *FRANC CFA (MILLIARDS)*
Agriculture, hunting, forestry and fishing	160	174	192	201	221	242	274	314	338	Agriculture, chasse, sylviculture et pêche
Mining and quarrying	2 774	2 172	3 027	2 738	4 102	4 786	4 670	4 136	4 310	Industries extractives
Manufacturing	145	162	181	199	202	149	268	296	337	Industries manufacturières
Electricity, gas & water	25	29	31	33	28	31	44	51	62	Electricité, gaz et eau
Construction & public works	109	124	139	158	232	293	231	304	394	Bâtiments et travaux publics
Wholesale & retail trade, restaurants, hotels	220	243	270	302	371	422	422	496	562	Commerce de gros et de détail, restaurants et hôtels
Finance, insurance, real estate, etc.	204	223	242	264	317	348	341	380	414	Banques, assurances, affaires immobilières
Transport and communications	162	181	202	223	277	299	310	351	400	Transport(s) et communications
Public administration and defense	173	181	192	206	224	264	284	314	369	Administrations publiques et défense
Education	-	...	...	...	...	...	...	...	...	Education
Health and Social Work	-	...	...	...	...	...	...	...	...	Santé et actions sociales
Other services	-	...	...	...	...	...	...	...	...	Autres services
Less Imputed Service Charges	-	...	...	...	...	...	...	...	...	Moins services d'intermédiation financière
Gross domestic product at factor cost / basic prices	3 971	3 489	4 476	4 323	5 974	6 834	6 842	6 642	7 186	Produit intérieur brut aux couts des facteurs / prix de base
Plus: indirect taxes / taxes on products, less subsidies	71	74	81	86	109	149	130	174	201	Plus taxes indirectes/impôts sur les produits, moins les subventions
EXPENDITURE ON GROSS DOMESTIC PRODUCT AT CURRENT PURCHASER'S VALUES *CFA FRANC (BILLIONS)*										**EMPLOI DU PRODUIT INTÉRIEUR BRUT AUX PRIX COURANTS D'ACQUISITION** *FRANC CFA (MILLIARDS)*
Government final consumption	370	413	448	469	484	512	992	981	1 208	Consommation finale des administrations publiques
Private final consumption	969	1 003	1 329	1 348	1 468	1 553	1 729	1 887	2 032	Consommation finale privée
Gross fixed capital formation	1 152	1 688	1 570	1 853	1 805	2 406	2 827	3 647	4 442	Formation brute de capital fixe
Change in inventories	9	20	13	10	-	-	-	-	-	Variation des stocks
Exports of goods and services	3 207	2 719	4 207	3 438	5 609	5 930	5 605	5 195	5 337	Exportations de biens et services
Less imports of goods and services	1 664	2 279	3 010	2 708	3 283	3 419	4 182	4 894	5 631	Moins importations de biens et services
GDP at purchasers' values	4 043	3 564	4 557	4 410	6 083	6 982	6 972	6 816	7 388	PIB aux prix d'acquisition
GROSS DOMESTIC PRODUCT BY KIND OF ECONOMIC ACTIVITY AT CONSTANT PRICES *ANNUAL GROWTH RATES (%)*										**PRODUIT INTÉRIEUR BRUT PAR BRANCHE D'ACTIVITÉ ECONOMIQUE AUX PRIX CONSTANTS** *TAUX DE CROISSANCE ANNUEL (%)*
Agriculture, hunting, forestry and fishing	5.4	5.0	5.4	- 3.0	6.2	7.1	7.3	7.9	7.9	Agriculture, chasse, sylviculture et pêche
Mining and quarrying	6.8	- 17.2	7.4	16.1	13.7	- 4.8	- 9.6	- 10.0	10.2	Industries extractives
Manufacturing	7.7	9.3	7.0	5.5	5.9	8.6	8.6	9.0	9.8	Industries manufacturières
Electricity, gas & water	8.6	10.9	3.6	1.3	5.5	7.4	7.5	7.0	10.1	Electricité, gaz et eau
Construction & public works	7.4	10.3	7.6	8.7	8.8	10.5	10.5	10.2	12.1	Bâtiments et travaux publics
Wholesale & retail trade, restaurants, hotels	5.9	7.1	6.0	7.5	7.4	9.2	9.5	9.2	- 13.7	Commerce de gros et de détail, restaurants et hôtels
Finance, insurance, real estate, etc.	5.8	5.9	4.1	4.8	4.9	6.7	6.0	4.4	6.2	Banques, assurances, affaires immobilières
Transport and communications	6.6	8.1	6.7	6.1	6.9	9.2	9.1	9.1	6.6	Transport(s) et communications
Public administration and defense	4.8	4.9	3.0	2.9	3.2	3.2	17.7	7.9	15.6	Administrations publiques et défense
Education	...	...	...	...	...	...	...	...	...	Education
Health and Social Work	...	...	...	...	...	...	...	...	...	Santé et actions sociales
Other services	...	...	...	...	...	...	...	...	...	Autres services
Less Imputed Service Charges	...	...	...	...	...	...	...	...	...	Moins services d'intermédiation financière
Gross domestic product at factor cost / basic prices	6.3	- 1.7	6.0	7.6	8.5	3.3	3.7	3.2	6.3	Produit intérieur brut aux couts des facteurs / prix de base
Plus: indirect taxes / taxes on products, less subsidies	4.0	1.9	4.2	4.5	16.0	6.6	8.1	8.1	- 0.8	Plus taxes indirectes/impôts sur les produits, moins les subventions
Gross domestic product at market prices	6.2	- 1.6	5.9	7.5	8.7	3.4	3.8	3.3	6.1	Produit intérieur brut aux prix du marché
EXPENDITURE ON GROSS DOMESTIC PRODUCT AT CONSTANT PURCHASERS' VALUES *ANNUAL GROWTH RATES (%)*										**EMPLOIS DU PRODUIT INTÉRIEUR BRUT AUX PRIX CONSTANTS D'ACQUISITION** *TAUX DE CROISSANCE ANNUEL (%)*
Government final consumption	5.4	- 1.0	6.3	4.6	3.2	3.2	50.5	- 4.4	14.9	Consommation finale des administrations publiques
Private final consumption	5.1	9.1	6.5	4.8	6.3	9.9	6.9	1.3	- 0.8	Consommation finale privée
Gross fixed capital formation	32.3	20.9	4.7	5.2	34.1	13.3	14.5	24.4	13.8	Formation brute de capital fixe
Exports of goods and services	2.7	- 17.2	9.8	0.1	7.1	- 5.9	- 3.4	7.9	1.9	Exportations de biens et services
Less imports of goods and services	13.9	6.9	8.5	- 0.3	17.0	10.3	26.3	16.3	9.0	Moins importations de biens et services
Notes	NA Data: 2011-2013:Estimates;2014:Projections				Données des CN: 2011-2013:Estimées;2014:Projections					Notes

III INFLATION

	2006	2007	2008	2009	2010	2011	2012	2013	2014	
ANNUAL GROWTH RATES (%)										**TAUX DE CROISSANCE ANNUEL (%)**
All items	4.9	2.6	4.5	5.8	0.3	2.1	6.1	6.0	-0.1	Ensemble
of which:										dont:
Food and Non-alcoholic beverages	6.9	2.3	1.4	11.0	-0.8	1.5	10.9	7.4	-2.3	Alimentation et boissons non alcoolisés
Alcoholic beverages & tobacco	...	...	...	...	...	...	5.8	5.9	-6.5	Boissons alcoolisées et tabacs
Clothing and Footwear	...	2.9	0.9	4.6	10.7	-1.3	3.8	3.7	-2.6	Habillement et chaussures
Housing, Water, Electricity, Gas and Other Fuels	9.1	2.7	-3.2	4.8	7.7	4.9	0.6	5.7	6.2	Logement, eau, electricité, gas et autres combustibles
Furnishing, household equipment	...	...	...	...	...	...	4.7	2.4	2.0	Meubles, articles de ménage et entretien courant
Health	4.8	3.3	33.5	-15.8	0.2	2.7	-0.9	1.4	8.8	Santé
Transport	-2.5	3.1	9.7	6.2	-1.2	-0.5	0.4	0.7	-0.6	Transport
Communication	...	...	...	...	...	...	-15.6	30.4	14.3	Communication
Recreation & culture	...	...	...	...	...	...	-0.6	0.9	-4.8	Loisirs et culture
Education	...	...	...	...	...	...	-14.2	1.3	25.2	Enseignement
Restaurants & hotels	...	...	...	...	...	...	2.0	9.0	-5.5	Restaurants et hôtels
Miscellaneous goods & services	...	...	...	...	...	...	3.6	1.3	-2.9	Biens et services divers

IV AGRICULTURAL PRODUCTION - PRODUCTION AGRICOLE	2006	2007	2008	2009	2010	2011	2012	2013	2014	
TONNES *(THOUSAND)*										**TONNES** *(MILLIERS)*
Cassava	1 072	1 140	1 196	1 231	1 149	1 150	1 200	1 250	...	Manioc
Sugar cane	550	540	565	600	650	650	650	650	...	Canne à sucre
Bananas	75	77	80	81	85	92	100	104	...	Banane
Plantains	70	73	79	80	81	82	84	86	...	Bananes, Plantains
Mangoes, mangosteens, guavas	34	36	37	38	39	38	40	41	...	Mangues, mangoustans, goyaves

V MINING PRODUCTION - PRODUCTION MINIERE	2006	2007	2008	2009	2010	2011	2012	2013	2014	
Crude petroleum, metric tons (thousands)	...	...	87 537	102 348	112 000	113 000	104 000	...	...	Pétrole brut, tonnes métriques (milliers)
Natural gas (terajoules)	...	...	1 610	2 469	1 300	1 400	1 400	...	...	Gaz naturel (térajoules)
Gold ores and concentrates (Kilograms)	...	...	100	100	150	150	150	...	...	Minerais d'or et concentrés (Kilogrammes)

VI ENERGY - ENERGIE	2006	2007	2008	2009	2010	2011	2012	2013	2014	
Total electricity generation (GWh)	448	407	461	526	781	1 293	1 349	1 407	...	Production d'électricité totale (GWh)
of which:										dont:
Production of electricity from fossil fuels (GWh)	76	72	86	196	355	502	522	543	...	Production d'électricité à partir de combustibles fossiles (GWh)
Production of hydro electricity (GWh)	372	335	375	330	426	791	827	864	...	Production d'électricité d'origine hydraulique (GWh)
Production of electricity from solar, wind, tide, wave and other sources (GWh)	...	...	...	...	...	...	...	...	...	Production d'électricité d'origine solaire, éolienne, marée motrice et autres (GWh)

VII TOURISM AND INFRASTRUCTURE - TOURISME ET INFRASTRUCTURE	2006	2007	2008	2009	2010	2011	2012	2013	2014	
VII-1 TOURISM										**VII-1 TOURISME**
International tourist arrivals (thousands)	46	55	62	94	194	218	256	257	252	Arrivées de touristes internationaux (milliers)
Rooms in hotels and similar establishments (thousands)	5	5.2	6.5	7	...	...	...	...	...	Chambres d'hotels et établissements assimilés (milliers)
Overnight stays (thousands)	247	333	384	382	423	725	1 108	1 111	1 093	Nuitées (milliers)
Tourism receipts (US$ thousand)	45 300	54 500	72 515	58 510	62 301	71 331	70 333	69 100	70 510	Recettes touristiques (milliers de $ EU)
Total contribution to GDP (%)	3.2	3.8	4.6	4.4	3.7	3.9	4.0	4.0	3.9	Contribution totale au PIB (%)
Total contribution to Employment (%)	2.9	3.4	3.6	3.6	2.6	3.6	3.6	3.8	3.7	Contribution totale à l'emploi (%)
VII-2 INFRASTRUCTURE										**VII-2 INFRASTRUCTURE**
Paved roads (% of total)	7	7	7	7	...	...	...	...	...	Routes asphaltées (% du total)
Total Network (Railways-km)	795	795	795	...	...	...	...	...	...	Réseau total voies ferrées-Km
Main Telephone Lines (per 100 inhabitants)	0	0	0	0	0	0	0	0	...	Lignes téléphoniques fixes (pour 100 habitants)
Mobile Cellular Subscribers (per 100 inhabitants)	25	34	47	74	90	92	99	105	...	Abonnés aux téléphones mobiles (pour 100 habitants)

VIII EXTERNAL TRADE - COMMERCE EXTERIEUR	2006	2007	2008	2009	2010	2011	2012	2013	2014	
CFA FRANC (MILLIONS) EXPORTS, FOB										**FRANC CFA (MILLIONS) EXPORTATIONS, FÀB**
Exports - Total	3 421 785	3 008 407	4 112 031	3 856 297	5 375 345	6 518 526	5 897 888	5 741 406	...	Exportations - Total
Exports to AFRICA	328 044	302 092	3 255 520	689 937	1 539 357	1 081 345	714 934	917 063	...	Exportations vers l'AFRIQUE
Main Products										**Principaux produits**
Crude oil	2 954 855	2 618 046	3 458 057	2 726 114	4 264 597	5 062 273	4 919 389	4 358 733	...	Pétrole brut
Wood	103 281	102 134	101 121	79 845	60 617	50 975	61 323	57 296	...	Bois
Sugar	11 553	8 101	10 633	11 337	11 207	2 477	...	...	...	Sucre
Cocoa	82	92	105	70	70	200	145	575	...	Cacao
Fish and Shrimp	79	91	21	103	103	14	32	209	...	Poissons et Crevettes
Main Destinations										**Principales destinations**
France	58 855	30 743	532 047	479 118	772 173	480 038	427 162	277 557	...	France
USA	183 010	673 106	769 103	529 389	622 493	843 248	90 092	340 608	...	Etats-Unis
Italy	102 338	75 742	127 695	71 182	26 836	134 147	37 665	340	...	Italie
Netherlands	106 532	6 378	3 937	33 281	421 843	326 579	418 805	194 464	...	Pays Bas
Belgium	18 407	4 460	3 064	2 514	3 263	3 035	21 918	16 870	...	Belgique
IMPORTS, CIF										**IMPORTATIONS, CAF**
Imports - Total	1 035 974	1 884 950	1 583 550	2 101 660	2 019 670	3 158 383	3 806 558	4 159 491	...	Importations - Total (millions)
Imports from Africa	5 225 538	99 885	847 707	882 583	1 164 714	2 012 429	1 984 931	2 117 268	...	Importations en provenance de l'Afrique
Main Products										**Principaux produits**
Meat and offal	15 349	18 480	25 395	41 803	18 953	31 629	47 439	65 431	...	Viandes et Abats
Mechanical Machinery	115 872	118 768	94 089	137 956	151 339	207 631	97 571	130 683	...	Machine mécanique
Book in Box	4 591	11 534	69 521	34 187	41 356	54 418	124 618	155 719	...	Ouvrage en Boite
Electrical Machinery	54 105	58 936	57 431	65 225	65 945	75 548	340 298	2 785 224	...	Machine et app électrique
Cars and automobile	24 181	42 593	46 198	49 308	49 167	66 357	1 322 910	146 899	...	Voitures et automobile
Main Origin										**Principales provenances**
France	175 577	240 167	158 703	264 564	264 074	251 711	307 830	378 164	...	France
USA	33 347	44 371	32 083	80 988	82 192	69 968	92 781	66 300	...	Etats-Unis
Hungary	252	13	25	94	94	1 430	1 454	1 346	...	Hongrie
Netherlands	19 533	38 299	25 683	78 004	83 215	32 086	28 874	93 451	...	Pays Bas
Belgium and Luxembourg	72 201	108 756	73 465	69 199	81 368	129 288	185 227	198 308	...	Belgique et Luxembourg

IX FINANCIAL AND MONETARY STATISTICS - FINANCES ET STATISTIQUES MONETAIRES

	2006	2007	2008	2009	2010	2011	2012	2013	2014	
IX-1 MONETARY STATISTICS *CFA FRANC (MILLIONS)*										**IX-1 STATISTIQUES MONÉTAIRES** *FRANC CFA (MILLIONS)*
Money supply (M1)	664 960	710 920	969 750	1 018 660	1 414 520	1 901 960	2 303 040	2 318 560	2 559 040	Masse monétaire (M1)
Quasi-money	82 660	90 943	126 800	137 609	165 147	209 735	260 481	333 603	345 426	Quasi-monnaie
of which Demand Deposit	...	...	...	...	...	...	...	...	...	dont Monnaie scripturale
Net foreign assets	1 035 063	1 102 412	1 867 790	1 830 931	2 325 304	3 058 686	3 096 264	3 015 377	2 783 546	Avoirs extérieurs nets
Domestic credit	- 334 688	- 275 628	- 809 643	- 650 551	- 852 927	-1 098 254	- 623 791	- 503 550	57 093	Crédit intérieur
of which claims on private sector	84 783	91 221	166 958	222 798	389 027	528 927	669 611	787 521	987 401	dont créances sur le secteur privé
of which claims on government sector, net	- 443 345	- 387 133	-1 012 923	- 893 102	-1 267 971	-1 641 869	-1 315 943	-1 312 975	- 971 576	dont créances nettes sur le gouvernement
International reserves (millions US$)	1 842	2 175	3 872	3 806	4 447	5 641	5 550	...	...	Réserves internationales (millions $EU)
Average Exchange Rate (National Currency per US$)	522.89	479.27	447.81	472.19	495.28	471.87	510.53	494.04	493.38	Taux de change (moyen) (monnaie nationale par $ EU)
IX-2 PUBLIC FINANCE *CFA FRANC (MILLIONS)*										**IX-2 FINANCES PUBLIQUES** *FRANC CFA (MILLIONS)*
Total Revenues and Grants	1 796 000	1 578 900	2 497 000	1 335 000	2 231 000	2 894 000	2 976 000	3 123 000	2 787 181	Recettes totales et dons
Tax Revenue	1 767 200	1 548 500	2 442 000	1 307 000	2 203 000	2 832 000	2 911 000	3 060 000	2 729 238	Recettes fiscales
Non Tax Revenue	23 800	15 200	20 000	13 000	24 000	27 000	55 000	37 000	20 624	Recettes non fiscales
Grants	5 000	15 200	35 000	15 000	4 000	35 000	10 000	26 000	37 320	Dons
Total Expenditures and Net Lending	1 105 700	1 171 400	1 256 000	1 118 400	1 275 000	1 774 000	2 526 000	2 555 000	3 179 037	Dépenses totales et prêts nets
Current expenditure	741 900	783 600	785 000	627 400	680 000	690 000	1 023 000	943 000	1 509 478	Dépenses courantes
Of which Wages and Salaries	134 900	141 900	166 000	175 000	180 000	207 000	248 000	275 000	316 234	Dont rémunérations et salaires
Capital expenditure	359 300	387 800	471 000	490 000	595 000	1 084 000	1 503 000	1 612 000	1 669 559	Dépenses d'équipement
Net Lending	4 500	-	-	1 000	-	-	-	-	-	Prêts nets
Fiscal Balance	690 300	407 500	1 241 000	216 600	956 000	1 120 000	450 000	568 000	- 391 855	Solde global y compris les dons
IX-3 BALANCE OF PAYMENTS *CFA FRANC (BILLIONS)*										**IX-3 BALANCE DES PAIEMENTS** *FRANC CFA (MILLIARDS)*
Trade balance	2 125	1 487	2 509	1 859	3 016	3 340	3 106	2 300	2 016	Balance commerciale
Services Balance	- 1 131	- 1 316	- 1 014	- 943	- 1 502	- 1 498	- 1 342	- 1 227	- 1 223	Balance des services
Net Income	- 916	- 835	- 1 378	- 1 231	- 1 134	- 1 304	- 1 659	- 1 202	- 1 134	Revenus nets
Compensation of employees	- 31	- 32	- 27	- 35	- 52	- 59	- 70	...	...	Rémunération des salariés
Investment Income	- 885	- 802	- 932	- 762	- 1 091	- 1 249	- 1 438	...	...	Revenus des investissements
Current transfers, net total	- 13	- 18	5	- 19	- 151	- 138	- 196	- 190	- 190	Transferts courants
Net official transfers	...	...	...	...	...	...	...	...	...	Transferts officiels nets
Workers' remittances	- 1	- 2	- 2	- 2	- 2	- 2	- 2	...	...	Envois de fonds des travailleurs
Other private transfers	...	...	...	...	...	...	...	...	...	Autres transferts privés
Current account balance	65	- 682	122	- 334	229	400	- 91	- 319	- 531	Solde du compte courant
Capital & financial account	275	826	1 093	427	1 218	1 459	2 208	...	...	Comptes de capital et financier
Capital account	5	15	18	15	1 312	35	181	...	...	Compte de capital
Financial account	270	811	1 075	413	- 94	1 423	2 027	...	...	Compte financier
Errors & omissions	- 7	- 49	64	44	- 23	- 43	-	...	...	Erreurs et omissions
Overall balance	333	96	1 278	137	1 424	1 815	2 117	...	...	Balance générale

X DEBT AND FINANCIAL FLOWS - DETTE ET FLUX FINANCIERS										
	2006	2007	2008	2009	2010	2011	2012	2013	2014	
X-1 DEBT *US$ (MILLIONS)*										**X-1 DETTE EXTÉRIEURE** *$ E.U (MILLIONS)*
Total external debt	6 644	7 401	6 541	5 501	2 425	3 207	3 583	4 452	4 767	Dette extérieure totale
Private	1 692	2 715	2 597	4 457	322	640	174	680	715	Privée
Public	4 952	4 686	3 945	1 044	2 102	2 567	3 409	3 772	4 053	Publique
Total external debt service	564	389	218	539	145	139	137	305	361	Service de la dette extérieure
Present value of External debt	...	...	...	...	...	...	...	...	...	Valeur actuelle de la dette extérieure
Total government domestic debt (in local currency)	...	...	...	...	...	...	...	...	...	Dette publique intérieure
X-2 FINANCIAL FLOWS *US$ (MILLIONS)*										**X-2 FLUX FINANCIERS** *$ E.U (MILLIONS)*
Net Foreign Direct Investment Inflows	1 925	2 275	2 526	1 862	2 211	3 056	2 758	2 038	...	Investissement étranger direct (flux nets entrants)
Main origin of FDI Inflows										**Principales origines de l'IDE entrant:**
France	403	341	550	315	- 9.3	318.9	335.5	...	...	France
Belgium	- 3	884	- 77	1 200	132.5	- 189.4	167.1	...	...	Belgique
Sweden	...	...	...	...	- 21.9	193.0	179.9	...	...	Suède
Luxembourg	36	30	...	- 3	1.5	...	...	...	...	Luxembourg
Korea	...	...	1	...	...	...	0.6	...	...	Corée
African countries	...	...	...	...	...	...	...	...	...	Pays africains
Net total Official Development Assistance	258	119	485	283	1 312	260	139	150	...	Aide publique au développement (nette totale)
Main origin of Net ODA										**Principales origines de l'APD nette**
France	123	19	368	93	909.4	61.3	16.4	...	...	France
IDA	16	14	17	9	20.7	25.4	29.3	...	...	IDA
Germany	4	6	0	26	9.4	97.1	88.8	...	...	Allemagne
Italy	24	- 1	- 1	29	97.5	...	...	...	...	Italie
Spain	- 2	1	1	44	0.5	0.5	1.5	...	...	Espagne

CONGO, DEM. REPUBLIC — RÉP. DÉMOCRATIQUE DU CONGO

AREA (km²)	2 345 409		SUPERFICIE (km²)
CAPITAL CITY	Kinshasa	Kinshasa	CAPITALE
CURRENCY	Congolese Franc	Franc Congolais	MONNAIE

I SOCIAL AND DEMOGRAPHIC INDICATORS – INDICATEURS DEMOGRAPHIQUES ET SOCIAUX

	Year / Année	Value / Valeur	
POPULATION			**POPULATION**
Population ('000)			Population ('000)
Both sexes	2014	69 360	Les deux sexes
Male	2014	34 455	Masculin
Female	2014	34 906	Féminin
Average annual growth rate	2014	2.7	Taux de croissance annuel
Active Population ('000)	2014	27 546	Population active ('000)
Population by age group ('000)			Population par groupe d'âge ('000)
0-14 years	2014	31 072	0-14 ans
15-64 years	2014	36 302	15-64 ans
65+ years	2014	1 986	65+ ans
Economically. active population. in agriculture (%)	2014	55.1	Participation de la population active agricole (%)
Crude birth rate	2014	42.3	Taux brut de natalité
Crude death rate	2014	15.2	Taux brut de mortalité
Total fertility rate	2014	5.8	Indice synthétique de fécondité
Proportion of urban population	2014	35.9	Part de la population urbaine
Life Expectancy at Birth - Total (years)	2014	50.3	Espérance de vie à la naissance - Totale (ans)
Dependency Ratio - Total (%)	2014	91.6	Taux de dépendance - Total (%)
HEALTH			**SANTÉ**
Percentage of children under-five and underweight	2010	24.2	% d'enfants de moins de cinq ans avec insuffisance pondérale
Prevalence of undernourishment	...	...	Prévalence de la malnutrition
Under five mortality rate (both sexes, per 1000)	2013	118.5	Taux de mortalité de moins de 5 ans (les deux sexes, pour 1000)
Infant mortality rate (both sexes) per 1000	2013	86.1	Taux de mortalité infantile (les deux sexes) par 1000
Percentage of children provided the vaccines :			Pourcentage d'enfants vaccinés :
BCG	2013	78.0	BCG
DPT3	2013	72.0	DTC3
Polio	2011	78.0	Polio
Measles	2013	73.0	Rougeole
Percentage of mothers provided at least one antenatal care (%)	...	...	Pourcentage de mères ayant au moins reçu un soin prénatal (%)
Percentage of deliveries attended by skilled health personnel	2010	80.4	% d'accouchements assistés par un personnel de santé qualifié
Number of doctors (per 10 000 population)	2004	1.1	Nombre de médecins (pour 10 000 habitants)
Number of nurses (per 10 000 population)	2004	5.3	Nombre d'infirmières (pour 10 000 habitants)
Hospital beds - Total (per 10 000 population)	2006	8.0	Nombre de lits d'hôpitaux - Total (pour 10 000)
Births registered (per 1 000)	2014	42.3	Naiss.s enregistrées (pour 1 000)
Deaths registered (per 1 000)	2014	15.2	Décès enregistrés (pour 1 000)
Public expenditure on Health (% of budget)	2009	17.0	Dépenses publiques consacrées à la santé (% du budget)
EDUCATION			**EDUCATION**
Enrolment in primary education (both sexes) (000)	2012	12 005	Scolarisation dans le primaire (les deux sexes) (000)
Female	2012	5 591	Féminin
Enrolment in secondary education (both sexes) (000)	2012	3 894	Scolarisation dans le secondaire (les deux sexes) (000)
Female	2012	1 441	Féminin
Enrolment in tertiary education (both sexes) (000)	2013	437.5	Scolarisation dans le tertiaire (les deux sexes) (000)
Female	2012	181.2	Féminin
Literacy rate (both sexes)	2007	61.2	Taux d'alphabétisation (deux sexes)
Male	2007	76.9	Masculin
Female	2007	46.1	Féminin
Pupil-teacher ratio	2011	37.4	Ratio élève-enseignant
Public expenditure on education (% of budget)	2010	9.2	Dépenses publiques consacrées à l'enseignement (% du budget)
POVERTY			**PAUVRETÉ**
GNI Per Capita (US$)	2013	430.0	RNB par habitant ($EU)
Human Poverty Index (HPI-1) Value (%)	2007	24.3	Valeur de l'Indice de pauvreté (IPH-1) (%)
Population below International Poverty Line ($2/day) (%)	2006	95.2	Population sous le seuil international de pauvreté (2$/J) (%)
Share of Income Held by Richest 10%	2006	34.7	% de revenu des 10% plus riches
Share of Income Held by Poorest 10%	2011	2.2	% de revenu des 10% plus pauvres
Gini index	2011	40.2	Indice de Gini

Charts / Graphiques

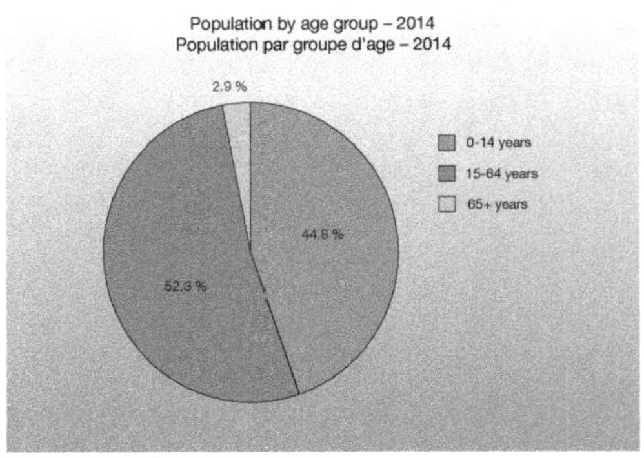

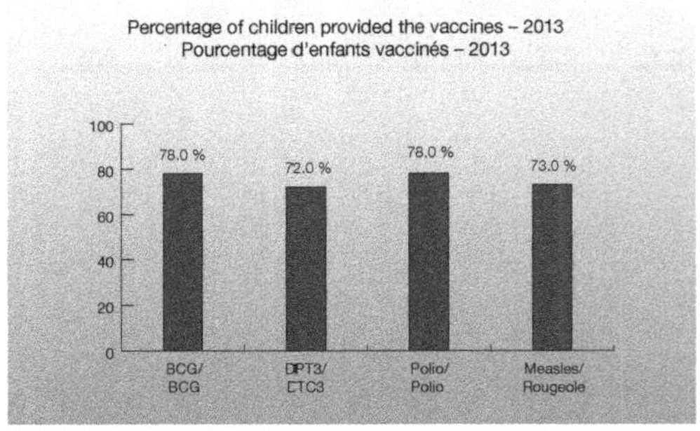

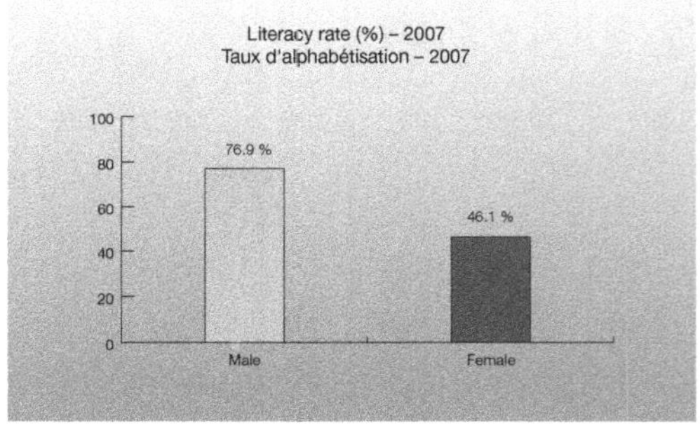

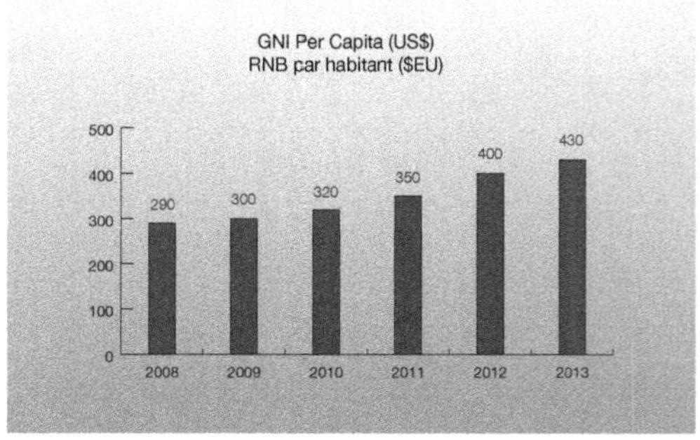

	2006	2007	2008	2009	2010	2011	2012	2013	2014	
II NATIONAL ACCOUNTS — COMPTES NATIONAUX										
GROSS DOMESTIC PRODUCT BY KIND OF ECONOMIC ACTIVITY AT CURRENT PRICES *CONGOLESE FRANC (MILLIONS)*										**PRODUIT INTÉRIEUR BRUT PAR BRANCHE D'ACTIVITÉ ÉCONOMIQUE AUX PRIX COURANTS** *FRANC CONGOLAIS (MILLIONS)*
Agriculture, hunting, forestry and fishing	1 435 395	1 868 348	2 503 338	3 575 156	4 186 415	4 969 777	5 509 797	5 804 886	6 167 209	Agriculture, chasse, sylviculture et pêche
Mining and quarrying	587 598	676 443	1 439 139	1 356 595	3 388 941	4 790 423	5 186 984	6 057 094	7 332 235	Industries extractives
Manufacturing	1 047 111	1 470 831	1 650 953	2 850 452	3 169 171	3 649 184	4 140 583	4 623 444	5 167 797	Industries manufacturières
Electricity, gas & water	84 129	104 648	143 710	165 381	788 881	1 055 675	1 264 563	1 448 505	1 485 564	Electricité, gaz et eau
Construction & public works	293 453	360 643	443 228	613 367	211 581	232 476	258 361	277 992	299 540	Bâtiments et travaux publics
Wholesale & retail trade, restaurants, hotels	920 832	1 167 412	1 168 894	1 708 910	2 080 030	2 391 108	2 842 133	3 110 795	3 299 680	Commerce de gros et de détail, restaurants et hôtels
Finance, insurance, real estate, etc.	747 984	892 888	852 624	1 183 700	1 487 205	1 697 813	1 889 869	2 027 803	2 268 802	Banques, assurances, affaires immobilières
Transport and communications	943 633	1 152 617	1 416 717	1 795 067	2 092 047	2 360 802	2 701 538	2 985 170	3 208 974	Transport(s) et communications
Public administration and defense	378 125	521 851	815 796	1 062 356	1 212 268	1 400 159	1 497 674	1 578 932	1 735 135	Administrations publiques et défense
Education	17 711	25 738	24 498	31 901	29 970	9 244	9 589	10 109	10 909	Education
Health and Social Work	4 300	6 996	7 576	9 866	10 053	8 620	3 275	3 453	3 764	Santé et actions sociales
Other services	...	...	...	...	...	...	...	...	...	Autres services
Less Imputed Service Charges	- 34 526	- 70 364	- 108 826	- 145 615	- 170 885	- 193 894	- 213 797	- 203 254	- 236 428	Moins services d'intermédiation financière
Gross domestic product at factor cost / basic prices	6 425 745	8 178 050	10 357 646	14 207 135	18 485 677	22 371 387	25 090 569	27 724 927	30 743 183	Produit intérieur brut aux couts des facteurs / prix de base
Plus: indirect taxes / taxes on products, less subsidies	341 775	470 829	709 923	894 052	1 051 000	1 388 038	1 863 988	2 326 252	2 481 098	Plus taxes indirectes/impôts sur les produits, moins les subventions
EXPENDITURE ON GROSS DOMESTIC PRODUCT AT CURRENT PURCHASER'S VALUES *CONGOLESE FRANC (MILLIONS)*										**EMPLOI DU PRODUIT INTÉRIEUR BRUT AUX PRIX COURANTS D'ACQUISITION** *FRANC CONGOLAIS (MILLIONS)*
Government final consumption	632 295	747 534	792 651	1 692 459	2 312 825	2 559 922	3 491 076	3 770 362	3 954 177	Consommation finale des administrations publiques
Private final consumption	5 803 906	7 050 222	10 200 873	12 954 512	16 741 724	20 011 417	22 204 437	22 882 539	25 583 570	Consommation finale privée
Gross fixed capital formation	987 034	1 177 323	1 189 344	2 188 625	2 309 233	2 763 433	3 215 125	4 609 657	4 771 085	Formation brute de capital fixe
Change in inventories	4 160	8 290	12 274	10 627	11 612	18 236	21 635	31 019	-	Variation des stocks
Exports of goods and services	3 137 626	6 540 374	7 697 856	5 021 005	8 866 530	10 211 300	9 031 062	11 176 309	12 257 997	Exportations de biens et services
Less imports of goods and services	3 797 502	6 874 864	8 825 428	6 766 041	10 705 248	11 804 884	11 008 777	12 418 706	13 342 594	Moins importations de biens et services
GDP at purchasers' values	6 767 520	8 648 879	11 067 569	15 101 188	19 536 677	23 759 425	26 954 557	30 051 179	33 224 281	PIB aux prix d'acquisition
GROSS DOMESTIC PRODUCT BY KIND OF ECONOMIC ACTIVITY AT CONSTANT PRICES *ANNUAL GROWTH RATES (%)*										**PRODUIT INTÉRIEUR BRUT PAR BRANCHE D'ACTIVITÉ ECONOMIQUE AUX PRIX CONSTANTS** *TAUX DE CROISSANCE ANNUEL (%)*
Agriculture, hunting, forestry and fishing	5.6	2.8	2.8	2.8	3.6	3.6	3.5	4.2	3.4	Agriculture, chasse, sylviculture et pêche
Mining and quarrying	- 10.7	2.5	11.4	0.9	235.2	23.8	9.8	10.1	12.4	Industries extractives
Manufacturing	8.2	5.1	2.7	1.9	- 35.5	1.8	5.2	10.1	7.2	Industries manufacturières
Electricity, gas & water	5.9	1.8	- 2.0	- 16.0	6.4	- 3.2	6.8	7.2	6.3	Electricité, gaz et eau
Construction & public works	- 0.4	5.4	3.8	5.8	1.3	17.9	15.1	14.1	8.0	Bâtiments et travaux publics
Wholesale & retail trade, restaurants, hotels	9.5	12.0	10.5	9.5	- 2.7	0.8	11.2	8.2	14.4	Commerce de gros et de détail, restaurants et hôtels
Finance, insurance, real estate, etc.	- 10.1	7.0	6.9	3.6	- 5.3	1.9	4.3	6.5	7.7	Banques, assurances, affaires immobilières
Transport and communications	7.0	16.3	9.4	- 2.5	- 5.3	0.6	5.9	9.5	10.0	Transport(s) et communications
Public administration and defense	178.4	5.8	14.9	7.2	- 6.7	1.9	- 1.5	3.9	5.1	Administrations publiques et défense
Education	- 88.7	119.1	- 0.6	45.4	- 11.2	- 13.5	6.4	15.4	4.1	Education
Health and Social Work	- 97.4	97.1	- 36.5	22.6	60.2	- 28.1	3.3	5.6	5.1	Santé et actions sociales
Other services	...	...	...	...	...	...	...	...	...	Autres services
Less Imputed Service Charges	5.6	69.2	40.5	16.6	- 3.4	1.3	2.3	- 6.0	1.4	Moins services d'intermédiation financière
Gross domestic product at factor cost / basic prices	4.9	7.1	6.3	2.9	7.3	6.9	7.0	8.3	9.3	Produit intérieur brut aux couts des facteurs / prix de base
Plus: indirect taxes / taxes on products, less subsidies	16.0	- 15.3	3.1	1.7	1.9	6.3	11.5	14.1	15.0	Plus taxes indirectes/impôts sur les produits, moins les subventions
Gross domestic product at market prices	5.3	6.3	6.2	2.9	7.1	6.9	7.1	8.5	9.5	Produit intérieur brut aux prix du marché
EXPENDITURE ON GROSS DOMESTIC PRODUCT AT CONSTANT PURCHASERS' VALUES *ANNUAL GROWTH RATES (%)*										**EMPLOIS DU PRODUIT INTÉRIEUR BRUT AUX PRIX CONSTANTS D'ACQUISITION** *TAUX DE CROISSANCE ANNUEL (%)*
Government final consumption	24.9	7.8	20.0	- 17.2	63.6	- 19.3	80.4	12.4	3.4	Consommation finale des administrations publiques
Private final consumption	0.1	7.3	0.6	2.2	16.0	2.5	- 8.1	6.1	9.6	Consommation finale privée
Gross fixed capital formation	19.1	12.3	6.4	66.2	20.8	21.9	- 42.1	17.0	10.7	Formation brute de capital fixe
Exports of goods and services	- 9.4	26.7	4.7	- 28.3	1.1	16.0	90.0	11.6	2.9	Exportations de biens et services
Less imports of goods and services	- 11.7	30.1	- 6.9	0.2	59.3	2.9	- 10.8	12.3	0.7	Moins importations de biens et services
Notes	NA Data: 2011-2014:Estimates						Données des CN: 2011-2014:Estimées			Notes

	2006	2007	2008	2009	2010	2011	2012	2013	2014	
III INFLATION										
ANNUAL GROWTH RATES (%)										**TAUX DE CROISSANCE ANNUEL (%)**
All items	21.4	22.3	44.7	29.0	17.2	12.6	3.7	1.3	1.3	Ensemble
of which:										dont:
Food and Non-alcoholic beverages	23.8	22.8	53.4	30.3	20.1	5.3	4.2	1.2	1.6	Alimentation et boissons non alcoolisés
Alcoholic beverages & tobacco	...	...	...	...	...	...	5.6	0.1	0.9	Boissons alcoolisées et tabacs
Clothing and Footwear	15.8	15.9	23.3	53.7	14.5	7.5	2.2	2.2	1.4	Habillement et chaussures
Housing, Water, Electricity, Gas and Other Fuels	26.8	11.5	79.1	20.2	21.4	12.4	0.4	0.3	1.2	Logement, eau, electricité, gas et autres combustibles
Furnishing, household equipment	...	...	...	...	...	...	4.6	0.6	0.3	Meubles, articles de ménage et entretien courant
Health	37.7	15.0	19.4	15.7	11.8	22.1	1.6	1.6	0.9	Santé
Transport	4.2	62.6	-3.9	53.6	12.5	2.8	13.3	1.8	1.1	Transport
Communication	-1.6	13.8	11.9	29.6	1.8	12.8	0.8	-	0.2	Communication
Recreation & culture	...	...	...	...	...	...	5.0	0.9	0.3	Loisirs et culture
Education	...	...	...	...	...	...	3.7	3.7	0.4	Enseignement
Restaurants & hotels	...	...	...	...	...	...	4.5	0.2	0.9	Restaurants et hôtels
Miscellaneous goods & services	...	...	...	...	...	...	3.2	0.8	1.1	Biens et services divers

IV AGRICULTURAL PRODUCTION - PRODUCTION AGRICOLE

	2006	2007	2008	2009	2010	2011	2012	2013	2014	
TONNES (THOUSAND)										**TONNES (MILLIERS)**
Cassava	14 989	15 004	15 013	15 054	15 014	15 024	16 000	16 500	...	Manioc
Maize	1 155	1 156	1 156	1 156	1 156	1 156	1 375	1 373	...	Maïs
Plantains	1 200	1 205	1 207	1 200	1 300	1 300	1 350	1 350	...	Banane plantain
Groundnuts, with shell	369	369	370	371	388	394	371	370	...	Arachides en coques
Rice, paddy	316	316	317	317	318	319	350	355	...	Riz

V MINING PRODUCTION - PRODUCTION MINIERE

	2006	2007	2008	2009	2010	2011	2012	2013	2014	
Copper, Tons (thousands)	22	185	337	310	438	499	620	659	...	Cuivre, tonnes (milliers)
Diamond, carats (thousands)	28 990	28 452	33 402	21 298	20 166	19 249	21 524	15 514	...	Diamants, carat (milliers)
Cobalt, Tons (thousands)	15	17	42	56	97	99	85	74	46	Cobalt, tonnes (milliers)

VI ENERGY - ENERGIE

	2006	2007	2008	2009	2010	2011	2012	2013	2014	
Total electricity generation (GWh)	7 312	7 582	7 228	7 526	7 600	7 273	7 274	7 278	...	Production d'électricité totale (GWh)
of which:										dont:
Production of electricity from fossil fuels (GWh)	24	7	17	6	9	35	36	38	...	Production d'électricité à partir de combustibles fossiles (GWh)
Production of hydro electricity (GWh)	7 288	7 575	7 211	7 520	7 591	7 235	7 235	7 235	...	Production d'électricité d'origine hydraulique (GWh)
Production of electricity from solar, wind, tide, wave and other sources (GWh)	...	...	...	...	...	3	3	5	...	Production d'électricité d'origine solaire, éolienne, marée motrice et autres (GWh)

VII TOURISM AND INFRASTRUCTURE - TOURISME ET INFRASTRUCTURE

	2006	2007	2008	2009	2010	2011	2012	2013	2014	
VII-1 TOURISM										**VII-1 TOURISME**
International tourist arrivals (thousands)	55	47	50	53	81	186	167	191	199	Arrivées de touristes internationaux (milliers)
Rooms in hotels and similar establishments (thousands)	...	...	...	...	1.1	1.1	2.3	3.1	...	Chambres d'hotels et établissements assimilés (milliers)
Overnight stays (thousands)	189	126	144	156	113	103	113	102	109	Nuitées (milliers)
Tourism receipts (US$ thousand)	2 370	535	535	18 345	8 179	8 714	5 274	612	752	Recettes touristiques (milliers de $ EU)
Total contribution to GDP (%)	2.5	2.5	2.9	3.1	2.5	2.2	2.0	1.8	1.7	Contribution totale au PIB (%)
Total contribution to Employment (%)	2.2	2.2	2.5	2.7	2.0	1.8	1.7	1.5	1.4	Contribution totale à l'emploi (%)
VII-2 INFRASTRUCTURE										**VII-2 INFRASTRUCTURE**
Paved roads (% of total)	...	...	...	...	...	...	...	6	...	Routes asphaltées (% du total)
Total Network (Railways-km)	3 641	3 641	4 007	3 641	3 641	3 641	3 641	...	...	Réseau total voies ferrées-Km
Main Telephone Lines (per 100 inhabitants)	0	0	0	0	0	0	0	-	...	Lignes téléphoniques fixes (pour 100 habitants)
Mobile Cellular Subscribers (per 100 inhabitants)	8	12	17	16	19	24	31	42	...	Abonnés aux téléphones mobiles (pour 100 habitants)

VIII EXTERNAL TRADE - COMMERCE EXTERIEUR

	2006	2007	2008	2009	2010	2011	2012	2013	2014	
CONGOLESE FRANC (MILLIONS) EXPORTS, FOB										**FRANC CONGOLAIS (MILLIONS) EXPORTATIONS, FÀB**
Exports - Total	1 294 769	1 982 307	3 657 966	4 601 750	8 031 800	9 388 700	8 110 500	...	...	Exportations - Total
Exports to AFRICA	...	...	...	...	...	...	...	...	...	Exportations vers l'AFRIQUE
Main Products										**Principaux produits**
Diamonds	302 220	349 599	268 679	175 113	281 411	335 242	373 000	...	...	Diamants
Crude oil	316 593	371 024	468 014	450 663	594 472	903 942	...	...	...	Pétrole brut
Cobalt	73 297	98 793	153 987	...	3 438 333	3 395 232	...	...	...	Cobalt
Copper	53 966	305 906	1 489 724	...	2 816 141	3 772 701	4 197 419	...	...	Cuivre
Log	5 944	268 306	44 219	...	58 231	59 960	32 196	...	...	Grumes
Main Destinations										**Principales destinations**
China	309 682	349 282	1 024 309	1 138 392	2 160 510	3 668 791	3 292 980	...	...	Chine
Belgium	428 309	380 801	329 666	234 966	253 542	423 707	124 010	...	...	Belgique
United States	72 385	158 256	174 994	339 532	470 940	722 966	1 258	...	...	États-Unis
Zambia	25 585	109 316	368 803	522 853	1 115 056	...	555 779	...	...	Zambie
Finland	105 321	146 382	210 808	102 095	112 486	103 735	34 581	...	...	Finlande
IMPORTS, CIF										**IMPORTATIONS, CAF**
Imports - Total	1 354 075	1 756 950	2 404 958	3 158 165	9 697 200	10 853 900	9 786 300	...	...	Importations - Total (millions)
Imports from Africa	...	...	...	...	...	...	...	...	...	Importations en provenance de l'Afrique
Main Products										**Principaux produits**
Petroleum, petroleum products and related materials	134 333	139 489	230 123	257 644	292 471	219 034	...	...	...	Pétrole et produits dérivés
Road vehicles	84 867	121 371	164 710	190 230	267 959	391 629	...	...	...	Véhicules routiers
Specialised machinery	72 196	100 348	154 559	155 454	182 579	345 451	...	...	...	Machines et appareils spécialisés
Cereals and cereal preparations	74 034	105 930	140 371	189 404	223 849	229 011	...	...	...	Céréales et préparations à base de céréales
Other industrial machinery and parts	42 289	68 679	115 944	130 759	192 518	...	...	...	...	Autres machines industrielles et pièces détachées
Main Origin										**Principales provenances**
South Africa	239 132	383 209	642 262	534 997	761 760	1 302 520	...	...	...	Afrique du Sud
Belgium	127 026	159 290	221 130	282 192	329 881	543 305	...	...	...	Belgique
China	39 570	53 775	132 803	280 668	441 356	1 027 595	...	...	...	Chine
Zambia	85 803	174 204	186 038	290 364	352 646	...	...	...	...	Zambie
France	101 128	108 263	104 055	200 611	211 579	303 016	...	...	...	France

IX FINANCIAL AND MONETARY STATISTICS - FINANCES ET STATISTIQUES MONETAIRES	2006	2007	2008	2009	2010	2011	2012	2013	2014	
IX-1 MONETARY STATISTICS *CONGOLESE FRANC (MILLIONS)*										**IX-1 STATISTIQUES MONÉTAIRES** *FRANC CONGOLAIS (MILLIONS)*
Money supply (M1)	428 790	641 240	998 440	1 501 870	1 964 600	2 419 420	2 930 110	3 255 340	3 654 410	Masse monétaire (M1)
Quasi-money	30 093	59 725	130 589	228 270	259 737	528 870	724 484	920 250	1 233 789	Quasi-monnaie
of which Demand Deposit	...	...	...	...	...	...	...	...	...	dont Monnaie scripturale
Net foreign assets	- 384 787	- 247 210	- 297 056	- 48 762	880 890	849 517	1 403 482	1 455 234	1 548 201	Avoirs extérieurs nets
Domestic credit	193 861	307 938	651 355	772 437	157 966	1 878 078	1 760 158	2 186 805	2 610 460	Crédit intérieur
of which claims on private sector	140 985	228 924	552 157	800 396	729 249	955 836	1 296 874	1 576 636	1 891 863	dont créances sur le secteur privé
of which claims on government sector, net	48 937	73 159	90 843	- 70 169	- 658 424	765 945	304 318	462 530	535 589	dont créances nettes sur le gouvernement
International reserves (millions US$)	155	181	78	1 035	1 300	1 268	1 633	1 678	1 557	Réserves internationales (millions $EU)
Average Exchange Rate (National Currency per US$)	468.28	516.75	559.29	809.79	905.91	919.49	919.76	919.79	925.28	Taux de change (moyen) (monnaie nationale par $ EU)
IX-2 PUBLIC FINANCE *CONGOLESE FRANC (MILLIONS)*										**IX-2 FINANCES PUBLIQUES** *FRANC CONGOLAIS (MILLIONS)*
Total Revenues and Grants	856 800	837 100	1 326 900	2 207 000	3 929 000	3 940 000	5 069 000	4 796 000	5 216 730	Recettes totales et dons
Tax Revenue	528 700	761 100	1 205 400	1 528 000	2 253 000	2 714 000	3 763 000	3 584 000	4 102 519	Recettes fiscales
Non Tax Revenue	-	-	-	-	-	-	-	-	-	Recettes non fiscales
Grants	328 100	76 000	121 500	679 000	1 676 000	1 226 000	1 306 000	1 212 000	1 114 211	Dons
Total Expenditures and Net Lending	883 978	966 600	1 478 700	2 586 000	3 342 000	4 194 000	4 922 000	5 275 000	6 384 181	Dépenses totales et prêts nets
Current expenditure	749 878	845 500	1 235 000	1 882 000	2 073 000	2 941 000	3 160 000	3 146 000	3 852 951	Dépenses courantes
Of which Wages and Salaries	218 898	301 000	452 200	548 000	697 000	1 091 000	1 256 000	1 398 000	1 969 430	Dont rémunérations et salaires
Capital expenditure	134 100	121 100	243 700	704 000	1 269 000	1 253 000	1 762 000	2 129 000	2 531 230	Dépenses d'équipement
Net Lending	-	0	-	-	-	-	-	-	-	Prêts nets
Fiscal Balance	- 27 178	- 129 500	- 151 800	- 379 000	587 000	- 254 000	147 000	- 479 000	-1 167 451	Solde global y compris les dons
IX-3 BALANCE OF PAYMENTS *CONGOLESE FRANC (BILLIONS)*										**IX-3 BALANCE DES PAIEMENTS** *FRANC CONGOLAIS (MILLIARDS)*
Trade balance	- 87	460	81	- 466	394	511	164	81	...	Balance commerciale
Services Balance	- 221	- 633	- 713	- 941	- 2 060	- 1 977	- 1 840	- 1 646	...	Balance des services
Net Income	- 214	- 342	- 515	- 628	- 948	- 1 009	- 956	- 877	...	Revenus nets
Compensation of employees	- 9	- 9	- 13	- 9	- 38	69	...	...	...	Rémunération des salariés
Investment Income	...	...	...	- 619	- 910	- 1 078	...	...	...	Revenus des investissements
Current transfers, net total	338	445	559	1 130	763	1 297	1 072	322	...	Transferts courants
Net official transfers	319	382	584	1 056	629	1 077	...	...	...	Transferts officiels nets
Workers' remittances	...	...	...	...	...	...	...	...	...	Envois de fonds des travailleurs
Other private transfers	15	63	- 25	74	135	221	...	...	...	Autres transferts privés
Current account balance	- 185	- 69	- 589	- 906	- 1 850	- 1 177	- 1 560	- 2 121	...	Solde du compte courant
Capital & financial account	...	...	...	...	...	...	...	...	...	Comptes de capital et financier
Capital account	38	- 1	62	116	144	858	...	...	...	Compte de capital
Financial account	- 32	51	164	253	760	361	...	...	...	Compte financier
Errors & omissions	...	...	...	...	151	28	...	...	...	Erreurs et omissions
Overall balance	- 196	- 140	- 355	- 736	- 1 085	69	...	...	...	Balance générale

X DEBT AND FINANCIAL FLOWS - DETTE ET FLUX FINANCIERS	2006	2007	2008	2009	2010	2011	2012	2013	2014	
X-1 DEBT *US$ (MILLIONS)*										**X-1 DETTE EXTÉRIEURE** *$ E.U (MILLIONS)*
Total external debt	12 228	12 976	13 591	13 705	4 997	5 110	5 515	6 675	8 202	Dette extérieure totale
Private	386	374	350	689	1 935	2 213	2 621	3 321	4 143	Privée
Public	11 842	12 602	13 241	13 016	3 062	2 897	2 894	3 354	4 059	Publique
Total external debt service	213	171	254	188	177	160	182	195	189	Service de la dette extérieure
Present value of External debt	...	...	...	...	...	...	...	...	...	Valeur actuelle de la dette extérieure
Total government domestic debt (in local currency)	...	...	...	...	...	...	...	...	...	Dette publique intérieure
X-2 FINANCIAL FLOWS *US$ (MILLIONS)*										**X-2 FLUX FINANCIERS** *$ E.U (MILLIONS)*
Net Foreign Direct Investment Inflows	256	1 808	1 727	664	2 939	1 687	3 312	2 098	...	Investissement étranger direct (flux nets entrants)
Main origin of FDI Inflows										**Principales origines de l'IDE entrant:**
Belgium	...	...	...	...	...	...	...	...	...	Belgique
Netherlands	...	...	...	...	...	...	...	...	...	Pays-Bas
Sweden	...	...	...	...	...	...	...	...	...	Suède
Luxembourg	...	...	...	...	...	...	...	...	...	Luxembourg
United Kingdom	...	...	...	...	...	...	...	...	...	Royaume-Uni
African countries	...	...	...	...	...	...	...	...	...	Pays africains
Net total Official Development Assistance	2 197	1 357	1 766	2 357	3 486	5 534	2 859	2 572	...	Aide publique au développement (nette totale)
Main origin of Net ODA										**Principales origines de l'APD nette**
United States	838	132	197	239	277.9	1 293.2	291.8	262.6	...	Etats-Unis
IDA	274	223	291	397	295.6	394.2	383.6	...	...	IDA
Belgium	222	210	174	177	648.8	180.3	87.3	158.4	...	Belgique
France	57	28	31	30	13.5	11.3	28.3	63.1	...	France
United Kingdom	140	121	193	225	250.8	383.1	220.2	...	...	Royaume-Uni

CÔTE D'IVOIRE

CÔTE D'IVOIRE

AREA (km²)	322 463		SUPERFICIE (km²)
CAPITAL CITY	Yamoussoukro	Yamoussoukro	CAPITALE
CURRENCY	CFA Franc	Franc CFA	MONNAIE

I SOCIAL AND DEMOGRAPHIC INDICATORS – INDICATEURS DEMOGRAPHIQUES ET SOCIAUX

	Year / Année	Value / Valeur	
POPULATION			**POPULATION**
Population ('000)			Population ('000)
Both sexes	2014	20 805	Les deux sexes
Male	2014	10 595	Masculin
Female	2014	10 209	Féminin
Average annual growth rate	2014	2.2	Taux de croissance annuel
Active Population ('000)	2014	8 252	Population active ('000)
Population by age group ('000)			Population par groupe d'âge ('000)
0-14 years	2014	8 567	0-14 ans
15-64 years	2014	11 578	15-64 ans
65+ years	2014	660	65+ ans
Economically. active population. in agriculture (%)	2014	34.1	Participation de la population active agricole (%)
Crude birth rate	2014	36.4	Taux brut de natalité
Crude death rate	2014	14.0	Taux brut de mortalité
Total fertility rate	2014	4.8	Indice synthétique de fécondité
Proportion of urban population	2014	53.5	Part de la population urbaine
Life Expectancy at Birth - Total (years)	2014	51.1	Espérance de vie à la naissance - Totale (ans)
Dependency Ratio - Total (%)	2014	77.6	Taux de dépendance - Total (%)
HEALTH			**SANTÉ**
Percentage of children under-five and underweight	2012	15.7	% d'enfants de moins de cinq ans avec insuffisance pondérale
Prevalence of undernourishment	2013	14.7	Prévalence de la malnutrition
Under five mortality rate (both sexes, per 1000)	2013	100.0	Taux de mortalité de moins de 5 ans (les deux sexes, pour 1000)
Infant mortality rate (both sexes) per 1000	2013	71.3	Taux de mortalité infantile (les deux sexes) par 1000
Percentage of children provided the vaccines :			Pourcentage d'enfants vaccinés :
BCG	2013	84.0	BCG
DPT3	2013	88.0	DTC3
Polio	2011	58.0	Polio
Measles	2013	74.0	Rougeole
Percentage of mothers provided at least one antenatal care (%)	2006	84.8	Pourcentage de mères ayant au moins reçu un soin prénatal (%)
Percentage of deliveries attended by skilled health personnel	2012	59.4	% d'accouchements assistés par un personnel de santé qualifié
Number of doctors (per 10 000 population)	2008	1.4	Nombre de médecins (pour 10 000 habitants)
Number of nurses (per 10 000 population)	2008	4.8	Nombre d'infirmières (pour 10 000 habitants)
Hospital beds - Total (per 10 000 population)	2014	1.8	Nombre de lits d'hôpitaux - Total (pour 10 000)
Births registered (per 1 000)	2014	36.4	Naiss.s enregistrées (pour 1 000)
Deaths registered (per 1 000)	2014	14.0	Décès enregistrés (pour 1 000)
Public expenditure on Health (% of budget)	2009	4.4	Dépenses publiques consacrées à la santé (% du budget)
EDUCATION			**EDUCATION**
Enrolment in primary education (both sexes) (000)	2013	3 021	Scolarisation dans le primaire (les deux sexes) (000)
Female	2013	1 394	Féminin
Enrolment in secondary education (both sexes) (000)	2013	1 245	Scolarisation dans le secondaire (les deux sexes) (000)
Female	2013	498	Féminin
Enrolment in tertiary education (both sexes) (000)	2013	80.3	Scolarisation dans le tertiaire (les deux sexes) (000)
Female	2013	64.4	Féminin
Literacy rate (both sexes)	2012	41.0	Taux d'alphabétisation (deux sexes)
Male	2012	51.6	Masculin
Female	2012	30.5	Féminin
Pupil-teacher ratio	...	...	Ratio élève-enseignant
Public expenditure on education (% of budget)	2008	21.9	Dépenses publiques consacrées à l'enseignement (% du budget)
Poverty			Pauvreté
GNI Per Capita (US$)	2013	1 450.0	RNB par habitant ($EU)
Human Poverty Index (HPI-1) Value (%)	2007	37.4	Valeur de l'Indice de pauvreté (IPH-1) (%)
Population below International Poverty Line ($2/day) (%)	2008	59.7	Population sous le seuil international de pauvreté (2$/J) (%)
Share of Income Held by Richest 10%	2008	32.9	% de revenu des 10% plus riches
Share of Income Held by Poorest 10%	2008	2.0	% de revenu des 10% plus pauvres
Gini index	2008	43.2	Indice de Gini

Charts / Graphiques

Population by age group – 2014
Population par groupe d'age – 2014

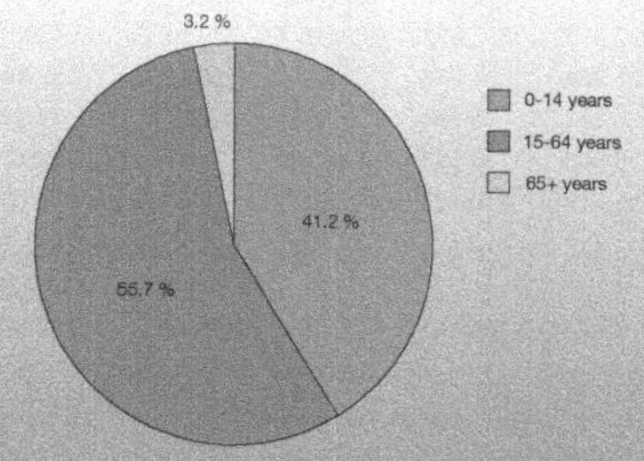

Percentage of children provided the vaccines – 2013
Pourcentage d'enfants vaccinés – 2013

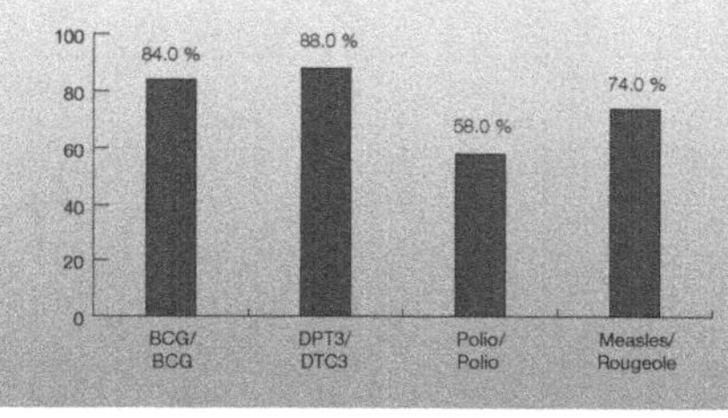

Literacy rate (%) – 2012
Taux d'alphabétisation – 2012

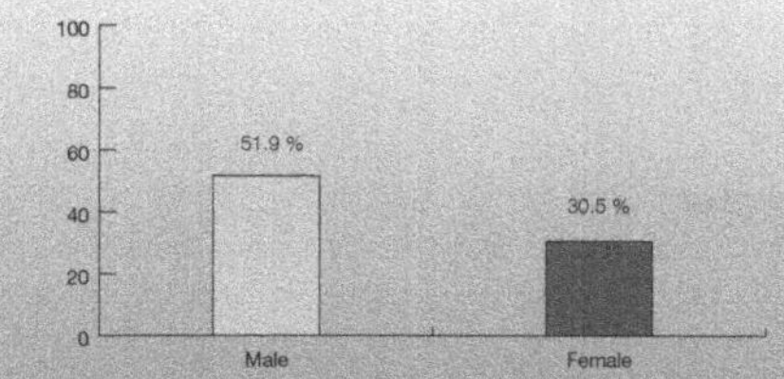

GNI Per Capita (US$)
RNB par habitant ($EU)

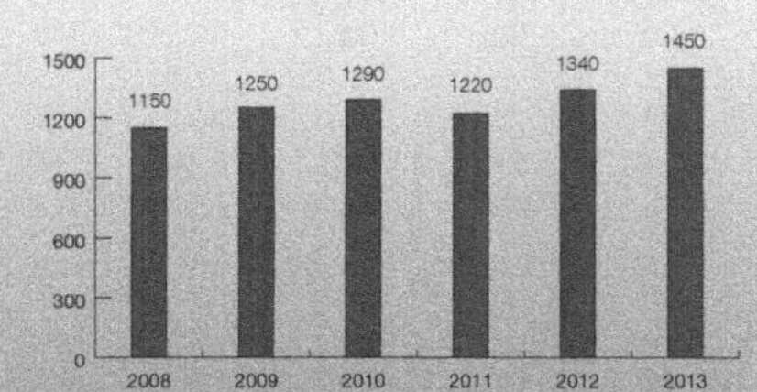

II NATIONAL ACCOUNTS — COMPTES NATIONAUX

	2006	2007	2008	2009	2010	2011	2012	2013	2014	
GROSS DOMESTIC PRODUCT BY KIND OF ECONOMIC ACTIVITY AT CURRENT PRICES *CFA FRANC (MILLIONS)*										**PRODUIT INTÉRIEUR BRUT PAR BRANCHE D'ACTIVITÉ ÉCONOMIQUE AUX PRIX COURANTS** *FRANC CFA (MILLIONS)*
Agriculture, hunting, forestry and fishing	2 105 934	2 144 500	2 460 015	2 430 287	3 023 184	3 190 749	3 079 625	3 376 044	...	Agriculture, chasse, sylviculture et pêche
Mining and quarrying	547 000	513 514	794 439	1 057 522	926 216	1 057 976	1 010 134	1 104 860	...	Industries extractives
Manufacturing	1 324 580	1 419 312	1 550 899	1 534 341	1 556 096	1 594 544	1 867 273	2 046 033	...	Industries manufacturières
Electricity, gas & water	105 765	125 496	117 521	87 499	69 231	29 487	85 925	104 834	...	Electricité, gaz et eau
Construction & public works	213 007	210 677	183 092	191 851	210 214	216 524	264 207	346 707	...	Bâtiments et travaux publics
Wholesale & retail trade, restaurants, hotels	881 415	851 258	1 013 456	1 173 391	1 335 464	1 370 255	1 346 505	1 515 242	...	Commerce de gros et de détail, restaurants et hôtels
Finance, insurance, real estate, etc.	1 778 499	1 849 890	2 041 560	2 103 950	2 244 438	1 900 509	2 214 741	2 413 305	...	Banques, assurances, affaires immobilières
Transport and communications	679 339	827 777	815 842	877 600	894 940	943 856	1 331 340	1 431 804	...	Transport(s) et communications
Public administration and defense	612 653	626 325	657 251	687 977	745 733	643 087	899 054	961 988	...	Administrations publiques et défense
Education	284 022	291 224	337 418	352 677	399 269	398 880	416 512	434 923	...	Education
Health and Social Work	61 298	68 382	75 962	80 831	86 781	93 999	110 163	129 107	...	Santé et actions sociales
Other services	87 417	99 965	109 593	111 749	123 852	122 166	211 697	366 842	...	Autres services
Less Imputed Service Charges	- 341 596	- 351 719	- 416 109	- 401 831	- 433 978	- 367 723	- 399 026	- 430 948	...	Moins services d'intermédiation financière
Gross domestic product at factor cost / basic prices	8 339 333	8 676 601	9 740 939	10 287 844	11 181 440	11 194 309	12 438 150	13 800 741	...	Produit intérieur brut aux couts des facteurs / prix de base
Plus: indirect taxes / taxes on products, less subsidies	968 575	1 073 428	1 107 101	1 175 656	1 143 283	918 377	1 390 845	1 678 160	...	Plus taxes indirectes/impôts sur les produits, moins les subventions
EXPENDITURE ON GROSS DOMESTIC PRODUCT AT CURRENT PURCHASER'S VALUES *CFA FRANC (MILLIONS)*										**EMPLOI DU PRODUIT INTÉRIEUR BRUT AUX PRIX COURANTS D'ACQUISITION** *FRANC CFA (MILLIONS)*
Government final consumption	1 265 095	1 300 515	1 374 421	1 448 453	1 500 854	1 346 919	2 025 396	2 037 380	...	Consommation finale des administrations publiques
Private final consumption	6 436 682	6 994 264	7 409 617	7 765 162	8 267 366	8 298 425	9 155 067	10 097 581	...	Consommation finale privée
Gross fixed capital formation	911 057	1 132 444	1 186 632	1 246 199	1 517 979	1 072 051	1 671 335	2 257 650	...	Formation brute de capital fixe
Change in inventories	- 204 577	- 166 093	122 637	- 249 235	138 098	- 582 782	405 096	683 280	...	Variation des stocks
Exports of goods and services	4 874 327	4 604 547	5 111 172	5 829 699	6 240 333	6 449 568	6 692 101	6 765 009	...	Exportations de biens et services
Less imports of goods and services	3 974 676	4 115 648	4 356 439	4 576 778	5 339 907	4 471 495	6 120 000	6 362 000	...	Moins importations de biens et services
GDP at purchasers' values	9 307 908	9 750 029	10 848 040	11 463 500	12 324 723	-2 112 686	13 828 995	15 478 901	...	PIB aux prix d'acquisition
GROSS DOMESTIC PRODUCT BY KIND OF ECONOMIC ACTIVITY AT CONSTANT PRICES *ANNUAL GROWTH RATES (%)*										**PRODUIT INTÉRIEUR BRUT PAR BRANCHE D'ACTIVITÉ ECONOMIQUE AUX PRIX CONSTANTS** *TAUX DE CROISSANCE ANNUEL (%)*
Agriculture, hunting, forestry and fishing	3.4	- 0.9	- 1.0	- 2.9	- 4.1	5.0	- 4.5	6.8	...	Agriculture, chasse, sylviculture et pêche
Mining and quarrying	- 4.6	- 15.2	39.5	5.5	- 13.3	1.2	- 5.6	6.6	...	Industries extractives
Manufacturing	3.0	7.0	- 6.7	- 0.2	- 1.0	- 11.1	11.6	6.8	...	Industries manufacturières
Electricity, gas & water	0.7	22.7	10.1	26.0	19.6	- 10.6	307.2	19.5	...	Electricité, gaz et eau
Construction & public works	13.9	- 9.0	5.9	17.2	12.2	- 20.7	5.3	27.9	...	Bâtiments et travaux publics
Wholesale & retail trade, restaurants, hotels	- 4.4	- 8.8	2.7	8.0	5.1	- 0.7	0.1	9.7	...	Commerce de gros et de détail, restaurants et hôtels
Finance, insurance, real estate, etc.	83.0	2.3	9.3	2.6	6.1	- 8.0	18.1	8.1	...	Banques, assurances, affaires immobilières
Transport and communications	- 0.4	20.7	- 3.7	15.6	20.8	2.6	22.8	7.5	...	Transport(s) et communications
Public administration and defense	- 34.2	1.0	4.6	4.0	8.8	- 14.0	15.1	- 4.9	...	Administrations publiques et défense
Education	3.2	- 2.8	14.7	1.7	14.9	- 1.6	2.2	1.5	...	Education
Health and Social Work	6.0	13.8	8.3	2.9	11.3	9.0	15.1	12.3	...	Santé et actions sociales
Other services	155.8	15.8	6.9	1.2	9.0	- 6.3	73.1	81.9	...	Autres services
Less Imputed Service Charges	6.4	3.0	18.3	- 3.4	6.0	- 10.3	7.4	8.0	...	Moins services d'intermédiation financière
Gross domestic product at factor cost / basic prices	1.2	1.3	3.4	3.5	2.6	- 2.6	7.4	8.2	...	Produit intérieur brut aux couts des facteurs / prix de base
Plus: indirect taxes / taxes on products, less subsidies	4.2	5.7	- 4.4	1.0	- 2.9	- 18.1	47.2	17.6	...	Plus taxes indirectes/impôts sur les produits, moins les subventions
Gross domestic product at market prices	1.5	1.8	2.5	3.3	2.0	- 4.1	10.4	9.2	...	Produit intérieur brut aux prix du marché
EXPENDITURE ON GROSS DOMESTIC PRODUCT AT CONSTANT PURCHASERS' VALUES *ANNUAL GROWTH RATES (%)*										**EMPLOIS DU PRODUIT INTÉRIEUR BRUT AUX PRIX CONSTANTS D'ACQUISITION** *TAUX DE CROISSANCE ANNUEL (%)*
Government final consumption	- 2.9	1.0	5.2	4.7	4.1	- 10.6	35.6	- 2.2	...	Consommation finale des administrations publiques
Private final consumption	1.8	6.3	- 0.2	3.8	4.6	- 3.7	8.9	7.5	...	Consommation finale privée
Gross fixed capital formation	12.0	21.0	6.2	3.6	22.8	- 38.5	47.0	31.8	...	Formation brute de capital fixe
Exports of goods and services	5.8	- 10.6	- 7.8	18.1	- 4.3	1.7	- 1.7	5.7	...	Exportations de biens et services
Less imports of goods and services	- 3.9	- 0.8	- 5.2	14.7	12.4	- 21.4	34.8	5.8	...	Moins importations de biens et services
Notes	The serie is revised from 2011						La série a été révisée à partir de 2011			Notes

III INFLATION

	2006	2007	2008	2009	2010	2011	2012	2013	2014	
ANNUAL GROWTH RATES (%)										**TAUX DE CROISSANCE ANNUEL (%)**
All items	2.5	1.9	6.3	0.5	1.7	4.9	1.3	2.6	0.5	Ensemble
of which:										dont:
Food and Non-alcoholic beverages	3.0	5.4	11.6	2.5	6.5	10.5	-0.3	1.9	-2.1	Alimentation et boissons non alcoolisés
Alcoholic beverages & tobacco	-2.9	3.1	5.1	0.2	-0.8	3.6	-0.3	0.2	0.4	Boissons alcoolisées et tabacs
Clothing and Footwear	-0.5	-0.4	-0.8	-1.5	-0.1	3.4	3.0	6.9	3.4	Habillement et chaussures
Housing, Water, Electricity, Gas and Other Fuels	1.7	-0.4	4.5	0.1	1.1	1.8	2.0	2.1	1.6	Logement, eau, electricité, gas et autres combustibles
Furnishing, household equipment	0.6	1.6	8.1	-0.2	-0.8	5.9	4.5	3.3	2.6	Meubles, articles de ménage et entretien courant
Health	1.8	2.8	1.5	0.2	0.2	0.9	-0.9	-1.7	0.7	Santé
Transport	8.8	-0.7	7.4	0.2	1.7	1.1	1.0	1.0	-0.4	Transport
Communication	2.8	-4.7	-6.9	-3.1	-7.4	-3.6	-3.3	-0.5	0.9	Communication
Recreation & culture	0.2	0.7	0.7	-0.8	-0.3	1.4	1.6	1.3	3.2	Loisirs et culture
Education	2.7	2.1	1.1	0.0	0.9	2.5	9.3	18.1	-0.5	Enseignement
Restaurants & hotels	1.5	3.2	3.3	2.1	3.1	8.8	2.8	0.8	1.3	Restaurants et hôtels
Miscellaneous goods & services	1.9	4.0	4.5	0.0	1.2	3.7	1.8	1.8	0.4	Biens et services divers

	2006	2007	2008	2009	2010	2011	2012	2013	2014	
IV AGRICULTURAL PRODUCTION - PRODUCTION AGRICOLE										
	2006	2007	2008	2009	2010	2011	2012	2013	2014	
TONNES *(THOUSAND)*										**TONNES** *(MILLIERS)*
Yams	5 569	5 502	5 945	5 313	5 392	5 532	5 675	5 732	...	Ignames
Cassava	2 267	2 342	2 531	2 262	2 307	2 359	2 412	2 436	...	Manioc
Rice, paddy	716	606	680	688	1 206	873	1 562	1 934	...	Riz
Plantains	1 540	1 511	1 675	1 497	1 542	1 559	1 577	1 624	...	Banane plantin
Cocoa, beans	1 409	1 230	1 382	1 223	1 301	1 511	1 486	1 449	...	Fèves de Cacao
V MINING PRODUCTION - PRODUCTION MINIERE										
	2006	2007	2008	2009	2010	2011	2012	2013	2014	
Crude petroleum, metric tons (thousands)	3 550	2 411	2 284	2 712	2 237	2 019	...	...	...	Pétrole brut, tonnes métriques (milliers)
Gold ores and concentrates (Kilograms)	1 327	1 466	2 884	7 055	5 201	12 357	29 360	31 360	33 428	Minerais d'or et concentrés (kilogrammes)
Natural gas, cubic meters (million)	1 740	1 574	1 657	1 699	1 756	1 800	1 860	2 160	2 162	Gaz naturel (nette, million de mètres cube)
VI ENERGY - ENERGIE										
	2006	2007	2008	2009	2010	2011	2012	2013	2014	
Total electricity generation (GWh)	5 768	5 746	5 918	5 953	6 052	6 208	8 977	9 102	...	Production d'électricité totale (GWh)
of which:										dont:
Production of electricity from fossil fuels (GWh)	4 034	3 719	3 784	3 656	4 278	4 261	7 016	7 016	...	Production d'électricité à partir de combustibles fossiles (GWh)
Production of hydro electricity (GWh)	1 510	1 797	1 898	2 117	1 602	1 774	1 789	1 914	...	Production d'électricité d'origine hydraulique (GWh)
Production of electricity from solar, wind, tide, wave and other sources (GWh)	112	115	118	107	109	109	109	109	...	Production d'électricité d'origine solaire, éolienne, marée motrice et autres (GWh)
VII TOURISM AND INFRASTRUCTURE - TOURISME ET INFRASTRUCTURE										
	2006	2007	2008	2009	2010	2011	2012	2013	2014	
VII-1 TOURISM										**VII-1 TOURISME**
International tourist arrivals (thousands)	428	406	379	353	348	344	361	381	396	Arrivées de touristes internationaux (milliers)
Rooms in hotels and similar establishments (thousands)	...	...	...	...	...	...	...	...	...	Chambres d'hotels et établissements assimilés (milliers)
Overnight stays (thousands)	4 613	4 454	2 460	2 249	2 121	2 082	2 211	4 019	4 162	Nuitées (milliers)
Tourism receipts (US$ thousand)	92 900	102 700	115 300	150 800	200 700	234 597	237 297	249 432	265 824	Recettes touristiques (milliers de $ EU)
Total contribution to GDP (%)	5.9	6.5	5.7	5.0	5.4	5.9	5.3	4.6	4.4	Contribution totale au PIB (%)
Total contribution to Employment (%)	4.9	5.4	4.8	4.2	4.6	5.2	4.7	4.0	3.9	Contribution totale à l'emploi (%)
VII-2 INFRASTRUCTURE										**VII-2 INFRASTRUCTURE**
Paved roads (% of total)	8	8	8	8	...	...	...	...	...	Routes asphaltées (% du total)
Total Network (Railways-km)	82 639	82 639	82 639	82 639	...	...	...	...	...	Réseau total voies ferrées-Km
Main Telephone Lines (per 100 inhabitants)	2	1	2	2	1	1	1	1	...	Lignes téléphoniques fixes (pour 100 habitants)
Mobile Cellular Subscribers (per 100 inhabitants)	23	42	57	71	82	89	91	95	...	Abonnés aux téléphones mobiles (pour 100 habitants)
VIII EXTERNAL TRADE - COMMERCE EXTERIEUR										
	2006	2007	2008	2009	2010	2011	2012	2013	2014	
CFA FRANC EXPORTS, FOB										**FRANC CFA (MILLIARDS) EXPORTATIONS, FÀB**
Exports - Total	4 256	3 856	4 400	4 847	5 063	5 232	5 538	6 782	...	Exportations - Total
Exports to AFRICA	1 253	1 234	1 411	1 450	1 610	1 572	1 933	3 034	...	Exportations vers l'AFRIQUE
Main Products										**Principaux produits**
Cocoa beans	743	688	789	1 224	1 227	1 429	1 186	1 322	...	Fèves de Cacao
Petroleum Products	1 569	1 257	1 632	1 423	1 196	1 272	1 611	1 393	...	Produits pétroliers
Cocoa transformed	320	366	474	532	657	541	536	609	...	Cacao transformé
Lumber	113	118	117	70	78	59	65	67	...	Bois débités
Cotton mass	59	47	36	32	62	65	114	134	...	Coton masse
Main Destinations										**Principales destinations**
France	780	788	610	527	349	298	251	397	...	France
Netherlands	411	352	495	673	720	614	484	573	...	Pays-Bas
U.S.A	386	262	425	373	522	624	448	463	...	Etats-Unis
Nigeria	307	308	281	337	329	314	442	441	...	Nigéria
Italy	166	134	171	155	157	148	122	115	...	Italie
IMPORTS, CIF										**IMPORTATIONS, CAF**
Imports - Total	3 041	3 198	3 527	3 280	3 881	3 174	4 987	6 276	...	Importations - Total (millions)
Imports from Africa	1 004	1 006	1 290	938	1 313	1 042	1 676	2 168	...	Importations en provenance de l'Afrique
Main Products										**Principaux produits**
Petroleum products	963	959	1 256	807	894	874	1 491	1 530	...	Produits pétroliers
Electrical Machinery	57	77	77	103	121	81	134	168	...	Machines électriques
Fish, crustaceans, molluscs	119	131	175	169	139	156	170	180	...	Poissons, crustacés, molusques
Rice	152	156	210	281	228	268	349	233	...	Riz
Vehicles and trucks	144	172	150	133	170	122	211	225	...	Véhicules et camions
Main Origin										**Principales provenances**
Nigeria	838	769	1 035	676	1 021	741	1 281	1 427	...	Nigéria
France	776	695	447	468	461	375	620	679	...	France
China	131	210	243	236	270	217	365	713	...	Chine
Germany	76	87	100	97	107	87	123	133	...	Allemagne
U.S.A	71	86	94	108	117	61	130	153	...	Etats-Unis

CÔTE D'IVOIRE

IX FINANCIAL AND MONETARY STATISTICS - FINANCES ET STATISTIQUES MONETAIRES										
	2006	2007	2008	2009	2010	2011	2012	2013	2014	
IX-1 MONETARY STATISTICS *CFA FRANC (MILLIONS)*										**IX-1 STATISTIQUES MONÉTAIRES** *FRANC CFA (MILLIONS)*
Money supply (M1)	1 002 280	1 254 830	1 302 580	1 620 200	1 933 540	2 265 700	2 093 380	2 297 250	2 596 880	Masse monétaire (M1)
Quasi-money	743 718	853 324	997 883	1 170 101	1 415 573	1 453 577	1 653 004	1 800 248	2 141 300	Quasi-monnaie
of which Demand Deposit	...	...	...	...	...	...	...	...	...	dont Monnaie scripturale
Net foreign assets	838 617	1 060 075	1 007 954	1 157 726	1 406 547	1 795 552	1 563 873	1 602 710	1 814 814	Avoirs extérieurs nets
Domestic credit	1 636 299	1 962 479	2 103 664	2 506 395	2 836 267	2 874 757	3 439 609	4 134 642	4 936 964	Crédit intérieur
of which claims on private sector	1 290 078	1 531 740	1 704 020	1 883 902	2 044 983	2 052 075	2 304 818	2 828 902	3 443 830	dont créances sur le secteur privé
of which claims on government sector, net	345 309	430 739	399 645	621 893	788 300	822 682	1 131 304	1 304 109	1 490 271	dont créances nettes sur le gouvernement
International reserves (millions US$)	1 798	2 519	2 253	3 267	3 624	4 316	3 928	4 243	4 268	Réserves internationales (millions $EU)
Average Exchange Rate (National Currency per US$)	522.90	478.89	446.87	471.07	494.68	471.42	510.18	493.94	493.76	Taux de change (moyen) (monnaie nationale par $ EU)
IX-2 PUBLIC FINANCE *CFA FRANC (MILLIONS)*										**IX-2 FINANCES PUBLIQUES** *FRANC CFA (MILLIONS)*
Total Revenues and Grants	1 615 542	1 871 200	2 160 100	2 368 628	2 282 694	1 725 919	2 621 300	3 039 000	3 279 174	Recettes totales et dons
Tax Revenue	1 364 011	1 468 100	1 626 400	1 795 600	1 928 500	1 493 200	2 212 900	2 408 000	2 559 763	Recettes fiscales
Non Tax Revenue	236 394	349 500	350 400	262 100	247 654	199 858	327 200	429 500	401 531	Recettes non fiscales
Grants	15 137	53 600	183 300	310 928	106 540	32 861	81 200	201 500	317 879	Dons
Total Expenditures and Net Lending	1 650 743	1 848 100	2 086 050	2 147 253	2 343 978	2 208 163	3 054 100	3 385 700	3 647 244	Dépenses totales et prêts nets
Current expenditure	1 389 603	1 565 700	1 748 750	1 800 522	1 960 714	1 923 343	2 436 000	2 449 200	2 593 224	Dépenses courantes
Of which Wages and Salaries	588 991	640 400	711 700	745 000	800 475	719 700	934 600	1 039 200	1 137 673	Dont rémunérations et salaires
Capital expenditure	239 040	253 600	319 600	334 331	349 864	285 720	615 800	934 200	1 054 020	Dépenses d'équipement
Net Lending	22 100	28 800	17 700	12 400	33 400	- 900	2 300	2 300	-	Prêts nets
Fiscal Balance	- 35 201	23 100	74 050	221 375	- 61 284	- 482 244	- 432 800	- 346 700	- 368 071	Solde global y compris les dons
IX-3 BALANCE OF PAYMENTS *CFA FRANC (BILLIONS)*										**IX-3 BALANCE DES PAIEMENTS** *FRANC CFA (MILLIARDS)*
Trade balance	1 626	1 229	1 487	2 003	1 782	2 771	1 788	1 884	1 730	Balance commerciale
Services Balance	- 726	- 743	- 733	- 750	- 881	- 841	- 1 131	- 1 442	- 1 402	Balance des services
Net Income	- 371	- 388	- 404	- 442	- 453	- 462	- 510	- 548	- 726	Revenus nets
Compensation of employees	...	...	...	...	...	...	...	...	...	Rémunération des salariés
Investment Income	...	...	...	...	...	...	...	...	...	Revenus des investissements
Current transfers, net total	- 278	- 165	- 149	- 47	- 218	- 252	- 305	- 134	- 135	Transferts courants
Net official transfers	...	...	...	...	...	...	...	...	...	Transferts officiels nets
Workers' remittances	...	...	...	...	...	...	...	...	...	Envois de fonds des travailleurs
Other private transfers	...	...	...	...	...	...	...	...	...	Autres transferts privés
Current account balance	250	- 67	202	764	814	1 329	- 158	- 240	- 533	Solde du compte courant
Capital & financial account	...	...	...	...	...	...	...	...	...	Comptes de capital et financier
Capital account	...	...	...	...	...	...	...	...	...	Compte de capital
Financial account	...	...	...	...	...	...	...	...	...	Compte financier
Errors & omissions	...	...	...	...	...	...	...	...	...	Erreurs et omissions
Overall balance	113	213	- 13	128	235	429	- 256	- 71	...	Balance générale

X DEBT AND FINANCIAL FLOWS - DETTE ET FLUX FINANCIERS										
	2006	2007	2008	2009	2010	2011	2012	2013	2014	
X-1 Debt *US$ (MILLIONS)*										**X-1 DETTE EXTÉRIEURE** *$ E.U (MILLIONS)*
Total external debt	18 626	19 160	18 743	17 428	16 499	16 954	11 955	12 471	13 264	Dette extérieure totale
Private	8 334	8 522	8 500	8 290	7 547	7 093	6 812	6 657	8 019	Privée
Public	10 292	10 638	10 244	9 138	8 952	9 861	5 143	5 814	5 246	Publique
Total external debt service	854	1 030	1 361	1 972	1 759	3 098	1 236	1 657	1 141	Service de la dette extérieure
Present value of External debt	...	...	...	...	...	...	...	...	...	Valeur actuelle de la dette extérieure
Total government domestic debt (in local currency)	1 166	1 024	1 405	1 371	1 793.0	1 718.7	1 779.9	...	...	Dette publique intérieure
X-2 FINANCIAL FLOWS *US$ (MILLIONS)*										**X-2 FLUX FINANCIERS** *$ E.U (MILLIONS)*
Net Foreign Direct Investment Inflows	319	427	446	377	339	302	322	371	...	Investissement étranger direct (flux nets entrants)
Main origin of FDI Inflows										**Principales origines de l'IDE entrant:**
France	73	60	73	114	91.4	- 11.1	117.0	...	...	France
Luxembourg	14	15	10	28	...	- 2.8	- 178.5	...	...	Luxembourg
Switzerland	61	66	3	105	113.6	18.7	43.4	128.6	...	Suisse
United Kingdom	13	26	121	...	- 4.6	1.6	7.9	...	...	Royaume-Uni
Belgium	1	48	-	3	6.6	11.1	2.6	...	...	Belgique
African countries	...	...	...	...	...	...	...	...	...	Pays africains
Net total Official Development Assistance	247	171	626	2 402	845	1 436	2 636	1 262	...	Aide publique au développement (nette totale)
Main origin of Net ODA										**Principales origines de l'APD nette**
France	107	51	39	1 199	138.5	553.2	1 279.0	86.9	...	France
IDA	-	- 16	235	184	184.7	163.9	84.5	...	...	IDA
United States	31	37	89	231	76.3	74.3	139.6	252.6	...	Etats-Unis
AfDF	1	-	13	60	9.3	148.9	0.6	...	...	FAfD
Germany	12	20	17	15	92.6	5.3	2.9	4.5	...	Allemagne

AREA (km²)	23 200		SUPERFICIE (km²)
CAPITAL CITY	Djibouti	Djibouti	CAPITALE
CURRENCY	Djibouti Franc	Franc Djiboutien	MONNAIE

I SOCIAL AND DEMOGRAPHIC INDICATORS — INDICATEURS DEMOGRAPHIQUES ET SOCIAUX

	Year / Année	Value / Valeur	
POPULATION			**POPULATION**
Population ('000)			Population ('000)
Both sexes	2013	914	Les deux sexes
Male	2013	492	Masculin
Female	2013	422	Féminin
Average annual growth rate	2013	2.8	Taux de croissance annuel
Active Population ('000)	2013	325	Population active ('000)
Population by age group ('000)			Population par groupe d'âge ('000)
0-14 years	2013	306	0-14 ans
15-64 years	2013	577	15-64 ans
65+ years	2013	30	65+ ans
Economically. active population. in agriculture (%)	2013	95.9	Participation de la population active agricole (%)
Crude birth rate	2013	27.5	Taux brut de natalité
Crude death rate	2013	8.7	Taux brut de mortalité
Total fertility rate	2013	3.4	Indice synthétique de fécondité
Proportion of urban population	2013	77.2	Part de la population urbaine
Life Expectancy at Birth - Total (years)	2014	62.3	Espérance de vie à la naissance - Totale (ans)
Dependency Ratio - Total (%)	2013	62.3	Taux de dépendance - Total (%)
HEALTH			**SANTÉ**
Percentage of children under-five and underweight	2012	29.8	% d'enfants de moins de cinq ans avec insuffisance pondérale
Prevalence of undernourishment	2011	19.8	Prévalence de la malnutrition
Under five mortality rate (both sexes, per 1000)	2013	69.6	Taux de mortalité de moins de 5 ans (les deux sexes, pour 1000)
Infant mortality rate (both sexes) per 1000	2013	57.4	Taux de mortalité infantile (les deux sexes) par 1000
Percentage of children provided the vaccines :			Pourcentage d'enfants vaccinés :
BCG	2013	86.0	BCG
DPT3	2013	82.0	DTC3
Polio	2013	94.4	Polio
Measles	2013	80.0	Rougeole
Percentage of mothers provided at least one antenatal care (%)	2012	87.7	Pourcentage de mères ayant au moins reçu un soin prénatal (%)
Percentage of deliveries attended by skilled health personnel	2006	92.9	% d'accouchements assistés par un personnel de santé qualifié
Number of doctors (per 10 000 population)	2006	2.3	Nombre de médecins (pour 10 000 habitants)
Number of nurses (per 10 000 population)	2008	8.0	Nombre d'infirmières (pour 10 000 habitants)
Hospital beds - Total (per 10 000 population)	2010	14.0	Nombre de lits d'hôpitaux - Total (pour 10 000)
Births registered (per 1 000)	2014	27.1	Naiss.s enregistrées (pour 1 000)
Deaths registered (per 1 000)	2014	8.6	Décès enregistrés (pour 1 000)
Public expenditure on Health (% of budget)	2013	9.2	Dépenses publiques consacrées à la santé (% du budget)
EDUCATION			**EDUCATION**
Enrolment in primary education (both sexes) (000)	2014	64	Scolarisation dans le primaire (les deux sexes) (000)
Female	2014	30	Féminin
Enrolment in secondary education (both sexes) (000)	2014	59	Scolarisation dans le secondaire (les deux sexes) (000)
Female	2014	26	Féminin
Enrolment in tertiary education (both sexes) (000)	2011	4.7	Scolarisation dans le tertiaire (les deux sexes) (000)
Female	2011	1.9	Féminin
Literacy rate (both sexes)	...	...	Taux d'alphabétisation (deux sexes)
Male	...	...	Masculin
Female	...	...	Féminin
Pupil-teacher ratio	2013	33.2	Ratio élève-enseignant
Public expenditure on education (% of budget)	2013	8.8	Dépenses publiques consacrées à l'enseignement (% du budget)
POVERTY			**PAUVRETÉ**
GNI Per Capita (US$)	2013	1 882.0	RNB par habitant ($EU)
Human Poverty Index (HPI-1) Value (%)	2007	25.6	Valeur de l'Indice de pauvreté (IPH-1) (%)
Population below International Poverty Line ($2/day) (%)	2002	41.2	Population sous le seuil international de pauvreté (2$/J) (%)
Share of Income Held by Richest 10%	2002	30.9	% de revenu des 10% plus riches
Share of Income Held by Poorest 10%	2002	2.4	% de revenu des 10% plus pauvres
Gini index	2002	40.0	Indice de Gini

Charts / Graphiques

Population by age group – 2013
Population par groupe d'age – 2013

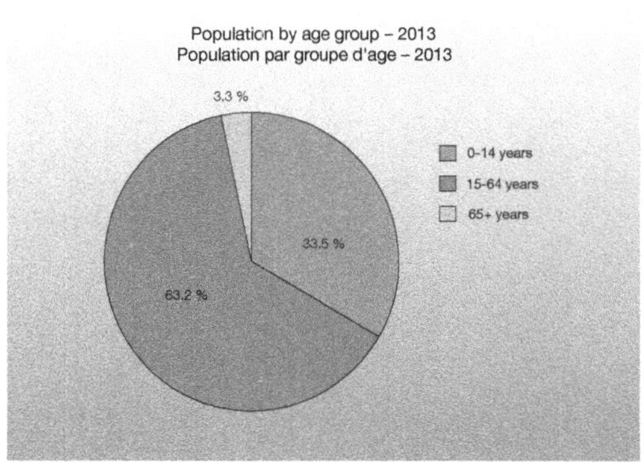

Percentage of children provided the vaccines – 2013
Pourcentage d'enfants vaccinés – 2013

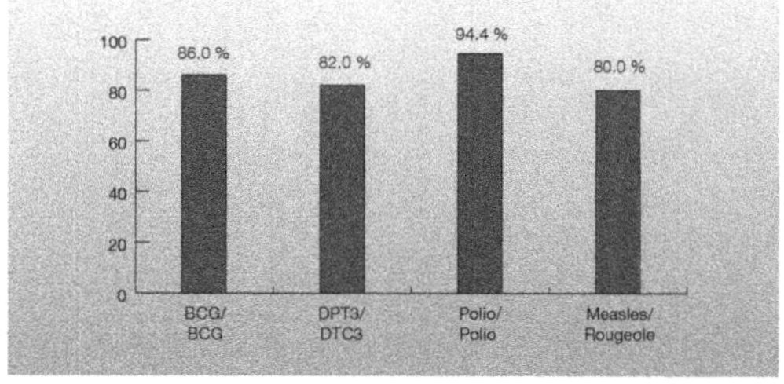

GNI Per Capita (US$)
RNB par habitant ($EU)

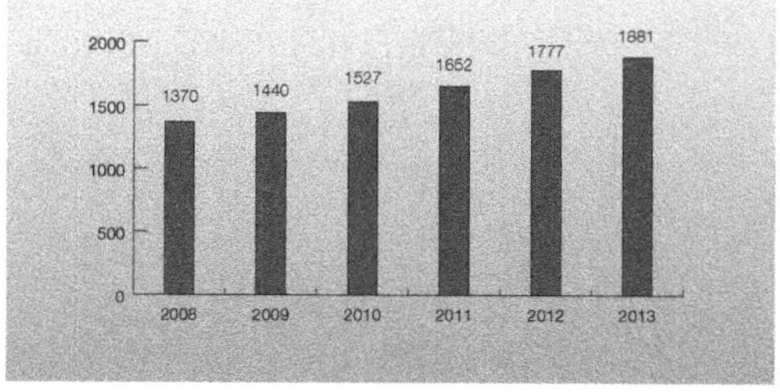

II NATIONAL ACCOUNTS — COMPTES NATIONAUX

	2006	2007	2008	2009	2010	2011	2012	2013	2014	
GROSS DOMESTIC PRODUCT BY KIND OF ECONOMIC ACTIVITY AT CURRENT PRICES *DJIBOUTI FRANC (MILLIONS)*										**PRODUIT INTÉRIEUR BRUT PAR BRANCHE D'ACTIVITÉ ÉCONOMIQUE AUX PRIX COURANTS** *FRANC DJIBOUTIEN (MILLIONS)*
Agriculture, hunting, forestry and fishing	4 367	5 475	5 551	6 613	6 819	7 006	7 777	8 664	...	Agriculture, chasse, sylviculture et pêche
Mining and quarrying	206	221	539	606	654	577	594	612	...	Industries extractives
Manufacturing	3 168	3 422	5 542	5 934	6 326	6 640	7 069	7 542	...	Industries manufacturières
Electricity, gas & water	7 006	7 691	6 791	4 884	5 446	6 328	10 295	12 029	...	Electricité, gaz et eau
Construction & public works	9 960	12 744	19 142	21 532	23 198	21 908	22 529	26 324	...	Bâtiments et travaux publics
Wholesale & retail trade, restaurants, hotels	27 261	30 653	30 576	39 332	45 207	51 069	55 819	53 673	...	Commerce de gros et de détail, restaurants et hôtels
Finance, insurance, real estate, etc.	16 119	17 905	18 385	19 836	18 440	19 141	24 205	26 871	...	Banques, assurances, affaires immobilières
Transport and communications	32 232	36 028	50 707	45 764	48 427	54 773	59 258	65 785	...	Transport(s) et communications
Public administration and defense	22 809	22 478	24 569	28 551	32 323	34 738	37 794	41 141	...	Administrations publiques et défense
Education	...	...	...	...	...	...	...	...	...	Education
Health and Social Work	...	...	...	...	...	...	...	...	...	Santé et actions sociales
Other services	2 241	2 487	1 622	1 540	1 570	1 609	1 657	1 804	...	Autres services
Less Imputed Service Charges	- 4 237	- 4 706	- 4 968	- 5 466	- 4 921	- 4 332	- 5 950	- 6 477	...	Moins services d'intermédiation financière
Gross domestic product at factor cost / basic prices	121 132	134 398	158 456	169 126	183 489	199 457	221 047	237 968	...	Produit intérieur brut aux couts des facteurs / prix de base
Plus: indirect taxes / taxes on products, less subsidies	15 472	16 260	16 345	17 323	17 089	20 765	19 522	20 690	...	Plus taxes indirectes/impôts sur les produits, moins les subventions
EXPENDITURE ON GROSS DOMESTIC PRODUCT AT CURRENT PURCHASER'S VALUES *DJIBOUTI FRANC (MILLIONS)*										**EMPLOI DU PRODUIT INTÉRIEUR BRUT AUX PRIX COURANTS D'ACQUISITION** *FRANC DJIBOUTIEN (MILLIONS)*
Government final consumption	40 169	38 193	39 102	40 635	47 786	51 383	57 143	61 191	...	Consommation finale des administrations publiques
Private final consumption	81 107	97 882	116 631	115 594	124 497	162 501	180 199	200 662	...	Consommation finale privée
Gross fixed capital formation	29 937	40 400	50 721	58 729	54 998	54 116	69 088	77 651	...	Formation brute de capital fixe
Change in inventories	16 766	22 626	28 406	3 284	- 13 879	- 2 509	- 3 203	- 3 600	...	Variation des stocks
Exports of goods and services	55 504	57 070	64 993	70 983	74 798	74 584	81 297	85 062	...	Exportations de biens et services
Less imports of goods and services	86 879	105 513	125 052	102 776	87 622	119 853	143 954	162 307	...	Moins importations de biens et services
GDP at purchasers' values	136 604	150 658	174 801	186 449	200 578	220 222	240 569	258 658	...	PIB aux prix d'acquisition
GROSS DOMESTIC PRODUCT BY KIND OF ECONOMIC ACTIVITY AT CONSTANT PRICES *ANNUAL GROWTH RATES (%)*										**PRODUIT INTÉRIEUR BRUT PAR BRANCHE D'ACTIVITÉ ECONOMIQUE AUX PRIX CONSTANTS** *TAUX DE CROISSANCE ANNUEL (%)*
Agriculture, hunting, forestry and fishing	6.5	6.0	7.0	10.6	- 4.1	- 2.7	...	...	...	Agriculture, chasse, sylviculture et pêche
Mining and quarrying	3.0	4.0	4.0	12.1	4.0	- 8.1	...	...	...	Industries extractives
Manufacturing	4.0	5.0	7.0	1.1	0.7	- 1.5	...	...	...	Industries manufacturières
Electricity, gas & water	8.6	6.0	7.0	4.7	4.1	5.8	...	...	...	Electricité, gaz et eau
Construction & public works	13.0	15.0	12.0	12.0	3.8	- 8.1	...	...	...	Bâtiments et travaux publics
Wholesale & retail trade, restaurants, hotels	6.8	7.0	7.2	19.1	7.9	6.7	...	...	...	Commerce de gros et de détail, restaurants et hôtels
Finance, insurance, real estate, etc.	5.0	5.5	6.0	6.0	- 9.4	0.4	...	...	...	Banques, assurances, affaires immobilières
Transport and communications	4.5	5.0	6.0	- 10.2	1.7	11.6	...	...	...	Transport(s) et communications
Public administration and defense	- 2.6	- 1.0	- 3.3	14.3	8.9	2.3	...	...	...	Administrations publiques et défense
Education	...	...	...	...	...	...	...	...	...	Education
Health and Social Work	...	...	...	...	...	...	...	...	...	Santé et actions sociales
Other services	...	3.0	- 2.3	3.0	1.8	2.2	...	...	...	Autres services
Less Imputed Service Charges	...	...	- 1.3	8.2	- 13.4	- 16.2	...	...	...	Moins services d'intermédiation financière
Gross domestic product at factor cost / basic prices	4.7	5.4	5.4	5.2	3.6	4.6	...	...	...	Produit intérieur brut aux couts des facteurs / prix de base
Plus: indirect taxes / taxes on products, less subsidies	64.3	3.4	3.4	3.4	2.0	3.4	...	...	...	Plus taxes indirectes/impôts sur les produits, moins les subventions
Gross domestic product at market prices	12.7	5.0	5.4	5.0	3.5	4.5	4.8	5.0	...	Produit intérieur brut aux prix du marché
EXPENDITURE ON GROSS DOMESTIC PRODUCT AT CONSTANT PURCHASERS' VALUES *ANNUAL GROWTH RATES (%)*										**EMPLOIS DU PRODUIT INTÉRIEUR BRUT AUX PRIX CONSTANTS D'ACQUISITION** *TAUX DE CROISSANCE ANNUEL (%)*
Government final consumption	22.3	- 6.7	6.3	2.2	13.1	2.3	4.9	...	...	Consommation finale des administrations publiques
Private final consumption	2.7	15.8	17.5	2.7	9.1	13.1	- 4.5	...	...	Consommation finale privée
Gross fixed capital formation	70.3	26.3	16.4	15.3	- 9.7	- 8.7	2.2	...	...	Formation brute de capital fixe
Exports of goods and services	12.7	- 1.6	9.6	6.6	0.6	- 1.3	9.1	...	...	Exportations de biens et services
Less imports of goods and services	30.0	17.1	26.2	- 20.8	- 15.6	28.5	3.5	...	...	Moins importations de biens et services
Notes	NA Data: 2012:Semi-Final;2013:Provisional				Données des CN: 2012:Semi-définitif;2013:Provisoire					Notes

III INFLATION

	2006	2007	2008	2009	2010	2011	2012	2013	2014	
ANNUAL GROWTH RATES (%)										**TAUX DE CROISSANCE ANNUEL (%)**
All items	3.5	5.0	12.0	1.7	4.0	5.1	3.7	2.4	3.2	Ensemble
of which:										dont:
Food and Non-alcoholic beverages	4.0	7.8	16.8	3.5	4.1	6.8	6.7	3.3	...	Alimentation et boissons non alcoolisés
Alcoholic beverages & tobacco	...	...	...	...	...	...	...	...	...	Boissons alcoolisées et tabacs
Clothing and Footwear	-2.2	-1.1	1.2	3.3	3.6	3.9	1.9	-0.1	...	Habillement et chaussures
Housing, Water, Electricity, Gas and Other Fuels	6.6	4.8	6.6	-3.3	4.1	4.5	-4.9	1.7	...	Logement, eau, electricité, gas et autres combustibles
Furnishing, household equipment	1.5	0.0	2.2	0.4	2.0	1.0	2.6	0.1	...	Meubles, articles de ménage et entretien courant
Health	-3.0	0.3	8.2	3.8	3.7	2.8	-1.7	-3.0	...	Santé
Transport	1.4	-0.5	10.4	0.0	4.9	1.7	2.1	0.3	...	Transport
Communication	...	...	...	...	...	...	...	...	...	Communication
Recreation & culture	-0.8	2.6	2.4	-2.9	-2.3	-0.7	-2.5	-0.9	...	Loisirs et culture
Education	1.3	0.4	-2.3	-2.2	3.6	0.2	1.0	2.9	...	Enseignement
Restaurants & hotels	0.4	-1.1	4.0	4.9	1.7	-1.1	2.2	-0.8	...	Restaurants et hôtels
Miscellaneous goods & services	-0.6	4.0	13.4	2.5	4.6	4.8	12.8	6.3	...	Biens et services divers

IV AGRICULTURAL PRODUCTION - PRODUCTION AGRICOLE										
	2006	2007	2008	2009	2010	2011	2012	2013	2014	
TONNES *(THOUSAND)*										**TONNES** *(MILLIERS)*
Beans, dry	2	2	1	2	2	2	3	3	...	Haricots secs
Lemons and limes	2	2	1	2	2	2	2	2	...	Citrons
Tomatoes	2	1	1	1	1	1	1	1	...	Tomates
Mangoes, mangosteens, guavas	1	0	1	1	1	1	1	1	...	Mangue
Chillies and peppers, dry	0	0	1	0	0	0	1	1	...	Piments et poivrons, secs

V MINING PRODUCTION - PRODUCTION MINIERE										
	2006	2007	2008	2009	2010	2011	2012	2013	2014	
Salt and pure sodium chloride, metric tons (thousands)	...	...	12	12	12	12	12	...	...	Sel et chlorure de sodium pur, tonnes métriques (milliers)
	...	...	...	...	...	...	...	...	...	
	...	...	...	...	...	...	...	...	...	

VI ENERGY - ENERGIE										
	2006	2007	2008	2009	2010	2011	2012	2013	2014	
Total electricity generation (GWh)	263	274	315	319	325	327	348	82	...	Production d'électricité totale (GWh)
of which:										dont:
Production of electricity from fossil fuels (GWh)	263	274	315	319	325	325	345	80	...	Production d'électricité à partir de combustibles fossiles (GWh)
Production of hydro electricity (GWh)	...	...	...	...	...	...	...	...	...	Production d'électricité d'origine hydraulique (GWh)
Production of electricity from solar, wind, tide, wave and other sources (GWh)	...	...	...	...	...	2	2	2	...	Production d'électricité d'origine solaire, éolienne, marée motrice et autres (GWh)

VII TOURISM AND INFRASTRUCTURE - TOURISME ET INFRASTRUCTURE										
	2006	2007	2008	2009	2010	2011	2012	2013	2014	
VII-1 TOURISM										**VII-1 TOURISME**
International tourist arrivals (thousands)	40	49	54	58	51	32	...	...	...	Arrivées de touristes internationaux (milliers)
Rooms in hotels and similar establishments (thousands)	0.45	0.677	0.677	0.721	0.726	0.726	0.878	1.107	...	Chambres d'hotels et établissements assimilés (milliers)
Overnight stays (thousands)	246	294	294	355	355	355	458	535	...	Nuitées (milliers)
Tourism receipts (US$ thousand)	...	...	...	...	...	...	...	...	...	Recettes touristiques (milliers de $ EU)
Total contribution to GDP (%)	...	...	...	...	...	...	...	...	...	Contribution totale au PIB (%)
Total contribution to Employment (%)	...	...	...	...	...	...	...	...	...	Contribution totale à l'emploi (%)
VII-2 INFRASTRUCTURE										**VII-2 INFRASTRUCTURE**
Paved roads (% of total)	...	...	...	...	...	...	...	...	...	Routes asphaltées (% du total)
Total Network (Railways-km)	...	...	...	...	...	...	...	...	...	Réseau total voies ferrées-Km
Main Telephone Lines (per 100 inhabitants)	1	2	2	2	2	2	2	2	...	Lignes téléphoniques fixes (pour 100 habitants)
Mobile Cellular Subscribers (per 100 inhabitants)	6	9	14	16	20	23	25	28	...	Abonnés aux téléphones mobiles (pour 100 habitants)

VIII EXTERNAL TRADE - COMMERCE EXTERIEUR										
	2006	2007	2008	2009	2010	2011	2012	2013	2014	
US$ (MILLIONS) **EXPORTS, FOB**										**$ E.U (MILLIONS)** **EXPORTATIONS, FÀB**
Exports - Total	36	36	44	38	47	53	52	54	...	Exportations - Total
Exports to AFRICA	...	...	...	...	...	...	...	...	...	Exportations vers l'AFRIQUE
Main Products										**Principaux produits**
Live animals other than animals of division 03	4	25	29	12	29	23	18	...	...	Animaux vivants autres que ceux aquatiques
Gold, non-monetary (excluding gold ores and concentrates)	2	3	4	2	13	8	6	...	...	Or, à usage non monétaire
Milk, cream and milk products (excluding butter, cheese)	0	1	0	3	1	1	1	...	...	Lait et produits laitiers (sauf beurre, fromages)
Coffee and coffee substitutes	8	1	2	0	5	3	2	...	...	Café et succédanés du café
Motor vehicles for the transport of persons	5	0	0	2	0	5	6	...	...	Véhicules automobiles pour transport de personnes
Main Destinations										**Principales destinations**
Ethiopia	32	3	4	0	6	7	7	...	...	Éthiopie
United Arab Emirates	4	7	8	3	1	15	15	...	...	Émirats arabes unis
Egypt	2	3	5	3	24	16	11	...	...	Égypte
Saudi Arabia	0	16	14	8	4	2	1	...	...	Arabie saoudite
Yemen	3	6	6	2	10	11	11	...	...	Yémen
IMPORTS, CIF										**IMPORTATIONS, CAF**
Imports - Total	158	200	254	236	277	351	410	398	...	Importations - Total (millions)
Imports from AFRICA	...	...	...	...	...	...	...	...	...	Importations en provenance de l'AFRIQUE
Main Products										**Principaux produits**
Petroleum, petroleum products and related materials	109	143	27	40	90	60	395	...	...	Pétrole et produits dérivés
Fixed vegetable oils and fats, crude, refined or fractionated	5	17	41	32	37	35	34	...	...	Graisses et huiles végétales fixes, raffinées ou fractionnées
Iron and steel	17	36	48	30	25	20	15	...	...	Fer et acier
Cereals and cereal preparations	8	12	54	33	15	27	50	...	...	Céréales et préparations à base de céréales
Road vehicles	14	20	24	22	19	21	23	...	...	Véhicules routiers
Main Origin										**Principales provenances**
India	56	92	116	54	56	59	61	...	...	Inde
Saudi Arabia	...	...	...	...	...	...	...	...	...	Arabie saoudite
China	29	38	74	64	81	63	49	...	...	Chine
United States	9	14	42	42	24	17	13	...	...	États-Unis
Malaysia	6	17	40	32	33	20	12	...	...	Malaisie

IX FINANCIAL AND MONETARY STATISTICS - FINANCES ET STATISTIQUES MONETAIRES	2006	2007	2008	2009	2010	2011	2012	2013	2014	
IX-1 MONETARY STATISTICS *DJIBOUTI FRANC (MILLIONS)*										**IX-1 STATISTIQUES MONÉTAIRES** *FRANC DJIBOUTIEN (MILLIONS)*
Money supply (M1)	107 720	118 030	142 310	167 190	187 590	179 210	206 180	220 400	244 410	Masse monétaire (M1)
Quasi-money	51 419	50 491	60 074	64 514	60 298	56 114	71 301	64 528	65 218	Quasi-monnaie
of which Demand Deposit	...	...	...	...	...	...	...	...	...	dont Monnaie scripturale
Net foreign assets	92 001	95 113	117 189	127 472	134 428	119 898	136 887	174 890	177 992	Avoirs extérieurs nets
Domestic credit	32 972	39 925	47 965	60 250	72 218	75 754	85 918	87 819	89 272	Crédit intérieur
of which claims on private sector	27 579	33 939	43 211	54 717	66 412	68 068	69 599	80 467	85 820	dont créances sur le secteur privé
of which claims on government sector, net	4 442	4 243	3 236	2 908	3 161	5 347	11 634	4 090	- 1 690	dont créances nettes sur le gouvernement
International reserves (millions US$)	120	132	175	242	249	244	249	425	376	Réserves internationales (millions $EU)
Average Exchange Rate (National Currency per US$)	177.72	177.72	177.72	177.72	177.72	177.72	177.72	177.72	177.72	Taux de change (moyen) (monnaie nationale par $ EU)
IX-2 PUBLIC FINANCE *DJIBOUTI FRANC (MILLIONS)*										**IX-2 FINANCES PUBLIQUES** *FRANC DJIBOUTIEN (MILLIONS)*
Total Revenues and Grants	47 742	53 002	73 091	68 953	71 124	75 992	82 572	90 537	96 387	Recettes totales et dons
Tax Revenue	27 690	30 901	35 004	37 449	40 582	44 630	44 451	52 630	57 772	Recettes fiscales
Non Tax Revenue	14 775	14 632	15 249	19 556	19 837	18 047	17 547	20 877	23 269	Recettes non fiscales
Grants	5 277	7 469	22 838	11 948	10 705	13 315	20 574	17 030	15 346	Dons
Total Expenditures and Net Lending	51 118	56 885	70 903	78 980	72 198	78 434	89 131	98 514	103 751	Dépenses totales et prêts nets
Current expenditure	40 816	40 026	46 738	46 859	48 707	54 015	57 828	60 558	61 172	Dépenses courantes
Of which Wages and Salaries	19 926	20 801	19 857	22 911	22 911	24 584	26 144	25 234	26 532	Dont rémunérations et salaires
Capital expenditure	10 302	16 859	24 164	32 121	23 491	24 419	31 303	37 956	42 579	Dépenses d'équipement
Net Lending	-	-	-	-	-	-	-	-	-	Prêts nets
Fiscal Balance	- 3 376	- 3 883	2 189	- 10 027	- 1 074	- 2 442	- 6 559	- 7 977	- 7 364	Solde global y compris les dons
IX-3 BALANCE OF PAYMENTS *DJIBOUTI FRANC (MILLIONS)*										**IX-3 BALANCE DES PAIEMENTS** *FRANC DJIBOUTIEN (MILLIONS)*
Trade balance	- 59 859	- 80 064	- 109 654	- 66 351	- 51 318	- 74 266	- 79 341	- 106 601	...	Balance commerciale
Services Balance	28 484	30 795	30 390	51 717	68 561	28 997	31 889	30 573	...	Balance des services
Net Income	15 021	16 722	15 995	12 618	20 997	1 172	4 911	4 679	...	Revenus nets
Compensation of employees	...	...	...	...	...	...	...	...	...	Rémunération des salariés
Investment Income	...	...	...	...	...	...	...	...	...	Revenus des investissements
Current transfers, net total	- 3 692	- 3 692	- 5 154	- 5 332	- 2 950	13 175	16 244	16 516	...	Transferts courants
Net official transfers	...	...	...	...	...	...	...	...	...	Transferts officiels nets
Workers' remittances	...	...	...	...	...	...	...	...	...	Envois de fonds des travailleurs
Other private transfers	...	...	...	...	...	...	...	...	...	Autres transferts privés
Current account balance	- 20 046	- 36 238	- 68 423	- 12 635	8 973	- 30 922	- 26 297	- 54 833	...	Solde du compte courant
Capital & financial account	...	...	...	...	...	...	12 552	22 131	...	Comptes de capital et financier
Capital account	...	...	...	...	...	...	9 313	8 969	...	Compte de capital
Financial account	...	...	...	...	...	...	3 239	13 162	...	Compte financier
Errors & omissions	...	...	...	...	...	...	13 745	32 702	...	Erreurs et omissions
Overall balance	...	...	...	...	...	...	-	-	...	Balance générale

X DEBT AND FINANCIAL FLOWS - DETTE ET FLUX FINANCIERS	2006	2007	2008	2009	2010	2011	2012	2013	2014	
X-1 DEBT *US$ (MILLIONS)*										**X-1 DETTE EXTÉRIEURE** *$ E.U (MILLIONS)*
Total external debt	437	540	591	628	634	648	666	704	818	Dette extérieure totale
Private	1	-	-	-	-	-	-	-	-	Privée
Public	436	540	591	628	634	648	666	704	818	Publique
Total external debt service	23	24	26	32	28	33	39	40	72	Service de la dette extérieure
Present value of External debt	...	...	...	...	...	...	...	...	...	Valeur actuelle de la dette extérieure
Total government domestic debt (in local currency)	...	...	...	...	...	...	...	...	...	Dette publique intérieure
X-2 FINANCIAL FLOWS *US$ (MILLIONS)*										**X-2 FLUX FINANCIERS** *$ E.U (MILLIONS)*
Net Foreign Direct Investment Inflows	108	195	229	100	27	78	110	286	...	Investissement étranger direct (flux nets entrants)
Main origin of FDI Inflows										**Principales origines de l'IDE entrant:**
France	18	...	...	...	...	...	...	...	...	France
Norway	...	...	- 1	17	- 2.2	...	...	...	...	Norvège
Luxembourg	...	...	...	...	...	...	...	...	...	Luxembourg
Slovenia	...	...	...	...	...	...	...	...	...	Slovénie
Netherlands	...	...	...	...	...	...	...	...	...	Pays-Bas
African countries	...	...	...	...	...	...	...	...	...	Pays africains
Net total Official Development Assistance	115	113	141	167	132	142	147	153	...	Aide publique au développement (nette totale)
Main origin of Net ODA										**Principales origines de l'APD nette**
France	72	57	51	42	46.2	44.0	40.4	50.4	...	France
Japan	5	4	4	29	38.0	16.6	24.8	6.2	...	Japon
IDA	12	11	8	7	- 0.2	0.8	5.3	...	...	IDA
United States	10	10	9	6	13.3	16.5	9.2	7.4	...	Etats-Unis
AfDF	- 1	2	8	20	4.0	6.6	0.8	...	...	FAfD

EGYPT — ÉGYPTE

AREA (km²)		**1 001 449**	**SUPERFICIE (km²)**
CAPITAL CITY	Cairo	Le Caire	**CAPITALE**
CURRENCY	Egyptian Pound	Livre egyptienne	**MONNAIE**

I SOCIAL AND DEMOGRAPHIC INDICATORS — INDICATEURS DEMOGRAPHIQUES ET SOCIAUX

	Year / Année	Value / Valeur	
POPULATION			**POPULATION**
Population ('000)			Population ('000)
Both sexes	2014	86 814	Les deux sexes
Male	2014	44 305	Masculin
Female	2014	42 509	Féminin
Average annual growth rate	2014	2.5	Taux de croissance annuel
Active Population ('000)	2013	29 185	Population active ('000)
Population by age group ('000)			Population par groupe d'âge ('000)
0-14 years	2014	27 622.0	0-14 ans
15-64 years	2014	55 942	15-64 ans
65+ years	2014	3 732	65+ ans
Economically. active population. in agriculture (%)	2004	29.0	Participation de la population active agricole (%)
Crude birth rate	2013	31.0	Taux brut de natalité
Crude death rate	2013	6.0	Taux brut de mortalité
Total fertility rate	2014	3.5	Indice synthétique de fécondité
Proportion of urban population	2014	42.7	Part de la population urbaine
Life Expectancy at Birth - Total (years)	2014	71.4	Espérance de vie à la naissance - Totale (ans)
Dependency Ratio - Total (%)	2014	55.0	Taux de dépendance - Total (%)
HEALTH			**SANTÉ**
Percentage of children under-five and underweight	2008	6.8	% d'enfants de moins de cinq ans avec insuffisance pondérale
Prevalence of undernourishment	2004	5.0	Prévalence de la malnutrition
Under five mortality rate (both sexes, per 1000)	2013	21.8	Taux de mortalité de moins de 5 ans (les deux sexes, pour 1000)
Infant mortality rate (both sexes) per 1000	2013	18.6	Taux de mortalité infantile (les deux sexes) par 1000
Percentage of children provided the vaccines :			Pourcentage d'enfants vaccinés :
BCG	2013	98.0	BCG
DPT3	2013	97.0	DTC3
Polio	2011	94.2	Polio
Measles	2013	96.0	Rougeole
Percentage of mothers provided at least one antenatal care (%)	2012	56.9	Pourcentage de mères ayant au moins reçu un soin prénatal (%)
Percentage of deliveries attended by skilled health personnel	2008	78.9	% d'accouchements assistés par un personnel de santé qualifié
Number of doctors (per 10 000 population)	2009	28.3	Nombre de médecins (pour 10 000 habitants)
Number of nurses (per 10 000 population)	2009	35.2	Nombre d'infirmières (pour 10 000 habitants)
Hospital beds - Total (per 10 000 population)	2013	14.8	Nombre de lits d'hôpitaux - Total (pour 10 000)
Births registered (per 1 000)	2014	22.8	Naiss.s enregistrées (pour 1 000)
Deaths registered (per 1 000)	2014	6.4	Décès enregistrés (pour 1 000)
Public expenditure on Health (% of budget)	2011	5.1	Dépenses publiques consacrées à la santé (% du budget)
EDUCATION			**EDUCATION**
Enrolment in primary education (both sexes) (000)	2012	10 820	Scolarisation dans le primaire (les deux sexes) (000)
Female	2012	5 179	Féminin
Enrolment in secondary education (both sexes) (000)	2012	7 850	Scolarisation dans le secondaire (les deux sexes) (000)
Female	2012	3 806	Féminin
Enrolment in tertiary education (both sexes) (000)	2013	2.3	Scolarisation dans le tertiaire (les deux sexes) (000)
Female	2012	1109.7	Féminin
Literacy rate (both sexes)	2012	73.9	Taux d'alphabétisation (deux sexes)
Male	2012	81.7	Masculin
Female	2012	65.8	Féminin
Pupil-teacher ratio	2014	2510.0	Ratio élève-enseignant
Public expenditure on education (% of budget)	2013	11.9	Dépenses publiques consacrées à l'enseignement (% du budget)
POVERTY			**PAUVRETÉ**
GNI Per Capita (US$)	2013	3 140.0	RNB par habitant ($EU)
Human Poverty Index (HPI-1) Value (%)	2007	23.4	Valeur de l'Indice de pauvreté (IPH-1) (%)
Population below International Poverty Line ($2/day) (%)	2008	15.4	Population sous le seuil international de pauvreté (2$/J) (%)
Share of Income Held by Richest 10%	2008	26.6	% de revenu des 10% plus riches
Share of Income Held by Poorest 10%	2008	4.0	% de revenu des 10% plus pauvres
Gini index	2008	30.8	Indice de Gini

Charts / Graphiques

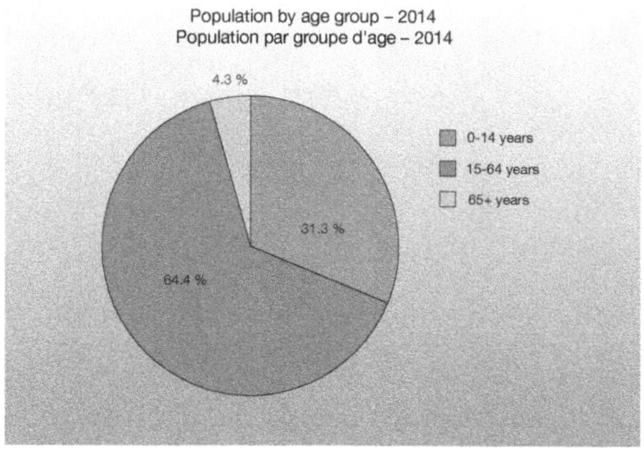

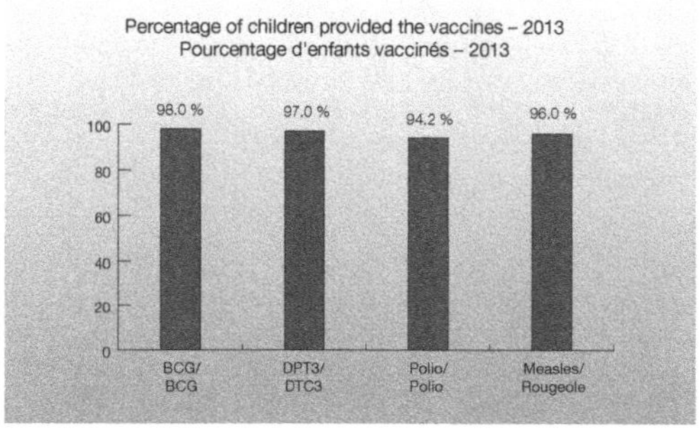

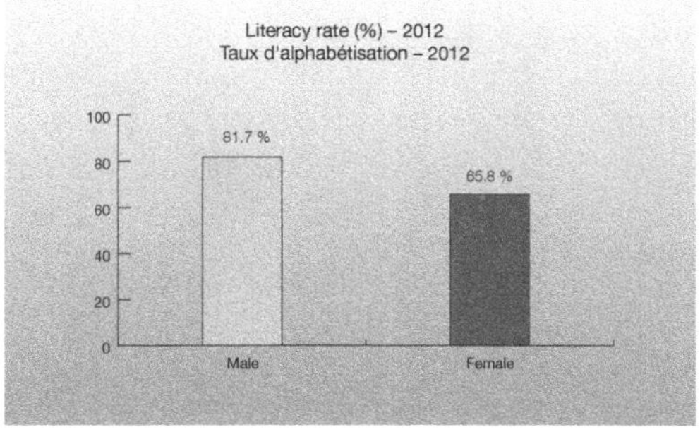

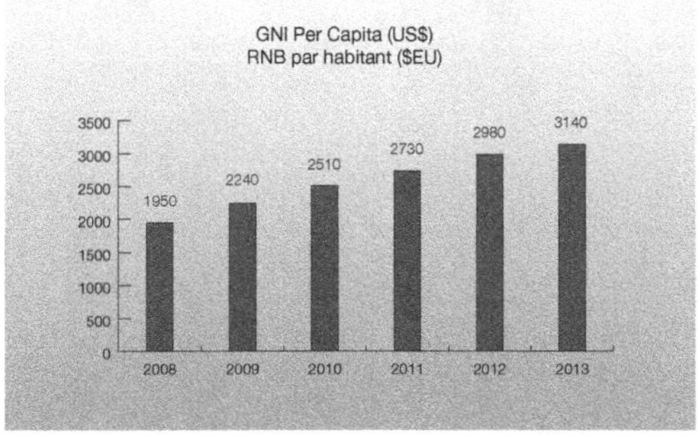

II NATIONAL ACCOUNTS — COMPTES NATIONAUX

	2006	2007	2008	2009	2010	2011	2012	2013	2014	
GROSS DOMESTIC PRODUCT BY KIND OF ECONOMIC ACTIVITY AT CURRENT PRICES *EGYPTIAN POUND (MILLIONS)*										**PRODUIT INTÉRIEUR BRUT PAR BRANCHE D'ACTIVITÉ ÉCONOMIQUE AUX PRIX COURANTS** *LIVRE EGYPTIENNE (MILLIONS)*
Agriculture, hunting, forestry and fishing	81 766	99 953	113 104	135 465	160 970	190 159	218 216	243 356	276 732	Agriculture, chasse, sylviculture et pêche
Mining and quarrying	89 834	103 656	133 674	147 966	165 747	195 136	261 671	290 739	329 815	Industries extractives
Manufacturing	98 693	114 475	139 003	164 523	194 290	216 184	238 283	262 505	314 077	Industries manufacturières
Electricity, gas & water	11 038	12 270	14 166	16 020	18 287	21 544	23 319	25 904	29 126	Electricité, gaz et eau
Construction & public works	23 763	30 175	36 780	44 026	52 609	60 070	67 382	76 747	88 934	Bâtiments et travaux publics
Wholesale & retail trade, restaurants, hotels	82 381	102 081	125 806	147 780	173 802	192 413	212 113	236 592	251 565	Commerce de gros et de détail, restaurants et hôtels
Finance, insurance, real estate, etc.	60 350	75 179	86 465	98 389	112 957	126 527	141 439	157 801	180 857	Banques, assurances, affaires immobilières
Transport and communications	59 892	76 735	90 669	101 103	110 448	122 681	133 438	144 115	161 957	Transport(s) et communications
Public administration and defense	56 930	64 220	79 737	98 575	114 944	133 688	153 984	174 713	202 949	Administrations publiques et défense
Education	3 496	8 376	9 492	11 133	12 828	14 558	16 229	17 950	20 684	Education
Health and Social Work	6 563	9 647	10 961	12 971	14 797	16 595	18 560	20 610	23 568	Santé et actions sociales
Other services	6 439	13 621	15 446	16 105	18 912	20 350	22 839	25 161	29 066	Autres services
Less Imputed Service Charges	...	...	...	...	...	...	...	...	...	Moins services d'intermédiation financière
Gross domestic product at factor cost / basic prices	581 144	710 388	855 302	994 055	1 150 590	1 309 906	1 507 473	1 676 193	1 909 328	Produit intérieur brut aux couts des facteurs / prix de base
Plus: indirect taxes / taxes on products, less subsidies	49 856	34 812	40 198	48 245	56 010	61 094	68 027	77 107	88 272	Plus taxes indirectes/impôts sur les produits, moins les subventions
EXPENDITURE ON GROSS DOMESTIC PRODUCT AT CURRENT PURCHASER'S VALUES *EGYPTIAN POUND (MILLIONS)*										**EMPLOI DU PRODUIT INTÉRIEUR BRUT AUX PRIX COURANTS D'ACQUISITION** *LIVRE EGYPTIENNE (MILLIONS)*
Government final consumption	75 900	84 400	97 500	118 300	134 700	157 000	179 000	204 800	240 000	Consommation finale des administrations publiques
Private final consumption	441 200	539 600	647 600	793 200	899 800	1 036 000	1 271 000	1 417 800	1 654 100	Consommation finale privée
Gross fixed capital formation	115 700	155 300	199 500	197 100	231 800	229 100	246 100	241 600	265 100	Formation brute de capital fixe
Change in inventories	-	-	1 000	2 900	3 500	5 400	12 000	7 000	15 500	Variation des stocks
Exports of goods and services	193 200	225 300	295 900	260 100	257 600	282 000	274 600	316 600	303 400	Exportations de biens et services
Less imports of goods and services	195 000	259 400	346 000	329 300	320 800	338 500	407 200	434 500	480 500	Moins importations de biens et services
GDP at purchasers' values	631 000	745 200	895 500	1 042 300	1 206 600	1 371 000	1 575 500	1 753 300	1 997 600	PIB aux prix d'acquisition
GROSS DOMESTIC PRODUCT BY KIND OF ECONOMIC ACTIVITY AT CONSTANT PRICES *ANNUAL GROWTH RATES (%)*										**PRODUIT INTÉRIEUR BRUT PAR BRANCHE D'ACTIVITÉ ECONOMIQUE AUX PRIX CONSTANTS** *TAUX DE CROISSANCE ANNUEL (%)*
Agriculture, hunting, forestry and fishing	3.2	3.7	3.3	3.2	3.5	2.7	2.9	3.0	3.0	Agriculture, chasse, sylviculture et pêche
Mining and quarrying	20.8	3.9	3.6	5.9	0.9	0.6	0.1	- 2.7	- 5.5	Industries extractives
Manufacturing	5.8	7.3	8.0	3.7	5.1	- 0.9	0.7	2.3	8.3	Industries manufacturières
Electricity, gas & water	8.2	6.5	7.6	10.6	6.4	4.5	5.6	4.5	2.9	Electricité, gaz et eau
Construction & public works	14.0	15.8	15.7	11.4	13.2	3.7	3.3	5.9	5.6	Bâtiments et travaux publics
Wholesale & retail trade, restaurants, hotels	6.0	9.4	11.2	2.4	7.7	- 0.5	2.8	3.6	- 3.3	Commerce de gros et de détail, restaurants et hôtels
Finance, insurance, real estate, etc.	4.8	11.5	6.2	4.6	5.3	3.0	3.9	3.3	4.6	Banques, assurances, affaires immobilières
Transport and communications	8.7	6.2	12.7	6.4	6.2	6.1	2.6	1.9	4.0	Transport(s) et communications
Public administration and defense	3.4	3.4	2.7	7.1	4.2	3.7	3.2	3.0	4.1	Administrations publiques et défense
Education	...	...	...	...	...	...	2.6	2.8	4.5	Education
Health and Social Work	...	...	...	...	...	...	62.7	3.1	4.5	Santé et actions sociales
Other services	4.9	6.8	5.1	- 2.4	5.0	2.8	2.6	2.6	5.7	Autres services
Less Imputed Service Charges	...	...	...	...	...	...	...	...	...	Moins services d'intermédiation financière
Gross domestic product at factor cost / basic prices	6.9	7.1	7.2	4.7	5.1	4.5	2.2	2.1	2.1	Produit intérieur brut aux couts des facteurs / prix de base
Plus: indirect taxes / taxes on products, less subsidies	5.5	7.6	8.3	10.2	- 2.2	- 53.8	1.8	3.0	4.0	Plus taxes indirectes/impôts sur les produits, moins les subventions
Gross domestic product at market prices	6.8	7.1	7.2	4.9	4.8	1.8	2.2	2.1	2.2	Produit intérieur brut aux prix du marché
EXPENDITURE ON GROSS DOMESTIC PRODUCT AT CONSTANT PURCHASERS' VALUES *ANNUAL GROWTH RATES (%)*										**EMPLOIS DU PRODUIT INTÉRIEUR BRUT AUX PRIX CONSTANTS D'ACQUISITION** *TAUX DE CROISSANCE ANNUEL (%)*
Government final consumption	3.1	0.2	2.1	5.6	4.5	3.8	3.1	3.5	5.8	Consommation finale des administrations publiques
Private final consumption	6.4	6.9	5.7	5.7	4.1	5.5	5.9	2.6	4.1	Consommation finale privée
Gross fixed capital formation	13.8	23.8	15.5	- 9.1	5.8	- 5.6	0.7	- 7.8	1.4	Formation brute de capital fixe
Exports of goods and services	21.3	23.3	28.8	- 14.5	- 3.0	1.2	22.3	5.9	- 12.6	Exportations de biens et services
Less imports of goods and services	21.8	28.8	26.3	- 17.9	- 3.2	8.4	10.8	- 0.6	0.9	Moins importations de biens et services
Notes	2014:Provisional								2014:Provisoire!	Notes

III INFLATION

	2006	2007	2008	2009	2010	2011	2012	2013	2014	
ANNUAL GROWTH RATES (%)										**TAUX DE CROISSANCE ANNUEL (%)**
All items	7.7	9.5	18.3	11.8	11.1	10.1	7.1	9.5	10.1	Ensemble
of which:										dont:
Food and Non-alcoholic beverages	10.1	13.0	24.0	16.2	19.7	15.5	9.2	12.4	12.3	Alimentation et boissons non alcoolisés
Alcoholic beverages & tobacco	4.3	3.0	11.0	8.9	21.9	40.6	17.7	7.9	17.3	Boissons alcoolisées et tabacs
Clothing and Footwear	1.7	5.3	7.7	8.8	1.7	1.9	4.3	4.3	2.5	Habillement et chaussures
Housing, Water, Electricity, Gas and Other Fuels	3.7	4.5	7.5	4.1	3.0	3.3	6.4	4.6	3.6	Logement, eau, electricité, gas et autres combustibles
Furnishing, household equipment	4.6	5.8	12.5	9.1	3.6	3.8	6.6	9.2	9.1	Meubles, articles de ménage et entretien courant
Health	3.7	2.4	10.4	6.3	0.5	1.5	1.4	10.5	12.7	Santé
Transport	5.0	5.8	16.2	7.6	0.8	1.4	2.3	4.3	15.4	Transport
Communication	16.0	5.2	6.8	2.4	-0.1	-1.4	-3.2	0.1	1.5	Communication
Recreation & culture	16.0	11.4	19.9	13.6	4.5	7.9	8.0	11.7	14.0	Loisirs et culture
Education	6.3	18.4	27.5	5.6	13.4	20.1	10.3	9.3	9.1	Enseignement
Restaurants & hotels	4.2	5.0	41.5	15.7	7.6	9.2	3.3	19.8	11.9	Restaurants et hôtels
Miscellaneous hotels & services	5.7	9.3	9.7	12.2	12.6	2.6	1.6	0.6	2.5	Biens et services divers

	2006	2007	2008	2009	2010	2011	2012	2013	2014	
IV AGRICULTURAL PRODUCTION - PRODUCTION AGRICOLE										
TONNES *(THOUSAND)*										**TONNES** *(MILLIERS)*
Wheat	8 274	7 379	7 977	8 523	7 169	8 371	8 795	9 460	...	Blé
Maize	6 909	6 930	7 401	7 686	7 183	6 876	8 094	7 966	...	Maise
Tomato	8 648	8 695	9 233	10 304	8 564	8 105	8 625	8 291	...	Tomates
Rice	6 755	6 877	7 253	5 520	4 329	5 675	5 911	5 724	...	Riz
Betterave à sucre	3 905	5 458	5 133	5 334	7 840	7 486	9 126	10 044	...	Pommes de terre
V MINING PRODUCTION - PRODUCTION MINIERE										
	2006	2007	2008	2009	2010	2011	2012	2013	2014	
Crude petroleum, metric tons (thousands)	31 303	32 102	33 966	33 210	33 841	33 221	33 463	31 799	...	Pétrole brut, tonnes métriques (milliers)
Natural gas (mill terajoules)	1857 158	1929 518	2124 234	2100 879	2088 639	2088 639	2072 933	44 201	...	Gaz naturel (térajoules)
Iron Ore (000 tons)	665	773	1 780	2 314	3 321	3 930	...	...	...	Minerai De Fer
VI ENERGY - ENERGIE										
	2006	2007	2008	2009	2010	2011	2012	2013	2014	
Total electricity generation (GWh)	115 407	125 129	125 129	139 000	146 795	146 668	157 024	157 930	...	Production d'électricité totale (GWh)
of which:										dont:
Production of electricity from fossil fuels (GWh)	101 866	108 788	108 788	125 004	132 045	132 045	142 468	142 468	...	Production d'électricité à partir de combustibles fossiles (GWh)
Production of hydro electricity (GWh)	12 925	15 510	15 510	12 863	13 046	13 046	12 935	13 840	...	Production d'électricité d'origine hydraulique (GWh)
Production of electricity from solar, wind, tide, wave and other sources (GWh)	616	831	831	1 133	1 704	1 577	1 621	1 621	...	Production d'électricité d'origine solaire, éolienne, marée motrice et autres (GWh)
VII TOURISM AND INFRASTRUCTURE - TOURISME ET INFRASTRUCTURE										
	2006	2007	2008	2009	2010	2011	2012	2013	2014	
VII-1 TOURISM										**VII-1 TOURISME**
International tourist arrivals (thousands)	8 646	10 610	12 296	11 914	14 051	9 497	11 196	9 189	9 756	Arrivées de touristes internationaux (milliers)
Rooms in hotels and similar establishments (thousands)	135.3	142.8	143.9	160.0	153.1	139.8	130.3	...	...	Chambres d'hotels et établissements assimilés (milliers)
Overnight stays (thousands)	115 527	144 633	165 856	163 835	185 720	143 922	173 666	118 966	125 412	Nuitées (milliers)
Tourism receipts (US$ thousand)	7417 850	9091 330	10734 600	10510 300	12282 600	8462 040	9695 140	5804 570	5996 120	Recettes touristiques (milliers de $ EU)
Total contribution to GDP (%)	19.0	19.5	19.0	17.1	16.7	13.7	14.1	11.8	11.6	Contribution totale au PIB (%)
Total contribution to Employment (%)	16.7	17.2	16.7	15.1	14.8	12.1	12.8	10.8	10.6	Contribution totale à l'emploi (%)
VII-2 INFRASTRUCTURE										**VII-2 INFRASTRUCTURE**
Paved roads (% of total)	81	82	83	89	90	90	...	...	...	Routes asphaltées (% du total)
Total Network (Railways-km)	9 556	9 570	9 570	9 570	9 570	9 570	9 570	9 570	...	Réseau total voies ferrées-Km
Main Telephone Lines (per 100 inhabitants)	15	15	16	13	12	11	11	8	...	Lignes téléphoniques fixes (pour 100 habitants)
Mobile Cellular Subscribers (per 100 inhabitants)	25	41	55	72	91	105	120	122	...	Abonnés aux téléphones mobiles (pour 100 habitants)
VIII EXTERNAL TRADE - COMMERCE EXTERIEUR										
	2006	2007	2008	2009	2010	2011	2012	2013	2014	
US$ EXPORTS, FOB										**$ E.U EXPORTATIONS, FÀB**
Exports - Total	13 720	16 167	26 244	24 193	27 335	31 582	30 627	29 009	26 756	Exportations - Total
Exports to AFRICA	...	...	...	...	...	...	...	...	...	Exportations vers l'AFRIQUE
Main Products										**Principaux produits**
Crude Oil	2 915	2 678	3 591	2 173	1 965	3 014	3 008	3 050	3 044	Pétrole brut
Petroleum Products	1 603	2 642	2 195	1 566	1 776	1 963	1 847	1 338	1 118	Produits pétroliers
Cotton	1 484	1 871	2 113	1 135	1 734	1 774	1 637	1 269	685	Coton
Carbon	884	1 051	895	1 070	1 074	1 714	1 377	1 024	678	Carbon
Rice	803	1 003	717	831	1 029	1 299	1 138	893	651	Riz
Main Destinations										**Principales destinations**
United States	1 592	2 576	2 708	1 613	2 235	2 719	2 355	2 687	2 449	États-Unis
Italy	1 383	1 777	1 659	1 588	1 691	2 265	2 135	2 137	1 977	Italie
Spain	1 257	1 545	1 499	1 585	1 677	1 978	2 096	2 021	1 919	Espagne
United Kingdom	1 182	1 011	1 488	1 455	1 664	1 819	1 948	1 777	1 448	Royaume-Uni
India	1 028	945	1 303	1 382	1 269	1 529	1 603	1 287	1 126	Inde
IMPORTS, CIF										**IMPORTATIONS, CAF**
Imports - Total	20 594	27 033	52 773	44 921	53 021	62 283	72 470	66 180	71 186	Importations - Total (millions)
Imports from Africa	144	168	961	597	739	931	969	688	687	Importations en provenance de l'Afrique
Main Products										**Principaux produits**
Wheat nes and meslin	2 916	4 118	2 108	1 539	2 141	3 500	5 348	3 585	3 056	Blé nda et méteil
Petroleum oils & oils obtained from bituminous minerals,o/than crude etc	1 042	1 562	2 014	1 432	2 075	3 195	3 497	2 022	3 038	Huiles de pétrole, bitumineux, distilles, sauf brut
Automobiles w reciprocatg piston engine displacg > 1500 cc to 3000 cc	1 041	1 295	1 554	1 287	1 806	2 107	2 919	1 939	2 790	Automobiles w reciprocatg moteur à piston displacg> 1500 cc à 3000 cc
Ferrous waste and scrap, iron or steel, nes	964	1 136	1 514	1 068	1 380	2 056	2 220	1 938	1 942	Déchets et débris de fonte, fer ou acier, nda
Maize, nes	945	1 109	1 465	981	1 321	1 700	1 986	1 568	1 924	Maïs, nda
Main Origin										**Principales provenances**
United States	2 896	4 015	5 673	4 743	4 962	6 469	6 771	6 952	8 041	États-Unis
China	1 592	2 508	4 432	3 907	4 902	5 708	5 451	5 193	5 528	Chine
Germany	1 415	2 182	3 262	3 601	4 024	3 930	4 772	5 167	5 187	Allemagne
Italy	1 188	1 734	3 102	2 652	2 963	3 124	4 051	3 530	3 508	Italie
France	1 076	1 593	3 020	2 346	2 120	2 787	3 971	3 138	3 258	France

IX FINANCIAL AND MONETARY STATISTICS - FINANCES ET STATISTIQUES MONETAIRES	2006	2007	2008	2009	2010	2011	2012	2013	2014	
IX-1 MONETARY STATISTICS *EGYPTIAN POUND (MILLIONS)*										**IX-1 STATISTIQUES MONÉTAIRES** *POUND EGYPTIEN (MILLIONS)*
Money supply (M1)	561 160	663 770	766 660	831 210	917 460	1 010 300	1 094 410	1 295 690	1 517 430	Masse monétaire (M1)
Quasi-money	458 708	537 599	591 029	640 257	716 434	742 440	828 237	956 770	1 099 997	Quasi-monnaie
of which Demand Deposit	...	...	...	...	...	...	...	...	...	dont Monnaie scripturale
Net foreign assets	187 997	231 587	247 440	255 846	305 209	190 209	132 822	117 592	84 397	Avoirs extérieurs nets
Domestic credit	574 256	626 722	695 790	782 844	837 646	1 022 981	1 223 477	1 511 332	1 854 288	Crédit intérieur
of which claims on private sector	304 470	338 997	383 252	376 158	399 050	427 165	458 674	487 842	545 422	dont créances sur le secteur privé
of which claims on government sector, net	191 057	196 026	229 002	311 935	333 250	501 884	663 851	912 637	1 172 147	dont créances nettes sur le gouvernement
International reserves (millions US$)	24 590	30 322	32 347	32 386	33 743	15 046	11 758	13 739	12 636	Réserves internationales (millions $EU)
Average Exchange Rate (National Currency per US$)	5.74	5.64	5.43	5.54	5.62	5.93	6.06	6.87	7.08	Taux de change (moyen) (monnaie nationale par $ EU)
IX-2 PUBLIC FINANCE *EGYPTIAN POUND (MILLIONS)*										**IX-2 FINANCES PUBLIQUES** *POUND EGYPTIEN (MILLIONS)*
Total Revenues and Grants	99 613	118 213	138 658	171 206	268 115	194 775	217 513	256 326	356 145	Recettes totales et dons
Tax Revenue	48 122	52 324	54 449	51 923	170 494	121 561	121 301	157 122	159 646	Recettes fiscales
Non Tax Revenue	49 907	62 003	82 746	111 299	93 288	70 927	86 109	93 996	100 643	Recettes non fiscales
Grants	1 584	3 886	1 463	7 984	4 333	2 287	10 103	5 208	95 856	Dons
Total Expenditures and Net Lending	204 463	222 029	282 291	351 499	365 986	401 866	470 992	588 188	701 514	Dépenses totales et prêts nets
Current expenditure	184 776	196 803	248 100	308 069	317 636	361 985	435 074	548 672	648 632	Dépenses courantes
Of which Wages and Salaries	45 918	52 153	62 839	76 147	85 369	96 271	122 818	142 956	178 589	Dont rémunérations et salaires
Capital expenditure	19 687	25 498	34 191	43 430	48 350	39 881	35 918	39 516	52 882	Dépenses d'équipement
Net Lending	-	- 272	-	-	-	-	-	-	-	Prêts nets
Fiscal Balance	- 104 850	- 103 816	- 143 633	- 180 293	- 97 871	- 207 092	- 253 479	- 331 862	- 345 369	Solde global y compris les dons
IX-3 BALANCE OF PAYMENTS *US$ (MILLIONS)*										**IX-3 BALANCE DES PAIEMENTS** *$ E.U (MILLIONS)*
Trade balance	- 11 986	- 16 291	- 23 415	- 25 173	- 25 120	- 27 103	- 20 675	- 21 088	- 23 854	Balance commerciale
Services Balance	8 191	11 498	14 966	12 502	10 339	7 878	7 306	8 551	5 856	Balance des services
Net Income	4 975	6 261	8 377	7 632	9 509	12 384	- 3 924	- 5 088	- 5 164	Revenus nets
Compensation of employees	...	...	...	...	...	...	...	...	...	Rémunération des salariés
Investment Income	...	...	...	...	...	...	...	...	...	Revenus des investissements
Current transfers, net total	572	800	961	614	954	753	11 148	13 373	20 494	Transferts courants
Net official transfers	800	961	614	954	753	632	...	...	...	Transferts officiels nets
Workers' remittances	6 261	8 377	7 632	9 509	12 384	17 776	...	...	...	Envois de fonds des travailleurs
Other private transfers	...	...	...	...	...	...	...	...	...	Autres transferts privés
Current account balance	1 752	2 269	888	- 4 424	- 4 318	- 6 088	- 6 145	- 4 253	- 2 668	Solde du compte courant
Capital & financial account	853	7 558	2 285	8 980	- 4 199	1 023	9 687	...	...	Comptes de capital et financier
Capital account	- 39	2	- 3	- 36	- 32	- 96	- 87	...	...	Compte de capital
Financial account	892	7 555	2 287	9 016	- 4 166	1 119	9 774	...	...	Compte financier
Errors & omissions	1 453	- 3 025	- 1 238	- 1 306	533	- 1 946	...	...	...	Erreurs et omissions
Overall balance	5 282	5 420	- 3 378	3 356	- 9 754	- 11 278	237	...	...	Balance générale

X DEBT AND FINANCIAL FLOWS - DETTE ET FLUX FINANCIERS	2006	2007	2008	2009	2010	2011	2012	2013	2014	
X-1 DEBT *US$ (MILLIONS)*										**X-1 DETTE EXTÉRIEURE** *$ E.U (MILLIONS)*
Total external debt	29 593	29 898	33 893	31 531	33 694	34 906	39 123	44 404	53 376	Dette extérieure totale
Private	4 431	4 209	3 746	3 317	3 328	3 265	3 258	3 211	3 211	Privée
Public	25 162	25 689	30 147	28 214	30 366	31 641	35 865	41 193	50 165	Publique
Total external debt service	5 150	4 159	4 451	5 509	4 525	5 621	5 330	5 732	11 547	Service de la dette extérieure
Present value of External debt	597	675	621	554	553.6	544.7	- 521.2	8 848.9	2 833.7	Valeur actuelle de la dette extérieure
Total government domestic debt (in local currency)	587 405	630 966	658 307	755 297	888 715.0	1 044 898.0	1 238 137.0	1 527 378.0	1 816 578.0	Dette publique intérieure
X-2 FINANCIAL FLOWS *US$ (MILLIONS)*										**X-2 FLUX FINANCIERS** *$ E.U (MILLIONS)*
Net Foreign Direct Investment Inflows	10 043	11 578	9 495	6 712	6 386	- 483	6 881	5 553	...	Investissement étranger direct (flux nets entrants)
Main origin of FDI Inflows										**Principales origines de l'IDE entrant:**
United States	54	996	1 617	1 512	1 919.0	2 333.0	2 160.0	...	...	États-Unis
United Kingdom	806	1 287	602	1 180	1 938.5	1 067.3	- 88.7	...	...	Royaume-Uni
France	299	590	12 918	- 7 533	- 53.0	196.4	144.0	...	...	France
Italy	1 538	37	791	534	615.4	1 541.9	1 373.0	...	...	Italie
Germany	161	638	168	568	421.2	649.0	144.0	...	...	Allemagne
African countries	...	...	...	...	...	...	...	...	...	Pays africains
Net total Official Development Assistance	899	1 133	1 742	1 005	597	414	1 807	5 506	...	Aide publique au développement (nette totale)
Main origin of Net ODA										**Principales origines de l'APD nette**
United States	196	462	471	185	52.7	- 98.2	- 13.4	57.2	...	Etats-Unis
France	63	77	142	112	140.1	115.8	140.3	54.9	...	France
Germany	141	154	170	139	104.5	100.4	9.5	0.8	...	Allemagne
United Arab Emirates	48	43	365	61	22.3	11.7	11.0	...	...	Emirats arabes unis
Kuwait (KFAED)	20	60	88	60	54.5	94.7	90.5	...	...	Koweit (FKDEA)

EQUATORIAL GUINEA — GUINÉE EQUATORIALE

AREA (km²)	28 051		SUPERFICIE (km²)
CAPITAL CITY	Malabo	Malabo	CAPITALE
CURRENCY	CFA Franc	Franc CFA	MONNAIE

I SOCIAL AND DEMOGRAPHIC INDICATORS — INDICATEURS DEMOGRAPHIQUES ET SOCIAUX

	Year / Année	Value / Valeur	
POPULATION			**POPULATION**
Population ('000)			Population ('000)
Both sexes	2014	778	Les deux sexes
Male	2014	398	Masculin
Female	2014	380	Féminin
Average annual growth rate	2014	2.2	Taux de croissance annuel
Active Population ('000)	2014	404	Population active ('000)
Population by age group ('000)			Population par groupe d'âge ('000)
0-14 years	2014	301	0-14 ans
15-64 years	2014	456	15-64 ans
65+ years	2014	22	65+ ans
Economically. active population. in agriculture (%)	2014	47.5	Participation de la population active agricole (%)
Crude birth rate	2014	34.9	Taux brut de natalité
Crude death rate	2014	12.9	Taux brut de mortalité
Total fertility rate	2014	4.7	Indice synthétique de fécondité
Proportion of urban population	2014	40.0	Part de la population urbaine
Life Expectancy at Birth - Total (years)	2014	53.5	Espérance de vie à la naissance - Totale (ans)
Dependency Ratio - Total (%)	2014	70.9	Taux de dépendance - Total (%)
HEALTH			**SANTÉ**
Percentage of children under-five and underweight	2010	5.6	% d'enfants de moins de cinq ans avec insuffisance pondérale
Prevalence of undernourishment	...	...	Prévalence de la malnutrition
Under five mortality rate (both sexes, per 1000)	2013	95.8	Taux de mortalité de moins de 5 ans (les deux sexes, pour 1000)
Infant mortality rate (both sexes) per 1000	2013	69.3	Taux de mortalité infantile (les deux sexes) par 1000
Percentage of children provided the vaccines :			Pourcentage d'enfants vaccinés :
BCG	2013	71.0	BCG
DPT3	2013	3.0	DTC3
Polio	2014	64.0	Polio
Measles	2013	42.0	Rougeole
Percentage of mothers provided at least one antenatal care (%)	2014	91.0	Pourcentage de mères ayant au moins reçu un soin prénatal (%)
Percentage of deliveries attended by skilled health personnel	2000	64.6	% d'accouchements assistés par un personnel de santé qualifié
Number of doctors (per 10 000 population)	2004	3.0	Nombre de médecins (pour 10 000 habitants)
Number of nurses (per 10 000 population)	2004	5.4	Nombre d'infirmières (pour 10 000 habitants)
Hospital beds - Total (per 10 000 population)	2010	21.0	Nombre de lits d'hôpitaux - Total (pour 10 000)
Births registered (per 1 000)	2014	34.9	Naiss.s enregistrées (pour 1 000)
Deaths registered (per 1 000)	2014	12.9	Décès enregistrés (pour 1 000)
Public expenditure on Health (% of budget)	2009	7.0	Dépenses publiques consacrées à la santé (% du budget)
EDUCATION			**EDUCATION**
Enrolment in primary education (both sexes) (000)	2014	86	Scolarisation dans le primaire (les deux sexes) (000)
Female	2014	42	Féminin
Enrolment in secondary education (both sexes) (000)	2014	34	Scolarisation dans le secondaire (les deux sexes) (000)
Female	2014	16	Féminin
Enrolment in tertiary education (both sexes) (000)	...	...	Scolarisation dans le tertiaire (les deux sexes) (000)
Female	2000	0.3	Féminin
Literacy rate (both sexes)	2014	88.7	Taux d'alphabétisation (deux sexes)
Male	2014	90.8	Masculin
Female	2014	86.7	Féminin
Pupil-teacher ratio	2010	27.2	Ratio élève-enseignant
Public expenditure on education (% of budget)	2003	4.0	Dépenses publiques consacrées à l'enseignement (% du budget)
POVERTY			**PAUVRETÉ**
GNI Per Capita (US$)	2013	14 320.0	RNB par habitant ($EU)
Human Poverty Index (HPI-1) Value (%)	2007	31.9	Valeur de l'Indice de pauvreté (IPH-1) (%)
Population below International Poverty Line ($2/day) (%)	...	...	Population sous le seuil international de pauvreté (2$/J) (%)
Share of Income Held by Richest 10%	...	...	% de revenu des 10% plus riches
Share of Income Held by Poorest 10%	...	...	% de revenu des 10% plus pauvres
Gini index	...	...	Indice de Gini

Charts / Graphiques

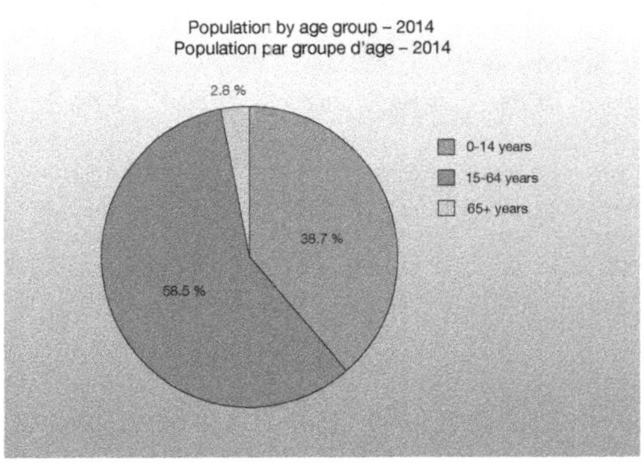

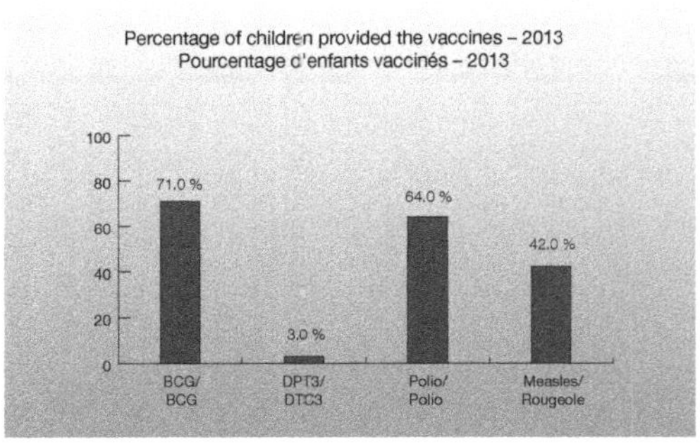

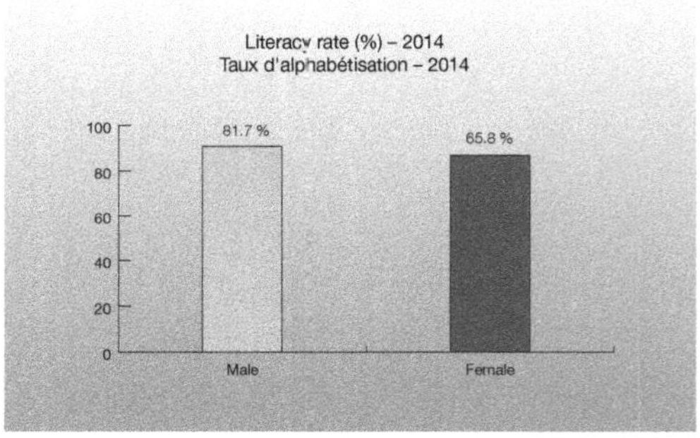

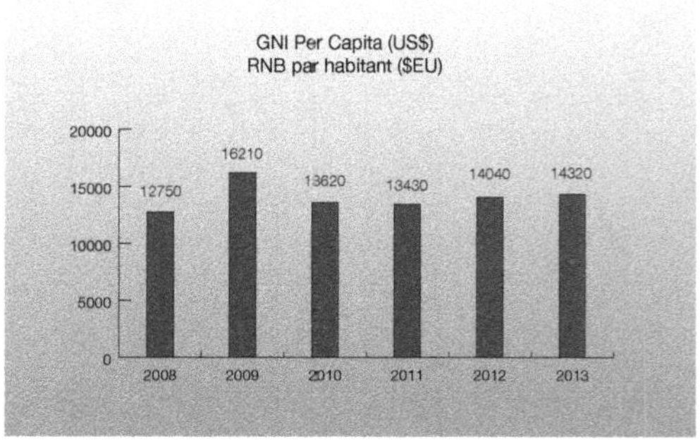

II NATIONAL ACCOUNTS — COMPTES NATIONAUX

	2006	2007	2008	2009	2010	2011	2012	2013	2014	
GROSS DOMESTIC PRODUCT BY KIND OF ECONOMIC ACTIVITY AT CURRENT PRICES *CFA FRANC (MILLIONS)*										**PRODUIT INTÉRIEUR BRUT PAR BRANCHE D'ACTIVITÉ ÉCONOMIQUE AUX PRIX COURANTS** *FRANC CFA (MILLIONS)*
Agriculture, hunting, forestry and fishing	86 392	101 334	84 213	84 821	107 596	114 867	128 479	132 588	135 472	Agriculture, chasse, sylviculture et pêche
Mining and quarrying	4 080 635	4 716 587	6 782 930	4 518 403	5 707 363	7 431 632	8 431 960	7 411 136	7 113 236	Industries extractives
Manufacturing	4 837	5 921	7 150	8 783	10 945	9 325	7 945	9 900	12 335	Industries manufacturières
Electricity, gas & water	19 994	25 792	30 950	36 521	43 825	52 590	63 108	69 419	84 060	Electricité, gaz et eau
Construction & public works	118 976	157 827	218 727	347 516	440 439	508 815	720 211	398 245	460 454	Bâtiments et travaux publics
Wholesale & retail trade, restaurants, hotels	33 836	37 754	41 292	46 807	56 369	64 203	72 828	78 033	93 986	Commerce de gros et de détail, restaurants et hôtels
Finance, insurance, real estate, etc.	14 123	17 314	24 806	30 156	43 993	63 092	77 516	68 325	75 705	Banques, assurances, affaires immobilières
Transport and communications	5 426	5 755	6 294	7 082	9 772	12 264	14 956	16 025	17 247	Transport(s) et communications
Public administration and defense	46 613	57 481	58 866	74 654	87 800	89 822	109 818	109 375	115 739	Administrations publiques et défense
Education	...	...	...	...	...	...	...	...	...	Education
Health and Social Work	...	...	...	...	...	...	...	...	...	Santé et actions sociales
Other services	14 276	16 329	18 359	20 467	25 462	29 742	34 421	36 881	39 694	Autres services
Less Imputed Service Charges	...	...	...	...	...	...	...	...	...	Moins services d'intermédiation financière
Gross domestic product at factor cost / basic prices	4 425 107	5 142 094	7 273 587	5 175 211	6 533 564	8 376 352	9 661 241	8 329 927	8 147 930	Produit intérieur brut aux couts des facteurs / prix de base
Plus: indirect taxes / taxes on products, less subsidies	39 061	47 061	58 879	76 817	99 144	113 366	147 514	110 255	124 163	Plus taxes indirectes/impôts sur les produits, moins les subventions
EXPENDITURE ON GROSS DOMESTIC PRODUCT AT CURRENT PURCHASER'S VALUES *CFA FRANC (MILLIONS)*										**EMPLOI DU PRODUIT INTÉRIEUR BRUT AUX PRIX COURANTS D'ACQUISITION** *FRANC CFA (MILLIONS)*
Government final consumption	128 125	137 874	195 586	224 841	264 352	290 410	532 617	430 373	466 917	Consommation finale des administrations publiques
Private final consumption	308 964	345 463	378 820	369 127	619 425	968 389	836 213	677 589	793 845	Consommation finale privée
Gross fixed capital formation	1 200 936	1 594 519	2 155 570	3 354 468	3 145 392	3 602 824	4 803 135	3 114 021	2 951 894	Formation brute de capital fixe
Change in inventories	200	200	200	200	200	200	200	200	200	Variation des stocks
Exports of goods and services	4 327 676	4 983 532	7 052 243	4 781 772	6 001 044	7 629 513	8 790 878	7 744 523	7 434 632	Exportations de biens et services
Less imports of goods and services	1 501 733	1 872 433	2 449 954	3 478 381	3 397 706	4 001 617	5 154 288	3 526 525	3 375 395	Moins importations de biens et services
GDP at purchasers' values	4 464 168	5 189 155	7 332 466	5 252 028	6 632 708	8 489 718	9 808 755	8 440 182	8 272 093	PIB aux prix d'acquisition
GROSS DOMESTIC PRODUCT BY KIND OF ECONOMIC ACTIVITY AT CONSTANT PRICES *ANNUAL GROWTH RATES (%)*										**PRODUIT INTÉRIEUR BRUT PAR BRANCHE D'ACTIVITÉ ECONOMIQUE AUX PRIX CONSTANTS** *TAUX DE CROISSANCE ANNUEL (%)*
Agriculture, hunting, forestry and fishing	4.7	23.4	- 20.2	- 2.5	13.4	- 3.4	8.5	0.4	0.5	Agriculture, chasse, sylviculture et pêche
Mining and quarrying	- 1.4	25.6	23.4	19.3	- 8.2	5.2	1.5	- 2.7	- 1.6	Industries extractives
Manufacturing	17.7	14.4	14.8	16.9	20.6	- 18.8	- 17.4	22.7	22.6	Industries manufacturières
Electricity, gas & water	44.2	20.0	13.5	11.5	16.0	16.0	16.4	7.0	18.0	Electricité, gaz et eau
Construction & public works	77.8	30.8	26.6	27.1	25.7	14.3	37.9	- 46.7	14.8	Bâtiments et travaux publics
Wholesale & retail trade, restaurants, hotels	0.0	6.1	3.4	7.6	18.4	11.9	10.8	5.2	18.4	Commerce de gros et de détail, restaurants et hôtels
Finance, insurance, real estate, etc.	11.2	17.1	39.8	18.6	42.9	40.4	19.2	- 14.8	7.8	Banques, assurances, affaires immobilières
Transport and communications	0.0	1.1	2.4	7.5	36.0	23.5	19.3	5.2	5.6	Transport(s) et communications
Public administration and defense	9.3	22.3	1.4	16.8	16.6	1.3	20.6	- 1.4	4.8	Administrations publiques et défense
Education	...	...	...	...	...	...	...	...	...	Education
Health and Social Work	...	...	...	...	...	...	...	...	...	Santé et actions sociales
Other services	0.0	8.4	7.2	5.5	23.4	15.8	14.1	6.2	6.6	Autres services
Less Imputed Service Charges	...	...	...	...	...	...	...	...	...	Moins services d'intérmediation financière
Gross domestic product at factor cost / basic prices	5.2	24.9	20.9	19.1	- 0.8	7.7	9.6	- 12.2	2.3	Produit intérieur brut aux couts des facteurs / prix de base
Plus: indirect taxes / taxes on products, less subsidies	17.0	3.1	9.8	4.7	3.3	0.0	0.0	12.5	2.2	Plus taxes indirectes/impôts sur les produits, moins les subventions
Gross domestic product at market prices	5.3	24.8	20.8	19.0	- 0.8	7.7	9.5	- 12.1	2.3	Produit intérieur brut aux prix du marché
EXPENDITURE ON GROSS DOMESTIC PRODUCT AT CONSTANT PURCHASERS' VALUES *ANNUAL GROWTH RATES (%)*										**EMPLOIS DU PRODUIT INTÉRIEUR BRUT AUX PRIX CONSTANTS D'ACQUISITION** *TAUX DE CROISSANCE ANNUEL (%)*
Government final consumption	3.0	2.1	35.9	9.0	12.0	5.0	79.8	- 22.2	5.5	Consommation finale des administrations publiques
Private final consumption	4.6	7.9	9.6	82.8	- 6.2	68.4	26.5	- 20.4	4.7	Consommation finale privée
Gross fixed capital formation	24.2	28.4	33.4	32.4	1.0	3.5	19.9	- 24.7	- 3.6	Formation brute de capital fixe
Exports of goods and services	- 3.8	12.9	12.8	3.7	- 10.7	0.1	6.0	- 6.4	- 1.3	Exportations de biens et services
Less imports of goods and services	21.0	16.2	30.8	45.8	- 3.0	18.1	30.1	- 28.0	- 3.9	Moins importations de biens et services
Notes	NA Data : 2013-2014:Estimates						Données des CN: 2013-2014:Estimées			Notes

III INFLATION

	2006	2007	2008	2009	2010	2011	2012	2013	2014	
ANNUAL GROWTH RATES (%)										**TAUX DE CROISSANCE ANNUEL (%)**
All items	4.4	2.8	6.0	5.5	4.7	7.3	3.6	3.6	3.6	Ensemble
of which:										dont:
Food and Non-alcoholic beverages	...	...	...	...	...	...	...	...	...	Alimentation et boissons non alcoolisés
Alcoholic beverages & tobacco	...	...	...	...	...	...	...	...	...	Boissons alcoolisées et tabacs
Clothing and Footwear	...	...	...	...	...	...	...	...	...	Habillement et chaussures
Housing, Water, Electricity, Gas and Other Fuels	...	...	...	...	...	...	...	...	...	Logement, eau, electricité, gas et autres combustibles
Furnishing, household equipment	...	...	...	...	...	...	...	...	...	Meubles, articles de ménage et entretien courant
Health	...	...	...	...	...	...	...	...	...	Santé
Transport	...	...	...	...	...	...	...	...	...	Transport
Communication	...	...	...	...	...	...	...	...	...	Communication
Recreation & culture	...	...	...	...	...	...	...	...	...	Loisirs et culture
Education	...	...	...	...	...	...	...	...	...	Enseignement
Restaurants & hotels	...	...	...	...	...	...	...	...	...	Restaurants et hôtels
Miscellaneous goods & services	...	...	...	...	...	...	...	...	...	Biens et services divers

IV AGRICULTURAL PRODUCTION - PRODUCTION AGRICOLE	2006	2007	2008	2009	2010	2011	2012	2013	2014	
TONNES *(THOUSAND)*										**TONNES** *(MILLIERS)*
Sweet potatoes	68	83	77	92	90	91	95	92	...	Patates douces
Cassava	55	57	58	73	64	66	68	70	...	Manioc
Plantains	36	37	38	40	42	42	43	44	...	Banane-Plantain
Bananas	27	29	30	27	27	28	29	30	...	Banane
Coconuts	7	6	7	6	7	7	7	8	...	Noix de coco

V MINING PRODUCTION - PRODUCTION MINIERE	2006	2007	2008	2009	2010	2011	2012	2013	2014	
Crude petroleum, metric tons (thousands)	17 153	17 750	17 825	15 406	14 250	13 927	14 940	13 006	...	Pétrole brut, tonnes métriques (milliers) (Bariles)
Natural gas (terajoules)	2 036	4 134	6 800	7 900	6 500	7 200	7 800	...	...	Gaz naturel (térajoules)(Bariles)
Gold ores and concentrates, Kilograms	...	...	...	...	...	...	...	...	...	Minerais d'or et concentrés (Kilogrammes)

VI ENERGY - ENERGIE	2006	2007	2008	2009	2010	2011	2012	2013	2014	
Total electricity generation (GWh)	90	94	94	94	410	410	410	413	...	Production d'électricité totale (GWh)
of which:										dont:
Production of electricity from fossil fuels (GWh)	83	87	87	87	396	396	396	396	...	Production d'électricité à partir de combustibles fossiles (GWh)
Production of hydro electricity (GWh)	7	7	7	7	14	14	14	18	...	Production d'électricité d'origine hydraulique (GWh)
Production of electricity from solar, wind, tide, wave and other sources (GWh)	...	...	...	...	...	...	...	...	...	Production d'électricité d'origine solaire, éolienne, marée motrice et autres (GWh)

VII TOURISM AND INFRASTRUCTURE - TOURISME ET INFRASTRUCTURE	2006	2007	2008	2009	2010	2011	2012	2013	2014	
VII-1 TOURISM										**VII-1 TOURISME**
International tourist arrivals (thousands)	...	...	...	...	...	...	...	...	...	Arrivées de touristes internationaux (milliers)
Rooms in hotels and similar establishments (thousands)	...	...	...	...	...	...	...	...	...	Chambres d'hotels et établissements assimilés (milliers)
Overnight stays (thousands)	...	...	...	...	...	...	...	...	...	Nuitées (milliers)
Tourism receipts (US$ thousand)	...	...	...	...	...	...	...	...	...	Recettes touristiques (milliers de $ EU)
Total contribution to GDP (%)	...	...	...	...	...	...	...	...	...	Contribution totale au PIB (%)
Total contribution to Employment (%)	...	...	...	...	...	...	...	...	...	Contribution totale à l'emploi (%)
VII-2 INFRASTRUCTURE										**VII-2 INFRASTRUCTURE**
Paved roads (% of total)	...	...	...	...	...	...	...	...	...	Routes asphaltées (% du total)
Total Network (Railways-km)	...	...	...	...	...	...	...	...	...	Réseau total voies ferrées-Km
Main Telephone Lines (per 100 inhabitants)	2	2	2	1	2	2	2	2	...	Lignes téléphoniques fixes (pour 100 habitants)
Mobile Cellular Subscribers (per 100 inhabitants)	19	23	27	30	57	67	68	67	...	Abonnés aux téléphones mobiles (pour 100 habitants)

VIII EXTERNAL TRADE - COMMERCE EXTERIEUR	2006	2007	2008	2009	2010	2011	2012	2013	2014	
US$ (MILLIONS) EXPORTS, FOB										**$ E.U (MILLIONS) EXPORTATIONS, FÀB**
Exports - Total	7 459	8 418	14 568	8 088	8 393	11 663	14 162	12 603	...	Exportations - Total
Exports to AFRICA	1 119	1 230	...	...	...	...	...	...	...	Exportations vers l'AFRIQUE
Main Products										**Principaux produits**
Crude oil	744	849	1 167	655	778	987	1 039	2 433	...	Pétrole brut
Methanol and Other Gases	686	162	316	156	190	336	372	1 283	...	Méthanol et Autres Gaz
Lumber	48	71	21	5	39	43	43	61	...	Bois
Cocoa	17	9	13	11	12	9	5	5	...	Cacao
Coffee	15	20	25	20	23	33	32	11	...	Café
Main Destinations										**Principales destinations**
United States	1 785	1 979	3 176	2 607	2 432	1 683	...	...	...	États-Unis
China	2 482	1 804	2 061	1 063	635	2 301	...	...	...	Chine
Spain	1 021	1 317	2 534	644	1 015	-	...	...	...	Espagne
China, Taiwan	851	1 290	1 488	490	489	1 102	...	...	...	Taïwan, Chine
Japan	314	622	1 032	787	381	1 819	...	...	...	Japon
IMPORTS, CIF										**IMPORTATIONS, CAF**
Imports - Total	1 625	1 353	1 736	2 030	2 492	2 435	2 299	2 979	...	Importations - Total (millions)
Imports from Africa	...	...	...	...	...	...	...	...	...	Importations en provenance de l'Afrique
Main Products										**Principaux produits**
Petroleum, petroleum products and related materials	164	301	442	2 029	1 712	583	...	...	...	Pétrole et produits dérivés
Specialised machinery	585	460	480	489	493	598	...	...	...	Machines et appareils spécialisés
Other industrial machinery and parts	160	266	224	288	354	518	...	...	...	Autres machines industrielles et pièces détachées
Manufactures of metal, n.e.s.	81	146	248	232	320	686	...	...	...	Articles manufacturés en métal, n.d.a.
Road vehicles	81	225	335	288	314	275	...	...	...	Véhicules routiers
Main Origin										**Principales provenances**
United States	747	495	422	538	476	975	...	...	...	États-Unis
Nigeria	...	2	17	1 807	1 446	...	...	...	...	Nigéria
China	56	194	634	631	800	907	...	...	...	Chine
France	122	241	388	290	410	923	...	...	...	France
Spain	197	365	488	477	524	...	...	...	...	Espagne

IX FINANCIAL AND MONETARY STATISTICS - FINANCES ET STATISTIQUES MONETAIRES	2006	2007	2008	2009	2010	2011	2012	2013	2014	
IX-1 MONETARY STATISTICS *CFA FRANC (MILLIONS)*										**IX-1 STATISTIQUES MONÉTAIRES** *FRANC CFA (MILLIONS)*
Money supply (M1)	312 240	438 290	572 760	744 180	993 560	1 069 870	1 688 620	1 811 990	1 975 160	Masse monétaire (M1)
Quasi-money	57 627	77 776	63 057	75 786	101 777	109 027	208 515	216 840	269 904	Quasi-monnaie
of which Demand Deposit	...	...	...	...	...	...	...	1 338 177	1 405 231	dont Monnaie scripturale
Net foreign assets	1 573 628	1 800 338	2 243 465	1 561 541	1 155 807	1 588 327	2 274 278	2 382 217	1 790 247	Avoirs extérieurs nets
Domestic credit	-1 223 561	-1 339 393	-1 685 721	- 690 276	86 203	- 282 806	- 312 403	- 270 031	1 218 469	Crédit intérieur
of which claims on private sector	125 152	175 583	362 967	412 944	539 111	704 847	608 999	817 723	1 513 085	dont créances sur le secteur privé
of which claims on government sector, net	-1 353 661	-1 523 724	-2 071 098	-1 131 055	- 496 718	-1 021 986	- 934 852	-1 103 645	- 314 300	dont créances nettes sur le gouvernement
International reserves (millions US$)	3 067	3 846	4 431	3 252	2 346	3 054	4 397	...	...	Réserves internationales (millions $EU)
Average Exchange Rate (National Currency per US$)	522.90	478.89	446.87	471.07	494.68	471.42	512.43	500.72	495.96	Taux de change (moyen) (monnaie nationale par $ EU)
IX-2 PUBLIC FINANCE *CFA FRANC (MILLIONS)*										**IX-2 FINANCES PUBLIQUES** *FRANC CFA (MILLIONS)*
Total Revenues and Grants	2 244 727	2 519 661	3 222 163	2 608 087	2 150 932	2 849 081	3 552 287	2 020 000	1 942 203	Recettes totales et dons
Tax Revenue	2 042 600	2 174 744	2 956 302	2 336 483	2 095 503	2 820 439	3 060 537	1 909 000	1 830 481	Recettes fiscales
Non Tax Revenue	202 127	344 917	265 861	271 604	55 429	28 642	491 750	111 000	111 722	Recettes non fiscales
Grants	-	-	-	-	-	-	-	-	-	Dons
Total Expenditures and Net Lending	957 464	1 236 509	1 759 224	2 827 494	2 516 843	2 767 018	4 065 898	2 396 435	2 539 153	Dépenses totales et prêts nets
Current expenditure	197 627	217 663	367 714	345 234	453 915	500 581	817 830	609 998	604 552	Dépenses courantes
Of which Wages and Salaries	40 613	52 481	56 366	70 654	77 800	79 822	99 754	105 000	118 965	Dont rémunérations et salaires
Capital expenditure	759 837	1 018 846	1 391 510	2 482 260	2 062 928	2 266 437	3 248 068	1 786 437	1 934 601	Dépenses d'équipement
Net Lending	-	-	-	-	-	-	-	-	-	Prêts nets
Fiscal Balance	1 287 263	1 283 152	1 462 939	- 219 407	- 365 911	82 063	- 513 611	- 376 435	- 596 949	Solde global y compris les dons
IX-3 BALANCE OF PAYMENTS *CFA FRANC (MILLIONS)*										**IX-3 BALANCE DES PAIEMENTS** *FRANC CFA (MILLIONS)*
Trade balance	2 539	3 096	4 594	1 509	2 319	4 092	5 140	5 344	5 167	Balance commerciale
Services Balance	- 506	- 717	- 838	- 828	- 1 031	- 1 129	- 1 542	- 1 126	- 1 048	Balance des services
Net Income	- 2 059	- 2 507	- 3 802	- 1 500	- 2 682	- 3 739	- 5 103	- 4 824	- 4 534	Revenus nets
Compensation of employees	...	...	...	...	...	...	...	...	...	Rémunération des salariés
Investment Income	...	...	...	...	...	...	...	...	...	Revenus des investissements
Current transfers, net total	- 18	- 22	- 36	- 50	- 52	- 49	- 61	- 75	- 91	Transferts courants
Net official transfers	...	...	...	...	...	...	...	...	...	Transferts officiels nets
Workers' remittances	...	...	...	...	...	...	...	...	...	Envois de fonds des travailleurs
Other private transfers	...	...	...	...	...	...	...	...	...	Autres transferts privés
Current account balance	- 44	- 150	- 82	- 868	- 1 446	- 826	- 1 567	- 681	- 506	Solde du compte courant
Capital & financial account	...	...	...	...	...	...	...	...	...	Comptes de capital et financier
Capital account	...	...	...	...	...	...	...	...	...	Compte de capital
Financial account	...	...	...	...	...	...	...	...	...	Compte financier
Errors & omissions	...	...	...	...	...	...	...	...	...	Erreurs et omissions
Overall balance	...	...	...	...	...	...	...	...	...	Balance générale

X DEBT AND FINANCIAL FLOWS - DETTE ET FLUX FINANCIERS										
	2006	2007	2008	2009	2010	2011	2012	2013	2014	
X-1 DEBT *US$ (MILLIONS)*										**X-1 DETTE EXTÉRIEURE** *$ E.U (MILLIONS)*
Total external debt	156	136	120	623	727	1 242	1 677	1 400	1 075	Dette extérieure totale
Private	1	1	1	11	16	-	-	-	-	Privée
Public	155	135	119	613	711	1 242	1 677	1 400	1 075	Publique
Total external debt service	97	37	10	20	34	19	119	398	359	Service de la dette extérieure
Present value of External debt	...	...	...	...	...	...	...	...	...	Valeur actuelle de la dette extérieure
Total government domestic debt (in local currency)	...	...	...	...	...	...	...	...	...	Dette publique intérieure
X-2 FINANCIAL FLOWS *US$ (MILLIONS)*										**X-2 FLUX FINANCIERS** *$ E.U (MILLIONS)*
Net Foreign Direct Investment Inflows	470	1 243	- 794	1 636	2 734	1 975	2 015	1 914	...	Investissement étranger direct (flux nets entrants)
Main origin of FDI Inflows										**Principales origines de l'IDE entrant:**
United States	678	- 93	- 913	56	- 88.0	40.0	269.0	...	...	États-Unis
Korea	...	...	...	...	62.4	17.4	1.7	...	...	Corée
France	30	...	...	...	...	...	...	...	...	France
Sweden	...	...	...	...	...	6.6	6.2	...	...	Suède
Luxembourg	...	...	...	...	...	...	...	...	...	Luxembourg
African countries	...	...	...	...	...	...	...	...	...	Pays africains
Net total Official Development Assistance	26	31	32	31	85	24	14	6	...	Aide publique au développement (nette totale)
Main origin of Net ODA										**Principales origines de l'APD nette**
Spain	15	20	14	22	19.7	15.4	9.3	1.8	...	Espagne
Italy	...	...	0	...	54.7	...	...	0.2	...	Italie
France	4	4	4	3	3.1	3.7	3.2	4.6	...	France
Global Fund	4	2	7	3	6.8	3.2	- 0.3	...	...	Fonds mondial
UNFPA	1	1	1	1	1.1	1.1	1.8	...	...	UNFPA

ERITREA — ÉRYTHRÉE

AREA (km²)	117 600	SUPERFICIE (km²)
CAPITAL CITY	Asmara	CAPITALE
CURRENCY	Nakfa	MONNAIE

I SOCIAL AND DEMOGRAPHIC INDICATORS — INDICATEURS DEMOGRAPHIQUES ET SOCIAUX

POPULATION	Year Année	Value Valeur	POPULATION
Population ('000)			Population ('000)
Both sexes	2014	6 536	Les deux sexes
Male	2014	3 263	Masculin
Female	2014	3 273	Féminin
Average annual growth rate	2014	2.9	Taux de croissance annuel
Active Population ('000)	2014	2 878	Population active ('000)
Population by age group ('000)			Population par groupe d'âge ('000)
0-14 years	2014	2 820	0-14 ans
15-64 years	2014	3 566	15-64 ans
65+ years	2014	150	65+ ans
Economically. active population. in agriculture (%)	2014	60.0	Participation de la population active agricole (%)
Crude birth rate	2014	36.0	Taux brut de natalité
Crude death rate	2014	6.5	Taux brut de mortalité
Total fertility rate	2014	4.6	Indice synthétique de fécondité
Proportion of urban population	2014	22.7	Part de la population urbaine
Life Expectancy at Birth - Total (years)	2014	63.4	Espérance de vie à la naissance - Totale (ans)
Dependency Ratio - Total (%)	2014	78.4	Taux de dépendance - Total (%)

Charts / Graphiques

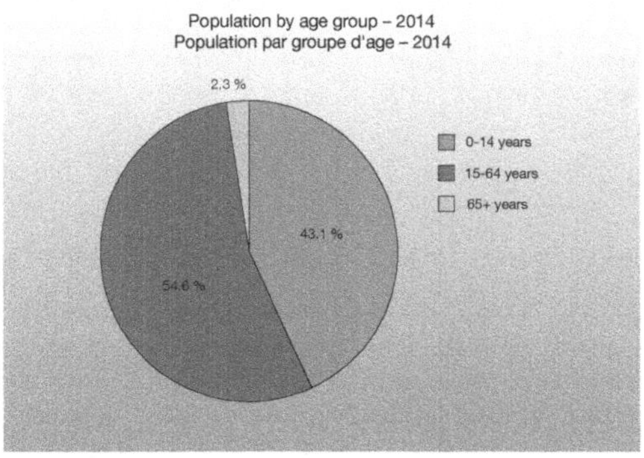

HEALTH	Year Année	Value Valeur	SANTÉ
Percentage of children under-five and underweight	2002	34.5	% d'enfants de moins de cinq ans avec insuffisance pondérale
Prevalence of undernourishment	...	...	Prévalence de la malnutrition
Under five mortality rate (both sexes, per 1000)	2013	49.9	Taux de mortalité de moins de 5 ans (les deux sexes, pour 1000)
Infant mortality rate (both sexes) per 1000	2013	36.1	Taux de mortalité infantile (les deux sexes) par 1000
Percentage of children provided the vaccines :			Pourcentage d'enfants vaccinés :
BCG	2013	97.0	BCG
DPT3	2013	94.0	DTC3
Polio	2012	99.0	Polio
Measles	2013	96.0	Rougeole
Percentage of mothers provided at least one antenatal care (%)	2002	70.0	Pourcentage de mères ayant au moins reçu un soin prénatal (%)
Percentage of deliveries attended by skilled health personnel	2002	28.3	% d'accouchements assistés par un personnel de santé qualifié
Number of doctors (per 10 000 population)	2004	0.5	Nombre de médecins (pour 10 000 habitants)
Number of nurses (per 10 000 population)	2004	5.8	Nombre d'infirmières (pour 10 000 habitants)
Hospital beds - Total (per 10 000 population)	2011	7.0	Nombre de lits d'hôpitaux - Total (pour 10 000)
Births registered (per 1 000)	2014	36.0	Naiss.s enregistrées (pour 1 000)
Deaths registered (per 1 000)	2014	6.5	Décès enregistrés (pour 1 000)
Public expenditure on Health (% of budget)	2009	3.1	Dépenses publiques consacrées à la santé (% du budget)

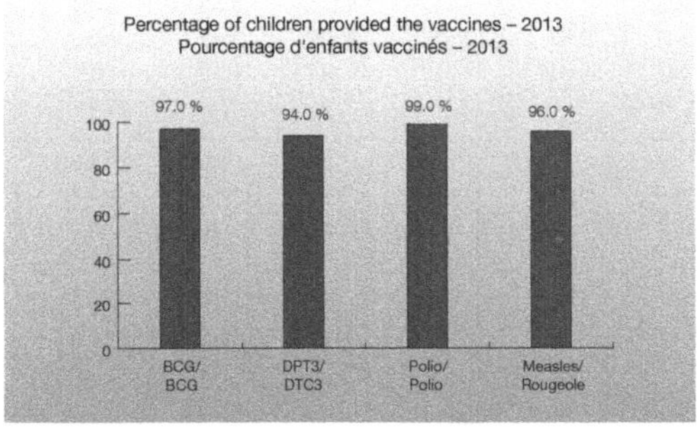

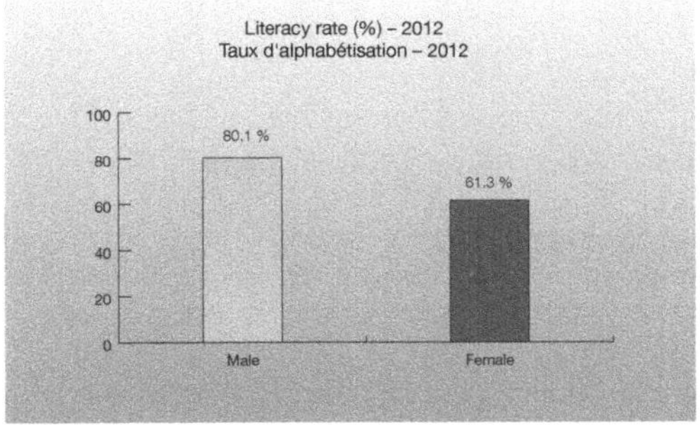

EDUCATION	Year Année	Value Valeur	EDUCATION
Enrolment in primary education (both sexes) (000)	2012	334	Scolarisation dans le primaire (les deux sexes) (000)
Female	2012	150	Féminin
Enrolment in secondary education (both sexes) (000)	2012	266	Scolarisation dans le secondaire (les deux sexes) (000)
Female	2012	116	Féminin
Enrolment in tertiary education (both sexes) (000)	...	...	Scolarisation dans le tertiaire (les deux sexes) (000)
Female	2014	4.1	Féminin
Literacy rate (both sexes)	2012	70.5	Taux d'alphabétisation (deux sexes)
Male	2012	80.1	Masculin
Female	2012	61.3	Féminin
Pupil-teacher ratio	...	...	Ratio élève-enseignant
Public expenditure on education (% of budget)	2005	5.2	Dépenses publiques consacrées à l'enseignement (% du budget)

POVERTY	Year Année	Value Valeur	PAUVRETÉ
GNI Per Capita (US$)	2013	490.0	RNB par habitant ($EU)
Human Poverty Index (HPI-1) Value (%)	2007	33.7	Valeur de l'Indice de pauvreté (IPH-1) (%)
Population below International Poverty Line ($2/day) (%)	...	...	Population sous le seuil international de pauvreté (2$/J) (%)
Share of Income Held by Richest 10%	...	...	% de revenu des 10% plus riches
Share of Income Held by Poorest 10%	...	...	% de revenu des 10% plus pauvres
Gini index	...	...	Indice de Gini

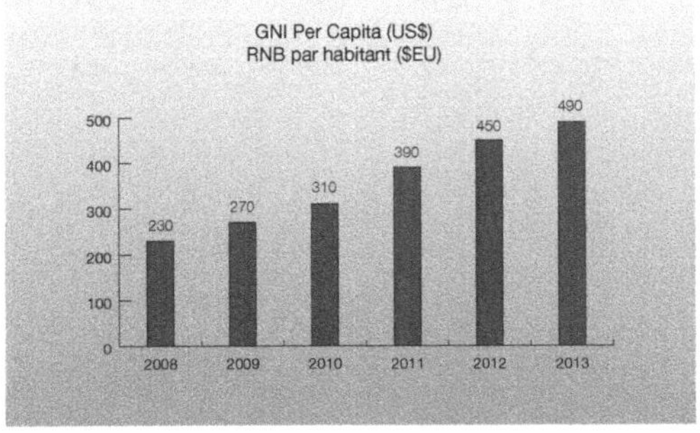

II NATIONAL ACCOUNTS — COMPTES NATIONAUX	2006	2007	2008	2009	2010	2011	2012	2013	2014	
GROSS DOMESTIC PRODUCT BY KIND OF ECONOMIC ACTIVITY AT CURRENT PRICES *NAKFA (MILLIONS)*										**PRODUIT INTÉRIEUR BRUT PAR BRANCHE D'ACTIVITÉ ÉCONOMIQUE AUX PRIX COURANTS** *NAKFA (MILLIONS)*
Agriculture, hunting, forestry and fishing	4 581	4 917	3 560	4 032	5 985	6 588	7 756	9 009	...	Agriculture, chasse, sylviculture et pêche
Mining and quarrying	229	280	415	471	541	704	803	900	...	Industries extractives
Manufacturing	1 114	1 107	1 384	1 568	1 897	2 385	2 736	3 088	...	Industries manufacturières
Electricity, gas & water	...	...	...	...	...	...	...	...	...	Electricité, gaz et eau
Construction & public works	2 036	2 502	3 700	4 190	4 824	6 273	7 154	8 018	...	Bâtiments et travaux publics
Wholesale & retail trade, restaurants, hotels	3 102	3 424	3 702	5 667	5 880	7 399	8 933	9 744	...	Commerce de gros et de détail, restaurants et hôtels
Finance, insurance, real estate, etc.	-	-	-	-	-	-	-	-	...	Banques, assurances, affaires immobilières
Transport and communications	1 987	2 193	2 371	3 629	3 766	4 739	5 721	6 241	...	Transport(s) et communications
Public administration and defense	4 495	4 948	5 348	8 195	8 498	10 694	12 913	14 084	...	Administrations publiques et défense
Education	...	...	...	...	...	...	...	...	...	Education
Health and Social Work	...	...	...	...	...	...	...	...	...	Santé et actions sociales
Other services	...	...	...	...	...	...	...	...	...	Autres services
Less Imputed Service Charges	...	...	...	...	...	...	...	...	...	Moins services d'intermédiation financière
Gross domestic product at factor cost / basic prices	17 546	19 372	20 480	27 752	31 391	38 781	46 015	51 084	...	Produit intérieur brut aux couts des facteurs / prix de base
Plus: indirect taxes / taxes on products, less subsidies	1 076	892	740	795	1 158	1 314	1 524	1 769	...	Plus taxes indirectes/impôts sur les produits, moins les subventions
EXPENDITURE ON GROSS DOMESTIC PRODUCT AT CURRENT PURCHASER'S VALUES *NAKFA (MILLIONS)*										**EMPLOI DU PRODUIT INTÉRIEUR BRUT AUX PRIX COURANTS D'ACQUISITION** *NAKFA (MILLIONS)*
Government final consumption	4 827	5 195	5 594	5 741	7 764	8 439	9 148	10 138	...	Consommation finale des administrations publiques
Private final consumption	17 106	17 165	17 534	25 561	27 799	31 167	35 601	40 689	...	Consommation finale privée
Gross fixed capital formation	2 548	2 568	2 698	2 645	3 027	4 008	4 536	4 637	...	Formation brute de capital fixe
Change in inventories	...	...	...	...	...	...	...	...	...	Variation des stocks
Exports of goods and services	1 285	1 170	940	1 293	1 559	5 764	9 080	9 028	...	Exportations de biens et services
Less imports of goods and services	7 144	5 834	5 545	6 692	7 599	9 283	10 826	11 640	...	Moins importations de biens et services
GDP at purchasers' values	18 622	20 264	21 220	28 547	32 549	40 095	47 539	52 853	...	PIB aux prix d'acquisition
GROSS DOMESTIC PRODUCT BY KIND OF ECONOMIC ACTIVITY AT CONSTANT PRICES *ANNUAL GROWTH RATES (%)*										**PRODUIT INTÉRIEUR BRUT PAR BRANCHE D'ACTIVITÉ ECONOMIQUE AUX PRIX CONSTANTS** *TAUX DE CROISSANCE ANNUEL (%)*
Agriculture, hunting, forestry and fishing	7.8	0.0	- 37.6	- 12.5	33.1	- 2.9	6.3	5.7	...	Agriculture, chasse, sylviculture et pêche
Mining and quarrying	- 11.0	13.9	27.5	- 12.4	3.1	14.7	3.0	1.9	...	Industries extractives
Manufacturing	- 13.2	- 7.4	7.7	- 12.5	8.4	10.9	3.6	2.7	...	Industries manufacturières
Electricity, gas & water	...	...	...	...	...	...	...	...	...	Electricité, gaz et eau
Construction & public works	- 11.7	14.5	27.4	- 12.5	3.2	14.7	2.9	2.0	...	Bâtiments et travaux publics
Wholesale & retail trade, restaurants, hotels	1.1	2.9	- 6.9	18.2	- 7.0	11.0	9.0	- 0.8	...	Commerce de gros et de détail, restaurants et hôtels
Finance, insurance, real estate, etc.	...	...	...	...	...	...	...	...	...	Banques, assurances, affaires immobilières
Transport and communications	1.1	2.9	- 6.9	18.2	- 7.0	11.0	9.0	- 0.8	...	Transport(s) et communications
Public administration and defense	1.7	2.6	- 6.9	18.3	- 7.1	11.0	9.0	- 0.8	...	Administrations publiques et défense
Education	...	...	...	...	...	...	...	...	...	Education
Health and Social Work	...	...	...	...	...	...	...	...	...	Santé et actions sociales
Other services	...	...	...	...	...	...	...	...	...	Autres services
Less Imputed Service Charges	...	...	...	...	...	...	...	...	...	Moins services d'intermédiation financière
Gross domestic product at factor cost / basic prices	0.0	2.9	- 8.9	4.6	1.4	9.0	7.1	1.0	...	Produit intérieur brut aux couts des facteurs / prix de base
Plus: indirect taxes / taxes on products, less subsidies	- 13.9	- 22.7	- 28.5	- 17.0	30.6	0.1	4.7	5.6	...	Plus taxes indirectes/impôts sur les produits, moins les subventions
Gross domestic product at market prices	- 1.0	1.4	- 9.8	3.9	2.2	8.7	7.0	1.1	...	Produit intérieur brut aux prix du marché
EXPENDITURE ON GROSS DOMESTIC PRODUCT AT CONSTANT PURCHASERS' VALUES *ANNUAL GROWTH RATES (%)*										**EMPLOIS DU PRODUIT INTÉRIEUR BRUT AUX PRIX CONSTANTS D'ACQUISITION** *TAUX DE CROISSANCE ANNUEL (%)*
Government final consumption	- 28.9	- 0.6	1.1	- 4.8	30.0	- 9.5	- 5.6	2.3	...	Consommation finale des administrations publiques
Private final consumption	- 5.3	- 6.9	- 12.8	12.1	- 5.0	- 6.7	- 0.8	5.5	...	Consommation finale privée
Gross fixed capital formation	- 40.0	- 12.1	- 5.7	- 13.0	7.5	14.5	2.0	- 2.3	...	Formation brute de capital fixe
Exports of goods and services	15.1	- 13.1	- 21.4	36.2	17.5	233.1	47.3	- 1.4	...	Exportations de biens et services
Less imports of goods and services	- 38.8	- 29.8	- 10.0	20.5	11.3	10.6	9.5	7.1	...	Moins importations de biens et services

III INFLATION	2006	2007	2008	2009	2010	2011	2012	2013	2014	
ANNUAL GROWTH RATES (%)										**TAUX DE CROISSANCE ANNUEL (%)**
All items	15.1	9.3	19.9	34.7	20.5	13.3	12.3	12.3	11.4	Ensemble
of which:										dont:
Food and Non-alcoholic beverages	...	...	...	...	...	...	...	...	...	Alimentation et boissons non alcoolisés
Alcoholic beverages & tobacco	...	...	...	...	...	...	...	...	...	Boissons alcoolisées et tabacs
Clothing and Footwear	...	...	...	...	...	...	...	...	...	Habillement et chaussures
Housing, Water, Electricity, Gas and Other Fuels	...	...	...	...	...	...	...	...	...	Logement, eau, electricité, gas et autres combustibles
Furnishing, household equipment	...	...	...	...	...	...	...	...	...	Meubles, articles de ménage et entretien courant
Health	...	...	...	...	...	...	...	...	...	Santé
Transport	...	...	...	...	...	...	...	...	...	Transport
Communication	...	...	...	...	...	...	...	...	...	Communication
Recreation & culture	...	...	...	...	...	...	...	...	...	Loisirs et culture
Education	...	...	...	...	...	...	...	...	...	Enseignement
Restaurants & hotels	...	...	...	...	...	...	...	...	...	Restaurants et hôtels
Miscellaneous goods & services	...	...	...	...	...	...	...	...	...	Biens et services divers

	2006	2007	2008	2009	2010	2011	2012	2013	2014	
IV AGRICULTURAL PRODUCTION - PRODUCTION AGRICOLE										
TONNES *(THOUSAND)*										**TONNES** *(MILLIERS)*
Sorghum	222	303	68	59	64	75	80	80	...	Sorgho
Barley	52	39	6	65	67	65	70	65	...	Orge
Wheat	22	27	5	26	33	29	33	30	...	Blé
Millet	33	63	12	17	17	20	20	20	...	Millet
Sesame seed	6	11	1	0	0	0	0	0	...	Graine de sésame
V MINING PRODUCTION - PRODUCTION MINIERE	2006	2007	2008	2009	2010	2011	2012	2013	2014	
Gold ores and concentrates, Kilograms	...	87	30	30	50	12	...	...	...	Minerais d'or et concentrés (Kilogrammes)
Salt and pure sodium chloride, metric tons (thousands)	...	7	8	8	8	8	...	...	...	Sel et chorure de sodium pur, tonnes métriques (milliers)
	...	...	...	...	...	...	...	...	...	
VI ENERGY - ENERGIE	2006	2007	2008	2009	2010	2011	2012	2013	2014	
Total electricity generation (GWh)	268	288	287	295	311	339	387	404	...	Production d'électricité totale (GWh)
of which:										dont:
Production of electricity from fossil fuels (GWh)	267	286	285	293	309	335	383	398	...	Production d'électricité à partir de combustibles fossiles (GWh)
Production of hydro electricity (GWh)	...	...	...	...	...	...	...	...	...	Production d'électricité d'origine hydraulique (GWh)
Production of electricity from solar, wind, tide, wave and other sources (GWh)	1	2	2	2	2	4	4	6	...	Production d'électricité d'origine solaire, éolienne, marée motrice et autres (GWh)
VII TOURISM AND INFRASTRUCTURE - TOURISME ET INFRASTRUCTURE	2006	2007	2008	2009	2010	2011	2012	2013	2014	
VII-1 TOURISM										**VII-1 TOURISME**
International tourist arrivals (thousands)	78	81	70	79	...	...	...	...	...	Arrivées de touristes internationaux (milliers)
Rooms in hotels and similar establishments (thousands)	5	...	...	...	...	...	...	...	...	Chambres d'hotels et établissements assimilés (milliers)
Overnight stays (thousands)	...	...	...	...	...	...	...	...	...	Nuitées (milliers)
Tourism receipts (US$ thousand)	...	...	...	...	...	...	...	...	...	Recettes touristiques (milliers de $ EU)
Total contribution to GDP (%)	...	...	...	...	...	...	...	...	...	Contribution totale au PIB (%)
Total contribution to Employment (%)	...	...	...	...	...	...	...	...	...	Contribution totale à l'emploi (%)
VII-2 INFRASTRUCTURE										**VII-2 INFRASTRUCTURE**
Paved roads (% of total)	...	...	...	...	...	...	...	...	...	Routes asphaltées (% du total)
Total Network (Railways-km)	...	...	...	...	...	...	...	...	...	Réseau total voies ferrées-Km
Main Telephone Lines (per 100 inhabitants)	1	1	1	1	1	1	1	1	...	Lignes téléphoniques fixes (pour 100 habitants)
Mobile Cellular Subscribers (per 100 inhabitants)	1	2	2	3	3	4	5	6	...	Abonnés aux téléphones mobiles (pour 100 habitants)
VIII EXTERNAL TRADE - COMMERCE EXTERIEUR	2006	2007	2008	2009	2010	2011	2012	2013	2014	
US$ (MILLIONS) **EXPORTS, FOB**										**$ E.U (MILLIONS)** **EXPORTATIONS, FÀB**
Exports - Total	13	14	14	19	23	26	47	46	60	Exportations - Total
Exports to AFRICA	...	...	...	...	...	...	...	...	...	Exportations vers l'AFRIQUE
Main Products										**Principaux produits**
Gold, non-monetary (excluding gold ores and concentrates)	...	...	...	...	...	...	...	...	...	Or, à usage non monétaire
Leather	1	1	1	1	1	3	...	...	...	Cuirs et peaux préparés
Radioactive and associated materials	...	6	...	0	0	5	...	...	...	Matières radioactives et produits associés
Oil seeds and oleaginous fruits (excluding flour)	0	1	1	0	0	1	...	...	...	Graines et fruits oléagineux (sauf farines)
Live animals other than animals of division 03	0	0	1	1	1	9	...	...	...	Animaux vivants autres que ceux aquatiques
Main Destinations										**Principales destinations**
Canada	...	...	...	...	...	...	...	...	...	Canada
Italy	...	...	...	...	...	...	...	...	...	Italie
Germany	...	...	...	...	...	...	...	...	...	Allemagne
India	...	...	...	...	...	...	...	...	...	Inde
Saudi Arabia	...	...	...	...	...	...	...	...	...	Arabie saoudite
IMPORTS, CIF										**IMPORTATIONS, CAF**
Imports - Total	367	333	318	389	438	530	610	650	810	Importations - Total (millions)
Imports from Africa	...	...	...	...	...	...	...	...	...	Importations en provenance de l'Afrique
Main Products										**Principaux produits**
Cereals and cereal preparations	68	101	91	57	92	98	...	...	...	Céréales et préparations à base de céréales
Sugar, sugar preparations and honey	27	32	37	62	77	42	...	...	...	Sucres, préparations à base de sucre, et miel
Specialised machinery	31	29	34	33	26	108	...	...	...	Machines et appareils spécialisés
Road vehicles	29	23	33	33	32	105	...	...	...	Véhicules routiers
Petroleum, petroleum products and related materials	18	61	25	33	21	14	...	...	...	Pétrole et produits dérivés
Main Origin										**Principales provenances**
Saudi Arabia	68	56	130	78	88	127	150	...	...	Arabie saoudite
China	79	42	56	66	58	246	96	...	...	Chine
Italy	80	58	71	67	37	58	96	...	...	Italie
India	15	142	67	13	65	37	53	...	...	Inde
Egypt	2	1	28	61	85	100	117	...	...	Égypte

IX FINANCIAL AND MONETARY STATISTICS - FINANCES ET STATISTIQUES MONETAIRES										
	2006	2007	2008	2009	2010	2011	2012	2013	2014	
IX-1 MONETARY STATISTICS *NAKFA (MILLIONS)*										**IX-1 STATISTIQUES MONÉTAIRES** *NAKFA (MILLIONS)*
Money supply (M1)	23 080	25 870	29 980	34 700	40 120	45 990	52 480	60 780	69 410	Masse monétaire (M1)
Quasi-money	12 211	13 159	14 656	17 397	20 388	23 635	26 444	30 279	28 489	Quasi-monnaie
of which Demand Deposit	...	...	...	...	...	...	...	...	...	dont Monnaie scripturale
Net foreign assets	2 747	2 488	2 898	4 031	5 744	7 017	8 253	8 158	8 719	Avoirs extérieurs nets
Domestic credit	23 175	24 548	28 669	32 293	37 224	41 679	46 641	56 074	58 547	Crédit intérieur
of which claims on private sector	4 839	4 202	4 681	4 787	5 201	5 577	6 665	15 307	18 755	dont créances sur le secteur privé
of which claims on government sector, net	17 743	19 778	23 391	26 949	31 328	35 400	39 283	40 040	39 152	dont créances nettes sur le gouvernement
International reserves (millions US$)	25	34	58	90	114	115	...	...	...	Réserves internationales (millions $EU)
Average Exchange Rate (National Currency per US$)	15.38	15.38	15.38	15.38	15.38	15.38	15.38	15.38	15.38	Taux de change (moyen) (monnaie nationale par $ EU)
IX-2 PUBLIC FINANCE *NAKFA*										**IX-2 FINANCES PUBLIQUES** *NAKFA*
Total Revenues and Grants	...	...	...	...	...	...	...	...	...	Recettes totales et dons
Tax Revenue	...	...	...	...	...	...	...	...	...	Recettes fiscales
Non Tax Revenue	...	...	...	...	...	...	...	...	...	Recettes non fiscales
Grants	...	...	...	...	...	...	...	...	...	Dons
Total Expenditures and Net Lending	...	...	...	...	...	...	...	...	...	Dépenses totales et prêts nets
Current expenditure	...	...	...	...	...	...	...	...	...	Dépenses courantes
Of which Wages and Salaries	...	...	...	...	...	...	...	...	...	Dont rémunérations et salaires
Capital expenditure	...	...	...	...	...	...	...	...	...	Dépenses d'équipement
Net Lending	...	...	...	...	...	...	...	...	...	Prêts nets
Fiscal Balance	...	...	...	...	...	...	...	...	...	Solde global y compris les dons
IX-3 BALANCE OF PAYMENTS *NAKFA (MILLIONS)*										**IX-3 BALANCE DES PAIEMENTS** *NAKFA (MILLIONS)*
Trade balance	- 5 442	- 4 902	- 4 671	- 5 691	- 6 377	- 4 141	- 2 240	...	...	Balance commerciale
Services Balance	- 416	238	65	292	337	620	431	...	...	Balance des services
Net Income	- 134	- 111	- 181	- 248	- 302	- 455	- 622	...	...	Revenus nets
Compensation of employees	...	...	...	...	...	...	...	...	...	Rémunération des salariés
Investment Income	...	...	...	...	...	...	...	...	...	Revenus des investissements
Current transfers, net total	5 325	3 537	3 626	3 474	4 512	4 196	3 451	...	...	Transferts courants
Net official transfers	768	628	604	737	1 707	1 275	560	...	...	Transferts officiels nets
Workers' remittances	...	...	...	...	...	...	...	...	...	Envois de fonds des travailleurs
Other private transfers	...	...	...	...	...	...	...	...	...	Autres transferts privés
Current account balance	- 667	- 1 238	- 1 160	- 2 174	- 1 830	220	1 021	...	...	Solde du compte courant
Capital & financial account	...	...	...	...	...	...	...	...	...	Comptes de capital et financier
Capital account	...	...	...	...	...	...	...	...	...	Compte de capital
Financial account	...	...	...	...	...	...	...	...	...	Compte financier
Errors & omissions	...	...	...	...	...	...	...	...	...	Erreurs et omissions
Overall balance	...	...	...	...	...	...	...	...	...	Balance générale

X DEBT AND FINANCIAL FLOWS - DETTE ET FLUX FINANCIERS										
	2006	2007	2008	2009	2010	2011	2012	2013	2014	
X-1 DEBT *US$ (MILLIONS)*										**X-1 DETTE EXTÉRIEURE** *$ E.U (MILLIONS)*
Total external debt	702	764	855	912	969	935	900	883	894	Dette extérieure totale
Private	-	-	-	-	-	-	-	-	-	Privée
Public	702	764	855	912	969	935	900	883	894	Publique
Total external debt service	25	27	28	30	34	49	49	49	50	Service de la dette extérieure
Present value of External debt	...	...	...	...	...	...	...	...	...	Valeur actuelle de la dette extérieure
Total government domestic debt (in local currency)	...	...	...	...	...	...	...	...	...	Dette publique intérieure
X-2 FINANCIAL FLOWS *US$ (MILLIONS)*										**X-2 FLUX FINANCIERS** *$ E.U (MILLIONS)*
Net Foreign Direct Investment Inflows	15	7	39	91	91	39	41	44	...	Investissement étranger direct (flux nets entrants)
Main origin of FDI Inflows										**Principales origines de l'IDE entrant:**
Italy	...	...	21	- 15	- 0.8	0.6	- 1.7	...	...	Italie
Germany	...	...	...	...	2.6	...	...	...	...	Allemagne
Netherlands	...	...	...	...	...	...	...	...	...	Pays-Bas
Poland	...	...	...	...	...	...	...	...	...	Pologne
Belgium	...	...	...	...	...	...	...	...	...	Belgique
African countries	...	...	...	...	...	...	...	...	...	Pays africains
Net total Official Development Assistance	126	158	143	144	161	130	134	84	...	Aide publique au développement (nette totale)
Main origin of Net ODA										**Principales origines de l'APD nette**
United States	7	2	3	4	0.9	0.1	0.2	0.2	...	Etats-Unis
IDA	24	32	30	5	1.4	12.4	1.1	...	...	IDA
Norway	18	10	9	10	9.6	8.1	3.2	0.0	...	Norvège
Italy	4	2	2	1	0.2	1.9	0.5	1.9	...	Italie
Global Fund	6	11	15	13	41.1	14.1	28.2	...	...	Fonds mondial

ETHIOPIA — ÉTHIOPIE

AREA (km²)	1 104 300		SUPERFICIE (km²)
CAPITAL CITY	Addis Ababa	Addis-Abeba	CAPITALE
CURRENCY	Ethiopian Birr	Birr Éthiopien	MONNAIE

I SOCIAL AND DEMOGRAPHIC INDICATORS – INDICATEURS DEMOGRAPHIQUES ET SOCIAUX

	Year / Année	Value / Valeur	
POPULATION			**POPULATION**
Population ('000)			Population ('000)
Both sexes	2014	96 506	Les deux sexes
Male	2014	48 276	Masculin
Female	2014	48 230	Féminin
Average annual growth rate	2014	2.5	Taux de croissance annuel
Active Population ('000)	2014	44 659	Population active ('000)
Population by age group ('000)			Population par groupe d'âge ('000)
0-14 years	2014	40 588	0-14 ans
15-64 years	2014	52 583	15-64 ans
65+ years	2014	3 335	65+ ans
Economically. active population. in agriculture (%)	2014	77.4	Participation de la population active agricole (%)
Crude birth rate	2014	32.5	Taux brut de natalité
Crude death rate	2014	7.3	Taux brut de mortalité
Total fertility rate	2014	4.4	Indice synthétique de fécondité
Proportion of urban population	2014	17.8	Part de la population urbaine
Life Expectancy at Birth - Total (years)	2014	64.2	Espérance de vie à la naissance - Totale (ans)
Dependency Ratio - Total (%)	2014	73.5	Taux de dépendance - Total (%)
HEALTH			**SANTÉ**
Percentage of children under-five and underweight	2011	29.2	% d'enfants de moins de cinq ans avec insuffisance pondérale
Prevalence of undernourishment	2013	35.0	Prévalence de la malnutrition
Under five mortality rate (both sexes, per 1000)	2013	64.4	Taux de mortalité de moins de 5 ans (les deux sexes, pour 1000)
Infant mortality rate (both sexes) per 1000	2013	44.4	Taux de mortalité infantile (les deux sexes) par 1000
Percentage of children provided the vaccines :			Pourcentage d'enfants vaccinés :
BCG	2013	71.0	BCG
DPT3	2013	72.0	DTC3
Polio	2011	62.0	Polio
Measles	2013	62.0	Rougeole
Percentage of mothers provided at least one antenatal care (%)	2011	33.9	Pourcentage de mères ayant au moins reçu un soin prénatal (%)
Percentage of deliveries attended by skilled health personnel	2011	10.0	% d'accouchements assistés par un personnel de santé qualifié
Number of doctors (per 10 000 population)	2009	0.3	Nombre de médecins (pour 10 000 habitants)
Number of nurses (per 10 000 population)	2009	2.5	Nombre d'infirmières (pour 10 000 habitants)
Hospital beds - Total (per 10 000 population)	2011	63.0	Nombre de lits d'hôpitaux - Total (pour 10 000)
Births registered (per 1 000)	2014	32.5	Naiss.s enregistrées (pour 1 000)
Deaths registered (per 1 000)	2014	7.3	Décès enregistrés (pour 1 000)
Public expenditure on Health (% of budget)	2009	11.4	Dépenses publiques consacrées à la santé (% du budget)
EDUCATION			**EDUCATION**
Enrolment in primary education (both sexes) (000)	2012	14 532	Scolarisation dans le primaire (les deux sexes) (000)
Female	2012	6 920	Féminin
Enrolment in secondary education (both sexes) (000)	2012	4 736	Scolarisation dans le secondaire (les deux sexes) (000)
Female	2012	2 231	Féminin
Enrolment in tertiary education (both sexes) (000)	2013	584.0	Scolarisation dans le tertiaire (les deux sexes) (000)
Female	2012	218.2	Féminin
Literacy rate (both sexes)	2007	39.0	Taux d'alphabétisation (deux sexes)
Male	2007	49.1	Masculin
Female	2007	28.9	Féminin
Pupil-teacher ratio	2011	55.1	Ratio élève-enseignant
Public expenditure on education (% of budget)	2013	25.2	Dépenses publiques consacrées à l'enseignement (% du budget)
POVERTY			**PAUVRETÉ**
GNI Per Capita (US$)	2013	470.0	RNB par habitant ($EU)
Human Poverty Index (HPI-1) Value (%)	2007	50.9	Valeur de l'Indice de pauvreté (IPH-1) (%)
Population below International Poverty Line ($2/day) (%)	2011	72.2	Population sous le seuil international de pauvreté (2$/J) (%)
Share of Income Held by Richest 10%	2011	27.5	% de revenu des 10% plus riches
Share of Income Held by Poorest 10%	2011	3.2	% de revenu des 10% plus pauvres
Gini index	2011	33.6	Indice de Gini

Charts / Graphiques

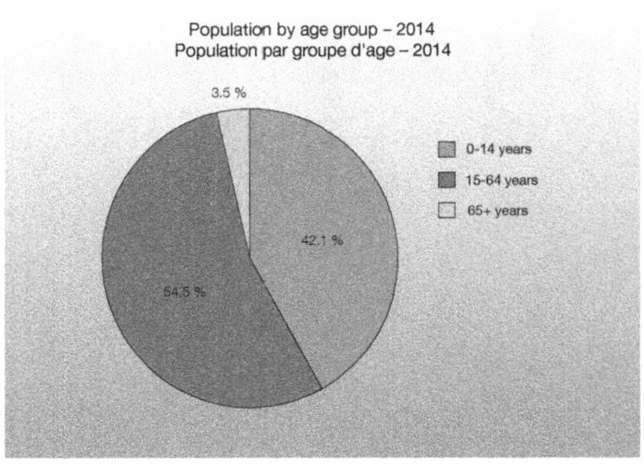

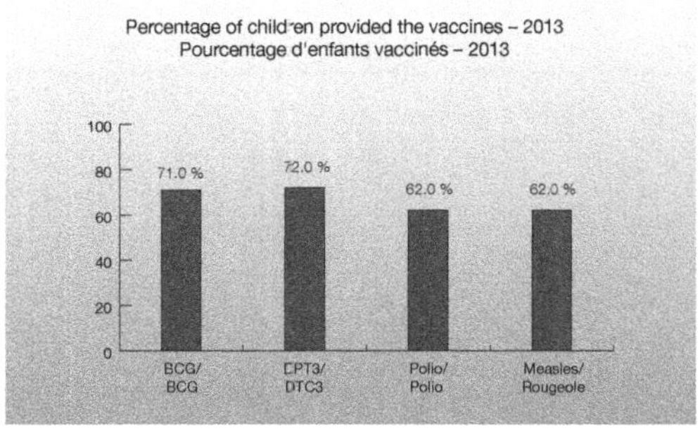

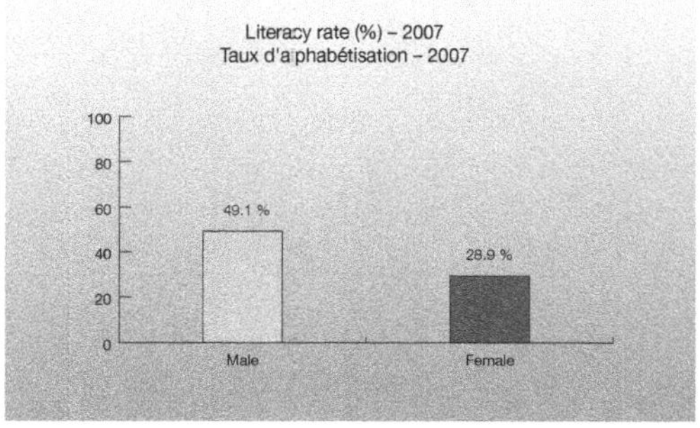

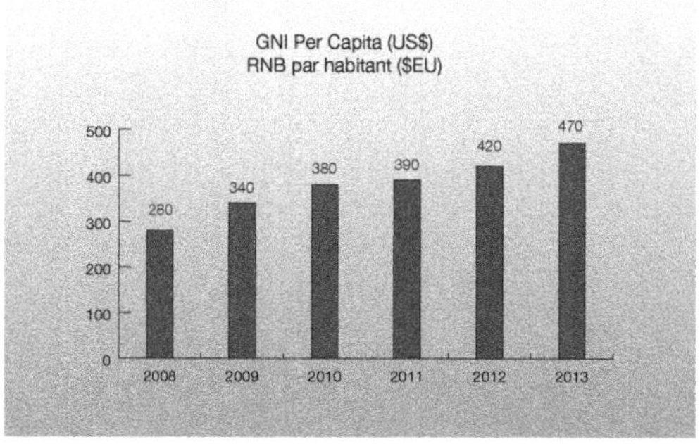

II NATIONAL ACCOUNTS — COMPTES NATIONAUX	2006	2007	2008	2009	2010	2011	2012	2013	2014	
GROSS DOMESTIC PRODUCT BY KIND OF ECONOMIC ACTIVITY AT CURRENT PRICES *ETHIOPIAN BIRR (MILLIONS)*										**PRODUIT INTÉRIEUR BRUT PAR BRANCHE D'ACTIVITÉ ÉCONOMIQUE AUX PRIX COURANTS** *BIRR ÉTHIOPIEN (MILLIONS)*
Agriculture, hunting, forestry and fishing	58 431	75 875	117 108	160 627	165 668	212 470	331 297	357 514	408 610	Agriculture, chasse, sylviculture et pêche
Mining and quarrying	676	636	944	1 270	2 475	6 810	9 301	9 687	9 955	Industries extractives
Manufacturing	5 533	7 136	9 251	11 813	14 467	18 968	25 559	32 095	40 223	Industries manufacturières
Electricity, gas & water	2 316	3 136	3 481	3 717	4 457	4 902	6 187	7 355	7 740	Electricité, gaz et eau
Construction & public works	6 921	9 269	12 000	16 074	15 882	19 100	29 771	45 744	91 041	Bâtiments et travaux publics
Wholesale & retail trade, restaurants, hotels	18 177	25 474	36 913	56 629	66 432	87 937	126 427	145 478	180 999	Commerce de gros et de détail, restaurants et hôtels
Finance, insurance, real estate, etc.	11 328	16 050	23 596	30 068	42 947	55 992	70 576	83 850	95 687	Banques, assurances, affaires immobilières
Transport and communications	6 863	7 928	9 350	12 766	15 967	19 891	29 721	38 608	45 702	Transport(s) et communications
Public administration and defense	5 447	6 343	8 370	10 320	11 577	25 736	29 274	34 546	39 681	Administrations publiques et défense
Education	3 793	4 831	6 516	7 390	8 841	10 772	13 283	16 415	19 827	Education
Health and Social Work	1 070	1 304	1 733	2 085	2 422	4 132	4 999	6 125	7 704	Santé et actions sociales
Other services	2 395	3 024	4 215	6 026	6 659	12 157	17 915	24 521	27 500	Autres services
Less Imputed Service Charges	- 1 007	- 1 200	- 1 657	- 2 544	- 2 843	- 3 219	- 3 864	- 7 918	- 9 259	Moins services d'intermédiation financière
Gross domestic product at factor cost / basic prices	121 943	159 803	231 820	316 241	354 952	475 648	690 444	794 019	965 408	Produit intérieur brut aux couts des facteurs / prix de base
Plus: indirect taxes / taxes on products, less subsidies	9 698	12 186	16 785	19 139	28 412	39 431	56 882	70 654	81 985	Plus taxes indirectes/impôts sur les produits, moins les subventions
EXPENDITURE ON GROSS DOMESTIC PRODUCT AT CURRENT PURCHASER'S VALUES *ETHIOPIAN BIRR (MILLIONS)*										**EMPLOI DU PRODUIT INTÉRIEUR BRUT AUX PRIX COURANTS D'ACQUISITION** *BIRR ÉTHIOPIEN (MILLIONS)*
Government final consumption	16 080	18 072	24 364	29 810	32 888	53 147	62 045	71 704	83 305	Consommation finale des administrations publiques
Private final consumption	112 272	149 108	216 976	290 436	330 131	373 089	541 536	626 774	728 373	Consommation finale privée
Gross fixed capital formation	33 176	38 044	55 512	76 185	94 497	165 380	277 244	309 527	421 786	Formation brute de capital fixe
Change in inventories	...	...	...	...	...	...	...	...	...	Variation des stocks
Exports of goods and services	18 205	21 854	28 317	35 233	52 168	85 950	102 887	107 969	122 632	Exportations de biens et services
Less imports of goods and services	48 092	55 088	76 564	96 285	126 319	162 487	236 385	251 301	308 703	Moins importations de biens et services
GDP at purchasers' values	131 641	171 989	248 605	335 380	383 364	515 079	747 326	864 673	1 047 393	PIB aux prix d'acquisition
GROSS DOMESTIC PRODUCT BY KIND OF ECONOMIC ACTIVITY AT CONSTANT PRICES *ANNUAL GROWTH RATES (%)*										**PRODUIT INTÉRIEUR BRUT PAR BRANCHE D'ACTIVITÉ ECONOMIQUE AUX PRIX CONSTANTS** *TAUX DE CROISSANCE ANNUEL (%)*
Agriculture, hunting, forestry and fishing	10.9	9.4	7.5	6.4	7.6	9.0	4.9	7.1	5.4	Agriculture, chasse, sylviculture et pêche
Mining and quarrying	7.2	- 15.4	21.4	12.8	44.2	57.7	12.7	6.3	- 3.4	Industries extractives
Manufacturing	10.6	8.3	10.3	9.1	10.0	12.1	11.8	16.9	11.3	Industries manufacturières
Electricity, gas & water	8.8	13.6	4.8	5.0	5.1	19.1	13.5	10.0	7.5	Electricité, gaz et eau
Construction & public works	10.5	10.9	11.3	11.7	10.9	12.8	31.5	38.7	36.4	Bâtiments et travaux publics
Wholesale & retail trade, restaurants, hotels	17.9	18.5	17.2	14.0	11.7	10.0	12.0	11.8	17.2	Commerce de gros et de détail, restaurants et hôtels
Finance, insurance, real estate, etc.	17.2	15.2	19.6	16.0	18.5	22.4	8.0	0.9	7.0	Banques, assurances, affaires immobilières
Transport and communications	5.7	9.3	11.5	8.9	13.8	9.7	12.6	15.2	13.7	Transport(s) et communications
Public administration and defense	6.4	11.8	12.5	18.4	3.4	9.4	3.1	6.5	5.0	Administrations publiques et défense
Education	8.6	21.2	14.8	13.0	17.0	9.4	4.5	10.6	11.8	Education
Health and Social Work	9.8	15.8	15.5	19.3	8.3	9.4	9.4	7.4	12.0	Santé et actions sociales
Other services	8.8	7.9	10.9	6.1	7.5	4.9	12.7	17.4	3.6	Autres services
Less Imputed Service Charges	40.3	13.5	30.0	12.5	8.7	11.1	- 10.6	22.2	19.2	Moins services d'intermédiation financière
Gross domestic product at factor cost / basic prices	11.5	11.8	11.2	10.0	10.4	11.4	8.7	9.8	10.3	Produit intérieur brut aux couts des facteurs / prix de base
Plus: indirect taxes / taxes on products, less subsidies	2.7	7.2	5.6	- 8.3	45.4	8.6	8.0	18.6	5.3	Plus taxes indirectes/impôts sur les produits, moins les subventions
Gross domestic product at market prices	10.8	11.5	10.8	8.8	12.4	11.2	8.6	10.5	9.9	Produit intérieur brut aux prix du marché
EXPENDITURE ON GROSS DOMESTIC PRODUCT AT CONSTANT PURCHASERS' VALUES *ANNUAL GROWTH RATES (%)*										**EMPLOIS DU PRODUIT INTÉRIEUR BRUT AUX PRIX CONSTANTS D'ACQUISITION** *TAUX DE CROISSANCE ANNUEL (%)*
Government final consumption	9.0	- 4.2	4.4	- 9.0	12.6	11.2	8.5	...	...	Consommation finale des administrations publiques
Private final consumption	12.5	8.6	16.7	7.3	12.4	11.2	8.7	...	...	Consommation finale privée
Gross fixed capital formation	16.6	14.2	- 5.3	15.0	12.6	11.2	8.5	...	...	Formation brute de capital fixe
Exports of goods and services	1.3	2.6	0.3	- 0.7	12.6	11.2	8.5	...	...	Exportations de biens et services
Less imports of goods and services	14.0	- 2.0	7.7	- 0.3	12.6	11.2	8.5	...	...	Moins importations de biens et services
Notes	National accounts:The accounts are based on fiscal year. Break in the serie from 2011.				Comptes Nationaux: Les comptes sont exprimés en années fiscales. Rupture dans la série à partir de 2011.					Notes

III INFLATION	2006	2007	2008	2009	2010	2011	2012	2013	2014	
ANNUAL GROWTH RATES (%)										**TAUX DE CROISSANCE ANNUEL (%)**
All items	12.3	17.0	25.5	36.4	2.8	33.2	23.0	7.7	7.4	Ensemble
of which:										dont:
Food and Non-alcoholic beverages	20.1	17.3	44.8	9.1	13.5	23.8	25.9	5.1	5.4	Alimentation et boissons non alcoolisés
Alcoholic beverages & tobacco	...	...	...	...	...	30.5	6.3	13.1	15.5	Boissons alcoolisées et tabacs
Clothing and Footwear	...	...	...	...	...	33.4	28.9	12.0	10.3	Habillement et chaussures
Housing, Water, Electricity, Gas and Other Fuels	23.5	16.1	27.0	18.6	23.3	20.7	15.4	12.0	11.0	Logement, eau, electricité, gas et autres combustibles
Furnishing, household equipment	...	...	...	...	...	25.5	26.6	12.8	8.8	Meubles, articles de ménage et entretien courant
Health	1.1	10.2	12.9	20.4	11.5	11.4	15.1	20.5	12.0	Santé
Transport	24.1	11.4	9.2	27.1	20.8	35.6	2.6	-2.7	3.7	Transport
Communication	...	...	...	...	...	...	...	0.0	0.0	Communication
Recreation & culture	...	...	...	...	...	36.8	22.0	10.8	1.1	Loisirs et culture
Education	...	...	...	...	...	25.4	15.2	4.1	0.8	Enseignement
Restaurants & hotels	...	...	...	...	...	...	...	10.2	8.2	Restaurants et hôtels
Miscellaneous goods & services	...	...	...	...	...	12.2	17.1	10.1	3.4	Biens et services divers

IV AGRICULTURAL PRODUCTION - PRODUCTION AGRICOLE	2006	2007	2008	2009	2010	2011	2012	2013	2014	
TONNES *(THOUSAND)*										**TONNES** *(MILLIERS)*
Maize	4 030	3 337	3 776	3 897	4 986	6 069	6 158	6 674	...	Mais
Sorghum	2 174	2 316	2 659	2 971	3 960	3 951	3 604	4 338	...	Sorgho
Wheat	2 219	2 463	2 314	3 076	2 856	2 916	3 435	4 039	...	Blé
Barley	1 410	1 271	1 352	1 750	1 703	1 585	1 782	1 933	...	Orge
Coffee, green	241	273	260	265	371	377	276	270	...	Graine de café

V MINING PRODUCTION - PRODUCTION MINIERE	2006	2007	2008	2009	2010	2011	2012	2013	2014	
Gold ores and concentrates, Kilograms	...	4 368	3 465	6 251	5 936	10 700	...	...	...	Minerais et concentrés d'or, Kilogrammes
Silver ores and concentrates, Kilograms	109 000	707	1 026	1 400	1 400	1 400	...	...	...	Minerais d'argent et concentrés, Kilogrammes
Tantalum, Ton	1	1	1	1	...	...	...	...	...	Tantale, Ton

VI ENERGY - ENERGIE	2006	2007	2008	2009	2010	2011	2012	2013	2014	
Total electricity generation (GWh)	3 332	3 532	3 728	3 982	4 931	7 308	7 567	8 461	...	Production d'électricité totale (GWh)
of which:										dont:
Production of electricity from fossil fuels (GWh)	40	162	418	434	31	564	564	564	...	Production d'électricité à partir de combustibles fossiles (GWh)
Production of hydro electricity (GWh)	3 292	3 370	3 296	3 524	4 882	6 485	6 485	7 306	...	Production d'électricité d'origine hydraulique (GWh)
Production of electricity from solar, wind, tide, wave and other sources (GWh)	...	...	...	...	...	126	294	489	...	Production d'électricité d'origine solaire, éolienne, marée motrice et autres (GWh)

VII TOURISM AND INFRASTRUCTURE - TOURISME ET INFRASTRUCTURE	2006	2007	2008	2009	2010	2011	2012	2013	2014	
VII-1 TOURISM										**VII-1 TOURISME**
International tourist arrivals (thousands)	330	358	383	427	468	523	596	659	693	Arrivées de touristes internationaux (milliers)
Rooms in hotels and similar establishments (thousands)	...	...	...	...	...	...	...	...	...	Chambres d'hotels et établissements assimilés (milliers)
Overnight stays (thousands)	1 305	1 018	1 075	1 391	1 577	1 771	1 966	2 198	2 331	Nuitées (milliers)
Tourism receipts (US$ thousand)	161 125	175 300	355 400	316 500	519 200	750 700	604 300	664 452	709 903	Recettes touristiques (milliers de $ EU)
Total contribution to GDP (%)	10.7	11.4	10.4	9.2	11.1	12.5	9.8	9.5	9.6	Contribution totale au PIB (%)
Total contribution to Employment (%)	9.4	9.9	9.0	8.1	9.8	10.7	9.1	8.7	8.8	Contribution totale à l'emploi (%)
VII-2 INFRASTRUCTURE										**VII-2 INFRASTRUCTURE**
Paved roads (% of total)	12	14	11	12	14	13	13	13	12	Routes asphaltées (% du total)
Total Network (Railways-km)	781	781	781	781	781	...	...	...	...	Réseau total voies ferrées-Km
Main Telephone Lines (per 100 inhabitants)	1	1	1	1	1	1	1	1	1	Lignes téléphoniques fixes (pour 100 habitants)
Mobile Cellular Subscribers (per 100 inhabitants)	1	2	2	5	8	16	22	27	33	Abonnés aux téléphones mobiles (pour 100 habitants)

VIII EXTERNAL TRADE - COMMERCE EXTERIEUR	2006	2007	2008	2009	2010	2011	2012	2013	2014	
ETHIOPIAN BIRR (MILLIONS) EXPORTS, FOB										**BIRR ÉTHIOPIEN (MILLIONS) EXPORTATIONS, FÀB**
Exports - Total	...	16 354	22 851	27 124	47 120	61 939	71 742	75 279	105 023	Exportations - Total
Exports to AFRICA	...	3 181	3 883	5 978	13 487	16 389	17 949	20 096	21 685	Exportations vers l'AFRIQUE
Main Products										**Principaux produits**
Coffee, not roasted or decaffeinated	29	5 804	8 708	6 469	14 228	18 392	...	14 228	...	Café non torréfié ou décaféiné
Sesame seeds	...	1 490	2 705	4 789	5 546	6 347	...	9 136	...	graines de sésame
Fresh chat	...	...	1 560	3 778	6 651	5 337	...	10 317	...	Frais de chat
Roses	...	250	1 964	3 562	4 937	6 682	...	8 908	...	Roses
Semi-manufactured gold (incl. gold plated with platinum), non-monetary	...	312	769	1 075	2 570	2 100	...	2 905	...	Produits semi-ouvrés d'or (y compris l'or platiné), non monétaire
Main Destinations										**Principales destinations**
Germany	...	1 920	2 978	2 563	5 938	7 389	8 075	4 834	5 935	Allemagne
Somalia	...	1 307	1 495	3 144	6 357	8 147	9 235	12 022	13 107	Somalie
Netherlands	...	1 367	2 268	3 595	5 010	7 069	8 831	8 678	9 759	Pays-Bas
China	...	743	980	3 359	4 240	5 071	6 094	6 076	9 881	Chine
Saudi Arabia	...	1 099	1 588	1 859	2 775	3 508	4 581	7 303	10 599	Arabie saoudite
IMPORTS, CIF										**IMPORTATIONS, CAF**
Imports - Total	46 583	52 486	82 959	94 482	124 919	161 671	253 020	275 331	406 203	Importations - Total (millions)
Imports from Africa	3 432	3 171	3 871	5 959	13 443	16 326	...	...	...	Importations en provenance de l'Afrique
Main Products										**Principaux produits**
Durum wheat	462	522	3 296	2 591	3 604	3 783	...	3 908	...	Blé dur
Spelt, common wheat and meslin	345	678	1 222	1 192	752	3 017	...	5 841	...	Épeautre, blé tendre et méteil
Other petroleum oils & oils obtained from bituminous minerals	...	...	826	307	584	258	...	1 877	...	Combustibles et huiles de pétrole
Other medicaments of mixed/unmixed products	57	111	185	281	346	453	...	4 266	...	Autres médicaments de produits mélangés / non mélangés
Iron/Steel bars & rods	72	76	93	152	252	427	...	2 340	...	Fer et tiges
Main Origin										**Principales provenances**
China	5 684	10 208	17 032	22 696	29 823	29 794	...	59 934	...	Chine
Saudi Arabia	8 534	5 945	11 842	10 983	14 650	15 163	...	22 080	...	Arabie saoudite
India	2 617	3 845	6 137	7 528	8 886	13 346	...	11 786	...	Inde
Japan	2 015	3 924	3 769	4 372	7 335	8 252	...	11 045	...	Japon
United States	1 434	2 498	3 751	5 605	6 924	8 674	...	10 890	...	États-Unis

IX FINANCIAL AND MONETARY STATISTICS - FINANCES ET STATISTIQUES MONETAIRES										
	2006	2007	2008	2009	2010	2011	2012	2013	2014	
IX-1 MONETARY STATISTICS *ETHIOPIAN BIRR (MILLIONS)*										**IX-1 STATISTIQUES MONÉTAIRES** *BIRR ÉTHIOPIEN (MILLIONS)*
Money supply (M1)	47 490	56 840	69 850	83 740	104 140	142 110	188 840	234 330	293 150	Masse monétaire (M1)
Quasi-money	24 303	29 974	35 882	-	-	-	-	-	-	Quasi-monnaie
of which Demand Deposit	...	...	...	...	...	...	...	...	...	dont Monnaie scripturale
Net foreign assets	13 746	16 277	13 118	...	...	...	...	...	...	Avoirs extérieurs nets
Domestic credit	58 770	72 516	92 232	-	-	-	-	-	-	Crédit intérieur
of which claims on private sector	27 126	32 106	44 312	...	...	...	...	...	...	dont créances sur le secteur privé
of which claims on government sector, net	28 056	35 302	37 006	...	...	...	...	...	...	dont créances nettes sur le gouvernement
International reserves (millions US$)	867	1 290	871	1 781	...	...	...	...	...	Réserves internationales (millions $EU)
Average Exchange Rate (National Currency per US$)	8.70	8.97	9.60	11.78	14.41	16.90	17.70	18.57	19.68	Taux de change (moyen) (monnaie nationale par $ EU)
IX-2 PUBLIC FINANCE *ETHIOPIAN BIRR (MILLIONS)*										**IX-2 FINANCES PUBLIQUES** *BIRR ÉTHIOPIEN (MILLIONS)*
Total Revenues and Grants	17 890	24 937	33 712	43 461	55 694	75 472	93 926	124 077	146 174	Recettes totales et dons
Tax Revenue	8 787	12 910	17 807	17 831	32 772	48 842	57 398	93 895	121 215	Recettes fiscales
Non Tax Revenue	5 371	4 444	5 993	11 176	10 546	10 139	13 887	17 067	13 055	Recettes non fiscales
Grants	3 732	7 583	9 911	14 454	12 376	16 491	22 641	13 115	11 904	Dons
Total Expenditures and Net Lending	29 425	35 607	46 915	57 774	72 598	93 831	106 333	154 009	184 974	Dépenses totales et prêts nets
Current expenditure	15 334	17 165	22 794	27 176	32 537	40 500	46 068	62 746	77 766	Dépenses courantes
Of which Wages and Salaries	8 094	10 349	13 438	16 282	20 125	27 387	30 464	...	...	Dont rémunérations et salaires
Capital expenditure	14 042	18 398	24 121	30 599	40 061	53 297	60 265	91 263	107 208	Dépenses d'équipement
Net Lending	50	44	-	-	-	35	-	-	...	Prêts nets
Fiscal Balance	- 11 535	- 10 670	- 13 203	- 14 313	- 16 904	- 18 359	- 12 407	- 29 931	- 38 801	Solde global y compris les dons
IX-3 BALANCE OF PAYMENTS *US$ (MILLIONS)*										**IX-3 BALANCE DES PAIEMENTS** *$ E.U (MILLIONS)*
Trade balance	- 3 592	- 3 941	- 5 345	- 6 279	- 6 266	- 5 506	- 7 909	- 8 386	- 10 467	Balance commerciale
Services Balance	...	...	...	...	...	...	...	572	712	Balance des services
Net Income	- 10	30	17	- 33	- 55	- 70	- 96	- 113	- 153	Revenus nets
Compensation of employees	...	...	...	...	...	...	...	...	...	Rémunération des salariés
Investment Income	...	...	...	...	...	...	...	...	...	Revenus des investissements
Current transfers, net total	1 982	2 928	3 701	4 258	4 615	4 607	5 034	5 107	5 204	Transferts courants
Net official transfers	756	1 199	1 312	1 551	1 906	1 861	1 788	1 530	1 162	Transferts officiels nets
Workers' remittances	...	...	...	...	...	...	...	...	...	Envois de fonds des travailleurs
Other private transfers	...	...	...	...	...	...	...	...	...	Autres transferts privés
Current account balance	...	...	...	...	...	...	...	- 2 820	- 4 704	Solde du compte courant
Capital & financial account	...	...	...	...	...	...	...	3 226	3 902	Comptes de capital et financier
Capital account	...	...	...	...	...	...	...	3 226	3 902	Compte de capital
Financial account	...	...	...	...	...	...	...	...	...	Compte financier
Errors & omissions	491	199	59	374	84	- 510	- 62	- 413	711	Erreurs et omissions
Overall balance	...	...	...	...	...	...	...	- 7	- 91	Balance générale

X DEBT AND FINANCIAL FLOWS - DETTE ET FLUX FINANCIERS	2006	2007	2008	2009	2010	2011	2012	2013	2014	
X-1 DEBT *US$ (MILLIONS)*										**X-1 DETTE EXTÉRIEURE** *$ E.U (MILLIONS)*
Total external debt	5 999	2 185	2 924	4 134	5 373	6 974	7 630	9 434	11 219	Dette extérieure totale
Private	-	-	-	-	-	-	-	-	-	Privée
Public	5 999	2 185	2 924	4 134	5 373	6 974	7 630	9 434	11 219	Publique
Total external debt service	168	182	89	79	131	230	394	503	756	Service de la dette extérieure
Present value of External debt	...	...	...	...	...	...	...	...	...	Valeur actuelle de la dette extérieure
Total government domestic debt (in local currency)	39	45	52	51	53.0	53.3	61.8	...	...	Dette publique intérieure
X-2 FINANCIAL FLOWS *US$ (MILLIONS)*										**X-2 FLUX FINANCIERS** *$ E.U (MILLIONS)*
Net Foreign Direct Investment Inflows	545	222	109	221	288	627	279	953	...	Investissement étranger direct (flux nets entrants)
Main origin of FDI Inflows										**Principales origines de l'IDE entrant:**
Italy	...	...	41	32	9.7	8.0	- 38.8	...	...	Italie
United Kingdom	...	...	...	...	...	...	11.1	...	...	Royaume-Uni
Slovak Republic	...	...	...	...	...	...	...	...	...	République slovaque
United States	...	...	...	...	5.0	4.0	4.0	...	...	États-Unis
Turkey	...	...	5	...	...	...	1.0	3.0	...	Turquie
African countries	...	...	...	...	...	...	...	...	...	Pays africains
Net total Official Development Assistance	2 034	2 558	3 329	3 819	3 525	3 539	3 261	3 826	...	Aide publique au développement (nette totale)
Main origin of Net ODA										**Principales origines de l'APD nette**
United States	316	372	811	726	875.3	706.7	732.6	619.4	...	Etats-Unis
IDA	354	324	546	1 038	664.9	708.5	741.0	...	...	IDA
United Kingdom	165	291	254	343	407.0	552.3	421.1	...	...	Royaume-Uni
AfDF	190	154	131	307	149.5	233.3	97.4	...	...	FAfD
Global Fund	131	162	144	130	256.7	194.6	93.9	...	...	Fonds mondial

AREA (km²)	267 667		SUPERFICIE (km²)
CAPITAL CITY	Libreville	Libreville	CAPITALE
CURRENCY	CFA Franc	Franc CFA	MONNAIE

I SOCIAL AND DEMOGRAPHIC INDICATORS — INDICATEURS DEMOGRAPHIQUES ET SOCIAUX

	Year / Année	Value / Valeur	
POPULATION			**POPULATION**
Population ('000)			Population ('000)
Both sexes	2014	1 711	Les deux sexes
Male	2014	860	Masculin
Female	2014	851	Féminin
Average annual growth rate	2014	2.3	Taux de croissance annuel
Active Population ('000)	2014	630	Population active ('000)
Population by age group ('000)			Population par groupe d'âge ('000)
0-14 years	2014	657	0-14 ans
15-64 years	2014	967	15-64 ans
65+ years	2014	87	65+ ans
Economically. active population. in agriculture (%)	2014	29.8	Participation de la population active agricole (%)
Crude birth rate	2014	31.5	Taux brut de natalité
Crude death rate	2014	8.9	Taux brut de mortalité
Total fertility rate	2014	4.0	Indice synthétique de fécondité
Proportion of urban population	2014	87.1	Part de la population urbaine
Life Expectancy at Birth - Total (years)	2014	63.8	Espérance de vie à la naissance - Totale (ans)
Dependency Ratio - Total (%)	2014	62.5	Taux de dépendance - Total (%)
HEALTH			**SANTÉ**
Percentage of children under-five and underweight	2012	6.5	% d'enfants de moins de cinq ans avec insuffisance pondérale
Prevalence of undernourishment	2013	5.0	Prévalence de la malnutrition
Under five mortality rate (both sexes, per 1000)	2013	56.1	Taux de mortalité de moins de 5 ans (les deux sexes, pour 1000)
Infant mortality rate (both sexes) per 1000	2013	39.1	Taux de mortalité infantile (les deux sexes) par 1000
Percentage of children provided the vaccines :			Pourcentage d'enfants vaccinés :
BCG	2013	92.0	BCG
DPT3	2013	79.0	DTC3
Polio	2014	68.0	Polio
Measles	2013	70.0	Rougeole
Percentage of mothers provided at least one antenatal care (%)	2012	94.7	Pourcentage de mères ayant au moins reçu un soin prénatal (%)
Percentage of deliveries attended by skilled health personnel	2012	89.3	% d'accouchements assistés par un personnel de santé qualifié
Number of doctors (per 10 000 population)	2004	2.9	Nombre de médecins (pour 10 000 habitants)
Number of nurses (per 10 000 population)	2004	50.2	Nombre d'infirmières (pour 10 000 habitants)
Hospital beds - Total (per 10 000 population)	2010	63.0	Nombre de lits d'hôpitaux - Total (pour 10 000)
Births registered (per 1 000)	2014	31.5	Naiss.s enregistrées (pour 1 000)
Deaths registered (per 1 000)	2014	8.9	Décès enregistrés (pour 1 000)
Public expenditure on Health (% of budget)	2009	8.3	Dépenses publiques consacrées à la santé (% du budget)
EDUCATION			**EDUCATION**
Enrolment in primary education (both sexes) (000)	2011	318	Scolarisation dans le primaire (les deux sexes) (000)
Female	2011	155	Féminin
Enrolment in secondary education (both sexes) (000)	2002	105	Scolarisation dans le secondaire (les deux sexes) (000)
Female	...	...	Féminin
Enrolment in tertiary education (both sexes) (000)	...	...	Scolarisation dans le tertiaire (les deux sexes) (000)
Female	2003	3.7	Féminin
Literacy rate (both sexes)	2012	82.3	Taux d'alphabétisation (deux sexes)
Male	2012	84.9	Masculin
Female	2012	79.9	Féminin
Pupil-teacher ratio	2011	24.5	Ratio élève-enseignant
Public expenditure on education (% of budget)	...	...	Dépenses publiques consacrées à l'enseignement (% du budget)
POVERTY			**PAUVRETÉ**
GNI Per Capita (US$)	2013	10 650.0	RNB par habitant ($EU)
Human Poverty Index (HPI-1) Value (%)	2007	17.5	Valeur de l'Indice de pauvreté (IPH-1) (%)
Population below International Poverty Line ($2/day) (%)	2005	2.9	Population sous le seuil international de pauvreté (2$/J) (%)
Share of Income Held by Richest 10%	2005	33.2	% de revenu des 10% plus riches
Share of Income Held by Poorest 10%	2005	2.4	% de revenu des 10% plus pauvres
Gini index	2005	42.2	Indice de Gini

Charts / Graphiques

Population by age group – 2014
Population par groupe d'age – 2014

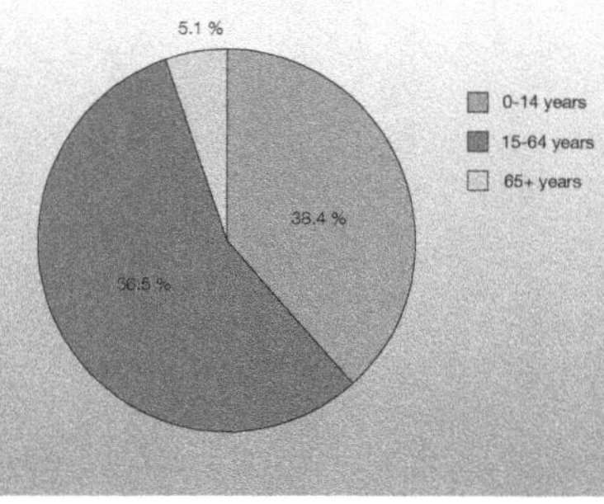

Percentage of children provided the vaccines – 2013
Pourcentage d'enfants vaccinés – 2013

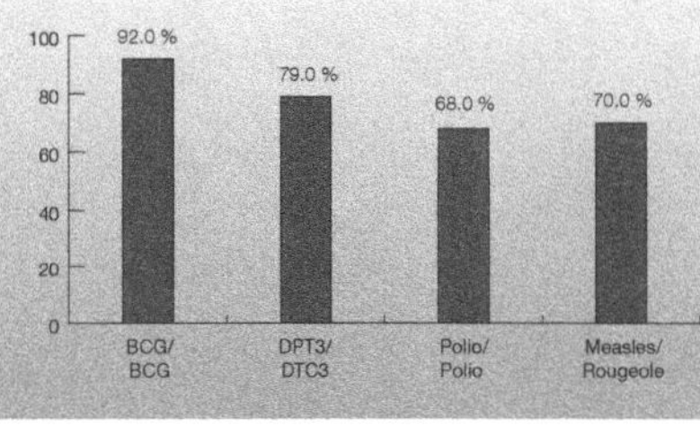

Literacy rate (%) – 2012
Taux d'alphabétisation – 2012

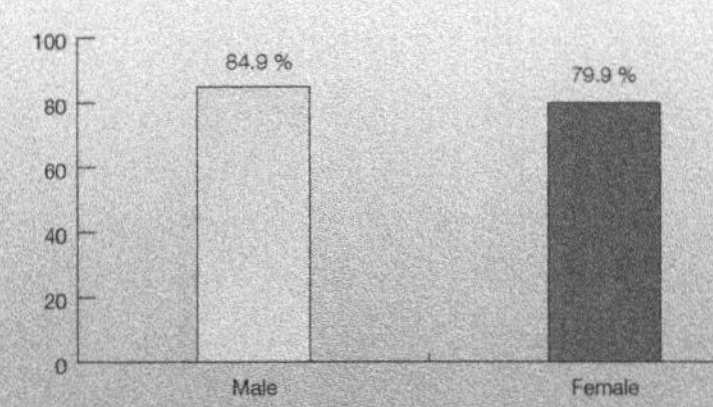

GNI Per Capita (US$)
RNB par habitant ($EU)

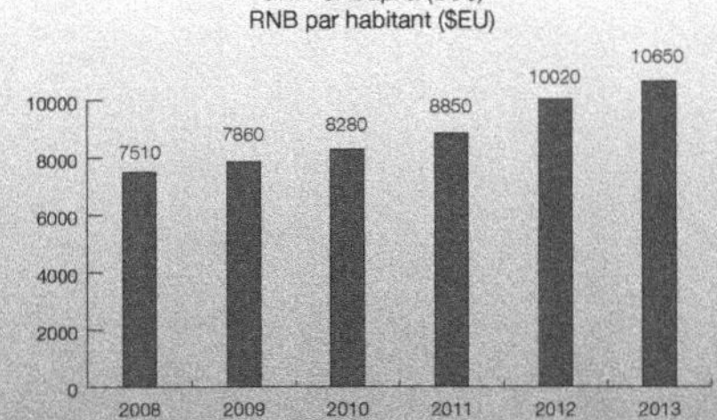

II NATIONAL ACCOUNTS — COMPTES NATIONAUX	2006	2007	2008	2009	2010	2011	2012	2013	2014	
GROSS DOMESTIC PRODUCT BY KIND OF ECONOMIC ACTIVITY AT CURRENT PRICES *CFA FRANC (BILLIONS)*										**PRODUIT INTÉRIEUR BRUT PAR BRANCHE D'ACTIVITÉ ÉCONOMIQUE AUX PRIX COURANTS** *FRANC CFA (MILLIARDS)*
Agriculture, hunting, forestry and fishing	265	296	294	310	275	288	287	290	316	Agriculture, chasse, sylviculture et pêche
Mining and quarrying	2 779	2 955	3 784	2 333	2 706	3 662	3 428	3 254	2 984	Industries extractives
Manufacturing	238	273	279	339	306	442	481	500	557	Industries manufacturières
Electricity, gas & water	49	26	45	46	53	61	67	70	78	Electricité, gaz et eau
Construction & public works	143	158	181	182	266	438	472	565	510	Bâtiments et travaux publics
Wholesale & retail trade, restaurants, hotels	238	265	281	299	321	353	399	435	497	Commerce de gros et de détail, restaurants et hôtels
Finance, insurance, real estate, etc.	608	705	773	733	918	1 138	1 207	1 338	1 470	Banques, assurances, affaires immobilières
Transport and communications	272	281	307	294	332	375	410	439	485	Transport(s) et communications
Public administration and defense	443	493	523	562	643	685	787	847	966	Administrations publiques et défense
Education	64	76	81	101	109	113	130	139	161	Education
Health and Social Work	44	48	48	60	64	67	72	78	83	Santé et actions sociales
Other services	...	...	...	...	...	...	...	...	...	Autres services
Less Imputed Service Charges	-	-	-	-	-	-	-	-	-	Moins services d'intermédiation financière
Gross domestic product at factor cost / basic prices	5 142	5 576	6 594	5 259	5 993	7 622	7 740	7 954	8 106	Produit intérieur brut aux couts des facteurs / prix de base
Plus: indirect taxes / taxes on products, less subsidies	254	386	350	261	387	390	413	458	502	Plus taxes indirectes/impôts sur les produits, moins les subventions
EXPENDITURE ON GROSS DOMESTIC PRODUCT AT CURRENT PURCHASER'S VALUES *CFA FRANC (BILLIONS)*										**EMPLOI DU PRODUIT INTÉRIEUR BRUT AUX PRIX COURANTS D'ACQUISITION** *FRANC CFA (MILLIARDS)*
Government final consumption	720	815	863	926	1 046	1 109	1 376	1 463	1 510	Consommation finale des administrations publiques
Private final consumption	1 625	1 760	1 881	1 820	1 985	2 142	2 394	2 600	2 953	Consommation finale privée
Gross fixed capital formation	1 250	1 410	1 738	1 601	1 995	2 176	2 127	2 480	2 659	Formation brute de capital fixe
Change in inventories	47	74	62	25	-	13	- 35	-	-	Variation des stocks
Exports of goods and services	3 268	3 489	4 262	2 973	3 498	4 681	4 652	4 175	3 671	Exportations de biens et services
Less imports of goods and services	1 515	1 586	1 861	1 825	2 144	2 108	2 362	2 307	2 185	Moins importations de biens et services
GDP at purchasers' values	5 395	5 962	6 945	5 520	6 380	8 012	8 152	8 412	8 609	PIB aux prix d'acquisition
GROSS DOMESTIC PRODUCT BY KIND OF ECONOMIC ACTIVITY AT CONSTANT PRICES *ANNUAL GROWTH RATES (%)*										**PRODUIT INTÉRIEUR BRUT PAR BRANCHE D'ACTIVITÉ ECONOMIQUE AUX PRIX CONSTANTS** *TAUX DE CROISSANCE ANNUEL (%)*
Agriculture, hunting, forestry and fishing	4.0	5.9	- 6.8	- 0.7	- 6.7	1.6	6.7	3.4	6.9	Agriculture, chasse, sylviculture et pêche
Mining and quarrying	- 18.3	2.4	- 18.1	14.8	13.1	0.9	- 1.7	2.0	0.2	Industries extractives
Manufacturing	- 0.6	15.6	- 3.6	4.5	10.0	2.8	6.4	2.4	10.7	Industries manufacturières
Electricity, gas & water	25.7	- 41.3	50.6	- 36.8	9.1	4.9	6.4	5.9	5.4	Electricité, gaz et eau
Construction & public works	4.4	6.4	16.3	- 10.0	23.3	68.0	- 2.4	12.7	- 4.5	Bâtiments et travaux publics
Wholesale & retail trade, restaurants, hotels	8.4	6.7	0.2	- 16.8	2.7	3.4	7.6	7.1	7.2	Commerce de gros et de détail, restaurants et hôtels
Finance, insurance, real estate, etc.	8.9	6.2	9.1	- 15.0	5.0	11.8	10.9	8.2	8.1	Banques, assurances, affaires immobilières
Transport and communications	16.6	5.3	5.0	- 7.4	5.3	7.0	11.1	10.2	6.2	Transport(s) et communications
Public administration and defense	10.9	4.2	5.8	5.5	5.1	7.3	11.8	7.6	9.6	Administrations publiques et défense
Education	3.9	10.9	6.8	0.4	3.9	5.2	9.5	- 2.0	7.9	Education
Health and Social Work	20.4	2.6	- 1.8	0.7	3.9	4.4	7.9	- 0.3	6.2	Santé et actions sociales
Other services	...	...	...	...	...	...	...	...	...	Autres services
Less Imputed Service Charges	...	...	...	...	...	...	...	...	...	Moins services d'intermédiation financière
Gross domestic product at factor cost / basic prices	- 2.8	4.5	- 3.4	0.0	7.8	7.2	5.1	5.5	5.0	Produit intérieur brut aux couts des facteurs / prix de base
Plus: indirect taxes / taxes on products, less subsidies	- 1.9	22.6	- 2.2	- 5.1	- 2.9	6.2	6.6	6.1	4.9	Plus taxes indirectes/impôts sur les produits, moins les subventions
Gross domestic product at market prices	- 2.8	6.0	- 3.3	- 0.5	6.8	7.1	5.3	5.6	5.0	Produit intérieur brut aux prix du marché
EXPENDITURE ON GROSS DOMESTIC PRODUCT AT CONSTANT PURCHASERS' VALUES *ANNUAL GROWTH RATES (%)*										**EMPLOIS DU PRODUIT INTÉRIEUR BRUT AUX PRIX CONSTANTS D'ACQUISITION** *TAUX DE CROISSANCE ANNUEL (%)*
Government final consumption	11.0	6.5	4.9	2.2	2.3	8.1	11.4	3.5	- 6.9	Consommation finale des administrations publiques
Private final consumption	6.2	3.6	3.3	- 5.0	7.5	6.5	8.8	8.1	9.0	Consommation finale privée
Gross fixed capital formation	6.9	9.8	10.3	- 4.8	14.5	5.2	13.3	4.0	2.6	Formation brute de capital fixe
Exports of goods and services	- 6.8	3.1	- 6.1	- 11.8	8.1	8.6	- 4.9	- 1.5	- 2.3	Exportations de biens et services
Less imports of goods and services	17.2	3.6	12.5	- 21.6	6.0	12.6	8.0	- 2.1	- 7.8	Moins importations de biens et services
Notes	2014:Provisional								2014: Provisoire	Notes

III INFLATION	2006	2007	2008	2009	2010	2011	2012	2013	2014	
ANNUAL GROWTH RATES (%)										**TAUX DE CROISSANCE ANNUEL (%)**
All items	-1.4	5.0	5.3	1.9	1.4	1.3	2.7	0.5	4.5	Ensemble
of which:										dont:
Food and Non-alcoholic beverages	0.9	2.2	7.8	3.7	4.4	4.0	5.3	-0.4	3.2	Alimentation et boissons non alcoolisés
Alcoholic beverages & tobacco	-1.3	0.7	1.5	1.7	11.1	1.7	0.3	2.9	-1.6	Boissons alcoolisées et tabacs
Clothing and Footwear	5.6	1.8	-0.2	-2.1	-1.9	1.4	2.1	1.5	4.8	Habillement et chaussures
Housing, Water, Electricity, Gas and Other Fuels	2.8	9.1	9.1	4.1	0.5	0.5	0.8	2.2	8.0	Logement, eau, electricité, gas et autres combustibles
Furnishing, household equipment	-1.2	10.6	2.3	-0.7	-3.3	-5.5	0.5	4.6	12.3	Meubles, articles de ménage et entretien courant
Health	9.5	-2.0	1.9	2.9	0.9	3.8	-0.1	1.2	1.2	Santé
Transport	3.0	13.5	3.3	-6.3	1.1	3.5	4.8	-1.1	4.5	Transport
Communication	-38.6	20.1	1.6	4.4	-8.7	-13.4	-3.8	-10.0	0.1	Communication
Recreation & culture	-10.1	-8.8	-1.8	1.7	1.7	-0.8	2.0	0.9	2.5	Loisirs et culture
Education	2.9	0.5	-0.9	2.7	6.4	-4.2	-6.2	9.8	1.5	Enseignement
Restaurants & hotels	-1.4	2.3	3.7	2.3	4.6	2.9	3.0	0.7	3.2	Restaurants et hôtels
Miscellaneous goods & services	-3.2	0.6	5.8	3.9	-2.9	-0.5	-4.7	0.1	1.3	Biens et services divers

IV AGRICULTURAL PRODUCTION - PRODUCTION AGRICOLE										
	2006	2007	2008	2009	2010	2011	2012	2013	2014	
TONNES *(THOUSAND)*										**TONNES** *(MILLIERS)*
Cassava	235	240	243	245	250	255	300	315	...	Manioc
Sugar cane	215	220	220	240	245	265	260	280	...	Canne à sucre
Plantains	273	275	275	317	325	295	285	272	...	Banane-Plantain
Yams	170	180	185	188	190	195	200	210	...	Ignames
Taro (cocoyam)	55	56	55	58	58	60	63	65	...	Taro
V MINING PRODUCTION - PRODUCTION MINIERE										
	2006	2007	2008	2009	2010	2011	2012	2013	2014	
Crude petroleum, metric tons (thousands)	11 930	12 130	12 700	11 829	12 431	12 512	12 655	11 270	10 900	Pétrole brut (1000 tonnes)
Gas natural, cubic meter (million)	155	167	187	258	338	336	...	...	...	Gaz naturel (millions de m3)
Gold (kilograms)	...	...	...	...	...	628	683	1 192	...	Or (en kilogrammes)
VI ENERGY - ENERGIE										
	2006	2007	2008	2009	2010	2011	2012	2013	2014	
Total electricity generation (GWh)	1 484	1 548	1 661	1 674	1 776	1 845	2 017	2 113	...	Production d'électricité totale (GWh)
of which:										dont:
Production of electricity from fossil fuels (GWh)	527	735	756	718	855	851	974	1 017	...	Production d'électricité à partir de combustibles fossiles (GWh)
Production of hydro electricity (GWh)	949	806	898	948	912	981	1 030	1 082	...	Production d'électricité d'origine hydraulique (GWh)
Production of electricity from solar, wind, tide, wave and other sources (GWh)	...	...	...	...	...	4	4	4	...	Production d'électricité d'origine solaire, éolienne, marée motrice et autres (GWh)
VII TOURISM AND INFRASTRUCTURE - TOURISME ET INFRASTRUCTURE										
	2006	2007	2008	2009	2010	2011	2012	2013	2014	
VII-1 TOURISM										**VII-1 TOURISME**
International tourist arrivals (thousands)	296	325	358	368	398	448	517	542	571	Arrivées de touristes internationaux (milliers)
Rooms in hotels and similar establishments (thousands)	...	4.2	...	...	...	...	...	...	...	Chambres d'hotels et établissements assimilés (milliers)
Overnight stays (thousands)	1 423	1 563	1 721	1 769	1 914	2 152	2 487	2 606	2 745	Nuitées (milliers)
Tourism receipts (US$ thousand)	8 598	8 402	7 565	7 099	7 129	10 100	10 889	11 507	12 036	Recettes touristiques (milliers de $ EU)
Total contribution to GDP (%)	2.7	2.9	3.5	3.5	2.9	2.3	2.4	2.3	2.4	Contribution totale au PIB (%)
Total contribution to Employment (%)	3.5	3.0	3.2	3.8	3.2	2.5	2.1	2.0	2.1	Contribution totale à l'emploi (%)
VII-2 INFRASTRUCTURE										**VII-2 INFRASTRUCTURE**
Paved roads (% of total)	...	12	...	...	...	...	...	...	...	Routes asphaltées (% du total)
Total Network (Railways-km)	810	1 098	...	...	...	...	...	...	...	Réseau total voies ferrées-Km
Main Telephone Lines (per 100 inhabitants)	3	2	2	2	2	1	1	1	...	Lignes téléphoniques fixes (pour 100 habitants)
Mobile Cellular Subscribers (per 100 inhabitants)	64	81	88	95	103	149	179	215	...	Abonnés aux téléphones mobiles (pour 100 habitants)
VIII EXTERNAL TRADE - COMMERCE EXTERIEUR										
	2006	2007	2008	2009	2010	2011	2012	2013	2014	
CFA FRANC EXPORTS, FOB										**FRANC CFA (MILLIARDS) EXPORTATIONS, FÀB**
Exports - Total	2 773	3 225	3 896	3 215	3 307	3 873	3 598	3 680	3 706	Exportations - Total
Exports to AFRICA	...	...	162	137	131	...	...	...	...	Exportations vers l'AFRIQUE
Main Products										**Principaux produits**
Crude oil	2 653	2 485	3 707	2 170	3 716	...	...	...	...	Pétrole brut
Rough lumber	159	192	165	197	73	...	...	...	...	Bois en grumes
Manganese	98	107	92	148	103	...	...	...	...	Manganèse
Lumber	103	127	107	86	129	...	...	...	...	Bois ouvrés
	...	...	...	...	...	...	...	...	...	
Main Destinations										**Principales destinations**
United States	1 836	1 605	2 204	1 493	2 485	1 682	1 805	...	...	Etats-Unis
France	222	341	255	115	163	306	329	...	...	France
China	332	288	561	205	218	738	783	...	...	Chine
Trinidad and Tobago	118	136	187	172	224	259	280	...	...	Trinité-et-Tobago
Spain	94	55	182	158	199	234	253	...	...	Espagne
IMPORTS, CIF										**IMPORTATIONS, CAF**
Imports - Total	3 432	4 344	5 001	4 873	5 488	7 112	6 751	7 085	6 608	Importations - Total (millions)
Imports from Africa	...	...	124	105	148	...	...	...	...	Importations en provenance de l'Afrique
Main Products										**Principaux produits**
Tools and materials non-electric	185	205	250	211	324	...	...	...	...	Outillage et matériels non électriques
Food	151	185	202	...	...	...	...	...	...	Produits alimentaires
Consumer Products nonfood	132	149	210	...	...	...	...	...	...	Produits de consommation non alimentaires
Vehicles	91	97	102	87	103	...	...	...	...	Véhicules
Electrical machinery and apparatus	80	90	79	95	101	...	...	...	...	Machines et appareils électriques
Main Origin										**Principales provenances**
France	362	365	404	389	452	483	...	...	...	France
United States	66	60	85	84	160	114	...	...	...	Etats-Unis
Chine	24	39	45	58	104	112	...	...	...	Chine
Netherlands	25	32	39	49	60	110	...	...	...	Pays-Bas
Cameroon	31	31	27	25	24	26	...	...	...	Cameroun

GABON

IX FINANCIAL AND MONETARY STATISTICS - FINANCES ET STATISTIQUES MONETAIRES	2006	2007	2008	2009	2010	2011	2012	2013	2014	
IX-1 MONETARY STATISTICS *CFA FRANC (MILLIONS)*										**IX-1 STATISTIQUES MONÉTAIRES** *FRANC CFA (MILLIONS)*
Money supply (M1)	977 830	1 047 780	1 139 650	1 165 150	1 389 190	1 757 160	2 033 580	2 260 890	2 472 920	Masse monétaire (M1)
Quasi-money	350 553	348 566	360 905	393 408	465 067	540 012	731 987	734 554	718 796	Quasi-monnaie
of which Demand Deposit	...	...	...	...	...	...	...	...	...	dont Monnaie scripturale
Net foreign assets	697 417	1 097 304	967 735	973 962	896 436	1 046 542	1 097 428	1 420 204	1 319 437	Avoirs extérieurs nets
Domestic credit	465 312	138 097	420 922	449 821	745 382	982 873	1 236 393	1 117 640	1 141 997	Crédit intérieur
of which claims on private sector	515 424	593 310	601 503	574 890	583 852	817 625	990 797	1 304 694	1 234 552	dont créances sur le secteur privé
of which claims on government sector, net	- 71 267	- 489 914	- 201 044	- 151 789	121 475	131 845	169 459	- 311 125	- 245 355	dont créances nettes sur le gouvernement
International reserves (millions US$)	1 114	1 228	1 924	1 993	1 736	2 157	2 352	...	...	Réserves internationales (millions $EU)
Average Exchange Rate (National Currency per US$)	522.89	479.27	447.81	472.19	495.28	471.87	510.53	494.04	493.38	Taux de change (moyen) (monnaie nationale par $ EU)
IX-2 PUBLIC FINANCE *CFA FRANC (BILLIONS)*										**IX-2 FINANCES PUBLIQUES** *FRANC CFA (MILLIARDS)*
Total Revenues and Grants	1 583	1 636	2 078	1 685	1 834	2 469	2 546	2 547	2 625	Recettes totales et dons
Tax Revenue	1 549	1 602	2 003	1 581	1 745	2 367	2 475	2 420	2 485	Recettes fiscales
Non Tax Revenue	33	34	75	103	89	102	71	127	140	Recettes non fiscales
Grants	-	0	-	1	-	-	-	-	-	Dons
Total Expenditures and Net Lending	1 122	1 166	1 336	1 348	1 707	2 269	2 641	2 847	2 967	Dépenses totales et prêts nets
Current expenditure	883	909	1 016	988	1 041	1 250	1 523	1 590	1 677	Dépenses courantes
Of which Wages and Salaries	252	302	324	380	412	450	529	551	552	Dont rémunérations et salaires
Capital expenditure	239	247	299	309	601	1 000	1 044	1 217	1 250	Dépenses d'équipement
Net Lending	-	10	21	51	65	19	74	40	40	Prêts nets
Fiscal Balance	460	471	742	337	127	200	- 95	- 300	- 342	Solde global y compris les dons
IX-3 BALANCE OF PAYMENTS *CFA FRANC (BILLIONS)*										**IX-3 BALANCE DES PAIEMENTS** *FRANC CFA (MILLIARDS)*
Trade balance	2 351	2 576	3 344	1 965	2 677	3 345	3 262	3 296	...	Balance commerciale
Services Balance	- 567	- 617	- 644	- 523	- 883	- 899	- 918	- 939	...	Balance des services
Net Income	- 810	- 961	- 1 148	- 697	- 1 025	- 1 543	- 922	- 1 055	...	Revenus nets
Compensation of employees	...	...	...	...	...	...	...	...	...	Rémunération des salariés
Investment Income	...	...	...	...	...	...	...	...	...	Revenus des investissements
Current transfers, net total	- 106	- 118	- 136	- 92	- 99	- 119	- 148	- 149	...	Transferts courants
Net official transfers	...	...	...	...	...	...	...	...	...	Transferts officiels nets
Workers' remittances	...	...	...	...	...	...	...	...	...	Envois de fonds des travailleurs
Other private transfers	...	...	...	...	...	...	...	...	...	Autres transferts privés
Current account balance	868	880	1 417	653	670	785	1 274	1 153	...	Solde du compte courant
Capital & financial account	...	...	...	...	...	...	...	...	...	Comptes de capital et financier
Capital account	...	...	...	...	...	...	...	...	...	Compte de capital
Financial account	...	...	...	...	...	...	...	...	...	Compte financier
Errors & omissions	...	...	...	...	...	...	...	...	...	Erreurs et omissions
Overall balance	...	...	...	...	...	...	...	...	...	Balance générale

X DEBT AND FINANCIAL FLOWS - DETTE ET FLUX FINANCIERS	2006	2007	2008	2009	2010	2011	2012	2013	2014	
X-1 DEBT *CFA FRANC (MILLIONS)*										**X-1 DETTE EXTÉRIEURE** *FRANC CFA (MILLIONS)*
Total external debt	3 117	4 294	2 181	2 150	2 291	2 477	2 745	3 473	3 844	Dette extérieure totale
Private	37	1 231	881	946	891	785	832	1 079	1 031	Privée
Public	3 080	3 063	1 300	1 204	1 400	1 692	1 913	2 394	2 812	Publique
Total external debt service	639	718	2 577	523	646	473	704	1 682	594	Service de la dette extérieure
Present value of External debt	...	...	...	...	...	...	...	...	...	Valeur actuelle de la dette extérieure
Total government domestic debt (in local currency)	93	141	148	256	89.4	56.6	57.0	244.2	206.4	Dette publique intérieure
X-2 FINANCIAL FLOWS *CFA FRANC (MILLIONS)*										**X-2 FLUX FINANCIERS** *FRANC CFA (MILLIONS)*
Net Foreign Direct Investment Inflows	268	269	773	573	499	696	696	856	...	Investissement étranger direct (flux nets entrants)
Main origin of FDI Inflows										**Principales origines de l'IDE entrant:**
France	158	275	382	54	- 7.9	26.5	206.9	...	...	France
Belgium	- 18	31	- 13	13	29.1	58.5	75.8	...	...	Belgique
Spain	73	...	...	...	...	...	...	...	...	Espagne
Italy	...	...	1	41	- 9.6	5.7	10.7	...	...	Italie
Germany	...	8	3	1	7.9	...	...	...	...	Allemagne
African countries	...	...	...	...	...	...	...	...	...	Pays africains
Net total Official Development Assistance	29	51	62	77	104	73	73	91	...	Aide publique au développement (nette totale)
Main origin of Net ODA										**Principales origines de l'APD nette**
France	30	32	37	54	58.1	51.4	56.6	63.9	...	France
Japan	...	...	2	0	24.8	11.0	3.2	3.7	...	Japon
Global Fund	6	6	3	7	2.2	1.0	- 0.9	...	...	Fonds mondial
United States	1	1	...	1	1.5	0.7	2.1	5.9	...	Etats-Unis
UNHCR	...	...	1	1	0.6	...	...	...	...	FNUAP

GAMBIA — GAMBIE

AREA (km²)		11 295	SUPERFICIE (km²)
CAPITAL CITY	Banjul	Banjul	CAPITALE
CURRENCY	Gambian Dalasi	Dalasi Gambien	MONNAIE

I SOCIAL AND DEMOGRAPHIC INDICATORS — INDICATEURS DEMOGRAPHIQUES ET SOCIAUX

	Year / Année	Value / Valeur	
POPULATION			**POPULATION**
Population ('000)			Population ('000)
Both sexes	2014	1 915	Les deux sexes
Male	2014	947	Masculin
Female	2014	968	Féminin
Average annual growth rate	2014	3.3	Taux de croissance annuel
Active Population ('000)	2014	825	Population active ('000)
Population by age group ('000)			Population par groupe d'âge ('000)
0-14 years	2014	816	0-14 ans
15-64 years	2014	1 036	15-64 ans
65+ years	2014	62	65+ ans
Economically. active population. in agriculture (%)	2014	82.1	Participation de la population active agricole (%)
Crude birth rate	2014	40.5	Taux brut de natalité
Crude death rate	2014	7.2	Taux brut de mortalité
Total fertility rate	2014	5.6	Indice synthétique de fécondité
Proportion of urban population	2014	58.8	Part de la population urbaine
Life Expectancy at Birth - Total (years)	2014	59.0	Espérance de vie à la naissance - Totale (ans)
Dependency Ratio - Total (%)	2014	81.4	Taux de dépendance - Total (%)
HEALTH			**SANTÉ**
Percentage of children under-five and underweight	2010	17.4	% d'enfants de moins de cinq ans avec insuffisance pondérale
Prevalence of undernourishment	2013	6.0	Prévalence de la malnutrition
Under five mortality rate (both sexes, per 1000)	2013	91.8	Taux de mortalité de moins de 5 ans (les deux sexes, pour 1000)
Infant mortality rate (both sexes) per 1000	2013	69.7	Taux de mortalité infantile (les deux sexes) par 1000
Percentage of children provided the vaccines :			Pourcentage d'enfants vaccinés :
BCG	2013	98.0	BCG
DPT3	2013	97.0	DTC3
Polio	2010	92.1	Polio
Measles	2013	96.0	Rougeole
Percentage of mothers provided at least one antenatal care (%)	2013	93.6	Pourcentage de mères ayant au moins reçu un soin prénatal (%)
Percentage of deliveries attended by skilled health personnel	2010	56.6	% d'accouchements assistés par un personnel de santé qualifié
Number of doctors (per 10 000 population)	2008	1.1	Nombre de médecins (pour 10 000 habitants)
Number of nurses (per 10 000 population)	2008	8.7	Nombre d'infirmières (pour 10 000 habitants)
Hospital beds - Total (per 10 000 population)	2013	264.3	Nombre de lits d'hôpitaux - Total (pour 10 000)
Births registered (per 1 000)	2014	42.4	Naiss.s enregistrées (pour 1 000)
Deaths registered (per 1 000)	2014	9.5	Décès enregistrés (pour 1 000)
Public expenditure on Health (% of budget)	2013	11.6	Dépenses publiques consacrées à la santé (% du budget)
EDUCATION			**EDUCATION**
Enrolment in primary education (both sexes) (000)	2014	275	Scolarisation dans le primaire (les deux sexes) (000)
Female	2014	139	Féminin
Enrolment in secondary education (both sexes) (000)	2014	137	Scolarisation dans le secondaire (les deux sexes) (000)
Female	2014	68	Féminin
Enrolment in tertiary education (both sexes) (000)	2008	6.5	Scolarisation dans le tertiaire (les deux sexes) (000)
Female	2014	21.7	Féminin
Literacy rate (both sexes)	2012	52.0	Taux d'alphabétisation (deux sexes)
Male	2012	61.4	Masculin
Female	2012	43.1	Féminin
Pupil-teacher ratio	2011	37.6	Ratio élève-enseignant
Public expenditure on education (% of budget)	2014	46.4	Dépenses publiques consacrées à l'enseignement (% du budget)
POVERTY			**PAUVRETÉ**
GNI Per Capita (US$)	2013	500.0	RNB par habitant ($EU)
Human Poverty Index (HPI-1) Value (%)	2007	40.9	Valeur de l'Indice de pauvreté (IPH-1) (%)
Population below International Poverty Line ($2/day) (%)	2003	55.9	Population sous le seuil international de pauvreté (2$/J) (%)
Share of Income Held by Richest 10%	2003	36.9	% de revenu des 10% plus riches
Share of Income Held by Poorest 10%	2003	2.0	% de revenu des 10% plus pauvres
Gini index	2003	47.3	Indice de Gini

Charts / Graphiques

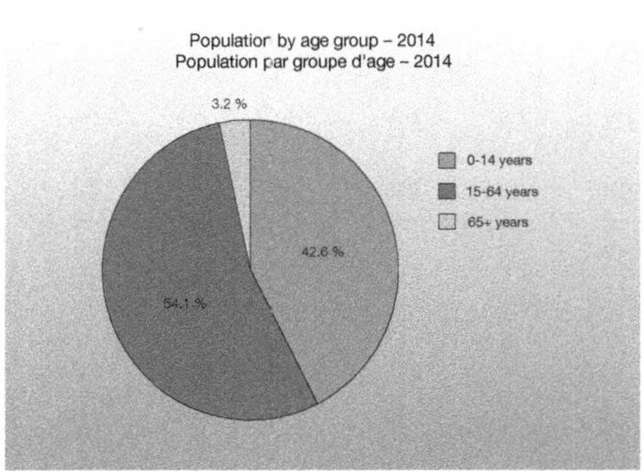

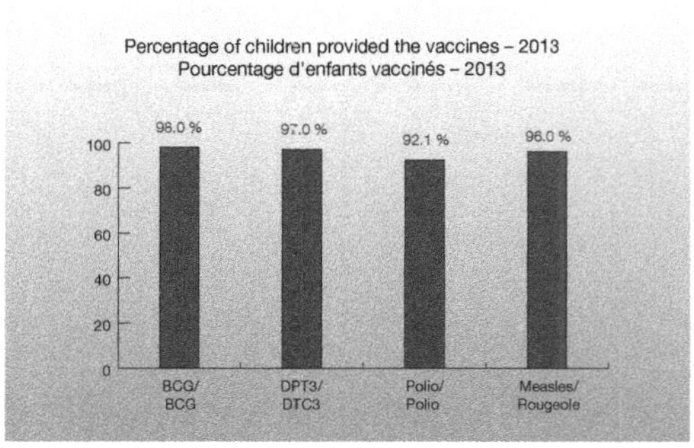

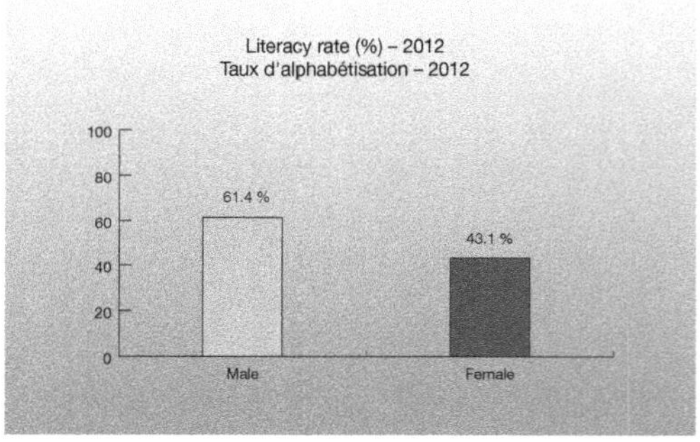

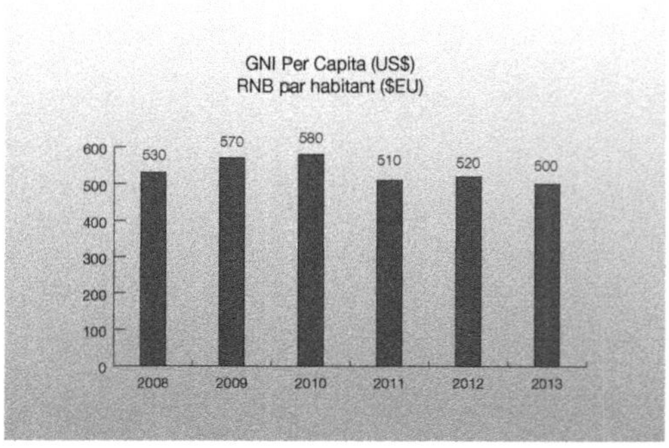

II NATIONAL ACCOUNTS — COMPTES NATIONAUX	2006	2007	2008	2009	2010	2011	2012	2013	2014	
GROSS DOMESTIC PRODUCT BY KIND OF ECONOMIC ACTIVITY AT CURRENT PRICES *GAMBIAN DALASI (MILLIONS)*										**PRODUIT INTÉRIEUR BRUT PAR BRANCHE D'ACTIVITÉ ÉCONOMIQUE AUX PRIX COURANTS** *DALASI GAMBIEN (MILLIONS)*
Agriculture, hunting, forestry and fishing	4 011	4 066	5 401	6 292	7 719	5 942	6 533	6 929	...	Agriculture, chasse, sylviculture et pêche
Mining and quarrying	447	394	524	603	705	792	897	1 014	...	Industries extractives
Manufacturing	1 259	1 327	1 241	1 195	1 260	1 460	1 671	1 724	...	Industries manufacturières
Electricity, gas & water	188	256	281	299	331	331	335	376	...	Electricité, gaz et eau
Construction & public works	777	744	845	910	992	1 131	1 324	1 457	...	Bâtiments et travaux publics
Wholesale & retail trade, restaurants, hotels	5 358	6 272	6 212	6 460	6 659	7 154	7 778	7 993	...	Commerce de gros et de détail, restaurants et hôtels
Finance, insurance, real estate, etc.	2 016	2 047	2 427	3 034	3 193	3 668	3 936	4 263	...	Banques, assurances, affaires immobilières
Transport and communications	2 249	2 463	2 410	2 653	3 114	3 464	3 939	4 879	...	Transport(s) et communications
Public administration and defense	412	313	323	440	526	565	608	687	...	Administrations publiques et défense
Education	201	213	235	249	276	297	321	366	...	Education
Health and Social Work	206	206	207	253	283	293	295	323	...	Santé et actions sociales
Other services	90	93	96	100	104	108	114	121	...	Autres services
Less Imputed Service Charges	- 684	- 676	- 749	- 1 017	- 848	- 1 058	- 1 126	- 1 228	...	Moins services d'intermédiation financière
Gross domestic product at factor cost / basic prices	16 529	17 716	19 453	21 470	24 314	24 147	26 623	28 904	-	Produit intérieur brut aux couts des facteurs / prix de base
Plus: indirect taxes / taxes on products, less subsidies	1 856	2 154	1 980	2 527	2 349	2 494	2 645	3 143	...	Plus taxes indirectes/impôts sur les produits, moins les subventions
EXPENDITURE ON GROSS DOMESTIC PRODUCT AT CURRENT PURCHASER'S VALUES *GAMBIAN DALASI (MILLIONS)*										**EMPLOI DU PRODUIT INTÉRIEUR BRUT AUX PRIX COURANTS D'ACQUISITION** *DALASI GAMBIEN (MILLIONS)*
Government final consumption	1 164	1 440	2 086	2 511	2 676	2 694	2 201	2 395	...	Consommation finale des administrations publiques
Private final consumption	17 549	18 019	18 705	19 576	23 204	20 798	24 470	27 454	...	Consommation finale privée
Gross fixed capital formation	5 643	5 844	5 723	6 421	4 903	6 755	6 839	6 649	...	Formation brute de capital fixe
Change in inventories	...	...	...	...	...	...	...	...	...	Variation des stocks
Exports of goods and services	266	1 378	1 014	2 418	2 770	5 029	6 209	6 328	...	Exportations de biens et services
Less imports of goods and services	6 237	6 809	6 095	6 929	6 890	8 636	10 451	10 780	...	Moins importations de biens et services
GDP at purchasers' values	18 385	19 871	21 433	23 997	26 663	26 641	29 268	32 047	-	PIB aux prix d'acquisition
GROSS DOMESTIC PRODUCT BY KIND OF ECONOMIC ACTIVITY AT CONSTANT PRICES *ANNUAL GROWTH RATES (%)*										**PRODUIT INTÉRIEUR BRUT PAR BRANCHE D'ACTIVITÉ ECONOMIQUE AUX PRIX CONSTANTS** *TAUX DE CROISSANCE ANNUEL (%)*
Agriculture, hunting, forestry and fishing	- 14.6	- 1.8	26.0	11.7	11.2	- 24.2	6.2	- 1.8	...	Agriculture, chasse, sylviculture et pêche
Mining and quarrying	1.2	- 14.1	29.8	12.1	14.2	7.6	9.0	7.4	...	Industries extractives
Manufacturing	4.1	3.9	- 8.3	- 4.3	0.4	3.9	2.5	3.2	...	Industries manufacturières
Electricity, gas & water	3.6	33.5	5.2	2.2	7.7	- 3.9	- 4.1	2.2	...	Electricité, gaz et eau
Construction & public works	3.9	- 9.2	8.8	3.0	3.8	9.2	12.7	4.5	...	Bâtiments et travaux publics
Wholesale & retail trade, restaurants, hotels	10.4	11.5	- 5.2	- 0.6	- 2.1	2.4	4.5	2.6	...	Commerce de gros et de détail, restaurants et hôtels
Finance, insurance, real estate, etc.	7.6	- 3.0	14.7	19.9	1.2	10.6	3.9	3.7	...	Banques, assurances, affaires immobilières
Transport and communications	7.1	8.9	- 3.7	8.0	11.4	5.5	9.2	18.3	...	Transport(s) et communications
Public administration and defense	3.1	- 27.8	- 1.4	30.5	13.8	2.4	3.2	7.0	...	Administrations publiques et défense
Education	10.4	5.9	10.2	5.4	10.5	4.7	7.0	13.7	...	Education
Health and Social Work	18.6	- 0.5	0.5	21.2	11.6	3.7	0.1	9.1	...	Santé et actions sociales
Other services	2.7	2.7	2.7	2.7	2.7	2.7	2.7	3.2	...	Autres services
Less Imputed Service Charges	11.7	- 6.2	6.0	29.9	- 20.6	19.0	2.1	3.2	...	Moins services d'intérmediation financière
Gross domestic product at factor cost / basic prices	1.1	3.6	5.7	6.4	6.5	- 4.3	5.9	4.8	...	Produit intérieur brut aux couts des facteurs / prix de base
Plus: indirect taxes / taxes on products, less subsidies	1.1	3.6	5.7	6.4	6.5	- 4.3	5.9	4.8	...	Plus taxes indirectes/impôts sur les produits, moins les subventions
Gross domestic product at market prices	1.1	3.6	5.7	6.4	6.5	- 4.3	5.9	4.8	...	Produit intérieur brut aux prix du marché
EXPENDITURE ON GROSS DOMESTIC PRODUCT AT CONSTANT PURCHASERS' VALUES *ANNUAL GROWTH RATES (%)*										**EMPLOIS DU PRODUIT INTÉRIEUR BRUT AUX PRIX CONSTANTS D'ACQUISITION** *TAUX DE CROISSANCE ANNUEL (%)*
Government final consumption	- 9.6	17.4	38.7	15.1	1.5	- 3.9	- 21.6	3.0	...	Consommation finale des administrations publiques
Private final consumption	5.0	- 1.3	2.0	- 0.6	13.4	- 13.9	13.1	7.0	...	Consommation finale privée
Gross fixed capital formation	8.4	0.3	- 6.5	8.0	- 29.8	33.5	- 3.4	- 8.3	...	Formation brute de capital fixe
Exports of goods and services	- 78.2	394.8	- 29.1	131.0	7.0	74.3	18.0	- 2.3	...	Exportations de biens et services
Less imports of goods and services	- 0.2	6.2	- 14.5	9.6	- 9.3	21.8	15.1	- 3.0	...	Moins importations de biens et services
Notes	2012-2013: Revised								2012-2013: Révisée	Notes

III INFLATION	2006	2007	2008	2009	2010	2011	2012	2013	2014	
ANNUAL GROWTH RATES (%)										**TAUX DE CROISSANCE ANNUEL (%)**
All items	2.1	5.4	4.4	4.6	5.0	4.8	4.3	5.7	5.7	Ensemble
of which:										dont:
Food and Non-alcoholic beverages	1.8	7.9	6.0	5.3	6.6	6.4	5.0	6.7	6.5	Alimentation et boissons non alcoolisés
Alcoholic beverages & tobacco	1.2	1.4	1.1	1.6	0.9	1.0	1.5	2.3	1.7	Boissons alcoolisées et tabacs
Clothing and Footwear	1.7	1.9	3.1	3.6	1.8	0.9	2.1	2.9	3.3	Habillement et chaussures
Housing, Water, Electricity, Gas and Other Fuels	7.8	2.0	3.5	4.0	2.1	3.9	8.9	11.6	5.6	Logement, eau, electricité, gas et autres combustibles
Furnishing, household equipment	2.5	3.7	2.3	2.8	1.3	1.7	1.8	2.5	2.3	Meubles, articles de ménage et entretien courant
Health	-0.3	0.3	0.3	0.7	0.1	0.1	0.3	0.4	17.9	Santé
Transport	-0.4	0.5	3.0	2.0	13.3	13.4	7.7	16.6	12.2	Transport
Communication	-0.4	0.8	0.6	0.5	0.4	0.1	0.3	0.4	0.3	Communication
Recreation & culture	1.2	1.0	0.4	0.9	1.2	1.9	2.2	2.8	2.8	Loisirs et culture
Education	-1.4	0.0	0.1	0.6	1.3	1.9	0.8	0.5	0.5	Enseignement
Restaurants & hotels	-1.0	2.6	4.8	4.8	6.6	7.7	5.3	6.5	4.4	Restaurants et hôtels
Miscellaneous goods & services	1.7	7.8	3.7	9.6	6.7	4.1	4.9	5.5	5.8	Biens et services divers

IV AGRICULTURAL PRODUCTION - PRODUCTION AGRICOLE

TONNES (THOUSAND)	2006	2007	2008	2009	2010	2011	2012	2013	2014	TONNES (MILLIERS)
Groundnuts, with shell	115	73	110	122	138	84	120	94	...	Arachides en coques
Millet	126	89	126	145	158	87	116	94	...	Millet
Rice, paddy	31	11	38	79	100	51	54	70	...	Riz
Maize	28	31	45	55	66	24	30	33	...	Maïs
Sorghum	30	18	26	32	39	21	23	30	...	Sorgho

V MINING PRODUCTION - PRODUCTION MINIERE

	2006	2007	2008	2009	2010	2011	2012	2013	2014	
Gravel and crushed stone, metric tons (thousands)	...	...	...	...	498	368	...	...	...	Graviers et pierres concentrés, tonnes métriques (milliers)
Clays, metric tons (thousands)	...	...	...	...	...	...	...	...	...	Argiles, tonnes métriques (milliers)
	...	...	...	...	...	...	...	...	...	

VI ENERGY - ENERGIE

	2006	2007	2008	2009	2010	2011	2012	2013	2014	
Total electricity generation (GWh)	163	220	222	155	205	205	238	238	...	Production d'électricité totale (GWh)
of which:										dont:
Production of electricity from fossil fuels (GWh)	163	220	222	155	203	203	236	236	...	Production d'électricité à partir de combustibles fossiles (GWh)
Production of hydro electricity (GWh)	...	...	...	...	...	...	...	...	...	Production d'électricité d'origine hydraulique (GWh)
Production of electricity from solar, wind, tide, wave and other sources (GWh)	...	...	...	...	2	2	2	2	...	Production d'électricité d'origine solaire, éolienne, marée motrice et autres (GWh)

VII TOURISM AND INFRASTRUCTURE - TOURISME ET INFRASTRUCTURE

	2006	2007	2008	2009	2010	2011	2012	2013	2014	
VII-1 TOURISM										**VII-1 TOURISME**
International tourist arrivals (thousands)	125	143	147	142	91	106	157	171	178	Arrivées de touristes internationaux (milliers)
Rooms in hotels and similar establishments (thousands)	8.0	8.6	8.6	8.6	8.6	8.6	8.6	8.6	...	Chambres d'hotels et établissements assimilés (milliers)
Overnight stays (thousands)	1 678	1 564	1 589	1 488	934	1 117	1 430	1 429	1 525	Nuitées (milliers)
Tourism receipts (US$ thousand)	61 480	78 568	74 574	58 043	65 247	69 786	74 086	89 430	92 832	Recettes touristiques (milliers de $ EU)
Total contribution to GDP (%)	18.9	20.2	19.0	17.5	17.3	19.8	18.8	21.5	22.1	Contribution totale au PIB (%)
Total contribution to Employment (%)	17.3	18.5	17.4	16.1	15.9	17.1	16.3	18.4	19.0	Contribution totale à l'emploi (%)
VII-2 INFRASTRUCTURE										**VII-2 INFRASTRUCTURE**
Paved roads (% of total)	...	...	...	1	1	1	1	1	...	Routes asphaltées (% du total)
Total Network (Railways-km)	780	780	...	...	...	...	...	...	...	Réseau total voies ferrées-Km
Main Telephone Lines (per 100 inhabitants)	3	3	3	3	3	3	4	3	...	Lignes téléphoniques fixes (pour 100 habitants)
Mobile Cellular Subscribers (per 100 inhabitants)	27	52	74	81	88	81	85	100	...	Abonnés aux téléphones mobiles (pour 100 habitants)

VIII EXTERNAL TRADE - COMMERCE EXTERIEUR

	2006	2007	2008	2009	2010	2011	2012	2013	2014	
US$ (THOUSANDS) EXPORTS, FOB										**$ E.U (MILLIERS) EXPORTATIONS, FÀB**
Exports - Total	288 197	312 167	277 282	712 544	953 850	332 557	594 716	426 688	...	Exportations - Total
Exports to AFRICA	103 747	112 753	65 887	712 544	127 540	241 197	30 142	29 826	...	Exportations vers l'AFRIQUE
Main Products										**Principaux produits**
Groundnuts oil and its fraction, Crude	2 653	78 696	1 198	172 097	239 435	43 426	99 766	...	...	Huiles d'arachide et ses fractions, brutes
Groundnuts, not roasted or otherwise cooked, shelled	154 372	28 585	19 817	80 868	179 509	55 946	52 064	...	...	Arachides, non grillées ni autrement cuites, décortiquées
Man-made filaments. Other woven fabrics :-- Printed	184	357	1 706	2 821	...	167	108	...	...	Filaments artificiels ou synthétiques, imprimés
Groundnuts, not roasted or otherwise cooked, in shell	...	...	312	2 444	35 659	697	152	...	...	Arachides, non grillées ni autrement cuites, en coques
Cashew nuts :-- In shell	...	487	43 666	87 623	93 860	61 324	91 201	188 657	...	Noix de cajou, en coques
Main Destinations										**Principales destinations**
Senegal	98 629	78 909	50 339	95 410	99 499	16 325	13 254	11 134	...	Sénégal
United Kingdom	157 314	66 154	29 087	131 353	261 077	62 934	139 009	31 464	...	Royaume Uni
Guinea	141	293	402	129	1 211	840	722	...	...	Guinée
France	223	35 232	2 799	170 055	185 359	43 451	192	3 149	...	France
Guinea-Bissau	533	206	132	1 364	1 314	390	2 369	651	...	Guinée-Bissau
IMPORTS, CIF										**IMPORTATIONS, CAF**
Imports - Total	7 277 285	7 945 367	7 111 605	8 084 622	8 049 760	10 450 792	12 154 846	12 394 622	...	Importations - Total (millions)
Imports from AFRICA	1 098 181	978 818	1 071 157	1 630 081	2 201 338	3 130 216	4 363 010	3 879 117	...	Importations en provenance de l'AFRIQUE
Main Products										**Principaux produits**
Petroleum oils and oils obtained from bituminous minerals, other than crude	1 239 622	1 322 966	1 390 296	1 249 250	1 621 721	2 227 715	3 277 561	2 949 546	...	Huiles de pétrole ou de minéraux bitumineux, autres que les huiles brutes
Sugar and sugar confectionery, other than raw	422 877	416 601	265 576	343 300	460 340	455 168	545 723	376 707	...	Sucre et des confiseries, autres que bruts
Broken rice	130 193	272 061	312 124	803 223	658 755	1 046 592	1 158 176	573 981	...	Riz brisé
Linseed oil and its fractions :-- Other than crude	374 852	441 630	334 306	571 039	502 211	514 904	575 254	587 151	...	Huile de lin et ses fractions: - Autres que les huiles brutes
Automobiles and other vehicles principally for the transport of persons, with spark-ignition	697 599	827 811	685 951	571 461	483 991	496 754	657 138	985 741	...	Moteurs voitures et autres véhicules, destinés au transport de personnes, à allumage par étincelles
Main Origin										**Principales provenances**
China	675 445	841 956	765 714	929 072	692 964	890 174	838 466	859 069	...	Chine
Senegal	288 291	218 306	213 520	148 095	216 466	502 758	442 660	731 285	...	Sénégal
Brazil	284 009	281 278	304 716	460 716	794 915	1 165 922	1 039 401	1 289 729	...	Brésil
Ivory Coast	628 961	533 001	635 832	1 156 277	1 534 674	2 134 192	3 237 243	2 875 220	...	Côte d'Ivoire
Netherlands	198 824	445 350	500 763	458 685	404 163	418 023	307 244	272 385	...	Pays-Bas

	2006	2007	2008	2009	2010	2011	2012	2013	2014	
IX FINANCIAL AND MONETARY STATISTICS - FINANCES ET STATISTIQUES MONETAIRES										
IX-1 MONETARY STATISTICS *GAMBIAN DALASI (MILLIONS)*										**IX-1 STATISTIQUES MONÉTAIRES** *DALASI GAMBIEN (MILLIONS)*
Money supply (M1)	7 760	8 270	9 800	11 700	13 290	14 750	15 900	18 310	21 060	Masse monétaire (M1)
Quasi-money	3 533	3 976	4 584	5 941	7 096	7 914	8 255	8 493	9 243	Quasi-monnaie
of which Demand Deposit	...	...	...	...	...	...	...	...	...	dont Monnaie scripturale
Net foreign assets	3 778	3 715	3 087	3 023	3 571	4 307	4 552	4 049	3 535	Avoirs extérieurs nets
Domestic credit	4 301	4 142	6 025	7 480	10 389	11 601	12 912	16 057	19 063	Crédit intérieur
of which claims on private sector	2 134	2 403	3 027	3 542	4 103	4 322	4 575	4 937	4 531	dont créances sur le secteur privé
of which claims on government sector, net	2 036	1 647	2 661	3 247	5 394	6 455	7 559	10 299	13 796	dont créances nettes sur le gouvernement
International reserves (millions US$)	121	143	117	224	202	223	236	211	159	Réserves internationales (millions $EU)
Average Exchange Rate (National Currency per US$)	28.17	24.92	22.29	26.56	27.74	28.37	31.11	33.38	32.46	Taux de change (moyen) (monnaie nationale par $ EU)
IX-2 PUBLIC FINANCE *GAMBIAN DALASI (MILLIONS)*										**IX-2 FINANCES PUBLIQUES** *DALASI GAMBIEN (MILLIONS)*
Total Revenues and Grants	3 190	3 651	3 848	4 909	5 026	5 619	7 397	5 992	7 520	Recettes totales et dons
Tax Revenue	2 710	3 025	3 146	3 518	3 528	3 780	4 221	4 579	5 086	Recettes fiscales
Non Tax Revenue	301	431	354	371	433	484	565	688	763	Recettes non fiscales
Grants	180	194	348	1 021	1 065	1 355	2 611	725	1 671	Dons
Total Expenditures and Net Lending	4 211	3 639	4 154	5 684	6 403	6 871	8 675	8 753	9 700	Dépenses totales et prêts nets
Current expenditure	2 574	2 586	3 010	3 622	4 059	4 579	5 068	6 451	7 302	Dépenses courantes
Of which Wages and Salaries	652	680	983	1 192	1 516	1 693	1 804	1 889	2 066	Dont rémunérations et salaires
Capital expenditure	1 574	977	1 047	1 924	2 344	2 292	3 607	2 302	2 411	Dépenses d'équipement
Net Lending	63	76	96	138	-	-	-	-	- 13	Prêts nets
Fiscal Balance	- 1 021	12	- 306	- 775	- 1 377	- 1 252	- 1 278	- 2 760	- 2 180	Solde global y compris les dons
IX-3 BALANCE OF PAYMENTS *GAMBIAN DALASI (MILLIONS)*										**IX-3 BALANCE DES PAIEMENTS** *DALASI GAMBIEN (MILLIONS)*
Trade balance	- 3 879	- 4 266	- 4 921	- 5 372	- 6 006	- 6 334	- 6 855	- 7 849	...	Balance commerciale
Services Balance	1 420	1 649	1 398	1 532	1 029	1 651	2 553	2 202	...	Balance des services
Net Income	- 1 347	- 1 166	- 1 023	- 1 147	- 830	- 939	- 874	- 1 083	...	Revenus nets
Compensation of employees	...	...	...	...	...	...	...	...	...	Rémunération des salariés
Investment Income	...	...	...	...	...	...	...	...	...	Revenus des investissements
Current transfers, net total	2 169	1 789	1 634	2 294	1 526	1 642	1 399	2 272	...	Transferts courants
Net official transfers	...	...	...	...	...	...	...	...	...	Transferts officiels nets
Workers' remittances	...	...	...	...	...	...	...	...	...	Envois de fonds des travailleurs
Other private transfers	...	...	...	...	...	...	...	...	...	Autres transferts privés
Current account balance	- 1 636	- 1 994	- 2 912	- 2 692	- 4 281	- 3 980	- 3 777	- 4 459	...	Solde du compte courant
Capital & financial account	...	...	...	...	...	...	...	...	...	Comptes de capital et financier
Capital account	...	...	...	...	...	...	...	...	...	Compte de capital
Financial account	...	...	...	...	...	...	...	...	...	Compte financier
Errors & omissions	...	...	...	...	...	...	...	...	...	Erreurs et omissions
Overall balance	...	...	...	...	...	...	...	...	...	Balance générale

X DEBT AND FINANCIAL FLOWS - DETTE ET FLUX FINANCIERS										
	2006	2007	2008	2009	2010	2011	2012	2013	2014	
X-1 DEBT *US$ (MILLIONS)*										**X-1 DETTE EXTÉRIEURE** *$ E.U (MILLIONS)*
Total external debt	759	338	366	389	406	403	415	425	438	Dette extérieure totale
Private	-	-	-	-	-	-	-	-	-	Privée
Public	759	338	366	389	406	403	415	425	438	Publique
Total external debt service	69	71	69	72	76	80	86	88	90	Service de la dette extérieure
Present value of External debt	...	...	...	...	...	...	...	...	...	Valeur actuelle de la dette extérieure
Total government domestic debt (in local currency)	...	...	4 773	7 239	8 706.7	9 651.6	10 737.0	13 520.0	15 320.0	Dette publique intérieure
X-2 FINANCIAL FLOWS *US$ (MILLIONS)*										**X-2 FLUX FINANCIERS** *$ E.U (MILLIONS)*
Net Foreign Direct Investment Inflows	71	76	70	40	37	36	25	25	...	Investissement étranger direct (flux nets entrants)
Main origin of FDI Inflows										**Principales origines de l'IDE entrant:**
Germany	...	...	...	...	...	...	...	...	...	Allemagne
France	...	...	...	...	...	...	...	...	...	France
Denmark	...	1	...	...	...	...	...	...	...	Danemark
Poland	...	...	...	...	...	...	...	...	...	Pologne
Hungary	...	...	...	...	...	...	- 0.1	...	...	Hongrie
African countries	...	...	...	...	...	...	...	...	...	Pays africains
Net total Official Development Assistance	75	97	94	127	120	135	139	111	...	Aide publique au développement (nette totale)
Main origin of Net ODA										**Principales origines de l'APD nette**
IDA	7	3	8	16	11.4	11.1	29.1	...	...	IDA
AfDF	8	35	11	15	5.4	5.8	10.4	...	...	FAfD
Japan	11	6	1	11	17.2	11.5	7.5	7.0	...	Japon
Global Fund	6	10	9	13	18.6	15.7	11.5	...	...	Fonds mondial
Islamic Dev. Bank	8	2	2	9	9.8	11.8	10.5	...	...	Banque de Dev.Isl.

GHANA

AREA (km²)		238 533	SUPERFICIE (km²)
CAPITAL CITY	Accra	Accra	CAPITALE
CURRENCY	Cedi	Cedi	MONNAIE

I SOCIAL AND DEMOGRAPHIC INDICATORS — INDICATEURS DEMOGRAPHIQUES ET SOCIAUX

	Year / Année	Value / Valeur	
POPULATION			**POPULATION**
Population ('000)			Population ('000)
Both sexes	2014	26 442	Les deux sexes
Male	2014	13 126	Masculin
Female	2014	13 317	Féminin
Average annual growth rate	2014	2.2	Taux de croissance annuel
Active Population ('000)	2014	11 050	Population active ('000)
Population by age group ('000)			Population par groupe d'âge ('000)
0-14 years	2014	10 116	0-14 ans
15-64 years	2014	15 411	15-64 ans
65+ years	2014	915	65+ ans
Economically. active population. in agriculture (%)	2014	60.8	Participation de la population active agricole (%)
Crude birth rate	2014	30.4	Taux brut de natalité
Crude death rate	2014	8.9	Taux brut de mortalité
Total fertility rate	2014	3.8	Indice synthétique de fécondité
Proportion of urban population	2014	53.9	Part de la population urbaine
Life Expectancy at Birth - Total (years)	2014	61.3	Espérance de vie à la naissance - Totale (ans)
Dependency Ratio - Total (%)	2014	72.1	Taux de dépendance - Total (%)
HEALTH			**SANTÉ**
Percentage of children under-five and underweight	2011	13.4	% d'enfants de moins de cinq ans avec insuffisance pondérale
Prevalence of undernourishment	2013	5.0	Prévalence de la malnutrition
Under five mortality rate (both sexes, per 1000)	2013	78.4	Taux de mortalité de moins de 5 ans (les deux sexes, pour 1000)
Infant mortality rate (both sexes) per 1000	2013	52.3	Taux de mortalité infantile (les deux sexes) par 1000
Percentage of children provided the vaccines :			Pourcentage d'enfants vaccinés :
BCG	2013	98.0	BCG
DPT3	2013	90.0	DTC3
Polio	2011	90.7	Polio
Measles	2013	89.0	Rougeole
Percentage of mothers provided at least one antenatal care (%)	2011	96.7	Pourcentage de mères ayant au moins reçu un soin prénatal (%)
Percentage of deliveries attended by skilled health personnel	2011	68.4	% d'accouchements assistés par un personnel de santé qualifié
Number of doctors (per 10 000 population)	2010	1.0	Nombre de médecins (pour 10 000 habitants)
Number of nurses (per 10 000 population)	2010	9.3	Nombre d'infirmières (pour 10 000 habitants)
Hospital beds - Total (per 10 000 population)	2011	9.0	Nombre de lits d'hôpitaux - Total (pour 10 000)
Births registered (per 1 000)	2014	30.4	Naiss.s enregistrées (pour 1 000)
Deaths registered (per 1 000)	2014	8.9	Décès enregistrés (pour 1 000)
Public expenditure on Health (% of budget)	2014	6.2	Dépenses publiques consacrées à la santé (% du budget)
EDUCATION			**EDUCATION**
Enrolment in primary education (both sexes) (000)	2014	4 117	Scolarisation dans le primaire (les deux sexes) (000)
Female	2014	2 015	Féminin
Enrolment in secondary education (both sexes) (000)	2014	2 266	Scolarisation dans le secondaire (les deux sexes) (000)
Female	2014	1 073	Féminin
Enrolment in tertiary education (both sexes) (000)	2014	258.7	Scolarisation dans le tertiaire (les deux sexes) (000)
Female	2012	111.4	Féminin
Literacy rate (both sexes)	2010	71.5	Taux d'alphabétisation (deux sexes)
Male	2010	78.3	Masculin
Female	2010	65.3	Féminin
Pupil-teacher ratio	2014	32.0	Ratio élève-enseignant
Public expenditure on education (% of budget)	2014	13.8	Dépenses publiques consacrées à l'enseignement (% du budget)
POVERTY			**PAUVRETÉ**
GNI Per Capita (US$)	2013	1 770.0	RNB par habitant ($EU)
Human Poverty Index (HPI-1) Value (%)	2007	28.1	Valeur de l'Indice de pauvreté (IPH-1) (%)
Population below International Poverty Line ($2/day) (%)	2006	51.8	Population sous le seuil international de pauvreté (2$/J) (%)
Share of Income Held by Richest 10%	2006	32.8	% de revenu des 10% plus riches
Share of Income Held by Poorest 10%	2006	2.0	% de revenu des 10% plus pauvres
Gini index	2006	42.8	Indice de Gini

Charts / Graphiques

Population by age group – 2014
Population par groupe d'age – 2014

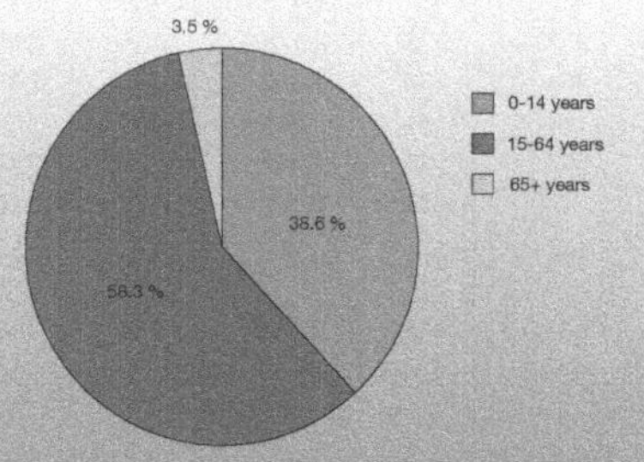

Percentage of children provided the vaccines – 2013
Pourcentage d'enfants vaccinés – 2013

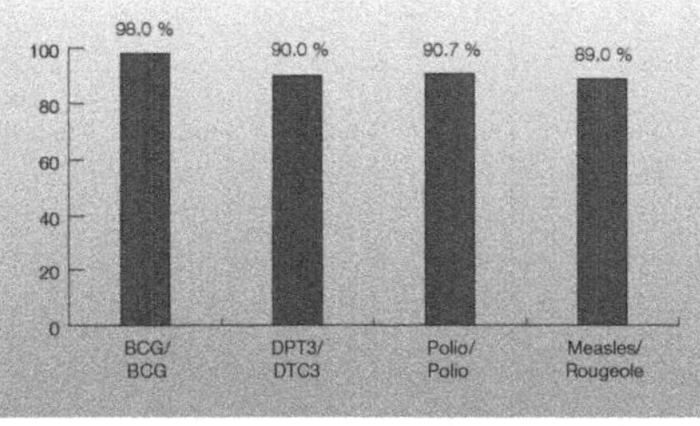

Literacy rate (%) – 2010
Taux d'alphabétisation – 2010

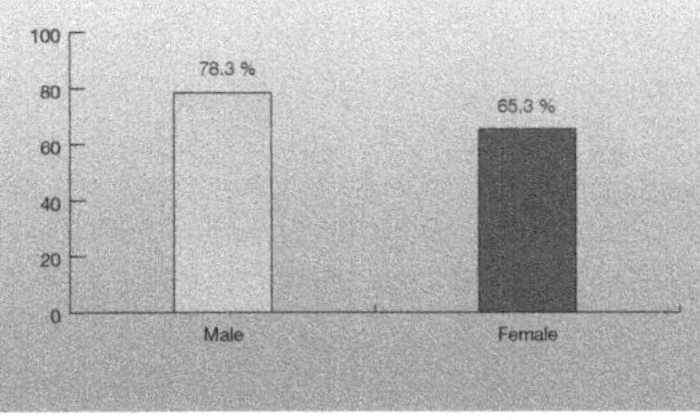

GNI Per Capita (US$)
RNB par habitant ($EU)

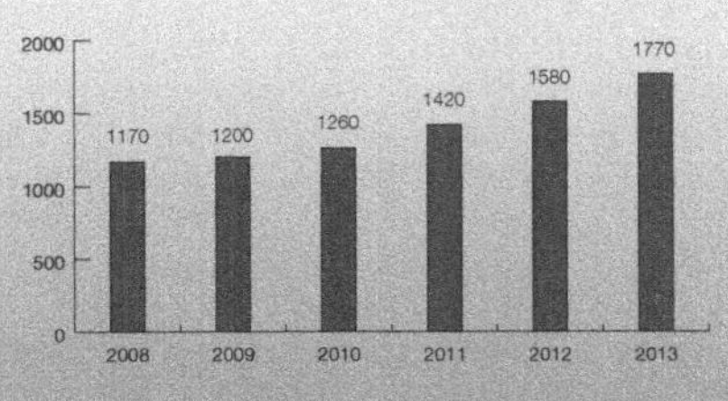

II NATIONAL ACCOUNTS — COMPTES NATIONAUX

	2006	2007	2008	2009	2010	2011	2012	2013	2014	
GROSS DOMESTIC PRODUCT BY KIND OF ECONOMIC ACTIVITY AT CURRENT PRICES *CEDI (MILLIONS)*										**PRODUIT INTÉRIEUR BRUT PAR BRANCHE D'ACTIVITÉ ÉCONOMIQUE AUX PRIX COURANTS** *CEDI (MILLIONS)*
Agriculture, hunting, forestry and fishing	5 415	6 320	8 875	11 342	12 910	14 155	16 669	19 970	21 643	Agriculture, chasse, sylviculture et pêche
Mining and quarrying	497	602	693	740	1 013	4 690	6 961	9 036	9 891	Industries extractives
Manufacturing	1 824	1 991	2 277	2 478	2 941	3 842	4 263	4 849	6 445	Industries manufacturières
Electricity, gas & water	367	357	384	413	634	747	843	987	1 171	Electricité, gaz et eau
Construction & public works	1 016	1 565	2 500	3 144	3 706	4 995	8 370	10 765	13 327	Bâtiments et travaux publics
Wholesale & retail trade, restaurants, hotels	2 949	3 562	4 611	5 767	7 239	8 880	11 079	13 359	14 560	Commerce de gros et de détail, restaurants et hôtels
Finance, insurance, real estate, etc.	473	739	1 089	1 547	2 240	2 466	3 452	5 954	7 468	Banques, assurances, affaires immobilières
Transport and communications	2 840	3 360	3 884	4 415	5 409	6 986	9 631	12 366	14 507	Transport(s) et communications
Public administration and defense	862	1 289	1 799	2 479	3 024	3 897	4 952	6 319	8 839	Administrations publiques et défense
Education	655	856	1 132	1 506	1 877	2 307	3 101	3 789	4 628	Education
Health and Social Work	250	308	381	513	674	728	921	1 132	1 363	Santé et actions sociales
Other services	662	807	1 039	1 318	1 722	2 159	2 701	3 886	4 871	Autres services
Less Imputed Service Charges	...	...	- 689	- 1 192	- 1 512	- 1 458	- 2 317	- 3 419	- 4 229	Moins services d'intermédiation financière
Gross domestic product at factor cost / basic prices	17 810	21 755	27 975	34 470	41 877	54 394	70 626	88 993	104 484	Produit intérieur brut aux couts des facteurs / prix de base
Plus: indirect taxes / taxes on products, less subsidies	895	1 400	2 204	2 128	4 166	5 422	4 689	5 946	8 954	Plus taxes indirectes/impôts sur les produits, moins les subventions
EXPENDITURE ON GROSS DOMESTIC PRODUCT AT CURRENT PURCHASER'S VALUES *CEDI (MILLIONS)*										**EMPLOI DU PRODUIT INTÉRIEUR BRUT AUX PRIX COURANTS D'ACQUISITION** *CEDI (MILLIONS)*
Government final consumption	2 114	2 676	3 393	4 294	4 768	9 955	15 732	15 606	-	Consommation finale des administrations publiques
Private final consumption	15 450	19 597	26 183	29 500	37 003	37 441	39 953	62 813	-	Consommation finale privée
Gross fixed capital formation	4 047	4 656	6 474	7 216	11 354	15 317	23 334	21 280	-	Formation brute de capital fixe
Change in inventories	...	-	-	349	480	440	-	-	-	Variation des stocks
Exports of goods and services	4 712	5 679	7 554	10 720	13 572	26 390	36 069	39 578	-	Exportations de biens et services
Less imports of goods and services	7 619	9 454	13 425	15 482	21 134	29 727	39 773	44 338	-	Moins importations de biens et services
GDP at purchasers' values	18 705	23 155	30 179	36 598	46 042	59 816	75 315	94 939	113 436	PIB aux prix d'acquisition
GROSS DOMESTIC PRODUCT BY KIND OF ECONOMIC ACTIVITY AT CONSTANT PRICES *ANNUAL GROWTH RATES (%)*										**PRODUIT INTÉRIEUR BRUT PAR BRANCHE D'ACTIVITÉ ECONOMIQUE AUX PRIX CONSTANTS** *TAUX DE CROISSANCE ANNUEL (%)*
Agriculture, hunting, forestry and fishing	4.5	- 1.7	7.4	7.2	5.3	0.9	2.3	5.2	5.2	Agriculture, chasse, sylviculture et pêche
Mining and quarrying	4.5	7.0	2.3	6.7	18.8	206.7	16.4	11.6	2.9	Industries extractives
Manufacturing	4.5	- 1.2	3.7	- 1.3	7.6	17.0	1.9	- 0.5	1.0	Industries manufacturières
Electricity, gas & water	4.5	- 6.0	7.2	7.6	7.8	1.6	5.7	5.6	2.1	Electricité, gaz et eau
Construction & public works	4.5	23.2	38.9	9.3	2.5	17.2	16.4	8.6	7.4	Bâtiments et travaux publics
Wholesale & retail trade, restaurants, hotels	4.5	4.2	9.3	1.4	9.0	8.1	9.3	18.1	- 1.4	Commerce de gros et de détail, restaurants et hôtels
Finance, insurance, real estate, etc.	4.5	8.5	3.9	3.8	15.0	8.5	19.8	- 0.5	9.1	Banques, assurances, affaires immobilières
Transport and communications	4.5	8.3	6.4	4.3	11.0	12.2	16.1	6.0	1.5	Transport(s) et communications
Public administration and defense	4.5	11.4	12.7	11.7	3.4	7.4	4.2	9.1	11.3	Administrations publiques et défense
Education	...	9.9	13.1	12.4	5.2	3.8	6.7	6.8	7.2	Education
Health and Social Work	4.5	3.7	4.6	15.2	11.2	4.9	11.0	7.7	1.1	Santé et actions sociales
Other services	...	8.8	9.2	7.5	10.8	12.9	4.2	37.4	9.2	Autres services
Less Imputed Service Charges	...	...	...	...	7.8	13.4	12.3	29.6	6.8	Moins services d'intermédiation financière
Gross domestic product at factor cost / basic prices	4.5	4.5	9.3	2.1	7.9	14.1	9.3	7.3	4.2	Produit intérieur brut aux couts des facteurs / prix de base
Plus: indirect taxes / taxes on products, less subsidies	4.5	45.6	- 4.2	24.5	7.9	14.1	9.3	7.4	4.2	Plus taxes indirectes/impôts sur les produits, moins les subventions
Gross domestic product at market prices	4.5	6.5	8.4	3.4	7.9	14.0	9.3	7.3	4.2	Produit intérieur brut aux prix du marché
EXPENDITURE ON GROSS DOMESTIC PRODUCT AT CONSTANT PURCHASERS' VALUES *ANNUAL GROWTH RATES (%)*										**EMPLOIS DU PRODUIT INTÉRIEUR BRUT AUX PRIX CONSTANTS D'ACQUISITION** *TAUX DE CROISSANCE ANNUEL (%)*
Government final consumption	- 3.4	1.5	13.0	20.0	14.0	49.8	12.9	- 14.3	...	Consommation finale des administrations publiques
Private final consumption	7.8	8.0	7.9	- 3.2	3.1	14.8	- 6.7	14.1	...	Consommation finale privée
Gross fixed capital formation	23.6	18.3	30.1	- 21.4	24.4	37.6	27.5	- 4.7	...	Formation brute de capital fixe
Exports of goods and services	10.3	18.2	16.7	7.6	24.6	30.1	29.9	8.4	...	Exportations de biens et services
Less imports of goods and services	13.7	21.7	24.6	- 12.6	21.0	47.7	12.0	2.3	...	Moins importations de biens et services
Notes	NA Data: 2012:Final; 2013:Revised ; 2014:Provisional!							Données des CN: 2012:Définitives;2013:Revisées;2014:Provisoires		Notes

III INFLATION

	2006	2007	2008	2009	2010	2011	2012	2013	2014	
ANNUAL GROWTH RATES (%)										**TAUX DE CROISSANCE ANNUEL (%)**
All items	11.7	10.7	16.5	19.2	10.7	8.7	9.2	11.8	16.0	Ensemble
of which:										dont:
Food and Non-alcoholic beverages	9.9	9.5	15.2	15.7	6.1	4.0	4.6	7.3	8.4	Alimentation et boissons non alcoolisés
Alcoholic beverages & tobacco	13.2	11.6	14.9	29.2	18.5	14.0	12.8	15.6	12.0	Boissons alcoolisées et tabacs
Clothing and Footwear	6.0	3.5	11.4	20.9	16.0	12.9	13.8	17.0	16.7	Habillement et chaussures
Housing, Water, Electricity, Gas and Other Fuels	20.0	16.1	17.8	4.6	10.3	10.6	7.9	22.6	46.1	Logement, eau, electricité, gas et autres combustibles
Furnishing, household equipment	8.6	3.6	16.0	31.6	15.3	11.9	13.8	14.6	10.6	Meubles, articles de ménage et entretien courant
Health	20.7	31.7	19.6	48.3	10.3	7.8	8.9	10.5	12.9	Santé
Transport	28.0	17.4	23.1	2.8	9.7	22.2	19.7	12.9	17.4	Transport
Communication	13.2	32.4	1.3	6.0	-0.1	0.2	0.5	0.5	7.6	Communication
Recreation & culture	16.6	14.5	14.1	74.2	20.8	8.5	13.4	13.5	13.6	Loisirs et culture
Education	9.1	4.2	15.9	11.9	1.1	2.5	15.1	11.4	6.1	Enseignement
Restaurants & hotels	10.3	16.1	21.6	29.4	18.3	8.6	7.5	9.9	8.3	Restaurants et hôtels
Miscellaneous goods & services	12.9	13.5	12.5	14.3	8.6	16.5	15.7	14.7	13.3	Biens et services divers

	2006	2007	2008	2009	2010	2011	2012	2013	2014	
IV AGRICULTURAL PRODUCTION - PRODUCTION AGRICOLE										
TONNES *(THOUSAND)*										**TONNES** *(MILLIERS)*
Cassava	9 638	10 218	11 351	12 231	13 504	14 241	14 547	15 990	...	Manioc
Yams	4 288	4 376	4 895	5 778	5 960	6 295	6 639	7 075	...	Ignames
Plantains	2 900	3 234	3 338	3 563	3 538	3 620	3 557	3 675	...	Banane-Plantain
Maize	1 189	1 220	1 470	1 620	1 872	1 684	1 950	1 764	...	Mais
Taro (cocoyam)	1 660	1 690	1 688	1 504	1 355	1 300	1 270	1 261	...	Macabo/Taro
V MINING PRODUCTION - PRODUCTION MINIERE										
	2006	2007	2008	2009	2010	2011	2012	2013	2014	
Crude petroleum, metric tons (thousands)	23	27	32	25	199	3 466	4 208	5 404	...	Pétrole brut, tonnes métriques (milliers)
Gold ores and concentrates, Kilograms	600	895	643	376	334	302	...	...	...	Minerais d'or et concentrés, Kilogrammes
Marble, travertines, etc., metric tons (thousands)	...	...	...	...	...	...	...	...	...	Marbles, travertins, etc., tonnes métriques (milliers)
VI ENERGY - ENERGIE										
	2006	2007	2008	2009	2010	2011	2012	2013	2014	
Total electricity generation (GWh)	...	...	8 324	...	...	...	...	...	...	Production d'électricité totale (GWh)
of which:										dont:
Production of electricity from fossil fuels (GWh)	2 811	3 251	2 129	2 081	3 171	3 639	3 953	4 635	...	Production d'électricité à partir de combustibles fossiles (GWh)
Production of hydro electricity (GWh)	5 619	3 727	6 195	6 877	6 925	7 561	8 070	8 233	...	Production d'électricité d'origine hydraulique (GWh)
Production of electricity from solar, wind, tide, wave and other sources (GWh)	...	...	...	...	...	...	...	3	...	Production d'électricité d'origine solaire, éolienne, marée motrice et autres (GWh)
VII TOURISM AND INFRASTRUCTURE - TOURISME ET INFRASTRUCTURE										
	2006	2007	2008	2009	2010	2011	2012	2013	2014	
VII-1 TOURISM										**VII-1 TOURISME**
International tourist arrivals (thousands)	497	587	698	803	931	1 005	1 234	1 061	1 123	Arrivées de touristes internationaux (milliers)
Rooms in hotels and similar establishments (thousands)	...	...	26.9	27.2	...	...	...	...	...	Chambres d'hotels et établissements assimilés (milliers)
Overnight stays (thousands)	6 269	6 530	7 777	8 903	10 274	11 152	14 265	12 097	13 080	Nuitées (milliers)
Tourism receipts (US$ thousand)	861 300	908 200	918 700	768 000	619 500	679 669	891 368	831 807	869 135	Recettes touristiques (milliers de $ EU)
Total contribution to GDP (%)	8.7	9.2	8.5	8.4	6.9	6.8	7.2	6.8	7.4	Contribution totale au PIB (%)
Total contribution to Employment (%)	8.2	8.7	8.0	7.9	6.5	6.1	5.9	5.5	6.0	Contribution totale à l'emploi (%)
VII-2 INFRASTRUCTURE										**VII-2 INFRASTRUCTURE**
Paved roads (% of total)	58	60	...	...	5	...	...	...	...	Routes asphaltées (% du total)
Total Network (Railways-km)	982	974	...	...	...	...	...	...	...	Réseau total voies ferrées-Km
Main Telephone Lines (per 100 inhabitants)	2	2	1	1	1	1	1	1	...	Lignes téléphoniques fixes (pour 100 habitants)
Mobile Cellular Subscribers (per 100 inhabitants)	24	34	50	64	72	85	101	108	...	Abonnés aux téléphones mobiles (pour 100 habitants)
VIII EXTERNAL TRADE - COMMERCE EXTERIEUR										
	2006	2007	2008	2009	2010	2011	2012	2013	2014	
CEDI (MILLIONS) EXPORTS, FOB										**CEDI (MILLIONS) EXPORTATIONS, FÀB**
Exports - Total	1 953	2 045	2 285	1 700	2 235	2 029	...	...	...	Exportations - Total
Exports to AFRICA	...	...	...	...	...	...	...	...	...	Exportations vers l'AFRIQUE
Main Products										**Principaux produits**
Petroleum oils, crude	928	878	1 115	686	698	761	...	...	...	Huiles brutes de pétrole
Fuel, lubricant	226	314	288	170	247	346	...	...	...	Carburants et lubrifiants
Wood	184	234	219	100	123	136	...	...	...	Bois sciés
Cocoa beans	116	88	120	255	301	242	...	...	...	Cacao brut en fèves
Aluminium, crude	79	79	74	32	48	45	...	...	...	Aluminium brut
Main Destinations										**Principales destinations**
Spain	483	...	362	142	354	331	...	...	...	Espagne
Italy	430	104	92	54	74	66	...	...	...	Italie
France	197	171	145	107	119	115	...	...	...	France
Netherlands	118	99	178	232	232	196	...	...	...	Pays bas
USA	119	...	106	70	134	129	...	...	...	Etats Unis
IMPORTS, CIF										**IMPORTATIONS, CAF**
Imports - Total	1 648	1 773	2 096	2 013	2 339	2 929	...	...	...	Importations - Total (millions)
Imports from Africa	...	...	...	...	...	...	...	...	...	Importations en provenance de l'Afrique
Main Products										**Principaux produits**
Hydrocarbons	527	734	714	370	662	825	...	...	...	Hydrocarbures
Cereals	121	124	199	182	161	222	...	...	...	Céréales
Machinery, mechanical	101	172	187	198	217	269	...	...	...	Machines et app. Mécaniques
Vehicles; tractors	96	126	144	146	192	217	...	...	...	Véhicules automobiles; tracteurs
Machinery, electrical	84	96	117	136	134	201	...	...	...	Machines et appareils électriques
Main Origin										**Principales provenances**
Nigeria	383	...	590	255	462	724	...	...	...	Nigéria
France	288	349	372	326	361	399	...	...	...	France
China	104	147	179	208	268	341	...	...	...	Chine
USA	47	121	120	70	84	102	...	...	...	Etats Unis
Belgium	67	74	75	81	75	76	...	...	...	Belgique

IX FINANCIAL AND MONETARY STATISTICS - FINANCES ET STATISTIQUES MONETAIRES	2006	2007	2008	2009	2010	2011	2012	2013	2014	
IX-1 MONETARY STATISTICS *CEDI (MILLIONS)*										**IX-1 STATISTIQUES MONÉTAIRES** *CEDI (MILLIONS)*
Money supply (M1)	4 230	5 750	8 130	10 230	13 770	18 200	22 620	26 940	35 350	Masse monétaire (M1)
Quasi-money	1 389	1 986	2 756	3 955	4 998	6 216	7 051	8 665	11 025	Quasi-monnaie
of which Demand Deposit	...	...	...	...	...	...	...	...	...	dont Monnaie scripturale
Net foreign assets	2 088	2 431	2 686	3 600	5 436	7 336	6 976	5 464	9 285	Avoirs extérieurs nets
Domestic credit	3 948	5 294	8 420	10 504	13 062	16 438	23 601	32 622	42 947	Crédit intérieur
of which claims on private sector	2 075	3 355	4 793	5 730	7 040	9 002	11 783	15 947	22 776	dont créances sur le secteur privé
of which claims on government sector, net	1 533	1 323	2 641	3 577	4 787	6 289	9 740	13 409	16 143	dont créances nettes sur le gouvernement
International reserves (millions US$)	2 105	2 000	1 785	3 402	4 778	5 498	5 383	5 264	4 253	Réserves internationales (millions $EU)
Average Exchange Rate (National Currency per US$)	0.92	0.94	1.06	1.41	1.43	1.51	1.80	1.95	2.55	Taux de change (moyen) (monnaie nationale par $ EU)
IX-2 PUBLIC FINANCE *CEDI (MILLIONS)*										**IX-2 FINANCES PUBLIQUES** *CEDI (MILLIONS)*
Total Revenues and Grants	3 330	4 656	5 564	5 812	7 145	11 157	14 155	15 921	15 498	Recettes totales et dons
Tax Revenue	2 603	3 486	3 932	4 647	6 437	10 441	12 857	15 325	14 832	Recettes fiscales
Non Tax Revenue	92	338	812	64	- 373	- 493	138	159	141	Recettes non fiscales
Grants	635	833	821	1 101	1 080	1 210	1 160	438	525	Dons
Total Expenditures and Net Lending	4 077	5 609	7 361	8 582	12 008	14 568	23 022	24 969	24 343	Dépenses totales et prêts nets
Current expenditure	2 677	3 592	5 163	5 995	8 501	12 269	18 997	20 666	19 823	Dépenses courantes
Of which Wages and Salaries	1 132	1 412	2 190	2 730	4 144	6 543	8 387	10 512	8 241	Dont rémunérations et salaires
Capital expenditure	1 096	1 630	2 198	2 587	3 506	2 299	4 025	4 303	4 520	Dépenses d'équipement
Net Lending	304	387	-	-	-	-	-	-	-	Prêts nets
Fiscal Balance	- 747	- 953	- 1 797	- 2 770	- 4 863	- 3 411	- 8 868	- 9 048	- 8 845	Solde global y compris les dons
IX-3 BALANCE OF PAYMENTS *US$ (MILLIONS)*										**IX-3 BALANCE DES PAIEMENTS** *$ E.U (MILLIONS)*
Trade balance	- 278	- 362	- 541	- 316	- 425	- 492	- 782	- 752	...	Balance commerciale
Services Balance	- 12	- 15	- 54	- 168	- 229	- 288	- 181	- 478	...	Balance des services
Net Income	- 12	- 13	- 28	- 55	- 77	- 190	- 395	- 264	...	Revenus nets
Compensation of employees	...	...	...	...	...	...	...	...	...	Rémunération des salariés
Investment Income	...	...	...	...	...	...	...	...	...	Revenus des investissements
Current transfers, net total	206	191	239	298	333	402	446	406	...	Transferts courants
Net official transfers	...	...	...	...	...	...	...	...	...	Transferts officiels nets
Workers' remittances	...	...	...	...	...	...	...	...	...	Envois de fonds des travailleurs
Other private transfers	...	...	...	...	...	...	...	...	...	Autres transferts privés
Current account balance	- 95	- 199	- 384	- 242	- 397	- 568	- 912	- 1 088	...	Solde du compte courant
Capital & financial account	136	248	304	620	615	693	677	...	...	Comptes de capital et financier
Capital account	21	18	50	81	48	69	53	...	...	Compte de capital
Financial account	115	225	254	539	566	624	624	...	...	Compte financier
Errors & omissions	- 3	- 11	- 22	- 212	- 8	- 40	11	...	...	Erreurs et omissions
Overall balance	38	39	- 102	166	210	85	- 224	...	...	Balance générale

X DEBT AND FINANCIAL FLOWS - DETTE ET FLUX FINANCIERS	2006	2007	2008	2009	2010	2011	2012	2013	2014	
X-1 DEBT *US$ (MILLIONS)*										**X-1 DETTE EXTÉRIEURE** *$ E.U (MILLIONS)*
Total external debt	4 088	5 757	6 075	6 980	8 752	9 938	10 556	13 883	13 644	Dette extérieure totale
Private	1 911	2 171	2 040	1 973	2 498	2 285	1 402	2 541	829	Privée
Public	2 177	3 586	4 035	5 008	6 255	7 653	9 154	11 342	12 815	Publique
Total external debt service	602	226	358	316	370	463	633	733	990	Service de la dette extérieure
Present value of External debt	...	...	...	...	...	...	...	...	...	Valeur actuelle de la dette extérieure
Total government domestic debt (in local currency)	...	...	4 800	6 083	8 280.1	11 841.1	18 535.2	26 665.8	...	Dette publique intérieure
X-2 FINANCIAL FLOWS *US$ (MILLIONS)*										**X-2 FLUX FINANCIERS** *$ E.U (MILLIONS)*
Net Foreign Direct Investment Inflows	435	855	1 220	2 897	2 527	3 222	3 293	3 226	...	Investissement étranger direct (flux nets entrants)
Main origin of FDI Inflows										**Principales origines de l'IDE entrant:**
United States	729	...	...	205	- 313.0	328.0	461.0	...	...	États-Unis
United Kingdom	53	90	99	97	126.7	158.7	161.6	...	...	Royaume-Uni
Sweden	12	13	48	64	65.7	54.6	65.4	...	...	Suède
Belgium	1	56	15	- 25	72.8	- 90.5	428.0	...	...	Belgique
France	6	...	...	...	...	...	...	...	...	France
African countries	...	...	...	...	...	...	...	...	...	Pays africains
Net total Official Development Assistance	1 243	1 165	1 307	1 582	1 693	1 810	1 808	1 331	...	Aide publique au développement (nette totale)
Main origin of Net ODA										**Principales origines de l'APD nette**
IDA	265	240	273	247	318.7	422.4	365.3	...	...	IDA
United Kingdom	167	152	151	154	166.6	130.5	83.5	...	...	Royaume-Uni
United States	68	71	80	151	208.1	314.4	220.6	114.5	...	Etats-Unis
Netherlands	97	142	120	98	72.9	63.1	40.7	21.5	...	Pays-Bas
AfDF	133	22	86	101	134.2	134.7	204.4	...	...	FAfD

AREA (km²)	245 857		SUPERFICIE (km²)
CAPITAL CITY	Conakry	Conakry	CAPITALE
CURRENCY	Guinea Franc	Franc Guinéen	MONNAIE

I SOCIAL AND DEMOGRAPHIC INDICATORS — INDICATEURS DEMOGRAPHIQUES ET SOCIAUX

	Year / Année	Value / Valeur	
POPULATION			**POPULATION**
Population ('000)			Population ('000)
Both sexes	2014	12 044	Les deux sexes
Male	2014	6 033	Masculin
Female	2014	6 011	Féminin
Average annual growth rate	2014	2.5	Taux de croissance annuel
Active Population ('000)	2014	4 432	Population active ('000)
Population by age group ('000)			Population par groupe d'âge ('000)
0-14 years	2014	5 067	0-14 ans
15-64 years	2014	6 604	15-64 ans
65+ years	2014	373	65+ ans
Economically. active population. in agriculture (%)	2014	94.5	Participation de la population active agricole (%)
Crude birth rate	2014	36.5	Taux brut de natalité
Crude death rate	2014	11.3	Taux brut de mortalité
Total fertility rate	2014	4.8	Indice synthétique de fécondité
Proportion of urban population	2014	36.9	Part de la population urbaine
Life Expectancy at Birth - Total (years)	2014	56.4	Espérance de vie à la naissance - Totale (ans)
Dependency Ratio - Total (%)	2014	83.4	Taux de dépendance - Total (%)
HEALTH			Santé
Percentage of children under-five and underweight	2012	35.0	% d'enfants de moins de cinq ans avec insuffisance pondérale
Prevalence of undernourishment	2013	18.1	Prévalence de la malnutrition
Under five mortality rate (both sexes, per 1000)	2013	100.7	Taux de mortalité de moins de 5 ans (les deux sexes, pour 1000)
Infant mortality rate (both sexes) per 1000	2013	64.9	Taux de mortalité infantile (les deux sexes) par 1000
Percentage of children provided the vaccines :			Pourcentage d'enfants vaccinés :
BCG	2013	66.0	BCG
DPT3	2013	63.0	DTC3
Polio	2011	97.4	Polio
Measles	2013	62.0	Rougeole
Percentage of mothers provided at least one antenatal care (%)	2011	63.2	Pourcentage de mères ayant au moins reçu un soin prénatal (%)
Percentage of deliveries attended by skilled health personnel	2012	45.3	% d'accouchements assistés par un personnel de santé qualifié
Number of doctors (per 10 000 population)	2005	1.0	Nombre de médecins (pour 10 000 habitants)
Number of nurses (per 10 000 population)	2004	5.1	Nombre d'infirmières (pour 10 000 habitants)
Hospital beds - Total (per 10 000 population)	2011	3.0	Nombre de lits d'hôpitaux - Total (pour 10 000)
Births registered (per 1 000)	2014	36.5	Naiss.s enregistrées (pour 1 000)
Deaths registered (per 1 000)	2014	11.3	Décès enregistrés (pour 1 000)
Public expenditure on Health (% of budget)	2012	2.0	Dépenses publiques consacrées à la santé (% du budget)
EDUCATION			**EDUCATION**
Enrolment in primary education (both sexes) (000)	2012	1 600	Scolarisation dans le primaire (les deux sexes) (000)
Female	2012	726	Féminin
Enrolment in secondary education (both sexes) (000)	2012	657	Scolarisation dans le secondaire (les deux sexes) (000)
Female	2011	245	Féminin
Enrolment in tertiary education (both sexes) (000)	...	...	Scolarisation dans le tertiaire (les deux sexes) (000)
Female	2012	27.0	Féminin
Literacy rate (both sexes)	2010	25.3	Taux d'alphabétisation (deux sexes)
Male	2010	36.8	Masculin
Female	2010	12.2	Féminin
Pupil-teacher ratio	...	...	Ratio élève-enseignant
Public expenditure on education (% of budget)	2012	9.5	Dépenses publiques consacrées à l'enseignement (% du budget)
Poverty			Pauvreté
GNI Per Capita (US$)	2013	460.0	RNB par habitant ($EU)
Human Poverty Index (HPI-1) Value (%)	2007	50.5	Valeur de l'Indice de pauvreté (IPH-1) (%)
Population below International Poverty Line ($2/day) (%)	2012	72.7	Population sous le seuil international de pauvreté (2$/J) (%)
Share of Income Held by Richest 10%	2012	26.5	% de revenu des 10% plus riches
Share of Income Held by Poorest 10%	2012	3.1	% de revenu des 10% plus pauvres
Gini index	2012	33.7	Indice de Gini

Charts / Graphiques

Population by age group – 2014
Population par groupe d'age – 2014

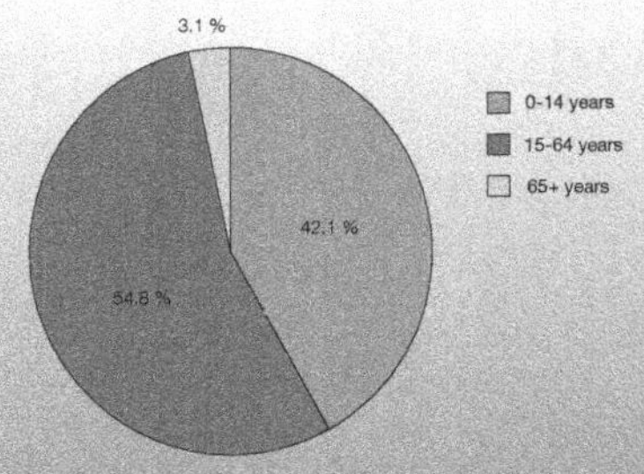

Percentage of children provided the vaccines – 2013
Pourcentage d'enfants vaccinés – 2013

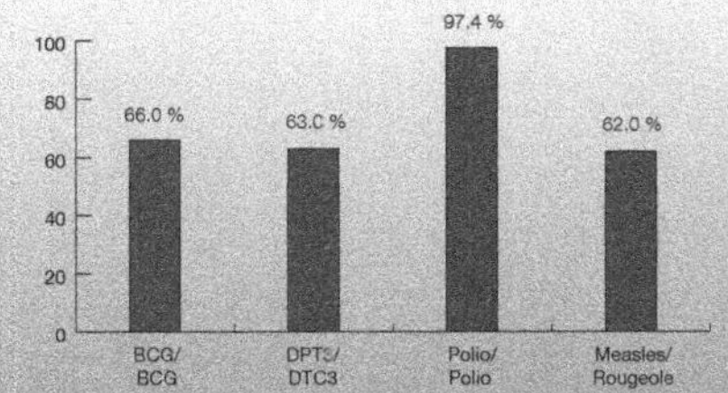

Literacy rate (%) – 2010
Taux d'alphabétisation – 2010

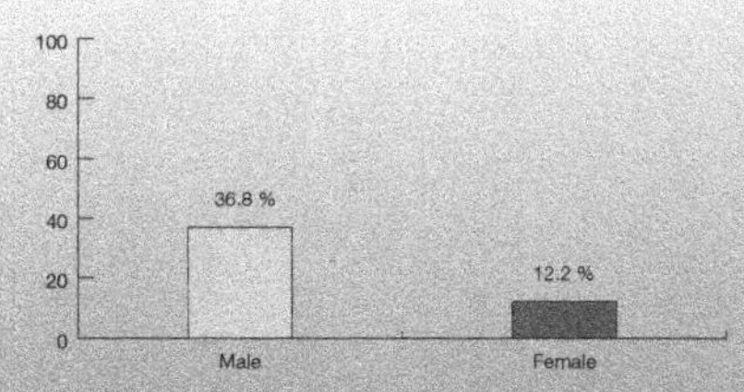

GNI Per Capita (US$)
RNB par habitant ($EU)

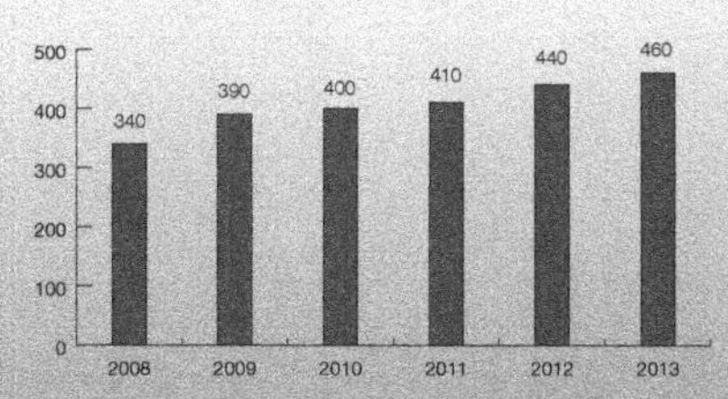

II NATIONAL ACCOUNTS — COMPTES NATIONAUX

	2006	2007	2008	2009	2010	2011	2012	2013	2014	
GROSS DOMESTIC PRODUCT BY KIND OF ECONOMIC ACTIVITY AT CURRENT PRICES *GUINEA FRANC (MILLIONS)*										**PRODUIT INTÉRIEUR BRUT PAR BRANCHE D'ACTIVITÉ ÉCONOMIQUE AUX PRIX COURANTS** *FRANC GUINÉEN (MILLIONS)*
Agriculture, hunting, forestry and fishing	3 312 611	4 056 952	4 741 217	5 232 139	5 490 562	6 349 485	7 523 879	8 462 508	7 342 922	Agriculture, chasse, sylviculture et pêche
Mining and quarrying	3 312 436	3 391 578	4 611 290	4 265 911	6 322 869	7 761 235	7 476 326	7 248 270	6 876 173	Industries extractives
Manufacturing	855 182	1 123 440	1 297 652	1 492 445	1 806 384	2 268 696	2 741 245	3 177 652	3 491 921	Industries manufacturières
Electricity, gas & water	57 268	69 210	78 128	90 706	109 775	126 850	194 644	189 048	228 729	Electricité, gaz et eau
Construction & public works	1 318 210	1 742 054	2 063 721	2 304 933	2 883 160	3 620 672	4 548 848	5 519 369	6 256 757	Bâtiments et travaux publics
Wholesale & retail trade, restaurants, hotels	2 212 357	2 911 528	3 240 893	3 579 839	4 429 155	6 620 589	7 990 885	9 088 082	9 696 983	Commerce de gros et de détail, restaurants et hôtels
Finance, insurance, real estate, etc.	-	-	-	-	-	-	-	-	-	Banques, assurances, affaires immobilières
Transport and communications	783 704	998 329	1 067 334	1 193 685	1 428 268	1 734 292	2 103 263	2 371 429	2 533 160	Transport(s) et communications
Public administration and defense	1 671 152	1 275 979	1 458 569	1 511 512	1 691 511	1 847 981	1 956 000	2 368 229	2 634 620	Administrations publiques et défense
Education	...	...	...	...	...	...	...	...	...	Education
Health and Social Work	...	...	...	...	...	...	...	...	...	Santé et actions sociales
Other services	369 516	437 243	447 356	559 419	708 364	1 109 540	1 330 217	1 548 239	1 689 748	Autres services
Less Imputed Service Charges	...	...	...	...	...	...	...	...	...	Moins services d'intermédiation financière
Gross domestic product at factor cost / basic prices	13 892 437	16 006 314	19 006 160	20 230 587	24 870 048	31 439 339	35 865 306	39 972 825	40 751 014	Produit intérieur brut aux couts des facteurs / prix de base
Plus: indirect taxes / taxes on products, less subsidies	1 201 768	1 347 920	1 774 270	1 902 040	2 211 574	2 881 130	4 217 270	4 810 230	5 393 300	Plus taxes indirectes/impôts sur les produits, moins les subventions
EXPENDITURE ON GROSS DOMESTIC PRODUCT AT CURRENT PURCHASER'S VALUES *GUINEA FRANC (MILLIONS)*										**EMPLOI DU PRODUIT INTÉRIEUR BRUT AUX PRIX COURANTS D'ACQUISITION** *FRANC GUINÉEN (MILLIONS)*
Government final consumption	1 065 135	1 156 306	1 270 764	1 889 117	3 550 620	3 355 311	4 118 231	4 959 034	5 641 049	Consommation finale des administrations publiques
Private final consumption	11 262 116	13 859 268	16 253 045	17 904 005	20 539 721	31 303 665	36 413 698	40 938 178	42 794 544	Consommation finale privée
Gross fixed capital formation	3 385 086	3 339 048	4 429 171	3 631 802	4 634 382	6 741 409	8 786 184	8 567 296	10 013 876	Formation brute de capital fixe
Change in inventories	123 896	93 870	140 854	- 8 473	2 407	5 054	5 451	3 663	7 167	Variation des stocks
Exports of goods and services	5 769 804	5 231 391	7 008 952	5 356 929	9 135 236	10 951 297	11 291 214	11 423 166	11 392 250	Exportations de biens et services
Less imports of goods and services	6 511 832	6 325 649	8 322 357	6 640 753	10 780 743	18 036 267	20 532 202	21 108 282	23 704 572	Moins importations de biens et services
GDP at purchasers' values	15 094 205	17 354 234	20 780 430	22 132 627	27 081 622	34 320 469	40 082 576	44 783 055	46 144 314	PIB aux prix d'acquisition
GROSS DOMESTIC PRODUCT BY KIND OF ECONOMIC ACTIVITY AT CONSTANT PRICES *ANNUAL GROWTH RATES (%)*										**PRODUIT INTÉRIEUR BRUT PAR BRANCHE D'ACTIVITÉ ECONOMIQUE AUX PRIX CONSTANTS** *TAUX DE CROISSANCE ANNUEL (%)*
Agriculture, hunting, forestry and fishing	3.9	2.8	3.6	3.2	3.2	4.5	3.8	5.1	3.3	Agriculture, chasse, sylviculture et pêche
Mining and quarrying	- 1.6	2.4	14.2	- 7.3	1.1	4.3	- 2.1	- 6.8	3.9	Industries extractives
Manufacturing	1.8	- 0.1	1.5	1.6	1.2	4.4	4.7	3.5	- 1.0	Industries manufacturières
Electricity, gas & water	0.5	5.1	5.5	4.5	1.7	- 4.5	34.6	- 7.5	9.0	Electricité, gaz et eau
Construction & public works	8.0	1.5	7.5	- 0.1	4.5	5.0	8.7	8.5	4.0	Bâtiments et travaux publics
Wholesale & retail trade, restaurants, hotels	1.5	1.0	2.3	- 1.2	1.0	5.3	4.5	2.5	- 3.0	Commerce de gros et de détail, restaurants et hôtels
Finance, insurance, real estate, etc.	...	...	...	...	...	...	...	...	...	Banques, assurances, affaires immobilières
Transport and communications	0.5	1.1	2.8	- 0.5	1.4	5.0	5.0	2.5	- 2.0	Transport(s) et communications
Public administration and defense	1.0	- 0.2	2.5	3.5	1.7	- 0.3	1.0	2.0	2.0	Administrations publiques et défense
Education	...	...	...	...	...	...	...	...	...	Education
Health and Social Work	...	...	...	...	...	...	...	...	...	Santé et actions sociales
Other services	2.5	0.5	1.3	2.5	1.3	3.8	3.8	3.0	2.0	Autres services
Less Imputed Service Charges	...	...	...	...	...	...	...	...	...	Moins services d'intermédiation financière
Gross domestic product at factor cost / basic prices	2.2	1.5	5.1	- 0.1	2.1	3.9	3.5	2.5	1.6	Produit intérieur brut aux couts des facteurs / prix de base
Plus: indirect taxes / taxes on products, less subsidies	6.3	5.2	2.8	- 2.5	- 0.2	3.1	8.4	0.1	- 1.6	Plus taxes indirectes/impôts sur les produits, moins les subventions
Gross domestic product at market prices	2.5	1.8	4.9	- 0.3	1.9	3.9	3.9	2.3	1.3	Produit intérieur brut aux prix du marché
EXPENDITURE ON GROSS DOMESTIC PRODUCT AT CONSTANT PURCHASERS' VALUES *ANNUAL GROWTH RATES (%)*										**EMPLOIS DU PRODUIT INTÉRIEUR BRUT AUX PRIX CONSTANTS D'ACQUISITION** *TAUX DE CROISSANCE ANNUEL (%)*
Government final consumption	88.3	4.4	5.7	42.9	80.7	- 9.1	18.0	8.9	3.6	Consommation finale des administrations publiques
Private final consumption	- 6.6	12.0	7.1	- 12.4	- 22.9	19.5	5.1	4.7	23.0	Consommation finale privée
Gross fixed capital formation	26.4	- 4.9	26.8	- 14.8	26.6	33.5	4.3	2.0	- 14.3	Formation brute de capital fixe
Exports of goods and services	- 2.1	14.0	- 7.2	- 3.6	11.6	25.2	- 0.1	- 6.6	8.1	Exportations de biens et services
Less imports of goods and services	20.0	22.4	19.6	- 23.2	29.4	48.7	10.0	3.7	10.8	Moins importations de biens et services
Notes	NA:2008-2013 Estimates;2014:Provisional					CN: 2008-2013 Estimées ;2014:Provisoire				Notes

III INFLATION

	2006	2007	2008	2009	2010	2011	2012	2013	2014	
ANNUAL GROWTH RATES (%)										**TAUX DE CROISSANCE ANNUEL (%)**
All items	34.7	22.9	18.4	4.7	15.5	21.4	15.2	8.0	13.6	Ensemble
of which:										dont:
Food and Non-alcoholic beverages	42.5	28.5	20.6	7.1	20.4	27.4	15.6	8.5	14.8	Alimentation et boissons non alcoolisés
Alcoholic beverages & tobacco	...	...	...	...	...	...	...	...	...	Boissons alcoolisées et tabacs
Clothing and Footwear	24.3	24.3	13.4	8.1	13.2	12.5	19.3	8.8	19.3	Habillement et chaussures
Housing, Water, Electricity, Gas and Other Fuels	22.5	33.9	17.3	7.2	9.5	9.9	12.7	11.6	10.5	Logement, eau, electricité, gas et autres combustibles
Furnishing, household equipment	26.9	23.0	19.4	11.8	5.0	21.3	16.9	7.1	12.7	Meubles, articles de ménage et entretien courant
Health	19.2	25.2	12.3	9.0	7.9	13.1	24.2	10.4	22.7	Santé
Transport	42.0	4.7	21.8	-16.0	19.2	16.5	7.5	1.2	2.0	Transport
Communication	...	...	...	...	...	...	...	...	...	Communication
Recreation & culture	22.4	19.7	4.6	2.9	2.5	13.2	16.8	5.8	8.5	Loisirs et culture
Education	16.5	14.8	18.4	16.8	5.0	12.4	19.9	2.7	7.5	Enseignement
Restaurants & hotels	40.0	21.5	18.4	9.5	8.2	22.9	16.1	13.2	5.1	Restaurants et hôtels
Miscellaneous goods & services	19.4	18.7	6.4	3.7	6.8	10.3	6.0	4.1	11.2	Biens et services divers

IV AGRICULTURAL PRODUCTION - PRODUCTION AGRICOLE	2006	2007	2008	2009	2010	2011	2012	2013	2014	
TONNES *(THOUSAND)*										**TONNES** *(MILLIERS)*
Rice	1 340	1 402	1 534	1 456	1 499	1 670	1 919	2 053	...	Riz
Maize	270	280	285	290	297	310	285	272	...	Maïs
Fonio	231	243	324	345	389	409	429	429	...	Fonio
Groundnuts	294	305	315	300	292	290	300	260	...	Arachide
Cassava	1 069	1 122	1 052	1 051	1 100	1 113	1 200	1 200	...	Manioc

V MINING PRODUCTION - PRODUCTION MINIERE	2006	2007	2008	2009	2010	2011	2012	2013	2014	
Aluminium ores and concentrates (Bauxite), metric tons (thousands)	17 502	17 242	18 521	15 285	16 666	18 224	17 900	...	...	Minerais d'aluminium et concentrés (Bauxite), tonnes (milliers)
Gold ores and concentrates (Kilograms)	18	19	20	21	23	15	14	...	...	Minerais d'or et concentrés, Kilogrammes
Diamonds, carat (thousands)	469	495	445	417	311	235	400	...	...	Diamant (milliers carats)

VI ENERGY - ENERGIE	2006	2007	2008	2009	2010	2011	2012	2013	2014	
Total electricity generation (GWh)	843	942	967	962	969	973	1 145	1 183	...	Production d'électricité totale (GWh)
of which:										dont:
Production of electricity from fossil fuels (GWh)	387	409	443	445	450	450	598	598	...	Production d'électricité à partir de combustibles fossiles (GWh)
Production of hydro electricity (GWh)	456	533	524	517	519	519	542	580	...	Production d'électricité d'origine hydraulique (GWh)
Production of electricity from solar, wind, tide, wave and other sources (GWh)	...	...	...	...	...	4	4	4	...	Production d'électricité d'origine solaire, éolienne, marée motrice et autres (GWh)

VII TOURISM AND INFRASTRUCTURE - TOURISME ET INFRASTRUCTURE	2006	2007	2008	2009	2010	2011	2012	2013	2014	
VII-1 TOURISM										**VII-1 TOURISME**
International tourist arrivals (thousands)	46	30	24	18	12	131	96	98	104	Arrivées de touristes internationaux (milliers)
Rooms in hotels and similar establishments (thousands)	4.3	...	...	...	...	...	...	...	...	Chambres d'hotels et établissements assimilés (milliers)
Overnight stays (thousands)	959	704	654	559	455	5 581	3 306	3 439	3 640	Nuitées (milliers)
Tourism receipts (US$ thousand)	49	43	321	600	600	700	400	458	498	Recettes touristiques (milliers de $ EU)
Total contribution to GDP (%)	4.4	5.2	5.2	5.2	5.3	4.7	4.7	4.6	4.7	Contribution totale au PIB (%)
Total contribution to Employment (%)	3.7	4.4	4.3	4.4	4.5	3.6	3.6	3.7	3.8	Contribution totale à l'emploi (%)
VII-2 INFRASTRUCTURE										**VII-2 INFRASTRUCTURE**
Paved roads (% of total)	...	...	...	...	...	...	...	...	...	Routes asphaltées (% du total)
Total Network (Railways-km)	...	...	...	...	...	...	...	...	...	Réseau total voies ferrées-Km
Main Telephone Lines (per 100 inhabitants)	0	0	0	0	0	0	-	-	...	Lignes téléphoniques fixes (pour 100 habitants)
Mobile Cellular Subscribers (per 100 inhabitants)	...	20	27	33	37	44	49	63	...	Abonnés aux téléphones mobiles (pour 100 habitants)

VIII EXTERNAL TRADE - COMMERCE EXTERIEUR	2006	2007	2008	2009	2010	2011	2012	2013	2014	
US$ (MILLIONS) EXPORTS, FOB										**$ E.U (MILLIONS) EXPORTATIONS, FÀB**
Exports - Total	1 033	1 203	1 417	1 050	1 471	1 601	1 925	2 161	...	Exportations - Total
Exports to AFRICA	...	...	...	...	...	...	...	...	...	Exportations vers l'AFRIQUE
Main Products										**Principaux produits**
Bauxite	405	425	501	241	387	436	561	...	...	Bauxite
Allumine	147	166	166	97	163	189	240	...	...	Allumine
Diamonds	43	51	102	62	51	57	97	...	...	Diamant
Gold	327	375	534	640	797	890	1 024	...	...	Or
Coffee	28	27	66	36	25	25	26	...	...	Café
Main Destinations										**Principales destinations**
Europe	217	300	133	517	784	1 090	1 463	1 556	...	Europe
East African / Southern	8	12	86	1	1	1	4	...	...	Afrique de l'est/Australe
Liberia	6	11	41	...	...	...	16	...	...	Liberia
North Africa	2	1	3	2	3	2	7	...	...	Afrique du Nord
China	7	12	40	2	36	...	5	30	...	Chine
IMPORTS, CIF										**IMPORTATIONS, CAF**
Imports - Total	1 066	1 260	1 488	1 134	1 596	1 841	2 370	6 509	...	Importations - Total (millions)
Imports from Africa	...	...	...	...	...	...	...	...	...	Importations en provenance de l'Afrique
Main Products										**Principaux produits**
Food	160	230	247	218	206	213	287	...	...	Produits alimentaires
Other consumer goods	147	206	223	204	257	269	357	...	...	Autres biens de consommation
Petroleum Products	202	346	387	278	339	393	501	...	...	Produits pétroliers
Intermediate goods	230	247	294	239	332	316	413	...	...	Biens intermédiaires
Equipment goods	327	230	336	194	462	650	812	...	...	Biens d'équipement
Main Origin										**Principales provenances**
Europe	39	39	35	18	66	39	45	171	...	Europe
European Union	338	492	473	426	622	996	1 081	...	...	Union Européenne
Other Asian countries	244	88	286	270	305	702	764	...	...	Autres Pays d' Asie
Ivory Coast	237	131	120	...	...	...	11	108	...	Côte d'Ivoire
North America	52	58	-	46	39	82	84	...	...	Amérique du Nord

IX FINANCIAL AND MONETARY STATISTICS - FINANCES ET STATISTIQUES MONETAIRES	2006	2007	2008	2009	2010	2011	2012	2013	2014	
IX-1 MONETARY STATISTICS *GUINEA FRANC (MILLIONS)*										**IX-1 STATISTIQUES MONÉTAIRES** *FRANC GUINÉEN (MILLIONS)*
Money supply (M1)	3 247 290	3 398 490	4 723 920	5 945 120	10 366 380	11 337 950	11 450 220	13 067 410	14 384 690	Masse monétaire (M1)
Quasi-money	1 262 095	1 001 437	1 615 854	1 203 057	1 561 738	2 485 029	...	...	...	Quasi-monnaie
of which Demand Deposit	...	...	...	...	...	...	...	...	...	dont Monnaie scripturale
Net foreign assets	423 647	254 008	686 268	1 169 908	- 200 745	4 871 762	...	...	...	Avoirs extérieurs nets
Domestic credit	3 331 271	3 106 731	3 951 887	4 682 363	10 116 304	10 869 001	...	...	...	Crédit intérieur
of which claims on private sector	1 000 514	860 356	1 038 141	857 766	1 547 252	3 080 028	...	...	...	dont créances sur le secteur privé
of which claims on government sector, net	2 326 581	2 221 234	2 862 817	3 781 953	8 490 836	7 691 250	...	...	...	dont créances nettes sur le gouvernement
International reserves (millions US$)	...	...	...	...	...	104	155	174	293	Réserves internationales (millions $EU)
Average Exchange Rate (National Currency per US$)	5 148.75	4 197.75	4 601.69	4 801.08	5 726.07	6 658.03	6 986.12	6 995.89	7 004.56	Taux de change (moyen) (monnaie nationale par $ EU)
IX-2 PUBLIC FINANCE *GUINEA FRANC (MILLIONS)*										**IX-2 FINANCES PUBLIQUES** *FRANC GUINÉEN (MILLIONS)*
Total Revenues and Grants	2 658 392	2 726 610	3 368 120	3 492 790	4 263 028	6 824 189	9 659 136	10 863 368	12 696 704	Recettes totales et dons
Tax Revenue	2 141 782	2 347 350	3 060 140	3 303 880	3 975 004	5 177 820	7 600 540	8 033 440	9 259 786	Recettes fiscales
Non Tax Revenue	271 530	129 930	204 970	108 330	179 874	484 030	375 020	442 790	501 606	Recettes non fiscales
Grants	245 080	249 330	103 010	80 580	108 150	1 162 339	1 683 576	2 387 138	2 935 311	Dons
Total Expenditures and Net Lending	2 710 304	2 641 329	3 617 920	5 240 240	8 041 100	6 919 919	10 146 047	11 788 797	14 822 113	Dépenses totales et prêts nets
Current expenditure	2 029 810	1 956 165	2 777 660	3 655 320	5 562 120	5 320 414	6 112 010	7 445 190	9 738 911	Dépenses courantes
Of which Wages and Salaries	444 420	607 210	856 270	1 109 230	1 551 190	1 764 234	1 756 890	2 190 170	2 714 982	Dont rémunérations et salaires
Capital expenditure	672 350	682 440	837 290	1 577 180	2 478 860	1 598 991	3 783 457	3 387 357	4 243 253	Dépenses d'équipement
Net Lending	8 144	2 724	2 970	7 740	120	514	250 580	956 250	839 949	Prêts nets
Fiscal Balance	- 51 912	85 281	- 249 800	-1 747 450	-3 778 072	- 95 730	- 486 911	- 925 429	-2 125 410	Solde global y compris les dons
IX-3 BALANCE OF PAYMENTS *GUINEA FRANC (MILLIONS)*										**IX-3 BALANCE DES PAIEMENTS** *FRANC GUINÉEN (MILLIONS)*
Trade balance	407 544	- 60 490	- 110 395	- 49 787	379 352	-3 740 931	-6 693 790	-7 344 421	...	Balance commerciale
Services Balance	-1 147 160	-1 113 002	-1 540 954	-1 284 118	-1 887 279	-3 329 086	-2 525 202	-2 463 068	...	Balance des services
Net Income	- 297 067	- 284 076	-2 390 671	-2 507 946	-2 555 123	-3 098 809	-3 134 738	- 850 878	...	Revenus nets
Compensation of employees	...	...	...	...	...	...	...	...	...	Rémunération des salariés
Investment Income	...	...	...	...	...	...	...	...	...	Revenus des investissements
Current transfers, net total	- 105 659	- 548 184	1 339 092	1 190 669	1 442 970	926 653	561 156	806 095	...	Transferts courants
Net official transfers	...	...	...	...	...	...	...	...	...	Transferts officiels nets
Workers' remittances	...	...	...	...	...	...	...	...	...	Envois de fonds des travailleurs
Other private transfers	...	...	...	...	...	...	...	...	...	Autres transferts privés
Current account balance	-1 162 254	-1 986 764	- 682 923	- 950 971	- 506 494	-7 035 696	-9 539 653	-9 852 272	...	Solde du compte courant
Capital & financial account	...	...	...	...	...	...	...	...	...	Comptes de capital et financier
Capital account	...	...	...	...	...	...	...	...	...	Compte de capital
Financial account	...	...	...	...	...	...	...	...	...	Compte financier
Errors & omissions	...	...	...	...	...	...	...	...	...	Erreurs et omissions
Overall balance	...	...	...	...	...	...	...	...	...	Balance générale

X DEBT AND FINANCIAL FLOWS - DETTE ET FLUX FINANCIERS	2006	2007	2008	2009	2010	2011	2012	2013	2014	
X-1 DEBT *US$ (MILLIONS)*										**X-1 DETTE EXTÉRIEURE** *$ E.U (MILLIONS)*
Total external debt	3 188	3 242	3 130	3 224	3 155	3 214	1 306	1 480	1 495	Dette extérieure totale
Private	-	-	-	-	-	-	-	-	-	Privée
Public	3 188	3 242	3 130	3 224	3 155	3 214	1 306	1 480	1 495	Publique
Total external debt service	139	139	158	93	58	145	3 960	55	236	Service de la dette extérieure
Present value of External debt	...	...	...	...	...	...	...	...	...	Valeur actuelle de la dette extérieure
Total government domestic debt (in local currency)	...	...	...	...	...	...	...	...	...	Dette publique intérieure
X-2 FINANCIAL FLOWS *US$ (MILLIONS)*										**X-2 FLUX FINANCIERS** *$ E.U (MILLIONS)*
Net Foreign Direct Investment Inflows	125	386	382	141	101	956	606	25	...	Investissement étranger direct (flux nets entrants)
Main origin of FDI Inflows										**Principales origines de l'IDE entrant:**
Belgium	1	21	18	4	37.1	44.6	88.7	...	...	Belgique
France	8	...	...	...	...	...	...	...	...	France
Italy	...	1	2	...	0.3	- 0.3	...	...	...	Italie
Denmark	...	...	...	...	...	...	...	...	...	Danemark
Korea	...	0	...	...	0.2	...	...	...	...	Corée
African countries	...	...	...	...	...	...	...	...	...	Pays africains
Net total Official Development Assistance	170	228	328	214	218	204	340	500	...	Aide publique au développement (nette totale)
Main origin of Net ODA										**Principales origines de l'APD nette**
France	21	55	73	82	36.0	36.4	80.0	133.5	...	France
United States	35	25	43	35	21.7	17.3	20.0	27.2	...	Etats-Unis
IDA	22	22	14	- 25	0.1	20.0	27.0	...	...	IDA
Germany	14	16	24	19	13.3	- 3.5	- 1.3	0.8	...	Allemagne
Japan	17	12	17	18	10.8	2.0	22.6	69.9	...	Japon

GUINEA-BISSAU | GUINÉE-BISSAU

AREA (km²)		**36 125**	**SUPERFICIE (km²)**
CAPITAL CITY	Bissau	Bissau	**CAPITALE**
CURRENCY	CFA Franc	Franc CFA	**MONNAIE**

I SOCIAL AND DEMOGRAPHIC INDICATORS — INDICATEURS DEMOGRAPHIQUES ET SOCIAUX

	Year / Année	Value / Valeur	
POPULATION			**POPULATION**
Population ('000)			Population ('000)
Both sexes	2014	1 514	Les deux sexes
Male	2014	741	Masculin
Female	2014	774	Féminin
Average annual growth rate	2014	2.2	Taux de croissance annuel
Active Population ('000)	2014	690	Population active ('000)
Population by age group ('000)			Population par groupe d'âge ('000)
0-14 years	2014	658	0-14 ans
15-64 years	2014	821	15-64 ans
65+ years	2014	36	65+ ans
Economically. active population. in agriculture (%)	2014	69.4	Participation de la population active agricole (%)
Crude birth rate	2014	41.0	Taux brut de natalité
Crude death rate	2014	12.7	Taux brut de mortalité
Total fertility rate	2014	4.9	Indice synthétique de fécondité
Proportion of urban population	2014	41.7	Part de la population urbaine
Life Expectancy at Birth - Total (years)	2014	52.4	Espérance de vie à la naissance - Totale (ans)
Dependency Ratio - Total (%)	2014	85.0	Taux de dépendance - Total (%)
HEALTH			**SANTÉ**
Percentage of children under-five and underweight	2014	16.8	% d'enfants de moins de cinq ans avec insuffisance pondérale
Prevalence of undernourishment	2013	17.7	Prévalence de la malnutrition
Under five mortality rate (both sexes, per 1000)	2014	88.8	Taux de mortalité de moins de 5 ans (les deux sexes, pour 1000)
Infant mortality rate (both sexes) per 1000	2014	55.4	Taux de mortalité infantile (les deux sexes) par 1000
Percentage of children provided the vaccines :			Pourcentage d'enfants vaccinés :
BCG	2014	93.5	BCG
DPT3	2014	82.9	DTC3
Polio	2014	83.2	Polio
Measles	2014	81.3	Rougeole
Percentage of mothers provided at least one antenatal care (%)	2014	92.4	Pourcentage de mères ayant au moins reçu un soin prénatal (%)
Percentage of deliveries attended by skilled health personnel	2014	45.0	% d'accouchements assistés par un personnel de santé qualifié
Number of doctors (per 10 000 population)	2014	2.0	Nombre de médecins (pour 10 000 habitants)
Number of nurses (per 10 000 population)	2014	14.0	Nombre d'infirmières (pour 10 000 habitants)
Hospital beds - Total (per 10 000 population)	2014	96.5	Nombre de lits d'hôpitaux - Total (pour 10 000)
Births registered (per 1 000)	2014	38.0	Naiss.s enregistrées (pour 1 000)
Deaths registered (per 1 000)	2014	14.6	Décès enregistrés (pour 1 000)
Public expenditure on Health (% of budget)	2014	10.0	Dépenses publiques consacrées à la santé (% du budget)
EDUCATION			**EDUCATION**
Enrolment in primary education (both sexes) (000)	2014	350	Scolarisation dans le primaire (les deux sexes) (000)
Female	2014	208	Féminin
Enrolment in secondary education (both sexes) (000)	2014	93	Scolarisation dans le secondaire (les deux sexes) (000)
Female	2014	34	Féminin
Enrolment in tertiary education (both sexes) (000)	2006	3.7	Scolarisation dans le tertiaire (les deux sexes) (000)
Female	...	...	Féminin
Literacy rate (both sexes)	2014	53.4	Taux d'alphabétisation (deux sexes)
Male	2014	58.2	Masculin
Female	2014	41.2	Féminin
Pupil-teacher ratio	2014	48.2	Ratio élève-enseignant
Public expenditure on education (% of budget)	2014	10.0	Dépenses publiques consacrées à l'enseignement (% du budget)
Poverty			Pauvreté
GNI Per Capita (US$)	2013	590.0	RNB par habitant ($EU)
Human Poverty Index (HPI-1) Value (%)	2007	34.9	Valeur de l'Indice de pauvreté (IPH-1) (%)
Population below International Poverty Line ($2/day) (%)	2002	78.0	Population sous le seuil international de pauvreté (2$/J) (%)
Share of Income Held by Richest 10%	2002	28.1	% de revenu des 10% plus riches
Share of Income Held by Poorest 10%	2002	3.1	% de revenu des 10% plus pauvres
Gini index	2002	35.5	Indice de Gini

Charts / Graphiques

Population by age group – 2014
Population par groupe d'age – 2014

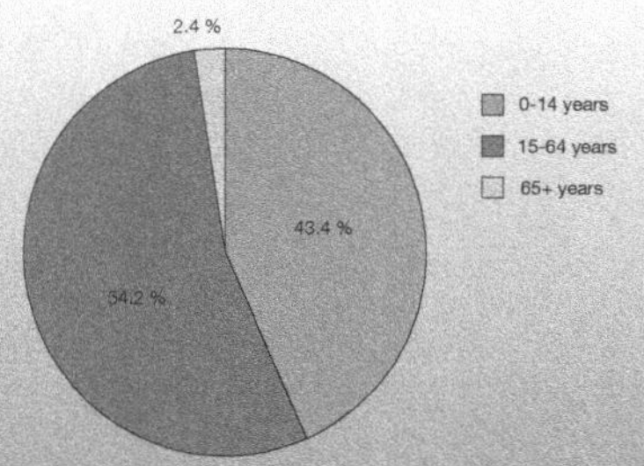

Percentage of children provided the vaccines – 2014
Pourcentage d'enfants vaccinés – 2014

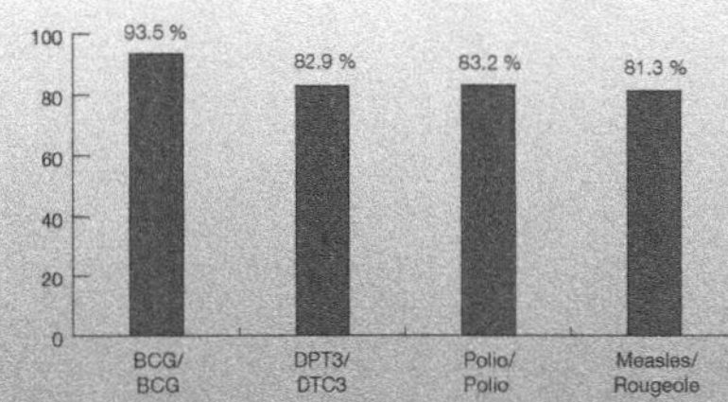

Literacy rate (%) – 2014
Taux d'alphabétisation – 2014

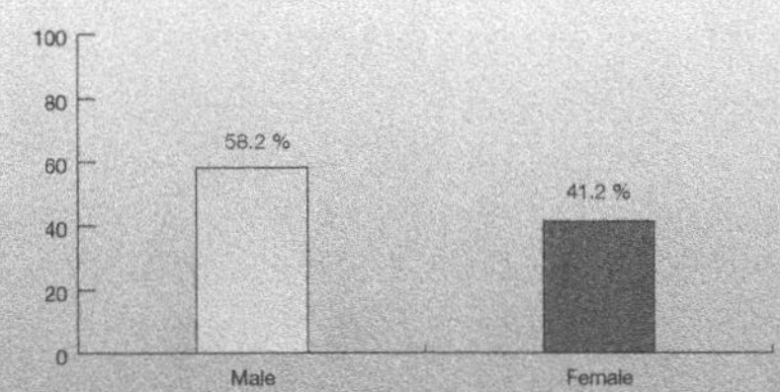

GNI Per Capita (US$)
RNB par habitant ($EU)

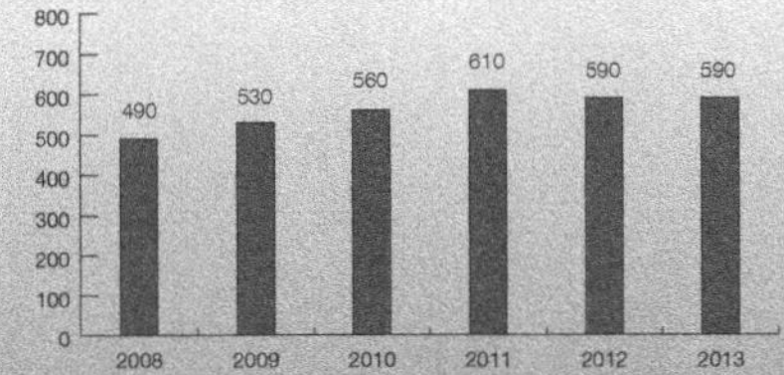

II NATIONAL ACCOUNTS — COMPTES NATIONAUX

	2006	2007	2008	2009	2010	2011	2012	2013	2014	
GROSS DOMESTIC PRODUCT BY KIND OF ECONOMIC ACTIVITY AT CURRENT PRICES *CFA FRANC (MILLIONS)*										**PRODUIT INTÉRIEUR BRUT PAR BRANCHE D'ACTIVITÉ ÉCONOMIQUE AUX PRIX COURANTS** *FRANC CFA (MILLIONS)*
Agriculture, hunting, forestry and fishing	129 649	142 903	179 410	170 410	188 296	231 764	254 440	267 837	279 868	Agriculture, chasse, sylviculture et pêche
Mining and quarrying	83	147	105	110	165	84	94	97	100	Industries extractives
Manufacturing	37 355	37 400	47 389	44 936	46 844	55 882	69 652	71 713	72 672	Industries manufacturières
Electricity, gas & water	1 316	1 119	1 502	1 605	1 642	7 214	5 474	5 636	5 944	Electricité, gaz et eau
Construction & public works	2 740	4 326	3 064	3 227	4 742	2 938	3 648	3 756	4 260	Bâtiments et travaux publics
Wholesale & retail trade, restaurants, hotels	63 837	69 682	74 134	80 114	75 377	102 131	97 174	100 267	102 324	Commerce de gros et de détail, restaurants et hôtels
Finance, insurance, real estate, etc.	17 679	18 355	21 631	19 654	22 760	27 101	28 027	33 630	34 583	Banques, assurances, affaires immobilières
Transport and communications	12 312	14 112	16 480	15 604	16 815	21 970	26 413	27 254	27 893	Transport(s) et communications
Public administration and defense	32 036	34 350	33 623	40 545	45 869	50 163	41 539	42 861	45 501	Administrations publiques et défense
Education	...	...	...	...	...	...	...	...	...	Education
Health and Social Work	...	...	...	...	...	...	...	...	...	Santé et actions sociales
Other services	...	...	...	...	...	...	...	...	...	Autres services
Less Imputed Service Charges	- 1 395	- 3 099	- 5 308	- 5 386	- 6 272	- 6 863	- 5 802	- 5 768	- 5 768	Moins services d'intermédiation financière
Gross domestic product at factor cost / basic prices	295 612	319 295	372 030	370 819	396 238	492 384	520 660	547 283	567 377	Produit intérieur brut aux couts des facteurs / prix de base
Plus: indirect taxes / taxes on products, less subsidies	13 850	14 086	14 932	19 111	23 505	28 392	26 524	24 749	25 923	Plus taxes indirectes/impôts sur les produits, moins les subventions
EXPENDITURE ON GROSS DOMESTIC PRODUCT AT CURRENT PURCHASER'S VALUES *CFA FRANC (MILLIONS)*										**EMPLOI DU PRODUIT INTÉRIEUR BRUT AUX PRIX COURANTS D'ACQUISITION** *FRANC CFA (MILLIONS)*
Government final consumption	46 000	48 500	40 500	54 000	57 500	58 650	61 583	51 385	71 493	Consommation finale des administrations publiques
Private final consumption	289 469	304 506	373 023	375 227	397 736	455 334	509 765	535 668	547 414	Consommation finale privée
Gross fixed capital formation	21 545	25 773	23 235	23 224	27 242	32 417	27 367	26 481	32 001	Formation brute de capital fixe
Change in inventories	- 1 900	500	300	1 400	900	1 400	100	100	100	Variation des stocks
Exports of goods and services	39 762	67 350	76 861	73 588	84 464	133 369	78 162	82 500	91 815	Exportations de biens et services
Less imports of goods and services	85 415	113 248	126 967	137 510	148 099	160 395	129 794	124 102	149 524	Moins importations de biens et services
GDP at purchasers' values	309 462	333 381	386 962	389 930	419 743	520 776	547 183	572 032	593 299	PIB aux prix d'acquisition
GROSS DOMESTIC PRODUCT BY KIND OF ECONOMIC ACTIVITY AT CONSTANT PRICES *ANNUAL GROWTH RATES (%)*										**PRODUIT INTÉRIEUR BRUT PAR BRANCHE D'ACTIVITÉ ECONOMIQUE AUX PRIX CONSTANTS** *TAUX DE CROISSANCE ANNUEL (%)*
Agriculture, hunting, forestry and fishing	- 1.1	2.5	2.9	3.1	0.2	8.7	- 0.1	3.1	2.3	Agriculture, chasse, sylviculture et pêche
Mining and quarrying	- 14.3	96.2	- 34.6	6.0	43.4	- 48.0	8.9	1.9	3.4	Industries extractives
Manufacturing	1.9	- 9.4	9.1	- 0.1	2.7	- 0.1	5.4	1.9	- 1.9	Industries manufacturières
Electricity, gas & water	- 11.5	- 15.0	34.1	6.9	2.3	261.2	- 21.0	1.9	3.8	Electricité, gaz et eau
Construction & public works	- 5.9	86.1	- 40.7	20.0	34.7	- 46.5	10.0	1.9	7.0	Bâtiments et travaux publics
Wholesale & retail trade, restaurants, hotels	9.6	9.7	5.4	- 5.1	- 0.5	8.4	- 2.0	- 1.1	3.5	Commerce de gros et de détail, restaurants et hôtels
Finance, insurance, real estate, etc.	5.6	1.0	11.4	- 6.7	12.6	17.6	- 5.5	- 8.0	0.9	Banques, assurances, affaires immobilières
Transport and communications	7.7	15.7	20.0	4.8	12.8	8.3	8.2	- 1.1	3.8	Transport(s) et communications
Public administration and defense	- 3.9	4.4	- 8.7	23.0	13.2	5.6	- 20.3	- 1.1	4.9	Administrations publiques et défense
Education	...	...	...	...	...	...	...	...	...	Education
Health and Social Work	...	...	...	...	...	...	...	...	...	Santé et actions sociales
Other services	...	...	...	...	...	...	...	...	...	Autres services
Less Imputed Service Charges	85.3	116.9	43.2	16.0	14.0	1.6	- 36.7	- 21.7	2.9	Moins services d'intérmediation financière
Gross domestic product at factor cost / basic prices	1.4	3.3	3.1	2.2	3.4	8.2	- 1.9	1.0	2.4	Produit intérieur brut aux couts des facteurs / prix de base
Plus: indirect taxes / taxes on products, less subsidies	26.8	1.7	6.0	28.0	23.0	20.8	- 6.6	0.1	3.5	Plus taxes indirectes/impôts sur les produits, moins les subventions
Gross domestic product at market prices	2.3	3.2	3.2	3.3	4.4	9.0	- 2.2	0.9	2.5	Produit intérieur brut aux prix du marché
EXPENDITURE ON GROSS DOMESTIC PRODUCT AT CONSTANT PURCHASERS' VALUES *ANNUAL GROWTH RATES (%)*										**EMPLOIS DU PRODUIT INTÉRIEUR BRUT AUX PRIX CONSTANTS D'ACQUISITION** *TAUX DE CROISSANCE ANNUEL (%)*
Government final consumption	8.8	1.0	- 25.7	36.6	3.8	- 3.3	2.6	- 17.3	40.5	Consommation finale des administrations publiques
Private final consumption	8.0	0.8	8.9	3.1	2.8	- 0.6	4.4	1.2	3.3	Consommation finale privée
Gross fixed capital formation	17.6	14.6	- 19.8	2.4	14.3	12.8	- 17.5	- 5.2	18.8	Formation brute de capital fixe
Exports of goods and services	- 18.6	62.3	1.5	- 1.9	11.8	49.7	- 42.7	3.4	- 6.4	Exportations de biens et services
Less imports of goods and services	12.2	27.0	- 0.3	11.0	5.0	2.6	- 20.9	- 6.4	19.0	Moins importations de biens et services

Notes: NA Data: 2013:Estimates;2014:Projections — Données des CN: 2013:Estimées;2014:Projections Notes

III INFLATION

	2006	2007	2008	2009	2010	2011	2012	2013	2014	
ANNUAL GROWTH RATES (%)										**TAUX DE CROISSANCE ANNUEL (%)**
All items	2.0	4.6	7.9	-2.8	2.2	4.8	2.3	1.2	-1.5	Ensemble
of which:										dont:
Food and Non-alcoholic beverages	0.5	5.9	12.4	-2.4	1.9	6.8	3.5	2.1	-2.5	Alimentation et boissons non alcoolisés
Alcoholic beverages & tobacco	0.3	3.5	5.9	-4.8	1.2	0.7	1.6	0.7	-0.3	Boissons alcoolisées et tabacs
Clothing and Footwear	9.2	3.7	0.8	-4.3	5.0	4.1	-	0.3	-3.9	Habillement et chaussures
Housing, Water, Electricity, Gas and Other Fuels	3.0	6.2	8.2	2.4	-1.3	-0.4	-0.1	2.0	2.0	Logement, eau, electricité, gas et autres combustibles
Furnishing, household equipment	-3.2	2.6	-4.2	0.3	2.0	2.1	0.3	0.2	0.3	Meubles, articles de ménage et entretien courant
Health	7.7	1.6	-4.2	-1.6	3.5	8.5	-0.1	0.7	1.9	Santé
Transport	3.6	-2.9	-4.7	-1.9	2.3	3.5	4.3	0.1	1.5	Transport
Communication	3.9	0.2	-	-8.1	0.9	5.3	0.2	1.0	-9.2	Communication
Recreation & culture	0.4	3.8	-15.3	-1.8	1.9	0.3	-0.2	0.6	-2.7	Loisirs et culture
Education	15.2	0.3	-10.8	-4.6	0.5	5.7	-	1.8	4.6	Enseignement
Restaurants & hotels	6.6	-4.4	4.3	13.0	3.7	-1.8	3.1	1.2	4.5	Restaurants et hôtels
Miscellaneous goods & services	4.9	5.0	2.0	-0.3	-3.0	4.5	4.1	0.5	-1.9	Biens et services divers

IV AGRICULTURAL PRODUCTION - PRODUCTION AGRICOLE

	2006	2007	2008	2009	2010	2011	2012	2013	2014	
TONNES *(THOUSAND)*										**TONNES** *(MILLIERS)*
Rice	113	129	128	154	137	200	210	232	255	Riz
Cashew nuts	106	131	153	182	209	175	199	210	229	Noix de cajou
Palm nuts	80	80	80	80	80	80	80	80	80	Noix de palme
Coconuts	40	43	48	45	49	50	50	46	45	Noix de coco
Millet	24	25	46	31	36	35	45	53	62	Millet

V MINING PRODUCTION - PRODUCTION MINIERE

	2006	2007	2008	2009	2010	2011	2012	2013	2014	
	...	...	...	...	...	...	...	...	...	
	...	...	...	...	...	...	...	...	...	
	...	...	...	...	...	...	...	...	...	

VI ENERGY - ENERGIE

	2006	2007	2008	2009	2010	2011	2012	2013	2014	
Total electricity generation (GWh)	62	66	65	67	67	101	75	75	...	Production d'électricité totale (GWh)
of which:										dont:
Production of electricity from fossil fuels (GWh)	62	66	65	67	67	101	75	75	...	Production d'électricité à partir de combustibles fossiles (GWh)
Production of hydro electricity (GWh)	...	...	...	...	...	...	...	...	...	Production d'électricité d'origine hydraulique (GWh)
Production of electricity from solar, wind, tide, wave and other sources (GWh)	...	...	...	...	...	...	...	...	...	Production d'électricité d'origine solaire, éolienne, marée motrice et autres (GWh)

VII TOURISM AND INFRASTRUCTURE - TOURISME ET INFRASTRUCTURE

	2006	2007	2008	2009	2010	2011	2012	2013	2014	
VII-1 TOURISM										**VII-1 TOURISME**
International tourist arrivals (thousands)	...	...	...	...	...	...	...	...	...	Arrivées de touristes internationaux (milliers)
Rooms in hotels and similar establishments (thousands)	3.7	3.7	3.7	3.7	3.7	3.7	3.7	3.7	...	Chambres d'hotels et établissements assimilés (milliers)
Overnight stays (thousands)	...	...	...	...	...	...	...	...	...	Nuitées (milliers)
Tourism receipts (US$ thousand)	...	...	...	...	...	...	...	...	...	Recettes touristiques (milliers de $ EU)
Total contribution to GDP (%)	...	...	...	...	...	...	...	...	...	Contribution totale au PIB (%)
Total contribution to Employment (%)	...	...	...	...	...	...	...	...	...	Contribution totale à l'emploi (%)
VII-2 INFRASTRUCTURE										**VII-2 INFRASTRUCTURE**
Paved roads (% of total)	33	33	33	33	33	33	33	33	33	Routes asphaltées (% du total)
Total Network (Railways-km)	...	...	...	...	...	...	...	...	...	Réseau total voies ferrées-Km
Main Telephone Lines (per 100 inhabitants)	0	0	0	0	0	0	0	0	0	Lignes téléphoniques fixes (pour 100 habitants)
Mobile Cellular Subscribers (per 100 inhabitants)	11	20	33	36	43	45	63	74	43	Abonnés aux téléphones mobiles (pour 100 habitants)

VIII EXTERNAL TRADE - COMMERCE EXTERIEUR

	2006	2007	2008	2009	2010	2011	2012	2013	2014	
CFA FRANC (MILLIONS) EXPORTS, FOB										**FRANC CFA (MILLIONS) EXPORTATIONS, FÀB**
Exports - Total	42 787	67 267	76 978	73 076	83 742	139 392	78 595	98 070	121 397	Exportations - Total
Exports to AFRICA	1 284	2 018	2 309	2 192	2 512	4 182	2 358	2 942	3 642	Exportations vers l'AFRIQUE
Main Products										**Principaux produits**
Cashew nut	18 020	41 037	46 195	45 800	48 195	105 619	64 404	82 066	93 234	Noix de cajou
Cotton	100	86	21	10	7	655	765	141	256	Coton
Woods	...	...	...	...	...	...	...	...	...	Bois
	...	...	...	...	...	...	...	...	...	
	...	...	...	...	...	...	...	...	...	
Main Destinations										**Principales destinations**
India	14 416	32 830	36 956	36 640	38 556	84 495	51 523	65 653	74 587	Inde
United States	1 802	4 104	4 620	4 580	4 820	10 562	6 440	8 207	9 323	États-Unis
Singapore	...	...	...	...	...	...	...	...	...	Singapour
Portugal	...	...	...	...	...	...	...	...	...	Portugal
Pakistan	...	...	...	...	...	...	...	...	...	Pakistan
IMPORTS, CIF										**IMPORTATIONS, CAF**
Imports - Total	...	113 148	127 214	136 563	148 173	160 409	129 817	136 187	149 954	Importations - Total (millions)
Imports from Africa	...	63 363	71 240	76 475	82 977	89 829	72 698	76 265	83 974	Importations en provenance de l'Afrique
Main Products										**Principaux produits**
Petroleum, petroleum products and related materials	...	22 370	28 709	29 400	30 125	35 085	19 368	20 388	21 408	Pétrole et produits dérivés
Cereals and cereal preparations	...	14 894	16 679	17 231	17 656	20 563	18 139	19 095	20 051	Céréales et préparations à base de céréales
beverages	...	3 928	4 448	5 501	5 312	5 056	6 694	7 287	7 880	Boissons
Iron and steel	...	3 720	4 737	6 751	6 807	7 373	3 700	3 852	4 004	Fer et acier
Road vehicles	...	4 007	4 144	3 893	3 989	4 646	5 722	6 023	6 324	Véhicules routiers
Main Origin										**Principales provenances**
Portugal	...	...	...	...	...	...	...	...	...	Portugal
Senegal	...	...	...	...	...	...	...	...	...	Sénégal
Italy	...	...	...	...	...	...	...	...	...	Italie
Netherlands	...	...	...	...	...	...	...	...	...	Pays-Bas
China	...	...	...	...	...	...	...	...	...	Chine

IX FINANCIAL AND MONETARY STATISTICS - FINANCES ET STATISTIQUES MONETAIRES	2006	2007	2008	2009	2010	2011	2012	2013	2014	
IX-1 MONETARY STATISTICS *CFA FRANC (MILLIONS)*										**IX-1 STATISTIQUES MONÉTAIRES** *FRANC CFA (MILLIONS)*
Money supply (M1)	55 010	71 630	92 100	96 110	124 580	173 300	162 830	186 910	206 850	Masse monétaire (M1)
Quasi-money	1 892	5 367	8 481	7 807	13 637	28 253	31 020	29 988	32 195	Quasi-monnaie
of which Demand Deposit	...	...	...	...	...	...	...	...	...	dont Monnaie scripturale
Net foreign assets	43 303	51 911	66 373	82 270	93 048	132 522	87 594	95 173	159 992	Avoirs extérieurs nets
Domestic credit	16 732	20 693	27 750	19 378	31 980	62 060	85 369	88 280	86 496	Crédit intérieur
of which claims on private sector	6 329	10 469	18 621	22 070	25 756	54 110	64 224	66 561	61 090	dont créances sur le secteur privé
of which claims on government sector, net	10 403	10 224	9 129	- 2 692	6 224	7 950	21 145	21 719	25 406	dont créances nettes sur le gouvernement
International reserves (millions US$)	82	113	125	169	156	220	165	186	299	Réserves internationales (millions $EU)
Average Exchange Rate (National Currency per US$)	522.90	478.89	446.87	471.07	494.68	471.42	510.18	493.94	493.76	Taux de change (moyen) (monnaie nationale par $ EU)
IX-2 PUBLIC FINANCE *CFA FRANC (MILLIONS)*										**IX-2 FINANCES PUBLIQUES** *FRANC CFA (MILLIONS)*
Total Revenues and Grants	50 599	53 700	65 400	98 485	91 196	87 002	58 100	59 959	110 225	Recettes totales et dons
Tax Revenue	18 474	18 800	20 900	26 578	33 086	40 253	38 900	37 428	40 326	Recettes fiscales
Non Tax Revenue	12 977	7 800	13 700	8 801	11 510	12 349	7 100	4 730	23 636	Recettes non fiscales
Grants	19 149	27 100	30 800	63 107	46 600	34 400	12 100	17 800	46 263	Dons
Total Expenditures and Net Lending	56 369	62 200	80 759	86 688	90 427	94 200	69 400	68 000	122 323	Dépenses totales et prêts nets
Current expenditure	38 969	38 200	53 459	45 600	49 900	57 200	62 200	49 700	89 390	Dépenses courantes
Of which Wages and Salaries	12 762	12 200	20 138	20 100	26 200	23 600	25 100	24 300	34 053	Dont rémunérations et salaires
Capital expenditure	17 400	24 000	27 300	41 088	40 527	37 000	7 200	18 300	32 933	Dépenses d'équipement
Net Lending	-	-	-	-	-	-	0	-	-	Prêts nets
Fiscal Balance	- 5 770	- 8 500	- 15 359	11 797	768	- 7 198	- 11 300	- 8 041	- 12 098	Solde global y compris les dons
IX-3 BALANCE OF PAYMENTS *CFA FRANC (MILLIONS)*										**IX-3 BALANCE DES PAIEMENTS** *FRANC CFA (MILLIONS)*
Trade balance	- 27 665	- 29 171	- 31 640	- 38 097	- 34 655	- 1 046	- 27 570	- 19 902	...	Balance commerciale
Services Balance	- 18 904	- 16 693	- 18 541	- 25 378	- 29 003	- 25 879	- 23 040	- 21 700	...	Balance des services
Net Income	- 4 619	- 4 669	- 6 577	- 5 197	- 1 144	- 8 734	- 3 785	- 7 500	...	Revenus nets
Compensation of employees	...	...	...	...	...	...	...	...	...	Rémunération des salariés
Investment Income	...	...	...	...	...	...	...	...	...	Revenus des investissements
Current transfers, net total	30 232	35 929	43 883	46 251	29 752	29 129	22 684	25 500	...	Transferts courants
Net official transfers	...	...	...	...	...	...	...	...	...	Transferts officiels nets
Workers' remittances	...	...	...	...	...	...	...	...	...	Envois de fonds des travailleurs
Other private transfers	...	...	...	...	...	...	...	...	...	Autres transferts privés
Current account balance	- 20 956	- 14 604	- 12 875	- 22 421	- 35 050	- 6 530	- 31 710	- 23 602	...	Solde du compte courant
Capital & financial account	...	...	...	...	...	...	...	...	...	Comptes de capital et financier
Capital account	...	...	...	...	...	...	...	...	...	Compte de capital
Financial account	...	...	...	...	...	...	...	...	...	Compte financier
Errors & omissions	...	...	...	...	...	...	...	...	...	Erreurs et omissions
Overall balance	...	...	...	...	...	...	...	...	...	Balance générale

X DEBT AND FINANCIAL FLOWS - DETTE ET FLUX FINANCIERS	2006	2007	2008	2009	2010	2011	2012	2013	2014	
X-1 DEBT *US$ (MILLIONS)*										**X-1 DETTE EXTÉRIEURE** *$ E.U (MILLIONS)*
Total external debt	1 025	1 031	1 040	1 067	200	351	420	423	427	Dette extérieure totale
Private	1	1	1	0	0	1	1	1	0	Privée
Public	1 024	1 031	1 039	1 066	200	350	419	422	427	Publique
Total external debt service	5	6	4	11	896	2	0	0	6	Service de la dette extérieure
Present value of External debt	...	...	...	...	...	...	...	...	...	Valeur actuelle de la dette extérieure
Total government domestic debt (in local currency)	...	...	...	...	...	...	...	...	...	Dette publique intérieure
X-2 FINANCIAL FLOWS *US$ (MILLIONS)*										**X-2 FLUX FINANCIERS** *$ E.U (MILLIONS)*
Net Foreign Direct Investment Inflows	17	19	5	17	33	25	7	15	...	Investissement étranger direct (flux nets entrants)
Main origin of FDI Inflows										**Principales origines de l'IDE entrant:**
Norway	...	...	...	...	...	...	...	...	...	Norvège
Luxembourg	...	...	...	...	...	...	...	...	...	Luxembourg
Korea	...	...	...	...	...	...	...	...	...	Corée
Slovenia	...	...	...	...	...	...	...	...	...	Slovénie
Czech Republic	...	...	...	...	...	...	...	...	...	République tchèque
African countries	...	...	...	...	...	...	...	...	...	Pays africains
Net total Official Development Assistance	87	122	134	147	125	120	79	104	...	Aide publique au développement (nette totale)
Main origin of Net ODA										**Principales origines de l'APD nette**
Portugal	15	16	18	14	15.7	13.7	9.5	8.0	...	Portugal
IDA	8	14	16	14	7.3	11.7	9.5	...	...	IDA
Italy	1	1	2	2	0.3	0.8	0.3	0.4	...	Italie
Spain	5	13	16	13	8.3	6.4	4.2	5.0	...	Espagne
France	10	3	6	6	1.8	14.4	1.4	1.0	...	France

AREA (km²)	610 000		SUPERFICIE (km²)
CAPITAL CITY	Nairobi	Nairobi	CAPITALE
CURRENCY	Kenyan Shilling	Shilling Kenyan	MONNAIE

I SOCIAL AND DEMOGRAPHIC INDICATORS — INDICATEURS DEMOGRAPHIQUES ET SOCIAUX

POPULATION	Year / Année	Value / Valeur	POPULATION
Population ('000)			Population ('000)
Both sexes	2014	42 961	Les deux sexes
Male	2014	21 290	Masculin
Female	2014	21 671	Féminin
Average annual growth rate	2014	2.9	Taux de croissance annuel
Active Population ('000)	2013	16 801	Population active ('000)
Population by age group ('000)			Population par groupe d'âge ('000)
0-14 years	2014	17 831	0-14 ans
15-64 years	2014	23 701	15-64 ans
65+ years	2014	1 391	65+ ans
Economically. active population. in agriculture (%)	2013	81.9	Participation de la population active agricole (%)
Crude birth rate	2014	38.4	Taux brut de natalité
Crude death rate	2014	10.4	Taux brut de mortalité
Total fertility rate	2014	3.9	Indice synthétique de fécondité
Proportion of urban population	2014	32.0	Part de la population urbaine
Life Expectancy at Birth - Total (years)	2014	61.0	Espérance de vie à la naissance - Totale (ans)
Dependency Ratio - Total (%)	2014	82.5	Taux de dépendance - Total (%)

Charts / Graphiques

Population by age group – 2014
Population par groupe d'age – 2014

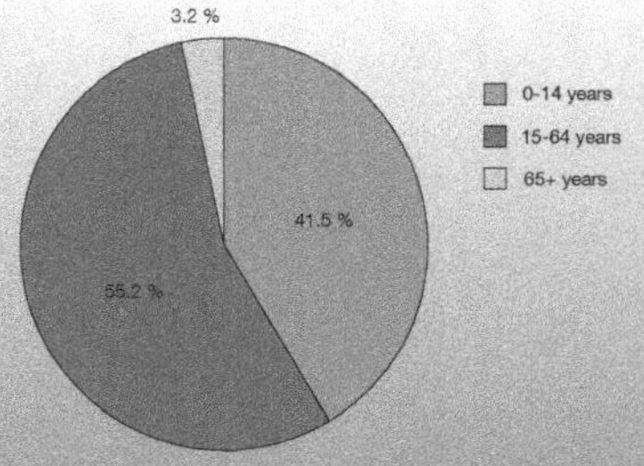

HEALTH	Year / Année	Value / Valeur	SANTÉ
Percentage of children under-five and underweight	2009	16.4	% d'enfants de moins de cinq ans avec insuffisance pondérale
Prevalence of undernourishment	2005	51.0	Prévalence de la malnutrition
Under five mortality rate (both sexes, per 1000)	2011	74.0	Taux de mortalité de moins de 5 ans (les deux sexes, pour 1000)
Infant mortality rate (both sexes) per 1000	2011	52.0	Taux de mortalité infantile (les deux sexes) par 1000
Percentage of children provided the vaccines :			Pourcentage d'enfants vaccinés :
BCG	2011	92.0	BCG
DPT3	2011	88.0	DTC3
Polio	2011	88.0	Polio
Measles	2011	87.0	Rougeole
Percentage of mothers provided at least one antenatal care (%)	2011	91.5	Pourcentage de mères ayant au moins reçu un soin prénatal (%)
Percentage of deliveries attended by skilled health personnel	2011	43.8	% d'accouchements assistés par un personnel de santé qualifié
Number of doctors (per 10 000 population)	2013	2.0	Nombre de médecins (pour 10 000 habitants)
Number of nurses (per 10 000 population)	2013	16.0	Nombre d'infirmières (pour 10 000 habitants)
Hospital beds - Total (per 10 000 population)	2006	140.0	Nombre de lits d'hôpitaux - Total (pour 10 000)
Births registered (per 1 000)	2012	37.1	Naiss.s enregistrées (pour 1 000)
Deaths registered (per 1 000)	2012	10.0	Décès enregistrés (pour 1 000)
Public expenditure on Health (% of budget)	2012	5.0	Dépenses publiques consacrées à la santé (% du budget)

Percentage of children provided the vaccines – 2011
Pourcentage d'enfants vaccinés – 2011

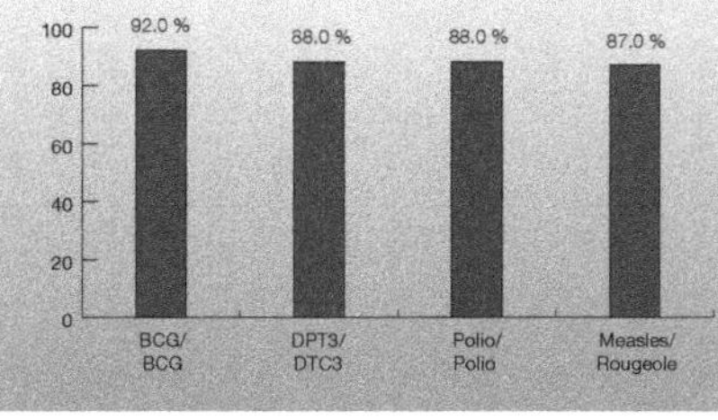

Literacy rate (%) – 2014
Taux d'alphabétisation – 2014

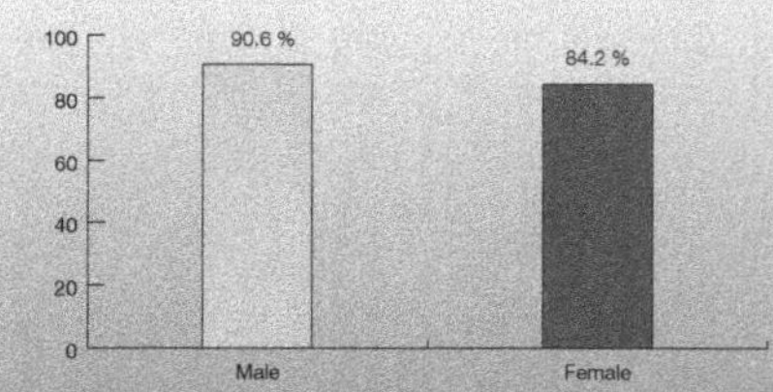

EDUCATION	Year / Année	Value / Valeur	EDUCATION
Enrolment in primary education (both sexes) (000)	2014	9 857	Scolarisation dans le primaire (les deux sexes) (000)
Female	2014	4 852	Féminin
Enrolment in secondary education (both sexes) (000)	2014	2 310	Scolarisation dans le secondaire (les deux sexes) (000)
Female	2014	1 108	Féminin
Enrolment in tertiary education (both sexes) (000)	2014	653.9	Scolarisation dans le tertiaire (les deux sexes) (000)
Female	2014	272.4	Féminin
Literacy rate (both sexes)	2010	87.4	Taux d'alphabétisation (deux sexes)
Male	2010	90.6	Masculin
Female	2010	84.2	Féminin
Pupil-teacher ratio	2014	42.0	Ratio élève-enseignant
Public expenditure on education (% of budget)	2013	19.8	Dépenses publiques consacrées à l'enseignement (% du budget)

GNI Per Capita (US$)
RNB par habitant ($EU)

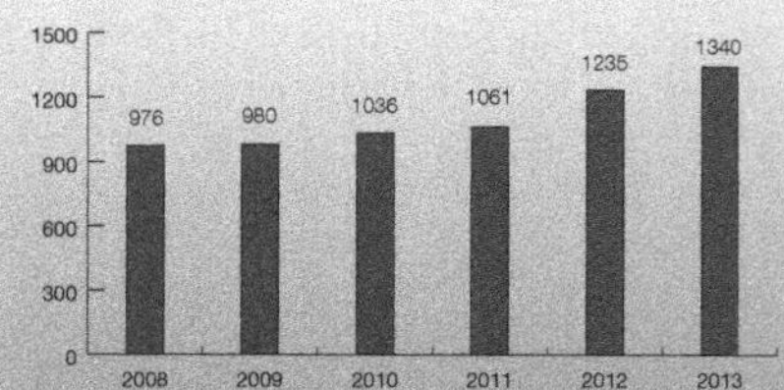

POVERTY	Year / Année	Value / Valeur	PAUVRETÉ
GNI Per Capita (US$)	2013	1 339.9	RNB par habitant ($EU)
Human Poverty Index (HPI-1) Value (%)	2004	35.5	Valeur de l'Indice de pauvreté (IPH-1) (%)
Population below International Poverty Line ($2/day) (%)	2006	19.7	Population sous le seuil international de pauvreté (2$/J) (%)
Share of Income Held by Richest 10%	2009	26.1	% de revenu des 10% plus riches
Share of Income Held by Poorest 10%	2009	2.6	% de revenu des 10% plus pauvres
Gini index	2009	44.5	Indice de Gini

II NATIONAL ACCOUNTS — COMPTES NATIONAUX

	2006	2007	2008	2009	2010	2011	2012	2013	2014	
GROSS DOMESTIC PRODUCT BY KIND OF ECONOMIC ACTIVITY AT CURRENT PRICES *KENYAN SHILLING (MILLIONS)*										**PRODUIT INTÉRIEUR BRUT PAR BRANCHE D'ACTIVITÉ ÉCONOMIQUE AUX PRIX COURANTS** *SHILLING KENYAN (MILLIONS)*
Agriculture, hunting, forestry and fishing	382 085	442 891	551 148	668 969	786 826	980 063	1 113 572	1 249 700	...	Agriculture, chasse, sylviculture et pêche
Mining and quarrying	10 027	13 770	16 785	18 134	26 027	32 506	46 576	38 680	...	Industries extractives
Manufacturing	236 281	275 167	300 345	342 532	356 717	437 798	463 998	496 313	...	Industries manufacturières
Electricity, gas & water	40 413	39 901	51 293	64 031	62 483	69 475	85 830	91 811	...	Electricité, gaz et eau
Construction & public works	74 219	86 419	92 998	112 220	142 668	164 622	190 852	212 103	...	Bâtiments et travaux publics
Wholesale & retail trade, restaurants, hotels	165 560	200 592	220 665	251 542	292 917	350 949	388 916	432 007	...	Commerce de gros et de détail, restaurants et hôtels
Finance, insurance, real estate, etc.	333 299	373 419	382 542	474 193	497 436	500 889	631 366	723 934	...	Banques, assurances, affaires immobilières
Transport and communications	162 492	195 261	234 907	279 465	285 331	327 181	396 934	419 661	...	Transport(s) et communications
Public administration and defense	83 437	96 829	113 517	127 807	138 929	159 085	189 748	228 523	...	Administrations publiques et défense
Education	118 459	130 803	163 456	177 993	174 480	199 110	228 761	258 406	...	Education
Health and Social Work	39 385	45 001	50 099	58 686	66 040	67 827	69 931	75 257	...	Santé et actions sociales
Other services	34 022	36 181	39 310	42 594	45 797	49 575	56 272	61 601	...	Autres services
Less Imputed Service Charges	- 30 692	- 35 248	- 45 749	- 59 373	- 71 891	- 90 687	- 111 631	- 122 407	...	Moins services d'intermédiation financière
Gross domestic product at factor cost / basic prices	1 648 987	1 900 986	2 171 316	2 558 793	2 803 760	3 248 393	3 751 125	4 165 589	...	Produit intérieur brut aux couts des facteurs / prix de base
Plus: indirect taxes / taxes on products, less subsidies	212 044	247 878	271 611	304 896	341 865	377 910	443 008	523 214	...	Plus taxes indirectes/impôts sur les produits, moins les subventions
EXPENDITURE ON GROSS DOMESTIC PRODUCT AT CURRENT PURCHASER'S VALUES *KENYAN SHILLING (MILLIONS)*										**EMPLOI DU PRODUIT INTÉRIEUR BRUT AUX PRIX COURANTS D'ACQUISITION** *SHILLING KENYAN (MILLIONS)*
Government final consumption	267 147	314 734	389 194	435 695	449 064	522 062	596 065	668 246	...	Consommation finale des administrations publiques
Private final consumption	1 419 467	1 610 385	1 870 427	2 183 599	2 445 295	2 936 351	3 344 408	3 807 184	...	Consommation finale privée
Gross fixed capital formation	361 691	429 511	468 427	529 927	645 647	759 746	903 740	971 203	...	Formation brute de capital fixe
Change in inventories	- 14 726	10 590	18 568	23 699	14 871	48 881	14 166	- 23 414	...	Variation des stocks
Exports of goods and services	427 989	471 554	563 010	573 672	654 689	805 766	844 425	843 490	...	Exportations de biens et services
Less imports of goods and services	600 537	687 911	866 700	882 904	1 063 942	1 446 502	1 508 672	1 577 905	...	Moins importations de biens et services
GDP at purchasers' values	1 861 033	2 148 863	2 442 927	2 863 688	3 145 624	3 626 304	4 194 132	4 688 803	...	PIB aux prix d'acquisition
GROSS DOMESTIC PRODUCT BY KIND OF ECONOMIC ACTIVITY AT CONSTANT PRICES *ANNUAL GROWTH RATES (%)*										**PRODUIT INTÉRIEUR BRUT PAR BRANCHE D'ACTIVITÉ ECONOMIQUE AUX PRIX CONSTANTS** *TAUX DE CROISSANCE ANNUEL (%)*
Agriculture, hunting, forestry and fishing	4.5	5.1	- 5.0	- 2.3	10.0	2.4	2.9	5.1	...	Agriculture, chasse, sylviculture et pêche
Mining and quarrying	4.1	17.6	0.0	11.3	31.7	19.0	19.0	- 9.0	...	Industries extractives
Manufacturing	6.3	4.4	1.1	- 1.1	4.5	7.2	- 0.5	5.9	...	Industries manufacturières
Electricity, gas & water	- 1.7	9.8	- 4.0	7.0	6.3	9.4	9.6	5.8	...	Electricité, gaz et eau
Construction & public works	6.3	8.5	- 1.7	17.5	19.1	4.0	11.2	5.5	...	Bâtiments et travaux publics
Wholesale & retail trade, restaurants, hotels	12.0	9.4	- 6.1	9.9	7.5	7.5	6.3	6.8	...	Commerce de gros et de détail, restaurants et hôtels
Finance, insurance, real estate, etc.	4.8	5.6	3.4	4.7	8.7	4.5	4.6	5.8	...	Banques, assurances, affaires immobilières
Transport and communications	11.4	10.1	4.5	7.9	8.2	11.4	2.6	5.1	...	Transport(s) et communications
Public administration and defense	- 1.6	2.4	6.9	7.1	1.5	2.5	5.9	0.2	...	Administrations publiques et défense
Education	0.3	6.5	9.2	5.3	10.2	7.5	11.6	6.9	...	Education
Health and Social Work	3.3	6.2	4.7	4.7	6.2	- 2.6	- 3.2	6.8	...	Santé et actions sociales
Other services	4.1	2.1	1.3	1.2	3.6	1.5	2.3	4.4	...	Autres services
Less Imputed Service Charges	5.1	3.6	4.5	10.6	15.9	9.1	10.1	5.7	...	Moins services d'intermédiation financière
Gross domestic product at factor cost / basic prices	5.6	6.3	- 0.1	3.3	8.3	5.4	4.3	5.3	...	Produit intérieur brut aux couts des facteurs / prix de base
Plus: indirect taxes / taxes on products, less subsidies	11.2	12.3	3.0	3.0	9.2	12.6	6.0	9.2	...	Plus taxes indirectes/impôts sur les produits, moins les subventions
Gross domestic product at market prices	6.3	6.9	0.2	3.3	8.4	6.1	4.5	5.7	...	Produit intérieur brut aux prix du marché
EXPENDITURE ON GROSS DOMESTIC PRODUCT AT CONSTANT PURCHASERS' VALUES *ANNUAL GROWTH RATES (%)*										**EMPLOIS DU PRODUIT INTÉRIEUR BRUT AUX PRIX CONSTANTS D'ACQUISITION** *TAUX DE CROISSANCE ANNUEL (%)*
Government final consumption	2.2	8.1	8.6	8.7	3.7	4.1	7.3	1.1	...	Consommation finale des administrations publiques
Private final consumption	9.8	5.7	- 0.4	4.9	8.4	8.4	4.2	7.8	...	Consommation finale privée
Gross fixed capital formation	22.5	2.2	12.9	10.0	14.1	4.5	12.7	1.4	...	Formation brute de capital fixe
Exports of goods and services	3.1	6.2	2.4	- 5.2	8.7	9.2	- 0.2	- 0.8	...	Exportations de biens et services
Less imports of goods and services	17.8	4.4	12.7	8.3	8.1	13.2	5.4	0.3	...	Moins importations de biens et services
Notes	The Accounts are calculated using the new base year 2009 from 2006				Les comptes sont calculées selon la nouvelle année de base 2009 à partir 2006					Notes

III INFLATION

	2006	2007	2008	2009	2010	2011	2012	2013	2014	
ANNUAL GROWTH RATES (%)										**TAUX DE CROISSANCE ANNUEL (%)**
All items	6.0	4.3	16.2	9.5	4.1	14.0	9.4	5.7	6.9	Ensemble
of which:										dont:
Food and Non-alcoholic beverages	7.5	4.2	23.1	15.4	5.9	20.5	10.0	7.3	8.9	Alimentation et boissons non alcoolisés
Alcoholic beverages & tobacco	7.0	5.7	13.6	9.4	7.5	9.4	9.0	6.0	5.5	Boissons alcoolisées et tabacs
Clothing and Footwear	2.1	2.3	4.7	4.3	3.4	7.1	9.6	5.2	4.8	Habillement et chaussures
Housing, Water, Electricity, Gas and Other Fuels	6.8	6.8	12.3	4.4	3.2	11.4	9.3	4.6	5.6	Logement, eau, electricité, gas et autres combustibles
Furnishing, household equipment	2.9	4.8	8.7	6.4	3.2	8.6	10.1	4.3	5.1	Meubles, articles de ménage et entretien courant
Health	1.9	3.0	7.0	9.5	4.4	7.3	5.8	4.3	6.1	Santé
Transport	6.9	4.8	13.9	4.6	5.3	21.3	7.4	4.8	9.2	Transport
Communication	5.5	0.8	0.5	-0.3	-10.3	-15.8	5.8	-1.5	-0.9	Communication
Recreation & culture	-0.6	1.8	3.4	2.7	1.2	8.0	9.6	6.1	10.6	Loisirs et culture
Education	0.5	1.1	0.5	0.1	1.4	4.4	6.7	5.2	5.4	Enseignement
Restaurants & hotels	2.0	4.8	15.4	8.6	4.0	14.7	14.4	7.1	6.7	Restaurants et hôtels
Miscellaneous goods & services	1.9	2.7	7.0	7.3	2.2	7.3	9.4	4.6	4.4	Biens et services divers

IV AGRICULTURAL PRODUCTION - PRODUCTION AGRICOLE

	2006	2007	2008	2009	2010	2011	2012	2013	2014	
TONNES *(THOUSAND)*										**TONNES** *(MILLIERS)*
Maize	3 114	2 925	2 349	2 250	3 060	3 096	3 573	3 501	...	Maïs
Tea	311	370	346	314	399	378	369	432	...	Thé
Sugar cane	4 933	5 204	5 112	5 611	5 695	5 307	5 824	6 671	...	Canne à sucre
Coffee green	51	52	39	57	42	36	49	40	...	Café vert
Wheat	99	108	86	129	200	106	163	195	...	Blé

V MINING PRODUCTION - PRODUCTION MINIERE

	2006	2007	2008	2009	2010	2011	2012	2013	2014	
Soda Ash, Tons (thousands)	0	0	1	0	0	0	0	0	...	Carbonate de soude, tonnes (milliers)
Fluorspar, Tons (thousands)	0	0	0	0	0	0	0	0	...	Spath fluor, tonnes (milliers)
Gold (Kilograms)	432	3 023	343	1 135	2 035	1 642	3 643	2 100	...	Minerai d'or et concentrés (Kilogrammes)

VI ENERGY - ENERGIE

	2006	2007	2008	2009	2010	2011	2012	2013	2014	
Total electricity generation (GWh)	6 785	6 670	6 776	6 875	7 467	7 875	8 540	8 989	...	Production d'électricité totale (GWh)
of which:										dont:
Production of electricity from fossil fuels (GWh)	2 299	1 840	2 426	3 029	2 287	2 569	3 274	3 405	...	Production d'électricité à partir de combustibles fossiles (GWh)
Production of hydro electricity (GWh)	3 278	3 488	2 849	2 170	3 393	3 451	2 402	2 498	...	Production d'électricité d'origine hydraulique (GWh)
Production of electricity from solar, wind, tide, wave and other sources (GWh)	1	1	1	16	18	21	35	42	...	Production d'électricité d'origine solaire, éolienne, marée motrice et autres (GWh)

VII TOURISM AND INFRASTRUCTURE - TOURISME ET INFRASTRUCTURE

	2006	2007	2008	2009	2010	2011	2012	2013	2014	
VII-1 TOURISM										**VII-1 TOURISME**
International tourist arrivals (thousands)	1 464	1 686	1 141	1 392	1 470	1 750	1 619	1 440	1 257	Arrivées de touristes internationaux (milliers)
Rooms in hotels and similar establishments (thousands)	7.2	8.3	8.1	10.3	10.2	10.6	11.5	11.4	...	Chambres d'hotels et établissements assimilés (milliers)
Overnight stays (thousands)	8 978	9 948	4 055	8 042	8 236	12 291	11 415	10 084	8 818	Nuitées (milliers)
Tourism receipts (US$ thousand)	687 500	916 700	752 200	689 900	800 100	925 900	934 800	867 155	820 068	Recettes touristiques (milliers de $ EU)
Total contribution to GDP (%)	13.2	13.1	11.7	10.4	11.2	11.7	11.4	10.9	10.4	Contribution totale au PIB (%)
Total contribution to Employment (%)	11.5	11.4	10.2	9.1	9.8	10.3	10.0	9.5	9.1	Contribution totale à l'emploi (%)
VII-2 INFRASTRUCTURE										**VII-2 INFRASTRUCTURE**
Paved roads (% of total)	14	14	14	14	14	14	16	18	...	Routes asphaltées (% du total)
Total Network (Railways-km)	66 169	66 172	66 172	66 945	61 946	61 954	62 043	...	...	Réseau total voies ferrées-Km
Main Telephone Lines (per 100 inhabitants)	1	1	2	2	1	1	1	0	1	Lignes téléphoniques fixes (pour 100 habitants)
Mobile Cellular Subscribers (per 100 inhabitants)	20	30	42	49	61	67	71	72	78	Abonnés aux téléphones mobiles (pour 100 habitants)

VIII EXTERNAL TRADE - COMMERCE EXTERIEUR

	2006	2007	2008	2009	2010	2011	2012	2013	2014	
KENYAN SHILLING (MILLIONS) EXPORTS, FOB										**SHILLING KENYAN (MILLIONS) EXPORTATIONS, FÀB**
Exports - Total	247 900	274 596	342 955	344 949	408 202	511 037	517 847	502 286	...	Exportations - Total
Exports to AFRICA	108 306	124 010	162 541	162 732	188 914	247 600	250 589	231 474	...	Exportations vers l'AFRIQUE
Main Products										**Principaux produits**
Tea	47 349	46 784	63 825	68 766	91 617	102 235	101 441	104 648	...	Thé
Cutflowers	19 547	21 094	30 698	32 574	31 413	83 331	81 129	89 339	...	Fleurs coupées
beverages and tobacco	9 160	10 760	11 809	13 991	14 528	22 260	22 271	24 379	...	Boissons et tabac
Coffee, not roasted	9 138	10 425	10 126	15 309	16 244	19 296	20 676	16 328	...	Café non torréfié
Sodium carbonate (Soda ash)	3 976	5 419	13 185	8 305	7 265	18 633	16 615	15 560	...	Carbonate de sodium
Main Destinations										**Principales destinations**
Uganda	26 689	31 731	35 716	37 996	45 922	54 208	67 450	65 362	...	Ouganda
United Kingdom	29 429	30 555	37 156	40 457	39 905	44 657	46 036	40 496	...	Royaume-Uni
Netherlands	22 556	26 039	31 947	33 664	34 148	46 207	40 630	37 613	...	Pays-Bas
United Republic of Tanzania	19 634	20 987	30 693	29 654	35 706	52 810	31 056	32 578	...	République-Unie de Tanzanie
United States	23 732	21 212	22 901	20 948	25 075	33 821	28 608	25 144	...	États-Unis
IMPORTS, CIF										**IMPORTATIONS, CAF**
Imports - Total	526 870	605 121	766 743	788 097	959 434	1 315 656	1 374 587	1 413 316	...	Importations - Total (millions)
Imports from Africa	63 613	72 038	85 991	104 672	115 096	151 254	140 755	147 839	...	Importations en provenance de l'Afrique
Main Products										**Principaux produits**
Petroleum, petroleum products and related materials	136 186	133 481	187 934	145 793	214 663	308 784	237 557	252 673	...	Pétrole et produits dérivés
Road vehicles	42 217	51 820	57 594	62 916	67 192	90 677	194 666	231 440	...	Véhicules routiers
Cereals and cereal preparations	16 087	18 749	30 038	60 024	33 392	72 928	73 768	83 330	...	Céréales et préparations à base de céréales
Iron and steel	21 634	27 694	37 803	34 345	46 575	64 189	68 086	80 749	...	Fer et acier
Telecommunication and sound recording apparatus	14 863	22 040	28 159	31 967	45 354	47 703	56 667	55 182	...	Équipements pour les télécommunications et le son
Main Origin										**Principales provenances**
India	70 500	83 023	101 229	97 257	136 971	179 839	195 230	258 230	...	Inde
China	39 402	55 870	78 260	90 860	129 058	165 749	167 206	182 356	...	Chine
United Arab Emirates	54 438	62 776	81 027	67 912	84 106	117 724	149 879	117 360	...	Émirats arabes unis
South Africa	32 734	39 272	47 249	66 841	70 814	99 242	66 841	83 720	...	Afrique du Sud
Saudi Arabia	37 413	35 980	53 634	44 076	55 765	77 620	65 966	57 412	...	Arabie saoudite

IX FINANCIAL AND MONETARY STATISTICS - FINANCES ET STATISTIQUES MONETAIRES										
	2006	2007	2008	2009	2010	2011	2012	2013	2014	
IX-1 MONETARY STATISTICS *KENYAN SHILLING (MILLIONS)*										**IX-1 STATISTIQUES MONÉTAIRES** *SHILLING KENYAN (MILLIONS)*
Money supply (M1)	653 110	777 770	901 060	1 045 660	1 271 640	1 514 150	1 727 430	1 996 240	2 376 150	Masse monétaire (M1)
Quasi-money	299 258	331 042	372 685	515 682	597 485	764 029	886 752	996 984	1 216 988	Quasi-monnaie
of which Demand Deposit	...	...	...	...	...	...	...	...	...	dont Monnaie scripturale
Net foreign assets	206 968	255 265	258 391	243 450	269 412	294 295	328 307	390 135	483 262	Avoirs extérieurs nets
Domestic credit	596	669	842	1 019	1 302	1 553	1 800	2 037	2 389	Crédit intérieur
of which claims on private sector	426	496	630	717	863	1 139	1 259	1 505	1 844	dont créances sur le secteur privé
of which claims on government sector, net	123 999	129 199	154 368	228 125	361 825	314 659	419 853	409 199	394 960	dont créances nettes sur le gouvernement
International reserves (millions US$)	2 416	3 355	2 879	3 849	4 320	4 264	5 711	6 598	7 911	Réserves internationales (millions $EU)
Average Exchange Rate (National Currency per US$)	72.10	67.32	69.18	77.35	79.23	88.81	84.53	86.12	87.76	Taux de change (moyen) (monnaie nationale par $ EU)
IX-2 PUBLIC FINANCE *KENYAN SHILLING (MILLIONS)*										**IX-2 FINANCES PUBLIQUES** *SHILLING KENYAN (MILLIONS)*
Total Revenues and Grants	331 321	388 525	453 920	507 593	568 872	686 500	844 900	906 000	1 211 900	Recettes totales et dons
Tax Revenue	283 804	338 061	399 304	449 467	466 572	557 300	660 700	718 780	1 017 683	Recettes fiscales
Non Tax Revenue	27 447	34 970	32 916	38 426	81 600	110 400	143 100	146 100	117 400	Recettes non fiscales
Grants	20 070	15 494	21 700	19 700	20 700	18 800	41 100	41 120	76 817	Dons
Total Expenditures and Net Lending	382 818	403 031	535 549	604 678	725 400	811 800	1 000 400	1 154 808	1 481 764	Dépenses totales et prêts nets
Current expenditure	311 126	322 677	404 076	438 378	510 700	592 400	668 100	855 678	1 123 388	Dépenses courantes
Of which Wages and Salaries	112 277	127 258	145 996	155 220	172 800	198 500	222 600	294 300	382 300	Dont rémunérations et salaires
Capital expenditure	67 692	80 354	131 473	166 300	213 500	216 900	329 700	296 730	356 076	Dépenses d'équipement
Net Lending	4 000	-	-	-	1 200	2 500	2 600	2 400	2 300	Prêts nets
Fiscal Balance	- 51 497	- 14 506	- 81 629	- 97 085	- 156 528	- 125 300	- 155 500	- 248 808	- 269 864	Solde global y compris les dons
IX-3 BALANCE OF PAYMENTS *KENYAN SHILLING (MILLIONS)*										**IX-3 BALANCE DES PAIEMENTS** *SHILLING KENYAN (MILLIONS)*
Trade balance	- 234 562	- 286 506	- 390 235	- 384 017	- 498 563	- 746 052	- 790 737	- 607 451	- 520 066	Balance commerciale
Services Balance	76 398	84 805	98 255	85 478	138 190	173 912	207 980	228 284	224 191	Balance des services
Net Income	- 5 053	- 9 706	- 2 190	- 3 454	- 11 697	- 5 266	- 14 418	- 29 124	- 58 831	Revenus nets
Compensation of employees	...	...	...	...	...	...	...	...	...	Rémunération des salariés
Investment Income	...	...	...	...	...	...	...	...	...	Revenus des investissements
Current transfers, net total	128 693	141 931	161 265	177 853	184 393	237 227	237 712	270 748	189 523	Transferts courants
Net official transfers	...	...	...	...	...	...	...	...	...	Transferts officiels nets
Workers' remittances	...	...	...	...	...	...	...	...	...	Envois de fonds des travailleurs
Other private transfers	...	...	...	...	...	...	...	...	...	Autres transferts privés
Current account balance	- 34 524	- 69 476	- 132 906	- 124 140	- 187 677	- 340 179	- 359 463	- 137 543	- 165 183	Solde du compte courant
Capital & financial account	12 142	10 558	6 535	20 178	19 030	20 861	19 890	...	...	Comptes de capital et financier
Capital account	...	...	...	...	...	...	...	...	...	Compte de capital
Financial account	...	...	...	...	...	...	...	...	...	Compte financier
Errors & omissions	15 190	- 17 364	16 547	8 835	13 901	29 457	44 610	...	...	Erreurs et omissions
Overall balance	44 446	63 250	- 33 162	75 182	12 226	21 847	123 184	...	...	Balance générale

X DEBT AND FINANCIAL FLOWS - DETTE ET FLUX FINANCIERS	2006	2007	2008	2009	2010	2011	2012	2013	2014	
X-1 DEBT *US$ (MILLIONS)*										**X-1 DETTE EXTÉRIEURE** *$ E.U (MILLIONS)*
Total external debt	6 305	6 508	7 144	7 748	8 607	9 316	9 090	9 759	12 123	Dette extérieure totale
Private	482	287	312	243	243	238	863	676	2 066	Privée
Public	5 823	6 221	6 831	7 505	8 364	9 078	8 227	9 083	10 057	Publique
Total external debt service	431	327	344	338	388	340	418	453	1 182	Service de la dette extérieure
Present value of External debt	...	...	...	...	...	...	...	...	...	Valeur actuelle de la dette extérieure
Total government domestic debt (in local currency)	381 298	417 650	471 980	585 536	711 122.9	807 830.9	768 569.3	889 120.8	...	Dette publique intérieure
X-2 FINANCIAL FLOWS *US$ (MILLIONS)*										**X-2 FLUX FINANCIERS** *$ E.U (MILLIONS)*
Net Foreign Direct Investment Inflows	51	729	96	115	178	335	259	514	...	Investissement étranger direct (flux nets entrants)
Main origin of FDI Inflows										**Principales origines de l'IDE entrant:**
United Kingdom	114	192	123	179	301.2	76.9	- 9.5	...	...	Royaume-Uni
France	6	606	- 192	10	- 1.3	16.7	45.0	...	...	France
Belgium	3	3	1	215	123.2	19.5	- 331.6	...	...	Belgique
Germany	- 3	3	31	- 13	5.3	...	...	...	...	Allemagne
Sweden	2	3	29	27	...	- 16.0	- 10.8	...	...	Suède
African countries	...	...	...	...	...	...	...	...	...	Pays africains
Net total Official Development Assistance	947	1 327	1 366	1 776	1 629	2 482	2 654	3 236	...	Aide publique au développement (nette totale)
Main origin of Net ODA										**Principales origines de l'APD nette**
United States	282	325	439	590	565.9	715.4	817.8	819.9	...	Etats-Unis
United Kingdom	108	111	91	131	105.2	142.0	161.3	...	...	Royaume-Uni
IDA	- 5	101	114	83	132.8	165.3	192.9	...	...	IDA
Germany	45	62	85	86	79.8	99.3	78.6	56.7	...	Allemagne
Japan	105	57	9	34	36.7	79.7	132.1	270.3	...	Japon

LESOTHO — LÉSOTHO

AREA (km²)		30 355	**SUPERFICIE (km²)**
CAPITAL CITY	Maseru	Maseru	**CAPITALE**
CURRENCY	Loti	Loti	**MONNAIE**

I SOCIAL AND DEMOGRAPHIC INDICATORS — INDICATEURS DEMOGRAPHIQUES ET SOCIAUX

	Year / Année	Value / Valeur	
POPULATION			**POPULATION**
Population ('000)			Population ('000)
Both sexes	2014	1 917	Les deux sexes
Male	2014	918	Masculin
Female	2014	999	Féminin
Average annual growth rate	2014	0.4	Taux de croissance annuel
Active Population ('000)	2014	921	Population active ('000)
Population by age group ('000)			Population par groupe d'âge ('000)
0-14 years	2014	689	0-14 ans
15-64 years	2014	1 129	15-64 ans
65+ years	2014	99	65+ ans
Economically. active population. in agriculture (%)	2014	40.6	Participation de la population active agricole (%)
Crude birth rate	2014	30.8	Taux brut de natalité
Crude death rate	2014	2 028.0	Taux brut de mortalité
Total fertility rate	2014	3.2	Indice synthétique de fécondité
Proportion of urban population	2014	26.6	Part de la population urbaine
Life Expectancy at Birth - Total (years)	2014	49.8	Espérance de vie à la naissance - Totale (ans)
Dependency Ratio - Total (%)	2014	68.2	Taux de dépendance - Total (%)
HEALTH			**SANTÉ**
Percentage of children under-five and underweight	2010	13.5	% d'enfants de moins de cinq ans avec insuffisance pondérale
Prevalence of undernourishment	2013	11.5	Prévalence de la malnutrition
Under five mortality rate (both sexes, per 1000)	2013	98.0	Taux de mortalité de moins de 5 ans (les deux sexes, pour 1000)
Infant mortality rate (both sexes) per 1000	2013	73.0	Taux de mortalité infantile (les deux sexes) par 1000
Percentage of children provided the vaccines :			Pourcentage d'enfants vaccinés :
BCG	2013	87.0	BCG
DPT3	2013	96.0	DTC3
Polio	2013	95.0	Polio
Measles	2013	92.0	Rougeole
Percentage of mothers provided at least one antenatal care (%)	2009	91.8	Pourcentage de mères ayant au moins reçu un soin prénatal (%)
Percentage of deliveries attended by skilled health personnel	2009	61.5	% d'accouchements assistés par un personnel de santé qualifié
Number of doctors (per 10 000 population)	2003	0.5	Nombre de médecins (pour 10 000 habitants)
Number of nurses (per 10 000 population)	2003	6.2	Nombre d'infirmières (pour 10 000 habitants)
Hospital beds - Total (per 10 000 population)	2006	13.3	Nombre de lits d'hôpitaux - Total (pour 10 000)
Births registered (per 1 000)	2014	27.3	Naiss.s enregistrées (pour 1 000)
Deaths registered (per 1 000)	2014	14.8	Décès enregistrés (pour 1 000)
Public expenditure on Health (% of budget)	2011	11.3	Dépenses publiques consacrées à la santé (% du budget)
EDUCATION			**EDUCATION**
Enrolment in primary education (both sexes) (000)	2013	369 469	Scolarisation dans le primaire (les deux sexes) (000)
Female	2013	181 419	Féminin
Enrolment in secondary education (both sexes) (000)	2013	127 121	Scolarisation dans le secondaire (les deux sexes) (000)
Female	2013	72 476	Féminin
Enrolment in tertiary education (both sexes) (000)	2011	25.5	Scolarisation dans le tertiaire (les deux sexes) (000)
Female	2011	15.2	Féminin
Literacy rate (both sexes)	2011	87.4	Taux d'alphabétisation (deux sexes)
Male	2011	...	Masculin
Female	2011	...	Féminin
Pupil-teacher ratio	2013	33.0	Ratio élève-enseignant
Public expenditure on education (% of budget)	2011	21.5	Dépenses publiques consacrées à l'enseignement (% du budget)
POVERTY			**PAUVRETÉ**
GNI Per Capita (US$)	2013	1 500.0	RNB par habitant ($EU)
Human Poverty Index (HPI-1) Value (%)	2007	34.3	Valeur de l'Indice de pauvreté (IPH-1) (%)
Population below International Poverty Line ($2/day) (%)	2010	73.4	Population sous le seuil international de pauvreté (2$/J) (%)
Share of Income Held by Richest 10%	2010	41.0	% de revenu des 10% plus riches
Share of Income Held by Poorest 10%	2010	1.0	% de revenu des 10% plus pauvres
Gini index	2010	54.2	Indice de Gini

Charts / Graphiques

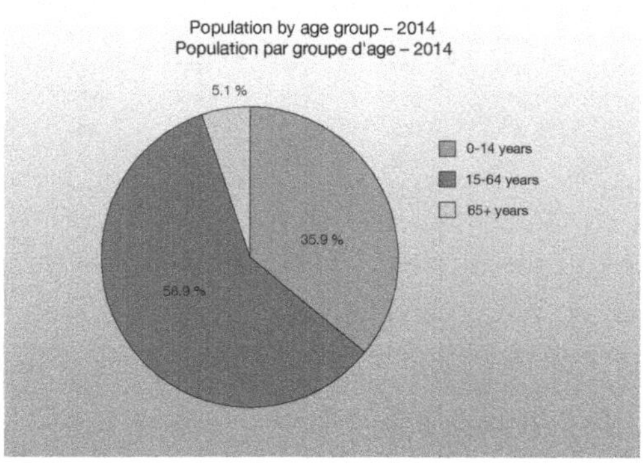

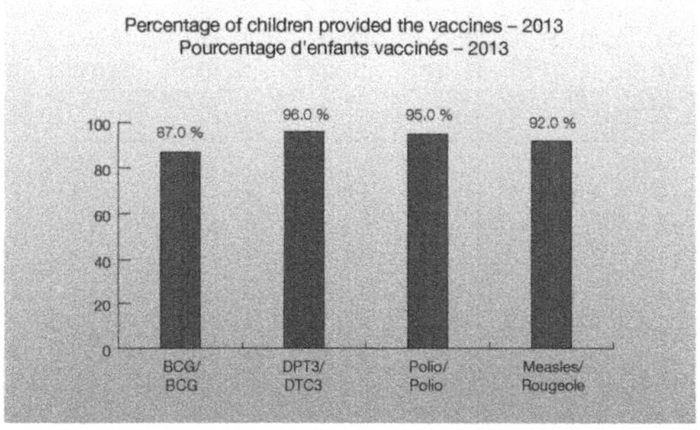

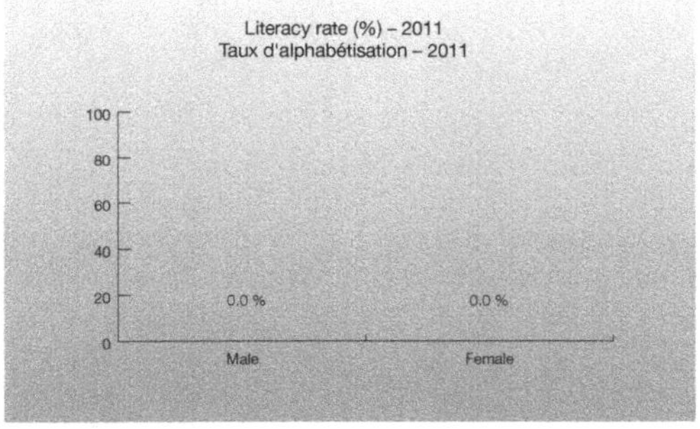

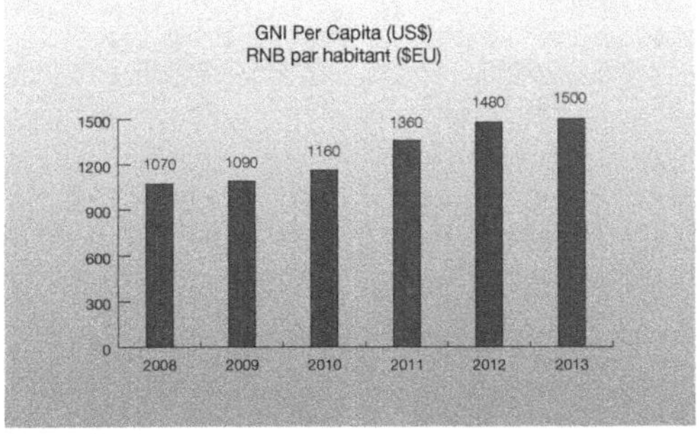

II NATIONAL ACCOUNTS – COMPTES NATIONAUX

	2006	2007	2008	2009	2010	2011	2012	2013	2014	
GROSS DOMESTIC PRODUCT BY KIND OF ECONOMIC ACTIVITY AT CURRENT PRICES *LOTI (MILLIONS)*										**PRODUIT INTÉRIEUR BRUT PAR BRANCHE D'ACTIVITÉ ÉCONOMIQUE AUX PRIX COURANTS** *LOTI (MILLIONS)*
Agriculture, hunting, forestry and fishing	709	790	992	1 025	1 212	1 385	1 300	1 571	1 574	Agriculture, chasse, sylviculture et pêche
Mining and quarrying	420	828	1 145	915	930	1 684	1 291	893	1 914	Industries extractives
Manufacturing	1 888	1 957	2 350	2 117	2 019	1 916	1 981	1 983	2 312	Industries manufacturières
Electricity, gas & water	459	477	510	552	653	759	841	824	995	Electricité, gaz et eau
Construction & public works	410	441	615	721	942	1 026	1 352	1 750	1 782	Bâtiments et travaux publics
Wholesale & retail trade, restaurants, hotels	817	945	1 180	1 175	1 326	1 534	1 830	2 053	2 156	Commerce de gros et de détail, restaurants et hôtels
Finance, insurance, real estate, etc.	1 202	1 630	2 288	2 429	3 089	3 311	4 220	4 810	4 500	Banques, assurances, affaires immobilières
Transport and communications	580	660	757	852	983	1 087	1 194	1 285	1 498	Transport(s) et communications
Public administration and defense	1 015	1 136	1 354	1 745	1 814	1 859	1 999	1 968	2 659	Administrations publiques et défense
Education	745	872	1 005	1 333	1 473	1 697	1 714	1 768	1 961	Education
Health and Social Work	172	187	205	276	292	422	569	673	687	Santé et actions sociales
Other services	106	121	134	146	156	165	178	193	208	Autres services
Less Imputed Service Charges	- 90	- 170	- 270	- 304	- 297	- 304	- 293	- 315	- 568	Moins services d'intermédiation financière
Gross domestic product at factor cost / basic prices	8 433	9 874	12 267	12 981	14 591	16 541	18 177	19 458	21 676	Produit intérieur brut aux couts des facteurs / prix de base
Plus: indirect taxes / taxes on products, less subsidies	1 094	1 313	1 530	1 625	1 813	2 061	2 306	2 427	2 643	Plus taxes indirectes/impôts sur les produits, moins les subventions
EXPENDITURE ON GROSS DOMESTIC PRODUCT AT CURRENT PURCHASER'S VALUES *LOTI (MILLIONS)*										**EMPLOI DU PRODUIT INTÉRIEUR BRUT AUX PRIX COURANTS D'ACQUISITION** *LOTI (MILLIONS)*
Government final consumption	3 426	4 017	4 959	5 740	6 070	6 420	7 361	7 526	9 132	Consommation finale des administrations publiques
Private final consumption	10 445	11 863	13 808	14 884	16 409	18 174	19 390	20 288	22 276	Consommation finale privée
Gross fixed capital formation	2 083	2 471	3 756	3 697	4 413	4 630	5 937	7 538	6 954	Formation brute de capital fixe
Change in inventories	- 85	253	- 36	- 1	243	- 526	- 610	- 446	-	Variation des stocks
Exports of goods and services	5 181	5 864	7 547	6 632	7 107	8 864	8 597	8 657	10 422	Exportations de biens et services
Less imports of goods and services	11 523	13 281	16 237	16 348	17 838	18 960	20 192	21 677	24 466	Moins importations de biens et services
GDP at purchasers' values	9 527	11 187	13 797	14 605	16 404	18 602	20 483	21 885	24 319	PIB aux prix d'acquisition
GROSS DOMESTIC PRODUCT BY KIND OF ECONOMIC ACTIVITY AT CONSTANT PRICES *ANNUAL GROWTH RATES (%)*										**PRODUIT INTÉRIEUR BRUT PAR BRANCHE D'ACTIVITÉ ECONOMIQUE AUX PRIX CONSTANTS** *TAUX DE CROISSANCE ANNUEL (%)*
Agriculture, hunting, forestry and fishing	- 10.3	- 0.9	16.2	- 5.1	10.3	9.2	- 13.8	17.1	- 4.2	Agriculture, chasse, sylviculture et pêche
Mining and quarrying	19.6	50.1	0.6	22.1	4.0	18.6	22.6	- 5.3	5.4	Industries extractives
Manufacturing	8.5	2.1	2.2	- 6.4	14.0	- 11.8	- 3.4	- 10.1	17.7	Industries manufacturières
Electricity, gas & water	5.1	3.5	0.7	4.1	0.8	2.5	2.0	2.2	4.2	Electricité, gaz et eau
Construction & public works	- 1.4	0.8	28.8	5.1	28.0	3.5	24.6	21.5	15.9	Bâtiments et travaux publics
Wholesale & retail trade, restaurants, hotels	4.7	5.4	6.6	0.3	6.5	6.5	11.2	9.5	- 1.2	Commerce de gros et de détail, restaurants et hôtels
Finance, insurance, real estate, etc.	6.0	4.9	3.2	8.4	2.7	6.5	5.3	7.1	- 1.9	Banques, assurances, affaires immobilières
Transport and communications	11.0	12.1	11.3	13.1	9.1	7.6	5.5	5.6	11.6	Transport(s) et communications
Public administration and defense	4.8	3.4	2.9	- 1.2	4.0	1.7	2.2	- 3.1	3.6	Administrations publiques et défense
Education	3.5	- 3.2	- 1.5	10.1	5.8	1.6	- 0.9	1.0	2.7	Education
Health and Social Work	2.8	- 1.0	1.7	8.5	2.6	48.3	28.2	18.4	- 1.7	Santé et actions sociales
Other services	2.7	1.7	1.9	1.1	0.6	3.1	2.3	4.1	3.2	Autres services
Less Imputed Service Charges	39.5	36.2	28.3	18.7	18.7	10.7	2.7	2.9	7.2	Moins services d'intermédiation financière
Gross domestic product at factor cost / basic prices	4.4	4.2	5.1	3.0	7.7	3.5	4.9	4.5	4.7	Produit intérieur brut aux couts des facteurs / prix de base
Plus: indirect taxes / taxes on products, less subsidies	3.8	10.1	11.8	6.5	9.7	8.9	6.0	5.1	3.1	Plus taxes indirectes/impôts sur les produits, moins les subventions
Gross domestic product at market prices	4.3	4.7	5.7	3.4	7.9	4.0	5.0	4.6	4.5	Produit intérieur brut aux prix du marché
EXPENDITURE ON GROSS DOMESTIC PRODUCT AT CONSTANT PURCHASERS' VALUES *ANNUAL GROWTH RATES (%)*										**EMPLOIS DU PRODUIT INTÉRIEUR BRUT AUX PRIX CONSTANTS D'ACQUISITION** *TAUX DE CROISSANCE ANNUEL (%)*
Government final consumption	2.8	5.1	8.9	- 1.2	2.9	0.0	12.3	- 0.9	...	Consommation finale des administrations publiques
Private final consumption	0.2	3.2	3.9	4.5	5.5	10.3	- 1.1	1.8	...	Consommation finale privée
Gross fixed capital formation	7.7	11.6	40.5	- 8.7	14.8	1.2	21.2	16.9	...	Formation brute de capital fixe
Exports of goods and services	12.7	4.3	10.5	- 4.3	7.5	3.1	- 1.2	- 4.7	...	Exportations de biens et services
Less imports of goods and services	2.7	7.0	11.5	- 2.6	7.8	2.2	2.5	1.4	...	Moins importations de biens et services
Notes	NA: 2012-2013:Estimates		2014:Projection			CN: 2012-2013:Estimées		2014:Projection!		Notes

III INFLATION

	2006	2007	2008	2009	2010	2011	2012	2013	2014	
ANNUAL GROWTH RATES (%)										**TAUX DE CROISSANCE ANNUEL (%)**
All items	6.1	8.0	10.7	7.3	3.6	5.0	6.0	5.0	5.4	Ensemble
of which:										dont:
Food and Non-alcoholic beverages	9.0	14.0	15.7	9.4	4.0	7.0	9.8	5.4	5.3	Alimentation et boissons non alcoolisés
Alcoholic beverages & tobacco	6.2	5.5	5.4	6.6	9.1	6.5	6.9	5.6	6.5	Boissons alcoolisées et tabacs
Clothing and Footwear	2.5	2.9	6.4	4.8	3.3	1.4	1.0	1.6	3.7	Habillement et chaussures
Housing, Water, Electricity, Gas and Other Fuels	8.5	8.1	14.6	2.2	3.2	11.5	8.3	5.7	7.8	Logement, eau, electricité, gas et autres combustibles
Furnishing, household equipment	4.1	1.6	4.0	6.0	3.1	3.3	2.9	3.6	2.8	Meubles, articles de ménage et entretien courant
Health	1.3	-1.3	1.5	1.9	2.4	1.4	0.4	0.6	1.0	Santé
Transport	3.9	3.5	10.4	5.8	4.0	3.0	6.5	4.1	10.5	Transport
Communication	1.7	1.4	-	0.4	1.3	0.9	-0.3	-	-	Communication
Recreation & culture	1.3	-0.8	2.0	5.8	2.1	1.5	2.0	0.9	1.2	Loisirs et culture
Education	1.0	2.4	2.6	3.1	6.1	0.8	0.9	13.5	7.1	Enseignement
Restaurants & hotels	8.4	18.7	13.5	8.4	5.0	4.2	-0.1	0.8	2.2	Restaurants et hôtels
Miscellaneous goods & services	2.6	3.0	5.8	6.6	3.7	2.4	2.4	2.7	4.4	Biens et services divers

IV AGRICULTURAL PRODUCTION - PRODUCTION AGRICOLE	2006	2007	2008	2009	2010	2011	2012	2013	2014	
TONNES *(THOUSAND)*										TONNES *(MILLIERS)*
Maize	60	60	57	128	84	70	42	86	90	Maïs
Sorghum	8	10	11	24	14	19	6	21	13	Sorgho
Wheat	1	2	5	20	16	13	5	13	10	Blé
Beans	1	4	3	9	2	4	11	3	2	Haricots
Peas	0	0	1	1	3	1	1	1	0	Pois

V MINING PRODUCTION - PRODUCTION MINIERE	2006	2007	2008	2009	2010	2011	2012	2013	2014	
Diamonds and other precious stones, unworked, carat (thousands)	0	0	0	0	0	0	0	0	...	Diamants et autres pierres précieuses, bruts, carat (milliers)
	...	...	...	...	...	...	...	...	...	
	...	...	...	...	...	...	...	...	...	

VI ENERGY - ENERGIE	2006	2007	2008	2009	2010	2011	2012	2013	2014	
Total electricity generation (GWh)	525	554	584	648	694	566	280	385	...	Production d'électricité totale (GWh)
of which:										dont:
Production of electricity from fossil fuels (GWh)	-	-	-	-	-	-	-	-	...	Production d'électricité à partir de combustibles fossiles (GWh)
Production of hydro electricity (GWh)	525	554	584	648	694	566	280	385	...	Production d'électricité d'origine hydraulique (GWh)
Production of electricity from solar, wind, tide, wave and other sources (GWh)	...	...	...	...	...	...	...	...	...	Production d'électricité d'origine solaire, éolienne, marée motrice et autres (GWh)

VII TOURISM AND INFRASTRUCTURE - TOURISME ET INFRASTRUCTURE	2006	2007	2008	2009	2010	2011	2012	2013	2014	
VII-1 TOURISM										**VII-1 TOURISME**
International tourist arrivals (thousands)	347	292	285	320	414	397	422	432	457	Arrivées de touristes internationaux (milliers)
Rooms in hotels and similar establishments (thousands)	...	...	2.3	2.4	2.5	2.8	3.0	2.6	...	Chambres d'hotels et établissements assimilés (milliers)
Overnight stays (thousands)	778	788	769	903	1 181	1 135	1 205	1 231	1 303	Nuitées (milliers)
Tourism receipts (US$ thousand)	28 700	30 600	29 600	29 600	24 600	28 600	45 600	39 054	34 720	Recettes touristiques (milliers de $ EU)
Total contribution to GDP (%)	10.3	10.3	10.5	16.4	11.6	11.8	11.6	11.9	12.1	Contribution totale au PIB (%)
Total contribution to Employment (%)	9.7	9.8	10.2	16.5	12.0	10.6	9.9	10.2	10.5	Contribution totale à l'emploi (%)
VII-2 INFRASTRUCTURE										**VII-2 INFRASTRUCTURE**
Paved roads (% of total)	25	...	...	20	...	...	...	...	...	Routes asphaltées (% du total)
Total Network (Railways-km)	5 020	...	...	7 091	...	...	...	...	...	Réseau total voies ferrées-Km
Main Telephone Lines (per 100 inhabitants)	3	2	2	2	2	2	2	3	...	Lignes téléphoniques fixes (pour 100 habitants)
Mobile Cellular Subscribers (per 100 inhabitants)	18	25	30	33	49	61	75	86	...	Abonnés aux téléphones mobiles (pour 100 habitants)

VIII EXTERNAL TRADE - COMMERCE EXTERIEUR	2006	2007	2008	2009	2010	2011	2012	2013	2014	
LOTI (MILLIONS) EXPORTS, FOB										**LOTI (MILLIONS) EXPORTATIONS, FÀB**
Exports - Total	701 653	614 253	726 692	770 757	679 071	852 025	770 757	...	...	Exportations - Total
Exports to AFRICA	114 668	265 552	296 396	313 428	1 464	364 006	332 966	...	...	Exportations vers l'AFRIQUE
Main Products										**Principaux produits**
Clothing	476 885	224 060	239 818	83 469	41 638	135 645	102 730	...	...	Vêtements
Diamonds	...	...	...	...	...	...	...	...	...	Diamants
Television Sets	...	66 510	52 862	34 984	77 984	32 287	...	...	...	Ensembles Televisions
Eletrical Components	...	...	...	36 504	39 688	...	...	...	...	Composants életriques
Water	...	...	...	29 583	60 043	67 595	64 543	...	...	Eau
Main Destinations										**Principales destinations**
United States	586 473	323 166	385 601	199 124	...	313 636	...	...	...	États-Unis
Belgium	...	...	38 112	10 188	...	23 278	...	...	...	Belgique
South Africa	114 190	265 411	289 768	306 124	...	346 365	321 306	...	...	Afrique du Sud
Canada	428 381	...	3 528	94 616	107 665	43 268	...	...	...	Canada
Madagascar	...	...	3 058	3 591	...	...	...	...	...	Madagascar
IMPORTS, CIF										**IMPORTATIONS, CAF**
Imports - Total	1 092 831	1 245 165	1 070 498	1 347 501	1 273 894	1 464 297	1 598 362	...	...	Importations - Total (millions)
Imports from Africa	1 079 342	1 212 627	1 022 714	1 287 740	1 015 911	1 426 641	1 428 385	...	...	Importations en provenance de l'Afrique
Main Products										**Principaux produits**
Textile yarn and related products	34 674	34 751	17 801	22 034	22 807	15 784	20 169	...	...	Fils, tissus et articles façonnés
Telecommunication and sound recording apparatus	30 904	64 879	86 385	71 259	118 040	77 095	89 451	...	...	Équipements pour les télécommunications et le son
Cereals and cereal preparations	19 938	29 497	27 066	28 594	27 506	32 422	38 275	...	...	Céréales et préparations à base de céréales
Petroleum, petroleum products and related materials	98 618	134 794	115 438	147 175	133 214	202 973	196 172	...	...	Pétrole et produits dérivés
Road vehicles	51 790	86 209	79 282	137 215	88 252	91 190	115 668	...	...	Véhicules routiers
Main Origin										**Principales provenances**
South Africa	1 065 348	1 212 473	1 019 321	1 283 356	1 004 335	1 411 398	1 421 427	...	...	Afrique du Sud
China, Hong Kong SAR	74	490	...	...	13 761	2 374	11 616	...	...	Chine (RAS de Hong Kong)
China	16	547	1 237	1 994	33 679	5 967	44 585	...	...	Chine
Taiwan	131	...	...	...	67 010	4 047	75 197	...	...	Taiwan
Republic of Korea	127	305	133	350	44 650	42	169	...	...	République de Corée

LÉSOTHO

IX FINANCIAL AND MONETARY STATISTICS - FINANCES ET STATISTIQUES MONETAIRES	2006	2007	2008	2009	2010	2011	2012	2013	2014	
IX-1 MONETARY STATISTICS *LOTI (MILLIONS)*										**IX-1 STATISTIQUES MONÉTAIRES** *LOTI (MILLIONS)*
Money supply (M1)	3 510	4 080	4 880	5 750	6 580	6 680	7 150	8 660	9 920	Masse monétaire (M1)
Quasi-money	819	1 091	1 006	1 568	1 589	3 859	3 672	4 673	4 907	Quasi-monnaie
of which Demand Deposit	...	...	...	...	...	...	...	...	...	dont Monnaie scripturale
Net foreign assets	6 166	8 480	11 237	10 840	10 104	9 906	10 141	12 835	13 964	Avoirs extérieurs nets
Domestic credit	- 577	- 2 071	- 2 466	- 2 136	- 1 001	127	640	390	171	Crédit intérieur
of which claims on private sector	897	1 184	1 463	1 860	2 194	2 687	3 778	4 556	5 121	dont créances sur le secteur privé
of which claims on government sector, net	- 1 499	- 3 324	- 3 973	- 3 996	- 3 198	- 2 572	- 3 149	- 4 178	- 4 963	dont créances nettes sur le gouvernement
International reserves (millions US$)	658	1 003	972	1 180	1 071	919	1 028	1 055	1 118	Réserves internationales (millions $EU)
Average Exchange Rate (National Currency per US$)	6.77	7.05	8.26	8.41	7.32	7.26	8.21	9.65	10.92	Taux de change (moyen) (monnaie nationale par $ EU)
IX-2 PUBLIC FINANCE *LOTI (MILLIONS)*										**IX-2 FINANCES PUBLIQUES** *LOTI (MILLIONS)*
Total Revenues and Grants	4 560	6 432	7 512	8 265	9 377	9 203	9 592	12 191	14 793	Recettes totales et dons
Tax Revenue	4 003	5 784	6 441	7 229	7 913	6 771	7 012	9 603	12 564	Recettes fiscales
Non Tax Revenue	473	555	823	847	873	1 232	1 143	885	1 031	Recettes non fiscales
Grants	84	92	248	189	590	1 200	1 437	1 703	1 198	Dons
Total Expenditures and Net Lending	4 293	5 138	6 471	8 004	9 281	9 172	10 094	11 724	11 978	Dépenses totales et prêts nets
Current expenditure	3 591	4 363	4 974	5 975	7 618	7 141	8 177	8 241	9 633	Dépenses courantes
Of which Wages and Salaries	1 264	1 359	1 604	1 864	3 016	2 881	3 136	3 226	3 855	Dont rémunérations et salaires
Capital expenditure	702	775	1 510	2 029	1 664	2 031	1 917	3 483	2 345	Dépenses d'équipement
Net Lending	-	-	- 13	- 1	-	-	-	-	-	Prêts nets
Fiscal Balance	267	1 294	1 041	262	96	31	- 501	467	2 815	Solde global y compris les dons
IX-3 BALANCE OF PAYMENTS *LOTI (MILLIONS)*										**IX-3 BALANCE DES PAIEMENTS** *LOTI (MILLIONS)*
Trade balance	- 628	- 719	- 643	- 845	- 1 093	- 981	- 1 273	- 999	- 1 030	Balance commerciale
Services Balance	- 336	- 354	- 350	- 385	- 400	- 423	- 392	- 310	- 283	Balance des services
Net Income	681	730	642	571	659	530	434	365	321	Revenus nets
Compensation of employees	604	671	563	539	603	640	548	443	391	Rémunération des salariés
Investment Income	- 3	- 23	6	- 30	- 15	- 130	- 134	- 103	- 97	Revenus des investissements
Current transfers, net total	575	738	685	717	662	605	860	780	798	Transferts courants
Net official transfers	436	603	564	585	500	426	696	638	660	Transferts officiels nets
Workers' remittances	6	7	6	5	6	6	5	4	4	Envois de fonds des travailleurs
Other private transfers	133	128	115	127	155	172	159	138	133	Autres transferts privés
Current account balance	293	395	334	58	- 173	- 269	- 372	- 164	- 194	Solde du compte courant
Capital & financial account	- 283	- 100	- 137	87	- 48	393	527	300	325	Comptes de capital et financier
Capital account	7	26	18	70	135	190	196	113	45	Compte de capital
Financial account	...	- 126	- 155	17	- 184	203	331	187	281	Compte financier
Errors & omissions	128	6	- 43	- 84	91	- 142	- 58	42	- 47	Erreurs et omissions
Overall balance	191	282	266	- 76	- 170	81	149	241	127	Balance générale

X DEBT AND FINANCIAL FLOWS - DETTE ET FLUX FINANCIERS										
	2006	2007	2008	2009	2010	2011	2012	2013	2014	
X-1 DEBT *US$ (MILLIONS)*										**X-1 DETTE EXTÉRIEURE** *$ E.U (MILLIONS)*
Total external debt	773	673	658	684	730	5 766	7 253	8 796	9 339	Dette extérieure totale
Private	-	-	-	-	-	5 015	6 495	7 957	8 424	Privée
Public	773	673	658	684	730	752	758	839	915	Publique
Total external debt service	34	23	32	43	37	38	37	41	50	Service de la dette extérieure
Present value of External debt	683	758	565	744	1 200.7	1 033.7	1 065.2	883.9	824.9	Valeur actuelle de la dette extérieure
Total government domestic debt (in local currency)	680	654	564	507	745.3	1 000.0	1 144.6	1 000.0	639.1	Dette publique intérieure
X-2 FINANCIAL FLOWS *US$ (MILLIONS)*										**X-2 FLUX FINANCIERS** *$ E.U (MILLIONS)*
Net Foreign Direct Investment Inflows	58	104	194	178	51	53	50	44	...	Investissement étranger direct (flux nets entrants)
Main origin of FDI Inflows										**Principales origines de l'IDE entrant:**
Italy	...	...	...	...	...	...	...	...	...	Italie
Korea	...	...	...	...	...	...	...	...	...	Corée
Spain	...	...	...	...	...	...	...	...	...	Espagne
Poland	...	...	...	...	...	...	...	...	...	Pologne
African countries	...	...	...	...	...	...	...	...	...	Pays africains
Other countries	...	...	...	...	...	...	...	...	...	Autres pays
Net total Official Development Assistance	71	129	144	122	256	265	283	320	...	Aide publique au développement (nette totale)
Main origin of Net ODA										**Principales origines de l'APD nette**
United States	3	19	14	25	57.5	106.2	131.7	170.4	...	Etats-Unis
Ireland	14	19	21	17	15.7	15.9	11.2	2.6	...	Irlande
IDA	6	12	20	11	34.1	16.6	- 3.6	...	...	IDA
Global Fund	5	9	19	16	21.8	19.8	23.5	...	...	Fonds mondial
Japan	5	5	13	3	8.8	20.2	3.2	2.6	...	Japon

LIBERIA — LIBÉRIA

	Year / Année	Value / Valeur	
AREA (km²)		111 369	SUPERFICIE (km²)
CAPITAL CITY		Monrovia	CAPITALE
CURRENCY		Liberian Dollar / Dollar Liberien	MONNAIE
I SOCIAL AND DEMOGRAPHIC INDICATORS – INDICATEURS DEMOGRAPHIQUES ET SOCIAUX			
POPULATION	Year / Année	Value / Valeur	**POPULATION**
Population ('000)			Population ('000)
Both sexes	2014	4 397	Les deux sexes
Male	2014	2 215	Masculin
Female	2014	2 182	Féminin
Average annual growth rate	2014	2.6	Taux de croissance annuel
Active Population ('000)	2014	1 505	Population active ('000)
Population by age group ('000)			Population par groupe d'âge ('000)
0-14 years	2014	1 874	0-14 ans
15-64 years	2014	2 390	15-64 ans
65+ years	2014	133	65+ ans
Economically. active population. in agriculture (%)	2014	65.2	Participation de la population active agricole (%)
Crude birth rate	2014	35.0	Taux brut de natalité
Crude death rate	2014	8.7	Taux brut de mortalité
Total fertility rate	2014	4.7	Indice synthétique de fécondité
Proportion of urban population	2014	49.3	Part de la population urbaine
Life Expectancy at Birth - Total (years)	2014	60.9	Espérance de vie à la naissance - Totale (ans)
Dependency Ratio - Total (%)	2014	85.0	Taux de dépendance - Total (%)
HEALTH			**SANTÉ**
Percentage of children under-five and underweight	2007	20.4	% d'enfants de moins de cinq ans avec insuffisance pondérale
Prevalence of undernourishment	2013	29.6	Prévalence de la malnutrition
Under five mortality rate (both sexes, per 1000)	2013	71.1	Taux de mortalité de moins de 5 ans (les deux sexes, pour 1000)
Infant mortality rate (both sexes) per 1000	2013	53.6	Taux de mortalité infantile (les deux sexes) par 1000
Percentage of children provided the vaccines :			Pourcentage d'enfants vaccinés :
BCG	2013	87.0	BCG
DPT3	2013	89.0	DTC3
Polio	2013	84.0	Polio
Measles	2013	74.0	Rougeole
Percentage of mothers provided at least one antenatal care (%)	2013	75.8	Pourcentage de mères ayant au moins reçu un soin prénatal (%)
Percentage of deliveries attended by skilled health personnel	2007	46.3	% d'accouchements assistés par un personnel de santé qualifié
Number of doctors (per 10 000 population)	2008	0.1	Nombre de médecins (pour 10 000 habitants)
Number of nurses (per 10 000 population)	2008	2.7	Nombre d'infirmières (pour 10 000 habitants)
Hospital beds - Total (per 10 000 population)	2010	8.0	Nombre de lits d'hôpitaux - Total (pour 10 000)
Births registered (per 1 000)	2014	35.0	Naiss.s enregistrées (pour 1 000)
Deaths registered (per 1 000)	2014	8.7	Décès enregistrés (pour 1 000)
Public expenditure on Health (% of budget)	2013	8.4	Dépenses publiques consacrées à la santé (% du budget)
EDUCATION			**EDUCATION**
Enrolment in primary education (both sexes) (000)	2014	684	Scolarisation dans le primaire (les deux sexes) (000)
Female	2014	321	Féminin
Enrolment in secondary education (both sexes) (000)	2014	223	Scolarisation dans le secondaire (les deux sexes) (000)
Female	2014	96	Féminin
Enrolment in tertiary education (both sexes) (000)	...	...	Scolarisation dans le tertiaire (les deux sexes) (000)
Female	2012	16.7	Féminin
Literacy rate (both sexes)	2007	42.9	Taux d'alphabétisation (deux sexes)
Male	2007	60.8	Masculin
Female	2007	27.0	Féminin
Pupil-teacher ratio	...	...	Ratio élève-enseignant
Public expenditure on education (% of budget)	...	...	Dépenses publiques consacrées à l'enseignement (% du budget)
POVERTY			**PAUVRETÉ**
GNI Per Capita (US$)	2013	410.0	RNB par habitant ($EU)
Human Poverty Index (HPI-1) Value (%)	2007	35.2	Valeur de l'Indice de pauvreté (IPH-1) (%)
Population below International Poverty Line ($2/day) (%)	2007	94.9	Population sous le seuil international de pauvreté (2$/J) (%)
Share of Income Held by Richest 10%	2007	30.1	% de revenu des 10% plus riches
Share of Income Held by Poorest 10%	2007	2.4	% de revenu des 10% plus pauvres
Gini index	2007	38.2	Indice de Gini

Charts / Graphiques

Population by age group – 2014
Population par groupe d'age – 2014

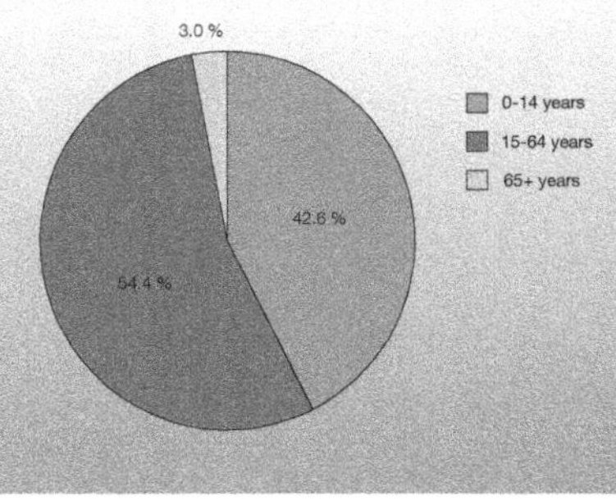

Percentage of children provided the vaccines – 2013
Pourcentage d'enfants vaccinés – 2013

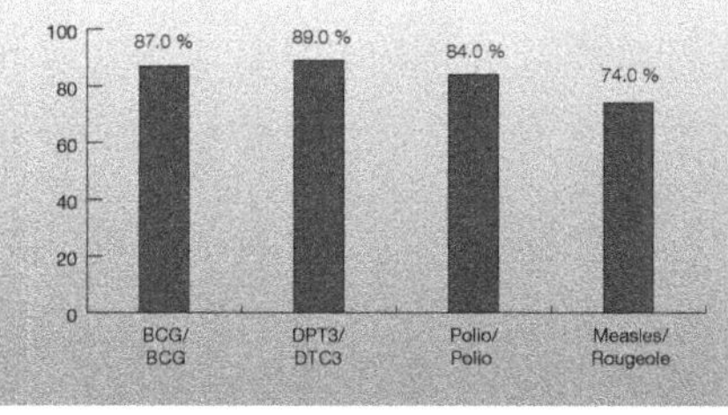

Literacy rate (%) – 2007
Taux d'alphabétisation – 2007

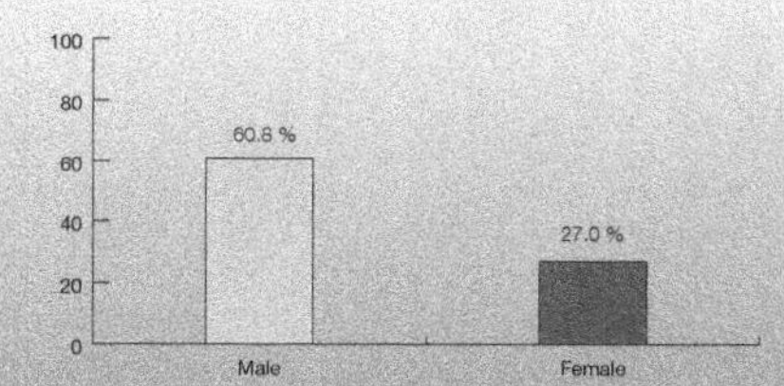

GNI Per Capita (US$)
RNB par habitant ($EU)

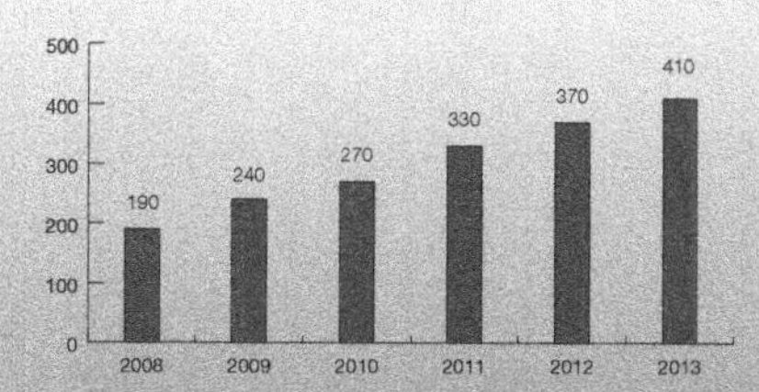

II NATIONAL ACCOUNTS — COMPTES NATIONAUX

	2006	2007	2008	2009	2010	2011	2012	2013	2014	
GROSS DOMESTIC PRODUCT BY KIND OF ECONOMIC ACTIVITY AT CURRENT PRICES *LIBERIAN DOLLAR (MILLIONS)*										**PRODUIT INTÉRIEUR BRUT PAR BRANCHE D'ACTIVITÉ ÉCONOMIQUE AUX PRIX COURANTS** *DOLLAR LIBERIEN (MILLIONS)*
Agriculture, hunting, forestry and fishing	488	648	766	794	914	1 135	1 210	1 255	1 168	Agriculture, chasse sylviculture et pêche
Mining and quarrying	4	8	20	22	23	25	32	42	54	Industries extractives
Manufacturing	44	49	51	54	57	61	79	103	133	Industries manufacturières
Electricity, gas & water	5	5	6	6	6	7	9	11	15	Electricité, gaz et eau
Construction & public works	20	22	23	25	26	28	36	47	61	Bâtiments et travaux publics
Wholesale & retail trade, restaurants, hotels	36	43	45	48	50	53	68	89	116	Commerce de gros et de détail, restaurants et hôtels
Finance, insurance, real estate, etc.	36	40	42	44	47	50	65	84	110	Banques, assurances, affaires immobilières
Transport and communications	41	44	48	53	54	58	75	98	127	Transport(s) et communications
Public administration and defense	26	29	31	33	35	37	49	63	82	Administrations publiques et défense
Education	...	...	...	...	...	...	...	...	...	Education
Health and Social Work	...	...	...	...	...	...	...	...	...	Santé et actions sociales
Other services	...	...	...	...	...	...	...	...	...	Autres services
Less Imputed Service Charges	- 7	- 8	- 8	- 8	- 9	- 9	- 12	- 16	- 21	Moins services d'intermédiation financière
Gross domestic product at factor cost / basic prices	692	880	1 025	1 070	1 203	1 443	1 611	1 776	1 845	Produit intérieur brut aux couts des facteurs / prix de base
Plus: indirect taxes / taxes on products, less subsidies	53	69	76	85	89	95	123	160	208	Plus taxes indirectes/impôts sur les produits, moins les subventions
EXPENDITURE ON GROSS DOMESTIC PRODUCT AT CURRENT PURCHASER'S VALUES *LIBERIAN DOLLAR (MILLIONS)*										**EMPLOI DU PRODUIT INTÉRIEUR BRUT AUX PRIX COURANTS D'ACQUISITION** *DOLLAR LIBERIEN (MILLIONS)*
Government final consumption	96	149	189	222	280	374	461	456	481	Consommation finale des administrations publiques
Private final consumption	621	823	1 175	1 147	1 229	1 218	1 123	961	1 498	Consommation finale privée
Gross fixed capital formation	235	269	192	208	242	569	738	1 107	466	Formation brute de capital fixe
Change in inventories	...	...	...	...	...	...	...	...	...	Variation des stocks
Exports of goods and services	158	208	254	153	215	374	479	558	613	Exportations de biens et services
Less imports of goods and services	366	499	709	574	674	996	1 067	1 146	1 006	Moins importations de biens et services
GDP at purchasers' values	745	949	1 101	1 155	1 292	1 538	1 734	1 936	2 053	PIB aux prix d'acquisition
GROSS DOMESTIC PRODUCT BY KIND OF ECONOMIC ACTIVITY AT CONSTANT PRICES *ANNUAL GROWTH RATES (%)*										**PRODUIT INTÉRIEUR BRUT PAR BRANCHE D'ACTIVITÉ ECONOMIQUE AUX PRIX CONSTANTS** *TAUX DE CROISSANCE ANNUEL (%)*
Agriculture, hunting, forestry and fishing	- 6.8	17.3	4.3	1.6	4.5	6.0	4.8	12.7	- 2.0	Agriculture, chasse sylviculture et pêche
Mining and quarrying	323.2	8.7	213.3	6.7	6.7	7.3	11.1	4.4	5.1	Industries extractives
Manufacturing	29.7	8.7	5.1	6.7	6.7	7.3	11.1	4.4	5.1	Industries manufacturières
Electricity, gas & water	3.9	8.7	3.7	6.7	6.7	7.3	11.1	4.4	5.1	Electricité, gaz et eau
Construction & public works	0.4	8.7	6.5	6.7	6.7	7.3	11.1	4.4	5.1	Bâtiments et travaux publics
Wholesale & retail trade, restaurants, hotels	29.8	8.7	3.7	6.7	6.7	7.3	11.1	4.4	5.1	Commerce de gros et de détail,restaurants et hôtels
Finance, insurance, real estate, etc.	42.2	- 21.0	4.0	6.7	6.7	7.3	11.1	4.4	5.1	Banques, assurances, affaires immobilières
Transport and communications	- 2.9	8.7	11.0	6.7	6.7	7.3	11.1	4.4	5.1	Transport(s) et communications
Public administration and defense	3.6	8.7	8.3	6.7	6.7	7.3	11.1	4.4	5.1	Administrations publiques et défense
Education	...	...	...	...	...	...	...	...	...	Education
Health and Social Work	...	...	...	...	...	...	...	...	...	Santé et actions sociales
Other services	...	...	...	...	...	...	...	...	...	Autres services
Less Imputed Service Charges	...	...	...	...	...	...	...	...	...	Moins services d'intermédiation financière
Gross domestic product at factor cost / basic prices	2.3	11.2	5.7	3.7	5.4	6.6	7.5	9.0	1.0	Produit intérieur brut aux couts des facteurs / prix de base
Plus: indirect taxes / taxes on products, less subsidies	187.2	30.2	10.4	18.1	12.2	16.2	13.1	6.8	6.4	Plus taxes indirectes/impôts sur les produits, moins les subventions
Gross domestic product at market prices	9.1	13.0	6.2	5.4	6.3	7.9	8.3	8.7	1.8	Produit intérieur brut aux prix du marché
EXPENDITURE ON GROSS DOMESTIC PRODUCT AT CONSTANT PURCHASERS' VALUES *ANNUAL GROWTH RATES (%)*										**EMPLOIS DU PRODUIT INTÉRIEUR BRUT AUX PRIX CONSTANTS D'ACQUISITION** *TAUX DE CROISSANCE ANNUEL (%)*
Government final consumption	...	...	...	...	...	...	...	...	...	Consommation finale des administrations publiques
Private final consumption	...	...	...	...	...	...	...	...	...	Consommation finale privée
Gross fixed capital formation	...	...	...	...	...	...	...	...	...	Formation brute de capital fixe
Exports of goods and services	...	...	...	...	...	...	...	...	...	Exportations de biens et services
Less imports of goods and services	...	...	...	...	...	...	...	...	...	Moins importations de biens et services
Notes	NA Data : The data is in US$					Les données des CN sont exprimées en $ EU				Notes

III INFLATION

	2006	2007	2008	2009	2010	2011	2012	2013	2014	
ANNUAL GROWTH RATES (%)										**TAUX DE CROISSANCE ANNUEL (%)**
All items	6.1	11.4	17.5	7.4	7.3	8.5	6.8	7.6	9.7	Ensemble
of which:										dont:
Food and Non-alcoholic beverages	...	18.7	25.0	2.6	7.2	11.4	10.2	10.3	8.1	Alimentation et boissons non alcoolisés
Alcoholic beverages & tobacco	...	4.3	3.8	12.8	10.5	10.2	3.7	6.1	11.6	Boissons alcoolisées et tabacs
Clothing and Footwear	...	7.8	4.6	16.1	8.6	5.9	3.3	5.0	20.6	Habillement et chaussures
Housing, Water, Electricity, Gas and Other Fuels	...	8.4	7.6	-2.1	3.3	5.7	4.0	1.1	-0.4	Logement, eau, électricité, gas et autres combustibles
Furnishing, household equip	...	5.7	16.0	25.6	6.9	1.8	4.2	5.7	10.2	Meubles, articles de ménage et entretien courant
Health	...	-0.6	0.3	3.1	0.8	-0.1	-0.6	0.1	16.1	Santé
Transport	...	8.3	43.4	3.9	4.7	18.2	5.4	5.6	20.7	Transport
Communication	...	-5.6	-0.8	-0.2	3.3	2.9	0.2	0.6	1.2	Communication
Recreation & culture	...	5.9	8.8	4.4	2.4	4.4	2.8	8.6	9.1	Loisirs et culture
Education	...	-	-	-	-	-	-	-	-	Enseignement
Restaurants & hotels	...	3.0	3.5	67.4	23.5	2.8	2.0	7.0	11.2	Restaurants et hôtels
Miscellaneous goods & services	...	1.9	8.3	8.6	4.5	-0.3	4.1	6.8	15.8	Biens et services divers

IV AGRICULTURAL PRODUCTION - PRODUCTION AGRICOLE

	2006	2007	2008	2009	2010	2011	2012	2013	2014	
TONNES *(THOUSAND)*										**TONNES** *(MILLIERS)*
Cassava	500	530	510	495	493	515	500	520	...	Manioc
Rice	164	232	295	293	296	298	291	238	...	Riz
Banana	116	120	120	123	125	125	127	132	...	Banane
Plantain	50	43	44	47	46	47	47	48	...	Banane-Plantain
Taro	27	25	30	27	26	27	28	28	...	Taros

V MINING PRODUCTION - PRODUCTION MINIERE

	2006	2007	2008	2009	2010	2011	2012	2013	2014	
Gold ores and concentrates (Kilograms)	...	...	624	524	666	448	641	...	...	Minerais d'or et concentrés (Kilogrammes)
Diamonds and other precious stones, unworked, carat (thousands)	...	...	47	28	27	42	34	...	...	Diamants et autres pierres précieuses, bruts, carat (milliers)
Cement,hydraulic (Metric tons)	...	...	94 037	70 584	71 733	80 594	108 840	...	...	Ciment (tonne)

VI ENERGY - ENERGIE

	2006	2007	2008	2009	2010	2011	2012	2013	2014	
Total electricity generation (GWh)	33	33	12	20	30	39	40	40	...	Production d'électricité totale (GWh)
of which:										dont:
Production of electricity from fossil fuels (GWh)	33	33	12	20	30	39	40	40	...	Production d'électricité à partir de combustibles fossiles (GWh)
Production of hydro electricity (GWh)	...	...	...	...	...	...	...	...	...	Production d'électricité d'origine hydraulique (GWh)
Production of electricity from solar, wind, tide, wave and other sources (GWh)	...	...	...	...	...	...	...	...	...	Production d'électricité d'origine solaire, éolienne, marée motrice et autres (GWh)

VII TOURISM AND INFRASTRUCTURE - TOURISME ET INFRASTRUCTURE

	2006	2007	2008	2009	2010	2011	2012	2013	2014	
VII-1 TOURISM										**VII-1 TOURISME**
International tourist arrivals (thousands)	...	...	...	...	...	...	...	...	...	Arrivées de touristes internationaux (milliers)
Rooms in hotels and similar establishments (thousands)	0.178	...	...	...	...	...	...	...	...	Chambres d'hotels et établissements assimilés (milliers)
Overnight stays (thousands)	...	...	...	...	...	...	...	...	...	Nuitées (milliers)
Tourism receipts (US$ thousand)	...	...	...	...	...	...	...	...	...	Recettes touristiques (milliers de $ EU)
Total contribution to GDP (%)	...	...	...	...	...	...	...	...	...	Contribution totale au PIB (%)
Total contribution to Employment (%)	...	...	...	...	...	...	...	...	...	Contribution totale à l'emploi (%)
VII-2 INFRASTRUCTURE										**VII-2 INFRASTRUCTURE**
Paved roads (% of total)	...	...	...	...	...	...	...	...	...	Routes asphaltées (% du total)
Total Network (Railways-km)	...	...	...	...	...	...	...	...	...	Réseau total voies ferrées-Km
Main Telephone Lines (per 100 inhabitants)	...	0	0	0	0	0	0	0	...	Lignes téléphoniques fixes (pour 100 habitants)
Mobile Cellular Subscribers (per 100 inhabitants)	8	16	23	28	40	50	57	59	...	Abonnés aux téléphones mobiles (pour 100 habitants)

VIII EXTERNAL TRADE - COMMERCE EXTERIEUR

	2006	2007	2008	2009	2010	2011	2012	2013	2014	
US$ (MILLIONS) **EXPORTS, FOB**										**$ E.U (MILLIONS)** **EXPORTATIONS, FÀB**
Exports - Total	158	208	254	160	200	774	829	544	...	Exportations - Total
Exports to AFRICA	...	...	...	...	...	27	12	50	...	Exportations vers l'AFRIQUE
Main Products										**Principaux produits**
Rubber	153	191	207	93	157	22	22	121	...	Caoutchouc
Coffee	...	...	...	...	...	22	22	...	...	Café
Iron Ore	1	1	2	1	3	22	117	312	...	Minerai de fer
Gold	0	6	13	12	20	17	26	22	...	Or
Cocoa Beans	0	1	3	4	5	14	7	10	...	Cacao en fèves
Main Destinations										**Principales destinations**
Poland	19	37	30	37	53	283	303	...	...	Pologne
United States	14	21	33	9	44	51	55	...	...	États-Unis
Germany	57	23	19	41	9	124	132	...	...	Allemagne
India	9	24	59	3	4	44	47	...	...	Inde
Malaysia	1	54	2	4	3	39	42	...	...	Malaisie
IMPORTS, CIF										**IMPORTATIONS, CAF**
Imports - Total	467	530	849	563	719	1 044	1 123	1 211	...	Importations - Total (millions)
Imports from Africa	...	...	...	...	...	121	170	195	...	Importations en provenance de l'Afrique
Main Products										**Principaux produits**
Other transport equipment	354	378	532	421	524	902	...	...	...	Autres matériels de transport
Petroleum, petroleum products and related materials	13	12	36	20	22	51	...	...	...	Pétrole et produits dérivés
Manufactures of metal, n.e.s.	3	3	14	12	7	18	...	...	...	Articles manufacturés en métal, n.d.a.
Cereals and cereal preparations	5	4	7	3	4	7	...	...	...	Céréales et préparations à base de céréales
Road vehicles	2	3	7	3	3	5	...	...	...	Véhicules routiers
Main Origin										**Principales provenances**
Korea, Republic of	218	159	208	230	234	436	...	...	...	Corée, République de
China	36	51	84	89	191	293	...	...	...	Chine
Japan	59	76	91	70	85	26	26	...	...	Japon
Singapore	66	112	195	77	125	...	...	...	...	Singapour
Germany	7	17	20	5	6	26	7	...	...	Allemagne

IX FINANCIAL AND MONETARY STATISTICS - FINANCES ET STATISTIQUES MONETAIRES	2006	2007	2008	2009	2010	2011	2012	2013	2014	
IX-1 MONETARY STATISTICS *LIBERIAN DOLLAR (MILLIONS)*										**IX-1 STATISTIQUES MONÉTAIRES** *DOLLAR LIBERIEN (MILLIONS)*
Money supply (M1)	150	200	270	360	460	650	630	680	590	Masse monétaire (M1)
Quasi-money	1 947	3 118	4 183	5 884	7 573	11 356	13 273	16 252	17 125	Quasi-monnaie
of which Demand Deposit	...	...	...	...	...	...	...	...	...	dont Monnaie scripturale
Net foreign assets	- 43 519	- 45 252	- 41 400	- 44 804	25 574	28 005	25 162	26 185	28 388	Avoirs extérieurs nets
Domestic credit	65 100	72 323	76 953	89 441	29 458	38 655	43 233	57 001	59 664	Crédit intérieur
of which claims on private sector	3 080	4 503	6 646	9 626	13 676	18 356	20 415	29 548	32 240	dont créances sur le secteur privé
of which claims on government sector, net	61 784	67 607	70 242	78 551	15 187	19 479	21 046	25 476	24 488	dont créances nettes sur le gouvernement
International reserves (millions US$)	72	119	161	372	466	513	497	493	543	Réserves internationales (millions $EU)
Average Exchange Rate (National Currency per US$)	58.01	61.27	63.21	68.29	71.40	72.23	73.51	75.51	76.85	Taux de change (moyen) (monnaie nationale par $ EU)
IX-2 PUBLIC FINANCE *LIBERIAN DOLLAR (MILLIONS)*										**IX-2 FINANCES PUBLIQUES** *DOLLAR LIBERIEN (MILLIONS)*
Total Revenues and Grants	7 223	12 083	15 644	20 882	28 411	35 142	45 123	42 245	46 029	Recettes totales et dons
Tax Revenue	6 965	10 652	13 021	16 607	21 771	27 641	34 552	31 047	34 629	Recettes fiscales
Non Tax Revenue	215	1 198	1 684	3 025	4 738	5 023	7 851	8 098	5 672	Recettes non fiscales
Grants	44	233	939	1 250	1 903	2 477	2 720	3 100	5 729	Dons
Total Expenditures and Net Lending	5 694	9 807	14 098	18 134	23 745	32 394	39 213	44 595	47 708	Dépenses totales et prêts nets
Current expenditure	5 030	8 566	12 275	15 897	19 989	26 980	33 905	34 421	36 980	Dépenses courantes
Of which Wages and Salaries	2 120	3 327	5 038	7 010	9 015	11 556	14 446	15 540	17 157	Dont rémunérations et salaires
Capital expenditure	664	1 241	1 824	2 236	3 756	5 413	5 308	10 175	10 727	Dépenses d'équipement
Net Lending	-	-	-	-	-	-	-	-	-	Prêts nets
Fiscal Balance	1 529	2 276	1 545	2 749	4 666	2 748	5 911	- 2 350	- 1 678	Solde global y compris les dons
IX-3 BALANCE OF PAYMENTS *US$ (MILLIONS)*										**IX-3 BALANCE DES PAIEMENTS** *$ E.U (MILLIONS)*
Trade balance	- 279	- 290	- 455	- 421	- 459	- 677	- 632	- 667	...	Balance commerciale
Services Balance	- 938	- 903	- 1 007	- 741	- 830	- 865	- 658	- 668	...	Balance des services
Net Income	- 152	- 154	- 160	- 145	- 182	- 688	- 944	- 634	...	Revenus nets
Compensation of employees	...	...	...	...	...	...	...	...	...	Rémunération des salariés
Investment Income	...	...	...	...	...	...	...	...	...	Revenus des investissements
Current transfers, net total	1 286	1 135	1 134	970	1 041	1 233	1 097	681	...	Transferts courants
Net official transfers	...	...	...	...	...	...	...	...	...	Transferts officiels nets
Workers' remittances	...	...	...	...	...	...	...	...	...	Envois de fonds des travailleurs
Other private transfers	...	...	...	...	...	...	...	...	...	Autres transferts privés
Current account balance	- 84	- 213	- 488	- 337	- 430	- 996	- 1 137	- 1 288	...	Solde du compte courant
Capital & financial account	...	...	...	...	...	1 231	1 871	1 529	...	Comptes de capital et financier
Capital account	...	...	...	...	...	...	...	...	...	Compte de capital
Financial account	...	...	...	...	...	...	...	...	...	Compte financier
Errors & omissions	...	...	...	...	...	- 1 508	- 519	- 316	...	Erreurs et omissions
Overall balance	...	...	...	...	...	- 20	44	- 177	...	Balance générale

X DEBT AND FINANCIAL FLOWS - DETTE ET FLUX FINANCIERS	2006	2007	2008	2009	2010	2011	2012	2013	2014	
X-1 DEBT *US$ (MILLIONS)*										**X-1 DETTE EXTÉRIEURE** *$ E.U (MILLIONS)*
Total external debt	4 732	4 399	3 203	1 680	114	185	201	273	412	Dette extérieure totale
Private	-	-	-	-	-	-	-	-	-	Privée
Public	4 732	4 399	3 203	1 680	114	185	201	273	412	Publique
Total external debt service	147	148	1 301	1 645	928	27	40	21	36	Service de la dette extérieure
Present value of External debt	...	...	...	...	...	...	...	...	...	Valeur actuelle de la dette extérieure
Total government domestic debt (in local currency)	...	...	...	...	...	...	...	...	...	Dette publique intérieure
X-2 FINANCIAL FLOWS *US$ (MILLIONS)*										**X-2 FLUX FINANCIERS** *$ E.U (MILLIONS)*
Net Foreign Direct Investment Inflows	108	132	284	218	450	508	985	1 061	...	Investissements étranger direct (flux nets entrants)
Main origin of FDI Inflows										**Principales origines de l'IDE entrant:**
Luxembourg	- 1	4	1	210	-	-	92.0	...	...	Luxembourg
United States	- 128	207	61	12	228.0	109.0	- 19.0	...	...	États-Unis
Slovenia	...	...	...	...	0.0	0.0	0.0	...	...	Slovénie
Japan	- 100	- 68	- 6	40	136.7	412.1	149.1	...	...	Japon
Germany	- 1	1	-	-	17.2	11.1	- 6.4	...	...	Allemagne
African countries	...	...	...	...	...	...	...	...	...	Pays africains
Net total Official Development Assistance	260	701	1 251	513	1 417	765	571	534	...	Aide publique au développement (nette totale)
Main origin of Net ODA										**Principales origines de l'APD nette**
United States	88	103	276	97	131.4	153.1	180.2	157.5	...	Etats-Unis
IMF (Concessional Trust Funds)	-	-	320	28	539.7	14.0	18.1	...	...	FMI (Fonds fiduciaires concessionnels)
IDA	1	407	5	42	40.1	62.8	41.5	...	...	IDA
Germany	9	10	317	28	50.1	1.3	1.0	0.4	...	Allemagne
France	2	1	27	0	232.0	1.3	0.9	0.7	...	France

LIBYA — LIBYE

AREA (KM²)		1 759 540	SUPERFICIE (KM²)
CAPITAL CITY	Tripoli	Tripoli	CAPITALE
CURRENCY	Libyan Dinar	Dinar Libyen	MONNAIE

I SOCIAL AND DEMOGRAPHIC INDICATORS — INDICATEURS DEMOGRAPHIQUES ET SOCIAUX

	Year / Année	Value / Valeur	
POPULATION			**POPULATION**
Population ('000)			Population ('000)
Both sexes	2014	6 253	Les deux sexes
Male	2014	3 109	Masculin
Female	2014	3 145	Féminin
Average annual growth rate	2014	1.6	Taux de croissance annuel
Active Population ('000)	2014	670	Population active ('000)
Population by age group ('000)			Population par groupe d'âge ('000)
0-14 years	2014	2 261	0-14 ans
15-64 years	2014	4 108	15-64 ans
65+ years	2014	305	65+ ans
Economically active population in agriculture (%)	2014	2.5	Participation de la population active agricole (%)
Crude birth rate	2014	20.2	Taux brut de natalité
Crude death rate	2014	4.2	Taux brut de mortalité
Total fertility rate	2014	2.3	Indice synthétique de fécondité
Proportion of urban population	2014	78.2	Part de la population urbaine
Life Expectancy at Birth - Total (years)	2014	75.5	Espérance de vie à la naissance - Totale (ans)
Dependency Ratio - Total (%)	2014	56.4	Taux de dépendance - Total (%)
HEALTH			**SANTÉ**
Percentage of children under-five and underweight	2007	5.6	% d'enfants de moins de cinq ans avec insuffisance pondérale
Prevalence of undernourishment	...	...	Prévalence de la malnutrition
Under five mortality rate (both sexes, per 1000)	2013	14.5	Taux de mortalité de moins de 5 ans (les deux sexes, pour 1000)
Infant mortality rate (both sexes) per 1000	2013	12.4	Taux de mortalité infantile (les deux sexes) par 1000
Percentage of children provided the vaccines :			Pourcentage d'enfants vaccinés :
BCG	2013	99.0	BCG
DPT3	2013	98.0	DTC3
Polio	2012	98.0	Polio
Measles	2013	98.0	Rougeole
Percentage of mothers provided at least one antenatal care (%)	2007	93.1	Pourcentage de mères ayant au moins reçu un soin prénatal (%)
Percentage of deliveries attended by skilled health personnel	2008	99.8	% d'accouchements assistés par un personnel de santé qualifié
Number of doctors (per 10 000 population)	2009	19.0	Nombre de médecins (pour 10 000 habitants)
Number of nurses (per 10 000 population)	2009	68.0	Nombre d'infirmières (pour 10 000 habitants)
Hospital beds - Total (per 10 000 population)	2009	37.0	Nombre de lits d'hôpitaux - Total (pour 10 000)
Births registered (per 1 000)	2014	20.2	Naiss.s enregistrées (pour 1 000)
Deaths registered (per 1 000)	2014	4.2	Décès enregistrés (pour 1 000)
Public expenditure on Health (% of budget)	2009	5.5	Dépenses publiques consacrées à la santé (% du budget)
EDUCATION			**EDUCATION**
Enrolment in primary education (both sexes) (000)	2006	755	Scolarisation dans le primaire (les deux sexes) (000)
Female	2006	360	Féminin
Enrolment in secondary education (both sexes) (000)	2006	733	Scolarisation dans le secondaire (les deux sexes) (000)
Female	2006	388	Féminin
Enrolment in tertiary education (both sexes) (000)	...	...	Scolarisation dans le tertiaire (les deux sexes) (000)
Female	2003	192.7	Féminin
Literacy rate (both sexes)	2012	89.9	Taux d'alphabétisation (deux sexes)
Male	2012	96.1	Masculin
Female	2012	83.7	Féminin
Pupil-teacher ratio	...	...	Ratio élève-enseignant
Public expenditure on education (% of budget)	...	...	Dépenses publiques consacrées à l'enseignement (% du budget)
POVERTY			**PAUVRETÉ**
GNI Per Capita (US$)	2013	14 476.9	RNB par habitant ($EU)
Human Poverty Index (HPI-1) Value (%)	2007	13.4	Valeur de l'Indice de pauvreté (IPH-1) (%)
Population below International Poverty Line ($2/day) (%)	...	...	Population sous le seuil international de pauvreté (2$/J) (%)
Share of Income Held by Richest 10%	...	...	% de revenu des 10% plus riches
Share of Income Held by Poorest 10%	...	...	% de revenu des 10% plus pauvres
Gini index	...	...	Indice de Gini

Charts / Graphiques

Population by age group – 2014
Population par groupe d'age – 2014

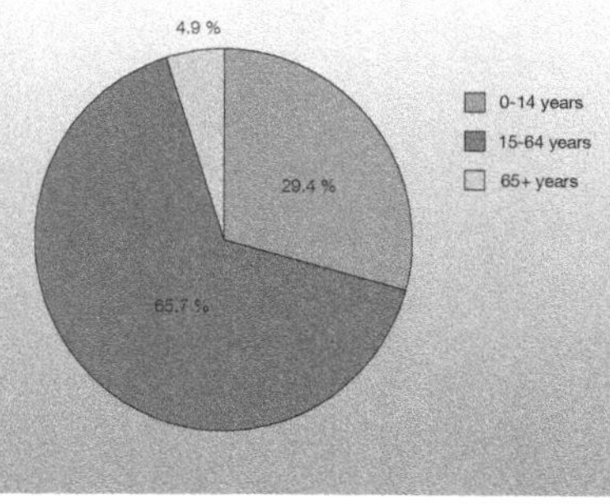

Percentage of children provided the vaccines – 2013
Pourcentage d'enfants vaccinés – 2013

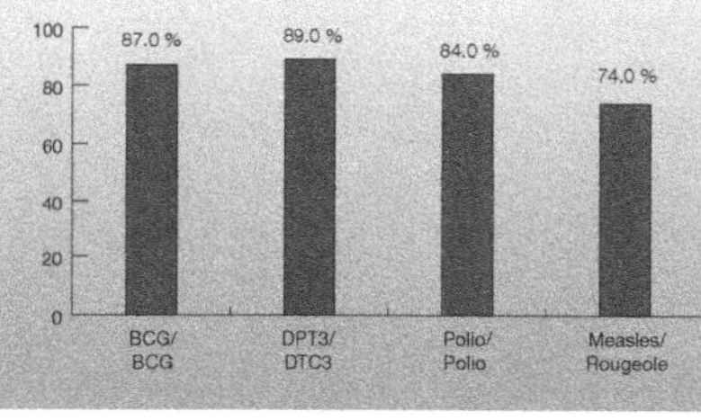

Literacy rate (%) – 2012
Taux d'alphabétisation – 2012

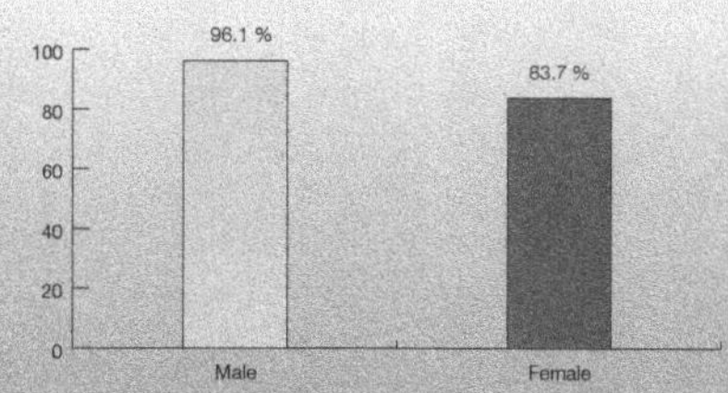

GNI Per Capita (US$)
RNB par habitant ($EU)

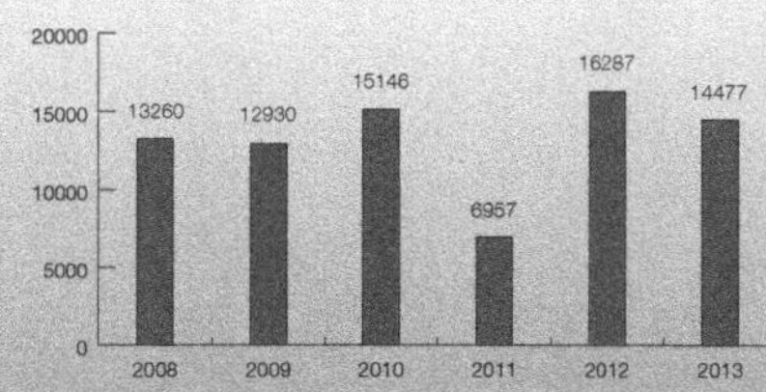

LIBYA

II NATIONAL ACCOUNTS — COMPTES NATIONAUX

	2006	2007	2008	2009	2010	2011	2012	2013	2014	
GROSS DOMESTIC PRODUCT BY KIND OF ECONOMIC ACTIVITY AT CURRENT PRICES *LIBYAN DINAR (MILLIONS)*										**PRODUIT INTÉRIEUR BRUT PAR BRANCHE D'ACTIVITÉ ÉCONOMIQUE AUX PRIX COURANTS** *DINAR LIBYEN (MILLIONS)*
Agriculture, hunting, forestry and fishing	1 643	1 905	2 248	2 383	2 544	844	929	838	...	Agriculture, chasse sylviculture et pêche
Mining and quarrying	45 476	54 296	70 483	38 872	51 619	14 802	62 615	56 533	...	Industries extractives
Manufacturing	3 603	4 032	4 889	5 448	5 810	978	3 776	3 409	...	Industries manufacturières
Electricity, gas & water	973	1 019	1 205	1 335	1 421	561	1 435	1 295	...	Electricité, gaz et eau
Construction & public works	3 129	4 198	5 995	7 578	8 067	1 392	1 531	1 382	...	Bâtiments et travaux publics
Wholesale & retail trade, restaurants, hotels	2 863	3 396	3 950	4 298	4 608	2 923	4 875	4 402	...	Commerce de gros et de détail, restaurants et hôtels
Finance, insurance, real estate, etc.	5 460	6 200	6 805	7 337	7 898	5 293	6 887	6 218	...	Banques, assurances, affaires immobilières
Transport and communications	2 724	3 300	3 884	4 126	4 432	3 318	3 553	3 208	...	Transport(s) et communications
Public administration and defense	4 935	6 288	6 671	6 871	7 129	12 319	17 406	15 711	...	Administrations publiques et défense
Education	85	99	122	134	141	40	113	102	...	Education
Health and Social Work	132	154	156	165	175	87	140	126	...	Santé et actions sociales
Other services	62	69	82	91	98	34	98	89	...	Autres services
Less Imputed Service Charges	- 533	- 364	- 643	- 706	- 753	- 436	- 364	- 328	...	Moins services d'intermédiation financière
Gross domestic product at factor cost / basic prices	70 553	84 593	105 845	77 930	93 187	42 155	102 994	92 985	...	Produit intérieur brut aux couts des facteurs / prix de base
Plus: indirect taxes / taxes on products, less subsidies	1 206	653	780	1 077	1 535	325	346	317	...	Plus taxes indirectes/impôts sur les produits, moins les subventions
EXPENDITURE ON GROSS DOMESTIC PRODUCT AT CURRENT PURCHASER'S VALUES *LIBYAN DINAR (MILLIONS)*										**EMPLOI DU PRODUIT INTÉRIEUR BRUT AUX PRIX COURANTS D'ACQUISITION** *DINAR LIBYEN (MILLIONS)*
Government final consumption	7 610	10 278	11 413	20 288	19 534	16 580	29 753	39 061	...	Consommation finale des administrations publiques
Private final consumption	12 277	13 746	11 601	13 844	18 045	15 343	21 081	18 368	...	Consommation finale privée
Gross fixed capital formation	15 364	24 437	37 866	31 877	36 341	6 280	16 437	19 751	...	Formation brute de capital fixe
Change in inventories	...	...	...	...	...	...	...	...	...	Variation des stocks
Exports of goods and services	56 489	61 941	76 205	46 901	59 838	23 365	77 178	58 723	...	Exportations de biens et services
Less imports of goods and services	19 982	25 157	30 460	33 904	39 036	19 089	41 109	42 601	...	Moins importations de biens et services
GDP at purchasers' values	71 759	85 246	106 625	79 006	94 723	42 479	103 340	93 302	...	PIB aux prix d'acquisition
GROSS DOMESTIC PRODUCT BY KIND OF ECONOMIC ACTIVITY AT CONSTANT PRICES *ANNUAL GROWTH RATES (%)*										**PRODUIT INTÉRIEUR BRUT PAR BRANCHE D'ACTIVITÉ ECONOMIQUE AUX PRIX CONSTANTS** *TAUX DE CROISSANCE ANNUEL (%)*
Agriculture, hunting, forestry and fishing	9.8	4.0	2.4	2.5	- 0.9	- 69.0	...	...	...	Agriculture, chasse sylviculture et pêche
Mining and quarrying	3.9	0.9	- 0.5	- 7.7	4.0	- 72.0	...	...	...	Industries extractives
Manufacturing	4.7	7.6	- 1.6	3.5	1.2	- 77.0	...	...	...	Industries manufacturières
Electricity, gas & water	8.4	13.9	10.0	7.0	4.7	- 61.0	...	...	...	Electricité, gaz et eau
Construction & public works	7.6	20.9	12.0	9.0	5.8	- 79.0	...	...	...	Bâtiments et travaux publics
Wholesale & retail trade, restaurants, hotels	8.4	11.0	8.1	6.5	6.5	- 60.0	...	...	...	Commerce de gros et de détail,restaurants et hôtels
Finance, insurance, real estate, etc.	4.7	8.9	7.8	7.3	6.2	- 51.1	...	...	...	Banques, assurances, affaires immobilières
Transport and communications	12.6	12.3	9.0	7.0	6.8	- 58.0	...	...	...	Transport(s) et communications
Public administration and defense	7.8	2.0	0.1	2.0	2.1	1.4	...	...	...	Administrations publiques et défense
Education	7.2	7.1	3.0	5.1	6.1	- 67.0	...	...	...	Education
Health and Social Work	7.2	7.1	5.0	6.1	6.6	- 64.0	...	...	...	Santé et actions sociales
Other services	6.6	6.4	8.0	8.5	5.6	- 59.0	...	...	...	Autres services
Less Imputed Service Charges	- 1.1	8.0	5.0	8.0	5.1	- 77.0	...	...	...	Moins services d'intermédiation financière
Gross domestic product at factor cost / basic prices	5.9	5.5	3.1	0.1	4.4	- 60.0	...	...	...	Produit intérieur brut aux couts des facteurs / prix de base
Plus: indirect taxes / taxes on products, less subsidies	30.3	35.1	- 8.3	- 25.3	30.2	- 126.1	...	...	...	Plus taxes indirectes/impôts sur les produits, moins les subventions
Gross domestic product at market prices	6.5	6.4	2.7	- 0.8	5.0	- 62.1	104.5	- 13.6	...	Produit intérieur brut aux prix du marché
EXPENDITURE ON GROSS DOMESTIC PRODUCT AT CONSTANT PURCHASERS' VALUES *ANNUAL GROWTH RATES (%)*										**EMPLOIS DU PRODUIT INTÉRIEUR BRUT AUX PRIX CONSTANTS D'ACQUISITION** *TAUX DE CROISSANCE ANNUEL (%)*
Government final consumption	...	...	...	...	...	...	...	...	...	Consommation finale des administrations publiques
Private final consumption	...	...	...	...	...	...	...	...	...	Consommation finale privée
Gross fixed capital formation	...	...	...	...	...	...	...	...	...	Formation brute de capital fixe
Exports of goods and services	...	...	...	...	...	...	...	...	...	Exportations de biens et services
Less imports of goods and services	...	...	...	...	...	...	...	...	...	Moins importations de biens et services
Notes	2012-2013:Estimates							2012-2013 :Estimée		Notes

III INFLATION

	2006	2007	2008	2009	2010	2011	2012	2013	2014	
ANNUAL GROWTH RATES (%)										**TAUX DE CROISSANCE ANSSNUEL (%)**
All items	1.5	6.3	10.4	2.5	2.5	15.9	6.1	2.6	2.7	Ensemble
of which:										dont:
Food and Non-alcoholic beverages	1.2	15.2	19.7	3.1	2.8	13.6	...	...	...	Alimentation et boissons non alcoolisés
Alcoholic beverages & tobacco	...	...	...	...	...	...	...	...	...	Boissons alcoolisées et tabacs
Clothing and Footwear	2.2	-1.6	2.3	3.6	8.9	2.2	...	...	...	Habillement et chaussures
Housing, Water, Electricity, Gas and Other Fuels	0.8	0.5	5.5	0.3	0.1	0.6	...	...	...	Logement, eau, électricité, gas et autres combustibles
Furnishing, household equip	1.3	-1.0	3.7	4.6	3.1	9.8	...	...	...	Meubles, articles de ménage et entretien courant
Health	6.1	12.3	0.2	-0.1	-	0.1	...	...	...	Santé
Transport	0.4	-0.4	3.6	2.2	-0.4	3.4	...	...	...	Transport
Communication	...	...	...	...	...	...	...	...	...	Communication
Recreation & culture	...	...	...	...	...	...	...	...	...	Loisirs et culture
Education	-2.1	0.2	3.4	6.2	5.4	1.5	...	...	...	Enseignement
Restaurants & hotels	...	...	...	...	...	...	...	...	...	Restaurants et hôtels
Miscellaneous goods & services	8.6	4.3	8.7	2.2	7.1	16.4	...	...	...	Biens et services divers

	2006	2007	2008	2009	2010	2011	2012	2013	2014	
IV AGRICULTURAL PRODUCTION - PRODUCTION AGRICOLE										
TONNES *(THOUSAND)*										**TONNES** *(MILLIERS)*
Potato	300	290	290	291	290	352	291	295	...	Pommes de terre
Tomato	160	213	213	220	230	223	225	221	...	Tomates
Dates	150	150	150	155	161	166	170	174	...	Dattes
Olive	180	180	180	171	180	139	135	138	...	Olive
Onions, dry	182	182	182	186	195	206	208	211	...	Oignons, sec
V MINING PRODUCTION - PRODUCTION MINIERE										
	2006	2007	2008	2009	2010	2011	2012	2013	2014	
Crude petroleum, metric tons (thousands)	83 310	81 114	90 628	82 262	82 611	23 852	75 141	...	...	Pétrole brut, tonnes métriques (milliers)
Natural gas (terajoules)	562 400	625 480	1128 720	1090 699	1126 746	367 216	872 701	...	...	Gaz naturel (térajoules)
Salt and sodium chloride, metric tons (thousands)	40	40	40	40	40	20	30	...	...	Sel et chlorure de sodium pur, tonnes métriques (milliers)
VI ENERGY - ENERGIE										
	2006	2007	2008	2009	2010	2011	2012	2013	2014	
Total electricity generation (GWh)	23 992	25 694	28 667	30 426	32 753	28 657	31 183	31 183	...	Production d'électricité totale (GWh)
of which:										dont:
Production of electricity from fossil fuels (GWh)	23 992	25 694	28 667	30 426	32 753	28 649	31 174	31 174	...	Production d'électricité à partir de combustibles fossiles (GWh)
Production of hydro electricity (GWh)	...	...	...	...	...	...	...	...	...	Production d'électricité d'origine hydraulique (GWh)
Production of electricity from solar, wind, tide, wave and other sources (GWh)	...	...	...	...	...	9	9	9	...	Production d'électricité d'origine solaire, éolienne, marée motrice et autres (GWh)
VII TOURISM AND INFRASTRUCTURE - TOURISME ET INFRASTRUCTURE										
	2006	2007	2008	2009	2010	2011	2012	2013	2014	
VII-1 TOURISM										**VII-1 TOURISME**
International tourist arrivals (thousands)	42	38	34	73	91	83	79	85	91	Arrivées de touristes internationaux (milliers)
Rooms in hotels and similar establishments (thousands)	7	8	8	...	...	...	...	...	...	Chambres d'hotels et établissements assimilés (milliers)
Overnight stays (thousands)	308	282	251	462	507	888	1 266	1 223	1 217	Nuitées (milliers)
Tourism receipts (US$ thousand)	190 000	74 200	74 200	50 000	60 000	26 949	34 151	27 172	23 158	Recettes touristiques (milliers de $ EU)
Total contribution to GDP (%)	3.8	3.8	3.1	5.1	4.2	5.7	3.9	3.9	4.1	Contribution totale au PIB (%)
Total contribution to Employment (%)	3.5	3.3	3.0	4.9	4.0	3.9	5.3	2.5	2.7	Contribution totale à l'emploi (%)
VII-2 INFRASTRUCTURE										**VII-2 INFRASTRUCTURE**
Paved roads (% of total)	...	...	...	...	...	...	...	...	...	Routes asphaltées (% du total)
Total Network (Railways-km)	...	...	...	...	...	...	...	...	...	Réseau total voies ferrées-Km
Main Telephone Lines (per 100 inhabitants)	16	17	16	18	20	16	13	13	...	Lignes téléphoniques fixes (pour 100 habitants)
Mobile Cellular Subscribers (per 100 inhabitants)	69	78	126	160	180	164	156	165	...	Abonnés aux téléphones mobiles (pour 100 habitants)
VIII EXTERNAL TRADE - COMMERCE EXTERIEUR										
	2006	2007	2008	2009	2010	2011	2012	2013	2014	
LIBYAN DINAR (MILLIONS) EXPORTS, FOB										**DINAR LIBYEN (MILLIONS) EXPORTATIONS, FÀB**
Exports - Total	42 844	48 989	62 119	37 055	48 935	19 796	21 254	...	...	Exportations - Total
Exports to AFRICA	...	...	...	...	...	...	...	...	...	Exportations vers l'AFRIQUE
Main Products										**Principaux produits**
Crude petroleum	33 085	38 435	50 677	29 381	39 023	...	...	...	...	Pétrole brut
Natural gas	5 195	5 610	5 242	3 472	3 493	...	...	...	...	Gaz naturel
	...	...	...	...	...	...	...	...	...	
	...	...	...	...	...	...	...	...	...	
	...	...	...	...	...	...	...	...	...	
Main Destinations										**Principales destinations**
Italy	19 066	23 471	28 848	17 834	18 950	7 232	7 776	...	...	Italie
Germany	7 354	7 367	9 476	5 070	6 191	1 314	1 417	...	...	Allemagne
Spain	4 726	4 855	5 879	3 893	6 125	3 173	3 372	...	...	Espagne
France	2 828	3 551	5 314	3 471	7 212	1 114	1 208	...	...	France
United States	3 326	4 547	5 178	2 474	2 989	1 008	1 089	...	...	États-Unis
IMPORTS, CIF										**IMPORTATIONS, CAF**
Imports - Total	7 931	8 506	11 126	12 550	13 276	6 046	8 060	...	...	Importations - Total (millions)
Imports from Africa	...	...	...	...	...	...	...	...	...	Importations en provenance de l'Afrique
Main Products										**Principaux produits**
Petroleum, petroleum products and related materials	675	897	1 430	1 055	1 273	406	...	...	...	Pétrole et produits dérivés
Road vehicles	800	839	905	1 206	1 103	335	...	...	...	Véhicules routiers
Cereals and cereal preparations	469	611	718	659	814	685	...	...	...	Céréales et préparations à base de céréales
Iron and steel	518	566	625	888	833	302	...	...	...	Fer et acier
Electrical machinery, apparatus and appliances, n.e.s.	648	488	648	820	892	343	...	...	...	Machines et appareils électriques, n.d.a.
Main Origin										**Principales provenances**
Italy	1 593	1 743	2 647	2 418	2 440	...	...	...	...	Italie
Germany	683	716	984	1 112	940	...	...	...	...	Allemagne
China	524	552	885	1 127	1 189	305	305	...	...	Chine
Turkey	362	405	583	997	1 096	...	...	...	...	Turquie
France	490	556	489	720	974	305	...	...	...	France

IX FINANCIAL AND MONETARY STATISTICS - FINANCES ET STATISTIQUES MONETAIRES	2006	2007	2008	2009	2010	2011	2012	2013	2014	
IX-1 MONETARY STATISTICS *LIBYAN DINAR (MILLIONS)*										**IX-1 STATISTIQUES MONÉTAIRES** *DINAR LIBYEN (MILLIONS)*
Money supply (M1)	19 560	26 720	39 740	44 720	46 350	57 940	65 610	70 150	72 950	Masse monétaire (M1)
Quasi-money	3 313	3 894	5 330	7 992	5 030	4 504	5 655	4 707	3 097	Quasi-monnaie
of which Demand Deposit	...	...	...	...	...	...	...	...	...	dont Monnaie scripturale
Net foreign assets	79 318	100 484	124 714	128 810	134 192	140 155	158 549	154 232	131 735	Avoirs extérieurs nets
Domestic credit	- 42 891	- 48 728	- 56 989	- 51 560	- 57 220	- 48 721	- 59 346	- 48 262	- 23 958	Crédit intérieur
of which claims on private sector	4 742	5 286	7 744	8 521	8 843	8 363	10 903	13 163	13 811	dont créances sur le secteur privé
of which claims on government sector, net	- 53 668	- 60 961	- 70 642	- 69 953	- 78 831	- 69 067	- 82 995	- 74 034	- 51 072	dont créances nettes sur le gouvernement
International reserves (millions US$)	59 533	79 660	92 563	98 979	99 894	104 999	118 609	115 399	93 485	Réserves internationales (millions $EU)
Average Exchange Rate (National Currency per US$)	1.31	1.26	1.22	1.25	1.27	1.22	1.26	1.27	1.27	Taux de change (moyen) (monnaie nationale par $ EU)
IX-2 PUBLIC FINANCE *LIBYAN DINAR (MILLIONS)*										**IX-2 FINANCES PUBLIQUES** *DINAR LIBYEN (MILLIONS)*
Total Revenues and Grants	47 088	53 366	72 741	41 785	61 503	16 614	74 714	54 762	23 393	Recettes totales et dons
Tax Revenue	45 352	50 542	67 707	38 729	59 354	16 257	74 264	54 462	23 236	Recettes fiscales
Non Tax Revenue	1 735	2 824	5 035	3 057	2 149	285	450	300	157	Recettes non fiscales
Grants	-	-	-	-	-	72	-	-	-	Dons
Total Expenditures and Net Lending	20 909	27 415	39 078	37 351	53 942	23 367	45 978	60 583	48 869	Dépenses totales et prêts nets
Current expenditure	9 613	12 140	13 891	17 568	28 486	18 964	40 278	51 283	40 408	Dépenses courantes
Of which Wages and Salaries	4 323	6 305	5 229	6 075	11 383	12 800	16 570	20 150	17 772	Dont rémunérations et salaires
Capital expenditure	11 217	15 040	24 837	18 984	24 176	3 403	4 800	8 700	6 461	Dépenses d'équipement
Net Lending	80	235	350	800	1 280	1 000	900	600	2 000	Prêts nets
Fiscal Balance	26 178	25 952	33 663	4 434	7 561	- 6 752	28 736	- 5 821	- 25 476	Solde global y compris les dons
IX-3 BALANCE OF PAYMENTS *LIBYAN DINAR (MILLIONS)*										**IX-3 BALANCE DES PAIEMENTS** *DINAR LIBYEN (MILLIONS)*
Trade balance	39 574	40 088	50 344	18 866	29 777	9 590	44 650	25 389	45 240	Balance commerciale
Services Balance	- 3 057	- 3 223	- 4 613	- 5 860	- 7 510	- 5 326	- 8 623	- 9 268	- 9 838	Balance des services
Net Income	- 50	1 050	850	723	- 37	68	- 2 434	- 150	- 100	Revenus nets
Compensation of employees	...	...	...	...	...	...	...	...	...	Rémunération des salariés
Investment Income	...	...	...	...	...	...	...	...	...	Revenus des investissements
Current transfers, net total	436	- 275	- 1 271	- 1 970	- 2 303	- 460	- 3 559	- 3 291	- 3 949	Transferts courants
Net official transfers	...	...	...	...	...	...	...	...	...	Transferts officiels nets
Workers' remittances	...	...	...	...	...	...	...	...	...	Envois de fonds des travailleurs
Other private transfers	...	...	...	...	...	...	...	...	...	Autres transferts privés
Current account balance	36 903	37 641	45 310	11 759	19 927	3 872	30 034	12 681	31 353	Solde du compte courant
Capital & financial account	...	...	...	...	...	...	...	...	...	Comptes de capital et financier
Capital account	...	...	...	...	...	...	...	...	...	Compte de capital
Financial account	...	...	...	...	...	...	...	...	...	Compte financier
Errors & omissions	...	...	...	...	...	...	...	...	...	Erreurs et omissions
Overall balance	...	...	...	...	...	...	...	...	...	Balance générale

X DEBT AND FINANCIAL FLOWS - DETTE ET FLUX FINANCIERS	2006	2007	2008	2009	2010	2011	2012	2013	2014	
X-1 DEBT *US$ (MILLIONS)*										**X-1 DETTE EXTÉRIEURE** *$ E.U (MILLIONS)*
Total external debt	5 574	5 574	5 574	5 574	5 574	5 574	5 574	5 574	5 574	Dette extérieure totale
Private	2 374	2 374	2 374	2 374	2 374	2 374	2 374	2 374	2 374	Privée
Public	3 200	3 200	3 200	3 200	3 200	3 200	3 200	3 200	3 200	Publique
Total external debt service	...	...	...	...	...	...	...	...	...	Service de la dette extérieure
Present value of External debt	...	...	...	...	...	...	...	...	...	Valeur actuelle de la dette extérieure
Total government domestic debt (in local currency)	...	...	...	...	...	...	...	...	...	Dette publique intérieure
X-2 FINANCIAL FLOWS *US$ (MILLIONS)*										**X-2 FLUX FINANCIERS** *$ E.U (MILLIONS)*
Net Foreign Direct Investment Inflows	2 064	3 850	3 180	3 310	1 909	-	1 425	702	...	Investissements étranger direct (flux nets entrants)
Main origin of FDI Inflows										**Principales origines de l'IDE entrant:**
United States	1 493	371	...	...	...	314.0	353.0	...	...	États-Unis
Germany	- 623	832	804	104	- 193.4	174.1	- 172.2	...	...	Allemagne
France	...	...	...	...	0.1	- 0.6	- 0.5	...	...	France
Norway	...	...	273	62	- 54.6	...	...	...	...	Norvège
Spain	...	...	190	...	...	...	- 724.9	...	...	Espagne
African countries	...	...	...	...	...	...	...	...	...	Pays africains
Net total Official Development Assistance	38	19	74	41	9	642	87	129	...	Aide publique au développement (nette totale)
Main origin of Net ODA										**Principales origines de l'APD nette**
United States	25	4	14	6	6.6	290.3	38.5	12.4	...	Etats-Unis
France	2	1	29	19	3.8	14.3	4.3	6.9	...	France
Turkey	1	1	2	1	1.0	53.1	3.1	...	...	Turquie
United Arab Emirates	...	...	...	...	...	57.6	0.0	...	...	Emirats arabes unis
Australia	...	...	...	...	...	41.0	1.0	0.1	...	Australie

AREA (KM²)	587 041		SUPERFICIE (KM²)
CAPITAL CITY	Antananarivo	Tananarive	CAPITALE
CURRENCY	Ariary	Ariary	MONNAIE

I SOCIAL AND DEMOGRAPHIC INDICATORS – INDICATEURS DEMOGRAPHIQUES ET SOCIAUX

POPULATION	Year / Année	Value / Valeur	POPULATION
Population ('000)			Population ('000)
Both sexes	2014	23 572	Les deux sexes
Male	2014	11 750	Masculin
Female	2014	11 822	Féminin
Average annual growth rate	2014	2.8	Taux de croissance annuel
Active Population ('000)	2014	11 149	Population active ('000)
Population by age group ('000)			Population par groupe d'âge ('000)
0-14 years	2014	9 910	0-14 ans
15-64 years	2014	12 997	15-64 ans
65+ years	2014	665	65+ ans
Economically active population in agriculture (%)	2014	73.6	Participation de la population active agricole (%)
Crude birth rate	2014	34.4	Taux brut de natalité
Crude death rate	2014	6.7	Taux brut de mortalité
Total fertility rate	2014	4.4	Indice synthétique de fécondité
Proportion of urban population	2014	34.5	Part de la population urbaine
Life Expectancy at Birth - Total (years)	2014	65.2	Espérance de vie à la naissance - Totale (ans)
Dependency Ratio - Total (%)	2014	81.3	Taux de dépendance - Total (%)

Charts / Graphiques

Population by age group – 2014
Population par groupe d'age – 2014

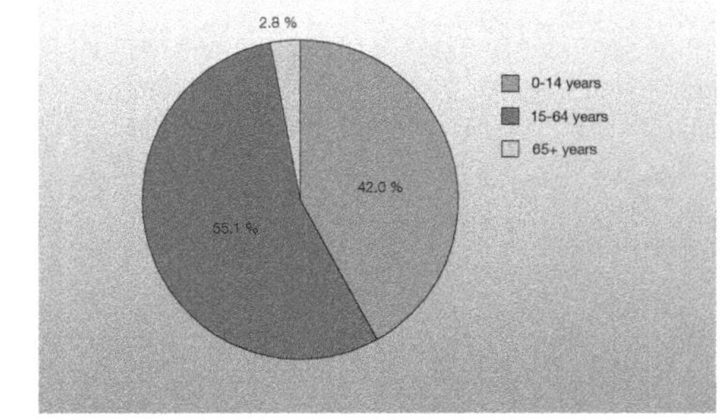

HEALTH	Year / Année	Value / Valeur	SANTÉ
Percentage of children under-five and underweight	2004	36.8	% d'enfants de moins de cinq ans avec insuffisance pondérale
Prevalence of undernourishment	2013	30.5	Prévalence de la malnutrition
Under five mortality rate (both sexes, per 1000)	2013	56.0	Taux de mortalité de moins de 5 ans (les deux sexes, pour 1000)
Infant mortality rate (both sexes) per 1000	2013	39.6	Taux de mortalité infantile (les deux sexes) par 1000
Percentage of children provided the vaccines :			Pourcentage d'enfants vaccinés :
BCG	2013	77.0	BCG
DPT3	2013	74.0	DTC3
Polio	2012	86.0	Polio
Measles	2013	63.0	Rougeole
Percentage of mothers provided at least one antenatal care (%)	2009	86.3	Pourcentage de mères ayant au moins reçu un soin prénatal (%)
Percentage of deliveries attended by skilled health personnel	2009	43.9	% d'accouchements assistés par un personnel de santé qualifié
Number of doctors (per 10 000 population)	2007	1.6	Nombre de médecins (pour 10 000 habitants)
Number of nurses (per 10 000 population)	2004	3.2	Nombre d'infirmières (pour 10 000 habitants)
Hospital beds - Total (per 10 000 population)	2010	2.0	Nombre de lits d'hôpitaux - Total (pour 10 000)
Births registered (per 1 000)	2014	34.4	Naiss.s enregistrées (pour 1 000)
Deaths registered (per 1 000)	2014	6.7	Décès enregistrés (pour 1 000)
Public expenditure on Health (% of budget)	2009	15.1	Dépenses publiques consacrées à la santé (% du budget)

Percentage of children provided the vaccines – 2013
Pourcentage d'enfants vaccinés – 2013

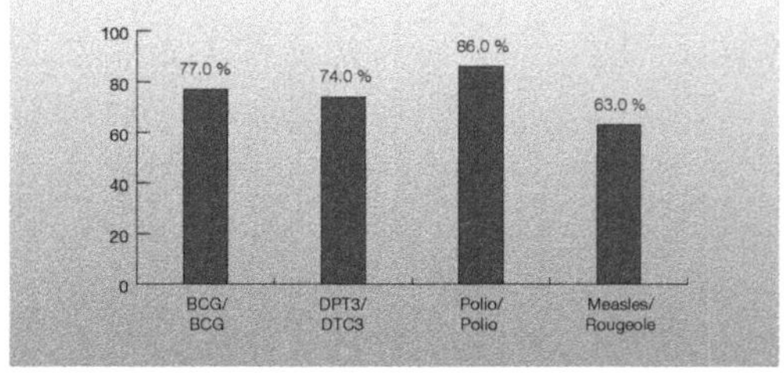

Literacy rate (%) – 2009
Taux d'alphabétisation – 2009

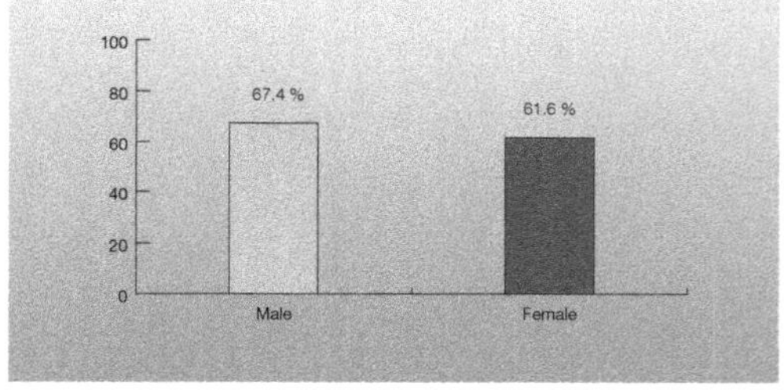

EDUCATION	Year / Année	Value / Valeur	EDUCATION
Enrolment in primary education (both sexes) (000)	2013	4 483	Scolarisation dans le primaire (les deux sexes) (000)
Female	2013	2 223	Féminin
Enrolment in secondary education (both sexes) (000)	2013	1 457	Scolarisation dans le secondaire (les deux sexes) (000)
Female	2013	715	Féminin
Enrolment in tertiary education (both sexes) (000)	2005	74.4	Scolarisation dans le tertiaire (les deux sexes) (000)
Female	2012	43.3	Féminin
Literacy rate (both sexes)	2009	64.5	Taux d'alphabétisation (deux sexes)
Male	2009	67.4	Masculin
Female	2009	61.6	Féminin
Pupil-teacher ratio	2006	43.2	Ratio élève-enseignant
Public expenditure on education (% of budget)	2012	20.3	Dépenses publiques consacrées à l'enseignement (% du budget)

GNI Per Capita (US$)
RNB par habitant ($EU)

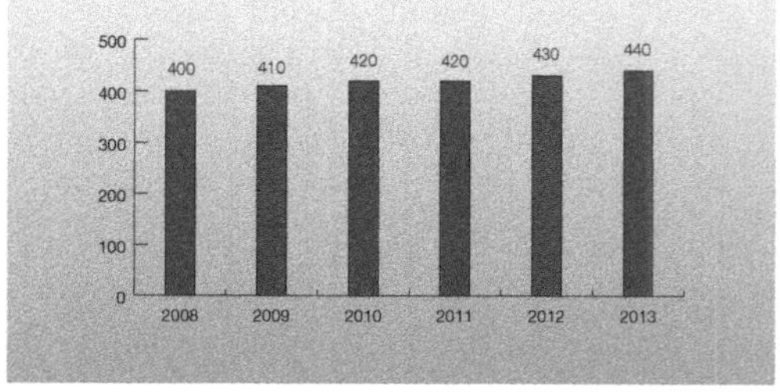

POVERTY	Year / Année	Value / Valeur	PAUVRETÉ
GNI Per Capita (US$)	2013	440.0	RNB par habitant ($EU)
Human Poverty Index (HPI-1) Value (%)	2007	36.1	Valeur de l'Indice de pauvreté (IPH-1) (%)
Population below International Poverty Line ($2/day) (%)	2010	95.1	Population sous le seuil international de pauvreté (2$/J) (%)
Share of Income Held by Richest 10%	2010	33.2	% de revenu des 10% plus riches
Share of Income Held by Poorest 10%	2010	2.6	% de revenu des 10% plus pauvres
Gini index	2010	40.6	Indice de Gini

II NATIONAL ACCOUNTS — COMPTES NATIONAUX

	2006	2007	2008	2009	2010	2011	2012	2013	2014	
GROSS DOMESTIC PRODUCT BY KIND OF ECONOMIC ACTIVITY AT CURRENT PRICES *ARIARY (BILLIONS)*										**PRODUIT INTÉRIEUR BRUT PAR BRANCHE D'ACTIVITÉ ÉCONOMIQUE AUX PRIX COURANTS** *ARIARY (MILLIARDS)*
Agriculture, hunting, forestry and fishing	2 969	3 219	3 589	4 490	4 701	5 201	5 612	5 684	6 276	Agriculture, chasse sylviculture et pêche
Mining and quarrying	19	16	17	16	24	29	40	62	89	Industries extractives
Manufacturing	1 597	1 877	2 131	2 250	2 431	2 682	2 908	3 116	3 419	Industries manufacturières
Electricity, gas & water	128	144	192	191	215	222	245	271	284	Electricité, gaz et eau
Construction & public works	403	547	709	647	654	703	718	724	760	Bâtiments et travaux publics
Wholesale & retail trade, restaurants, hotels	1 435	1 636	1 909	2 085	2 250	2 492	2 675	2 844	3 109	Commerce de gros et de détail, restaurants et hôtels
Finance, insurance, real estate, etc.	122	150	203	208	288	374	437	604	632	Banques, assurances, affaires immobilières
Transport and communications	2 111	2 977	3 100	3 071	3 534	3 863	4 366	5 192	5 617	Transport(s) et communications
Public administration and defense	522	619	650	664	769	876	952	1 097	1 345	Administrations publiques et défense
Education	223	262	286	280	317	349	376	421	501	Education
Health and Social Work	316	368	414	390	434	463	493	537	619	Santé et actions sociales
Other services	1 067	1 232	1 436	1 297	1 406	1 441	1 511	1 584	1 735	Autres services
Less Imputed Service Charges	- 108	- 135	- 187	- 182	- 267	- 360	- 432	- 623	- 656	Moins services d'intermédiation financière
Gross domestic product at factor cost / basic prices	10 805	12 913	14 451	15 407	16 755	18 333	19 900	21 514	23 729	Produit intérieur brut aux couts des facteurs / prix de base
Plus: indirect taxes / taxes on products, less subsidies	1 012	1 229	1 630	1 319	1 491	1 701	1 873	1 883	2 049	Plus taxes indirectes/impôts sur les produits, moins les subventions
EXPENDITURE ON GROSS DOMESTIC PRODUCT AT CURRENT PURCHASER'S VALUES *ARIARY (BILLIONS)*										**EMPLOI DU PRODUIT INTÉRIEUR BRUT AUX PRIX COURANTS D'ACQUISITION** *ARIARY (MILLIARDS)*
Government final consumption	1 058	1 691	1 492	1 581	1 941	2 041	2 100	2 269	2 806	Consommation finale des administrations publiques
Private final consumption	9 666	10 986	12 989	14 224	15 812	17 588	19 156	20 528	21 704	Consommation finale privée
Gross fixed capital formation	2 989	4 456	6 483	5 815	3 790	3 528	3 774	3 650	3 782	Formation brute de capital fixe
Change in inventories	...	...	...	...	...	...	...	...	...	Variation des stocks
Exports of goods and services	3 513	4 172	4 268	3 742	4 557	5 358	6 317	7 043	8 440	Exportations de biens et services
Less imports of goods and services	5 408	7 164	9 151	8 635	7 854	8 481	9 573	10 092	10 953	Moins importations de biens et services
GDP at purchasers' values	11 817	14 142	16 081	16 726	18 245	20 034	21 774	23 397	25 779	PIB aux prix d'acquisition
GROSS DOMESTIC PRODUCT BY KIND OF ECONOMIC ACTIVITY AT CONSTANT PRICES *ANNUAL GROWTH RATES (%)*										**PRODUIT INTÉRIEUR BRUT PAR BRANCHE D'ACTIVITÉ ECONOMIQUE AUX PRIX CONSTANTS** *TAUX DE CROISSANCE ANNUEL (%)*
Agriculture, hunting, forestry and fishing	2.1	2.2	2.9	8.5	- 3.4	0.7	1.5	- 6.1	3.3	Agriculture, chasse sylviculture et pêche
Mining and quarrying	9.1	- 7.2	9.0	- 8.9	55.3	31.1	183.2	219.2	26.2	Industries extractives
Manufacturing	3.3	10.8	3.0	- 8.8	- 2.1	3.9	2.7	1.7	2.8	Industries manufacturières
Electricity, gas & water	4.4	5.6	6.9	- 0.4	7.5	- 0.9	3.9	5.6	4.2	Electricité, gaz et eau
Construction & public works	27.6	21.8	27.6	- 17.7	2.6	3.7	3.4	- 2.2	3.1	Bâtiments et travaux publics
Wholesale & retail trade, restaurants, hotels	4.5	4.6	4.2	0.5	- 1.0	1.5	1.8	- 2.7	2.5	Commerce de gros et de détail,restaurants et hôtels
Finance, insurance, real estate, etc.	14.1	8.8	4.2	16.5	9.9	1.5	5.2	8.1	5.1	Banques, assurances, affaires immobilières
Transport and communications	7.8	8.2	8.1	- 9.0	2.9	- 2.3	5.1	4.5	2.2	Transport(s) et communications
Public administration and defense	2.1	3.0	3.0	- 5.0	1.0	1.0	1.1	1.0	2.0	Administrations publiques et défense
Education	3.4	4.9	5.1	- 8.9	0.9	0.0	1.0	0.9	1.7	Education
Health and Social Work	4.4	6.4	6.7	- 11.7	0.8	- 0.7	0.9	0.9	1.5	Santé et actions sociales
Other services	5.5	7.9	8.3	- 14.4	0.7	- 1.5	0.8	0.8	1.2	Autres services
Less Imputed Service Charges	14.2	8.9	4.0	16.7	9.7	1.3	5.3	8.1	5.3	Moins services d'intermédiation financière
Gross domestic product at factor cost / basic prices	4.9	6.1	6.0	- 3.0	- 0.6	0.6	3.2	1.4	3.5	Produit intérieur brut aux couts des facteurs / prix de base
Plus: indirect taxes / taxes on products, less subsidies	6.2	7.2	16.2	- 11.4	7.2	7.8	2.0	8.5	2.1	Plus taxes indirectes/impôts sur les produits, moins les subventions
Gross domestic product at market prices	5.0	6.2	7.1	- 4.0	0.3	1.5	3.0	2.3	3.3	Produit intérieur brut aux prix du marché
EXPENDITURE ON GROSS DOMESTIC PRODUCT AT CONSTANT PURCHASERS' VALUES *ANNUAL GROWTH RATES (%)*										**EMPLOIS DU PRODUIT INTÉRIEUR BRUT AUX PRIX CONSTANTS D'ACQUISITION** *TAUX DE CROISSANCE ANNUEL (%)*
Government final consumption	- 11.6	41.5	- 16.9	- 0.3	7.6	- 5.6	- 3.4	- 4.1	6.4	Consommation finale des administrations publiques
Private final consumption	1.5	0.3	7.6	0.1	0.8	1.6	3.3	0.5	1.4	Consommation finale privée
Gross fixed capital formation	19.3	20.8	52.8	- 18.9	- 12.3	1.3	5.8	- 2.7	2.2	Formation brute de capital fixe
Exports of goods and services	17.2	32.7	- 6.9	- 11.3	3.1	7.8	1.8	32.4	8.0	Exportations de biens et services
Less imports of goods and services	4.9	28.3	26.1	- 12.1	- 6.1	3.4	3.6	10.3	1.8	Moins importations de biens et services
Notes	NA data: 2013: Revised;2014:Provisional								Données des CN: 2013: Révisées;2014:Provisoires	Notes

III INFLATION

	2006	2007	2008	2009	2010	2011	2012	2013	2014	
ANNUAL GROWTH RATES (%)										**TAUX DE CROISSANCE ANNUEL (%)**
All items	10.8	10.3	9.2	9.0	9.2	9.5	5.7	5.8	6.1	Ensemble
of which:										dont:
Food and Non-alcoholic beverages	4.2	14.1	10.5	8.3	6.5	13.3	5.2	5.0	5.4	Alimentation et boissons non alcoolisés
Alcoholic beverages & tobacco	...	...	...	...	...	...	...	...	...	Boissons alcoolisées et tabacs
Clothing and Footwear	11.6	6.0	6.7	15.6	15.2	3.6	6.6	8.4	8.7	Habillement et chaussures
Housing, Water, Electricity, Gas and Other Fuels	23.0	5.8	9.2	11.6	12.4	6.7	7.6	6.1	6.6	Logement, eau, électricité, gas et autres combustibles
Furnishing, household equip	13.9	7.2	5.6	14.7	20.4	-0.8	4.5	4.2	3.3	Meubles, articles de ménage et entretien courant
Health	8.4	9.5	10.8	9.8	19.1	8.1	7.6	5.6	6.1	Santé
Transport	19.6	6.9	8.0	2.5	3.0	3.1	2.6	4.5	4.6	Transport
Communication	...	...	...	...	...	...	...	...	...	Communication
Recreation & culture	11.2	7.9	5.4	4.6	13.3	-5.7	2.6	6.8	7.2	Loisirs et culture
Education	7.3	9.9	6.7	6.9	14.5	14.7	11.1	13.6	9.9	Enseignement
Restaurants & hotels	25.3	6.1	8.0	9.5	17.1	8.2	3.8	8.5	8.0	Restaurants et hôtels
Miscellaneous goods & services	10.3	7.4	6.8	8.4	8.6	10.1	9.4	9.8	11.7	Biens et services divers

IV AGRICULTURAL PRODUCTION - PRODUCTION AGRICOLE

	2006	2007	2008	2009	2010	2011	2012	2013	2014	
TONNES *(THOUSAND)*										**TONNES** *(MILLIERS)*
Rice	3 488	3 596	3 914	4 540	4 738	4 300	4 551	3 611	...	Riz
Cassava	2 982	2 994	3 021	3 020	3 009	3 490	3 621	3 115	...	Manioc
Bananas	315	325	306	352	361	350	356	355	...	Bananes
Maize	405	417	430	425	412	428	448	381	...	Maïs
Sugar cane	2 691	2 600	2 500	3 000	3 000	3 050	3 270	3 250	...	Canne à sucre

V MINING PRODUCTION - PRODUCTION MINIERE

	2006	2007	2008	2009	2010	2011	2012	2013	2014	
Gold ores and concentrates (Kilograms)	...	5 695	25 148	...	...	...	...	...	...	Minerais d'or et leurs concentrés (Kilogrammes)
Chromium ores and concentrates, metric tons (thousands)	...	0	2	...	...	...	...	...	...	Minerai de chrome et concentrés, tonnes métriques (milliers)
Ilmenite, metric tons (thousands)	490	530	315	...	...	...	...	...	...	Ilménite, tonnes métriques (milliers)

VI ENERGY - ENERGIE

	2006	2007	2008	2009	2010	2011	2012	2013	2014	
Total electricity generation (GWh)	1 008	1 056	1 247	1 242	1 196	3 469	2 349	2 422	...	Production d'électricité totale (GWh)
of which:										dont:
Production of electricity from fossil fuels (GWh)	366	333	540	501	478	1 482	1 512	1 542	...	Production d'électricité à partir de combustibles fossiles (GWh)
Production of hydro electricity (GWh)	638	719	700	734	711	1 967	817	858	...	Production d'électricité d'origine hydraulique (GWh)
Production of electricity from solar, wind, tide, wave and other sources (GWh)	4	4	7	7	7	19	20	21	...	Production d'électricité d'origine solaire, éolienne, marée motrice et autres (GWh)

VII TOURISM AND INFRASTRUCTURE - TOURISME ET INFRASTRUCTURE

	2006	2007	2008	2009	2010	2011	2012	2013	2014	
VII-1 TOURISM										**VII-1 TOURISME**
International tourist arrivals (thousands)	312	344	375	163	196	225	256	196	218	Arrivées de touristes internationaux (milliers)
Rooms in hotels and similar establishments (thousands)	11.9	13.3	14.4	16.1	17.6	19.1	20.5	...	...	Chambres d'hotels et établissements assimilés (milliers)
Overnight stays (thousands)	10 570	11 060	11 336	4 777	6 376	7 481	8 571	6 518	7 289	Nuitées (milliers)
Tourism receipts (US$ thousand)	236 000	261 000	350 000	307 000	320 000	397 386	426 976	447 292	679 929	Recettes touristiques (milliers de $ EU)
Total contribution to GDP (%)	11.9	13.4	13.1	13.0	14.8	14.4	15.4	15.2	19.5	Contribution totale au PIB (%)
Total contribution to Employment (%)	10.1	11.5	11.2	11.2	12.3	11.9	12.9	12.7	16.4	Contribution totale à l'emploi (%)
VII-2 INFRASTRUCTURE										**VII-2 INFRASTRUCTURE**
Paved roads (% of total)	...	...	...	16	16	16	...	...	...	Routes asphaltées (% du total)
Total Network (Railways-km)	...	848	...	...	...	...	...	...	...	Réseau total voies ferrées-Km
Main Telephone Lines (per 100 inhabitants)	1	1	1	1	1	1	1	1	...	Lignes téléphoniques fixes (pour 100 habitants)
Mobile Cellular Subscribers (per 100 inhabitants)	6	11	24	31	37	40	39	37	...	Abonnés aux téléphones mobiles (pour 100 habitants)

VIII EXTERNAL TRADE - COMMERCE EXTERIEUR

	2006	2007	2008	2009	2010	2011	2012	2013	2014	
ARIARY EXPORTS, FOB										**ARIARY (MILLIARDS) EXPORTATIONS, FÀB**
Exports - Total	2 112	2 518	2 866	2 146	2 246	2 983	3 299	...	...	Exportations - Total
Exports to AFRICA	...	...	...	...	...	...	...	...	...	Exportations vers l'AFRIQUE
Main Products										**Principaux produits**
Petroleum products	89	167	104	167	95	65	65	...	...	Produits pétroliers
Shrimps and prawns	203	256	233	187	153	65	65	...	...	Crevettes
Shirts, blouses	36	48	69	155	66	65	59	...	...	Chemises, chemisettes
Chrome ore	21	28	22	56	33	51	37	...	...	Minerai de chrome
Vanilla	95	101	104	86	87	37	30	...	...	Vanille
Main Destinations										**Principales destinations**
France	800	1 037	1 241	674	704	1 682	1 805	...	...	France
Germany	127	127	185	137	164	306	329	...	...	Allemagne
China	47	50	90	103	118	738	783	...	...	Chine
United States	318	436	624	384	92	259	280	...	...	Etats-Unis
Italy	87	88	70	55	64	234	253	...	...	Italie
IMPORTS, CIF										**IMPORTATIONS, CAF**
Imports - Total	3 724	4 528	6 532	6 189	5 305	1 406	1 871	...	...	Importations - Total (millions)
Imports from Africa	...	...	...	...	...	...	...	...	...	Importations en provenance de l'Afrique
Main Products										**Principaux produits**
Other petroleum products	650	710	800	600	750	1 127	1 191	...	...	Autres produits pétroliers
Plastics	117	129	171	120	155	152	171	...	...	Matières plastiques
Pharmaceutical products	98	94	113	118	138	128	125	...	...	Produits pharmaceutiques
Rebars and laminates	94	91	207	136	113	129	116	...	...	Fers à béton et laminés
Rice	86	114	126	93	112	173	184	...	...	Riz
Main Origin										Principales provenances
France	485	474	577	599	710	...	...	...	...	France
China	662	864	1 374	695	646	...	...	...	...	Chine
South Africa	216	240	405	277	410	77	77	...	...	Afrique du Sud
Mauritius	115	135	145	288	278	...	...	...	...	Maurice, île
Germany	92	110	274	136	119	77	129	...	...	Allemagne

IX FINANCIAL AND MONETARY STATISTICS - FINANCES ET STATISTIQUES MONETAIRES

	2006	2007	2008	2009	2010	2011	2012	2013	2014	
IX-1 MONETARY STATISTICS *ARIARY (MILLIONS)*										**IX-1 STATISTIQUES MONÉTAIRES** *ARIARY (MILLIONS)*
Money supply (M1)	1 062 990	1 404 650	1 585 390	1 643 170	1 893 280	2 378 250	2 612 110	2 452 810	5 894 420	Masse monétaire (M1)
Quasi-money	818 249	1 031 676	1 241 245	1 497 797	1 661 577	1 749 856	1 963 858	2 026 697	2 320 599	Quasi-monnaie
of which Demand Deposit	...	...	...	...	...	...	...	...	...	dont Monnaie scripturale
Net foreign assets	1 525 576	1 846 135	2 098 270	1 924 641	2 307 952	2 625 962	2 530 094	1 779 374	2 087 203	Avoirs extérieurs nets
Domestic credit	1 138 300	1 371 321	1 507 689	1 951 522	1 911 702	2 368 453	2 827 916	3 662 433	4 300 956	Crédit intérieur
of which claims on private sector	1 191 327	1 397 752	1 796 359	1 926 169	2 133 735	2 206 138	2 398 532	2 792 644	3 319 051	dont créances sur le secteur privé
of which claims on government sector, net	- 57 582	- 31 128	- 293 687	19 764	- 228 821	154 566	420 739	860 753	973 625	dont créances nettes sur le gouvernement
International reserves (millions US$)	583	847	982	982	1 023	1 135	1 053	776	774	Réserves internationales (millions $EU)
Average Exchange Rate (National Currency per US$)	2 182.84	1 857.65	1 714.47	1 978.40	2 112.59	2 027.12	2 199.10	2 218.26	2 267.95	Taux de change (moyen) (monnaie nationale par $ EU)
IX-2 PUBLIC FINANCE *ARIARY (BILLIONS)*										**IX-2 FINANCES PUBLIQUES** *ARIARY (MILLIARDS)*
Total Revenues and Grants	1 888	2 201	2 488	1 927	2 404	2 339	2 358	2 550	3 075	Recettes totales et dons
Tax Revenue	1 261	1 573	1 890	1 570	1 781	1 912	1 978	2 183	2 480	Recettes fiscales
Non Tax Revenue	62	35	50	80	268	36	118	71	75	Recettes non fiscales
Grants	565	593	548	278	355	390	263	296	521	Dons
Total Expenditures and Net Lending	2 515	2 570	2 999	2 353	2 562	2 817	2 927	3 483	3 571	Dépenses totales et prêts nets
Current expenditure	1 302	1 520	1 754	1 540	1 648	1 975	2 332	2 753	2 604	Dépenses courantes
Of which Wages and Salaries	590	711	759	803	945	1 060	1 167	1 342	1 587	Dont rémunérations et salaires
Capital expenditure	1 214	1 050	1 245	813	915	842	595	731	992	Dépenses d'équipement
Net Lending	-	-	-	0	-	-	-	-	- 25	Prêts nets
Fiscal Balance	- 627	- 369	- 511	- 426	- 159	- 478	- 569	- 933	- 496	Solde global y compris les dons
IX-3 BALANCE OF PAYMENTS *ARIARY (BILLIONS)*										**IX-3 BALANCE DES PAIEMENTS** *ARIARY (MILLIARDS)*
Trade balance	- 1 211	- 1 873	- 3 251	- 3 262	- 2 246	- 1 905	- 1 970	- 1 814	...	Balance commerciale
Services Balance	- 258	- 330	- 664	- 697	- 299	- 313	- 531	- 108	...	Balance des services
Net Income	- 177	- 105	- 86	- 179	- 181	- 350	- 560	- 743	...	Revenus nets
Compensation of employees	...	...	...	...	...	...	...	...	...	Rémunération des salariés
Investment Income	...	...	...	...	...	...	...	...	...	Revenus des investissements
Current transfers, net total	455	567	692	599	1 016	1 192	1 238	1 399	...	Transferts courants
Net official transfers	...	...	...	...	...	...	...	...	...	Transferts officiels nets
Workers' remittances	...	...	...	...	...	...	...	...	...	Envois de fonds des travailleurs
Other private transfers	...	...	...	...	...	...	...	...	...	Autres transferts privés
Current account balance	- 1 191	- 1 741	- 3 309	- 3 538	- 1 710	- 1 376	- 1 823	- 1 267	...	Solde du compte courant
Capital & financial account	...	...	...	...	...	...	...	...	...	Comptes de capital et financier
Capital account	...	...	...	...	...	...	...	...	...	Compte de capital
Financial account	...	...	...	...	...	...	...	...	...	Compte financier
Errors & omissions	...	...	...	...	...	...	...	...	...	Erreurs et omissions
Overall balance	...	...	...	...	...	...	...	...	...	Balance générale

X DEBT AND FINANCIAL FLOWS - DETTE ET FLUX FINANCIERS										
	2006	2007	2008	2009	2010	2011	2012	2013	2014	
X-1 DEBT *US$ (MILLIONS)*										**X-1 DETTE EXTÉRIEURE** *$ E.U (MILLIONS)*
Total external debt	1 964	2 627	3 660	4 749	5 135	3 894	4 384	4 651	4 728	Dette extérieure totale
Private	374	722	1 453	2 235	2 632	1 755	2 084	2 276	2 129	Privée
Public	1 590	1 906	2 206	2 514	2 503	2 139	2 301	2 375	2 599	Publique
Total external debt service	2 212	99	129	195	302	607	711	769	772	Service de la dette extérieure
Present value of External debt	...	...	...	...	...	...	...	...	...	Valeur actuelle de la dette extérieure
Total government domestic debt (in local currency)	...	...	...	...	...	...	...	...	...	Dette publique intérieure
X-2 FINANCIAL FLOWS *US$ (MILLIONS)*										**X-2 FLUX FINANCIERS** *$ E.U (MILLIONS)*
Net Foreign Direct Investment Inflows	295	773	1 169	1 066	808	810	812	838	...	Investissements étranger direct (flux nets entrants)
Main origin of FDI Inflows										**Principales origines de l'IDE entrant:**
Korea	30	134	110	286	162.0	293.9	270.1	...	...	Corée
France	74	...	...	...	...	...	...	...	...	France
Japan	...	...	...	...	...	...	...	...	...	Japon
Italy	...	1	44	- 31	- 0.5	0.4	30.6	...	...	Italie
Germany	...	...	...	- 1	1.3	5.6	3.9	...	...	Allemagne
African countries	...	...	...	...	...	...	...	...	...	Pays africains
Net total Official Development Assistance	782	894	843	444	470	443	379	500	...	Aide publique au développement (nette totale)
Main origin of Net ODA										**Principales origines de l'APD nette**
IDA	178	209	216	36	79.0	44.2	46.8	...	...	IDA
France	104	142	88	97	84.0	89.3	73.4	75.4	...	France
United States	61	67	84	77	77.0	66.4	52.4	55.9	...	Etats-Unis
AfDF	122	42	79	33	13.8	22.4	8.0	...	...	FAfD
Japan	39	111	20	19	9.6	10.7	13.7	50.6	...	Japon

AREA (KM²)	118 484		**SUPERFICIE (KM²)**
CAPITAL CITY	Lilongwe	Lilongwe	**CAPITALE**
CURRENCY	Kwacha	Kwacha	**MONNAIE**

I SOCIAL AND DEMOGRAPHIC INDICATORS — INDICATEURS DEMOGRAPHIQUES ET SOCIAUX

	Year / Année	Value / Valeur	
POPULATION			**POPULATION**
Population ('000)			Population ('000)
Both sexes	2014	16 829	Les deux sexes
Male	2014	8 440	Masculin
Female	2014	8 390	Féminin
Average annual growth rate	2014	2.8	Taux de croissance annuel
Active Population ('000)	2014	7 121	Population active ('000)
Population by age group ('000)			Population par groupe d'âge ('000)
0-14 years	2014	7 576	0-14 ans
15-64 years	2014	8 708	15-64 ans
65+ years	2014	545	65+ ans
Economically active population in agriculture (%)	2014	78.2	Participation de la population active agricole (%)
Crude birth rate	2014	39.4	Taux brut de natalité
Crude death rate	2014	11.1	Taux brut de mortalité
Total fertility rate	2014	5.3	Indice synthétique de fécondité
Proportion of urban population	2014	16.1	Part de la population urbaine
Life Expectancy at Birth - Total (years)	2014	55.8	Espérance de vie à la naissance - Totale (ans)
Dependency Ratio - Total (%)	2014	96.7	Taux de dépendance - Total (%)
HEALTH			**SANTÉ**
Percentage of children under-five and underweight	2010	13.8	% d'enfants de moins de cinq ans avec insuffisance pondérale
Prevalence of undernourishment	2013	21.8	Prévalence de la malnutrition
Under five mortality rate (both sexes, per 1000)	2013	67.9	Taux de mortalité de moins de 5 ans (les deux sexes, pour 1000)
Infant mortality rate (both sexes) per 1000	2013	44.2	Taux de mortalité infantile (les deux sexes) par 1000
Percentage of children provided the vaccines :			Pourcentage d'enfants vaccinés :
BCG	2013	96.0	BCG
DPT3	2013	89.0	DTC3
Polio	2013	79.0	Polio
Measles	2013	88.0	Rougeole
Percentage of mothers provided at least one antenatal care (%)	2010	94.7	Pourcentage de mères ayant au moins reçu un soin prénatal (%)
Percentage of deliveries attended by skilled health personnel	2010	71.4	% d'accouchements assistés par un personnel de santé qualifié
Number of doctors (per 10 000 population)	2009	0.2	Nombre de médecins (pour 10 000 habitants)
Number of nurses (per 10 000 population)	2009	3.4	Nombre d'infirmières (pour 10 000 habitants)
Hospital beds - Total (per 10 000 population)	2011	13.0	Nombre de lits d'hôpitaux - Total (pour 10 000)
Births registered (per 1 000)	2014	39.4	Naiss.s enregistrées (pour 1 000)
Deaths registered (per 1 000)	2014	11.1	Décès enregistrés (pour 1 000)
Public expenditure on Health (% of budget)	2014	10.0	Dépenses publiques consacrées à la santé (% du budget)
EDUCATION			**EDUCATION**
Enrolment in primary education (both sexes) (000)	2013	3 952	Scolarisation dans le primaire (les deux sexes) (000)
Female	2013	1 989	Féminin
Enrolment in secondary education (both sexes) (000)	2013	853	Scolarisation dans le secondaire (les deux sexes) (000)
Female	2013	403	Féminin
Enrolment in tertiary education (both sexes) (000)	2013	8.7	Scolarisation dans le tertiaire (les deux sexes) (000)
Female	2011	4.8	Féminin
Literacy rate (both sexes)	2010	61.3	Taux d'alphabétisation (deux sexes)
Male	2010	72.1	Masculin
Female	2010	51.3	Féminin
Pupil-teacher ratio	2014	70.0	Ratio élève-enseignant
Public expenditure on education (% of budget)	2014	24.0	Dépenses publiques consacrées à l'enseignement (% du budget)
POVERTY			**PAUVRETÉ**
GNI Per Capita (US$)	2013	270.0	RNB par habitant ($EU)
Human Poverty Index (HPI-1) Value (%)	2007	28.2	Valeur de l'Indice de pauvreté (IPH-1) (%)
Population below International Poverty Line ($2/day) (%)	2010	88.1	Population sous le seuil international de pauvreté (2$/J) (%)
Share of Income Held by Richest 10%	2010	37.5	% de revenu des 10% plus riches
Share of Income Held by Poorest 10%	2010	2.2	% de revenu des 10% plus pauvres
Gini index	2010	46.2	Indice de Gini

Charts / Graphiques

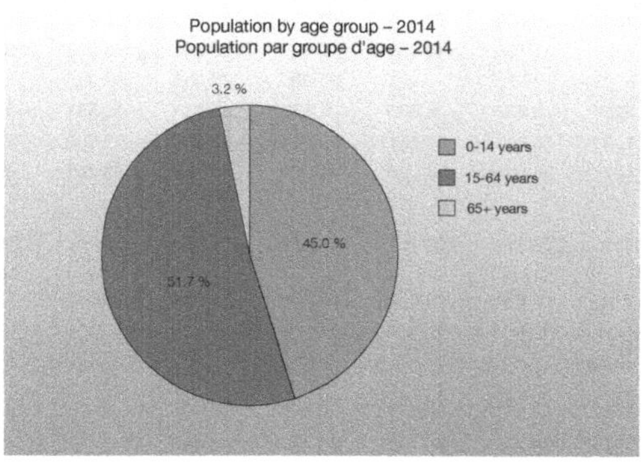

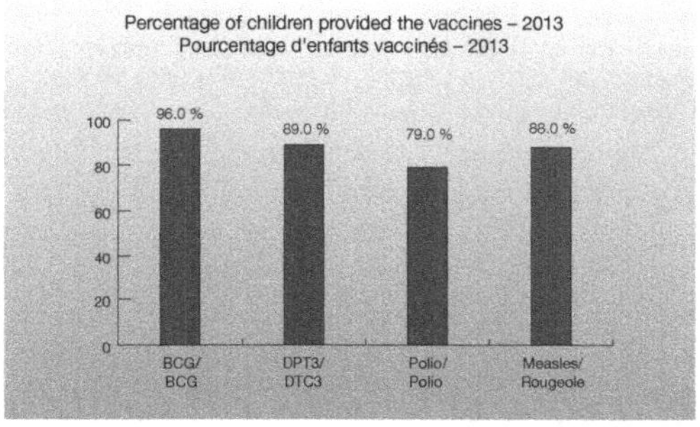

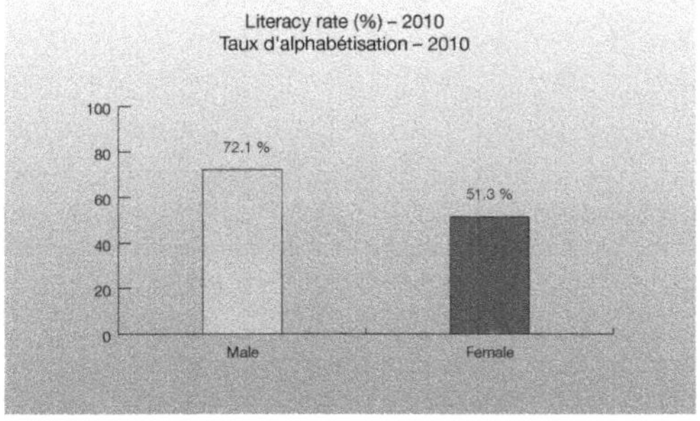

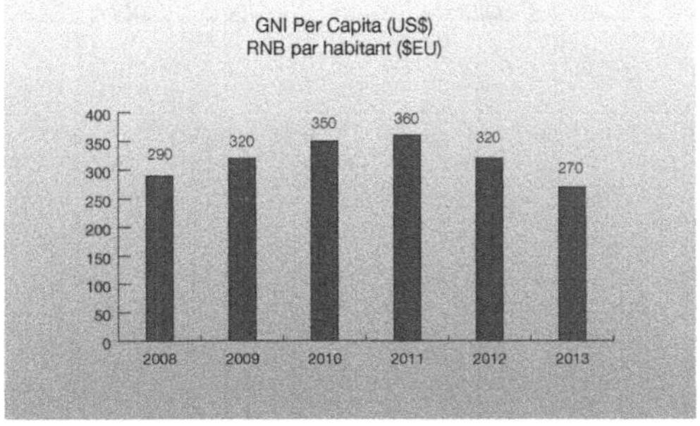

II NATIONAL ACCOUNTS — COMPTES NATIONAUX

	2006	2007	2008	2009	2010	2011	2012	2013	2014	
GROSS DOMESTIC PRODUCT BY KIND OF ECONOMIC ACTIVITY AT CURRENT PRICES *KWACHA (MILLIONS)*										**PRODUIT INTÉRIEUR BRUT PAR BRANCHE D'ACTIVITÉ ÉCONOMIQUE AUX PRIX COURANTS** *KWACHA (MILLIONS)*
Agriculture, hunting, forestry and fishing	167 852	170 686	224 136	265 944	310 167	360 446	381 562	491 554	...	Agriculture, chasse sylviculture et pêche
Mining and quarrying	3 747	4 647	4 460	7 156	10 528	12 393	16 816	19 098	...	Industries extractives
Manufacturing	67 451	86 544	87 620	90 708	103 789	126 146	105 091	163 572	...	Industries manufacturières
Electricity, gas & water	4 785	6 913	9 749	11 738	13 640	17 374	21 894	22 576	...	Electricité, gaz et eau
Construction & public works	12 659	14 019	18 318	24 385	31 393	37 183	45 786	87 398	...	Bâtiments et travaux publics
Wholesale & retail trade, restaurants, hotels	74 666	99 694	146 651	156 761	181 450	229 580	274 545	370 651	...	Commerce de gros et de détail, restaurants et hôtels
Finance, insurance, real estate, etc.	56 185	68 639	79 318	103 875	134 876	156 253	237 298	299 750	...	Banques, assurances, affaires immobilières
Transport and communications	26 842	31 738	40 028	49 608	65 576	75 000	93 802	113 774	...	Transport(s) et communications
Public administration and defense	20 610	18 977	13 153	13 960	20 058	39 303	34 802	38 257	...	Administrations publiques et défense
Education	12 398	13 632	18 665	22 668	25 135	28 551	33 480	59 742	...	Education
Health and Social Work	18 120	18 047	17 351	22 713	27 229	32 009	36 405	45 638	...	Santé et actions sociales
Other services	22 492	25 081	33 702	40 964	47 768	39 261	69 049	77 987	...	Autres services
Less Imputed Service Charges	...	...	...	...	...	...	...	...	...	Moins services d'intermédiation financière
Gross domestic product at factor cost / basic prices	487 806	558 617	693 151	810 479	971 608	1 153 499	1 350 529	1 789 995	...	Produit intérieur brut aux couts des facteurs / prix de base
Plus: indirect taxes / taxes on products, less subsidies	55 979	61 805	54 572	63 504	75 728	99 251	74 597	111 109	...	Plus taxes indirectes/impôts sur les produits, moins les subventions
EXPENDITURE ON GROSS DOMESTIC PRODUCT AT CURRENT PURCHASER'S VALUES *KWACHA (MILLIONS)*										**EMPLOI DU PRODUIT INTÉRIEUR BRUT AUX PRIX COURANTS D'ACQUISITION** *KWACHA (MILLIONS)*
Government final consumption	59 481	75 781	92 270	107 993	95 281	...	...	...	...	Consommation finale des administrations publiques
Private final consumption	482 452	559 378	665 123	813 241	1 021 561	...	...	...	...	Consommation finale privée
Gross fixed capital formation	90 109	95 537	158 401	142 538	159 734	...	...	...	...	Formation brute de capital fixe
Change in inventories	20 046	- 21 688	24 897	- 25 796	10 129	...	...	...	...	Variation des stocks
Exports of goods and services	91 310	124 100	140 932	187 363	183 055	...	...	...	...	Exportations de biens et services
Less imports of goods and services	199 614	212 687	333 899	351 357	422 425	...	...	...	...	Moins importations de biens et services
GDP at purchasers' values	543 784	620 422	747 723	873 982	1 047 336	1 252 750	1 425 126	1 901 104	...	PIB aux prix d'acquisition
GROSS DOMESTIC PRODUCT BY KIND OF ECONOMIC ACTIVITY AT CONSTANT PRICES *ANNUAL GROWTH RATES (%)*										**PRODUIT INTÉRIEUR BRUT PAR BRANCHE D'ACTIVITÉ ECONOMIQUE AUX PRIX CONSTANTS** *TAUX DE CROISSANCE ANNUEL (%)*
Agriculture, hunting, forestry and fishing	0.4	11.2	3.6	4.0	6.8	4.3	1.0	6.2	...	Agriculture, chasse sylviculture et pêche
Mining and quarrying	82.2	8.6	- 8.2	17.6	23.9	1.4	5.3	6.9	...	Industries extractives
Manufacturing	7.8	17.1	11.0	29.1	11.4	1.4	- 0.9	5.6	...	Industries manufacturières
Electricity, gas & water	- 7.0	2.0	- 4.0	2.3	2.9	6.0	- 0.9	5.5	...	Electricité, gaz et eau
Construction & public works	12.9	13.9	12.9	1.8	- 2.4	2.3	0.7	2.0	...	Bâtiments et travaux publics
Wholesale & retail trade, restaurants, hotels	10.2	22.6	13.5	8.7	3.1	3.8	1.2	7.6	...	Commerce de gros et de détail,restaurants et hôtels
Finance, insurance, real estate, etc.	10.6	2.7	11.3	7.6	10.0	7.2	3.8	3.0	...	Banques, assurances, affaires immobilières
Transport and communications	14.6	12.3	15.3	3.9	9.3	3.7	5.5	6.6	...	Transport(s) et communications
Public administration and defense	4.0	- 4.0	- 5.1	7.3	8.9	80.2	- 38.4	2.7	...	Administrations publiques et défense
Education	- 31.0	1.5	12.5	11.1	7.6	4.3	7.3	5.4	...	Education
Health and Social Work	- 25.0	- 2.8	- 2.2	14.1	11.7	6.0	1.9	5.1	...	Santé et actions sociales
Other services	- 2.0	5.6	9.2	9.0	5.1	- 25.2	49.2	5.5	...	Autres services
Less Imputed Service Charges	...	...	...	...	...	...	...	...	...	Moins services d'intérmediation financière
Gross domestic product at factor cost / basic prices	3.0	10.9	8.0	8.3	7.0	4.3	2.0	5.7	...	Produit intérieur brut aux couts des facteurs / prix de base
Plus: indirect taxes / taxes on products, less subsidies	26.6	- 4.2	3.2	8.7	5.2	11.4	- 32.3	17.0	...	Plus taxes indirectes/impôts sur les produits, moins les subventions
Gross domestic product at market prices	4.7	9.6	7.6	8.3	6.9	4.9	- 0.6	6.3	...	Produit intérieur brut aux prix du marché
EXPENDITURE ON GROSS DOMESTIC PRODUCT AT CONSTANT PURCHASERS' VALUES *ANNUAL GROWTH RATES (%)*										**EMPLOIS DU PRODUIT INTÉRIEUR BRUT AUX PRIX CONSTANTS D'ACQUISITION** *TAUX DE CROISSANCE ANNUEL (%)*
Government final consumption	- 3.2	37.3	10.2	3.3	- 26.9	...	...	...	...	Consommation finale des administrations publiques
Private final consumption	7.9	3.3	2.9	9.8	3.5	...	...	...	...	Consommation finale privée
Gross fixed capital formation	50.0	15.9	22.2	- 32.5	- 7.0	...	...	...	...	Formation brute de capital fixe
Exports of goods and services	0.1	23.8	- 5.5	13.6	- 2.3	...	...	...	...	Exportations de biens et services
Less imports of goods and services	16.7	17.1	18.7	- 19.6	- 9.4	...	...	...	...	Moins importations de biens et services

III INFLATION

	2006	2007	2008	2009	2010	2011	2012	2013	2014	
ANNUAL GROWTH RATES (%)										**TAUX DE CROISSANCE ANNUEL (%)**
All items	13.9	8.0	8.7	8.4	7.4	7.6	21.3	27.3	23.8	Ensemble
of which:										dont:
Food and Non-alcoholic beverages	15.5	7.5	6.9	7.4	5.1	3.2	18.8	23.3	21.2	Alimentation et boissons non alcoolisés
Alcoholic beverages & tobacco	13.7	10.6	9.4	11.5	13.1	10.4	18.1	27.0	11.9	Boissons alcoolisées et tabacs
Clothing and Footwear	8.3	5.9	7.4	9.0	7.9	10.2	12.9	24.2	20.0	Habillement et chaussures
Housing, Water, Electricity, Gas and Other Fuels	12.7	9.2	9.5	2.9	6.7	12.1	33.9	41.5	32.3	Logement, eau, électricité, gas et autres combustibles
Furnishing, household equip	16.5	7.2	14.1	18.1	13.1	10.2	20.7	25.0	34.3	Meubles, articles de ménage et entretien courant
Health	...	...	...	...	...	...	...	18.7	17.4	Santé
Transport	13.7	10.5	17.3	12.1	12.7	17.0	21.0	23.5	22.5	Transport
Communication	...	...	...	...	...	...	...	30.6	30.8	Communication
Recreation & culture	...	...	...	...	...	...	...	39.5	38.7	Loisirs et culture
Education	...	...	...	...	...	...	...	26.9	4.0	Enseignement
Restaurants & hotels	...	...	...	...	...	...	...	94.4	19.2	Restaurants et hôtels
Miscellaneous goods & services	8.2	7.1	9.8	13.3	9.4	14.6	18.1	18.1	12.0	Biens et services divers

	2006	2007	2008	2009	2010	2011	2012	2013	2014	
IV AGRICULTURAL PRODUCTION - PRODUCTION AGRICOLE										
TONNES *(THOUSAND)*										**TONNES** *(MILLIERS)*
Maize	2 611	3 445	2 777	3 767	3 419	3 895	3 624	3 640	3 978	Maïs
Tobacco	155	111	195	232	220	237	73	133	139	Tabac
Tea	45	48	42	53	52	47	42	46	...	Thé
Sugar cane	2 450	2 500	2 750	2 600	2 500	2 500	2 800	2 900	...	Cane à sucre
Rice	91	113	115	301	110	118	110	125	115	Riz
V MINING PRODUCTION - PRODUCTION MINIERE										
	2006	2007	2008	2009	2010	2011	2012	2013	2014	
Coal, metric tons (thousands)	60	59	61	59	79	77	71	67	64	Houilles, tonnes métriques (milliers)
Gemstones (kilograms)	24 208	31 490	57 477	47 150	57 296	60 161	64 100	60 895	57 850	Pierres précieuses (kilogrammes)
Cement, metric tons (thousands)	21	21	23	26	32	33	22	21	20	Ciments, tonnes métriques (milliers)
VI ENERGY - ENERGIE										
	2006	2007	2008	2009	2010	2011	2012	2013	2014	
Total electricity generation (GWh)	1 551	1 585	1 763	1 899	1 943	1 745	2 180	2 442	...	Production d'électricité totale (GWh)
of which:										dont:
Production of electricity from fossil fuels (GWh)	212	218	242	240	210	6	7	43	...	Production d'électricité à partir de combustibles fossiles (GWh)
Production of hydro electricity (GWh)	1 339	1 367	1 521	1 659	1 733	1 733	2 164	2 380	...	Production d'électricité d'origine hydraulique (GWh)
Production of electricity from solar, wind, tide, wave and other sources (GWh)	...	...	...	...	...	3	3	12	...	Production d'électricité d'origine solaire, éolienne, marée motrice et autres (GWh)
VII TOURISM AND INFRASTRUCTURE - TOURISME ET INFRASTRUCTURE										
	2006	2007	2008	2009	2010	2011	2012	2013	2014	
VII-1 TOURISM										**VII-1 TOURISME**
International tourist arrivals (thousands)	638	735	742	755	746	767	751	679	756	Arrivées de touristes internationaux (milliers)
Rooms in hotels and similar establishments (thousands)	...	...	...	...	...	...	...	...	...	Chambres d'hotels et établissements assimilés (milliers)
Overnight stays (thousands)	5 570	5 460	5 864	5 167	6 057	5 821	5 395	4 771	5 294	Nuitées (milliers)
Tourism receipts (US$ thousand)	23 912	27 100	29 100	31 000	31 100	31 600	31 800	29 178	31 020	Recettes touristiques (milliers de $ EU)
Total contribution to GDP (%)	6.8	7.7	7.1	8.0	7.9	7.6	7.2	7.4	7.2	Contribution totale au PIB (%)
Total contribution to Employment (%)	5.5	6.6	5.7	6.5	6.4	6.6	6.2	6.4	6.2	Contribution totale à l'emploi (%)
VII-2 INFRASTRUCTURE										**VII-2 INFRASTRUCTURE**
Paved roads (% of total)	23	23	25	26	...	...	...	...	...	Routes asphaltées (% du total)
Total Network (Railways-km)	767	767	767	767	767	767	...	...	...	Réseau total voies ferrées-Km
Main Telephone Lines (per 100 inhabitants)	1	1	1	1	1	1	1	0	...	Lignes téléphoniques fixes (pour 100 habitants)
Mobile Cellular Subscribers (per 100 inhabitants)	5	8	11	17	21	26	29	32	...	Abonnés aux téléphones mobiles (pour 100 habitants)
VIII EXTERNAL TRADE - COMMERCE EXTERIEUR										
	2006	2007	2008	2009	2010	2011	2012	2013	2014	
KWACHA (MILLIONS) **EXPORTS, FOB**										**KWACHA (MILLIONS)** **EXPORTATIONS, FÀB**
Exports - Total	73 804	99 804	123 399	167 688	159 214	222 386	302 333	434 797	...	Exportations - Total
Exports to AFRICA	35 052	48 649	32 947	54 164	50 049	84 183	79 564	112 984	...	Exportations vers l'AFRIQUE
Main Products										**Principaux produits**
Tobacco	...	...	...	...	...	...	...	...	...	Tabac
Tea	6 752	7 817	5 188	11 051	12 079	13 518	17 318	31 013	...	Thé
Sugar	5 191	8 480	7 138	9 907	10 324	30 401	10 171	41 176	...	Sucre
Cotton	1 986	3 227	3 102	3 776	2 301	7 360	13 331	22	...	Coton
Nuts	3 189	3 347	1 503	3 915	2 424	6 447	13 366	26 769	...	Noix
Main Destinations										**Principales destinations**
South Africa	20 367	17 979	12 454	17 175	9 154	18 090	22 400	32 839	...	Afrique du Sud
USA	7 914	5 014	6 687	6 786	9 472	11 847	11 957	27 831	...	Etats-Unis
Germany	10 766	6 989	5 158	5 435	9 828	7 250	16 759	16 519	...	Allemagne
UK	11 996	8 000	11 024	7 116	7 281	17 132	9 912	25 466	...	Royaume-Uni
Japan	296	152	47	155	347	241	506	508	...	Japon
IMPORTS, CIF										**IMPORTATIONS, CAF**
Imports - Total	162 505	156 387	278 477	255 118	325 790	380 545	661 179	1 031 020	...	Importations - Total (millions)
Imports from Africa	111 229	111 092	163 427	175 178	147 483	157 651	292 933	...	...	Importations en provenance de l'Afrique
Main Products										**Principaux produits**
Fertilizer	8 550	26 509	47 399	23 795	30 827	29 187	71 697	125 444	...	Engrais
Diesel and other	9 742	11 427	14 979	14 170	17 491	17 675	50 466	87 342	...	Diesel et autres
Petrol	4 389	6 011	7 334	8 029	8 702	9 358	22 471	43 968	...	Essence
Paraffin	942	1 317	1 360	1 149	978	737	1 191	740	...	Paraffine
Coal	163	120	96	148	139	182	368	1 085	...	Charbon
Main Origin										**Principales provenances**
South Africa	59 804	54 941	78 879	100 205	97 761	94 998	146 342	224 496	...	Afrique du Sud
Zimbabwe	5 797	7 157	5 459	5 334	9 318	7 823	7 243	13 347	...	Zimbabwe
UK	9 696	9 021	10 881	16 235	12 413	12 957	15 903	26 663	...	Royaume-Uni
Japan	1 440	2 013	4 581	3 103	3 766	4 841	15 162	30 276	...	Japon
Germany	2 550	3 257	3 375	5 066	9 086	20 041	11 742	34 439	...	Allemagne

IX FINANCIAL AND MONETARY STATISTICS - FINANCES ET STATISTIQUES MONETAIRES										
	2006	2007	2008	2009	2010	2011	2012	2013	2014	
IX-1 MONETARY STATISTICS *KWACHA (MILLIONS)*										**IX-1 STATISTIQUES MONÉTAIRES** *KWACHA (MILLIONS)*
Money supply (M1)	78 010	104 880	139 640	173 050	231 710	314 330	386 460	521 960	626 610	Masse monétaire (M1)
Quasi-money	27 170	35 130	69 047	92 132	124 841	172 396	233 082	324 190	348 782	Quasi-monnaie
of which Demand Deposit	...	...	...	...	...	...	...	...	...	dont Monnaie scripturale
Net foreign assets	19 300	28 034	19 667	- 2 045	21 234	3 968	32 819	116 207	242 824	Avoirs extérieurs nets
Domestic credit	47 080	56 890	157 107	213 801	243 602	334 320	377 907	421 544	389 159	Crédit intérieur
of which claims on private sector	27 747	33 988	68 143	95 044	144 843	174 538	218 866	250 446	293 038	dont créances sur le secteur privé
of which claims on government sector, net	18 121	19 164	82 919	112 517	94 096	139 757	139 673	153 257	92 186	dont créances nettes sur le gouvernement
International reserves (millions US$)	134	217	243	150	308	198	224	414	371	Réserves internationales (millions $EU)
Average Exchange Rate (National Currency per US$)	136.00	140.00	140.52	141.07	150.53	156.92	253.09	370.22	405.74	Taux de change (moyen) (monnaie nationale par $ EU)
IX-2 PUBLIC FINANCE *KWACHA (MILLIONS)*										**IX-2 FINANCES PUBLIQUES** *KWACHA (MILLIONS)*
Total Revenues and Grants	112 534	140 658	155 987	197 944	220 203	240 024	230 880	472 389	518 248	Recettes totales et dons
Tax Revenue	52 453	70 347	87 820	106 696	104 459	143 818	161 869	268 941	388 360	Recettes fiscales
Non Tax Revenue	7 431	6 974	8 567	15 269	37 296	31 877	26 196	27 683	53 236	Recettes non fiscales
Grants	52 650	63 337	59 600	75 979	78 448	64 329	42 815	175 765	76 652	Dons
Total Expenditures and Net Lending	120 009	153 580	179 288	247 520	257 098	296 197	340 043	501 164	648 798	Dépenses totales et prêts nets
Current expenditure	93 746	99 463	115 621	200 780	195 862	230 226	262 478	397 201	648 798	Dépenses courantes
Of which Wages and Salaries	20 209	23 778	30 018	37 595	44 792	58 092	70 178	97 166	140 026	Dont rémunérations et salaires
Capital expenditure	26 263	53 665	63 775	46 740	60 086	64 971	77 565	103 963	99 788	Dépenses d'équipement
Net Lending	-	452	- 108	-	1 150	1 000	-	-	-	Prêts nets
Fiscal Balance	- 7 475	- 12 922	- 23 301	- 49 576	- 36 895	- 56 173	- 109 163	- 204 540	- 207 202	Solde global y compris les dons
IX-3 BALANCE OF PAYMENTS *KWACHA (MILLIONS)*										**IX-3 BALANCE DES PAIEMENTS** *KWACHA (MILLIONS)*
Trade balance	- 440	- 582	- 868	- 740	- 695	- 1 089	- 1 078	- 1 437	- 1 387	Balance commerciale
Services Balance	- 95	- 79	- 114	- 150	- 149	- 146	- 118	- 115	- 145	Balance des services
Net Income	- 73	- 79	- 148	- 122	- 190	- 377	- 41	- 262	- 285	Revenus nets
Compensation of employees	- 7	- 7	- 6	- 7	- 6	- 6	- 6	- 5	- 6	Rémunération des salariés
Investment Income	- 66	- 72	- 142	- 116	- 184	- 371	- 36	- 257	- 279	Revenus des investissements
Current transfers, net total	301	322	437	469	641	519	470	585	601	Transferts courants
Net official transfers	136	97	232	216	379	242	189	320	304	Transferts officiels nets
Workers' remittances	14	18	12	10	13	13	16	23	26	Envois de fonds des travailleurs
Other private transfers	151	207	193	242	250	263	265	242	271	Autres transferts privés
Current account balance	- 307	- 418	- 693	- 544	- 394	- 1 093	- 767	- 1 230	- 1 217	Solde du compte courant
Capital & financial account	295	353	858	647	716	1 485	420	1 399	1 281	Comptes de capital et financier
Capital account	2 481	191	439	409	710	458	360	603	574	Compte de capital
Financial account	- 2 186	162	420	238	6	1 026	60	796	707	Compte financier
Errors & omissions	11	65	- 165	- 103	- 322	- 392	348	- 168	- 65	Erreurs et omissions
Overall balance	0	-	-	-	-	-	-	-	-	Balance générale

X DEBT AND FINANCIAL FLOWS - DETTE ET FLUX FINANCIERS	2006	2007	2008	2009	2010	2011	2012	2013	2014	
X-1 DEBT *US$ (MILLIONS)*										**X-1 DETTE EXTÉRIEURE** *$ E.U (MILLIONS)*
Total external debt	528	575	709	799	866	908	961	1 185	1 185	Dette extérieure totale
Private	-	-	-	-	-	-	-	-	-	Privée
Public	528	575	709	799	866	908	961	1 185	1 185	Publique
Total external debt service	1 950	399	13	13	18	20	28	20	35	Service de la dette extérieure
Present value of External debt	...	...	...	...	...	...	...	...	...	Valeur actuelle de la dette extérieure
Total government domestic debt (in local currency)	64	85	148	172	154.3	206.4	254.2	...	...	Dette publique intérieure
X-2 FINANCIAL FLOWS *US$ (MILLIONS)*										**X-2 FLUX FINANCIERS** *$ E.U (MILLIONS)*
Net Foreign Direct Investment Inflows	36	124	195	49	97	129	129	118	...	Investissements étranger direct (flux nets entrants)
Main origin of FDI Inflows										**Principales origines de l'IDE entrant:**
United Kingdom	13	10	11	14	- 27.8	3.2	...	...	...	Royaume-Uni
Netherlands	...	...	...	...	...	...	...	...	...	Pays-Bas
France	...	...	...	...	...	...	...	...	...	France
Denmark	...	...	4	4	...	...	...	...	...	Danemark
Germany	...	...	...	...	...	...	1.3	...	...	Allemagne
African countries	...	...	...	...	...	...	...	...	...	Pays africains
Net total Official Development Assistance	723	744	924	771	1 023	800	1 175	1 126	...	**Aide publique au développement (nette totale)**
Main origin of Net ODA										**Principales origines de l'APD nette**
United Kingdom	171	134	147	112	148.0	104.1	196.9	...	...	Royaume-Uni
IDA	67	78	53	82	131.8	70.0	157.3	...	...	IDA
United States	64	79	88	111	126.3	154.6	185.9	196.7	...	Etats-Unis
Norway	50	55	64	64	64.7	66.9	69.4	107.4	...	Norvège
Global Fund	29	79	92	67	49.8	118.6	71.8	...	...	Fonds mondial

AREA (KM²)		1 241 238	SUPERFICIE (KM²)
CAPITAL CITY	Bamako	Bamako	CAPITALE
CURRENCY	CFA Franc	Franc CFA	MONNAIE

I SOCIAL AND DEMOGRAPHIC INDICATORS – INDICATEURS DEMOGRAPHIQUES ET SOCIAUX

	Year / Année	Value / Valeur	
POPULATION			**POPULATION**
Population ('000)			Population ('000)
Both sexes	2013	16 737	Les deux sexes
Male	2013	8 301	Masculin
Female	2013	8 435	Féminin
Average annual growth rate	2014	3.6	Taux de croissance annuel
Active Population ('000)	2012	4 843	Population active ('000)
Population by age group ('000)			Population par groupe d'âge ('000)
0-14 years	2014	8 113	0-14 ans
15-64 years	2014	8 831	15-64 ans
65+ years	2014	364	65+ ans
Economically active population in agriculture (%)	2014	69.3	Participation de la population active agricole (%)
Crude birth rate	2014	43.9	Taux brut de natalité
Crude death rate	2014	12.5	Taux brut de mortalité
Total fertility rate	2014	6.2	Indice synthétique de fécondité
Proportion of urban population	2013	42.0	Part de la population urbaine
Life Expectancy at Birth - Total (years)	2014	55.4	Espérance de vie à la naissance - Totale (ans)
Dependency Ratio - Total (%)	2014	96.0	Taux de dépendance - Total (%)
HEALTH			**SANTÉ**
Percentage of children under-five and underweight	2006	27.9	% d'enfants de moins de cinq ans avec insuffisance pondérale
Prevalence of undernourishment	2013	5.0	Prévalence de la malnutrition
Under five mortality rate (both sexes, per 1000)	2013	122.7	Taux de mortalité de moins de 5 ans (les deux sexes, pour 1000)
Infant mortality rate (both sexes) per 1000	2013	77.6	Taux de mortalité infantile (les deux sexes) par 1000
Percentage of children provided the vaccines :			Pourcentage d'enfants vaccinés :
BCG	2013	87.0	BCG
DPT3	2013	74.0	DTC3
Polio	2013	79.0	Polio
Measles	2013	72.0	Rougeole
Percentage of mothers provided at least one antenatal care (%)	2006	70.4	Pourcentage de mères ayant au moins reçu un soin prénatal (%)
Percentage of deliveries attended by skilled health personnel	2010	56.1	% d'accouchements assistés par un personnel de santé qualifié
Number of doctors (per 10 000 population)	2010	0.8	Nombre de médecins (pour 10 000 habitants)
Number of nurses (per 10 000 population)	2010	4.3	Nombre d'infirmières (pour 10 000 habitants)
Hospital beds - Total (per 10 000 population)	2010	1.2	Nombre de lits d'hôpitaux - Total (pour 10 000)
Births registered (per 1 000)	2014	46.9	Naiss.s enregistrées (pour 1 000)
Deaths registered (per 1 000)	2014	12.7	Décès enregistrés (pour 1 000)
Public expenditure on Health (% of budget)	2012	7.9	Dépenses publiques consacrées à la santé (% du budget)
EDUCATION			**EDUCATION**
Enrolment in primary education (both sexes) (000)	2013	2 668	Scolarisation dans le primaire (les deux sexes) (000)
Female	2013	1 204	Féminin
Enrolment in secondary education (both sexes) (000)	2011	570	Scolarisation dans le secondaire (les deux sexes) (000)
Female	2012	271	Féminin
Enrolment in tertiary education (both sexes) (000)	2010	81.2	Scolarisation dans le tertiaire (les deux sexes) (000)
Female	2010	23.3	Féminin
Literacy rate (both sexes)	2013	35.0	Taux d'alphabétisation (deux sexes)
Male	2013	...	Masculin
Female	2013	...	Féminin
Pupil-teacher ratio	2013	45.7	Ratio élève-enseignant
Public expenditure on education (% of budget)	2012	20.0	Dépenses publiques consacrées à l'enseignement (% du budget)
POVERTY			**PAUVRETÉ**
GNI Per Capita (US$)	2013	670.0	RNB par habitant ($EU)
Human Poverty Index (HPI-1) Value (%)	2007	54.5	Valeur de l'Indice de pauvreté (IPH-1) (%)
Population below International Poverty Line ($2/day) (%)	2010	78.8	Population sous le seuil international de pauvreté (2$/J) (%)
Share of Income Held by Richest 10%	2010	25.8	% de revenu des 10% plus riches
Share of Income Held by Poorest 10%	2010	3.5	% de revenu des 10% plus pauvres
Gini index	2010	33.0	Indice de Gini

Charts / Graphiques

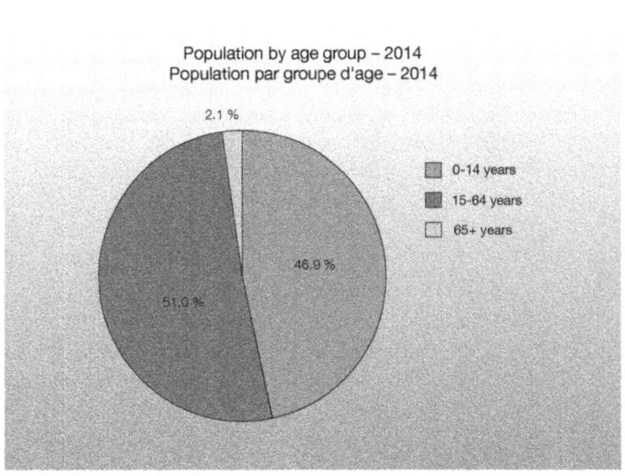

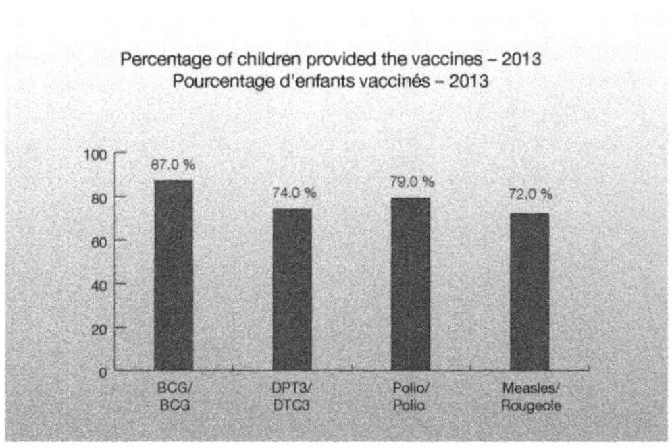

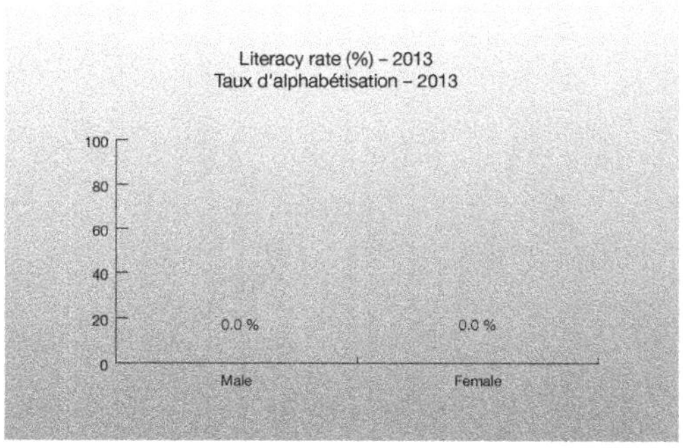

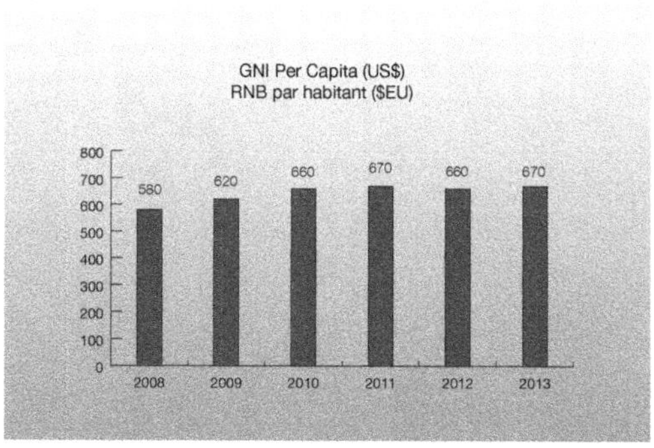

	2006	2007	2008	2009	2010	2011	2012	2013	2014	
II NATIONAL ACCOUNTS — COMPTES NATIONAUX										
GROSS DOMESTIC PRODUCT BY KIND OF ECONOMIC ACTIVITY AT CURRENT PRICES *CFA FRANC (BILLIONS)*										**PRODUIT INTÉRIEUR BRUT PAR BRANCHE D'ACTIVITÉ ÉCONOMIQUE AUX PRIX COURANTS** *FRANC CFA (MILLIARDS)*
Agriculture, hunting, forestry and fishing	1 064	1 115	1 412	1 486	1 698	1 773	2 005	1 865	2 085	Agriculture, chasse sylviculture et pêche
Mining and quarrying	240	229	242	284	287	351	422	385	353	Industries extractives
Manufacturing	259	236	207	219	227	287	333	346	346	Industries manufacturières
Electricity, gas & water	60	66	75	83	91	100	101	116	130	Electricité, gaz et eau
Construction & public works	145	169	191	216	238	263	215	249	271	Bâtiments et travaux publics
Wholesale & retail trade, restaurants, hotels	421	490	560	611	669	713	756	841	880	Commerce de gros et de détail, restaurants et hôtels
Finance, insurance, real estate, etc.	243	263	293	315	333	350	254	300	317	Banques, assurances, affaires immobilières
Transport and communications	156	192	221	233	250	268	279	315	347	Transport(s) et communications
Public administration and defense	325	332	359	378	399	427	427	468	505	Administrations publiques et défense
Education	...	...	...	...	...	...	...	...	...	Education
Health and Social Work	...	...	...	...	...	...	...	...	...	Santé et actions sociales
Other services	...	...	...	...	...	...	...	...	...	Autres services
Less Imputed Service Charges	- 14	- 13	- 15	- 15	- 16	- 23	- 22	- 23	- 24	Moins services d'intermédiation financière
Gross domestic product at factor cost / basic prices	2 899	3 079	3 545	3 810	4 176	4 509	4 769	4 861	5 209	Produit intérieur brut aux couts des facteurs / prix de base
Plus: indirect taxes / taxes on products, less subsidies	303	345	368	423	480	515	510	545	620	Plus taxes indirectes/impôts sur les produits, moins les subventions
EXPENDITURE ON GROSS DOMESTIC PRODUCT AT CURRENT PURCHASER'S VALUES *CFA FRANC (BILLIONS)*										**EMPLOI DU PRODUIT INTÉRIEUR BRUT AUX PRIX COURANTS D'ACQUISITION** *FRANC CFA (MILLIARDS)*
Government final consumption	553	597	688	734	788	859	861	948	1 011	Consommation finale des administrations publiques
Private final consumption	2 091	2 215	2 495	2 633	2 831	3 097	3 362	3 543	3 722	Consommation finale privée
Gross fixed capital formation	529	664	716	868	986	1 114	856	1 168	1 455	Formation brute de capital fixe
Change in inventories	123	74	75	31	155	44	288	- 56	79	Variation des stocks
Exports of goods and services	958	996	896	914	1 105	1 254	1 409	1 484	1 418	Exportations de biens et services
Less imports of goods and services	1 053	1 122	957	947	1 209	1 345	1 497	1 680	1 856	Moins importations de biens et services
GDP at purchasers' values	3 201	3 425	3 913	4 233	4 656	5 024	5 279	5 406	5 829	PIB aux prix d'acquisition
GROSS DOMESTIC PRODUCT BY KIND OF ECONOMIC ACTIVITY AT CONSTANT PRICES *ANNUAL GROWTH RATES (%)*										**PRODUIT INTÉRIEUR BRUT PAR BRANCHE D'ACTIVITÉ ECONOMIQUE AUX PRIX CONSTANTS** *TAUX DE CROISSANCE ANNUEL (%)*
Agriculture, hunting, forestry and fishing	4.3	2.5	13.2	5.6	11.4	- 1.3	8.6	- 7.4	9.4	Agriculture, chasse sylviculture et pêche
Mining and quarrying	17.8	- 8.4	- 6.4	1.5	- 14.3	0.0	9.2	1.5	0.3	Industries extractives
Manufacturing	0.9	- 12.0	- 14.4	1.0	0.1	20.8	3.6	4.8	- 2.9	Industries manufacturières
Electricity, gas & water	10.0	9.7	10.0	10.0	10.0	8.0	- 2.0	9.9	10.0	Electricité, gaz et eau
Construction & public works	3.0	8.7	4.5	6.0	7.0	5.0	- 25.0	10.0	5.0	Bâtiments et travaux publics
Wholesale & retail trade, restaurants, hotels	14.0	12.0	4.4	4.5	5.4	4.0	1.0	8.0	3.0	Commerce de gros et de détail,restaurants et hôtels
Finance, insurance, real estate, etc.	4.2	7.6	1.1	5.1	3.9	2.1	- 32.4	13.6	3.1	Banques, assurances, affaires immobilières
Transport and communications	16.0	20.9	10.0	1.9	5.0	5.2	-	9.0	7.4	Transport(s) et communications
Public administration and defense	2.5	1.2	2.0	1.9	3.0	4.0	- 4.7	7.4	6.8	Administrations publiques et défense
Education	...	...	...	...	...	...	...	...	...	Education
Health and Social Work	...	...	...	...	...	...	...	...	...	Santé et actions sociales
Other services	...	...	...	...	...	...	...	...	...	Autres services
Less Imputed Service Charges	4.3	- 12.3	5.5	4.0	5.0	9.0	- 10.0	3.0	3.0	Moins services d'intermédiation financière
Gross domestic product at factor cost / basic prices	7.2	3.9	5.5	4.4	5.9	2.5	0.1	1.3	6.0	Produit intérieur brut aux couts des facteurs / prix de base
Plus: indirect taxes / taxes on products, less subsidies	- 15.0	9.5	- 2.0	5.9	4.2	6.0	- 1.1	7.5	3.8	Plus taxes indirectes/impôts sur les produits, moins les subventions
Gross domestic product at market prices	5.3	4.3	5.0	4.5	5.8	2.7	0.0	1.7	5.8	Produit intérieur brut aux prix du marché
EXPENDITURE ON GROSS DOMESTIC PRODUCT AT CONSTANT PURCHASERS' VALUES *ANNUAL GROWTH RATES (%)*										**EMPLOIS DU PRODUIT INTÉRIEUR BRUT AUX PRIX CONSTANTS D'ACQUISITION** *TAUX DE CROISSANCE ANNUEL (%)*
Government final consumption	9.7	4.3	8.0	3.0	5.0	3.8	- 5.0	8.5	4.0	Consommation finale des administrations publiques
Private final consumption	3.2	4.5	1.9	3.1	4.4	4.0	2.5	6.0	3.0	Consommation finale privée
Gross fixed capital formation	4.0	15.2	- 0.8	14.0	6.9	5.6	- 30.8	24.0	19.2	Formation brute de capital fixe
Exports of goods and services	1.3	0.5	- 13.0	1.0	6.0	3.2	7.0	7.5	- 2.5	Exportations de biens et services
Less imports of goods and services	1.8	1.2	- 19.1	- 3.4	12.0	2.0	1.2	9.0	5.2	Moins importations de biens et services
Notes	NA Data: 2013:Semi-final;2014:Provisional				Données des CN: 2013:Semi-définitives;2014:Provisoires					Notes

	2006	2007	2008	2009	2010	2011	2012	2013	2014	
III INFLATION										
ANNUAL GROWTH RATES (%)										**TAUX DE CROISSANCE ANNUEL (%)**
All items	1.5	1.4	9.2	2.4	1.2	3.0	5.3	-0.6	0.9	Ensemble
of which:										dont:
Food and Non-alcoholic beverages	-0.4	1.9	13.0	3.8	3.4	5.1	8.0	-3.3	-0.2	Alimentation et boissons non alcoolisés
Alcoholic beverages & tobacco	-1.3	-3.0	11.2	0.5	7.0	-0.4	-0.4	5.9	13.1	Boissons alcoolisées et tabacs
Clothing and Footwear	1.9	-0.8	8.8	0.5	1.9	0.0	3.6	-0.4	2.1	Habillement et chaussures
Housing, Water, Electricity, Gas and Other Fuels	2.4	2.0	5.2	1.5	-2.8	2.9	2.1	3.8	3.1	Logement, eau, électricité, gas et autres combustibles
Furnishing, household equip	-0.5	1.4	9.1	4.4	-0.5	2.7	4.1	-2.3	-0.4	Meubles, articles de ménage et entretien courant
Health	0.6	0.8	1.0	0.7	-0.9	1.6	-1.2	-0.2	0.9	Santé
Transport	6.5	2.1	4.6	0.2	2.1	2.1	2.1	4.1	3.3	Transport
Communication	-11.9	-1.3	-7.3	-2.0	-4.3	-3.7	3.8	3.4	-0.8	Communication
Recreation & culture	0.8	-0.3	-0.1	0.2	-2.2	1.0	0.5	-0.8	-1.6	Loisirs et culture
Education	29.2	-1.1	7.1	2.4	2.8	0.8	-0.9	0.5	1.2	Enseignement
Restaurants & hotels	0.0	2.5	10.6	3.5	-2.8	-0.4	7.8	1.9	-1.4	Restaurants et hôtels
Miscellaneous goods & services	2.5	0.4	7.7	5.4	-6.3	0.0	6.0	2.0	0.4	Biens et services divers

	2006	2007	2008	2009	2010	2011	2012	2013	2014	
IV AGRICULTURAL PRODUCTION - PRODUCTION AGRICOLE										
	2006	2007	2008	2009	2010	2011	2012	2013	2014	
TONNES *(THOUSAND)*										**TONNES** *(MILLIERS)*
Cotton seed	509	242	210	229	243	445	453	440	505	Graines de coton
Rice	946	108	1 624	1 074	1 296	1 741	1 915	2 212	2 202	Riz paddy
Millet	1 158	1 175	1 414	1 390	1 373	1 462	1 772	1 152	2 073	Millet
Sorghum	629	901	1 027	1 466	1 251	1 191	1 212	820	1 181	Sorgho
Maize	707	690	695	1 477	1 404	1 298	1 714	1 488	941	Maïs
V MINING PRODUCTION - PRODUCTION MINIERE										
	2006	2007	2008	2009	2010	2011	2012	2013	2014	
Gold ores and concentrates (Kilograms)	62 382	56 753	49 700	53 726	46 033	46 038	50 272	50 994	51 147	Minerais d'or et concentrés (Kilogrammes)
Silver ores and concentrates (Kilograms)	6 000	6 000	...	...	...	187 514	267 530	149 356	604 400	Minerais de fer (Kilogrammes)
Salt and pure sodium chloride, metric tons (thousands)	...	...	...	...	...	...	...	...	...	Sel et chlorure de sodium pur, tonnes métriques (milliers)
VI ENERGY - ENERGIE										
	2006	2007	2008	2009	2010	2011	2012	2013	2014	
Total electricity generation (GWh)	1 331	1 408	1 482	1 575	1 691	1 729	1 682	1 736	...	Production d'électricité totale (GWh)
of which:										dont:
Production of electricity from fossil fuels (GWh)	611	698	764	844	944	953	864	864	...	Production d'électricité à partir de combustibles fossiles (GWh)
Production of hydro electricity (GWh)	668	658	666	679	695	724	766	820	...	Production d'électricité d'origine hydraulique (GWh)
Production of electricity from solar, wind, tide, wave and other sources (GWh)	...	...	...	...	...	0	0	0	...	Production d'électricité d'origine solaire, éolienne, marée motrice et autres (GWh)
VII TOURISM AND INFRASTRUCTURE - TOURISME ET INFRASTRUCTURE										
	2006	2007	2008	2009	2010	2011	2012	2013	2014	
VII-1 TOURISM										**VII-1 TOURISME**
International tourist arrivals (thousands)	153	164	190	160	169	160	32	57	...	Arrivées de touristes internationaux (milliers)
Rooms in hotels and similar establishments (thousands)	5.2	6.0	7.8	8.4	8.9	9.5	9.9	9.5	...	Chambres d'hotels et établissements assimilés (milliers)
Overnight stays (thousands)	642	757	906	699	563	564	122	214	251	Nuitées (milliers)
Tourism receipts (US$ thousand)	173 000	219 000	272 400	169 900	186 100	242 860	193 821	133 059	138 803	Recettes touristiques (milliers de $ EU)
Total contribution to GDP (%)	9.9	9.0	10.3	9.2	10.2	9.7	10.2	10.1	10.1	Contribution totale au PIB (%)
Total contribution to Employment (%)	8.6	7.8	8.9	8.0	8.0	7.5	8.4	7.2	6.9	Contribution totale à l'emploi (%)
VII-2 INFRASTRUCTURE										**VII-2 INFRASTRUCTURE**
Paved roads (% of total)	25	20	30	32	...	...	...	...	...	Routes asphaltées (% du total)
Total Network (Railways-km)	734	729	729	729	729	723	723	643	643	Réseau total voies ferrées-Km
Main Telephone Lines (per 100 inhabitants)	1	1	1	1	1	1	1	1	...	Lignes téléphoniques fixes (pour 100 habitants)
Mobile Cellular Subscribers (per 100 inhabitants)	12	20	26	33	53	75	98	129	...	Abonnés aux téléphones mobiles (pour 100 habitants)
VIII EXTERNAL TRADE - COMMERCE EXTERIEUR										
	2006	2007	2008	2009	2010	2011	2012	2013	2014	
CFA FRANC (MILLIONS) EXPORTS, FOB										**FRANC CFA (MILLIONS) EXPORTATIONS, FÀB**
Exports - Total	795 504	685 636	862 095	841 308	989 174	1 132 206	1 340 804	1 371 672	...	Exportations - Total
Exports to AFRICA	627 883	529 458	744 925	671 800	667 393	827 058	861 855	1 014 446	...	Exportations vers l'AFRIQUE
Main Products										**Principaux produits**
Gold	588 315	515 178	645 871	668 198	782 246	797 938	875 994	928 836	...	Or
Cotton	134 160	94 509	91 041	66 842	69 057	70 494	190 725	172 989	...	Coton
Live Animals	22 555	27 933	35 754	22 962	24 095	47 428	51 000	56 718	...	Animaux vivants
	...	...	...	...	...	...	...	...	...	
	...	...	...	...	...	...	...	...	...	
Main Destinations										**Principales destinations**
Switzerland	563 451	459 740	624 734	573 085	564 465	637 020	692 794	804 007	...	Suisse
South Africa	49 125	31 200	58 915	62 461	119 706	131 838	155 588	109 997	...	Afrique du Sud
Senegal	21 104	29 085	22 084	47 989	59 479	54 389	104 050	70 754	...	Sénégal
Ivory Coast	...	...	...	...	...	...	...	...	...	Côte d'Ivoire
China	...	...	...	...	...	...	...	...	...	Chine
IMPORTS, CIF										**IMPORTATIONS, CAF**
Imports - Total	951 798	1 047 858	1 488 790	1 174 067	1 696 780	1 581 985	1 769 539	1 888 424	...	Importations - Total (millions)
Imports from Africa	441 694	533 908	583 299	505 430	689 184	772 137	902 245	859 925	...	Importations en provenance de l'Afrique
Main Products										**Principaux produits**
Petroleum Products	188 597	186 223	248 077	205 216	269 309	384 332	412 345	442 794	...	Produits petroliers
Building Materials	40 337	53 793	69 762	80 570	99 597	93 275	85 893	80 246	...	Matériaux de Construction & public workss
Chemical products	33 518	46 656	62 798	45 036	85 707	69 186	79 824	71 201	...	Produits chimiques
Vehicles and machinery	29 600	39 290	37 593	41 482	55 305	38 208	65 515	55 121	...	Véhicules et machines
Food	22 565	17 679	24 485	23 893	26 105	29 774	31 591	43 299	...	Produits alimentaires
Main Origin										**Principales provenances**
France	145 036	207 269	256 691	162 307	256 799	338 237	443 458	414 655	...	France
Senegal	115 367	156 293	207 107	142 778	239 645	169 540	191 288	226 359	...	Sénégal
Ivory Coast	103 352	132 873	154 689	133 561	209 042	162 605	187 697	175 236	...	Côte-d'Ivoire
Togo	...	...	...	...	...	...	...	...	...	Togo
Benin	...	...	...	...	...	...	...	...	...	Bénin

IX FINANCIAL AND MONETARY STATISTICS - FINANCES ET STATISTIQUES MONETAIRES	2006	2007	2008	2009	2010	2011	2012	2013	2014	
IX-1 MONETARY STATISTICS *CFA FRANC (MILLIONS)*										**IX-1 STATISTIQUES MONÉTAIRES** *FRANC CFA (MILLIONS)*
Money supply (M1)	931 950	1 018 260	1 023 630	1 187 900	1 294 460	1 491 950	1 718 050	1 845 370	2 025 400	Masse monétaire (M1)
Quasi-money	208 867	288 854	264 404	344 368	361 834	392 209	428 865	497 181	555 999	Quasi-monnaie
of which Demand Deposit	...	...	...	...	...	...	...	...	...	dont Monnaie scripturale
Net foreign assets	542 833	546 833	524 423	769 405	760 875	710 798	713 300	808 215	662 617	Avoirs extérieurs nets
Domestic credit	447 063	494 786	516 194	453 007	572 083	846 128	1 045 033	1 127 274	1 372 574	Crédit intérieur
of which claims on private sector	575 228	618 331	671 225	740 711	841 666	1 049 320	1 099 195	1 232 166	1 458 174	dont créances sur le secteur privé
of which claims on government sector, net	- 128 166	- 123 545	- 155 031	- 287 704	- 269 583	- 203 192	- 54 162	- 104 892	- 85 601	dont créances nettes sur le gouvernement
International reserves (millions US$)	970	1 087	1 072	1 604	1 344	1 379	1 341	1 306	717	Réserves internationales (millions $EU)
Average Exchange Rate (National Currency per US$)	522.90	478.89	446.87	471.07	494.68	471.42	510.18	493.94	493.76	Taux de change (moyen) (monnaie nationale par $ EU)
IX-2 PUBLIC FINANCE *CFA FRANC (MILLIONS)*										**IX-2 FINANCES PUBLIQUES** *FRANC CFA (MILLIONS)*
Total Revenues and Grants	1 740 600	671 600	674 870	825 400	861 360	960 960	830 656	1 099 400	740 100	Recettes totales et dons
Tax Revenue	470 200	487 200	519 870	625 000	681 860	733 860	769 770	865 200	699 400	Recettes fiscales
Non Tax Revenue	25 900	22 200	20 800	28 900	45 800	33 100	47 886	34 200	26 200	Recettes non fiscales
Grants	1 244 500	162 200	134 200	171 500	133 700	194 000	13 000	200 000	14 500	Dons
Total Expenditures and Net Lending	768 000	785 100	772 800	943 900	982 600	1 149 500	844 600	1 188 300	557 270	Dépenses totales et prêts nets
Current expenditure	433 200	437 100	458 800	548 800	601 200	714 900	713 200	800 600	445 100	Dépenses courantes
Of which Wages and Salaries	147 900	162 900	185 600	213 500	231 800	265 100	291 100	290 800	223 400	Dont rémunérations et salaires
Capital expenditure	340 800	395 600	305 900	376 200	366 700	437 800	134 200	393 900	112 600	Dépenses d'équipement
Net Lending	- 6 000	- 47 600	8 100	18 900	14 700	- 3 200	- 2 800	- 6 200	- 430	Prêts nets
Fiscal Balance	972 600	- 113 500	- 97 930	- 118 500	- 121 240	- 188 540	- 13 944	- 88 900	182 830	Solde global y compris les dons
IX-3 BALANCE OF PAYMENTS *CFA FRANC (MILLIONS)*										**IX-3 BALANCE DES PAIEMENTS** *FRANC CFA (MILLIONS)*
Trade balance	39 201	- 138 858	- 284 681	- 100 410	- 334 373	- 157 057	57 014	- 176 608	...	Balance commerciale
Services Balance	- 143 700	- 141 959	...	...	- 313 689	- 338 553	- 367 225	- 927 514	...	Balance des services
Net Income	- 134 643	- 139 679	- 139 986	- 215 955	- 207 517	- 217 906	- 234 831	- 213 687	...	Revenus nets
Compensation of employees	4 802	3 511	4 758	1 065	1 680	- 4 265	- 1 505	1 117	...	Rémunération des salariés
Investment Income	- 139 445	- 143 190	- 144 744	- 217 020	- 209 200	- 208 302	- 235 131	- 213 447	...	Revenus des investissements
Current transfers, net total	169 999	191 680	203 697	229 650	266 227	403 770	405 837	1 168 708	...	Transferts courants
Net official transfers	86 120	56 769	47 515	82 344	98 110	81 045	29 003	776 500	...	Transferts officiels nets
Workers' remittances	83 879	134 911	156 182	147 306	168 117	322 725	376 834	392 208	...	Envois de fonds des travailleurs
Other private transfers	...	...	...	...	...	...	...	...	...	Autres transferts privés
Current account balance	- 69 143	- 228 816	- 220 970	- 86 715	- 589 352	- 309 746	- 139 206	- 149 101	...	Solde du compte courant
Capital & financial account	225 083	254 965	423 015	- 41 058	- 300 410	78 347	- 41 058	- 8 562	...	Comptes de capital et financier
Capital account	1 158 710	144 631	147 254	181 344	124 730	184 333	56 346	129 334	...	Compte de capital
Financial account	- 933 627	110 334	275 761	414 937	- 425 140	- 105 986	- 97 404	- 137 896	...	Compte financier
Errors & omissions	- 25 795	12 866	19 899	- 35 033	18 998	- 25 186	- 10 464	- 18 014	...	Erreurs et omissions
Overall balance	130 145	39 015	221 944	- 162 806	- 870 764	- 256 585	- 190 728	- 175 677	...	Balance générale

X DEBT AND FINANCIAL FLOWS - DETTE ET FLUX FINANCIERS	2006	2007	2008	2009	2010	2011	2012	2013	2014	
X-1 DEBT *US$ (MILLIONS)*										**X-1 DETTE EXTÉRIEURE** *$ E.U (MILLIONS)*
Total external debt	1 221	1 296	1 802	1 984	2 524	2 474	2 713	2 940	3 520	Dette extérieure totale
Private	-	-	-	-	-	-	-	-	-	Privée
Public	1 221	1 296	1 802	1 984	2 524	2 474	2 713	2 940	3 520	Publique
Total external debt service	2 046	87	89	110	109	165	153	148	179	Service de la dette extérieure
Present value of External debt	...	...	...	...	...	...	...	...	...	Valeur actuelle de la dette extérieure
Total government domestic debt (in local currency)	45	80	99	128	168.9	186.2	171.6	494.2	...	Dette publique intérieure
X-2 FINANCIAL FLOWS *US$ (MILLIONS)*										**X-2 FLUX FINANCIERS** *$ E.U (MILLIONS)*
Net Foreign Direct Investment Inflows	83	73	180	748	406	556	398	410	...	Investissements étranger direct (flux nets entrants)
Main origin of FDI Inflows										**Principales origines de l'IDE entrant:**
France	13	8	6	4	5.3	25.1	2.6	...	...	France
Sweden	-	-	...	1	3.1	0.8	0.7	...	...	Suède
Belgium	-	-	-	-	-	0.0	0.0	...	...	Belgique
Italy	-	-	...	...	1.0	0.1	1.0	...	...	Italie
Luxembourg	-	-	-	-	...	...	0.3	...	...	Luxembourg
African countries	...	...	...	...	...	...	...	...	...	Pays africains
Net total Official Development Assistance	866	1 019	964	984	1 089	1 281	1 001	1 391	...	Aide publique au développement (nette totale)
Main origin of Net ODA										**Principales origines de l'APD nette**
IDA	106	151	113	167	153.2	150.6	68.9	...	...	IDA
France	82	214	82	75	77.6	73.5	41.2	95.0	...	France
United States	65	54	53	111	197.9	273.8	348.2	146.3	...	Etats-Unis
Netherlands	66	65	80	77	56.7	59.4	46.1	60.3	...	Pays-Bas
Canada	27	56	99	83	96.0	116.2	93.9	64.8	...	Canada

MAURITANIA — MAURITANIE

AREA (KM²)	1 025 520		SUPERFICIE (KM²)
CAPITAL CITY	Nouakchott	Nouakchott	CAPITALE
CURRENCY	Ouguiya	Ouguiya	MONNAIE

I SOCIAL AND DEMOGRAPHIC INDICATORS – INDICATEURS DEMOGRAPHIQUES ET SOCIAUX

	Year Année	Value Valeur	
POPULATION			**POPULATION**
Population ('000)			Population ('000)
Both sexes	2014	3 984	Les deux sexes
Male	2014	2 007	Masculin
Female	2014	1 978	Féminin
Average annual growth rate	2014	2.5	Taux de croissance annuel
Active Population ('000)	2014	1 216	Population active ('000)
Population by age group ('000)			Population par groupe d'âge ('000)
0-14 years	2014	1 590	0-14 ans
15-64 years	2014	2 268	15-64 ans
65+ years	2014	127	65+ ans
Economically active population in agriculture (%)	2014	67.4	Participation de la population active agricole (%)
Crude birth rate	2014	33.7	Taux brut de natalité
Crude death rate	2014	8.6	Taux brut de mortalité
Total fertility rate	2014	4.6	Indice synthétique de fécondité
Proportion of urban population	2014	42.3	Part de la population urbaine
Life Expectancy at Birth - Total (years)	2014	61.7	Espérance de vie à la naissance - Totale (ans)
Dependency Ratio - Total (%)	2014	71.8	Taux de dépendance - Total (%)
HEALTH			**SANTÉ**
Percentage of children under-five and underweight	2012	19.5	% d'enfants de moins de cinq ans avec insuffisance pondérale
Prevalence of undernourishment	2013	6.5	Prévalence de la malnutrition
Under five mortality rate (both sexes, per 1000)	2013	90.1	Taux de mortalité de moins de 5 ans (les deux sexes, pour 1000)
Infant mortality rate (both sexes) per 1000	2013	67.1	Taux de mortalité infantile (les deux sexes) par 1000
Percentage of children provided the vaccines :			Pourcentage d'enfants vaccinés :
BCG	2013	95.0	BCG
DPT3	2013	80.0	DTC3
Polio	2012	80.0	Polio
Measles	2013	80.0	Rougeole
Percentage of mothers provided at least one antenatal care (%)	2007	72.3	Pourcentage de mères ayant au moins reçu un soin prénatal (%)
Percentage of deliveries attended by skilled health personnel	2011	65.1	% d'accouchements assistés par un personnel de santé qualifié
Number of doctors (per 10 000 population)	2009	1.3	Nombre de médecins (pour 10 000 habitants)
Number of nurses (per 10 000 population)	2009	6.7	Nombre d'infirmières (pour 10 000 habitants)
Hospital beds - Total (per 10 000 population)	2006	4.0	Nombre de lits d'hôpitaux - Total (pour 10 000)
Births registered (per 1 000)	2014	33.7	Naiss.s enregistrées (pour 1 000)
Deaths registered (per 1 000)	2014	8.6	Décès enregistrés (pour 1 000)
Public expenditure on Health (% of budget)	2009	4.9	Dépenses publiques consacrées à la santé (% du budget)
EDUCATION			**EDUCATION**
Enrolment in primary education (both sexes) (000)	2013	569	Scolarisation dans le primaire (les deux sexes) (000)
Female	2013	287	Féminin
Enrolment in secondary education (both sexes) (000)	2013	171	Scolarisation dans le secondaire (les deux sexes) (000)
Female	2013	82	Féminin
Enrolment in tertiary education (both sexes) (000)	...	...	Scolarisation dans le tertiaire (les deux sexes) (000)
Female	2013	5.8	Féminin
Literacy rate (both sexes)	2007	45.5	Taux d'alphabétisation (deux sexes)
Male	2007	57.4	Masculin
Female	2007	35.3	Féminin
Pupil-teacher ratio	...	...	Ratio élève-enseignant
Public expenditure on education (% of budget)	2011	13.0	Dépenses publiques consacrées à l'enseignement (% du budget)
POVERTY			**PAUVRETÉ**
GNI Per Capita (US$)	2013	1 060.0	RNB par habitant ($EU)
Human Poverty Index (HPI-1) Value (%)	2007	36.2	Valeur de l'Indice de pauvreté (IPH-1) (%)
Population below International Poverty Line ($2/day) (%)	2008	47.7	Population sous le seuil international de pauvreté (2$/J) (%)
Share of Income Held by Richest 10%	2008	31.6	% de revenu des 10% plus riches
Share of Income Held by Poorest 10%	2008	2.4	% de revenu des 10% plus pauvres
Gini index	2008	40.5	Indice de Gini

Charts
Graphiques

Population by age group – 2014
Population par groupe d'age – 2014

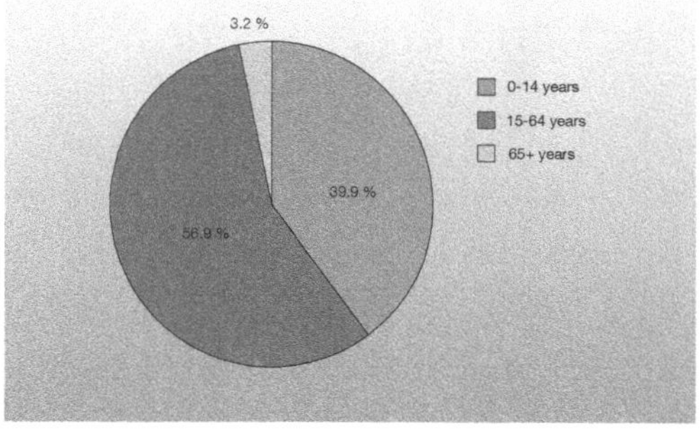

Percentage of children provided the vaccines – 2013
Pourcentage d'enfants vaccinés – 2013

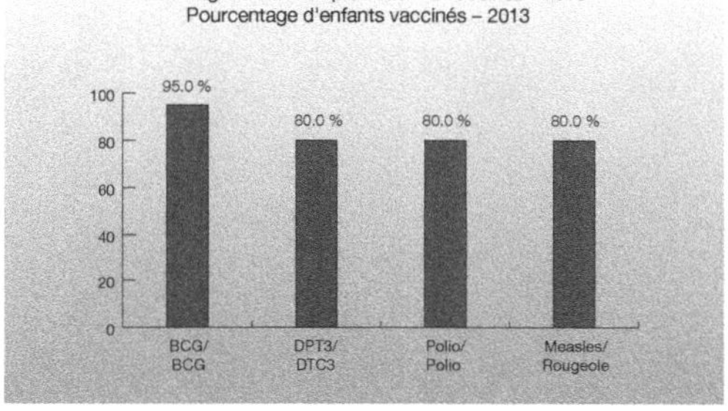

Literacy rate (%) – 2007
Taux d'alphabétisation – 2007

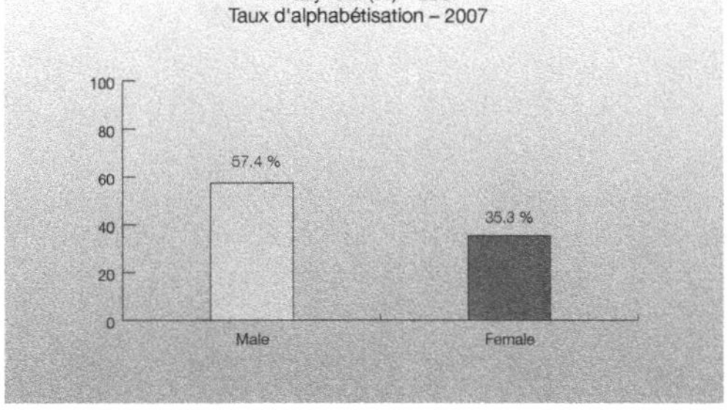

GNI Per Capita (US$)
RNB par habitant ($EU)

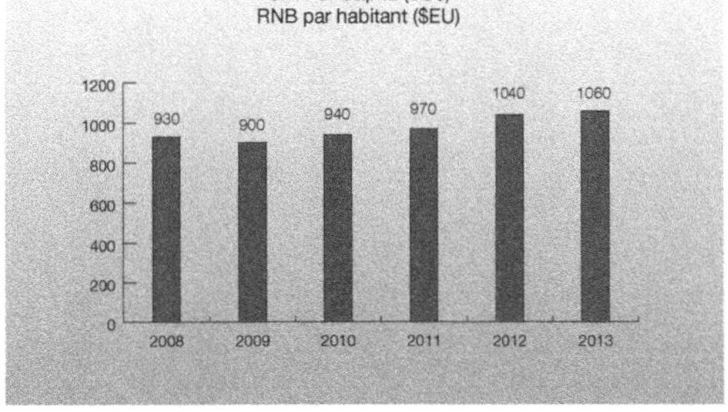

II NATIONAL ACCOUNTS — COMPTES NATIONAUX	2006	2007	2008	2009	2010	2011	2012	2013	2014	
GROSS DOMESTIC PRODUCT BY KIND OF ECONOMIC ACTIVITY AT CURRENT PRICES *OUGUIYA (MILLIONS)*										**PRODUIT INTÉRIEUR BRUT PAR BRANCHE D'ACTIVITÉ ÉCONOMIQUE AUX PRIX COURANTS** *OUGUIYA (MILLIONS)*
Agriculture, hunting, forestry and fishing	174 917	205 012	225 061	231 680	242 864	281 593	284 520	295 616	324 998	Agriculture, chasse sylviculture et pêche
Mining and quarrying	242 847	210 629	249 149	181 251	304 345	476 515	381 403	365 691	280 756	Industries extractives
Manufacturing	53 745	51 154	47 835	77 064	85 219	94 331	102 092	111 170	109 335	Industries manufacturières
Electricity, gas & water	3 521	- 2 270	2 500	5 554	5 562	5 272	5 907	6 425	6 939	Electricité, gaz et eau
Construction & public works	54 758	57 937	52 911	53 775	71 772	74 950	100 525	110 511	135 580	Bâtiments et travaux publics
Wholesale & retail trade, restaurants, hotels	58 690	68 246	79 973	82 136	86 825	90 234	105 879	119 631	132 587	Commerce de gros et de détail, restaurants et hôtels
Finance, insurance, real estate, etc.	79 828	95 786	117 674	145 863	171 293	184 146	197 312	221 197	246 024	Banques, assurances, affaires immobilières
Transport and communications	40 088	48 977	42 939	38 994	53 403	53 266	58 861	64 711	70 707	Transport(s) et communications
Public administration and defense	65 144	82 183	90 304	96 233	120 179	128 989	137 094	150 187	154 734	Administrations publiques et défense
Education	...	...	...	...	...	...	...	...	...	Education
Health and Social Work	...	...	...	...	...	...	...	...	...	Santé et actions sociales
Other services	...	...	...	...	...	...	...	...	...	Autres services
Less Imputed Service Charges	- 10 888	- 16 021	- 15 017	- 13 832	- 19 813	- 22 428	- 25 120	- 27 329	- 29 897	Moins services d'intermédiation financière
Gross domestic product at factor cost / basic prices	762 650	801 633	893 329	898 718	1 121 649	1 366 867	1 348 473	1 417 811	1 431 763	Produit intérieur brut aux couts des facteurs / prix de base
Plus: indirect taxes / taxes on products, less subsidies	54 087	66 380	66 880	62 140	75 122	73 330	88 700	102 981	112 465	Plus taxes indirectes/impôts sur les produits, moins les subventions
EXPENDITURE ON GROSS DOMESTIC PRODUCT AT CURRENT PURCHASER'S VALUES *OUGUIYA (MILLIONS)*										**EMPLOI DU PRODUIT INTÉRIEUR BRUT AUX PRIX COURANTS D'ACQUISITION** *OUGUIYA (MILLIONS)*
Government final consumption	150 626	137 535	152 986	154 933	165 566	173 758	198 483	214 952	237 292	Consommation finale des administrations publiques
Private final consumption	634 578	818 958	891 174	868 293	1 077 508	1 262 980	1 603 369	1 688 070	1 452 782	Consommation finale privée
Gross fixed capital formation	63 768	71 996	98 353	83 336	67 237	74 063	52 754	3 334	3 386	Formation brute de capital fixe
Change in inventories	...	...	...	...	...	...	...	...	...	Variation des stocks
Exports of goods and services	390 348	384 663	467 899	399 747	606 225	858 454	829 166	910 839	900 288	Exportations de biens et services
Less imports of goods and services	422 583	545 140	650 203	545 451	719 766	929 060	1 246 599	1 296 403	1 049 519	Moins importations de biens et services
GDP at purchasers' values	816 737	868 013	960 209	960 858	1 196 771	1 440 197	1 437 173	1 520 792	1 544 229	PIB aux prix d'acquisition
GROSS DOMESTIC PRODUCT BY KIND OF ECONOMIC ACTIVITY AT CONSTANT PRICES *ANNUAL GROWTH RATES (%)*										**PRODUIT INTÉRIEUR BRUT PAR BRANCHE D'ACTIVITÉ ECONOMIQUE AUX PRIX CONSTANTS** *TAUX DE CROISSANCE ANNUEL (%)*
Agriculture, hunting, forestry and fishing	0.0	9.7	8.0	1.3	5.2	- 2.0	6.4	4.0	7.3	Agriculture, chasse sylviculture et pêche
Mining and quarrying	142.7	- 20.8	4.9	- 3.4	1.9	- 3.1	- 2.4	0.3	1.8	Industries extractives
Manufacturing	- 16.9	1.1	9.3	0.1	- 1.1	20.7	5.6	4.6	- 5.0	Industries manufacturières
Electricity, gas & water	33.1	- 54.9	- 24.6	- 5.2	- 2.3	7.2	4.6	8.8	8.0	Electricité, gaz et eau
Construction & public works	32.0	3.4	- 10.7	- 8.9	3.9	11.9	12.7	5.6	18.5	Bâtiments et travaux publics
Wholesale & retail trade, restaurants, hotels	- 8.4	3.6	- 7.0	6.5	7.4	9.4	9.8	8.5	7.1	Commerce de gros et de détail,restaurants et hôtels
Finance, insurance, real estate, etc.	4.2	7.3	4.2	11.0	6.6	6.2	2.8	7.7	7.4	Banques, assurances, affaires immobilières
Transport and communications	26.9	24.3	- 7.3	- 16.2	15.1	6.1	7.0	9.9	9.4	Transport(s) et communications
Public administration and defense	22.0	17.8	- 15.0	- 8.5	5.3	1.6	1.3	4.5	2.0	Administrations publiques et défense
Education	...	...	...	...	...	...	...	...	...	Education
Health and Social Work	...	...	...	...	...	...	...	...	...	Santé et actions sociales
Other services	...	...	...	...	...	...	...	...	...	Autres services
Less Imputed Service Charges	- 12.8	37.1	- 12.4	- 9.8	34.7	7.1	6.7	5.8	6.9	Moins services d'intermediation financière
Gross domestic product at factor cost / basic prices	19.6	1.8	1.2	- 0.7	4.4	3.1	4.9	5.0	6.2	Produit intérieur brut aux couts des facteurs / prix de base
Plus: indirect taxes / taxes on products, less subsidies	10.1	15.7	0.3	- 5.4	9.1	18.7	16.7	11.5	8.3	Plus taxes indirectes/impôts sur les produits, moins les subventions
Gross domestic product at market prices	18.9	2.8	1.1	- 1.0	4.8	4.4	6.0	5.7	6.4	Produit intérieur brut aux prix du marché
EXPENDITURE ON GROSS DOMESTIC PRODUCT AT CONSTANT PURCHASERS' VALUES *ANNUAL GROWTH RATES (%)*										**EMPLOIS DU PRODUIT INTÉRIEUR BRUT AUX PRIX CONSTANTS D'ACQUISITION** *TAUX DE CROISSANCE ANNUEL (%)*
Government final consumption	12.0	13.5	- 8.1	- 4.5	10.0	4.2	2.0	5.2	2.2	Consommation finale des administrations publiques
Private final consumption	56.3	7.4	9.1	- 2.9	16.0	2.8	26.9	3.4	1.4	Consommation finale privée
Gross fixed capital formation	- 84.9	9.2	24.8	- 16.2	- 32.1	- 4.5	- 24.4	- 93.7	6.4	Formation brute de capital fixe
Exports of goods and services	63.5	- 3.7	- 1.7	2.2	3.2	19.1	- 4.4	5.4	2.4	Exportations de biens et services
Less imports of goods and services	- 19.2	12.2	12.2	- 6.1	19.0	7.5	29.5	- 2.1	- 4.2	Moins importations de biens et services
Notes	NA Data: 2013:Provisional;2014:Projection				Données des CN: 2013:Provisoires;2014:Projections					Notes

III INFLATION	2006	2007	2008	2009	2010	2011	2012	2013	2014	
ANNUAL GROWTH RATES (%)										**TAUX DE CROISSANCE ANNUEL (%)**
All items	6.2	7.3	7.3	2.2	5.7	6.2	4.9	4.1	3.5	Ensemble
of which:										dont:
Food and Non-alcoholic beverages	5.4	10.5	9.6	2.6	7.6	6.5	4.3	4.4	5.1	Alimentation et boissons non alcoolisés
Alcoholic beverages & tobacco	...	...	20.1	15.9	12.8	12.8	16.5	-2.9	1.8	Boissons alcoolisées et tabacs
Clothing and Footwear	8.8	4.3	1.9	6.9	6.8	6.4	7.8	5.1	1.3	Habillement et chaussures
Housing, Water, Electricity, Gas and Other Fuels	5.8	8.5	7.8	-2.9	4.4	4.1	3.4	3.9	1.6	Logement, eau, électricité, gas et autres combustibles
Furnishing, household equip	5.6	1.5	4.9	7.0	4.3	4.0	3.0	1.5	2.3	Meubles, articles de ménage et entretien courant
Health	10.6	7.5	0.6	3.3	1.2	0.0	3.8	2.0	-0.1	Santé
Transport	3.7	0.6	1.9	-0.9	3.0	6.6	10.9	5.9	1.0	Transport
Communication	...	...	-	-	-	-	-	-	-	Communication
Recreation & culture	-8.7	-4.1	-10.7	0.2	0.5	3.7	1.1	1.1	1.2	Loisirs et culture
Education	-4.1	-1.5	0.1	0.1	0.5	0.9	0.3	0.2	-	Enseignement
Restaurants & hotels	5.8	-1.4	5.7	2.3	4.4	3.3	4.8	3.4	-	Restaurants et hôtels
Miscellaneous goods & services	3.0	40.7	3.3	2.3	2.9	1.1	2.7	6.8	3.0	Biens et services divers

IV AGRICULTURAL PRODUCTION - PRODUCTION AGRICOLE	2006	2007	2008	2009	2010	2011	2012	2013	2014	
TONNES *(THOUSAND)*										**TONNES** *(MILLIERS)*
Sorghum	74	80	86	94	114	25	30	94	...	Sorgho
Rice	70	82	82	54	134	161	243	192	...	Riz paddy
Maize	17	17	15	12	20	12	19	6	...	Maïs
Beans, dry	10	10	10	10	12	12	12	12	...	Haricots secs
Dates	20	20	19	20	21	21	22	19	...	Dattes

V MINING PRODUCTION - PRODUCTION MINIERE	2006	2007	2008	2009	2010	2011	2012	2013	2014	
Iron ores and concentrates, metric tons (thousands)	11 155	11 233	11 296	10 524	11 534	11 160	11 200	...	...	Minerais de fer, tonnes (milliers)
Gold ores and concentrates (Kilograms)	10	8	6	8	8	8	8	...	...	Minerais d'or (Kilogrammes)
Copper, Tons (thousands)	5	29	33	37	37	40	38	...	...	Cuivre, tonnes (milliers)

VI ENERGY - ENERGIE	2006	2007	2008	2009	2010	2011	2012	2013	2014	
Total electricity generation (GWh)	586	606	679	712	701	378	383	391	...	Production d'électricité totale (GWh)
of which:										dont:
Production of electricity from fossil fuels (GWh)	535	552	619	602	585	268	268	268	...	Production d'électricité à partir de combustibles fossiles (GWh)
Production of hydro electricity (GWh)	51	54	60	110	116	110	115	123	...	Production d'électricité d'origine hydraulique (GWh)
Production of electricity from solar, wind, tide, wave and other sources (GWh)	...	...	...	...	...	...	...	...	...	Production d'électricité d'origine solaire, éolienne, marée motrice et autres (GWh)

VII TOURISM AND INFRASTRUCTURE - TOURISME ET INFRASTRUCTURE	2006	2007	2008	2009	2010	2011	2012	2013	2014	
VII-1 TOURISM										**VII-1 TOURISME**
International tourist arrivals (thousands)	...	...	...	...	...	...	...	...	...	Arrivées de touristes internationaux (milliers)
Rooms in hotels and similar establishments (thousands)	...	...	...	...	...	...	...	...	...	Chambres d'hotels et établissements assimilés (milliers)
Overnight stays (thousands)	...	...	...	...	...	...	...	...	...	Nuitées (milliers)
Tourism receipts (US$ thousand)	...	...	...	...	...	...	...	...	...	Recettes touristiques (milliers de $ EU)
Total contribution to GDP (%)	...	...	...	...	...	...	...	...	...	Contribution totale au PIB (%)
Total contribution to Employment (%)	...	...	...	...	...	...	...	...	...	Contribution totale à l'emploi (%)
VII-2 INFRASTRUCTURE										**VII-2 INFRASTRUCTURE**
Paved roads (% of total)	27	27	...	28	30	35	...	...	...	Routes asphaltées (% du total)
Total Network (Railways-km)	...	...	728	728	728	728	728	...	...	Réseau total voies ferrées-Km
Main Telephone Lines (per 100 inhabitants)	1	1	2	2	2	2	2	1	...	Lignes téléphoniques fixes (pour 100 habitants)
Mobile Cellular Subscribers (per 100 inhabitants)	33	42	61	62	77	90	106	103	...	Abonnés aux téléphones mobiles (pour 100 habitants)

VIII EXTERNAL TRADE - COMMERCE EXTERIEUR	2006	2007	2008	2009	2010	2011	2012	2013	2014	
OUGUIYA (MILLIONS) **EXPORTS, FOB**										**OUGUIYA (MILLIONS)** **EXPORTATIONS, FÀB**
Exports - Total	367 069	379 063	422 917	357 908	572 080	780 959	782 725	801 090	...	Exportations - Total
Exports to AFRICA	...	...	...	...	...	...	...	...	...	Exportations vers l'AFRIQUE
Main Products										**Principaux produits**
Iron Ore	122 209	144 403	175 837	137 024	275 069	360 878	378 475	410 211	...	Minerai de fer
Fishing Products	45 993	64 032	70 406	70 561	76 058	104 688	113 744	99 683	...	Produits de pêche
Petroleum Products	170 504	88 105	81 726	57 269	82 019	39 316	60 763	65 549	...	Produits pétroliers
	...	...	...	...	...	...	...	...	...	
	...	...	...	...	...	...	...	...	...	
Main Destinations										**Principales destinations**
China	70 207	106 877	152 908	156 109	223 497	359 412	381 837	...	...	Chine
France	37 241	36 783	39 873	13 939	53 122	63 733	44 457	...	...	France
Italy	40 162	30 523	25 879	34 280	34 431	69 093	61 499	...	...	Italie
Spain	24 962	30 988	27 814	20 670	32 306	37 152	35 762	...	...	Espagne
Japan	24 994	19 332	17 211	27 034	33 852	35 734	53 814	...	...	Japon
IMPORTS, CIF										**IMPORTATIONS, CAF**
Imports - Total	288 295	369 887	468 413	350 804	476 340	485 759	726 930	919 501	...	Importations - Total (millions)
Imports from Africa	...	...	...	...	...	...	...	...	...	Importations en provenance de l'Afrique
Main Products										**Principaux produits**
Equipment goods	52 526	68 126	55 807	78 686	134 825	224 826	...	...	...	Biens d'équipement
Petroleum Products	77 825	113 300	138 549	70 855	125 956	74 287	108 405	191 512	...	Produits pétroliers
Food	64 963	84 015	105 271	96 049	86 542	92 818	113 309	113 880	...	Produits alimentaires
Cars / spare parts	20 141	26 033	27 139	26 024	37 801	48 671	...	...	...	Voitures/pieces détachées
Construction & public works Equipment	24 326	31 293	24 068	26 536	38 755	64 886	...	...	...	Matériel Construction & public works
Main Origin										**Principales provenances**
France	41 484	69 461	86 958	53 081	59 640	64 906	84 588	...	...	France
China	27 667	33 986	45 053	47 583	62 735	88 710	123 610	...	...	Chine
Netherlands	7 562	12 684	34 123	36 898	63 518	64 242	...	...	...	Pays-Bas
United States	23 022	25 348	25 916	11 346	18 736	55 750	72 718	...	...	États-Unis
Spain	19 300	27 569	31 153	14 669	23 474	45 392	51 163	...	...	Espagne

IX FINANCIAL AND MONETARY STATISTICS - FINANCES ET STATISTIQUES MONETAIRES	2006	2007	2008	2009	2010	2011	2012	2013	2014	
IX-1 MONETARY STATISTICS *OUGUIYA (MILLIONS)*										**IX-1 STATISTIQUES MONÉTAIRES** *OUGUIYA (MILLIONS)*
Money supply (M1)	177 920	211 560	240 630	276 520	312 060	374 150	413 440	469 670	527 750	Masse monétaire (M1)
Quasi-money	29 177	40 501	37 576	45 924	48 810	50 329	51 620	-	-	Quasi-monnaie
of which Demand Deposit	...	...	...	...	...	...	...	...	...	dont Monnaie scripturale
Net foreign assets	- 3 034	11 438	- 5 258	- 3 516	9 281	71 296	193 288	...	...	Avoirs extérieurs nets
Domestic credit	266 075	305 043	379 916	420 031	465 860	502 786	458 854	-	-	Crédit intérieur
of which claims on private sector	153 892	183 182	238 221	247 114	283 812	315 551	358 537	...	...	dont créances sur le secteur privé
of which claims on government sector, net	112 183	121 861	141 695	172 917	182 047	187 235	100 317	-	-	dont créances nettes sur le gouvernement
International reserves (millions US$)	188	198	189	226	272	485	950	831	...	Réserves internationales (millions $EU)
Average Exchange Rate (National Currency per US$)	271.33	262.49	243.09	263.22	276.09	281.35	296.62	302.07	306.00	Taux de change (moyen) (monnaie nationale par $ EU)
IX-2 PUBLIC FINANCE *OUGUIYA (MILLIONS)*										**IX-2 FINANCES PUBLIQUES** *OUGUIYA (MILLIONS)*
Total Revenues and Grants	405 959	185 058	189 000	188 500	248 550	301 170	356 920	509 870	515 531	Recettes totales et dons
Tax Revenue	97 093	106 126	114 666	106 605	155 652	185 024	248 100	268 880	254 683	Recettes fiscales
Non Tax Revenue	56 345	62 641	67 849	75 781	83 038	108 440	101 450	229 690	250 868	Recettes non fiscales
Grants	252 521	16 291	6 485	6 114	9 860	7 706	7 370	11 300	9 981	Dons
Total Expenditures and Net Lending	206 247	217 357	262 023	242 880	254 603	311 753	414 520	436 740	495 190	Dépenses totales et prêts nets
Current expenditure	157 799	158 878	206 421	186 656	176 503	226 713	277 570	267 060	308 655	Dépenses courantes
Of which Wages and Salaries	52 816	64 582	71 268	76 970	83 680	89 140	94 670	103 700	118 476	Dont rémunérations et salaires
Capital expenditure	44 648	58 479	55 602	51 794	64 750	85 040	136 950	169 580	186 380	Dépenses d'équipement
Net Lending	3 800	-	-	4 430	13 350	-	-	100	155	Prêts nets
Fiscal Balance	199 712	- 32 299	- 73 023	- 54 380	- 6 053	- 10 583	- 57 600	73 130	20 341	Solde global y compris les dons
IX-3 BALANCE OF PAYMENTS *OUGUIYA (MILLIONS)*										**IX-3 BALANCE DES PAIEMENTS** *OUGUIYA (MILLIONS)*
Trade balance	53 613	5 962	- 29 973	- 28 507	38 132	86 749	- 156 886	- 118 653	...	Balance commerciale
Services Balance	- 85 845	- 143 632	- 151 127	- 104 093	- 151 996	- 155 243	- 255 800	- 245 794	...	Balance des services
Net Income	- 20 160	- 20 748	7 414	13 577	- 18 912	- 43 772	- 56 502	- 59 266	...	Revenus nets
Compensation of employees	...	...	...	...	...	...	...	...	...	Rémunération des salariés
Investment Income	...	...	...	...	...	...	...	...	...	Revenus des investissements
Current transfers, net total	43 061	30 302	47 791	34 430	44 729	42 574	94 788	75 669	...	Transferts courants
Net official transfers	...	...	...	...	...	...	...	...	...	Transferts officiels nets
Workers' remittances	...	...	...	...	...	...	...	...	...	Envois de fonds des travailleurs
Other private transfers	...	...	...	...	...	...	...	...	...	Autres transferts privés
Current account balance	- 9 332	- 128 116	- 125 895	- 84 594	- 88 047	- 69 690	- 374 402	- 348 045	...	Solde du compte courant
Capital & financial account	...	...	...	...	151 925	140 464	519 584	...	...	Comptes de capital et financier
Capital account	...	...	...	...	57 663	...	...	...	...	Compte de capital
Financial account	...	...	...	...	94 262	...	...	...	...	Compte financier
Errors & omissions	...	...	...	...	1 206	422	- 16 944	...	...	Erreurs et omissions
Overall balance	...	...	...	...	65 083	71 196	144 835	...	...	Balance générale

X DEBT AND FINANCIAL FLOWS - DETTE ET FLUX FINANCIERS	2006	2007	2008	2009	2010	2011	2012	2013	2014	
X-1 DEBT *US$ (MILLIONS)*										**X-1 DETTE EXTÉRIEURE** *$ E.U (MILLIONS)*
Total external debt	2 541	2 700	2 911	3 197	3 432	3 747	4 225	4 550	3 830	Dette extérieure totale
Private	196	100	67	67	67	67	67	67	67	Privée
Public	2 345	2 600	2 844	3 131	3 366	3 680	4 158	4 484	3 763	Publique
Total external debt service	80	81	112	102	122	127	167	161	265	Service de la dette extérieure
Present value of External debt	...	...	...	...	...	...	...	...	...	Valeur actuelle de la dette extérieure
Total government domestic debt (in local currency)	...	...	...	...	...	...	...	...	...	Dette publique intérieure
X-2 FINANCIAL FLOWS *US$ (MILLIONS)*										**X-2 FLUX FINANCIERS** *$ E.U (MILLIONS)*
Net Foreign Direct Investment Inflows	155	139	343	- 3	131	589	1 383	1 154	...	Investissements étranger direct (flux nets entrants)
Main origin of FDI Inflows										**Principales origines de l'IDE entrant:**
Netherlands	-	-	...	...	...	...	...	...	...	Pays-Bas
Germany	...	...	-	1	4.0	...	...	...	...	Allemagne
Luxembourg	-	0	0	6	...	...	19.9	...	...	Luxembourg
France	- 1	...	...	...	...	...	...	...	...	France
Denmark	...	...	...	...	...	...	...	...	...	Danemark
African countries	...	...	...	...	...	...	...	...	...	Pays africains
Net total Official Development Assistance	226	347	452	373	374	382	408	291	...	Aide publique au développement (nette totale)
Main origin of Net ODA										**Principales origines de l'APD nette**
IDA	50	72	45	38	38.3	33.4	37.6	...	...	IDA
France	32	38	29	35	32.2	57.2	84.1	45.4	...	France
Spain	13	39	34	45	34.7	35.1	9.1	14.8	...	Espagne
Japan	12	23	14	10	14.6	10.0	13.4	23.6	...	Japon
United States	12	10	26	10	11.4	11.6	22.0	21.5	...	Etats-Unis
General notes	National Account: The accounts are calculated using the new base year 2004				Comptes Nationaux: Les comptes sont calculées selon la nouvelle année de base 2004					Notes générales

MAURITIUS — MAURICE

AREA (KM²)	2 040		SUPERFICIE (KM²)
CAPITAL CITY	Port Louis	Port Louis	CAPITALE
CURRENCY	Mauritian Rupee	Roupie Mauricienne	MONNAIE

I SOCIAL AND DEMOGRAPHIC INDICATORS — INDICATEURS DEMOGRAPHIQUES ET SOCIAUX

	Year / Année	Value / Valeur	
POPULATION			**POPULATION**
Population ('000)			Population ('000)
Both sexes	2014	1 249	Les deux sexes
Male	2014	616	Masculin
Female	2014	633	Féminin
Average annual growth rate	2014	0.3	Taux de croissance annuel
Active Population ('000)	2014	621	Population active ('000)
Population by age group ('000)			Population par groupe d'âge ('000)
0-14 years	2014	242	0-14 ans
15-64 years	2014	893	15-64 ans
65+ years	2014	114	65+ ans
Economically active population in agriculture (%)	2014	6.8	Participation de la population active agricole (%)
Crude birth rate	2014	11.4	Taux brut de natalité
Crude death rate	2014	8.1	Taux brut de mortalité
Total fertility rate	2014	1.5	Indice synthétique de fécondité
Proportion of urban population	2014	41.8	Part de la population urbaine
Life Expectancy at Birth - Total (years)	2014	73.8	Espérance de vie à la naissance - Totale (ans)
Dependency Ratio - Total (%)	2014	39.5	Taux de dépendance - Total (%)
HEALTH			**SANTÉ**
Percentage of children under-five and underweight	...	...	% d'enfants de moins de cinq ans avec insuffisance pondérale
Prevalence of undernourishment	2013	5.0	Prévalence de la malnutrition
Under five mortality rate (both sexes, per 1000)	2013	14.3	Taux de mortalité de moins de 5 ans (les deux sexes, pour 1000)
Infant mortality rate (both sexes) per 1000	2013	12.5	Taux de mortalité infantile (les deux sexes) par 1000
Percentage of children provided the vaccines :			Pourcentage d'enfants vaccinés :
BCG	2013	99.0	BCG
DPT3	2013	98.0	DTC3
Polio	2012	99.0	Polio
Measles	2013	99.0	Rougeole
Percentage of mothers provided at least one antenatal care (%)	2003	93.0	Pourcentage de mères ayant au moins reçu un soin prénatal (%)
Percentage of deliveries attended by skilled health personnel	2003	98.4	% d'accouchements assistés par un personnel de santé qualifié
Number of doctors (per 10 000 population)	2004	10.6	Nombre de médecins (pour 10 000 habitants)
Number of nurses (per 10 000 population)	2004	37.3	Nombre d'infirmières (pour 10 000 habitants)
Hospital beds - Total (per 10 000 population)	2011	34.0	Nombre de lits d'hôpitaux - Total (pour 10 000)
Births registered (per 1 000)	2014	11.4	Naiss.s enregistrées (pour 1 000)
Deaths registered (per 1 000)	2014	8.1	Décès enregistrés (pour 1 000)
Public expenditure on Health (% of budget)	2011	9.0	Dépenses publiques consacrées à la santé (% du budget)
EDUCATION			**EDUCATION**
Enrolment in primary education (both sexes) (000)	2013	109	Scolarisation dans le primaire (les deux sexes) (000)
Female	2013	54	Féminin
Enrolment in secondary education (both sexes) (000)	2012	127	Scolarisation dans le secondaire (les deux sexes) (000)
Female	2012	64	Féminin
Enrolment in tertiary education (both sexes) (000)	...	...	Scolarisation dans le tertiaire (les deux sexes) (000)
Female	2013	22.7	Féminin
Literacy rate (both sexes)	2011	89.2	Taux d'alphabétisation (deux sexes)
Male	2011	92.0	Masculin
Female	2011	86.7	Féminin
Pupil-teacher ratio	...	...	Ratio élève-enseignant
Public expenditure on education (% of budget)	2013	14.8	Dépenses publiques consacrées à l'enseignement (% du budget)
POVERTY			**PAUVRETÉ**
GNI Per Capita (US$)	2013	9 290.0	RNB par habitant ($EU)
Human Poverty Index (HPI-1) Value (%)	2007	9.5	Valeur de l'Indice de pauvreté (IPH-1) (%)
Population below International Poverty Line ($2/day) (%)	2012	1.9	Population sous le seuil international de pauvreté (2$/J) (%)
Share of Income Held by Richest 10%	2012	28.9	% de revenu des 10% plus riches
Share of Income Held by Poorest 10%	2012	3.0	% de revenu des 10% plus pauvres
Gini index	2012	35.9	Indice de Gini

Charts / Graphiques

Population by age group – 2014
Population par groupe d'age – 2014

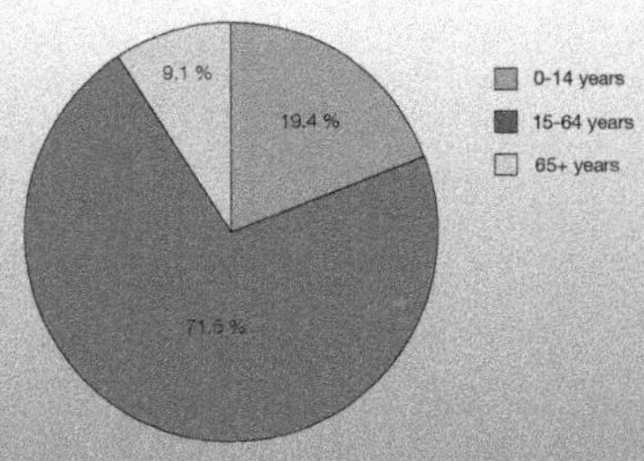

Percentage of children provided the vaccines – 2013
Pourcentage d'enfants vaccinés – 2013

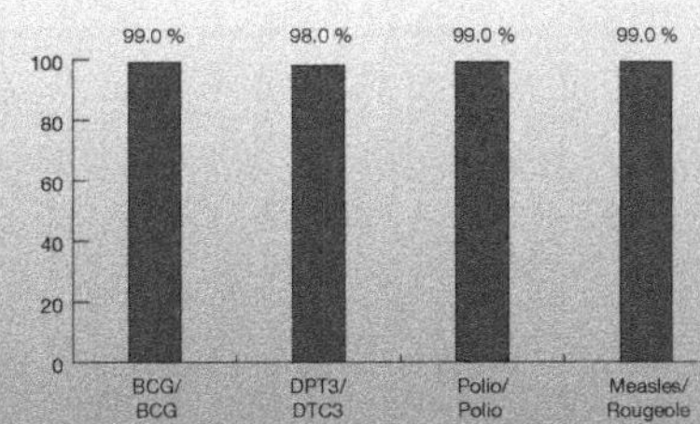

Literacy rate (%) – 2011
Taux d'alphabétisation – 2011

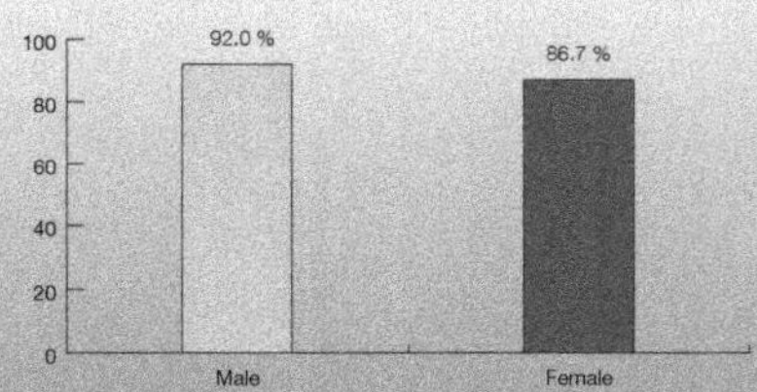

GNI Per Capita (US$)
RNB par habitant ($EU)

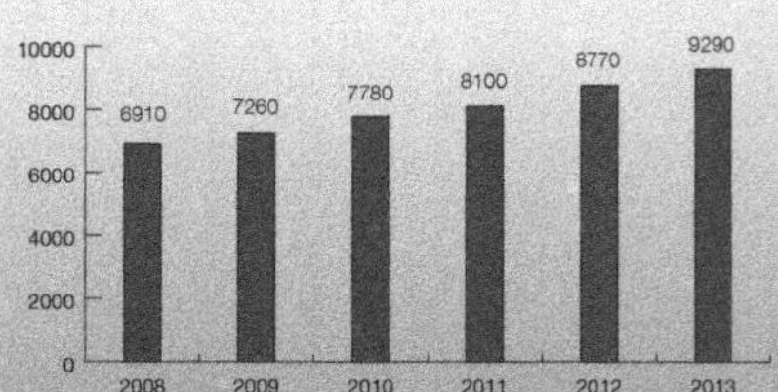

II NATIONAL ACCOUNTS — COMPTES NATIONAUX

	2006	2007	2008	2009	2010	2011	2012	2013	2014	
GROSS DOMESTIC PRODUCT BY KIND OF ECONOMIC ACTIVITY AT CURRENT PRICES *MAURITIAN RUPEE (MILLIONS)*										**PRODUIT INTÉRIEUR BRUT PAR BRANCHE D'ACTIVITÉ ÉCONOMIQUE AUX PRIX COURANTS** *ROUPIE MAURICIENNE (MILLIONS)*
Agriculture, hunting, forestry and fishing	9 759	9 653	9 942	9 539	9 440	10 253	10 494	10 405	10 757	Agriculture, chasse sylviculture et pêche
Mining and quarrying	85	79	108	1 040	1 173	1 041	1 000	990	1 030	Industries extractives
Manufacturing	36 818	41 409	47 128	44 909	45 180	48 182	50 537	55 021	56 930	Industries manufacturières
Electricity, gas & water	3 239	3 321	4 590	5 615	5 635	5 368	5 285	5 755	6 182	Electricité, gaz et eau
Construction & public works	10 242	13 282	16 473	17 756	18 544	18 922	19 034	17 680	16 993	Bâtiments et travaux publics
Wholesale & retail trade, restaurants, hotels	37 623	44 365	48 198	45 332	49 407	53 739	58 056	59 402	64 470	Commerce de gros et de détail, restaurants et hôtels
Finance, insurance, real estate, etc.	36 741	43 609	51 167	54 548	57 947	63 804	69 449	74 483	80 697	Banques, assurances, affaires immobilières
Transport and communications	21 544	23 790	23 922	27 513	29 298	30 730	31 275	32 721	34 737	Transport(s) et communications
Public administration and defense	11 650	12 041	13 780	15 322	16 159	17 189	17 984	21 283	22 280	Administrations publiques et défense
Education	8 268	8 947	10 273	11 098	11 707	12 622	13 413	15 428	16 354	Education
Health and Social Work	6 143	6 712	7 729	8 810	9 529	10 583	11 698	13 768	15 062	Santé et actions sociales
Other services	7 013	8 240	9 805	10 133	11 198	12 846	14 392	16 022	17 749	Autres services
Less Imputed Service Charges	...	...	...	...	...	...	...	...	...	Moins services d'intermédiation financière
Gross domestic product at factor cost / basic prices	189 125	215 449	243 115	251 615	265 216	285 279	302 617	322 958	343 241	Produit intérieur brut aux couts des facteurs / prix de base
Plus: indirect taxes / taxes on products, less subsidies	24 319	28 549	31 201	30 739	33 956	37 731	41 218	43 270	45 058	Plus taxes indirectes/impôts sur les produits, moins les subventions
EXPENDITURE ON GROSS DOMESTIC PRODUCT AT CURRENT PURCHASER'S VALUES *MAURITIAN RUPEE (MILLIONS)*										**EMPLOI DU PRODUIT INTÉRIEUR BRUT AUX PRIX COURANTS D'ACQUISITION** *ROUPIE MAURICIENNE (MILLIONS)*
Government final consumption	30 124	31 492	34 789	39 751	41 625	43 705	45 917	52 748	54 769	Consommation finale des administrations publiques
Private final consumption	148 766	169 522	200 760	208 879	220 305	237 166	254 468	270 261	288 467	Consommation finale privée
Gross fixed capital formation	51 695	61 240	67 529	74 430	74 396	77 565	79 185	77 618	79 115	Formation brute de capital fixe
Change in inventories	5 299	4 453	7 352	- 14 294	- 3 412	6 340	5 977	10 274	7 669	Variation des stocks
Exports of goods and services	128 994	141 187	145 204	138 243	157 036	172 564	187 688	198 893	213 329	Exportations de biens et services
Less imports of goods and services	151 434	163 896	181 319	164 655	190 777	214 328	229 399	243 567	255 052	Moins importations de biens et services
GDP at purchasers' values	213 444	243 998	274 316	282 354	299 172	323 011	343 835	366 228	388 297	PIB aux prix d'acquisition
GROSS DOMESTIC PRODUCT BY KIND OF ECONOMIC ACTIVITY AT CONSTANT PRICES *ANNUAL GROWTH RATES (%)*										**PRODUIT INTÉRIEUR BRUT PAR BRANCHE D'ACTIVITÉ ECONOMIQUE AUX PRIX CONSTANTS** *TAUX DE CROISSANCE ANNUEL (%)*
Agriculture, hunting, forestry and fishing	0.9	- 5.4	3.0	9.1	- 0.8	4.1	- 0.2	0.4	6.4	Agriculture, chasse sylviculture et pêche
Mining and quarrying	- 14.1	- 15.1	22.2	- 5.4	4.4	- 18.9	- 8.3	- 4.6	-	Industries extractives
Manufacturing	5.0	2.4	3.2	2.4	1.9	0.7	2.2	4.4	1.9	Industries manufacturières
Electricity, gas & water	0.0	2.7	6.1	-	4.6	4.1	4.0	4.0	4.8	Electricité, gaz et eau
Construction & public works	6.0	15.9	11.6	5.9	4.3	- 2.0	- 3.0	- 9.4	- 6.7	Bâtiments et travaux publics
Wholesale & retail trade, restaurants, hotels	7.1	7.5	3.5	- 1.8	5.0	3.6	2.5	2.9	3.3	Commerce de gros et de détail,restaurants et hôtels
Finance, insurance, real estate, etc.	6.3	8.4	9.4	4.2	4.8	5.5	4.9	4.9	4.7	Banques, assurances, affaires immobilières
Transport and communications	7.2	7.5	6.1	6.5	5.0	5.3	4.9	4.1	4.3	Transport(s) et communications
Public administration and defense	3.8	0.4	1.1	1.0	3.3	5.0	2.2	2.2	3.1	Administrations publiques et défense
Education	3.6	2.3	3.0	2.5	3.9	3.9	2.9	2.7	2.9	Education
Health and Social Work	8.0	5.6	4.6	6.4	5.9	6.4	7.4	6.4	6.4	Santé et actions sociales
Other services	6.7	8.0	8.4	9.2	7.1	7.0	8.3	8.0	6.9	Autres services
Less Imputed Service Charges	...	...	...	...	...	...	...	...	...	Moins services d'intérmediation financière
Gross domestic product at factor cost / basic prices	5.7	5.7	5.5	3.4	4.0	3.7	3.3	3.2	3.4	Produit intérieur brut aux couts des facteurs / prix de base
Plus: indirect taxes / taxes on products, less subsidies	- 3.3	7.1	5.9	- 1.1	4.8	5.6	2.3	2.7	3.0	Plus taxes indirectes/impôts sur les produits, moins les subventions
Gross domestic product at market prices	4.9	5.8	5.5	3.0	4.1	3.9	3.2	3.2	3.4	Produit intérieur brut aux prix du marché
EXPENDITURE ON GROSS DOMESTIC PRODUCT AT CONSTANT PURCHASERS' VALUES *ANNUAL GROWTH RATES (%)*										**EMPLOIS DU PRODUIT INTÉRIEUR BRUT AUX PRIX CONSTANTS D'ACQUISITION** *TAUX DE CROISSANCE ANNUEL (%)*
Government final consumption	4.3	0.6	- 1.4	5.1	3.4	2.9	2.9	0.7	2.7	Consommation finale des administrations publiques
Private final consumption	6.5	4.4	6.6	- 6.2	2.5	6.4	3.4	7.4	3.0	Consommation finale privée
Gross fixed capital formation	17.5	5.4	1.3	8.9	- 0.7	1.4	- 0.8	- 3.3	- 1.0	Formation brute de capital fixe
Exports of goods and services	4.8	1.7	- 0.6	- 3.4	14.3	4.7	3.1	4.5	6.1	Exportations de biens et services
Less imports of goods and services	12.6	2.5	1.8	- 10.7	9.5	6.2	1.4	5.9	3.8	Moins importations de biens et services
Notes	NA Data: 2013:Semi-final ;2014:Provisional				Données des CN: 2013:Semi-définitives;2014:Provisoires					Notes

III INFLATION

	2006	2007	2008	2009	2010	2011	2012	2013	2014	
ANNUAL GROWTH RATES (%)										**TAUX DE CROISSANCE ANNUEL (%)**
All items	8.9	8.8	9.7	2.5	2.9	6.5	3.9	2.9	4.2	Ensemble
of which:										dont:
Food and Non-alcoholic beverages	5.4	10.5	9.6	2.6	6.9	8.0	3.1	2.1	4.7	Alimentation et boissons non alcoolisés
Alcoholic beverages & tobacco	13.0	-9.0	-14.7	4.6	2.8	18.4	13.2	10.1	5.2	Boissons alcoolisées et tabacs
Clothing and Footwear	8.8	4.3	1.9	6.9	6.4	8.0	6.5	2.6	0.9	Habillement et chaussures
Housing, Water, Electricity, Gas and Other Fuels	5.8	8.5	7.8	-3.2	3.8	5.3	2.8	0.9	-0.2	Logement, eau, électricité, gas et autres combustibles
Furnishing, household equip	6.6	-3.5	-5.2	4.6	3.7	2.7	2.7	2.5	5.1	Meubles, articles de ménage et entretien courant
Health	10.6	7.5	0.6	3.3	1.1	0.1	3.8	3.2	2.2	Santé
Transport	3.7	0.6	1.9	-0.9	2.7	9.9	7.8	1.8	-0.1	Transport
Communication	-3.2	-11.6	-15.3	-2.1	-0.3	-2.2	-1.8	0.0	3.5	Communication
Recreation & culture	5.8	-2.7	-6.6	0.9	2.3	1.4	2.9	0.1	1.6	Loisirs et culture
Education	3.4	-3.9	-9.5	3.5	1.2	5.3	1.9	2.6	4.3	Enseignement
Restaurants & hotels	16.6	-8.8	-8.2	4.1	3.7	9.7	6.9	4.7	2.3	Restaurants et hôtels
Miscellaneous goods & services	4.5	-3.7	-7.9	5.7	4.1	2.6	2.1	2.5	3.1	Biens et services divers

IV AGRICULTURAL PRODUCTION - PRODUCTION AGRICOLE	2006	2007	2008	2009	2010	2011	2012	2013	2014	
TONNES *(THOUSAND)*										**TONNES** *(MILLIERS)*
Potato	11	15	15	20	22	22	20	16	...	Pommes de terre
Tomato	15	11	12	13	12	11	13	11	...	Tomates
Pumpkins, squash and gourds	18	15	14	17	19	19	19	20	...	Citrouilles, courges et calebasses
Sugar cane	4 749	4 236	4 533	4 667	4 366	4 230	3 947	3 816	...	Cane à sucre
Bananas	11	9	10	11	12	11	10	10	...	Bananes

V MINING PRODUCTION - PRODUCTION MINIERE	2006	2007	2008	2009	2010	2011	2012	2013	2014	
Salt and pure sodium chloride, metric tons (thousands)	7	7	5	2	3	3	4	4	...	Sel et chlorure de sodium pur, tonnes métriques (milliers)
...	...	...	...	...	...	...	...	...	...	...
...	...	...	...	...	...	...	...	...	...	...

VI ENERGY - ENERGIE	2006	2007	2008	2009	2010	2011	2012	2013	2014	
Total electricity generation (GWh)	2 218	2 325	2 417	2 436	2 689	2 506	2 537	2 886	...	Production d'électricité totale (GWh)
of which:										dont:
Production of electricity from fossil fuels (GWh)	1 718	1 798	1 845	1 850	2 035	1 736	1 757	2 291	...	Production d'électricité à partir de combustibles fossiles (GWh)
Production of hydro electricity (GWh)	76	83	107	121	101	98	98	95	...	Production d'électricité d'origine hydraulique (GWh)
Production of electricity from solar, wind, tide, wave and other sources (GWh)	4	4	5	5	3	7	7	6	...	Production d'électricité d'origine solaire, éolienne, marée motrice et autres (GWh)

VII TOURISM AND INFRASTRUCTURE - TOURISME ET INFRASTRUCTURE	2006	2007	2008	2009	2010	2011	2012	2013	2014	
VII-1 TOURISM										**VII-1 TOURISME**
International tourist arrivals (thousands)	788	907	930	871	935	965	965	993	1 036	Arrivées de touristes internationaux (milliers)
Rooms in hotels and similar establishments (thousands)	10.9	10.9	11.5	11.5	12.1	11.9	12.5	12.4	...	Chambres d'hotels et établissements assimilés (milliers)
Overnight stays (thousands)	7 761	8 987	9 218	8 639	9 651	10 000	10 461	10 835	11 341	Nuitées (milliers)
Tourism receipts (US$ thousand)	1004 220	1302 300	1452 240	1118 900	1283 800	1482 400	1477 670	1320 430	1438 190	Recettes touristiques (milliers de $ EU)
Total contribution to GDP (%)	31.1	35.4	33.0	27.3	28.9	28.6	27.9	25.3	25.5	Contribution totale au PIB (%)
Total contribution to Employment (%)	28.9	33.0	30.8	25.6	27.1	27.1	26.3	23.9	24.2	Contribution totale à l'emploi (%)
VII-2 INFRASTRUCTURE										**VII-2 INFRASTRUCTURE**
Paved roads (% of total)	98	98	98	98	...	...	...	...	...	Routes asphaltées (% du total)
Total Network (Railways-km)	...	...	...	...	...	...	...	...	...	Réseau total voies ferrées-Km
Main Telephone Lines (per 100 inhabitants)	29	30	30	31	32	30	28	29	...	Lignes téléphoniques fixes (pour 100 habitants)
Mobile Cellular Subscribers (per 100 inhabitants)	63	76	84	89	97	105	120	123	...	Abonnés aux téléphones mobiles (pour 100 habitants)

VIII EXTERNAL TRADE - COMMERCE EXTERIEUR	2006	2007	2008	2009	2010	2011	2012	2013	2014	
MAURITIUS RUPEE (MILLIONS) EXPORTS, FOB										**ROUPIE MAURICIENNE (MILLIONS) EXPORTATIONS, FÀB**
Exports - Total	74 037	69 708	67 970	61 681	69 550	73 586	79 658	88 048	96 733	Exportations - Total
Exports to AFRICA	8 155	9 629	9 826	10 516	11 399	13 140	15 916	15 040	...	Exportations vers l'AFRIQUE
Main Products										**Principaux produits**
Prepared or preserved tuna, skipjack and atlantic bonito	4 981	6 140	6 009	6 712	7 546	7 484	9 988	10 977	...	Préparations et conserves de thon, la bonite et la bonite atlantique
Raw cane sugar	11 198	9 578	8 268	6 828	7 708	8 226	8 135	9 480	...	Sucre de canne brut
T-shirt, singlet & other vest of other textile excl cotton, knitted/crocheted	12 360	12 523	10 357	9 659	9 915	8 920	7 415	6 389	...	T-shirt, singlet et autres gilet d'autres textile excluant coton, tricot / bonneterie
Men's or boys' shirts of cotton, not knitted or crochetd	3 591	4 057	3 487	3 382	3 753	4 032	4 367	5 133	...	Chemises de coton pour hommes ou garçonnets, autres qu'en bonneterie
Men's/boys' trouser, short etc. of cotton, not knitted/crocheted	1 736	2 278	2 284	2 521	2 476	2 697	3 343	3 157	...	Pantalon pour Hommes / garçons, short, etc., de coton, autres qu'en bonneterie
Main Destinations										**Principales destinations**
France	8 704	8 889	7 915	9 317	10 517	8 797	8 720	8 553	...	France
Italy	2 754	3 568	2 686	3 090	4 609	5 159	4 892	6 663	...	Italie
Madagascar	3 288	3 865	3 451	3 587	3 562	3 973	4 641	4 503	...	Madagascar
UK	22 362	21 924	20 134	15 280	13 373	12 644	12 497	11 935	...	Royaume-Uni
USA	5 754	4 760	3 926	4 624	6 189	6 667	6 714	7 242	...	Etats-Unis
IMPORTS, CIF										**IMPORTATIONS, CAF**
Imports - Total	115 502	121 037	132 165	118 444	134 882	147 815	160 996	157 673	162 746	Importations - Total (millions)
Imports from Africa	12 881	13 983	16 986	14 799	16 910	16 925	17 383	17 739	...	Importations en provenance de l'Afrique
Main Products										**Principaux produits**
Fish and fish preparation	6 687	7 066	8 474	7 055	10 182	9 280	10 968	11 880	...	Poisson et préparation de poisson
Refined petroleum products	17 025	18 969	24 042	15 293	21 302	26 977	29 269	31 263	...	Produits petrolier raffinés
Textile yarn and fabrics	8 441	8 989	7 489	6 391	7 267	8 166	7 523	8 299	...	Fils textiles et de tissus
Telecommunications and sound recording	10 678	5 430	4 901	3 483	4 357	3 925	4 781	5 879	...	Telecommunications et enregistrements sonors
Road vehicles	4 505	5 228	6 057	5 446	6 824	7 149	8 658	7 866	...	Vehicules routiers
Main Origin										**Principales provenances**
China	9 988	13 768	15 288	14 903	18 033	20 780	25 834	24 312	...	Chine
France	16 440	12 813	10 159	13 812	11 787	13 158	13 363	13 368	...	France
India	15 687	35 633	31 699	22 336	29 629	34 666	37 191	39 896	...	Inde
Japan	3 254	4 334	5 221	3 823	4 520	3 701	4 086	3 913	...	Japan
South Africa	8 433	8 910	10 723	10 236	11 433	10 457	10 535	10 230	...	Afrique du Sud

IX FINANCIAL AND MONETARY STATISTICS - FINANCES ET STATISTIQUES MONETAIRES										
	2006	2007	2008	2009	2010	2011	2012	2013	2014	
IX-1 MONETARY STATISTICS *MAURITIUS RUPEE (MILLIONS)*										**IX-1 STATISTIQUES MONÉTAIRES** *ROUPIE MAURICIENNE (MILLIONS)*
Money supply (M1)	207 520	239 320	274 310	280 830	300 230	319 540	345 620	365 610	390 210	Masse monétaire (M1)
Quasi-money	153 493	173 661	197 188	194 053	213 064	227 842	246 842	258 832	276 088	Quasi-monnaie
of which Demand Deposit	...	...	...	...	...	...	...	...	...	dont Monnaie scripturale
Net foreign assets	238 553	265 990	285 142	336 656	396 026	370 755	401 321	396 300	457 823	Avoirs extérieurs nets
Domestic credit	218 007	242 190	296 098	281 514	308 855	341 302	391 022	448 175	446 806	Crédit intérieur
of which claims on private sector	153 085	183 106	232 514	233 629	262 857	295 286	346 603	395 882	387 243	dont créances sur le secteur privé
of which claims on government sector, net	46 181	45 524	46 967	30 192	29 843	30 173	26 748	34 759	44 771	dont créances nettes sur le gouvernement
International reserves (millions US$)	1 273	1 784	1 746	2 186	2 449	2 589	2 844	3 347	3 628	Réserves internationales (millions $EU)
Average Exchange Rate (National Currency per US$)	31.71	31.31	28.45	31.96	30.78	28.71	30.05	30.70	30.62	Taux de change (moyen) (monnaie nationale par $ EU)
IX-2 PUBLIC FINANCE *MAURITIUS RUPEE (MILLIONS)*										**IX-2 FINANCES PUBLIQUES** *ROUPIE MAURICIENNE (MILLIONS)*
Total Revenues and Grants	44 024	49 431	57 719	62 893	64 471	68 203	73 794	78 211	92 460	Recettes totales et dons
Tax Revenue	38 585	43 942	50 082	52 085	55 209	59 180	64 919	67 990	79 805	Recettes fiscales
Non Tax Revenue	5 033	5 101	6 019	6 036	7 271	6 678	6 477	8 826	10 414	Recettes non fiscales
Grants	406	388	1 618	4 773	1 991	2 344	2 398	1 394	2 241	Dons
Total Expenditures and Net Lending	49 957	55 557	65 261	73 803	75 059	79 570	80 045	91 058	108 305	Dépenses totales et prêts nets
Current expenditure	42 547	43 130	46 435	50 207	50 360	54 251	52 657	59 355	72 706	Dépenses courantes
Of which Wages and Salaries	16 145	14 606	14 474	17 087	17 541	18 001	18 684	22 717	26 798	Dont rémunérations et salaires
Capital expenditure	6 879	9 970	13 784	16 063	16 623	16 686	17 772	20 541	24 160	Dépenses d'équipement
Net Lending	532	2 457	5 043	7 533	8 076	8 632	9 616	11 162	11 439	Prêts nets
Fiscal Balance	- 5 933	- 6 126	- 7 542	- 10 910	- 10 588	- 11 367	- 6 251	- 12 847	- 15 845	Solde global y compris les dons
IX-3 BALANCE OF PAYMENTS *MAURITIUS RUPEE (MILLIONS)*										**IX-3 BALANCE DES PAIEMENTS** *ROUPIE MAURICIENNE (MILLIONS)*
Trade balance	- 34 532	- 43 939	- 56 597	- 49 473	- 58 289	- 67 585	- 73 098	- 69 590	- 72 250	Balance commerciale
Services Balance	11 231	19 786	17 655	20 050	21 949	22 869	27 008	24 916	25 974	Balance des services
Net Income	1 633	7 023	4 900	1 678	- 274	- 1 953	6 231	9 134	9 080	Revenus nets
Compensation of employees	- 298	- 289	- 343	- 307	- 235	- 256	...	...	...	Rémunération des salariés
Investment Income	1 931	7 312	5 243	1 985	- 39	- 1 697	...	...	...	Revenus des investissements
Current transfers, net total	2 269	3 882	6 409	6 909	5 629	3 795	3 943	2 776	2 809	Transferts courants
Net official transfers	357	545	2 509	3 049	1 699	2 463	...	...	...	Transferts officiels nets
Workers' remittances	...	...	...	...	...	...	...	...	...	Envois de fonds des travailleurs
Other private transfers	1 912	3 337	3 900	3 860	3 930	1 332	...	...	...	Autres transferts privés
Current account balance	- 19 399	- 13 248	- 27 633	- 20 836	- 30 985	- 42 874	- 35 916	- 32 764	- 34 387	Solde du compte courant
Capital & financial account	10 362	1 916	21 073	11 626	26 138	34 476	...	...	...	Comptes de capital et financier
Capital account	- 83	- 51	- 40	- 59	- 148	- 53	...	...	...	Compte de capital
Financial account	10 445	1 967	21 113	11 685	26 286	34 529	...	...	...	Compte financier
Errors & omissions	9 037	11 332	6 560	9 210	4 847	8 397	...	...	...	Erreurs et omissions
Overall balance	-	0	0	-	0	-	...	...	...	Balance générale

X DEBT AND FINANCIAL FLOWS - DETTE ET FLUX FINANCIERS	2006	2007	2008	2009	2010	2011	2012	2013	2014	
X-1 DEBT *US$ (MILLIONS)*										**X-1 DETTE EXTÉRIEURE** *$ E.U (MILLIONS)*
Total external debt	...	...	...	135 433	174 984	229 911	233 847	153 363	145 556	Dette extérieure totale
Private	...	...	...	134 460	173 818	228 464	232 319	151 458	143 588	Privée
Public	720	795	675	973	1 167	1 447	1 528	1 905	1 969	Publique
Total external debt service	295	322	196	130	217	209	224	233	290	Service de la dette extérieure
Present value of External debt	...	...	...	...	...	...	...	...	...	Valeur actuelle de la dette extérieure
Total government domestic debt (in local currency)	104 829	108 668	107 744	125 644	128 557.0	137 219.0	140 806.0	149 960.0	165 285.0	Dette publique intérieure
X-2 FINANCIAL FLOWS *US$ (MILLIONS)*										**X-2 FLUX FINANCIERS** *$ E.U (MILLIONS)*
Net Foreign Direct Investment Inflows	105	339	383	248	430	433	589	259	...	Investissements étranger direct (flux nets entrants)
Main origin of FDI Inflows										**Principales origines de l'IDE entrant:**
United States	16	38	41	73	51.9	141.7	142.9	88.2	...	États-Unis
Luxembourg	121	89	72	47	150.5	80.6	135.6	16.4	...	Luxembourg
Japan	5	76	37	21	4.3	8.0	13.0	6.9	...	Japon
France	1	16	50	16	47.7	104.6	177.8	48.8	...	France
Netherlands	7	19	67	10	93.8	18.1	23.5	2.4	...	Pays-Bas
African countries	9	36	68	33	65.6	122.7	194.8	66.5	...	Pays africains
Net total Official Development Assistance	19	69	110	155	125	185	178	148	...	Aide publique au développement (nette totale)
Main origin of Net ODA										**Principales origines de l'APD nette**
France	3	40	16	43	54.0	100.5	83.7	62.3	...	France
United Kingdom	...	...	1	21	5.5	13.5	0.0	...	...	Royaume-Uni
Japan	4	3	0	- 2	- 2.9	- 2.4	1.1	- 0.6	...	Japon
UNTA	1	2	1	-	...	...	...	...	...	ATNU
UNDP	...	1	2	1	1.1	0.6	0.5	...	...	PNUD

MOROCCO — MAROC

AREA (KM²)	710 850	SUPERFICIE (KM²)
CAPITAL CITY	Rabat	CAPITALE
CURRENCY	Dirham	MONNAIE

I SOCIAL AND DEMOGRAPHIC INDICATORS — INDICATEURS DEMOGRAPHIQUES ET SOCIAUX

	Year Année	Value Valeur	
POPULATION			**POPULATION**
Population ('000)			Population ('000)
Both sexes	2014	33 493	Les deux sexes
Male	2014	16 563	Masculin
Female	2014	16 930	Féminin
Average annual growth rate	2014	1.6	Taux de croissance annuel
Active Population ('000)	2014	11 685	Population active ('000)
Population by age group ('000)			Population par groupe d'âge ('000)
0-14 years	2014	9 354	0-14 ans
15-64 years	2014	22 462	15-64 ans
65+ years	2014	1 677	65+ ans
Economically active population in agriculture (%)	2014	24.5	Participation de la population active agricole (%)
Crude birth rate	2014	22.5	Taux brut de natalité
Crude death rate	2014	6.3	Taux brut de mortalité
Total fertility rate	2014	2.7	Indice synthétique de fécondité
Proportion of urban population	2014	58.1	Part de la population urbaine
Life Expectancy at Birth - Total (years)	2014	71.2	Espérance de vie à la naissance - Totale (ans)
Dependency Ratio - Total (%)	2014	48.3	Taux de dépendance - Total (%)
HEALTH			**SANTÉ**
Percentage of children under-five and underweight	2011	3.1	% d'enfants de moins de cinq ans avec insuffisance pondérale
Prevalence of undernourishment	2013	5.0	Prévalence de la malnutrition
Under five mortality rate (both sexes. per 1000)	2013	30.4	Taux de mortalité de moins de 5 ans (les deux sexes. pour 1000)
Infant mortality rate (both sexes) per 1000	2013	26.1	Taux de mortalité infantile (les deux sexes) par 1000
Percentage of children provided the vaccines :			Pourcentage d'enfants vaccinés :
BCG	2013	99.0	BCG
DPT3	2013	99.0	DTC3
Polio	2011	98.0	Polio
Measles	2013	99.0	Rougeole
Percentage of mothers provided at least one antenatal care (%)	2011	77.1	Pourcentage de mères ayant au moins reçu un soin prénatal (%)
Percentage of deliveries attended by skilled health personnel	2011	73.6	% d'accouchements assistés par un personnel de santé qualifié
Number of doctors (per 10 000 population)	2009	6.2	Nombre de médecins (pour 10 000 habitants)
Number of nurses (per 10 000 population)	2009	8.9	Nombre d'infirmières (pour 10 000 habitants)
Hospital beds - Total (per 10 000 population)	2013	8.4	Nombre de lits d'hôpitaux - Total (pour 10 000)
Births registered (per 1 000)	2014	22.5	Naiss.s enregistrées (pour 1 000)
Deaths registered (per 1 000)	2014	6.3	Décès enregistrés (pour 1 000)
Public expenditure on Health (% of budget)	2013	4.8	Dépenses publiques consacrées à la santé (% du budget)
EDUCATION			**EDUCATION**
Enrolment in primary education (both sexes) (000)	2014	4 030	Scolarisation dans le primaire (les deux sexes) (000)
Female	2014	1 918	Féminin
Enrolment in secondary education (both sexes) (000)	2013	2 555	Scolarisation dans le secondaire (les deux sexes) (000)
Female	2013	1 166	Féminin
Enrolment in tertiary education (both sexes) (000)	...	...	Scolarisation dans le tertiaire (les deux sexes) (000)
Female	2010	210.5	Féminin
Literacy rate (both sexes)	2011	67.1	Taux d'alphabétisation (deux sexes)
Male	2011	76.1	Masculin
Female	2011	57.6	Féminin
Pupil-teacher ratio	2013	25.9	Ratio élève-enseignant
Public expenditure on education (% of budget)	2013	20.0	Dépenses publiques consacrées à l'enseignement (% du budget)
POVERTY			**PAUVRETÉ**
GNI Per Capita (US$)	2013	3 020.0	RNB par habitant ($EU)
Human Poverty Index (HPI-1) Value (%)	2007	31.1	Valeur de l'Indice de pauvreté (IPH-1) (%)
Population below International Poverty Line ($2/day) (%)	2007	14.2	Population sous le seuil international de pauvreté (2$/J) (%)
Share of Income Held by Richest 10%	2007	33.2	% de revenu des 10% plus riches
Share of Income Held by Poorest 10%	2007	2.7	% de revenu des 10% plus pauvres
Gini index	2007	40.9	Indice de Gini

Charts
Graphiques

Population by age group – 2014
Population par groupe d'age – 2014

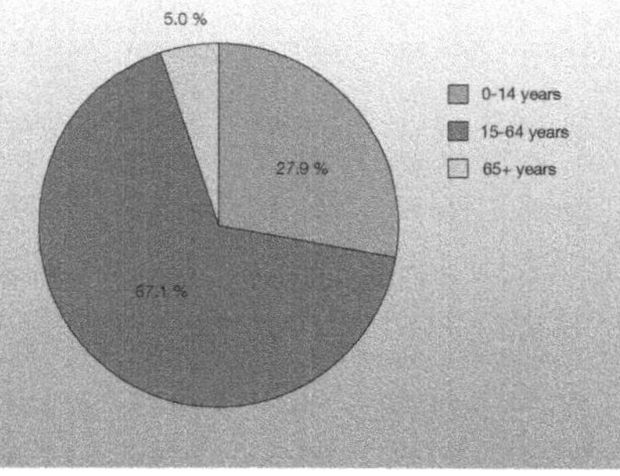

Percentage of children provided the vaccines – 2013
Pourcentage d'enfants vaccinés – 2013

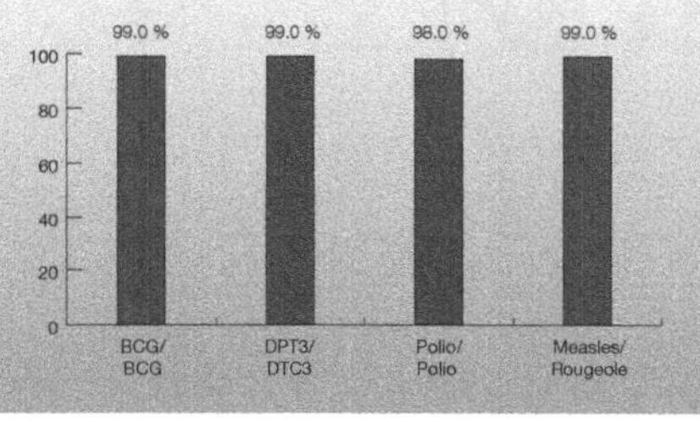

Literacy rate (%) – 2011
Taux d'alphabétisation – 2011

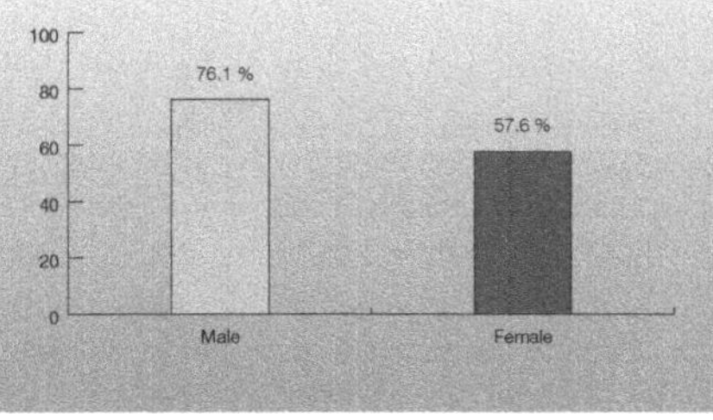

GNI Per Capita (US$)
RNB par habitant ($EU)

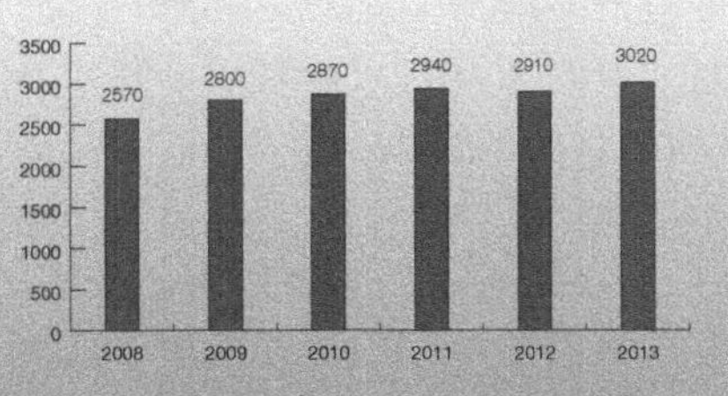

II NATIONAL ACCOUNTS — COMPTES NATIONAUX

	2006	2007	2008	2009	2010	2011	2012	2013	2014	
GROSS DOMESTIC PRODUCT BY KIND OF ECONOMIC ACTIVITY AT CURRENT PRICES *DIRHAM (MILLIONS)*										**PRODUIT INTÉRIEUR BRUT PAR BRANCHE D'ACTIVITÉ ÉCONOMIQUE AUX PRIX COURANTS** *DIRHAM (MILLIONS)*
Agriculture, hunting, forestry and fishing	87 482	74 928	90 690	107 050	105 534	114 866	110 575	132 465	...	Agriculture, chasse sylviculture et pêche
Mining and quarrying	10 534	13 155	45 121	16 925	29 579	41 355	40 343	30 808	...	Industries extractives
Manufacturing	82 498	82 915	87 959	105 088	108 049	116 298	122 386	123 396	...	Industries manufacturières
Electricity, gas & water	14 687	15 749	16 123	18 953	19 362	18 962	20 044	21 042	...	Electricité, gaz et eau
Construction & public works	32 912	37 233	38 663	45 776	47 085	47 941	50 099	52 833	...	Bâtiments et travaux publics
Wholesale & retail trade, restaurants, hotels	74 221	81 352	86 875	88 829	92 261	95 829	99 569	103 486	...	Commerce de gros et de détail, restaurants et hôtels
Finance, insurance, real estate, etc.	96 167	113 454	119 778	125 276	129 419	137 454	146 793	150 450	...	Banques, assurances, affaires immobilières
Transport and communications	36 491	43 151	45 262	47 892	50 545	50 897	50 487	49 604	...	Transport(s) et communications
Public administration and defense	50 664	51 910	54 000	59 875	62 600	69 611	74 830	77 937	...	Administrations publiques et défense
Education	49 997	54 271	59 360	62 293	66 604	75 512	79 902	84 194	...	Education
Health and Social Work	-	-	-	-	-	-	-	-	...	Santé et actions sociales
Other services	8 246	8 664	9 126	9 502	10 566	10 650	10 912	11 396	...	Autres services
Less Imputed Service Charges	- 25 951	- 31 089	- 33 325	- 34 302	- 33 882	- 36 956	- 38 210	- 38 206	...	Moins services d'intermédiation financière
Gross domestic product at factor cost / basic prices	517 948	545 693	619 632	653 157	687 722	742 419	767 730	799 405	...	Produit intérieur brut aux couts des facteurs / prix de base
Plus: indirect taxes / taxes on products, less subsidies	59 396	70 561	69 211	79 292	76 309	60 188	59 767	73 386	...	Plus taxes indirectes/impôts sur les produits, moins les subventions
EXPENDITURE ON GROSS DOMESTIC PRODUCT AT CURRENT PURCHASER'S VALUES *DIRHAM (MILLIONS)*										**EMPLOI DU PRODUIT INTÉRIEUR BRUT AUX PRIX COURANTS D'ACQUISITION** *DIRHAM (MILLIONS)*
Government final consumption	107 071	112 234	118 132	133 397	133 938	146 332	159 118	165 559	...	Consommation finale des administrations publiques
Private final consumption	331 996	360 008	400 395	418 461	437 547	472 938	495 655	524 395	...	Consommation finale privée
Gross fixed capital formation	162 456	192 573	227 465	226 177	234 407	246 394	258 859	263 272	...	Formation brute de capital fixe
Change in inventories	7 446	7 614	35 095	34 898	33 251	42 168	33 006	34 893	...	Variation des stocks
Exports of goods and services	197 459	220 302	258 165	210 241	253 941	285 530	297 170	293 670	...	Exportations de biens et services
Less imports of goods and services	229 084	276 477	350 409	290 725	329 053	390 755	416 311	408 998	...	Moins importations de biens et services
GDP at purchasers' values	577 344	616 254	688 843	732 449	764 031	802 607	827 497	872 791	...	PIB aux prix d'acquisition
GROSS DOMESTIC PRODUCT BY KIND OF ECONOMIC ACTIVITY AT CONSTANT PRICES *ANNUAL GROWTH RATES (%)*										**PRODUIT INTÉRIEUR BRUT PAR BRANCHE D'ACTIVITÉ ECONOMIQUE AUX PRIX CONSTANTS** *TAUX DE CROISSANCE ANNUEL (%)*
Agriculture, hunting, forestry and fishing	24.5	- 20.4	16.4	29.7	- 2.1	5.3	- 8.2	18.9	- 1.6	Agriculture, chasse sylviculture et pêche
Mining and quarrying	1.6	9.1	- 5.9	- 23.8	38.6	5.9	- 2.4	- 2.9	4.2	Industries extractives
Manufacturing	3.9	4.4	2.0	0.1	2.8	2.2	1.7	0.1	2.9	Industries manufacturières
Electricity, gas & water	6.9	5.8	5.9	3.5	7.1	6.0	6.9	0.4	3.5	Electricité, gaz et eau
Construction & public works	8.7	11.7	9.4	3.4	2.6	4.2	2.1	1.4	0.4	Bâtiments et travaux publics
Wholesale & retail trade, restaurants, hotels	5.2	2.7	3.9	2.8	0.8	3.7	2.3	1.6	1.7	Commerce de gros et de détail,restaurants et hôtels
Finance, insurance, real estate, etc.	46.7	15.2	0.6	- 9.7	4.1	2.7	- 0.7	- 3.9	8.4	Banques, assurances, affaires immobilières
Transport and communications	7.9	9.4	5.9	2.8	5.6	13.0	15.8	2.6	5.4	Transport(s) et communications
Public administration and defense	3.2	2.4	3.9	9.3	2.9	5.8	6.7	3.4	2.2	Administrations publiques et défense
Education	2.6	8.0	8.7	3.2	4.8	8.4	4.9	3.8	5.2	Education
Health and Social Work	...	...	...	...	...	...	...	...	...	Santé et actions sociales
Other services	3.0	3.9	1.7	2.3	1.1	1.0	0.8	2.1	...	Autres services
Less Imputed Service Charges	8.9	17.5	3.2	1.5	- 2.2	8.3	2.5	- 1.9	- 0.8	Moins services d'intérmediation financière
Gross domestic product at factor cost / basic prices	12.8	1.7	5.7	4.8	3.2	5.3	2.3	4.1	1.9	Produit intérieur brut aux couts des facteurs / prix de base
Plus: indirect taxes / taxes on products, less subsidies	- 20.4	10.6	5.0	4.6	6.7	2.7	5.4	6.0	2.8	Plus taxes indirectes/impôts sur les produits, moins les subventions
Gross domestic product at market prices	7.8	2.7	5.6	4.8	3.6	5.0	2.7	4.4	2.0	Produit intérieur brut aux prix du marché
EXPENDITURE ON GROSS DOMESTIC PRODUCT AT CONSTANT PURCHASERS' VALUES *ANNUAL GROWTH RATES (%)*										**EMPLOIS DU PRODUIT INTÉRIEUR BRUT AUX PRIX CONSTANTS D'ACQUISITION** *TAUX DE CROISSANCE ANNUEL (%)*
Government final consumption	2.9	4.4	4.8	12.1	- 0.9	4.6	7.9	3.7	...	Consommation finale des administrations publiques
Private final consumption	4.9	2.9	5.1	7.2	1.6	7.7	2.5	4.4	...	Consommation finale privée
Gross fixed capital formation	9.7	14.3	11.5	2.6	- 0.7	2.5	1.6	0.2	...	Formation brute de capital fixe
Exports of goods and services	11.6	5.2	7.3	- 14.8	16.6	2.1	2.6	2.4	...	Exportations de biens et services
Less imports of goods and services	8.2	15.0	12.2	- 6.0	3.6	5.0	1.7	- 1.5	...	Moins importations de biens et services
Notes	NA Data: 2012: Semi-final; 2013:Provisional				Données des CN: 2012 semi-définitives;2013:Provisoires					Notes

III INFLATION

	2006	2007	2008	2009	2010	2011	2012	2013	2014	
ANNUAL GROWTH RATES (%)										**TAUX DE CROISSANCE ANNUEL (%)**
All items	3.3	2.0	3.7	1.0	0.9	0.9	1.3	1.9	0.4	Ensemble
of which:										dont:
Food and Non-alcoholic beverages	3.9	2.7	7.4	0.5	0.6	1.4	2.4	2.2	-1.2	Alimentation et boissons non alcoolisés
Alcoholic beverages & tobacco	...	...	...	...	...	-	0.1	5.4	1.7	Boissons alcoolisées et tabacs
Clothing and Footwear	...	1.1	1.8	1.4	0.7	1.7	2.0	1.5	2.1	Habillement et chaussures
Housing, Water, Electricity, Gas and Other Fuels	3.0	2.2	1.3	0.7	0.5	0.4	0.5	1.1	2.5	Logement, eau, électricité, gas et autres combustibles
Furnishing, household equip	...	1.6	2.9	1.4	0.8	0.9	0.1	0.2	0.8	Meubles, articles de ménage et entretien courant
Health	0.8	0.6	0.5	1.0	0.4	0.2	0.7	0.9	-0.2	Santé
Transport	8.9	-2.3	0.9	0.7	-0.3	-0.1	3.2	3.2	2.6	Transport
Communication	...	...	...	...	...	-5.4	-19.7	-9.2	-4.6	Communication
Recreation & culture	...	0.9	2.0	1.8	-	-0.7	0.5	0.5	-0.9	Loisirs et culture
Education	...	...	...	...	...	4.1	3.9	5.5	3.4	Enseignement
Restaurants & hotels	...	...	...	...	...	1.7	2.0	3.2	2.5	Restaurants et hôtels
Miscellaneous goods & services	...	1.2	2.6	2.2	1.8	2.0	1.3	1.3	1.2	Biens et services divers

IV AGRICULTURAL PRODUCTION - PRODUCTION AGRICOLE

	2006	2007	2008	2009	2010	2011	2012	2013	2014	
TONNES *(THOUSAND)*										**TONNES** *(MILLIERS)*
Wheat	6 327	1 583	3 769	6 371	4 876	6 018	3 878	6 934	...	Blé tendre
Potatoes	1 569	1 437	1 537	1 234	1 605	1 721	1 657	1 929	...	pomme de terre
Tomatoes	1 245	1 237	1 312	1 230	1 434	1 218	1 219	1 293	...	Tomates
Olives	631	659	765	850	1 506	1 416	1 316	1 182	...	Olives
Onions, dry	882	700	662	802	821	861	856	930	...	Oignons

V MINING PRODUCTION - PRODUCTION MINIERE

	2006	2007	2008	2009	2010	2011	2012	2013	2014	
Zinc, Tons	148 690	111 081	161 493	88 398	83 328	72 239	91 630	82 484	...	Zinc, tonnes
Copper, Tons	17 811	19 891	27 619	42 051	37 689	39 927	58 969	46 319	...	Cuivre, tonnes
Phosphates (dry), Tons (thousands)	27 386	27 834	24 788	18 307	26 628	28 052	27 060	26 400	...	Phosphates secs, tonnes (milliers)

VI ENERGY - ENERGIE

	2006	2007	2008	2009	2010	2011	2012	2013	2014	
Total electricity generation (GWh)	23 215	20 497	20 815	21 345	23 637	25 005	26 356	26 689	...	Production d'électricité totale (GWh)
of which:										dont:
Production of electricity from fossil fuels (GWh)	21 408	19 312	19 597	18 412	19 545	22 308	23 812	22 483	...	Production d'électricité à partir de combustibles fossiles (GWh)
Production of hydro electricity (GWh)	1 601	906	920	2 542	3 433	2 005	1 816	2 990	...	Production d'électricité d'origine hydraulique (GWh)
Production of electricity from solar, wind, tide, wave and other sources (GWh)	206	279	298	391	659	692	728	1 215	...	Production d'électricité d'origine solaire, éolienne, marée motrice et autres (GWh)

VII TOURISM AND INFRASTRUCTURE - TOURISME ET INFRASTRUCTURE

	2006	2007	2008	2009	2010	2011	2012	2013	2014	
VII-1 TOURISM										**VII-1 TOURISME**
International tourist arrivals (thousands)	6 558	7 408	7 879	8 341	9 288	9 342	9 375	10 047	10 398	Arrivées de touristes internationaux (milliers)
Rooms in hotels and similar establishments (thousands)	64.0	68.0	73.0	78.0	...	...	91.5	97.2	...	Chambres d'hotels et établissements assimilés (milliers)
Overnight stays (thousands)	17 265	17 780	16 771	16 212	17 585	15 649	15 812	17 472	18 540	Nuitées (milliers)
Tourism receipts (US$ thousand)	5948 130	7138 380	7177 740	6585 040	6658 580	7277 780	6654 280	6807 290	7051 050	Recettes touristiques (milliers de $ EU)
Total contribution to GDP (%)	20.8	22.4	21.0	19.2	19.5	19.2	19.3	18.0	18.3	Contribution totale au PIB (%)
Total contribution to Employment (%)	18.5	19.9	18.7	17.2	17.3	17.2	17.2	16.0	16.3	Contribution totale à l'emploi (%)
VII-2 INFRASTRUCTURE										**VII-2 INFRASTRUCTURE**
Paved roads (% of total)	62	62	62	70	70	71	...	...	...	Routes asphaltées (% du total)
Total Network (Railways-km)	...	...	...	...	2 109	2 109	2 109	2 109	...	Réseau total voies ferrées-Km
Main Telephone Lines (per 100 inhabitants)	4	8	10	11	12	11	10	9	...	Lignes téléphoniques fixes (pour 100 habitants)
Mobile Cellular Subscribers (per 100 inhabitants)	53	65	74	81	101	114	120	129	...	Abonnés aux téléphones mobiles (pour 100 habitants)

VIII EXTERNAL TRADE - COMMERCE EXTERIEUR

	2006	2007	2008	2009	2010	2011	2012	2013	2014	
DIRHAM (MILLIONS) EXPORTS, FOB										**DIRHAM (MILLIONS) EXPORTATIONS, FÀB**
Exports - Total	104 785	123 941	155 740	113 020	149 583	174 994	184 885	184 685	...	Exportations - Total
Exports to AFRICA	...	...	...	...	...	...	...	...	...	Exportations vers l'AFRIQUE
Main Products										**Principaux produits**
Clothing finished	20 699	20 474	18 924	17 796	18 041	18 430	18 954	18 720	...	Vêtements finis
Hosiery	7 192	7 882	6 659	6 461	6 973	7 742	7 601	7 254	...	Articles de bonneterie
Crustaceans, molluscs and shellfish	4 266	5 165	2 108	4 439	4 564	5 486	5 636	5 970	...	Crustacés, mollusques et coquillages
Phosphoric acid	7 891	9 069	22 831	8 042	13 753	16 392	...	12 053	...	Acide phosphorique
Phosphates	545	712	2 306	4 453	8 984	12 610	12 827	9 097	...	Phosphates
Main Destinations										**Principales destinations**
France	32 518	35 054	31 384	27 464	33 558	35 743	39 696	39 543	...	France
Spain	22 620	25 559	27 862	23 574	25 297	31 618	30 528	34 827	...	Espagne
Italy	5 587	6 480	7 261	5 286	6 725	7 249	6 745	6 977	...	Italie
United Kingdom	6 867	6 388	5 350	3 764	4 341	4 413	5 148	4 991	...	Royaume Uni
India	4 456	4 853	10 520	5 852	9 056	11 786	10 006	6 849	...	Inde
IMPORTS, CIF										**IMPORTATIONS, CAF**
Imports - Total	210 554	261 288	326 042	263 982	297 963	357 770	386 949	379 919	...	Importations - Total (millions)
Imports from Africa	...	...	...	...	...	...	...	...	...	Importations en provenance de l'Afrique
Main Products										**Principaux produits**
Petroleum oils, crude	2 866	3 217	3 983	17 166	25 090	31 423	36 424	36 326	...	Huile brute de pétrole
Gaz-oils & fuel-oils	7 365	10 024	17 685	15 414	19 575	31 519	36 036	35 596	...	Gaz-oils et fuel-oils
Machinery and apparatus, diverse	8 693	9 636	11 087	10 187	10 869	...	...	...	...	Machines et appareils divers
Fabrics	8 223	7 732	7 191	6 501	6 611	7 905	7 808	7 978	...	Tissus
Passenger Cars	6 235	7 691	9 873	8 314	9 501	9 001	10 576	9 249	...	Voitures de tourisme
Main Origin										**Principales provenances**
France	37 140	41 607	48 950	41 584	41 080	51 146	47 919	49 123	...	France
Spain	24 128	27 544	36 447	32 141	32 141	39 174	50 906	51 451	...	Espagne
Italy	13 299	16 695	21 742	17 290	17 290	18 614	18 934	20 286	...	Italie
USA	9 492	15 442	16 624	18 289	20 981	28 953	24 598	28 524	...	Etats-Unis
China	11 069	15 146	18 538	20 610	24 993	23 331	25 585	20 286	...	Chine

IX FINANCIAL AND MONETARY STATISTICS - FINANCES ET STATISTIQUES MONETAIRES	2006	2007	2008	2009	2010	2011	2012	2013	2014	
IX-1 MONETARY STATISTICS *DIRHAM (MILLIONS)*										**IX-1 STATISTIQUES MONÉTAIRES** *DIRHAM (MILLIONS)*
Money supply (M1)	600 560	705 940	799 910	855 950	891 870	949 290	992 180	1 020 400	1 066 320	Masse monétaire (M1)
Quasi-money	199 442	226 892	287 344	298 490	319 022	329 717	339 099	353 000	385 142	Quasi-monnaie
of which Demand Deposit	...	...	...	...	...	...	...	...	...	dont Monnaie scripturale
Net foreign assets	191 537	208 069	197 099	192 714	192 491	168 456	140 403	141 661	172 672	Avoirs extérieurs nets
Domestic credit	448 508	557 214	674 106	731 954	796 465	891 970	955 366	1 008 380	1 040 055	Crédit intérieur
of which claims on private sector	280 706	359 732	435 151	473 778	524 623	577 761	607 405	612 429	634 990	dont créances sur le secteur privé
of which claims on government sector, net	89 655	94 791	96 806	87 797	81 218	102 143	125 402	149 281	143 959	dont créances nettes sur le gouvernement
International reserves (millions US$)	20 378	24 162	22 142	22 836	22 651	19 564	16 394	18 442	19 591	Réserves internationales (millions $EU)
Average Exchange Rate (National Currency per US$)	8.80	8.22	7.73	8.13	8.43	8.10	8.64	8.42	8.25	Taux de change (moyen) (monnaie nationale par $ EU)
IX-2 PUBLIC FINANCE *DIRHAM (MILLIONS)*										**IX-2 FINANCES PUBLIQUES** *DIRHAM (MILLIONS)*
Total Revenues and Grants	132 999	168 271	211 602	199 619	193 767	213 046	224 520	232 104	263 388	Recettes totales et dons
Tax Revenue	113 579	150 124	185 733	167 376	173 562	184 981	198 504	195 760	214 162	Recettes fiscales
Non Tax Revenue	16 492	15 347	16 269	28 625	20 105	23 065	25 560	31 344	34 540	Recettes non fiscales
Grants	2 928	2 800	9 600	3 618	100	5 000	456	5 000	14 685	Dons
Total Expenditures and Net Lending	144 300	177 000	212 400	215 475	227 751	269 301	289 517	279 815	310 935	Dépenses totales et prêts nets
Current expenditure	127 384	143 207	166 708	169 256	181 578	215 610	238 059	231 545	256 800	Dépenses courantes
Of which Wages and Salaries	63 164	65 665	70 315	75 527	78 768	88 973	96 673	98 641	105 961	Dont rémunérations et salaires
Capital expenditure	23 846	26 300	37 740	46 219	46 173	53 691	51 458	48 270	54 135	Dépenses d'équipement
Net Lending	- 6 930	7 493	7 952	-	-	0	-	0	0	Prêts nets
Fiscal Balance	- 11 301	- 8 729	- 798	- 15 856	- 33 984	- 56 255	- 64 997	- 47 711	- 47 547	Solde global y compris les dons
IX-3 BALANCE OF PAYMENTS *DIRHAM (MILLIONS)*										**IX-3 BALANCE DES PAIEMENTS** *DIRHAM (MILLIONS)*
Trade balance	- 85 652	- 115 327	- 150 963	- 131 163	- 126 033	- 155 943	- 172 518	- 184 064	- 171 295	Balance commerciale
Services Balance	46 770	55 179	51 475	43 450	42 837	43 079	46 075	45 279	46 712	Balance des services
Net Income	- 4 203	- 3 320	- 4 070	- 11 770	- 12 555	- 16 473	- 19 762	- 19 230	- 14 890	Revenus nets
Compensation of employees	...	...	...	...	...	...	...	...	...	Rémunération des salariés
Investment Income	...	...	...	...	...	...	...	...	...	Revenus des investissements
Current transfers, net total	55 508	62 897	67 622	59 609	61 429	64 734	63 759	66 350	76 000	Transferts courants
Net official transfers	...	...	...	...	...	...	...	...	...	Transferts officiels nets
Workers' remittances	...	...	...	...	...	...	...	...	...	Envois de fonds des travailleurs
Other private transfers	...	...	...	...	...	...	...	...	...	Autres transferts privés
Current account balance	12 423	- 571	- 35 937	- 39 874	- 34 322	- 64 603	- 82 446	- 91 665	- 63 473	Solde du compte courant
Capital & financial account	15 697	16 635	39 100	44 038	37 193	67 396	84 432	...	...	Comptes de capital et financier
Capital account	- 26	- 25	- 15	- 4	- 1	- 2	1	...	...	Compte de capital
Financial account	15 723	16 660	39 115	44 042	37 194	67 398	84 431	...	...	Compte financier
Errors & omissions	- 4 485	873	- 3 163	- 4 164	- 2 871	- 2 793	- 1 987	...	...	Erreurs et omissions
Overall balance	23 635	16 937	...	...	...	...	...	...	...	Balance générale

X DEBT AND FINANCIAL FLOWS - DETTE ET FLUX FINANCIERS	2006	2007	2008	2009	2010	2011	2012	2013	2014	
X-1 DEBT *US$ (MILLIONS)*										**X-1 DETTE EXTÉRIEURE** *$ E.U (MILLIONS)*
Total external debt	16 391	18 853	19 392	22 213	23 457	24 928	28 612	32 314	36 974	Dette extérieure totale
Private	4 506	5 071	4 088	4 294	4 947	5 258	6 035	6 815	7 798	Privée
Public	11 885	13 781	15 305	17 919	18 510	19 671	22 578	25 499	29 176	Publique
Total external debt service	2 351	2 777	2 667	1 979	1 979	2 254	2 412	2 825	2 999	Service de la dette extérieure
Present value of External debt	...	...	...	...	...	...	...	...	...	Valeur actuelle de la dette extérieure
Total government domestic debt (in local currency)	...	...	...	...	...	...	...	...	...	Dette publique intérieure
X-2 FINANCIAL FLOWS *US$ (MILLIONS)*										**X-2 FLUX FINANCIERS** *$ E.U (MILLIONS)*
Net Foreign Direct Investment Inflows	2 449	2 805	2 487	1 952	1 574	2 568	2 728	3 358	...	Investissements étranger direct (flux nets entrants)
Main origin of FDI Inflows										**Principales origines de l'IDE entrant:**
France	541	496	1 604	1 364	527.2	188.0	611.8	...	...	France
Spain	975	398	1 048	...	- 749.7	161.6	115.7	...	...	Espagne
Belgium	- 31	- 52	19	44	921.9	51.5	- 45.0	...	...	Belgique
Switzerland	27	37	58	100	55.4	39.9	- 1.6	...	...	Suisse
United Kingdom	7	24	26	6	- 1.5	- 41.7	- 17.4	...	...	Royaume-Uni
African countries	...	...	...	...	...	...	...	...	...	Pays africains
Net total Official Development Assistance	1 102	1 221	1 451	930	993	1 456	1 480	1 966	...	Aide publique au développement (nette totale)
Main origin of Net ODA										**Principales origines de l'APD nette**
France	301	219	163	238	254.4	523.9	507.3	...	...	France
United Arab Emirates	151	228	331	- 125	- 4.6	9.3	2.7	...	...	Emirats arabes unis
Japan	61	65	106	98	121.2	30.1	76.4	...	...	Japon
Spain	73	85	117	191	90.6	36.8	34.0	...	...	Espagne
Germany	104	143	91	82	38.9	56.1	11.5	...	...	Allemagne
General notes	* The accounts at constant prices are based on chained prices with 1998 as reference year				* les comptes en prix constant sont publiés aux prix chaines - les données en volumes sont chainées (1998 année de référence)					Notes générales

AREA (KM²)		799 380	SUPERFICIE (KM²)
CAPITAL CITY	Maputo	Maputo	CAPITALE
CURRENCY	Metical	Metical	MONNAIE

I SOCIAL AND DEMOGRAPHIC INDICATORS – INDICATEURS DEMOGRAPHIQUES ET SOCIAUX

	Year Année	Value Valeur	
POPULATION			**POPULATION**
Population ('000)			Population ('000)
Both sexes	2014	26 473	Les deux sexes
Male	2014	12 957	Masculin
Female	2014	13 516	Féminin
Average annual growth rate	2014	2.5	Taux de croissance annuel
Active Population ('000)	2014	11 494	Population active ('000)
Population by age group ('000)			Population par groupe d'âge ('000)
0-14 years	2014	11 989	0-14 ans
15-64 years	2014	13 612	15-64 ans
65+ years	2014	872	65+ ans
Economically active population in agriculture (%)	2014	82.3	Participation de la population active agricole (%)
Crude birth rate	2014	38.4	Taux brut de natalité
Crude death rate	2014	13.9	Taux brut de mortalité
Total fertility rate	2014	5.1	Indice synthétique de fécondité
Proportion of urban population	2014	32.0	Part de la population urbaine
Life Expectancy at Birth - Total (years)	2014	53.5	Espérance de vie à la naissance - Totale (ans)
Dependency Ratio - Total (%)	2014	87.6	Taux de dépendance - Total (%)
HEALTH			**SANTÉ**
Percentage of children under-five and underweight	2011	15.6	% d'enfants de moins de cinq ans avec insuffisance pondérale
Prevalence of undernourishment	2013	27.9	Prévalence de la malnutrition
Under five mortality rate (both sexes, per 1000)	2013	87.2	Taux de mortalité de moins de 5 ans (les deux sexes, pour 1000)
Infant mortality rate (both sexes) per 1000	2013	61.5	Taux de mortalité infantile (les deux sexes) par 1000
Percentage of children provided the vaccines :			Pourcentage d'enfants vaccinés :
BCG	2013	93.0	BCG
DPT3	2013	78.0	DTC3
Polio	2013	94.0	Polio
Measles	2013	85.0	Rougeole
Percentage of mothers provided at least one antenatal care (%)	2011	90.6	Pourcentage de mères ayant au moins reçu un soin prénatal (%)
Percentage of deliveries attended by skilled health personnel	2011	54.3	% d'accouchements assistés par un personnel de santé qualifié
Number of doctors (per 10 000 population)	2012	0.4	Nombre de médecins (pour 10 000 habitants)
Number of nurses (per 10 000 population)	2012	4.1	Nombre d'infirmières (pour 10 000 habitants)
Hospital beds - Total (per 10 000 population)	2013	8.3	Nombre de lits d'hôpitaux - Total (pour 10 000)
Births registered (per 1 000)	2014	38.4	Naiss.s enregistrées (pour 1 000)
Deaths registered (per 1 000)	2014	13.9	Décès enregistrés (pour 1 000)
Public expenditure on Health (% of budget)	2014	8.3	Dépenses publiques consacrées à la santé (% du budget)
EDUCATION			**EDUCATION**
Enrolment in primary education (both sexes) (000)	2014	5 670	Scolarisation dans le primaire (les deux sexes) (000)
Female	2014	2 706	Féminin
Enrolment in secondary education (both sexes) (000)	2014	987	Scolarisation dans le secondaire (les deux sexes) (000)
Female	2014	475	Féminin
Enrolment in tertiary education (both sexes) (000)	2013	128.1	Scolarisation dans le tertiaire (les deux sexes) (000)
Female	2013	52.5	Féminin
Literacy rate (both sexes)	2009	50.6	Taux d'alphabétisation (deux sexes)
Male	2009	67.4	Masculin
Female	2009	36.5	Féminin
Pupil-teacher ratio	2014	56.1	Ratio élève-enseignant
Public expenditure on education (% of budget)	2014	17.4	Dépenses publiques consacrées à l'enseignement (% du budget)
POVERTY			**PAUVRETÉ**
GNI Per Capita (US$)	2013	610.0	RNB par habitant ($EU)
Human Poverty Index (HPI-1) Value (%)	2007	46.8	Valeur de l'Indice de pauvreté (IPH-1) (%)
Population below International Poverty Line ($2/day) (%)	2009	82.5	Population sous le seuil international de pauvreté (2$/J) (%)
Share of Income Held by Richest 10%	2009	36.7	% de revenu des 10% plus riches
Share of Income Held by Poorest 10%	2009	1.9	% de revenu des 10% plus pauvres
Gini index	2009	45.7	Indice de Gini

Charts
Graphiques

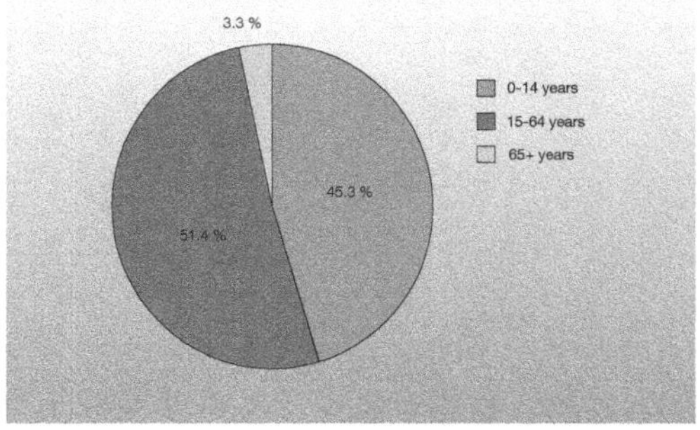

Population by age group – 2014
Population par groupe d'age – 2014

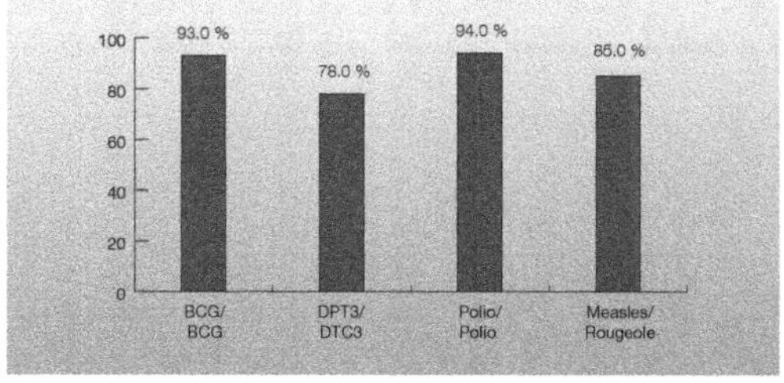

Percentage of children provided the vaccines – 2013
Pourcentage d'enfants vaccinés – 2013

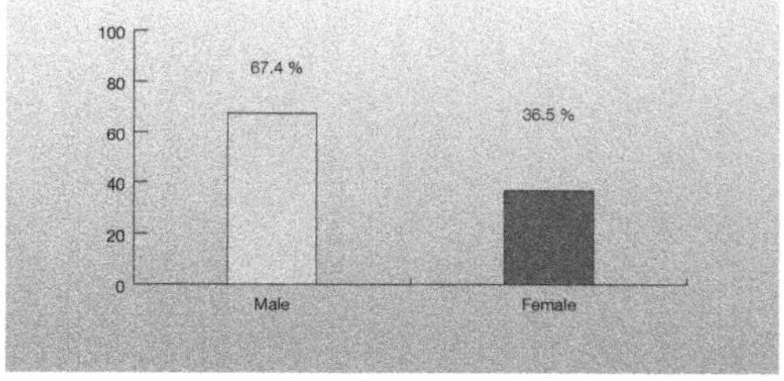

Literacy rate (%) – 2009
Taux d'alphabétisation – 2009

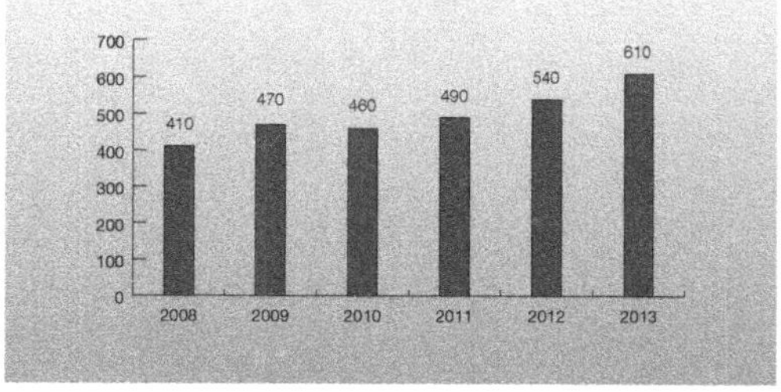

GNI Per Capita (US$)
RNB par habitant ($EU)

II NATIONAL ACCOUNTS — COMPTES NATIONAUX

	2006	2007	2008	2009	2010	2011	2012	2013	2014	
GROSS DOMESTIC PRODUCT BY KIND OF ECONOMIC ACTIVITY AT CURRENT PRICES *METICAL (MILLIONS)*										**PRODUIT INTÉRIEUR BRUT PAR BRANCHE D'ACTIVITÉ ÉCONOMIQUE AUX PRIX COURANTS** *METICAL (MILLIONS)*
Agriculture, hunting, forestry and fishing	45 852	60 233	74 848	84 521	96 322	105 719	111 184	121 880	...	Agriculture, chasse sylviculture et pêche
Mining and quarrying	2 337	3 665	4 040	4 489	5 744	8 663	13 333	15 405	...	Industries extractives
Manufacturing	26 355	36 322	35 742	35 860	40 797	43 682	45 577	47 851	...	Industries manufacturières
Electricity, gas & water	9 579	7 723	7 971	10 197	12 369	12 402	13 571	15 100	...	Electricité, gaz et eau
Construction & public works	5 213	3 960	5 014	6 014	8 160	9 613	11 273	11 570	...	Bâtiments et travaux publics
Wholesale & retail trade, restaurants, hotels	25 579	30 038	33 625	36 944	45 773	50 986	53 813	58 459	...	Commerce de gros et de détail, restaurants et hôtels
Finance, insurance, real estate, etc.	19 318	25 215	28 937	32 089	36 555	41 520	46 803	55 069	...	Banques, assurances, affaires immobilières
Transport and communications	16 458	21 204	24 555	27 002	32 183	32 910	36 780	39 842	...	Transport(s) et communications
Public administration and defense	6 640	9 747	11 105	13 579	16 749	20 125	22 674	26 163	...	Administrations publiques et défense
Education	6 521	15 253	18 424	20 041	22 202	26 726	32 452	33 158	...	Education
Health and Social Work	2 396	3 475	4 191	4 790	5 248	6 417	7 945	8 396	...	Santé et actions sociales
Other services	3 066	2 297	2 518	2 703	2 975	3 257	3 363	3 511	...	Autres services
Less Imputed Service Charges	- 4 732	- 2 044	- 3 610	- 4 928	- 6 275	- 7 104	- 8 444	- 11 241	...	Moins services d'intermédiation financière
Gross domestic product at factor cost / basic prices	164 582	217 088	247 360	273 301	318 802	354 916	390 324	425 163	...	Produit intérieur brut aux couts des facteurs / prix de base
Plus: indirect taxes / taxes on products, less subsidies	15 658	18 461	21 167	21 654	24 845	28 695	33 411	40 162	...	Plus taxes indirectes/impôts sur les produits, moins les subventions
EXPENDITURE ON GROSS DOMESTIC PRODUCT AT CURRENT PURCHASER'S VALUES *METICAL (MILLIONS)*										**EMPLOI DU PRODUIT INTÉRIEUR BRUT AUX PRIX COURANTS D'ACQUISITION** *METICAL (MILLIONS)*
Government final consumption	22 228	40 544	47 120	54 258	65 333	75 971	90 943	103 401	...	Consommation finale des administrations publiques
Private final consumption	143 382	178 165	201 091	223 663	254 297	280 306	302 689	328 264	...	Consommation finale privée
Gross fixed capital formation	31 819	28 613	35 765	42 340	52 983	67 081	64 722	73 890	...	Formation brute de capital fixe
Change in inventories	- 1 187	4 499	- 336	2 261	- 91	3 668	8 538	8 063	...	Variation des stocks
Exports of goods and services	54 861	74 638	77 627	85 694	103 228	113 343	119 030	129 575	...	Exportations de biens et services
Less imports of goods and services	70 861	90 912	92 738	113 261	132 101	156 761	162 188	177 867	...	Moins importations de biens et services
GDP at purchasers' values	180 242	235 547	268 528	294 955	343 648	383 608	423 734	465 326	...	PIB aux prix d'acquisition
GROSS DOMESTIC PRODUCT BY KIND OF ECONOMIC ACTIVITY AT CONSTANT PRICES *ANNUAL GROWTH RATES (%)*										**PRODUIT INTÉRIEUR BRUT PAR BRANCHE D'ACTIVITÉ ECONOMIQUE AUX PRIX CONSTANTS** *TAUX DE CROISSANCE ANNUEL (%)*
Agriculture, hunting, forestry and fishing	10.2	8.2	6.1	6.0	5.5	4.3	2.0	3.6	6.3	Agriculture, chasse sylviculture et pêche
Mining and quarrying	27.9	19.2	7.6	5.9	2.8	27.2	66.5	15.7	13.0	Industries extractives
Manufacturing	3.0	3.1	- 3.0	- 1.2	3.7	1.8	9.5	2.1	11.3	Industries manufacturières
Electricity, gas & water	13.1	8.6	27.0	14.1	1.5	5.3	- 1.5	5.5	7.1	Electricité, gaz et eau
Construction & public works	10.4	11.8	7.0	16.0	21.4	12.3	8.4	10.0	10.5	Bâtiments et travaux publics
Wholesale & retail trade, restaurants, hotels	19.9	9.4	11.6	1.9	9.1	8.8	8.0	5.8	6.7	Commerce de gros et de détail,restaurants et hôtels
Finance, insurance, real estate, etc.	1.9	9.7	15.2	10.3	10.8	9.7	11.2	16.0	13.2	Banques, assurances, affaires immobilières
Transport and communications	10.4	3.4	6.9	10.9	11.7	2.1	4.5	9.9	3.5	Transport(s) et communications
Public administration and defense	11.2	5.1	8.0	10.1	15.0	12.9	7.7	10.4	12.2	Administrations publiques et défense
Education	8.3	7.4	2.2	15.5	3.3	17.1	13.8	10.2	6.2	Education
Health and Social Work	14.5	8.0	11.1	6.5	6.8	8.6	8.0	7.5	6.2	Santé et actions sociales
Other services	2.4	10.6	6.0	5.6	5.4	5.1	4.9	4.8	0.9	Autres services
Less Imputed Service Charges	27.7	2.9	70.7	34.5	22.5	8.6	20.8	33.8	37.5	Moins services d'intermédiation financière
Gross domestic product at factor cost / basic prices	8.7	7.6	6.4	6.3	7.2	7.0	7.4	6.8	7.3	Produit intérieur brut aux couts des facteurs / prix de base
Plus: indirect taxes / taxes on products, less subsidies	8.6	4.5	4.7	3.6	1.8	13.0	3.4	13.9	7.7	Plus taxes indirectes/impôts sur les produits, moins les subventions
Gross domestic product at market prices	8.7	7.3	6.3	6.1	6.8	7.4	7.1	7.3	7.4	Produit intérieur brut aux prix du marché
EXPENDITURE ON GROSS DOMESTIC PRODUCT AT CONSTANT PURCHASERS' VALUES *ANNUAL GROWTH RATES (%)*										**EMPLOIS DU PRODUIT INTÉRIEUR BRUT AUX PRIX CONSTANTS D'ACQUISITION** *TAUX DE CROISSANCE ANNUEL (%)*
Government final consumption	10.2	7.2	8.3	6.9	12.1	9.8	12.4	14.4	...	Consommation finale des administrations publiques
Private final consumption	4.5	7.5	5.7	5.6	4.6	5.3	5.6	6.3	...	Consommation finale privée
Gross fixed capital formation	6.2	5.8	35.3	12.4	7.1	15.7	7.6	3.7	...	Formation brute de capital fixe
Exports of goods and services	12.2	15.9	7.0	10.0	2.7	9.1	12.9	5.0	...	Exportations de biens et services
Less imports of goods and services	1.2	12.8	7.2	17.3	- 2.1	12.8	13.6	3.9	...	Moins importations de biens et services
Notes	The Accounts are calculated using the new base year 2009 from 2007				Les comptes sont calculés selon la nouvelle année de base 2009 à partir de 2007					Notes

III INFLATION

	2006	2007	2008	2009	2010	2011	2012	2013	2014	
ANNUAL GROWTH RATES (%)										**TAUX DE CROISSANCE ANNUEL (%)**
All items	13.6	9.2	14.5	3.8	12.4	11.2	2.6	4.3	2.6	Ensemble
of which:										dont:
Food and Non-alcoholic beverages	17.0	10.3	18.9	7.0	15.3	13.2	3.1	5.4	3.8	Alimentation et boissons non alcoolisés
Alcoholic beverages & tobacco	12.0	11.0	5.3	6.3	13.3	6.8	3.8	7.7	2.2	Boissons alcoolisées et tabacs
Clothing and Footwear	3.1	2.1	2.9	2.6	2.8	5.7	3.5	2.7	2.2	Habillement et chaussures
Housing, Water, Electricity, Gas and Other Fuels	12.6	14.2	15.0	-7.4	10.8	8.9	4.3	4.8	3.4	Logement, eau, électricité, gas et autres combustibles
Furnishing, household equip	5.7	5.0	5.9	3.1	6.1	8.2	2.0	1.9	0.0	Meubles, articles de ménage et entretien courant
Health	10.0	5.8	7.9	6.1	6.1	1.0	1.1	4.6	3.0	Santé
Transport	12.0	3.1	8.5	-3.5	7.2	6.3	0.7	3.5	0.2	Transport
Communication	-1.4	4.7	-0.7	-0.1	-0.3	-0.1	-1.2	1.6	-1.1	Communication
Recreation & culture	5.5	3.4	0.2	1.5	3.9	5.7	-2.9	-0.4	-0.7	Loisirs et culture
Education	10.3	9.1	5.0	9.0	5.3	22.1	6.2	9.7	5.8	Enseignement
Restaurants & hotels	10.0	10.7	8.7	10.4	11.3	14.9	3.2	4.7	3.9	Restaurants et hôtels
Miscellaneous goods & services	10.4	6.0	7.6	5.6	10.0	13.5	1.8	2.4	0.6	Biens et services divers

	2006	2007	2008	2009	2010	2011	2012	2013	2014	
IV AGRICULTURAL PRODUCTION - PRODUCTION AGRICOLE										
TONNES *(THOUSAND)*										**TONNES** *(MILLIERS)*
Cassava	5 481	4 959	4 055	5 670	9 738	10 094	10 051	10 000	...	Manioc
Sugar cane	2 060	2 061	2 451	2 207	2 720	3 396	3 394	3 800	...	Canne à sucre
Maize	1 418	1 582	1 676	1 612	2 090	2 179	1 177	1 631	...	Maïs
Sweet potatoes	678	861	903	900	920	860	900	890	...	Patates douces
Bananas	175	209	245	280	321	341	470	450	...	Bananes
V MINING PRODUCTION - PRODUCTION MINIERE										
	2006	2007	2008	2009	2010	2011	2012	2013	2014	
NaturalCoal tons (thousands)	...	...	...	...	...	658	4 583	7 274	4 469	NaturalCoal tons (thousands)
Natural Gas (thousands)	...	...	...	...	...	3 241	3 504	3 914	3 506	Natural Gas (thousands)
Heavy Sand (thousands)	...	...	...	...	...	1 711	1 708	1 478	717	Heavy Sand (thousands)
VI ENERGY - ENERGIE										
	2006	2007	2008	2009	2010	2011	2012	2013	2014	
Total electricity generation (GWh)	14 739	16 083	15 127	16 967	16 658	16 734	16 744	15 026	...	Production d'électricité totale (GWh)
of which:										dont:
Production of electricity from fossil fuels (GWh)	22	13	13	17	18	20	21	318	...	Production d'électricité à partir de combustibles fossiles (GWh)
Production of hydro electricity (GWh)	14 717	16 070	15 114	16 950	16 640	16 567	16 567	14 542	...	Production d'électricité d'origine hydraulique (GWh)
Production of electricity from solar, wind, tide, wave and other sources (GWh)	...	...	...	...	...	2	5	7	...	Production d'électricité d'origine solaire, éolienne, marée motrice et autres (GWh)
VII TOURISM AND INFRASTRUCTURE - TOURISME ET INFRASTRUCTURE										
	2006	2007	2008	2009	2010	2011	2012	2013	2014	
VII-1 TOURISM										**VII-1 TOURISME**
International tourist arrivals (thousands)	664	771	1 193	1 461	1 718	1 902	2 113	1 886	2 060	Arrivées de touristes internationaux (milliers)
Rooms in hotels and similar establishments (thousands)	9.8	11.6	13.5	16.4	20.8	21.1	22.1	22.3	...	Chambres d'hotels et établissements assimilés (milliers)
Overnight stays (thousands)	1 033	945	889	972	1 001	1 151	851	904	1 327	Nuitées (milliers)
Tourism receipts (US$ thousand)	137 800	162 300	187 500	193 500	194 800	224 200	245 700	240 200	262 291	Recettes touristiques (milliers de $ EU)
Total contribution to GDP (%)	6.9	7.4	7.6	8.1	6.8	7.3	6.9	7.1	7.0	Contribution totale au PIB (%)
Total contribution to Employment (%)	6.0	6.4	6.6	7.0	5.3	5.5	6.0	6.0	6.0	Contribution totale à l'emploi (%)
VII-2 INFRASTRUCTURE										**VII-2 INFRASTRUCTURE**
Paved roads (% of total)	18	18	18	18	18	18	18	21	...	Routes asphaltées (% du total)
Total Network (Railways-km)	30 400	30 400	30 331	30 331	30 331	30 331	30 562	30 464	...	Réseau total voies ferrées-Km
Main Telephone Lines (per 100 inhabitants)	0	0	0	0	0	0	0	0	...	Lignes téléphoniques fixes (pour 100 habitants)
Mobile Cellular Subscribers (per 100 inhabitants)	11	14	19	26	30	32	35	48	...	Abonnés aux téléphones mobiles (pour 100 habitants)
VIII EXTERNAL TRADE - COMMERCE EXTERIEUR										
	2006	2007	2008	2009	2010	2011	2012	2013	2014	
US$ (MILLIONS) EXPORTS, FOB										**$ E.U (MILLIONS) EXPORTATIONS, FÀB**
Exports - Total	2 381	2 412	2 653	2 147	2 333	3 118	3 856	4 123	4 725	Exportations - Total
Exports to AFRICA	480	546	365	611	623	776	994	1 020	1 153	Exportations vers l'AFRIQUE
Main Products										**Principaux produits**
Aluminium	1 401	1 480	1 452	868	1 160	1 357	1 092	1 063	1 046	Aluminium
Electricity	178	240	221	274	277	299	233	270	301	Electricite
Natural Gas	110	121	152	123	134	162	175	230	549	Gas natural
Tobaco	110	52	195	181	153	180	238	251	258	Tabac
Cotton	46	42	48	26	29	39	49	99	77	Coton
Main Destinations										**Principales destinations**
Scandinavian countries	1 422	1 492	1 472	894	1 189	1 357	931	1 124	1 111	Pays Scandinaves
South Africa	362	414	245	460	504	584	764	812	948	Afrique du Sud
India	30	17	22	57	35	57	172	679	388	India
China	33	40	42	74	90	168	703	101	204	China
United Arab Emirates	7	5	14	41	20	26	97	148	53	Emirats Arabes Unis
IMPORTS, CIF										**IMPORTATIONS, CAF**
Imports - Total	2 649	2 811	3 643	3 422	3 512	5 368	7 903	8 480	8 747	Importations - Total (millions)
Imports from Africa	1 047	979	1 144	1 311	1 869	1 999	2 413	2 433	3 119	Importations en provenance de l'Afrique
Main Products										**Principaux produits**
Machinery	362	380	484	536	502	1 106	1 485	2 052	1 832	Machines
Vehicles	152	197	273	301	292	431	535	508	624	Vehicules
Patrol	314	370	574	324	492	872	1 012	1 112	1 186	Patrol
Cereais	202	176	222	251	183	280	249	356	371	Cereales
Energy	76	108	111	117	143	286	279	262	270	Energy
Main Origin										**Principales provenances**
South Africa	960	911	1 059	1 213	1 798	1 824	2 152	2 176	2 892	Afrique du Sud
China	70	97	142	157	200	375	419	638	700	Chine
Singapore	11	7	9	61	1	37	49	625	110	Singapour
Portugal	87	99	105	129	282	226	320	482	456	Portugal
Japan	17	86	116	129	195	185	173	223	275	Japan

IX FINANCIAL AND MONETARY STATISTICS - FINANCES ET STATISTIQUES MONETAIRES	2006	2007	2008	2009	2010	2011	2012	2013	2014	
IX-1 MONETARY STATISTICS *METICAL (MILLIONS)*										**IX-1 STATISTIQUES MONÉTAIRES** *METICAL (MILLIONS)*
Money supply (M1)	35 170	42 770	53 890	72 540	85 280	105 700	132 720	160 840	191 400	Masse monétaire (M1)
Quasi-money	13 437	18 620	26 652	33 174	42 274	46 223	56 817	70 404	82 868	Quasi-monnaie
of which Demand Deposit	...	...	...	...	...	...	...	...	...	dont Monnaie scripturale
Net foreign assets	47 607	54 283	56 957	63 737	79 875	72 999	94 333	99 960	104 726	Avoirs extérieurs nets
Domestic credit	14 558	20 894	33 520	60 111	80 170	92 601	117 768	137 637	185 709	Crédit intérieur
of which claims on private sector	23 898	28 055	43 995	65 981	83 901	88 898	106 211	135 963	170 162	dont créances sur le secteur privé
of which claims on government sector, net	- 11 932	- 9 983	- 11 523	- 11 330	- 12 202	- 5 650	- 62	- 14 026	- 8 876	dont créances nettes sur le gouvernement
International reserves (millions US$)	1 161	1 450	1 583	2 103	2 163	2 473	2 776	3 152	3 019	Réserves internationales (millions $EU)
Average Exchange Rate (National Currency per US$)	23 060.97	25 400.78	25 840.34	24 300.64	27 518.30	33 960.10	29 067.60	28 372.98	30 104.11	Taux de change (moyen) (monnaie nationale par $ EU)
IX-2 PUBLIC FINANCE *METICAL (MILLIONS)*										**IX-2 FINANCES PUBLIQUES** *METICAL (MILLIONS)*
Total Revenues and Grants	47 499	56 531	64 010	74 390	90 885	108 493	125 911	157 141	177 362	Recettes totales et dons
Tax Revenue	23 407	29 510	34 205	41 761	53 709	68 263	84 607	108 150	135 006	Recettes fiscales
Non Tax Revenue	5 904	6 730	6 794	6 858	9 858	12 851	13 972	18 758	21 238	Recettes non fiscales
Grants	18 188	20 291	23 010	25 771	27 318	27 380	27 332	30 233	21 118	Dons
Total Expenditures and Net Lending	56 696	68 412	76 737	97 661	120 559	141 526	140 920	163 256	189 756	Dépenses totales et prêts nets
Current expenditure	32 711	40 428	49 016	56 478	75 172	88 616	95 755	100 877	116 782	Dépenses courantes
Of which Wages and Salaries	12 909	15 545	18 797	23 877	29 469	35 679	40 157	45 686	55 280	Dont rémunérations et salaires
Capital expenditure	15 868	20 052	20 596	28 078	31 914	39 319	31 148	35 627	44 032	Dépenses d'équipement
Net Lending	8 117	7 932	7 125	13 105	13 474	13 591	14 017	26 753	28 942	Prêts nets
Fiscal Balance	- 9 197	- 11 881	- 12 727	- 23 270	- 29 675	- 33 033	- 15 009	- 6 115	- 12 394	Solde global y compris les dons
IX-3 BALANCE OF PAYMENTS *US$ (MILLIONS)*										**IX-3 BALANCE DES PAIEMENTS** *$ E.U (MILLIONS)*
Trade balance	- 268	- 399	- 990	- 1 275	- 1 179	- 2 249	- 4 048	- 4 357	- 4 035	Balance commerciale
Services Balance	- 364	- 398	- 423	- 457	- 685	- 1 436	- 3 136	- 3 259	- 2 932	Balance des services
Net Income	- 634	- 592	- 642	- 282	- 336	- 204	- 16	- 59	- 202	Revenus nets
Compensation of employees	50	49	63	55	77	101	88	55	- 17	Rémunération des salariés
Investment Income	- 471	- 549	- 542	- 238	- 213	- 305	- 104	- 114	- 185	Revenus des investissements
Current transfers, net total	501	602	862	763	682	891	829	1 421	1 372	Transferts courants
Net official transfers	453	515	768	682	605	792	713	1 088	1 087	Transferts officiels nets
Workers' remittances	4	5	5	- 9	- 14	1	33	- 3	- 22	Envois de fonds des travailleurs
Other private transfers	44	82	88	90	92	99	84	336	307	Autres transferts privés
Current account balance	- 765	- 786	- 1 193	- 1 251	- 1 518	- 2 997	- 6 371	- 6 253	- 5 797	Solde du compte courant
Capital & financial account	632	725	1 075	6 352	1 410	3 018	6 352	6 231	5 771	Comptes de capital et financier
Capital account	2 278	542	421	424	352	445	456	423	372	Compte de capital
Financial account	- 1 646	183	654	670	1 058	2 573	5 897	5 808	5 399	Compte financier
Errors & omissions	134	62	118	152	113	- 21	18	22	26	Erreurs et omissions
Overall balance	-	-	0	5 254	5	0	0	0	0	Balance générale

X DEBT AND FINANCIAL FLOWS - DETTE ET FLUX FINANCIERS	2006	2007	2008	2009	2010	2011	2012	2013	2014	
X-1 DEBT *US$ (MILLIONS)*										**X-1 DETTE EXTÉRIEURE** *$ E.U (MILLIONS)*
Total external debt	7 698	6 071	6 320	6 964	7 540	7 460	8 008	9 634	12 817	Dette extérieure totale
Private	4 416	2 754	2 681	2 984	3 687	3 203	3 137	3 978	6 002	Privée
Public	3 282	3 317	3 639	3 980	3 853	4 258	4 870	5 656	6 815	Publique
Total external debt service	2 108	244	721	519	1 010	667	517	613	733	Service de la dette extérieure
Present value of External debt	...	...	...	...	...	...	...	...	...	Valeur actuelle de la dette extérieure
Total government domestic debt (in local currency)	6 932	8 042	7 446	11 914	18 747.4	22 330.2	23 738.3	...	...	Dette publique intérieure
X-2 FINANCIAL FLOWS *US$ (THOUSANDS)*										**X-2 FLUX FINANCIERS** *$ E.U (MILLIERS)*
Net Foreign Direct Investment Inflows	113	399	592	898	1 018	3 559	5 629	6 175	4 902	Investissements étranger direct (flux nets entrants)
Main origin of FDI Inflows										**Principales origines de l'IDE entrant:**
Brazil	6	81	101	375	608.3	907.9	1 299.6	24.3	20.2	Brésil
United States of America	2	- 1	3	4	1.3	35.5	914.8	1 207.1	1 749.8	Etats Unis
United Arab Emirates	-	-	0	6	6.7	43.9	217.0	1 651.9	1 505.4	Emirates Arabes
Mauritius	30	29	71	197	234.4	460.9	472.8	145.5	500.1	Maurice, île
India	-	25	15	2	- 1.7	9.6	409.4	898.5	4.3	Inde
African countries	...	...	...	...	...	...	...	...	...	Pays africains
Net total Official Development Assistance	1 059	1 120	1 195	1 605	1 677	1 719	1 730	1 904	...	Aide publique au développement (nette totale)
Main origin of Net ODA										**Principales origines de l'APD nette**
World Bank	250	266	258	255	194.7	101.4	231.7	53.9	...	Banque mondiale
United States	...	...	...	263	237.8	445.5	406.5	507.4	...	Etats Unis
European Union	138	150	145	106	186.1	124.3	181.2	106.2	...	Union Européenne
AfDB	107	75	73	102	76.1	58.0	89.4	375.9	...	BAD
DFID	88	106	113	147	96.2	200.1	131.8	109.8	...	DFID
General notes	National Accounts : The annual Growth Rates for 2014 are estimates based on the sum of four quarters of 2014.					Comptes Nationaux: Les croissances annuelles de L'année 2014 sont estimées à partir des comptes trimestriels				Notes générales

AREA (KM²)	824 292		SUPERFICIE (KM²)
CAPITAL CITY	Windhoek	Windhoek	CAPITALE
CURRENCY	Namibian Dollar	Dollar Namibien	MONNAIE

I SOCIAL AND DEMOGRAPHIC INDICATORS – INDICATEURS DEMOGRAPHIQUES ET SOCIAUX

	Year / Année	Value / Valeur	
POPULATION			**POPULATION**
Population ('000)			Population ('000)
Both sexes	2014	2 348	Les deux sexes
Male	2014	1 141	Masculin
Female	2014	1 207	Féminin
Average annual growth rate	2014	1.9	Taux de croissance annuel
Active Population ('000)	2014	1 005	Population active ('000)
Population by age group ('000)			Population par groupe d'âge ('000)
0-14 years	2014	834	0-14 ans
15-64 years	2014	1 430	15-64 ans
65+ years	2014	84	65+ ans
Economically active population in agriculture (%)	2014	27.3	Participation de la population active agricole (%)
Crude birth rate	2014	25.7	Taux brut de natalité
Crude death rate	2014	7.1	Taux brut de mortalité
Total fertility rate	2014	3.0	Indice synthétique de fécondité
Proportion of urban population	2014	40.1	Part de la population urbaine
Life Expectancy at Birth - Total (years)	2014	64.8	Espérance de vie à la naissance - Totale (ans)
Dependency Ratio - Total (%)	2014	62.8	Taux de dépendance - Total (%)
HEALTH			**SANTÉ**
Percentage of children under-five and underweight	2007	17.5	% d'enfants de moins de cinq ans avec insuffisance pondérale
Prevalence of undernourishment	2013	37.2	Prévalence de la malnutrition
Under five mortality rate (both sexes, per 1000)	2013	49.8	Taux de mortalité de moins de 5 ans (les deux sexes, pour 1000)
Infant mortality rate (both sexes) per 1000	2013	35.2	Taux de mortalité infantile (les deux sexes) par 1000
Percentage of children provided the vaccines :			Pourcentage d'enfants vaccinés :
BCG	2013	94.0	BCG
DPT3	2013	89.0	DTC3
Polio	2011	85.0	Polio
Measles	2013	82.0	Rougeole
Percentage of mothers provided at least one antenatal care (%)	2007	94.6	Pourcentage de mères ayant au moins reçu un soin prénatal (%)
Percentage of deliveries attended by skilled health personnel	2007	81.4	% d'accouchements assistés par un personnel de santé qualifié
Number of doctors (per 10 000 population)	2007	3.7	Nombre de médecins (pour 10 000 habitants)
Number of nurses (per 10 000 population)	2007	27.8	Nombre d'infirmières (pour 10 000 habitants)
Hospital beds - Total (per 10 000 population)	2009	26.7	Nombre de lits d'hôpitaux - Total (pour 10 000)
Births registered (per 1 000)	2014	25.7	Naiss.s enregistrées (pour 1 000)
Deaths registered (per 1 000)	2014	7.1	Décès enregistrés (pour 1 000)
Public expenditure on Health (% of budget)	2009	12.1	Dépenses publiques consacrées à la santé (% du budget)
EDUCATION			**EDUCATION**
Enrolment in primary education (both sexes) (000)	2012	415	Scolarisation dans le primaire (les deux sexes) (000)
Female	2012	204	Féminin
Enrolment in secondary education (both sexes) (000)	2007	158	Scolarisation dans le secondaire (les deux sexes) (000)
Female	2007	85	Féminin
Enrolment in tertiary education (both sexes) (000)	2013	36.1	Scolarisation dans le tertiaire (les deux sexes) (000)
Female	2008	11.2	Féminin
Literacy rate (both sexes)	2007	76.5	Taux d'alphabétisation (deux sexes)
Male	2007	74.3	Masculin
Female	2007	78.4	Féminin
Pupil-teacher ratio	2013	27.2	Ratio élève-enseignant
Public expenditure on education (% of budget)	2013	22.6	Dépenses publiques consacrées à l'enseignement (% du budget)
POVERTY			**PAUVRETÉ**
GNI Per Capita (US$)	2013	5 870.0	RNB par habitant ($EU)
Human Poverty Index (HPI-1) Value (%)	2007	17.1	Valeur de l'Indice de pauvreté (IPH-1) (%)
Population below International Poverty Line ($2/day) (%)	2010	43.2	Population sous le seuil international de pauvreté (2$/J) (%)
Share of Income Held by Richest 10%	2010	51.8	% de revenu des 10% plus riches
Share of Income Held by Poorest 10%	2010	1.5	% de revenu des 10% plus pauvres
Gini index	2010	61.3	Indice de Gini

Charts / Graphiques

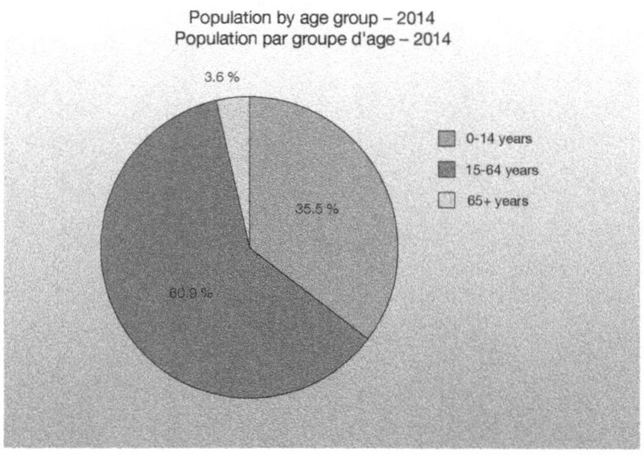

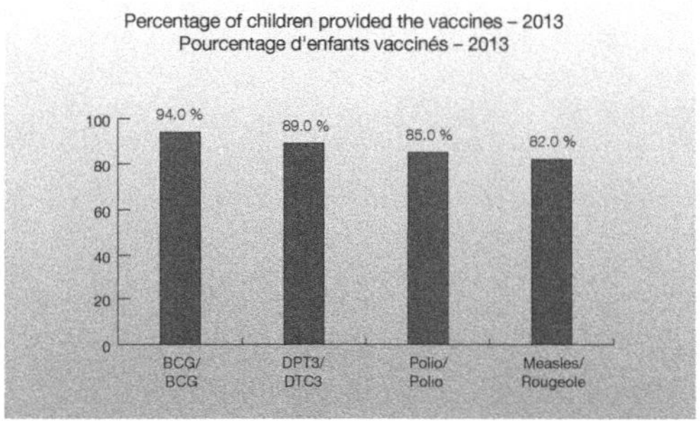

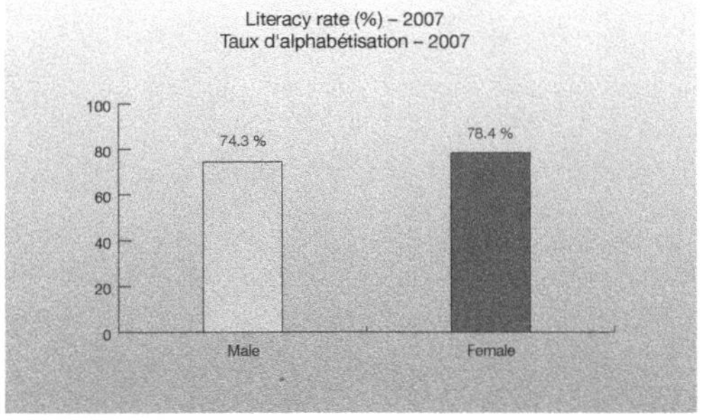

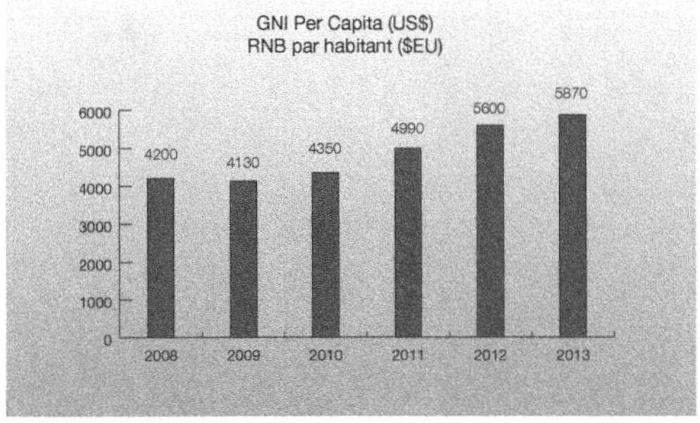

II NATIONAL ACCOUNTS — COMPTES NATIONAUX

	2006	2007	2008	2009	2010	2011	2012	2013	2014	
GROSS DOMESTIC PRODUCT BY KIND OF ECONOMIC ACTIVITY AT CURRENT PRICES *NAMIBIAN DOLLAR (MILLIONS)*										**PRODUIT INTÉRIEUR BRUT PAR BRANCHE D'ACTIVITÉ ÉCONOMIQUE AUX PRIX COURANTS** *DOLLAR NAMIBIEN (MILLIONS)*
Agriculture, hunting, forestry and fishing	5 223	5 264	5 350	6 207	7 085	7 417	8 607	7 217	...	Agriculture, chasse sylviculture et pêche
Mining and quarrying	6 654	7 833	12 034	8 178	8 598	7 832	13 412	16 492	...	Industries extractives
Manufacturing	7 792	8 401	8 005	9 800	10 306	12 302	13 027	15 451	...	Industries manufacturières
Electricity, gas & water	1 012	1 467	1 418	1 497	1 538	1 818	2 022	2 406	...	Electricité, gaz et eau
Construction & public works	1 826	2 136	2 826	2 429	2 618	3 127	3 554	4 835	...	Bâtiments et travaux publics
Wholesale & retail trade, restaurants, hotels	6 819	7 820	8 672	9 613	10 705	11 897	13 226	16 280	...	Commerce de gros et de détail, restaurants et hôtels
Finance, insurance, real estate, etc.	8 520	10 144	10 360	12 326	13 964	15 357	16 473	19 966	...	Banques, assurances, affaires immobilières
Transport and communications	2 535	2 595	3 275	3 891	4 238	4 606	5 011	5 648	...	Transport(s) et communications
Public administration and defense	4 423	5 547	6 305	7 624	9 100	8 769	12 119	15 325	...	Administrations publiques et défense
Education	3 703	4 244	4 844	5 546	5 872	7 403	8 829	10 463	...	Education
Health and Social Work	1 647	1 834	2 015	2 225	2 531	2 923	3 202	3 713	...	Santé et actions sociales
Other services	384	424	630	749	853	972	1 126	1 110	...	Autres services
Less Imputed Service Charges	- 644	- 649	- 764	- 795	- 1 011	- 1 100	- 1 315	- 1 462	...	Moins services d'intermédiation financière
Gross domestic product at factor cost / basic prices	49 894	57 060	64 970	69 290	76 397	83 323	99 293	117 444	...	Produit intérieur brut aux couts des facteurs / prix de base
Plus: indirect taxes / taxes on products, less subsidies	4 133	4 522	5 137	5 920	6 202	6 805	7 745	9 164	...	Plus taxes indirectes/impôts sur les produits, moins les subventions
EXPENDITURE ON GROSS DOMESTIC PRODUCT AT CURRENT PURCHASER'S VALUES *NAMIBIAN DOLLAR (MILLIONS)*										**EMPLOI DU PRODUIT INTÉRIEUR BRUT AUX PRIX COURANTS D'ACQUISITION** *DOLLAR NAMIBIEN (MILLIONS)*
Government final consumption	10 526	14 695	15 282	17 945	21 107	20 895	27 498	34 929	...	Consommation finale des administrations publiques
Private final consumption	29 361	35 169	43 740	52 407	52 221	59 841	68 519	83 573	...	Consommation finale privée
Gross fixed capital formation	11 686	13 554	17 751	21 025	20 884	20 453	27 636	32 525	...	Formation brute de capital fixe
Change in inventories	342	1 450	2 103	- 529	- 958	- 291	1 043	- 1 558	...	Variation des stocks
Exports of goods and services	24 566	31 089	38 108	39 372	39 447	41 023	46 390	54 453	...	Exportations de biens et services
Less imports of goods and services	22 454	34 374	46 871	55 005	50 102	51 789	64 051	77 314	...	Moins importations de biens et services
GDP at purchasers' values	54 028	61 582	70 107	75 210	82 599	90 128	107 038	126 608	-	PIB aux prix d'acquisition
GROSS DOMESTIC PRODUCT BY KIND OF ECONOMIC ACTIVITY AT CONSTANT PRICES *ANNUAL GROWTH RATES (%)*										**PRODUIT INTÉRIEUR BRUT PAR BRANCHE D'ACTIVITÉ ECONOMIQUE AUX PRIX CONSTANTS** *TAUX DE CROISSANCE ANNUEL (%)*
Agriculture, hunting, forestry and fishing	- 0.7	- 9.3	- 15.9	17.7	4.9	- 1.3	2.0	- 16.9	...	Agriculture, chasse sylviculture et pêche
Mining and quarrying	27.6	0.5	2.6	- 31.7	22.2	- 5.4	25.1	0.6	...	Industries extractives
Manufacturing	2.7	8.5	4.9	2.0	7.5	5.7	- 6.8	1.9	...	Industries manufacturières
Electricity, gas & water	5.6	4.4	- 8.9	- 16.4	2.3	3.1	17.8	- 0.7	...	Electricité, gaz et eau
Construction & public works	37.2	14.6	15.4	- 17.5	6.8	15.9	8.6	29.8	...	Bâtiments et travaux publics
Wholesale & retail trade, restaurants, hotels	7.6	8.2	- 3.0	9.4	7.4	6.3	4.8	13.1	...	Commerce de gros et de détail,restaurants et hôtels
Finance, insurance, real estate, etc.	3.6	5.4	8.4	2.9	4.1	6.6	1.7	6.0	...	Banques, assurances, affaires immobilières
Transport and communications	14.2	7.2	10.7	16.0	6.7	4.9	8.0	9.7	...	Transport(s) et communications
Public administration and defense	3.9	10.4	11.8	5.3	2.8	5.3	2.9	8.9	...	Administrations publiques et défense
Education	3.6	6.0	4.9	3.0	- 0.2	17.4	4.5	3.3	...	Education
Health and Social Work	1.0	5.7	- 8.0	5.5	9.5	5.6	5.8	8.8	...	Santé et actions sociales
Other services	2.3	3.4	8.6	8.6	8.7	8.6	8.5	- 6.7	...	Autres services
Less Imputed Service Charges	14.3	9.9	2.1	- 7.3	23.3	10.7	4.5	9.4	...	Moins services d'intérmediation financière
Gross domestic product at factor cost / basic prices	7.3	5.4	2.7	- 0.3	6.6	5.1	4.9	4.9	...	Produit intérieur brut aux couts des facteurs / prix de base
Plus: indirect taxes / taxes on products, less subsidies	4.1	4.8	1.8	8.0	0.0	5.3	8.9	7.4	...	Plus taxes indirectes/impôts sur les produits, moins les subventions
Gross domestic product at market prices	7.1	5.4	2.6	0.3	6.0	5.1	5.2	5.1	...	Produit intérieur brut aux prix du marché
EXPENDITURE ON GROSS DOMESTIC PRODUCT AT CONSTANT PURCHASERS' VALUES *ANNUAL GROWTH RATES (%)*										**EMPLOIS DU PRODUIT INTÉRIEUR BRUT AUX PRIX CONSTANTS D'ACQUISITION** *TAUX DE CROISSANCE ANNUEL (%)*
Government final consumption	11.0	12.6	10.2	3.8	1.0	6.7	3.3	8.6	...	Consommation finale des administrations publiques
Private final consumption	1.3	18.8	11.9	13.8	- 4.4	8.8	8.3	13.1	...	Consommation finale privée
Gross fixed capital formation	29.8	12.1	18.0	14.5	- 1.2	- 4.4	31.8	13.5	...	Formation brute de capital fixe
Exports of goods and services	15.3	6.4	- 4.4	1.8	2.8	- 3.3	1.0	9.6	...	Exportations de biens et services
Less imports of goods and services	16.3	31.8	18.7	15.4	- 10.2	- 0.8	18.2	17.5	...	Moins importations de biens et services
Notes	The Accounts are calculated using the new base year 2010 from 2007					Les comptes sont calculés selon la nouvelle année de base 2010 à partir de 2007				Notes

III INFLATION

	2006	2007	2008	2009	2010	2011	2012	2013	2014	
ANNUAL GROWTH RATES (%)										**TAUX DE CROISSANCE ANNUEL (%)**
All items	5.0	6.6	9.1	9.5	4.9	5.0	6.7	5.6	5.4	Ensemble
of which:										dont:
Food and Non-alcoholic beverages	6.3	11.9	16.8	10.7	3.2	4.9	9.1	6.5	8.3	Alimentation et boissons non alcoolisés
Alcoholic beverages & tobacco	7.1	7.6	10.5	12.3	10.2	6.4	8.7	8.7	6.6	Boissons alcoolisées et tabacs
Clothing and Footwear	-0.9	3.5	0.4	10.0	3.2	1.2	0.5	3.5	3.4	Habillement et chaussures
Housing, Water, Electricity, Gas and Other Fuels	2.0	3.9	3.6	7.8	4.5	7.8	5.8	5.2	3.2	Logement, eau, électricité, gas et autres combustibles
Furnishing, household equip	1.5	4.0	9.0	11.7	2.0	1.7	6.0	6.1	4.7	Meubles, articles de ménage et entretien courant
Health	0.5	2.8	2.7	5.8	5.0	4.9	3.3	3.1	2.1	Santé
Transport	7.5	5.6	13.2	5.1	5.5	5.2	7.1	5.3	7.2	Transport
Communication	0.6	1.4	5.0	6.1	1.1	1.3	0.7	2.3	-0.5	Communication
Recreation & culture	2.4	3.9	10.3	8.0	2.3	3.4	7.5	4.4	5.7	Loisirs et culture
Education	5.3	6.2	6.5	3.8	5.0	4.3	4.5	4.0	8.1	Enseignement
Restaurants & hotels	5.6	6.4	11.6	10.8	7.9	4.5	4.9	8.9	5.9	Restaurants et hôtels
Miscellaneous goods & services	6.9	1.7	5.0	10.6	3.3	2.5	2.5	1.8	4.4	Biens et services divers

IV AGRICULTURAL PRODUCTION - PRODUCTION AGRICOLE										
	2006	2007	2008	2009	2010	2011	2012	2013	2014	
TONNES *(THOUSAND)*										**TONNES** *(MILLIERS)*
Millet	106	45	36	37	73	41	56	25	37	Millet
Maize	64	56	58	57	70	88	87	40	67	Maïs
Wheat	13	12	15	12	13	16	15	15	15	Blé
Grapes	19	20	20	20	22	22	23	24	...	Raisins
Sorghum	10	4	4	5	8	6	8	2	3	Sorgho
V MINING PRODUCTION - PRODUCTION MINIERE										
	2006	2007	2008	2009	2010	2011	2012	2013	2014	
Silver ores and concentrates (thousand Kilograms)	21	22	20	20	19	16	145	128	119	Minerais d'argent et concentrés (kilogrammes)
Lead ores and concentrates, metric tons (thousands)	31	8	11	8	6	4	6	5	5	Minerais de plomb et concentrés, tonnes métriques (milliers)
Uranium ores and concentrates, metric tons (thousands)	4	4	5	6	5	4	2	2	2	Minerais et concentrés d'uranium, tonnes métriques (milliers)
VI ENERGY - ENERGIE										
	2006	2007	2008	2009	2010	2011	2012	2013	2014	
Total electricity generation (GWh)	1 512	1 694	1 545	1 510	1 293	1 424	1 454	1 496	...	Production d'électricité totale (GWh)
of which:										dont:
Production of electricity from fossil fuels (GWh)	-	130	130	81	58	39	41	41	...	Production d'électricité à partir de combustibles fossiles (GWh)
Production of hydro electricity (GWh)	1 512	1 564	1 415	1 429	1 235	1 386	1 413	1 442	...	Production d'électricité d'origine hydraulique (GWh)
Production of electricity from solar, wind, tide, wave and other sources (GWh)	...	...	...	...	...	...	...	5	...	Production d'électricité d'origine solaire, éolienne, marée motrice et autres (GWh)
VII TOURISM AND INFRASTRUCTURE - TOURISME ET INFRASTRUCTURE										
	2006	2007	2008	2009	2010	2011	2012	2013	2014	
VII-1 TOURISM										**VII-1 TOURISME**
International tourist arrivals (thousands)	833	929	931	980	984	1 027	1 063	974	1 072	Arrivées de touristes internationaux (milliers)
Rooms in hotels and similar establishments (thousands)	10.8	11.5	12.1	13.0	12.0	9.7	12.1	12.5	15.5	Chambres d'hotels et établissements assimilés (milliers)
Overnight stays (thousands)	1 372	1 557	1 341	1 292	1 296	1 247	1 389	1 298	1 320	Nuitées (milliers)
Tourism receipts (US$ thousand)	520 270	992 660	874 660	831 220	1003 870	1184 510	813 782	493 600	461 338	Recettes touristiques (milliers de $ EU)
Total contribution to GDP (%)	15.3	15.5	13.2	11.6	14.2	14.8	15.3	14.9	14.9	Contribution totale au PIB (%)
Total contribution to Employment (%)	21.8	21.4	18.2	15.7	19.1	19.7	20.1	19.5	19.2	Contribution totale à l'emploi (%)
VII-2 INFRASTRUCTURE										**VII-2 INFRASTRUCTURE**
Paved roads (% of total)	13	13	14	14	15	15	15	15	15	Routes asphaltées (% du total)
Total Network (Railways-km)	2 409	2 409	2 409	2 409	2 409	2 409	2 467	2 467	2 467	Réseau total voies ferrées-Km
Main Telephone Lines (per 100 inhabitants)	7	7	7	7	7	7	8	8	...	Lignes téléphoniques fixes (pour 100 habitants)
Mobile Cellular Subscribers (per 100 inhabitants)	30	38	50	76	89	99	95	118	...	Abonnés aux téléphones mobiles (pour 100 habitants)
VIII EXTERNAL TRADE - COMMERCE EXTERIEUR										
	2006	2007	2008	2009	2010	2011	2012	2013	2014	
US$ (MILLIONS) **EXPORTS, FOB**										**$ E.U (MILLIONS)** **EXPORTATIONS, FÀB**
Exports - Total	3 376	4 040	4 729	5 255	5 283	5 365	5 480	5 418	4 416	Exportations - Total
Exports to AFRICA	1 233	1 723	2 259	2 541	2 199	2 142	2 457	2 974	1 861	Exportations vers l'AFRIQUE
Main Products										Principaux produits
Diamonds, non-industrial, unworked or simply sawn, cleaved or bruted	895	703	728	753	1 033	1 055	1 145	1 660	543	Diamants, non industriels, bruts ou simplement sciés, clivés ou débrutés
Printed books, newspapers, pictures & other products	292	357	806	2 000	1 000	-	679	5 000	295	Livres imprimés, journaux, images et autres produits
Uranium ores and concentrates	163	350	742	601	721	623	275	948	291	Minerais et concentrés d'uranium
Fish, frozen, excluding fish fillets and other fish meat	191	224	215	343	316	394	216	737	240	Poissons congelés, à l'exclusion des filets de poissons et autre chair de poissons
Zinc, not alloyed	539	580	276	287	353	326	198	279	192	Zinc, non alliage
Main Destinations										**Principales destinations**
South Africa	830	1 172	1 505	1 360	1 040	1 146	937	1 222	708	Afrique du Sud
United Kingdom	865	683	710	626	743	846	643	125	545	Royaume Uni
Angola	193	261	406	686	566	496	503	442	526	Angola
Spain	202	243	242	281	285	248	444	214	428	Espagne
United States	82	102	261	190	264	419	353	209	241	Etats-Unis
IMPORTS, CIF										**IMPORTATIONS, CAF**
Imports - Total	2 799	4 026	4 689	6 476	6 499	6 623	7 320	7 344	7 534	Importations - Total (millions)
Imports from Africa	2 616	3 568	3 716	4 616	4 892	5 288	5 689	5 432	5 126	Importations en provenance de l'Afrique
Main Products										**Principaux produits**
Petroleum oils & oils obtained from bituminous minerals,o/than crude etc	76	392	603	506	552	593	520	657	550	Huiles de pétrole ou de minéraux bitumineux, sauf brut
Pharmaceutical products: Medicaments	46	51	75	168	165	187	377	148	331	Produits pharmaceutiques: Médicaments
Portland cement, other than white cement	25	36	43	67	61	20	359	27	248	Ciment Portland, autre que du ciment blanc
Sugars and sugar confectionery: other, including invert sugar	18	96	24	29	27	25	357	98	224	Sucres et sucreries: autres, y compris le sucre inverti
Other articles of iron or steel	17	83	37	47	46	42	294	272	152	Autres ouvrages en fer ou en acier
Main Origin										**Principales provenances**
South Africa	2 305	3 143	3 180	4 456	4 630	5 038	5 103	4 640	4 669	Afrique du Sud
United Kingdom	24	45	373	340	292	227	438	118	560	Royaume Uni
China	97	101	153	268	215	195	290	229	296	Chine
Germany	62	84	97	239	179	145	181	115	254	Allemagne
United States	42	55	95	62	67	63	179	114	191	Etats-Unis

IX FINANCIAL AND MONETARY STATISTICS - FINANCES ET STATISTIQUES MONETAIRES										
	2006	2007	2008	2009	2010	2011	2012	2013	2014	
IX-1 MONETARY STATISTICS *NAMIBIAN DOLLAR (MILLIONS)*										**IX-1 STATISTIQUES MONÉTAIRES** *DOLLAR NAMIBIEN (MILLIONS)*
Money supply (M1)	22 520	24 810	46 220	49 470	53 190	57 290	67 080	73 890	81 620	Masse monétaire (M1)
Quasi-money	8 833	10 166	11 239	27 180	28 506	31 391	36 381	35 078	37 650	Quasi-monnaie
of which Demand Deposit	...	...	...	...	...	...	...	...	...	dont Monnaie scripturale
Net foreign assets	4 845	7 463	13 659	24 600	19 635	23 172	20 902	23 332	19 516	Avoirs extérieurs nets
Domestic credit	28 398	30 092	31 919	34 504	42 738	46 365	53 160	62 866	77 065	Crédit intérieur
of which claims on private sector	26 225	29 758	33 297	36 591	40 589	44 441	51 970	59 486	69 282	dont créances sur le secteur privé
of which claims on government sector, net	113	- 2 264	- 4 693	- 5 227	- 1 721	- 554	- 1 306	269	4 002	dont créances nettes sur le gouvernement
International reserves (millions US$)	450	896	1 293	2 051	1 696	1 787	1 746	1 511	1 209	Réserves internationales (millions $EU)
Average Exchange Rate (National Currency per US$)	6.77	7.05	8.26	8.47	7.32	7.26	8.21	9.66	10.82	Taux de change (moyen) (monnaie nationale par $ EU)
IX-2 PUBLIC FINANCE *NAMIBIAN DOLLAR (MILLIONS)*										**IX-2 FINANCES PUBLIQUES** *DOLLAR NAMIBIEN (MILLIONS)*
Total Revenues and Grants	13 108	17 593	20 688	23 416	24 047	23 254	32 917	38 049	45 954	Recettes totales et dons
Tax Revenue	11 963	15 843	19 183	21 224	22 273	21 528	30 053	35 276	42 973	Recettes fiscales
Non Tax Revenue	1 105	1 701	1 427	2 109	1 573	1 702	2 685	2 605	2 477	Recettes non fiscales
Grants	39	50	78	83	201	24	179	168	504	Dons
Total Expenditures and Net Lending	13 198	15 373	17 510	21 024	24 209	29 121	32 907	39 282	39 886	Dépenses totales et prêts nets
Current expenditure	11 547	12 697	14 215	17 241	19 700	24 401	27 604	35 314	36 953	Dépenses courantes
Of which Wages and Salaries	5 889	6 214	6 725	7 559	9 045	10 801	10 290	15 948	13 536	Dont rémunérations et salaires
Capital expenditure	1 443	2 026	2 075	2 647	3 834	4 143	4 060	3 248	2 923	Dépenses d'équipement
Net Lending	208	651	1 219	1 136	675	577	1 243	720	10	Prêts nets
Fiscal Balance	- 90	2 220	3 178	2 392	- 162	- 5 867	10	- 1 233	6 068	Solde global y compris les dons
IX-3 BALANCE OF PAYMENTS *US$ (MILLIONS)*										**IX-3 BALANCE DES PAIEMENTS** *$ E.U (MILLIONS)*
Trade balance	1 438	- 1 429	- 581	- 7 246	- 7 380	- 8 532	- 13 401	- 18 965	- 24 565	Balance commerciale
Services Balance	674	615	- 492	641	1 437	193	277	117	573	Balance des services
Net Income	- 658	- 1 244	- 1 797	- 1 825	- 2 441	887	- 2 927	- 3 811	- 7 242	Revenus nets
Compensation of employees	...	...	...	...	...	...	...	...	...	Rémunération des salariés
Investment Income	...	...	...	...	...	...	...	...	...	Revenus des investissements
Current transfers, net total	6 733	7 052	9 278	10 614	9 018	11 760	13 285	16 590	19 725	Transferts courants
Net official transfers	...	...	...	...	...	...	...	...	...	Transferts officiels nets
Workers' remittances	...	...	...	...	...	...	...	...	...	Envois de fonds des travailleurs
Other private transfers	...	...	...	...	...	...	...	...	...	Autres transferts privés
Current account balance	8 187	4 994	6 408	2 184	634	4 308	- 2 766	- 6 069	- 11 509	Solde du compte courant
Capital & financial account	...	...	...	...	...	...	...	...	...	Comptes de capital et financier
Capital account	...	...	...	...	...	...	...	...	...	Compte de capital
Financial account	...	...	...	...	...	...	...	...	...	Compte financier
Errors & omissions	...	...	...	...	...	...	...	...	...	Erreurs et omissions
Overall balance	...	...	...	...	...	...	...	...	...	Balance générale

X DEBT AND FINANCIAL FLOWS - DETTE ET FLUX FINANCIERS										
	2006	2007	2008	2009	2010	2011	2012	2013	2014	
X-1 DEBT *US$ (MILLIONS)*										**X-1 DETTE EXTÉRIEURE** *$ E.U (MILLIONS)*
Total external debt	2 245	2 261	2 002	2 506	3 481	4 861	4 905	4 935	5 011	Dette extérieure totale
Private	1 883	1 815	1 624	2 073	2 998	4 071	3 835	3 959	3 780	Privée
Public	362	446	377	433	483	790	1 071	976	1 231	Publique
Total external debt service	891	1 085	921	585	666	1 007	1 456	1 011	1 075	Service de la dette extérieure
Present value of External debt	180	167	186	138	241.6	451.8	372.0	371.6	...	Valeur actuelle de la dette extérieure
Total government domestic debt (in local currency)	10 988	8 782	9 490	10 177	9 982.5	16 029.4	17 277.9	19 023.4	...	Dette publique intérieure
X-2 FINANCIAL FLOWS *US$ (MILLIONS)*										**X-2 FLUX FINANCIERS** *$ E.U (MILLIONS)*
Net Foreign Direct Investment Inflows	387	733	720	522	793	816	861	699	...	Investissements étranger direct (flux nets entrants)
Main origin of FDI Inflows										**Principales origines de l'IDE entrant:**
Spain	...	...	...	168	...	71.0	- 127.2	...	...	Espagne
Germany	3	4	- 7	176	- 107.3	37.6	33.4	...	...	Allemagne
United Kingdom	...	...	...	...	...	...	...	...	...	Royaume-Uni
France	...	...	...	...	...	...	...	...	...	France
Italy	...	...	...	4	...	1.3	- 0.1	...	...	Italie
African countries	...	...	...	...	...	...	...	...	...	Pays africains
Net total Official Development Assistance	152	217	210	326	256	291	265	262	...	Aide publique au développement (nette totale)
Main origin of Net ODA										**Principales origines de l'APD nette**
United States	51	59	71	90	117.2	121.8	148.9	162.5	...	Etats-Unis
Germany	14	21	22	37	24.0	91.9	60.4	62.7	...	Allemagne
Global Fund	23	31	15	38	29.5	8.1	35.6	...	...	Fonds mondial
Japan	1	6	10	40	40.6	25.2	- 6.7	- 4.3	...	Japon
Spain	8	28	15	12	8.5	4.3	1.0	0.5	...	Espagne

NIGER

NIGER

	Year / Année	Value / Valeur	
AREA (KM²)		1 267 000	SUPERFICIE (KM²)
CAPITAL CITY	Niamey	Niamey	CAPITALE
CURRENCY	CFA Franc	Franc CFA	MONNAIE
I SOCIAL AND DEMOGRAPHIC INDICATORS — INDICATEURS DEMOGRAPHIQUES ET SOCIAUX			
POPULATION			**POPULATION**
Population ('000)			Population ('000)
Both sexes	2014	18 535	Les deux sexes
Male	2014	9 344	Masculin
Female	2014	9 191	Féminin
Average annual growth rate	2014	3.9	Taux de croissance annuel
Active Population ('000)	2014	5 737	Population active ('000)
Population by age group ('000)			Population par groupe d'âge ('000)
0-14 years	2014	9 289	0-14 ans
15-64 years	2014	8 760	15-64 ans
65+ years	2014	486	65+ ans
Economically active population in agriculture (%)	2014	84.3	Participation de la population active agricole (%)
Crude birth rate	2014	49.5	Taux brut de natalité
Crude death rate	2014	10.6	Taux brut de mortalité
Total fertility rate	2014	7.5	Indice synthétique de fécondité
Proportion of urban population	2014	18.6	Part de la population urbaine
Life Expectancy at Birth - Total (years)	2014	58.9	Espérance de vie à la naissance - Totale (ans)
Dependency Ratio - Total (%)	2014	104.3	Taux de dépendance - Total (%)
HEALTH			**SANTÉ**
Percentage of children under-five and underweight	2012	37.9	% d'enfants de moins de cinq ans avec insuffisance pondérale
Prevalence of undernourishment	2013	11.3	Prévalence de la malnutrition
Under five mortality rate (both sexes, per 1000)	2013	104.2	Taux de mortalité de moins de 5 ans (les deux sexes, pour 1000)
Infant mortality rate (both sexes) per 1000	2013	59.9	Taux de mortalité infantile (les deux sexes) par 1000
Percentage of children provided the vaccines :			Pourcentage d'enfants vaccinés :
BCG	2013	49.0	BCG
DPT3	2013	70.0	DTC3
Polio	2012	74.7	Polio
Measles	2013	67.0	Rougeole
Percentage of mothers provided at least one antenatal care (%)	2013	88.5	Pourcentage de mères ayant au moins reçu un soin prénatal (%)
Percentage of deliveries attended by skilled health personnel	2012	29.3	% d'accouchements assistés par un personnel de santé qualifié
Number of doctors (per 10 000 population)	2008	0.2	Nombre de médecins (pour 10 000 habitants)
Number of nurses (per 10 000 population)	2008	1.4	Nombre d'infirmières (pour 10 000 habitants)
Hospital beds - Total (per 10 000 population)	2005	3.1	Nombre de lits d'hôpitaux - Total (pour 10 000)
Births registered (per 1 000)	2014	49.5	Naiss.s enregistrées (pour 1 000)
Deaths registered (per 1 000)	2014	10.6	Décès enregistrés (pour 1 000)
Public expenditure on Health (% of budget)	2013	5.6	Dépenses publiques consacrées à la santé (% du budget)
EDUCATION			**EDUCATION**
Enrolment in primary education (both sexes) (000)	2014	2 227	Scolarisation dans le primaire (les deux sexes) (000)
Female	2014	1 026	Féminin
Enrolment in secondary education (both sexes) (000)	2014	473	Scolarisation dans le secondaire (les deux sexes) (000)
Female	2014	188	Féminin
Enrolment in tertiary education (both sexes) (000)	2014	31.1	Scolarisation dans le tertiaire (les deux sexes) (000)
Female	2014	6.5	Féminin
Literacy rate (both sexes)	2012	15.5	Taux d'alphabétisation (deux sexes)
Male	2012	23.2	Masculin
Female	2012	8.9	Féminin
Pupil-teacher ratio	2014	36.0	Ratio élève-enseignant
Public expenditure on education (% of budget)	2014	9.9	Dépenses publiques consacrées à l'enseignement (% du budget)
POVERTY			**PAUVRETÉ**
GNI Per Capita (US$)	2013	400.0	RNB par habitant ($EU)
Human Poverty Index (HPI-1) Value (%)	2007	55.8	Valeur de l'Indice de pauvreté (IPH-1) (%)
Population below International Poverty Line ($2/day) (%)	2011	76.1	Population sous le seuil international de pauvreté (2$/J) (%)
Share of Income Held by Richest 10%	2011	26.3	% de revenu des 10% plus riches
Share of Income Held by Poorest 10%	2011	4.0	% de revenu des 10% plus pauvres
Gini index	2011	31.2	Indice de Gini

Charts / Graphiques

Population by age group – 2014
Population par groupe d'age – 2014

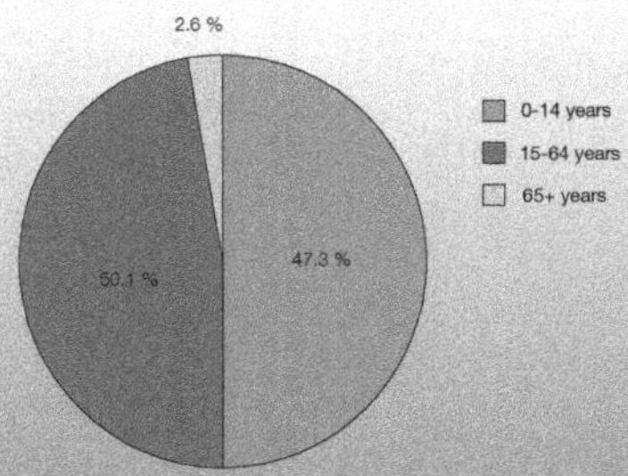

Percentage of children provided the vaccines – 2013
Pourcentage d'enfants vaccinés – 2013

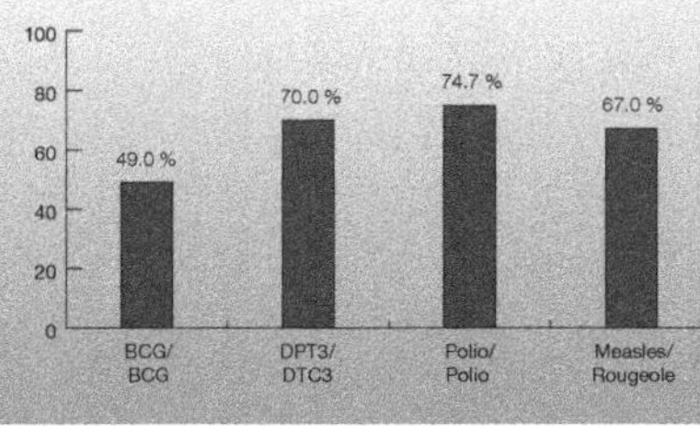

Literacy rate (%) – 2012
Taux d'alphabétisation – 2012

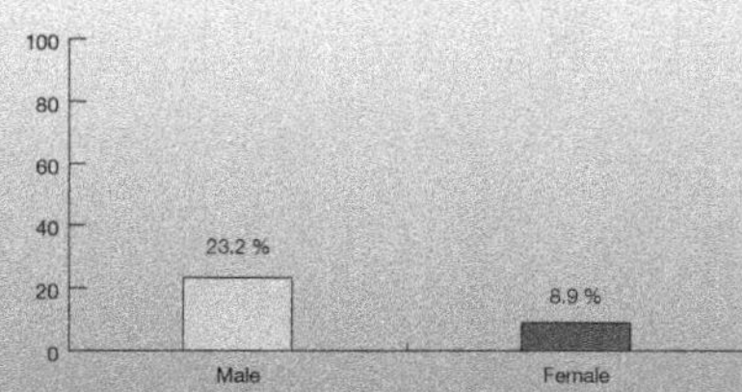

GNI Per Capita (US$)
RNB par habitant ($EU)

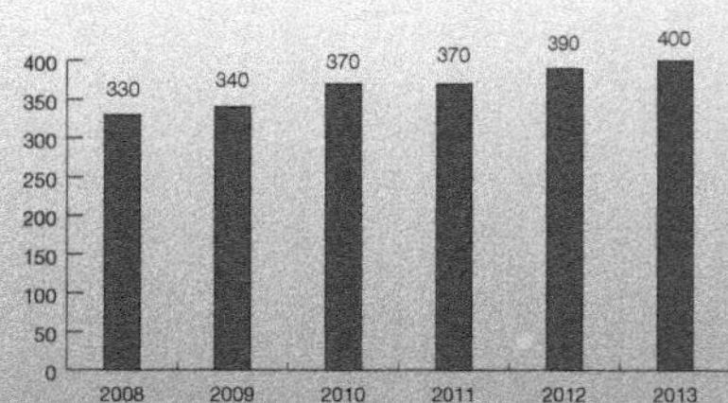

II NATIONAL ACCOUNTS — COMPTES NATIONAUX

	2006	2007	2008	2009	2010	2011	2012	2013	2014	
GROSS DOMESTIC PRODUCT BY KIND OF ECONOMIC ACTIVITY AT CURRENT PRICES *CFA FRANC (MILLIONS)*										**PRODUIT INTÉRIEUR BRUT PAR BRANCHE D'ACTIVITÉ ÉCONOMIQUE AUX PRIX COURANTS** *FRANC CFA (MILLIONS)*
Agriculture, hunting, forestry and fishing	817 662	842 593	1 045 424	999 357	1 158 359	1 156 647	1 330 031	1 361 315	1 498 051	Agriculture, chasse sylviculture et pêche
Mining and quarrying	40 096	90 775	144 399	162 627	203 462	221 494	338 810	360 667	376 864	Industries extractives
Manufacturing	102 635	106 578	117 559	128 256	134 918	143 942	192 081	223 452	236 508	Industries manufacturières
Electricity, gas & water	24 590	22 158	24 289	28 600	32 293	40 498	38 918	36 972	39 848	Electricité, gaz et eau
Construction & public works	47 471	51 584	58 096	64 096	71 643	76 173	83 447	90 289	98 379	Bâtiments et travaux publics
Wholesale & retail trade, restaurants, hotels	273 886	290 831	323 308	384 236	403 338	435 528	460 419	492 768	525 011	Commerce de gros et de détail, restaurants et hôtels
Finance, insurance, real estate, etc.	81 572	112 770	118 318	128 504	138 232	151 186	157 070	171 684	185 994	Banques, assurances, affaires immobilières
Transport and communications	124 105	134 886	147 359	156 493	171 911	193 196	209 863	235 091	254 700	Transport(s) et communications
Public administration and defense	166 930	181 111	193 400	225 082	215 784	251 651	282 597	327 623	349 746	Administrations publiques et défense
Education	32 689	32 845	34 242	37 082	40 197	43 413	47 521	49 507	52 850	Education
Health and Social Work	36 266	35 978	37 160	39 390	42 620	46 243	46 254	52 874	56 444	Santé et actions sociales
Other services	35 820	24 352	28 830	30 884	30 117	32 053	35 247	38 863	39 562	Autres services
Less Imputed Service Charges	- 15 081	- 18 235	- 19 165	- 21 690	- 22 668	- 24 341	- 26 960	- 29 419	- 32 197	Moins services d'intermédiation financière
Gross domestic product at factor cost / basic prices	1 768 641	1 908 226	2 253 219	2 362 917	2 620 206	2 767 683	3 195 298	3 411 686	3 681 760	Produit intérieur brut aux couts des facteurs / prix de base
Plus: indirect taxes / taxes on products, less subsidies	138 196	144 737	166 435	185 530	212 080	256 588	218 971	247 875	299 500	Plus taxes indirectes/impôts sur les produits, moins les subventions
EXPENDITURE ON GROSS DOMESTIC PRODUCT AT CURRENT PURCHASER'S VALUES *CFA FRANC (MILLIONS)*										**EMPLOI DU PRODUIT INTÉRIEUR BRUT AUX PRIX COURANTS D'ACQUISITION** *FRANC CFA (MILLIONS)*
Government final consumption	286 186	321 865	363 080	412 978	386 440	436 487	431 328	496 571	556 300	Consommation finale des administrations publiques
Private final consumption	1 389 307	1 517 062	1 714 569	1 926 410	2 076 008	2 239 687	2 413 479	2 563 839	2 735 400	Consommation finale privée
Gross fixed capital formation	430 199	467 984	746 513	883 824	1 101 631	1 159 074	1 178 708	1 260 479	1 505 900	Formation brute de capital fixe
Change in inventories	19 502	2 981	29 996	1 464	29 912	2 082	13 038	- 350	-	Variation des stocks
Exports of goods and services	344 704	358 453	429 008	517 883	628 718	632 144	830 646	854 028	817 461	Exportations de biens et services
Less imports of goods and services	563 059	615 383	863 512	1 194 112	1 390 424	1 445 203	1 452 930	1 515 007	1 633 800	Moins importations de biens et services
GDP at purchasers' values	1 906 837	2 052 962	2 419 654	2 548 447	2 832 285	3 024 271	3 414 269	3 659 560	3 981 261	PIB aux prix d'acquisition
GROSS DOMESTIC PRODUCT BY KIND OF ECONOMIC ACTIVITY AT CONSTANT PRICES *ANNUAL GROWTH RATES (%)*										**PRODUIT INTÉRIEUR BRUT PAR BRANCHE D'ACTIVITÉ ECONOMIQUE AUX PRIX CONSTANTS** *TAUX DE CROISSANCE ANNUEL (%)*
Agriculture, hunting, forestry and fishing	10.3	4.6	16.2	- 9.5	15.8	- 3.0	13.2	0.0	8.2	Agriculture, chasse sylviculture et pêche
Mining and quarrying	0.7	- 5.8	- 2.1	39.5	17.2	16.4	106.5	7.2	1.7	Industries extractives
Manufacturing	2.4	0.3	3.9	4.4	3.3	4.1	30.6	9.9	4.0	Industries manufacturières
Electricity, gas & water	- 1.1	- 13.5	8.8	8.4	9.7	- 12.1	5.7	- 5.7	5.0	Electricité, gaz et eau
Construction & public works	5.1	3.6	5.0	7.9	9.5	4.3	7.5	6.0	7.1	Bâtiments et travaux publics
Wholesale & retail trade, restaurants, hotels	44.9	1.2	4.8	5.8	1.6	4.7	3.8	5.1	4.7	Commerce de gros et de détail,restaurants et hôtels
Finance, insurance, real estate, etc.	...	26.7	4.8	6.6	4.6	3.2	2.6	7.5	2.0	Banques, assurances, affaires immobilières
Transport and communications	0.2	2.3	4.8	5.0	4.3	6.8	8.1	5.7	6.6	Transport(s) et communications
Public administration and defense	5.0	3.2	2.1	8.2	- 3.3	5.9	5.4	12.8	4.9	Administrations publiques et défense
Education	...	0.3	1.4	- 1.4	4.6	16.1	6.4	2.4	4.9	Education
Health and Social Work	...	- 5.2	1.9	1.5	1.7	15.8	8.0	4.4	4.9	Santé et actions sociales
Other services	- 53.5	- 19.5	1.5	1.7	1.7	1.0	0.3	- 2.1	6.4	Autres services
Less Imputed Service Charges	...	19.9	10.6	13.2	9.2	16.5	0.6	10.8	- 6.0	Moins services d'intermédiation financière
Gross domestic product at factor cost / basic prices	12.2	3.1	9.5	- 1.3	8.8	1.4	13.6	3.7	6.3	Produit intérieur brut aux couts des facteurs / prix de base
Plus: indirect taxes / taxes on products, less subsidies	- 39.1	3.2	10.4	7.1	3.8	13.2	- 16.7	10.8	18.6	Plus taxes indirectes/impôts sur les produits, moins les subventions
Gross domestic product at market prices	5.8	3.1	9.6	- 0.7	8.4	2.3	11.1	4.1	7.1	Produit intérieur brut aux prix du marché
EXPENDITURE ON GROSS DOMESTIC PRODUCT AT CONSTANT PURCHASERS' VALUES *ANNUAL GROWTH RATES (%)*										**EMPLOIS DU PRODUIT INTÉRIEUR BRUT AUX PRIX CONSTANTS D'ACQUISITION** *TAUX DE CROISSANCE ANNUEL (%)*
Government final consumption	5.7	3.7	9.0	10.6	- 7.5	6.0	3.7	7.6	13.3	Consommation finale des administrations publiques
Private final consumption	3.3	4.9	4.4	5.8	5.2	5.3	5.0	3.9	4.7	Consommation finale privée
Gross fixed capital formation	7.6	4.2	49.7	9.6	17.1	0.9	- 2.1	3.9	16.9	Formation brute de capital fixe
Exports of goods and services	5.5	2.7	15.1	18.0	19.7	- 0.9	27.2	1.4	- 5.8	Exportations de biens et services
Less imports of goods and services	- 0.8	4.9	33.2	32.2	11.5	3.1	- 0.9	2.2	4.8	Moins importations de biens et services
Notes	NA data: 2013 : Provisional;2014:Estimates					Données des CN: 2013:Provisoires;2014:Estimations				Notes

III INFLATION

	2006	2007	2008	2009	2010	2011	2012	2013	2014	
ANNUAL GROWTH RATES (%)										**TAUX DE CROISSANCE ANNUEL (%)**
All items	-	0.1	11.3	0.5	0.9	2.9	0.5	2.3	-0.9	Ensemble
of which:										dont:
Food and Non-alcoholic beverages	-2.1	-0.6	20.6	8.4	2.1	3.4	3.2	4.4	-1.3	Alimentation et boissons non alcoolisés
Alcoholic beverages & tobacco	-2.5	-0.3	4.0	6.4	-11.8	8.5	6.7	-9.6	-0.8	Boissons alcoolisées et tabacs
Clothing and Footwear	1.2	0.5	5.0	0.9	1.0	0.2	1.1	-0.6	-	Habillement et chaussures
Housing, Water, Electricity, Gas and Other Fuels	1.2	0.5	5.0	-0.4	-0.8	5.7	-2.7	1.2	0.7	Logement, eau, électricité, gas et autres combustibles
Furnishing, household equip	2.5	2.0	3.2	4.4	-5.1	-2.6	5.2	0.6	-0.1	Meubles, articles de ménage et entretien courant
Health	-2.6	-0.5	-3.3	-2.5	0.9	2.7	0.7	1.7	1.1	Santé
Transport	7.5	-1.7	3.8	-13.4	0.4	11.1	-2.9	-0.4	1.6	Transport
Communication	-3.4	-3.3	-	-14.1	-9.5	-8.1	-6.8	-2.7	-16.1	Communication
Recreation & culture	-4.1	-2.7	-0.5	5.7	-1.0	1.0	-0.7	-0.6	1.0	Loisirs et culture
Education	6.1	6.1	1.9	-	0.6	0.6	0.1	-	2.5	Enseignement
Restaurants & hotels	-0.5	4.7	4.7	-12.8	16.8	1.9	-7.3	7.1	-0.8	Restaurants et hôtels
Miscellaneous goods & services	-1.2	1.3	1.9	10.2	-8.1	-4.3	4.6	-2.2	-0.1	Biens et services divers

IV AGRICULTURAL PRODUCTION - PRODUCTION AGRICOLE	2006	2007	2008	2009	2010	2011	2012	2013	2014	
TONNES *(THOUSAND)*										**TONNES** *(MILLIERS)*
Millet	3 015	2 782	3 489	2 678	3 838	2 926	3 862	2 816	2 922	Millet
Sorghum	935	975	1 311	739	1 305	770	1 376	1 222	1 320	Sorgho
Rice	7	7	32	20	30	12	5	5	13	Riz paddy
Cow pea	693	1 001	1 548	787	1 773	1 569	1 330	1 634	1 790	Niébé
Groundnuts in shells	136	148	305	254	406	396	292	331	343	Arachides en coques

V MINING PRODUCTION - PRODUCTION MINIERE	2006	2007	2008	2009	2010	2011	2012	2013	2014	
Uranium, Tons	3 434	3 153	2 993	3 245	4 199	4 264	4 773	4 277	...	Uranium (tonnes)
Gold, industrial (Kilograms)	1 481	2 467	2 168	1 985	1 950	1 957	1 662	1 041	...	Or industriel (Kilogrammes)
Hard Coal, metric tons (thousands)	176	171	183	225	247	246	235	242	...	Charbon minéral, tonne (milliers)

VI ENERGY - ENERGIE	2006	2007	2008	2009	2010	2011	2012	2013	2014	
Total electricity generation (GWh)	218	2 141	230	248	250	342	399	452	...	Production d'électricité totale (GWh)
of which:										dont:
Production of electricity from fossil fuels (GWh)	218	2 141	230	248	250	342	399	448	...	Production d'électricité à partir de combustibles fossiles (GWh)
Production of hydro electricity (GWh)	...	...	...	...	...	...	...	...	...	Production d'électricité d'origine hydraulique (GWh)
Production of electricity from solar, wind, tide, wave and other sources (GWh)	...	...	...	...	...	...	...	4	...	Production d'électricité d'origine solaire, éolienne, marée motrice et autres (GWh)

VII TOURISM AND INFRASTRUCTURE - TOURISME ET INFRASTRUCTURE	2006	2007	2008	2009	2010	2011	2012	2013	2014	
VII-1 TOURISM										**VII-1 TOURISME**
International tourist arrivals (thousands)	60	48	73	66	74	82	85	80	84	Arrivées de touristes internationaux (milliers)
Rooms in hotels and similar establishments (thousands)	1.9	2.0	2.0	2.0	2.1	2.1	2.2	2.2	...	Chambres d'hotels et établissements assimilés (milliers)
Overnight stays (thousands)	293	288	314	337	344	417	157	304	310	Nuitées (milliers)
Tourism receipts (US$ thousand)	35 800	40 900	78 200	66 000	104 900	50 800	49 500	51 212	54 472	Recettes touristiques (milliers de $ EU)
Total contribution to GDP (%)	4.9	4.9	4.7	4.3	4.9	3.8	3.1	2.9	3.0	Contribution totale au PIB (%)
Total contribution to Employment (%)	4.2	4.2	3.8	3.5	4.1	3.3	2.7	2.5	2.6	Contribution totale à l'emploi (%)
VII-2 INFRASTRUCTURE										**VII-2 INFRASTRUCTURE**
Paved roads (% of total)	20	21	21	21	21	21	21	21	...	Routes asphaltées (% du total)
Total Network (Railways-km)	...	...	...	...	...	...	...	...	...	Réseau total voies ferrées-Km
Main Telephone Lines (per 100 inhabitants)	0	0	0	0	1	1	1	1	...	Lignes téléphoniques fixes (pour 100 habitants)
Mobile Cellular Subscribers (per 100 inhabitants)	4	6	13	17	23	29	31	39	...	Abonnés aux téléphones mobiles (pour 100 habitants)

VIII EXTERNAL TRADE - COMMERCE EXTERIEUR	2006	2007	2008	2009	2010	2011	2012	2013	2014	
US$ (MILLIONS) EXPORTS, FOB										**$ E.U (MILLIONS) EXPORTATIONS, FÀB**
Exports - Total	330	494	759	693	811	974	1 279	1 380	1 071	Exportations - Total
Exports to AFRICA	90	96	228	190	198	121	376	548	357	Exportations vers l'AFRIQUE
Main Products										**Principaux produits**
Uranium	152	298	442	413	461	664	662	613	488	Uranium
Gold	37	59	43	44	75	97	85	54	28	Or
Hydrocarbons	5	7	8	7	8	11	221	383	277	Hydraucarbures
Onions	23	27	30	32	38	31	49	81	14	Oignons
Cattle, live	20	18	67	51	67	22	30	20	8	Bovins sur pieds
Main Destinations										**Principales destinations**
France	114	208	199	199	251	389	464	482	391	France
Nigeria	49	41	179	139	134	52	145	228	136	Nigeria
United States	138	143	135	146	58	120	2	3	80	Etats-Unis
Switzerland	38	60	43	44	75	97	85	55	33	Suisse
Japan	37	66	73	64	79	96	64	50	2	Japon
IMPORTS, CIF										**IMPORTATIONS, CAF**
Imports - Total	854	943	1 229	1 606	2 278	1 892	1 687	1 745	2 174	Importations - Total (millions)
Imports from Africa	237	248	269	287	300	320	369	409	425	Importations en provenance de l'Afrique
Main Products										**Principaux produits**
Petroleum products	106	143	180	170	257	304	37	52	46	Produits pétroliers
Rice	64	56	112	67	71	55	169	195	162	Riz
Medicaments	31	69	112	54	30	107	44	53	58	Médicaments
Hydraulic cements	32	37	51	49	59	63	66	81	107	Ciments hydrauliques
Cigars	19	24	25	32	38	46	41	51	49	Cigares
Main Origin										**Principales provenances**
China	107	65	157	492	995	508	358	417	492	Chine
France	130	177	156	216	252	230	199	175	317	France
United States	86	85	95	78	138	111	112	105	114	Etats-Unis
Côte d'Ivoire	55	75	61	62	51	61	57	62	58	Côte d'Ivoire
Nigeria	52	45	58	81	89	88	102	88	83	Nigeria

IX FINANCIAL AND MONETARY STATISTICS - FINANCES ET STATISTIQUES MONETAIRES	2006	2007	2008	2009	2010	2011	2012	2013	2014	
IX-1 MONETARY STATISTICS *CFA FRANC (MILLIONS)*										**IX-1 STATISTIQUES MONÉTAIRES** *FRANC CFA (MILLIONS)*
Money supply (M1)	289 050	355 670	399 200	472 300	576 020	611 560	802 500	882 300	1 000 530	Masse monétaire (M1)
Quasi-money	59 998	86 307	106 894	116 182	124 196	132 630	161 964	173 190	209 992	Quasi-monnaie
of which Demand Deposit	...	...	...	...	...	...	...	...	...	dont Monnaie scripturale
Net foreign assets	169 660	255 667	320 813	238 383	342 947	316 336	487 341	615 092	795 030	Avoirs extérieurs nets
Domestic credit	151 741	142 089	147 761	311 277	351 213	418 432	454 863	433 319	498 510	Crédit intérieur
of which claims on private sector	159 630	191 922	262 603	310 891	347 148	402 607	499 986	519 768	573 597	dont créances sur le secteur privé
of which claims on government sector, net	- 7 889	- 49 833	- 114 842	386	4 065	15 825	- 45 123	- 86 449	- 75 087	dont créances nettes sur le gouvernement
International reserves (millions US$)	371	593	705	656	760	673	1 015	1 167	1 191	Réserves internationales (millions $EU)
Average Exchange Rate (National Currency per US$)	522.84	479.57	448.33	471.52	495.86	473.70	512.43	500.72	495.96	Taux de change (moyen) (monnaie nationale par $ EU)
IX-2 PUBLIC FINANCE *CFA FRANC (MILLIONS)*										**IX-2 FINANCES PUBLIQUES** *FRANC CFA (MILLIONS)*
Total Revenues and Grants	330 300	455 600	584 100	474 500	515 800	627 600	759 341	825 570	956 851	Recettes totales et dons
Tax Revenue	204 000	233 200	281 200	343 000	361 700	485 900	495 700	577 349	591 375	Recettes fiscales
Non Tax Revenue	43 400	75 800	160 900	20 600	23 900	28 200	47 100	51 166	54 186	Recettes non fiscales
Grants	82 900	146 600	142 000	110 900	130 200	113 500	216 541	197 055	311 290	Dons
Total Expenditures and Net Lending	352 300	435 900	501 900	609 900	584 100	684 800	799 173	910 103	1 175 984	Dépenses totales et prêts nets
Current expenditure	169 700	199 300	254 800	300 800	366 300	477 200	404 978	511 600	555 736	Dépenses courantes
Of which Wages and Salaries	83 300	88 500	102 700	114 900	125 400	157 200	170 100	188 213	201 826	Dont rémunérations et salaires
Capital expenditure	182 600	236 600	247 100	309 100	217 800	207 600	394 195	398 503	422 989	Dépenses d'équipement
Net Lending	-	-	-	-	-	-	-	-	197 259	Prêts nets
Fiscal Balance	- 22 000	19 700	82 200	- 135 400	- 68 300	- 57 200	- 39 832	- 84 533	- 219 133	Solde global y compris les dons
IX-3 BALANCE OF PAYMENTS *CFA FRANC (MILLIONS)*										**IX-3 BALANCE DES PAIEMENTS** *FRANC CFA (MILLIONS)*
Trade balance	- 125 668	- 120 500	- 195 900	- 376 500	- 402 700	- 435 000	- 218 700	- 241 400	- 359 700	Balance commerciale
Services Balance	- 124 432	- 136 500	- 210 512	- 299 700	- 397 100	- 378 000	- 403 600	- 419 600	- 456 600	Balance des services
Net Income	634	- 4 700	- 8 482	- 16 352	- 21 245	- 24 100	- 66 800	- 90 980	- 198 952	Revenus nets
Compensation of employees	...	...	...	...	...	...	...	...	...	Rémunération des salariés
Investment Income	...	...	...	...	...	...	...	...	...	Revenus des investissements
Current transfers, net total	85 421	88 791	103 147	71 274	222 000	161 900	167 800	145 000	207 800	Transferts courants
Net official transfers	...	...	...	...	...	...	...	...	...	Transferts officiels nets
Workers' remittances	...	...	...	...	...	...	...	...	...	Envois de fonds des travailleurs
Other private transfers	...	...	...	...	...	...	...	...	...	Autres transferts privés
Current account balance	- 164 045	- 172 909	- 311 747	- 621 277	- 599 045	- 675 200	- 521 300	- 606 980	- 807 452	Solde du compte courant
Capital & financial account	...	...	...	...	...	...	...	...	...	Comptes de capital et financier
Capital account	...	...	...	...	...	...	...	...	...	Compte de capital
Financial account	...	...	...	...	...	...	...	...	...	Compte financier
Errors & omissions	...	...	...	...	...	...	...	...	...	Erreurs et omissions
Overall balance	...	...	...	...	...	...	...	...	...	Balance générale

X DEBT AND FINANCIAL FLOWS - DETTE ET FLUX FINANCIERS	2006	2007	2008	2009	2010	2011	2012	2013	2014	
X-1 DEBT *US$ (MILLIONS)*										**X-1 DETTE EXTÉRIEURE** *$ E.U (MILLIONS)*
Total external debt	630	818	1 225	2 156	2 855	3 124	3 508	3 717	5 282	Dette extérieure totale
Private	54	136	468	1 097	1 888	2 130	2 323	2 321	2 587	Privée
Public	575	682	757	1 059	967	994	1 185	1 396	2 695	Publique
Total external debt service	20	31	28	26	29	58	39	73	88	Service de la dette extérieure
Present value of External debt	...	...	...	...	...	...	...	...	...	Valeur actuelle de la dette extérieure
Total government domestic debt (in local currency)	...	...	...	...	...	...	...	...	...	Dette publique intérieure
X-2 FINANCIAL FLOWS *US$ (MILLIONS)*										**X-2 FLUX FINANCIERS** *$ E.U (MILLIONS)*
Net Foreign Direct Investment Inflows	51	129	340	791	940	1 066	841	631	...	Investissements étranger direct (flux nets entrants)
Main origin of FDI Inflows										**Principales origines de l'IDE entrant:**
Czech Republic	...	...	...	...	...	23.2	...	...	...	République tchèque
Korea	...	...	...	15	...	...	...	...	...	Corée
Italy	...	...	...	...	...	...	...	...	...	Italie
Japan	...	...	...	3	1.1	- 1.3	...	...	...	Japon
Sweden	...	...	...	...	0.8	1.5	1.5	...	...	Suède
African countries	...	...	...	...	...	...	...	...	...	Pays africains
Net total Official Development Assistance	544	544	612	469	745	650	902	773	...	Aide publique au développement (nette totale)
Main origin of Net ODA										**Principales origines de l'APD nette**
France	89	57	68	57	50.0	47.3	102.0	67.3	...	France
IDA	83	80	62	39	71.8	102.9	112.9	...	...	IDA
United States	31	41	46	37	102.6	92.4	112.7	64.5	...	Etats-Unis
AfDF	67	36	23	27	24.5	47.2	26.2	...	...	FAfD
Germany	21	21	21	22	22.6	68.7	43.1	26.6	...	Allemagne

NIGERIA — NIGÉRIA

AREA (KM²)	923 768		SUPERFICIE (KM²)
CAPITAL CITY	Abuja	Abuja	CAPITALE
CURRENCY	Naira	Naira	MONNAIE

I SOCIAL AND DEMOGRAPHIC INDICATORS — INDICATEURS DEMOGRAPHIQUES ET SOCIAUX

	Year / Année	Value / Valeur	
POPULATION			**POPULATION**
Population ('000)			Population ('000)
Both sexes	2014	178 517	Les deux sexes
Male	2014	90 887	Masculin
Female	2014	87 630	Féminin
Average annual growth rate	2014	2.8	Taux de croissance annuel
Active Population ('000)	2014	53 030	Population active ('000)
Population by age group ('000)			Population par groupe d'âge ('000)
0-14 years	2014	79 259	0-14 ans
15-64 years	2014	94 377	15-64 ans
65+ years	2014	4 880	65+ ans
Economically active population in agriculture (%)	2014	23.3	Participation de la population active agricole (%)
Crude birth rate	2014	40.9	Taux brut de natalité
Crude death rate	2014	12.9	Taux brut de mortalité
Total fertility rate	2014	5.9	Indice synthétique de fécondité
Proportion of urban population	2014	51.5	Part de la population urbaine
Life Expectancy at Birth - Total (years)	2014	52.9	Espérance de vie à la naissance - Totale (ans)
Dependency Ratio - Total (%)	2014	85.8	Taux de dépendance - Total (%)
HEALTH			**SANTÉ**
Percentage of children under-five and underweight	2013	31.0	% d'enfants de moins de cinq ans avec insuffisance pondérale
Prevalence of undernourishment	2013	6.4	Prévalence de la malnutrition
Under five mortality rate (both sexes, per 1000)	2013	117.4	Taux de mortalité de moins de 5 ans (les deux sexes, pour 1000)
Infant mortality rate (both sexes) per 1000	2013	74.3	Taux de mortalité infantile (les deux sexes) par 1000
Percentage of children provided the vaccines :			Pourcentage d'enfants vaccinés :
BCG	2013	80.0	BCG
DPT3	2013	58.0	DTC3
Polio	2011	48.8	Polio
Measles	2013	59.0	Rougeole
Percentage of mothers provided at least one antenatal care (%)	2011	56.6	Pourcentage de mères ayant au moins reçu un soin prénatal (%)
Percentage of deliveries attended by skilled health personnel	2011	48.7	% d'accouchements assistés par un personnel de santé qualifié
Number of doctors (per 10 000 population)	2009	4.1	Nombre de médecins (pour 10 000 habitants)
Number of nurses (per 10 000 population)	2008	16.1	Nombre d'infirmières (pour 10 000 habitants)
Hospital beds - Total (per 10 000 population)	2004	5.3	Nombre de lits d'hôpitaux - Total (pour 10 000)
Births registered (per 1 000)	2014	40.9	Naiss.s enregistrées (pour 1 000)
Deaths registered (per 1 000)	2014	12.9	Décès enregistrés (pour 1 000)
Public expenditure on Health (% of budget)	2009	6.4	Dépenses publiques consacrées à la santé (% du budget)
EDUCATION			**EDUCATION**
Enrolment in primary education (both sexes) (000)	2010	21 558	Scolarisation dans le primaire (les deux sexes) (000)
Female	2010	10 060	Féminin
Enrolment in secondary education (both sexes) (000)	2010	9 057	Scolarisation dans le secondaire (les deux sexes) (000)
Female	2010	4 152	Féminin
Enrolment in tertiary education (both sexes) (000)	2005	1 391.5	Scolarisation dans le tertiaire (les deux sexes) (000)
Female	2005	566.5	Féminin
Literacy rate (both sexes)	2008	51.1	Taux d'alphabétisation (deux sexes)
Male	2008	61.3	Masculin
Female	2008	41.4	Féminin
Pupil-teacher ratio	2010	58.0	Ratio élève-enseignant
Public expenditure on education (% of budget)	...	...	Dépenses publiques consacrées à l'enseignement (% du budget)
POVERTY			**PAUVRETÉ**
GNI Per Capita (US$)	2013	2 710.0	RNB par habitant ($EU)
Human Poverty Index (HPI-1) Value (%)	2007	36.2	Valeur de l'Indice de pauvreté (IPH-1) (%)
Population below International Poverty Line ($2/day) (%)	2010	82.2	Population sous le seuil international de pauvreté (2$/J) (%)
Share of Income Held by Richest 10%	2010	32.9	% de revenu des 10% plus riches
Share of Income Held by Poorest 10%	2010	2.2	% de revenu des 10% plus pauvres
Gini index	2010	43.0	Indice de Gini

Charts / Graphiques

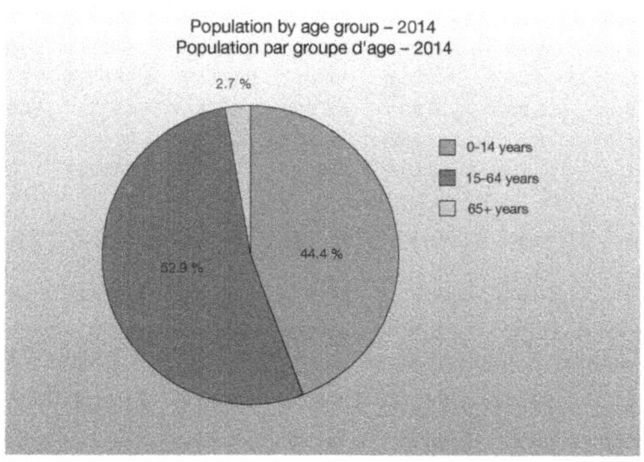

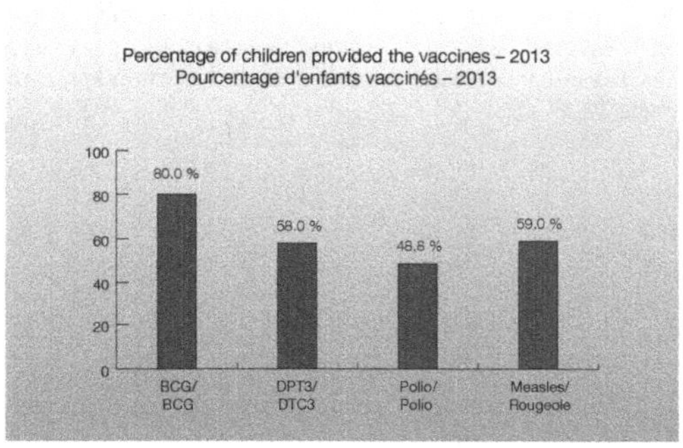

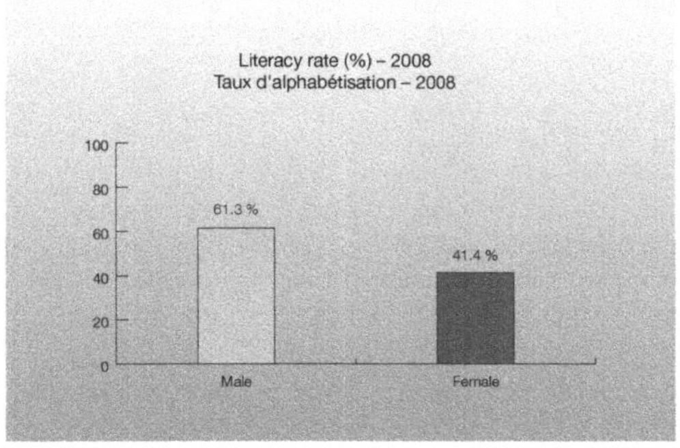

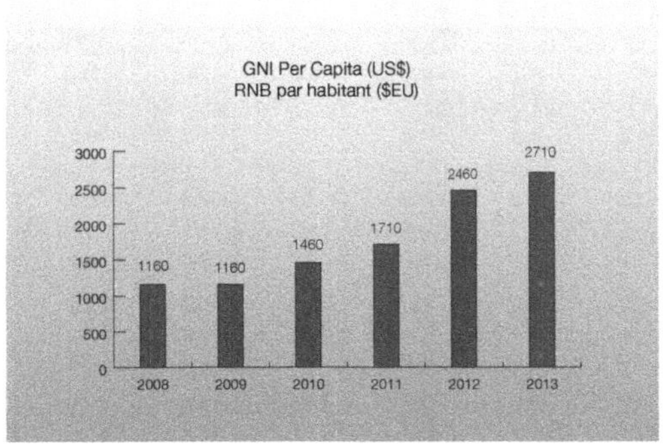

II NATIONAL ACCOUNTS — COMPTES NATIONAUX

	2006	2007	2008	2009	2010	2011	2012	2013	2014	
GROSS DOMESTIC PRODUCT BY KIND OF ECONOMIC ACTIVITY AT CURRENT PRICES *NAIRA (MILLIONS)*										**PRODUIT INTÉRIEUR BRUT PAR BRANCHE D'ACTIVITÉ ÉCONOMIQUE AUX PRIX COURANTS** *NAIRA (MILLIONS)*
Agriculture, hunting, forestry and fishing	5 940 237	6 757 868	7 981 397	9 186 306	13 048 893	14 037 826	15 815 998	16 816 553	18 018 613	Agriculture, chasse sylviculture et pêche
Mining and quarrying	7 010 197	7 564 470	9 133 941	7 458 762	8 454 554	11 098 978	11 386 523	10 380 972	9 716 761	Industries extractives
Manufacturing	478 524	520 883	585 573	612 309	3 578 642	4 527 445	5 588 822	7 233 322	8 685 430	Industries manufacturières
Electricity, gas & water	42 615	45 778	52 671	62 148	222 265	321 116	423 658	563 267	621 992	Electricité, gaz et eau
Construction & public works	250 332	266 464	306 582	347 691	1 570 973	1 905 575	2 188 719	2 676 284	3 188 823	Bâtiments et travaux publics
Wholesale & retail trade, restaurants, hotels	2 799 406	3 117 613	3 589 240	4 181 313	9 238 411	10 608 942	12 196 752	14 351 227	16 523 912	Commerce de gros et de détail, restaurants et hôtels
Finance, insurance, real estate, etc.	1 105 260	1 266 503	1 456 478	1 657 246	7 761 631	8 269 246	10 222 163	12 039 975	13 688 206	Banques, assurances, affaires immobilières
Transport and communications	607 346	716 996	729 010	762 725	6 649 832	7 158 914	8 184 038	9 410 628	10 786 011	Transport(s) et communications
Public administration and defense	131 329	151 330	174 030	197 262	1 998 471	2 471 239	2 210 046	2 384 904	2 644 232	Administrations publiques et défense
Education	29 690	33 357	39 394	47 096	826 672	1 110 721	1 252 722	1 549 934	1 804 405	Education
Health and Social Work	7 778	8 738	9 962	11 086	330 964	387 195	442 939	518 736	615 026	Santé et actions sociales
Other services	161 858	207 290	238 052	270 295	930 958	1 083 201	1 801 556	2 166 761	2 750 204	Autres services
Less Imputed Service Charges	...	...	...	...	...	...	...	...	...	Moins services d'intermédiation financière
Gross domestic product at factor cost / basic prices	18 564 572	20 657 290	24 296 329	24 794 239	54 612 264	62 980 397	71 713 935	80 092 563	89 043 615	Produit intérieur brut aux couts des facteurs / prix de base
Plus: indirect taxes / taxes on products, less subsidies	145 214	283 620	368 915	441 818	857 086	732 962	885 695	917 401	1 093 369	Plus taxes indirectes/impôts sur les produits, moins les subventions
EXPENDITURE ON GROSS DOMESTIC PRODUCT AT CURRENT PURCHASER'S VALUES *NAIRA (MILLIONS)*										**EMPLOI DU PRODUIT INTÉRIEUR BRUT AUX PRIX COURANTS D'ACQUISITION** *NAIRA (MILLIONS)*
Government final consumption	1 283 403	2 608 600	2 871 376	3 269 928	4 832 148	5 412 006	5 953 206	6 548 527	-	Consommation finale des administrations publiques
Private final consumption	11 834 578	15 682 906	16 090 499	18 980 959	36 676 905	41 686 511	42 394 482	58 440 391	-	Consommation finale privée
Gross fixed capital formation	1 546 526	1 935 040	2 053 006	3 050 576	9 424 691	10 180 859	10 618 680	11 723 097	-	Formation brute de capital fixe
Change in inventories	1 470	1 571	1 564	1 626	166 371	148 339	204 248	201 440	-	Variation des stocks
Exports of goods and services	8 066 038	7 063 060	9 837 271	7 764 785	14 013 841	19 961 271	22 824 414	14 615 287	-	Exportations de biens et services
Less imports of goods and services	4 022 227	6 350 266	6 188 471	7 831 818	9 644 605	13 675 626	9 395 401	10 518 778	-	Moins importations de biens et services
GDP at purchasers' values	18 709 786	20 940 911	24 665 244	25 236 056	55 469 350	63 713 359	72 599 630	81 009 965	90 136 985	PIB aux prix d'acquisition
GROSS DOMESTIC PRODUCT BY KIND OF ECONOMIC ACTIVITY AT CONSTANT PRICES *ANNUAL GROWTH RATES (%)*										**PRODUIT INTÉRIEUR BRUT PAR BRANCHE D'ACTIVITÉ ECONOMIQUE AUX PRIX CONSTANTS** *TAUX DE CROISSANCE ANNUEL (%)*
Agriculture, hunting, forestry and fishing	7.4	7.2	6.3	5.9	5.8	2.9	6.7	2.9	4.3	Agriculture, chasse sylviculture et pêche
Mining and quarrying	- 4.3	- 4.3	- 5.9	0.7	5.4	2.4	- 4.8	- 12.8	- 1.1	Industries extractives
Manufacturing	9.4	9.6	8.9	7.9	7.6	17.8	13.5	21.8	14.7	Industries manufacturières
Electricity, gas & water	4.9	4.9	3.7	3.2	3.3	32.5	13.0	18.8	- 3.3	Electricité, gaz et eau
Construction & public works	13.0	13.0	13.1	12.0	11.9	15.7	9.4	14.2	13.0	Bâtiments et travaux publics
Wholesale & retail trade, restaurants, hotels	15.2	15.1	14.0	11.5	11.2	7.3	2.6	8.7	6.5	Commerce de gros et de détail,restaurants et hôtels
Finance, insurance, real estate, etc.	6.7	6.9	6.8	6.1	22.6	- 2.3	9.0	9.0	5.8	Banques, assurances, affaires immobilières
Transport and communications	16.4	17.9	19.5	21.0	6.8	2.5	2.4	7.8	6.7	Transport(s) et communications
Public administration and defense	4.5	4.5	4.4	4.4	4.2	15.5	- 20.3	- 0.5	2.5	Administrations publiques et défense
Education	10.8	10.8	10.8	10.0	9.8	31.6	1.7	15.6	8.9	Education
Health and Social Work	10.3	10.4	10.3	10.0	10.0	13.0	4.3	9.6	10.5	Santé et actions sociales
Other services	10.4	10.4	10.5	9.8	9.6	8.6	48.2	11.0	17.5	Autres services
Less Imputed Service Charges	...	...	...	...	...	...	...	...	...	Moins services d'intérmediation financière
Gross domestic product at factor cost / basic prices	6.0	6.4	6.0	7.0	8.0	5.3	4.2	5.5	6.2	Produit intérieur brut aux couts des facteurs / prix de base
Plus: indirect taxes / taxes on products, less subsidies	6.0	6.4	19.9	5.9	2.0	- 21.9	10.6	- 2.2	13.9	Plus taxes indirectes/impôts sur les produits, moins les subventions
Gross domestic product at market prices	6.0	6.4	6.3	6.9	7.8	4.9	4.3	5.4	6.3	Produit intérieur brut aux prix du marché
EXPENDITURE ON GROSS DOMESTIC PRODUCT AT CONSTANT PURCHASERS' VALUES *ANNUAL GROWTH RATES (%)*										**EMPLOIS DU PRODUIT INTÉRIEUR BRUT AUX PRIX CONSTANTS D'ACQUISITION** *TAUX DE CROISSANCE ANNUEL (%)*
Government final consumption	35.8	21.4	60.2	0.7	11.9	4.6	- 2.0	1.4	...	Consommation finale des administrations publiques
Private final consumption	- 18.2	60.2	- 24.4	31.7	- 9.0	2.6	0.3	29.1	...	Consommation finale privée
Gross fixed capital formation	27.8	- 51.3	55.3	34.8	18.3	- 29.8	1.9	10.5	...	Formation brute de capital fixe
Exports of goods and services	70.4	- 15.5	17.9	- 30.7	53.5	25.8	- 3.6	- 45.8	...	Exportations de biens et services
Less imports of goods and services	36.0	39.9	- 4.1	11.7	12.7	- 7.8	- 32.9	12.1	...	Moins importations de biens et services
Notes	National Account: The accounts are calculated using the new base year 2010					Comptes Nationaux : Les comptes sont calculés selon la nouvelle année de base 2010				Notes

III INFLATION

	2006	2007	2008	2009	2010	2011	2012	2013	2014	
ANNUAL GROWTH RATES (%)										**TAUX DE CROISSANCE ANNUEL (%)**
All items	8.2	5.4	11.6	12.5	13.7	10.8	12.2	8.5	8.1	Ensemble
of which:										dont:
Food and Non-alcoholic beverages	3.9	8.2	15.9	14.7	14.9	10.2	11.0	9.6	9.5	Alimentation et boissons non alcoolisés
Alcoholic beverages & tobacco	...	...	3.3	1.3	8.2	6.8	7.1	6.3	6.7	Boissons alcoolisées et tabacs
Clothing and Footwear	...	...	8.2	6.7	10.6	8.9	12.7	8.5	7.4	Habillement et chaussures
Housing, Water, Electricity, Gas and Other Fuels	18.3	8.4	6.1	8.3	10.0	15.5	17.7	9.6	5.8	Logement, eau, électricité, gas et autres combustibles
Furnishing, household equip	...	...	9.8	11.4	15.2	8.3	10.9	7.3	7.2	Meubles, articles de ménage et entretien courant
Health	9.9	-6.5	7.4	10.8	8.3	9.3	9.7	6.9	6.8	Santé
Transport	23.6	7.2	-0.5	7.1	13.9	10.6	13.5	7.3	6.8	Transport
Communication	...	...	0.2	5.8	2.6	4.4	7.9	3.9	4.3	Communication
Recreation & culture	...	...	4.4	6.3	8.9	5.1	7.8	6.3	7.5	Loisirs et culture
Education	...	...	11.8	18.3	13.2	5.2	10.9	7.0	6.4	Enseignement
Restaurants & hotels	...	...	27.1	10.7	7.2	6.5	7.6	5.6	7.1	Restaurants et hôtels
Miscellaneous goods & services	...	...	5.0	12.7	11.5	8.9	11.8	6.6	6.9	Biens et services divers

	2006	2007	2008	2009	2010	2011	2012	2013	2014	
IV AGRICULTURAL PRODUCTION - PRODUCTION AGRICOLE										
TONNES *(THOUSAND)*										**TONNES** *(MILLIERS)*
Cassava	45 721	43 410	44 582	36 822	42 533	46 190	50 950	53 000	...	Manioc
Yams	36 720	31 136	35 017	29 092	37 328	33 134	32 319	40 500	...	Ignames
Sorghun	9 866	9 058	9 318	5 279	7 141	5 690	5 837	6 700	...	Sorgho
Maize	7 100	6 724	7 525	7 358	7 677	8 878	8 695	10 400	...	Maïs
Millet	7 705	8 090	9 064	4 930	5 170	1 271	1 281	5 000	...	Millet
V MINING PRODUCTION - PRODUCTION MINIERE										
	2006	2007	2008	2009	2010	2011	2012	2013	2014	
Crude Petroleun (million Barrels)	1 183	1 093	1 047	1 062	1 219	1 180	1 160	1 080	...	Pétrole brut (millions de barils)
Limestone (Thousand Tons)	15 281	3 323	3 473	3 243	5 125	...	...	...	...	Calcaire (milliers de tonnes)
Natural Gas (million standard Cubic Feet)	2 252	2 416	2 282	1 837	...	...	...	...	...	Gaz naturel (millions de pieds cubes)
VI ENERGY - ENERGIE										
	2006	2007	2008	2009	2010	2011	2012	2013	2014	
Total electricity generation (GWh)	23 110	22 978	21 110	19 777	26 057	27 034	25 391	25 200	...	Production d'électricité totale (GWh)
of which:										dont:
Production of electricity from fossil fuels (GWh)	15 396	16 751	15 389	15 248	19 747	21 384	20 084	19 934	...	Production d'électricité à partir de combustibles fossiles (GWh)
Production of hydro electricity (GWh)	7 714	6 227	5 721	4 529	6 310	5 650	5 307	5 267	...	Production d'électricité d'origine hydraulique (GWh)
Production of electricity from solar, wind, tide, wave and other sources (GWh)	...	...	...	...	...	...	...	...	...	Production d'électricité d'origine solaire, éolienne, marée motrice et autres (GWh)
VII TOURISM AND INFRASTRUCTURE - TOURISME ET INFRASTRUCTURE										
	2006	2007	2008	2009	2010	2011	2012	2013	2014	
VII-1 TOURISM										**VII-1 TOURISME**
International tourist arrivals (thousands)	1 111	1 212	1 313	1 414	1 555	715	768	813	834	Arrivées de touristes internationaux (milliers)
Rooms in hotels and similar establishments (thousands)	40.8	42.7	43.8	...	...	...	...	...	...	Chambres d'hotels et établissements assimilés (milliers)
Overnight stays (thousands)	6 754	7 493	8 247	8 498	9 569	3 269	3 783	4 060	4 121	Nuitées (milliers)
Tourism receipts (US$ thousand)	184 200	213 300	569 000	601 800	571 200	623 300	557 000	597 487	600 421	Recettes touristiques (milliers de $ EU)
Total contribution to GDP (%)	2.6	4.2	5.4	4.6	2.9	2.8	2.7	3.5	3.4	Contribution totale au PIB (%)
Total contribution to Employment (%)	2.3	3.7	4.6	4.0	2.7	2.6	2.4	3.1	3.0	Contribution totale à l'emploi (%)
VII-2 INFRASTRUCTURE										**VII-2 INFRASTRUCTURE**
Paved roads (% of total)	69	72	...	...	...	...	...	...	...	Routes asphaltées (% du total)
Total Network (Railways-km)	3 505	3 505	3 505	3 505	3 505	3 505	...	...	...	Réseau total voies ferrées-Km
Main Telephone Lines (per 100 inhabitants)	1	1	1	1	1	0	0	0	...	Lignes téléphoniques fixes (pour 100 habitants)
Mobile Cellular Subscribers (per 100 inhabitants)	23	27	42	48	55	58	67	73	...	Abonnés aux téléphones mobiles (pour 100 habitants)
VIII EXTERNAL TRADE - COMMERCE EXTERIEUR										
	2006	2007	2008	2009	2010	2011	2012	2013	2014	
NAIRA (MILLIONS) EXPORTS, FOB										**NAIRA (MILLIONS) EXPORTATIONS, FÀB**
Exports - Total	7 555 141	8 309 758	10 161 490	8 356 386	11 490 298	14 826 063	15 003 021	19 358 569	19 589 626	Exportations - Total
Exports to AFRICA	...	...	...	...	...	...	...	...	...	Exportations vers l'AFRIQUE
Main Products										**Principaux produits**
Crude petroleum	7 006 591	7 256 604	8 751 759	7 321 426	10 120 578	14 326 519	14 526 833	...	...	Pétrole Brut
Natural Gas	...	853 896	1 161 892	745 807	973 343	...	...	...	...	Gaz naturel
Palm Nuts & Kernels	...	...	...	...	...	...	...	...	...	Noix de palme et noix
Light Vessels etc, nes	35 478	18 914	5 972	1 319	16 577	...	...	...	...	Bâtiments légers etc, nda
Sesame Seeds	3 347	15 079	17 695	28 941	95 872	...	...	...	...	Graines de sésame
Main Destinations										**Principales destinations**
United States	3 497 119	3 884 770	4 110 705	2 424 333	4 204 063	19 586 180	20 216 253	...	...	États-Unis
India	671 211	808 854	983 114	725 138	1 354 760	5 691 806	4 132 659	...	...	Inde
Brazil	462 537	623 982	720 605	640 090	847 638	2 305 000	2 422 690	...	...	Brésil
Spain	585 467	483 641	633 516	462 883	673 303	1 517 110	1 511 542	...	...	Espagne
France	334 046	279 292	476 203	352 711	461 852	1 401 961	1 509 042	...	...	France
IMPORTS, CIF										**IMPORTATIONS, CAF**
Imports - Total	2 922 248	3 911 953	5 189 803	5 102 534	7 614 656	10 229 426	5 624 870	7 015 815	7 231 422	Importations - Total (millions)
Imports from Africa	...	...	...	...	...	...	245 605	673 256	522 032	Importations en provenance de l'Afrique
Main Products										**Principaux produits**
Spelt,Wheat & Meslin	163 189	233 061	73 553	159 894	119 525	...	...	...	...	Epeautre, blé et méteil
Urea	19 655	18 857	24 169	8 799	8 845	...	...	...	...	Urée
F/cold rolled iron steel	18 787	36 445	24 350	27 755	127	...	...	...	...	F / acier laminé à froid en acier
Coffee Products	445	1 368	480	302	107	...	...	...	...	Produits du café
Paper	472	...	...	...	...	...	...	...	...	Papier
Main Origin										**Principales provenances**
China	449 532	633 231	788 804	822 234	1 100 746	1 463 293	1 362 480	...	...	Chine
United States	393 240	513 389	469 490	478 833	802 029	1 018 943	948 003	...	...	États-Unis
Netherlands	217 267	369 654	464 136	379 275	528 776	517 741	538 082	...	...	Pays-Bas
United Kingdom	277 609	301 526	289 964	266 189	280 641	328 655	327 245	...	...	Royaume-Uni
France	212 941	227 787	248 844	262 147	354 463	349 620	363 300	...	...	France

IX FINANCIAL AND MONETARY STATISTICS - FINANCES ET STATISTIQUES MONETAIRES										
	2006	2007	2008	2009	2010	2011	2012	2013	2014	
IX-1 MONETARY STATISTICS *NAIRA (MILLIONS)*										**IX-1 STATISTIQUES MONÉTAIRES** *NAIRA (MILLIONS)*
Money supply (M1)	4 027 900	5 832 490	9 208 460	10 780 630	11 525 530	11 987 100	15 480 440	15 612 170	16 162 930	Masse monétaire (M1)
Quasi-money	1 739 637	2 686 841	4 247 826	5 707 989	5 941 368	6 526 685	8 021 190	9 603 453	11 313 513	Quasi-monnaie
of which Demand Deposit	...	...	...	...	...	...	...	...	...	dont Monnaie scripturale
Net foreign assets	6 188 683	7 310 444	8 597 230	7 287 925	6 195 141	6 643 739	8 715 632	8 262 158	6 892 254	Avoirs extérieurs nets
Domestic credit	918 539	4 020 620	6 549 586	9 363 895	10 426 949	14 112 185	15 102 802	17 702 702	19 510 822	Crédit intérieur
of which claims on private sector	2 466 574	5 287 334	8 324 791	9 687 254	8 554 239	7 949 079	8 569 594	10 202 487	13 168 097	dont créances sur le secteur privé
of which claims on government sector, net	-1 812 022	-1 855 726	-3 082 386	-1 844 274	446 896	749 633	760 129	1 838 341	518 020	dont créances nettes sur le gouvernement
International reserves (millions US$)	42 335	51 372	53 039	44 800	34 956	35 249	46 442	...	...	Réserves internationales (millions $EU)
Average Exchange Rate (National Currency per US$)	128.65	125.81	118.55	148.90	150.30	154.74	157.50	157.31	165.16	Taux de change (moyen) (monnaie nationale par $ EU)
IX-2 PUBLIC FINANCE *NAIRA (MILLIONS)*										**IX-2 FINANCES PUBLIQUES** *NAIRA (MILLIONS)*
Total Revenues and Grants	6 069 800	5 715 600	7 866 600	4 844 600	7 303 700	11 116 900	10 654 700	13 190 000	13 537 726	Recettes totales et dons
Tax Revenue	6 036 500	5 173 100	7 508 700	4 502 200	6 980 100	10 661 400	10 177 900	12 071 000	12 106 836	Recettes fiscales
Non Tax Revenue	33 300	284 800	114 000	73 200	153 600	182 500	206 800	782 000	870 890	Recettes non fiscales
Grants	-	257 700	243 900	269 200	170 000	273 000	270 000	337 000	560 000	Dons
Total Expenditures and Net Lending	4 290 700	5 832 837	7 913 980	5 654 608	8 409 101	12 295 796	11 839 324	12 331 187	13 462 530	Dépenses totales et prêts nets
Current expenditure	2 952 706	4 031 037	4 874 480	2 787 908	5 370 801	9 469 296	8 583 813	9 478 971	10 314 609	Dépenses courantes
Of which Wages and Salaries	629 100	1 691 000	1 080 700	1 148 300	1 564 000	1 854 000	1 811 000	1 860 000	1 954 116	Dont rémunérations et salaires
Capital expenditure	1 090 000	1 757 900	2 979 200	2 800 000	2 942 900	2 715 500	3 144 400	2 739 994	3 067 921	Dépenses d'équipement
Net Lending	247 994	43 900	60 300	66 700	95 400	111 000	111 111	112 222	80 000	Prêts nets
Fiscal Balance	1 779 100	- 117 237	- 47 380	- 810 008	-1 105 401	-1 178 896	-1 184 624	858 813	75 196	Solde global y compris les dons
IX-3 BALANCE OF PAYMENTS *NAIRA (MILLIONS)*										IX-3 Balance des paiements *NAIRA (MILLIONS)*
Trade balance	4 495 928	4 749 881	5 438 770	3 773 346	4 546 102	5 340 962	6 393 803	6 829 086	...	Balance commerciale
Services Balance	-1 495 584	-2 126 813	-2 621 053	-2 453 708	-2 743 227	-3 259 469	-3 392 667	-3 137 628	...	Balance des services
Net Income	- 591 999	-1 478 203	-1 784 947	-2 144 671	-2 921 789	-3 505 308	-3 478 448	-4 014 681	...	Revenus nets
Compensation of employees	16 153	23 933	10 904	17 789	22 213	21 108	26 116	...	...	Rémunération des salariés
Investment Income	- 608 152	-1 502 135	-1 795 851	-2 162 460	-2 944 002	-3 526 416	-3 513 231	...	...	Revenus des investissements
Current transfers, net total	2 289 702	2 333 509	2 417 820	2 882 980	3 111 920	3 355 220	3 435 092	3 466 996	...	Transferts courants
Net official transfers	125 493	97 818	205 007	219 407	215 078	264 024	276 879	...	...	Transferts officiels nets
Workers' remittances	2 153 647	2 235 634	2 258 678	2 710 253	2 938 239	3 139 423	3 203 293	...	...	Envois de fonds des travailleurs
Other private transfers	10 562	56	- 45 865	- 46 680	- 41 397	- 48 227	- 45 046	...	...	Autres transferts privés
Current account balance	4 698 047	3 478 375	3 450 590	2 057 948	1 993 006	1 931 404	2 957 781	3 143 772	...	Solde du compte courant
Capital & financial account	-2 491 547	-1 666 525	- 992 280	1 862 598	305 561	- 831 406	-1 949 198	...	...	Comptes de capital et financier
Capital account	1 357 984	...	...	...	...	...	...	...	...	Compte de capital
Financial account	-3 849 530	-1 666 525	- 992 280	1 862 598	305 561	- 831 406	-1 949 198	...	...	Compte financier
Errors & omissions	2 206 501	1 811 849	2 458 310	-3 920 550	- 247 729	-1 099 997	-1 242 324	...	...	Erreurs et omissions
Overall balance	4 413 001	3 623 699	4 916 620	...	2 050 839	...	- 233 742	...	...	Balance générale

X DEBT AND FINANCIAL FLOWS - DETTE ET FLUX FINANCIERS										
	2006	2007	2008	2009	2010	2011	2012	2013	2014	
X-1 DEBT *US$ (MILLIONS)*										**X-1 DETTE EXTÉRIEURE** *$ E.U (MILLIONS)*
Total external debt	3 544	4 040	4 460	3 951	5 134	5 625	6 523	8 168	9 984	Dette extérieure totale
Private	509	-	-	-	-	-	-	-	-	Privée
Public	3 035	4 040	4 460	3 951	5 134	5 625	6 523	8 168	9 984	Publique
Total external debt service	17 575	1 272	596	537	482	529	482	648	653	Service de la dette extérieure
Present value of External debt	...	...	...	...	...	...	...	...	...	Valeur actuelle de la dette extérieure
Total government domestic debt (in local currency)	...	2 170	2 320	3 228	4 551.8	5 622.8	...	...	...	Dette publique intérieure
X-2 FINANCIAL FLOWS *US$ (MILLIONS)*										**X-2 FLUX FINANCIERS** *$ E.U (MILLIONS)*
Net Foreign Direct Investment Inflows	4 898	6 087	8 249	8 650	6 099	8 915	7 127	5 609	...	Investissements étranger direct (flux nets entrants)
Main origin of FDI Inflows										**Principales origines de l'IDE entrant:**
Netherlands	896	1 700	674	- 1 916	...	...	...	...	...	Pays-Bas
United States	144	- 596	1 772	5 170	81.0	157.0	2 762.0	...	...	États-Unis
France	...	1	- 2	1	0.7	...	- 0.6	...	...	France
United Kingdom	81	1 343	500	1 190	352.2	567.3	142.6	...	...	Royaume-Uni
Italy	- 1	...	234	22	97.7	464.1	- 83.0	...	...	Italie
African countries	...	...	...	...	...	...	...	...	...	Pays africains
Net total Official Development Assistance	11 428	1 956	1 290	1 657	2 062	1 769	1 916	2 529	...	Aide publique au développement (nette totale)
Main origin of Net ODA										**Principales origines de l'APD nette**
United Kingdom	3 186	286	47	189	264.6	298.9	312.7	...	...	Royaume-Uni
France	2 027	12	12	9	8.9	10.6	7.2	56.6	...	France
IDA	343	315	333	476	975.4	604.3	479.3	...	...	IDA
Germany	1 710	25	28	27	39.0	29.9	39.4	22.5	...	Allemagne
United States	787	241	364	354	445.9	409.2	419.1	551.1	...	Etats-Unis

AREA (KM²)	26 340		SUPERFICIE (KM²)
CAPITAL CITY	Kigali	Kigali	CAPITALE
CURRENCY	Rwandan Franc	Franc Rwandais	MONNAIE

I SOCIAL AND DEMOGRAPHIC INDICATORS – INDICATEURS DEMOGRAPHIQUES ET SOCIAUX

	Year / Année	Value / Valeur	
POPULATION			**POPULATION**
Population ('000)			Population ('000)
Both sexes	2014	10 997	Les deux sexes
Male	2014	5 279	Masculin
Female	2014	5 718	Féminin
Average annual growth rate	2014	2.4	Taux de croissance annuel
Active Population ('000)	2014	5 679	Population active ('000)
Population by age group ('000)			Population par groupe d'âge ('000)
0-14 years	2014	4 451	0-14 ans
15-64 years	2014	6 200	15-64 ans
65+ years	2014	346	65+ ans
Economically active population in agriculture (%)	2014	86.0	Participation de la population active agricole (%)
Crude birth rate	2014	30.8	Taux brut de natalité
Crude death rate	2014	7.1	Taux brut de mortalité
Total fertility rate	2014	3.9	Indice synthétique de fécondité
Proportion of urban population	2014	21.1	Part de la population urbaine
Life Expectancy at Birth - Total (years)	2014	64.5	Espérance de vie à la naissance - Totale (ans)
Dependency Ratio - Total (%)	2014	0.8	Taux de dépendance - Total (%)
HEALTH			**SANTÉ**
Percentage of children under-five and underweight	2011	11.7	% d'enfants de moins de cinq ans avec insuffisance pondérale
Prevalence of undernourishment	2013	33.8	Prévalence de la malnutrition
Under five mortality rate (both sexes, per 1000)	2013	52.0	Taux de mortalité de moins de 5 ans (les deux sexes, pour 1000)
Infant mortality rate (both sexes) per 1000	2013	37.1	Taux de mortalité infantile (les deux sexes) par 1000
Percentage of children provided the vaccines :			Pourcentage d'enfants vaccinés :
BCG	2013	99.0	BCG
DPT3	2013	98.0	DTC3
Polio	2012	98.0	Polio
Measles	2013	97.0	Rougeole
Percentage of mothers provided at least one antenatal care (%)	2010	98.0	Pourcentage de mères ayant au moins reçu un soin prénatal (%)
Percentage of deliveries attended by skilled health personnel	2010	69.0	% d'accouchements assistés par un personnel de santé qualifié
Number of doctors (per 10 000 population)	2013	0.6	Nombre de médecins (pour 10 000 habitants)
Number of nurses (per 10 000 population)	2013	8.3	Nombre d'infirmières (pour 10 000 habitants)
Hospital beds - Total (per 10 000 population)	2013	17.6	Nombre de lits d'hôpitaux - Total (pour 10 000)
Births registered (per 1 000)	2014	34.5	Naiss.s enregistrées (pour 1 000)
Deaths registered (per 1 000)	2014	6.9	Décès enregistrés (pour 1 000)
Public expenditure on Health (% of budget)	2009	16.8	Dépenses publiques consacrées à la santé (% du budget)
EDUCATION			**EDUCATION**
Enrolment in primary education (both sexes) (000)	2013	2 402	Scolarisation dans le primaire (les deux sexes) (000)
Female	2013	1 219	Féminin
Enrolment in secondary education (both sexes) (000)	2013	566	Scolarisation dans le secondaire (les deux sexes) (000)
Female	2013	298	Féminin
Enrolment in tertiary education (both sexes) (000)	2013	84.4	Scolarisation dans le tertiaire (les deux sexes) (000)
Female	2013	37.2	Féminin
Literacy rate (both sexes)	2010	65.9	Taux d'alphabétisation (deux sexes)
Male	2010	71.1	Masculin
Female	2010	61.5	Féminin
Pupil-teacher ratio	2013	60.0	Ratio élève-enseignant
Public expenditure on education (% of budget)	2013	19.4	Dépenses publiques consacrées à l'enseignement (% du budget)
POVERTY			**PAUVRETÉ**
GNI Per Capita (US$)	2013	630.0	RNB par habitant ($EU)
Human Poverty Index (HPI-1) Value (%)	2007	32.9	Valeur de l'Indice de pauvreté (IPH-1) (%)
Population below International Poverty Line ($2/day) (%)	2011	82.3	Population sous le seuil international de pauvreté (2$/J) (%)
Share of Income Held by Richest 10%	2011	43.2	% de revenu des 10% plus riches
Share of Income Held by Poorest 10%	2011	2.1	% de revenu des 10% plus pauvres
Gini index	2011	50.8	Indice de Gini

Charts / Graphiques

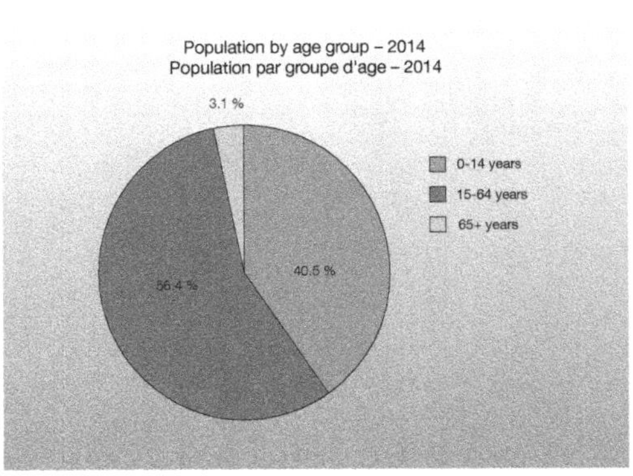

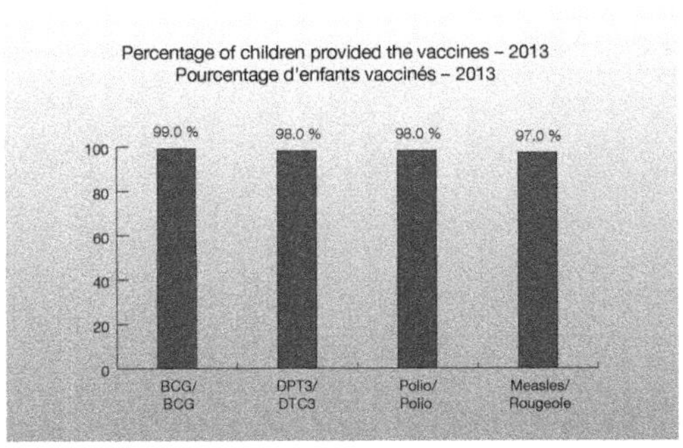

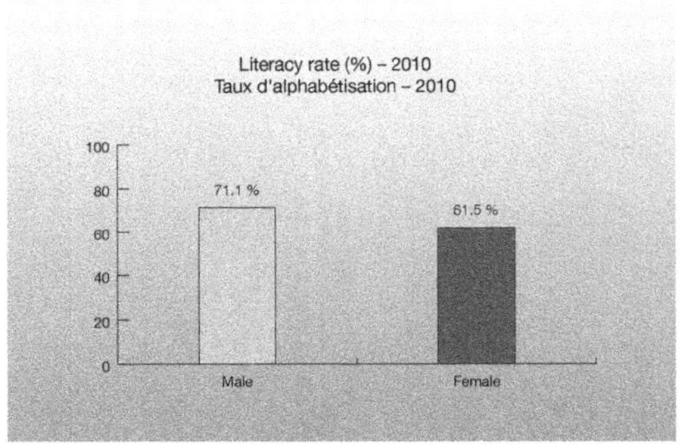

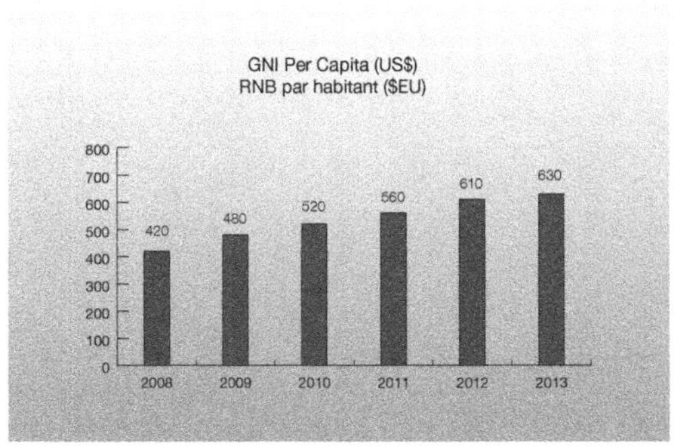

II NATIONAL ACCOUNTS — COMPTES NATIONAUX

	2006	2007	2008	2009	2010	2011	2012	2013	2014	
GROSS DOMESTIC PRODUCT BY KIND OF ECONOMIC ACTIVITY AT CURRENT PRICES *RWANDAN FRANC (MILLIONS)*										**PRODUIT INTÉRIEUR BRUT PAR BRANCHE D'ACTIVITÉ ÉCONOMIQUE AUX PRIX COURANTS** *FRANC RWANDAIS (MILLIONS)*
Agriculture, hunting, forestry and fishing	675 000	725 000	858 000	1 022 000	1 082 000	1 244 000	1 483 000	1 624 000	1 785 000	Agriculture, chasse sylviculture et pêche
Mining and quarrying	16 000	31 000	37 000	24 000	33 000	74 000	70 000	89 000	96 000	Industries extractives
Manufacturing	91 000	100 000	128 000	159 000	181 000	204 000	234 000	253 000	261 000	Industries manufacturières
Electricity, gas & water	10 000	24 000	16 000	18 000	22 000	25 000	30 000	32 000	35 000	Electricité, gaz et eau
Construction & public works	81 000	102 000	150 000	171 000	193 000	251 000	304 000	350 000	383 000	Bâtiments et travaux publics
Wholesale & retail trade, restaurants, hotels	238 000	296 000	423 000	459 000	517 000	585 000	680 000	722 000	792 000	Commerce de gros et de détail, restaurants et hôtels
Finance, insurance, real estate, etc.	224 000	324 000	431 000	510 000	547 000	593 000	646 000	687 000	752 000	Banques, assurances, affaires immobilières
Transport and communications	79 000	99 000	134 000	155 000	179 000	200 000	250 000	263 000	295 000	Transport(s) et communications
Public administration and defense	53 000	60 000	70 000	81 000	95 000	115 000	147 000	166 000	182 000	Administrations publiques et défense
Education	43 000	54 000	64 000	81 000	98 000	122 000	150 000	201 000	227 000	Education
Health and Social Work	16 000	21 000	26 000	32 000	37 000	39 000	49 000	56 000	65 000	Santé et actions sociales
Other services	89 000	104 000	117 000	119 000	130 000	137 000	156 000	182 000	224 000	Autres services
Less Imputed Service Charges	...	...	...	...	...	...	...	...	...	Moins services d'intermédiation financière
Gross domestic product at factor cost / basic prices	1 615 000	1 940 000	2 454 000	2 831 000	3 114 000	3 589 000	4 199 000	4 625 000	5 097 000	Produit intérieur brut aux couts des facteurs / prix de base
Plus: indirect taxes / taxes on products, less subsidies	101 000	124 000	169 000	188 000	209 000	258 000	237 000	239 000	293 000	Plus taxes indirectes/impôts sur les produits, moins les subventions
EXPENDITURE ON GROSS DOMESTIC PRODUCT AT CURRENT PURCHASER'S VALUES *RWANDAN FRANC (MILLIONS)*										**EMPLOI DU PRODUIT INTÉRIEUR BRUT AUX PRIX COURANTS D'ACQUISITION** *FRANC RWANDAIS (MILLIONS)*
Government final consumption	312 000	333 000	368 000	435 000	494 000	525 000	638 000	689 000	815 000	Consommation finale des administrations publiques
Private final consumption	1 341 000	1 518 000	2 018 000	2 318 000	2 585 000	3 000 000	3 438 000	3 616 000	3 997 000	Consommation finale privée
Gross fixed capital formation	275 000	377 000	616 000	693 000	748 000	879 000	1 111 000	1 242 000	1 363 000	Formation brute de capital fixe
Change in inventories	12 000	14 000	18 000	21 000	23 000	26 000	37 000	48 000	54 000	Variation des stocks
Exports of goods and services	212 000	328 000	334 000	359 000	402 000	555 000	628 000	761 000	804 000	Exportations de biens et services
Less imports of goods and services	434 000	505 000	729 000	808 000	929 000	1 138 000	1 416 000	1 491 000	1 646 000	Moins importations de biens et services
GDP at purchasers' values	1 716 000	2 065 000	2 623 000	3 017 000	3 323 000	3 846 000	4 435 000	4 864 000	5 389 000	PIB aux prix d'acquisition
GROSS DOMESTIC PRODUCT BY KIND OF ECONOMIC ACTIVITY AT CONSTANT PRICES *ANNUAL GROWTH RATES (%)*										**PRODUIT INTÉRIEUR BRUT PAR BRANCHE D'ACTIVITÉ ECONOMIQUE AUX PRIX CONSTANTS** *TAUX DE CROISSANCE ANNUEL (%)*
Agriculture, hunting, forestry and fishing	2.8	2.6	6.5	7.7	4.9	4.7	6.4	3.3	5.3	Agriculture, chasse sylviculture et pêche
Mining and quarrying	- 13.8	42.9	- 16.3	- 17.9	- 10.9	51.0	- 8.1	20.6	11.0	Industries extractives
Manufacturing	13.4	0.6	5.7	2.4	9.9	7.9	5.9	4.6	0.9	Industries manufacturières
Electricity, gas & water	- 13.3	7.7	21.4	11.8	15.8	13.6	12.0	3.6	10.3	Electricité, gaz et eau
Construction & public works	13.1	15.2	27.8	1.6	8.6	23.6	14.7	10.8	8.2	Bâtiments et travaux publics
Wholesale & retail trade, restaurants, hotels	19.0	12.0	16.4	2.2	8.8	7.3	12.5	5.2	8.4	Commerce de gros et de détail,restaurants et hôtels
Finance, insurance, real estate, etc.	22.5	7.3	19.9	12.3	10.5	8.6	4.6	3.6	5.9	Banques, assurances, affaires immobilières
Transport and communications	14.1	15.9	22.9	9.3	8.5	4.7	25.0	3.6	12.4	Transport(s) et communications
Public administration and defense	9.2	5.4	5.1	7.3	13.6	15.0	21.7	9.3	7.2	Administrations publiques et défense
Education	...	14.9	7.8	15.7	8.3	17.3	7.4	4.6	7.3	Education
Health and Social Work	...	13.6	12.0	17.9	15.2	2.6	23.1	4.2	10.0	Santé et actions sociales
Other services	9.6	13.7	2.3	- 5.1	7.0	- 0.7	10.9	11.8	19.4	Autres services
Less Imputed Service Charges	...	...	...	...	...	...	...	...	...	Moins services d'intermédiation financière
Gross domestic product at factor cost / basic prices	9.3	7.9	11.1	6.0	7.5	8.3	9.3	5.2	7.2	Produit intérieur brut aux couts des facteurs / prix de base
Plus: indirect taxes / taxes on products, less subsidies	8.7	4.2	11.6	9.5	5.0	1.6	1.6	- 3.1	2.4	Plus taxes indirectes/impôts sur les produits, moins les subventions
Gross domestic product at market prices	9.2	7.6	11.2	6.3	7.3	7.9	8.8	4.7	7.0	Produit intérieur brut aux prix du marché
EXPENDITURE ON GROSS DOMESTIC PRODUCT AT CONSTANT PURCHASERS' VALUES *ANNUAL GROWTH RATES (%)*										**EMPLOIS DU PRODUIT INTÉRIEUR BRUT AUX PRIX CONSTANTS D'ACQUISITION** *TAUX DE CROISSANCE ANNUEL (%)*
Government final consumption	9.4	1.0	2.5	11.7	10.2	3.8	14.7	1.0	14.5	Consommation finale des administrations publiques
Private final consumption	14.2	- 4.9	15.8	14.3	5.1	9.0	6.9	2.9	5.4	Consommation finale privée
Gross fixed capital formation	17.6	27.8	32.7	2.9	6.9	9.3	21.8	7.2	9.4	Formation brute de capital fixe
Exports of goods and services	3.0	- 1.5	16.8	- 22.8	13.5	40.5	17.7	13.3	4.2	Exportations de biens et services
Less imports of goods and services	29.8	- 25.9	49.1	12.9	4.3	24.4	21.4	5.6	7.2	Moins importations de biens et services
Notes	The Accounts are calculated using the new base year 2011					Les comptes sont calculés selon la nouvelle année de base 2011				Notes

III INFLATION

	2006	2007	2008	2009	2010	2011	2012	2013	2014	
ANNUAL GROWTH RATES (%)										**TAUX DE CROISSANCE ANNUEL (%)**
All items	8.9	9.1	15.4	10.3	2.3	5.6	6.3	4.2	1.8	Ensemble
of which:										dont:
Food and Non-alcoholic beverages	9.9	7.8	16.3	16.3	1.7	6.5	12.4	5.1	1.2	Alimentation et boissons non alcoolisés
Alcoholic beverages & tobacco	3.5	10.4	20.0	18.0	7.3	2.1	4.1	5.1	7.2	Boissons alcoolisées et tabacs
Clothing and Footwear	-0.6	0.8	4.2	3.0	1.4	6.8	3.7	1.2	5.5	Habillement et chaussures
Housing, Water, Electricity, Gas and Other Fuels	17.7	17.3	18.2	6.7	1.0	3.7	4.8	0.9	0.9	Logement, eau, électricité, gas et autres combustibles
Furnishing, household equip	1.7	1.6	18.2	7.4	-1.9	2.1	4.4	2.7	1.0	Meubles, articles de ménage et entretien courant
Health	1.1	13.7	9.2	3.2	1.1	0.6	1.3	0.5	10.3	Santé
Transport	5.6	6.2	20.2	3.2	8.0	9.0	1.8	1.3	-0.8	Transport
Communication	6.7	16.6	-9.9	-3.7	-	-1.6	-5.3	-1.0	-1.1	Communication
Recreation & culture	2.7	-3.5	0.1	4.3	0.9	4.2	-1.0	1.6	0.9	Loisirs et culture
Education	21.2	10.8	13.6	16.6	6.6	20.3	1.9	35.2	7.1	Enseignement
Restaurants & hotels	3.3	20.5	13.0	8.8	2.4	0.8	1.8	4.1	7.5	Restaurants et hôtels
Miscellaneous goods & services	1.5	0.3	7.7	2.0	-0.9	6.0	3.4	3.4	3.5	Biens et services divers

IV AGRICULTURAL PRODUCTION - PRODUCTION AGRICOLE

	2006	2007	2008	2009	2010	2011	2012	2013	2014	
TONNES *(THOUSAND)*										**TONNES** *(MILLIERS)*
Banana	2 653	2 698	2 604	1 857	2 749	3 036	3 219	3 292	...	Banane-Plantain
Cassava	1 285	777	1 682	1 137	2 377	2 579	2 716	2 948	...	Pommes de terre
Irish potatoes	777	967	1 162	893	1 789	2 172	2 172	2 241	...	Patates douces
Sweet potatoes	765	845	826	540	840	845	1 005	1 081	...	Manioc
Maize	215	102	167	262	432	526	573	668	...	Citrouilles, courges et calebasses

V MINING PRODUCTION - PRODUCTION MINIERE

	2006	2007	2008	2009	2010	2011	2012	2013	2014	
Cassiterite	...	...	...	...	...	695	4 637	4 895	...	Cassiterite
Coltan	...	...	...	...	...	890	1 145	2 466	...	Coltan
Wolfram	...	...	...	...	...	1 006	1 751	2 218	...	Wolfram

VI ENERGY - ENERGIE

	2006	2007	2008	2009	2010	2011	2012	2013	2014	
Total electricity generation (GWh)	160	158	183	238	280	340	348	769	...	Production d'électricité totale (GWh)
of which:										dont:
Production of electricity from fossil fuels (GWh)	122	116	115	140	170	190	196	256	...	Production d'électricité à partir de combustibles fossiles (GWh)
Production of hydro electricity (GWh)	38	42	68	98	110	149	150	214	...	Production d'électricité d'origine hydraulique (GWh)
Production of electricity from solar, wind, tide, wave and other sources (GWh)	...	...	...	...	...	131	263	298	...	Production d'électricité d'origine solaire, éolienne, marée motrice et autres (GWh)

VII TOURISM AND INFRASTRUCTURE - TOURISME ET INFRASTRUCTURE

	2006	2007	2008	2009	2010	2011	2012	2013	2014	
VII-1 TOURISM										**VII-1 TOURISME**
International tourist arrivals (thousands)	494	566	507	502	504	688	815	851	944	Arrivées de touristes internationaux (milliers)
Rooms in hotels and similar establishments (thousands)	...	...	...	4.0	4.7	6.5	6.8	8.0	...	Chambres d'hotels et établissements assimilés (milliers)
Overnight stays (thousands)	3 003	3 499	3 184	3 017	3 102	4 174	5 021	4 637	5 366	Nuitées (milliers)
Tourism receipts (US$ thousand)	131 800	151 600	185 900	174 200	201 000	251 100	281 100	292 900	316 145	Recettes touristiques (milliers de $ EU)
Total contribution to GDP (%)	8.8	10.5	10.6	9.1	8.5	8.8	9.1	9.0	9.4	Contribution totale au PIB (%)
Total contribution to Employment (%)	7.7	9.3	9.3	8.1	7.3	7.6	7.8	7.8	8.1	Contribution totale à l'emploi (%)
VII-2 INFRASTRUCTURE										**VII-2 INFRASTRUCTURE**
Paved roads (% of total)	...	...	...	...	25	25	26	...	...	Routes asphaltées (% du total)
Total Network (Railways-km)	...	...	...	...	...	...	...	...	...	Réseau total voies ferrées-Km
Main Telephone Lines (per 100 inhabitants)	0	0	0	0	0	0	0	0	...	Lignes téléphoniques fixes (pour 100 habitants)
Mobile Cellular Subscribers (per 100 inhabitants)	3	6	13	23	33	40	50	57	...	Abonnés aux téléphones mobiles (pour 100 habitants)

VIII EXTERNAL TRADE - COMMERCE EXTERIEUR

	2006	2007	2008	2009	2010	2011	2012	2013	2014	
US$ (MILLIONS) **EXPORTS, FOB**										**$ E.U (MILLIONS)** **EXPORTATIONS, FÀB**
Exports - Total	147	177	268	235	234	418	509	480	...	Exportations - Total
Exports to AFRICA	...	...	...	...	95	150	474	319	...	Exportations vers l'AFRIQUE
Main Products										**Principaux produits**
Ores and concentrates of base metals, n.e.s.	40	76	79	49	72	148	53	135	...	Minerais de métaux communs et concentrés, n.d.a.
Coffee and coffee substitutes	58	48	30	29	46	65	...	49	...	Café et succédanés du café
Tea and mate	14	18	4	63	85	100	81	62	...	Thé et maté
Petroleum oils, oils from bitumin. materials, crude	...	...	...	...	...	...	...	...	...	Huiles brutes de pétrole ou minéraux bitumineux
Petroleum oils or bituminous minerals > 70 % oil	...	...	...	...	...	...	...	...	...	Huiles de pétrole ou minéraux bitumineux > 70%
Main Destinations										**Principales destinations**
Kenya	30	34	32	83	39	64	96	73	...	Kenya
Belgium	23	26	65	29	27	47	4	36	...	Belgique
United Kingdom	29	34	13	5	11	17	11	6	...	Royaume Uni
Switzerland	13	13	7	12	54	76	8	113	...	Suisse
Bouvet Island	...	...	...	...	...	...	...	...	...	Ile Bouvet
IMPORTS, CIF										**IMPORTATIONS, CAF**
Imports - Total	591	679	1 174	1 308	1 254	1 360	1 646	2 487	...	Importations - Total (millions)
Imports from Africa	...	...	...	...	440	579	548	480	...	Importations en provenance de l'Afrique
Main Products										**Principaux produits**
Petroleum oils and oils obtained from bituminous minerals, other than crude; preparation	36	44	94	77	91	118	108	299	...	Fer et acier
Portland cement, aluminous cement, slag cement, supersulphate cement and similar hydraulic	31	32	74	129	75	64	67	68	...	Équipements pour les télécommunications et le son
Electrical apparatus for line telephony or line telegraphy, including line telephone set	16	26	75	77	89	99	47	60	...	Articles minéraux non métalliques manufacturés, n.d.a.
Road vehicles	41	53	65	63	77	91	50	51	...	Véhicules routiers
Cereals and cereal preparation	25	33	89	56	65	93	51	49	...	Céréales et préparations à base de céréales
Main Origin										**Principales provenances**
Kenya	66	86	130	123	122	118	135	119	...	Kenya
Uganda	31	83	137	135	151	159	225	200	...	Ouganda
United Arab Emirates	116	99	134	91	61	55	120	115	...	Émirats arabes unis
Belgium	28	43	55	49	43	46	53	64	...	Belgique
Germany	45	43	45	46	39	44	50	51	...	Allemagne

IX FINANCIAL AND MONETARY STATISTICS - FINANCES ET STATISTIQUES MONETAIRES	2006	2007	2008	2009	2010	2011	2012	2013	2014	
IX-1 MONETARY STATISTICS *RWANDAN FRANC (MILLIONS)*										**IX-1 STATISTIQUES MONÉTAIRES** *FRANC RWANDAIS (MILLIONS)*
Money supply (M1)	287 460	375 900	466 390	527 100	615 940	780 380	889 920	1 028 190	1 161 090	Masse monétaire (M1)
Quasi-money	...	...	...	...	...	...	...	...	...	Quasi-monnaie
of which Demand Deposit	...	...	...	...	...	...	...	...	...	dont Monnaie scripturale
Net foreign assets	...	...	...	...	...	...	...	...	...	Avoirs extérieurs nets
Domestic credit	...	...	...	...	...	...	...	...	...	Crédit intérieur
of which claims on private sector	...	...	...	...	...	...	...	...	...	dont créances sur le secteur privé
of which claims on government sector, net	...	...	...	...	...	...	...	...	...	dont créances nettes sur le gouvernement
International reserves (millions US$)	440	553	596	743	813	1 050	848	1 070	934	Réserves internationales (millions $EU)
Average Exchange Rate (National Currency per US$)	551.71	546.96	546.85	568.28	583.13	600.31	614.30	646.64	679.03	Taux de change (moyen) (monnaie nationale par $ EU)
IX-2 PUBLIC FINANCE *RWANDAN FRANC (MILLIONS)*										**IX-2 FINANCES PUBLIQUES** *FRANC RWANDAIS (MILLIONS)*
Total Revenues and Grants	409 150	533 350	659 359	747 959	814 250	913 000	1 082 700	1 043 400	1 258 400	Recettes totales et dons
Tax Revenue	199 950	249 950	311 336	353 836	402 300	458 750	545 550	645 800	707 000	Recettes fiscales
Non Tax Revenue	14 450	33 300	34 422	15 772	17 800	33 000	34 950	52 100	92 200	Recettes non fiscales
Grants	194 750	250 100	313 600	378 350	394 150	421 250	502 200	345 500	459 200	Dons
Total Expenditures and Net Lending	437 650	570 650	700 350	777 600	876 250	1 026 950	1 218 300	1 174 600	1 454 400	Dépenses totales et prêts nets
Current expenditure	284 400	340 900	396 400	441 850	475 150	543 650	638 100	641 500	672 100	Dépenses courantes
Of which Wages and Salaries	68 000	79 000	90 800	102 150	114 450	126 600	158 900	158 700	179 100	Dont rémunérations et salaires
Capital expenditure	152 500	227 050	279 850	304 300	377 650	473 600	574 950	513 900	649 500	Dépenses d'équipement
Net Lending	750	2 700	24 100	31 450	23 450	9 700	5 250	19 200	132 800	Prêts nets
Fiscal Balance	- 28 500	- 37 300	- 40 992	- 29 642	- 62 000	- 113 950	- 135 600	- 131 200	- 196 000	Solde global y compris les dons
IX-3 BALANCE OF PAYMENTS *RWANDAN FRANC (MILLIONS)*										**IX-3 BALANCE DES PAIEMENTS** *FRANC RWANDAIS (MILLIONS)*
Trade balance	- 299	- 404	- 625	- 764	- 787	- 1 101	- 1 268	- 1 148	...	Balance commerciale
Services Balance	- 132	- 123	- 101	- 182	- 246	- 187	- 93	- 122	...	Balance des services
Net Income	- 29	- 17	- 35	- 37	- 43	- 52	- 74	- 114	...	Revenus nets
Compensation of employees	...	...	...	...	...	...	...	...	...	Rémunération des salariés
Investment Income	...	...	...	...	...	...	...	...	...	Revenus des investissements
Current transfers, net total	326	461	519	604	657	881	722	848	...	Transferts courants
Net official transfers	...	...	...	...	...	...	...	...	...	Transferts officiels nets
Workers' remittances	...	...	...	...	...	...	...	...	...	Envois de fonds des travailleurs
Other private transfers	...	...	...	...	...	...	...	...	...	Autres transferts privés
Current account balance	- 2	40	- 242	- 379	- 418	- 460	- 713	- 537	...	Solde du compte courant
Capital & financial account	216	197	316	-	499	683	512	773	...	Comptes de capital et financier
Capital account	1 400	92	210	200	286	197	171	235	...	Compte de capital
Financial account	- 1 184	105	106	227	214	486	340	539	...	Compte financier
Errors & omissions	0	- 3	- 20	5	- 9	12	11	- 7	...	Erreurs et omissions
Overall balance	214	234	54	53	72	235	- 212	229	...	Balance générale

X DEBT AND FINANCIAL FLOWS - DETTE ET FLUX FINANCIERS	2006	2007	2008	2009	2010	2011	2012	2013	2014	
X-1 DEBT *US$ (MILLIONS)*										**X-1 DETTE EXTÉRIEURE** *$ E.U (MILLIONS)*
Total external debt	486	574	677	737	776	1 007	1 027	1 498	1 741	Dette extérieure totale
Private	-	-	-	-	-	-	-	-	-	Privée
Public	486	574	677	737	776	1 007	1 027	1 498	1 741	Publique
Total external debt service	91	10	9	10	14	34	95	208	69	Service de la dette extérieure
Present value of External debt	...	...	...	...	...	...	...	...	...	Valeur actuelle de la dette extérieure
Total government domestic debt (in local currency)	190	239	170	254	288.3	298.2	398.9	...	...	Dette publique intérieure
X-2 FINANCIAL FLOWS *US$ (MILLIONS)*										**X-2 FLUX FINANCIERS** *$ E.U (MILLIONS)*
Net Foreign Direct Investment Inflows	31	82	102	119	42	106	160	111	...	Investissements étranger direct (flux nets entrants)
Main origin of FDI Inflows										**Principales origines de l'IDE entrant:**
Germany	...	5	3	- 3	1.3	...	...	...	...	Allemagne
United States	1	1	1	...	...	...	...	...	...	États-Unis
France	...	...	...	...	...	...	...	...	...	France
Luxembourg	...	...	...	3	...	...	...	...	...	Luxembourg
Belgium	- 3	1	1	...	...	...	1.3	...	...	Belgique
African countries	...	...	...	...	...	...	...	...	...	Pays africains
Net total Official Development Assistance	603	723	934	934	1 032	1 264	879	1 081	...	Aide publique au développement (nette totale)
Main origin of Net ODA										**Principales origines de l'APD nette**
IDA	59	101	140	114	145.5	289.0	95.1	...	...	IDA
United States	78	91	117	146	140.6	179.2	159.6	153.3	...	Etats-Unis
United Kingdom	95	95	100	90	106.2	135.6	44.8	...	...	Royaume-Uni
Global Fund	52	37	82	81	142.9	125.7	146.4	...	...	Fonds mondial
Belgium	36	43	65	82	70.3	65.3	27.1	31.4	...	Belgique

SÃO TOMÉ & PRÍNCIPE

AREA (KM²)	964		**SUPERFICIE (KM²)**
CAPITAL CITY	São Tomé	São Tomé	**CAPITALE**
CURRENCY	Dobra	Dobra	**MONNAIE**

I SOCIAL AND DEMOGRAPHIC INDICATORS — INDICATEURS DEMOGRAPHIQUES ET SOCIAUX

	Year / Année	Value / Valeur	
POPULATION			**POPULATION**
Population ('000)			Population ('000)
Both sexes	2014	198	Les deux sexes
Male	2014	98	Masculin
Female	2014	100	Féminin
Average annual growth rate	2014	2.6	Taux de croissance annuel
Active Population ('000)	2014	65	Population active ('000)
Population by age group ('000)			Population par groupe d'âge ('000)
0-14 years	2014	82	0-14 ans
15-64 years	2014	109	15-64 ans
65+ years	2014	7	65+ ans
Economically active population in agriculture (%)	2014	53.5	Participation de la population active agricole (%)
Crude birth rate	2014	33.1	Taux brut de natalité
Crude death rate	2014	6.7	Taux brut de mortalité
Total fertility rate	2014	4.0	Indice synthétique de fécondité
Proportion of urban population	2014	64.7	Part de la population urbaine
Life Expectancy at Birth - Total (years)	2014	66.5	Espérance de vie à la naissance - Totale (ans)
Dependency Ratio - Total (%)	2014	72.7	Taux de dépendance - Total (%)
HEALTH			**SANTÉ**
Percentage of children under-five and underweight	2009	14.4	% d'enfants de moins de cinq ans avec insuffisance pondérale
Prevalence of undernourishment	2013	6.8	Prévalence de la malnutrition
Under five mortality rate (both sexes, per 1000)	2013	51.0	Taux de mortalité de moins de 5 ans (les deux sexes, pour 1000)
Infant mortality rate (both sexes) per 1000	2013	36.7	Taux de mortalité infantile (les deux sexes) par 1000
Percentage of children provided the vaccines :			Pourcentage d'enfants vaccinés :
BCG	2013	97.0	BCG
DPT3	2013	97.0	DTC3
Polio	2011	96.0	Polio
Measles	2013	91.0	Rougeole
Percentage of mothers provided at least one antenatal care (%)	2009	97.5	Pourcentage de mères ayant au moins reçu un soin prénatal (%)
Percentage of deliveries attended by skilled health personnel	2009	81.7	% d'accouchements assistés par un personnel de santé qualifié
Number of doctors (per 10 000 population)	2004	4.9	Nombre de médecins (pour 10 000 habitants)
Number of nurses (per 10 000 population)	2004	18.7	Nombre d'infirmières (pour 10 000 habitants)
Hospital beds - Total (per 10 000 population)	2011	29.0	Nombre de lits d'hôpitaux - Total (pour 10 000)
Births registered (per 1 000)	2014	33.1	Naiss.s enregistrées (pour 1 000)
Deaths registered (per 1 000)	2014	6.7	Décès enregistrés (pour 1 000)
Public expenditure on Health (% of budget)	2009	13.2	Dépenses publiques consacrées à la santé (% du budget)
EDUCATION			**EDUCATION**
Enrolment in primary education (both sexes) (000)	2013	35	Scolarisation dans le primaire (les deux sexes) (000)
Female	2013	17	Féminin
Enrolment in secondary education (both sexes) (000)	2013	16	Scolarisation dans le secondaire (les deux sexes) (000)
Female	2013	8	Féminin
Enrolment in tertiary education (both sexes) (000)	...	...	Scolarisation dans le tertiaire (les deux sexes) (000)
Female	2012	0.7	Féminin
Literacy rate (both sexes)	2008	69.5	Taux d'alphabétisation (deux sexes)
Male	2008	80.3	Masculin
Female	2008	60.1	Féminin
Pupil-teacher ratio	...	...	Ratio élève-enseignant
Public expenditure on education (% of budget)	2010	19.3	Dépenses publiques consacrées à l'enseignement (% du budget)
POVERTY			**PAUVRETÉ**
GNI Per Capita (US$)	2013	1 470.0	RNB par habitant ($EU)
Human Poverty Index (HPI-1) Value (%)	2007	12.6	Valeur de l'Indice de pauvreté (IPH-1) (%)
Population below International Poverty Line ($2/day) (%)	2010	73.8	Population sous le seuil international de pauvreté (2$/J) (%)
Share of Income Held by Richest 10%	2010	26.0	% de revenu des 10% plus riches
Share of Income Held by Poorest 10%	2010	3.2	% de revenu des 10% plus pauvres
Gini index	2010	33.9	Indice de Gini

Charts / Graphiques

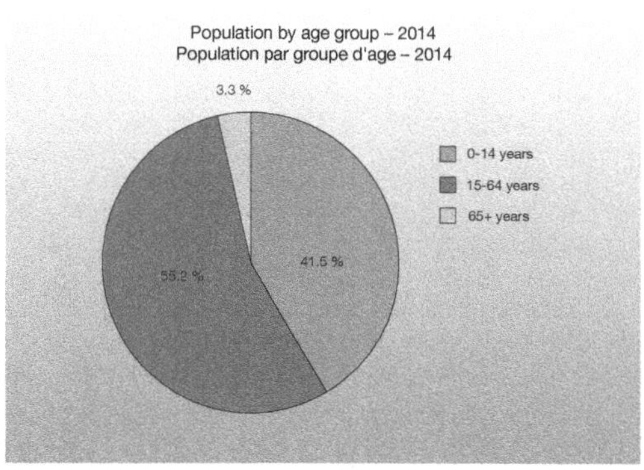

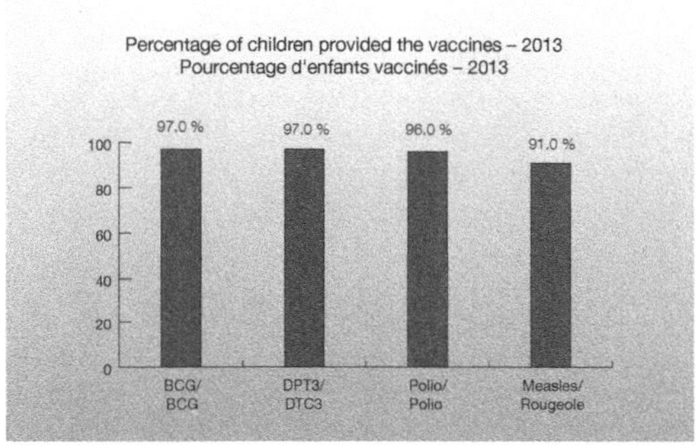

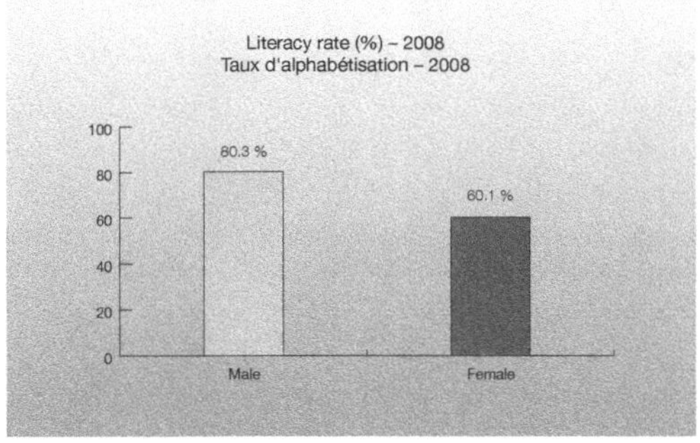

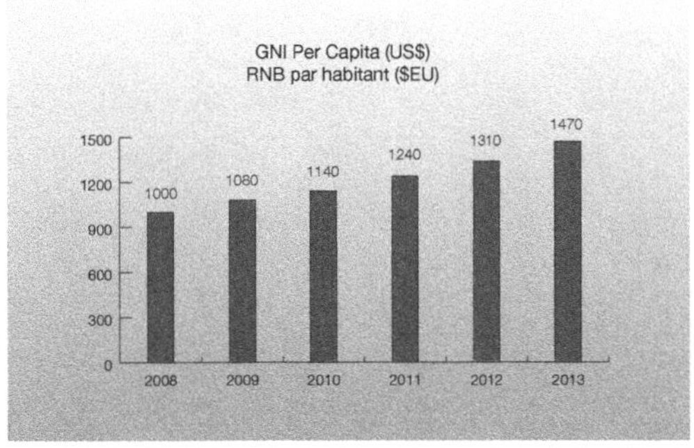

II NATIONAL ACCOUNTS — COMPTES NATIONAUX										
	2006	2007	2008	2009	2010	2011	2012	2013	2014	
GROSS DOMESTIC PRODUCT BY KIND OF ECONOMIC ACTIVITY AT CURRENT PRICES *DOBRA (MILLIONS)*										**PRODUIT INTÉRIEUR BRUT PAR BRANCHE D'ACTIVITÉ ÉCONOMIQUE AUX PRIX COURANTS** *DOBRA (MILLIONS)*
Agriculture, hunting, forestry and fishing	304 791	371 998	511 201	716 786	835 421	1 040 185	1 166 254	1 302 769	1 452 681	Agriculture, chasse sylviculture et pêche
Mining and quarrying	8 189	10 718	16 478	18 451	19 791	21 582	20 953	23 405	26 098	Industries extractives
Manufacturing	115 262	133 458	240 659	261 356	314 143	376 591	457 935	511 536	570 401	Industries manufacturières
Electricity, gas & water	42 136	50 441	83 629	93 742	102 214	134 474	177 508	198 285	221 102	Electricité, gaz et eau
Construction & public works	123 046	160 503	245 614	272 494	285 265	313 200	297 197	331 986	370 187	Bâtiments et travaux publics
Wholesale & retail trade, restaurants, hotels	444 774	527 071	813 582	929 803	1 080 545	1 289 747	1 479 917	1 653 146	1 843 376	Commerce de gros et de détail, restaurants et hôtels
Finance, insurance, real estate, etc.	176 892	218 313	303 391	546 992	576 868	623 985	656 729	733 599	818 016	Banques, assurances, affaires immobilières
Transport and communications	286 194	342 483	468 617	505 983	554 989	717 889	920 446	1 028 187	1 146 501	Transport(s) et communications
Public administration and defense	116 810	107 004	111 908	109 455	110 682	115 249	115 629	129 164	144 027	Administrations publiques et défense
Education	9 422	10 208	10 960	14 237	17 127	19 611	20 362	22 746	25 363	Education
Health and Social Work	6 580	7 271	7 895	9 005	11 100	12 365	14 170	15 829	17 651	Santé et actions sociales
Other services	67 740	85 872	119 870	149 173	179 313	227 971	290 159	324 124	361 421	Autres services
Less Imputed Service Charges	- 80 037	- 94 882	- 141 650	- 298 248	- 312 154	- 319 565	- 323 371	- 361 223	- 402 789	Moins services d'intermédiation financière
Gross domestic product at factor cost / basic prices	1 621 799	1 930 458	2 792 154	3 329 229	3 775 304	4 573 284	5 293 888	5 913 553	6 594 035	Produit intérieur brut aux couts des facteurs / prix de base
Plus: indirect taxes / taxes on products, less subsidies	97 112	112 583	154 548	188 159	234 768	256 009	277 572	310 063	345 744	Plus taxes indirectes/impôts sur les produits, moins les subventions
EXPENDITURE ON GROSS DOMESTIC PRODUCT AT CURRENT PURCHASER'S VALUES *DOBRA (MILLIONS)*										**EMPLOI DU PRODUIT INTÉRIEUR BRUT AUX PRIX COURANTS D'ACQUISITION** *DOBRA (MILLIONS)*
Government final consumption	179 470	297 427	490 732	511 643	558 908	2 568 345	1 247 471	1 504 484	1 540 700	Consommation finale des administrations publiques
Private final consumption	1 956 929	2 182 569	3 286 690	2 959 067	3 408 070	4 147 546	4 598 521	5 490 847	5 738 143	Consommation finale privée
Gross fixed capital formation	386 921	547 994	716 139	1 473 348	1 864 833	258 609	2 041 214	1 656 863	2 521 019	Formation brute de capital fixe
Change in inventories	- 84 135	- 97 480	- 133 915	- 74 559	- 27 861	- 47 363	- 132 943	- 143 930	- 164 192	Variation des stocks
Exports of goods and services	277 103	274 390	285 821	344 592	486 639	554 110	591 520	680 225	730 561	Exportations de biens et services
Less imports of goods and services	997 372	1 161 860	1 698 765	1 696 701	2 280 520	2 651 953	2 774 323	2 964 873	3 426 451	Moins importations de biens et services
GDP at purchasers' values	1 718 916	2 043 040	2 946 702	3 517 390	4 010 069	4 829 294	5 571 460	6 223 616	6 939 780	PIB aux prix d'acquisition
GROSS DOMESTIC PRODUCT BY KIND OF ECONOMIC ACTIVITY AT CONSTANT PRICES *ANNUAL GROWTH RATES (%)*										**PRODUIT INTÉRIEUR BRUT PAR BRANCHE D'ACTIVITÉ ECONOMIQUE AUX PRIX CONSTANTS** *TAUX DE CROISSANCE ANNUEL (%)*
Agriculture, hunting, forestry and fishing	5.9	2.8	8.6	3.9	- 1.3	1.0	0.3	4.3	4.8	Agriculture, chasse sylviculture et pêche
Mining and quarrying	6.7	2.8	3.9	4.6	5.0	0.8	- 3.9	4.3	4.8	Industries extractives
Manufacturing	5.0	3.2	7.7	2.7	0.5	7.8	7.2	4.3	4.8	Industries manufacturières
Electricity, gas & water	9.6	3.8	5.9	8.0	9.6	12.7	12.7	4.3	4.8	Electricité, gaz et eau
Construction & public works	7.0	5.1	4.2	5.3	6.7	0.6	- 4.7	4.3	4.8	Bâtiments et travaux publics
Wholesale & retail trade, restaurants, hotels	13.7	1.6	12.5	1.1	1.1	0.7	0.2	4.3	4.8	Commerce de gros et de détail,restaurants et hôtels
Finance, insurance, real estate, etc.	9.3	1.0	7.1	- 1.1	0.1	3.9	3.0	4.3	4.8	Banques, assurances, affaires immobilières
Transport and communications	16.5	3.1	14.9	1.5	2.0	4.9	4.6	4.3	4.8	Transport(s) et communications
Public administration and defense	2.1	1.6	1.0	1.1	1.1	2.0	1.0	4.3	4.8	Administrations publiques et défense
Education	4.0	0.5	5.0	2.2	4.6	5.5	2.8	4.3	4.8	Education
Health and Social Work	2.0	5.6	1.5	0.7	- 3.4	1.9	- 0.7	4.3	4.8	Santé et actions sociales
Other services	4.5	7.0	5.8	6.4	6.1	6.2	5.1	4.3	4.8	Autres services
Less Imputed Service Charges	17.2	23.1	34.1	28.9	10.2	- 3.1	- 4.5	4.3	4.8	Moins services d'intérmediation financière
Gross domestic product at factor cost / basic prices	9.3	1.0	7.1	- 1.1	0.1	3.9	3.0	4.3	4.8	Produit intérieur brut aux couts des facteurs / prix de base
Plus: indirect taxes / taxes on products, less subsidies	52.1	19.4	24.7	38.3	26.1	8.7	10.0	4.3	4.8	Plus taxes indirectes/impôts sur les produits, moins les subventions
Gross domestic product at market prices	12.3	2.7	9.1	3.9	4.6	4.9	4.5	4.3	4.8	Produit intérieur brut aux prix du marché
EXPENDITURE ON GROSS DOMESTIC PRODUCT AT CONSTANT PURCHASERS' VALUES *ANNUAL GROWTH RATES (%)*										**EMPLOIS DU PRODUIT INTÉRIEUR BRUT AUX PRIX CONSTANTS D'ACQUISITION** *TAUX DE CROISSANCE ANNUEL (%)*
Government final consumption	12.3	2.7	9.1	3.9	4.6	4.9	5.5	4.3	4.8	Consommation finale des administrations publiques
Private final consumption	12.3	2.7	9.1	3.9	4.6	4.9	4.6	4.3	4.8	Consommation finale privée
Gross fixed capital formation	12.3	2.7	9.1	3.9	4.6	4.9	5.5	4.3	4.8	Formation brute de capital fixe
Exports of goods and services	12.3	2.7	9.1	3.9	4.6	4.9	5.5	4.3	4.8	Exportations de biens et services
Less imports of goods and services	12.3	2.7	9.1	3.9	4.6	4.9	5.5	4.3	4.8	Moins importations de biens et services
Notes	NA data: 2011-2012:Provisional; 2013- 2014:Estimates					Données des CN: 2011-2012:Provisoires; 2013-2014:Estimations				Notes

III INFLATION										
	2006	2007	2008	2009	2010	2011	2012	2013	2014	
ANNUAL GROWTH RATES (%)										**TAUX DE CROISSANCE ANNUEL (%)**
All items	23.1	18.6	32.0	17.0	13.3	14.3	10.6	8.1	6.3	Ensemble
of which:										dont:
Food and Non-alcoholic beverages	26.9	38.3	28.9	20.6	14.9	11.8	12.3	...	...	Alimentation et boissons non alcoolisés
Alcoholic beverages & tobacco	...	...	...	...	...	...	...	...	...	Boissons alcoolisées et tabacs
Clothing and Footwear	...	...	...	...	...	...	...	...	...	Habillement et chaussures
Housing, Water, Electricity, Gas and Other Fuels	6.5	10.2	47.4	-6.2	5.5	8.6	1.4	...	...	Logement, eau, électricité, gas et autres combustibles
Furnishing, household equip	...	...	...	...	...	...	...	...	...	Meubles, articles de ménage et entretien courant
Health	4.4	3.5	17.6	9.5	6.1	-8.8	1.6	...	...	Santé
Transport	20.9	13.8	-6.8	2.1	1.1	25.1	0.8	...	...	Transport
Communication	...	...	...	...	...	...	...	...	...	Communication
Recreation & culture	...	...	...	...	...	...	...	...	...	Loisirs et culture
Education	...	...	...	...	...	...	...	...	...	Enseignement
Restaurants & hotels	...	...	...	...	...	...	...	...	...	Restaurants et hôtels
Miscellaneous goods & services	...	...	...	...	...	...	...	...	...	Biens et services divers

IV AGRICULTURAL PRODUCTION - PRODUCTION AGRICOLE										
	2006	2007	2008	2009	2010	2011	2012	2013	2014	
TONNES *(THOUSAND)*										**TONNES** *(MILLIERS)*
Maize	3	3	3	3	4	4	4	4	...	Maïs
Cassava	2	2	2	2	2	2	2	2	...	Manioc
Coconuts	28	25	28	31	32	34	38	54	...	Noix de coco
Banana	32	32	33	34	33	40	41	41	...	Banane (ton)
Taro	23	20	19	16	13	10	9	8	...	Tarau (ton)
V MINING PRODUCTION - PRODUCTION MINIERE										
	2006	2007	2008	2009	2010	2011	2012	2013	2014	
	...	...	...	...	...	...	...	...	...	
	...	...	...	...	...	...	...	...	...	
	...	...	...	...	...	...	...	...	...	
VI ENERGY - ENERGIE										
	2006	2007	2008	2009	2010	2011	2012	2013	2014	
Total electricity generation (GWh)	12	38	28	27	25	28	28	28	...	Production d'électricité totale (GWh)
of which:										dont:
Production of electricity from fossil fuels (GWh)	8	31	20	20	20	18	18	18	...	Production d'électricité à partir de combustibles fossiles (GWh)
Production of hydro electricity (GWh)	4	7	8	7	5	10	11	11	...	Production d'électricité d'origine hydraulique (GWh)
Production of electricity from solar, wind, tide, wave and other sources (GWh)	...	...	...	...	...	...	...	0	...	Production d'électricité d'origine solaire, éolienne, marée motrice et autres (GWh)
VII TOURISM AND INFRASTRUCTURE - TOURISME ET INFRASTRUCTURE										
	2006	2007	2008	2009	2010	2011	2012	2013	2014	
VII-1 TOURISM										**VII-1 TOURISME**
International tourist arrivals (thousands)	12	12	15	15	8	12	12	24	22	Arrivées de touristes internationaux (milliers)
Rooms in hotels and similar establishments (thousands)	...	...	...	...	...	...	...	...	...	Chambres d'hotels et établissements assimilés (milliers)
Overnight stays (thousands)	75	73	91	91	49	82	82	162	149	Nuitées (milliers)
Tourism receipts (US$ thousand)	6 700	5 000	7 700	8 300	11 100	15 900	15 000	30 600	27 985	Recettes touristiques (milliers de $ EU)
Total contribution to GDP (%)	10.7	10.1	11.4	12.0	11.3	12.6	11.8	16.2	14.0	Contribution totale au PIB (%)
Total contribution to Employment (%)	9.3	8.9	9.8	10.4	9.7	10.9	10.5	14.6	13.1	Contribution totale à l'emploi (%)
VII-2 INFRASTRUCTURE										**VII-2 INFRASTRUCTURE**
Paved roads (% of total)	...	...	...	...	...	...	...	...	...	Routes asphaltées (% du total)
Total Network (Railways-km)	...	...	...	...	...	...	...	...	...	Réseau total voies ferrées-Km
Main Telephone Lines (per 100 inhabitants)	5	5	5	4	4	4	4	4	...	Lignes téléphoniques fixes (pour 100 habitants)
Mobile Cellular Subscribers (per 100 inhabitants)	12	18	30	47	58	63	65	65	...	Abonnés aux téléphones mobiles (pour 100 habitants)
VIII EXTERNAL TRADE - COMMERCE EXTERIEUR										
	2006	2007	2008	2009	2010	2011	2012	2013	2014	
DOBRA (MILLIONS) **EXPORTS, FOB**										**DOBRA (MILLIONS)** **EXPORTATIONS, FÀB**
Exports - Total	95 990	92 191	115 084	149 217	202 263	192 878	288 388	237 765	299 409	Exportations - Total
Exports to AFRICA	419	310	727	1 420	1 388	1 779	12 744	9 563	...	Exportations vers l'AFRIQUE
Main Products										**Principaux produits**
Cocoa beans, whole or broken, raw or roasted	42 237	47 549	74 075	89 054	99 891	92 038	92 040	...	...	Cacao en fèves, entières ou en morceaux, bruts ou torréfiés
Oils petroleum, bituminous, distillates, except crude	...	30 375	72 675	29 995	...	610	200	...	...	Huiles de pétrole bitumineux, distillées, à l'exception du brut
Coconuts, fresh or dried	442	297	329	1 409	1 648	1 644	1 821	...	...	Noix de coco, fraîches ou sèches
Chocolate/cocoa food preparations, nes	224	198	1 333	1 992	3 873	1 052	4 374	...	...	Chocolat / cacao préparations alimentaires, nda
Central heating boilers, nes	...	3 946	...	...	...	...	...	...	...	Chaudières de chauffage central, nda
Main Destinations										**Principales destinations**
Netherlands	12 983	6 993	23 307	27 079	18 751	39 829	49 847	37 429	...	Pays-Bas
Portugal	16 100	24 190	40 829	33 138	50 406	13 036	8 160	8 042	...	Portugal
Belgium	6 859	9 252	6 546	19 025	25 052	30 289	6 806	26 304	...	Belgique
Angola	730	659	791	1 125	1 556	2 080	2 344	4 747	...	Angola
France	4 563	9 131	5 667	2 646	368	3 120	10 558	15 298	...	France
IMPORTS, CIF										**IMPORTATIONS, CAF**
Imports - Total	737 453	878 077	1 354 212	1 357 682	1 779 490	2 038 641	2 271 818	2 366 682	2 379 847	Importations - Total (millions)
Imports from Africa	176 928	220 675	384 053	246 142	324 951	258 433	604 899	698 620	...	Importations en provenance de l'Afrique
Main Products										**Principaux produits**
Oils petroleum, bituminous, distillates, except crude	176 212	215 237	384 080	248 008	326 517	66 680	88 475	...	...	Huiles de pétrole bitumineux, les distillats, à l'exception brut
Rice, husked (brown)	19 599	26 658	57 875	71 194	82 752	111 059	100 309	...	...	Riz, décortiqué (marron)
Grape wines nes, fortified wine or must, pack < 2l	45 009	43 540	49 451	41 435	48 836	191 269	197 656	...	...	Vins de raisins nda, vin fortifié ou moût de vin, pacquet <2l
Wheat or meslin flour	26 534	42 406	52 053	46 890	64 207	14 782	16 741	...	...	Farine de blé ou de méteil
Refined soya-bean oil, not chemically modified	15 710	27 083	51 739	79 895	39 371	30 987	43 432	...	...	Huiles de soja raffinées, non chimiquement modifiées
Main Origin										**Principales provenances**
Portugal	572	743	1 032	946	1 345	1 410	1 401	1 662	...	Portugal
Netherlands	7	16	2	7	14	9	7	7	...	Pays-Bas
Belgium	39	22	28	32	56	44	93	54	...	Belgium
France	7	3	3	6	7	61	...	19	...	France
Angola	...	...	...	...	...	...	...	...	...	Angola

IX FINANCIAL AND MONETARY STATISTICS - FINANCES ET STATISTIQUES MONETAIRES	2006	2007	2008	2009	2010	2011	2012	2013	2014	
IX-1 MONETARY STATISTICS *DOBRA (MILLIONS)*										**IX-1 STATISTIQUES MONÉTAIRES** *DOBRA (MILLIONS)*
Money supply (M1)	553 110	763 830	1 044 820	1 130 350	1 414 600	1 561 890	1 879 480	2 140 380	2 369 470	Masse monétaire (M1)
Quasi-money	116 776	151 165	209 703	266 164	331 373	433 626	640 270	556 082	681 935	Quasi-monnaie
of which Demand Deposit	...	...	...	...	...	...	...	...	...	dont Monnaie scripturale
Net foreign assets	737 513	1 029 500	1 417 830	1 278 631	1 364 142	1 262 714	1 487 478	1 647 562	2 066 173	Avoirs extérieurs nets
Domestic credit	353 080	459 993	333 622	809 573	1 465 504	1 727 691	1 765 270	1 651 328	1 561 750	Crédit intérieur
of which claims on private sector	464 243	621 697	763 303	1 063 451	1 444 314	1 667 451	1 820 799	1 789 752	1 765 294	dont créances sur le secteur privé
of which claims on government sector, net	- 123 394	- 178 056	- 449 995	- 280 124	- 60 444	- 22 072	- 123 437	- 250 177	- 320 023	dont créances nettes sur le gouvernement
International reserves (millions US$)	34	39	61	67	48	52	52	64	64	Réserves internationales (millions $EU)
Average Exchange Rate (National Currency per US$)	12 364.91	13 536.76	14 695.20	16 208.45	18 498.60	17 622.94	19 068.42	18 449.95	18 447.68	Taux de change (moyen) (monnaie nationale par $ EU)
IX-2 PUBLIC FINANCE *DOBRA (MILLIONS)*										**IX-2 FINANCES PUBLIQUES** *DOBRA (MILLIONS)*
Total Revenues and Grants	570 156	3 211 592	1 224 542	994 860	1 458 718	1 764 502	1 612 058	1 492 878	1 676 480	Recettes totales et dons
Tax Revenue	266 617	319 777	411 008	461 570	646 946	726 000	703 724	870 887	961 645	Recettes fiscales
Non Tax Revenue	39 318	434 205	33 467	67 296	59 989	61 220	66 983	99 638	111 022	Recettes non fiscales
Grants	264 221	2 457 610	780 068	465 994	751 783	977 282	841 351	522 353	603 814	Dons
Total Expenditures and Net Lending	783 262	761 893	789 245	1 546 099	1 847 161	2 316 808	2 225 811	2 140 486	2 276 056	Dépenses totales et prêts nets
Current expenditure	440 830	484 713	569 445	646 275	766 281	850 538	875 811	1 047 486	1 126 061	Dépenses courantes
Of which Wages and Salaries	133 334	174 344	219 099	252 090	338 383	369 185	419 418	485 517	522 689	Dont rémunérations et salaires
Capital expenditure	342 433	277 179	271 800	934 823	1 080 879	1 466 270	1 350 000	1 093 000	1 149 995	Dépenses d'équipement
Net Lending	-	-	- 52 000	- 35 000	-	-	-	-	-	Prêts nets
Fiscal Balance	- 213 106	2 449 699	435 298	- 551 239	- 388 443	- 552 306	- 613 753	- 647 608	- 599 576	Solde global y compris les dons
IX-3 BALANCE OF PAYMENTS *DOBRA (MILLIONS)*										**IX-3 BALANCE DES PAIEMENTS** *DOBRA (MILLIONS)*
Trade balance	- 52	- 58	- 84	- 75	- 85	- 105	- 103	- 107	...	Balance commerciale
Services Balance	- 9	- 12	- 12	- 9	- 11	- 13	- 8	- 11	...	Balance des services
Net Income	3	5	0	0	0	0	- 3	- 4	...	Revenus nets
Compensation of employees	...	...	...	...	...	...	...	...	...	Rémunération des salariés
Investment Income	...	...	...	...	...	...	...	...	...	Revenus des investissements
Current transfers, net total	0	1	3	5	9	12	14	6	...	Transferts courants
Net official transfers	1	2	3	6	6	10	9	1	...	Transferts officiels nets
Workers' remittances	...	...	...	...	...	...	...	...	...	Envois de fonds des travailleurs
Other private transfers	...	...	...	...	...	...	...	...	...	Autres transferts privés
Current account balance	- 58	- 64	- 94	- 79	- 88	- 106	- 100	- 115	...	Solde du compte courant
Capital & financial account	67	75	125	88	88	113	106	117	...	Comptes de capital et financier
Capital account	24	225	56	40	42	47	40	51	...	Compte de capital
Financial account	43	- 151	70	49	56	66	66	66	...	Compte financier
Errors & omissions	- 9	- 10	- 32	- 10	- 10	- 7	- 7	- 1	...	Erreurs et omissions
Overall balance	9	10	32	10	0	7	7	1	...	Balance générale

X DEBT AND FINANCIAL FLOWS - DETTE ET FLUX FINANCIERS										
	2006	2007	2008	2009	2010	2011	2012	2013	2014	
X-1 DEBT *US$ (MILLIONS)*										**X-1 DETTE EXTÉRIEURE** *$ E.U (MILLIONS)*
Total external debt	359	150	110	136	157	182	222	231	259	Dette extérieure totale
Private	-	-	-	-	-	-	17	16	15	Privée
Public	359	150	110	136	157	182	205	215	244	Publique
Total external debt service	9	9	9	4	3	2	2	5	7	Service de la dette extérieure
Present value of External debt	...	...	...	...	...	...	...	...	...	Valeur actuelle de la dette extérieure
Total government domestic debt (in local currency)	...	...	...	...	...	...	...	...	...	Dette publique intérieure
X-2 FINANCIAL FLOWS *US$ (MILLIONS)*										**X-2 FLUX FINANCIERS** *$ E.U (MILLIONS)*
Net Foreign Direct Investment Inflows	38	36	79	16	25	18	...	...	...	Investissements étranger direct (flux nets entrants)
Main origin of FDI Inflows										**Principales origines de l'IDE entrant:**
United States	...	...	...	1	...	1.0	...	...	...	États-Unis
Netherlands	...	...	...	...	...	...	...	...	...	Pays-Bas
Luxembourg	...	...	...	...	...	...	...	...	...	Luxembourg
Slovenia	...	...	...	...	...	...	...	...	...	Slovénie
Chile	...	...	...	...	...	...	...	...	...	Chili
African countries	...	...	...	...	...	...	...	...	...	Pays africains
Net total Official Development Assistance	23	51	47	31	50	0	...	...	...	**Aide publique au développement (nette totale)**
Main origin of Net ODA										Principales origines de l'APD nette
Portugal	11	13	13	15	25.7	29.1	21.5	...	...	Portugal
IDA	2	3	9	1	2.2	18.8	5.9	...	...	IDA
France	3	4	3	2	2.4	2.2	2.2	...	...	France
Japan	0	3	7	0	3.6	3.5	3.7	...	...	Japon
AfDF	- 5	15	0	1	0.3	3.3	3.0	...	...	FAfD

SENEGAL — SÉNÉGAL

AREA (KM²)		**196 722**	**SUPERFICIE (KM²)**
CAPITAL CITY	**Dakar**	**Dakar**	**CAPITALE**
CURRENCY	**CFA Franc**	**Franc CFA**	**MONNAIE**

I SOCIAL AND DEMOGRAPHIC INDICATORS – INDICATEURS DEMOGRAPHIQUES ET SOCIAUX

	Year / Année	Value / Valeur	
POPULATION			**POPULATION**
Population ('000)			Population ('000)
Both sexes	2014	14 548	Les deux sexes
Male	2014	7 141	Masculin
Female	2014	7 408	Féminin
Average annual growth rate	2014	3.0	Taux de croissance annuel
Active Population ('000)	2014	5 922	Population active ('000)
Population by age group ('000)			Population par groupe d'âge ('000)
0-14 years	2014	6 319	0-14 ans
15-64 years	2014	7 800	15-64 ans
65+ years	2014	429	65+ ans
Economically active population in agriculture (%)	2014	72.4	Participation de la population active agricole (%)
Crude birth rate	2014	37.3	Taux brut de natalité
Crude death rate	2014	7.5	Taux brut de mortalité
Total fertility rate	2014	4.9	Indice synthétique de fécondité
Proportion of urban population	2014	43.4	Part de la population urbaine
Life Expectancy at Birth - Total (years)	2014	63.6	Espérance de vie à la naissance - Totale (ans)
Dependency Ratio - Total (%)	2014	82.5	Taux de dépendance - Total (%)
HEALTH			**SANTÉ**
Percentage of children under-five and underweight	2013	16.8	% d'enfants de moins de cinq ans avec insuffisance pondérale
Prevalence of undernourishment	2013	16.7	Prévalence de la malnutrition
Under five mortality rate (both sexes, per 1000)	2013	55.3	Taux de mortalité de moins de 5 ans (les deux sexes, pour 1000)
Infant mortality rate (both sexes) per 1000	2013	43.9	Taux de mortalité infantile (les deux sexes) par 1000
Percentage of children provided the vaccines :			Pourcentage d'enfants vaccinés :
BCG	2013	97.0	BCG
DPT3	2013	92.0	DTC3
Polio	2013	83.0	Polio
Measles	2013	84.0	Rougeole
Percentage of mothers provided at least one antenatal care (%)	2012	4.0	Pourcentage de mères ayant au moins reçu un soin prénatal (%)
Percentage of deliveries attended by skilled health personnel	2011	65.1	% d'accouchements assistés par un personnel de santé qualifié
Number of doctors (per 10 000 population)	2008	0.6	Nombre de médecins (pour 10 000 habitants)
Number of nurses (per 10 000 population)	2008	4.2	Nombre d'infirmières (pour 10 000 habitants)
Hospital beds - Total (per 10 000 population)	2008	3.4	Nombre de lits d'hôpitaux - Total (pour 10 000)
Births registered (per 1 000)	2014	37.3	Naiss.s enregistrées (pour 1 000)
Deaths registered (per 1 000)	2014	7.5	Décès enregistrés (pour 1 000)
Public expenditure on Health (% of budget)	2009	11.6	Dépenses publiques consacrées à la santé (% du budget)
EDUCATION			**EDUCATION**
Enrolment in primary education (both sexes) (000)	2014	1.888	Scolarisation dans le primaire (les deux sexes) (000)
Female	2014	974	Féminin
Enrolment in secondary education (both sexes) (000)	2011	834	Scolarisation dans le secondaire (les deux sexes) (000)
Female	2011	396	Féminin
Enrolment in tertiary education (both sexes) (000)	...	...	Scolarisation dans le tertiaire (les deux sexes) (000)
Female	2010	34.3	Féminin
Literacy rate (both sexes)	2011	52.1	Taux d'alphabétisation (deux sexes)
Male	2011	66.3	Masculin
Female	2011	40.4	Féminin
Pupil-teacher ratio	...	...	Ratio élève-enseignant
Public expenditure on education (% of budget)	2010	20.7	Dépenses publiques consacrées à l'enseignement (% du budget)
POVERTY			**PAUVRETÉ**
GNI Per Capita (US$)	2013	1 050.0	RNB par habitant ($EU)
Human Poverty Index (HPI-1) Value (%)	2007	41.6	Valeur de l'Indice de pauvreté (IPH-1) (%)
Population below International Poverty Line ($2/day) (%)	2011	6.3	Population sous le seuil international de pauvreté (2$/J) (%)
Share of Income Held by Richest 10%	2011	31.1	% de revenu des 10% plus riches
Share of Income Held by Poorest 10%	2011	2.5	% de revenu des 10% plus pauvres
Gini index	2011	40.3	Indice de Gini

Charts / Graphiques

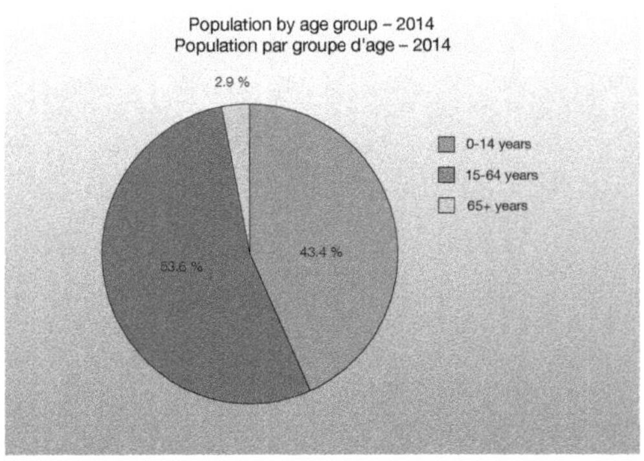

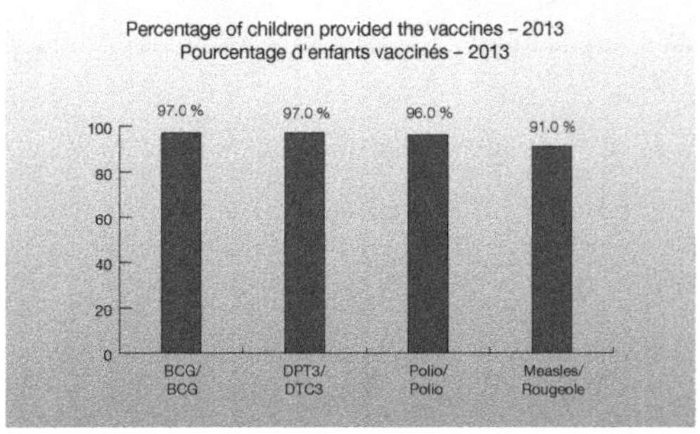

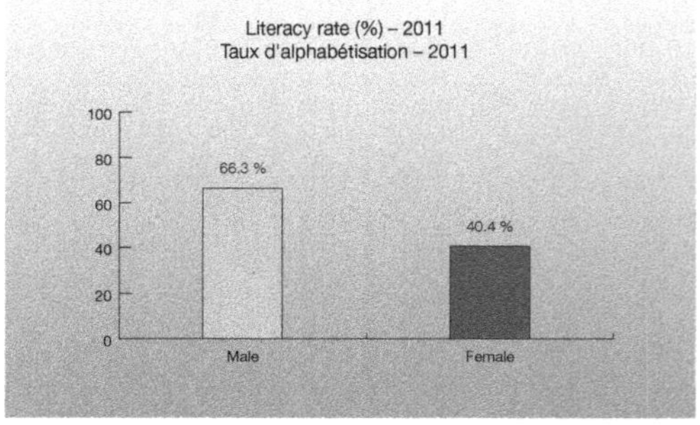

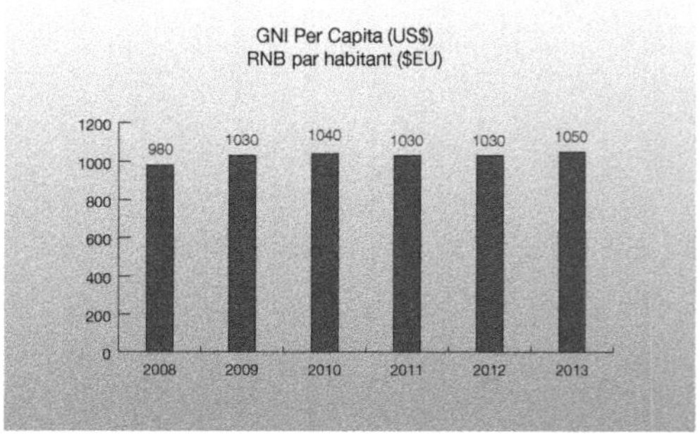

II NATIONAL ACCOUNTS — COMPTES NATIONAUX	2006	2007	2008	2009	2010	2011	2012	2013	2014	
GROSS DOMESTIC PRODUCT BY KIND OF ECONOMIC ACTIVITY AT CURRENT PRICES *CFA FRANC (MILLIONS)*										**PRODUIT INTÉRIEUR BRUT PAR BRANCHE D'ACTIVITÉ ÉCONOMIQUE AUX PRIX COURANTS** *FRANC CFA (MILLIONS)*
Agriculture, hunting, forestry and fishing	634 000	642 000	838 113	919 213	978 872	864 580	995 195	1 038 131	1 096 890	Agriculture, chasse sylviculture et pêche
Mining and quarrying	52 000	52 000	50 692	101 667	117 822	141 866	193 497	146 869	126 186	Industries extractives
Manufacturing	612 000	675 000	737 881	739 848	773 460	854 886	865 314	808 349	846 028	Industries manufacturières
Electricity, gas & water	115 000	136 000	154 282	153 232	171 795	171 766	174 888	165 102	172 664	Electricité, gaz et eau
Construction & public works	234 000	262 000	262 933	244 185	246 447	284 111	282 984	303 480	347 198	Bâtiments et travaux publics
Wholesale & retail trade, restaurants, hotels	886 000	983 000	1 092 128	1 054 130	1 105 001	1 193 459	1 256 676	1 261 576	1 321 525	Commerce de gros et de détail, restaurants et hôtels
Finance, insurance, real estate, etc.	651 548	727 000	822 392	805 098	850 248	926 703	956 239	1 016 836	1 095 242	Banques, assurances, affaires immobilières
Transport and communications	526 000	591 000	668 230	641 809	666 206	701 247	749 046	834 387	885 120	Transport(s) et communications
Public administration and defense	296 000	332 000	361 731	369 624	392 589	442 024	482 028	499 529	526 639	Administrations publiques et défense
Education	175 000	206 000	216 547	222 892	242 858	266 178	285 052	304 111	318 593	Education
Health and Social Work	59 000	67 000	77 361	78 811	81 566	88 014	93 750	104 365	113 729	Santé et actions sociales
Other services	94 000	102 000	109 722	110 266	111 896	116 653	119 661	123 408	131 329	Autres services
Less Imputed Service Charges	- 103 000	- 110 000	- 132 496	- 133 088	- 132 725	- 151 651	- 166 670	- 182 502	- 207 700	Moins services d'intermédiation financière
Gross domestic product at factor cost / basic prices	4 231 548	4 665 000	5 259 516	5 307 685	5 606 034	5 899 836	6 287 659	6 423 640	6 773 443	Produit intérieur brut aux couts des facteurs / prix de base
Plus: indirect taxes / taxes on products, less subsidies	662 000	743 000	734 960	719 863	789 321	874 751	876 940	884 051	952 945	Plus taxes indirectes/impôts sur les produits, moins les subventions
EXPENDITURE ON GROSS DOMESTIC PRODUCT AT CURRENT PURCHASER'S VALUES *CFA FRANC (MILLIONS)*										**EMPLOI DU PRODUIT INTÉRIEUR BRUT AUX PRIX COURANTS D'ACQUISITION** *FRANC CFA (MILLIONS)*
Government final consumption	668 000	767 098	806 425	861 020	947 438	1 040 612	1 091 394	1 131 021	1 204 150	Consommation finale des administrations publiques
Private final consumption	3 872 000	4 270 600	4 889 981	4 857 682	5 024 020	5 243 112	5 495 013	5 727 562	5 969 952	Consommation finale privée
Gross fixed capital formation	1 280 000	1 414 078	1 607 562	1 386 191	1 421 476	1 658 334	1 717 501	1 830 971	1 980 777	Formation brute de capital fixe
Change in inventories	- 71 000	167 970	267 128	- 58 870	- 12 447	86 460	414 962	156 370	89 864	Variation des stocks
Exports of goods and services	1 254 000	1 376 220	1 566 250	1 471 790	1 592 644	1 787 320	1 835 625	2 049 359	2 095 606	Exportations de biens et services
Less imports of goods and services	2 109 000	2 587 630	3 142 870	2 490 265	2 577 776	3 041 252	3 389 896	3 587 592	3 613 962	Moins importations de biens et services
GDP at purchasers' values	4 894 000	5 408 336	5 994 476	6 027 548	6 395 355	6 774 586	7 164 598	7 307 691	7 726 388	PIB aux prix d'acquisition
GROSS DOMESTIC PRODUCT BY KIND OF ECONOMIC ACTIVITY AT CONSTANT PRICES *ANNUAL GROWTH RATES (%)*										**PRODUIT INTÉRIEUR BRUT PAR BRANCHE D'ACTIVITÉ ECONOMIQUE AUX PRIX CONSTANTS** *TAUX DE CROISSANCE ANNUEL (%)*
Agriculture, hunting, forestry and fishing	- 8.6	- 5.5	19.3	13.0	5.8	- 14.8	8.9	3.3	3.2	Agriculture, chasse sylviculture et pêche
Mining and quarrying	- 16.7	- 5.7	2.0	51.2	6.5	9.0	7.9	- 24.7	- 16.6	Industries extractives
Manufacturing	- 2.9	6.4	- 2.9	5.4	2.6	6.7	1.3	- 4.3	4.0	Industries manufacturières
Electricity, gas & water	5.0	8.6	3.9	- 4.6	7.5	- 2.7	5.6	3.4	3.5	Electricité, gaz et eau
Construction & public works	12.9	9.3	- 0.4	- 4.5	4.7	7.3	- 1.2	10.3	12.2	Bâtiments et travaux publics
Wholesale & retail trade, restaurants, hotels	3.8	3.9	1.8	2.2	2.0	2.6	3.2	- 0.5	3.3	Commerce de gros et de détail,restaurants et hôtels
Finance, insurance, real estate, etc.	2.6	5.4	5.3	- 0.7	5.3	7.3	4.1	7.2	6.7	Banques, assurances, affaires immobilières
Transport and communications	16.1	11.5	8.5	1.4	7.1	2.5	5.2	15.9	6.7	Transport(s) et communications
Public administration and defense	4.6	5.6	- 0.7	1.0	2.4	5.4	3.4	2.9	3.9	Administrations publiques et défense
Education	2.9	9.8	4.0	1.6	1.8	5.0	2.4	4.0	3.7	Education
Health and Social Work	2.9	11.1	2.8	1.3	3.3	4.3	2.0	7.8	7.9	Santé et actions sociales
Other services	2.4	4.8	0.6	0.6	1.2	1.5	1.6	2.4	4.8	Autres services
Less Imputed Service Charges	7.3	5.7	17.2	- 0.3	1.5	15.4	13.3	8.7	12.7	Moins services d'intermédiation financière
Gross domestic product at factor cost / basic prices	2.2	5.0	4.3	3.4	4.3	1.1	3.7	3.9	4.7	Produit intérieur brut aux couts des facteurs / prix de base
Plus: indirect taxes / taxes on products, less subsidies	3.7	5.1	- 1.1	- 4.9	3.1	5.9	0.7	0.1	6.2	Plus taxes indirectes/impôts sur les produits, moins les subventions
Gross domestic product at market prices	2.4	5.0	3.7	2.4	4.2	1.7	3.4	3.5	4.8	Produit intérieur brut aux prix du marché
EXPENDITURE ON GROSS DOMESTIC PRODUCT AT CONSTANT PURCHASERS' VALUES *ANNUAL GROWTH RATES (%)*										**EMPLOIS DU PRODUIT INTÉRIEUR BRUT AUX PRIX CONSTANTS D'ACQUISITION** *TAUX DE CROISSANCE ANNUEL (%)*
Government final consumption	4.9	7.3	0.7	1.7	2.6	5.4	2.9	2.9	3.9	Consommation finale des administrations publiques
Private final consumption	4.7	5.0	5.6	3.9	2.1	1.2	3.2	3.2	3.2	Consommation finale privée
Gross fixed capital formation	13.2	7.4	8.1	- 4.3	1.5	9.0	1.6	5.5	6.7	Formation brute de capital fixe
Exports of goods and services	- 3.2	- 0.1	1.8	6.2	5.7	7.9	- 1.9	4.5	1.4	Exportations de biens et services
Less imports of goods and services	1.2	14.3	- 0.1	- 3.9	- 5.0	9.1	7.7	7.8	- 0.1	Moins importations de biens et services
Notes	NA data: 2012:Semi-final; 2013-2014:Provisional						Données des CN: 2012:Semi-définitives; 2013-2014:Provisoires			Notes

III INFLATION	2006	2007	2008	2009	2010	2011	2012	2013	2014	
ANNUAL GROWTH RATES (%)										**TAUX DE CROISSANCE ANNUEL (%)**
All items	2.1	5.9	5.8	-1.0	1.2	3.4	1.4	0.7	-1.1	Ensemble
of which:										dont:
Food and Non-alcoholic beverages	1.4	7.3	9.6	-3.0	4.0	6.7	2.5	1.3	-1.9	Alimentation et boissons non alcoolisés
Alcoholic beverages & tobacco	0.2	0.7	1.4	-0.3	4.3	-1.0	-2.2	11.7	0.0	Boissons alcoolisées et tabacs
Clothing and Footwear	-2.4	0.5	0.8	-2.4	0.3	-1.1	-0.2	-0.7	-0.4	Habillement et chaussures
Housing, Water, Electricity, Gas and Other Fuels	3.5	10.0	1.5	1.3	2.1	3.1	0.2	-0.3	-1.1	Logement, eau, électricité, gas et autres combustibles
Furnishing, household equip	-0.2	4.4	4.0	3.2	-1.2	0.4	1.1	-0.3	0.5	Meubles, articles de ménage et entretien courant
Health	17.2	1.8	0.0	2.9	1.0	0.8	1.0	3.0	1.0	Santé
Transport	8.5	2.5	9.6	-1.4	2.9	5.5	1.8	0.4	1.7	Transport
Communication	0.0	-	0.1	0.1	-7.9	0.2	0.4	-5.3	3.8	Communication
Recreation & culture	1.2	-0.1	-1.7	-0.9	-3.8	0.3	0.5	-1.4	1.0	Loisirs et culture
Education	1.3	8.9	6.8	3.4	1.1	2.6	2.7	2.6	0.8	Enseignement
Restaurants & hotels	2.2	13.4	7.7	4.1	0.3	1.2	2.3	6.6	0.6	Restaurants et hôtels
Miscellaneous goods & services	-2.5	0.5	0.8	-0.3	-2.8	2.8	0.9	0.1	-0.2	Biens et services divers

IV AGRICULTURAL PRODUCTION - PRODUCTION AGRICOLE

	2006	2007	2008	2009	2010	2011	2012	2013	2014	
TONNES *(THOUSAND)*										**TONNES** *(MILLIERS)*
Sugar	830	836	836	836	850	880	900	890	...	Sucre
Groundnuts	460	331	731	1 033	1 287	528	673	710	...	Arachides
Millet	494	319	678	810	813	481	662	572	...	Millet
Rice	190	193	408	502	604	406	631	423	...	Riz
Maize	60	142	150	160	160	190	210	225	...	Maïs

V MINING PRODUCTION - PRODUCTION MINIERE

	2006	2007	2008	2009	2010	2011	2012	2013	2014	
Phosphate, Tons (thousands)	584	691	645	949	1 131	1 437	1 416	...	...	Phosphate (Milliers de tonnes)
Sea salt iodizes, Tons (thousands)	199	212	241	222	232	258	237	...	...	Sel marin iodé (Milliers de tonnes)
Attapulgite, Tons (thousands)	234	138	200	234	166	193	181	...	...	Attapulgite (Milliers de tonnes)

VI ENERGY - ENERGIE

	2006	2007	2008	2009	2010	2011	2012	2013	2014	
Total electricity generation (GWh)	2 248	2 347	2 434	2 811	3 032	2 965	2 932	2 952	...	Production d'électricité totale (GWh)
of which:										dont:
Production of electricity from fossil fuels (GWh)	1 958	2 125	2 172	2 519	2 724	2 651	2 586	2 586	...	Production d'électricité à partir de combustibles fossiles (GWh)
Production of hydro electricity (GWh)	237	181	229	239	253	257	290	311	...	Production d'électricité d'origine hydraulique (GWh)
Production of electricity from solar, wind, tide, wave and other sources (GWh)	2	3	3	3	3	3	4	4	...	Production d'électricité d'origine solaire, éolienne, marée motrice et autres (GWh)

VII TOURISM AND INFRASTRUCTURE - TOURISME ET INFRASTRUCTURE

	2006	2007	2008	2009	2010	2011	2012	2013	2014	
VII-1 TOURISM										**VII-1 TOURISME**
International tourist arrivals (thousands)	866	875	867	810	900	1 001	989	1 012	1 039	Arrivées de touristes internationaux (milliers)
Rooms in hotels and similar establishments (thousands)	15.8	15.8	...	...	...	...	...	...	...	Chambres d'hotels et établissements assimilés (milliers)
Overnight stays (thousands)	2 844	2 633	3 566	3 342	3 685	4 108	3 798	3 895	4 007	Nuitées (milliers)
Tourism receipts (US$ thousand)	249 200	503 300	508 300	430 500	432 300	439 200	466 301	516 081	559 975	Recettes touristiques (milliers de $ EU)
Total contribution to GDP (%)	11.7	14.9	12.3	11.5	11.1	10.7	10.9	11.1	11.3	Contribution totale au PIB (%)
Total contribution to Employment (%)	9.9	12.6	10.5	9.7	9.4	9.1	9.2	9.7	9.9	Contribution totale à l'emploi (%)
VII-2 INFRASTRUCTURE										**VII-2 INFRASTRUCTURE**
Paved roads (% of total)	33	33	...	32	36	...	...	...	...	Routes asphaltées (% du total)
Total Network (Railways-km)	...	...	...	...	...	...	...	...	...	Réseau total voies ferrées-Km
Main Telephone Lines (per 100 inhabitants)	2	2	2	2	3	3	2	2	...	Lignes téléphoniques fixes (pour 100 habitants)
Mobile Cellular Subscribers (per 100 inhabitants)	26	30	44	55	64	70	84	93	...	Abonnés aux téléphones mobiles (pour 100 habitants)

VIII EXTERNAL TRADE - COMMERCE EXTERIEUR

	2006	2007	2008	2009	2010	2011	2012	2013	2014	
CFA FRANC (MILLIONS) **EXPORTS, FOB**										**FRANC CFA (MILLIONS)** **EXPORTATIONS, FÀB**
Exports - Total	833 471	802 211	987 862	990 062	1 071 901	1 200 354	1 216 272	1 207 150	...	Exportations - Total
Exports to AFRICA	322 163	356 087	434 278	393 221	500 017	487 362	536 424	...	...	Exportations vers l'AFRIQUE
Main Products										**Principaux produits**
Phosphoric acid	40 327	46 959	106 905	69 815	98 481	160 695	140 353	89 602	...	Acide phosphoriques
Gas oil	60 167	88 426	155 651	82 191	134 423	73 378	22 281	...	...	Gaz oil
Jet fuel	100 863	27 983	150 040	102 643	78 584	98 694	104 226	...	...	Carburéacteur
Frozen and fresh fish	83 514	86 466	58 988	73 531	78 862	89 466	132 213	49 266	...	Autres poissons frais/réfrigérés
Groundnut oil, crude	27 843	32 353	7 889	18 141	28 609	37 440	13 727	11 076	...	Huiles d'arachide brutes & ses fractions
Main Destinations										**Principales destinations**
Mali	137 132	159 966	213 112	171 117	247 134	180 990	173 965	...	...	Mali
India	41 351	49 699	121 151	73 158	103 789	168 169	148 349	...	...	Inde
France	60 936	70 878	56 203	50 579	47 166	53 041	56 803	...	...	France
Italy	37 024	37 562	17 100	24 427	23 186	32 604	29 259	...	...	Italie
Spain	38 980	37 082	21 592	20 394	28 877	34 960	29 200	...	...	Espagne
IMPORTS, CIF										**IMPORTATIONS, CAF**
Imports - Total	1 890 992	2 264 100	2 842 500	2 211 900	2 297 600	2 673 152	3 005 463	2 994 700	...	Importations - Total (millions)
Imports from Africa	257 209	381 725	571 623	404 149	395 492	473 865	627 289	...	...	Importations en provenance de l'Afrique
Main Products										**Principaux produits**
Petroleum oils,crude	85 777	193 249	343 243	186 706	224 362	255 068	385 654	...	...	Huiles brutes de petrole
Broken rice	121 289	168 322	199 466	160 512	129 806	174 505	203 486	...	...	Brisures de riz
Gas oil	248 606	218 782	109 379	168 944	268 875	332 769	137 628	...	...	Gaz oil
Medicaments for retail sale, nes	48 224	53 426	56 922	58 272	57 870	66 708	74 906	...	...	Autres médicaments pour la vente au détail
Wheat & meslin, nes	41 148	61 993	70 660	52 638	63 017	80 450	96 663	...	...	Autres blés & méteil
Main Origin										**Principales provenances**
France	448 864	498 942	455 122	425 484	441 273	460 349	486 074	...	...	France
Nigeria	62 808	196 645	345 321	197 430	230 842	256 297	388 143	...	...	Nigeria
Thailand	85 372	113 401	153 052	116 901	73 863	96 824	54 840	...	...	Thaïlande
China	80 219	128 247	165 001	191 989	195 124	177 914	187 967	...	...	Chine
Spain	72 100	68 290	73 839	92 185	84 887	93 680	103 102	...	...	Espagne

IX FINANCIAL AND MONETARY STATISTICS - FINANCES ET STATISTIQUES MONETAIRES	2006	2007	2008	2009	2010	2011	2012	2013	2014	
IX-1 MONETARY STATISTICS *CFA FRANC (MILLIONS)*										**IX-1 STATISTIQUES MONÉTAIRES** *FRANC CFA (MILLIONS)*
Money supply (M1)	1 751 200	1 973 020	2 006 600	2 226 000	2 540 250	2 711 430	2 894 660	3 127 080	3 366 690	Masse monétaire (M1)
Quasi-money	644 160	703 531	753 459	867 492	991 161	1 062 657	1 118 402	1 139 869	1 358 756	Quasi-monnaie
of which Demand Deposit	...	...	...	...	...	...	...	...	...	dont Monnaie scripturale
Net foreign assets	841 398	892 270	775 051	896 442	1 028 641	903 926	928 052	910 169	1 109 485	Avoirs extérieurs nets
Domestic credit	1 122 402	1 323 435	1 467 718	1 606 811	1 847 310	2 122 292	2 241 881	2 565 366	2 637 585	Crédit intérieur
of which claims on private sector	1 111 277	1 230 254	1 439 551	1 491 992	1 646 988	1 953 001	2 140 772	2 414 262	2 567 737	dont créances sur le secteur privé
of which claims on government sector, net	11 125	93 182	28 167	114 819	200 322	169 291	101 109	151 104	69 848	dont créances nettes sur le gouvernement
International reserves (millions US$)	1 334	1 660	1 602	2 123	2 047	1 946	2 082	2 253	2 012	Réserves internationales (millions $EU)
Average Exchange Rate (National Currency per US$)	522.90	478.89	446.87	471.07	494.68	471.42	510.18	493.94	493.76	Taux de change (moyen) (monnaie nationale par $ EU)
IX-2 PUBLIC FINANCE *CFA FRANC (MILLIONS)*										**IX-2 FINANCES PUBLIQUES** *FRANC CFA (MILLIONS)*
Total Revenues and Grants	1 036 040	1 231 339	1 291 750	1 304 700	1 398 330	1 486 400	1 629 300	1 620 580	1 559 311	Recettes totales et dons
Tax Revenue	921 900	1 041 400	1 087 150	1 084 600	1 194 740	1 286 900	1 352 000	1 342 840	1 256 961	Recettes fiscales
Non Tax Revenue	40 740	58 600	64 900	37 300	41 740	49 500	71 000	90 200	89 082	Recettes non fiscales
Grants	73 400	131 339	139 700	182 800	161 850	150 000	206 300	187 540	213 268	Dons
Total Expenditures and Net Lending	1 327 993	1 435 608	1 578 500	1 616 970	1 741 110	1 942 310	2 048 110	2 025 251	1 924 529	Dépenses totales et prêts nets
Current expenditure	825 953	864 940	978 720	1 006 870	1 007 540	1 195 510	1 215 110	1 229 051	1 138 434	Dépenses courantes
Of which Wages and Salaries	286 150	328 600	347 700	364 350	392 340	427 500	461 500	464 700	461 335	Dont rémunérations et salaires
Capital expenditure	474 940	565 268	594 680	606 900	735 670	718 400	813 700	801 300	779 565	Dépenses d'équipement
Net Lending	27 100	5 400	5 100	3 200	- 2 100	28 400	19 300	- 5 100	6 531	Prêts nets
Fiscal Balance	- 291 953	- 204 269	- 286 750	- 312 270	- 342 780	- 455 910	- 418 810	- 404 671	- 365 219	Solde global y compris les dons
IX-3 BALANCE OF PAYMENTS *CFA FRANC (MILLIONS)*										**IX-3 BALANCE DES PAIEMENTS** *FRANC CFA (MILLIONS)*
Trade balance	- 836 529	-1 193 289	-1 522 538	- 957 738	- 950 499	-1 184 000	-1 468 917	-1 481 477	...	Balance commerciale
Services Balance	- 18 501	- 18 072	- 54 087	- 60 773	- 34 627	- 65 168	- 55 000	- 56 800	...	Balance des services
Net Income	- 33 171	- 35 388	- 21 416	- 80 149	- 71 286	- 120 832	- 153 840	- 158 475	...	Revenus nets
Compensation of employees	33 870	34 318	37 601	38 421	38 075	38 604	...	...	...	Rémunération des salariés
Investment Income	119 681	125 543	145 400	153 802	164 818	196 155	...	...	...	Revenus des investissements
Current transfers, net total	437 466	618 022	754 355	695 636	767 536	833 000	897 551	907 314	...	Transferts courants
Net official transfers	28 166	52 006	32 514	23 147	33 441	23 867	...	...	...	Transferts officiels nets
Workers' remittances	399 517	468 218	558 880	516 857	586 582	599 458	...	...	...	Envois de fonds des travailleurs
Other private transfers	9 783	97 798	162 961	155 632	147 513	150 849	...	...	...	Autres transferts privés
Current account balance	- 450 735	- 628 727	- 843 686	- 403 024	- 288 876	- 537 000	- 780 206	- 789 438	...	Solde du compte courant
Capital & financial account	544 400	694 000	751 000	496 800	409 614	462 700	...	...	...	Comptes de capital et financier
Capital account	1 185 878	95 163	107 807	145 087	151 600	118 686	...	...	...	Compte de capital
Financial account	- 639 600	534 500	643 800	352 700	260 100	342 000	...	...	...	Compte financier
Errors & omissions	5 401	5 543	4 204	2 586	- 4 748	...	...	...	...	Erreurs et omissions
Overall balance	99 029	70 800	- 88 400	96 386	115 966	- 57 300	...	...	...	Balance générale

X DEBT AND FINANCIAL FLOWS - DETTE ET FLUX FINANCIERS	2006	2007	2008	2009	2010	2011	2012	2013	2014	
X-1 DEBT US$ (MILLIONS)										**X-1 DETTE EXTÉRIEURE** *$ E.U (MILLIONS)*
Total external debt	3 483	4 526	5 861	6 651	6 866	7 615	8 887	10 265	11 483	Dette extérieure totale
Private	1 751	2 380	3 428	3 238	3 547	5 622	6 666	7 898	8 734	Privée
Public	1 732	2 146	2 433	3 413	3 319	1 993	2 221	2 368	2 749	Publique
Total external debt service	4 682	176	167	193	207	519	301	292	461	Service de la dette extérieure
Present value of External debt	...	...	...	...	...	...	...	...	...	Valeur actuelle de la dette extérieure
Total government domestic debt (in local currency)	...	...	...	...	...	...	...	...	...	Dette publique intérieure
X-2 FINANCIAL FLOWS *US$ (MILLIONS)*										**X-2 FLUX FINANCIERS** *$ E.U (MILLIONS)*
Net Foreign Direct Investment Inflows	220	297	398	320	266	338	276	298	...	Investissements étranger direct (flux nets entrants)
Main origin of FDI Inflows										**Principales origines de l'IDE entrant:**
France	25	120	64	117	94.0	- 59.9	- 25.7	...	...	France
Luxembourg	39	1	- 16	1	...	...	14.0	...	...	Luxembourg
Italy	3	3	28	- 22	- 2.1	4.4	- 2.3	...	...	Italie
Turkey	...	...	1	...	6.0	...	6.0	...	...	Turquie
Germany	- 11	...	1	- 4	4.0	...	...	...	...	Allemagne
African countries	...	...	...	...	...	...	...	...	...	Pays africains
Net total Official Development Assistance	865	870	1 069	1 016	928	1 060	1 080	983	...	Aide publique au développement (nette totale)
Main origin of Net ODA										**Principales origines de l'APD nette**
France	287	177	189	141	157.2	177.3	304.3	191.8	...	France
IDA	125	133	133	134	110.4	172.1	137.2	...	...	IDA
United States	38	39	72	68	101.4	119.5	129.7	203.4	...	Etats-Unis
AfDF	89	56	86	40	63.6	94.0	52.8	...	...	FAfD
Japan	34	32	25	47	55.2	82.8	80.5	42.1	...	Japon

SEYCHELLES

AREA (KM²)	455		SUPERFICIE (KM²)
CAPITAL CITY	Victoria	Victoria	CAPITALE
CURRENCY	Seychelles Rupee	Rupee	MONNAIE

I SOCIAL AND DEMOGRAPHIC INDICATORS – INDICATEURS DEMOGRAPHIQUES ET SOCIAUX

	Year / Année	Value / Valeur	
POPULATION			**POPULATION**
Population ('000)			Population ('000)
Both sexes	2014	93	Les deux sexes
Male	2014	47	Masculin
Female	2014	46	Féminin
Average annual growth rate	2014	0.8	Taux de croissance annuel
Active Population ('000)	2014	...	Population active ('000)
Population by age group ('000)			Population par groupe d'âge ('000)
0-14 years	2014	21	0-14 ans
15-64 years	2014	65	15-64 ans
65+ years	2014	7	65+ ans
Economically active population in agriculture (%)	...	...	Participation de la population active agricole (%)
Crude birth rate	2014	16.1	Taux brut de natalité
Crude death rate	2014	7.9	Taux brut de mortalité
Total fertility rate	2014	2.2	Indice synthétique de fécondité
Proportion of urban population	2014	54.8	Part de la population urbaine
Life Expectancy at Birth - Total (years)	2014	73.4	Espérance de vie à la naissance - Totale (ans)
Dependency Ratio - Total (%)	...	...	Taux de dépendance - Total (%)
HEALTH			**SANTÉ**
Percentage of children under-five and underweight	...	...	% d'enfants de moins de cinq ans avec insuffisance pondérale
Prevalence of undernourishment	...	...	Prévalence de la malnutrition
Under five mortality rate (both sexes, per 1000)	2013	14.2	Taux de mortalité de moins de 5 ans (les deux sexes, pour 1000)
Infant mortality rate (both sexes) per 1000	2013	12.2	Taux de mortalité infantile (les deux sexes) par 1000
Percentage of children provided the vaccines :			Pourcentage d'enfants vaccinés :
BCG	2013	99.0	BCG
DPT3	2013	98.0	DTC3
Polio	2011	99.0	Polio
Measles	2013	97.0	Rougeole
Percentage of mothers provided at least one antenatal care (%)	2009	99.8	Pourcentage de mères ayant au moins reçu un soin prénatal (%)
Percentage of deliveries attended by skilled health personnel	...	...	% d'accouchements assistés par un personnel de santé qualifié
Number of doctors (per 10 000 population)	2004	15.1	Nombre de médecins (pour 10 000 habitants)
Number of nurses (per 10 000 population)	2004	79.3	Nombre d'infirmières (pour 10 000 habitants)
Hospital beds - Total (per 10 000 population)	2011	36.0	Nombre de lits d'hôpitaux - Total (pour 10 000)
Births registered (per 1 000)	2014	16.1	Naiss.s enregistrées (pour 1 000)
Deaths registered (per 1 000)	2014	7.9	Décès enregistrés (pour 1 000)
Public expenditure on Health (% of budget)	2011	14.8	Dépenses publiques consacrées à la santé (% du budget)
EDUCATION			**EDUCATION**
Enrolment in primary education (both sexes) (000)	2012	9	Scolarisation dans le primaire (les deux sexes) (000)
Female	2012	4	Féminin
Enrolment in secondary education (both sexes) (000)	2012	8	Scolarisation dans le secondaire (les deux sexes) (000)
Female	2012	4	Féminin
Enrolment in tertiary education (both sexes) (000)	...	...	Scolarisation dans le tertiaire (les deux sexes) (000)
Female	2012	0.1	Féminin
Literacy rate (both sexes)	2012	91.8	Taux d'alphabétisation (deux sexes)
Male	2012	91.4	Masculin
Female	2012	92.3	Féminin
Pupil-teacher ratio	...	...	Ratio élève-enseignant
Public expenditure on education (% of budget)	2011	10.4	Dépenses publiques consacrées à l'enseignement (% du budget)
POVERTY			**PAUVRETÉ**
GNI Per Capita (US$)	2013	13 210.0	RNB par habitant ($EU)
Human Poverty Index (HPI-1) Value (%)	...	...	Valeur de l'Indice de pauvreté (IPH-1) (%)
Population below International Poverty Line ($2/day) (%)	2007	1.8	Population sous le seuil international de pauvreté (2$/J) (%)
Share of Income Held by Richest 10%	2007	60.2	% de revenu des 10% plus riches
Share of Income Held by Poorest 10%	2007	1.6	% de revenu des 10% plus pauvres
Gini index	2007	65.8	Indice de Gini

Charts / Graphiques

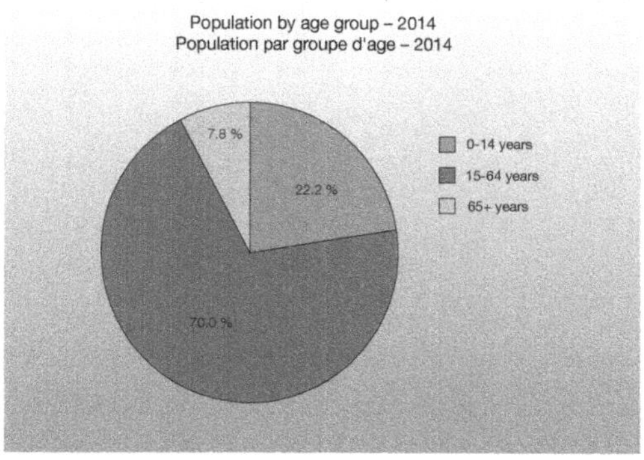

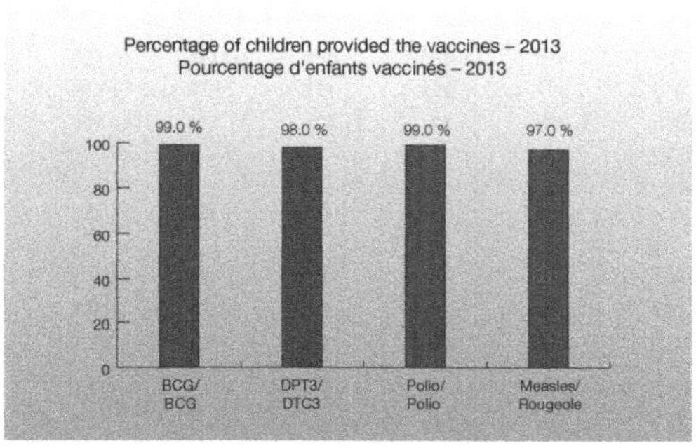

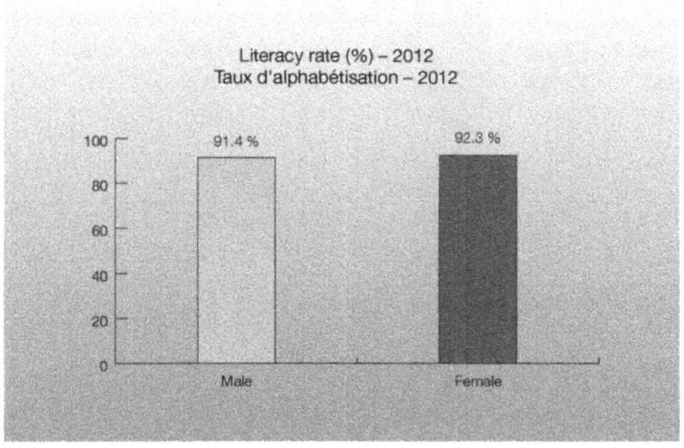

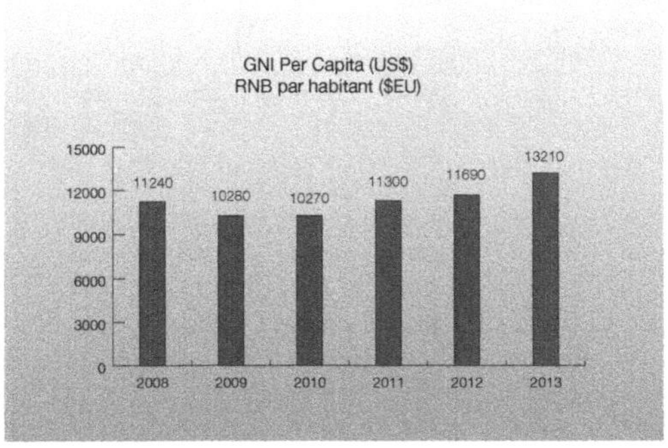

SEYCHELLES

II NATIONAL ACCOUNTS — COMPTES NATIONAUX

	2006	2007	2008	2009	2010	2011	2012	2013	2014	
GROSS DOMESTIC PRODUCT BY KIND OF ECONOMIC ACTIVITY AT CURRENT PRICES *SEYCHELLES RUPEE (MILLIONS)*										**PRODUIT INTÉRIEUR BRUT PAR BRANCHE D'ACTIVITÉ ÉCONOMIQUE AUX PRIX COURANTS** *RUPEE (MILLIONS)*
Agriculture, hunting, forestry and fishing	167	190	235	260	265	293	304	427	399	Agriculture, chasse sylviculture et pêche
Mining and quarrying	-	-	-	-	-	-	-	-	-	Industries extractives
Manufacturing	503	663	850	902	940	964	1 217	1 327	1 644	Industries manufacturières
Electricity, gas & water	104	90	93	147	167	57	210	409	436	Electricité, gaz et eau
Construction & public works	305	361	486	568	534	788	634	457	543	Bâtiments et travaux publics
Wholesale & retail trade, restaurants, hotels	914	1 523	2 264	2 955	2 788	3 171	4 059	3 928	4 452	Commerce de gros et de détail, restaurants et hôtels
Finance, insurance, real estate, etc.	1 081	1 316	1 797	2 619	2 798	3 070	3 709	3 981	4 464	Banques, assurances, affaires immobilières
Transport and communications	842	948	1 183	1 453	1 269	1 388	1 455	2 469	2 280	Transport(s) et communications
Public administration and defense	518	590	622	559	604	731	852	1 012	1 263	Administrations publiques et défense
Education	212	231	258	243	261	305	342	361	399	Education
Health and Social Work	150	145	157	161	170	208	237	272	361	Santé et actions sociales
Other services	79	83	93	121	126	144	176	179	225	Autres services
Less Imputed Service Charges	- 100	- 132	- 188	- 225	- 182	- 205	- 275	- 255	- 227	Moins services d'intermédiation financière
Gross domestic product at factor cost / basic prices	4 775	6 010	7 850	9 765	9 740	10 913	12 920	14 568	16 240	Produit intérieur brut aux couts des facteurs / prix de base
Plus: indirect taxes / taxes on products, less subsidies	835	916	1 298	1 768	1 965	2 283	2 623	2 447	3 017	Plus taxes indirectes/impôts sur les produits, moins les subventions
EXPENDITURE ON GROSS DOMESTIC PRODUCT AT CURRENT PURCHASER'S VALUES *SEYCHELLES RUPEE (MILLIONS)*										**EMPLOI DU PRODUIT INTÉRIEUR BRUT AUX PRIX COURANTS D'ACQUISITION** *RUPEE (MILLIONS)*
Government final consumption	2 210	2 652	2 497	3 308	3 183	3 496	4 045	4 797	4 682	Consommation finale des administrations publiques
Private final consumption	2 797	2 935	5 951	7 221	6 908	7 915	9 006	7 595	11 188	Consommation finale privée
Gross fixed capital formation	1 510	1 884	2 249	2 934	4 142	4 569	5 812	6 398	6 500	Formation brute de capital fixe
Change in inventories	...	...	...	...	...	...	...	...	...	Variation des stocks
Exports of goods and services	4 733	5 813	8 705	11 566	10 146	11 730	12 776	13 300	13 967	Exportations de biens et services
Less imports of goods and services	5 640	6 357	10 255	13 495	12 673	14 514	16 095	15 074	17 079	Moins importations de biens et services
GDP at purchasers' values	5 610	6 926	9 147	11 533	11 705	13 196	15 544	17 015	19 258	PIB aux prix d'acquisition
GROSS DOMESTIC PRODUCT BY KIND OF ECONOMIC ACTIVITY AT CONSTANT PRICES *ANNUAL GROWTH RATES (%)*										**PRODUIT INTÉRIEUR BRUT PAR BRANCHE D'ACTIVITÉ ECONOMIQUE AUX PRIX CONSTANTS** *TAUX DE CROISSANCE ANNUEL (%)*
Agriculture, hunting, forestry and fishing	- 5.4	0.8	4.6	- 16.5	- 6.2	3.5	- 1.0	26.1	- 5.2	Agriculture, chasse sylviculture et pêche
Mining and quarrying	...	...	...	...	...	...	...	...	...	Industries extractives
Manufacturing	3.2	3.5	- 12.4	- 11.3	8.4	7.0	0.6	25.6	- 6.3	Industries manufacturières
Electricity, gas & water	3.9	12.0	- 3.6	- 2.3	12.9	10.9	185.7	- 53.3	0.0	Electricité, gaz et eau
Construction & public works	15.8	10.0	11.4	- 4.9	- 5.3	27.6	- 14.5	- 42.1	17.6	Bâtiments et travaux publics
Wholesale & retail trade, restaurants, hotels	13.3	20.5	- 10.6	3.3	12.8	6.8	3.9	16.4	2.5	Commerce de gros et de détail,restaurants et hôtels
Finance, insurance, real estate, etc.	13.1	13.0	6.7	9.2	8.2	7.6	8.7	5.1	7.3	Banques, assurances, affaires immobilières
Transport and communications	7.9	10.3	2.4	- 1.9	3.5	5.1	2.9	16.1	23.9	Transport(s) et communications
Public administration and defense	14.8	2.1	1.3	- 12.6	- 15.2	12.5	1.5	5.0	2.5	Administrations publiques et défense
Education	3.1	1.2	- 3.2	2.4	5.1	- 2.4	1.7	3.3	5.4	Education
Health and Social Work	3.4	2.2	- 2.4	- 9.1	5.0	- 9.1	3.2	21.3	3.2	Santé et actions sociales
Other services	4.5	2.4	- 18.4	9.7	5.5	11.1	2.8	11.9	8.8	Autres services
Less Imputed Service Charges	11.9	14.4	23.6	- 0.2	- 13.0	7.3	15.5	- 21.4	- 2.0	Moins services d'intérmediation financière
Gross domestic product at factor cost / basic prices	9.6	10.1	- 1.5	- 0.7	5.2	7.7	7.1	5.9	7.5	Produit intérieur brut aux couts des facteurs / prix de base
Plus: indirect taxes / taxes on products, less subsidies	8.5	12.4	- 5.5	- 3.6	10.3	9.0	5.5	13.8	15.0	Plus taxes indirectes/impôts sur les produits, moins les subventions
Gross domestic product at market prices	9.4	10.4	- 2.1	- 1.1	5.9	7.9	6.8	7.0	8.7	Produit intérieur brut aux prix du marché
EXPENDITURE ON GROSS DOMESTIC PRODUCT AT CONSTANT PURCHASERS' VALUES *ANNUAL GROWTH RATES (%)*										**EMPLOIS DU PRODUIT INTÉRIEUR BRUT AUX PRIX CONSTANTS D'ACQUISITION** *TAUX DE CROISSANCE ANNUEL (%)*
Government final consumption	24.8	0.2	- 26.8	0.8	- 1.6	10.5	6.1	7.0	8.7	Consommation finale des administrations publiques
Private final consumption	- 1.8	7.6	39.3	- 20.1	26.5	21.4	7.0	7.0	8.7	Consommation finale privée
Gross fixed capital formation	- 6.8	- 4.8	- 15.3	- 5.1	47.8	0.6	11.4	7.0	8.7	Formation brute de capital fixe
Exports of goods and services	17.9	9.5	- 10.3	14.3	- 15.5	- 5.2	0.6	7.0	8.7	Exportations de biens et services
Less imports of goods and services	10.0	0.2	- 0.6	- 2.8	4.3	6.2	3.6	7.0	8.7	Moins importations de biens et services
Notes	NA: 2014 Provisional							CN: 2014 Provisoire		Notes

III INFLATION

	2006	2007	2008	2009	2010	2011	2012	2013	2014	
ANNUAL GROWTH RATES (%)										**TAUX DE CROISSANCE ANNUEL (%)**
All items	-1.9	5.3	37.0	31.7	-2.4	2.6	7.1	4.3	1.4	Ensemble
of which:										dont:
Food and Non-alcoholic beverages	1.6	5.8	34.9	51.2	-4.7	-0.1	11.3	5.5	-0.3	Alimentation et boissons non alcoolisés
Alcoholic beverages & tobacco	...	5.7	32.9	41.5	-4.0	0.1	4.5	4.2	0.1	Boissons alcoolisées et tabacs
Clothing and Footwear	...	10.7	31.4	26.8	2.5	3.7	6.1	6.4	9.6	Habillement et chaussures
Housing, Water, Electricity, Gas and Other Fuels	-0.7	0.4	63.2	12.0	3.4	1.0	14.4	2.4	1.1	Logement, eau, électricité, gas et autres combustibles
Furnishing, household equip	...	7.5	18.0	25.1	-0.2	1.1	3.7	6.1	1.5	Meubles, articles de ménage et entretien courant
Health	4.0	10.9	18.3	13.6	0.4	1.9	5.8	3.9	2.4	Santé
Transport	1.1	9.4	52.3	32.8	-7.3	5.0	9.9	0.7	1.0	Transport
Communication	...	-5.1	10.6	25.1	-0.3	0.0	0.4	0.0	0.3	Communication
Recreation & culture	...	10.8	27.8	30.8	-7.1	5.6	8.7	5.4	8.4	Loisirs et culture
Education	...	0.8	0.3	19.8	4.4	-	15.2	7.9	-	Enseignement
Restaurants & hotels	...	14.0	29.2	17.5	3.3	4.5	13.9	9.4	1.7	Restaurants et hôtels
Miscellaneous goods & services	...	3.9	22.1	24.2	-6.0	1.5	4.8	2.6	3.3	Biens et services divers

IV AGRICULTURAL PRODUCTION - PRODUCTION AGRICOLE	2006	2007	2008	2009	2010	2011	2012	2013	2014	
TONNES *(THOUSAND)*										**TONNES** *(MILLIERS)*
Coconuts	3	2	2	2	2	2	3	3	...	Noix de coco
Banana	2	2	2	2	2	2	2	2	...	Banane
cassava	0	0	0	0	0	0	0	0	...	Manioc
Tomato	0	0	0	0	0	0	0	0	...	Tomates
Pineapple	...	...	...	...	...	...	...	...	...	Ananas

V MINING PRODUCTION - PRODUCTION MINIERE	2006	2007	2008	2009	2010	2011	2012	2013	2014	
	...	...	...	...	...	...	...	...	...	
	...	...	...	...	...	...	...	...	...	
	...	...	...	...	...	...	...	...	...	

VI ENERGY - ENERGIE	2006	2007	2008	2009	2010	2011	2012	2013	2014	
Total electricity generation (GWh)	821	903	947	825	283	401	405	409	...	Production d'électricité totale (GWh)
of which:										dont:
Production of electricity from fossil fuels (GWh)	237	255	253	259	283	400	404	408	...	Production d'électricité à partir de combustibles fossiles (GWh)
Production of hydro electricity (GWh)	...	...	...	...	...	...	...	...	...	Production d'électricité d'origine hydraulique (GWh)
Production of electricity from solar, wind, tide, wave and other sources (GWh)	...	...	...	...	...	1	1	1	...	Production d'électricité d'origine solaire, éolienne, marée motrice et autres (GWh)

VII TOURISM AND INFRASTRUCTURE - TOURISME ET INFRASTRUCTURE	2006	2007	2008	2009	2010	2011	2012	2013	2014	
VII-1 TOURISM										**VII-1 TOURISME**
International tourist arrivals (thousands)	141	161	159	158	175	194	208	230	232	Arrivées de touristes internationaux (milliers)
Rooms in hotels and similar establishments (thousands)	2	3	3	2	3	3	3	...	...	Chambres d'hotels et établissements assimilés (milliers)
Overnight stays (thousands)	1 378	1 597	1 605	1 607	1 815	1 945	2 060	2 349	2 515	Nuitées (milliers)
Tourism receipts (US$ thousand)	227 800	325 800	308 700	256 500	274 400	291 000	310 300	343 600	340 767	Recettes touristiques (milliers de $ EU)
Total contribution to GDP (%)	60.5	68.5	67.4	69.7	64.3	64.2	62.8	58.1	57.5	Contribution totale au PIB (%)
Total contribution to Employment (%)	58.8	68.3	69.5	69.9	63.5	65.5	63.0	58.2	57.9	Contribution totale à l'emploi (%)
VII-2 INFRASTRUCTURE										**VII-2 INFRASTRUCTURE**
Paved roads (% of total)	96	96	96	96	96	96	...	...	...	Routes asphaltées (% du total)
Total Network (Railways-km)	...	...	...	...	...	...	...	...	...	Réseau total voies ferrées-Km
Main Telephone Lines (per 100 inhabitants)	23	25	25	29	24	30	23	23	...	Lignes téléphoniques fixes (pour 100 habitants)
Mobile Cellular Subscribers (per 100 inhabitants)	80	87	104	122	129	138	148	147	...	Abonnés aux téléphones mobiles (pour 100 habitants)

VIII EXTERNAL TRADE - COMMERCE EXTERIEUR	2006	2007	2008	2009	2010	2011	2012	2013	2014	
US$ (MILLIONS) **EXPORTS, FOB**										**$ E.U (MILLIONS)** **EXPORTATIONS, FÀB**
Exports - Total	420	398	437	431	402	439	497	578	539	Exportations - Total
Exports to AFRICA	...	...	...	...	...	...	...	3	...	Exportations vers l'AFRIQUE
Main Products										**Principaux produits**
Canned tuna	184	215	219	197	242	242	249	351	...	Thon en conserve
Crustaceans	2	2	...	...	...	...	...	...	...	Crustacés
Frozen and fresh fish	2	2	2	2	2	2	1	1	...	Poissons frais et congelés
Shark Fins (Dried)	...	...	...	...	...	...	...	...	...	Requin Fins (Séché)
Cinnamon bark	...	...	...	...	...	...	...	...	...	Écorce de cannelle
Main Destinations										**Principales destinations**
United Kingdom	88	79	93	118	76	88	143	113	...	Royaume-Uni
France	59	66	87	88	71	106	155	162	...	France
Italy	40	20	30	45	45	39	67	61	...	Italie
Japan	23	21	29	33	43	0	2	3	...	Japon
Spain	29	13	14	23	13	0	0	0	...	Espagne
IMPORTS, CIF										**IMPORTATIONS, CAF**
Imports - Total	855	696	1 089	796	984	1 006	1 020	1 078	1 081	Importations - Total (millions)
Imports from Africa	82	168	117	110	210	128	104	108	...	Importations en provenance de l'Afrique
Main Products										**Principaux produits**
Petroleum, petroleum products and related materials	200	214	125	180	172	246	327	275	...	Pétrole et produits dérivés
Other transport equipment	27	95	88	81	74	85	76	80	...	Autres matériels de transport
Fish, crustaceans, molluscs and preparations thereof	95	103	63	74	68	132	161	171	...	Poissons, crustacés, mollusques et préparations
Road vehicles	24	32	42	31	29	38	29	23	...	Véhicules routiers
Manufactures of metal, n.e.s.	39	34	41	32	27	32	30	30	...	Articles manufacturés en métal, n.d.a.
Main Origin										**Principales provenances**
Spain	70	97	68	65	107	107	116	129	...	Espagne
France	78	123	56	58	60	63	72	82	...	France
Singapore	53	152	46	57	60	63	38	40	...	Singapour
South Africa	58	57	58	61	70	72	56	54	...	Afrique du Sud
Saudi Arabia	0	0	0	1	1	1	1	1	...	Arabie Saoudite

IX FINANCIAL AND MONETARY STATISTICS - FINANCES ET STATISTIQUES MONETAIRES	2006	2007	2008	2009	2010	2011	2012	2013	2014	
IX-1 MONETARY STATISTICS *SEYCHELLES RUPEE (MILLIONS)*										**IX-1 STATISTIQUES MONÉTAIRES** *RUPEE (MILLIONS)*
Money supply (M1)	5 040	4 640	5 980	6 400	7 270	7 600	7 550	9 340	10 500	Masse monétaire (M1)
Quasi-money	2 387	1 372	1 211	1 617	1 921	1 264	1 204	1 398	1 529	Quasi-monnaie
of which Demand Deposit	...	...	...	...	...	...	...	...	...	dont Monnaie scripturale
Net foreign assets	530	421	2 094	2 751	3 489	4 262	5 072	7 081	9 146	Avoirs extérieurs nets
Domestic credit	4 799	5 282	6 037	4 966	5 807	5 796	5 306	6 047	5 985	Crédit intérieur
of which claims on private sector	1 277	1 717	2 550	2 315	2 861	2 936	3 114	3 412	4 273	dont créances sur le secteur privé
of which claims on government sector, net	3 228	3 178	2 931	2 235	2 559	2 380	1 760	2 335	1 414	dont créances nettes sur le gouvernement
International reserves (millions US$)	113	41	64	191	256	279	308	426	465	Réserves internationales (millions $EU)
Average Exchange Rate (National Currency per US$)	5.52	6.70	9.46	13.61	12.07	12.38	13.70	12.07	12.27	Taux de change (moyen) (monnaie nationale par $ EU)
IX-2 PUBLIC FINANCE *SEYCHELLES RUPEE (MILLIONS)*										**IX-2 FINANCES PUBLIQUES** *RUPEE (MILLIONS)*
Total Revenues and Grants	2 476	2 209	3 137	4 109	4 108	5 054	6 074	5 816	5 955	Recettes totales et dons
Tax Revenue	1 371	1 636	2 456	3 295	3 533	4 165	4 600	4 676	4 747	Recettes fiscales
Non Tax Revenue	1 033	556	412	497	474	569	772	796	835	Recettes non fiscales
Grants	73	17	268	317	101	319	702	343	372	Dons
Total Expenditures and Net Lending	2 302	2 805	2 856	4 179	4 704	5 824	7 046	5 656	5 785	Dépenses totales et prêts nets
Current expenditure	1 900	2 494	2 398	3 942	4 084	4 755	5 440	4 490	4 320	Dépenses courantes
Of which Wages and Salaries	760	779	725	736	677	866	965	1 068	1 081	Dont rémunérations et salaires
Capital expenditure	404	374	341	608	1 009	1 061	1 613	1 160	1 341	Dépenses d'équipement
Net Lending	- 2	- 63	117	- 372	- 389	9	- 6	6	124	Prêts nets
Fiscal Balance	174	- 596	281	- 70	- 596	- 771	- 972	159	169	Solde global y compris les dons
IX-3 BALANCE OF PAYMENTS *SEYCHELLES RUPEE (MILLIONS)*										**IX-3 BALANCE DES PAIEMENTS** *RUPEE (MILLIONS)*
Trade balance	- 1 602	- 1 894	- 3 820	- 4 087	- 4 361	- 5 147	- 6 441	- 5 128	- 6 668	Balance commerciale
Services Balance	862	1 149	2 322	2 949	1 929	2 412	3 130	3 353	3 556	Balance des services
Net Income	- 241	- 429	- 641	- 631	- 567	- 630	- 834	- 916	- 819	Revenus nets
Compensation of employees	- 41	- 30	- 58	- 105	- 26	- 25	...	...	...	Rémunération des salariés
Investment Income	- 200	- 400	- 584	- 526	- 542	- 605	- 592	...	...	Revenus des investissements
Current transfers, net total	243	98	308	651	306	430	328	- 133	146	Transferts courants
Net official transfers	...	...	...	...	...	...	...	...	...	Transferts officiels nets
Workers' remittances	...	...	...	...	...	...	...	...	...	Envois de fonds des travailleurs
Other private transfers	...	...	...	...	...	...	...	...	...	Autres transferts privés
Current account balance	- 738	- 1 077	- 1 832	- 1 119	- 2 693	- 2 935	- 3 817	- 2 823	- 3 785	Solde du compte courant
Capital & financial account	1 074	1 414	- 1 146	2 059	5 791	2 832	3 038	...	...	Comptes de capital et financier
Capital account	73	55	48	712	3 321	751	828	...	...	Compte de capital
Financial account	1 001	1 359	- 1 194	1 347	2 470	2 081	2 210	...	...	Compte financier
Errors & omissions	9	74	143	335	710	457	529	...	...	Erreurs et omissions
Overall balance	- 583	411	- 2 835	1 275	3 808	354	402	...	...	Balance générale

X DEBT AND FINANCIAL FLOWS - DETTE ET FLUX FINANCIERS	2006	2007	2008	2009	2010	2011	2012	2013	2014	
X-1 DEBT *US$ (MILLIONS)*										**X-1 DETTE EXTÉRIEURE** *$ E.U (MILLIONS)*
Total external debt	521	710	798	761	478	490	512	521	549	Dette extérieure totale
Private	295	454	496	509	238	230	238	230	222	Privée
Public	226	256	302	252	240	260	274	291	327	Publique
Total external debt service	119	94	106	115	72	22	22	42	45	Service de la dette extérieure
Present value of External debt	...	...	...	...	...	...	...	...	...	Valeur actuelle de la dette extérieure
Total government domestic debt (in local currency)	...	...	...	...	...	...	...	...	...	Dette publique intérieure
X-2 FINANCIAL FLOWS *US$ (MILLIONS)*										**X-2 FLUX FINANCIERS** *$ E.U (MILLIONS)*
Net Foreign Direct Investment Inflows	146	239	130	171	211	207	166	178	...	Investissements étranger direct (flux nets entrants)
Main origin of FDI Inflows										**Principales origines de l'IDE entrant:**
Belgium	...	...	9	...	2.6	9.7	- 12.9	...	...	Belgique
Netherlands	3	1	...	...	...	...	...	...	...	Pays-Bas
United States	...	...	...	...	...	...	...	...	...	États-Unis
United Kingdom	...	...	...	- 8	...	8.0	...	...	...	Royaume-Uni
Hungary	...	4	1	3	2.3	- 0.5	- 3.3	...	...	Hongrie
African countries	...	...	...	...	...	...	...	...	...	Pays africains
Net total Official Development Assistance	14	11	13	23	56	22	36	25	...	Aide publique au développement (nette totale)
Main origin of Net ODA										**Principales origines de l'APD nette**
United Arab Emirates	...	2	...	...	17.4	5.9	12.0	...	...	Emirats arabes unis
France	3	1	3	2	10.5	2.4	1.6	4.1	...	France
Japan	2	1	2	9	9.6	1.2	1.8	0.6	...	Japon
GEF	...	6	6	1	3.4	1.4	2.1	...	...	FEM
BADEA	1	...	...	- 1	2.4	2.4	1.5	...	...	BADEA
General notes	National Accounts : The data for 2014 are estimates based on the sum of four quarters of 2014.					Comptes Nationaux: Les données de L'année 2014 sont estimées à partir des comptes trimestriels				Notes générales

SEYCHELLES

SIERRA LEONE

AREA (KM²)		71 740	SUPERFICIE (KM²)
CAPITAL CITY	Freetown	Freetown	CAPITALE
CURRENCY	Leone	Leone	MONNAIE

I SOCIAL AND DEMOGRAPHIC INDICATORS — INDICATEURS DEMOGRAPHIQUES ET SOCIAUX

	Year / Année	Value / Valeur	
POPULATION			**POPULATION**
Population ('000)			Population ('000)
Both sexes	2014	6 205	Les deux sexes
Male	2014	3 082	Masculin
Female	2014	3 123	Féminin
Average annual growth rate	2014	1.9	Taux de croissance annuel
Active Population ('000)	2014	2 456	Population active ('000)
Population by age group ('000)			Population par groupe d'âge ('000)
0-14 years	2014	2 559	0-14 ans
15-64 years	2014	3 480	15-64 ans
65+ years	2014	166	65+ ans
Economically active population in agriculture (%)	2014	56.8	Participation de la population active agricole (%)
Crude birth rate	2014	36.0	Taux brut de natalité
Crude death rate	2014	17.0	Taux brut de mortalité
Total fertility rate	2014	4.6	Indice synthétique de fécondité
Proportion of urban population	2014	40.4	Part de la population urbaine
Life Expectancy at Birth - Total (years)	2014	45.8	Espérance de vie à la naissance - Totale (ans)
Dependency Ratio - Total (%)	2014	78.9	Taux de dépendance - Total (%)
HEALTH			**SANTÉ**
Percentage of children under-five and underweight	2010	39.7	% d'enfants de moins de cinq ans avec insuffisance pondérale
Prevalence of undernourishment	2013	25.5	Prévalence de la malnutrition
Under five mortality rate (both sexes, per 1000)	2013	160.6	Taux de mortalité de moins de 5 ans (les deux sexes, pour 1000)
Infant mortality rate (both sexes) per 1000	2013	107.2	Taux de mortalité infantile (les deux sexes) par 1000
Percentage of children provided the vaccines :			Pourcentage d'enfants vaccinés :
BCG	2013	99.0	BCG
DPT3	2013	92.0	DTC3
Polio	2012	81.0	Polio
Measles	2013	83.0	Rougeole
Percentage of mothers provided at least one antenatal care (%)	2008	59.1	Pourcentage de mères ayant au moins reçu un soin prénatal (%)
Percentage of deliveries attended by skilled health personnel	2010	62.5	% d'accouchements assistés par un personnel de santé qualifié
Number of doctors (per 10 000 population)	2010	0.2	Nombre de médecins (pour 10 000 habitants)
Number of nurses (per 10 000 population)	2010	1.7	Nombre d'infirmières (pour 10 000 habitants)
Hospital beds - Total (per 10 000 population)	2006	4.0	Nombre de lits d'hôpitaux - Total (pour 10 000)
Births registered (per 1 000)	2014	36.0	Naiss.s enregistrées (pour 1 000)
Deaths registered (per 1 000)	2014	17.0	Décès enregistrés (pour 1 000)
Public expenditure on Health (% of budget)	2012	8.9	Dépenses publiques consacrées à la santé (% du budget)
EDUCATION			**EDUCATION**
Enrolment in primary education (both sexes) (000)	2013	1 300	Scolarisation dans le primaire (les deux sexes) (000)
Female	2013	651	Féminin
Enrolment in secondary education (both sexes) (000)	2013	417	Scolarisation dans le secondaire (les deux sexes) (000)
Female	2013	195	Féminin
Enrolment in tertiary education (both sexes) (000)	...	...	Scolarisation dans le tertiaire (les deux sexes) (000)
Female	2002	2.6	Féminin
Literacy rate (both sexes)	2012	44.5	Taux d'alphabétisation (deux sexes)
Male	2012	55.5	Masculin
Female	2012	33.7	Féminin
Pupil-teacher ratio	...	...	Ratio élève-enseignant
Public expenditure on education (% of budget)	2012	14.1	Dépenses publiques consacrées à l'enseignement (% du budget)
POVERTY			**PAUVRETÉ**
GNI Per Capita (US$)	2013	660.0	RNB par habitant ($EU)
Human Poverty Index (HPI-1) Value (%)	2007	47.7	Valeur de l'Indice de pauvreté (IPH-1) (%)
Population below International Poverty Line ($2/day) (%)	2011	82.5	Population sous le seuil international de pauvreté (2$/J) (%)
Share of Income Held by Richest 10%	2011	28.7	% de revenu des 10% plus riches
Share of Income Held by Poorest 10%	2011	3.4	% de revenu des 10% plus pauvres
Gini index	2011	35.4	Indice de Gini

Charts / Graphiques

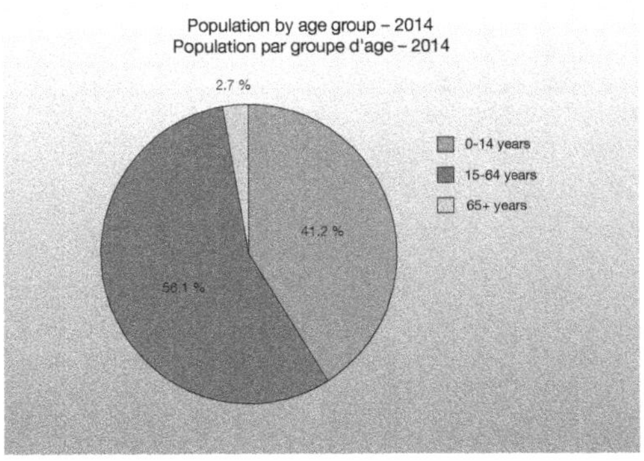

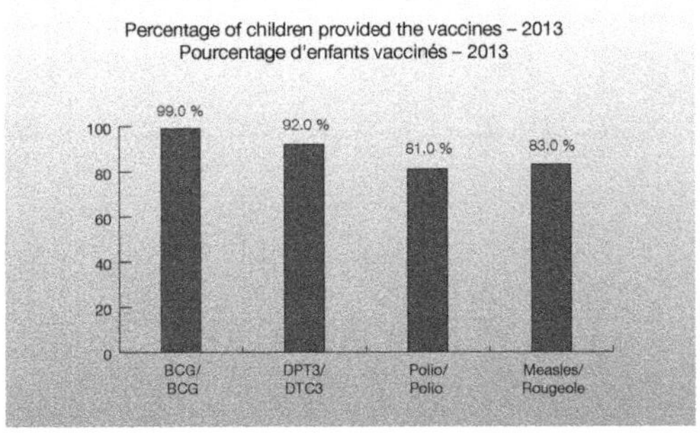

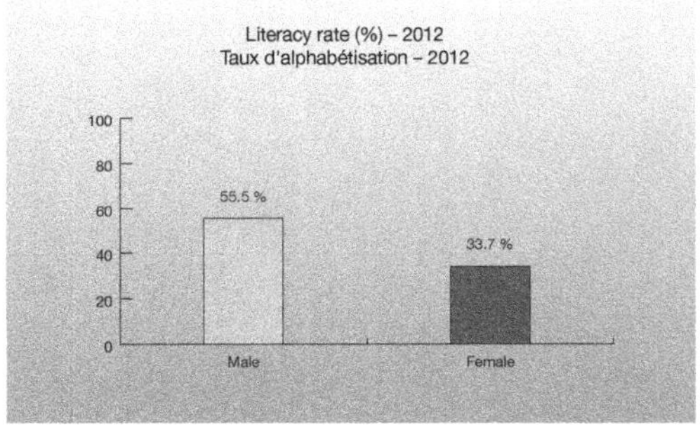

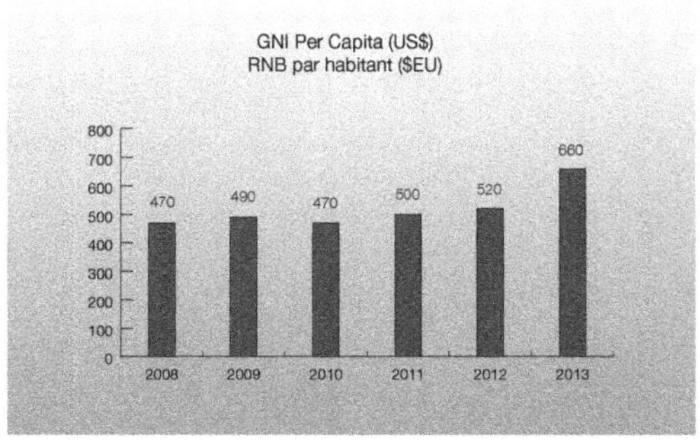

II NATIONAL ACCOUNTS — COMPTES NATIONAUX

	2006	2007	2008	2009	2010	2011	2012	2013	2014	
GROSS DOMESTIC PRODUCT BY KIND OF ECONOMIC ACTIVITY AT CURRENT PRICES *LEONE (MILLIONS)*										**PRODUIT INTÉRIEUR BRUT PAR BRANCHE D'ACTIVITÉ ÉCONOMIQUE AUX PRIX COURANTS** *LEONE (MILLIONS)*
Agriculture, hunting, forestry and fishing	2 808 186	3 361 971	4 007 950	4 591 100	5 429 597	6 986 661	8 355 508	10 215 233	11 530 750	Agriculture, chasse sylviculture et pêche
Mining and quarrying	302 038	326 583	265 961	240 340	410 642	528 777	1 831 856	4 130 680	4 607 057	Industries extractives
Manufacturing	146 348	159 175	182 041	176 800	223 299	288 488	333 221	349 867	373 744	Industries manufacturières
Electricity, gas & water	24 322	22 237	16 912	17 512	24 443	30 237	37 805	43 890	60 501	Electricité, gaz et eau
Construction & public works	114 733	113 222	120 307	109 294	139 643	159 623	197 533	209 255	204 493	Bâtiments et travaux publics
Wholesale & retail trade, restaurants, hotels	414 481	478 171	655 359	738 286	941 678	1 206 762	1 454 408	1 649 055	1 752 731	Commerce de gros et de détail, restaurants et hôtels
Finance, insurance, real estate, etc.	539 491	577 817	662 966	724 676	889 152	1 081 359	1 264 558	1 353 749	1 463 125	Banques, assurances, affaires immobilières
Transport and communications	347 047	390 587	473 909	528 442	586 426	688 455	733 836	804 167	866 843	Transport(s) et communications
Public administration and defense	246 741	257 834	259 292	292 214	421 261	582 853	768 132	901 388	1 013 589	Administrations publiques et défense
Education	114 017	137 794	214 918	203 609	237 666	290 722	350 979	379 766	411 435	Education
Health and Social Work	172 759	231 904	257 441	273 170	437 171	479 580	538 252	564 594	610 579	Santé et actions sociales
Other services	77 066	71 237	98 331	114 276	103 417	137 208	211 660	192 889	202 310	Autres services
Less Imputed Service Charges	- 71 068	- 81 357	- 102 208	- 121 928	- 152 963	- 186 728	- 224 582	- 252 006	- 275 308	Moins services d'intermédiation financière
Gross domestic product at factor cost / basic prices	5 236 162	6 047 174	7 113 179	7 887 791	9 691 432	12 273 997	15 853 166	20 542 527	22 821 849	Produit intérieur brut aux couts des facteurs / prix de base
Plus: indirect taxes / taxes on products, less subsidies	280 799	302 727	357 365	420 503	564 711	478 940	607 489	744 146	909 649	Plus taxes indirectes/impôts sur les produits, moins les subventions
EXPENDITURE ON GROSS DOMESTIC PRODUCT AT CURRENT PURCHASER'S VALUES *LEONE (MILLIONS)*										**EMPLOI DU PRODUIT INTÉRIEUR BRUT AUX PRIX COURANTS D'ACQUISITION** *LEONE (MILLIONS)*
Government final consumption	563 877	557 136	721 134	873 436	1 066 555	1 289 136	1 693 056	1 855 847	2 146 741	Consommation finale des administrations publiques
Private final consumption	4 834 028	5 772 042	6 944 974	7 804 027	7 815 188	11 161 180	13 414 129	16 957 725	15 680 489	Consommation finale privée
Gross fixed capital formation	552 922	580 756	684 423	799 404	3 150 100	5 315 874	4 082 899	2 968 030	3 017 591	Formation brute de capital fixe
Change in inventories	22 980	25 568	29 500	30 859	38 276	49 952	517 693	- 255 246	411 774	Variation des stocks
Exports of goods and services	941 684	1 005 419	1 009 892	1 121 567	1 722 427	2 081 749	5 394 184	9 515 288	15 452 990	Exportations de biens et services
Less imports of goods and services	1 398 530	1 591 020	1 919 379	2 320 999	3 536 401	7 144 955	8 641 304	9 754 969	12 978 090	Moins importations de biens et services
GDP at purchasers' values	5 516 961	6 349 901	7 470 544	8 308 293	10 256 144	12 752 935	16 460 656	21 286 675	23 731 496	PIB aux prix d'acquisition
GROSS DOMESTIC PRODUCT BY KIND OF ECONOMIC ACTIVITY AT CONSTANT PRICES *ANNUAL GROWTH RATES (%)*										**PRODUIT INTÉRIEUR BRUT PAR BRANCHE D'ACTIVITÉ ECONOMIQUE AUX PRIX CONSTANTS** *TAUX DE CROISSANCE ANNUEL (%)*
Agriculture, hunting, forestry and fishing	6.0	13.3	6.7	4.0	3.5	4.9	3.8	4.6	3.4	Agriculture, chasse sylviculture et pêche
Mining and quarrying	3.7	5.2	- 30.3	- 0.9	15.7	1.8	297.0	129.7	16.4	Industries extractives
Manufacturing	16.4	1.1	1.5	- 6.8	9.1	15.0	4.0	2.4	1.3	Industries manufacturières
Electricity, gas & water	- 3.2	- 37.6	187.8	- 8.8	2.7	3.9	5.6	- 18.6	3.1	Electricité, gaz et eau
Construction & public works	1.6	4.2	- 4.9	- 8.3	13.2	24.1	12.0	6.2	- 4.6	Bâtiments et travaux publics
Wholesale & retail trade, restaurants, hotels	0.6	3.5	19.7	3.4	8.5	8.1	5.5	7.3	3.2	Commerce de gros et de détail,restaurants et hôtels
Finance, insurance, real estate, etc.	3.0	- 4.9	0.8	4.0	4.0	2.8	3.4	3.4	3.7	Banques, assurances, affaires immobilières
Transport and communications	- 2.1	12.3	24.3	8.8	4.0	5.3	5.8	4.4	2.7	Transport(s) et communications
Public administration and defense	9.3	- 6.4	- 12.4	3.2	22.4	16.8	15.9	14.0	9.3	Administrations publiques et défense
Education	- 9.4	20.2	56.0	- 6.1	5.1	6.7	4.2	5.0	5.3	Education
Health and Social Work	2.2	1.4	3.3	3.3	4.8	3.2	4.1	2.8	6.6	Santé et actions sociales
Other services	- 0.4	- 7.3	16.2	11.0	2.6	4.4	5.6	5.3	5.9	Autres services
Less Imputed Service Charges	- 0.2	2.5	9.4	9.2	7.9	3.0	5.7	5.9	3.5	Moins services d'intermédiation financière
Gross domestic product at factor cost / basic prices	4.3	8.0	6.8	3.2	5.4	6.0	15.7	20.8	6.7	Produit intérieur brut aux couts des facteurs / prix de base
Plus: indirect taxes / taxes on products, less subsidies	4.3	8.0	5.5	3.2	5.3	5.8	5.3	5.5	3.5	Plus taxes indirectes/impôts sur les produits, moins les subventions
Gross domestic product at market prices	4.3	8.0	6.7	3.2	5.4	6.0	15.2	20.1	6.6	Produit intérieur brut aux prix du marché
EXPENDITURE ON GROSS DOMESTIC PRODUCT AT CONSTANT PURCHASERS' VALUES *ANNUAL GROWTH RATES (%)*										**EMPLOIS DU PRODUIT INTÉRIEUR BRUT AUX PRIX CONSTANTS D'ACQUISITION** *TAUX DE CROISSANCE ANNUEL (%)*
Government final consumption	9.2	- 11.5	12.7	10.9	3.7	2.0	15.5	6.5	12.4	Consommation finale des administrations publiques
Private final consumption	1.0	9.8	8.8	7.4	- 10.2	24.4	11.8	5.1	- 15.1	Consommation finale privée
Gross fixed capital formation	- 3.4	- 1.5	6.7	9.0	239.9	42.2	- 18.4	- 25.4	- 1.6	Formation brute de capital fixe
Exports of goods and services	7.7	1.1	- 15.9	8.0	18.8	- 1.3	152.2	91.5	61.2	Exportations de biens et services
Less imports of goods and services	- 5.6	- 2.1	2.2	28.8	39.8	73.9	18.0	8.7	20.7	Moins importations de biens et services
Notes	2012-2014:provisional								2012-2014:provisoire	Notes

III INFLATION

	2006	2007	2008	2009	2010	2011	2012	2013	2014	
ANNUAL GROWTH RATES (%)										**TAUX DE CROISSANCE ANNUEL (%)**
All items	9.7	11.6	14.8	9.3	17.8	18.5	13.8	9.9	8.3	Ensemble
of which:										dont:
Food and Non-alcoholic beverages	7.8	13.6	20.6	14.2	17.7	21.4	16.3	12.7	11.8	Alimentation et boissons non alcoolisés
Alcoholic beverages & tobacco	...	...	10.2	1.8	17.6	5.8	25.4	9.0	3.7	Boissons alcoolisées et tabacs
Clothing and Footwear	...	...	6.5	25.4	10.6	0.9	0.0	1.7	8.7	Habillement et chaussures
Housing, Water, Electricity, Gas and Other Fuels	14.0	9.6	6.5	-15.0	10.9	13.0	13.3	16.0	5.0	Logement, eau, électricité, gas et autres combustibles
Furnishing, household equip	...	...	0.1	9.2	19.6	17.1	23.6	3.0	-13.0	Meubles, articles de ménage et entretien courant
Health	9.2	16.6	10.7	7.1	16.7	18.4	25.1	0.9	0.5	Santé
Transport	15.2	7.0	12.7	-2.0	21.5	1.4	3.3	0.9	-0.9	Transport
Communication	...	...	14.4	-4.6	24.0	31.5	9.1	0.1	0.4	Communication
Recreation & culture	...	...	7.5	-12.1	16.7	20.6	8.9	2.6	3.2	Loisirs et culture
Education	...	...	-0.2	17.8	32.5	17.4	13.4	4.4	5.4	Enseignement
Restaurants & hotels	...	...	11.5	11.5	15.5	7.9	-0.5	14.3	11.0	Restaurants et hôtels
Miscellaneous goods & services	...	...	7.1	3.9	19.7	21.7	0.2	-1.2	-4.8	Biens et services divers

IV AGRICULTURAL PRODUCTION - PRODUCTION AGRICOLE

	2006	2007	2008	2009	2010	2011	2012	2013	2014	
TONNES *(THOUSAND)*										**TONNES** *(MILLIERS)*
Groundnuts	115	57	60	70	81	83	85	86	...	Arachides
Coffe	21	21	21	22	31	33	35	36	...	Café
Oilpalm Fruit	45	46	48	50	52	54	57	60	...	Huile de palme
Rice	1 062	588	680	888	1 027	1 078	1 141	1 256	...	Riz
Cassava	1 457	1 894	1 989	2 815	3 250	3 460	3 585	3 810	...	Manioc

V MINING PRODUCTION - PRODUCTION MINIERE

	2006	2007	2008	2009	2010	2011	2012	2013	2014	
Diamond, carats (thousands)	582	605	331	400	525	357	541	...	...	Diamants, carats (milliers)
Bauxite, metric tons (thousands)	1 071	1 169	954	743	905	1 300	776	...	...	Bauxite, tonnes métriques (milliers)
Rutile, metric tons (thousands)	74	83	79	64	73	...	...	...	...	Rutile, tonnes métriques (milliers)

VI ENERGY - ENERGIE

	2006	2007	2008	2009	2010	2011	2012	2013	2014	
Total electricity generation (GWh)	39	57	60	281	298	302	313	332	...	Production d'électricité totale (GWh)
of which:										dont:
Production of electricity from fossil fuels (GWh)	35	39	40	42	45	45	45	45	...	Production d'électricité à partir de combustibles fossiles (GWh)
Production of hydro electricity (GWh)	4	18	20	239	253	257	268	287	...	Production d'électricité d'origine hydraulique (GWh)
Production of electricity from solar, wind, tide, wave and other sources (GWh)	...	...	...	...	...	...	...	...	...	Production d'électricité d'origine solaire, éolienne, marée motrice et autres (GWh)

VII TOURISM AND INFRASTRUCTURE - TOURISME ET INFRASTRUCTURE

	2006	2007	2008	2009	2010	2011	2012	2013	2014	
VII-1 TOURISM										**VII-1 TOURISME**
International tourist arrivals (thousands)	34	32	36	37	39	52	60	82	50	Arrivées de touristes internationaux (milliers)
Rooms in hotels and similar establishments (thousands)	2.6	2.8	3.0	3.0	3.3	3.9	4.5	...	...	Chambres d'hotels et établissements assimilés (milliers)
Overnight stays (thousands)	471	446	487	509	522	729	837	1 185	1 051	Nuitées (milliers)
Tourism receipts (US$ thousand)	23 000	22 200	33 800	25 400	25 800	44 300	46 800	46 463	43 085	Recettes touristiques (milliers de $ EU)
Total contribution to GDP (%)	7.5	7.9	6.8	8.2	8.5	8.6	7.0	5.3	4.9	Contribution totale au PIB (%)
Total contribution to Employment (%)	7.2	7.3	6.5	7.8	8.3	8.4	7.1	5.6	5.4	Contribution totale à l'emploi (%)
VII-2 INFRASTRUCTURE										**VII-2 INFRASTRUCTURE**
Paved roads (% of total)	...	...	...	...	...	...	...	...	...	Routes asphaltées (% du total)
Total Network (Railways-km)	...	...	...	...	...	...	...	...	...	Réseau total voies ferrées-Km
Main Telephone Lines (per 100 inhabitants)	1	1	1	1	0	0	0	0	...	Lignes téléphoniques fixes (pour 100 habitants)
Mobile Cellular Subscribers (per 100 inhabitants)	...	14	18	21	35	36	37	66	...	Abonnés aux téléphones mobiles (pour 100 habitants)

VIII EXTERNAL TRADE - COMMERCE EXTERIEUR

	2006	2007	2008	2009	2010	2011	2012	2013	2014	
LEONE (MILLIONS) EXPORTS, FOB										**LEONE (MILLIONS) EXPORTATIONS, FÀB**
Exports - Total	676 225	729 894	641 797	788 564	1 357 289	2 596 748	4 697 568	8 169 666	8 007 254	Exportations - Total
Exports to AFRICA	...	...	...	...	...	...	...	...	...	Exportations vers l'AFRIQUE
Main Products										**Principaux produits**
Diamond	362 181	423 943	293 651	267 509	450 740	564 422	702 622	800 983	929 714	Diamant
Rutile	84 654	113 846	109 127	121 704	162 235	149 783	746 021	558 916	472 185	Rutile
Coffee	3 230	5 539	4 419	42 727	7 863	8 703	16 706	12 148	...	Café
Cocoa	34 408	33 926	44 807	66 385	145 657	191 475	97 867	38 674	...	Cacao
Bauxite	69 952	97 597	83 647	64 258	122 984	169 623	74 225	59 603	...	Bauxite
Main Destinations										**Principales destinations**
Belgium	302 005	339 411	226 773	197 015	284 822	378	870	...	...	Belgique
UK	23 477	30 759	54 561	32 552	13 660	55 597	...	...	...	Royaume-Uni
United States	195 196	224 274	213 633	237 106	367 672	129	90	...	...	Etats-Unis
Switzerland	5 236	42 494	8 614	65 644	151 011	139 596	...	...	...	Suisse
Germany	352	46	827	1 683	28	1 717	...	...	...	Allemagne
IMPORTS, CIF										**IMPORTATIONS, CAF**
Imports - Total	1 169 256	1 332 783	1 590 338	1 764 303	3 083 669	7 466 216	6 966 850	7 709 863	6 871 736	Importations - Total (millions)
Imports from Africa	...	...	...	...	...	...	...	...	...	Importations en provenance de l'Afrique
Main Products										**Principaux produits**
Fuels, lubricants, etc.	435 639	503 093	597 095	427 422	459 431	121 858	...	...	...	Carburants, lubrifiants, etc.
Food and live animals	166 293	202 741	345 636	353 744	244 389	71 097	...	...	...	Alimentaire et animaux vivants
Machines, transport equipments	204 517	224 160	225 184	323 038	236 919	60 230	...	...	...	Machines, équipements de transport
Manufactured goods	143 990	154 872	169 474	224 850	162 132	42 533	...	...	...	Biens manifacturés
Chemicals, related products nes	71 100	92 545	73 035	113 426	83 139	21 785	...	...	...	Produits chimiques, produits connexes nda
Main Origin										**Principales provenances**
Côte d'Ivoire	414 185	477 415	568 885	631 624	1 096 454	2 672 154	...	...	...	Côte d'Ivoire
Canada	73 619	84 837	101 081	112 236	194 831	474 819	...	...	...	Canada
Netherlands	66 598	77 131	92 093	102 130	177 338	432 198	...	...	...	Pays-Bas
United States	58 980	68 254	81 468	90 364	156 901	382 389	...	...	...	États-Unis
Japan	48 099	55 468	66 108	73 391	127 404	310 496	...	...	...	Japon

IX FINANCIAL AND MONETARY STATISTICS - FINANCES ET STATISTIQUES MONETAIRES										
	2006	2007	2008	2009	2010	2011	2012	2013	2014	
IX-1 MONETARY STATISTICS *LEONE (MILLIONS)*										**IX-1 STATISTIQUES MONÉTAIRES** *LEONE (MILLIONS)*
Money supply (M1)	900 480	1 135 320	1 431 200	1 878 990	2 413 930	2 958 290	3 623 230	4 161 230	4 900 180	Masse monétaire (M1)
Quasi-money	390 210	298 746	422 015	559 702	644 379	901 074	1 170 936	1 347 432	1 558 900	Quasi-monnaie
of which Demand Deposit	...	...	...	...	...	...	...	...	...	dont Monnaie scripturale
Net foreign assets	555 823	674 919	678 114	832 407	839 494	1 270 385	1 628 700	1 882 963	2 395 367	Avoirs extérieurs nets
Domestic credit	973 016	554 774	895 723	1 195 143	1 777 761	2 092 063	2 313 066	2 601 936	3 231 367	Crédit intérieur
of which claims on private sector	188 933	278 814	416 443	683 295	802 381	981 148	1 027 103	1 016 691	1 069 171	dont créances sur le secteur privé
of which claims on government sector, net	759 607	256 024	446 042	448 855	891 347	1 012 095	1 141 863	1 289 160	1 858 135	dont créances nettes sur le gouvernement
International reserves (millions US$)	184	217	220	405	409	439	478	533	572	Réserves internationales (millions $EU)
Average Exchange Rate (National Currency per US$)	2 961.91	2 985.19	2 981.51	3 385.65	3 978.09	4 349.16	4 344.04	4 332.50	4 434.11	Taux de change (moyen) (monnaie nationale par $ EU)
IX-2 PUBLIC FINANCE *LEONE (MILLIONS)*										**IX-2 FINANCES PUBLIQUES** *LEONE (MILLIONS)*
Total Revenues and Grants	842 194	2 129 282	948 410	1 257 997	1 560 742	2 170 759	2 506 070	2 827 586	3 288 207	Recettes totales et dons
Tax Revenue	454 504	493 024	622 603	689 076	899 423	1 180 756	1 550 673	1 875 826	2 047 495	Recettes fiscales
Non Tax Revenue	41 140	43 840	61 191	68 584	117 779	281 344	322 833	404 189	478 263	Recettes non fiscales
Grants	346 550	1 592 418	264 616	500 337	543 540	708 659	632 564	547 571	762 449	Dons
Total Expenditures and Net Lending	928 861	837 613	1 207 969	1 451 956	2 073 764	2 751 942	3 357 859	3 337 085	3 580 159	Dépenses totales et prêts nets
Current expenditure	714 305	660 949	848 274	999 678	1 286 477	1 602 816	2 094 916	2 190 552	2 233 276	Dépenses courantes
Of which Wages and Salaries	271 531	296 509	334 357	401 536	535 669	681 346	935 912	1 060 021	1 120 332	Dont rémunérations et salaires
Capital expenditure	214 557	173 764	359 058	452 278	787 287	1 149 126	1 262 944	1 146 533	1 346 883	Dépenses d'équipement
Net Lending	-	2 900	637	-	-	-	-	-	-	Prêts nets
Fiscal Balance	- 86 667	1 291 669	- 259 559	- 193 959	- 513 022	- 581 183	- 851 789	- 509 499	- 291 952	Solde global y compris les dons
IX-3 BALANCE OF PAYMENTS *LEONE (MILLIONS)*										**IX-3 BALANCE DES PAIEMENTS** *LEONE (MILLIONS)*
Trade balance	- 278 163	- 281 048	- 584 861	- 636 494	-2 009 594	-6 708 641	-4 388 478	-4 131 695	-4 391 136	Balance commerciale
Services Balance	383 888	438 335	555 831	571 038	1 076 642	2 623 459	-1 506 549	-2 254 602	-2 612 631	Balance des services
Net Income	- 171 391	- 103 428	- 222 476	- 118 523	- 195 364	- 153 612	- 579 126	-2 421 583	-2 772 095	Revenus nets
Compensation of employees	5 600	- 3 112	3 018	4 620	3 632	6 630	...	...	...	Rémunération des salariés
Investment Income	- 123 069	- 308 170	- 225 973	- 136 727	- 216 650	- 259 768	...	...	...	Revenus des investissements
Current transfers, net total	345 814	281 233	330 366	439 372	835 995	1 081 115	1 026 516	877 977	1 089 201	Transferts courants
Net official transfers	134 051	175 625	231 510	342 659	632 980	785 370	...	...	...	Transferts officiels nets
Workers' remittances	29 169	117 105	54 714	104 824	127 885	148 896	...	...	...	Envois de fonds des travailleurs
Other private transfers	65 749	15 877	44 850	52 524	63 482	73 405	...	...	...	Autres transferts privés
Current account balance	280 149	335 091	78 860	255 393	- 292 321	-3 157 680	-5 447 637	-7 929 904	-8 686 661	Solde du compte courant
Capital & financial account	363 239	523 156	764 433	690 389	1 783 338	2 346 235	...	...	...	Comptes de capital et financier
Capital account	767 202	1 893 181	197 922	248 887	575 274	686 925	...	...	...	Compte de capital
Financial account	- 403 964	-1 370 025	566 511	441 502	1 208 064	1 659 310	...	...	...	Compte financier
Errors & omissions	- 81 801	- 45 127	- 92 267	- 26 469	- 783 778	-1 784 561	...	...	...	Erreurs et omissions
Overall balance	...	...	...	...	...	...	...	...	...	Balance générale

X DEBT AND FINANCIAL FLOWS - DETTE ET FLUX FINANCIERS										
	2006	2007	2008	2009	2010	2011	2012	2013	2014	
X-1 DEBT *US$ (MILLIONS)*										**X-1 DETTE EXTÉRIEURE** *$ E.U (MILLIONS)*
Total external debt	1 565	529	608	693	783	955	981	1 045	1 236	Dette extérieure totale
Private	-	-	-	-	-	-	-	-	-	Privée
Public	1 565	529	608	693	783	955	981	1 045	1 236	Publique
Total external debt service	242	473	11	15	16	23	25	34	45	Service de la dette extérieure
Present value of External debt	...	...	...	...	...	...	...	...	...	Valeur actuelle de la dette extérieure
Total government domestic debt (in local currency)	...	...	...	...	...	...	...	...	...	Dette publique intérieure
X-2 FINANCIAL FLOWS *US$ (MILLIONS)*										**X-2 FLUX FINANCIERS** *$ E.U (MILLIONS)*
Net Foreign Direct Investment Inflows	59	97	58	111	238	950	548	579	...	Investissements étranger direct (flux nets entrants)
Main origin of FDI Inflows										**Principales origines de l'IDE entrant:**
Luxembourg	6	6	1	3	...	5.6	4.9	...	...	Luxembourg
Sweden	...	...	...	...	...	12.3	11.7	...	...	Suède
Denmark	...	...	...	...	...	...	...	...	...	Danemark
United Kingdom	...	...	...	...	...	6.4	...	...	...	Royaume-Uni
Italy	...	...	6	...	...	...	...	...	...	Italie
African countries	...	...	...	...	...	...	...	...	...	Pays africains
Net total Official Development Assistance	380	550	378	448	467	425	443	444	...	Aide publique au développement (nette totale)
Main origin of Net ODA										**Principales origines de l'APD nette**
United Kingdom	66	88	93	80	84.8	73.6	99.5	...	...	Royaume-Uni
IDA	46	33	51	36	57.3	60.5	64.8	...	...	IDA
United States	21	21	16	17	29.8	22.6	22.7	15.5	...	Etats-Unis
AfDF	51	4	24	21	17.6	27.6	35.2	...	...	FAfD
IMF (Concessional Trust Funds)	9	...	18	19	40.7	8.9	- 0.3	...	...	FMI (Fonds fiduciaires concessionnels)
General notes	National Accounts:annual accounts are based on new prices of 2006					Comptes Nationaux: publication des comptes annuels selon la nouvelle base des prix 2006				Notes générales

SOMALIA — SOMALIE

AREA (KM²)		**637 660**	**SUPERFICIE (KM²)**
CAPITAL CITY	**Mogadishu**	**Mogadiscio**	**CAPITALE**
CURRENCY	**Somali Shilling**	**Shilling Somalien**	**MONNAIE**

I SOCIAL AND DEMOGRAPHIC INDICATORS — INDICATEURS DEMOGRAPHIQUES ET SOCIAUX

	Year / Année	Value / Valeur	
POPULATION			**POPULATION**
Population ('000)			Population ('000)
Both sexes	2014	10 806	Les deux sexes
Male	2014	5 376	Masculin
Female	2014	5 429	Féminin
Average annual growth rate	2014	3.1	Taux de croissance annuel
Active Population ('000)	2014	3 175	Population active ('000)
Population by age group ('000)			Population par groupe d'âge ('000)
0-14 years	2014	5 072	0-14 ans
15-64 years	2014	5 428	15-64 ans
65+ years	2014	305	65+ ans
Economically active population in agriculture (%)	2014	84.1	Participation de la population active agricole (%)
Crude birth rate	2014	43.4	Taux brut de natalité
Crude death rate	2014	12.0	Taux brut de mortalité
Total fertility rate	2014	6.5	Indice synthétique de fécondité
Proportion of urban population	2014	39.2	Part de la population urbaine
Life Expectancy at Birth - Total (years)	2014	55.4	Espérance de vie à la naissance - Totale (ans)
Dependency Ratio - Total (%)	2014	90.4	Taux de dépendance - Total (%)
HEALTH			**SANTÉ**
Percentage of children under-five and underweight	2006	32.8	% d'enfants de moins de cinq ans avec insuffisance pondérale
Prevalence of undernourishment	...	...	Prévalence de la malnutrition
Under five mortality rate (both sexes, per 1000)	2013	145.6	Taux de mortalité de moins de 5 ans (les deux sexes, pour 1000)
Infant mortality rate (both sexes) per 1000	2013	89.8	Taux de mortalité infantile (les deux sexes) par 1000
Percentage of children provided the vaccines :			Pourcentage d'enfants vaccinés :
BCG	2013	33.0	BCG
DPT3	2013	42.0	DTC3
Polio	2012	47.0	Polio
Measles	2013	46.0	Rougeole
Percentage of mothers provided at least one antenatal care (%)	2006	22.0	Pourcentage de mères ayant au moins reçu un soin prénatal (%)
Percentage of deliveries attended by skilled health personnel	2006	33.0	% d'accouchements assistés par un personnel de santé qualifié
Number of doctors (per 10 000 population)	2006	0.4	Nombre de médecins (pour 10 000 habitants)
Number of nurses (per 10 000 population)	2006	1.1	Nombre d'infirmières (pour 10 000 habitants)
Hospital beds - Total (per 10 000 population)	...	...	Nombre de lits d'hôpitaux - Total (pour 10 000)
Births registered (per 1 000)	2014	43.4	Naiss.s enregistrées (pour 1 000)
Deaths registered (per 1 000)	2014	12.0	Décès enregistrés (pour 1 000)
Public expenditure on Health (% of budget)	...	...	Dépenses publiques consacrées à la santé (% du budget)
EDUCATION			**EDUCATION**
Enrolment in primary education (both sexes) (000)	2007	457	Scolarisation dans le primaire (les deux sexes) (000)
Female	2007	162	Féminin
Enrolment in secondary education (both sexes) (000)	2007	87	Scolarisation dans le secondaire (les deux sexes) (000)
Female	2007	27	Féminin
Enrolment in tertiary education (both sexes) (000)	...	...	Scolarisation dans le tertiaire (les deux sexes) (000)
Female	...	...	Féminin
Literacy rate (both sexes)	...	...	Taux d'alphabétisation (deux sexes)
Male	...	...	Masculin
Female	...	...	Féminin
Pupil-teacher ratio	...	...	Ratio élève-enseignant
Public expenditure on education (% of budget)	...	...	Dépenses publiques consacrées à l'enseignement (% du budget)
POVERTY			**PAUVRETÉ**
GNI Per Capita (US$)	...	...	RNB par habitant ($EU)
Human Poverty Index (HPI-1) Value (%)	...	...	Valeur de l'Indice de pauvreté (IPH-1) (%)
Population below International Poverty Line ($2/day) (%)	...	...	Population sous le seuil international de pauvreté (2$/J) (%)
Share of Income Held by Richest 10%	...	...	% de revenu des 10% plus riches
Share of Income Held by Poorest 10%	...	...	% de revenu des 10% plus pauvres
Gini index	...	...	Indice de Gini

Charts / Graphiques

Population by age group – 2014
Population par groupe d'age – 2014

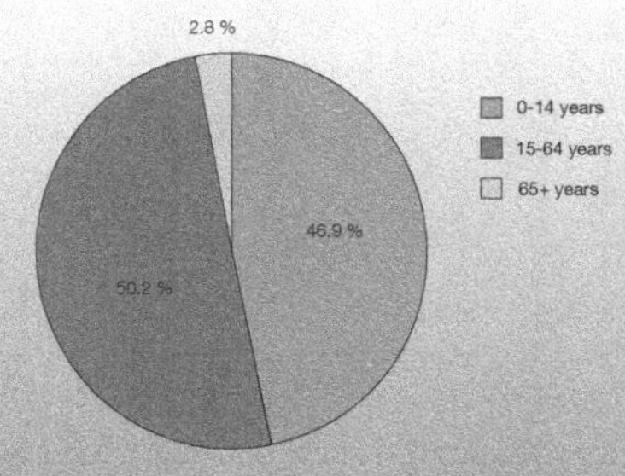

Percentage of children provided the vaccines – 2013
Pourcentage d'enfants vaccinés – 2013

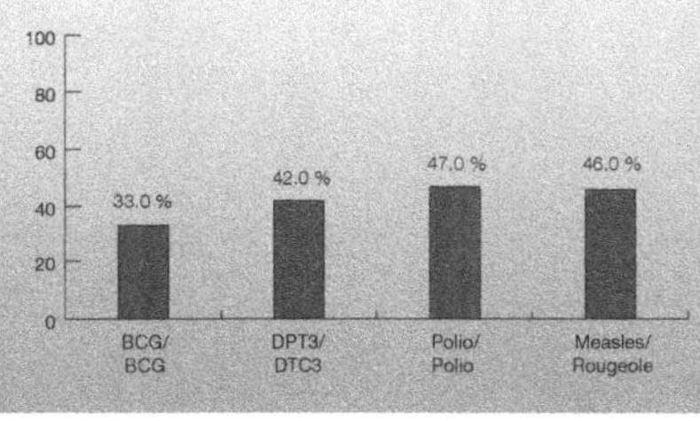

II NATIONAL ACCOUNTS — COMPTES NATIONAUX

	2006	2007	2008	2009	2010	2011	2012	2013	2014	
GROSS DOMESTIC PRODUCT BY KIND OF ECONOMIC ACTIVITY AT CURRENT PRICES *SOMALI SHILLING (MILLIONS)*										**PRODUIT INTÉRIEUR BRUT PAR BRANCHE D'ACTIVITÉ ÉCONOMIQUE AUX PRIX COURANTS** *SHILLING SOMALIEN (MILLIONS)*
Agriculture, hunting, forestry and fishing	17 785	18 945	19 795	20 802	18 075	18 001	18 092	17 975	...	Agriculture, chasse sylviculture et pêche
Mining and quarrying	200	212	222	233	203	202	203	202	...	Industries extractives
Manufacturing	735	782	817	859	746	743	747	742	...	Industries manufacturières
Electricity, gas & water	...	...	...	...	...	...	...	...	...	Electricité, gaz et eau
Construction & public works	1 239	1 322	1 381	1 451	1 261	1 256	1 262	1 254	...	Bâtiments et travaux publics
Wholesale & retail trade, restaurants, hotels	3 137	3 344	3 495	3 671	3 190	3 177	3 193	3 172	...	Commerce de gros et de détail, restaurants et hôtels
Finance, insurance, real estate, etc.	-	-	-	-	-	-	-	-	...	Banques, assurances, affaires immobilières
Transport and communications	2 732	2 955	3 103	3 234	2 821	2 810	2 820	2 804	...	Transport(s) et communications
Public administration and defense	3 703	3 921	4 088	4 311	3 740	3 724	3 745	3 720	...	Administrations publiques et défense
Education	...	...	...	...	...	...	...	...	...	Education
Health and Social Work	...	...	...	...	...	...	...	...	...	Santé et actions sociales
Other services	...	...	...	...	...	...	...	...	...	Autres services
Less Imputed Service Charges	...	...	...	...	...	...	...	...	...	Moins services d'intermédiation financière
Gross domestic product at factor cost / basic prices	29 531	31 481	32 901	34 561	30 036	29 913	30 063	29 869	...	Produit intérieur brut aux couts des facteurs / prix de base
Plus: indirect taxes / taxes on products, less subsidies	4 148	4 289	4 555	4 782	4 135	4 134	4 151	4 121	...	Plus taxes indirectes/impôts sur les produits, moins les subventions
EXPENDITURE ON GROSS DOMESTIC PRODUCT AT CURRENT PURCHASER'S VALUES *SOMALI SHILLING (MILLIONS)*										**EMPLOI DU PRODUIT INTÉRIEUR BRUT AUX PRIX COURANTS D'ACQUISITION** *SHILLING SOMALIEN (MILLIONS)*
Government final consumption	2 919	3 142	3 260	3 430	2 985	2 969	2 985	2 966	...	Consommation finale des administrations publiques
Private final consumption	24 378	26 078	27 176	28 569	24 839	24 725	24 854	24 694	...	Consommation finale privée
Gross fixed capital formation	6 825	7 023	7 512	7 863	6 797	6 802	6 826	6 778	...	Formation brute de capital fixe
Change in inventories	22	15	22	22	18	19	19	18	...	Variation des stocks
Exports of goods and services	106	106	115	120	104	104	104	104	...	Exportations de biens et services
Less imports of goods and services	570	595	631	661	573	572	574	571	...	Moins importations de biens et services
GDP at purchasers' values	33 679	35 770	37 456	39 343	34 171	34 047	34 214	33 990	...	PIB aux prix d'acquisition
GROSS DOMESTIC PRODUCT BY KIND OF ECONOMIC ACTIVITY AT CONSTANT PRICES *ANNUAL GROWTH RATES (%)*										**PRODUIT INTÉRIEUR BRUT PAR BRANCHE D'ACTIVITÉ ECONOMIQUE AUX PRIX CONSTANTS** *TAUX DE CROISSANCE ANNUEL (%)*
Agriculture, hunting, forestry and fishing	3.9	1.9	2.6	2.9	2.4	2.6	0.0	2.6	...	Agriculture, chasse sylviculture et pêche
Mining and quarrying	- 1.0	3.6	3.1	1.9	2.9	2.6	0.0	2.5	...	Industries extractives
Manufacturing	- 0.1	3.3	3.0	2.1	2.8	2.6	0.0	2.5	...	Industries manufacturières
Electricity, gas & water	...	...	...	...	...	...	...	...	...	Electricité, gaz et eau
Construction & public works	1.7	2.7	2.8	2.4	2.7	2.6	0.0	2.6	...	Bâtiments et travaux publics
Wholesale & retail trade, restaurants, hotels	1.8	2.6	2.8	2.5	2.6	2.6	0.0	2.6	...	Commerce de gros et de détail,restaurants et hôtels
Finance, insurance, real estate, etc.	...	...	...	...	...	...	...	...	...	Banques, assurances, affaires immobilières
Transport and communications	2.0	2.6	2.8	2.5	2.6	2.6	0.0	2.6	...	Transport(s) et communications
Public administration and defense	2.3	2.5	2.7	2.5	2.7	2.6	0.0	2.6	...	Administrations publiques et défense
Education	...	...	...	...	...	...	...	...	...	Education
Health and Social Work	...	...	...	...	...	...	...	...	...	Santé et actions sociales
Other services	...	...	...	...	...	...	...	...	...	Autres services
Less Imputed Service Charges	...	...	...	...	...	...	...	...	...	Moins services d'intermédiation financière
Gross domestic product at factor cost / basic prices	3.1	2.2	2.7	2.7	2.5	2.6	0.0	2.6	...	Produit intérieur brut aux couts des facteurs / prix de base
Plus: indirect taxes / taxes on products, less subsidies	- 2.5	5.7	2.1	1.7	3.3	2.6	21.8	2.5	...	Plus taxes indirectes/impôts sur les produits, moins les subventions
Gross domestic product at market prices	2.4	2.6	2.6	2.6	2.6	2.6	2.6	2.6	...	Produit intérieur brut aux prix du marché
EXPENDITURE ON GROSS DOMESTIC PRODUCT AT CONSTANT PURCHASERS' VALUES *ANNUAL GROWTH RATES (%)*										**EMPLOIS DU PRODUIT INTÉRIEUR BRUT AUX PRIX CONSTANTS D'ACQUISITION** *TAUX DE CROISSANCE ANNUEL (%)*
Government final consumption	4.5	1.9	2.4	3.0	2.4	2.6	2.7	2.6	...	Consommation finale des administrations publiques
Private final consumption	1.0	3.2	2.7	2.4	2.7	2.6	2.6	2.6	...	Consommation finale privée
Gross fixed capital formation	6.0	1.4	2.2	3.3	2.3	2.5	2.8	2.5	...	Formation brute de capital fixe
Exports of goods and services	3.9	2.1	4.5	6.6	- 0.6	3.4	3.2	2.0	...	Exportations de biens et services
Less imports of goods and services	- 5.1	9.3	2.9	5.3	0.7	2.9	3.0	2.2	...	Moins importations de biens et services

III INFLATION

	2006	2007	2008	2009	2010	2011	2012	2013	2014	
ANNUAL GROWTH RATES (%)										**TAUX DE CROISSANCE ANNUEL (%)**
All items	...	...	...	...	...	...	...	...	...	Ensemble
of which:										dont:
Food and Non-alcoholic beverages	...	...	...	...	...	...	...	...	...	Alimentation et boissons non alcoolisés
Alcoholic beverages & tobacco	...	...	...	...	...	...	...	...	...	Boissons alcoolisées et tabacs
Clothing and Footwear	...	...	...	...	...	...	...	...	...	Habillement et chaussures
Housing, Water, Electricity, Gas and Other Fuels	...	...	...	...	...	...	...	...	...	Logement, eau, électricité, gas et autres combustibles
Furnishing, household equip	...	...	...	...	...	...	...	...	...	Meubles, articles de ménage et entretien courant
Health	...	...	...	...	...	...	...	...	...	Santé
Transport	...	...	...	...	...	...	...	...	...	Transport
Communication	...	...	...	...	...	...	...	...	...	Communication
Recreation & culture	...	...	...	...	...	...	...	...	...	Loisirs et culture
Education	...	...	...	...	...	...	...	...	...	Enseignement
Restaurants & hotels	...	...	...	...	...	...	...	...	...	Restaurants et hôtels
Miscellaneous goods & services	...	...	...	...	...	...	...	...	...	Biens et services divers

IV AGRICULTURAL PRODUCTION - PRODUCTION AGRICOLE										
	2006	2007	2008	2009	2010	2011	2012	2013	2014	
TONNES *(THOUSAND)*										**TONNES** *(MILLIERS)*
Maize	200	200	200	230	230	230	220	220	...	Maïs
Sorghum	145	80	75	95	214	48	234	231	...	Sorgho
Cassava	100	100	100	129	133	65	145	149	...	Manioc
Banana	50	50	54	64	65	65	80	90	...	Banane
Sesame seed	16	18	13	16	19	18	19	20	...	Graines de sésame
V MINING PRODUCTION - PRODUCTION MINIERE										
	2006	2007	2008	2009	2010	2011	2012	2013	2014	
Salt and pure sodium chloride, metric tons (thousands)	1 000	1 000	...	...	...	...	...	...	...	Sel et chlorure de sodium pur, tonnes métriques (milliers)
VI ENERGY - ENERGIE										
	2006	2007	2008	2009	2010	2011	2012	2013	2014	
Total electricity generation (GWh)	282	292	301	305	310	323	342	362	...	Production d'électricité totale (GWh)
of which:										dont:
Production of electricity from fossil fuels (GWh)	282	292	301	305	310	312	331	351	...	Production d'électricité à partir de combustibles fossiles (GWh)
Production of hydro electricity (GWh)	...	...	...	...	...	11	11	11	...	Production d'électricité d'origine hydraulique (GWh)
Production of electricity from solar, wind, tide, wave and other sources (GWh)	...	...	...	...	...	...	...	...	...	Production d'électricité d'origine solaire, éolienne, marée motrice et autres (GWh)
VII TOURISM AND INFRASTRUCTURE - TOURISME ET INFRASTRUCTURE										
	2006	2007	2008	2009	2010	2011	2012	2013	2014	
VII-1 TOURISM										**VII-1 TOURISME**
International tourist arrivals (thousands)	...	...	...	...	...	...	...	...	...	Arrivées de touristes internationaux (milliers)
Rooms in hotels and similar establishments (thousands)	...	...	...	...	...	...	...	...	...	Chambres d'hotels et établissements assimilés (milliers)
Overnight stays (thousands)	...	...	...	...	...	...	...	...	...	Nuitées (milliers)
Tourism receipts (US$ thousand)	...	...	...	...	...	...	...	...	...	Recettes touristiques (milliers de $ EU)
Total contribution to GDP (%)	...	...	...	...	...	...	...	...	...	Contribution totale au PIB (%)
Total contribution to Employment (%)	...	...	...	...	...	...	...	...	...	Contribution totale à l'emploi (%)
VII-2 INFRASTRUCTURE										**VII-2 INFRASTRUCTURE**
Paved roads (% of total)	...	...	...	...	...	...	...	...	...	Routes asphaltées (% du total)
Total Network (Railways-km)	...	...	...	...	...	...	...	...	...	Réseau total voies ferrées-Km
Main Telephone Lines (per 100 inhabitants)	1	1	1	1	1	1	1	1	...	Lignes téléphoniques fixes (pour 100 habitants)
Mobile Cellular Subscribers (per 100 inhabitants)	6	7	7	7	7	18	23	49	...	Abonnés aux téléphones mobiles (pour 100 habitants)
VIII EXTERNAL TRADE - COMMERCE EXTERIEUR										
	2006	2007	2008	2009	2010	2011	2012	2013	2014	
US$ (MILLIONS) **EXPORTS, FOB**										**$ E.U (MILLIONS)** **EXPORTATIONS, FÀB**
Exports - Total	285	346	415	422	450	520	510	...	...	Exportations - Total
Exports to AFRICA	...	...	...	...	...	...	...	...	...	Exportations vers l'AFRIQUE
Main Products										**Principaux produits**
Live animals other than animals of division 03	110	91	82	162	216	397	346	...	...	Animaux vivants autres que ceux aquatiques
Gold, non-monetary (excluding gold ores and concentrates)	89	108	132	102	94	...	...	...	...	Or, à usage non monétaire
Fuel wood (excluding wood waste) and wood charcoal	21	39	65	65	59	32	35	...	...	Bois de chauffage (sauf déchets), charbon de bois
Other meat and edible meat offal	12	12	40	37	24	6	...	...	...	Autres viandes et abats comestibles
Hides and skins (except furskins), raw	7	10	20	6	5	16	30	...	...	Cuirs et peaux (sauf pelleteries), bruts
Main Destinations										**Principales destinations**
United Arab Emirates	136	169	248	229	206	...	...	...	...	Émirats arabes unis
Yemen	61	74	55	44	34	211	...	...	...	Yémen
Saudi Arabia	10	8	19	45	113	...	...	...	...	Arabie saoudite
Oman	7	8	16	69	65	...	...	...	...	Oman
Pakistan	4	7	13	5	3	55	...	...	...	Pakistan
IMPORTS, CIF										**IMPORTATIONS, CAF**
Imports - Total	793	887	890	750	940	880	...	...	...	Importations - Total (millions)
Imports from Africa	...	...	...	...	...	...	...	...	...	Importations en provenance de l'Afrique
Main Products										**Principaux produits**
Cereals and cereal preparations	121	128	236	160	123	301	...	...	...	Céréales et préparations à base de céréales
Vegetables and fruits	16	22	115	137	195	185	...	...	...	Légumes et fruits
Sugar, sugar preparations and honey	122	100	133	121	142	83	...	...	...	Sucres, préparations à base de sucre, et miel
Crude animal and vegetable materials, n.e.s.	100	117	108	36	28	1	...	...	...	Matières brutes d'origine animale ou végétale, n.d.a.
Fixed vegetable oils and fats, crude, refined or fractionated	31	44	88	23	27	18	...	...	...	Graisses et huiles végétales fixes, raffinées ou fractionnées
Main Origin										Principales provenances
United Arab Emirates	186	247	200	205	146	...	...	...	...	Émirats arabes unis
Ethiopia	82	93	107	135	211	342	...	...	...	Éthiopie
India	79	138	138	19	67	172	...	...	...	Inde
Kenya	99	115	164	100	116	...	...	...	...	Kenya
Oman	64	59	94	73	78	...	...	...	...	Oman

IX FINANCIAL AND MONETARY STATISTICS - FINANCES ET STATISTIQUES MONETAIRES	2006	2007	2008	2009	2010	2011	2012	2013	2014	
IX-1 MONETARY STATISTICS *SOMALI SHILLING (MILLIONS)*										**IX-1 STATISTIQUES MONÉTAIRES** *SHILLING SOMALIEN (MILLIONS)*
Money supply (M1)	...	...	...	...	...	...	...	...	...	Masse monétaire (M1)
Quasi-money	...	...	...	...	...	...	...	...	...	Quasi-monnaie
of which Demand Deposit	...	...	...	...	...	...	...	...	...	dont Monnaie scripturale
Net foreign assets	...	...	...	...	...	...	...	...	...	Avoirs extérieurs nets
Domestic credit	...	...	...	...	...	...	...	...	...	Crédit intérieur
of which claims on private sector	...	...	...	...	...	...	...	...	...	dont créances sur le secteur privé
of which claims on government sector, net	...	...	...	...	...	...	...	...	...	dont créances nettes sur le gouvernement
International reserves (millions US$)	...	...	...	...	...	...	...	...	...	Réserves internationales (millions $EU)
Average Exchange Rate (National Currency per US$)	...	...	...	...	...	...	...	...	...	Taux de change (moyen) (monnaie nationale par $ EU)
IX-2 PUBLIC FINANCE *SOMALI SHILLING (MILLIONS)*										**IX-2 FINANCES PUBLIQUES** *SHILLING SOMALIEN (MILLIONS)*
Total Revenues and Grants	...	...	...	...	...	...	...	...	...	Recettes totales et dons
Tax Revenue	...	...	...	...	...	...	...	...	...	Recettes fiscales
Non Tax Revenue	...	...	...	...	...	...	...	...	...	Recettes non fiscales
Grants	...	...	...	...	...	...	...	...	...	Dons
Total Expenditures and Net Lending	...	...	...	...	...	...	...	...	...	Dépenses totales et prêts nets
Current expenditure	...	...	...	...	...	...	...	...	...	Dépenses courantes
Of which Wages and Salaries	...	...	...	...	...	...	...	...	...	Dont rémunérations et salaires
Capital expenditure	...	...	...	...	...	...	...	...	...	Dépenses d'équipement
Net Lending	...	...	...	...	...	...	...	...	...	Prêts nets
Fiscal Balance	...	...	...	...	...	...	...	...	...	Solde global y compris les dons
IX-3 BALANCE OF PAYMENTS *SOMALI SHILLING (MILLIONS)*										**IX-3 BALANCE DES PAIEMENTS** *SHILLING SOMALIEN (MILLIONS)*
Trade balance	...	...	...	...	...	...	...	...	...	Balance commerciale
Services Balance	...	...	...	...	...	...	...	...	...	Balance des services
Net Income	...	...	...	...	...	...	...	...	...	Revenus nets
Compensation of employees	...	...	...	...	...	...	...	...	...	Rémunération des salariés
Investment Income	...	...	...	...	...	...	...	...	...	Revenus des investissements
Current transfers, net total	...	...	...	...	...	...	...	...	...	Transferts courants
Net official transfers	...	...	...	...	...	...	...	...	...	Transferts officiels nets
Workers' remittances	...	...	...	...	...	...	...	...	...	Envois de fonds des travailleurs
Other private transfers	...	...	...	...	...	...	...	...	...	Autres transferts privés
Current account balance	...	...	...	...	...	...	...	...	...	Solde du compte courant
Capital & financial account	...	...	...	...	...	...	...	...	...	Comptes de capital et financier
Capital account	...	...	...	...	...	...	...	...	...	Compte de capital
Financial account	...	...	...	...	...	...	...	...	...	Compte financier
Errors & omissions	...	...	...	...	...	...	...	...	...	Erreurs et omissions
Overall balance	...	...	...	...	...	...	...	...	...	Balance générale

X DEBT AND FINANCIAL FLOWS - DETTE ET FLUX FINANCIERS										
	2006	2007	2008	2009	2010	2011	2012	2013	2014	
X-1 DEBT *US$ (MILLIONS)*										**X-1 DETTE EXTÉRIEURE** *$ E.U (MILLIONS)*
Total external debt	...	...	...	...	...	...	...	...	...	Dette extérieure totale
Private	...	...	...	...	...	...	...	...	...	Privée
Public	...	...	...	...	...	...	...	...	...	Publique
Total external debt service	...	...	...	...	...	...	...	...	...	Service de la dette extérieure
Present value of External debt	...	...	...	...	...	...	...	...	...	Valeur actuelle de la dette extérieure
Total government domestic debt (in local currency)	...	...	...	...	...	...	...	...	...	Dette publique intérieure
X-2 FINANCIAL FLOWS *US$ (MILLIONS)*										**X-2 FLUX FINANCIERS** *$ E.U (MILLIONS)*
Net Foreign Direct Investment Inflows	96	141	87	108	112	102	107	107	...	Investissements étranger direct (flux nets entrants)
Main origin of FDI Inflows										**Principales origines de l'IDE entrant:**
Country 1	...	...	...	...	...	...	...	...	...	Pays 1
Country 2	...	...	...	...	...	...	...	...	...	Pays 2
Country 3	...	...	...	...	...	...	...	...	...	Pays 3
Country 4	...	...	...	...	...	...	...	...	...	Pays 4
Country 5	...	...	...	...	...	...	...	...	...	Pays 5
African countries	...	...	...	...	...	...	...	...	...	Pays africains
Net total Official Development Assistance	396	394	766	662	498	1 096	999	992	...	Aide publique au développement (nette totale)
Main origin of Net ODA										**Principales origines de l'APD nette**
United States	95	59	243	195	59.4	121.5	219.6	178.9	...	Etats-Unis
United Kingdom	53	26	76	44	62.3	152.1	142.2	...	...	Royaume-Uni
Norway	34	43	44	33	31.6	84.2	35.0	63.1	...	Norvège
Sweden	13	26	25	29	25.9	63.5	42.3	57.6	...	Suède
Netherlands	14	12	19	15	9.3	27.9	17.6	6.4	...	Pays-Bas
General notes	National Accounts:The data are estimated by the statistics division of the United Nations.				Comptes Nationaux:Les données sont estimées par la division des statistiques des Nations Unies.					Notes générales

SOUTH AFRICA — AFRIQUE DU SUD

AREA (KM²)	1 221 040		SUPERFICIE (KM²)
CAPITAL CITY	Pretoria	Pretoria	CAPITALE
CURRENCY	Rand	Rand	MONNAIE

I SOCIAL AND DEMOGRAPHIC INDICATORS — INDICATEURS DEMOGRAPHIQUES ET SOCIAUX

	Year / Année	Value / Valeur	
POPULATION			**POPULATION**
Population ('000)			Population ('000)
Both sexes	2014	53 140	Les deux sexes
Male	2014	25 809	Masculin
Female	2014	27 331	Féminin
Average annual growth rate	2014	0.8	Taux de croissance annuel
Active Population ('000)	2014	19 050	Population active ('000)
Population by age group ('000)			Population par groupe d'âge ('000)
0-14 years	2014	15 621	0-14 ans
15-64 years	2014	34 526	15-64 ans
65+ years	2014	2 993	65+ ans
Economically active population in agriculture (%)	2014	5.5	Participation de la population active agricole (%)
Crude birth rate	2014	20.6	Taux brut de natalité
Crude death rate	2014	12.9	Taux brut de mortalité
Total fertility rate	2014	2.4	Indice synthétique de fécondité
Proportion of urban population	2014	63.3	Part de la population urbaine
Life Expectancy at Birth - Total (years)	2014	57.4	Espérance de vie à la naissance - Totale (ans)
Dependency Ratio - Total (%)	2014	52.5	Taux de dépendance - Total (%)
HEALTH			**SANTÉ**
Percentage of children under-five and underweight	2008	8.7	% d'enfants de moins de cinq ans avec insuffisance pondérale
Prevalence of undernourishment	2013	5.0	Prévalence de la malnutrition
Under five mortality rate (both sexes, per 1000)	2013	50.0	Taux de mortalité de moins de 5 ans (les deux sexes, pour 1000)
Infant mortality rate (both sexes) per 1000	2013	38.0	Taux de mortalité infantile (les deux sexes) par 1000
Percentage of children provided the vaccines :			Pourcentage d'enfants vaccinés :
BCG	2013	84.0	BCG
DPT3	2013	65.0	DTC3
Polio	2013	66.0	Polio
Measles	2013	66.0	Rougeole
Percentage of mothers provided at least one antenatal care (%)	2003	91.7	Pourcentage de mères ayant au moins reçu un soin prénatal (%)
Percentage of deliveries attended by skilled health personnel	2003	91.2	% d'accouchements assistés par un personnel de santé qualifié
Number of doctors (per 10 000 population)	2013	7.8	Nombre de médecins (pour 10 000 habitants)
Number of nurses (per 10 000 population)	2012	49.0	Nombre d'infirmières (pour 10 000 habitants)
Hospital beds - Total (per 10 000 population)	2005	28.4	Nombre de lits d'hôpitaux - Total (pour 10 000)
Births registered (per 1 000)	2014	20.6	Naiss.s enregistrées (pour 1 000)
Deaths registered (per 1 000)	2014	12.9	Décès enregistrés (pour 1 000)
Public expenditure on Health (% of budget)	2009	9.3	Dépenses publiques consacrées à la santé (% du budget)
EDUCATION			**EDUCATION**
Enrolment in primary education (both sexes) (000)	2013	7 064	Scolarisation dans le primaire (les deux sexes) (000)
Female	2013	3 425	Féminin
Enrolment in secondary education (both sexes) (000)	2013	5 201	Scolarisation dans le secondaire (les deux sexes) (000)
Female	2013	2 698	Féminin
Enrolment in tertiary education (both sexes) (000)	...	...	Scolarisation dans le tertiaire (les deux sexes) (000)
Female	2012	583.5	Féminin
Literacy rate (both sexes)	2012	93.7	Taux d'alphabétisation (deux sexes)
Male	2012	95.0	Masculin
Female	2012	92.6	Féminin
Pupil-teacher ratio	...	...	Ratio élève-enseignant
Public expenditure on education (% of budget)	2013	19.1	Dépenses publiques consacrées à l'enseignement (% du budget)
POVERTY			**PAUVRETÉ**
GNI Per Capita (US$)	2013	7 190.0	RNB par habitant ($EU)
Human Poverty Index (HPI-1) Value (%)	2007	25.4	Valeur de l'Indice de pauvreté (IPH-1) (%)
Population below International Poverty Line ($2/day) (%)	2011	26.2	Population sous le seuil international de pauvreté (2$/J) (%)
Share of Income Held by Richest 10%	2011	53.8	% de revenu des 10% plus riches
Share of Income Held by Poorest 10%	2011	1.1	% de revenu des 10% plus pauvres
Gini index	2011	65.0	Indice de Gini

Charts / Graphiques

Population by age group – 2014
Population par groupe d'age – 2014

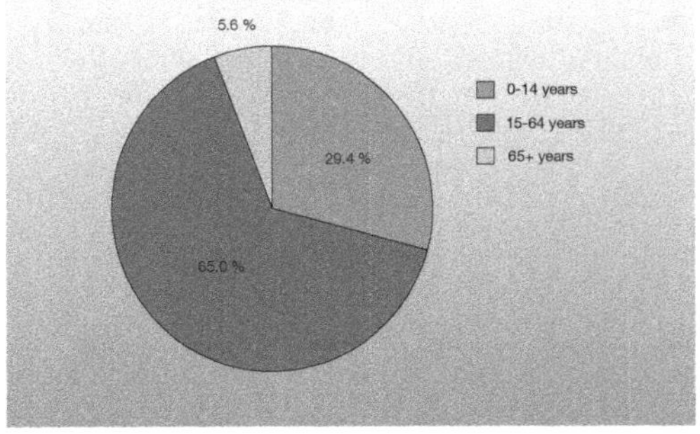

Percentage of children provided the vaccines – 2013
Pourcentage d'enfants vaccinés – 2013

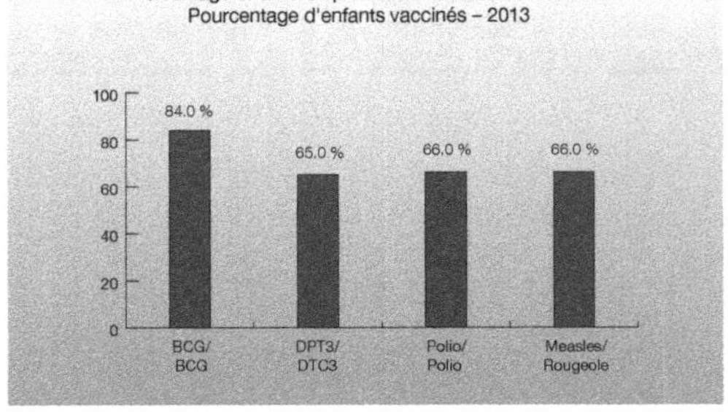

Literacy rate (%) – 2012
Taux d'alphabétisation – 2012

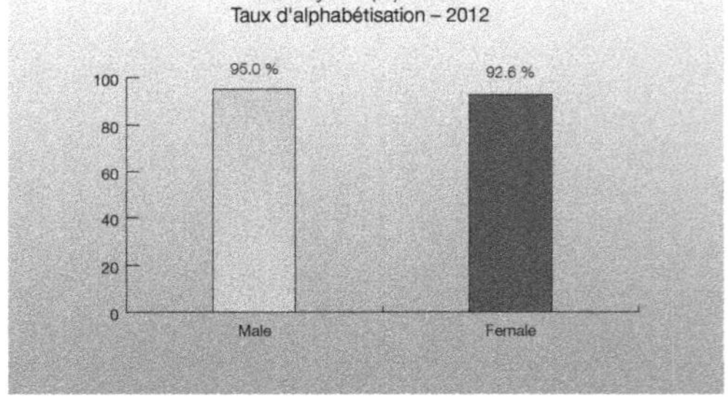

GNI Per Capita (US$)
RNB par habitant ($EU)

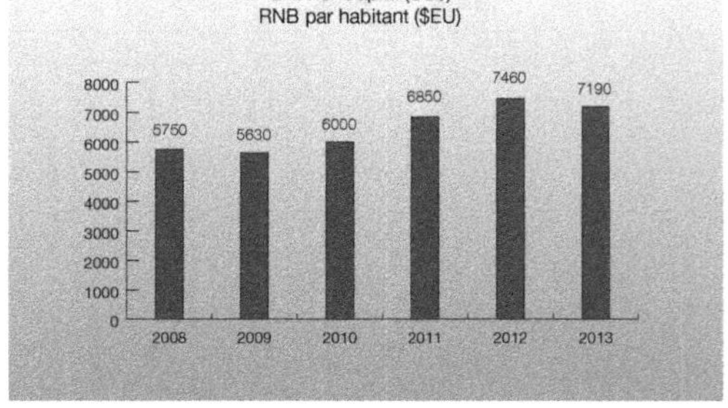

AFRIQUE DU SUD

II NATIONAL ACCOUNTS — COMPTES NATIONAUX	2006	2007	2008	2009	2010	2011	2012	2013	2014	
GROSS DOMESTIC PRODUCT BY KIND OF ECONOMIC ACTIVITY AT CURRENT PRICES *RAND (MILLIONS)*										**PRODUIT INTÉRIEUR BRUT PAR BRANCHE D'ACTIVITÉ ÉCONOMIQUE AUX PRIX COURANTS** *RAND (MILLIONS)*
Agriculture, hunting, forestry and fishing	42 884	55 762	67 743	68 044	65 605	68 591	70 245	73 458	84 662	Agriculture, chasse sylviculture et pêche
Mining and quarrying	132 843	157 672	197 643	200 824	230 350	262 391	271 410	284 802	286 607	Industries extractives
Manufacturing	269 769	302 991	341 697	341 658	358 699	363 174	385 654	419 931	452 326	Industries manufacturières
Electricity, gas & water	30 849	33 278	37 779	53 473	67 940	86 905	105 770	117 466	125 378	Electricité, gaz et eau
Construction & public works	49 117	65 631	92 953	95 753	95 453	103 302	111 040	126 435	138 917	Bâtiments et travaux publics
Wholesale & retail trade, restaurants, hotels	231 999	258 908	297 518	317 655	370 580	405 860	441 038	471 008	504 854	Commerce de gros et de détail, restaurants et hôtels
Finance, insurance, real estate, etc.	347 755	418 980	446 756	482 872	523 526	565 056	606 031	643 166	699 591	Banques, assurances, affaires immobilières
Transport and communications	196 054	210 995	221 549	223 427	229 499	258 731	292 841	317 974	339 930	Transport(s) et communications
Public administration and defense	236 104	264 777	309 629	356 819	404 647	449 360	482 144	532 122	578 030	Administrations publiques et défense
Education	...	...	...	...	...	...	...	...	...	Education
Health and Social Work	...	...	...	...	...	...	...	...	...	Santé et actions sociales
Other services	104 847	115 729	123 923	136 621	148 561	161 653	173 466	186 599	194 260	Autres services
Less Imputed Service Charges	...	...	...	...	...	...	...	...	...	Moins services d'intermédiation financière
Gross domestic product at factor cost / basic prices	1 642 221	1 884 723	2 137 190	2 277 146	2 494 860	2 725 023	2 939 639	3 172 961	3 404 555	Produit intérieur brut aux couts des facteurs / prix de base
Plus: indirect taxes / taxes on products, less subsidies	197 179	224 779	231 873	230 531	253 148	299 928	322 902	361 365	391 907	Plus taxes indirectes/impôts sur les produits, moins les subventions
EXPENDITURE ON GROSS DOMESTIC PRODUCT AT CURRENT PURCHASER'S VALUES *RAND (MILLIONS)*										**EMPLOI DU PRODUIT INTÉRIEUR BRUT AUX PRIX COURANTS D'ACQUISITION** *RAND (MILLIONS)*
Government final consumption	333 916	375 787	442 018	498 137	555 912	603 879	650 868	715 959	771 641	Consommation finale des administrations publiques
Private final consumption	1 136 725	1 296 996	1 421 795	1 492 269	1 621 836	1 796 841	1 974 588	2 143 324	2 299 426	Consommation finale privée
Gross fixed capital formation	348 105	435 548	556 997	539 440	529 431	566 676	614 505	708 357	769 230	Formation brute de capital fixe
Change in inventories	52 466	29 341	- 13 356	- 32 338	6 713	31 312	64 583	47 007	26 815	Variation des stocks
Exports of goods and services	538 464	657 613	843 918	699 940	786 349	920 928	969 814	1 094 771	1 186 640	Exportations de biens et services
Less imports of goods and services	570 276	685 783	882 309	689 771	752 233	894 685	1 011 813	1 175 091	1 257 292	Moins importations de biens et services
GDP at purchasers' values	1 839 400	2 109 502	2 369 063	2 507 677	2 748 008	3 024 951	3 262 545	3 534 327	3 796 460	PIB aux prix d'acquisition
GROSS DOMESTIC PRODUCT BY KIND OF ECONOMIC ACTIVITY AT CONSTANT PRICES *ANNUAL GROWTH RATES (%)*										**PRODUIT INTÉRIEUR BRUT PAR BRANCHE D'ACTIVITÉ ECONOMIQUE AUX PRIX CONSTANTS** *TAUX DE CROISSANCE ANNUEL (%)*
Agriculture, hunting, forestry and fishing	- 5.5	3.0	19.4	- 1.9	- 0.3	1.3	0.6	1.5	5.6	Agriculture, chasse sylviculture et pêche
Mining and quarrying	- 0.6	- 0.6	- 5.3	- 5.1	5.3	- 0.7	- 2.9	4.0	- 1.6	Industries extractives
Manufacturing	6.4	5.4	2.3	- 10.6	5.9	2.9	1.9	0.7	0.0	Industries manufacturières
Electricity, gas & water	3.4	3.4	- 3.5	- 1.8	2.4	1.4	- 0.1	- 0.6	- 0.9	Electricité, gaz et eau
Construction & public works	10.4	15.5	9.9	8.5	0.7	0.4	2.1	2.7	2.9	Bâtiments et travaux publics
Wholesale & retail trade, restaurants, hotels	6.0	5.6	1.8	- 1.1	4.4	3.8	3.6	1.9	1.3	Commerce de gros et de détail,restaurants et hôtels
Finance, insurance, real estate, etc.	7.7	6.1	5.6	2.0	1.9	4.3	3.2	3.1	2.6	Banques, assurances, affaires immobilières
Transport and communications	5.1	7.5	3.5	- 0.2	1.7	3.0	2.5	2.0	2.3	Transport(s) et communications
Public administration and defense	...	...	...	...	...	...	...	...	...	Administrations publiques et défense
Education	...	...	...	...	...	...	...	...	...	Education
Health and Social Work	...	...	...	...	...	...	...	...	...	Santé et actions sociales
Other services	5.2	5.5	3.8	- 0.8	0.4	2.4	2.1	1.8	1.4	Autres services
Less Imputed Service Charges	...	...	...	...	...	...	...	...	...	Moins services d'intérmediation financière
Gross domestic product at factor cost / basic prices	5.5	5.4	3.3	- 1.4	2.9	3.0	2.2	2.3	1.6	Produit intérieur brut aux couts des facteurs / prix de base
Plus: indirect taxes / taxes on products, less subsidies	6.2	4.9	2.3	- 2.6	4.2	5.1	2.5	1.3	1.1	Plus taxes indirectes/impôts sur les produits, moins les subventions
Gross domestic product at market prices	5.6	5.4	3.2	- 1.5	3.0	3.2	2.2	2.2	1.5	Produit intérieur brut aux prix du marché
EXPENDITURE ON GROSS DOMESTIC PRODUCT AT CONSTANT PURCHASERS' VALUES *ANNUAL GROWTH RATES (%)*										**EMPLOIS DU PRODUIT INTÉRIEUR BRUT AUX PRIX CONSTANTS D'ACQUISITION** *TAUX DE CROISSANCE ANNUEL (%)*
Government final consumption	1.9	4.0	5.8	4.6	3.0	1.7	3.4	3.3	1.9	Consommation finale des administrations publiques
Private final consumption	- 0.3	7.0	1.2	- 2.6	3.9	4.9	3.4	2.9	1.4	Consommation finale privée
Gross fixed capital formation	18.2	13.8	12.8	- 6.7	- 3.9	5.7	3.6	7.6	- 0.4	Formation brute de capital fixe
Exports of goods and services	25.6	7.8	1.5	- 17.0	7.7	4.3	0.1	4.6	2.6	Exportations de biens et services
Less imports of goods and services	13.5	9.4	2.8	- 17.7	10.8	10.5	6.0	1.8	- 0.5	Moins importations de biens et services
Notes	The Accounts are calculated using the new base year 2010					Les comptes Annuels sont élaborés selon la nouvelle année de base 2010				Notes

III INFLATION	2006	2007	2008	2009	2010	2011	2012	2013	2014	
ANNUAL GROWTH RATES (%)										**TAUX DE CROISSANCE ANNUEL (%)**
All items	3.2	6.2	9.9	7.2	4.1	5.0	5.6	5.7	6.1	Ensemble
of which:										dont:
Food and Non-alcoholic beverages	6.0	10.0	15.1	9.4	1.2	7.1	7.2	5.7	8.0	Alimentation et boissons non alcoolisés
Alcoholic beverages & tobacco	7.8	7.8	8.8	11.1	9.1	6.1	7.2	7.0	6.4	Boissons alcoolisées et tabacs
Clothing and Footwear	-8.6	-8.4	13.1	4.9	1.9	2.3	3.8	3.2	5.4	Habillement et chaussures
Housing, Water, Electricity, Gas and Other Fuels	4.4	10.9	11.4	8.1	6.7	6.8	6.4	5.7	5.7	Logement, eau, électricité, gas et autres combustibles
Furnishing, household equip	1.6	3.7	4.4	6.0	0.2	1.3	2.4	3.2	3.0	Meubles, articles de ménage et entretien courant
Health	3.8	4.4	9.6	10.8	7.6	5.9	5.3	4.6	5.3	Santé
Transport	3.0	2.7	8.0	-0.5	2.5	5.0	6.4	6.2	6.4	Transport
Communication	-2.4	-0.2	-0.2	0.5	-2.0	-1.9	-0.9	1.1	-0.7	Communication
Recreation & culture	-0.1	0.4	3.0	11.5	0.0	-0.6	0.9	3.3	2.7	Loisirs et culture
Education	6.2	6.4	6.8	9.6	9.5	9.0	8.9	9.0	8.8	Enseignement
Restaurants & hotels	...	...	...	10.5	9.4	8.7	8.2	7.3	8.4	Restaurants et hôtels
Miscellaneous goods & services	2.9	5.3	7.8	11.7	6.5	4.1	5.3	7.0	6.7	Biens et services divers

	2006	2007	2008	2009	2010	2011	2012	2013	2014	
IV AGRICULTURAL PRODUCTION - PRODUCTION AGRICOLE										
TONNES *(THOUSAND)*										**TONNES** *(MILLIERS)*
Sugar cane	20 275	19 724	19 255	18 655	16 016	16 800	17 278	18 000	...	Canne à sucre
Maize	6 935	7 125	12 700	12 050	12 815	10 360	11 830	12 486	...	Maïs
Potato	1 863	1 972	2 040	1 867	2 090	2 195	2 251	2 252	...	Pommes de terre
Wheat	2 105	1 905	2 130	1 958	1 430	2 005	1 915	1 879	...	Blé
Grapes	1 757	1 812	1 865	1 749	1 743	1 684	1 839	1 850	...	Raisins
V MINING PRODUCTION - PRODUCTION MINIERE										
	2006	2007	2008	2009	2010	2011	2012	2013	2014	
Hard Coal, metric tons (thousands)	244 784	247 666	252 699	250 538	254 522	252 757	...	...	...	Houille, tonnes métriques (milliers)
Iron ores and concentrates, metric tons (thousands)	41 195	42 083	48 983	55 313	58 709	58 056	...	...	...	Minerais de fer et concentrés, tonnes métriques (milliers)
Copper ores and concentrates, metric tons (thousands)	89 700	97 000	108 700	107 600	102 600	96 600	...	...	...	Minerais de cuivre et concentrés, tonnes métriques (milliers)
VI ENERGY - ENERGIE										
	2006	2007	2008	2009	2010	2011	2012	2013	2014	
Total electricity generation (GWh)	231 050	238 992	236 564	240 444	245 840	279 585	258 237	283 728	...	Production d'électricité totale (GWh)
of which:										dont:
Production of electricity from fossil fuels (GWh)	214 347	222 932	218 690	222 603	227 552	257 857	235 766	260 017	...	Production d'électricité à partir de combustibles fossiles (GWh)
Production of hydro electricity (GWh)	5 845	3 908	4 032	4 194	5 091	7 858	7 858	7 858	...	Production d'électricité d'origine hydraulique (GWh)
Production of electricity from solar, wind, tide, wave and other sources (GWh)	564	564	564	564	110	123	131	142	...	Production d'électricité d'origine solaire, éolienne, marée motrice et autres (GWh)
VII TOURISM AND INFRASTRUCTURE - TOURISME ET INFRASTRUCTURE										
	2006	2007	2008	2009	2010	2011	2012	2013	2014	
VII-1 TOURISM										**VII-1 TOURISME**
International tourist arrivals (thousands)	6 259	6 774	7 157	7 012	8 074	8 339	9 188	9 383	10 070	Arrivées de touristes internationaux (milliers)
Rooms in hotels and similar establishments (thousands)	...	...	...	...	...	...	...	...	...	Chambres d'hotels et établissements assimilés (milliers)
Overnight stays (thousands)	38 052	41 875	44 951	42 140	49 686	52 771	57 960	59 683	63 150	Nuitées (milliers)
Tourism receipts (US$ thousand)	7956 340	8601 880	7796 130	7471 010	8918 240	9337 370	9818 270	9080 320	9209 430	Recettes touristiques (milliers de $ EU)
Total contribution to GDP (%)	9.7	9.7	9.3	9.2	8.9	8.5	9.1	9.2	9.4	Contribution totale au PIB (%)
Total contribution to Employment (%)	10.1	10.2	9.9	9.6	9.5	9.2	9.7	9.7	9.9	Contribution totale à l'emploi (%)
VII-2 INFRASTRUCTURE										**VII-2 INFRASTRUCTURE**
Paved roads (% of total)	...	...	...	...	...	...	...	...	...	Routes asphaltées (% du total)
Total Network (Railways-km)	20 047	24 487	24 487	22 051	22 051	20 500	20 500	...	...	Réseau total voies ferrées-Km
Main Telephone Lines (per 100 inhabitants)	10	10	10	10	9	9	9	7	...	Lignes téléphoniques fixes (pour 100 habitants)
Mobile Cellular Subscribers (per 100 inhabitants)	81	85	90	91	98	123	131	146	...	Abonnés aux téléphones mobiles (pour 100 habitants)
VIII EXTERNAL TRADE - COMMERCE EXTERIEUR										
	2006	2007	2008	2009	2010	2011	2012	2013	2014	
US$ (MILLIONS) **EXPORTS, FOB**										**$ E.U (MILLIONS)** **EXPORTATIONS, FÀB**
Exports - Total	65 825	76 435	86 118	66 542	85 700	92 976	86 712	80 010	...	Exportations - Total
Exports to AFRICA	...	...	...	...	...	...	...	...	...	Exportations vers l'AFRIQUE
Main Products										**Principaux produits**
Silver, platinum, other metals of the platinum group	9 765	11 415	11 476	7 942	10 242	11 070	...	...	...	Argent, platine et métaux de la mine du platine
Coal, whether or not pulverized, not agglomerated	3 994	4 261	5 897	4 726	5 187	5 870	...	...	...	Houilles, même pulvérisées, mais non agglomérées
Pig iron & spiegeleisen, sponge iron, powder & granu	2 954	4 147	6 289	3 177	5 160	4 721	...	...	...	Fonte, fer spongieux, poudres de fer et d'acier
Gold, non-monetary (excluding gold ores and concentrates)	2 691	4 195	3 811	3 276	5 008	6 597	...	...	...	Or, à usage non monétaire
Pearls, precious & semi-precious stones	4 202	4 773	4 701	3 276	4 291	2 894	...	...	...	Perles fines ou de culture, pierres gemmes et similaires
Main Destinations										**Principales destinations**
China	3 419	5 620	6 636	7 389	11 450	16 733	10 139	...	...	Chine
United States	7 629	8 768	8 903	5 638	8 026	8 272	7 586	...	...	États-Unis
Japan	7 124	7 698	8 359	4 691	7 022	7 374	5 414	...	...	Japon
United Kingdom	6 897	7 363	7 682	5 884	6 951	4 656	3 358	...	...	Royaume-Uni
Germany	4 838	5 530	6 258	4 344	6 093	6 066	4 175	...	...	Allemagne
IMPORTS, CIF										**IMPORTATIONS, CAF**
Imports - Total	80 951	90 527	87 593	75 647	96 249	122 418	101 611	94 820	...	Importations - Total (millions)
Imports from Africa	...	...	...	...	...	...	...	...	...	Importations en provenance de l'Afrique
Main Products										**Principaux produits**
Petroleum, petroleum products and related materials	12 242	14 318	18 513	12 949	14 769	20 083	...	...	...	Pétrole et produits dérivés
Road vehicles	6 566	7 746	6 161	4 340	6 856	8 742	...	...	...	Véhicules routiers
Other industrial machinery and parts	3 378	3 882	4 272	3 342	3 796	4 793	...	...	...	Autres machines industrielles et pièces détachées
Telecommunication and sound recording apparatus	3 745	3 818	3 913	3 172	4 398	4 762	...	...	...	Équipements pour les télécommunications et le son
Specialised machinery	2 866	4 159	4 417	2 605	2 759	4 261	...	...	...	Machines et appareils spécialisés
Main Origin										**Principales provenances**
Germany	8 584	9 317	9 914	7 438	9 051	10 659	10 237	...	...	Allemagne
China	6 879	8 563	9 909	8 325	11 499	14 200	14 638	...	...	Chine
United States	5 216	6 166	7 038	4 949	5 838	7 955	7 497	...	...	États-Unis
Japan	4 458	5 249	4 883	3 094	4 245	4 726	4 623	...	...	Japon
Saudi Arabia	3 612	3 606	5 523	3 204	3 243	4 445	7 877	...	...	Arabie saoudite

IX FINANCIAL AND MONETARY STATISTICS - FINANCES ET STATISTIQUES MONETAIRES	2006	2007	2008	2009	2010	2011	2012	2013	2014	
IX-1 MONETARY STATISTICS *RAND (MILLIONS)*										**IX-1 STATISTIQUES MONÉTAIRES** *RAND (MILLIONS)*
Money supply (M1)	1 349 290	1 667 580	1 914 200	1 948 220	2 083 110	2 255 300	2 372 200	2 518 130	2 714 290	Masse monétaire (M1)
Quasi-money	796 297	962 436	1 150 864	1 154 303	1 217 424	1 420 874	1 475 003	1 552 370	1 690 421	Quasi-monnaie
of which Demand Deposit	...	...	...	...	...	...	...	...	...	dont Monnaie scripturale
Net foreign assets	271 460	302 579	387 441	333 510	337 781	504 824	504 105	641 393	600 239	Avoirs extérieurs nets
Domestic credit	1 433 677	1 735 551	2 000 012	2 108 473	2 238 120	2 292 052	2 524 945	2 586 829	2 833 667	Crédit intérieur
of which claims on private sector	1 354 286	1 651 656	1 816 799	1 870 685	1 933 351	2 043 637	2 233 178	2 381 470	2 551 944	dont créances sur le secteur privé
of which claims on government sector, net	- 38 623	- 49 506	- 50 957	55 124	51 900	- 16 724	- 24 842	- 115 106	- 108 153	dont créances nettes sur le gouvernement
International reserves (millions US$)	23 267	29 810	30 800	35 458	38 392	42 811	44 212	45 080	44 472	Réserves internationales (millions $EU)
Average Exchange Rate (National Currency per US$)	6.77	7.05	8.26	8.47	7.32	7.26	8.21	9.66	10.82	Taux de change (moyen) (monnaie nationale par $ EU)
IX-2 PUBLIC FINANCE *RAND (MILLIONS)*										**IX-2 FINANCES PUBLIQUES** *RAND (MILLIONS)*
Total Revenues and Grants	411 164	481 197	560 795	682 995	664 842	762 873	842 263	909 276	1 010 489	Recettes totales et dons
Tax Revenue	402 463	471 668	548 998	596 178	570 791	656 277	720 890	771 675	855 626	Recettes fiscales
Non Tax Revenue	8 701	9 529	11 797	86 817	94 051	106 596	121 374	137 601	154 863	Recettes non fiscales
Grants	-	-	-	-	-	-	-	-	-	Dons
Total Expenditures and Net Lending	416 784	470 193	541 445	674 643	782 227	874 047	947 408	1 041 742	1 144 273	Dépenses totales et prêts nets
Current expenditure	415 051	470 910	542 005	633 749	717 908	782 181	877 896	952 315	1 037 449	Dépenses courantes
Of which Wages and Salaries	140 202	154 687	177 012	211 164	248 612	281 651	314 711	341 079	373 861	Dont rémunérations et salaires
Capital expenditure	20 649	22 970	26 090	29 861	32 608	69 428	66 465	84 486	102 119	Dépenses d'équipement
Net Lending	- 18 916	- 23 688	- 26 650	11 033	31 711	22 438	3 048	4 940	4 704	Prêts nets
Fiscal Balance	- 5 620	11 004	19 349	8 352	- 117 385	- 111 174	- 105 145	- 132 466	- 133 784	Solde global y compris les dons
IX-3 BALANCE OF PAYMENTS *US$ (MILLIONS)*										**IX-3 BALANCE DES PAIEMENTS** *$ E.U (MILLIONS)*
Trade balance	- 324 935	- 5 157	- 4 304	268	3 716	2 257	- 31 545	- 68 341	- 115 806	Balance commerciale
Services Balance	- 2 065	- 2 672	- 4 059	- 2 760	- 4 437	- 4 738	- 10 454	- 11 979	- 21 904	Balance des services
Net Income	- 5 135	- 9 768	- 8 942	- 6 316	- 7 229	- 9 168	- 86 388	- 90 734	- 59 580	Revenus nets
Compensation of employees	...	...	...	...	...	...	...	...	...	Rémunération des salariés
Investment Income	...	...	...	...	...	...	...	...	...	Revenus des investissements
Current transfers, net total	- 2 329	- 2 353	- 2 289	- 2 647	- 2 290	- 1 955	- 33 301	- 32 668	- 26 811	Transferts courants
Net official transfers	...	...	...	...	...	...	...	...	...	Transferts officiels nets
Workers' remittances	...	...	...	...	...	...	...	...	...	Envois de fonds des travailleurs
Other private transfers	...	...	...	...	...	...	...	...	...	Autres transferts privés
Current account balance	- 13 852	- 19 949	- 19 594	- 11 455	- 10 238	- 13 605	- 161 688	- 203 722	- 224 102	Solde du compte courant
Capital & financial account	...	...	...	...	...	...	...	...	...	Comptes de capital et financier
Capital account	...	...	...	...	...	...	...	...	...	Compte de capital
Financial account	...	...	...	...	...	...	...	...	...	Compte financier
Errors & omissions	...	...	...	...	...	...	...	...	...	Erreurs et omissions
Overall balance	...	...	...	...	...	...	...	...	...	Balance générale

X DEBT AND FINANCIAL FLOWS - DETTE ET FLUX FINANCIERS										
	2006	2007	2008	2009	2010	2011	2012	2013	2014	
X-1 DEBT *US$ (MILLIONS)*										**X-1 DETTE EXTÉRIEURE** *$ E.U (MILLIONS)*
Total external debt	59 396	75 316	72 869	78 561	104 456	113 134	137 508	123 802	...	Dette extérieure totale
Private	54 334	70 244	67 786	73 467	97 352	105 020	129 384	115 668	...	Privée
Public	5 062	5 072	5 083	5 094	7 104	8 114	8 124	8 134	...	Publique
Total external debt service	29 290	30 848	45 724	38 931	31 471	34 215	36 656	41 880	...	Service de la dette extérieure
Present value of External debt	...	...	...	...	...	...	...	...	...	Valeur actuelle de la dette extérieure
Total government domestic debt (in local currency)	496	493	521	658	840.1	1 029.8	1 209.2	...	...	Dette publique intérieure
X-2 FINANCIAL FLOWS *US$ (MILLIONS)*										**X-2 FLUX FINANCIERS** *$ E.U (MILLIONS)*
Net Foreign Direct Investment Inflows	- 527	5 695	9 209	7 502	3 636	4 243	4 559	8 188	...	Investissements étranger direct (flux nets entrants)
Main origin of FDI Inflows										**Principales origines de l'IDE entrant:**
United Kingdom	2 698	2 211	2 412	1 550	3 798.3	2 899.0	8 061.8	...	...	Royaume-Uni
Switzerland	344	815	3 450	- 226	121.6	245.4	129.1	...	...	Suisse
United States	...	...	...	...	...	...	...	...	...	États-Unis
Germany	666	782	- 34	307	740.4	605.9	316.2	...	...	Allemagne
France	262	197	338	376	276.8	366.3	217.2	...	...	France
African countries	...	...	...	...	...	...	...	...	...	Pays africains
Net total Official Development Assistance	715	807	1 125	1 075	1 031	1 403	1 067	1 293	...	Aide publique au développement (nette totale)
Main origin of Net ODA										**Principales origines de l'APD nette**
United States	141	227	379	524	529.5	564.0	505.3	479.4	...	Etats-Unis
Germany	41	101	150	87	39.5	34.0	13.7	14.5	...	Allemagne
United Kingdom	1	- 23	113	67	39.3	46.6	- 21.7	...	...	Royaume-Uni
France	159	105	33	- 16	47.6	143.9	57.8	301.2	...	France
Netherlands	53	45	36	49	36.1	32.5	21.9	10.3	...	Pays-Bas

SOUTH SUDAN — SOUDAN DU SUD

AREA (KM²)		619 745	**SUPERFICIE (KM²)**
CAPITAL CITY	Juba	Djouba	**CAPITALE**
CURRENCY	South Sudanese Pound	Livre Sud-Soudanaise	**MONNAIE**

I SOCIAL AND DEMOGRAPHIC INDICATORS – INDICATEURS DEMOGRAPHIQUES ET SOCIAUX

	Year / Année	Value / Valeur	
POPULATION			**POPULATION**
Population ('000)			Population ('000)
Both sexes	2014	11 384	Les deux sexes
Male	2014	5 042	Masculin
Female	2014	6 343	Féminin
Average annual growth rate	2014	2.4	Taux de croissance annuel
Active Population ('000)	2014	...	Population active ('000)
Population by age group ('000)			Population par groupe d'âge ('000)
0-14 years	2014	5 012	0-14 ans
15-64 years	2014	5 362	15-64 ans
65+ years	2014	98	65+ ans
Economically active population in agriculture (%)	2014	42.6	Participation de la population active agricole (%)
Crude birth rate	2014	35.7	Taux brut de natalité
Crude death rate	2014	11.5	Taux brut de mortalité
Total fertility rate	2014	7.5	Indice synthétique de fécondité
Proportion of urban population	2014	19.4	Part de la population urbaine
Life Expectancy at Birth - Total (years)	2014	60.6	Espérance de vie à la naissance - Totale (ans)
Dependency Ratio - Total (%)	2014	52.2	Taux de dépendance - Total (%)
HEALTH			**SANTÉ**
Percentage of children under-five and underweight	2014	27.6	% d'enfants de moins de cinq ans avec insuffisance pondérale
Prevalence of undernourishment	...	...	Prévalence de la malnutrition
Under five mortality rate (both sexes, per 1000)	2014	66.0	Taux de mortalité de moins de 5 ans (les deux sexes, pour 1000)
Infant mortality rate (both sexes) per 1000	2014	102.0	Taux de mortalité infantile (les deux sexes) par 1000
Percentage of children provided the vaccines :			Pourcentage d'enfants vaccinés :
BCG	2013	38.0	BCG
DPT3	2013	38.0	DTC3
Polio	2013	39.0	Polio
Measles	2013	54.0	Rougeole
Percentage of mothers provided at least one antenatal care (%)	2014	27.6	Pourcentage de mères ayant au moins reçu un soin prénatal (%)
Percentage of deliveries attended by skilled health personnel	2010	19.4	% d'accouchements assistés par un personnel de santé qualifié
Number of doctors (per 10 000 population)	...	...	Nombre de médecins (pour 10 000 habitants)
Number of nurses (per 10 000 population)	...	...	Nombre d'infirmières (pour 10 000 habitants)
Hospital beds - Total (per 10 000 population)	...	...	Nombre de lits d'hôpitaux - Total (pour 10 000)
Births registered (per 1 000)	2014	35.7	Naiss.s enregistrées (pour 1 000)
Deaths registered (per 1 000)	2014	11.5	Décès enregistrés (pour 1 000)
Public expenditure on Health (% of budget)	2014	4.0	Dépenses publiques consacrées à la santé (% du budget)
EDUCATION			**EDUCATION**
Enrolment in primary education (both sexes) (000)	2013	1 311	Scolarisation dans le primaire (les deux sexes) (000)
Female	2013	511	Féminin
Enrolment in secondary education (both sexes) (000)	2013	47	Scolarisation dans le secondaire (les deux sexes) (000)
Female	2013	15	Féminin
Enrolment in tertiary education (both sexes) (000)	2011	0.0	Scolarisation dans le tertiaire (les deux sexes) (000)
Female	...	...	Féminin
Literacy rate (both sexes)	2013	39.0	Taux d'alphabétisation (deux sexes)
Male	2013	40.0	Masculin
Female	2013	16.0	Féminin
Pupil-teacher ratio	2013	47.3	Ratio élève-enseignant
Public expenditure on education (% of budget)	2014	7.0	Dépenses publiques consacrées à l'enseignement (% du budget)
POVERTY			**PAUVRETÉ**
GNI Per Capita (US$)	2013	950.0	RNB par habitant ($EU)
Human Poverty Index (HPI-1) Value (%)	...	...	Valeur de l'Indice de pauvreté (IPH-1) (%)
Population below International Poverty Line ($2/day) (%)	2014	50.6	Population sous le seuil international de pauvreté (2$/J) (%)
Share of Income Held by Richest 10%	...	...	% de revenu des 10% plus riches
Share of Income Held by Poorest 10%	...	...	% de revenu des 10% plus pauvres
Gini index	2014	45.0	Indice de Gini

Charts / Graphiques

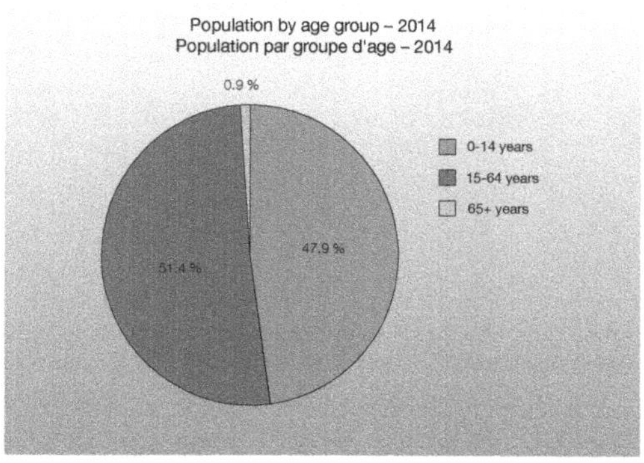

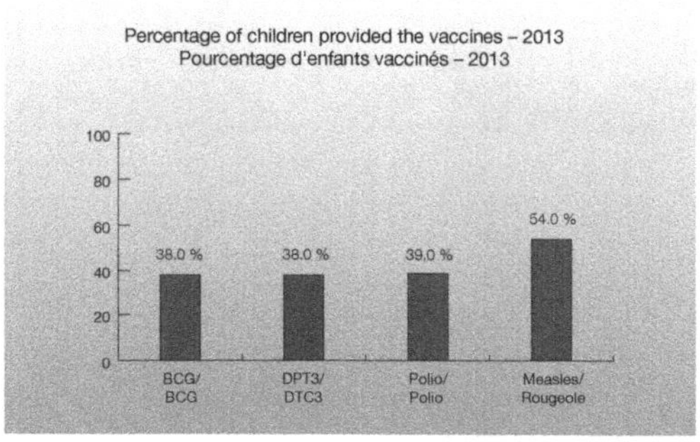

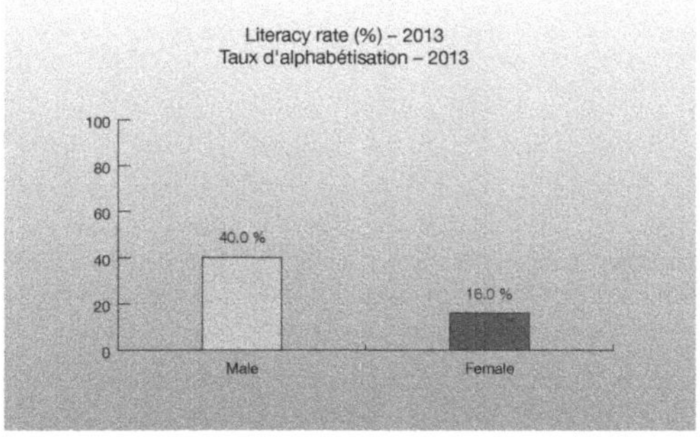

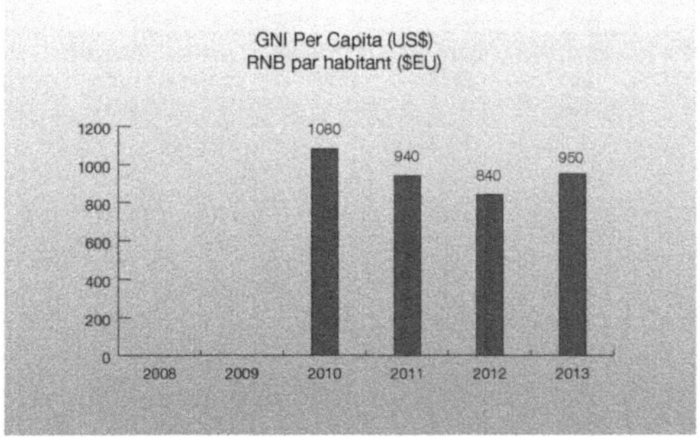

II NATIONAL ACCOUNTS — COMPTES NATIONAUX

	2006	2007	2008	2009	2010	2011	2012	2013	2014	
GROSS DOMESTIC PRODUCT BY KIND OF ECONOMIC ACTIVITY AT CURRENT PRICES *SOUTH SUDANESE POUND (MILLIONS)*										**PRODUIT INTÉRIEUR BRUT PAR BRANCHE D'ACTIVITÉ ÉCONOMIQUE AUX PRIX COURANTS** *LIVRE SUD-SOUDANAISE (MILLIONS)*
Agriculture, hunting, forestry and fishing	...	...	...	...	...	-	...	...	...	Agriculture, chasse sylviculture et pêche
Mining and quarrying	...	...	...	...	...	-	...	...	...	Industries extractives
Manufacturing	...	...	...	...	...	-	...	...	...	Industries manufacturières
Electricity, gas & water	...	...	...	...	...	-	...	...	...	Electricité, gaz et eau
Construction & public works	...	...	...	...	...	-	...	...	...	Bâtiments et travaux publics
Wholesale & retail trade, restaurants, hotels	...	...	...	...	...	-	...	...	...	Commerce de gros et de détail, restaurants et hôtels
Finance, insurance, real estate, etc.	...	...	...	...	...	-	...	...	...	Banques, assurances, affaires immobilières
Transport and communications	...	...	...	...	...	-	...	...	...	Transport(s) et communications
Public administration and defense	...	...	...	...	...	-	...	...	...	Administrations publiques et défense
Education	...	...	...	...	...	...	...	...	...	Education
Health and Social Work	...	...	...	...	...	...	...	...	...	Santé et actions sociales
Other services	...	...	...	...	...	-	...	...	...	Autres services
Less Imputed Service Charges	...	...	...	...	...	...	...	...	...	Moins services d'intermédiation financière
Gross domestic product at factor cost / basic prices	-	-	-	-	-	-	-	-	-	Produit intérieur brut aux couts des facteurs / prix de base
Plus: indirect taxes / taxes on products, less subsidies	...	...	...	...	...	-	...	...	...	Plus taxes indirectes/impôts sur les produits, moins les subventions
EXPENDITURE ON GROSS DOMESTIC PRODUCT AT CURRENT PURCHASER'S VALUES *SOUTH SUDANESE POUND (MILLIONS)*										**EMPLOI DU PRODUIT INTÉRIEUR BRUT AUX PRIX COURANTS D'ACQUISITION** *LIVRE SUD-SOUDANAISE (MILLIONS)*
Government final consumption	...	...	4 770	4 364	5 910	6 725	7 013	8 025	...	Consommation finale des administrations publiques
Private final consumption	...	...	11 916	13 132	15 027	20 754	30 906	31 232	...	Consommation finale privée
Gross fixed capital formation	...	...	4 478	3 857	3 730	5 056	3 402	4 128	...	Formation brute de capital fixe
Change in inventories	...	...	43	- 387	10	7	17	18	...	Variation des stocks
Exports of goods and services	...	...	21 472	17 040	22 270	35 208	3 096	6 334	...	Exportations de biens et services
Less imports of goods and services	...	...	10 159	9 753	10 697	14 467	13 844	14 914	...	Moins importations de biens et services
GDP at purchasers' values	-	-	32 520	28 252	36 250	53 284	30 588	34 823	-	PIB aux prix d'acquisition
GROSS DOMESTIC PRODUCT BY KIND OF ECONOMIC ACTIVITY AT CONSTANT PRICES *ANNUAL GROWTH RATES (%)*										**PRODUIT INTÉRIEUR BRUT PAR BRANCHE D'ACTIVITÉ ECONOMIQUE AUX PRIX CONSTANTS** *TAUX DE CROISSANCE ANNUEL (%)*
Agriculture, hunting, forestry and fishing	...	...	...	...	...	...	...	...	...	Agriculture, chasse sylviculture et pêche
Mining and quarrying	...	...	...	...	...	...	...	...	...	Industries extractives
Manufacturing	...	...	...	...	...	...	...	...	...	Industries manufacturières
Electricity, gas & water	...	...	...	...	...	...	...	...	...	Electricité, gaz et eau
Construction & public works	...	...	...	...	...	...	...	...	...	Bâtiments et travaux publics
Wholesale & retail trade, restaurants, hotels	...	...	...	...	...	...	...	...	...	Commerce de gros et de détail,restaurants et hôtels
Finance, insurance, real estate, etc.	...	...	...	...	...	...	...	...	...	Banques, assurances, affaires immobilières
Transport and communications	...	...	...	...	...	...	...	...	...	Transport(s) et communications
Public administration and defense	...	...	...	...	...	...	...	...	...	Administrations publiques et défense
Education	...	...	...	...	...	...	...	...	...	Education
Health and Social Work	...	...	...	...	...	...	...	...	...	Santé et actions sociales
Other services	...	...	...	...	...	...	...	...	...	Autres services
Less Imputed Service Charges	...	...	...	...	...	...	...	...	...	Moins services d'intérmediation financière
Gross domestic product at factor cost / basic prices	...	...	...	...	...	...	...	...	...	Produit intérieur brut aux couts des facteurs / prix de base
Plus: indirect taxes / taxes on products, less subsidies	...	...	...	...	...	...	...	...	...	Plus taxes indirectes/impôts sur les produits, moins les subventions
Gross domestic product at market prices	...	...	...	5.0	5.5	- 4.6	- 46.1	13.1	...	Produit intérieur brut aux prix du marché
EXPENDITURE ON GROSS DOMESTIC PRODUCT AT CONSTANT PURCHASERS' VALUES *ANNUAL GROWTH RATES (%)*										**EMPLOIS DU PRODUIT INTÉRIEUR BRUT AUX PRIX CONSTANTS D'ACQUISITION** *TAUX DE CROISSANCE ANNUEL (%)*
Government final consumption	...	...	...	- 11.3	27.8	- 15.6	- 6.8	10.9	...	Consommation finale des administrations publiques
Private final consumption	...	...	...	4.3	12.5	- 4.9	4.5	4.2	...	Consommation finale privée
Gross fixed capital formation	...	...	...	- 21.0	- 5.7	7.3	- 53.2	17.6	...	Formation brute de capital fixe
Exports of goods and services	...	...	...	10.8	- 1.6	- 2.1	- 91.9	99.5	...	Exportations de biens et services
Less imports of goods and services	...	...	...	- 10.6	12.4	- 2.6	- 35.3	10.7	...	Moins importations de biens et services
Notes	National Accounts data 2014 is projected					les données des comptes nationaux des années 2014 sont des projections				Notes

III INFLATION

	2006	2007	2008	2009	2010	2011	2012	2013	2014	
ANNUAL GROWTH RATES (%)										**TAUX DE CROISSANCE ANNUEL (%)**
All items	...	...	25.8	8.9	12.8	47.3	45.1	0.0	1.7	Ensemble
of which:										dont:
Food and Non-alcoholic beverages	...	...	-0.8	-6.9	8.8	53.6	44.0	-4.0	2.6	Alimentation et boissons non alcoolisés
Alcoholic beverages & tobacco	...	...	-1.7	-9.7	15.7	75.8	134.2	33.1	-13.2	Boissons alcoolisées et tabacs
Clothing and Footwear	...	...	22.1	2.3	-	...	30.0	10.5	-1.4	Habillement et chaussures
Housing, Water, Electricity, Gas and Other Fuels	...	...	...	...	...	25.7	40.2	-7.9	12.3	Logement, eau, électricité, gas et autres combustibles
Furnishing, household equip	...	...	2.0	-1.2	-5.0	58.5	46.0	-0.3	2.6	Meubles, articles de ménage et entretien courant
Health	...	...	7.6	-1.3	-2.2	...	7.0	-8.6	11.6	Santé
Transport	...	...	...	...	...	35.0	26.8	-2.5	-8.1	Transport
Communication	...	...	-5.0	-5.0	-	...	0.9	-1.0	-5.8	Communication
Recreation & culture	...	...	...	...	...	14.7	33.4	11.8	14.5	Loisirs et culture
Education	...	...	-1.9	-10.1	-	...	43.4	12.3	3.8	Enseignement
Restaurants & hotels	...	...	...	...	...	25.2	34.9	17.5	3.3	Restaurants et hôtels
Miscellaneous goods & services	...	...	-0.7	9.3	16.6	10.8	29.7	12.4	3.2	Biens et services divers

SOUDAN DU SUD

IV AGRICULTURAL PRODUCTION - PRODUCTION AGRICOLE	2006	2007	2008	2009	2010	2011	2012	2013	2014	
TONNES *(THOUSAND)*										**TONNES** *(MILLIERS)*
Cereals	709	711	1 068	660	695	...	...	...	...	Céréales
Olive oil	...	...	...	...	...	...	...	...	...	Huile d'olive
Dates	...	...	...	...	...	...	...	...	...	Dattes
Citrus	...	...	...	...	...	...	...	...	...	Agrumes
Milk	...	...	...	...	...	...	...	...	...	Lait

V MINING PRODUCTION - PRODUCTION MINIERE	2006	2007	2008	2009	2010	2011	2012	2013	2014	
Petroleum, Crude, Metric tons (thousands)	...	...	168	125	320	122	...	...	...	Pétrole, brut, tonnes métriques (milliers)
Lead ore, Tons (thousands)	...	...	...	...	...	...	...	...	...	Minerai de plomb, tonnes (milliers)
Iron ore, Tons (thousands)	...	...	...	...	...	...	...	...	...	Minerai de fer, tonnes (milliers)

VI ENERGY - ENERGIE	2006	2007	2008	2009	2010	2011	2012	2013	2014	
Total electricity generation (GWh)	...	...	...	...	...	172	193	271	...	Production d'électricité totale (GWh)
of which:										dont:
Production of electricity from fossil fuels (GWh)	-	-	-	-	-	158	175	250	...	Production d'électricité à partir de combustibles fossiles (GWh)
Production of hydro electricity (GWh)	...	...	...	...	...	14	18	21	...	Production d'électricité d'origine hydraulique (GWh)
Production of electricity from solar, wind, tide, wave and other sources (GWh)	...	...	...	...	...	0	0	0	...	Production d'électricité d'origine solaire, éolienne, marée motrice et autres (GWh)

VII TOURISM AND INFRASTRUCTURE - TOURISME ET INFRASTRUCTURE	2006	2007	2008	2009	2010	2011	2012	2013	2014	
VII-1 TOURISM										**VII-1 TOURISME**
International tourist arrivals (thousands)	...	...	...	...	...	...	...	...	...	Arrivées de touristes internationaux (milliers)
Rooms in hotels and similar establishments (thousands)	...	...	...	...	...	...	...	...	...	Chambres d'hotels et établissements assimilés (milliers)
Overnight stays (thousands)	...	...	...	...	...	...	...	...	...	Nuitées (milliers)
Tourism receipts (US$ thousand)	...	...	...	...	...	...	...	...	...	Recettes touristiques (milliers de $ EU)
Total contribution to GDP (%)	...	...	...	...	...	...	...	...	...	Contribution totale au PIB (%)
Total contribution to Employment (%)	...	...	...	...	...	...	...	...	...	Contribution totale à l'emploi (%)
VII-2 INFRASTRUCTURE										**VII-2 INFRASTRUCTURE**
Paved roads (% of total)	...	...	...	...	...	...	...	...	...	Routes asphaltées (% du total)
Total Network (Railways-km)	...	...	...	...	...	...	...	...	...	Réseau total voies ferrées-Km
Main Telephone Lines (per 100 inhabitants)	...	...	...	...	...	0	0	-	...	Lignes téléphoniques fixes (pour 100 habitants)
Mobile Cellular Subscribers (per 100 inhabitants)	...	...	...	...	...	17	21	25	...	Abonnés aux téléphones mobiles (pour 100 habitants)

VIII EXTERNAL TRADE - COMMERCE EXTERIEUR	2006	2007	2008	2009	2010	2011	2012	2013	2014	
SOUTH SUDANESE POUND (MILLIONS) EXPORTS, FOB										**LIVRE SUD-SOUDANAISE (MILLIONS) EXPORTATIONS, FÀB**
Exports - Total	...	...	...	...	...	...	...	...	...	Exportations - Total
Exports to AFRICA	...	...	...	...	...	...	...	...	...	Exportations vers l'AFRIQUE
Main Products										**Principaux produits**
Hosiery and Confection	...	...	...	...	...	...	...	...	...	Bonneterie et Confection
Crude oil	...	...	...	...	...	...	...	...	...	Pétrole brut
Threads and cables Electric	...	...	...	...	...	...	...	...	...	Fils et Câbles électriques
D.A.P (Diammonium phosphate)	...	...	...	...	...	...	...	...	...	D.A.P (Diammoniaque phosphaté)
Phosphoric acid	...	...	...	...	...	...	...	...	...	Acide phosphorique
Main Destinations										**Principales destinations**
France	...	...	...	...	...	...	...	...	...	France
Italy	...	...	...	...	...	...	...	...	...	Italie
Germany	...	...	...	...	...	...	...	...	...	Allemagne
Libya	...	...	...	...	...	...	...	...	...	Libye
United Kingdom	...	...	...	...	...	...	...	...	...	Royaume-Uni
IMPORTS, CIF										**IMPORTATIONS, CAF**
Imports - Total	...	...	...	...	...	...	...	...	...	Importations - Total (millions)
Imports from Africa	...	...	...	...	...	...	...	...	...	Importations en provenance de l'Afrique
Main Products										Principaux produits
Refined Products	...	...	...	...	...	...	...	...	...	**Produits raffinés**
Fabrics	...	...	...	...	...	...	...	...	...	Tissus
Iron & Steel	...	...	...	...	...	...	...	...	...	Fer & acier
Material structure and plastic	...	...	...	...	...	...	...	...	...	Matière et ouvrage en plastique
Crude petroleum	...	...	...	...	...	...	...	...	...	Pétrole brut
Main Origin										**Principales provenances**
France	...	...	...	...	...	...	...	...	...	France
Italy	...	...	...	...	...	...	...	...	...	Italie
Germany	...	...	...	...	...	...	...	...	...	Allemagne
Russia	...	...	...	...	...	...	...	...	...	Russie
Libya	...	...	...	...	...	...	...	...	...	Libye

IX FINANCIAL AND MONETARY STATISTICS - FINANCES ET STATISTIQUES MONETAIRES	2006	2007	2008	2009	2010	2011	2012	2013	2014	
IX-1 MONETARY STATISTICS *SOUTH SUDANESE POUND (MILLIONS)*										**IX-1 STATISTIQUES MONÉTAIRES** *LIVRE SUD-SOUDANAISE (MILLIONS)*
Money supply (M1)	-	-	-	-	-	4 780	6 580	6 470	7 010	Masse monétaire (M1)
Quasi-money	-	-	-	-	-	454	586	949	1 017	Quasi-monnaie
of which Demand Deposit	...	...	...	...	...	...	...	...	...	dont Monnaie scripturale
Net foreign assets	...	...	...	...	...	7 521	3 876	2 973	1 560	Avoirs extérieurs nets
Domestic credit	-	-	-	-	-	- 3 273	1 964	3 755	8 852	Crédit intérieur
of which claims on private sector	-	-	-	-	-	229	402	616	746	dont créances sur le secteur privé
of which claims on government sector, net	...	...	...	...	...	- 3 530	1 533	3 099	8 106	dont créances nettes sur le gouvernement
International reserves (millions US$)	...	...	...	...	...	...	...	948	417	Réserves internationales (millions $EU)
Average Exchange Rate (National Currency per US$)	...	...	...	...	...	...	...	...	...	Taux de change (moyen) (monnaie nationale par $ EU)
IX-2 PUBLIC FINANCE *SOUTH SUDANESE POUND (MILLIONS)*										**IX-2 FINANCES PUBLIQUES** *LIVRE SUD-SOUDANAISE (MILLIONS)*
Total Revenues and Grants	...	...	...	...	...	...	...	...	...	Recettes totales et dons
Tax Revenue	...	...	...	...	...	...	...	...	...	Recettes fiscales
Non Tax Revenue	...	...	...	...	...	...	...	...	...	Recettes non fiscales
Grants	...	...	...	...	...	...	...	...	...	Dons
Total Expenditures and Net Lending	...	...	...	...	...	...	...	...	...	Dépenses totales et prêts nets
Current expenditure	...	...	...	...	...	...	...	...	...	Dépenses courantes
Of which Wages and Salaries	...	...	...	...	...	...	...	...	...	Dont rémunérations et salaires
Capital expenditure	...	...	...	...	...	...	...	...	...	Dépenses d'équipement
Net Lending	...	...	...	...	...	...	...	...	...	Prêts nets
Fiscal Balance	...	...	...	...	...	...	...	...	...	Solde global y compris les dons
IX-3 BALANCE OF PAYMENTS *SOUTH SUDANESE POUND (MILLIONS)*										**IX-3 BALANCE DES PAIEMENTS** *LIVRE SUD-SOUDANAISE (MILLIONS)*
Trade balance	...	...	...	...	...	...	...	...	...	Balance commerciale
Services Balance	...	...	...	...	...	...	...	...	...	Balance des services
Net Income	...	...	...	...	...	...	...	...	...	Revenus nets
Compensation of employees	...	...	...	...	...	...	...	...	...	Rémunération des salariés
Investment Income	...	...	...	...	...	...	...	...	...	Revenus des investissements
Current transfers, net total	...	...	...	...	...	...	...	...	...	Transferts courants
Net official transfers	...	...	...	...	...	...	...	...	...	Transferts officiels nets
Workers' remittances	...	...	...	...	...	...	...	...	...	Envois de fonds des travailleurs
Other private transfers	...	...	...	...	...	...	...	...	...	Autres transferts privés
Current account balance	...	...	...	...	...	...	...	...	...	Solde du compte courant
Capital & financial account	...	...	...	...	...	...	...	...	...	Comptes de capital et financier
Capital account	...	...	...	...	...	...	...	...	...	Compte de capital
Financial account	...	...	...	...	...	...	...	...	...	Compte financier
Errors & omissions	...	...	...	...	...	...	...	...	...	Erreurs et omissions
Overall balance	...	...	...	...	...	...	...	...	...	Balance générale

X DEBT AND FINANCIAL FLOWS - DETTE ET FLUX FINANCIERS										
	2006	2007	2008	2009	2010	2011	2012	2013	2014	
X-1 DEBT *US$ (MILLIONS)*										**X-1 DETTE EXTÉRIEURE** *$ E.U (MILLIONS)*
Total external debt	...	...	...	...	...	...	...	...	...	Dette extérieure totale
Private	-	-	-	-	-	-	-	-	-	Privée
Public	...	...	...	...	...	...	...	...	...	Publique
Total external debt service	...	...	...	...	...	-	-	-	-	Service de la dette extérieure
Present value of External debt	...	...	...	...	...	...	...	...	...	Valeur actuelle de la dette extérieure
Total government domestic debt (in local currency)	...	...	...	...	...	...	...	...	...	Dette publique intérieure
X-2 FINANCIAL FLOWS *US$ (MILLIONS)*										**X-2 FLUX FINANCIERS** *$ E.U (MILLIONS)*
Net Foreign Direct Investment Inflows	...	...	...	...	...	...	...	...	...	Investissements étranger direct (flux nets entrants)
Main origin of FDI Inflows										**Principales origines de l'IDE entrant:**
Country 1	...	...	...	...	...	...	...	...	...	Pays 1
Country 2	...	...	...	...	...	...	...	...	...	Pays 2
Country 3	...	...	...	...	...	...	...	...	...	Pays 3
Country 4	...	...	...	...	...	...	...	...	...	Pays 4
Country 5	...	...	...	...	...	...	...	...	...	Pays 5
African countries	...	...	...	...	...	...	...	...	...	Pays africains
Net total Official Development Assistance	...	...	...	...	...	1 088	1 578	1 447	...	Aide publique au développement (nette totale)
Main origin of Net ODA										**Principales origines de l'APD nette**
United States	...	...	...	...	...	707.4	773.3	457.9	...	Etats-Unis
United Kingdom	...	...	...	...	83.0	172.0	...	...	...	Royaume-Uni
Norway	...	...	...	...	...	60.3	73.6	91.1	...	Norvège
Canada	...	...	...	...	...	49.0	65.6	66.1	...	Canada
Denmark	...	...	...	...	...	35.8	37.4	33.7	...	Danemark

AREA (KM²)		1 886 068		SUPERFICIE (KM²)
CAPITAL CITY	Khartoum		Khartoum	CAPITALE
CURRENCY	Sudanese Pound		Livre soudanaise	MONNAIE

I SOCIAL AND DEMOGRAPHIC INDICATORS – INDICATEURS DEMOGRAPHIQUES ET SOCIAUX

	Year / Année	Value / Valeur	
POPULATION			**POPULATION**
Population ('000)			Population ('000)
Both sexes	2014	37 300	Les deux sexes
Male	2014	18 613	Masculin
Female	2014	18 687	Féminin
Average annual growth rate	2014	2.8	Taux de croissance annuel
Active Population ('000)	2014	15 160	Population active ('000)
Population by age group ('000)			Population par groupe d'âge ('000)
0-14 years	2014	15 573	0-14 ans
15-64 years	2014	20 516	15-64 ans
65+ years	2014	1 200	65+ ans
Economically active population in agriculture (%)	2014	49.7	Participation de la population active agricole (%)
Crude birth rate	2014	39.7	Taux brut de natalité
Crude death rate	2014	9.5	Taux brut de mortalité
Total fertility rate	2014	5.3	Indice synthétique de fécondité
Proportion of urban population	2014	35.7	Part de la population urbaine
Life Expectancy at Birth - Total (years)	2014	62.6	Espérance de vie à la naissance - Totale (ans)
Dependency Ratio - Total (%)	2014	82.0	Taux de dépendance - Total (%)
HEALTH			**SANTÉ**
Percentage of children under-five and underweight	2014	12.6	% d'enfants de moins de cinq ans avec insuffisance pondérale
Prevalence of undernourishment	2010	24.3	Prévalence de la malnutrition
Under five mortality rate (both sexes, per 1000)	2013	76.6	Taux de mortalité de moins de 5 ans (les deux sexes, pour 1000)
Infant mortality rate (both sexes) per 1000	2013	51.2	Taux de mortalité infantile (les deux sexes) par 1000
Percentage of children provided the vaccines :			Pourcentage d'enfants vaccinés :
BCG	2013	93.0	BCG
DPT3	2013	93.0	DTC3
Polio	2011	93.0	Polio
Measles	2013	85.0	Rougeole
Percentage of mothers provided at least one antenatal care (%)	2006	70.0	Pourcentage de mères ayant au moins reçu un soin prénatal (%)
Percentage of deliveries attended by skilled health personnel	2010	23.1	% d'accouchements assistés par un personnel de santé qualifié
Number of doctors (per 10 000 population)	2008	2.8	Nombre de médecins (pour 10 000 habitants)
Number of nurses (per 10 000 population)	2008	8.4	Nombre d'infirmières (pour 10 000 habitants)
Hospital beds - Total (per 10 000 population)	2011	8.0	Nombre de lits d'hôpitaux - Total (pour 10 000)
Births registered (per 1 000)	2014	33.1	Naiss.s enregistrées (pour 1 000)
Deaths registered (per 1 000)	2014	8.3	Décès enregistrés (pour 1 000)
Public expenditure on Health (% of budget)	2010	17.8	Dépenses publiques consacrées à la santé (% du budget)
EDUCATION			**EDUCATION**
Enrolment in primary education (both sexes) (000)	2012	4 143	Scolarisation dans le primaire (les deux sexes) (000)
Female	2012	1 925	Féminin
Enrolment in secondary education (both sexes) (000)	2012	1 724	Scolarisation dans le secondaire (les deux sexes) (000)
Female	2012	812	Féminin
Enrolment in tertiary education (both sexes) (000)	2013	537.6	Scolarisation dans le tertiaire (les deux sexes) (000)
Female	2013	334.1	Féminin
Literacy rate (both sexes)	2012	73.4	Taux d'alphabétisation (deux sexes)
Male	2012	81.7	Masculin
Female	2012	65.3	Féminin
Pupil-teacher ratio	2009	38.4	Ratio élève-enseignant
Public expenditure on education (% of budget)	2010	12.9	Dépenses publiques consacrées à l'enseignement (% du budget)
POVERTY			**PAUVRETÉ**
GNI Per Capita (US$)	2013	1 550.0	RNB par habitant ($EU)
Human Poverty Index (HPI-1) Value (%)	2007	34.0	Valeur de l'Indice de pauvreté (IPH-1) (%)
Population below International Poverty Line ($2/day) (%)	2009	44.1	Population sous le seuil international de pauvreté (2$/J) (%)
Share of Income Held by Richest 10%	2009	26.7	% de revenu des 10% plus riches
Share of Income Held by Poorest 10%	2009	2.7	% de revenu des 10% plus pauvres
Gini index	2009	35.3	Indice de Gini

Charts / Graphiques

Population by age group – 2014
Population par groupe d'age – 2014

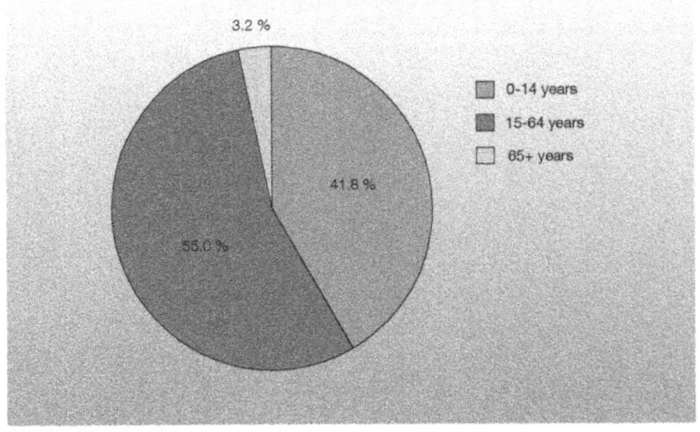

Percentage of children provided the vaccines – 2013
Pourcentage d'enfants vaccinés – 2013

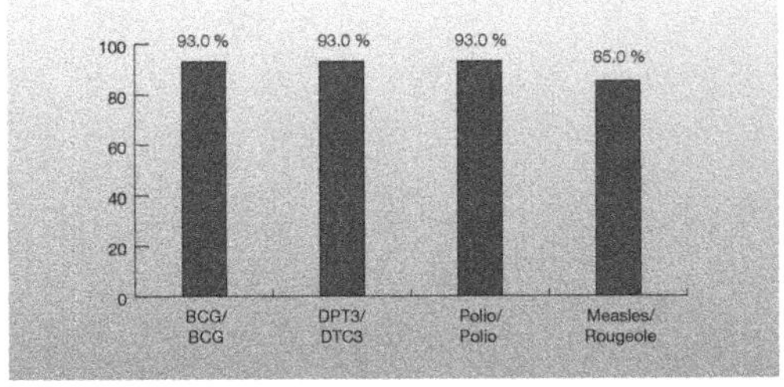

Literacy rate (%) – 2012
Taux d'alphabétisation – 2012

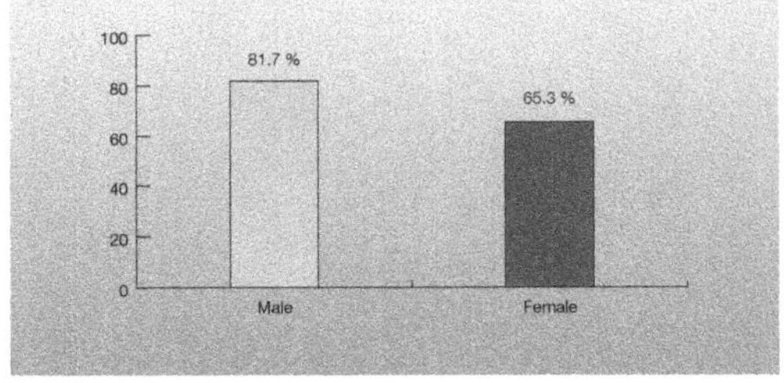

GNI Per Capita (US$)
RNB par habitant ($EU)

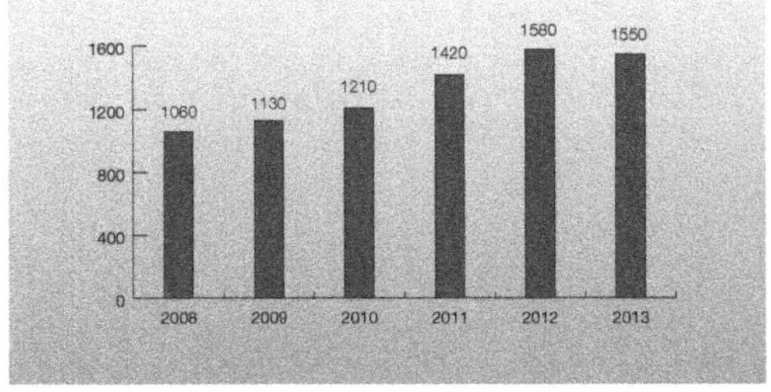

II NATIONAL ACCOUNTS — COMPTES NATIONAUX

	2006	2007	2008	2009	2010	2011	2012	2013	2014	
GROSS DOMESTIC PRODUCT BY KIND OF ECONOMIC ACTIVITY AT CURRENT PRICES *SUDANESE POUND (MILLIONS)*										**PRODUIT INTÉRIEUR BRUT PAR BRANCHE D'ACTIVITÉ ÉCONOMIQUE AUX PRIX COURANTS** *LIVRE SOUDANAISE (MILLIONS)*
Agriculture, hunting, forestry and fishing	31 191	32 985	37 481	44 971	54 465	63 609	80 675	99 681	117 143	Agriculture, chasse sylviculture et pêche
Mining and quarrying	9 302	17 824	20 064	15 777	14 943	11 428	12 847	14 770	18 092	Industries extractives
Manufacturing	8 042	8 782	9 726	11 769	12 975	16 285	21 677	26 101	30 590	Industries manufacturières
Electricity, gas & water	1 820	1 981	2 242	794	893	1 606	2 181	2 644	3 919	Electricité, gaz et eau
Construction & public works	4 243	4 651	5 239	6 087	7 340	8 718	11 525	13 866	16 264	Bâtiments et travaux publics
Wholesale & retail trade, restaurants, hotels	14 328	16 728	18 376	20 613	23 381	30 709	40 720	48 664	56 986	Commerce de gros et de détail, restaurants et hôtels
Finance, insurance, real estate, etc.	8 732	9 067	10 355	14 264	18 924	16 499	21 475	25 777	29 273	Banques, assurances, affaires immobilières
Transport and communications	14 147	13 781	15 046	14 252	15 633	24 426	32 511	39 178	46 270	Transport(s) et communications
Public administration and defense	5 297	5 944	6 681	9 370	10 157	9 998	15 248	18 466	21 623	Administrations publiques et défense
Education	...	...	...	...	...	...	...	...	...	Education
Health and Social Work	...	...	...	...	...	...	...	...	...	Santé et actions sociales
Other services	861	996	1 109	1 583	1 831	1 502	1 954	2 351	2 739	Autres services
Less Imputed Service Charges	- 1 026	- 720	- 789	- 1 707	- 1 719	- 1 625	- 2 123	- 2 549	- 2 980	Moins services d'intermédiation financière
Gross domestic product at factor cost / basic prices	96 935	112 020	125 530	137 773	158 823	183 155	238 690	288 949	339 919	Produit intérieur brut aux couts des facteurs / prix de base
Plus: indirect taxes / taxes on products, less subsidies	1 783	1 997	2 217	1 614	1 824	3 535	4 723	5 681	6 630	Plus taxes indirectes/impôts sur les produits, moins les subventions
EXPENDITURE ON GROSS DOMESTIC PRODUCT AT CURRENT PURCHASER'S VALUES *SUDANESE POUND (MILLIONS)*										**EMPLOI DU PRODUIT INTÉRIEUR BRUT AUX PRIX COURANTS D'ACQUISITION** *LIVRE SOUDANAISE (MILLIONS)*
Government final consumption	9 606	9 635	10 811	11 758	12 001	12 742	16 903	23 751	-	Consommation finale des administrations publiques
Private final consumption	74 698	82 089	88 669	105 783	112 731	129 986	187 875	228 162	-	Consommation finale privée
Gross fixed capital formation	19 616	22 839	24 165	25 376	31 705	41 616	54 118	54 261	-	Formation brute de capital fixe
Change in inventories	5 659	4 397	3 735	3 208	3 099	4 868	5 585	9 187	-	Variation des stocks
Exports of goods and services	12 718	18 665	25 401	19 119	27 522	27 198	9 411	30 306	-	Exportations de biens et services
Less imports of goods and services	23 580	23 607	25 035	25 859	26 411	29 719	30 480	51 036	-	Moins importations de biens et services
GDP at purchasers' values	98 719	114 018	127 747	139 387	160 647	186 690	243 413	294 630	346 550	PIB aux prix d'acquisition
GROSS DOMESTIC PRODUCT BY KIND OF ECONOMIC ACTIVITY AT CONSTANT PRICES *ANNUAL GROWTH RATES (%)*										**PRODUIT INTÉRIEUR BRUT PAR BRANCHE D'ACTIVITÉ ECONOMIQUE AUX PRIX CONSTANTS** *TAUX DE CROISSANCE ANNUEL (%)*
Agriculture, hunting, forestry and fishing	9.0	- 5.2	5.0	- 3.3	11.7	3.4	5.7	3.5	3.9	Agriculture, chasse sylviculture et pêche
Mining and quarrying	36.2	32.5	- 5.4	1.8	- 2.2	- 26.2	- 60.9	33.1	5.3	Industries extractives
Manufacturing	2.0	19.0	0.1	19.3	10.0	8.1	9.1	3.3	5.9	Industries manufacturières
Electricity, gas & water	9.8	6.0	8.2	7.4	7.0	6.3	6.3	3.0	8.5	Electricité, gaz et eau
Construction & public works	5.5	8.3	2.7	5.2	2.8	10.2	5.8	2.0	5.8	Bâtiments et travaux publics
Wholesale & retail trade, restaurants, hotels	6.1	6.3	6.7	3.9	5.5	5.3	2.1	2.6	5.4	Commerce de gros et de détail,restaurants et hôtels
Finance, insurance, real estate, etc.	6.0	1.2	5.8	7.1	5.3	- 3.6	2.8	2.4	- 2.8	Banques, assurances, affaires immobilières
Transport and communications	11.3	11.6	5.6	8.8	5.7	5.1	5.9	2.7	- 0.7	Transport(s) et communications
Public administration and defense	- 3.7	1.3	10.2	4.6	2.1	4.0	3.0	1.1	4.5	Administrations publiques et défense
Education	...	...	...	...	...	...	...	...	...	Education
Health and Social Work	...	...	...	...	...	...	...	...	...	Santé et actions sociales
Other services	3.0	2.7	1.3	4.4	3.1	3.3	2.1	1.0	4.8	Autres services
Less Imputed Service Charges	39.1	- 4.5	9.3	- 10.8	0.7	5.9	2.2	1.1	4.8	Moins services d'intermédiation financière
Gross domestic product at factor cost / basic prices	7.4	5.8	3.9	4.7	6.6	0.9	0.5	3.6	3.4	Produit intérieur brut aux couts des facteurs / prix de base
Plus: indirect taxes / taxes on products, less subsidies	19.9	2.9	2.8	- 5.6	1.6	2.1	3.0	0.8	4.9	Plus taxes indirectes/impôts sur les produits, moins les subventions
Gross domestic product at market prices	7.7	5.8	3.8	4.5	6.5	0.9	0.5	3.6	3.4	Produit intérieur brut aux prix du marché
EXPENDITURE ON GROSS DOMESTIC PRODUCT AT CONSTANT PURCHASERS' VALUES *ANNUAL GROWTH RATES (%)*										**EMPLOIS DU PRODUIT INTÉRIEUR BRUT AUX PRIX CONSTANTS D'ACQUISITION** *TAUX DE CROISSANCE ANNUEL (%)*
Government final consumption	3.4	- 0.6	- 3.8	- 14.8	1.1	0.9	0.5	3.6	...	Consommation finale des administrations publiques
Private final consumption	26.9	- 4.8	- 4.1	7.9	3.9	0.9	0.5	3.6	...	Consommation finale privée
Gross fixed capital formation	- 9.9	2.3	3.8	4.1	10.8	0.9	0.5	3.6	...	Formation brute de capital fixe
Exports of goods and services	- 1.6	52.3	21.2	- 90.8	30.5	0.9	0.5	3.6	...	Exportations de biens et services
Less imports of goods and services	6.5	- 8.0	- 8.9	- 90.3	8.4	0.9	0.5	3.6	...	Moins importations de biens et services
Notes	National Accounts data 2014 is projected					les données des comptes nationaux des années 2014 sont des projections				Notes

III INFLATION

	2006	2007	2008	2009	2010	2011	2012	2013	2014	
ANNUAL GROWTH RATES (%)										**TAUX DE CROISSANCE ANNUEL (%)**
All items	7.2	8.1	14.3	11.3	13.0	18.0	35.6	36.4	37.0	Ensemble
of which:										dont:
Food and Non-alcoholic beverages	2.1	5.4	18.5	12.2	15.6	20.4	38.8	30.7	28.9	Alimentation et boissons non alcoolisés
Alcoholic beverages & tobacco	...	...	...	4.3	8.3	11.3	41.9	24.4	33.8	Boissons alcoolisées et tabacs
Clothing and Footwear	...	...	...	10.0	9.9	17.4	49.5	54.7	49.3	Habillement et chaussures
Housing, Water, Electricity, Gas and Other Fuels	14.7	4.9	18.0	8.6	9.9	11.0	13.4	19.5	20.0	Logement, eau, électricité, gas et autres combustibles
Furnishing, household equip	...	...	...	9.1	8.3	20.5	39.6	91.9	45.9	Meubles, articles de ménage et entretien courant
Health	39.5	17.4	7.8	9.6	5.1	20.1	37.4	47.8	30.4	Santé
Transport	29.0	32.1	3.3	4.4	2.4	14.8	53.6	66.3	73.8	Transport
Communication	...	...	...	7.0	3.4	5.9	31.7	139.6	40.3	Communication
Recreation & culture	...	...	...	5.5	6.6	8.6	63.7	32.1	45.5	Loisirs et culture
Education	...	...	...	18.7	31.3	25.6	13.4	54.0	36.5	Enseignement
Restaurants & hotels	...	...	...	34.8	19.4	14.5	12.9	32.2	37.3	Restaurants et hôtels
Miscellaneous goods & services	...	...	...	11.6	10.3	17.1	36.5	53.8	45.3	Biens et services divers

IV AGRICULTURAL PRODUCTION - PRODUCTION AGRICOLE										
	2006	2007	2008	2009	2010	2011	2012	2013	2014	
TONNES *(THOUSAND)*										**TONNES** *(MILLIERS)*
Sugar cane	7 000	7 467	7 453	7 527	6 728	6 055	6 173	6 798	...	Canne à sucre
Sorghum	4 327	4 999	3 869	4 192	2 630	4 605	1 883	4 524	...	Sorgho
Groundnuts, with shell	555	564	716	942	763	1 185	1 032	1 767	...	Arachide, dont la coquille
Onions, dry	1 405	920	938	1 024	1 116	1 116	1 036	1 037	...	Oignons, sec
Bananas	519	540	562	624	684	687	750	758	...	Bananes

V MINING PRODUCTION - PRODUCTION MINIERE										
	2006	2007	2008	2009	2010	2011	2012	2013	2014	
Petroleum, Crude, Metric tons (thousands)	18	24	24	24	24	23	5	8	...	Pétrole, brut, tonnes métriques (milliers)
Gold Kilograms (thousand)	3	2	15	26	24	46	...	...	...	Or, Kilogrammes (milliers)
Gypsum, tons (thousand)	7	8	13	30	31	31	12	...	...	Gypse, tonnes (milliers)

VI ENERGY - ENERGIE										
	2006	2007	2008	2009	2010	2011	2012	2013	2014	
Total electricity generation (GWh)	4 720	4 720	6 017	6 883	8 009	11 508	11 554	11 599	...	Production d'électricité totale (GWh)
of which:										dont:
Production of electricity from fossil fuels (GWh)	2 841	2 841	4 041	3 137	1 297	3 416	3 460	3 504	...	Production d'électricité à partir de combustibles fossiles (GWh)
Production of hydro electricity (GWh)	1 369	1 369	1 466	3 236	6 202	7 884	7 884	7 884	...	Production d'électricité d'origine hydraulique (GWh)
Production of electricity from solar, wind, tide, wave and other sources (GWh)	...	...	...	...	...	5	7	9	...	Production d'électricité d'origine solaire, éolienne, marée motrice et autres (GWh)

VII TOURISM AND INFRASTRUCTURE - TOURISME ET INFRASTRUCTURE										
	2006	2007	2008	2009	2010	2011	2012	2013	2014	
VII-1 TOURISM										**VII-1 TOURISME**
International tourist arrivals (thousands)	328	436	440	420	495	536	814	772	792	Arrivées de touristes internationaux (milliers)
Rooms in hotels and similar establishments (thousands)	2.8	3.5	...	4.6	...	...	...	...	...	Chambres d'hotels et établissements assimilés (milliers)
Overnight stays (thousands)	1 994	2 695	2 764	2 524	3 046	2 938	3 594	3 894	4 059	Nuitées (milliers)
Tourism receipts (US$ thousand)	194 100	389 700	255 300	230 700	82 300	179 300	771 800	773 000	811 679	Recettes touristiques (milliers de $ EU)
Total contribution to GDP (%)	4.2	4.5	4.2	4.5	3.8	3.9	6.0	6.5	6.4	Contribution totale au PIB (%)
Total contribution to Employment (%)	3.7	3.9	3.7	3.9	3.4	3.5	4.8	5.2	5.2	Contribution totale à l'emploi (%)
VII-2 INFRASTRUCTURE										**VII-2 INFRASTRUCTURE**
Paved roads (% of total)	36	32	32	32	52	91	91	91	...	Routes asphaltées (% du total)
Total Network (Railways-km)	4 578	5 901	5 901	4 180	4 508	4 509	4 509	4 509	...	Réseau total voies ferrées-Km
Main Telephone Lines (per 100 inhabitants)	1	1	1	1	1	1	1	1	...	Lignes téléphoniques fixes (pour 100 habitants)
Mobile Cellular Subscribers (per 100 inhabitants)	12	20	29	36	42	69	74	73	...	Abonnés aux téléphones mobiles (pour 100 habitants)

VIII EXTERNAL TRADE - COMMERCE EXTERIEUR										
	2006	2007	2008	2009	2010	2011	2012	2013	2014	
SUDANESE POUND (MILLIONS) EXPORTS, FOB										**POUND SUDANAIS (MILLIONS) EXPORTATIONS, FÀB**
Exports - Total	11 875	18 029	24 684	17 261	26 866	23 974	11 225	18 141	...	Exportations - Total
Exports to AFRICA	...	...	...	...	...	...	...	...	...	Exportations vers l'AFRIQUE
Main Products										**Principaux produits**
Benzene	9 917	16 227	22 681	15 186	22 478	18 909	...	59 563	...	Benzene
Sesame	311	168	356	327	470	503	735	1 283	...	Sésame
Gum Arabic	109	137	146	136	161	188	222	654	...	Gomme arabique
Cotton	154	144	124	89	94	70	62	266	...	Coton
Gold	165	127	234	188	2 755	2 235	6 545	5 085	...	Or
Main Destinations										**Principales destinations**
China	9 364	16 164	20 275	13 111	21 490	18 650	266	5 964	...	Chine
Japan	647	123	1 464	340	649	311	19	5	...	Japon
Saudi Arabia	297	208	225	560	387	824	1 178	2 559	...	Arabie Saoudite
United Arab Emirates	455	289	457	756	3 041	2 550	6 429	5 551	...	Émirats Arabes Unis
United Kingdom	44	25	16	52	80	18	31	33	...	Royaume-Uni
IMPORTS, CIF										**IMPORTATIONS, CAF**
Imports - Total	19 112	19 254	25 931	19 064	28 311	25 768	25 183	27 129	...	Importations - Total (millions)
Imports from Africa	...	...	...	...	...	...	...	...	...	Importations en provenance de l'Afrique
Main Products										**Principaux produits**
Machinery & Equipment	5 450	5 774	5 274	4 007	5 841	5 003	4 523	5 436	...	Machines et équipements
Transport Equipment	3 847	4 266	6 800	3 260	4 070	3 464	3 034	3 775	...	Matériel de transport
Wheat & Wheat Flour	719	419	1 107	903	3 114	1 660	1 374	1 735	...	Blé et farine de blé
Iron, Steel & Articles Thereof	1 725	985	2 253	1 881	1 698	1 811	1 977	1 258	...	Fer, acier et ouvrages en ces matières
Petroleum Products	984	609	1 679	808	1 785	2 465	2 568	3 226	...	Produits pétroliers
Main Origin										**Principales provenances**
Saudi Arabia	1 712	2 420	4 504	1 438	1 574	2 085	1 961	1 920	...	Arabie Saoudite
United Arab Emirates	1 064	1 093	1 533	1 402	3 259	2 213	1 303	1 720	...	Émirats Arabes Unis
China	3 598	3 376	4 833	3 164	4 969	5 582	4 464	6 418	...	Chine
United Kingdom	900	891	487	425	1 090	357	716	764	...	Royaume-Uni
Japan	1 533	1 664	1 573	1 823	1 711	1 598	1 063	149	...	Japon

IX FINANCIAL AND MONETARY STATISTICS - FINANCES ET STATISTIQUES MONETAIRES	2006	2007	2008	2009	2010	2011	2012	2013	2014	
IX-1 MONETARY STATISTICS *SUDANESE POUND (MILLIONS)*										**IX-1 STATISTIQUES MONÉTAIRES** *LIVRE SOUDANAISE (MILLIONS)*
Money supply (M1)	17 890	19 750	22 980	28 520	35 610	41 910	58 790	66 450	79 140	Masse monétaire (M1)
Quasi-money	6 492	7 271	8 047	10 621	13 800	15 247	23 504	26 217	29 933	Quasi-monnaie
of which Demand Deposit	...	...	...	...	...	...	...	...	...	dont Monnaie scripturale
Net foreign assets	1 338	810	1 017	- 1 107	- 202	- 1 605	- 212	- 3 658	- 3 150	Avoirs extérieurs nets
Domestic credit	16 394	18 601	20 436	26 600	33 344	42 622	60 919	75 739	83 963	Crédit intérieur
of which claims on private sector	10 859	11 759	12 711	15 513	17 959	19 427	26 966	33 034	36 242	dont créances sur le secteur privé
of which claims on government sector, net	4 284	3 958	5 008	8 085	11 748	19 300	29 650	37 104	40 320	dont créances nettes sur le gouvernement
International reserves (millions US$)	1 660	1 378	1 399	1 094	1 036	193	193	193	181	Réserves internationales (millions $EU)
Average Exchange Rate (National Currency per US$)	2.17	2.02	2.09	2.30	2.31	2.67	3.57	4.76	5.70	Taux de change (moyen) (monnaie nationale par $ EU)
IX-2 PUBLIC FINANCE *SUDANESE POUND (MILLIONS)*										**IX-2 FINANCES PUBLIQUES** *LIVRE SOUDANAISE (MILLIONS)*
Total Revenues and Grants	17 451	20 242	27 378	18 986	29 245	32 357	22 305	31 309	47 173	Recettes totales et dons
Tax Revenue	5 879	6 529	7 680	8 619	10 008	11 426	13 879	19 428	31 111	Recettes fiscales
Non Tax Revenue	11 323	13 533	19 662	10 320	18 261	20 313	7 420	9 808	14 639	Recettes non fiscales
Grants	250	180	36	47	976	618	1 007	2 073	1 423	Dons
Total Expenditures and Net Lending	18 502	23 468	26 733	25 198	28 815	31 979	30 901	38 586	51 547	Dépenses totales et prêts nets
Current expenditure	17 029	19 746	23 071	22 398	26 772	29 716	28 842	35 655	47 430	Dépenses courantes
Of which Wages and Salaries	4 592	6 368	5 951	6 836	7 516	9 763	10 730	13 670	18 353	Dont rémunérations et salaires
Capital expenditure	3 535	6 030	3 756	7 876	2 591	4 525	5 643	3 331	4 738	Dépenses d'équipement
Net Lending	- 2 063	- 2 308	- 94	- 5 077	- 548	- 2 263	- 3 584	- 400	- 621	Prêts nets
Fiscal Balance	- 1 051	- 3 226	645	- 6 211	430	379	- 8 596	- 7 277	- 4 374	Solde global y compris les dons
IX-3 BALANCE OF PAYMENTS *SUDANESE POUND (MILLIONS)*										**IX-3 BALANCE DES PAIEMENTS** *LIVRE SOUDANAISE (MILLIONS)*
Trade balance	- 3 145	2 333	7 194	- 1 587	5 915	4 075	- 16 989	- 18 733	...	Balance commerciale
Services Balance	- 4 891	- 4 248	- 4 174	- 4 112	- 5 324	- 4 017	- 3 670	- 1 634	...	Balance des services
Net Income	- 8 708	- 6 784	- 11 589	- 9 476	- 9 729	- 6 657	- 5 684	- 12 122	...	Revenus nets
Compensation of employees	...	...	...	...	...	...	...	...	...	Rémunération des salariés
Investment Income	...	...	...	...	...	...	...	...	...	Revenus des investissements
Current transfers, net total	2 608	1 557	1 302	2 815	5 060	3 015	3 086	4 754	...	Transferts courants
Net official transfers	...	...	...	...	...	...	...	...	...	Transferts officiels nets
Workers' remittances	...	...	...	...	...	...	...	...	...	Envois de fonds des travailleurs
Other private transfers	...	...	...	...	...	...	...	...	...	Autres transferts privés
Current account balance	- 14 137	- 7 143	- 7 267	- 12 361	- 4 078	- 3 584	- 23 257	- 27 734	...	Solde du compte courant
Capital & financial account	6 006	4 461	2 629	4 747	2 672	749	4 010	...	...	Comptes de capital et financier
Capital account	205	173	177	236	314	190	320	...	...	Compte de capital
Financial account	5 800	4 288	2 452	4 511	2 357	559	3 690	...	...	Compte financier
Errors & omissions	294	- 1 201	868	- 376	- 983	- 89	2 491	...	...	Erreurs et omissions
Overall balance	- 209	- 282	21	- 556	- 27	- 680	- 24	...	...	Balance générale

X DEBT AND FINANCIAL FLOWS - DETTE ET FLUX FINANCIERS	2006	2007	2008	2009	2010	2011	2012	2013	2014	
X-1 DEBT *US$ (MILLIONS)*										**X-1 DETTE EXTÉRIEURE** *$ E.U (MILLIONS)*
Total external debt	28 216	31 052	32 561	34 866	39 486	41 445	43 189	45 010	46 429	Dette extérieure totale
Private	5 298	5 831	5 968	6 465	6 532	6 874	7 215	7 558	7 902	Privée
Public	22 918	25 221	26 593	28 401	32 953	34 571	35 974	37 452	38 527	Publique
Total external debt service	305	304	482	262	382	283	261	177	232	Service de la dette extérieure
Present value of External debt	...	...	...	...	...	...	...	...	...	Valeur actuelle de la dette extérieure
Total government domestic debt (in local currency)	8	10	11	14	16.5	19.8	27.4	...	...	Dette publique intérieure
X-2 FINANCIAL FLOWS *US$ (MILLIONS)*										**X-2 FLUX FINANCIERS** *$ E.U (MILLIONS)*
Net Foreign Direct Investment Inflows	2 589	2 436	2 600	2 572	2 894	2 692	2 488	3 094	...	Investissements étranger direct (flux nets entrants)
Main origin of FDI Inflows										**Principales origines de l'IDE entrant:**
Italy	...	...	23	...	0.8	1.6	2.6	...	...	Italie
France	4	...	...	...	...	...	...	...	...	France
Turkey	...	...	...	...	...	...	...	...	...	Turquie
Luxembourg	...	...	7	...	...	...	...	...	...	Luxembourg
Germany	1	1	3	...	...	...	...	...	...	Allemagne
African countries	...	...	...	...	...	...	...	...	...	Pays africains
Net total Official Development Assistance	2 048	2 121	2 566	2 351	2 076	1 099	975	1 163	...	Aide publique au développement (nette totale)
Main origin of Net ODA										**Principales origines de l'APD nette**
United States	739	710	848	955	726.4	16.5	63.5	373.5	...	Etats-Unis
United Kingdom	216	206	199	292	119.1	157.3	82.0	...	...	Royaume-Uni
Netherlands	96	203	158	97	86.7	45.4	14.9	10.8	...	Pays-Bas
Norway	107	120	120	92	116.7	47.0	33.3	33.9	...	Norvège
Canada	79	71	84	105	108.3	52.3	29.3	21.5	...	Canada

AREA (KM²)		17 364		SUPERFICIE (KM²)
CAPITAL CITY	Mbabane		Mbabane	CAPITALE
CURRENCY	Lilangeni		Lilangeni	MONNAIE

I SOCIAL AND DEMOGRAPHIC INDICATORS – INDICATEURS DEMOGRAPHIQUES ET SOCIAUX

	Year / Année	Value / Valeur	
POPULATION			**POPULATION**
Population ('000)			Population ('000)
Both sexes	2014	1 106	Les deux sexes
Male	2014	525	Masculin
Female	2014	581	Féminin
Average annual growth rate	2014	1.2	Taux de croissance annuel
Active Population ('000)	2013	442	Population active ('000)
Population by age group ('000)			Population par groupe d'âge ('000)
0-14 years	2014	408	0-14 ans
15-64 years	2014	660	15-64 ans
65+ years	2014	38	65+ ans
Economically active population in agriculture (%)	2014	30.8	Participation de la population active agricole (%)
Crude birth rate	2014	31.1	Taux brut de natalité
Crude death rate	2014	17.4	Taux brut de mortalité
Total fertility rate	2014	3.6	Indice synthétique de fécondité
Proportion of urban population	2014	23.1	Part de la population urbaine
Life Expectancy at Birth - Total (years)	2014	45.6	Espérance de vie à la naissance - Totale (ans)
Dependency Ratio - Total (%)	2014	72.5	Taux de dépendance - Total (%)
HEALTH			**SANTÉ**
Percentage of children under-five and underweight	2010	5.8	% d'enfants de moins de cinq ans avec insuffisance pondérale
Prevalence of undernourishment	2013	26.1	Prévalence de la malnutrition
Under five mortality rate (both sexes, per 1000)	2014	144.1	Taux de mortalité de moins de 5 ans (les deux sexes, pour 1000)
Infant mortality rate (both sexes) per 1000	2014	99.2	Taux de mortalité infantile (les deux sexes) par 1000
Percentage of children provided the vaccines :			Pourcentage d'enfants vaccinés :
BCG	2013	98.0	BCG
DPT3	2013	98.0	DTC3
Polio	2012	88.0	Polio
Measles	2013	85.0	Rougeole
Percentage of mothers provided at least one antenatal care (%)	2010	96.8	Pourcentage de mères ayant au moins reçu un soin prénatal (%)
Percentage of deliveries attended by skilled health personnel	2010	82.0	% d'accouchements assistés par un personnel de santé qualifié
Number of doctors (per 10 000 population)	2009	1.7	Nombre de médecins (pour 10 000 habitants)
Number of nurses (per 10 000 population)	2009	16.0	Nombre d'infirmières (pour 10 000 habitants)
Hospital beds - Total (per 10 000 population)	2011	19.0	Nombre de lits d'hôpitaux - Total (pour 10 000)
Births registered (per 1 000)	2014	29.5	Naiss.s enregistrées (pour 1 000)
Deaths registered (per 1 000)	2014	14.4	Décès enregistrés (pour 1 000)
Public expenditure on Health (% of budget)	2014	12.0	Dépenses publiques consacrées à la santé (% du budget)
EDUCATION			**EDUCATION**
Enrolment in primary education (both sexes) (000)	2014	245	Scolarisation dans le primaire (les deux sexes) (000)
Female	2014	116	Féminin
Enrolment in secondary education (both sexes) (000)	2014	93	Scolarisation dans le secondaire (les deux sexes) (000)
Female	2014	46	Féminin
Enrolment in tertiary education (both sexes) (000)	2014	10.4	Scolarisation dans le tertiaire (les deux sexes) (000)
Female	2014	5.1	Féminin
Literacy rate (both sexes)	2010	83.1	Taux d'alphabétisation (deux sexes)
Male	2010	83.9	Masculin
Female	2010	82.4	Féminin
Pupil-teacher ratio	2014	30.0	Ratio élève-enseignant
Public expenditure on education (% of budget)	2014	17.3	Dépenses publiques consacrées à l'enseignement (% du budget)
POVERTY			**PAUVRETÉ**
GNI Per Capita (US$)	2013	2 990.0	RNB par habitant ($EU)
Human Poverty Index (HPI-1) Value (%)	2007	35.1	Valeur de l'Indice de pauvreté (IPH-1) (%)
Population below International Poverty Line ($2/day) (%)	2010	59.1	Population sous le seuil international de pauvreté (2$/J) (%)
Share of Income Held by Richest 10%	2010	40.1	% de revenu des 10% plus riches
Share of Income Held by Poorest 10%	2010	1.7	% de revenu des 10% plus pauvres
Gini index	2010	51.5	Indice de Gini

Charts / Graphiques

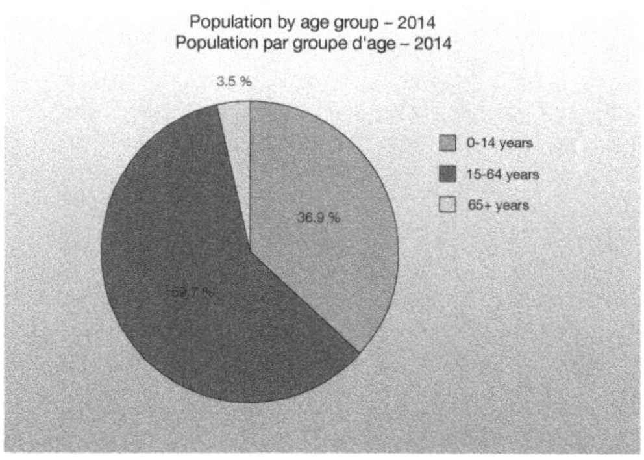

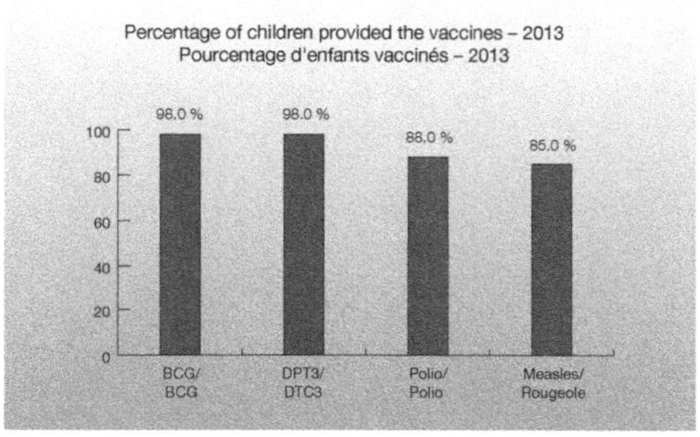

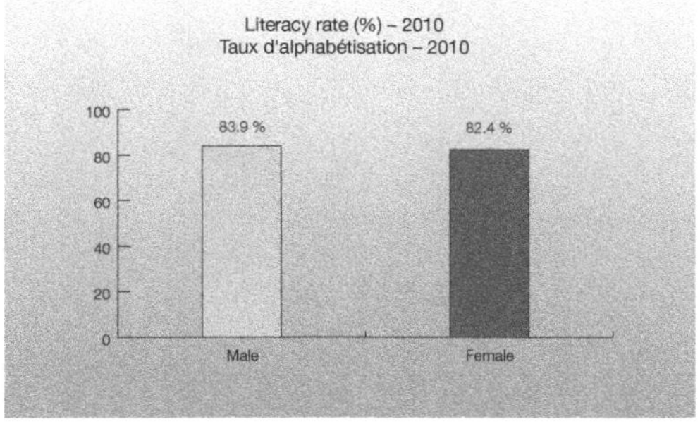

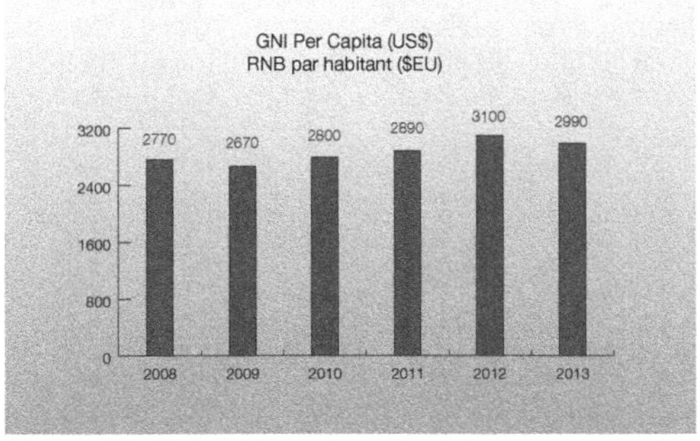

SWAZILAND

II NATIONAL ACCOUNTS — COMPTES NATIONAUX

	2006	2007	2008	2009	2010	2011	2012	2013	2014	
GROSS DOMESTIC PRODUCT BY KIND OF ECONOMIC ACTIVITY AT CURRENT PRICES *LILANGENI (MILLIONS)*										**PRODUIT INTÉRIEUR BRUT PAR BRANCHE D'ACTIVITÉ ÉCONOMIQUE AUX PRIX COURANTS** *LILANGENI (MILLIONS)*
Agriculture, hunting, forestry and fishing	1 152	1 277	1 460	1 588	1 630	2 009	2 215	2 235	2 252	Agriculture, chasse sylviculture et pêche
Mining and quarrying	57	54	52	57	73	69	93	94	95	Industries extractives
Manufacturing	6 078	6 686	7 816	8 519	9 371	10 466	11 961	13 397	15 272	Industries manufacturières
Electricity, gas & water	139	149	175	188	269	249	254	255	256	Electricité, gaz et eau
Construction & public works	588	568	551	535	519	623	1 447	1 449	1 450	Bâtiments et travaux publics
Wholesale & retail trade, restaurants, hotels	1 678	1 774	2 021	2 107	2 166	2 303	2 530	2 687	2 877	Commerce de gros et de détail, restaurants et hôtels
Finance, insurance, real estate, etc.	1 403	1 558	1 836	2 030	2 241	2 400	2 879	2 874	2 888	Banques, assurances, affaires immobilières
Transport and communications	972	1 199	1 363	1 446	1 549	1 596	1 718	1 844	1 993	Transport(s) et communications
Public administration and defense	2 342	2 459	2 887	3 263	3 687	3 575	4 117	4 118	4 119	Administrations publiques et défense
Education	225	243	286	309	347	369	401	437	476	Education
Health and Social Work	145	156	184	198	223	237	258	281	306	Santé et actions sociales
Other services	251	272	306	345	388	412	449	489	532	Autres services
Less Imputed Service Charges	- 332	- 372	- 432	- 431	- 474	- 559	- 486	- 423	- 368	Moins services d'intermédiation financière
Gross domestic product at factor cost / basic prices	14 698	16 024	18 506	20 154	21 990	23 748	27 837	29 735	32 148	Produit intérieur brut aux couts des facteurs / prix de base
Plus: indirect taxes / taxes on products, less subsidies	5 264	5 491	6 441	6 634	4 688	4 697	4 706	4 735	4 744	Plus taxes indirectes/impôts sur les produits, moins les subventions
EXPENDITURE ON GROSS DOMESTIC PRODUCT AT CURRENT PURCHASER'S VALUES *LILANGENI (MILLIONS)*										**EMPLOI DU PRODUIT INTÉRIEUR BRUT AUX PRIX COURANTS D'ACQUISITION** *LILANGENI (MILLIONS)*
Government final consumption	2 771	3 041	3 338	3 663	4 413	4 413	4 843	5 315	5 833	Consommation finale des administrations publiques
Private final consumption	16 949	18 405	22 640	24 806	23 682	23 904	27 669	29 122	31 024	Consommation finale privée
Gross fixed capital formation	2 558	2 644	2 756	2 757	2 759	2 759	2 760	2 761	2 762	Formation brute de capital fixe
Change in inventories	...	...	...	...	...	2	3	4	5	Variation des stocks
Exports of goods and services	13 179	13 996	14 814	15 762	15 102	15 797	17 512	17 512	17 512	Exportations de biens et services
Less imports of goods and services	15 495	16 572	18 602	20 200	19 277	18 429	20 245	20 245	20 245	Moins importations de biens et services
GDP at purchasers' values	19 962	21 515	24 947	26 788	26 678	28 446	32 543	34 470	36 892	PIB aux prix d'acquisition
GROSS DOMESTIC PRODUCT BY KIND OF ECONOMIC ACTIVITY AT CONSTANT PRICES *ANNUAL GROWTH RATES (%)*										**PRODUIT INTÉRIEUR BRUT PAR BRANCHE D'ACTIVITÉ ECONOMIQUE AUX PRIX CONSTANTS** *TAUX DE CROISSANCE ANNUEL (%)*
Agriculture, hunting, forestry and fishing	- 2.4	2.6	- 0.1	- 0.9	5.9	21.5	- 2.5	5.5	6.8	Agriculture, chasse sylviculture et pêche
Mining and quarrying	15.8	- 39.1	- 16.0	- 30.0	27.0	- 14.4	35.6	18.8	- 13.1	Industries extractives
Manufacturing	1.5	2.6	1.6	- 3.1	- 12.0	11.8	14.3	- 19.4	0.5	Industries manufacturières
Electricity, gas & water	5.1	4.8	2.4	5.7	- 6.0	- 7.0	1.9	5.3	- 7.0	Electricité, gaz et eau
Construction & public works	3.5	- 3.4	- 3.0	- 2.6	- 2.6	- 4.3	20.2	9.6	8.0	Bâtiments et travaux publics
Wholesale & retail trade, restaurants, hotels	10.6	9.6	4.4	4.7	2.5	4.8	9.3	5.7	3.0	Commerce de gros et de détail,restaurants et hôtels
Finance, insurance, real estate, etc.	3.2	3.6	4.1	4.6	1.0	8.5	- 2.5	- 2.5	4.8	Banques, assurances, affaires immobilières
Transport and communications	5.6	3.0	7.2	5.6	5.9	7.0	8.5	6.4	5.3	Transport(s) et communications
Public administration and defense	6.5	4.5	1.6	6.4	5.4	4.0	2.0	4.3	2.5	Administrations publiques et défense
Education	2.4	3.7	3.0	3.5	3.6	3.8	3.8	1.0	1.0	Education
Health and Social Work	2.4	3.7	3.0	3.5	3.6	3.8	3.8	1.0	0.9	Santé et actions sociales
Other services	2.4	3.7	3.0	3.5	3.6	3.8	3.8	1.0	1.0	Autres services
Less Imputed Service Charges	4.3	3.5	3.0	7.5	- 3.0	18.0	- 13.0	- 1.0	12.7	Moins services d'intermédiation financière
Gross domestic product at factor cost / basic prices	3.4	3.5	2.4	1.2	- 1.6	8.4	7.6	- 3.6	2.9	Produit intérieur brut aux couts des facteurs / prix de base
Plus: indirect taxes / taxes on products, less subsidies	2.8	3.4	2.1	1.6	- 2.9	6.8	0.2	- 2.3	1.0	Plus taxes indirectes/impôts sur les produits, moins les subventions
Gross domestic product at market prices	3.3	3.5	2.4	1.3	- 1.8	8.2	6.3	- 3.4	2.6	Produit intérieur brut aux prix du marché
EXPENDITURE ON GROSS DOMESTIC PRODUCT AT CONSTANT PURCHASERS' VALUES *ANNUAL GROWTH RATES (%)*										**EMPLOIS DU PRODUIT INTÉRIEUR BRUT AUX PRIX CONSTANTS D'ACQUISITION** *TAUX DE CROISSANCE ANNUEL (%)*
Government final consumption	...	...	...	...	...	...	...	...	...	Consommation finale des administrations publiques
Private final consumption	...	...	...	...	...	...	...	...	...	Consommation finale privée
Gross fixed capital formation	...	...	...	...	...	...	...	...	...	Formation brute de capital fixe
Exports of goods and services	...	...	...	...	...	...	...	...	...	Exportations de biens et services
Less imports of goods and services	...	...	...	...	...	...	...	...	...	Moins importations de biens et services
Notes	The data for 2013-2014 are provisional				Les données de 2013-2014 sont des prévisions					Notes

III INFLATION

	2006	2007	2008	2009	2010	2011	2012	2013	2014	
ANNUAL GROWTH RATES (%)										**TAUX DE CROISSANCE ANNUEL (%)**
All items	5.3	8.1	12.6	7.6	4.5	6.1	8.9	5.6	5.7	Ensemble
of which:										dont:
Food and Non-alcoholic beverages	14.6	16.6	18.9	10.2	0.4	6.0	13.1	5.7	6.3	Alimentation et boissons non alcoolisés
Alcoholic beverages & tobacco	-2.0	9.7	9.8	9.7	6.8	4.5	5.6	4.5	6.7	Boissons alcoolisées et tabacs
Clothing and Footwear	1.3	-0.5	1.8	6.1	6.8	1.1	4.6	3.6	7.4	Habillement et chaussures
Housing, Water, Electricity, Gas and Other Fuels	0.0	1.6	10.2	10.1	8.8	6.7	8.6	5.5	3.5	Logement, eau, électricité, gas et autres combustibles
Furnishing, household equip	...	2.5	8.3	9.6	5.0	3.3	5.2	5.0	4.6	Meubles, articles de ménage et entretien courant
Health	6.6	3.2	2.9	5.3	2.1	3.0	10.2	12.9	7.3	Santé
Transport	-	10.2	28.4	1.8	5.0	13.3	8.2	2.4	8.8	Transport
Communication	...	-4.6	4.5	7.2	7.5	0.4	0.0	0.0	-0.2	Communication
Recreation & culture	...	0.3	2.2	3.0	16.3	3.2	2.8	6.7	6.7	Loisirs et culture
Education	-1.5	-0.8	1.1	-1.7	12.0	12.3	7.5	9.4	9.6	Enseignement
Restaurants & hotels	3.2	7.4	15.1	13.4	1.4	2.6	5.9	-0.3	4.3	Restaurants et hôtels
Miscellaneous goods & services	1.2	1.5	5.1	3.8	5.0	6.1	2.4	0.3	4.0	Biens et services divers

IV AGRICULTURAL PRODUCTION - PRODUCTION AGRICOLE	2006	2007	2008	2009	2010	2011	2012	2013	2014	
TONNES *(THOUSAND)*										**TONNES** *(MILLIERS)*
Sugar cane	5 000	5 000	5 000	5 000	5 000	5 000	5 400	5 450	...	Canne à sucre
Maize	67	26	60	57	68	85	76	82	...	Maïs
Oranges	39	40	38	36	43	43	45	46	...	Oranges
Pineapples	21	20	24	25	27	31	32	34	...	Ananas
Grapefruit	37	35	35	36	37	37	38	33	...	Pamplemousse

V MINING PRODUCTION - PRODUCTION MINIERE	2006	2007	2008	2009	2010	2011	2012	2013	2014	
Coal, metric tons (thousands)	311	241	175	130	146	121	152	257	...	Houilles, tonnes métriques (milliers)
Iron Ore, metric tons (thousands)	...	...	...	...	...	1	1	1	...	Iron Ore, tonnes (milliers)
Quarry stone, metric tons (thousands)	1	0	0	0	0	0	0	0	...	Pierres taillées, tonnes métriques (milliers)

VI ENERGY - ENERGIE	2006	2007	2008	2009	2010	2011	2012	2013	2014	
Total electricity generation (GWh)	419	763	413	544	653	700	700	700	...	Production d'électricité totale (GWh)
of which:										dont:
Production of electricity from fossil fuels (GWh)	263	264	256	256	260	315	315	315	...	Production d'électricité à partir de combustibles fossiles (GWh)
Production of hydro electricity (GWh)	156	166	157	288	288	212	212	212	...	Production d'électricité d'origine hydraulique (GWh)
Production of electricity from solar, wind, tide, wave and other sources (GWh)	...	...	...	...	...	...	...	...	...	Production d'électricité d'origine solaire, éolienne, marée motrice et autres (GWh)

VII TOURISM AND INFRASTRUCTURE - TOURISME ET INFRASTRUCTURE	2006	2007	2008	2009	2010	2011	2012	2013	2014	
VII-1 TOURISM										**VII-1 TOURISME**
International tourist arrivals (thousands)	873	869	756	928	1.078	879	1.093	1.110	1.132	Arrivées de touristes internationaux (milliers)
Rooms in hotels and similar establishments (thousands)	...	...	...	...	...	...	...	...	...	Chambres d'hotels et établissements assimilés (milliers)
Overnight stays (thousands)	873	870	839	951	950	939	1 127	1 522	1 598	Nuitées (milliers)
Tourism receipts (US$ thousand)	72 500	28 900	17 700	28 300	31 700	10 600	17 900	5 900	6 603	Recettes touristiques (milliers de $ EU)
Total contribution to GDP (%)	5.6	4.0	5.1	5.5	5.5	4.5	4.9	4.3	4.4	Contribution totale au PIB (%)
Total contribution to Employment (%)	4.9	3.6	4.6	4.9	4.9	4.0	4.4	3.8	3.9	Contribution totale à l'emploi (%)
VII-2 INFRASTRUCTURE										**VII-2 INFRASTRUCTURE**
Paved roads (% of total)	38	38	38	38	38	42	44	45	45	Routes asphaltées (% du total)
Total Network (Railways-km)	297	297	297	297	297	297	297	332	332	Réseau total voies ferrées-Km
Main Telephone Lines (per 100 inhabitants)	4	4	4	4	4	6	4	4	5	Lignes téléphoniques fixes (pour 100 habitants)
Mobile Cellular Subscribers (per 100 inhabitants)	22	33	46	57	61	63	65	71	80	Abonnés aux téléphones mobiles (pour 100 habitants)

VIII EXTERNAL TRADE - COMMERCE EXTERIEUR	2006	2007	2008	2009	2010	2011	2012	2013	2014	
LILANGENI (MILLIONS) EXPORTS, FOB										**LILANGENI (MILLIONS) EXPORTATIONS, FÀB**
Exports - Total	11 260	12 293	12 959	13 270	13 217	13 838	15 813	18 295	...	Exportations - Total
Exports to AFRICA	6 862	8 352	8 906	8 909	10 826	9 897	11 877	14 867	...	Exportations vers l'AFRIQUE
Main Products										**Principaux produits**
Sugar	1 901	2 088	2 442	2 414	1 995	2 026	2 888	2 813	...	Sucre
Miscellaneous Edibles	4 994	5 851	6 602	7 536	7 464	7 543	7 806	8 729	...	Divers Comestibles
Textiles	916	954	1 031	797	792	558	1 226	1 454	...	Textiles
Canned fruits	193	212	236	193	173	178	178	222	...	Conserves de fruits
Minerals	120	103	119	103	126	126	816	1 344	...	Minéraux
Main Destinations										**Principales destinations**
South Africa	212	457	367	365	405	0	10 017	11 504	...	Afrique du Sud
United States	180	159	179	169	183	323	142	92	...	États-Unis
Thailand	229	38	105	97	100	50	3	3	...	Thaïlande
Australia	34	51	75	61	69	90	27	40	...	Australie
United Kingdom	67	65	75	69	76	75	107	103	...	Royaume-Uni
IMPORTS, CIF										**IMPORTATIONS, CAF**
Imports - Total	12 967	12 998	13 040	15 094	14 315	14 157	15 174	16 344	...	Importations - Total (millions)
Imports from Africa	7 214	8 243	10 310	11 121	13 625	13 018	12 836	14 564	...	Importations en provenance de l'Afrique
Main Products										**Principaux produits**
Food and Live Animals	1 075	1 596	1 706	1 849	2 195	2 905	1 614	1 723	...	Alimentaires et animaux vivants
Mineral Fuel and Lubricants	1 221	1 276	1 831	1 518	1 517	1 641	113	118	...	Carburants et lubrifiants
Chemicals and Chemical products	1 074	1 211	1 681	1 745	1 772	1 813	1 736	1 898	...	Produits chimiques
Manufactures classified by Material	1 741	1 846	1 956	2 018	2 473	2 342	2 239	2 945	...	Produits manufacturés selon la matière
Machinery and Equipments	1 898	1 723	1 987	2 333	2 577	2 384	1 816	2 337	...	Mechines et équipements
Main Origin										**Principales provenances**
South Africa	10 737	10 557	11 829	12 652	12 519	12 880	12 704	14 263	...	Afrique du Sud
India	76	109	100	112	112	4 263	142	169	...	Inde
China	140	263	248	267	269	1 522	577	653	...	Chine
China, Taiwan	333	212	288	303	295	825	171	225	...	Chine, Taiwan
United States	123	257	219	245	247	1 004	98	89	...	États-Unis

IX FINANCIAL AND MONETARY STATISTICS - FINANCES ET STATISTIQUES MONETAIRES	2006	2007	2008	2009	2010	2011	2012	2013	2014	
IX-1 MONETARY STATISTICS *LILANGENI (MILLIONS)*										**IX-1 STATISTIQUES MONÉTAIRES** *LILANGENI (MILLIONS)*
Money supply (M1)	4 340	5 270	6 080	7 710	8 320	8 780	9 660	11 200	12 450	Masse monétaire (M1)
Quasi-money	2 982	3 605	4 111	5 376	5 784	5 896	6 219	6 783	7 375	Quasi-monnaie
of which Demand Deposit	...	...	...	...	...	...	...	...	...	dont Monnaie scripturale
Net foreign assets	3 296	5 760	8 065	7 811	5 744	4 024	6 269	7 867	7 714	Avoirs extérieurs nets
Domestic credit	2 681	1 390	454	2 273	4 668	7 660	6 473	6 751	7 907	Crédit intérieur
of which claims on private sector	4 250	5 184	5 527	6 250	6 215	7 833	7 698	9 254	10 159	dont créances sur le secteur privé
of which claims on government sector, net	- 1 677	- 3 884	- 5 296	- 4 238	- 2 232	- 619	- 1 589	- 3 008	- 2 965	dont créances nettes sur le gouvernement
International reserves (millions US$)	373	774	752	959	756	601	741	763	691	Réserves internationales (millions $EU)
Average Exchange Rate (National Currency per US$)	6.77	7.05	8.25	8.44	7.32	7.25	8.21	9.65	10.37	Taux de change (moyen) (monnaie nationale par $ EU)
IX-2 PUBLIC FINANCE *LILANGENI (MILLIONS)*										**IX-2 FINANCES PUBLIQUES** *LILANGENI (MILLIONS)*
Total Revenues and Grants	5 499	8 020	9 410	9 642	6 831	7 184	12 036	12 850	14 258	Recettes totales et dons
Tax Revenue	5 179	7 667	9 019	8 717	6 585	7 045	11 715	12 400	13 204	Recettes fiscales
Non Tax Revenue	148	188	246	384	187	104	278	262	276	Recettes non fiscales
Grants	172	166	145	540	59	34	43	189	778	Dons
Total Expenditures and Net Lending	6 079	6 281	9 780	10 935	10 338	9 132	10 423	12 909	15 307	Dépenses totales et prêts nets
Current expenditure	4 670	4 845	7 308	8 465	8 465	8 114	9 076	10 300	11 551	Dépenses courantes
Of which Wages and Salaries	2 401	2 589	3 469	3 839	4 138	3 822	4 062	4 598	4 739	Dont rémunérations et salaires
Capital expenditure	1 410	1 437	2 472	2 470	1 873	1 019	1 347	2 609	3 756	Dépenses d'équipement
Net Lending	-	-	-	-	-	-	-	-	-	Prêts nets
Fiscal Balance	- 580	1 739	- 370	- 1 293	- 3 508	- 1 948	1 613	- 59	- 1 049	Solde global y compris les dons
IX-3 BALANCE OF PAYMENTS *LILANGENI (BILLIONS)*										**IX-3 BALANCE DES PAIEMENTS** *LILANGENI (MILLIARDS)*
Trade balance	- 1 707	- 705	- 82	- 1 028	- 1 097	- 319	641	2 462	1 667	Balance commerciale
Services Balance	- 610	- 1 871	- 3 706	- 3 411	- 3 078	- 4 344	- 4 799	- 5 310	- 5 801	Balance des services
Net Income	95	290	- 43	- 640	- 1 655	- 1 857	- 2 578	- 3 561	- 3 512	Revenus nets
Compensation of employees	...	...	...	...	...	...	...	...	...	Rémunération des salariés
Investment Income	...	...	...	...	...	...	...	...	...	Revenus des investissements
Current transfers, net total	890	1 290	1 964	1 601	2 968	3 845	8 006	8 347	7 965	Transferts courants
Net official transfers	...	...	...	...	...	...	...	...	...	Transferts officiels nets
Workers' remittances	...	...	...	...	...	...	...	...	...	Envois de fonds des travailleurs
Other private transfers	...	...	...	...	...	...	...	...	...	Autres transferts privés
Current account balance	- 1 332	- 996	- 1 867	- 3 478	- 2 868	- 2 675	1 270	1 939	319	Solde du compte courant
Capital & financial account	1 918	3 100	4 025	2 390	869	982	267	...	...	Comptes de capital et financier
Capital account	168	- 43	323	91	106	147	930	...	...	Compte de capital
Financial account	1 750	3 142	3 702	2 299	764	836	- 664	...	...	Compte financier
Errors & omissions	116	311	- 1 007	1 096	311	1 002	- 47	...	...	Erreurs et omissions
Overall balance	702	2 414	1 152	8	- 1 689	- 690	1 303	...	...	Balance générale

X DEBT AND FINANCIAL FLOWS - DETTE ET FLUX FINANCIERS	2006	2007	2008	2009	2010	2011	2012	2013	2014	
X-1 DEBT *US$ (MILLIONS)*										**X-1 DETTE EXTÉRIEURE** *$ E.U (MILLIONS)*
Total external debt	456	532	481	399	514	643	575	654	678	Dette extérieure totale
Private	456	532	481	399	514	643	575	654	678	Privée
Public	...	...	...	...	...	...	...	...	...	Publique
Total external debt service	107	63	34	27	51	430	158	261	198	Service de la dette extérieure
Present value of External debt	...	...	...	...	...	...	...	...	...	Valeur actuelle de la dette extérieure
Total government domestic debt (in local currency)	1	0	0	0	1.7	1.9	4.1	...	...	Dette publique intérieure
X-2 FINANCIAL FLOWS *US$ (MILLIONS)*										**X-2 FLUX FINANCIERS** *$ E.U (MILLIONS)*
Net Foreign Direct Investment Inflows	121	37	106	66	136	93	90	67	...	Investissements étranger direct (flux nets entrants)
Main origin of FDI Inflows										**Principales origines de l'IDE entrant:**
Italy	...	...	-6.8	-67.1	19.1	-1.0	-22.8	...	...	Italie
Poland	...	...	...	...	-23.6	28.9	0.3	...	...	Pologne
Luxembourg	...	...	-0.3	...	...	...	0.1	...	...	Luxembourg
Japan	...	-0.8	...	...	...	...	...	...	...	Japan
France	7.5	...	...	...	...	...	...	...	...	France
African countries	...	...	...	...	...	...	...	...	...	Pays africains
Net total Official Development Assistance	35	51	70	56	91	125	88	116	...	Aide publique au développement (nette totale)
Main origin of Net ODA										**Principales origines de l'APD nette**
Global Fund	11	15	11	17	36.6	15.5	6.6	...	...	Fonds mondial
United States	2	3	9	16	23.6	46.3	43.6	38.6	...	Etats-Unis
Japan	12	7	3	1	4.4	12.6	- 1.5	- 0.3	...	Japon
AfDF	- 3	- 1	21	- 1	- 1.5	3.2	- 1.8	...	...	FAfD
Italy	0	1	1	0	0.4	0.4	...	...	...	Italie

SWAZILAND

AREA (KM²)	945 090		**SUPERFICIE (KM²)**
CAPITAL CITY	Dar es Salaam	Dar es Salaam	**CAPITALE**
CURRENCY	Tanzanian Shilling	Shilling Tanzanien	**MONNAIE**

I SOCIAL AND DEMOGRAPHIC INDICATORS – INDICATEURS DEMOGRAPHIQUES ET SOCIAUX

	Year / Année	Value / Valeur	
POPULATION			**POPULATION**
Population ('000)			Population ('000)
Both sexes	2014	50 757	Les deux sexes
Male	2014	25 385	Masculin
Female	2014	25 372	Féminin
Average annual growth rate	2014	3.0	Taux de croissance annuel
Active Population ('000)	2012	23 748	Population active ('000)
Population by age group ('000)			Population par groupe d'âge ('000)
0-14 years	2014	22 732	0-14 ans
15-64 years	2014	26 388	15-64 ans
65+ years	2014	1 637	65+ ans
Economically active population in agriculture (%)	2014	79.4	Participation de la population active agricole (%)
Crude birth rate	2014	38.7	Taux brut de natalité
Crude death rate	2014	8.3	Taux brut de mortalité
Total fertility rate	2014	5.1	Indice synthétique de fécondité
Proportion of urban population	2014	28.1	Part de la population urbaine
Life Expectancy at Birth - Total (years)	2014	62.1	Espérance de vie à la naissance - Totale (ans)
Dependency Ratio - Total (%)	2014	93.1	Taux de dépendance - Total (%)
HEALTH			**SANTÉ**
Percentage of children under-five and underweight	2011	13.6	% d'enfants de moins de cinq ans avec insuffisance pondérale
Prevalence of undernourishment	2013	34.6	Prévalence de la malnutrition
Under five mortality rate (both sexes, per 1000)	2013	51.8	Taux de mortalité de moins de 5 ans (les deux sexes, pour 1000)
Infant mortality rate (both sexes) per 1000	2013	36.4	Taux de mortalité infantile (les deux sexes) par 1000
Percentage of children provided the vaccines :			Pourcentage d'enfants vaccinés :
BCG	2013	99.0	BCG
DPT3	2013	91.0	DTC3
Polio	2011	88.0	Polio
Measles	2013	99.0	Rougeole
Percentage of mothers provided at least one antenatal care (%)	2010	87.8	Pourcentage de mères ayant au moins reçu un soin prénatal (%)
Percentage of deliveries attended by skilled health personnel	2010	48.9	% d'accouchements assistés par un personnel de santé qualifié
Number of doctors (per 10 000 population)	2006	0.1	Nombre de médecins (pour 10 000 habitants)
Number of nurses (per 10 000 population)	2013	2.1	Nombre d'infirmières (pour 10 000 habitants)
Hospital beds - Total (per 10 000 population)	2013	5.0	Nombre de lits d'hôpitaux - Total (pour 10 000)
Births registered (per 1 000)	2014	38.7	Naiss.s enregistrées (pour 1 000)
Deaths registered (per 1 000)	2014	8.3	Décès enregistrés (pour 1 000)
Public expenditure on Health (% of budget)	2009	18.1	Dépenses publiques consacrées à la santé (% du budget)
EDUCATION			**EDUCATION**
Enrolment in primary education (both sexes) (000)	2013	8 232	Scolarisation dans le primaire (les deux sexes) (000)
Female	2013	4 166	Féminin
Enrolment in secondary education (both sexes) (000)	2013	1 804	Scolarisation dans le secondaire (les deux sexes) (000)
Female	2013	865	Féminin
Enrolment in tertiary education (both sexes) (000)	2005	51.6	Scolarisation dans le tertiaire (les deux sexes) (000)
Female	2012	58.7	Féminin
Literacy rate (both sexes)	2010	67.8	Taux d'alphabétisation (deux sexes)
Male	2010	75.5	Masculin
Female	2010	60.8	Féminin
Pupil-teacher ratio	2013	43.0	Ratio élève-enseignant
Public expenditure on education (% of budget)	2014	21.7	Dépenses publiques consacrées à l'enseignement (% du budget)
POVERTY			**PAUVRETÉ**
GNI Per Capita (US$)	2013	630.0	RNB par habitant ($EU)
Human Poverty Index (HPI-1) Value (%)	2007	30.0	Valeur de l'Indice de pauvreté (IPH-1) (%)
Population below International Poverty Line ($2/day) (%)	2012	73.0	Population sous le seuil international de pauvreté (2$/J) (%)
Share of Income Held by Richest 10%	2012	31.1	% de revenu des 10% plus riches
Share of Income Held by Poorest 10%	2012	3.2	% de revenu des 10% plus pauvres
Gini index	2012	37.8	Indice de Gini

Charts / Graphiques

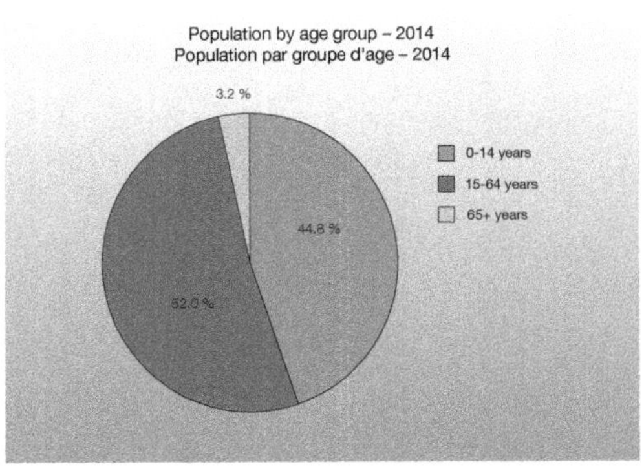

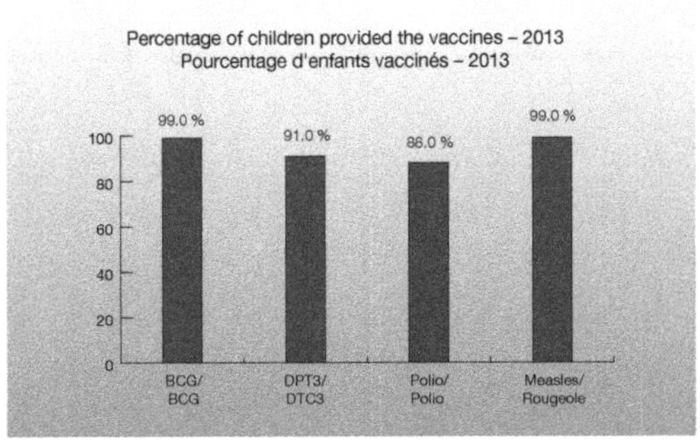

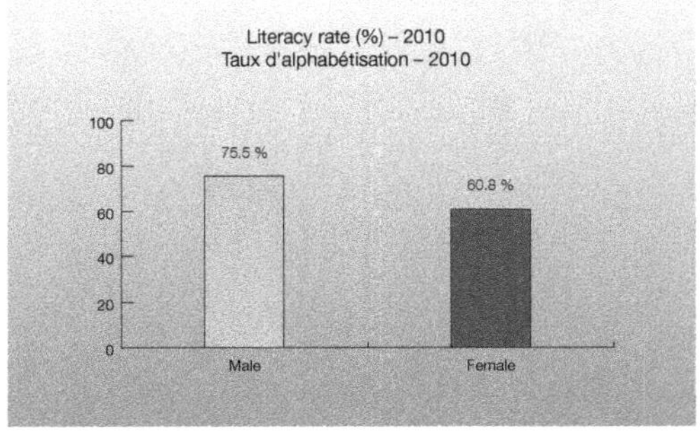

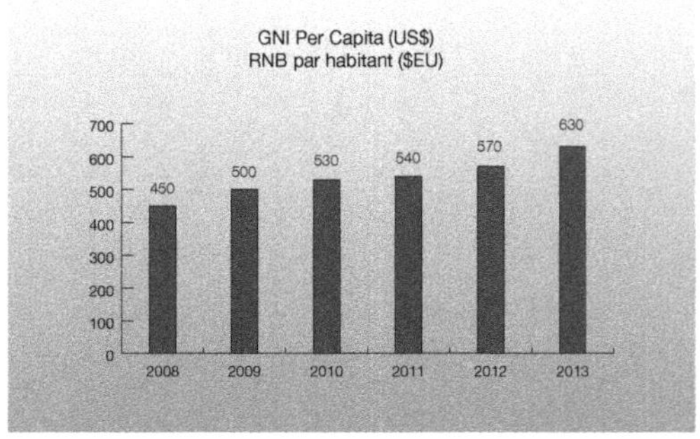

II NATIONAL ACCOUNTS — COMPTES NATIONAUX	2006	2007	2008	2009	2010	2011	2012	2013	2014	
GROSS DOMESTIC PRODUCT BY KIND OF ECONOMIC ACTIVITY AT CURRENT PRICES *TANZANIAN SHILLING (MILLIONS)*										**PRODUIT INTÉRIEUR BRUT PAR BRANCHE D'ACTIVITÉ ÉCONOMIQUE AUX PRIX COURANTS** *SHILLING TANZANIEN (MILLIONS)*
Agriculture, hunting, forestry and fishing	4 950 010	7 181 000	9 433 000	11 408 000	13 110 000	15 488 000	19 096 000	22 129 000	...	Agriculture, chasse sylviculture et pêche
Mining and quarrying	576 363	935 000	991 000	1 073 000	1 780 000	2 689 000	3 001 000	2 986 000	...	Industries extractives
Manufacturing	1 395 282	1 880 000	2 284 000	2 597 000	3 022 000	4 032 000	4 416 000	4 812 000	...	Industries manufacturières
Electricity, gas & water	352 724	474 000	555 000	620 000	667 000	551 000	808 000	873 000	...	Electricité, gaz et eau
Construction & public works	1 399 609	2 117 000	2 733 000	2 740 000	3 146 000	4 340 000	5 009 000	6 480 000	...	Bâtiments et travaux publics
Wholesale & retail trade, restaurants, hotels	2 504 005	3 127 000	3 762 000	4 440 000	5 163 000	6 330 000	7 312 000	8 282 000	...	Commerce de gros et de détail, restaurants et hôtels
Finance, insurance, real estate, etc.	2 023 305	3 469 000	3 971 000	4 480 000	3 877 000	4 615 000	5 748 000	9 215 000	...	Banques, assurances, affaires immobilières
Transport and communications	1 144 071	2 188 000	2 692 000	3 234 000	3 689 000	3 974 000	4 189 000	4 425 000	...	Transport(s) et communications
Public administration and defense	1 440 913	2 179 000	2 283 000	2 512 000	2 669 000	3 338 000	4 017 000	4 936 000	...	Administrations publiques et défense
Education	268 594	851 000	1 007 000	1 193 000	1 380 000	1 464 000	1 607 000	1 893 000	...	Education
Health and Social Work	275 726	438 000	532 000	664 000	736 000	821 000	919 000	1 020 000	...	Santé et actions sociales
Other services	117 284	439 000	505 000	572 000	613 000	679 000	782 000	872 000	...	Autres services
Less Imputed Service Charges	- 169 661	- 331 000	- 289 000	- 327 000	- 376 000	- 558 000	- 638 000	- 867 000	...	Moins services d'intermédiation financière
Gross domestic product at factor cost / basic prices	16 278 225	24 947 000	30 459 000	35 206 000	39 476 000	47 763 000	56 266 000	67 056 000	...	Produit intérieur brut aux couts des facteurs / prix de base
Plus: indirect taxes / taxes on products, less subsidies	1 663 043	1 822 000	2 173 000	2 481 000	2 815 000	3 261 000	3 871 000	4 480 000	...	Plus taxes indirectes/impôts sur les produits, moins les subventions
EXPENDITURE ON GROSS DOMESTIC PRODUCT AT CURRENT PURCHASER'S VALUES *TANZANIAN SHILLING (MILLIONS)*										**EMPLOI DU PRODUIT INTÉRIEUR BRUT AUX PRIX COURANTS D'ACQUISITION** *SHILLING TANZANIEN (MILLIONS)*
Government final consumption	3 144 881	4 968 000	5 276 000	6 599 000	6 452 000	7 294 000	9 055 000	11 580 000	...	Consommation finale des administrations publiques
Private final consumption	12 195 212	16 426 000	20 936 000	24 959 000	28 652 000	34 587 000	40 817 000	48 815 000	...	Consommation finale privée
Gross fixed capital formation	4 883 490	8 428 000	10 919 000	10 893 000	12 345 000	16 993 000	18 806 000	20 962 000	...	Formation brute de capital fixe
Change in inventories	74 292	366 000	- 521 000	-1 405 000	- 607 000	214 000	-1 276 000	- 300 000	...	Variation des stocks
Exports of goods and services	4 047 990	5 065 000	6 110 000	6 555 000	8 218 000	10 952 000	13 076 000	12 524 000	...	Exportations de biens et services
Less imports of goods and services	6 404 597	8 482 000	10 088 000	9 914 000	12 769 000	19 015 000	20 342 000	22 045 000	...	Moins importations de biens et services
GDP at purchasers' values	17 941 268	26 770 000	32 632 000	37 687 000	42 291 000	51 024 000	60 137 000	71 536 000	...	PIB aux prix d'acquisition
GROSS DOMESTIC PRODUCT BY KIND OF ECONOMIC ACTIVITY AT CONSTANT PRICES *ANNUAL GROWTH RATES (%)*										**PRODUIT INTÉRIEUR BRUT PAR BRANCHE D'ACTIVITÉ ECONOMIQUE AUX PRIX CONSTANTS** *TAUX DE CROISSANCE ANNUEL (%)*
Agriculture, hunting, forestry and fishing	3.9	4.0	7.5	5.1	2.7	3.5	3.2	3.2	...	Agriculture, chasse sylviculture et pêche
Mining and quarrying	15.6	10.7	- 9.7	18.7	7.2	6.3	6.7	3.9	...	Industries extractives
Manufacturing	8.5	8.7	11.4	4.7	8.9	7.0	4.1	6.6	...	Industries manufacturières
Electricity, gas & water	- 0.5	10.1	5.1	4.4	7.7	- 2.9	3.1	8.2	...	Electricité, gaz et eau
Construction & public works	9.5	9.7	9.7	- 3.7	10.3	22.9	3.2	18.9	...	Bâtiments et travaux publics
Wholesale & retail trade, restaurants, hotels	8.7	9.0	6.3	2.5	9.0	10.3	4.2	5.0	...	Commerce de gros et de détail,restaurants et hôtels
Finance, insurance, real estate, etc.	8.6	10.1	4.6	12.8	15.4	5.9	10.9	8.8	...	Banques, assurances, affaires immobilières
Transport and communications	7.9	7.5	7.1	7.1	9.4	6.5	6.0	5.0	...	Transport(s) et communications
Public administration and defense	6.5	6.7	- 6.2	- 0.7	- 5.0	15.9	9.1	7.8	...	Administrations publiques et défense
Education	5.0	...	9.5	9.2	6.4	5.5	7.4	4.3	...	Education
Health and Social Work	8.5	...	5.7	7.3	3.4	5.3	11.5	8.8	...	Santé et actions sociales
Other services	3.7	6.2	5.2	4.5	5.8	5.9	6.5	5.7	...	Autres services
Less Imputed Service Charges	14.9	15.3	6.9	19.8	8.0	22.5	1.2	0.2	...	Moins services d'intermédiation financière
Gross domestic product at factor cost / basic prices	6.7	7.2	5.6	4.9	6.5	7.6	5.5	6.7	...	Produit intérieur brut aux couts des facteurs / prix de base
Plus: indirect taxes / taxes on products, less subsidies	6.8	6.9	5.0	12.8	3.8	12.2	0.4	15.0	...	Plus taxes indirectes/impôts sur les produits, moins les subventions
Gross domestic product at market prices	6.7	7.1	5.6	5.4	6.4	7.9	5.1	7.3	...	Produit intérieur brut aux prix du marché
EXPENDITURE ON GROSS DOMESTIC PRODUCT AT CONSTANT PURCHASERS' VALUES *ANNUAL GROWTH RATES (%)*										**EMPLOIS DU PRODUIT INTÉRIEUR BRUT AUX PRIX CONSTANTS D'ACQUISITION** *TAUX DE CROISSANCE ANNUEL (%)*
Government final consumption	8.2	9.5	- 5.4	12.8	- 9.7	5.3	13.3	18.1	...	Consommation finale des administrations publiques
Private final consumption	8.1	6.0	7.9	8.0	7.4	5.7	3.3	6.9	...	Consommation finale privée
Gross fixed capital formation	16.0	14.5	12.5	- 0.8	11.5	21.7	1.0	6.7	...	Formation brute de capital fixe
Exports of goods and services	- 3.3	16.8	6.6	3.5	6.8	10.1	16.0	0.6	...	Exportations de biens et services
Less imports of goods and services	10.3	16.3	1.9	- 2.4	14.7	25.9	- 0.8	11.0	...	Moins importations de biens et services
Notes	The accounts are calculated using the new base year 2007					Les comptes annuels sont élaborés selon la nouvelle base des prix 2007				Notes

III INFLATION	2006	2007	2008	2009	2010	2011	2012	2013	2014	
ANNUAL GROWTH RATES (%)										**TAUX DE CROISSANCE ANNUEL (%)**
All items	7.3	7.0	10.3	12.1	8.2	12.7	16.0	7.9	6.1	Ensemble
of which:										dont:
Food and Non-alcoholic beverages	7.0	7.0	12.7	17.5	9.7	16.0	20.6	8.5	7.4	Alimentation et boissons non alcoolisés
Alcoholic beverages & tobacco	7.7	10.5	8.1	8.8	13.8	4.8	14.8	14.0	5.9	Boissons alcoolisées et tabacs
Clothing and Footwear	7.0	5.9	1.5	6.3	-0.3	9.5	13.8	5.7	3.0	Habillement et chaussures
Housing, Water, Electricity, Gas and Other Fuels	5.5	3.6	2.4	12.5	-0.9	18.7	16.3	14.2	10.7	Logement, eau, électricité, gas et autres combustibles
Furnishing, household equip	8.5	6.1	10.7	-1.6	18.6	13.8	9.0	4.1	1.9	Meubles, articles de ménage et entretien courant
Health	7.8	7.9	6.0	6.1	2.1	2.1	3.1	2.8	3.6	Santé
Transport	2.0	8.6	3.2	5.2	4.9	7.4	6.1	6.3	3.8	Transport
Communication	11.2	2.9	5.0	6.8	2.1	-1.5	-1.2	-0.3	0.7	Communication
Recreation & culture	5.0	8.9	5.5	9.2	2.7	3.0	9.9	2.1	0.7	Loisirs et culture
Education	9.1	7.0	6.9	-	5.9	4.1	4.6	2.4	5.3	Enseignement
Restaurants & hotels	2.5	9.6	7.0	10.1	4.9	8.1	16.6	5.5	2.7	Restaurants et hôtels
Miscellaneous goods & services	8.0	0.8	1.8	3.2	-0.7	4.7	10.7	5.7	6.1	Biens et services divers

	2006	2007	2008	2009	2010	2011	2012	2013	2014	
IV AGRICULTURAL PRODUCTION - PRODUCTION AGRICOLE										
TONNES *(THOUSAND)*										**TONNES** *(MILLIERS)*
Maize	3 423	3 659	5 441	3 326	4 733	4 341	5 104	5 356	...	Maïs
Cassava	6 158	5 199	5 392	5 916	4 548	4 647	5 462	4 755	...	Manioc
Sweet potatoes	1 396	1 322	1 379	1 417	2 424	3 573	3 018	3 470	...	Patates douces
Bananas	3 507	3 083	2 447	3 006	3 156	3 144	2 525	2 679	...	Bananes
Paddy	1 206	1 342	1 421	1 335	2 650	2 248	1 801	2 195	...	Riz
V MINING PRODUCTION - PRODUCTION MINIERE										
	2006	2007	2008	2009	2010	2011	2012	2013	2014	
Hard coal, metric tons (thousands)	18	27	15	0	0	81	79	85	...	Houilles, tonnes métriques (milliers)
Gold ores and concentrates, kilograms (thousands)	15	12	10	8	12	10	11	12	...	Minerais d'or et leurs concentrés, kilogrammes (milliers)
Silver ores and concentrates, kilograms (thousands)	40	40	36	39	39	37	39	43	...	Minerais d'argent et leurs concentrés, kilogrammes (milliers)
VI ENERGY - ENERGIE										
	2006	2007	2008	2009	2010	2011	2012	2013	2014	
Total electricity generation (GWh)	2 776	4 175	4 414	4 628	5 080	6 294	5 871	6 051	...	Production d'électricité totale (GWh)
of which:										dont:
Production of electricity from fossil fuels (GWh)	1 340	1 664	1 759	1 844	2 532	4 205	4 293	4 385	...	Production d'électricité à partir de combustibles fossiles (GWh)
Production of hydro electricity (GWh)	1 436	2 511	2 655	2 784	2 548	1 983	1 472	1 560	...	Production d'électricité d'origine hydraulique (GWh)
Production of electricity from solar, wind, tide, wave and other sources (GWh)	...	...	...	...	...	11	12	5	...	Production d'électricité d'origine solaire, éolienne, marée motrice et autres (GWh)
VII TOURISM AND INFRASTRUCTURE - TOURISME ET INFRASTRUCTURE										
	2006	2007	2008	2009	2010	2011	2012	2013	2014	
VII-1 TOURISM										**VII-1 TOURISME**
International tourist arrivals (thousands)	622	692	750	695	754	843	1 043	1 153	1 192	Arrivées de touristes internationaux (milliers)
Rooms in hotels and similar establishments (thousands)	31.7	31.9	32.0	32.3	...	...	...	...	...	Chambres d'hotels et établissements assimilés (milliers)
Overnight stays (thousands)	7 729	8 629	9 241	8 633	9 353	10 236	13 138	14 733	15 225	Nuitées (milliers)
Tourism receipts (US$ thousand)	950 200	1198 800	1288 700	1159 800	1254 500	1353 200	1712 700	1880 400	2006 390	Recettes touristiques (milliers de $ EU)
Total contribution to GDP (%)	15.3	15.8	13.5	13.8	13.2	13.9	14.7	14.5	14.0	Contribution totale au PIB (%)
Total contribution to Employment (%)	12.9	13.4	11.5	11.5	11.1	11.6	12.3	12.6	12.2	Contribution totale à l'emploi (%)
VII-2 INFRASTRUCTURE										**VII-2 INFRASTRUCTURE**
Paved roads (% of total)	...	...	7	15	...	...	...	...	...	Routes asphaltées (% du total)
Total Network (Railways-km)	4 460	4 460	4 460	4 460	3 682	3 682	3 682	3 682	...	Réseau total voies ferrées-Km
Main Telephone Lines (per 100 inhabitants)	0	0	0	0	0	0	0	0	...	Lignes téléphoniques fixes (pour 100 habitants)
Mobile Cellular Subscribers (per 100 inhabitants)	14	20	31	40	47	55	57	56	...	Abonnés aux téléphones mobiles (pour 100 habitants)
VIII EXTERNAL TRADE - COMMERCE EXTERIEUR										
	2006	2007	2008	2009	2010	2011	2012	2013	2014	
US$ (MILLIONS) **EXPORTS, FOB**										**$ E.U (MILLIONS)** **EXPORTATIONS, FÀB**
Exports - Total	1 743	2 024	3 112	2 859	3 760	4 433	5 121	4 572	...	Exportations - Total
Exports to AFRICA	...	...	...	...	...	...	...	...	...	Exportations vers l'AFRIQUE
Main Products										**Principaux produits**
Gold in unwrought forms non-monetary	483	403	545	657	574	...	...	...	...	Or non-monétaire, sous forme brute
Precious metal ores and concentrates except silver	178	201	350	498	461	...	...	...	...	Minerais de métaux précieux et leurs concentrés, excepté l'argent
Gold, semi-manufactured forms, non-monetary	127	151	214	161	392	...	...	...	...	Or non-monétaire, semi-ouvré
Tobacco, unmanufactured, stemmed or stripped	96	86	172	90	112	...	...	...	...	Tabac brut, tabac écôtés
Coffee, not roasted, not decaffeinated	74	113	100	111	102	143	...	...	...	Café, non torréfié, non décaféiné
Main Destinations										**Principales destinations**
China	172	279	267	373	645	669	521	309	...	Chine
India	106	93	170	184	222	206	477	749	...	Inde
Switzerland	156	509	622	679	676	928	792	404	...	Suisse
Japan	102	76	145	174	213	353	50	220	...	Japon
South Africa	119	235	228	179	424	843	975	764	...	Afrique du Sud
IMPORTS, CIF										**IMPORTATIONS, CAF**
Imports - Total	4 527	5 919	7 081	6 531	8 013	11 184	...	...	...	Importations - Total (millions)
Imports from Africa	...	...	...	...	...	...	...	...	...	Importations en provenance de l'Afrique
Main Products										**Principaux produits**
Petroleum, petroleum products and related materials	683	1 042	1 536	1 211	1 684	2 654	...	...	...	Pétrole et produits dérivés
Road vehicles	415	530	619	680	789	925	...	...	...	Véhicules routiers
Specialised machinery	250	239	404	424	449	631	...	...	...	Machines et appareils spécialisés
Iron and steel	195	226	338	295	348	472	...	...	...	Fer et acier
Cereals and cereal preparations	232	236	225	262	297	423	...	...	...	Céréales et préparations à base de céréales
Main Origin										**Principales provenances**
China	419	421	714	678	868	1 035	1 154	1 587	...	Chine
India	308	515	856	757	879	1 545	874	2 296	...	Inde
South Africa	507	666	820	673	76	973	928	726	...	Afrique du Sud
United Arab Emirates	402	163	193	471	662	1 220	1 018	233	...	Émirats arabes unis
Kenya	320	333	426	298	275	335	560	334	...	Kenya

IX FINANCIAL AND MONETARY STATISTICS - FINANCES ET STATISTIQUES MONETAIRES	2006	2007	2008	2009	2010	2011	2012	2013	2014	
IX-1 MONETARY STATISTICS *TANZANIAN SHILLING (MILLIONS)*										**IX-1 STATISTIQUES MONÉTAIRES** *SHILLING TANZANIEN (MILLIONS)*
Money supply (M1)	5 164 460	6 223 590	7 458 780	8 780 140	11 012 660	13 021 320	14 647 100	16 106 770	18 812 200	Masse monétaire (M1)
Quasi-money	2 245 621	2 642 802	3 169 028	3 924 470	4 715 501	5 219 938	5 795 699	6 458 737	7 711 642	Quasi-monnaie
of which Demand Deposit	...	...	...	...	...	...	...	...	...	dont Monnaie scripturale
Net foreign assets	3 613 809	3 674 845	4 076 152	4 930 809	6 086 780	6 296 384	6 371 084	6 572 437	6 562 003	Avoirs extérieurs nets
Domestic credit	2 027 507	2 831 367	4 221 201	5 120 245	6 798 432	9 093 572	11 045 512	12 947 217	16 090 155	Crédit intérieur
of which claims on private sector	2 285 717	3 119 092	3 984 318	4 326 349	5 235 706	6 668 738	7 988 285	9 149 395	10 988 864	dont créances sur le secteur privé
of which claims on government sector, net	- 282 629	- 319 844	- 334 967	128 358	806 665	1 471 255	2 035 131	2 554 554	3 678 330	dont créances nettes sur le gouvernement
International reserves (millions US$)	2 259	2 886	2 863	3 470	3 905	3 726	4 052	4 674	4 310	Réserves internationales (millions $EU)
Average Exchange Rate (National Currency per US$)	1 251.90	1 245.04	1 197.18	1 320.33	1 410.16	1 571.10	1 571.70	1 597.56	1 641.98	Taux de change (moyen) (monnaie nationale par $ EU)
IX-2 PUBLIC FINANCE *TANZANIAN SHILLING (MILLIONS)*										**IX-2 FINANCES PUBLIQUES** *SHILLING TANZANIEN (MILLIONS)*
Total Revenues and Grants	3 168 222	3 710 547	5 207 795	5 550 383	6 066 788	7 204 900	9 623 548	10 970 500	12 537 000	Recettes totales et dons
Tax Revenue	1 946 389	2 529 417	3 359 269	4 043 699	4 427 800	5 293 200	7 623 500	9 044 500	10 607 500	Recettes fiscales
Non Tax Revenue	178 411	209 583	275 331	249 401	233 700	284 700	208 500	268 000	387 000	Recettes non fiscales
Grants	1 043 422	971 547	1 573 195	1 257 283	1 405 288	1 627 000	1 791 548	1 658 000	1 542 500	Dons
Total Expenditures and Net Lending	4 005 564	4 474 669	5 209 024	6 811 859	8 311 300	9 439 000	12 154 000	13 750 500	15 625 000	Dépenses totales et prêts nets
Current expenditure	2 661 864	3 137 469	3 398 024	4 681 459	5 700 000	6 690 000	8 217 639	9 871 500	10 623 500	Dépenses courantes
Of which Wages and Salaries	656 789	976 094	1 134 709	1 608 591	1 723 000	2 346 000	3 036 000	3 659 500	4 351 000	Dont rémunérations et salaires
Capital expenditure	1 343 700	1 337 200	1 811 000	2 130 400	2 611 300	2 749 000	3 936 361	3 879 000	5 001 500	Dépenses d'équipement
Net Lending	-	-	-	-	-	-	-	-	-	Prêts nets
Fiscal Balance	- 837 342	- 764 122	- 1 229	-1 261 476	-2 244 512	-2 234 100	-2 530 452	-2 780 000	-3 088 000	Solde global y compris les dons
IX-3 BALANCE OF PAYMENTS *US$ (MILLIONS)*										**IX-3 BALANCE DES PAIEMENTS** *$ E.U (MILLIONS)*
Trade balance	- 1 947	- 2 634	- 3 434	- 2 540	- 2 842	- 4 730	- 4 430	- 5 680	...	Balance commerciale
Services Balance	279	462	350	146	157	92	428	700	...	Balance des services
Net Income	- 95	- 123	- 314	- 298	- 327	- 257	- 608	- 446	...	Revenus nets
Compensation of employees	- 23	- 46	- 55	- 81	12	24	21	...	...	Rémunération des salariés
Investment Income	...	...	...	...	...	...	...	...	...	Revenus des investissements
Current transfers, net total	589	652	834	891	1 051	902	- 608	- 446	...	Transferts courants
Net official transfers	...	...	...	...	...	...	...	...	...	Transferts officiels nets
Workers' remittances	...	...	...	...	...	...	...	...	...	Envois de fonds des travailleurs
Other private transfers	...	...	...	...	...	...	...	...	...	Autres transferts privés
Current account balance	- 1 174	- 1 643	- 2 595	- 1 768	- 1 960	- 3 992	- 3 792	- 4 651	...	Solde du compte courant
Capital & financial account	1 102	1 765	3 130	2 477	3 612	4 023	4 433	...	...	Comptes de capital et financier
Capital account	5 184	912	537	493	538	598	780	...	...	Compte de capital
Financial account	- 4 082	853	2 593	1 984	3 074	3 425	3 653	...	...	Compte financier
Errors & omissions	533	283	- 392	- 251	- 1 282	- 233	- 447	...	...	Erreurs et omissions
Overall balance	461	404	143	459	370	- 202	327	...	...	Balance générale

TANZANIE

X DEBT AND FINANCIAL FLOWS - DETTE ET FLUX FINANCIERS	2006	2007	2008	2009	2010	2011	2012	2013	2014	
X-1 DEBT *US$ (MILLIONS)*										**X-1 DETTE EXTÉRIEURE** *$ E.U (MILLIONS)*
Total external debt	5 207	3 963	4 983	5 996	7 177	8 358	9 893	11 831	13 700	Dette extérieure totale
Private	759	844	1 024	1 262	1 510	1 928	2 906	4 325	5 704	Privée
Public	4 448	3 119	3 959	4 734	5 667	6 430	6 987	7 506	7 996	Publique
Total external debt service	2 601	2 438	203	196	220	243	230	314	460	Service de la dette extérieure
Present value of External debt	...	...	...	...	...	...	...	...	...	Valeur actuelle de la dette extérieure
Total government domestic debt (in local currency)	1 820	1 940	2 055	2 495	3 231.6	3 891.9	4 318.3	...	...	Dette publique intérieure
X-2 FINANCIAL FLOWS *US$ (MILLIONS)*										**X-2 FLUX FINANCIERS** *$ E.U (MILLIONS)*
Net Foreign Direct Investment Inflows	403	582	1 383	953	1 813	1 229	1 800	1 872	...	Investissements étranger direct (flux nets entrants)
Main origin of FDI Inflows										**Principales origines de l'IDE entrant:**
United Kingdom	6	28	26	16	23.2	46.5	-	...	...	Royaume-Uni
Sweden	6	10	53	31	44.3	31.0	33.1	...	...	Suède
Netherlands	-	...	-	-	-	-	-	...	...	Pays-Bas
Norway	-	-	43	- 6	27.6	-	-	...	...	Norvège
Italy	-	1	80	- 35	11.9	- 17.2	0.9	...	...	Italie
African countries	...	...	...	...	...	...	...	...	...	Pays africains
Net total Official Development Assistance	1 883	2 822	2 331	2 933	2 958	2 446	2 832	3 430	...	Aide publique au développement (nette totale)
Main origin of Net ODA										**Principales origines de l'APD nette**
IDA	423	506	421	627	693.4	258.3	535.3	...	...	IDA
United Kingdom	219	231	254	217	240.9	158.9	250.0	...	...	Royaume-Uni
United States	122	167	247	284	457.4	541.3	568.7	734.1	...	Etats-Unis
Japan	39	722	71	120	104.6	119.4	147.9	196.9	...	Japon
AfDF	160	137	93	240	141.3	159.5	130.1	...	...	FAfD

TOGO

AREA (KM²)	56 790		SUPERFICIE (KM²)
CAPITAL CITY	Lomé	Lomé	CAPITALE
CURRENCY	CFA Franc	Franc CFA	MONNAIE

I SOCIAL AND DEMOGRAPHIC INDICATORS – INDICATEURS DEMOGRAPHIQUES ET SOCIAUX

	Year / Année	Value / Valeur	
POPULATION			**POPULATION**
Population ('000)			Population ('000)
Both sexes	2014	6 812	Les deux sexes
Male	2014	3 315	Masculin
Female	2014	3 497	Féminin
Average annual growth rate	2014	2.4	Taux de croissance annuel
Active Population ('000)	2014	3 156	Population active ('000)
Population by age group ('000)			Population par groupe d'âge ('000)
0-14 years	2014	2 799	0-14 ans
15-64 years	2014	3 775	15-64 ans
65+ years	2014	239	65+ ans
Economically active population in agriculture (%)	2014	43.3	Participation de la population active agricole (%)
Crude birth rate	2014	32.9	Taux brut de natalité
Crude death rate	2014	10.7	Taux brut de mortalité
Total fertility rate	2014	4.8	Indice synthétique de fécondité
Proportion of urban population	2014	2.4	Part de la population urbaine
Life Expectancy at Birth - Total (years)	2014	56.9	Espérance de vie à la naissance - Totale (ans)
Dependency Ratio - Total (%)	2014	80.5	Taux de dépendance - Total (%)
HEALTH			**SANTÉ**
Percentage of children under-five and underweight	2013	7.8	% d'enfants de moins de cinq ans avec insuffisance pondérale
Prevalence of undernourishment	2013	15.3	Prévalence de la malnutrition
Under five mortality rate (both sexes, per 1000)	2013	84.7	Taux de mortalité de moins de 5 ans (les deux sexes, pour 1000)
Infant mortality rate (both sexes) per 1000	2013	55.8	Taux de mortalité infantile (les deux sexes) par 1000
Percentage of children provided the vaccines :			Pourcentage d'enfants vaccinés :
BCG	2013	84.0	BCG
DPT3	2013	89.0	DTC3
Polio	2013	87.0	Polio
Measles	2013	82.0	Rougeole
Percentage of mothers provided at least one antenatal care (%)	2010	84.3	Pourcentage de mères ayant au moins reçu un soin prénatal (%)
Percentage of deliveries attended by skilled health personnel	2013	43.8	% d'accouchements assistés par un personnel de santé qualifié
Number of doctors (per 10 000 population)	2014	0.7	Nombre de médecins (pour 10 000 habitants)
Number of nurses (per 10 000 population)	2014	2.1	Nombre d'infirmières (pour 10 000 habitants)
Hospital beds - Total (per 10 000 population)	2014	6.8	Nombre de lits d'hôpitaux - Total (pour 10 000)
Births registered (per 1 000)	2014	35.9	Naiss.s enregistrées (pour 1 000)
Deaths registered (per 1 000)	2014	10.5	Décès enregistrés (pour 1 000)
Public expenditure on Health (% of budget)	2014	5.5	Dépenses publiques consacrées à la santé (% du budget)
EDUCATION			**EDUCATION**
Enrolment in primary education (both sexes) (000)	2013	1 421	Scolarisation dans le primaire (les deux sexes) (000)
Female	2013	669	Féminin
Enrolment in secondary education (both sexes) (000)	2013	534	Scolarisation dans le secondaire (les deux sexes) (000)
Female	2013	204	Féminin
Enrolment in tertiary education (both sexes) (000)	2012	65.6	Scolarisation dans le tertiaire (les deux sexes) (000)
Female	2013	18.3	Féminin
Literacy rate (both sexes)	2014	60.3	Taux d'alphabétisation (deux sexes)
Male	2014	74.0	Masculin
Female	2014	47.9	Féminin
Pupil-teacher ratio	2013	41.1	Ratio élève-enseignant
Public expenditure on education (% of budget)	2014	10.9	Dépenses publiques consacrées à l'enseignement (% du budget)
POVERTY			**PAUVRETÉ**
GNI Per Capita (US$)	2013	530.0	RNB par habitant ($EU)
Human Poverty Index (HPI-1) Value (%)	2007	36.6	Valeur de l'Indice de pauvreté (IPH-1) (%)
Population below International Poverty Line ($2/day) (%)	2011	72.8	Population sous le seuil international de pauvreté (2$/J) (%)
Share of Income Held by Richest 10%	2011	34.7	% de revenu des 10% plus riches
Share of Income Held by Poorest 10%	2011	2.0	% de revenu des 10% plus pauvres
Gini index	2011	46.0	Indice de Gini

Charts / Graphiques

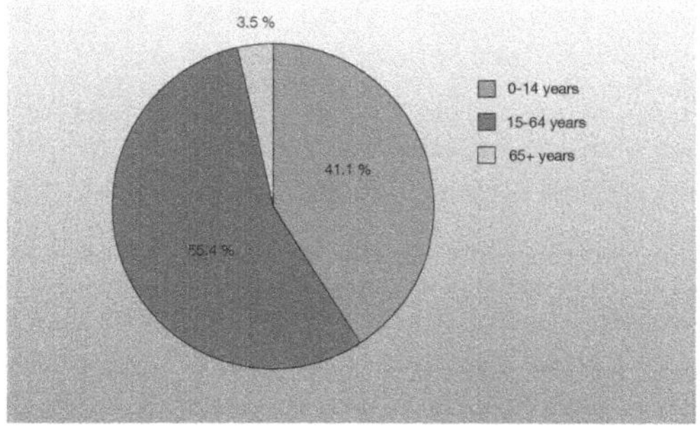

Population by age group – 2014
Population par groupe d'age – 2014

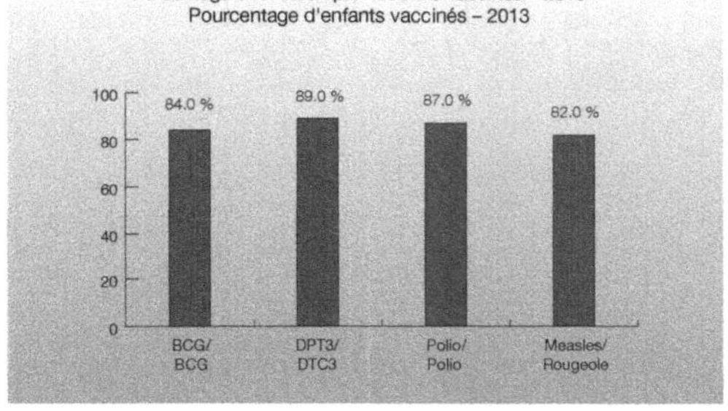

Percentage of children provided the vaccines – 2013
Pourcentage d'enfants vaccinés – 2013

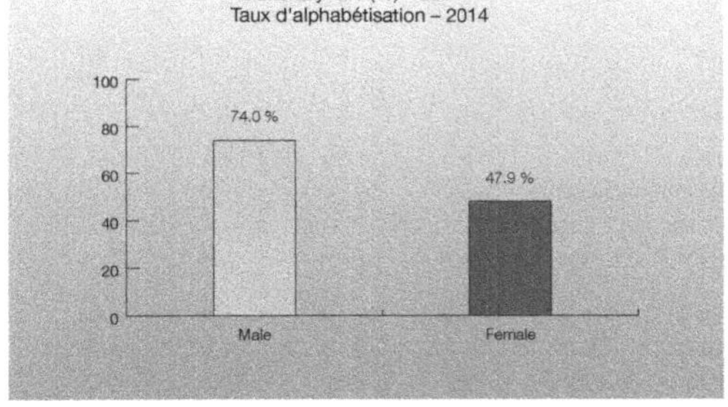

Literacy rate (%) – 2014
Taux d'alphabétisation – 2014

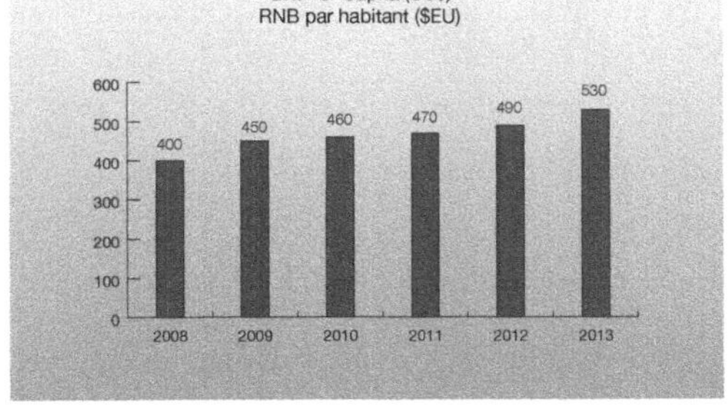

GNI Per Capita (US$)
RNB par habitant ($EU)

TOGO

II NATIONAL ACCOUNTS — COMPTES NATIONAUX										
	2006	2007	2008	2009	2010	2011	2012	2013	2014	
GROSS DOMESTIC PRODUCT BY KIND OF ECONOMIC ACTIVITY AT CURRENT PRICES *CFA FRANC (MILLIONS)*										**PRODUIT INTÉRIEUR BRUT PAR BRANCHE D'ACTIVITÉ ÉCONOMIQUE AUX PRIX COURANTS** *FRANC CFA (MILLIONS)*
Agriculture, hunting, forestry and fishing	421 603	436 667	578 603	639 378	644 255	714 866	840 928	800 668	931 673	Agriculture, chasse sylviculture et pêche
Mining and quarrying	32 522	31 818	59 114	48 187	40 290	57 513	79 844	77 537	74 412	Industries extractives
Manufacturing	106 649	111 084	120 089	118 087	122 315	129 553	136 293	129 233	134 305	Industries manufacturières
Electricity, gas & water	35 669	38 272	38 861	38 937	43 568	50 010	57 058	60 520	67 009	Electricité, gaz et eau
Construction & public works	37 362	44 855	39 382	33 508	48 003	75 383	90 719	109 018	117 198	Bâtiments et travaux publics
Wholesale & retail trade, restaurants, hotels	131 263	135 688	131 060	116 032	139 692	144 368	145 812	145 082	183 838	Commerce de gros et de détail, restaurants et hôtels
Finance, insurance, real estate, etc.	134 341	139 993	155 430	156 134	175 604	187 208	189 996	238 758	248 464	Banques, assurances, affaires immobilières
Transport and communications	69 094	71 267	73 285	78 626	91 519	94 823	94 058	104 171	112 275	Transport(s) et communications
Public administration and defense	96 222	94 668	103 204	138 932	119 946	141 414	157 960	168 349	183 233	Administrations publiques et défense
Education	...	...	...	...	...	...	...	...	...	Education
Health and Social Work	...	...	...	...	...	...	...	...	...	Santé et actions sociales
Other services	1 637	1 689	1 743	1 798	1 854	1 913	1 973	2 036	2 100	Autres services
Less Imputed Service Charges	- 20 629	- 21 643	- 25 482	- 26 783	- 28 297	- 31 979	- 40 284	- 50 006	- 60 590	Moins services d'intermédiation financière
Gross domestic product at factor cost / basic prices	1 045 734	1 084 358	1 275 289	1 342 836	1 398 750	1 565 072	1 754 357	1 785 365	1 993 918	Produit intérieur brut aux couts des facteurs / prix de base
Plus: indirect taxes / taxes on products, less subsidies	114 378	128 467	143 240	150 714	172 586	207 512	235 133	279 318	234 583	Plus taxes indirectes/impôts sur les produits, moins les subventions
EXPENDITURE ON GROSS DOMESTIC PRODUCT AT CURRENT PURCHASER'S VALUES *CFA FRANC (MILLIONS)*										**EMPLOI DU PRODUIT INTÉRIEUR BRUT AUX PRIX COURANTS D'ACQUISITION** *FRANC CFA (MILLIONS)*
Government final consumption	157 941	148 789	190 304	211 456	189 813	206 150	254 739	312 407	308 961	Consommation finale des administrations publiques
Private final consumption	1 086 463	1 109 618	1 215 199	1 236 263	1 349 161	1 547 912	1 666 281	1 689 674	1 833 802	Consommation finale privée
Gross fixed capital formation	194 845	174 195	203 294	248 678	283 250	309 201	476 147	493 269	472 297	Formation brute de capital fixe
Change in inventories	6 464	2 894	47 379	30 083	12 581	30 038	1 411	1 899	- 3 610	Variation des stocks
Exports of goods and services	507 415	451 979	508 641	565 007	642 070	744 891	860 992	950 108	1 125 870	Exportations de biens et services
Less imports of goods and services	793 016	674 650	746 288	797 938	905 539	1 065 607	1 270 079	1 382 674	1 508 819	Moins importations de biens et services
GDP at purchasers' values	1 160 112	1 212 824	1 418 529	1 493 550	1 571 336	1 772 584	1 989 491	2 064 682	2 228 501	PIB aux prix d'acquisition
GROSS DOMESTIC PRODUCT BY KIND OF ECONOMIC ACTIVITY AT CONSTANT PRICES *ANNUAL GROWTH RATES (%)*										**PRODUIT INTÉRIEUR BRUT PAR BRANCHE D'ACTIVITÉ ECONOMIQUE AUX PRIX CONSTANTS** *TAUX DE CROISSANCE ANNUEL (%)*
Agriculture, hunting, forestry and fishing	4.9	3.3	3.7	8.3	- 22.7	6.7	5.7	0.0	14.9	Agriculture, chasse sylviculture et pêche
Mining and quarrying	2.9	- 25.6	- 12.0	- 0.1	2.1	17.3	13.3	6.6	- 4.9	Industries extractives
Manufacturing	9.1	2.2	8.1	- 7.0	4.5	8.5	9.0	0.9	5.0	Industries manufacturières
Electricity, gas & water	- 9.3	- 11.0	10.4	12.8	10.1	- 31.1	15.9	3.8	5.2	Electricité, gaz et eau
Construction & public works	27.4	- 1.0	17.1	12.3	6.9	17.6	20.5	13.1	12.1	Bâtiments et travaux publics
Wholesale & retail trade, restaurants, hotels	- 22.3	- 0.2	- 8.6	2.6	7.2	36.4	4.0	10.9	13.1	Commerce de gros et de détail,restaurants et hôtels
Finance, insurance, real estate, etc.	66.4	2.0	- 1.2	- 0.6	124.4	- 11.4	- 19.7	10.1	3.1	Banques, assurances, affaires immobilières
Transport and communications	- 3.6	16.8	11.3	4.5	- 0.6	1.3	- 0.6	8.6	2.9	Transport(s) et communications
Public administration and defense	1.7	- 2.7	- 4.1	1.7	0.3	0.1	0.1	12.0	1.5	Administrations publiques et défense
Education	...	...	...	...	...	...	...	...	...	Education
Health and Social Work	...	...	...	...	...	...	...	...	...	Santé et actions sociales
Other services	92.1	2.2	- 5.1	4.6	2.0	15.1	13.4	8.5	0.8	Autres services
Less Imputed Service Charges	331.8	6.4	- 16.9	3.6	124.4	6.5	- 54.6	30.9	20.0	Moins services d'intérmédiation financière
Gross domestic product at factor cost / basic prices	2.5	0.7	3.0	4.1	3.0	3.3	4.9	5.0	7.9	Produit intérieur brut aux couts des facteurs / prix de base
Plus: indirect taxes / taxes on products, less subsidies	18.4	14.6	- 2.7	- 3.2	13.3	17.5	12.3	8.6	- 10.4	Plus taxes indirectes/impôts sur les produits, moins les subventions
Gross domestic product at market prices	3.9	2.1	2.4	3.4	4.1	4.8	5.8	5.4	5.5	Produit intérieur brut aux prix du marché
EXPENDITURE ON GROSS DOMESTIC PRODUCT AT CONSTANT PURCHASERS' VALUES *ANNUAL GROWTH RATES (%)*										**EMPLOIS DU PRODUIT INTÉRIEUR BRUT AUX PRIX CONSTANTS D'ACQUISITION** *TAUX DE CROISSANCE ANNUEL (%)*
Government final consumption	4.9	- 7.0	17.3	- 7.0	- 1.7	- 4.3	18.9	29.5	- 6.8	Consommation finale des administrations publiques
Private final consumption	8.2	5.3	- 15.8	7.9	5.0	7.0	- 2.7	13.8	4.8	Consommation finale privée
Gross fixed capital formation	10.7	- 12.3	12.2	24.6	15.0	7.4	50.0	3.1	- 8.9	Formation brute de capital fixe
Exports of goods and services	20.1	- 18.2	16.0	6.2	18.0	15.2	20.7	7.1	14.3	Exportations de biens et services
Less imports of goods and services	19.7	- 9.8	- 12.1	14.7	15.6	13.5	12.3	18.8	6.7	Moins importations de biens et services
Notes	NA data: 2012-2013 : Revised; 2014:Projection				Données des CN: 2012-2013: Révisées;2014:Projections					Notes
III INFLATION										
	2006	2007	2008	2009	2010	2011	2012	2013	2014	
ANNUAL GROWTH RATES (%)										**TAUX DE CROISSANCE ANNUEL (%)**
All items	2.2	0.9	8.7	3.7	1.5	3.6	2.6	1.8	0.2	Ensemble
of which:										dont:
Food and Non-alcoholic beverages	-1.1	2.8	20.4	9.5	-0.3	1.2	3.4	0.6	-4.3	Alimentation et boissons non alcoolisés
Alcoholic beverages & tobacco	2.4	3.9	5.7	5.4	4.1	-2.3	0.5	1.7	0.4	Boissons alcoolisées et tabacs
Clothing and Footwear	-0.6	-1.8	1.3	-1.2	1.2	1.6	0.9	1.6	0.5	Habillement et chaussures
Housing, Water, Electricity, Gas and Other Fuels	7.2	2.0	2.7	1.4	1.4	5.8	6.0	2.0	2.8	Logement, eau, électricité, gas et autres combustibles
Furnishing, household equip	1.0	-0.8	4.6	0.5	1.3	5.1	1.2	1.7	1.6	Meubles, articles de ménage et entretien courant
Health	-2.7	-0.6	2.5	1.6	0.7	3.5	-1.6	-1.6	-0.2	Santé
Transport	12.2	-0.4	6.9	1.4	6.2	5.2	4.9	-0.6	4.2	Transport
Communication	-5.0	-6.0	0.9	-0.5	-0.1	3.6	-4.6	3.1	-0.8	Communication
Recreation & culture	-	-0.4	1.9	-1.7	0.8	2.8	0.2	-1.9	-0.8	Loisirs et culture
Education	3.0	0.1	-2.1	3.7	-0.1	1.0	2.4	4.1	2.6	Enseignement
Restaurants & hotels	1.5	0.2	-0.1	3.7	3.2	5.8	1.3	5.2	2.6	Restaurants et hôtels
Miscellaneous goods & services	-0.8	0.1	1.0	0.9	-0.9	6.0	4.8	5.0	1.1	Biens et services divers

IV AGRICULTURAL PRODUCTION - PRODUCTION AGRICOLE										
	2006	2007	2008	2009	2010	2011	2012	2013	2014	
TONNES *(THOUSAND)*										**TONNES** *(MILLIERS)*
Cassava	767	773	795	896	909	999	960	903	...	Manioc
Maize	543	546	590	652	638	651	826	693	...	Maïs
Yams	621	618	648	704	710	728	864	661	...	Ignames
Sorghum	221	210	211	238	245	243	221	285	...	Sorgho
Paddy	76	75	86	121	110	112	161	165	...	Riz
V MINING PRODUCTION - PRODUCTION MINIERE										
	2006	2007	2008	2009	2010	2011	2012	2013	2014	
Limestone, thousand Tons	...	1 824	1 704	1 656	1 923	1 900	...	...	...	Calcaires, milliers de tonnes
Phosphate, thousand metric tons	1 170	750	840	730	700	870	1 110	1 510	...	Phosphate, milliers de tonnes métriques
Gold, thousand Kilogrammes	...	12	13	10	16	17	...	...	...	Or, milliers de Kilogrammes
VI ENERGY - ENERGIE										
	2006	2007	2008	2009	2010	2011	2012	2013	2014	
Total electricity generation (GWh)	221	194	123	126	132	139	202	208	...	Production d'électricité totale (GWh)
of which:										dont:
Production of electricity from fossil fuels (GWh)	127	92	30	31	32	34	111	111	...	Production d'électricité à partir de combustibles fossiles (GWh)
Production of hydro electricity (GWh)	91	92	91	93	98	103	89	95	...	Production d'électricité d'origine hydraulique (GWh)
Production of electricity from solar, wind, tide, wave and other sources (GWh)	...	...	...	...	...	...	...	...	...	Production d'électricité d'origine solaire, éolienne, marée motrice et autres (GWh)
VII TOURISM AND INFRASTRUCTURE - TOURISME ET INFRASTRUCTURE										
	2006	2007	2008	2009	2010	2011	2012	2013	2014	
VII-1 TOURISM										**VII-1 TOURISME**
International tourist arrivals (thousands)	94	86	74	150	202	300	235	250	263	Arrivées de touristes internationaux (milliers)
Rooms in hotels and similar establishments (thousands)	5.2	5.4	...	...	...	...	...	...	...	Chambres d'hotels et établissements assimilés (milliers)
Overnight stays (thousands)	417	379	407	630	814	1 338	1 031	1 108	1 167	Nuitées (milliers)
Tourism receipts (US$ thousand)	18 000	33 600	38 600	67 700	65 000	68 925	72 615	76 574	82 200	Recettes touristiques (milliers de $ EU)
Total contribution to GDP (%)	4.2	4.9	4.8	5.5	7.0	6.6	7.1	6.5	6.8	Contribution totale au PIB (%)
Total contribution to Employment (%)	3.4	3.9	3.9	4.5	5.3	5.4	5.8	5.6	5.8	Contribution totale à l'emploi (%)
VII-2 INFRASTRUCTURE										**VII-2 INFRASTRUCTURE**
Paved roads (% of total)	...	21	...	...	...	...	...	...	...	Routes asphaltées (% du total)
Total Network (Railways-km)	...	...	...	...	...	...	...	...	...	Réseau total voies ferrées-Km
Main Telephone Lines (per 100 inhabitants)	1	2	2	3	1	1	1	1	...	Lignes téléphoniques fixes (pour 100 habitants)
Mobile Cellular Subscribers (per 100 inhabitants)	12	20	26	36	41	42	50	63	...	Abonnés aux téléphones mobiles (pour 100 habitants)
VIII EXTERNAL TRADE - COMMERCE EXTERIEUR										
	2006	2007	2008	2009	2010	2011	2012	2013	2014	
CFA FRANC (MILLIONS) EXPORTS, FOB										**FRANC CFA (MILLIONS) EXPORTATIONS, FÀB**
Exports - Total	329 600	324 400	231 463	267 282	277 491	331 430	460 807	516 153	669 425	Exportations - Total
Exports to AFRICA	...	...	184 321	198 536	69 158	249 794	323 631	384 812	201 380	Exportations vers l'AFRIQUE
Main Products										**Principaux produits**
Cocoa	7 866	2 544	5 189	4 934	4 327	3 355	2 663	3 866	3 774	Cacao
Coffee	1 620	1 751	1 469	2 195	2 679	2 919	3 868	3 192	2 905	Café
Cotton	15 806	12 000	13 303	7 806	8 893	23 526	32 316	28 359	27 647	Coton
Phosphates	16 566	15 030	54 572	60 549	46 353	54 499	82 386	62 650	19 087	Phosphates
Cement	28 156	39 305	15 381	34 332	34 405	26 576	38 550	43 450	3 839	Ciment
Main Destinations										**Principales destinations**
Benin	20 769	14 607	27 281	41 037	11 628	49 699	56 359	59 321	41 092	Bénin
Burkina Faso	23 746	13 068	33 660	38 116	10 470	48 210	77 314	93 994	38 138	Burkina Faso
Mali	14 780	9 551	9 464	8 770	2 931	12 481	12 788	11 949	15 014	Mali
Ghana	37 649	7 847	15 003	39 139	11 928	27 197	21 738	56 560	19 533	Ghana
Netherlands	1 114	649	1 660	2 770	6 334	1 762	2 940	3 697	8 900	Pays-Bas
IMPORTS, CIF										**IMPORTATIONS, CAF**
Imports - Total	637 293	513 803	528 351	551 945	599 176	830 446	851 185	966 101	855 925	Importations - Total (millions)
Imports from Africa	...	...	101 976	85 895	101 875	118 757	125 940	133 018	107 822	Importations en provenance de l'Afrique
Main Products										**Principaux produits**
Food	49 527	53 813	60 469	66 051	76 968	98 637	109 924	117 110	113 037	Produits alimentaires
Other Consumer goods	84 535	86 683	95 351	108 549	113 477	...	...	...	...	Autres biens de consommation
Intermidiary goods	86 092	93 026	141 855	156 842	177 375	224 037	224 635	276 106	213 856	Biens intermédiaires
Equipment	77 555	80 695	111 841	152 858	140 844	248 341	200 640	218 367	226 937	Biens d'équipement
Petroleum products	237 245	97 310	119 875	74 671	92 299	138 390	184 883	213 679	160 178	Produits pétroliers
Main Origin										**Principales provenances**
Germany	10 788	7 464	7 545	18 355	16 349	24 434	15 127	24 225	32 973	Allemagne
Netherlands	12 983	41 774	39 256	32 749	21 689	28 086	29 111	72 806	41 614	Pays-Bas
Italy	14 313	8 359	7 002	7 629	13 177	11 101	13 656	14 971	16 400	Italie
France	79 694	72 223	86 469	64 310	81 007	79 159	80 166	75 916	78 960	France
Côte d'Ivoire	10 891	9 845	30 248	19 892	25 780	28 263	25 694	25 273	20 085	Côte d'Ivoire

TOGO

IX FINANCIAL AND MONETARY STATISTICS - FINANCES ET STATISTIQUES MONETAIRES	2006	2007	2008	2009	2010	2011	2012	2013	2014	
IX-1 MONETARY STATISTICS *CFA FRANC (MILLIONS)*										**IX-1 STATISTIQUES MONÉTAIRES** *FRANC CFA (MILLIONS)*
Money supply (M1)	383 820	459 280	530 920	616 690	717 030	831 300	905 580	978 180	1 062 820	Masse monétaire (M1)
Quasi-money	134 770	171 051	195 541	243 774	297 660	330 972	378 952	452 597	534 287	Quasi-monnaie
of which Demand Deposit	...	...	...	...	...	...	...	...	...	dont Monnaie scripturale
Net foreign assets	209 959	206 687	239 400	246 367	265 228	290 234	276 770	316 576	238 731	Avoirs extérieurs nets
Domestic credit	199 069	263 208	321 875	407 248	497 536	604 966	731 245	771 171	886 961	Crédit intérieur
of which claims on private sector	196 421	255 065	243 263	295 010	358 757	506 027	601 800	690 616	762 578	dont créances sur le secteur privé
of which claims on government sector, net	2 648	8 143	78 612	112 238	138 779	98 939	129 445	80 555	124 383	dont créances nettes sur le gouvernement
International reserves (millions US$)	375	438	582	703	715	774	442	507	444	Réserves internationales (millions $EU)
Average Exchange Rate (National Currency per US$)	522.89	479.27	447.81	472.19	495.28	471.87	510.53	494.04	493.91	Taux de change (moyen) (monnaie nationale par $ EU)
IX-2 PUBLIC FINANCE *CFA FRANC (MILLIONS)*										**IX-2 FINANCES PUBLIQUES** *FRANC CFA (MILLIONS)*
Total Revenues and Grants	211 888	223 909	240 985	275 812	359 143	401 144	419 584	522 112	518 416	Recettes totales et dons
Tax Revenue	179 121	195 865	211 240	229 597	246 673	291 412	327 697	403 517	409 682	Recettes fiscales
Non Tax Revenue	16 781	7 659	9 435	23 379	50 213	25 128	43 872	46 859	47 176	Recettes non fiscales
Grants	15 986	20 386	20 310	22 836	62 257	84 603	48 015	71 736	61 559	Dons
Total Expenditures and Net Lending	236 511	228 759	253 250	326 317	354 473	420 750	535 132	614 128	619 862	Dépenses totales et prêts nets
Current expenditure	196 889	204 690	203 123	234 150	230 905	276 113	359 637	424 501	427 065	Dépenses courantes
Of which Wages and Salaries	59 268	64 286	70 411	94 334	82 622	104 682	120 409	130 633	126 662	Dont rémunérations et salaires
Capital expenditure	39 576	24 068	49 867	92 169	123 558	144 250	175 221	188 957	192 797	Dépenses d'équipement
Net Lending	45	-	261	- 2	10	388	274	670	-	Prêts nets
Fiscal Balance	- 24 623	- 4 849	- 12 265	- 50 505	4 670	- 19 607	- 115 548	- 92 016	- 101 446	Solde global y compris les dons
IX-3 BALANCE OF PAYMENTS *CFA FRANC (MILLIONS)*										**IX-3 BALANCE DES PAIEMENTS** *FRANC CFA (MILLIONS)*
Trade balance	- 242 887	- 189 388	- 203 529	- 194 605	- 224 969	- 273 687	- 420 862	- 467 125	- 413 049	Balance commerciale
Services Balance	- 42 790	- 33 290	- 34 118	- 38 326	- 38 500	- 47 029	11 775	34 559	50 100	Balance des services
Net Income	- 19 763	- 14 492	- 6 750	- 8 991	- 11 700	- 11 393	107 662	105 505	110 463	Revenus nets
Compensation of employees	...	...	...	...	...	...	...	...	...	Rémunération des salariés
Investment Income	...	...	...	...	...	...	...	...	...	Revenus des investissements
Current transfers, net total	127 400	133 715	145 018	158 503	176 200	171 278	111 007	145 702	150 355	Transferts courants
Net official transfers	...	...	...	...	...	...	...	...	...	Transferts officiels nets
Workers' remittances	...	...	...	...	...	...	...	...	...	Envois de fonds des travailleurs
Other private transfers	...	...	...	...	...	...	...	...	...	Autres transferts privés
Current account balance	- 177 964	- 103 448	- 99 379	- 83 419	- 98 969	- 160 832	- 190 418	- 181 360	- 102 132	Solde du compte courant
Capital & financial account	...	...	...	...	...	...	...	...	...	Comptes de capital et financier
Capital account	...	...	...	...	...	...	...	...	...	Compte de capital
Financial account	...	...	...	...	...	...	...	...	...	Compte financier
Errors & omissions	...	...	...	...	...	...	...	...	...	Erreurs et omissions
Overall balance	...	...	...	...	...	...	...	...	...	Balance générale

X DEBT AND FINANCIAL FLOWS - DETTE ET FLUX FINANCIERS	2006	2007	2008	2009	2010	2011	2012	2013	2014	
X-1 DEBT *US$ (MILLIONS)*										**X-1 DETTE EXTÉRIEURE** *$ E.U (MILLIONS)*
Total external debt	1 820	2 185	1 777	1 748	546	577	721	865	976	Dette extérieure totale
Private	-	-	-	-	-	-	-	-	-	Privée
Public	1 820	2 185	1 777	1 748	546	577	721	865	976	Publique
Total external debt service	3	5	40	54	60	31	39	70	74	Service de la dette extérieure
Present value of External debt	7 400	-	193 200	0	0.0	0.0	0.0	0.0	0.0	Valeur actuelle de la dette extérieure
Total government domestic debt (in local currency)	...	...	...	...	467 370.0	592 430.0	629 070.0	687 020.0	...	Dette publique intérieure
X-2 FINANCIAL FLOWS *US$ (MILLIONS)*										**X-2 FLUX FINANCIERS** *$ E.U (MILLIONS)*
Net Foreign Direct Investment Inflows	77	49	24	49	86	728	94	84	...	Investissements étranger direct (flux nets entrants)
Main origin of FDI Inflows										**Principales origines de l'IDE entrant:**
France	10	...	...	...	...	...	-	...	...	France
Sweden	- 1	- 2	6	9	12.2	13.6	12.9	...	...	Suède
Germany	...	...	-	-	-	0.0	0.0	...	...	Allemagne
Greece	-	-	-	...	0.3	-	-	...	...	Grèce
Italy	-	-	1	- 1	0.4	- 0.1	- 0.2	...	...	Italie
African countries	...	...	...	...	...	...	...	...	...	Pays africains
Net total Official Development Assistance	80	122	330	499	404	543	241	221	...	Aide publique au développement (nette totale)
Main origin of Net ODA										**Principales origines de l'APD nette**
France	33	34	128	41	168.0	36.8	22.6	26.6	...	France
Switzerland	1	1	1	159	1.7	76.0	2.5	...	...	Suisse
Belgium	2	2	3	62	5.0	95.0	0.7	0.7	...	Belgique
Germany	8	12	8	24	8.8	93.5	109.7	75.1	...	Allemagne
IDA	-	-	48	6	7.9	55.9	36.9	...	...	IDA

AREA (KM²)	163 610		SUPERFICIE (KM²)
CAPITAL CITY	Tunis	Tunis	CAPITALE
CURRENCY	Tunisian Dinar	Dinar Tunisien	MONNAIE

I SOCIAL AND DEMOGRAPHIC INDICATORS – INDICATEURS DEMOGRAPHIQUES ET SOCIAUX

Indicator	Year / Année	Value / Valeur	Indicateur
POPULATION			**POPULATION**
Population ('000)			Population ('000)
Both sexes	2014	11 117	Les deux sexes
Male	2014	5 507	Masculin
Female	2014	5 610	Féminin
Average annual growth rate	2014	1.1	Taux de croissance annuel
Active Population ('000)	2014	3 957	Population active ('000)
Population by age group ('000)			Population par groupe d'âge ('000)
0-14 years	2014	2 578	0-14 ans
15-64 years	2014	7 726	15-64 ans
65+ years	2014	813	65+ ans
Economically active population in agriculture (%)	2014	20.4	Participation de la population active agricole (%)
Crude birth rate	2014	17.0	Taux brut de natalité
Crude death rate	2014	5.7	Taux brut de mortalité
Total fertility rate	2014	2.0	Indice synthétique de fécondité
Proportion of urban population	2014	67.0	Part de la population urbaine
Life Expectancy at Birth - Total (years)	2014	76.1	Espérance de vie à la naissance - Totale (ans)
Dependency Ratio - Total (%)	2014	43.1	Taux de dépendance - Total (%)
HEALTH			**SANTÉ**
Percentage of children under-five and underweight	2012	2.3	% d'enfants de moins de cinq ans avec insuffisance pondérale
Prevalence of undernourishment	2013	5.0	Prévalence de la malnutrition
Under five mortality rate (both sexes, per 1000)	2013	15.2	Taux de mortalité de moins de 5 ans (les deux sexes, pour 1000)
Infant mortality rate (both sexes) per 1000	2013	13.1	Taux de mortalité infantile (les deux sexes) par 1000
Percentage of children provided the vaccines :			Pourcentage d'enfants vaccinés :
BCG	2013	97.0	BCG
DPT3	2013	98.0	DTC3
Polio	2011	98.0	Polio
Measles	2013	94.0	Rougeole
Percentage of mothers provided at least one antenatal care (%)	2008	96.0	Pourcentage de mères ayant au moins reçu un soin prénatal (%)
Percentage of deliveries attended by skilled health personnel	2012	98.6	% d'accouchements assistés par un personnel de santé qualifié
Number of doctors (per 10 000 population)	2010	12.2	Nombre de médecins (pour 10 000 habitants)
Number of nurses (per 10 000 population)	2009	32.8	Nombre d'infirmières (pour 10 000 habitants)
Hospital beds - Total (per 10 000 population)	2010	18.3	Nombre de lits d'hôpitaux - Total (pour 10 000)
Births registered (per 1 000)	2014	17.0	Naiss.s enregistrées (pour 1 000)
Deaths registered (per 1 000)	2014	5.7	Décès enregistrés (pour 1 000)
Public expenditure on Health (% of budget)	2009	6.8	Dépenses publiques consacrées à la santé (% du budget)
EDUCATION			**EDUCATION**
Enrolment in primary education (both sexes) (000)	2013	1 063	Scolarisation dans le primaire (les deux sexes) (000)
Female	2013	511	Féminin
Enrolment in secondary education (both sexes) (000)	2013	1 072	Scolarisation dans le secondaire (les deux sexes) (000)
Female	2011	574	Féminin
Enrolment in tertiary education (both sexes) (000)	2011	336.0	Scolarisation dans le tertiaire (les deux sexes) (000)
Female	2012	215.7	Féminin
Literacy rate (both sexes)	2011	79.7	Taux d'alphabétisation (deux sexes)
Male	2011	87.8	Masculin
Female	2011	71.7	Féminin
Pupil-teacher ratio	2013	17.2	Ratio élève-enseignant
Public expenditure on education (% of budget)	2012	17.4	Dépenses publiques consacrées à l'enseignement (% du budget)
POVERTY			**PAUVRETÉ**
GNI Per Capita (US$)	2013	4 200.0	RNB par habitant ($EU)
Human Poverty Index (HPI-1) Value (%)	2007	15.6	Valeur de l'Indice de pauvreté (IPH-1) (%)
Population below International Poverty Line ($2/day) (%)	2010	4.5	Population sous le seuil international de pauvreté (2$/J) (%)
Share of Income Held by Richest 10%	2010	27.2	% de revenu des 10% plus riches
Share of Income Held by Poorest 10%	2010	2.7	% de revenu des 10% plus pauvres
Gini index	2010	35.8	Indice de Gini

Charts / Graphiques

Population by age group – 2014
Population par groupe d'age – 2014

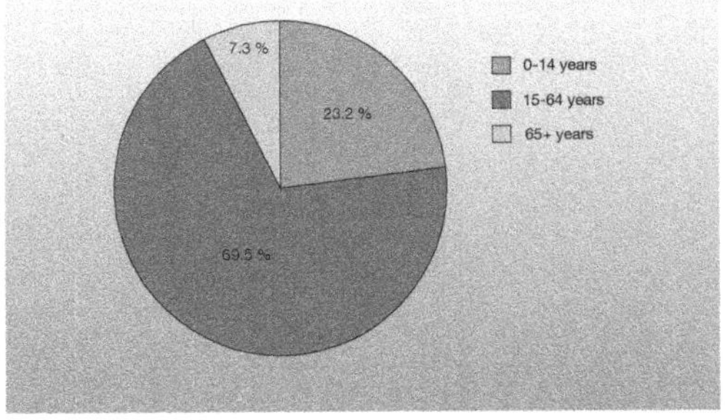

Percentage of children provided the vaccines – 2013
Pourcentage d'enfants vaccinés – 2013

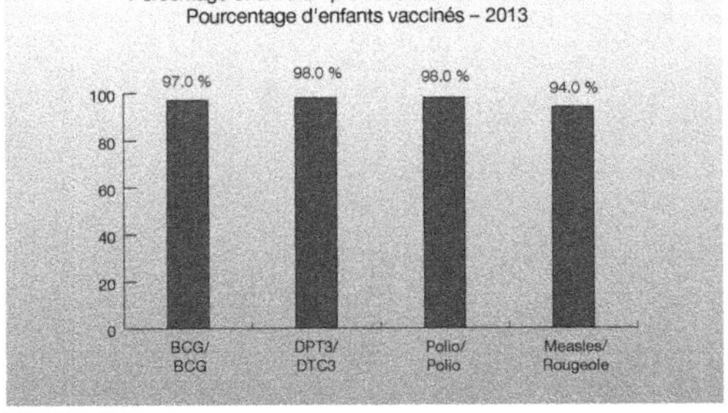

Literacy rate (%) – 2014
Taux d'alphabétisation – 2014

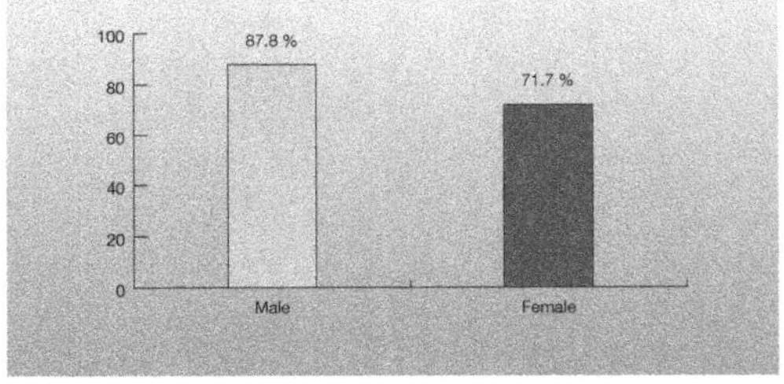

GNI Per Capita (US$)
RNB par habitant ($EU)

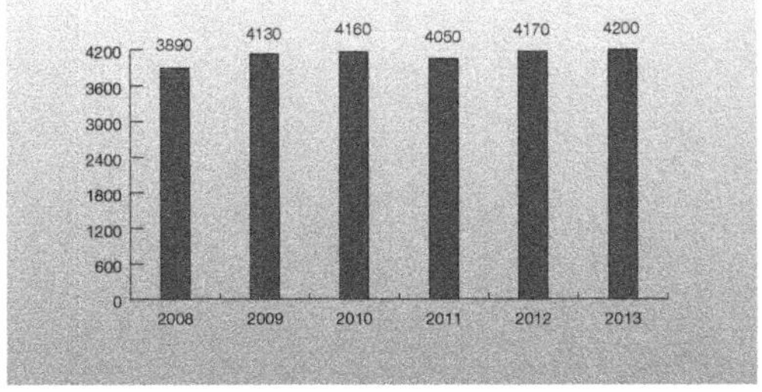

II NATIONAL ACCOUNTS — COMPTES NATIONAUX

	2006	2007	2008	2009	2010	2011	2012	2013	2014	
GROSS DOMESTIC PRODUCT BY KIND OF ECONOMIC ACTIVITY AT CURRENT PRICES *TUNISIAN DINAR (MILLIONS)*										**PRODUIT INTÉRIEUR BRUT PAR BRANCHE D'ACTIVITÉ ÉCONOMIQUE AUX PRIX COURANTS** *DINAR TUNISIEN (MILLIONS)*
Agriculture, hunting, forestry and fishing	4 246	4 309	4 338	4 962	4 751	5 504	6 397	6 689	...	Agriculture, chasse sylviculture et pêche
Mining and quarrying	2 424	3 237	4 388	3 274	4 304	4 751	5 323	5 253	...	Industries extractives
Manufacturing	7 295	8 397	10 026	9 938	10 422	10 681	11 302	11 837	...	Industries manufacturières
Electricity, gas & water	593	611	701	719	818	857	911	1 078	...	Electricité, gaz et eau
Construction & public works	2 079	2 170	2 268	2 523	2 727	2 908	3 123	3 248	...	Bâtiments et travaux publics
Wholesale & retail trade, restaurants, hotels	6 267	6 616	7 080	7 680	8 157	8 513	9 379	10 968	...	Commerce de gros et de détail, restaurants et hôtels
Finance, insurance, real estate, etc.	7 197	7 813	8 386	9 673	9 460	9 104	9 748	10 413	...	Banques, assurances, affaires immobilières
Transport and communications	5 410	5 949	6 800	7 327	8 295	7 913	8 610	8 622	...	Transport(s) et communications
Public administration and defense	3 774	4 101	4 370	4 370	5 266	6 098	6 877	7 587	...	Administrations publiques et défense
Education	2 307	2 508	2 672	2 672	3 220	3 645	3 950	4 234	...	Education
Health and Social Work	773	841	896	896	1 079	1 726	2 071	2 269	...	Santé et actions sociales
Other services	206	215	232	245	264	288	310	330	...	Autres services
Less Imputed Service Charges	- 750	- 885	- 813	- 762	- 822	- 875	- 1 042	- 1 078	...	Moins services d'intermédiation financière
Gross domestic product at factor cost / basic prices	41 821	45 881	51 345	53 517	57 940	61 113	66 958	71 450	-	Produit intérieur brut aux couts des facteurs / prix de base
Plus: indirect taxes / taxes on products, less subsidies	3 935	3 977	3 923	5 160	5 114	3 415	3 373	3 729	...	Plus taxes indirectes/impôts sur les produits, moins les subventions
EXPENDITURE ON GROSS DOMESTIC PRODUCT AT CURRENT PURCHASER'S VALUES *TUNISIAN DINAR (MILLIONS)*										**EMPLOI DU PRODUIT INTÉRIEUR BRUT AUX PRIX COURANTS D'ACQUISITION** *DINAR TUNISIEN (MILLIONS)*
Government final consumption	7 645	8 298	8 917	9 759	10 478	11 609	12 818	14 113	...	Consommation finale des administrations publiques
Private final consumption	28 243	30 699	33 922	36 390	39 665	42 804	46 967	51 822	...	Consommation finale privée
Gross fixed capital formation	10 333	11 490	13 060	14 278	15 502	14 066	15 458	15 960	...	Formation brute de capital fixe
Change in inventories	396	319	1 047	- 26	659	864	1 678	436	...	Variation des stocks
Exports of goods and services	21 061	25 470	30 761	26 428	31 210	31 299	34 204	35 293	...	Exportations de biens et services
Less imports of goods and services	21 923	26 419	32 440	28 152	34 460	36 114	40 795	42 444	...	Moins importations de biens et services
GDP at purchasers' values	45 756	49 857	55 268	58 677	63 055	64 528	70 331	75 179	-	PIB aux prix d'acquisition
GROSS DOMESTIC PRODUCT BY KIND OF ECONOMIC ACTIVITY AT CONSTANT PRICES *ANNUAL GROWTH RATES (%)*										**PRODUIT INTÉRIEUR BRUT PAR BRANCHE D'ACTIVITÉ ECONOMIQUE AUX PRIX CONSTANTS** *TAUX DE CROISSANCE ANNUEL (%)*
Agriculture, hunting, forestry and fishing	7.9	0.8	- 0.7	9.2	- 9.1	10.3	6.7	- 3.2	2.8	Agriculture, chasse sylviculture et pêche
Mining and quarrying	- 6.3	22.6	- 6.7	0.0	1.1	- 17.3	- 2.5	- 6.7	-12.4	Industries extractives
Manufacturing	3.2	8.8	3.1	- 1.4	3.0	- 3.2	1.0	0.6	-3.3	Industries manufacturières
Electricity, gas & water	- 0.1	- 4.3	12.5	- 2.8	15.1	1.8	0.8	2.6	-10.1	Electricité, gaz et eau
Construction & public works	6.5	4.0	3.1	3.7	3.5	- 1.2	3.5	1.0	-1.0	Bâtiments et travaux publics
Wholesale & retail trade, restaurants, hotels	5.6	3.6	5.7	2.2	3.1	- 5.8	1.3	0.2	-12.1	Commerce de gros et de détail,restaurants et hôtels
Finance, insurance, real estate, etc.	14.8	10.9	10.0	6.9	- 0.9	- 0.1	2.0	5.1	23.9	Banques, assurances, affaires immobilières
Transport and communications	8.0	8.0	10.8	5.5	9.0	- 6.9	7.3	10.2	15.1	Transport(s) et communications
Public administration and defense	2.7	2.0	- 0.1	3.0	12.5	10.9	7.3	5.3	4.4	Administrations publiques et défense
Education	0.7	0.0	- 2.0	1.0	10.3	8.7	3.0	1.5	-1.2	Education
Health and Social Work	2.6	4.0	2.5	2.7	3.0	4.0	13.0	2.9	-1.9	Santé et actions sociales
Other services	1.2	1.9	4.5	2.9	2.9	4.7	2.0	1.7	0.9	Autres services
Less Imputed Service Charges	8.2	6.6	- 9.0	6.2	4.8	17.0	6.1	5.9	4.3	Moins services d'intermédiation financière
Gross domestic product at factor cost / basic prices	5.9	6.7	4.4	3.1	3.2	- 1.6	3.4	2.1	2.3	Produit intérieur brut aux couts des facteurs / prix de base
Plus: indirect taxes / taxes on products, less subsidies	3.2	2.0	5.4	3.9	0.6	- 6.1	12.4	11.5	2.3	Plus taxes indirectes/impôts sur les produits, moins les subventions
Gross domestic product at market prices	5.7	6.3	4.5	3.1	3.0	- 1.9	3.9	2.5	2.3	Produit intérieur brut aux prix du marché
EXPENDITURE ON GROSS DOMESTIC PRODUCT AT CONSTANT PURCHASERS' VALUES *ANNUAL GROWTH RATES (%)*										**EMPLOIS DU PRODUIT INTÉRIEUR BRUT AUX PRIX CONSTANTS D'ACQUISITION** *TAUX DE CROISSANCE ANNUEL (%)*
Government final consumption	7.0	5.5	4.4	5.8	3.7	6.1	5.2	5.1	...	Consommation finale des administrations publiques
Private final consumption	4.5	5.5	4.8	3.6	4.3	4.1	4.0	4.1	...	Consommation finale privée
Gross fixed capital formation	9.5	6.3	5.3	3.5	4.3	- 12.7	4.9	1.1	...	Formation brute de capital fixe
Exports of goods and services	4.3	11.8	2.8	- 7.0	10.6	- 5.0	4.3	1.8	...	Exportations de biens et services
Less imports of goods and services	7.6	9.6	5.4	- 8.2	15.3	- 3.5	5.4	- 1.8	...	Moins importations de biens et services
Notes	NA: 2012 Semi-Final-2013 provisional. The annual Growth Rates for 2014 are estimates based on the sum of four quarters of 2014.					2012 Semi-Définitive-2013:provisoire. Les croissances annuelles de L'année 2014 sont estimées à partir des comptes trimestriels				Notes

III INFLATION

	2006	2007	2008	2009	2010	2011	2012	2013	2014	
ANNUAL GROWTH RATES (%)										**TAUX DE CROISSANCE ANNUEL (%)**
All items	4.1	3.4	4.9	3.5	4.2	3.5	5.1	5.8	4.9	Ensemble
of which:										dont:
Food and Non-alcoholic beverages	5.0	3.0	6.1	4.4	6.8	5.1	7.5	8.0	5.4	Alimentation et boissons non alcoolisés
Alcoholic beverages & tobacco	...	2.4	1.2	9.1	5.2	2.8	9.5	5.0	5.4	Boissons alcoolisées et tabacs
Clothing and Footwear	3.0	3.2	2.1	2.3	3.6	4.0	7.5	7.2	7.5	Habillement et chaussures
Housing, Water, Electricity, Gas and Other Fuels	5.6	4.0	6.1	2.8	3.0	3.2	3.0	4.0	5.3	Logement, eau, électricité, gas et autres combustibles
Furnishing, household equip	9.4	3.0	3.7	3.7	2.1	3.1	6.0	6.3	5.4	Meubles, articles de ménage et entretien courant
Health	3.4	1.5	4.1	2.7	1.4	1.9	2.1	2.1	2.7	Santé
Transport	6.4	6.8	6.6	3.0	3.4	2.9	2.6	6.3	3.6	Transport
Communication	-2.8	-2.2	-0.9	0.5	-0.4	1.5	0.4	1.0	-0.3	Communication
Recreation & culture	1.3	0.6	-2.3	0.5	1.1	-0.3	1.9	3.2	3.5	Loisirs et culture
Education	2.4	3.0	3.2	1.4	10.8	3.0	4.9	3.1	2.7	Enseignement
Restaurants & hotels	2.7	5.1	4.8	6.0	4.5	4.8	7.8	7.3	6.7	Restaurants et hôtels
Miscellaneous goods & services	3.1	5.0	5.7	3.6	3.1	2.9	5.1	5.2	5.9	Biens et services divers

IV AGRICULTURAL PRODUCTION - PRODUCTION AGRICOLE	2006	2007	2008	2009	2010	2011	2012	2013	2014	
TONNES *(THOUSAND)*										**TONNES** *(MILLIERS)*
Tomatoes	855	1 000	1 200	1 135	1 296	1 284	1 100	1 200	...	Tomates
Olives	1 218	998	1 183	800	873	562	963	1 100	...	Huile d'olive
Wheat	1 251	1 443	919	1 654	822	1 606	1 523	975	...	Blé
Potatoes	365	350	370	324	370	367	340	385	...	Pommes de terre
Chillies and peppers, green	256	278	291	281	304	268	373	275	...	Piments et Poivrons, verts

V MINING PRODUCTION - PRODUCTION MINIERE	2006	2007	2008	2009	2010	2011	2012	2013	2014	
Phosphates, Tons (thousands)	7 801	8 002	7 692	7 409	8 149	...	...	...	...	Phosphates de chaux, tonnes (milliers)
Iron ore, Tons (thousands)	214	180	207	151	181	171	279	...	...	Minerai de fer, tonnes (milliers)
	...	...	...	...	...	...	...	...	...	

VI ENERGY - ENERGIE	2006	2007	2008	2009	2010	2011	2012	2013	2014	
Total electricity generation (GWh)	13 420	13 968	14 585	15 251	16 521	17 909	18 056	18 369	...	Production d'électricité totale (GWh)
of which:										dont:
Production of electricity from fossil fuels (GWh)	13 291	13 876	14 508	15 075	15 907	16 332	17 746	17 944	...	Production d'électricité à partir de combustibles fossiles (GWh)
Production of hydro electricity (GWh)	92	49	38	79	50	54	196	60	...	Production d'électricité d'origine hydraulique (GWh)
Production of electricity from solar, wind, tide, wave and other sources (GWh)	38	43	39	97	139	109	113	365	...	Production d'électricité d'origine solaire, éolienne, marée motrice et autres (GWh)

VII TOURISM AND INFRASTRUCTURE - TOURISME ET INFRASTRUCTURE	2006	2007	2008	2009	2010	2011	2012	2013	2014	
VII-1 TOURISM										**VII-1 TOURISME**
International tourist arrivals (thousands)	6 550	6 762	7 049	6 901	6 903	4 785	5 950	6 269	6 069	Arrivées de touristes internationaux (milliers)
Rooms in hotels and similar establishments (thousands)	825	834	836	856	856	861	846	...	...	Chambres d'hotels et établissements assimilés (milliers)
Overnight stays (thousands)	44 095	44 825	44 981	40 860	40 495	21 684	32 663	32 463	32 049	Nuitées (milliers)
Tourism receipts (US$ thousand)	2256 000	2555 000	2931 000	2751 000	2624 000	1894 300	2203 800	2166 600	2290 580	Recettes touristiques (milliers de $ EU)
Total contribution to GDP (%)	19.9	19.5	19.0	18.3	17.6	14.6	15.7	14.9	15.1	Contribution totale au PIB (%)
Total contribution to Employment (%)	18.0	17.6	17.1	16.6	16.0	13.5	14.2	13.5	13.8	Contribution totale à l'emploi (%)
VII-2 INFRASTRUCTURE										**VII-2 INFRASTRUCTURE**
Paved roads (% of total)	74	...	75	75	76	76	...	...	...	Routes asphaltées (% du total)
Total Network (Railways-km)	2 165	2 165	2 165	2 165	2 165	...	...	...	...	Réseau total voies ferrées-Km
Main Telephone Lines (per 100 inhabitants)	12	12	12	12	12	11	10	9	...	Lignes téléphoniques fixes (pour 100 habitants)
Mobile Cellular Subscribers (per 100 inhabitants)	72	76	83	93	105	115	118	116	...	Abonnés aux téléphones mobiles (pour 100 habitants)

VIII EXTERNAL TRADE - COMMERCE EXTERIEUR	2006	2007	2008	2009	2010	2011	2012	2013	2014	
TUNISIAN DINAR (MILLIONS) EXPORTS, FOB										**DINAR TUNISIEN (MILLIONS) EXPORTATIONS, FÀB**
Exports - Total	15 558	19 410	23 637	19 469	23 519	25 092	26 548	27 701	28 407	Exportations - Total
Exports to AFRICA	1 518	1 893	2 428	2 554	2 759	2 844	3 163	3 315	...	Exportations vers l'AFRIQUE
Main Products										**Principaux produits**
Hosiery and Confection	3 972	4 523	3 852	3 426	3 679	...	...	4 499	...	Bonneterie et Confection
Crude oil	1 564	2 632	3 219	2 093	2 979	...	...	2 839	...	Pétrole brut
Threads and cables Electric	773	1 003	1 254	1 354	1 850	...	...	34 100	...	Fils et Câbles électriques
D.A.P (Diammonium phosphate)	389	509	1 074	502	768	...	...	491	...	D.A.P (Diammoniaque phosphaté)
Phosphoric acid	317	344	887	418	519	...	...	349	...	Acide phosphorique
Main Destinations										**Principales destinations**
France	5 021	6 239	6 735	5 771	6 750	7 695	7 154	7 306	...	France
Italy	3 437	4 519	4 884	4 095	4 675	5 432	5 013	5 117	...	Italie
Germany	1 220	1 597	1 637	1 712	1 987	2 271	2 183	2 490	...	Allemagne
Libya	826	893	1 065	1 121	1 049	1 103	...	1 411	...	Libye
United Kingdom	452	836	1 099	926	1 181	702	826	1 046	...	Royaume-Uni
IMPORTS, CIF										**IMPORTATIONS, CAF**
Imports - Total	20 004	24 437	30 241	25 878	31 817	33 695	38 228	39 509	...	Importations - Total (millions)
Imports from Africa	1 545	1 712	2 755	1 852	1 817	1 419	2 777	...	...	Importations en provenance de l'Afrique
Main Products										**Principaux produits**
Refined Products	1 932	1 936	3 084	1 691	3 033	...	...	3 550	42 043	Produits raffinés
Fabrics	1 735	2 120	2 121	1 901	2 069	...	...	2 128	...	Tissus
Iron & Steel	746	1 048	1 407	749	1 084	...	...	101	...	Fer & acier
Material structure and plastic	926	1 132	1 264	1 197	1 488	...	...	2 094	...	Matière et ouvrage en plastique
Crude petroleum	710	746	1 149	676	233	...	...	1 555	...	Pétrole brut
Main Origin										**Principales provenances**
France	4 526	5 227	5 586	5 334	6 019	6 165	6 281	7 215	...	France
Italy	3 858	4 764	5 213	4 184	5 596	5 332	5 415	5 722	...	Italie
Germany	1 574	0	2 109	2 251	2 430	2 488	2 631	2 827	...	Allemagne
Russia	756	1 042	2 280	962	1 481	1 937	1 671	1 064	...	Russie
Libya	966	827	1 319	754	406	32	493	665	...	Libye

IX FINANCIAL AND MONETARY STATISTICS - FINANCES ET STATISTIQUES MONETAIRES	2006	2007	2008	2009	2010	2011	2012	2013	2014	
IX-1 MONETARY STATISTICS *TUNISIAN DINAR (MILLIONS)*										**IX-1 STATISTIQUES MONÉTAIRES** *DINAR TUNISIEN (MILLIONS)*
Money supply (M1)	26 550	29 850	34 150	38 590	43 270	47 200	51 170	54 550	60 110	Masse monétaire (M1)
Quasi-money	14 674	16 539	19 278	21 427	23 961	24 524	26 838	29 124	31 322	Quasi-monnaie
of which Demand Deposit	...	...	...	...	...	...	...	...	...	dont Monnaie scripturale
Net foreign assets	6 837	6 698	8 216	9 785	9 230	6 131	7 648	4 458	2 510	Avoirs extérieurs nets
Domestic credit	28 028	30 777	34 825	38 413	44 615	51 261	55 985	60 839	66 704	Crédit intérieur
of which claims on private sector	25 070	27 525	31 669	34 805	41 459	46 958	50 976	54 957	59 969	dont créances sur le secteur privé
of which claims on government sector, net	2 958	3 253	3 156	3 608	3 157	4 304	5 009	5 882	6 735	dont créances nettes sur le gouvernement
International reserves (millions US$)	6 785	7 863	8 861	11 069	9 471	7 465	8 369	7 299	7 246	Réserves internationales (millions $EU)
Average Exchange Rate (National Currency per US$)	1.33	1.28	1.23	1.35	1.43	1.41	1.56	1.62	1.68	Taux de change (moyen) (monnaie nationale par $ EU)
IX-2 PUBLIC FINANCE *TUNISIAN DINAR (MILLIONS)*										**IX-2 FINANCES PUBLIQUES** *DINAR TUNISIEN (MILLIONS)*
Total Revenues and Grants	9 752	10 904	13 356	13 762	14 823	16 753	18 488	19 960	20 784	Recettes totales et dons
Tax Revenue	8 470	9 508	11 331	11 685	12 699	13 630	14 865	16 334	16 847	Recettes fiscales
Non Tax Revenue	1 238	1 358	1 834	1 899	2 071	2 916	2 991	3 405	3 526	Recettes non fiscales
Grants	44	38	192	178	54	207	633	221	411	Dons
Total Expenditures and Net Lending	11 104	12 248	13 934	15 355	15 420	18 333	20 410	23 427	24 452	Dépenses totales et prêts nets
Current expenditure	8 242	8 986	10 407	10 545	11 153	13 693	15 904	18 857	19 685	Dépenses courantes
Of which Wages and Salaries	4 932	5 328	5 761	6 299	6 785	7 679	8 656	9 608	9 740	Dont rémunérations et salaires
Capital expenditure	2 646	2 794	3 315	4 014	4 302	4 729	4 766	4 394	4 575	Dépenses d'équipement
Net Lending	216	468	213	796	- 36	- 89	- 260	176	192	Prêts nets
Fiscal Balance	- 1 352	- 1 345	- 578	- 1 593	- 596	- 1 580	- 1 921	- 3 467	- 3 668	Solde global y compris les dons
IX-3 BALANCE OF PAYMENTS *TUNISIAN DINAR (MILLIONS)*										**IX-3 BALANCE DES PAIEMENTS** *DINAR TUNISIEN (MILLIONS)*
Trade balance	- 3 345	- 3 685	- 4 941	- 4 995	- 6 548	- 6 756	- 9 535	- 9 635	- 6 506	Balance commerciale
Services Balance	2 450	2 699	3 257	3 409	3 521	2 102	3 053	2 634	3 647	Balance des services
Net Income	- 123	- 420	- 675	- 109	- 30	- 160	282	125	162	Revenus nets
Compensation of employees	1 988	2 179	2 417	2 635	2 934	2 795	...	...	...	Rémunération des salariés
Investment Income	9	8	9	6	10	9	...	...	...	Revenus des investissements
Current transfers, net total	194	231	250	28	44	48	387	574	612	Transferts courants
Net official transfers	...	...	...	...	...	...	...	...	...	Transferts officiels nets
Workers' remittances	...	...	...	...	...	...	...	...	...	Envois de fonds des travailleurs
Other private transfers	...	...	...	...	...	...	...	...	...	Autres transferts privés
Current account balance	- 824	- 1 175	- 2 109	- 1 666	- 3 012	- 4 766	- 5 812	- 6 302	- 2 085	Solde du compte courant
Capital & financial account	3 648	2 105	4 022	3 781	2 632	2 280	7 830	5 002	...	Comptes de capital et financier
Capital account	193	212	97	222	118	259	701	187	...	Compte de capital
Financial account	3 455	1 993	3 925	1 940	2 515	2 021	7 128	4 815	...	Compte financier
Errors & omissions	- 51	- 47	140	89	180	139	151	205	...	Erreurs et omissions
Overall balance	2 773	883	2 053	2 204	- 199	- 2 347	2 168	- 1 095	...	Balance générale

X DEBT AND FINANCIAL FLOWS - DETTE ET FLUX FINANCIERS										
	2006	2007	2008	2009	2010	2011	2012	2013	2014	
X-1 DEBT *US$ (MILLIONS)*										**X-1 DETTE EXTÉRIEURE** *$ E.U (MILLIONS)*
Total external debt	18 532	20 145	20 589	21 518	21 371	22 053	24 326	25 388	27 407	Dette extérieure totale
Private	7 946	8 816	9 446	9 281	9 342	9 626	11 026	11 511	12 488	Privée
Public	10 586	11 329	11 142	12 237	12 029	12 427	13 300	13 878	14 920	Publique
Total external debt service	2 916	2 629	2 147	2 334	2 289	12 597	12 837	14 416	14 663	Service de la dette extérieure
Present value of External debt	...	...	...	...	...	...	...	...	...	Valeur actuelle de la dette extérieure
Total government domestic debt (in local currency)	...	...	...	...	...	...	...	...	...	Dette publique intérieure
X-2 FINANCIAL FLOWS *US$ (MILLIONS)*										**X-2 FLUX FINANCIERS** *$ E.U (MILLIONS)*
Net Foreign Direct Investment Inflows	3 308	1 616	2 759	1 688	1 513	1 148	1 603	1 096	...	Investissements étranger direct (flux nets entrants)
Main origin of FDI Inflows										**Principales origines de l'IDE entrant:**
France	89	116	708	158	72.8	12.5	38.6	...	...	France
Italy	34	34	115	427	- 407.2	162.4	256.1	...	...	Italie
Germany	-	-	-	-	0.1	0.1	0.0	...	...	Allemagne
Sweden	28	38	199	21	-	19.1	- 260.5	...	...	Suède
Turkey	-	48	163	1	-	2.0	3.0	...	...	Turquie
African countries	...	...	...	...	...	...	...	...	...	Pays africains
Net total Official Development Assistance	431	321	375	503	550	921	1 017	714	...	Aide publique au développement (nette totale)
Main origin of Net ODA										**Principales origines de l'APD nette**
France	176	128	160	170	126.8	304.4	242.5	69.3	...	France
Japan	19	21	54	14	35.9	25.0	- 53.3	- 36.4	...	Japon
Spain	16	21	16	124	158.0	82.9	0.5	25.2	...	Espagne
Germany	40	27	27	31	23.9	33.7	8.3	18.5	...	Allemagne
GEF	1	-	3	14	7.0	3.3	1.6	...	...	FEM
General notes	National Accounts : The annual Growth Rates for 2014 are estimates based on the sum of four quarters of 2014.					Comptes Nationaux: Les croissances annuelles de L'année 2014 sont estimées à partir des comptes trimestriels				Notes générales

TUNISIA

AREA (KM²)	241 551		SUPERFICIE (KM²)
CAPITAL CITY	Kampala	Kampala	CAPITALE
CURRENCY	Uganda Shilling	Shilling Ugandais	MONNAIE

I SOCIAL AND DEMOGRAPHIC INDICATORS – INDICATEURS DEMOGRAPHIQUES ET SOCIAUX

	Year / Année	Value / Valeur	
POPULATION			**POPULATION**
Population ('000)			Population ('000)
Both sexes	2014	36 616	Les deux sexes
Male	2014	18 043	Masculin
Female	2014	18 573	Féminin
Average annual growth rate	2014	3.4	Taux de croissance annuel
Active Population ('000)	2014	14 674	Population active ('000)
Population by age group ('000)			Population par groupe d'âge ('000)
0-14 years	2014	18 711	0-14 ans
15-64 years	2014	17 466	15-64 ans
65+ years	2014	439	65+ ans
Economically active population in agriculture (%)	2014	83.4	Participation de la population active agricole (%)
Crude birth rate	2014	47.7	Taux brut de natalité
Crude death rate	2014	13.5	Taux brut de mortalité
Total fertility rate	2014	5.8	Indice synthétique de fécondité
Proportion of urban population	2014	17.5	Part de la population urbaine
Life Expectancy at Birth - Total (years)	2014	59.7	Espérance de vie à la naissance - Totale (ans)
Dependency Ratio - Total (%)	2014	109.6	Taux de dépendance - Total (%)
HEALTH			**SANTÉ**
Percentage of children under-five and underweight	2011	14.1	% d'enfants de moins de cinq ans avec insuffisance pondérale
Prevalence of undernourishment	2013	25.7	Prévalence de la malnutrition
Under five mortality rate (both sexes, per 1000)	2013	66.1	Taux de mortalité de moins de 5 ans (les deux sexes, pour 1000)
Infant mortality rate (both sexes) per 1000	2013	43.8	Taux de mortalité infantile (les deux sexes) par 1000
Percentage of children provided the vaccines :			Pourcentage d'enfants vaccinés :
BCG	2013	85.0	BCG
DPT3	2013	80.0	DTC3
Polio	2013	77.0	Polio
Measles	2013	80.0	Rougeole
Percentage of mothers provided at least one antenatal care (%)	2012	94.9	Pourcentage de mères ayant au moins reçu un soin prénatal (%)
Percentage of deliveries attended by skilled health personnel	2011	57.4	% d'accouchements assistés par un personnel de santé qualifié
Number of doctors (per 10 000 population)	2005	1.2	Nombre de médecins (pour 10 000 habitants)
Number of nurses (per 10 000 population)	2005	13.1	Nombre d'infirmières (pour 10 000 habitants)
Hospital beds - Total (per 10 000 population)	2011	5.0	Nombre de lits d'hôpitaux - Total (pour 10 000)
Births registered (per 1 000)	2014	42.6	Naiss.s enregistrées (pour 1 000)
Deaths registered (per 1 000)	2014	9.0	Décès enregistrés (pour 1 000)
Public expenditure on Health (% of budget)	2014	4.8	Dépenses publiques consacrées à la santé (% du budget)
EDUCATION			**EDUCATION**
Enrolment in primary education (both sexes) (000)	2013	8 459	Scolarisation dans le primaire (les deux sexes) (000)
Female	2013	4 240	Féminin
Enrolment in secondary education (both sexes) (000)	2013	1 421	Scolarisation dans le secondaire (les deux sexes) (000)
Female	2013	659	Féminin
Enrolment in tertiary education (both sexes) (000)	2012	138.0	Scolarisation dans le tertiaire (les deux sexes) (000)
Female	2011	61.3	Féminin
Literacy rate (both sexes)	2010	73.2	Taux d'alphabétisation (deux sexes)
Male	2010	82.6	Masculin
Female	2010	64.6	Féminin
Pupil-teacher ratio	...	...	Ratio élève-enseignant
Public expenditure on education (% of budget)	2014	6.8	Dépenses publiques consacrées à l'enseignement (% du budget)
POVERTY			**PAUVRETÉ**
GNI Per Capita (US$)	2013	440.0	RNB par habitant ($EU)
Human Poverty Index (HPI-1) Value (%)	2007	28.8	Valeur de l'Indice de pauvreté (IPH-1) (%)
Population below International Poverty Line ($2/day) (%)	2013	62.9	Population sous le seuil international de pauvreté (2$/J) (%)
Share of Income Held by Richest 10%	2013	35.8	% de revenu des 10% plus riches
Share of Income Held by Poorest 10%	2013	2.5	% de revenu des 10% plus pauvres
Gini index	2013	40.0	Indice de Gini

Charts / Graphiques

Population by age group – 2014
Population par groupe d'age – 2014

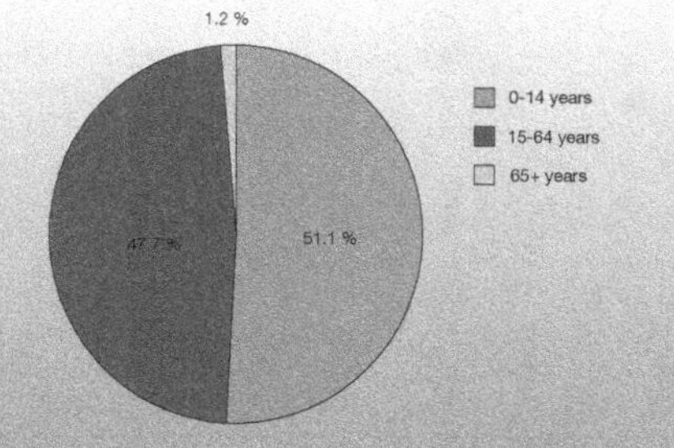

Percentage of children provided the vaccines – 2013
Pourcentage d'enfants vaccinés – 2013

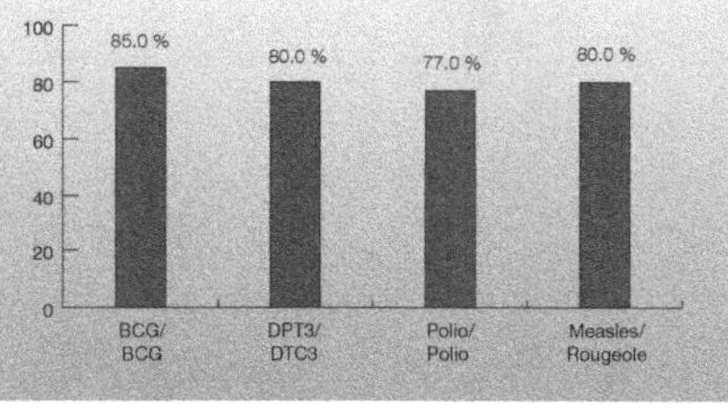

Literacy rate (%) – 2010
Taux d'alphabétisation – 2010

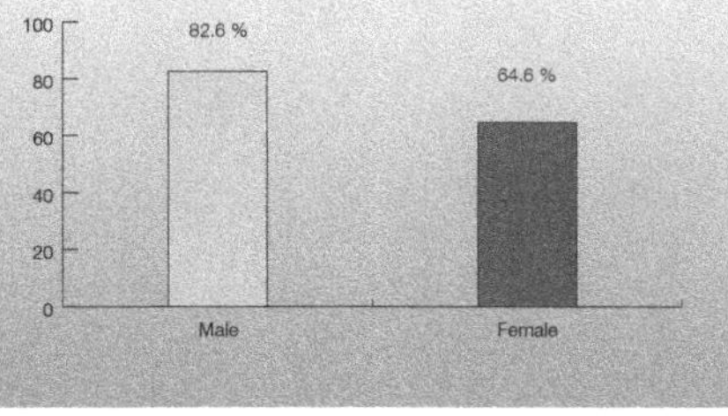

GNI Per Capita (US$)
RNB par habitant ($EU)

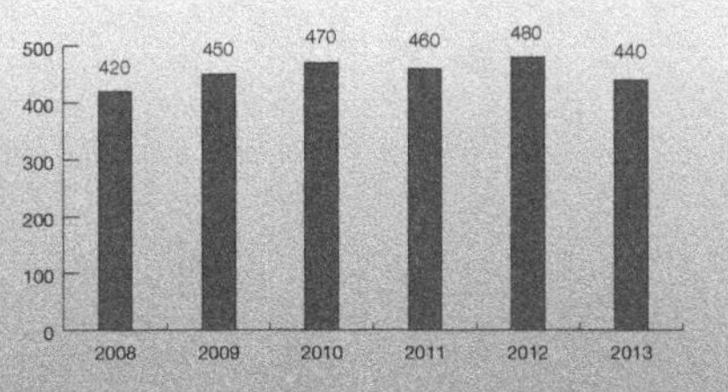

II NATIONAL ACCOUNTS — COMPTES NATIONAUX	2006	2007	2008	2009	2010	2011	2012	2013	2014	
GROSS DOMESTIC PRODUCT BY KIND OF ECONOMIC ACTIVITY AT CURRENT PRICES *UGANDA SHILLING (BILLIONS)*										**PRODUIT INTÉRIEUR BRUT PAR BRANCHE D'ACTIVITÉ ÉCONOMIQUE AUX PRIX COURANTS** *SHILLING UGANDAIS (MILLIARDS)*
Agriculture, hunting, forestry and fishing	4 553	4 827	7 568	10 523	10 399	14 488	15 908	16 481	...	Agriculture, chasse sylviculture et pêche
Mining and quarrying	55	67	380	485	402	448	597	546	...	Industries extractives
Manufacturing	1 394	1 616	3 092	3 249	4 051	6 034	6 134	6 448	...	Industries manufacturières
Electricity, gas & water	783	1 062	901	1 062	1 151	1 226	1 579	1 614	...	Electricité, gaz et eau
Construction & public works	2 256	2 840	1 677	2 144	2 493	3 943	4 285	4 971	...	Bâtiments et travaux publics
Wholesale & retail trade, restaurants, hotels	3 556	4 240	4 484	5 780	6 772	9 704	10 396	11 048	...	Commerce de gros et de détail, restaurants et hôtels
Finance, insurance, real estate, etc.	2 259	2 687	3 630	4 445	5 334	6 053	6 831	7 169	...	Banques, assurances, affaires immobilières
Transport and communications	1 218	1 474	2 475	3 139	3 506	2 680	3 429	3 967	...	Transport(s) et communications
Public administration and defense	720	747	893	1 061	1 380	1 626	1 802	1 869	...	Administrations publiques et défense
Education	1 419	1 474	1 695	1 904	2 204	2 514	3 163	3 672	...	Education
Health and Social Work	311	307	1 124	1 180	1 289	1 391	1 702	2 044	...	Santé et actions sociales
Other services	416	506	547	669	754	895	1 093	1 233	...	Autres services
Less Imputed Service Charges	- 330	- 408	...	...	...	...	...	...	...	Moins services d'intermédiation financière
Gross domestic product at factor cost / basic prices	18 611	21 440	28 466	35 641	39 735	51 002	56 919	61 062	...	Produit intérieur brut aux couts des facteurs / prix de base
Plus: indirect taxes / taxes on products, less subsidies	1 555	1 911	2 356	2 779	3 134	3 702	4 224	4 936	...	Plus taxes indirectes/impôts sur les produits, moins les subventions
EXPENDITURE ON GROSS DOMESTIC PRODUCT AT CURRENT PURCHASER'S VALUES *UGANDA SHILLING (BILLIONS)*										**EMPLOI DU PRODUIT INTÉRIEUR BRUT AUX PRIX COURANTS D'ACQUISITION** *SHILLING UGANDAIS (MILLIARDS)*
Government final consumption	2 692	2 609	3 013	3 325	4 968	5 717	4 973	5 422	...	Consommation finale des administrations publiques
Private final consumption	16 142	17 970	21 755	28 014	32 168	41 353	45 044	47 821	...	Consommation finale privée
Gross fixed capital formation	4 126	5 304	8 571	10 276	11 337	15 515	17 956	18 837	...	Formation brute de capital fixe
Change in inventories	53	62	107	133	129	187	228	301	...	Variation des stocks
Exports of goods and services	3 003	4 405	5 763	7 228	7 572	10 733	12 272	13 380	...	Exportations de biens et services
Less imports of goods and services	5 851	7 000	8 382	10 558	13 304	18 800	19 331	19 764	...	Moins importations de biens et services
GDP at purchasers' values	20 166	23 351	30 826	38 419	42 870	54 705	61 142	65 997	...	PIB aux prix d'acquisition
GROSS DOMESTIC PRODUCT BY KIND OF ECONOMIC ACTIVITY AT CONSTANT PRICES *ANNUAL GROWTH RATES (%)*										**PRODUIT INTÉRIEUR BRUT PAR BRANCHE D'ACTIVITÉ ECONOMIQUE AUX PRIX CONSTANTS** *TAUX DE CROISSANCE ANNUEL (%)*
Agriculture, hunting, forestry and fishing	- 1.8	1.7	2.3	6.5	2.6	2.0	- 0.2	3.3	...	Agriculture, chasse sylviculture et pêche
Mining and quarrying	18.2	5.0	10.4	- 0.7	19.4	12.6	6.7	2.4	...	Industries extractives
Manufacturing	3.5	7.6	7.2	4.8	5.8	6.1	- 1.2	0.6	...	Industries manufacturières
Electricity, gas & water	- 3.7	5.3	4.0	10.1	7.8	5.3	10.1	4.1	...	Electricité, gaz et eau
Construction & public works	10.0	8.8	21.6	11.7	5.3	19.0	- 0.7	9.6	...	Bâtiments et travaux publics
Wholesale & retail trade, restaurants, hotels	9.5	12.0	13.3	8.1	5.6	6.6	0.1	2.0	...	Commerce de gros et de détail,restaurants et hôtels
Finance, insurance, real estate, etc.	8.7	4.2	8.4	7.3	11.8	7.7	- 0.6	1.8	...	Banques, assurances, affaires immobilières
Transport and communications	21.7	12.6	22.7	21.9	24.8	5.9	18.6	17.4	...	Transport(s) et communications
Public administration and defense	3.0	3.7	8.7	10.8	23.7	11.0	- 4.3	- 3.5	...	Administrations publiques et défense
Education	10.0	1.5	9.7	0.9	4.1	8.6	4.7	5.2	...	Education
Health and Social Work	7.7	- 1.3	10.7	3.9	5.6	5.6	3.4	5.1	...	Santé et actions sociales
Other services	13.8	13.1	11.7	3.7	4.8	6.7	3.5	5.4	...	Autres services
Less Imputed Service Charges	33.8	- 17.5	...	...	...	...	...	...	...	Moins services d'intérmediation financière
Gross domestic product at factor cost / basic prices	6.4	6.9	10.2	7.8	7.9	6.4	2.2	4.6	...	Produit intérieur brut aux couts des facteurs / prix de base
Plus: indirect taxes / taxes on products, less subsidies	13.4	19.1	12.6	11.0	5.2	12.1	8.0	4.9	...	Plus taxes indirectes/impôts sur les produits, moins les subventions
Gross domestic product at market prices	7.0	8.1	10.4	8.1	7.7	6.8	2.6	4.7	...	Produit intérieur brut aux prix du marché
EXPENDITURE ON GROSS DOMESTIC PRODUCT AT CONSTANT PURCHASERS' VALUES *ANNUAL GROWTH RATES (%)*										**EMPLOIS DU PRODUIT INTÉRIEUR BRUT AUX PRIX CONSTANTS D'ACQUISITION** *TAUX DE CROISSANCE ANNUEL (%)*
Government final consumption	3.7	- 1.5	1.7	1.5	42.0	5.9	- 24.9	1.1	...	Consommation finale des administrations publiques
Private final consumption	12.3	2.9	7.8	14.7	9.1	7.2	2.1	3.0	...	Consommation finale privée
Gross fixed capital formation	11.0	15.1	5.9	10.7	4.9	14.2	3.7	3.0	...	Formation brute de capital fixe
Exports of goods and services	- 6.3	53.8	46.5	- 12.2	- 0.2	2.3	14.0	10.1	...	Exportations de biens et services
Less imports of goods and services	17.2	15.7	17.6	8.0	13.9	11.4	- 1.6	1.7	...	Moins importations de biens et services
Notes	The Annual accounts are based on new prices of 2009/2010 from 2008					Les comptes annuels sont élaborés selon la nouvelle base des prix 2009/2010 à partir de 2008				Notes

III INFLATION	2006	2007	2008	2009	2010	2011	2012	2013	2014	
ANNUAL GROWTH RATES (%)										**TAUX DE CROISSANCE ANNUEL (%)**
All items	7.2	6.1	12.1	13.0	4.0	18.7	14.0	5.5	4.3	Ensemble
of which:										dont:
Food and Non-alcoholic beverages	5.7	2.5	19.8	25.1	2.1	32.3	8.6	3.5	4.6	Alimentation et boissons non alcoolisés
Alcoholic beverages & tobacco	2.0	2.7	10.1	10.7	5.1	16.3	16.5	12.7	0.5	Boissons alcoolisées et tabacs
Clothing and Footwear	4.8	4.5	8.6	8.0	2.9	27.0	16.2	4.5	4.7	Habillement et chaussures
Housing, Water, Electricity, Gas and Other Fuels	8.7	16.6	9.9	6.7	5.2	16.4	20.2	4.9	2.9	Logement, eau, électricité, gas et autres combustibles
Furnishing, household equip	4.9	6.1	15.8	9.6	6.6	23.2	15.7	4.2	2.1	Meubles, articles de ménage et entretien courant
Health	3.5	4.6	7.9	13.0	9.7	15.8	15.8	8.8	6.2	Santé
Transport	9.9	6.4	9.9	2.4	-1.4	-4.6	13.7	4.5	4.2	Transport
Communication	...	...	...	...	...	...	...	...	...	Communication
Recreation & culture	...	...	...	...	...	...	...	...	...	Loisirs et culture
Education	4.8	4.8	6.7	7.8	6.6	8.1	15.4	6.8	4.9	Enseignement
Restaurants & hotels	...	...	...	...	...	...	...	...	...	Restaurants et hôtels
Miscellaneous goods & services	...	...	...	...	...	...	...	...	...	Biens et services divers

IV AGRICULTURAL PRODUCTION - PRODUCTION AGRICOLE										
	2006	2007	2008	2009	2010	2011	2012	2013	2014	
TONNES *(THOUSAND)*										**TONNES** *(MILLIERS)*
Plantains	9 054	9 231	9 371	9 512	9 550	9 600	9 200	8 926	...	Banane-Plantain
Cassava	4 926	4 973	5 072	5 179	5 282	4 758	4 925	5 228	...	Manioc
Maize	1 258	1 262	2 315	2 355	2 374	2 551	2 734	2 748	...	Maïs
Sweet potatoes	2 628	2 654	2 707	2 766	2 838	2 554	2 646	2 587	...	Patates douces
Bananas	563	574	583	592	600	580	570	578	...	Bananes

V MINING PRODUCTION - PRODUCTION MINIERE										
	2006	2007	2008	2009	2010	2011	2012	2013	2014	
Gold ores and concentrates (Kilograms)	...	25	20	...	...	...	...	...	...	Minerais d'or et concentrés (Kilogrammes)
Salt and pure sodium chloride, metric tons (thousands)	...	15	15	15	15	15	...	...	...	Sel et chlorure de sodium pur, tonnes métriques (milliers)
	...	...	...	...	...	...	...	...	...	

VI ENERGY - ENERGIE										
	2006	2007	2008	2009	2010	2011	2012	2013	2014	
Total electricity generation (GWh)	1 594	1 986	2 267	2 189	2 406	2 222	2 224	3 203	...	Production d'électricité totale (GWh)
of which:										dont:
Production of electricity from fossil fuels (GWh)	353	508	556	703	821	547	547	613	...	Production d'électricité à partir de combustibles fossiles (GWh)
Production of hydro electricity (GWh)	1 161	1 398	1 631	1 396	1 485	1 514	1 514	2 393	...	Production d'électricité d'origine hydraulique (GWh)
Production of electricity from solar, wind, tide, wave and other sources (GWh)	...	...	...	...	...	18	19	21	...	Production d'électricité d'origine solaire, éolienne, marée motrice et autres (GWh)

VII TOURISM AND INFRASTRUCTURE - TOURISME ET INFRASTRUCTURE										
	2006	2007	2008	2009	2010	2011	2012	2013	2014	
VII-1 TOURISM										**VII-1 TOURISME**
International tourist arrivals (thousands)	539	642	844	807	946	1 151	1 197	1 206	1 306	Arrivées de touristes internationaux (milliers)
Rooms in hotels and similar establishments (thousands)	...	...	...	...	...	...	...	...	...	Chambres d'hotels et établissements assimilés (milliers)
Overnight stays (thousands)	2 084	2 440	3 261	3 218	3 523	4 730	4 382	4 499	4 881	Nuitées (milliers)
Tourism receipts (US$ thousand)	318 200	372 800	470 400	636 700	747 100	926 300	1106 400	1153 400	1391 750	Recettes touristiques (milliers de $ EU)
Total contribution to GDP (%)	8.1	7.8	7.8	8.3	8.6	9.4	9.5	9.4	10.0	Contribution totale au PIB (%)
Total contribution to Employment (%)	7.1	6.9	6.8	7.4	7.7	7.8	7.3	8.2	8.7	Contribution totale à l'emploi (%)
VII-2 INFRASTRUCTURE										**VII-2 INFRASTRUCTURE**
Paved roads (% of total)	...	...	...	...	...	...	...	...	...	Routes asphaltées (% du total)
Total Network (Railways-km)	...	...	...	...	...	...	...	...	...	Réseau total voies ferrées-Km
Main Telephone Lines (per 100 inhabitants)	0	1	1	1	1	1	1	1	...	Lignes téléphoniques fixes (pour 100 habitants)
Mobile Cellular Subscribers (per 100 inhabitants)	7	14	27	29	38	48	45	44	...	Abonnés aux téléphones mobiles (pour 100 habitants)

VIII EXTERNAL TRADE - COMMERCE EXTERIEUR										
	2006	2007	2008	2009	2010	2011	2012	2013	2014	
US$ (MILLIONS) **EXPORTS, FOB**										**$ E.U (MILLIONS)** **EXPORTATIONS, FÀB**
Exports - Total	1 194	1 867	2 532	2 366	2 147	2 515	2 811	2 846	...	Exportations - Total
Exports to AFRICA	553	1 125	1 605	1 583	1 378	1 423	1 756	1 751	...	Exportations vers l'AFRIQUE
Main Products										**Principaux produits**
Coffee, not roasted, not decaffeinated	188	254	366	266	267	459	371	424	...	Café, non torréfié, non décaféiné
Fish fillets and other fish meat, minced or not, fresh or chilled	141	118	119	109	129	136	123	127	...	Filet de poisson ou de viande, hachée ou non, fraîches ou réfrigérées
Tobacco, unmanufactured, stemmed or stripped	27	66	66	57	62	46	58	115	...	Tabac, artisanal, filtre, ou emballe
Portland cement nes	6	19	78	83	71	94	107	103	...	Ciment Portland NDA
Cut flowers and flower buds for bouquets, etc., fresh	...	...	...	...	...	...	...	...	...	Cut flowers and flower buds for bouquets, etc., fresh
Main Destinations										**Principales destinations**
Belgium	40	53	64	42	42	64	47	59	...	Belgique
Netherlands	62	67	82	79	90	97	95	109	...	Pays-Bas
Rwanda	56	122	192	170	182	229	264	242	...	Rwanda
France	38	33	34	22	12	12	20	17	...	France
Germany	42	65	75	63	74	88	71	104	...	Allemagne
IMPORTS, CIF										**IMPORTATIONS, CAF**
Imports - Total	2 638	3 553	4 604	4 340	4 731	5 685	6 096	5 867	...	Importations - Total (millions)
Imports from Africa	720	860	1 050	958	993	1 148	1 161	1 016	...	Importations en provenance de l'Afrique
Main Products										**Principaux produits**
Medicaments nes, in dosage	83	117	175	154	154	186	203	291	...	Médicaments nda, en dosage
Portland cement nes	27	31	45	75	73	73	60	37	...	Ciment Portland NDA
Petroleum oils & oils obtained from bituminous minerals,o/than crude etc	518	634	822	711	897	1 255	1 309	1 281	...	Huiles de pétrole, bitumineux, distilles, sauf brut
Transmission apparatus,for radioteleph incorporatg reception apparatus	106	118	20	10	16	10	4	6	...	Appareils de transmission, pour les appareils de réception radioteleph incorporatg
Electrical apparatus for line telephony/ telegraphy nes	...	...	...	...	...	...	249	166	...	Appareils électriques pour la téléphonie ou la télégraphie NDA
Main Origin										**Principales provenances**
Kenya	465	523	552	546	549	672	615	587	...	Kenya
China	138	274	366	379	415	522	684	622	...	Chine
India	209	341	470	521	684	928	1 266	1 560	...	Inde
South Africa	156	207	305	245	250	264	298	251	...	Afrique du Sud
Japan	174	230	269	270	306	323	324	332	...	Japon

IX FINANCIAL AND MONETARY STATISTICS - FINANCES ET STATISTIQUES MONETAIRES	2006	2007	2008	2009	2010	2011	2012	2013	2014	
IX-1 MONETARY STATISTICS *UGANDA SHILLING (MILLIONS)*										**IX-1 STATISTIQUES MONÉTAIRES** *SHILLING UGANDAIS (MILLIONS)*
Money supply (M1)	3 626 250	4 422 790	5 785 730	6 745 060	9 544 420	10 550 480	12 123 130	13 270 540	14 767 340	Masse monétaire (M1)
Quasi-money	1 108 677	1 337 260	2 005 602	2 396 744	3 456 282	4 203 461	4 775 472	5 305 310	6 130 563	Quasi-monnaie
of which Demand Deposit	...	...	...	...	...	...	...	...	...	dont Monnaie scripturale
Net foreign assets	3 784 993	4 942 419	5 014 409	5 216 106	6 171 302	6 312 456	8 454 662	8 510 372	8 620 158	Avoirs extérieurs nets
Domestic credit	1 367 657	1 163 670	2 969 545	3 551 577	5 968 455	7 588 848	8 170 322	9 057 951	11 508 854	Crédit intérieur
of which claims on private sector	1 840 745	2 167 709	3 405 404	3 995 283	5 464 063	7 269 283	8 127 792	8 628 587	9 843 695	dont créances sur le secteur privé
of which claims on government sector, net	- 562 138	-1 109 940	- 553 311	- 567 572	436 860	239 382	- 28 987	346 004	1 584 225	dont créances nettes sur le gouvernement
International reserves (millions US$)	1 811	2 560	2 301	2 994	2 706	2 617	3 167	3 338	3 240	Réserves internationales (millions $EU)
Average Exchange Rate (National Currency per US$)	1 831.45	1 723.49	1 720.44	2 030.49	2 177.56	2 522.75	2 504.56	2 586.89	2 557.10	Taux de change (moyen) (monnaie nationale par $ EU)
IX-2 PUBLIC FINANCE *UGANDA SHILLING (MILLIONS)*										**IX-2 FINANCES PUBLIQUES** *SHILLING UGANDAIS (MILLIONS)*
Total Revenues and Grants	3 211 524	3 810 018	3 985 399	4 671 414	5 183 121	7 292 199	7 762 626	8 698 282	9 625 000	Recettes totales et dons
Tax Revenue	2 210 382	2 625 561	3 161 172	3 662 335	4 206 190	6 306 773	6 528 178	7 323 370	8 123 000	Recettes fiscales
Non Tax Revenue	103 627	96 666	85 727	124 279	113 910	95 062	105 195	132 127	403 000	Recettes non fiscales
Grants	897 515	1 087 791	738 500	884 800	863 021	890 364	1 129 253	1 242 785	1 099 000	Dons
Total Expenditures and Net Lending	3 549 000	4 207 800	4 439 200	5 175 100	6 831 100	8 972 500	9 273 436	10 100 307	12 663 000	Dépenses totales et prêts nets
Current expenditure	2 322 300	2 590 600	3 165 400	3 574 700	4 389 400	6 151 800	5 709 936	5 875 207	6 903 000	Dépenses courantes
Of which Wages and Salaries	866 500	986 500	1 106 100	1 183 600	1 308 400	1 659 500	1 831 800	2 160 500	2 653 000	Dont rémunérations et salaires
Capital expenditure	1 256 000	1 516 100	1 436 700	1 657 100	2 478 400	2 850 900	3 602 900	4 236 900	5 794 000	Dépenses d'équipement
Net Lending	- 29 300	101 100	- 162 900	- 56 700	- 36 700	- 30 200	- 39 400	- 11 800	- 34 000	Prêts nets
Fiscal Balance	- 337 476	- 397 782	- 453 801	- 503 686	-1 647 979	-1 680 301	-1 510 810	-1 402 025	-3 038 000	Solde global y compris les dons
IX-3 BALANCE OF PAYMENTS *US$ (MILLIONS)*										**IX-3 BALANCE DES PAIEMENTS** *$ E.U (MILLIONS)*
Trade balance	- 1 028	- 1 182	- 1 835	- 1 509	- 2 212	- 2 504	- 2 458	- 2 145	...	Balance commerciale
Services Balance	- 245	- 384	- 458	- 400	- 577	- 693	- 376	- 326	...	Balance des services
Net Income	- 239	- 243	- 261	- 374	- 297	- 407	- 404	- 713	...	Revenus nets
Compensation of employees	...	...	...	...	...	...	...	...	...	Rémunération des salariés
Investment income	102	119	157	78	3	3	-	...	...	Revenus des investissements
Current transfers, net total	1 173	1 176	1 287	1 192	1 362	1 475	1 612	1 266	...	Transferts courants
Net official transfers	...	...	...	...	...	...	...	...	...	Transferts officiels nets
Workers' remittances	...	...	...	...	...	...	...	...	...	Envois de fonds des travailleurs
Other private transfers	...	...	...	...	768	813	910	...	...	Autres transferts privés
Current account balance	- 338	- 633	- 1 268	- 1 090	- 1 724	- 2 129	- 1 627	- 1 920	...	Solde du compte courant
Capital & financial account	880	1 393	1 169	1 721	1 045	1 595	2 436	...	...	Comptes de capital et financier
Capital account	3 555	-	-	-	-	12	22	...	...	Compte de capital
Financial account	- 2 675	1 393	1 169	1 721	1 045	1 583	2 414	...	...	Compte financier
Errors & omissions	14	7	115	- 265	516	459	6	...	...	Erreurs et omissions
Overall balance	556	767	17	365	- 163	- 75	534	...	...	Balance générale

UGANDA

X DEBT AND FINANCIAL FLOWS - DETTE ET FLUX FINANCIERS	2006	2007	2008	2009	2010	2011	2012	2013	2014	
X-1 DEBT *US$ (MILLIONS)*										**X-1 DETTE EXTÉRIEURE** *$ E.U (MILLIONS)*
Total external debt	1 958	2 502	2 967	3 551	4 046	5 777	6 438	6 903	7 963	Dette extérieure totale
Private	905	875	1 064	1 372	1 524	2 782	2 917	2 860	3 052	Privée
Public	1 053	1 627	1 902	2 179	2 523	2 995	3 520	4 042	4 911	Publique
Total external debt service	389	375	374	382	373	451	624	738	799	Service de la dette extérieure
Present value of External debt	...	...	...	...	...	...	...	...	...	Valeur actuelle de la dette extérieure
Total government domestic debt (in local currency)	...	...	...	...	...	...	...	...	...	Dette publique intérieure
X-2 FINANCIAL FLOWS *US$ (MILLIONS)*										**X-2 FLUX FINANCIERS** *$ E.U (MILLIONS)*
Net Foreign Direct Investment Inflows	644	792	729	842	544	894	1 205	1 146	...	Investissements étranger direct (flux nets entrants)
Main origin of FDI Inflows										**Principales origines de l'IDE entrant:**
United Kingdom	13	44	75	39	61.8	81.7	-	...	...	Royaume-Uni
Belgium	1	-	104	111	- 58.3	- 39.0	- 6.4	...	...	Belgique
France	...	-	-	-	-	-	-	...	...	France
Netherlands	-	-	-	-	-	-	-	...	...	Pays-Bas
Japan	-	-	-	-	-	0.5	2.5	...	...	Japon
African countries	152	223	176	199	198.6	291.5	130.6	...	...	Pays africains
Net total Official Development Assistance	1 586	1 737	1 641	1 785	1 723	1 578	1 655	1 693	...	Aide publique au développement (nette totale)
Main origin of Net ODA										**Principales origines de l'APD nette**
IDA	270	374	180	395	325.7	171.2	186.9	...	...	IDA
United States	246	302	353	367	378.1	397.9	394.3	452.0	...	Etats-Unis
United Kingdom	214	166	66	117	179.3	143.0	149.2	...	...	Royaume-Uni
AfDF	136	124	106	111	101.0	139.0	146.3	...	...	FAfD
Denmark	79	110	83	93	77.0	68.2	62.9	55.2	...	Danemark

ZAMBIA — ZAMBIE

AREA (km²)	752 618		SUPERFICIE (km²)
CAPITAL CITY	Lusaka	Lusaka	CAPITALE
CURRENCY	Zambian Kwacha	Kwacha	MONNAIE

I SOCIAL AND DEMOGRAPHIC INDICATORS – INDICATEURS DEMOGRAPHIQUES ET SOCIAUX

	Year / Année	Value / Valeur	
POPULATION			**POPULATION**
Population ('000)			Population ('000)
Both sexes	2014	15 021	Les deux sexes
Male	2014	7 490	Masculin
Female	2014	7 531	Féminin
Average annual growth rate	2014	3.3	Taux de croissance annuel
Active Population ('000)	2014	5 861	Population active ('000)
Population by age group ('000)			Population par groupe d'âge ('000)
0-14 years	2014	6 982	0-14 ans
15-64 years	2014	7 648	15-64 ans
65+ years	2014	391	65+ ans
Economically. active population. in agriculture (%)	2014	61.1	Participation de la population active agricole (%)
Crude birth rate	2014	42.6	Taux brut de natalité
Crude death rate	2014	9.7	Taux brut de mortalité
Total fertility rate	2014	5.6	Indice synthétique de fécondité
Proportion of urban population	2014	40.5	Part de la population urbaine
Life Expectancy at Birth - Total (years)	2014	59.0	Espérance de vie à la naissance - Totale (ans)
Dependency Ratio - Total (%)	2014	100.1	Taux de dépendance - Total (%)
HEALTH			**SANTÉ**
Percentage of children under-five and underweight	2007	14.9	% d'enfants de moins de cinq ans avec insuffisance pondérale
Prevalence of undernourishment	2013	48.3	Prévalence de la malnutrition
Under five mortality rate (both sexes, per 1000)	2013	87.4	Taux de mortalité de moins de 5 ans (les deux sexes, pour 1000)
Infant mortality rate (both sexes) per 1000	2013	55.8	Taux de mortalité infantile (les deux sexes) par 1000
Percentage of children provided the vaccines :			Pourcentage d'enfants vaccinés :
BCG	2013	94.0	BCG
DPT3	2013	85.0	DTC3
Polio	2013	87.3	Polio
Measles	2013	85.0	Rougeole
Percentage of mothers provided at least one antenatal care (%)	2013	83.0	Pourcentage de mères ayant au moins reçu un soin prénatal (%)
Percentage of deliveries attended by skilled health personnel	2013	43.0	% d'accouchements assistés par un personnel de santé qualifié
Number of doctors (per 10 000 population)	2013	1.0	Nombre de médecins (pour 10 000 habitants)
Number of nurses (per 10 000 population)	2013	10.0	Nombre d'infirmières (pour 10 000 habitants)
Hospital beds - Total (per 10 000 population)	2013	18.0	Nombre de lits d'hôpitaux - Total (pour 10 000)
Births registered (per 1 000)	2014	42.6	Naiss.s enregistrées (pour 1 000)
Deaths registered (per 1 000)	2014	9.7	Décès enregistrés (pour 1 000)
Public expenditure on Health (% of budget)	2013	11.3	Dépenses publiques consacrées à la santé (% du budget)
EDUCATION			**EDUCATION**
Enrolment in primary education (both sexes) (000)	2013	3 075	Scolarisation dans le primaire (les deux sexes) (000)
Female	2013	1 534	Féminin
Enrolment in secondary education (both sexes) (000)	...	...	Scolarisation dans le secondaire (les deux sexes) (000)
Female	...	...	Féminin
Enrolment in tertiary education (both sexes) (000)	2013	91.3	Scolarisation dans le tertiaire (les deux sexes) (000)
Female	2000	7.8	Féminin
Literacy rate (both sexes)	2007	61.4	Taux d'alphabétisation (deux sexes)
Male	2007	71.9	Masculin
Female	2007	51.8	Féminin
Pupil-teacher ratio	...	...	Ratio élève-enseignant
Public expenditure on education (% of budget)	2008	5.7	Dépenses publiques consacrées à l'enseignement (% du budget)
POVERTY			**PAUVRETÉ**
GNI Per Capita (US$)	2013	1 810.0	RNB par habitant ($EU)
Human Poverty Index (HPI-1) Value (%)	2007	35.5	Valeur de l'Indice de pauvreté (IPH-1) (%)
Population below International Poverty Line ($2/day) (%)	2010	86.6	Population sous le seuil international de pauvreté (2$/J) (%)
Share of Income Held by Richest 10%	2010	47.4	% de revenu des 10% plus riches
Share of Income Held by Poorest 10%	2010	1.5	% de revenu des 10% plus pauvres
Gini index	2010	57.5	Indice de Gini

Charts / Graphiques

Population by age group – 2014
Population par groupe d'age – 2014

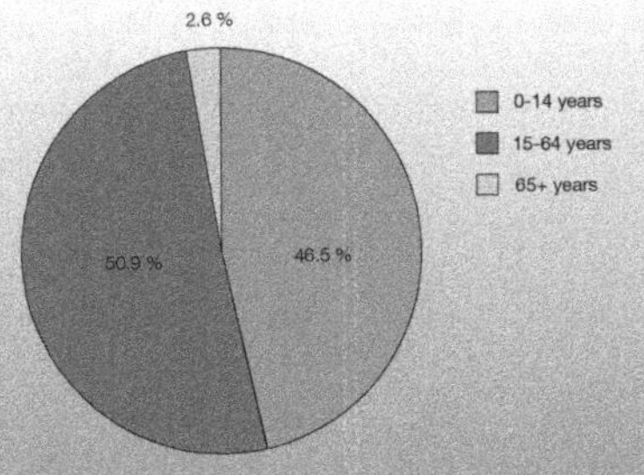

Percentage of children provided the vaccines – 2013
Pourcentage d'enfants vaccinés – 2013

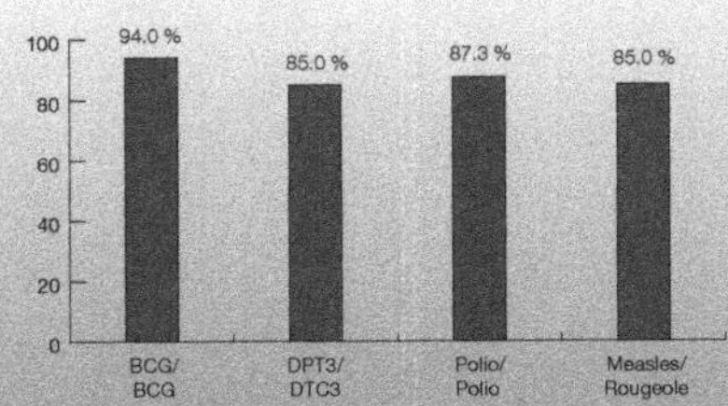

Literacy rate (%) – 2007
Taux d'alphabétisation – 2007

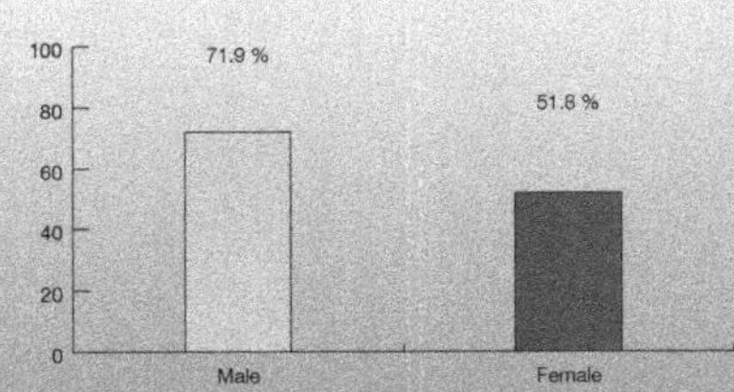

GNI Per Capita (US$)
RNB par habitant ($EU)

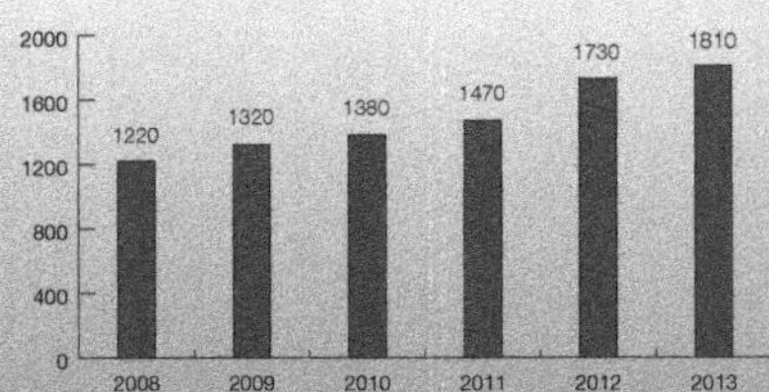

II NATIONAL ACCOUNTS — COMPTES NATIONAUX

	2006	2007	2008	2009	2010	2011	2012	2013	2014	
GROSS DOMESTIC PRODUCT BY KIND OF ECONOMIC ACTIVITY AT CURRENT PRICES *ZAMBIAN KWACHA (BILLIONS)*										**PRODUIT INTÉRIEUR BRUT PAR BRANCHE D'ACTIVITÉ ÉCONOMIQUE AUX PRIX COURANTS** *KWACHA (MILLIARDS)*
Agriculture, hunting, forestry and fishing	6 070	6 811	7 684	8 936	9 602	11 107	12 490	13 161	14 754	Agriculture, chasse sylviculture et pêche
Mining and quarrying	4 772	6 622	7 167	6 678	12 518	13 870	12 164	11 984	10 818	Industries extractives
Manufacturing	4 324	4 884	5 672	6 718	7 677	8 833	10 053	11 161	12 511	Industries manufacturières
Electricity, gas & water	1 051	1 193	1 317	1 515	1 825	2 413	2 642	3 030	3 374	Electricité, gaz et eau
Construction & public works	3 824	5 254	6 636	8 468	10 588	14 035	16 664	20 022	23 395	Bâtiments et travaux publics
Wholesale & retail trade, restaurants, hotels	9 797	11 546	13 855	16 422	19 486	22 755	25 037	28 100	32 140	Commerce de gros et de détail, restaurants et hôtels
Finance, insurance, real estate, etc.	5 754	6 645	7 912	9 599	11 480	13 735	15 446	17 745	20 371	Banques, assurances, affaires immobilières
Transport and communications	2 952	3 835	4 658	5 254	7 425	8 637	9 780	11 413	13 188	Transport(s) et communications
Public administration and defense	4 846	6 310	8 348	10 678	13 820	16 445	19 909	24 015	29 269	Administrations publiques et défense
Education	...	...	...	...	...	...	...	...	...	Education
Health and Social Work	...	...	...	...	...	...	...	...	...	Santé et actions sociales
Other services	...	...	...	...	...	...	...	...	...	Autres services
Less Imputed Service Charges	- 1 509	- 1 636	- 1 879	- 2 076	- 2 586	- 2 902	- 3 450	- 4 165	- 4 981	Moins services d'intermédiation financière
Gross domestic product at factor cost / basic prices	41 882	51 464	61 369	72 191	91 836	108 926	120 736	136 465	154 839	Produit intérieur brut aux couts des facteurs / prix de base
Plus: indirect taxes / taxes on products, less subsidies	4 083	4 799	5 720	5 158	5 380	6 427	7 634	8 258	11 694	Plus taxes indirectes/impôts sur les produits, moins les subventions
EXPENDITURE ON GROSS DOMESTIC PRODUCT AT CURRENT PURCHASER'S VALUES *ZAMBIAN KWACHA (BILLIONS)*										**EMPLOI DU PRODUIT INTÉRIEUR BRUT AUX PRIX COURANTS D'ACQUISITION** *KWACHA (MILLIARDS)*
Government final consumption	4 376	4 487	6 951	7 721	9 118	11 228	15 021	18 118	-	Consommation finale des administrations publiques
Private final consumption	28 043	36 146	39 910	45 469	53 072	61 707	67 188	72 328	-	Consommation finale privée
Gross fixed capital formation	10 728	13 553	19 753	21 303	25 174	34 306	42 837	50 329	-	Formation brute de capital fixe
Change in inventories	1 761	2 183	2 556	2 945	3 872	4 571	4 926	5 481	-	Variation des stocks
Exports of goods and services	14 236	19 494	19 776	22 592	35 995	44 735	50 589	60 336	-	Exportations de biens et services
Less imports of goods and services	13 178	19 600	21 857	22 683	30 015	41 195	52 190	61 870	-	Moins importations de biens et services
GDP at purchasers' values	45 964	56 263	67 089	77 348	97 216	115 353	128 370	144 722	166 533	PIB aux prix d'acquisition
GROSS DOMESTIC PRODUCT BY KIND OF ECONOMIC ACTIVITY AT CONSTANT PRICES *ANNUAL GROWTH RATES (%)*										**PRODUIT INTÉRIEUR BRUT PAR BRANCHE D'ACTIVITÉ ECONOMIQUE AUX PRIX CONSTANTS** *TAUX DE CROISSANCE ANNUEL (%)*
Agriculture, hunting, forestry and fishing	- 1.4	- 3.8	- 2.7	0.6	- 1.4	8.0	6.8	- 7.4	6.5	Agriculture, chasse sylviculture et pêche
Mining and quarrying	17.4	13.8	13.0	33.2	28.0	- 5.2	- 2.7	5.9	- 1.4	Industries extractives
Manufacturing	6.7	4.1	3.0	3.6	5.8	8.0	7.2	4.5	2.3	Industries manufacturières
Electricity, gas & water	9.0	- 0.6	- 3.1	4.4	4.6	8.2	4.1	5.9	2.7	Electricité, gaz et eau
Construction & public works	11.1	15.9	4.2	4.2	1.7	8.9	13.6	11.4	8.5	Bâtiments et travaux publics
Wholesale & retail trade, restaurants, hotels	6.4	6.5	6.6	4.8	9.4	7.5	3.4	5.0	6.0	Commerce de gros et de détail,restaurants et hôtels
Finance, insurance, real estate, etc.	4.1	4.1	5.9	4.3	4.6	3.6	6.7	6.6	7.1	Banques, assurances, affaires immobilières
Transport and communications	29.6	27.1	24.1	15.9	24.3	13.7	12.8	12.4	13.2	Transport(s) et communications
Public administration and defense	13.1	17.3	16.9	14.2	11.2	8.4	9.4	12.8	5.6	Administrations publiques et défense
Education	...	...	...	...	...	...	...	...	...	Education
Health and Social Work	...	...	...	...	...	...	...	...	...	Santé et actions sociales
Other services	...	...	...	...	...	...	...	...	...	Autres services
Less Imputed Service Charges	- 0.5	- 1.1	- 1.8	- 1.9	- 3.9	2.3	2.3	2.3	2.3	Moins services d'intermédiation financière
Gross domestic product at factor cost / basic prices	8.3	8.6	7.6	9.1	10.1	6.3	6.7	6.7	6.0	Produit intérieur brut aux couts des facteurs / prix de base
Plus: indirect taxes / taxes on products, less subsidies	0.9	4.2	10.9	12.2	14.0	6.3	6.7	6.7	6.1	Plus taxes indirectes/impôts sur les produits, moins les subventions
Gross domestic product at market prices	7.9	8.4	7.8	9.2	10.3	6.3	6.7	6.7	6.0	Produit intérieur brut aux prix du marché
EXPENDITURE ON GROSS DOMESTIC PRODUCT AT CONSTANT PURCHASERS' VALUES *ANNUAL GROWTH RATES (%)*										**EMPLOIS DU PRODUIT INTÉRIEUR BRUT AUX PRIX CONSTANTS D'ACQUISITION** *TAUX DE CROISSANCE ANNUEL (%)*
Government final consumption	- 3.7	- 30.7	- 9.9	- 49.8	1.9	21.6	...	...	...	Consommation finale des administrations publiques
Private final consumption	148.5	- 36.7	- 9.9	100.1	50.0	5.4	...	...	...	Consommation finale privée
Gross fixed capital formation	...	...	...	...	...	...	...	...	...	Formation brute de capital fixe
Exports of goods and services	- 70.4	-	- 9.9	2 456.6	13.3	21.0	...	...	...	Exportations de biens et services
Less imports of goods and services	-	-	- 9.9	1 021.3	45.3	38.5	...	...	...	Moins importations de biens et services
Notes	The Accounts are calculated using the new base year 2010						Les comptes Annuels sont élaborés selon la nouvelle année de base 2010			Notes

III INFLATION

	2006	2007	2008	2009	2010	2011	2012	2013	2014	
ANNUAL GROWTH RATES (%)										**TAUX DE CROISSANCE ANNUEL (%)**
All items	9.0	10.7	12.4	13.4	8.5	8.6	6.6	7.0	7.8	Ensemble
of which:										dont:
Food and Non-alcoholic beverages	-0.2	5.9	20.5	14.4	5.6	5.2	7.0	6.5	7.2	Alimentation et boissons non alcoolisés
Alcoholic beverages & tobacco	...	...	...	...	...	...	6.4	-5.3	13.4	Boissons alcoolisées et tabacs
Clothing and Footwear	...	...	...	...	...	...	5.2	-1.6	7.0	Habillement et chaussures
Housing, Water, Electricity, Gas and Other Fuels	13.0	11.2	15.2	11.4	20.8	8.4	7.3	21.5	9.7	Logement, eau, électricité, gas et autres combustibles
Furnishing, household equip	...	...	...	...	...	...	6.3	6.5	5.1	Meubles, articles de ménage et entretien courant
Health	25.1	9.1	9.9	15.9	8.3	6.7	6.2	4.7	6.0	Santé
Transport	15.2	13.6	15.9	-3.4	14.0	12.3	1.5	29.5	10.6	Transport
Communication	...	...	...	...	...	...	6.2	4.3	-11.8	Communication
Recreation & culture	...	...	...	...	...	...	9.0	11.8	-4.0	Loisirs et culture
Education	...	...	...	...	...	...	6.2	16.6	10.9	Enseignement
Restaurants & hotels	...	...	...	...	...	...	9.0	2.6	7.7	Restaurants et hôtels
Miscellaneous goods & services	...	...	...	...	...	...	3.9	7.2	5.8	Biens et services divers

	2006	2007	2008	2009	2010	2011	2012	2013	2014	
IV AGRICULTURAL PRODUCTION - PRODUCTION AGRICOLE										
TONNES *(THOUSAND)*										**TONNES** *(MILLIERS)*
Sugar cane	2 450	2 430	2 050	3 200	3 500	3 500	3 900	4 000	...	Canne à sucre
Maize	1 424	1 366	1 212	1 887	2 795	3 020	2 853	2 533	...	Maïs
Cassava	1 060	1 060	1 186	1 161	1 152	1 087	1 062	1 070	...	Manioc
Wheat	94	116	113	195	172	237	254	274	...	Blé
Soya beans	58	55	57	119	112	117	203	261	...	Feuilles de Soja
V MINING PRODUCTION - PRODUCTION MINIERE										
	2006	2007	2008	2009	2010	2011	2012	2013	2014	
Copper ores, Tons (thousands)	515 618	560 731	575 037	698 646	767 008	739 759	699 020	763 805	...	Minerais de cuivre, de tonnes (milliers)
Cobalt, Tons (thousands)	4 649	4 414	4 053	3 660	2 128	2 137	771	5 000	...	Cobalt, Tonnes (en milliers)
	...	...	...	...	...	...	...	...	...	
VI ENERGY - ENERGIE										
	2006	2007	2008	2009	2010	2011	2012	2013	2014	
Total electricity generation (GWh)	9 329	9 831	9 696	10 308	11 304	11 916	11 916	11 917	...	Production d'électricité totale (GWh)
of which:										dont
Production of electricity from fossil fuels (GWh)	-	30	30	32	31	781	781	781	...	Production d'électricité à partir de combustibles fossiles (GWh)
Production of hydro electricity (GWh)	9 329	9 801	9 666	10 276	11 273	11 134	11 134	11 134	...	Production d'électricité d'origine hydraulique (GWh)
Production of electricity from solar, wind, tide, wave and other sources (GWh)	...	...	...	...	...	2	2	3	...	Production d'électricité d'origine solaire, éolienne, marée motrice et autres (GWh)
VII TOURISM AND INFRASTRUCTURE - TOURISME ET INFRASTRUCTURE										
	2006	2007	2008	2009	2010	2011	2012	2013	2014	
VII-1 TOURISM										**VII-1 TOURISME**
International tourist arrivals (thousands)	757	897	812	710	815	920	859	886	929	Arrivées de touristes internationaux (milliers)
Rooms in hotels and similar establishments (thousands)	...	...	...	...	...	...	67	74	...	Chambres d'hotels et établissements assimilés (milliers)
Overnight stays (thousands)	5 383	6 574	5 612	4 996	5 654	6 824	5 418	5 691	6 142	Nuitées (milliers)
Tourism receipts (US$ thousand)	110 000	137 800	148 400	97 700	124 600	146 300	154 800	224 500	214 159	Recettes touristiques (milliers de $ EU)
Total contribution to GDP (%)	4.7	6.1	6.7	6.3	5.6	5.5	5.9	6.0	6.2	Contribution totale au PIB (%)
Total contribution to Employment (%)	3.3	3.5	3.7	3.9	3.8	4.0	4.5	4.2	4.3	Contribution totale à l'emploi (%)
VII-2 INFRASTRUCTURE										**VII-2 INFRASTRUCTURE**
Paved roads (% of total)	...	...	...	...	...	...	...	...	...	Routes asphaltées (% du total)
Total Network (Railways-km)	...	...	...	...	...	...	...	...	...	Réseau total voies ferrées-Km
Main Telephone Lines (per 100 inhabitants)	1	1	1	1	1	1	1	1	...	Lignes téléphoniques fixes (pour 100 habitants)
Mobile Cellular Subscribers (per 100 inhabitants)	14	22	28	34	41	60	75	72	...	Abonnés aux téléphones mobiles (pour 100 habitants)
VIII EXTERNAL TRADE - COMMERCE EXTERIEUR										
	2006	2007	2008	2009	2010	2011	2012	2013	2014	
ZAMBIAN KWACHA EXPORTS, FOB										**KWACHA (MILLIARDS) EXPORTATIONS, FÀB**
Exports - Total	13 411	18 399	18 654	21 377	34 500	42 915	48 206	57 176	...	Exportations - Total
Exports to AFRICA	...	...	...	...	...	...	...	...	...	Exportations vers l'AFRIQUE
Main Products										**Principaux produits**
Cathodes and sections of cathodes of refined copper	5 265	8 382	7 657	8 822	16 744	23 269	21 832	16 341	...	Cathodes et sections de cathodes de cuivre raffiné
Plates, sheets and strip, of refined copper, uncoi	3 227	3 284	3 543	2 631	3 247	1 883	1 140	350	...	Plaques, feuilles et bandes de cuivre raffiné, uncoi
Copper ores and concentrates	1 500	1 018	2 580	1 448	1 127	42	35	175	...	Minerais de cuivre et leurs concentrés
Other: articles of cobalt, nes	510	987	1 066	370	935	953	1 081	455	...	Autre: articles de cobalt, nda
Wire of refined copper, maximum cross-sectional dimension >6mm	531	595	492	486	707	871	773	465	...	Fil en cuivre raffiné, la plus grande dimension transversale> 6mm
Main Destinations										**Principales destinations**
Switzerland	5 332	7 769	9 274	10 051	17 594	22 273	20 378	13 558	...	Suisse
South Africa	1 478	2 208	1 943	1 937	3 161	4 228	4 362	4 024	...	Afrique du Sud
United Kingdom	364	224	429	428	640	1 683	1 610	518	...	Royaume-Uni
China	922	754	1 058	2 384	6 978	7 425	9 261	7 538	...	Chine
Congo, DR	481	982	1 053	1 500	1 600	1 971	3 732	4 191	...	Congo, RD
IMPORTS, CIF										**IMPORTATIONS, CAF**
Imports - Total	11 063	15 945	18 480	19 124	25 507	35 441	45 276	54 898	...	Importations - Total (millions)
Imports from Africa	...	...	...	...	...	...	...	...	...	Importations en provenance de l'Afrique
Main Products										**Principaux produits**
Petroleum oils and oils obtained from bituminous minerals, crude	833	916	1 747	2 164	2 439	1 814	2 797	480	...	Huiles de pétrole, les huiles de minéraux bitumineux, brut
Copper ores and concentrates	96	518	1 581	1 299	2 977	4 956	4 356	4 965	...	Minerais de cuivre et leurs concentrés
Gas oils.	397	536	676	183	41	291	748	1 669	...	Gas-oils
Diesel non dual purpose vehicles for either person	181	164	238	170	210	297	368	312	...	Diesel but non double pour les véhicules soit à la personne
Urea	108	161	146	329	309	556	372	355	...	Urée
Main Origin										**Principales provenances**
South Africa	5 196	7 547	7 844	7 598	8 781	12 593	15 273	10 470	...	Afrique du Sud
United Kingdom	405	639	573	685	509	941	1 132	1 242	...	Royaume-Uni
Congo, DR	113	517	1 986	2 416	6 064	6 481	6 517	6 560	...	Congo, DR
Zimbabwe	631	445	381	287	345	430	478	374	...	Zimbabwe
United Arab Emirates	1 159	1 028	448	536	558	1 178	1 135	875	...	Émirats Arabes Unis

IX FINANCIAL AND MONETARY STATISTICS - FINANCES ET STATISTIQUES MONETAIRES	2006	2007	2008	2009	2010	2011	2012	2013	2014	
IX-1 MONETARY STATISTICS *ZAMBIAN KWACHA (MILLIONS)*										**IX-1 STATISTIQUES MONÉTAIRES** *KWACHA (MILLIONS)*
Money supply (M1)	8 300	10 400	12 820	13 800	17 920	21 800	25 700	31 040	36 980	Masse monétaire (M1)
Quasi-money	2 528	3 281	4 325	4 700	5 647	7 479	9 432	11 913	13 562	Quasi-monnaie
of which Demand Deposit	...	...	...	...	...	...	...	...	...	dont Monnaie scripturale
Net foreign assets	3 498	4 552	4 985	4 913	6 690	9 393	12 014	11 663	15 306	Avoirs extérieurs nets
Domestic credit	6 423	7 572	10 338	11 976	14 689	16 850	19 739	28 404	31 987	Crédit intérieur
of which claims on private sector	3 755	5 460	8 209	7 741	8 942	11 454	15 707	17 675	22 335	dont créances sur le secteur privé
of which claims on government sector, net	2 402	1 678	1 886	3 963	5 548	5 200	3 242	10 335	9 182	dont créances nettes sur le gouvernement
International reserves (millions US$)	720	1 090	1 096	1 892	2 094	2 324	3 042	2 684	3 078	Réserves internationales (millions $EU)
Average Exchange Rate (National Currency per US$)	3.60	4.00	3.75	5.05	4.80	4.86	5.15	5.40	6.15	Taux de change (moyen) (monnaie nationale par $ EU)
IX-2 PUBLIC FINANCE *ZAMBIAN KWACHA (MILLIONS)*										**IX-2 FINANCES PUBLIQUES** *KWACHA (MILLIONS)*
Total Revenues and Grants	8 508 010	10 626 010	12 290 000	12 182 000	15 199 000	20 283 000	24 339 000	26 634 000	32 234 078	Recettes totales et dons
Tax Revenue	6 317 010	8 184 010	9 654 000	9 661 000	12 701 000	18 018 000	19 260 000	21 307 000	27 088 852	Recettes fiscales
Non Tax Revenue	1 171 000	338 000	567 000	654 000	1 109 000	1 551 000	2 842 000	3 175 000	4 099 358	Recettes non fiscales
Grants	1 020 000	2 104 000	2 069 000	1 867 000	1 389 000	714 000	2 237 000	2 152 000	1 045 869	Dons
Total Expenditures and Net Lending	9 157 000	11 210 000	13 096 977	13 849 000	17 585 000	22 297 000	28 392 000	36 313 788	42 633 188	Dépenses totales et prêts nets
Current expenditure	7 073 000	9 481 900	10 704 100	11 570 000	15 086 000	19 145 000	24 426 000	29 141 800	35 242 633	Dépenses courantes
Of which Wages and Salaries	2 833 000	3 531 000	4 465 000	5 274 000	6 325 000	7 402 000	9 393 000	11 897 000	14 346 245	Dont rémunérations et salaires
Capital expenditure	1 601 000	1 926 000	1 966 000	2 291 000	2 512 000	3 902 000	4 393 000	5 471 988	7 279 055	Dépenses d'équipement
Net Lending	483 000	- 197 900	426 877	- 12 000	- 13 000	- 750 000	- 427 000	1 700 000	111 500	Prêts nets
Fiscal Balance	- 648 990	- 583 990	- 806 977	-1 667 000	-2 386 000	-2 014 000	-4 053 000	-9 679 788	-10 399 110	Solde global y compris les dons
IX-3 BALANCE OF PAYMENTS *ZAMBIAN KWACHA (MILLIONS)*										**IX-3 BALANCE DES PAIEMENTS** *KWACHA (MILLIONS)*
Trade balance	1 307	899	407	906	2 704	2 206	1 437	1 451	...	Balance commerciale
Services Balance	- 358	- 640	- 607	- 420	- 567	- 724	- 783	- 874	...	Balance des services
Net Income	- 1 168	- 1 545	- 1 399	- 419	- 1 363	- 1 155	- 334	- 768	...	Revenus nets
Compensation of employees	- 23	- 28	- 29	- 29	- 29	- 29	- 29	...	...	Rémunération des salariés
Investment Income	- 1 146	- 1 517	- 1 371	- 390	- 1 334	- 1 126	- 1 098	...	...	Revenus des investissements
Current transfers, net total	362	531	560	516	432	378	391	...	...	Transferts courants
Net official transfers	209	303	321	304	237	146	454	389	...	Transferts officiels nets
Workers' remittances	- 23	- 28	- 29	- 29	- 29	- 29	- 29	...	...	Envois de fonds des travailleurs
Other private transfers	189	265	281	207	190	227	240	...	...	Autres transferts privés
Current account balance	143	- 755	- 1 039	583	1 206	705	774	198	...	Solde du compte courant
Capital & financial account	482	1 108	1 062	88	- 1 247	- 220	- 33	- 514	...	Comptes de capital et financier
Capital account	2 633	223	230	237	150	119	223	225	...	Compte de capital
Financial account	- 2 151	885	832	- 150	- 1 396	- 339	- 256	- 739	...	Compte financier
Errors & omissions	- 361	- 1	5	112	179	- 215	- 15	- 29	...	Erreurs et omissions
Overall balance	264	352	29	782	138	270	727	- 345	...	Balance générale

X DEBT AND FINANCIAL FLOWS - DETTE ET FLUX FINANCIERS	2006	2007	2008	2009	2010	2011	2012	2013	2014	
X-1 DEBT *US$ (MILLIONS)*										**X-1 DETTE EXTÉRIEURE** *$ E.U (MILLIONS)*
Total external debt	533	1 189	5 662	6 405	6 131	3 536	4 275	4 412	5 620	Dette extérieure totale
Private	-	-	4 403	4 828	4 377	1 444	1 429	1 078	1 960	Privée
Public	533	1 189	1 259	1 578	1 754	2 092	2 846	3 334	3 660	Publique
Total external debt service	66	69	264	628	299	187	552	304	429	Service de la dette extérieure
Present value of External debt	...	...	...	...	...	...	...	...	...	Valeur actuelle de la dette extérieure
Total government domestic debt (in local currency)	9	10	9	10	10.1	12.1	12.4	...	...	Dette publique intérieure
X-2 FINANCIAL FLOWS *US$ (MILLIONS)*										**X-2 FLUX FINANCIERS** *$ E.U (MILLIONS)*
Net Foreign Direct Investment Inflows	616	1 324	939	695	1 729	1 108	1 732	1 811	...	Investissements étranger direct (flux nets entrants)
Main origin of FDI Inflows										**Principales origines de l'IDE entrant:**
United Kingdom	20	10	251	27	78.8	107.4	-	...	...	Royaume-Uni
United States	15	5	- 1	3	18.0	- 3.0	-	...	...	États-Unis
Germany	-	-	...	...	0.0	0.0	0.0	...	...	Allemagne
Luxembourg	-	...	-	3	-	3.1	15.2	...	...	Luxembourg
Denmark	-	3	2	-	0.5	0.6	- 1.4	...	...	Danemark
African countries	...	...	...	...	...	...	...	...	...	Pays africains
Net total Official Development Assistance	1 468	1 008	1 116	1 267	914	1 035	958	1 142	...	Aide publique au développement (nette totale)
Main origin of Net ODA										**Principales origines de l'APD nette**
United States	310	165	226	232	225.1	276.7	305.1	313.2	...	Etats-Unis
IDA	61	71	59	43	33.5	72.1	78.9	...	...	IDA
United Kingdom	87	74	62	74	79.3	92.6	84.3	...	...	Royaume-Uni
Germany	288	41	45	56	33.3	39.6	34.1	35.8	...	Allemagne
Japan	32	95	37	37	46.1	46.1	47.8	66.6	...	Japon

AREA (km²)	**390 760**		**SUPERFICIE (km²)**
CAPITAL CITY	**Harare**	**Harare**	**CAPITALE**
CURRENCY	**Zimbabwe Dollar**	**Dollar Zimbabween**	**MONNAIE**

I SOCIAL AND DEMOGRAPHIC INDICATORS – INDICATEURS DEMOGRAPHIQUES ET SOCIAUX

	Year / Année	Value / Valeur	
POPULATION			**POPULATION**
Population ('000)			Population ('000)
Both sexes	2014	14 599	Les deux sexes
Male	2014	7 216	Masculin
Female	2014	7 384	Féminin
Average annual growth rate	2014	2.2	Taux de croissance annuel
Active Population ('000)	2014	7 121	Population active ('000)
Population by age group ('000)			Population par groupe d'âge ('000)
0-14 years	2014	5 688	0-14 ans
15-64 years	2014	8 351	15-64 ans
65+ years	2014	561	65+ ans
Economically. active population. in agriculture (%)	2014	46.9	Participation de la population active agricole (%)
Crude birth rate	2014	30.9	Taux brut de natalité
Crude death rate	2014	8.5	Taux brut de mortalité
Total fertility rate	2014	3.4	Indice synthétique de fécondité
Proportion of urban population	2014	40.1	Part de la population urbaine
Life Expectancy at Birth - Total (years)	2014	61.2	Espérance de vie à la naissance - Totale (ans)
Dependency Ratio - Total (%)	2014	68.5	Taux de dépendance - Total (%)
HEALTH			**SANTÉ**
Percentage of children under-five and underweight	2011	10.1	% d'enfants de moins de cinq ans avec insuffisance pondérale
Prevalence of undernourishment	2013	31.8	Prévalence de la malnutrition
Under five mortality rate (both sexes, per 1000)	2013	88.5	Taux de mortalité de moins de 5 ans (les deux sexes, pour 1000)
Infant mortality rate (both sexes) per 1000	2013	55.0	Taux de mortalité infantile (les deux sexes) par 1000
Percentage of children provided the vaccines :			Pourcentage d'enfants vaccinés :
BCG	2013	95.0	BCG
DPT3	2013	95.0	DTC3
Polio	2011	19.5	Polio
Measles	2013	93.0	Rougeole
Percentage of mothers provided at least one antenatal care (%)	2011	89.8	Pourcentage de mères ayant au moins reçu un soin prénatal (%)
Percentage of deliveries attended by skilled health personnel	2011	66.2	% d'accouchements assistés par un personnel de santé qualifié
Number of doctors (per 10 000 population)	2009	0.6	Nombre de médecins (pour 10 000 habitants)
Number of nurses (per 10 000 population)	2009	12.5	Nombre d'infirmières (pour 10 000 habitants)
Hospital beds - Total (per 10 000 population)	2011	17.0	Nombre de lits d'hôpitaux - Total (pour 10 000)
Births registered (per 1 000)	2014	30.9	Naiss.s enregistrées (pour 1 000)
Deaths registered (per 1 000)	2014	8.5	Décès enregistrés (pour 1 000)
Public expenditure on Health (% of budget)	2011	8.0	Dépenses publiques consacrées à la santé (% du budget)
EDUCATION			**EDUCATION**
Enrolment in primary education (both sexes) (000)	2012	2 666	Scolarisation dans le primaire (les deux sexes) (000)
Female	2012	1 321	Féminin
Enrolment in secondary education (both sexes) (000)	2012	937	Scolarisation dans le secondaire (les deux sexes) (000)
Female	2012	462	Féminin
Enrolment in tertiary education (both sexes) (000)	2013	91.3	Scolarisation dans le tertiaire (les deux sexes) (000)
Female	2013	43.6	Féminin
Literacy rate (both sexes)	2011	83.6	Taux d'alphabétisation (deux sexes)
Male	2011	87.8	Masculin
Female	2011	80.1	Féminin
Pupil-teacher ratio	...	...	Ratio élève-enseignant
Public expenditure on education (% of budget)	2010	8.7	Dépenses publiques consacrées à l'enseignement (% du budget)
POVERTY			**PAUVRETÉ**
GNI Per Capita (US$)	2013	860.0	RNB par habitant ($EU)
Human Poverty Index (HPI-1) Value (%)	2007	34.0	Valeur de l'Indice de pauvreté (IPH-1) (%)
Population below International Poverty Line ($2/day) (%)	...	...	Population sous le seuil international de pauvreté (2$/J) (%)
Share of Income Held by Richest 10%	...	...	% de revenu des 10% plus riches
Share of Income Held by Poorest 10%	...	...	% de revenu des 10% plus pauvres
Gini index	...	...	Indice de Gini

Charts / Graphiques

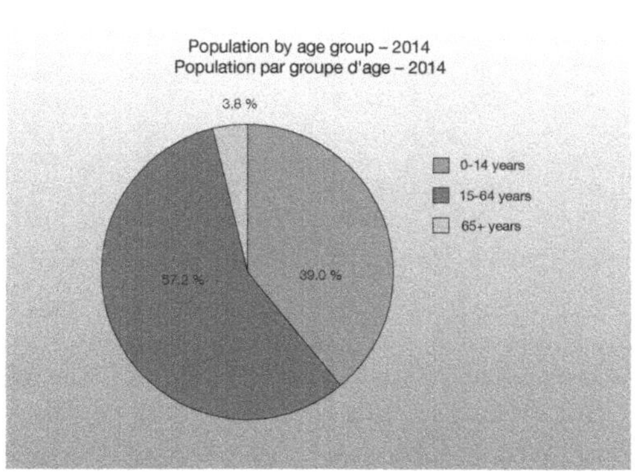

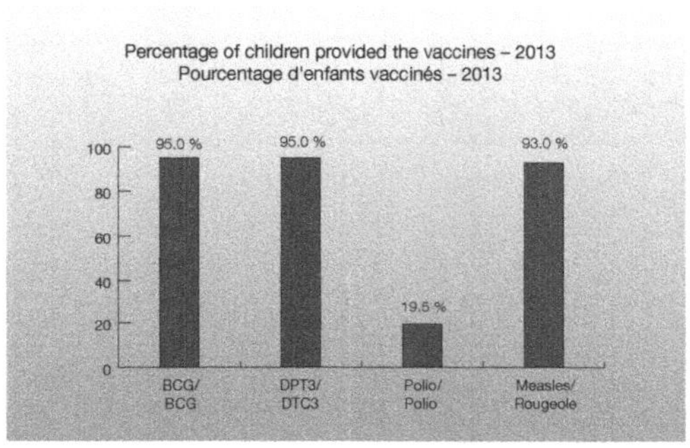

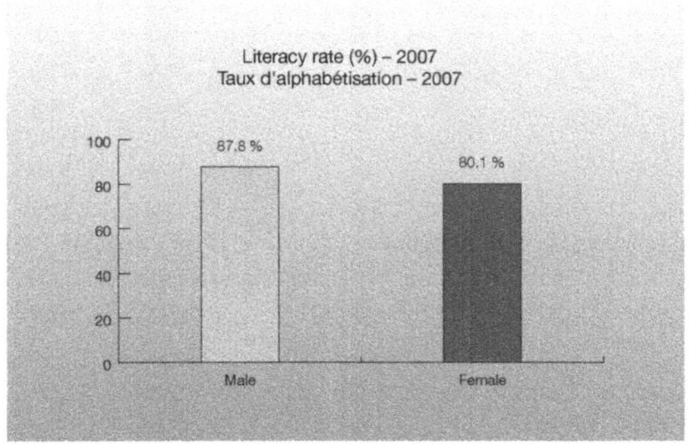

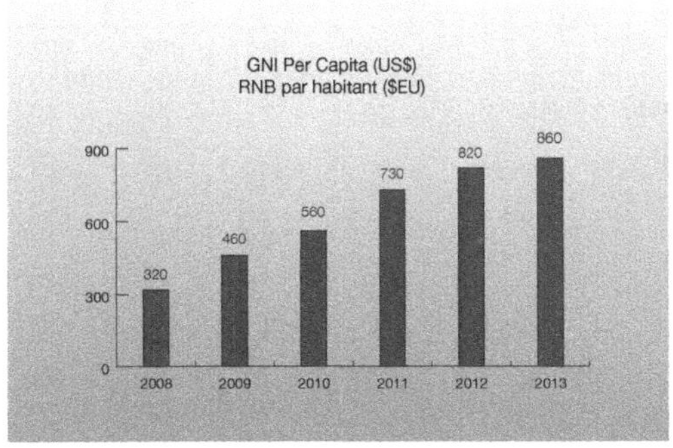

II NATIONAL ACCOUNTS — COMPTES NATIONAUX

	2006	2007	2008	2009	2010	2011	2012	2013	2014	
GROSS DOMESTIC PRODUCT BY KIND OF ECONOMIC ACTIVITY AT CURRENT PRICES *ZIMBABWE DOLLAR (BILLIONS)*										**PRODUIT INTÉRIEUR BRUT PAR BRANCHE D'ACTIVITÉ ÉCONOMIQUE AUX PRIX COURANTS** *DOLLAR ZIMBABWEEN (MILLIARDS)*
Agriculture, hunting, forestry and fishing	156	3 335	351 722 873	1 038	1 157	1 222	1 377	1 364	...	Agriculture, chasse sylviculture et pêche
Mining and quarrying	239	3 547	99 667 704	561	802	1 006	1 064	1 187	...	Industries extractives
Manufacturing	283	1 249	103 044 119	1 066	1 109	1 293	1 420	1 457	...	Industries manufacturières
Electricity, gas & water	27	1 777	113 993 074	279	359	436	448	492	...	Electricité, gaz et eau
Construction & public works	15	485	13 622 993	137	182	289	376	399	...	Bâtiments et travaux publics
Wholesale & retail trade, restaurants, hotels	169	1 711	384 243 165	1 207	1 376	1 397	1 601	1 909	...	Commerce de gros et de détail, restaurants et hôtels
Finance, insurance, real estate, etc.	42	308	2 405 787	682	745	897	1 246	1 413	...	Banques, assurances, affaires immobilières
Transport and communications	21	761	154 988 919	1 080	1 137	1 320	1 334	1 374	...	Transport(s) et communications
Public administration and defense	7	260	22 172 296	186	292	321	383	402	...	Administrations publiques et défense
Education	...	...	...	210	304	518	710	879	...	Education
Health and Social Work	...	...	...	87	102	109	119	123	...	Santé et actions sociales
Other services	37	2 220	207 053 386	378	429	494	457	443	...	Autres services
Less Imputed Service Charges	- 1	- 9	- 991 961	- 22	- 36	- 50	- 67	- 77	...	Moins services d'intermédiation financière
Gross domestic product at factor cost / basic prices	996	15 645	1451 922 357	6 889	7 958	9 254	10 467	11 365	...	Produit intérieur brut aux couts des facteurs / prix de base
Plus: indirect taxes / taxes on products, less subsidies	34	123	441	1 268	1 464	1 703	1 926	2 125	...	Plus taxes indirectes/impôts sur les produits, moins les subventions
EXPENDITURE ON GROSS DOMESTIC PRODUCT AT CURRENT PURCHASER'S VALUES *ZIMBABWE DOLLAR (BILLIONS)*										**EMPLOI DU PRODUIT INTÉRIEUR BRUT AUX PRIX COURANTS D'ACQUISITION** *DOLLAR ZIMBABWEEN (MILLIARDS)*
Government final consumption	18	733	8 256 310	672	1 112	1 805	1 979	2 113	...	Consommation finale des administrations publiques
Private final consumption	999	14 144	1410 943 484	10 210	8 670	11 737	12 327	13 816	...	Consommation finale privée
Gross fixed capital formation	98	455	12 778 596	960	2 048	2 064	2 079	1 753	...	Formation brute de capital fixe
Change in inventories	- 17	710	19 944 688	272	211	390	- 392	5	...	Variation des stocks
Exports of goods and services	364	182	193	2 250	3 245	3 557	3 884	3 507	...	Exportations de biens et services
Less imports of goods and services	432	456	472	6 207	5 865	8 596	7 484	7 704	...	Moins importations de biens et services
GDP at purchasers' values	1 030	15 768	1451 922 798	8 157	9 422	10 956	12 393	13 490	...	PIB aux prix d'acquisition
GROSS DOMESTIC PRODUCT BY KIND OF ECONOMIC ACTIVITY AT CONSTANT PRICES *ANNUAL GROWTH RATES (%)*										**PRODUIT INTÉRIEUR BRUT PAR BRANCHE D'ACTIVITÉ ECONOMIQUE AUX PRIX CONSTANTS** *TAUX DE CROISSANCE ANNUEL (%)*
Agriculture, hunting, forestry and fishing	- 4.0	- 7.0	- 35.8	...	7.2	1.4	7.8	- 2.6	...	Agriculture, chasse sylviculture et pêche
Mining and quarrying	- 6.0	- 3.0	- 29.5	...	37.4	24.4	8.0	11.7	...	Industries extractives
Manufacturing	- 2.8	- 5.0	- 12.3	...	2.0	13.8	5.3	- 0.6	...	Industries manufacturières
Electricity, gas & water	- 4.2	- 0.8	- 8.7	...	19.5	6.4	0.3	5.0	...	Electricité, gaz et eau
Construction & public works	- 4.5	- 3.0	- 3.3	...	14.1	65.1	23.5	3.9	...	Bâtiments et travaux publics
Wholesale & retail trade, restaurants, hotels	- 2.0	2.5	8.7	...	8.8	4.3	4.3	3.9	...	Commerce de gros et de détail,restaurants et hôtels
Finance, insurance, real estate, etc.	- 5.5	- 3.7	- 19.1	...	7.7	14.7	34.3	8.7	...	Banques, assurances, affaires immobilières
Transport and communications	- 1.0	- 2.0	11.4	...	4.7	0.0	6.7	7.0	...	Transport(s) et communications
Public administration and defense	...	...	...	...	30.3	19.6	19.1	3.4	...	Administrations publiques et défense
Education	...	...	...	...	37.0	63.9	38.1	2.9	...	Education
Health and Social Work	...	...	...	...	15.7	7.7	7.7	0.5	...	Santé et actions sociales
Other services	- 3.2	- 4.0	- 1.6	...	14.3	10.3	- 10.1	- 3.8	...	Autres services
Less Imputed Service Charges	- 4.4	- 2.0	- 23.7	...	32.9	38.7	9.8	11.3	...	Moins services d'intermédiation financière
Gross domestic product at factor cost / basic prices	- 3.6	- 3.7	- 11.3	...	11.4	11.9	10.6	3.8	...	Produit intérieur brut aux couts des facteurs / prix de base
Plus: indirect taxes / taxes on products, less subsidies	- 3.8	0.0	-	...	11.4	11.9	10.6	8.2	...	Plus taxes indirectes/impôts sur les produits, moins les subventions
Gross domestic product at market prices	- 3.6	- 3.3	- 9.9	...	11.4	11.9	10.6	4.5	...	Produit intérieur brut aux prix du marché
EXPENDITURE ON GROSS DOMESTIC PRODUCT AT CONSTANT PURCHASERS' VALUES *ANNUAL GROWTH RATES (%)*										**EMPLOIS DU PRODUIT INTÉRIEUR BRUT AUX PRIX CONSTANTS D'ACQUISITION** *TAUX DE CROISSANCE ANNUEL (%)*
Government final consumption	26.5	3 811.8	- 9.9	...	60.4	56.9	5.7	5.1	...	Consommation finale des administrations publiques
Private final consumption	- 3.7	- 30.7	- 9.9	...	- 22.9	20.9	17.5	6.6	...	Consommation finale privée
Gross fixed capital formation	148.5	- 36.7	- 9.9	...	84.3	- 5.6	- 22.2	22.4	...	Formation brute de capital fixe
Exports of goods and services	- 70.4	-	- 9.9	...	1.9	- 4.9	32.4	5.9	...	Exportations de biens et services
Less imports of goods and services	-	-	- 9.9	...	- 33.3	27.1	5.6	20.7	...	Moins importations de biens et services
Notes			2013:Projection					2013:Projection!		Notes

III INFLATION

	2006	2007	2008	2009	2010	2011	2012	2013	2014	
ANNUAL GROWTH RATES (%)										**TAUX DE CROISSANCE ANNUEL (%)**
All items	184101.1	12562581.0	5.3	11.5	3.0	3.3	3.9	1.6	-0.2	Ensemble
of which:										dont:
Food and Non-alcoholic beverages	14745627.0	...	...	10.6	3.7	4.0	4.6	1.7	-3.1	Alimentation et boissons non alcoolisés
Alcoholic beverages & tobacco	...	...	...	...	8.8	4.9	6.3	5.2	1.9	Boissons alcoolisées et tabacs
Clothing and Footwear	...	...	...	3.0	-5.1	1.6	0.8	-0.2	-0.4	Habillement et chaussures
Housing, Water, Electricity, Gas and Other Fuels	...	...	...	1.8	4.9	4.3	11.9	4.4	0.9	Logement, eau, électricité, gas et autres combustibles
Furnishing, household equip	...	...	...	3.4	2.4	3.5	2.1	-	-2.2	Meubles, articles de ménage et entretien courant
Health	595497.0	33011038.0	...	4.7	0.5	-0.3	1.6	2.8	0.7	Santé
Transport	225313.0	24890041.0	...	1.9	4.7	7.5	1.9	5.3	0.7	Transport
Communication	...	...	...	-0.1	-4.7	1.6	7.8	-10.2	-3.9	Communication
Recreation & culture	...	...	...	3.5	-2.0	0.2	0.5	-0.4	-1.0	Loisirs et culture
Education	...	...	...	3.5	4.9	4.0	9.2	10.4	15.8	Enseignement
Restaurants & hotels	...	...	...	8.4	9.6	4.9	6.1	1.6	0.8	Restaurants et hôtels
Miscellaneous goods & services	...	...	...	9.4	-0.8	6.0	1.3	0.8	-2.0	Biens et services divers

IV AGRICULTURAL PRODUCTION - PRODUCTION AGRICOLE										
	2006	2007	2008	2009	2010	2011	2012	2013	2014	
TONNES *(THOUSAND)*										**TONNES** *(MILLIERS)*
Sugar cane	3 682	2 897	2 582	2 338	2 692	3 058	3 929	3 880	...	Canne à sucre
Maize	1 485	953	496	700	1 192	1 452	968	799	...	Mais
Cassava	212	192	206	216	204	225	228	230	...	Manioc
Cottonseed	129	146	210	145	180	170	200	175	...	Coton
Groundnuts, with shell	83	125	80	79	106	85	93	102	...	Arachides en coques

V MINING PRODUCTION - PRODUCTION MINIERE										
	2006	2007	2008	2009	2010	2011	2012	2013	2014	
Coal, metric tons (thousands)	2 107	2 080	1 509	1 667	2 500	2 562	1 594	2 976	...	Houille, tonnes (milliers)
Chrome, metric tons (thousands)	104	79	3	194	517	599	408	355	...	Chrome, tonnes (milliers)
Platinum, metric tons (thousands)	97	85	11	7	9	11	11	13	...	Platinum, tonnes (milliers)

VI ENERGY - ENERGIE										
	2006	2007	2008	2009	2010	2011	2012	2013	2014	
Total electricity generation (GWh)	9 776	8 508	7 990	9 216	8 160	8 800	8 800	8 800	...	Production d'électricité totale (GWh)
of which:										dont:
Production of electricity from fossil fuels (GWh)	4 224	3 967	3 727	3 676	2 089	2 917	2 917	2 917	...	Production d'électricité à partir de combustibles fossiles (GWh)
Production of hydro electricity (GWh)	5 552	4 541	4 263	5 464	6 001	5 844	5 844	5 844	...	Production d'électricité d'origine hydraulique (GWh)
Production of electricity from solar, wind, tide, wave and other sources (GWh)	...	...	...	...	...	4	4	4	...	Production d'électricité d'origine solaire, éolienne, marée motrice et autres (GWh)

VII TOURISM AND INFRASTRUCTURE - TOURISME ET INFRASTRUCTURE										
	2006	2007	2008	2009	2010	2011	2012	2013	2014	
VII-1 TOURISM										**VII-1 TOURISME**
International tourist arrivals (thousands)	2 133	2 338	1 825	1 881	2 089	2 260	1 673	1 710	1 848	Arrivées de touristes internationaux (milliers)
Rooms in hotels and similar establishments (thousands)	...	...	5.7	4.9	8.0	6.0	...	...	5.8	Chambres d'hotels et établissements assimilés (milliers)
Overnight stays (thousands)	257	288	307	301	288	325	239	248	272	Nuitées (milliers)
Tourism receipts (US$ thousand)	338 000	306 780	336 940	389 730	351 090	367 104	410 963	418 978	447 240	Recettes touristiques (milliers de $ EU)
Total contribution to GDP (%)	17.4	11.1	14.5	12.0	9.5	10.6	10.3	10.4	10.7	Contribution totale au PIB (%)
Total contribution to Employment (%)	15.1	9.6	12.6	10.1	7.7	8.3	7.9	7.7	7.5	Contribution totale à l'emploi (%)
VII-2 INFRASTRUCTURE										**VII-2 INFRASTRUCTURE**
Paved roads (% of total)	...	...	...	...	...	...	...	...	...	Routes asphaltées (% du total)
Total Network (Railways-km)	...	...	2 583	...	...	...	...	...	...	Réseau total voies ferrées-Km
Main Telephone Lines (per 100 inhabitants)	3	3	3	3	3	3	2	2	...	Lignes téléphoniques fixes (pour 100 habitants)
Mobile Cellular Subscribers (per 100 inhabitants)	7	10	13	31	59	69	92	96	...	Abonnés aux téléphones mobiles (pour 100 habitants)

VIII EXTERNAL TRADE - COMMERCE EXTERIEUR										
	2006	2007	2008	2009	2010	2011	2012	2013	2014	
ZIMBABWE DOLLAR (MILLIONS) EXPORTS, FOB										**DOLLAR ZIMBABWEEN (MILLIONS) EXPORTATIONS, FÀB**
Exports - Total	1 588	1 721	1 694	2 190	3 204	3 516	3 838	3 416	3 009	Exportations - Total
Exports to AFRICA	...	...	...	1 453	2 069	2 700	3 087	3 080	2 732	Exportations vers l'AFRIQUE
Main Products										**Principaux produits**
Natural or cultured pearls, precious or semi-precious stones, precious metals, metals clad with precious metal and articles thereof; imitation jewellery; coin	188	203	47	148	669	717	1 436	970	905	Perles fines ou de culture, pierres précieuses ou semi-précieuses, métaux précieux, plaqués ou doublés de métaux précieux et leurs articles; bijouterie de fantaisie; pièce de monnaie
Tobacco and manufactured tobacco substitutes	212	266	100	276	478	717	827	908	840	Tabac, artisanal, filtre, ou emballe
Ores, slag and ash	169	211	149	181	310	364	367	337	361	Minerais, scories et cendres
Iron and steel	172	224	234	43	205	117	134	159	283	Fer et acier
Sugar and sugar confectionery	339	537	33	78	52	53	107	94	153	Sucres et sucreries
Main Destinations										**Principales destinations**
South Africa	686	854	759	1 146	1 774	2 396	2 649	2 534	2 015	Afrique du Sud
Mozambique	139	143	148	97	91	128	279	365	574	Mozambique
Belgium	131	226	118	61	61	60	48	27	125	Belgique
United Arab Emirates	176	112	107	18	329	209	482	229	96	Emirats Arabes Unis
Zambia	143	139	92	65	68	75	85	110	95	Zambie
IMPORTS, CIF										**IMPORTATIONS, CAF**
Imports - Total	2 577	3 442	2 832	6 207	5 865	8 596	7 484	7 704	6 380	Importations - Total (millions)
Imports from Africa	...	...	...	5 330	3 492	5 683	4 101	4 435	3 354	Importations en provenance de l'Afrique
Main Products										**Principaux produits**
Mineral fuels, mineral oils and products of their distillation; bituminous substances; mineral waxes	305	335	346	402	940	1 255	1 515	1 617	1 567	Pétrole et produits dérivés
Nuclear reactors, boilers, machinery and mechanical appliances; parts thereof	136	225	306	295	529	581	642	655	596	Réacteurs nucléaires, chaudières, machines, appareils et engins mécaniques et accessoires
Vehicles others than railway or tramway rolling-stock, and parts and accessories thereof	126	163	401	428	1 082	1 066	1 106	717	543	Véhicules autres que ferroviaires ou de tramway et accessoires
Electrical machinery and equipment and parts thereof; sound recorders and reproducers, television image and sound recorders and reproducers, and parts and accessories of such articles	136	172	122	232	463	411	394	428	389	Machines et matériels électriques et leurs accessoires, appareils d'enregistrement ou de reproduction, appareils d'enregistrement d'image télévisée et de reproduction du son, et accessoires.
Cereals	101	252	185	221	293	352	467	325	332	Céréales
Main Origin										**Principales provenances**
South Africa	1 065	1 195	1 689	4 809	2 820	4 833	3 206	3 659	2 736	Afrique du Sud
Singapore	253	370	219	7	20	32	32	63	1 168	Singapour
China	136	203	133	128	320	371	354	438	399	Chine
United Kingdom	369	-	-	71	159	188	1 262	1 416	208	Royaume Uni
Zambia	48	105	93	90	146	218	492	262	180	Zambie

IX FINANCIAL AND MONETARY STATISTICS - FINANCES ET STATISTIQUES MONETAIRES										
	2006	2007	2008	2009	2010	2011	2012	2013	2014	
IX-1 MONETARY STATISTICS *ZIMBABWE DOLLAR (MILLIONS)*										**IX-1 STATISTIQUES MONÉTAIRES** *DOLLAR ZIMBABWEEN (MILLIONS)*
Money supply (M1)	1 080	600	310	1 380	2 330	3 100	3 690	3 890	4 020	Masse monétaire (M1)
Quasi-money	270 556	123 289 054	50220623704 161 200	...	...	...	...	...	...	Quasi-monnaie
of which Demand Deposit	...	...	...	...	...	...	...	...	...	dont Monnaie scripturale
Net foreign assets	- 35 620	2 210 588	-1725225941 842 110	...	...	...	...	...	...	Avoirs extérieurs nets
Domestic credit	621 042	747 344 742	5423268787690 760 000	...	...	...	...	...	...	Crédit intérieur
of which claims on private sector	383 832	613 593 207	5427387512968 050 000	...	...	...	...	...	...	dont créances sur le secteur privé
of which claims on government sector, net	204 702	105 078 388	-23467218325 446 200	...	...	...	...	...	...	dont créances nettes sur le gouvernement
International reserves (millions US$)	155	146	76	822	732	659	574	475	484	Réserves internationales (millions $EU)
Average Exchange Rate (National Currency per US$)	164.55	9 686.77	6723 052 073.34	...	...	...	...	...	...	Taux de change (moyen) (monnaie nationale par $ EU)
IX-2 PUBLIC FINANCE *US$ (MILLIONS)*										**IX-2 FINANCES PUBLIQUES** *$ E.U (MILLIONS)*
Total Revenues and Grants	520	202	133	974	2 199	2 921	3 496	3 742	2 970	Recettes totales et dons
Tax Revenue	504	193	128	882	2 075	2 660	3 279	3 415	2 712	Recettes fiscales
Non Tax Revenue	17	9	5	51	124	261	217	327	258	Recettes non fiscales
Grants	-	-	-	41	-	-	-	-	-	Dons
Total Expenditures and Net Lending	696	384	258	1 145	2 310	3 180	3 658	4 069	3 225	Dépenses totales et prêts nets
Current expenditure	572	305	241	1 099	1 717	2 629	3 303	3 586	2 843	Dépenses courantes
Of which Wages and Salaries	211	89	52	518	1 064	1 834	2 504	2 767	2 188	Dont rémunérations et salaires
Capital expenditure	121	70	14	46	593	551	355	483	377	Dépenses d'équipement
Net Lending	2	9	3	-	-	-	-	-	5	Prêts nets
Fiscal Balance	- 175	- 183	- 125	- 171	- 111	- 259	- 162	- 328	- 255	Solde global y compris les dons
IX-3 BALANCE OF PAYMENTS *ZIMBABWE DOLLAR (BILLIONS)*										**IX-3 BALANCE DES PAIEMENTS** *DOLLAR ZIMBABWEEN (MILLIARDS)*
Trade balance	- 475	- 308	- 969	- 1 600	- 1 844	- 3 066	- 2 907	- 3 115	...	Balance commerciale
Services Balance	- 121	- 143	- 207	- 266	- 449	- 654	- 866	- 931	...	Balance des services
Net Income	- 209	- 364	- 337	- 284	- 278	- 299	- 959	- 1 018	...	Revenus nets
Compensation of employees	...	...	...	...	...	...	...	...	...	Rémunération des salariés
Investment Income	...	...	...	...	...	...	...	...	...	Revenus des investissements
Current transfers, net total	439	440	625	926	573	803	1 679	1 635	...	Transferts courants
Net official transfers	...	...	...	...	...	...	...	...	...	Transferts officiels nets
Workers' remittances	...	...	...	...	...	...	...	...	...	Envois de fonds des travailleurs
Other private transfers	...	...	...	...	...	...	...	...	...	Autres transferts privés
Current account balance	- 365	- 375	- 888	- 1 224	- 1 998	- 3 216	- 3 053	- 3 429	...	Solde du compte courant
Capital & financial account	...	...	...	- 657	617	1 564	...	...	...	Comptes de capital et financier
Capital account	...	...	...	...	...	...	...	...	...	Compte de capital
Financial account	...	...	...	...	...	...	...	...	...	Compte financier
Errors & omissions	...	...	...	- 70	888	964	...	...	...	Erreurs et omissions
Overall balance	...	...	...	- 1 867	- 412	- 593	...	...	...	Balance générale

X DEBT AND FINANCIAL FLOWS - DETTE ET FLUX FINANCIERS										
	2006	2007	2008	2009	2010	2011	2012	2013	2014	
X-1 DEBT *US$ (MILLIONS)*										**X-1 DETTE EXTÉRIEURE** *$ E.U (MILLIONS)*
Total external debt	4 874	5 280	6 383	7 930	7 974	8 231	9 057	10 660	12 826	Dette extérieure totale
Private	1 012	1 164	2 115	2 509	2 095	2 529	3 026	4 350	6 245	Privée
Public	3 862	4 116	4 268	5 421	5 879	5 702	6 032	6 309	6 581	Publique
Total external debt service	507	493	614	731	510	...	...	...	...	Service de la dette extérieure
Present value of External debt	...	...	...	...	...	...	...	...	...	Valeur actuelle de la dette extérieure
Total government domestic debt (in local currency)	...	...	...	...	...	...	...	...	...	Dette publique intérieure
X-2 FINANCIAL FLOWS *US$ (MILLIONS)*										**X-2 FLUX FINANCIERS** *$ E.U (MILLIONS)*
Net Foreign Direct Investment Inflows	40	69	52	105	166	387	400	400	...	Investissements étranger direct (flux nets entrants)
Main origin of FDI Inflows										**Principales origines de l'IDE entrant:**
United Kingdom	15	10	- 11	2	18.5	40.1	28.5	...	...	Royaume-Uni
United States	-	-	-	-	-	-	-	...	...	États-Unis
Italy	...	-	...	...	0.0	0.0	0.0	...	...	Italie
Sweden	2	3	9	- 1	2.4	-	1.8	...	...	Suède
Germany	4	1	-	- 1	-	- 2.8	- 2.6	...	...	Allemagne
African countries	...	...	...	...	...	...	...	...	...	Pays africains
Net total Official Development Assistance	278	478	612	736	732	716	1 001	811	...	Aide publique au développement (nette totale)
Main origin of Net ODA										**Principales origines de l'APD nette**
United States	36	139	223	250	175.2	180.1	174.1	156.2	...	Etats-Unis
United Kingdom	70	94	89	110	108.0	77.5	220.0	...	...	Royaume-Uni
Germany	10	19	25	35	33.1	58.5	56.7	31.6	...	Allemagne
Sweden	18	20	26	29	30.4	38.6	39.8	36.9	...	Suède
Japan	7	12	10	12	18.9	18.1	21.8	12.4	...	Japon
General notes	All figures in monetary values are in Zimbabwean Dollars (Z$) for the period 2000 - 2008. For 2009 and beyond, monetary values are in United States Dollars (US$).				Comptes Nationaux : Les données sont exprimées en $ EU à partir de 2009					Notes générales

ZIMBABWE